Contemporary Literary Criticism

Volume 16

Contemporary Literary Criticism

Excerpts from Criticism
of the Works of Today's
Novelists, Poets, Playwrights,
Short Story Writers, Filmmakers,
and Other Creative Writers

Sharon R. Gunton
Editor

Gale Research Company
Book Tower
Detroit, Michigan 48226

STAFF

Library of Congress Catalog Card Number 76-38938
ISBN 0-8103-0105-9

Contents

Filmmakers in this volume:

Preface

As the film industry has grown, its influence has also expanded. Now considered a major art form, the film has become the subject of extensive scholarly criticism, much of it focused on the literary qualities of outstanding productions in the medium, rather than on technical or cinematographic aspects.

To make some of the most important comment more readily available, this volume of *Contemporary Literary Criticism* is devoted to evaluations of filmmakers whose works have already received much critical acclaim or seem destined to attain significance in the future. In keeping with the literary direction of the series, criticism has been selected which considers film in relation to its theme, formal style, characterization, and intent. Most of the filmmakers included have functioned as writers as well as directors; all of them are responsible for the distinctive styles of their productions.

For this special volume, we have chosen criticism of artists such as Frank Capra, Alfred Hitchcock, and John Ford because of the magnitude of their work and their influence on their successors. Others, like Leni Riefenstahl and Francis Ford Coppola, have been chosen for coverage because of their limited, yet distinctive, contributions to the art.

This special volume of film criticism complements other volumes of *CLC* and follows the same format, with some slight variations. The list of filmmakers treated is international in scope and, as in the other *CLC* volumes, includes artists who are living now or have died after January 1, 1960. Since this volume of *CLC* is intended to provide a definitive overview of the careers of the filmmakers included, the editors have included approximately 40 filmmakers (compared to 150 authors in a standard *CLC*) in order to devote more attention to each filmmaker.

There are about 850 individual excerpts in this volume, taken from about 90 books and several hundred issues of some 100 general magazines, film reviews, and scholarly journals. The sources from which material has been reprinted have been listed in the appendix. The appendix does not, however, list books or periodicals merely consulted during preparation of the volume.

References and Notes

Page numbers appear after each fragment (unless the entire essay was contained on one page), and all credit lines include the complete essay title, volume and issue number of all journal entries, inclusive pagination for all essays, and total pagination for all books. An asterisk following a credit line indicates that the essay or book contains information on more than one author.

Notes in many entries directing the user to consult *Contemporary Authors* for detailed biographical and bibliographical information refer to a series of biographical reference books published by the Gale Research Company since 1962, which now includes detailed biographical sketches of more than 60,000 authors who have lived since 1960, many of whose careers began during the post-World War II period, or earlier.

Acknowledgments

The editors wish to thank the copyright holders of the excerpts included in this volume for their permission to use the material, and the staffs of the Detroit Public Library, Wayne State University Library, and the libraries of the University of Michigan for making their resources available to us.

Authors Forthcoming in *CLC*

With the publication of *Contemporary Literary Criticism,* Volume 12, the series expanded its scope to encompass songwriters, filmmakers, cartoonists, screenwriters, producers, and other creative writers whose work is often evaluated from a literary perspective. These writers take their place with the novelists, poets, dramatists, and short story writers who will continue to be the primary focus of *CLC.*

Volume 17 will be designed to be of special interest to young adult readers. Volume 18 will include criticism on a number of authors not previously listed, and will also feature criticism of newer works of authors included in earlier volumes.

To Be Included in Volume 17

Joy Adamson (British nature writer)—Best known for her chronicles of the lioness named Elsa, especially *Born Free*

Barbara Corcoran (American young adult novelist, nonfiction writer, short story writer, playwright, and journalist)—Her novel *May I Cross Your Golden River?,* written under the pseudonym of Paige Dixon, depicts the struggles of a young man faced with a fatal disease

Maureen Daly (American young adult novelist and nonfiction writer)—Author of the ground-breaking *Seventeenth Summer*

Roy A. Gallant (American young adult science writer, biographer, and editor)—Author of several introductory works on astronomy, as well as other natural sciences

Alan Garner (British novelist and editor)—Novels such as *The Owl Service* and *Red Shift* reflect his fascination with myth and legend

William Golding (British novelist)—Author of *Lord of the Flies,* a novel often compared with *Catcher in the Rye* for its popularity with young adults

Lorraine Hansberry (American playwright)—Author of *A Raisin in the Sun,* the first Broadway play written by a black woman

Mick Jagger and Keith Richard (British songwriters)—Founding members of the Rolling Stones

Jonathan Kozol (American novelist and education writer)—Critic of American school system and proponent of free school movement, best known for *Death at an Early Age*

Willie Nelson (American songwriter)—A veteran of the country-western music scene whose versatile style has led to his wide popularity

John Neufeld (American young adult novelist, editor, playwright, short story writer, and television scriptwriter)—He is a strong advocate of young adults and critic of adult social standards

Robert Newton Peck (American young adult novelist and poet)—Author of the *Soup* series

Françoise Sagan (French novelist)—The popular *Bonjour Tristesse,* published when Sagan was nineteen, portrays a young girl's attempt to prevent her father's remarriage

Alvin Silverstein and Virginia Silverstein (American science writers)—Their works cover a variety of scientific subjects, from *Allergies* to *The World of Bionics*

Zilpha Keatley Snyder (American young adult novelist)—Author of the award-winning *The Egypt Game*

Jessamyn West (American novelist)—Author of *Cress Delahanty* and *Leafy Rivers,* books which treat special times in a young woman's life

To Be Included in Volume 18

Richard Adams (British novelist)—Will feature criticism on new novel, *The Girl in a Swing*

Pearl S. Buck (American novelist, short story writer, and dramatist)

Arthur C. Clarke (British science fiction writer)

Roald Dahl (British short story writer, screenwriter, and novelist)—Will feature criticism on new novel, *My Uncle Oswald*

Henry De Montherlant (French novelist, dramatist, poet, and essayist)

E.L. Doctorow (American novelist and editor)—Will feature criticism on new novel, *Loon Lake*

Ronald L. Fair (Black American novelist)

William Faulkner (American novelist)

Max Frisch (Swiss novelist and dramatist)—Will feature criticism on new novel, *Man in the Holocene*

John Gardner (American novelist, short story writer, and essayist)—Will feature criticism on new novel, *Freddy's Book*

Nadine Gordimer (South African novelist, short story writer, and essayist)

Dashiell Hammett (American novelist and screenwriter)

Yasunari Kawabata (Japanese novelist, short story writer, and critic)

Thomas McGuane (American novelist)—Will feature criticism on new novel, *Panama*

Eugenio Montale (Italian poet)

Marge Piercy (American novelist and poet)—Will feature criticism on new novel, *Vida*

Varlam Shalamov (Russian short story writer)—Will feature criticism on new collection, *Kolyma Tales*

Joseph Wambaugh (American novelist and screenwriter)

Woody Allen

1935-

(Born Allen Stewart Konigsberg) American director, actor, author, playwright, and scriptwriter.

In his films, Woody Allen has created a persona as distinct as that of Charlie Chaplin's little tramp. The Allen character is typically a maligned, confused adolescent who becomes an isolated adult; an observer who finds it difficult to participate. Sexually and emotionally inadequate, he is the quintessential *schlemiel,* or Jewish underdog. However, his experiences reflect aspects of everyone's lives. While Allen's earlier films are gag-oriented and reminiscent of Chaplin's tradition of a little man dealing with an overwhelming society, later works are more introspective. Initially, Allen attacked society as a whole. This attitude evolved into a more personal view of his failure to deal with emotions and intimate relationships.

Born in Brooklyn, Allen claims as his earliest memories rejection and harassment by his peers, a situation that figures prominently in his comic routines. While studying cinema at New York University, Allen mailed jokes to newspaper columnists who in turn passed them on to local celebrities. Consequently, an advertising agency hired him as a jokewriter. This led to writing for standup comedians, until he began writing and performing his own material. Allen also experimented with playwriting before turning to cinema. His first film, *What's Up, Tiger Lily?,* is actually a Japanese spy film that Allen re-edited and supplied with new dialogue. The result, while referred to as a "one-gimmick" film, introduced his leading character: the lovable klutz. Like the Woody Allen character that followed, he is alienated, an observer.

***Take the Money and Run,* the first film in which he both starred and directed, reflected the misadventures of an unsuccessful bank robber; it relied on a comic sense that compensated for any structural difficulties, as did *Bananas,* his next film. They consist of verbal and visual "one-liners." Both are simplistic forms of the parodies he created later. *Everything You Always Wanted to Know About Sex* provided an innovative experiment for Allen. More than a comedy created from a sex manual, it not only parodied the book, but its concept and audience as well. *Sleeper* is a social satire as well as an amusing parody of futuristic science fiction. With this film, Allen began discussing his deprived childhood less while utilizing broader symbolism about man's blasé attitude towards life.**

With *Love and Death,* Allen chose an even more ambitious topic: the satirization of classic Russian literature and cinema. He draws from other sources, too, reflecting in particular his great admiration for Ingmar Bergman and Sergei Eisenstein. *Love and Death* is a black comedy of death, despair, and life in a godless universe. While still concerned with visual humor, Allen's films were developing thematic and visual sophistication.

***Annie Hall* is generally regarded as his masterpiece, and a landmark of his stylistic development. An autobiographical romantic comedy, *Annie Hall* examines Allen's failure in intimate relationships. For the first time, he consciously avoids excessive use of humor, so as not to destroy his tale's credibility. Significantly, this film was nearly called *Anhedonia,* meaning the inability to experience pleasure, a common failing of the Woody Allen character. By changing the name, Allen concentrates on the positive aspects of his relationship with Diane Keaton, his ex-girlfriend who costarred with him in the film, instead of emphasizing his ultimate failure. In this film, the *schlemiel* becomes more complex; he is beginning to search for permanence in the world, and finds it in art. *Annie Hall* met with resounding critical and popular success.**

After the success of *Annie Hall,* Allen undertook his biggest challenge: writing and directing a noncomic film in which he did not appear. Although *Interiors* met with mixed critical receptions, some critics found it Allen's most outstanding work. An austere, somber film, it reflects his taste for Bergman. *Interiors* treats human frailty in much the same manner as *Annie Hall;* however, this time he did not have his familiar network of visual and spoken humor to fall back on. *Manhattan* combines elements of both *Annie Hall* and *Interiors.* The style is sparse and more confident, reflected by his use of black and white film. It is a drama with comedy, instead of a comedy with drama. While some critics labeled the film superficial, disjointed, and boring, others pronounced it Allen's most mature work to date. (See also *Contemporary Authors,* Vols. 33-36, rev. ed.)

ARTHUR KNIGHT

[None] of [*What's Up, Tiger Lily?*] is precisely what used to be called boffo humor. No custard pies fill the air, and the climax contains no lunatic chase in break-away cars. Instead, Allen's sense of fun is at once low-keyed, far-out, and hip. . . . Allen's humor is without malice and without effort; and if some of his puns are terrible, there is an added fillip of fun in the realization that he is every bit as aware of it as we are.

Arthur Knight, "Fun Time," in Saturday Review *(© 1966 by Saturday Review; all rights reserved; reprinted with permission), Vol. XLIX, No. 5, November 5, 1966, p. 45.*

MICHAEL SHEDLIN

[*Take the Money and Run*] is a festival of [Woody Allen's] peculiar and prolific wit, a meld of ruthless satire, surrealism, and blatant absurdity. . . . The episodic nature of the movie is intrinsic and entirely suited to Allen's rapid-fire humor; the sight gags are numerous, unself-conscious, and are never allowed to perform as mere specula of the spoken jokes—an index of Allen's talent and promise as a director of comedy. Indeed, many of the most memorable scenes are purely visual. . . . The prevailing prison atmosphere in *Take the Money and Run* is effective, although a bit too benign and glossy. . . . Allen's comedy style, which is situational and considerably more sarcastic than slapstick, is a reflection of his favorite comedy films, "*Seduced and Abandoned,* and all of the Marx Brothers," and his highly regarded and influential stand-up colleague Mort Sahl. . . . [It] is altogether possible that Woody Allen will become the funniest filmmaker alive. (pp. 63-4)

Michael Shedlin, "Short Notices: 'Take the Money and Run'," in Film Quarterly *(copyright 1969 by The Regents of the University of California; reprinted by permission of the University of California Press), Vol. XXIII, No. 2, Winter, 1969-70, pp. 63-4.*

RICHARD DAVIS

We've seen countless comedies about incompetent crooks. In fact most screen comedians have used the format at some time or other; even the gags which turn up [in *Take the Money and Run*]—or many of them—aren't exactly new. But the measure of Woody Allen's talent is that he can impart an aura of novelty to even the most hackneyed situation.

Take the Money and Run is a joy. It's wry and sardonic. . . .

There are few belly-laughs. Allen's humour, except in a couple of instances, is firmly anchored in the offbeat and the sly nudge. His scene in the prison laundry, where he wrestles with the washing and drying machine, is perhaps the only concession to the more obvious humour, and is reminiscent of [Jacques] Tati or of Chaplin's classic *Modern Times* sequence with the forcible feeder, in its depiction of the 'little man' against the fearsome complexity of the Machine Age. But Man against Machine, a classic situation, a priceless gift to comedians, is one which, far from losing its efficacy, becomes more and more relevant by the hour. Apart from this Allen the observer can still find new things to say even when character and situation appear to have exhausted all possibilities.

Richard Davis, "Reviews: 'Take the Money and Run'" (© copyright Richard Davis 1971; reprinted with permission), in Films and Filming, *Vol. 17, No. 4, January, 1971, p. 53.*

PENELOPE GILLIATT

Woody Allen is deeply fascinated and affronted by the reign of jargon. Sociologists who write about the death of the word in America must have tin ears; American wits at the moment have the antennae for details of cliché that the English have for details of vernacular. In "Bananas," which is slightly about revolution in a banana republic, the plot is ropy and can seem flailingly right-wing when it probably thinks and means something reforming; the one-liners therefore run out of steam halfway through the picture, and too many scenes tend to come out on a bit of *l'esprit de l'escalier* when they would work better if the person on the staircase would shut up, but the film really *is* funny about automated language. (pp. 127-28)

But still, for all the odd glories of the film, it has to be said that the Castro jokes are often miles out of control, that the blackout lines get lame, and perhaps that the use of a comic personality dependent on being humbly distraught and henpecked may be holding back this wit from the soaring and fearless lunacy that he can sometimes flight to. (pp. 128-29)

Penelope Gilliatt, "Woody Allen," in The New Yorker *(© 1971 by The New Yorker Magazine, Inc.), Vol. XLVII, No. 13, May 15, 1971, pp. 127-29.*

DAVID DENBY

Woody Allen is probably the best comic talent working in American movies today, but also about the most erratic. . . . [*Bananas*] has some ideas that are so bad we may laugh simply because he's really going through with them. . . .

Much of his humor is intentionally "stupid," intentionally sophomoric; like an irrepressible college humorist who somehow never graduated, he is always freshly enthralled by the world's absurdity, always eager to prove the power of far-out humor to take the measure of that absurdity. Occasionally his stupid jokes have a rather sneaky force if you're aware of the reality behind them. . . .

At his best Allen mocks the dead language of television, movies, and advertising by placing the clichés in an absurd context or by gleefully exaggerating them. . . . Most of his ideas, however, are closer to free-flying nonsense humor, exhilarating and undisciplined, but without the aggressive force of the film's opening. One has to speak of separate ideas rather than an overall conception because Allen hasn't bothered to impose a unified style or theme on his material. Satire, burlesque, slapstick, and parody are all jumbled together. (p. 93)

Allen is so impatient that he can't sustain or develop anything, and his movie keeps darting off in odd directions or pausing demurely for little interludes. Some of the gags are linked by a kind of comic free association, and the plot . . . is so casual and intermittent that it seems to be there mainly to tease our assumption that a movie *needs* a plot. (pp. 93-4)

As a satirist, Allen is not without the diffidence of his screen character. It's good that he's not protecting any of the conventional pieties (he's free, for instance, to attack Castro *and* the CIA), and he has the originality to change an old emphasis or shift a familiar target (in a spoof of psychoanalysis he makes fun of the patient's revelations rather than the analyst's jargon). With the whole of American culture as his province he'll probably never run out of absurdities to work up into sharp little bits, but on the other hand, the lack of any moral or political position whatsoever prevents his work from having much bite. He has the sophistication for a truly cleansing American satire, but at present, not the guts. (p. 94)

David Denby, "It Only Hurts When We Laugh," in The Atlantic Monthly *(copyright © 1971, by The Atlantic Monthly Company, Boston, Mass.; reprinted with permission), Vol. 228, No. 2, August, 1971, pp. 92-4.*

ROBERT G. MICHELS

Woody Allen's movies have been so disorganized as to defy description and so hilarious as to merit them. The link between his free-associational wit and his casual manner of presentation has not been adventitious, as *Play It Again, Sam,* his extended excursion into nostalgia, conclusively demonstrates. Although Allen again stars in his own scenario, in leaving the directing to Herbert Ross he has chosen the wrong man at the wrong timing. Ross cannot capture Allen's humor. He can only contain it. . . . In *Play It Again, Sam* Allen has returned to gag writing. He has transferred rather than translated his play to the screen. The one-liners are integrated into a coherent story, but it suffers by comparison with the previous films, which became mired in *non sequiturs* whose very randomness evinced a certain fatalism. . . . With each successive film Allen has insisted upon specifying the ramifications of sexual frustration at the expense of developing his initial theme of social inadequacy. By doing so, he inevitably turns from contemplation of society to self, thus widening his appeal . . . while limiting his scope. Allen has not lost his comic vision, but he has blurred it perceptibly. The character he has created always was numbered among the walking wounded. In *Play It Again, Sam* the injuries seem to be self-inflicted. Of course, they remain incurable. . . . [To] survive is an accomplishment. To comprehend is an impossibility. It is this inarticulated assumption which provides the manic intensity that animates Allen's work and the resignation that informs it. His ever improbable sense of the ludicrous rescues him from the occupational hazard of repetitiveness, but his interest in a laugh a minute precludes raising his horizons noticeably beyond the next punch line. Within these bounds Allen's efforts can be no different than they have been. They cannot be any funnier than they already are. (pp. 57-8)

Robert G. Michels, "Short Notices: 'Play It Again, Sam'," in Film Quarterly *(copyright 1972 by The Regents of the University of California; reprinted by permission of the University of California Press), Vol. XXVI, No. 2, Winter, 1972-73, pp. 57-8.*

RICHARD SCHICKEL

Woody Allen is a walking compendium of a generation's concerns, comically stated. At every stage of his career he has demonstrated himself to be uncannily in touch with the things that are on the minds of the vast majority of his contemporaries. (p. 33)

"What's Up, Tiger Lily?" was . . . so modest that it passed very nearly without notice except among [Woody Allen's] devotees, though it is among his choicer lunacies. . . . There is in any of these Oriental imitations of American genre films a delicious element of unconscious parody, verging on the surreal, and thus there was a matching of visual material with the sensibility of the new soundtrack that seemed near miraculous, perhaps the best example of found art we've yet had in any medium. . . .

[In] fooling around with this ridiculous, throwaway project Allen for the first time tapped that great mother lode of a generation's sensibility—media memory. "Tiger Lily's" immediate reference point was the Bond subgenre, but it was also, in its little way, part of what can only be termed a tradition. *Our* tradition: some 30 years of slumping farther and farther down on our spines while the great screen before us flickered with uncounted tales of crime and espionage. College may have made us appreciators of literary modernism, but the matinees of childhood maddened us with movies—and were first on the scene. We have known from the start that we mustn't take them seriously. At the same time, of course, we have inescapably taken them seriously.

Which has led some into camp. And some to the *auteur* theory. And a few into satire and parody of these and other film forms—the only intellectually respectable way to resolve the contradictions inherent for us in this subject. "Tiger Lily" must have shown Allen what he could do in this vein; in a way it's his easiest, gooniest picture. But not, of course, his most delicious or subtle stuff. . . .

[Allen] does confine himself to the easy targets. "Take the Money and Run" is, to be sure, a full-length parody of a heist film. But in "Bananas" he takes on Ingmar Bergman . . . and Sergei Eisenstein. . . . On the other hand, he makes no big deal of this. Indeed, the basis of his visual style, like that of his verbal style, is understatement—very often in the form of the practical question intruding on the cosmic speculation. . . .

These, then, are his two basic tools—parody and the devastating understatement, the latter functioning as a sort of lightning rod, grounding the wild comic flashes of the former, conducting them back to earth, to the absurd reality we share. But they are, in his hands, marvelously versatile tools. . . .

[In] the course of these cheerful assaults he has managed to attack, in his oblique way, such major issues as mortality ("It is impossible to experience one's own death objectively and still carry a tune"), organized crime (Mafiosi "usually can be recognized by their large cufflinks and their failure to stop eating when the man sitting next to them is hit by a falling anvil"). . . .

By these quotations I don't mean to suggest that Allen's reputation must stand or fall on his one-liners. It is true that, excepting "Play It Again, Sam," his plays and movies are a bit raggle-taggle in organization, but then, what isn't these days, given the widespread belief that Donald Barthelme was right when he called the collage the basic art form of our time. (p. 36)

It is no accident, then, that so many of us should—without consulting one another (a thing we never do anyway)—choose Allen as comic culture hero. Like him, we have a peculiar sense of our individual worth, a kind of selfishness, really (which may account for his obsessive joking about food; the concern with being comfortably fed is a basic signal of egocentricity). Like him we are not merely apolitical, but in many cases antipolitical, at least partly on the grounds that politics is one of the most constricting metaphors ever embraced by man. . . . Like him, we find the characteristic quality of eclectic attention to be "a certain humorous remove from our experience," with media and literature, all intermingled, being one of the largest stores of that experience. And there is no doubt in our mind that an Allen parody of a Bergman or an Antonioni is, like our familiar laughter at it, a proper form of homage. Above all, however, we retain sensibilities which "seem to see the world still in words, as writers, arguers, archivists—even, perhaps even especially, those who do not write."

Truer words than these never having been spoken about my generation, his generation, the rise of Woody Allen seems to me inevitable given the simultaneous rise of his contemporaries in the tastemaking hierarchy. Or, as he himself puts it: "All of literature is a footnote to Faust. I have no idea what I mean by that." (p. 37)

Richard Schickel, "The Basic Woody Allen Joke: Not Only Is God Dead, but Try Getting a Plumber on Weekends," in The New York Times Magazine *(© 1971 by The New York Times Company; reprinted by permission), January 7, 1973, pp. 10, 33-7.*

RICHARD COMBS

For all the panache with which Woody Allen dashes off sight gags and cinematic puns (everything from *Potemkin* to *Casablanca*), his visual and verbal humour have always jostled for space on the screen. Allen's comedy is joke-oriented, and almost devoutly Jewish joke-oriented. His maladroit hero stumbles through life expecting social and sexual humiliation, and is usually rewarded with disaster. The world crashes about his ears with each mishap, and each gag seems to begin from scratch rather than building from previous situations.

Confessing his unfitness for survival in a constant, self-deprecating monologue, Allen's little man has neither the never-say-die spastic energy which inspired the visual contortions of Jerry Lewis' best comedies, nor the affected 'cool' of Peter Sellers' Inspector Clouseau, skating with a certain bumbling style over the thin ice of total incompetence. . . . Allen is not so much a man pitting his wits against impersonal forces as a physically inept creature going down under another onslaught. His comedy has little conventional timing and acrobatic inventiveness. The styleless, graceless collision of situations is precisely the point, and in defeat the hero always retreats with humility, almost gratefully.

Visual parody and throwaway gags follow rather limply in the train of Allen's wisecracking philosophy of frustration, and the parodies and the monologue have yet to meet in a complete movie. *Play It Again, Sam* . . . is perhaps the least inventive of his films, but it is the most consistent and developed in its humour. *Everything You Always Wanted to Know about Sex* . . . has been filmed in the direct and unfussy way that Allen has evolved since the first messy camera rovings of *Take the Money and Run.* It is a technique which quickly sets up and makes the most of each gag, but which only lends itself to very plain social satire when the verbal humour dries up. . . .

In other instances, Allen's parody is too straight and literal (the 'What's My Perversion?' TV panel game; the sexual research centre which looks like Frankenstein's laboratory) to be more than intermittently effective. The best episodes gain a lot from Allen's own presence. . . .

[*Everything You Always Wanted to Know about Sex*] undoubtedly has an advantage over his two previous features in that it lacks the inconvenience of a plot. But even in an episodic framework, his comic gifts are too wayward to escalate a joke with the convulsive intensity and visual surprise of Jerry Lewis at his best. The classically put-upon little man that is Allen's own screen persona never seems to develop as far as it might, for want of a consistently appropriate context.

Richard Combs, "Film Reviews: 'Everything You Always Wanted to Know About Sex . . .'," in Sight and Sound *(copyright © 1973 by The British Film Institute), Vol. 42, No. 3, Summer, 1973, p. 178.*

GARY ARNOLD

Woody Allen's *Sleeper* is fast, inventive and delightful: a slapstick chase comedy set two centuries in the future, the better to satirize the present. (p. 126)

Sleeper has some of the acceleration and momentum of a Mack Sennett comedy. The situations and gags accumulate and snowball for stretches of ten or fifteen minutes, usually climaxed by a renewal of the chase. Then Allen seems to take a breather for a few minutes before resuming his all-out, headlong comic attack. His machine doesn't have a classic, smooth-running hum, but it gets you where you want to go, and I think the brief rest stops are necessary in feature-length slapstick.

Despite occasional lapses—Allen shortchanges a few sight gags after setting them up quite nicely—*Sleeper* impresses me as the most incisive and consistently funny Woody Allen comedy to date. (p. 127)

If Woody Allen continues to leave certain segments of the mass audience cold, it won't be because he's seriously deficient as a funnyman but because his sense of humor offends some conventional tastes. On his part, Allen has reached out to a large public and met it more than halfway—symbolically, by slipping on a giant banana peel. *Sleeper* is a hip popular comedy, uniting broad slapstick gags with a tart, satirical, up-to-date point of view. (p. 128)

Gary Arnold, "'Sleeper'," in The Washington Post *(© 1973, The Washington Post Co.), December 19, 1973 (and reprinted in* The National Society of Film Critics on Movie Comedy, *edited by Stuart Byron and Elisabeth Weis, Grossman Publishers, 1977, pp. 126-28.*

PAULINE KAEL

Woody Allen appears before us as the battered adolescent, scarred forever, a little too nice and much too threatened to allow himself to be aggressive. He has the city-wise effrontery of a shrimp who began by using language to protect himself and then discovered that language has a life of its own. The running war between the tame and the surreal—between Woody Allen the frightened nice guy trying to keep the peace and Woody Allen the wiseacre whose subversive fantasies keep jumping out of his mouth—has been the source of the comedy in his films. Messy, tasteless, and crazily uneven (as the best talking comedies have often been), the last two pictures he directed—*Bananas* and *Everything You Always Wanted to Know About Sex*—had wild highs that suggested an erratic comic genius. The tension between his insecurity and his wit makes us empathize with him; we, too, are scared to show how smart we feel. . . . At his top, in parts of *Bananas* and *Sex,* the inexplicably funny took over; it might be grotesque, it almost always had the flippant, corny bawdiness of a frustrated sophomore running amok, but it seemed to burst out—as the most inspired comedy does—as if we had all been repressing it. We laughed as if he had let out what we couldn't hold in any longer.

The surreal is itself tamed in Woody Allen's *Sleeper,* the most stable and most sustained of his films. (It also has the best title.) Easily the slapstick comedy of the year—there hasn't been any other—*Sleeper* holds together, as his sharpest earlier films failed to do; it doesn't sputter and blow fuses, like *Bananas* and *Sex.* It's charming—a very even work, with almost no thudding bad lines and with no low stretches. I can't think of anything much the matter with it; it's a small classic. But it doesn't have the loose, manic highs of those other films. . . . Allen's new sense of control over the medium and over his own material seems to level out the abrasive energy. You can be with it all the way, and yet it doesn't impose itself on your imagination—it dissolves when it's finished. (pp. 240-41)

[So] far in his movies he's the only character, because his conception of himself keeps him alone. (p. 241)

When we see his films, all our emotions attach to him; his fear and his frailty are what everything revolves around. No one else in his pictures has a vivid presence, or any particular quality except being a threat to him, and even that quality isn't really characterized. Maybe the reason he doesn't invest others with comic character (or even villainous character) is that he's so hung up that he has no interest in other people's hangups; that could be why his stories never really build to the big climactic finish one expects from a comedy. His plots don't tie a gigantic knot and then explode it, because the other characters aren't strong enough to carry the threads. The end of *Sleeper* is just a mild cutoff point—not bad but unexciting. . . . (p. 242)

[One] might say that *Sleeper* is a sober comedy; it doesn't unhinge us, we never feel that our reason is being shredded. It has a businesslike, nine-to-five look about it, and a faint nine-to-five lethargy. For a comedian, the price of stability may be the loss of inspiration. (p. 243)

Pauline Kael, "Survivor" (originally published in The New Yorker, *Vol. XLIX, No. 45, December 31, 1973), in her* Reeling *(copyright © 1973 by Pauline Kael; reprinted by permission of Little, Brown and Company in association with the Atlantic Monthly Press), Atlantic-Little, Brown, 1976, pp. 240-47.**

LEONARD MALTIN

There are critics who have suggested that Woody Allen be named a national art treasure, and I certainly would pledge my support for such a designation. In America's barren wasteland of comedy, he stands out like a Coke machine in the Mojave Desert. Yet two of his latest films, *Everything You Always Wanted to Know About Sex,* which he wrote and directed, and *Play It Again, Sam,* which he wrote but Herbert Ross directed, provide an interesting contrast in exploring the strengths and weaknesses of his comic talent.

Sex, a multi-episode film, is for the most part brilliantly directed. . . . *Sex* is quite clearly the work of a talent laced with genius. Yet it is not nearly so funny as *Play It Again, Sam*. . . .

The humor in *Sam* falls into two categories: monologue and sight-gag. Woody spends a good deal of the film talking, either to himself or to his friend's wife . . . machine-gunning a non-stop series of Allenisms (e.g., he remembers the girl's birthday because it's the anniversary of his mother's hysterectomy). Other major comic sequences are built around slapstick type of material: an uproarious scene has him trying to act nonchalant when his friends bring him a blind date. (p. 42)

The film teeters on the edge of truth, managing to be poignantly real when it wants to be, and outrageously unreal when the situation calls for it. . . . (pp. 42-3)

What is it about *Sex* that, with all of its innovations, makes it less funny than *Sam,* a thoroughly enjoyable but more conventional film? Well, in *Sex,* Allen tosses off all conventions and lets his imagination run wild. In doing so, he comes up with devilishly clever material—but strays so far from reality that there is nothing tangible for the audience to grab onto and *feel.* Most of the humor is derived from shock value. In other scenes, Allen turns around and hits so close to home that the line between truth and satire becomes hopelessly blurred, for equally ineffectual results. (p. 43)

These problems stem from the fact that Woody Allen is still essentially a gag-writer trying to adapt his brand of humor to film. Try to picture Henny Youngman making a short subject out of "Take my wife—please," and you have the basic conflict of Allen's films.

A rare and happy exception is *What's Up Tiger Lily?,* a large-scale extension of a one-joke idea. . . . [Because] the Japanese footage was so engagingly bad, and Woody's ideas so consistently ludicrous, it all seemed to click. . . .

Allen's first directorial effort, *Take the Money and Run,* suffered from an excess of "limbo" humor, neither verbal nor visual. More than any other Woody Allen film, one suspects that *Money* must have been an excruciatingly funny script to *read.* It's just that much of it doesn't play out on-screen. . . .

Bananas has a firmer grip on screen comedy technique, although it has its share of "clever" gags which don't pay off —as when Miss America, testifying at a trial, bursts into a rendition of "Caro Nome," as if she were back at the talent trials of the beauty contest. . . .

Another of Allen's problems is that he can't resist a gag, even when it intrudes on the situation. In the opening medieval segment of *Sex,* he plays a court jester and does a sidesplitting impression of Bob Hope delivering a monologue which gets no laughs. Then, ignoring his own spoof, he clutters the following scene with throwaway lines which only detract from the impact of the sequence. . . .

Sex has at least one sequence which defies criticism, perhaps the only one in the entire film that succeeds on every point. It is the final segment, depicting the activity inside the male body as it engages in sex. Beginning with a fanciful premise . . . , Allen builds on it with clever dialogue, incredible visual ideas (a work team turning a giant wheel in order to effect an erection, eventually knee-deep in liquid), and the omnipresent gag lines (with Woody himself as one of the sperm about to take off into the "unknown"). The foundation of this delightful segment is a funny *idea;* with this as a starting-point, Allen's large heaping of comic ideas creates a richly funny episode. (p. 44)

Leonard Maltin, "Take Woody Allen—Please!" in Film Comment *(copyright © 1974 by Film Comment Publishing Corporation; all rights reserved), Vol. 10, No. 2, March-April, 1974, pp. 42-5.*

LEONARD FLEISCHER

For all of its borrowings from silent film and Keystone Kops harum scarum, Allen's art is often very private and parochial, emerging paradoxically out of a clearly-defined cultural context. What Allen has done then is to blend the autobiographical elements that form so great a portion of his comedy with the more accessible allusions to mass culture, the result being an engaging amalgam of parody and confession, satire and sentiment, hostility and affection.

Consider Allen's use of his Jewish middle-class origins. In three of his films we hear voices of what obviously are a New York Jewish middle-aged couple nagging and whining about their son. (pp. 51-2)

I suspect it is no accident that we never see the faces of Allen's parents, that we merely hear their nagging voices, their pained disappointment over their son's failures. Allen's portrait of them is devastating, but stops short of being malicious or cruel. Perhaps it is enough that the college drop-out has had the last word! Allen's reference to his Jewishness extends beyond these parental allusions. He seems fascinated—almost obsessed—by the rabbinate and appears to delight in mocking the solemnity and dignity of the rabbinical image. (p. 52)

[Though Allen comes] close to offensive caricature in [his] broad treatment of recognizable Jewish types, [he is] at the same time asserting the freedom to employ such ethnic material in non-ethnic situations. The Jewish comic may be exorcising personal dybukks through these routines, striking back against a Jewish background that may have been unfulfilling and restricting. Yet at the same time these comic bits are a joke on the gentiles who don't quite get the point. (p. 53)

Allen is not always on target in blending the obvious and the bizarre. At times his nervous imagination causes him to move too quickly from one bit to another, neglecting the careful rhythms that structure comic genius. The courtroom sequence in *Bananas*—a segment with some of his zaniest moments—is cut short before its comic possibilities have been exhausted. (This is the scene in which a large black woman, in taking the stand in the Federal government's loyalty case against Allen gives her name as J. Edgar Hoover.) His films tend to have a disjointed effect, with transitions missing and pieces dangling. . . . His films suffer from the absence of comic foils, for when his own inventiveness lags, there is no one else on screen to pick up the ball. Finally, the latter portions of the films inevitably are a let-down after the early hilarity. (pp. 56-7)

Leonard Fleischer, "Getting Even: The Comic Art of Woody Allen," in Midstream *(copyright © 1974 by The Theodor Herzl Foundation, Inc.), Vol. XX, No. 4, April, 1974, pp. 51-7.*

MOLLY HASKELL

[Woody Allen] has encouraged a "just fun" attitude toward his films while stealthily adding more elaborate sketches to his repertory in order to invite comparison with the great comedians of the past. . . .

But Allen's sense of his own identity is too strong and too obtrusive for him ever to successfully camouflage himself as a mechanical man, the way Chaplin does in *The Circus,* the way Keaton enters animistically into harmony with other organisms. Nor can he quite envision a world of "normal" people as Lewis does in *The Nutty Professor.* Allen clings tenaciously to the worm's-eye view which is the source of his humor and of his success, and which defines the limits of his vision. It is the humor of a stand-up comic, wit that plays off a given world, rather than inventing it. It is a verbal, parochial, ratty, ethnic, bargain-basement humor, sexist, conservative, self-centered, and the funniest lines in *Sleeper* are hangover lines, when the "morning after" happens to be two centuries later. . . .

In alien territory, Allen can just about survive. He lacks the ability of a Chaplin or a Keaton to turn expediency into poetry, and his overconcrete personality—Jewish ethnic, New York—is a cross he brandishes with bravado. . . . In this, Allen is very much in tune with the contemporary *Zeitgeist,* the vision of the alien as insider, the underdog as top banana. Whereas most comedians suggested, by their smallness or obesity, the plight of outsiders looking in, longing to join the beautiful people (and thus were universal), Allen, to his disadvantage and advantage, comes at a time when little of the decorum and ritual of an elitist society remains for the comedian to sabotage, and when the WASP establishment has been demoted, in movie mythology, with the ethnic occupying centerstage. (p. 130)

At the same time, Allen—and this is the source of the reactionary side of his wit—wants *in.* Like the traditionally upward-mobile Jewish kid, part of him wants to join the dumb goyim, the smiling blond middle-Americans whose surrogates are the lobotomized futuristic race of *Sleeper* who say "Green-witch Village" and never heard of Norman Mailer. But Allen never develops the tensions, and contradictions, inherent in this situation beyond showing a disinclination to become involved in a radical plot, by a group called Aries, to overthrow the government, and by showing a marked contentedness once he has been reconditioned as a member of the Establishment. He tries to have it both ways—the vernal paradise of the revolutionaries recalls *Fahrenheit 451,* but it also plays on the negative image of carnivores in Godard's *Weekend.*

Allen is too much a product of his own biography to make the leaps of association of which the great comedians were capable, or—and this is a more serious failing—to envision an adversary as a worthwhile opponent. Allen's vision of a futuristic society, despite the elaborateness of the sets under Dale Hennesy's art direction, makes one appreciate the authority of a Stanley Kubrick. The comedian lives in a symbiotic relationship with his enemy, and this is where we appreciate the genius of Chaplin and Keaton, not just in the sublime grace (or deliberate gracelessness) of their mimetic art, but on the conceptual level, in the instinct for investing the opponent with strength—the towering mass of the bully in *Easy Street,* the numerical advantage of the cops or the army of women in Keaton's films, which give rise to feats of grace and ingenuity and intimations of the spirit's immortality that are beyond the considerable talents of Woody Allen. (p. 131)

Molly Haskell, "'Sleeper'," in The Village Voice *(reprinted by permission of* The Village Voice; *copyright © The Village Voice, Inc., 1974), 1974 (and reprinted in* The National Society of Film Critics on Movie Comedy, *edited by Stuart Byron and Elisabeth Weis, Grossman Publishers, 1977, pp. 128-31).*

PENELOPE GILLIATT

Woody Allen's imperially funny new picture is named "Love and Death," a coupling of big concepts that says at once where the story is set. We are obviously going to be in the land of "War and Peace," of "Crime and Punishment," of "Fathers and Sons," though we turn out to be not really so much in Russia as in Russian literature. It is a literature seen through Woody Allen's unique prism of the grandiose but hesitant, as if it were being read by a student racked by anxieties about both the afterlife and the common cold. (p. 104)

For such a recklessly funny film, the impression is weirdly serene. The feeling comes not just from the photography and the editing and the stately Prokofieff music but, more fundamentally, from the cast of Woody Allen's mind. He is the only wit alive who could manage with such easy style the skiddy topics of some of the movie's best jokes. Comedians who deal in sexual uncertainty can be dire, like comedians who trade on pretending to be cowards, because both sorts profit by affecting to have qualities that they secretly despise; but Woody Allen makes haplessness about love seem one of the conditions laid down for loving, much as he makes fear of death seem one of the conditions laid down for living. No one who wasn't petrified by mortality could make a comedy that was so palliatively funny about the straits we inhabit. God, if he exists, is described as an underachiever, presumably because of the Deity's failure to put an end to the anguish that comedy tries to see us through. . . . [Boris' dance with death is a] scene of peculiar carnival respite, like the experience of watching the whole movie. "Love and Death" strikes me as majestically funny: the most shapely piece of cinema that Woody Allen has yet made, and one of comedy's hardiest ripostes to extinction. (p. 109)

Penelope Gilliatt, "The Current Cinema: 'Love and Death'," in The New Yorker *(© 1975 by The New Yorker Magazine, Inc.), Vol. LI, No. 17, June 16, 1975, pp. 104, 107-09.*

JOHN SIMON

"Love and Death" is a curious olio of nightclub patter, revue sketches and one-liners, most of them quite funny but uneasily stitched together. What comes out resembles a movie only as something midway between a crazy quilt and a potato sack resembles a suit of clothes. Now, there is nothing intrinsically wrong with that: like anything else, film can accommodate a great many forms or lacks of form of a madcap, one-shot, sui generis kind. But there is a grave problem with "Love and Death," hilarious as much of it may be. This sort of film wears thin too easily, laughter that is largely pointless becomes in the end exhausting. This does not necessarily happen within a single Woody Allen film, which, kept wisely short, can generally squeeze by without our realizing until later that we have been exercising our jaws in a vacuum—that we could have gotten roughly the same effect from laughing gas, sneezing powder or a mutual tickling session with a friendly prankster. (pp. 1, 15)

[For] the more discriminating viewer a certain, as it were, postcoital depression sets in even earlier: say, midway through the film. It is in the nature of gags not to be all as funny as the best of the lot: a set of perfectly matched jokes is infinitely harder to come by than a necklace of perfectly matched pearls. . . . What put "Sleeper" above Allen's other films so far is that it really was about something besides gags—about what was wrong with present-day society revealed in terms of a grimly caricatured but all too plausible future.

In "Love and Death," however, the joke is everything; if it misfires, we promptly begin to wonder what it is that we have been laughing at, anyway. The film starts out as a vague satire on Russian novels (do we need that?), but soon scatters toward all kinds of targets, from anti-Semitism to Jewish sexuality. . . . "Love and Death," says the title, and we think that the film may work its way up to some comic insights into these two big subjects or, better yet, about how they interrelate. Yet while it boasts gags galore about both, it has nothing much to say about either, let alone about the two of them together. . . .

This is particularly saddening because Woody Allen is more than merely funny: at his best, he exhibits a penetrating intelligence—indeed, intellect—well beyond the mental means of our run-of-the-mill farceurs. Such intelligence can uncover, ridicule, and perhaps help laugh out of existence genuine evils, and a little, a very little, of this elixir survives even in the anomic laugh-fest of "Love and Death." But the movie stoops far too often to such things as a facile sight gag about a convention of village idiots which, when you come right down to it, yields laughter that leaves you with a bad taste in the soul. (p. 15)

John Simon, "Our Movie Comedies Are No Laughing Matter," in The New York Times, *Section 2 (© 1975 by The New York Times Company; reprinted by permission), June 29, 1975, pp. 1, 15.*

PENELOPE GILLIATT

"Annie Hall" perfects a sort of humor that can best be described as psychoanalytic slapstick. It has a Geiger-counter ear for urban clichés. . . . (p. 137)

"Annie Hall" goes further than any earlier Woody Allen film in the purity of its romanticism. This is a love story told with piercing sweetness and grief, for all its funniness. . . . In "Annie Hall," Woody Allen technically pushes far ahead of anything he has done in the cinema before, playing with ideas in film which he has been experimenting with in prose. His ear for metropolitan speech has never been finer, his approach to character never so direct, his feeling about hypocrisy never so ringing, his sobriety never so witty. (p. 138)

Penelope Gilliatt, "Woody at His Best Yet," in The New Yorker *(© 1977 by The New Yorker Magazine, Inc.), Vol. LIII, No. 10, April 25, 1977, pp. 136-38.*

ANDREW SARRIS

Annie Hall is by far the most brilliant Woody Allen movie to date. . . . For the first time in his career Woody Allen has acknowledged his own power and eminence as a condition of his existence. The old Woody might have gone to a shrink, but he would not have had the wherewithal to pay for his girl friend's analysis. He would never have shown himself making hordes of people laugh. He would never have begun to reveal in himself all the ruthlessness any reasonably successful urban adult must exercise to survive. For the first time Woody Allen is telling it like it is—almost. And that almost seems to be the key to my persistent yes-but feelings about Allen.

It is nothing I can put my finger on exactly, and I have no advice to offer on the subject. It just strikes me from time to time that Allen is all nuance with very little substance, that much of what he says is not very original, and that he tries to play both ends against the middlebrow. . . .

In years to come *Annie Hall* may be fondly remembered as the *Romeo and Juliet* of the analysands. Allen uses the most outrageously literal devices to distinguish the past from the present, the conscious from the unconscious, the physical from the spiritual, the id from the superego, the drama from the essay. He manages to be so boring on the subject of death that he makes Bergman seem lighthearted. Yet, the whole movie hangs together through the power of its reminiscence.

Andrew Sarris, "Woody Allen's Funny Valentine," in The Village Voice *(reprinted by permission of* The Village Voice; *copyright © The Village Voice, Inc., 1977), Vol. XXII, No. 17, April 25, 1977, p. 45.*

M. J. SOBRAN, JR.

He who despises himself, Nietzsche says somewhere, nonetheless esteems the despiser within himself. Woody's soliloquies (and *Annie Hall* teems with them) address that despiser, trying to charm, appease, and outflank him. He treats the audience the same way, as if to anticipate its presumptive contempt for him. Why does he expect contempt? Because, apparently, he is a man of humble origins. . . . Sometimes he kids his anxiety by making Alvy paranoiacally touchy about antisemitism, and sometimes he indulges it by making Annie's family really antisemitic. Either way, *Annie Hall* expresses his own self-absorption: you never know whether you are seeing reality *à clef,* or Allen's perception of reality, or his *perception* of his perception of reality. But the jokes are funny even when it's not clear who their butt is. He traps you inside his quirky consciousness and unscrupulously tickles you to death. (p. 622)

Annie Hall is frequently funny; but not integrally funny. The slight story of a vapid affair is heavily festooned with *mots* and gags that run on without adding up; after a while they seem ad hoc, defensive, timid, merely tactical self-depreciations even when Woody is trying to lure us, as Alvy lures Annie, into his language-field. (pp. 622-23)

The whole movie, one feels, is his last word: it should have been called *Alvy Singer.* If Woody couldn't make the kind of chivalrous homage to a woman that (say) Truffaut or Rohmer might have given us, he should at least have had the courage of his neuroses and given us a comedy of miscegenation. . . . What it finally comes to is ninety minutes of coitus interruptus, fun but fruitless. *Annie Hall* may look like a comedy or a romance, but it's really a *tsuris* trap. (p. 623)

M. J. Sobran, Jr., "On the Screen: Boy Meets Shiksa," in National Review *(© National Review, Inc., 1977; 150 East 35th St., New York, N.Y. 10016), Vol. XXIX, No. 20, May 27, 1977, pp. 622-23.*

HARRY M. GEDULD

[Woody Allen in *Annie Hall*] is—delightfully—in top form exposing the cultural stereotypes and clichés, the pretensions, fatuities, and hangups, and above all the jargon, of urban American pseudo-intellectuals. . . . His Alvin Singer brilliantly expresses the absurdity of a contemporary Everyman trying to enact the role of *l'homme moyen sensuel* in the form of an inadequate, self-deprecatory paranoid runt. ("I'm the only guy I know who suffers from penis-envy.") Woody repeatedly reminds us that the modern American male is a *reductio ad absurdum* quivering helplessly under the combined weights of Sigmund Freud and Women's Lib. . . .

Annie Hall's satiric barbs lance a multiplicity of contemporary targets, but the film's essential concern is with the reworking of the old myth of Pygmalion and Galatea. At first, Annie forces a relationship with the reluctant Alvin; but gradually, despite his evident inadequacies, he assumes control and begins to transform her into an educated and self-confident woman. Soon the increasing success of the transformation produces a crucial dilemma: love or independence? . . .

The film offers some novel and topical variations on the old myth. . . . Woody Allen's "Pygmalion" is a divorcee who makes absurdly fumbling efforts to pass himself off as a latter-day worldly-wise Casanova. And while Alvin Singer is not destroyed by his "creation," his involvement with Annie Hall does, in fact, reveal his many weaknesses in contrast with her growing strength. Shaw's *Pygmalion* shows the gradual elevation of Eliza to equality with Higgins, but *Annie Hall* offers us instead a new Galatea nonchalantly turning her back on a Pygmalion who seems too ridiculous even to be pathetic. (p. 54)

Harry M. Geduld, "Woody Allen and Galatea," in The Humanist *(copyright 1977 by the American Humanist Association; reprinted by permission), Vol. XXXVII, No. 4, July-August, 1977, pp. 54-5.*

GEOFF BROWN

In some ways, *Annie Hall* . . . is Woody Allen's first film; . . . his technical and narrative assurance has reached a new level, and there has never before been so much concentration on the comic's own personality, outlook and phobias. . . .

Allen's concerns and comic apparatus have been drastically simplified. The elaborate parody mechanisms of *Sleeper* and *Love and Death* are here abandoned. . . . The setting in *Annie Hall* is largely Manhattan, its apartments, sidewalks, bookshops, tennis clubs, analysts' offices, restaurants, park benches and cinemas—all of which provide mainly neutral backgrounds for the verbal gymnastics of the leading couple. . . . Outside Manhattan, however, the environments are seen through more satirical eyes: Alvy's Brooklyn home, beneath a roller-coaster; Annie's home in Wisconsin, straight from a Norman Rockwell painting; and, especially, the scenes in Los Angeles. 'It's like living in Munchkinland!' Alvy tells his friend and manager Rob. . . . And so it seems all is fakery and sunbaked glitter. . . .

There is a simple reason for these changes in treatment: Manhattan is the home ground of Allen's humour, and under its inspiration the verbal gags completely dominate over the visual. The topics, however, are all as before: like his forerunners Alvy is haunted by love and death, depression and psychoanalysis, the fact of being a Jew, the importance of literature and learning . . . , the cultural hogwash talked in cinema queues and at parties. But these topics have never been so clearly centred round Allen himself. For the rise of the bespectacled, slight, nervous comedian Alvy Singer directly parallels the rise of Woody Allen. . . . Indeed, the concentration on Allen and the daily round of a New York Jewish comic makes one fear for the film's communicability, both now and in the future. (p. 256)

Yet behind this top layer of dazzling quips and their accompanying stylistic flourishes (ranging from a cartoon fantasy and thought-revealed subtitles to Alvy and Annie revisiting their past like characters out of Arthur Miller) there lies a solid foundation—the trials and tribulations of the comic outlook and its effect on human relationships. . . . When comedians mirror their own habits and frustrations without the customary distortions of invented characters and plots, the results are usually more embarrassing than funny. Woody Allen, however, has miraculously made his most personal film his funniest. (pp. 256-57)

Geoff Brown, "Film Reviews: 'Annie Hall'," in Sight and Sound *(copyright © 1977 by The British Film Institute), Vol. 46, No. 4, Autumn, 1977, pp. 256-57.*

OWEN S. RACHLEFF

Woody Allen's somber *Interiors* is unlike any other of his films and accordingly does not poke fun at Jewishness. It may, nevertheless, concern modern Jewish dynamics evident in the lives of a very urbane, arty family that forms the nucleus of this film. Theirs is the kind of supposed Jewish struggle with sexuality, venality, creativity, and psychoneurosis that appears in specifically Jewish characters described by Roth, Potok, and Bellow. (p. 59)

[The] almost stereotypical characters, usually grist for Woody Allen's pulverizing mill, are in no way reduced to the usual antics. Although it owes much to Ingmar Bergman, something to Chekhov, and a great deal more to Woody Allen's untapped sensitivities, the film does not belong in any way to the comedian's well-known satirical genre. As some have lamented, indeed, there are no jokes in the entire picture. . . . In fact, there is a great deal to mark this movie as a beautiful landmark, particularly in the way Allen—like a spider spinning a web—captures the fragile truth of the psychoanalytical seventies. True, there may be no jokes (there are some laughs, to be sure), but there are enough droplets of brilliance . . . to give the web a shimmering as well as delicate appearance. And there are subtle undercurrents as well, one of which, the possible Jewishness of the characters, still intrigues me.

Woody Allen is obviously very much affected by his Jewishness; it is an inevitable leitmotif that surfaces in all his work—literary, cinematic, on the nightclub stage. Even when it's clearly uncalled for, there it is. . . . So long as Woody is being jocular, Jewishness per se will emerge and range from charming and telling references to hints of offensiveness and scorn. . . . The Jewish tonality [in *Interiors*] is so subtle it might even be missed. Mostly it shows itself with Eve, a formidable character. . . .

Was Eve a rather more elegant but nonetheless hysterical version of Sophie Portnoy, the proverbial Jewish mama-monster of Philip Roth? The "television scene," with its unctuous evangelist, seems to hint at this and more, and consequently imputes Jewishness to the rest of the film. . . .

Interiors, as the title suggests, requires blueprints and much studying of corners and curves, for in those places lurk subtle symbols and shadows and old leitmotifs, newly lit. (p. 60)

Owen S. Rachleff, "Leitmotifs," in Midstream *(copyright © 1978 by The Theodor Herzl Foundation, Inc.), Vol. XXIV, No. 10, December, 1978, pp. 58-62.*

TED WHITEHEAD

For two years, reviewing theatre and cinema, I've managed to avoid the use of the word 'Art', because I believe that the word has come to signify little more than some vague cultural blessing and that there are other more specific criteria by which we can judge what any particular play or film is actually doing. But there's no avoiding Art with Woody Allen's new film *Interiors*. . . . After moving from the first phase of satiric farce with the poignant comedy of *Annie Hall,* Allen now strips off the joker's mask completely and reveals the face of the tortured artist beneath. But the face is not Woody Allen's, but Ingmar Bergman's. The debt to Bergman shows not only in the film's formal qualities, its austere composition and self-conscious elegance, but in its themes of personal isolation and death, and crucially in its attitude to art, which is seen as something refined, exquisite and in a sense inhuman. The story concerns a well-heeled WASP family in New England. . . . Arthur is a quiet, decent, responsible sort of man, while Eve is the perfect wife and mother—a little tense and introverted, perhaps, but then she's an artist. If Arthur provides the loot, she provides the aesthetic sense that makes their home a model of gracious affluence. (pp. 38-9)

The contrast between Eve and the new wife, Pearl . . . is at the heart of the film, Pearl is described by Joey as a 'vulgarian', and I suppose she is in the sense that her responses are simple and uncomplicated, more sensual than cerebral, and taste to her is a function of the tongue and not of the sensibility. She likes eating and drinking, and music and dancing, and she wows the boys with card tricks—in other words, she's a lot of fun, and that's something Arthur has had very little of. If for Arthur she represents an escape from bourgeois respectability, for Woody Allen she seems to offer an alternative to the neurotic, self-conscious, obsessive figure of the artist—or at least of his type of artist.

Her role as life-force is symbolised in the melodramatic finale. . . .

[If] the clouds that gather over the Long Island house seem peculiarly Swedish, the theme of the tension between the vulgar and the fine is authentically American and authentically Allen, now in the costume of tragedy. (p. 39)

Ted Whitehead, "Art Movie," in The Spectator *(© 1978 by* The Spectator; *reprinted by permission of* The Spectator*), Vol. 241, No. 7849, December 9, 1978, pp. 38-9.*

TIM PULLEINE

The increasing directorial ambition evinced by *Sleeper* and

Love and Death probably made it only to be expected that Woody Allen would seek to direct a movie not centred on himself as performer, and the elements of psychodrama in *Annie Hall* similarly made predictable a venture outside the realms of comedy. The evidence of *Interiors* . . . , however, may call into question his wisdom in attempting both aims at once.

As the title implies, *Interiors* is chamber drama. . . . The film's essentially theatrical construction . . . heightens the suspicion that the condition to which *Interiors* aspires is that of Long Island Chekhov, and that the three sisters at the heart of the picture represent a Chekhovian legacy as much as did the trio in *Cries and Whispers*. But where Bergman is able to use this as a starting point for his own inimitable concerns, it is by no means certain where Allen is headed (though it is clearly not in the direction of laughter). (p. 60)

Dramatically and thematically, it is with our response to Renata and Joey that the essential stumbling block to the movie presents itself. Involvement with them is crucially hindered by the fact that the family background is not elaborated in enough detail to let us judge for ourselves the validity of, for instance, Renata's claim that Joey feels guilty for rejecting her mother, or Joey's that Renata is wary of her (Joey) as a competitive threat. And more damagingly still, Allen's delineation of these literary-artistic lives sometimes verges uncomfortably close to unwitting parody. When Renata constantly seeks to convince her husband of his talent as a novelist, or declares that she is preoccupied with death but 'the intimacy of it embarrasses me', or when Joey voices 'a need to express myself, but I don't know what I want to express', we seem to be only a small step away from the memorably pompous culture-vulture of the cinema foyer scene in *Annie Hall*.

We may deduce that what links these characters is a preoccupation with a way of living rather than with living itself. . . . Joey fears that a job she has been offered would cause her to be 'swallowed up in some anonymous lifestyle'. But the implications are never worked through, and it seems significant that one has to turn to the movie's dialogue to evidence such concerns. . . .

[If] Allen has already appeared to stack the deck by making Eve something of a traditional Hollywood *monstre sacrée*, . . . he is guilty of sentimental condescension if he is seeking to posit Pearl as a life-enhancing antidote to the hermetic dilettantism of Renata, Joey and their mother. . . .

Interestingly enough, the themes adumbrated around Pearl are more succinctly developed in the treatment of Flyn, who—patronised overtly by her odious brother-in-law and implicitly by her sisters—proves not only to be more genuine in relating to them but also possesses, judging from her remarks about her career, a more practical and unresentful capacity for ironic self-awareness. This is one of the incidental felicities in *Interiors*. And, as well as the pleasure afforded by Gordon Willis' glowing images, there is in the film—however much it must be accounted a failure—a modesty and a refusal of the fashionable that leave scope for optimism about Allen's future in serious as well as comic movies. One must only hope that in future forays he will not, so to speak, wear a straight face so patently on his sleeve. (p. 61)

Tim Pulleine, "Film Reviews: 'Interiors'," in Sight and Sound *(copyright © 1978-79 by The British Film Institute), Vol. 48, No. 1, Winter, 1978-79, pp. 60-1.*

VERNON YOUNG

Woody Allen, since 1971, if no farther back, had thirsted to make what he thought of as a "European" film, preferably in the monastic style of Ingmar Bergman. Finally he has made it, and contingently it resembles (at least in outline) the particular Bergman number [*Autumn Sonata*] which arrived almost at the same hour of release. (p. 60)

Impressed by the austerity of Bergman's style and by what he reads as Bergman's tragic view of life, he endangered his project at the outset; he was faced with the problem of imposing a Swedish ethos on urban American material. Bergman, since *The Virgin Spring*, has as often as possible shut out not only the world of nature but also the world of things and the world of society at large, so that his agonists can battle nakedly with each other (or with a surrogate God), undistracted by the alternative points of view or the cultural frivolities which tempt the commonality of mankind. Allen's film is far more populous than *Autumn Sonata* or any late film of Bergman; our comprehension of it is not delayed by a level of symbolic reference; it can be summarized as a story line that holds together. Motivation, however, is another matter. If *Autumn Sonata* is ambivalent because Bergman is playing a game with appearances, *Interiors* is eventually ambiguous because the calamities represented are in excess of the cause alleged.

Interiors should have been the tragedy (or even the comedy) of a man's attempt, alternately assisted or opposed by his three daughters, to win his own soul by ridding himself of their mother, his wife. I say "should have been" because Allen's conception of that man is so feeble (in the Bergman tradition of the ineffectual male) . . . that he emerges far less sympathetically than the compulsively meticulous wife. . . . (p. 62)

[The] whole embroilment is distorted by Allen's insistence on telling his story in a style alien to the milieu he provides, transposing the key of an American metropolitan setting into that of the hushed and claustrophobic atmosphere of Bergman's Baltic. . . . [Too much of the dialogue is] the sort of talk which, in earlier Woody Allen vehicles, would have speedily led to a verbal pratfall.

Allen tries harder—perhaps too hard—to keep his settings from becoming as cluttered as his language, staging crucial scenes at the dining table, in the bedroom, in an empty church, at a beach house, as a means of exiling the everyday world. . . .

With every sequence he appears to have asked himself, not "How can I best shoot this?" but "How would Bergman shoot it?" And he ends his film with a strict reversion to the Bergman format which, at the same time, summons a whole repertory of understated curtain tableaux, post-Chekhov and Ibsen. (p. 63)

It has been said that the smothering family atmosphere in certain Bergman films appealed to Allen by reason of his special Jewish vulnerability to comparably oppressive parents in his own environment. I would not wish to pronounce on this probability, if probability it is, but I suspect that the driving force behind Allen's wistful Bergman-worship is rather a (Jewish?) love of perfection and a confusion of it with the Less-Is-More aesthetic of Scandinavian reductionism.

Be that as it may, the truth is that it takes more independent imagination, greater cinematic scope, a more vital sense of life-poetry to make *Bonnie and Clyde, Mean Streets,* or *Badlands* than it does to make *Interiors.* Centrally, what *is* Allen's film about? Certainly not about "the meaning of life"—a silly predication for any work of art. And though the rejected wife and mother kills herself, the film is in no awesome way about death. The people involved are not tragic, although some of them would like to be; they tend to be hysterical, obtuse, or pathetically abusive. . . . Is this what makes the film, for Allen, "more personal"?

Interiors is an embarrassing episode in Woody Allen's career, a feeble struggle to escape from his more authentic self, an incredible concession to the snobbish misgiving that comedy is an inferior art. (p. 64)

Vernon Young, "Autumn Interiors," in Commentary *(reprinted by permission; all rights reserved), Vol. 67, No. 1, January, 1979, pp. 60-4.*

ARTHUR SCHLESINGER, JR.

Allen's association with [*Interiors*] has distracted the critics. We read essays wondering why a great comedian should make a movie without a laugh in it or why a Jew should make a drama about a WASP family. All this is surely irrelevant. *Interiors* deserves, like any other movie, to be considered on its intrinsic merits.

Let us therefore purge Woody Allen from our minds and approach *Interiors* as if it had been written by the unknown but gifted X. For the real test is what one would say about it if one never knew that Woody Allen had any connection with it. And the first point a reviewer might well make is that it is a movie about a divorce. . . .

Interiors is certainly the first in a long time to take a hard, close look at this nerve-wracking chapter in so many American lives. . . .

The movie is occasionally too pat, as when the most hostile daughter is saved from drowning by her stepmother's kiss of life. But it is generally superb in its exactness of observation and its breadth of sympathy. I have seen no movie that explores the impact of divorce with such sensitivity to the dilemmas of everyone involved. . . .

Nor has Woody Allen—that name can't be excluded altogether—lost his satiric touch. The pseudo-intellectual cant he has used before to comic effect he uses to dramatic effect here, and his ear is as precise and devastating as ever. Of course his direction has been influenced by Ingmar Bergman. Why not? No one objected when movies were made, for example, in the manner of Lubitsch; and Bergman is a pretty good influence if your object is to render presumably civilized adults under acute emotional stress. *Interiors* seemed to me a remarkably intelligent movie. The unknown X has a considerable talent for high seriousness.

Arthur Schlesinger, Jr., "Days of High Seriousness," in Saturday Review *(© 1979 by Saturday Review; all rights reserved; reprinted with permission), Vol. VI, No. 1, January 6, 1979, p. 46.*

ANDREW SARRIS

Woody Allen's *Manhattan* has materialized out of the void as the one truly great American film of the '70s. It tops *Annie Hall* in brilliance, wit, feeling, and articulation, though it is less of a throbbing valentine to a lost love, and more of a meditation on an overexamined life. As a carnival of the sexes, it can be mentioned in the same breath with such previous masterpieces as Max Ophuls's *Madame de . . .* , Jean Renoir's *La Regle du Jeu,* Ingmar Bergman's *Smiles of a Summer Night,* and Preston Sturges's *The Lady Eve* and *The Palm Beach Story.* . . .

Manhattan is comparable to such epiphanies of my movie-reviewing career as Luis Buñuel's *Viridiana* in 1962, Richard Lester's and the Beatles's *A Hard Day's Night* in 1964, and Eric Rohmer's *My Night at Maud's* in 1970. At a time when even the most discerning film critics seem to be mesmerized by gaudy, growly, weepy, inarticulate firework displays masquerading as movies, Allen has returned us to square one with an authentic talking picture about recognizably motivated human beings. I now suspect that *Interiors,* far from being a detour, was a necessary step in Allen's artistic progression from *Annie Hall* to *Manhattan.* Never in *Manhattan* does Allen compromise his mise-en-scene by enslaving it to a transient and thus ultimately disorienting sight gag. Instead, an ironic counterpoint is established from the outset between the verbal and the visual, between the satire and the romance, between the intellectual perception and the emotional projection. For once, Allen's jokes do not jump off the screen so much as they remain embedded in the mise-en-scene. And yet the jokes are funnier than ever, though the loud guffaws of the past may be replaced by a rippling merriment now that the intervals of nonjokes are so much more engrossing psychologically and dramatically. . . .

Halfway through the movie Allen utters a devastating line that must take its place in film history alongside of Jean Renoir's "Tout le monde a ses raisons" from *La Regle du Jeu.* After Diane Keaton has turned out the lights to have sex, she asks Allen what he is thinking, and he replies that he is bothered by the fact that he has never had a relationship that lasted as long as Hitler's with Eva Braun. This is a blackout line of sorts, and we are not primed for a belly laugh, but as the idea sinks in, the ethical configuration of Manhattan emerges in broad relief, and the desperation of the characters finds its comic correlative.

Allen, like many contemporary directors, is obsessed with death, and he does not hesitate to do a Yorick number with a skeleton in a moment of crisis. Like a self-proclaimed Hebrew prophet, he endows his persona with both a theological and teleological dimension. He courts Keaton in the counterfeit lunar surfaces of the Planetarium. At times he is too much the tour guide to an ultra-touristy New York in which all the fashionable landmarks pop up too conveniently without any spatial logic. But by and large he gets away with the most self-conscious camera conceits imaginable because of the force and strength of the characterizations in their somber setting. (p. 51)

[*Manhattan*] has become a film for the ages by not seeking to be a film for the moment. It is universal by virtue of its being resolutely provincial. (p. 54)

Andrew Sarris, "'S Wonderful," in The Village Voice *(reprinted by permission of* The Village Voice; *copyright © News Group Publications, Inc., 1979), Vol. XXIV, No. 17, April 30, 1979, pp. 51, 54.*

ROBERT ASAHINA

Like most gagmen who earn their living by making fun of people, Woody Allen can recognize the ridiculous in everyone but himself. . . .

Allen's strained seriousness and inadvertent humor are . . . on display in his latest film, *Manhattan*. . . . As always, his writing and directing are aimed at marketing his own virtue, or rather that of his familiar persona, here christened Isaac Davis. . . .

Allen's persona was appealing in the past because he was such a loser; he reassured audiences about their own inadequacies—that nothing succeeds like failure. Beginning with *Annie Hall,* however, the filmmaker—perhaps sensitive to the declining status of "losers" and "victims" in our egocentric age—changed his formula. Now, winning seems to be all there is for his one-time schlemiel, who is unchanged in other respects. (p. 21)

[Davis scores with Mary Wilke] . . . , the on-again off-again mistress of his married best friend. . . . Because Isaac and Mary hate each other at first sight, we know they will presently fall in love. The reasons for their initial dislike, though, are an important clue to the hidden message of *Manhattan*.

When they first meet at an art gallery, Mary—a vaguely "literary" journalist—derides Isaac's preference for plexiglass sculptures she considers "purely derivative"; she also praises some minimalist steel cubes that he had found incomprehensible, expounding on their "negative capability." Later, she mocks what she calls "The Academy of the Overrated"—a group that includes Kierkegaard, Ingmar Bergman, Heinrich Böll, Isak Dinesen, and others who are all heroes to Isaac (and to Allen). It is clear we are supposed to regard her—at least at the start—as irritating or even downright unpleasant; her opinions are expressions of snobbery, rooted in cultural and psychological insecurity. But why should the director take pot shots at his own beliefs—especially by using as a mouthpiece a woman his persona ultimately loves?

A decade ago, when mores were rapidly changing, Allen successfully began to exploit his audiences' *social* insecurity by giving them someone to condescend to—his lovable and "nonthreatening" schlemiel. In the post-"New Sensibility" era, when artistic standards are in disarray or nonexistent, Allen is catering to the widespread *cultural* insecurity by providing—a target. Because the shnook has in the meantime been transformed into a "winner," he can hardly assume the role. The only possible solution is to create a pretentious, trendy intellectual who on the one hand is unsympathetic—so that the Allen persona and Allen himself are spared being labeled pretentious or trendy—and on the other hand speaks in properly highbrow rhetoric—so that Allen cannot be accused of philistinism. To top it all off, Isaac gets to bed Mary, thus establishing his superiority by conquest.

In other words, Allen is an anxious middlebrow. He wants to reassure both his audience and himself that it is really all right to be square, that one should not be intimidated by the highbrows. To this end, the best defense is a good offense—reverse snobbery (like the reverse chic of wearing fatigue jackets). For what counts is not genuine understanding, it is having the right attitudes—as prescribed by Allen, of course, who has a reasonably bright undergraduate's knowledge of art, literature and philosophy.

No wonder the inhabitants of his *Manhattan* are a homogeneous crowd of upper-middle-class, graduate-school-educated writers, critics, professors, and other middlebrows on the fringes of the literary world. These are the people who make it possible to read reviews instead of books, who predigest experience for vicarious intellectual thrill seekers. These are the people Allen pictures in his film because they are also the audience—and will therefore love this movie about themselves. (pp. 21-2)

At one point, Isaac-Allen describes himself perfectly: "He longed to be an artist but balked at the necessary sacrifices." Until he stops selling out by flattering his audiences, and until he can be serious without undercutting himself a moment later in a paroxysm of middlebrow anxiety, Woody Allen will continue to be a pathetic clown. (p. 22)

Robert Asahina, "Woody Allen's Rotten Apple," in The New Leader *(© 1979 by the American Labor Conference on International Affairs, Inc.), Vol. LXII, No. 12, June 4, 1979, pp. 21-2.*

STUART BYRON

Manhattan is ice cold—on the rocks rather than straight up. It is a movie about cruelty and betrayal among contemporary urban intellectuals, but I've yet to meet a c.u.i. who has flinched at any of it. And it is a movie that is flinchable or nothing; Woody Allen is incapable of the sculptural precision and timing which justify emotional distance in Dreyer or Bresson or even Lubitsch. Allen means to confront us with unpleasant truths—but there is no confrontation, only exposition.

Other recent c.u.i. films have succeeded where Allen fails. There were moments so raw and real in Mazursky's *Blume in Love* and Bergman's *Scenes From a Marriage* that friends of mine had to escape to the lobby for a few minutes. Yet watching *Manhattan,* not once are we moved to look away from the screen. To take one example: Has anyone who's ever broken with a best friend over a mutual lover experienced the matter as bloodlessly as Woody Allen and Michael Murphy do? Here is a film about passion which is wholly devoid of it. . . .

Manhattan's "liberalism" functions only so long as that word is defined along traditional lines, which have come to include "equal rights for women." In the ways that seem important to me in 1979, *Manhattan* is a profoundly conservative movie. In its *sexual* politics, it is shockingly conservative. In its understanding of women, in its view of the possibilities of man-woman relationships, in its attitudes toward sexual viewpoints different from Woody Allen's own, *Manhattan* is more than old-fashioned; it is reactionary. Which would be fine if one could feel that Allen's position on these matters was hard won. But his way of dealing with challenges to his stance is obtuse and superficial—prejudiced, really. And unless you're Griffith making *Birth of a Nation,* great art is unlikely to emerge from prejudice. . . .

From *Take the Money and Run* to *Manhattan,* there is a consistency in the Allen persona. Whether shy with women, as in the early films, or aggressive with them, as in the recent ones, the character Allen portrays always represents common sense. He is correct, morally virtuous, sensible; the others are selfish and ridiculous. . . .

One has only to compare Robert Altman's recent, and very

underrated, *A Perfect Couple,* with *Manhattan* to see the difference between the generosity of a great artist and the mean-spiritedness of a *petit maitre.* Altman, while expressing his commitment to serial heterosexual monogamy, *tries to understand the other options.* . . . Allen, by contrast, appears to believe that his way is the only way.

There is a word for Woody Allen's world-view. The word is "provincial."

Stuart Byron, "He'll Take Dubuque" (reprinted by permission; copyright © Stuart Byron, 1979), in The Village Voice, *Vol. XXIV, No. 23, June 4, 1979, p. 50.*

JOHN SIMON

Manhattan is a profoundly and multifariously dishonest picture. It can be read in both directions, as if it were written simultaneously in English and Hebrew. As *Manhattan,* it is the story of a decent little fellow who shakes off TV commercialism, moves into a more modest apartment, and tries to authenticate his life as an artist. . . .

Read backward, however—and the continuous flip humor demands that it be read thus—*Nattahnam* is all tongue-in-cheek cynicism. Isaac is a bit of a shnook, redeemed only partially by his wisecracks; Mary, though dazzling, is also a fool and a sickie; Tracy has previously had three affairs with boys and is, for all her extolled precocious perspicacity, also childishly uncomprehending—as when she comments about aging TV performers with face-lifts, "Why can't they just age naturally?" Jill and Connie are clever, cold women, obviously created during a milk-of-human-kindness strike; Emily is a cipher—of the kind, incidentally, that no true artist would allow in his film. . . .

Look at that closing speech of Tracy's, in response to Isaac's fear that she will lose her innocence and her love for him: "Six months isn't so long." Very sensible. "Everybody gets corrupted." Is that to be taken at face value—truth from an angel: Tracy's kind of corruption would be merely a civilizing old-world polish on her honesty and wisdom? Or as wry irony: even the cherub looks forward to the world, the flesh, and the devil? In which case, her "You must have a little faith in people" (this to Isaac, who has always had too much faith in people) is the final sardonic twist. Or is it? . . .

Art, to be sure, does not have to provide answers; indeed, the greatest art is probably always ultimately ambiguous, leaving us finally with a question mark. But it also leaves us with insights, epiphanies, a climate of elation in which it is easier to breathe in the perennial problems, more possible to live with them according to our individual lights. *Manhattan,* however, is two-faced rather than ambiguous: both a self-serving exaltation of Allen and his values, and, if one were to challenge them, a perfect set-up for Allen and his collaborator, Marshall Brickman, to snap back: "You simpleton! Don't you see that it's all satire, all a put-on?"

But is it? When Yale and Mary play a cocktail-party intellectuals' game of smirkingly nominating members for "the Academy of the Overrated" . . . , we are clearly to side with Isaac, who makes fun of this nonsense. But later, when Isaac himself dictates to his tape recorder the things that make life worth living . . . , we are patently invited to take this absurd hodgepodge seriously. . . .

Or is Isaac-Allen also a figure of fun? We are, for instance, constantly told about his successes with women, his good looks, his great amatory technique. This is meant partly in jest, but partly also, I am sure, as truth. . . .

But if the film and its hero are a joke, why all this self-adulation and Manhattan-boosting? And if the film is a "serious" comedy, why must Isaac, even at the height of his jealous grief and rage, wisecrack with Yale ("You think you're God!" "I've got to model myself after someone!")? Why must even semi-virginal Tracy accept universal corruption? Why must there be ludicrous dung in the enchanted lagoon? Because Allen is insecure, as no true artist is, but as a fellow who wants to be both Groucho Marx (or Woody Allen) and Bergman (or Mozart, or Cézanne's apples and pears) will be. Having it both ways is not having it at all. (p. 819)

I am not ambivalent. *Manhattan* and *Nattahnam* are bad movies both. (p. 820)

John Simon, "Nattahnam," in National Review *(© National Review, Inc., 1979; 150 East 35th St., New York, N.Y. 10016), Vol. XXXI, No. 25, June 22, 1979, pp. 818-20.*

JOAN DIDION

Self-absorption is general, as is self-doubt. In the large coastal cities of the United States this summer many people wanted to be dressed in "real linen," cut by Calvin Klein to wrinkle, which implies real money. In the large coastal cities of the United States this summer many people wanted to be served the perfect vegetable terrine. It was a summer in which only have-nots wanted a cigarette or a vodka-and-tonic or a charcoal-broiled steak. It was a summer in which the more hopeful members of the society wanted roller skates, and stood in line to see Woody Allen's *Manhattan,* a picture in which, toward the end, the Woody Allen character makes a list of reasons to stay alive. "Groucho Marx" is one reason, and "Willie Mays" is another. The second movement of Mozart's "Jupiter" Symphony. Louis Armstrong's "Potato Head Blues." Flaubert's *A Sentimental Education.* This list is modishly eclectic, a trace wry, definitely OK with real linen; and notable, as *raisons d'etre* go, in that every experience it evokes is essentially passive. This list of Woody Allen's is the ultimate consumer report, and the extent to which it has been quoted approvingly suggests a new class in America, a subworld of people rigid with apprehension that they will die wearing the wrong sneaker, naming the wrong symphony, preferring *Madame Bovary.*

What is arresting about these recent "serious" pictures of Woody Allen's, about *Annie Hall* and *Interiors* as well as *Manhattan,* is not the way they work as pictures but the way they work with audiences. The people who go to see these pictures, who analyze them and write about them and argue the deeper implications in their texts and subtexts, seem to agree that the world onscreen pretty much mirrors the world as they know it. This is interesting, and rather astonishing, since the peculiar and hermetic self-regard in *Annie Hall* and *Interiors* and *Manhattan* would seem nothing with which large numbers of people would want to identify. The characters in these pictures are, at best, trying. They are morose. They have bad manners. They seem to take long walks and go to smart restaurants only to ask one another hard questions. "Are you serious about Tracy?" the Michael Murphy character asks the Woody Allen character in *Manhattan.* "Are you still hung up on Yale?" the Woody Allen character asks the Diane Keaton character. "I think I'm still in love with Yale," she confesses several scenes later. "You are?" he counters, "or you think you are?" All of the characters in Woody Allen pictures not only ask these questions but actually answer them, on camera, and then, usually in another restaurant, listen raptly to third-party analyses of their own questions and answers.

"How come you guys got divorced?" they ask each other with real interest, and, on a more rhetorical level, "why are you so hostile," and "why can't you just once in a while consider my needs." ("I'm sick of your needs" is the way Diane Keaton answers this question in *Interiors,* one of the few lucid moments in the picture.) *What does she say,* these people ask incessantly, what does she say and what does he say and, finally, inevitably, "what does your analyst say." These people have, on certain subjects, extraordinary attention spans. When Natalie Gittelson of *The New York Times Magazine* recently asked Woody Allen how his own analysis was going after twenty-two years, he answered this way: "It's very slow. . .but an hour a day, talking about your emotions, hopes, angers, disappointments, with someone who's trained to evaluate this material—over a period of years, you're bound to get more in touch with feelings than someone who makes no effort."

Well, yes and (apparently) no. Over a period of twenty-two years "you're bound" only to get older, barring nasty surprises. This notion of oneself as a kind of continuing career—something to work at, work on, "make an effort" for and subject to an hour a day of emotional Nautilus training, all in the interests not of attaining grace but of improving one's "relationships"—is fairly recent in the world, at least in the world not inhabited entirely by adolescents. In fact the paradigm for the action in these recent Woody Allen movies is high school. The characters in *Manhattan* and *Annie Hall* and *Interiors* are, with one exception, presented as adults, as sentient men and women in the most productive years of their lives, but their concerns and conversations are those of clever children, "class brains," acting out a yearbook fantasy of adult life. (The one exception is "Tracy," the Mariel Hemingway part in *Manhattan,* another kind of adolescent fantasy. Tracy actually is a high-school senior, at the Dalton School, and has perfect skin, perfect wisdom, perfect sex, and no visible family. Tracy's mother and father are covered in a single line: they are said to be in London, finding Tracy an apartment. When Tracy wants to go to JFK she calls a limo. Tracy put me in mind of an American-International Pictures executive who once advised me, by way of pointing out the absence of adult characters in AIP beach movies, that nobody ever paid $3 to see a parent.)

These *faux* adults of Woody Allen's have dinner at Elaine's, and argue art versus ethics. They share sodas, and wonder "what love is." They have "interesting" occupations, none of which intrudes in any serious way on their dating. Many characters in these pictures "write," usually on tape recorders. In *Manhattan,* Woody Allen quits his job as a television writer and is later seen dictating an "idea" for a short story, an idea which, I am afraid, is also the "idea" for the picture itself: "People in Manhattan are constantly creating these real unnecessary neurotic problems for themselves that keep them from dealing with more terrifying unsolvable problems about the universe."

In *Annie Hall,* Diane Keaton sings from time to time, at a place like Reno Sweeney's. In *Interiors* she seems to be some kind of celebrity poet. In *Manhattan* she is a magazine writer, and we actually see her typing once, on a novelization, and talking on the telephone to "Harvey," who, given the counterfeit "insider" shine to the dialogue, we are meant to understand is Harvey Shapiro, the editor of *The New York Times Book Review.* (Similarly, we are meant to know that the "Jack and Anjelica" to whom Paul Simon refers in *Annie Hall* are Jack Nicholson and Anjelica Huston, and to feel somehow flattered by our inclusion in this little joke on those who fail to get it.) A writer in *Interiors* is said to be "taking his rage out in critical pieces." "Have you thought any more about having kids?" a wife asks her husband in *Manhattan.* "I've got to get the O'Neill book finished," the husband answers. "I could talk about my book all night," one character says. "Viking loved my book," another says.

These are not possible constructions, but they reflect exactly the false and desperate knowingness of the smartest kid in the class. "When it comes to relationships with women I'm the winner of the August Strindberg Award," the Woody Allen character tells us in *Manhattan*; later, in a frequently quoted and admired line, he says, to Diane Keaton, "I've never had a relationship with a woman that lasted longer than the one between Hitler and Eva Braun." These lines are meaningless, and not funny: they are simply "references," the way Harvey and Jack and Anjelica and *A Sentimental Education* are references, smart talk meant to convey the message that the speaker knows his way around Lit and History, not to mention Show Biz.

In fact the sense of social reality in these pictures is dim in the extreme, and derives more from show business than from anywhere else. The three sisters in *Interiors* are named, without comment, "Renata," "Joey," and "Flyn." That "Renata," "Joey," and "Flyn" are names from three different parts of town seems not to be a point in the picture, nor does the fact that all the characters, who are presented as overeducated, speak an odd and tortured English. "You implied that a lot," one says. "Political activity is not my interest." "Frederick has finished what I've already told him is his best work by far." The particular cadence here is common among actors but not, I think, in the world outside.

"Overeducation" is something Woody Allen seems to discern more often than the rest of us might. "I know so many people who are well-educated and super-educated," he told an interviewer for *Time* recently. "Their common problem is that they have no understanding and no wisdom; without that, their education can only take them so far." In other words they have problems with their "relationships," they have failed to "work through" the material of their lives with a trained evaluator, they have yet to perfect the quality of their emotional consumption. Wisdom is hard to find. Happiness takes research. The message that large numbers of people are getting from *Manhattan* and *Interiors* and *Annie Hall* is that this kind of emotional shopping around is the proper business of life's better students, that adolescence can now extend to middle age. Not long ago I shared, for three nights, a hospital room with a young woman named Linda. I was being watched for appendicitis and was captive to Linda's telephone conversations. which were constant. Linda had two problems, only one of which, her "relationship," had her attention. Linda spoke constantly about this relationship, about her "needs," about her "partner," about the "quality of his nurturance," about the "low frequency of his interaction." Linda's other problem, one which tried her patience because it was preventing her from working on her relationship, was acute and unexplained renal failure. "I'm not relating to this just now," she said to her doctor when he tried to discuss continuing dialysis.

You could call that "overeducation," or you could call it one more instance of "people constantly creating these real unnecessary neurotic problems for themselves that keep them from dealing with more terrifying unsolvable problems about the

universe," or you could call it something else. Woody Allen often tells interviewers that his original title for *Annie Hall* was "Anhedonia," which is a psychoanalytic term meaning the inability to experience pleasure. Wanting to call a picture "Anhedonia" is "cute," and implies that the *auteur* and his audience share a superiority to those jocks who need to ask what it means. Superior people suffer. "My emptiness set in a year ago," Diane Keaton is made to say in *Interiors.* "What do I care if a handful of my poems are read after I'm dead. . .is that supposed to be some compensation?" (The notion of compensation for dying is novel.)

Most of us remember very well these secret signals and sighs of adolescence, remember the dramatic apprehension of our own mortality and other "more terrifying unsolvable problems about the universe," but eventually we realize that we are not the first to notice that people die. "Even with all the distractions of my work and my life," Woody Allen was quoted as saying in a cover story (the cover line was "Woody Allen Comes of Age") in *Time,* "I spend a lot of time face to face with my own mortality." This is actually the first time I have ever heard anyone speak of his own life as a "distraction." (pp. 18-19)

Joan Didion, "Letter from 'Manhattan'" (reprinted by permission of Wallace & Sheil Agency, Inc.; copyright © 1979 by Joan Didion), in The New York Review of Books, *Vol. XXVI, No. 13, August 16, 1979, pp. 18-19.*

JAMES MONACO

As a filmmaker, Woody Allen has had to confront many of the same problems as Mel Brooks. There has been an element of spoofery in all his films except *Annie Hall.* In general, he's been able to keep it under better control. His films are about people and ideas as well as movies. Like Brooks, too, he has had to deal with his own comedian's persona. But he started as an actor, and he has appeared in all his films so far (except *What's Up Tiger Lily?,* a success, and *Interiors,* a failure). As a result, his films are not only more cohesive than Brooks's but also—at least in my view—more authentic. (p. 240)

His first directorial outing was *Take the Money and Run* (1969), in which he played the archetypal Allen bungler as crook. The film had a fresh, semidocumentary approach which set it immediately apart from the general comedic stream. Allen's films still benefit from this visual realism, much richer and more engaging than Brooks's glossy, glassy set constructions. *Take the Money and Run* worked as a showcase for the Allen comedy with which audiences had become familiar through his television appearances, but he was just beginning to discover how to translate the monologist's style into cinematic language. Again, the difference is between telling and seeing. During a prison sequence in *Take the Money,* our hero is sadistically sentenced to three days in a sweatbox, with an insurance salesman. Listening to this, you laugh; watching it, you say, "That's Funny."

Each of Allen's next three films had its experimental aspect. *Bananas* (1971 . . .) took the Allen schlemiel out of his native habitat, making him the unlikely hero of a South American revolution. Now the tenuous balance between visual and verbal jokes was further complicated by Woody's newly discovered interest in the art of film. He began sticking in parodic shots and scenes, such as the recreation of the famous *Potemkin* baby-carriage-on-the-steps sequence. Again, whatever laughter the scene elicits depends on recognition. Brooks moved further in this direction as his career progressed. Allen, conversely, discovered that the spoofery very often worked against the basic tone of his comedy. "Many times I've filmed terrific gags," he told an interviewer, "in a kind of arty way, but you always screw up the gag and you always cut it out of the picture." As a result, he developed a strictly functional visual style, to focus attention on the gags. (pp. 241-42)

Allen's film work is carefully thought out, and a close study of his films in sequence would make an excellent course in comic film technique. Each film has been measurably more efficient than its predecessor.

Sleeper (1973 . . .) is Allen as sketch comedian in top form. By now, he had developed some elaborate ideas about what he could and couldn't do with the medium. There are still visual gags (the giant fruit, for example), but most of the comedy depends on the concept. The framework of futurism—Miles Monroe wakes up in 2173, wrapped in aluminum foil—allows him to build a rapid-fire string of comments on the world of 1973, each of which has added humor because it's phrased in the past tense. (p. 243)

The most surprising fact about *Annie Hall* . . . is that it took Woody Allen so long to make it. It is the most obvious and effective solution to all his esthetic problems; it's much closer in spirit to Allen's monologues and prose humor than any of his previous films; and it marks a quantum jump for him as a filmmaker. Comedy as style is rightly superseding comedy as genre, and Allen's performance shtik—the persona he built on television and in night clubs—is neatly integrated into a classically structured, yet refreshingly contemporary narrative. (p. 244)

[We] need comedy, even from a schlump like Woody, who doesn't own a car, or a mantra. Somebody has to be in charge of keeping things in perspective, and Woody Allen does the job exceedingly well.

And *this* is why Allen's long-threatened "serious" film, *Interiors* (1978), is so heartbreakingly disappointing. Coming from another filmmaker, *Interiors* might just have some mild excuses to make for itself. But coming from Woody Allen it looks like a violent act of self-mutilation, and those of us who greatly value his other films, books, plays, articles, and performances react instinctively against the rigid—nearly catatonic—strained seriousness of *Interiors* as if to a personal betrayal. We have depended on Allen for more than ten years now as a champion against just this particular sort of bad-faith artiness and the midcult bourgeois sensibility from which it stems. Now, it seems, not only has Woody gone over to the enemy, but he's apparently been secretly enamored of the opposite camp during the very time we trusted him. (p. 245)

Even if it had been made by someone else—if it were, for example, Ingmar Bergman's first American film (and it is in a way), *Interiors* would be cause for concern. Allen's study in "beiges and earth tones" is the ultimate midcult American movie of the 1970s; it shares all of the failings of that bourgeois sensibility. For these reasons it has considerable historical significance. Fifteen years ago, when the reigning American cultural set was Philistine, *Interiors* wouldn't have been given a second thought by most critics, who would have dismissed it out of hand as some "egghead" nonsense. Now that the dominant cultural sensibility has reached the level of midcult—now that we all know about gourmet cuisine, study "films" rather than "movies" in college, and go to Europe regularly—now *Interiors* is not only acceptable, seeing it is a sign of our own seriousness (and therefore, our class). (pp. 246-47)

On a technical level, *Interiors* is clearly well made, and this is a primary criterion of midcult criticism. More important, it is full of allusions and symbolism of the sort dear to every English teacher's heart. All the colors are muted browns, tans, and grays, see, except this one lady, Pearl, the life force in the film. She wears red. Get it? And her name, too, see, that's symbolic: she gleams, like, among the rest of these tortured people. And there are three sisters. . . . There was this play this Russian writer wrote about these people who could never get to Moscow, and *that* was called *Three Sisters*. And at the end there, where the three sisters, so nicely composed, are staring out the window at the sea (please be ready to talk about Sea Symbolism on Tuesday's exam), and one of them says, "The water's so calm," and the other replies, "Yes, it's very peaceful," and that's the last line of the play—I mean film . . . well, that's an allusion to . . . well, I know it's an allusion to something. I'll think of it. Just a moment.

In the age of midcult, this is what we are taught is art, and no doubt *Interiors* will get steady play on the high-school and college circuit. (p. 247)

No doubt such people as the writers Allen concerns himself with in *Interiors* do exist. All sorts of people exist. The question is, why choose to build a movie around such characters? There is an ethical problem here, too. Except for Pearl . . . , Allen is merciless with his characters. He has designed them as perfect, finished neurotics. He gives them no room to act, to breathe. They can only think, and in thinking suffer. There is no sense of politics here; in fact, politics as a possibility of action is expressly denied: we hear that Fred is a filmmaker working on a film about politics, but the subject intentionally never comes into play.

Yes, *Interiors* is very much like a Bergman film, but in this case, imitation isn't the sincerest form of flattery. Allen's movie is so close to Bergman that it's eerie. . . . Allen's deathly clone has the net effect of making it difficult even to treat Bergman with respect again: we'll always hear the ghosts of *Interiors* murmuring just off-screen. (p. 248)

James Monaco, "The Importance of Being Funny: Comics and Comedians," in his American Film Now: The People, the Power, the Money, the Movies *(copyright © 1979 by James Monaco; reprinted by arrangement with The New American Library, Inc., New York, New York), The New American Library, New York, 1979, pp. 215-48.**

MAURICE YACOWAR

[*What's Up, Tiger Lily?*] abounds with clichés about Orientalism that relate to Allen's Jewish, sex, and loser jokes. All four patterns constitute a central theme: a narrow perspective is being imposed on an alien reality. (p. 116)

[Two] jokes converge when Wing Fat and Shepherd Wong argue over whether Wong looks Chinese or Japanese: the tradition of "But you don't *look* Jewish," and the Occidental's inability to distinguish among Orientals. All these Western-bias jokes about the East emphasize the fact that this film imposes an outsider's perspective on the action, and that such a perspective can only distort its material.

As though further to distort perspective, the film often refers to the fact that it is a film by offering film parodies. For example, Cobra Man not only speaks in a Peter Lorre voice but at one point complains, "Oh, my throat. This Peter Lorre imitation is killing me." . . .

This formal self-consciousness works in several ways. It is another example of the film's disjunction. Just as the soundtrack is always at madcap odds with the action, so the film references undercut any lingering pretense to realism. Furthermore, the obvious disparity between character and role is a variation on the basic point of the film's structure, which is the imposition of an Occidental viewpoint on the Oriental world. (p. 117)

Allen stands apart from the material which he presents in *What's Up, Tiger Lily?* Moreover, he transforms everything he shows by what he says. This interplay between the serious image and the reductive tone is the basic element in all his work—in his parodies, his mock-heroic pretenses, and his ironic persona projection. Seen in this light, almost everything in Allen's later comedy can be found in embryonic form in his first film. (p. 118)

Woody Allen's first complete feature film, *Take the Money and Run,* derived from the style of his monologues. It comprised a series of absurd skits depicting a nebbish's comic attempts to become a master criminal. . . .

More specifically, the film parodies the *cinéma-vérité* documentary film form. Popular in the 1960s, it characteristically attempted to convey the impression of recording life as it happened, without staging or distortion by editing. (p. 120)

[Although] Virgil Starkwell is Allen's familiar loser, the central tension in *Take the Money and Run* derives from Allen's juxtaposition of the supposed realism of *cinéma-vérité* with the romanticism of the gangster-film tradition. Allen contrasts the glories that his hero wishes to emulate with the failure that is his lot. The fact that Virgil may be vulnerable because he wants to be what his myopic eyes see may explain the running gag in which various people—urchins, an iceman, hoodlums, a judge, and finally Virgil himself—smash his glasses. . . .

In its structural similarity to the monologues, this film suggests that Allen was feeling his way into the medium. His parodic themes enable him to exercise the language of film rhetoric and conventions while he learned how film works. (p. 127)

Many of the comic turns [in *Bananas*] are variations on a single theme—the contrast between Inside and Outside. Allen plays his usual role of an outsider who wants to come in from the cold, but here this motif is varied and amplified to become the film's dominant theme. Thus Mellish is much concerned with doors and doorways, symbols of admission/exclusion. (p. 129)

The In and Out metaphor is most explicit in the scene in which Mellish regains consciousness in the rebel camp—"Blood! That should be on the inside"—but the motif occurs everywhere. (p. 130)

[The] film depicts a lunatic world, a world gone bananas. Thus President Mellish and the United States Ambassador converse in clear English but they accept the intercession of an awkward, accented translator—afterward identified as an escapee from an asylum. In addition to implying a general madness, the title relates the film to the noble tradition of banana-peel slapstick comedy.

The most important implication of the title, however, is its association with exploitative politics. San Marcos, a nation of marks or victims, is a banana republic. As the film details the political machinations between America and San Marcos, and between the mutually exploiting factions within the nation itself, this aspect of the title is the most important unifier. For *Bananas* satirizes different kinds of imperialist exploitation. The most obvious kind is political: the cyclical tyrannies of Vargas and Esposito; the American government's abuse of the nation's citizenry; and American interference in San Marcos affairs. Although Allen claims that "*Bananas* was coincidentally political," it has very clear political implications. From Mellish's first appearance in a red-white-and-blue striped shirt, he functions as the muddled, idealistic American citizen. For the bulk of the film he is manipulated and victimized by his own government and that of San Marcos. (pp. 132-33)

The nebbish hero of *Bananas* would like to live by [the idealism of loving, giving, and sunshine], but the bananas world does not nourish those values. *Bananas* satirizes the variety of ways that man conspires to exploit others—politically, religiously, culturally, and romantically. The sense that this exploitation is a lunatic waste of life gives this chaos of comedy its remarkable and sober cohesion. (p. 135)

[*Sleeper*] provides a hilarious slapstick adventure story with a serious underpinning. As the title alerts us, Allen's central metaphor is sleep, which can be taken to represent noncommitment either in one's political or emotional life. (p. 152)

In the tradition of negative utopias, the world to which Miles awakens in 2173 is a cautionary extension of our own; the country is called the Central Parallel of the Americas. The central parallel between Miles's new world and ours is its hedonistic apathy. Lost in the stupor of pleasure, Luna's society literally has a ball (large and silver) on drugs. Sex has been reduced to a mechanical convenience—the orgasmitron—to which a character can repair in mid-sentence for an orgasm—partner optional. As the characters are lost in their pursuit of pleasure, the joke about the cloning of the leader quite literally posits a society that is led by the nose.

Luna's pleasure-seeking friends are contrasted to the rebels and to the activists who revive Miles. While they do not convert Miles to political commitment, they do awaken him to the realization that his own survival depends on awareness and activity. . . .

Sleeper warns against the loss of human personality, individuality, and vulnerability, by positing an age of imposed equality, technological dominance, and the replacement of human responsibility with the debasing efficiency of the machine. (p. 153)

The Dostoyevskian opening [of *Love and Death*] dwindles into bathetic comedy. This device, bathos, is the primary source of unity and meaning in the film. Throughout *Love and Death,* an elevated expectation is established only to be comically deflated. As a result man seems too small a creature to assume the mantle of heroic philosophy woven by the great writers. (p. 159)

[The] film's title promises the profound ether of the Russian novel but Allen's literary expressions in the film are reductive. . . .

Allen's major theme in *Love and Death* [is that] philosophical and literary speculation are essentially irrelevant to the business of living. To this end Allen continually introduces philosophical passages only to turn away from them in favor of man's basic appetites—food and sex—the drives by which man ensures his survival both individually and generically.

Allen's deflation of profundity often involves religious subjects. Thus Boris demands that God prove His existence with a miracle, like the traditional parting of the seas or—more practically, perhaps—by making "my Uncle Sasha pick up a check." . . . What begins as a traditional statement of religious quest is deflated by the practical concerns of the modern, urban intellectual's struggle to reconcile old faith with his present education and needs. As in Bergman's work, the voice of God cannot be heard; but Allen fills the silence with one-liners. (pp. 162-63)

Annie Hall seems more fruitfully located in the myth of Pygmalion than in Allen's life story. It is the story of an artist who falls in love with his own creation and loses her when she blossoms into full life. (p. 172)

The power of art to compensate for the limitations of life is the primary theme of *Annie Hall.* This concern happens to be central to the first book that Alvy buys Annie, Ernest Becker's *The Denial of Death*. . . . Alvy's gift . . . raises the specter of man's death, of his inability to resist the processes of time and loss.

That Annie has not contemplated death is dramatized in her emotionally uncertain story about the old man who died in a fit of narcolepsy while waiting in line for his free war-veterans' turkey. In this anecdote, death is an amusing, puzzling, vaguely unsettling continuation of the sleepy, passive life. As Annie does not see death as a unique and overwhelming problem, she is confused by her own story and uncertain both as to what it means and why she feels compelled to tell it. (p. 179)

Even as a boy, Alvy was aware of man's doom. The lad's sense of not just man's mortality but the limited life of the universe resisted Dr. Flicker's advice that "We've got to try and enjoy ourselves while we're here, huh? Huh?"—he laughs, smokes, and coughs. Allen cuts to the Singer home, which quakes under the impact of hedonists blithely enjoying a roller coaster ride, while Alvy ponders his blood-red and quivering bowl of tomato soup. Alvy's consciousness of death prevents his enjoying the pleasures known by simpler souls. For Allen, the unexamined death is not worth living. Therefore he contemplates death and loss, and reaffirms the values of life, art, and love.

This theme is supported by the striking liberties that Allen takes with narrative convention in *Annie Hall.* As if to demonstrate man's need to control and to reshape reality, he violates various principles of film rhetoric. For example, his opening direct address denies the usual gap between film-image and audience. (pp. 179-80)

Alvy's statement on the fluid state of photographic rhetoric may also justify Allen's liberties with form: "The medium enters in as a condition of the art form itself." Both as he confronts death and loss, and as he contemplates his art form, Allen exercises the freedom of a life and art in flux. Alvy's young classmates admitting their adult failures, Annie's recollection of narcoleptic George, Alvy's closing montage of scenes with Annie from earlier in the film, Annie and Alvy revisiting scenes from their past, indeed all Allen's liberties with film rhetoric assert the power of art in the struggle against the transience of love and life. All are denials of death. (p. 180)

Alvy literally uses movies as a means of avoiding problems in his real life. A tension with Annie is deflected into a quarrel over whether or not to enter a theater showing Bergman's *Face to Face* . . . once the screening has begun. Later he prevents a useful opportunity for her to see Tony Lacy by going yet again to see Ophuls's *The Sorrow and the Pity*. . . .

Indeed one could take all the film references in *Annie Hall* as the coordinates of Allen's relationship to film. If the *Snow White* sequence expresses Alvy's infantilism, it also expresses the abiding influence that art has on one's life. The Ophuls film relates to the hero's Jewish sense of alienation, but also represents one function of film: to confront issues of political and historical significance, and to provide an understanding of the past. The Bergman references represent the use of the medium to explore the artist's psychological nature. (p. 182)

More generally, the *Snow White* and Ophuls inserts represent the artist's social function, in which he speaks to and for his community, while the Bergman and Fellini context represents the use of art to express and to explore the artist's private tensions. These four coordinates embody the balance between personal experience and general metaphor that makes *Annie Hall* the culmination of Allen's work, especially in its inflection of his persona. The film references also confirm the self-reflexive stance of the film: "the medium enters in as a condition of the art form itself."

Annie Hall deals with the use of art as a means of confronting man's helplessness before time, loss, and death. (pp. 182-83)

Allen's use of art as a means of confronting death is consistent with Becker's argument [in *The Denial of Death*] that the artist's work "justifies" him by "transcending death by qualifying for immortality": "he lives the fantasy of the control of life and death, of destiny, in the 'body' of his work." . . .

As Becker defines it, Annie would represent Alvy's "romantic solution" to his anxiety about death. Man fixes "his urge to cosmic heroism onto *another person* in the form of a love object" and looks to that love partner for "the self-glorification" that he needed in his innermost nature. (p. 184)

[The Becker context is confirmed by Allen's choice of title. We can read it as Alvy's dedication to Annie.] Alvy's treasuring homage to his lost love becomes Allen's melancholy but affirmative homage to lost life and time. Annie Hall is a character as charming, as absurd, and as elusive as life itself. She embodies Alvy's denial of death through romantic love, and Allen's through art. (p. 185)

[*Manhattan* is Woody Allen's] most lyrical and emotional film to date. Although it may not be as complex as *Annie Hall, Manhattan* is a magnificent film, subtle both in expression and feeling. (p. 197)

[The] film details the professional and romantic compromises by which man avoids confronting his insignificance in the cosmos and his inability to control his fate. Both concerns are familiar from Allen's earlier work.

The film's dominant theme is man's need for personal integrity in a decaying culture. (pp. 197-98)

In *Manhattan* Allen continues his satire against man's foolish applications of logic and culture. Hence the skulls when Yale rationalizes his betrayal of Isaac. Often there is a comical discrepancy between what the characters know and what they can effectively use in their lives. As Isaac admits, "When it comes to relationships with women I'm the winner of the August Strindberg Award." Although he still wants her himself, he warns Yale that Mary is "the winner of the Zelda Fitzgerald Emotional Maturity Award." Both quips combine intellectual knowledge with emotional deficiency. . . . Man's culture is no defense against his greatest dangers. Greater truths are told by the heart and the senses than by the mind. . . . Tracy's last line [to Isaac], "You have to have a little faith in people," is really a call to trust his instincts. Tracy's own faith in her relationship with Isaac overrides her sense that "maybe people weren't made for long relationships," but for a "series of relationships with different links."

Though unconventional, Isaac is a character of exemplary integrity. (pp. 200-01)

The theme of integrity relates to the feel of the film. As Isaac describes himself as "a non-compromiser" who is "living in the past," the film assumes a rigorous, classical spirit from its straightforward romantic narrative, its resolute black-and-white photography, and its George Gershwin score. (p. 202)

Manhattan opens with a three-minute abstract sequence. . . . In describing the city, Isaac's hero—and so Allen's—projects his various moods and conceptions of himself onto the setting. When in the mellow dawn Isaac tells Mary "This is really a great city. I don't care what people say, I'm really knocked out," this is a tribute not to any real Manhattan but to the mood between Mary and Isaac, which the city at that point seems to embody.

Similarly the setting offers both elegant beauty and the rough streets, with a citizenry "desensitized by noise, music, drugs, and garbage." The city is in constant change, as one scene of a demolition crew at work reveals. But which of the innumerable and contradictory aspects will characterize the setting is the individual's choice. (p. 203)

As an emblem of moral and aesthetic choices, Manhattan means something rather different in *Manhattan* than it meant when Annie Hall compared the insular Alvy Singer to it ("this island unto yourself"). In *Manhattan* Allen's hero reconciles a compromised, new Manhattan with his old idealized one and extends his rigorous ethics into a romance that exceeds logical and conventional limits. Despite the familiar Jewish, sexual and paranoia jokes, Isaac is Allen's most competent and confident role. (p. 205)

Maurice Yacowar, in his Loser Take All: The Comic Art of Woody Allen *(copyright © 1979 by Frederick Ungar Publishing Co., Inc.), Ungar, 1979, 243 p.*

Robert Altman

1925-

American filmmaker.

With the release of *M*A*S*H* in 1970, Altman won critical praise for his innovation and his artistry. However, the very techniques which brought him this acclaim, such as obscure themes and meandering plot lines, have also kept his films from wide audience appeal.

For ten years Altman directed, produced, and wrote for television, working on episodes for such popular series as *Alfred Hitchcock Presents* and *Bonanza*. In 1967 he directed a film called *Countdown*, starring a relatively unknown actor named James Caan. Even though he was not allowed final editing decisions on the film (and for this reason has subsequently disavowed it), it is generally considered far better than most of the other science fiction films of that era. After he directed *That Cold Day in the Park*, which also drew lukewarm notices from the critics, producer Otto Preminger asked him to direct *M*A*S*H*. According to some reports, however, Altman was chosen after fifteen other directors declined the offer. The popularity of *M*A*S*H*, an anti-war film brimming with satirical one-liners and dedicated but zany army doctors, was Altman's means to artistic and financial freedom. His later films have been praised for the qualities that are typically Altman: overlapping dialogue and sound effects, light humor, an iconoclastic view of traditions, and a camera which, moving constantly and recording from a distance, keeps the viewer somewhat emotionally remote from the characters.

Altman's popularity with actors is largely because of the artistic freedom he allows them. Much of the dialogue is improvised, either in rehearsals or during final shooting. In *Nashville* his actors and actresses wrote the songs they were to perform. It may be this personal attitude towards the actors, or his multitextured sound tracks, or his off-balance characters, or his iconoclastic attitude which has made Altman famous. For whatever reason, he has the admiration of film critics. As Andrew Sarris has written: "[Altman is] considered by many critics to be the quintessential director of the '70s." Yet although he speaks eloquently of the decade to the critics, the meagerness of his public following has always cast a shadow on that distinction. (See also *Contemporary Authors*, Vols. 73-76.)

DAVID ROBINSON

[*The James Dean Story*] breaks new ground by its purely documentary approach; the way with show-business life-stories has always previously been to avoid using the least fragment of authentic material. . . . Apart from a few staged details (most of them unsuccessful) all the material in this film is documentary—stills of Dean at various stages of his life, shots of the places in which he lived, interviews with the people who knew him and worked with him, a tape recording he made of a conversation with his family, a screen-test for *East of Eden*. The weakness of the film arises from the attempt to spin out this material—enough for a good thirty-minute short—to feature-length. In its repetitive analysis of Dean's personality and problems, its overlong interviews and excessive use of stills, the film becomes from time to time tedious, and is forced into pretentious over-writing. . . .

The film really convinces you that it is a serious attempt to probe the character of this extraordinary, talented and undoubtedly tormented young man, with his self-confessed longing for someone to love and for flamboyant success, his sense of isolation and of parental deprivation. If it rarely gets further than a lot of words, it is probably because Dean's real problems, socially and psychologically were at once too involved and too familiar for this sort of discussion.

David Robinson, "'The James Dean Story'," in Sight and Sound *(copyright © 1957 by The British Film Institute), Vol. 27, No. 2, Autumn, 1957, p. 93.*

HOWARD THOMPSON

Say one thing for "Countdown." . . . It makes the moon seem just as dull as Mother Earth.

[It] is simply stultifying. The bulk of it is a slack, cliché-ridden prelude to the climactic space ride, as we see the conditioning of three astronauts at a simulated Cape Kennedy. The lads bound home to their worried wives. "Hey there, give us a smile," is a sample of the dialogue. Finally, one of the men buckles in and roars aloft, thanks to some documentary footage, as the music rumbles ominously and the rest of the cast hang around a winking control board.

By then slow death has already set in, since Robert Altman's direction is almost as listless as the acting of a dreary cast.

Howard Thompson, "'Countdown'," in The New York Times *(© 1968 by The New York Times*

Company; reprinted by permission), May 2, 1968, p. 57.

MICHAEL DEMPSEY

Obscure dramas, laden with opaque relationships, carefully developed (yet still incomprehensible) motifs, latent themes, and inexplicable deeds, seem to be the newest cinematic fad. . . . The latest and by far the worst specimen is *That Cold Day in the Park*. . . . Altman's direction runs to fancy reflection shots, blurry transitions, and ponderous camera movement. He strains to be ornate but cannot relate his devices to his heroine's subjectivity. Whereas Losey gave us uneasy comedy, Clouzot compassionate dissection, and Chabrol cool elegance, Altman supplies logy murkraking. . . . [To] become a good director he must stop mistaking half-baked mannerisms for psychological profundity. It is one thing to stylize emotions or to seek metaphors, outlandish or otherwise, for their terrifying extremities; it is quite another to make freaks of your characters, as though loneliness were an exotic disease.

Michael Dempsey, "Short Notices: 'That Cold Day in the Park'," in Film Quarterly *(copyright 1969 by The Regents of the University of California; reprinted by permission of the University of California Press), Vol. XXIII, No. 1, Fall, 1969, p. 56.*

WILLIAM JOHNSON

Mash (as I'll call [*M*A*S*H*] for short) is a comedy at which you may very well do not just a double but a quadruple take. . . . (p. 38)

What makes *Mash* outstanding—and as something more than a wacky comedy—is the richness of its texture. The characters stroll, run, interweave among the tents of their unit; dust swirls around them; the camera pans and cuts to seemingly random details. Meanwhile, on the sound track, lines of dialogue overlap or are casually tossed away; the PA system continually breaks in with an odd announcement or the Japanese version of an American popular song. Many films these days impose quick cuts and overlapping dialogue on what are basically four-square, linear scripts, and thus produce an irritating effect of contrivance. *Mash* stands out because—with the exception of the fake suicide and Japanese sequences . . .—the incidents and dialogue in [Ring Lardner, Jr.'s] script are ideally suited to the dense, elliptical style with which Altman has put them on film. (p. 39)

The dialogue has an almost Proustian richness, with asides and fragmentary exchanges which may easily be missed at a first viewing. In a rapid throwaway line, the general refers to "the dark days before Pearl Harbor." . . .

With one or two exceptions, even the most broadly conceived characters are something more than stereotypes, and they create a sense of living their own lives beyond the context of the film. There is still more richness of variety among the characters as a group. . . .

The Mash personnel are seen in special, once-in-a-lifetime circumstances. They are in the army, yet insulated from the full rigor of its discipline. At the same time, thanks to the army, they are freed of their everyday responsibilities. . . . To the extent that military bureaucracy impinges on Mash, it only heightens the enchantment, creating an Alice in Wonderland setting in which there are continual cries of "Off with their heads!" but no executions.

The fragile uniqueness of these circumstances is reflected in Mash's physical setting: tents and huts which could be dismantled in a few hours, dusty tracks which a few days of wind and rain could obliterate. . . .

Underlying the film is the awareness that time changes all things. One of the Mash officers, a white Southerner, has become accustomed to living and working with a black surgeon; on being discharged he says goodbye with the casual words, "See you around," and the black replies, "It's possible." The exchange makes one realize that, in fact, they are unlikely ever to meet again. (p. 40)

In short, *Mash* is not really about army life or rebellion or any of its other ostensible topics: it is about the human condition. And that's why it is such an exciting comedy. (p. 41)

*William Johnson, "Reviews: 'M*A*S*H'," in* Film Quarterly *(copyright 1970 by The Regents of the University of California; reprinted by permission of the University of California Press), Vol. XXIII, No. 3, Spring, 1970, pp. 38-41.*

DAVID HUTCHISON

[In] their efforts to give [*That Cold Day in the Park*] what they believe to be contemporary audience appeal the makers have injected a vast dose of ill-assorted spices into what could have been a small, well-observed and unsentimentalised modern *Marty*. Included are the apparently essential ingredients of: nudity and sex, with a detailed examination at a birth control clinic, hints of incest, and prostitution; contemporary stock characters such as a draft dodger and hippie type drop-outs; and of course a pot smoking sequence. All these ingredients are in this context unnecessary embellishments which add little to the story and seem to have been included solely with an eye to the box office—a gesture which hasn't paid off. (p. 85)

Despite the weaknesses of the script the American director Robert Altman . . . keeps one's attention from wandering; although he is unable to create the necessary sense of tension and claustrophobia to make the plot's wilder flights of fancy believable. A number of his stylistic touches, including the unnecessary use of the hand-held camera and self-conscious and laboured crosscutting in the scene of the doctor's proposal to Frances, are irritating; but he uses colour intelligently to create atmosphere. . . . (p. 88)

David Hutchison, "'That Cold Day in the Park'" (© copyright David Hutchison 1970; reprinted with permission), in Films and Filming, *Vol. 16, No. 9, June, 1970, pp. 85, 88.*

JAN DAWSON

[If there's one moral that can safely be drawn from the succession of gags and incidents which provide M*A*S*H's] sprawling narrative structure, it's that inflexible attitudes to war (chauvinistic, religious, bureaucratic or heroic) lead straight to the strait-jacket. (p. 161)

[Much of M*A*S*H's] ironic tension derives from the contrast between the life-saving activity of the doctors and the destructive impulse of war. And this idea comes closer than most to being spelled out when two recalcitrant surgeons commandeer a Japanese military hospital to treat a local whore's baby: 'We stumbled on him. We didn't want him, but we couldn't back away from him.' But stronger though less explicit than the contrast between medicine and militarism is that between soldier and civilian. . . . And one suspects the real source of official displeasure with the film is the way its enlisted characters obdurately persist in behaving like civilians. (pp. 161-62)

It's not just the rhetoric of Church and Army that receives the considerable weight of the script's satire, but also that of traditional war films. Throughout the proceedings an incompetent Tannoy (the most fully developed machine-character since the *2001* computer) announces such movies as *Halls of Montezuma,* whose inflated publicity blurbs stand in sharp counterpoint to the matter-of-fact realism which even shifts from irony to caricature cannot obscure: the amazing throwaway performances from the trio of surgeons . . . ; the muted photography with its preponderant colours of camouflage-green and faded crimson (many of the gaudier scenes are shot through dirty windows) and marked preference for medium shots; the bedlam of the soundtrack, with overlapping dialogue and everybody talking at once.

But beyond analytic observations, M*A*S*H demands to be taken, on its own empirical terms, as probably one of the most irreducibly funny films ever made. (p. 162)

*Jan Dawson, "'M*A*S*H'," in* Sight and Sound *(copyright © 1970 by The British Film Institute), Vol. 39, No. 3, Summer, 1970, pp. 161-62.*

JAN DAWSON

Disconcertingly, after the tuneless rendering of the Star Spangled Banner that introduced *Brewster McCloud,* or the 'Tokyo Rose' transmissions that lent an insane kind of musical continuity to *M*A*S*H,* it is Leonard Cohen's gentle ballad 'The Stranger' that both introduces and accompanies Robert Altman's latest film, *McCabe and Mrs. Miller*. . . . Disconcertingly but appropriately, to the point where one suspects Altman of extrapolating his scenario from the song rather than from the Edmund Naughton novel on which he and Brian McKay based their script. The film stubbornly defies analogies or easy pigeon-holing; but its mood is closer to that of Cohen's writing, with its transitions from obscenity to finely wrought metaphor in the evocation of fear, tentatively raised hopes and final impenetrable loneliness, than to anything one had come to expect from Altman. . . .

The jovial black absurdity of Altman's earlier films, with their chaotic depiction of both licensed and unlawful lunacy, here darkens into a virtually existentialist notion of the Absurd. Though the jokes still fall as thick and fast, it is the film's muted but unanswerable sadness that predominates. . . .

Despite the stock characters of itinerant gambler and tough madam, both perversely refusing to conform to type, and the climactic gunfight that in the event proves disturbingly anti-climactic (photographed like much of the film through a pointilliste snow, and with none of the townsfolk even aware that it's happening), the West provides Altman with considerably more than a formal structure. . . .

There is a sense of the transitory about all the relationships in the film, and the sets echo this: makeshift buildings always in construction or collapse; a church which rises throughout the film only to be finally gutted by fire. The weather, too, is unusually capricious, conspiring with the giant forests and empty landscapes to emphasise man's precarious footing in nature, caught and held in our last glimpse of McCabe's body being transformed and then obliterated by the snow. The very accuracy of the turn of the century period detail implies not just that these things shall pass, but that they have passed. Even the consistent mistiness of the camerawork, like the opium to which Constance resorts to face the world, establishes the characters as lying just beyond our help or reach.

Then, too, the West provides Altman with material for extending his satire of American attitudes. It reveals an ideology and an economic system in the making, as McCabe's route from gambler to speculator, and final extinction at the hands of big business, takes him through a capsule version of the economic history of the United States. The exploitation of people and feelings is somehow an extension of a necessary exploitation of the land itself—an all too fragile and illusory defence against annihilation. . . .

As befits a hymn to vanquished individualism, *McCabe and Mrs. Miller* is built around the uneasy relationship between its title characters—a relationship as makeshift and ephemeral as everything else in the film.

Jan Dawson, "'McCabe and Mrs. Miller'," in Sight and Sound *(copyright © 1971 by The British Film Institute), Vol. 40, No. 4, Autumn, 1971, p. 221.*

ROBERTA RUBENSTEIN

[What] is Altman's *Brewster McCloud* really *about*? The most obvious idea of the film is, of course, the fantasy of flying. As the Lecturer intones at the film's opening, ". . . the desire to fly has been ever-present in the mind of Man. . . . Was the dream to attain the ability to fly, or was the dream the freedom that true flight seemed to offer Man?" This question is the "score," or major *leitmotif,* of the film—the main theme upon which subsequent variations are orchestrated. From the opening sequence, throughout nearly every scene of the film to its finale, the ideas of flight, freedom, and constraint are developed, each with its own further variations. (p. 46)

Even granted [the] asides on contemporary society and its ills, it would be easy enough to dismiss *Brewster McCloud* as an entertaining fantasy. It is that, of course, but it is more than that; the ultimate effect of the film, which emerges from the comedy itself, is serious. The fantasy of flying/freedom touches a yearning which we all share, in its promise of physical release and freedom from psychological restraint as well. Yet Brewster himself is a victim of his own cage. . . . His obsession with flight deludes him into believing that there are no social or ethical restraints upon him—that he is a kind of superman for whom murder is no more than removal of obstacles in the way of his goal. And, beneath the social implications of the film, one finds even deeper mythical themes: the hubris of the quest for flight/freedom which Brewster shares with his spiritual ancestors, Icarus and Daedalus, along with the initiation into adulthood, with its attendant necessary restraints on absolute freedom and the fantasy of omnipotence. (pp. 47-8)

It is not a simple film, nor is Brewster a simple "hero" who comes to a tragic end. He is ambiguously innocent and trusting and yet immoral and destructive. He is tempted by the superhuman urge to fly and destroyed by his own human weaknesses—his physical and psychic limitations.

The visual image of Brewster's first (and last) flight in the Astrodome expands the several themes of the film to their widest meanings, their greatest crescendos: even in flight, he is still inside a cage. In the mythical "fall" and in the actual fall which is Brewster's death, the audience comes to know that to destroy those who build cages does not insure that we ourselves can fly; the quest for pure freedom can never be fulfilled because we carry within us the seeds of our own destruction. (pp. 48-9)

Roberta Rubenstein, "Reviews: 'Brewster McCloud'," in Film Quarterly *(copyright 1971 by The Regents of the University of California; reprinted by permission of the University of California Press), Vol. XXV, No. 2, Winter, 1971-72, pp. 44-9.*

JACKSON BURGESS

The "spoof" . . . is only one form of American movies' film-consciousness. Somewhere this side of burlesque, connected to it, lies a distinctively American kind of film which also works with conventional film-styles but instead of deflating *or* inflating them tries to domesticate them. A stock plot and stock characters, even stock editing, are set forth with a wealth of gritty, sometimes squalid detail. At their best, these films set up a resonance between the ideal values of the convention and the homely ordinariness of their settings, properties, and dialogue. . . . The film convention thus enclosed is not shown up, debunked, burlesqued, or otherwise patronized: it is, if a word must be found, *actual*-ized—i.e., supplied with actuality. . . .

The comic strain is always important in the genre, and it is always a threat to the director's equilibrium. At best, two attitudes toward the characters are juxtaposed and kept in balance in a way that informs and complicates both of them. . . . (p. 49)

Robert Altman's *McCabe and Mrs. Miller* is a near-perfect example of the type. (p. 50)

Every image is an homage to the "it-ness" of life, to the feel and look and use and enjoyment of physical existence: rarely has the weather and the progress of the seasons been more meticulously attended to in a film *without* investing it with some symbolic or sentimental importance, and the same matter-of-fact respect is accorded to *things* such as underwear, furniture, and hats (the hats border on the bizarre, and yet every one of them is perfectly all right, or even just right). A footbridge, a suit of underwear, the very boards of McCabe's unfinished saloon, are relished and celebrated in their ordinariness, and lend their solidity to the quirks and "ideas" and actions of the characters—especially the minor characters. (p. 51)

[A certain] attitude toward the evil is another mark of the genre I have described. As the Christian believes that the Devil is an ass for preferring temporary self-importance to eternal bliss, these stories portray bad men as absurdly unaware of the simple pleasures. It is an attitude leading to comedy, rather than tragedy, and is the reason why films in this style often have trouble controlling their comic elements (*Butch Cassidy, Bonnie and Clyde,* as well as *Little Big Man*), for the style is not really one of comedy. However ridiculous the bully may be in some ultimate philosophical sense, at the moment he is kneeling on your chest, and your awareness that he's a fool only adds maddening unreasonableness to the situation, and it is just here, between theoretical laughter and actual tears, that these films, when successful, must balance. *McCabe* does it more adroitly than any of the others I've named. . . . (pp. 51-2)

Jackson Burgess, "Reviews: 'McCabe and Mrs. Miller'," in Film Quarterly *(copyright 1971 by The Regents of the University of California; reprinted by permission of the University of California Press), Vol. XXV, No. 2, Winter, 1971-72, pp. 49-53.*

GARY ENGLE

McCabe and Mrs. Miller tells two interrelated but recognizably distinct stories, each bearing some relationship to . . . [a Western theme]. One is the story of the founding and growth of a frontier town. The second is that of McCabe's personal struggle for survival. These two parts of the film can be separated and discussed individually to show how Altman creates a work which uses the forms and themes of the conventional Western to systematically undercut the meanings traditionally associated with them. (pp. 269-70)

Until the mid-point of *McCabe and Mrs. Miller* Altman seems unconcerned with characterizing the end toward which the town is moving. Upon reflection it can be seen that the town's progress has been measured by vast material changes. But here in the middle of the film Altman begins to analyze and evaluate the morality of the townspeople. The arrival of the representatives of the mining company signifies that Presbyterian Church has finally advanced enough to draw attention to itself from outside the community. The business monopoly, with its depersonalizing organization and concomitant financial and political power, has come to incorporate. For the first time we see the goal toward which the town is headed. The sympathy we feel for the town's progress throughout the first half of the film becomes suspect, for we see that the townspeople make no attempt to oppose the mining company's invasion. (p. 273)

Altman's treatment of the theme of social progress cannot be interpreted as an affirmation of the virtues of civilization. The goal of social progress is corrupt and brutal. There is no conflict between the townspeople and the forces of evil. Rather they condone them. . . . Portraying society as hypocritical, often childish, morally vacuous, insensitive, able to be manipulated and exploited with relative ease by both McCabe and the mining company, Altman undercuts our original response to the town's development. . . .

The second theme of the Western—the role of heroism in the development of civilization—is dealt with by Altman in his detailed analysis of McCabe's character. McCabe is nominally the *hero* of the film. I place emphasis upon the word *hero* in order to qualify the term; for a close inspection of McCabe's story reveals a disturbing lack of heroic qualities in his character. (p. 275)

We might be justified in identifying with McCabe, and thus in viewing his death as something lamentable and heroic, if he were to exhibit some degree of native intelligence, common sense, or insight in his conduct. If he were simply to show that he is good at what he undertakes, we might at least grant him the virtue of competence. But no such qualities are to be found. On the contrary, many of the central episodes of the film serve to reveal his incompetence. (p. 277)

Even though McCabe is portrayed in . . . a critical light, the Western tradition offers two distinct ways in which Altman could transform the character into a hero if such were his intentions. One possibility is that McCabe's worth could be redeemed through an abiding love for a good woman. The other is that McCabe could prove himself, could overcome his weaknesses and faults by committing some conclusive act of heroism—conventionally a shoot-out with the agents of evil—in which victory or a noble death might lift him above his former self. Altman seems keenly aware of each possibility because of the decisive way in which he rejects both. (p. 281)

If there is a form of redemption for McCabe in his love for Mrs. Miller, it is a redemption in terms contradictory to Western conventions. Mrs. Miller is simply not the typical Western woman. Nor does she perform the expected woman's function of taming the central male figure by bringing him, through love, into harmony with accepted cultural values. As his involvement with her increases, his role as a central figure in the social structure of the town decreases. This, however, does not fully explain why McCabe's love for her does not make him heroic. Part of the reason is apparent in the nature of their relationship. (p. 282)

Mrs. Miller appears admirably sensitive when compared with McCabe. His affection is totally self-serving and limited by his inability to sympathize with the sufferings of others. During their last night together Mrs. Miller is tormented by the realization that all chances of saving her share of the business are gone and that the killers will indeed get McCabe. He, blind to the assured loss of her dream of owning a boarding house in San Francisco, interprets her anguish only as evidence that she loves him. There is a powerful contrast between Mrs. Miller's almost speechless desperation over her and McCabe's futures and his dumb, smiling satisfaction. His self-centered reaction confirms his incapacity for the sympathy which characterizes Mrs. Miller's feelings for him. McCabe's last tearful confession to her—that he has never been so close to anyone before—is pathetically ironic. Obviously he never has been so close to anyone before; yet the closeness is so very much less than he imagines it to be. (p. 284)

McCabe's relationship with Mrs. Miller exposes him in a manner totally consistent with the general pattern of Altman's treatment of the character. McCabe begins the relationship with the possibility of providing for her ultimate happiness. Because of his irresponsibility, greed, vanity, and misjudgment, he ends the affair as the one person most directly responsible for her despair. The movement is an undeniable descent from the illusion of heroism.

The search for McCabe's heroic qualities must cease with an analysis of his last act. Certainly the shoot-out with the killers has the form of a conventional Western heroic struggle. One man is set alone against recognizable agents of evil. But it lacks heroic content. In comparison with a classic Western shoot-out the last sequence of the film reveals the degree to which Altman is undercutting McCabe's heroism and, in so doing, is attacking Western conventions.

The importance of a shoot-out in a Western resides in its dramatic impact. It is normally an intense moment in which all lines of theme and action converge into one concentrated confrontation; and as such it provides an appropriate climax to be followed by a release of tension. Altman attacks this Western cliché throughout the film. . . . By the time the final shoot-out occurs, the most common of all Western conventions has been totally divested of all heroic overtones. Altman completes his attack on the convention by undercutting its role as a unifying moment in the film. He has the lines of theme and action diverge instead of come together at this point. A tremendous contrast is achieved by intercutting shots of McCabe's fight with shots of the townspeople's struggle to put out the fire in the church. The effect underscores the town's indifference to McCabe's plight and points out the insignificance of the outcome of his struggle.

For McCabe's struggle to be heroic there must be some recognizable good operating in the contest. There are several reasons for arguing that there is none. First, nothing is gained by McCabe's elimination of the killers. The mining company remains. It is worth stressing that McCabe's own death leaves the company free to plunder the resources of the town. Secondly, McCabe does not fight on behalf of the community. Nor does he fight out of devotion to any ideal set of values. His only motive for accepting involvement with the company is financial gain; and his only motive for eventually fighting them is self-preservation. Finally, his actions cannot be considered heroic in the sense that he might represent the individual who achieves nobility by engaging in a futile attempt to wrestle with fate; for we are made to see that his death is unnecessary. If he had shown discretion in his earlier dealings, or if he had overcome his need to distance himself from others and only listened to Mrs. Miller's warnings, his confrontation with the killers could easily have been avoided. His character has not been exalted, but rather exposed and discredited throughout the course of the story. At the moment of his death he is not acting at the peak of heroism, but rather at the nadir of anti-heroism. (pp. 285-86)

Gary Engle, "'McCabe and Mrs. Miller': Robert Altman's Anti-Western," in Journal of Popular Film *(copyright © 1972 by Sam L. Grogg, Jr., Michael T. Marsden, and John G. Nachbar), Vol. I, No. 4, 1972, pp. 268-87.*

PAULINE KAEL

[*Images*] is a modern variant of the old *The Cabinet of Dr. Caligari* ploy—the world as seen through a mad person's eyes. A classy schizo (Susannah York) duplicates herself, confuses the living with the dead, and can't tell her husband . . . from her lovers. . . . Miss York's madness has no roots, no nourishment; it is a matter of tinkling wind chimes, slivers of glass, windows, lenses, mirrors—"images." To be effective, the movie needs to draw us in to identify with Susannah York's hallucinations, but the cold shine of the surfaces doesn't do it. . . . This is a psychological thriller with no psychological content, so there's no suspense and the climax has no power. We know from the heroine's dashingly casual clothes and the exquisitries of the super-modern décor that this film is concerned not with why she is going mad but with the coquetry of madness; that is, with suggestive objects (eyeglasses, camera, binoculars), with fragmentation, and with the bizarre situations a rich, sexy schizo can get into. . . . Altman is a fantastic technician; the rhythms of the cutting are seductive, and there are inventive moments. . . . Altman could probably turn, say, a Daphne du Maurier novel into a stylish screen terror, but he himself doesn't seem to have the gothic sensibility to make the scare effects matter. You stop being frightened as soon as you know that he takes it all seriously, and that it will be a hollow puzzle, a moviemaker's show-business view of schizophrenia, a prismatic *Repulsion*.

When he has a dramatic framework, Altman can do so much to affect us emotionally by virtuosity with visual images that he may at times think that words don't matter, that images do it all, and *Images* seems to have been made in that conviction. But this movie (from an original screenplay by Altman, plus improvisations) is not conceived to work without words; rather, it is indifferent to them. It is full of words, and they're runty words or they're the stupefyingly high-flown literary language we hear in Miss York's narration of the story for children, *In Search of Unicorns*, that her character is composing (and that Miss York has actually written). In this ornamental visual setting, with so much care given to twirling glassy baubles, the occasional flat improvised lines are like peanut shells stuck in jewelry. (pp. 80-1)

The style of this film is different from anything of Altman's I've seen before, and it's not like any other director's. It's an empty, trashy chic film, but, scene by scene, Altman doesn't do anything ordinary; *Images* is not remotely an example of hack work—it's an example of a conceptual failure. Altman often trusts a very bad instinct, the kind of instinct that some people may expect an artist of his stature to have outgrown. But artists, particularly in show business, often retain gaping areas of naïveté and of flossiness, and though sometimes they pull something out of those areas that seems miraculously right, other times we may wish to avert our eyes. It's possible that this formidably complicated man has as many facets as this gadgety movie's tiresome prisms, and that in reaching out instinctively and restlessly he's learning techniques that he hasn't yet found a use for. My bet is that he *will;* when he's bad he's very bad, but when he's good he's extraordinary. (pp. 81-2)

Pauline Kael, "Round Up the Usual Suspects" (originally published in The New Yorker, *Vol. XLVIII, No. 44, December 23, 1972), in her* Reeling *(copyright © 1972 by Pauline Kael; reprinted by permission of Little, Brown and Company in association with the Atlantic Monthly Press), Atlantic-Little, Brown, 1976, pp. 74-82.**

RICHARD SCHICKEL

[The] good guys of *M*A*S*H* are not just a bunch of merry pranksters on a spree. They are best understood, I think, as Robin Hoods of rationalism, robbing from the rich stockpiles of madness controlled by the people who make (and manage) wars and doling it out in inoculating life-saving doses to the little guys caught up in the mess. They may be vicious in their persecution of the pompous, the petty and the paranoid, but they have a wonderful tenderness with outcasts and underlings and innocents. (pp. 284-85)

I have nothing but awed admiration for the way Altman has managed what is obviously a precarious project, one which could have gone all black on him. Or, more likely, have been betrayed by a lack of courage on his part. The thing has a loose, improvisational quality about it—as if his actors were encouraged to be as inventive as possible. But it is never slack, careless or indulgent of their whims or the director's. Every scene is both tight in execution and rich in detail. (p. 285)

*Richard Schickel, "'M*A*S*H'" (originally published in* Life, *February 20, 1970), in his* Second Sight: Notes on Some Movies, 1965-70 *(copyright © 1972 by, Richard Schickel; reprinted by permission of Simon and Schuster, a Division of Gulf & Western Corporation), Simon and Schuster, 1972, pp. 283-85.*

RICHARD COMBS

Conceivably, schizophrenia is a malady to which all Robert Altman's major characters have been prone. Their behaviour is of little interest analysed on the level of clues or symptoms, but compelling where it gives evidence of large and dangerous attempts to comprehend an irrational world through personal experience, of minds which escape from the trap of an insane situation by going promptly, appropriately, healthily insane. Broad Laingian concepts of madness as socially conditioned, as a valid experience of a given situation, are as closely worked out in Altman's tragicomedies as in the explicit psychiatric challenge of *Family Life*. And perhaps just as such a theory opposes the psychiatric treatment of schizophrenia as a personal, functional disorder, so Altman has always opted for revealing his characters through complex situations rather than psychological puzzles. A precise and restless talent for experiment is evident in his switching through original combinations of comedy and drama, creating each time a complete universe, dense in detail and mood yet transparent to the passage of his characters from some rearguard delusion to eventual resignation and absorption. Self-destruction seems the inevitable conclusion, with the single exception of *M*A*S*H*, where a best possible adjustment is made through more vigorous comedy.

Confronting an absurd situation, Altman's heroes plainly have a right to their schizoid view of the world; while their heroism exists in contrast to those skittering creatures on the periphery—the miners in *McCabe*, the army types in *M*A*S*H*—more comically deluded in what they take to be a comfortable adjustment to a basically reasonable world. For *Images* . . . the population has been substantially reduced—to a vividly fragmenting personality, Cathryn . . . , her compulsive husband Hugh . . . , and the small cast of characters, both real and imaginary, who mediate their frighteningly exclusive attitudes and behaviour. Altman has insisted that his intention was not a clinical description of insanity but a reproduction of the world from Cathryn's point of view. And quite rightly—in keeping with Laing's dictum that it is possible to experience another's behaviour but not his experience—Hugh is insensitive to his wife's fantasies to a degree which reduces him to the comic grotesques of the earlier films and removes him to some remotely unfeeling corner of Cathryn's stage. (pp. 50-1)

An undeniable sense of frustration . . . infects the development of the film, which is eventually too direct in its communication and too abstract in its moods, insulating the spectator, as much as the other characters, from Cathryn and her predicament. . . . *Images* still requires melodrama on the order of [*That Cold Day in the Park*] to set the story off and keep it going—noticeably in the build-up of simple suspense during the opening scene, where Cathryn is persecuted over the telephone by a mysterious voice which she does not recognise as her own, and collapses in hysteria when the vision of a dead lover suddenly takes the place of her solicitous husband. Altman has grafted on to this his generalised conception of time and place, explicit points about Cathryn's present sexual frustration and past fears, and incorporated a materialised *alter ego* and other imaginary presences into a dramatic chamber piece. The result is a film which works in conventionally tight, psychological situations, rather than opening out into the landscape of the mind which the subject promises, and which *McCabe and Mrs. Miller* came closer to achieving. (p. 51)

Richard Combs, "'Images'," in Sight and Sound *(copyright © 1972 by The British Film Institute), Vol. 42, No. 1, Winter, 1972-73, pp. 50-2.*

CHARLES A. BAKER

[There] is in *Brewster McCloud* and *McCabe and Mrs. Miller,* as well as in *That Cold Day in the Park* and *M*A*S*H,* an underlying view of life and the world which, bypassing differences in subject matter, links these four films together as the work of a consistently serious and perceptive critic of certain conditions of contemporary society. . . . In the four films which are the subject of this study, Altman reserves his strongest disapproval and censure for those characters who, rather than maintaining their freedom of choice and action and a flexibility which permits them to alter their conduct according to the contingencies of a given situation, fall back on a structure, an established set of values, which, whether self-invented and self-imposed or applied by some outside agency and found to be acceptable by the characters involved, causes them to lose their options, become fixed in their response, no matter what the circumstances, and normally leads them to a disaster of varying degrees—whether it be failure, defeat, insanity, or death. (pp. 243-44)

A pessimistic film, *That Cold Day in the Park* is a chilling illustration of the tragic madness which can result from allowing oneself to become enmeshed in a structure imposed from outside and too readily and unquestioningly accepted. The result is a waning in one's ability to break loose from the habits of a lifetime, even when one most desires to do so. Altman clearly implies that when freedom has been so long compromised and surrendered the capacity to ever truly change has been lost. . . .

The youth, both in his mysterious silence and in his ultimate temptation, is an ancestor of Brewster McCloud. Free when the film begins, he is torn between maintaining a total freedom and accepting a new life where he believes he can keep the essence of his freedom and also the benefits of a luxury which is clearly beyond his means. Lured by the objects which Frances' structured existence confers, and ignoring the little warning signs of danger to come, he is unwilling to make a clean break and rechoose his freedom. Perhaps overconfident of his ability to control his situation, he hesitates too long and becomes one of the victims of the forces which he has half-knowingly unleashed. (p. 246)

*M*A*S*H* primarily attacks those who have substituted structured, established attitudes for freedom of choice. . . .

The best example of a character who is paralyzed by his rigid reactions to events and people is Major Frank Burns. A bigot who substitutes pithy homilies, prayers, and preachments for life and thought, Burns perfectly represents to many the institutional Christian. His religious principles find little place in his actions and attitudes toward others, and, in fact, give him justification for his narrow and unfeeling view of his fellow men. Basically elitist in his orientation and wearing religion as an armored protection against those whom he considers inferior or whose humanity offends him, he is effectively insulated from human exchange with those to whom, in his righteousness, he feels superior. Perhaps his intolerant misanthropy could have been ignored, if it had been buttressed by medical proficiency; unfortunately, he is clearly a less skillful surgeon than his colleagues. (p. 247)

It should be made clear that Burns is not condemned by Altman because he bedded Hotlips—Altman is clearly in favor of alternatives to self-abuse. Burns is satirized and scoffed at because, by allowing himself to become the puppet of a rigidly authoritarian set of principles, he has seriously shortcircuited his ability to accept alternative action in a given situation. (pp. 248-49)

One cannot view Hotlips' adjustment to reality without answering those women's liberationists for whom Hotlips' redemption is decidedly male chauvinist in its orientation. In their view, Hotlips is reduced to the level of the male theory that all most females need to straighten them out is a good screw. To this criticism one can only reply that Hotlips should not be considered as representative of universal womanhood and that she is treated more kindly and is more professionally esteemed than Burns. In Altman's universe the opposition is between structure and flexibility and not between male chauvinism and women's liberation; it is one's ability or inability to adjust and accept humanity in preference to mechanical response which is important—not partisan views of the male and female role. (p. 249)

If there can be uncertainty as to exactly what specific aspects of contemporary American life most perturb Altman in *Brewster,* and if it can be said that he asks far more questions than he supplies answers, there is certainly no difficulty in recognizing Altman's continuing antipathy toward structure and the disaster lurking in the path of those who depend upon it. (p. 251)

Brewster, a modern Icarus, is a mysterious and quiet young man whose consuming interest is to learn to fly like a bird. All who would obstruct him are found mysteriously murdered. He lives in a forgotten fallout shelter under that largest of man-made bird cages, the Houston Astrodome. Guided by the otherworldly Louise, who may or may not be a fallen angel or a former bird, he spends all his time studying birds, their techniques, and the aerodynamics of bird-like flight. His preparations also include building up his muscles for the day when he will soar like a bird and avoiding such earthly pleasures as sex. (p. 252)

In many ways, he is reminiscent of the youth in *That Cold Day in the Park.* Brewster fails [to fly] not because he has constantly depended upon and been wedded to structure, but because, having a clear choice between structure and freedom, he has allowed himself to be tempted and seduced by structure in the person of Suzanne. The fact that he is so swiftly and harshly punished reveals all too clearly the extent of Altman's repugnance with structure. (p. 253)

[There] is no doubt that *McCabe and Mrs. Miller* is another example of Altman's consistent view on the undesirability of structure. In no place in this film is this antipathy better demonstrated than in his depiction of the two principal characters. Their careers plainly reveal that those who structure their existence or allow others to regulate it risk not only their freedom but also their lives. The happiness which lies at the end of the structured rainbow is a chimerical illusion which easily turns into a nightmare. (p. 254)

Even though [McCabe's] business operations do not possess the tight control and carefully regulated accounting system which are the traditional cornerstone of the American business establishment, they are totally in harmony with his relaxed and flexible personality and the unstable, unstructured ambience of Presbyterian Church. Let others worry about the rainy days to come, McCabe is content to enjoy today's sunlight.

Unfortunately, his freewheeling existence does not last. Mrs. Miller . . . , a whore with ambitious aspirations and a penchant for well-ordered businesses, arrives in town. She convinces a doubting and reluctant McCabe that his enterprises can be better run, his girls more easily handled, and his profits increased; they establish an uneasy partnership. Flexibility and structure confront one another; flexibility, tempted by both greed and the hope of attaining rights to Mrs. Miller's clearly defined charms, capitulates. (pp. 254-55)

[McCabe] dies alone in the swirling snow as the town saves its church and its hope for established respectability. The cumulative weight of the attractions of ordered regularity has proved too strong for the individual to overcome. (p. 256)

It is evident that the sloppily run business which he had before Mrs. Miller appeared would never have interested the mining company. Their more efficient methods would have successfully negated any threat his enterprises might have offered. And surely such a failure would have been of little consequence to the freewheeling gambler of the beginning of the film. McCabe is doomed by his acquiescence in Mrs. Miller's ambitious hoping. It is the success of their partnership which attracts the mining company and makes them a threat which must be eliminated. Although one cannot help but admire McCabe's return to a belief in his resourcefulness as an individual, one can only regret that this reaffirmation of self came too late to save them.

Clearly Altman's *weltanschauung,* as seen in the four films discussed, is highly pessimistic; obviously, "the road that leads to life is small and narrow." The pressures on individuals, like McCabe, to conform and subjugate their individuality will not lessen. It is evident that Altman believes that few will be able to withstand the lonely solitude which acting as a freely choosing, flexible individual entails in a world in which structure reigns. . . . And yet it is the existence of this small group that is the sole source of light in Altman's world. (pp. 256-57)

Charles A. Baker, "The Theme of Structure in the Films of Robert Altman," in Journal of Popular Film *(copyright © 1973 by Sam L. Grogg, Jr., Michael T. Marsden, and John G. Nachbar), Vol. II, No. 3, 1973, pp. 243-61.*

ROBERT B. MEYERS

[In his "'McCabe and Mrs. Miller': Robert Altman's Anti-Western" (see excerpt above), Gary Engle's] purpose is to praise [Altman] for having succeeded in producing the best Anti-western of a current outpouring which includes films such as *Doc* and *Little Big Man.* Engle does not elaborate on the worth of the Anti-western as a genre. He seems, rather, to assume that the reader will recognize the sense and value of having produced an anti-something. (p. 301)

[Engle is also] so preoccupied with making all the parts he mentions subordinate to the theme of social progress that he gives short shrift to the film's sensual immediacy and the impact it makes. For one thing, he neglects the leisureliness of the opening. The film is several minutes old before the characters engage in intelligible social intercourse which reveals who they are and how they are related. The delay creates a kind of suspense which is uniquely cinematic in that the audience is deprived of fundamental social information but thoroughly engrossed at the same time in the visual wealth which sets the initial mood of gloom. Giving an adequate verbal account of this richness of existence and how it functions is one of the overwhelming difficulties of adequate film criticism. But the difficulty is surely not rectified by reducing all the visual detail to a meaning, to a proposition in the development of a theme. Engle also neglects to mention the haunting Cohen song which accompanies the "action" of the beginning of the film. My discussion, of course, is no more adequate than Engle's. I simply wish to suggest that what makes the initial section of the film a pleasure to experience is more bound up with these sensuous dimensions of the film, all of which are difficult to verbalize. In conjunction with them, the story of McCabe begins to unfold. Wherever we place it, the theme of social development which Engle wishes to promote seems hardly to merit the primary place in the audience's consciousness that Engle grants it. (p. 305)

Much of the film's ingenuity—and much of the reason that it is not a conventional Western—stems from the comic treatment of the "world" of Presbyterian Church. Contrary to Engle, the "world" built by McCabe is not one of "social progress" in any usual sense. Instead, the world evoked is a never-never land of the highest order. If genre Westerns romanticize the civilization of the frontier, this film does nothing to undercut that romanticizing tendency. Instead, *McCabe and Mrs. Miller* directs the romanticizing in an unusual direction. To be sure, there are realistic elements in the world evoked in the film. Probably a mining town was more whore houses than school houses, but the pleasure world conjured in the film, with its idealized whore house and utopian sense of community, is surely fantasy. (p. 307)

For a while at the start of the film it appears that Altman will present the West as it "really" was. Engle rightly points out that Sheehan's saloon is wretched and the townspeople totally cloddish. When the characters begin to interact with McCabe and each other, however, they transform into a pack of lovable clods. Their innocence is overwhelming if they are compared, say, to the backwoodsmen in *Deliverance*. . . .

[Engle talks] at one point of the "sympathy" generated for the townspeople in the first half of the film. What he does not seem to realize is that the sympathy we feel results from the evocation of a sympathetic, wish-fulfilling world, whose existence integrally depends on the occurrence of "characters" devoid of most of the psychological and moral complications that beset the minds of even the simplest "real" people. (pp. 307-08)

[When handling the "theme of hero,"] Engle specifically sets out to analyze McCabe in terms of heroic qualities, which he thinks McCabe sorely lacks. . . . As in the first half, the point seems to be that Altman's film is particularly strong, effective, and good simply because it turns everything upside down. But as was the case in the first half, Engle's it's-exactly-the-opposite orientation leads to some conclusions that do not necessarily accord with response to the work not mediated by intellectualistic expectations and special value hypotheses.

Just as he thought that the audience's reaction to the townspeople would be overwhelmingly negative, so here he thinks that the audience will sour on McCabe. . . . Engle cannot conceive of degrees between extremes. His assumption here seems to be that McCabe is either a hero, with whom the audience will identify, or else he has no heroic qualities, and the audience will feel nothing for him. The notion of "identification," a complex idea under any circumstances, is here collapsed completely to suggest that it only operates when the main character is a success. Engle comes close to positing an arrogant audience, one whose sympathies are drastically narrow. He seems utterly to overlook any inclination to sympathize with an underdog, just as he forgets that even in Aristotelian tragedy the audience experiences katharsis in relation to a hero who has flaws and makes mistakes. . . . Granted a wider idea of heroic behavior, McCabe does not emerge as the inadequate creature that Engle sees. (pp. 308-09)

Engle's discussion of McCabe's general ineptitude is, then, a particular instance of his inability to perceive the comic elements in the film as a whole. But his obliviousness to the comic element is further complicated by his opacity to the multiple presentation of McCabe in the film. The comic representation of the townspeople is essentially dependent on their representation in the ironic mode, i.e., as worse or less than we are. They are low characters, mainly tending toward the ineffectual when they witness the higher characters in conflict. From the very start, these people view McCabe as their leader and hero, and they maintain a simple allegiance to him throughout the film, with the exception of Sheehan and the preacher. The outsiders—Mrs. Miller, Sears and Hollander, the senator, and Butler—are, on the other hand, "higher" characters, more serious characters, from whose perspective McCabe is not so much a hero as he is a fool. McCabe develops from an essentially comic figure, a hero among the low characters, to a serious character of some merit, a development which Engle entirely ignores. At the start of the film, among the low characters, McCabe emerges as the ascendent figure, totally in control. With the arrival of Mrs. Miller he begins to come in contact with people of greater capability. These contacts begin on a rather light note but become more and more serious as the film progresses. . . . Much of the film's ingenuity comes from this multiple vision in which McCabe is seen as a hero of fools, a fool among shrewder men, and finally a hero, though a hero in a low key, consistent with the kind of character McCabe has been throughout the film. (pp. 310-11)

In the last analysis, Engle's interpretation suffers from a chain of wrong assumptions which utterly destroy the possibility of a proper response to the film. He begins by conceiving of invention in utterly dualistic terms: either the presentation of material is stereotyped or else it is totally inverted into an anti-something. This extreme conception of valuing dulls Engle to the conventions which do work in the film. He maintains a stony demeanor before the work's clear comic inclinations, even though it is the nature of comedy to make its objects of imitation sympathetic. Even mustache-twirling villains take on a certain likeability in comedy. He misses the double characterization of McCabe, with his shift from the ironic to the serious mode. Much of this shift, by the way, is cinematic, visual rather than verbal. McCabe's change in perspective appears in his manner more than anything he says. . . . Besides having overlooked the impact of comic elements and the development of McCabe from one level of character to another, Engle also misses the many similarities between McCabe's behavior and that of other clearly heroic types. In many ways, Engle simply refuses to accept the film as a work of art, a created world which resembles but significantly distorts the world of everyday life. For this reason, his many judgments of action in the film in terms of everyday morality are totally inappropriate. Ironically, he nominally has a high awareness of conventions in Westerns, as evidenced by his many references to [John Cawelti, author of *The Six-Gun Mystique*]. But he uses Cawelti's theory, along with . . . intellectualizations and other twists . . . , to mould the film into an anti-Western which evokes severe negative reactions in the audience. In general, the difficulty with the analysis is that Engle uses all his critical tools to report whether something in the film is black or white, a convention or its antithesis. Somewhere in the process, the film gets lost. (pp. 314-15)

Robert B. Meyers, "Theory Number One: Dissecting an Interpretation," in Journal of Popular Film *(copyright © 1973 by Sam L. Grogg, Jr., Michael T. Marsden, and John G. Nachbar), Vol. II, No. 3, 1973, pp. 300-15.*

CHARLES GREGORY

Philip Marlowe's back and the Seventies got him. Raymond Chandler's private eye, who survived threats from gangsters, gamblers, karate experts, cops, treacherous women, sadistic killers, has finally been defeated—by his own code and an age that doesn't need it. At least, so says Robert Altman in the latest Marlowe movie, *The Long Goodbye*. . . .

Altman's ambition . . . was more sweeping than most of his audience realised, for Marlowe and his fellow shamuses, gumshoes and dicks are not the only target for the director's satire and anger. An entire genre of tightlipped, cynical but grimly romantic films is being criticised and parodied in *The Long Goodbye*. The plot and characters come, albeit loosely, from Chandler's 1953 novel, but the characterisation and the ambience come from films like *Double Indemnity, The Postman Always Rings Twice, Nightmare Alley, Scarlet Street* and the like, as well as from the 1940s private eye movies. (p. 155)

What particularly bothers Altman is Marlowe as hero, the defiantly poor individualist surviving in a corrupt world. . . . Altman has survived the sixties by learning to distrust heroes and heroics; his romanticism takes a different direction. The overwhelming competence and control of Marlowe is too much for him, because his vision does not include the possibility of control. The moment is all that survives in his work. . . .

Altman's pre-release publicity and interviews stressed that he wanted to say 'a long goodbye' to the Marlowe hero; and the Chandler novel has been warped to make Marlowe's major virtues little more than mere vices. He sees the private eye as just another narrow American moralist who would be judge and jury for everyone. In Altman's view, Marlowe's admired integrity is limited, suspect, even dangerous. How can one dare to dispense justice in an unjust world? . . . Altman probably cherishes the line from *Raymond Chandler Speaking* (which he distributed to the entire cast and crew) which says, '. . . any man who tried to be honest looks in the end either sentimental or plain foolish.' Altman is determined to be neither. . . .

Altman has taken Marlowe more seriously than other film-makers have done. Chandler and even the worst of the Marlowe films never suffered from the righteousness that rises in Altman when he talks about his film, or in the film itself. (p. 156)

Some of Altman's best inventions have always been on the fringes of his films: the throwaway dialogue in *McCabe,* the PA system in *M*A*S*H,* the small moments in *Brewster McCloud* and the décor in *Images.* In *The Long Goodbye,* the satiric elements still function well away from Marlowe. The nubile, nude candle-makers in the next-door apartment; the star-crazy guard at the expensive enclave of the rich; David Carradine as the slogan-spouting hippie sharing a cell with Marlowe; the crazy people wandering around in the sanatorium, and the submerged animosity in the black/white detective team all give the film insight and wit at the edges. . . .

[Altman's Marlowe does not resemble] in any direct way the continuing line of Marlowe interpretations: he is too bewildered, too manipulated, too misled. And that is perhaps the fatal mistake in the film. [He] never acts, only reacts—until the final shocking moment when he kills Terry Lennox and skips down the road playing a harmonica and dancing to the tune of 'Hooray for Hollywood'. To satirise Marlowe effectively, the character must be in more assumed control of the action. . . .

All the locations from the old films appear, but Marlowe's vacuous stare hurts the intended parodies. No one could be so out of touch. He lacks even the naïve confidence that carries McCabe through so much of his movie, and Altman's criticism of the Western hero is far more successful, because fuller, than his criticism of the private eye.

While it is valid to question Marlowe's position in a world that seems devoid of meaning, Altman fails to do so honestly. He too readily condemns a hero that he fails to understand; he changes the game and loads things against Marlowe to the point where one feels an unintended sympathy for him. Although Marlowe may well look as ludicrous as the knight of La Mancha, the need and the longing remain. The world grows increasingly difficult and even more corrupt, but Marlowe will survive as he has for thirty years. (p. 159)

Charles Gregory, "Knight Without Meaning?" in Sight and Sound *(copyright © 1973 by The British Film Institute), Vol. 42, No. 3, Summer, 1973, pp. 155-59.*

PAULINE KAEL

*M*A*S*H* is a marvellously unstable comedy, a tough, funny, and sophisticated burlesque of military attitudes that is at the same time a tale of chivalry. It's a sick joke, but it's also generous and romantic—an erratic, episodic film, full of the pleasures of the unexpected. I think it's the closest an American movie has come to the kind of constantly surprising mixture in *Shoot the Piano Player,* though *M*A*S*H* moves so fast that it's over before you have time to think of comparisons. (p. 92)

What holds the disparate elements of *M*A*S*H* together in the precarious balance that is the movie's chief charm is a free-for-all, throwaway attitude. The picture looks as if the people who made it had a good time, as if they played with it and improvised and took some chances. It's elegantly made, and yet it doesn't have that overplanned rigidity of so many Hollywood movies. . . . The throwaway stuff isn't really thrown away; it all helps to create the free, graceful atmosphere that sustains the movie and keeps it consistently funny. The director, Robert Altman, has a great feel for low-keyed American humor. . . . Altman has made a real sport of a movie which combines traditional roustabout comedy with modern attitudes. As in other good comedies, there's often a mixture of what seems perfectly straight stuff and what seems incredible fantasy, and yet when we try to say which is which we can't. *M*A*S*H* affects us on a bewildering number of levels, like the Radio Tokyo versions of American songs on the camp loudspeaker system. All this may sound more like a testimonial than a review, but I don't know when I've had such a good time at a movie. Many of the best recent American movies leave you feeling that there's nothing to do but get stoned and die, that that's your proper fate as an American. This movie heals a breach in American movies: it's hip but it isn't hopeless. A surgical hospital where the doctors' hands are lost in chests and guts is certainly an unlikely subject for a comedy, but I think *M*A*S*H* is the best American war comedy since sound came in, and the sanest American movie of recent years. (pp. 94-5)

Pauline Kael, "Blessed Profanity" (originally published in The New Yorker, *Vol. XLV, No. 49, January 24, 1970), in her* Deeper into Movies *(copyright © 1970 by Pauline Kael; reprinted by permission of Little, Brown and Company in association with the Atlantic Monthly Press), Atlantic-Little, Brown, 1973, pp. 92-7.**

PAULINE KAEL

In other Altman films, there is always something that people can complain about; they ask, "What's that there for?" In *Thieves Like Us,* there's nothing to stumble over. It's a serenely simple film—contained and complete. You feel elated by the chasteness of the technique, and the film engages your senses and stays with you, like a single vision. It's beautiful right from the first, pearly-green long shot. Robert Altman finds a sureness of tone and never loses it; *Thieves Like Us* has the pensive, delicate romanticism of *McCabe*, but it isn't hesitant or precarious. It isn't a heady, whirling sideshow of a movie, like *The Long Goodbye;* it has perfect clarity. I wouldn't say that I respond to it more than to *McCabe* or that I enjoy it more than the loony *The Long Goodbye*, but *Thieves Like Us* seems to achieve beauty without artifice. It's the closest to flawless of Altman's films—a masterpiece.

Altman breaks the pattern of what American directors are commonly supposed to be good at; this picture has the relaxed awareness that we honor Europeans for and that still mystifies Hollywood. . . . The movie has the ambience of a novel; it is the most literary of all Altman's films, yet the most freely intuitive. *Thieves Like Us* is so sensuous and lucid that it is as if William Faulkner and the young Jean Renoir had collaborated. (pp. 268-69)

You can see that Altman doesn't have to prove to anybody that he can re-create the thirties. The movie isn't a work of nostalgia; it's not a glorification of the past. It's localized in an era, and the people can be understood only in terms of that era. They are part of the age of radio, and Altman uses radio programs of the thirties for his score, and Coca-Cola for his motif. . . . For the last two years now, friends of mine have been shouting that Altman must do *The Wild Palms* or *As I Lay Dying;* they've been convinced that he is the man to bring Faulkner to the screen. Maybe he knew it all along, and maybe he was smart enough to know that he could do it best by using someone else's material for his text. . . . *Thieves Like Us* comes closer to the vision and sensibility of Faulkner's novels than any of the movie adaptations of them do. Altman didn't start from Faulkner, but he wound up there. If he did a Faulkner novel, he might not be able to achieve what people want him to. But *Thieves Like Us* is *his* Faulkner novel. (p. 271)

Pauline Kael, "Love and Coca-Cola" (originally published in The New Yorker, *Vol. XLIX, No. 50, February 4, 1974), in her* Reeling *(copyright © 1974 by Pauline Kael; reprinted by permission of Little, Brown and Company in association with the Atlantic Monthly Press), Atlantic-Little, Brown, 1976, pp. 267-71.*

STANLEY KAUFFMANN

[The close-up of the body at the end of *Thieves Like Us*] and the choice of the puddle are typical of the heaviness, the fundamentally mawkish fatalism with which Robert Altman has loaded this film. (p. 263)

[The book by Edward Anderson, on which the film is based,] does exactly what Altman's film does not do: it fixes its hero and heroine, Bowie and his girl Keechie, as creatures of circumstance, helpless and overpowered, grasping frantically for some truth—a paradox of the possibility of spirit in a drastically degraded moral landscape. We accept Bowie's values, given his conditioning, and accept the fate of Bowie and his girl as Zola-Dreiser specks of human grit bursting into flower for a few moments before the juggernaut of society rolls over them.

Almost all of this is missing from Altman's film. His only attempts to connect Bowie with society are in terms of minutiae. . . . (p. 264)

[Altman's script is so far removed from any social or Freudian motivation] that we almost get two cleaned-off clinical specimens. We cannot feel that these two are products of the Depression or of environment, only that Bowie is a moral idiot and that Keechie is a mollusk clinging to him. Then Altman the director emphasizes the script's coldness and bareness by going exactly the opposite way in execution; he and his cinematographer Jean Boffety have worked with wistful visual sentiment from the opening shot. He misses few chances of any kind to blunder artily. A mirror cracks fortuitously and symbolically. When the young pair first make love, a radio gives us *Romeo and Juliet*, and keeps repeating the same bit, like a stuck phonograph. (It's the one purposely unreal touch.) Altman couldn't have been satirizing his lovers, so he must have thought he was embellishing the scene. And to pile on the art for us, he alters Anderson's ending. . . . The blasting of the cabin is itself superfluous; there's no reason why the hidden cops couldn't have shot the boy the moment he stepped out of his car before he went inside. That wasn't done so we could have the protracted shooting in which the cabin is nearly blown apart, and he dies alone so we could have a fancy epilogue in which Keechie melts into the crowd. Art has rarely seemed longer, or life shorter. (pp. 264-65)

Again Altman proves that he has little security except in satire like *M*A*S*H* and *The Long Goodbye.* He has no grip on the center of *Thieves Like Us,* so it never grips us. (p. 265)

Stanley Kauffmann, "'Thieves Like Us'" (originally published in The New Republic, *Vol. 170, No. 9, March 2, 1974), in his* Living Images: Film Comment and Criticism *(copyright © 1971, 1972, 1973, 1974 by Stanley Kauffmann; reprinted by permission of Harper & Row, Publishers, Inc.), Harper, 1975, pp. 263-65.*

JOSEPH KANON

Altman is a director who works on the periphery: he can take a tired motif and move around it with such precision and freshness that the very form seems altered, expanded. He looks at his subjects sideways. His talent is an original one, but it's probably the most erratic now at work in American movies. The technique can jell to extraordinary effect (*McCabe & Mrs. Miller*) or get lost in muddle (*The Long Goodbye*) and occasionally even fall apart completely (*Brewster McCloud*). *Thieves Like Us* is one of Altman's more successful movies, coherent and rich in detail, and it plays without a hitch. It has the rhythm of a hazy Mississippi heat cut with flashes of rain and it's so firmly set in its period that it can't be accused of cashing in on the nostalgia run. (p. 115)

Thieves Like Us isn't condescending about its characters, though it scores a few laughs off the dumb redneck Dee Mobley (who can't find the wrench before his eyes). . . . The people here are not so much mean-spirited as mindless —they don't have the brains to be, say, the Snopeses. . . . It's as surprising to them as Keechie's pregnancy or the door that falls off its loose hinges—they can't leap from cause to effect, they just take things as they come. But neither are they victims, except in the most general sense. . . . [We're] not meant to respond to the characters as victims of social upheaval. They're more like victims of social inertia.

Thieves Like Us shares with *Bonnie and Clyde* its emphasis on the role of the mass media in stunted fantasy lives (the soundtrack plays "Gangbusters" as the robbers march into a bank), but it drops the edginess, the excitement, and the investigation into pop mythology that made *Bonnie and Clyde* a landmark movie. It may be interesting to play a crime movie in low-key, but it's also odd, as if whole snatches of notes were missing. For a movie so well made and so well acted, *Thieves Like Us* is curiously uninvolving. In part, this is a function of Altman's peripheral vision—he skirts the violence so much that we never see how it shapes the characters' lives—but it also has a good deal to do with the ordinariness of the material itself. We don't get very far into the heads of the characters because they're so simple-minded there's nowhere to go. . . . *Thieves Like Us* is like an old master's commissioned portrait of an anemic royal cousin—the background is wonderful, full of skill and a sense of the period, but the subject is unworthy and since the artist never managed to get a new fix on it, we have to keep looking around the head, squinting at art. (pp. 116-17)

Joseph Kanon, "Peripheral Vision," in The Atlantic Monthly *(copyright © 1974, by The Atlantic Monthly Company, Boston, Mass.; reprinted with permission), Vol. 233, No. 4, April, 1974, pp. 115-18.**

PENELOPE GILLIATT

Like gambling itself, the impulses of Altman's characters [in "California Split"] seem a matter of luck or catastrophe, resting on choices ungoverned by rehearsal. The film gives us the sense that it is being improvised. We catch at events and personalities by the ends of threads. Everything seems to be going on in some tight corner of life that is off the direct route, inhabited by something musky, dangerous, and surprisingly poetic. The characters suffer the fierce aloneness that Altman identifies in American living. His film is an implacable and minatory one. It is sometimes very funny, in a mood of not caring whether you find it so or not. . . . Using the overlapping talk that has always been so potent in his movies, Altman again shows that he has a mysterious feeling for the low-toned energy of American humor. His films have a supple genius for the awkward in speech. It is the kind of awkwardness that makes small kids giggle about riddles, or newcomers to English who live here suddenly express the heart of America in a one-legged phrase. . . .

The imagery of risk in the film works like a spell. One is drawn into the heroes' universe, where they are sometimes opiate-lidded with fatigue, sometimes pepped up by a red-hot winning streak and superstitious that the streak can be broken as though by an evil eye if an onlooker gets too interested. (p. 78)

[Multiple] conversations crowd the film with a peculiar vivacity, which is part of its lack of natural repose. Their quality of incompleteness characterizes the world of gambling, with its emptied one-room homes where even the toaster has gone to the pawnshop and which seem inhabited only by cards and the craving to win. . . .

"California Split" has, as any film about gambling must, some of the concentrated wildness of Dostoevski's great short novel "The Gambler," but it also achieves a kind of complicity in near-casual leisure. Complicity has always interested this warm, original director. In "California Split," Altman, as usual, has wanted to fill his dangerous, somnambulistic world with humor and with eddies of talk and mood, so that anecdotal happenings are always breaking up the ferocity of the main topic. The wish softens the film. So do the jack-in-the-box wit and the restful acceptance of eccentricity. (p. 79)

Altman always gives his out-of-step figures something poised and venturesome. He respects strong character and finds it in odd places. With each film he makes, he becomes more eloquent in his innovative way of fragmenting narrative and of burying personality so that no more of it shows than a hipbone sticking out of the sand in a mound made over someone by children on the beach. This is the way life is, of course. We are always coming in at the end of things and picking up what we can of characters formed by unknown events. But what Altman is doing is strange to the American cinema tradition. People accustomed to foreign films will latch on to his work in a second; I hope large enough audiences of others will be excited by his ambitious, imperfect, edgy dreams, which keep growing more intense and more expressive of America. One of the interesting things about "California Split" is that people who get nervous at the mere sight of someone betting a dollar in real life will find his image of hothead gamblers composing. The phenomenon maybe has to do with the remove at which art happens. (p. 80)

Penelope Gilliatt, "Dreams of Tight Corners," in The New Yorker *(© 1974 by The New Yorker Magazine, Inc.), Vol. L, No. 26, August 19, 1974, pp. 78-80.*

ROBERT PHILLIP KOLKER

[In *Thieves Like Us*] Altman re-creates the depression Thirties . . . , but despite the clothing, cars, buildings, the ubiquitous Coca-Cola bottles, and the 1930s radio programmes that Altman uses almost as a music track, he has not made just another 'evocation' film. Rather, by using the basic plot of the novel, he has made an alternative to [Nicholas Ray's *film noir, They Live By Night,* based on Edward Anderson's novel *Thieves Like Us*] in which the entrapment and destruction of innocents takes place in the open country, in the light instead of the dark, in a world that appears to be free and pure. Altman's distancing effect is therefore quite different from Ray's. *They Live By Night* is contemporary in time, and its *film noir* elements remove us from any intense identification with its characters. *Thieves Like Us* is a re-creation of a distant time, but a re-creation done with such a high degree of stylisation and self-consciousness that we cannot be absolutely sure how far our sentiments and sympathies should extend. (p. 238)

Ray guides our affections and sympathies all the way. If we can't 'identify' with his Bowie and Keechie, we are at least certain that they are the central characters and certain of our own sense of their despair and isolation. But Altman feels affection for, or at least an attraction to, almost all his characters. He is too much like Jean Renoir, and since he condemns almost no one, he offers us little in the way of directed sympathy or, more accurately, gives us little moral direction. If we are all thieves, the only pity is that some of us get caught. Altman's world and its people remain brave and open, quite the opposite of those of the Ray film. . . .

Ray indicates a spiritual death for his Keechie. Altman, almost in defiance of Ray's dark point of view, allows Keechie strength to enter the world—a grim, faceless, depression-ridden world to be sure—but at least a world in which some sad flow of life continues.

It is not a question of hope. Altman's vision (even as it was in *McCabe and Mrs. Miller*) is as hopeless as Ray's. What Ray adds and Altman subtracts, the factor inherent in the *film noir* genre as a whole, is despair. *Film noir* allows no one to win, particularly not the audience. They see only their own defencelessness magnified and their darkness and fears reinforced. The new genre that has risen from the night still lacks hope, but allows for defence and reduces fear. Penn's Bonnie and Clyde were merry folk in a bright, hungry world. Innocents in the garden of evil. Their deaths only reinforced the vitality of their lives. The whole crop of *Bonnie and Clyde* spin-offs, as divergent as *Bloody Mama, Dillinger,* and more recently *Badlands* and *The Sugarland Express* as well as *Thieves Like Us,* add the vitality missing from the *film noir* genre. . . . In the new *film lumière* we are in no doubt that these are people of spirit, even kindness, who, however lost and beaten, however amoral, are allowed a certain triumph to their lives. (p. 239)

Robert Phillip Kolker, "Night to Day," in Sight and Sound *(copyright © 1974 by The British Film Institute), Vol. 43, No. 4, Autumn, 1974, pp. 236-39.**

ROBIN WOOD

Apart from their intrinsic quality (often very high indeed) Altman's films are interesting by virtue of their centrality to the development of the American cinema, their synthesis of contemporary tendencies. First, Altman is very conscious of his legacy; a number of his films are overtly retrospective, establishing their significance through their relation (half-homage, half-sardonic critique) to the Hollywood past. . . .

Second, that awareness of the European cinema that marks one of the decisive differences between the American cinema of today and the Hollywood of the studio/star/genre system—the increase in artistic consciousness or self-consciousness and the rise of the director as the *recognized* prime determinant of quality—is especially strong in Altman. One can recognize an Altman film as one can a Fellini or Antonioni—from its stylistic self-assertion.

Third, an equally conscious contemporaneity, a desire to capture impressionistically the mood of the age, dominates those films (*MASH* and *California Split*) that one guesses Altman takes least seriously (though we need not necessarily follow suit). If several Altman films are critiques of past genres, *California Split* belongs very plainly to a currently fashionable one, the "male duo" picture initiated by *Midnight Cowboy* and *Easy Rider*. . . .

Every new development in a collective art form produces its own general stylistic and formal procedures; the major artist is not so much the man who invents forms as the man who learns how to control them. Above all other contemporary American directors Altman has made artistic sense of the dominant technical devices of the modern cinema, the telephoto and zoom lenses—as the superb opening shot of *Thieves Like Us* alone suggests. . . . Screen space today, instead of appearing stable and three-dimensional, is a matter of flattened or shifting perspectives as background and foreground move into and out of focus and distance is squeezed into flatness. Such technique lends itself to the expression of a sense of dream-like unreality; in Altman's films this is intensified by his fascination (going right back to *That Cold Day in the Park*) with glass surfaces—characters seen in mirrors or through windows, with spatial relationships often confused or ambiguous.

Altman's movies reveal a very consistent recurrent pattern: the protagonist, confident of his ability to cope with what he undertakes, gradually discovers that his control is an illusion and that he has involved himself in a process of which his understanding is far from complete and which usually culminates in his own destruction. . . .

What is intermittently worrying about Altman is a tendency to look down on his characters. In fact, he is perhaps closer to them than he realizes. For all the stylistic consciousness his films exhibit, he often seems only partially in control of the effects he creates—witness the use of "Hurray for Hollywood" at the end of *The Long Goodbye*, the "Romeo and Juliet" sequence of *Thieves Like Us*, and the whole of *MASH* and *Images*, his worst two films which mark, interestingly, the polar extremes (popular and esoteric) of his work so far.

Robin Wood, "Controlling the Situation," in The Times Educational Supplement *(© Times Newspapers Ltd. (London) 1975; reproduced from* The Times Educational Supplement *by permission), No. 3118, February 28, 1975, p. 126.*

JONATHAN ROSENBAUM

[An assorted array of cranks] populate *McCabe* and *The Long Goodbye*, each riding on an autonomous wavelength that runs at an oblique angle to everyone else's. Consider, for instance, Harvey in *California Split*, an old friend whom Bill looks up in a paint store:

> Harvey: Wait a minute! Don't tell anybody you came, I'm getting a flash. You see, I have a good amount of ESP. I'm blessed with it—my wife kids me about it—but you should catch it when I get these flashes. Let me see how close I can get to what's goin' on here. I get—I get that you're probably back with your old lady . . . an-n-n that you probably want to paint your garage door—perhaps even the whole front of your house —I'm gettin' the colour . . . it's a greenish colour. Right, how close did I get?
> Bill: I need a loan, Harvey.
> Harvey: A loan?
> Bill: Yeah.

And that's all we ever see of Harvey. Like some of the Flemish peasants in Brueghel's landscapes and certain topics and individual chapters in *Tristram Shandy*, he emerges briefly in apparent non-relation to his immediate surroundings, but retrospectively blends into an overall pattern of awkward everyday cussedness that comprises an appropriate setting for absurdist-humanist drama. . . .

The pathos of these characters—and countless other examples could be picked from Altman's menagerie—is directly related to the way that they momentarily take the plot away from the films' equally displaced heroes; their fumblings are only condensed versions of the clumsy, uncertain relationships of McCabe, Marlowe, the bank robbers of *Thieves* and the gamblers of *California Split* to their respective worlds. (p. 93)

[Inarticulateness] and clarity can often register as moral positions in Altman's films—at least until *California Split*, where the whole question of a moral context becomes largely suspended. In the absurdist terrains traversed by McCabe and Marlowe, a hired gun . . . describing how to make profits out of dead Chinamen can be a lot more articulate than the leading citizen of First Presbyterian Church, talking to himself. . . . (pp. 93-4)

Altman's apparent preference here for his tongue-tied characters over their smooth-talking counterparts . . . seems to rest on the notion that emotions speak louder than words. And the most serious reproaches that have been levelled against the director—whether for 'laziness', lack of intellectual rigour or incoherent rambling—can mainly be traced back to this bias. But on Altman's behalf, it is worth noting that rigour and clean articulation is not really what he is after: the vagaries of behaviour, the indulging of certain moods and the staging of chance encounters, can be enormously expressive even without the dividends of what critics like to call 'an organic whole'. It is rather like censuring a jazz musician because his improvisations lack the polished form and execution of a classical musician performing a written piece. While it is certainly true that the former is less likely to *achieve* a finished form, there is a different kind of excitement in the way that he tries to achieve it—a way of regarding 'form' as a verb rather than a noun, a process rather than a postulate. And the baselines established by Altman for isolating and relating different kinds and degrees of coherence are anything but loose.

In Michael Tarantino's accompanying article [see excerpt below], a persuasive case is made through concrete evidence that the nearly constant movement of the camera in *The Long Goodbye* affects both our relationship to the film and Marlowe's relationship to the world around him. In what I hope might serve as complementary evidence of that film's formal interest (which surpasses, I believe, that of Altman's other works to date), I would like to show how roughly comparable parameters are at work on the soundtrack, above and beyond the overlapping dialogue—particularly in the extraordinary use of the title tune, a facet of the film that many commentators have taken to be nothing more than a trivial joke.

'The Long Goodbye' is a 32-bar standard by John T. Williams and Johnny Mercer that is performed throughout the film in countless versions, none of which is ever heard in its entirety. . . . (p. 94)

In simplest thematic terms, [the lyrics of the song are] a commentary on the broken encounters that punctuate the film. . . .

The continuities and discontinuities that are established or implied in [the scenes where strains of the theme are heard] are not merely reflections but active instruments of the divisions being set up between these discrete entities, at the same time that a common tune is binding them all together. And the spectator's relationship to the action is being further played with by the multiple shifts in the music's volume throughout most of the above examples, as melody and/or words fade in and out of the soundtrack in relation to the dialogue, passing from 'foreground' to 'background' in a manner somewhat analogous to the camera movements in so far as they repeatedly redefine our focus on and distance from the events taking place—thus continually altering and varying our grasp of them. . . .

The shifting volumes of other sound elements—the miaow of Marlowe's cat, the voices of his spaced-out neighbours—are simultaneously altering our impressions of spatial depth and physical separations in these scenes. . . .

But the spatial and spiritual distances suggested in the above are modest indeed compared to those which accumulate in the movie's later scenes, beginning with the Wades' disastrous party. . . .

For all its jokey overtones, the scene [in which Marlowe finds himself in the hospital] is decidedly the most nightmarish in the entire film. On the bed opposite Marlowe's lies a figure wrapped mummy-like, from head to toe, in bandages. . . . [The] figure grunts at him incoherently but insistently, beckoning him over. 'Hey listen, you tell that guy that it don't hurt to die,' Marlowe remarks to the virtual corpse that might as well be him—indeed, *is* him if we consider how Marlowe stalks senselessly through the remainder of the film. 'Hey, that's the smallest one I've seen,' he goes on, picking up the mummy's miniature harmonica. 'No, listen, I can't,' he explains, 'I gotta tin ear.' He blows a plaintive whine on the harmonica, adds, 'I'll practise—see you later,' and beats his retreat from the room. . . .

In this crucial scene, we have Altman's 'universe', themes and formal procedures reduced to their barest expressions. And if the harmonica and Marlowe's cryptic adoption of it—he is blowing on it again in the movie's closing shot—immediately recalls the harmonica wails of Jean-Pierre Léaud in Jacques Rivette's *Out I: Spectre* for its reduction of communication itself and the production of 'meaning' to stark essentials, the relationship may not be entirely fortuitous. Rivette has recently expressed an interest in Altman's work which began with *The Long Goodbye*. . . .

Central to the concept of modernism in all the arts is the idea of collaboration—the notion that artist and audience conspire to create the work in its living form, that the experience of making it is in some way coterminous (if far from identical) to the experience of hearing, seeing or reading it. Even at his most venturesome and 'experimental', Altman cannot be described as a director who pursues this notion unequivocally and consistently, in the sense that Tati does in *Playtime* (through visual options) and Rivette does in *Spectre* (through interpretative options); considering the fairly constant way he has remained active in the commercial cinema since *MASH* in 1969—and all the conditions that this fact implies—he cannot really be considered in the same league at all. But virtually alone among his peers, he has opened up the American illusionist cinema to a few of the *possibilities* inherent in this sort of game—played for limited stakes in controlled situations, but played none the less (p. 95)

Jonathan Rosenbaum, "Improvisations and Interactions in Altmanville," in Sight and Sound *(copyright © 1975 by The British Film Institute), Vol. 44, No. 2, Spring, 1975, pp. 90-5.*

KURT VONNEGUT, JR.

I have often hoped that the arts could be wonderfully useful in times of trouble. I have seen few examples of that. *Nashville,* however, fulfills my dream. It is a spiritual inventory of America, splendidly frank and honest.

The movie shows us a system of yearnings and rewards and punishments and physical objects which we have tacked together over the years. . . .

Mr. Altman implies that our understanding of our curious civilization must come from ourselves. He has an actress portray a British documentary filmmaker on a visit to Nashville, fresh from Israel and darkest Africa. She confidently misinterprets all she sees. She has European brilliance and sophistication which, when applied to the city of Nashville, render her asinine. She says of a country-music star's mansion built of logs, "It's pure Bergman." And then she adds, "But of course these are the wrong people for Bergman."

And I must say that, when the movie was over, not only did I want to cry but I was thunderstruck by how discontinuous with the rest of the world our culture is. It is pure and recent invention, inspired by random opportunities to gain money or power or fame. Even the past is faked. And those who partake of that culture, especially the weak or simple-minded, feel compelled to invent personalities as novel and arbitrary and commercial as the inventions with which they hope to harmonize. . . .

[Everything] goes wrong at the end of the movie. There is maximum ugliness and insanity and meaninglessness. And no great human being or idea or miracle appears to heal the horrified witnesses, a crowd revealed to be childlike in bewilderment and hope. We are not beasts, says Altman. The American people are made by the camera to appear innocent and beautiful.

And leaderless.

And idealess.

And all that can be given to them for comfort by our culture is an enchantingly catchy and heartbreakingly inane ditty played over the public-address system. Everyone is invited to sing along.

Its refrain is this one: "It don't worry me."

Kurt Vonnegut, Jr., "'Nashville'—A Shadow Play of What We Have Become and Where We Might Look for Wisdom" (copyright © 1975 by the Condé Nast Publications, Inc.; reprinted with permission of Donald C. Farber, attorney for Kurt Vonnegut, Jr.), in Vogue, *Vol. 165, No. 6, June, 1975, p. 103.*

JOHN SIMON

Paramount Pictures has, I suspect, done Robert Altman a grave disservice in not releasing his *Nashville* in some longer version. . . . From an eight-hour version to a six-hour one to be released in two parts, from a three-and-a-half- to its present two-and-a-half-hour version, the film kept shrinking with nothing reaching us except rumors of its decrease. . . . What has finally been vouchsafed us strikes me as highly interesting but ultimately insufficient. . . .

In a sense, the film resembles Joyce's *Ulysses:* more or less interconnected, self-important but essentially humdrum lives strutting in a brief time span against the more important backdrop of an exceptionally raucous but second-rate city, and the whole thing functioning on two levels. But there are two sizable differences: the non-literal level in the book is mythic, not merely allegorical; and the novel is a work of genius, the film only of talent.

Still, this is an absorbing film, Altman's best so far, and look what the drastic cutting has done to it. We encounter, for instance, a mismated married couple: an elderly farmer husband . . . and his flighty young wife . . . who keeps eluding him to take stabs at becoming a country-and-western singer. We see so little of their relationship . . . that the surprise climax, in which [the wife] against all probability gets a sensational start on the road to stardom, lacks the petty beginnings against which to resonate. Such fragmentation diminishes most of the characters and relationships in the released *Nashville,* which now comes across rather like a huge novel turned into a telegram. . . .

The biggest problem, however, despite the flavorousness, humor, and even excitement of the literal level, is the uneasy symbolism. We are led to the symbolic level adroitly enough, to be sure. (p. 34)

[But] how does the symbology work? Easy fame, easy money, easy sex, uneasy competitiveness, all stemming from a dubious commodity, C. & W. music—meaning presumably that our materialistic, appetitive and competitive society produces unwholesome social climates and political ideologies. Yet does the fanatical production of musical claptrap really parallel the political, let alone the cultural situation? Does one become a politician the way one becomes a C. & W. musician? And isn't our culture to a large extent, alas, precisely C. &. W. and rock music—in which case, how can the thing symbolized do double duty as the symbol? And what is the point of symbolizing unless new light is shed on the thing symbolized, yet I cannot find anything new about America in the movie, however much it may hold my interest. But maybe a fuller version would have yielded something more. (p. 38)

Altman's previously irritatingly distracting multiple sound track works here: where there is no plot-advancing dialogue to follow, we don't care what we miss by tuning in on one conversation to the exclusion of another: they are all equally unimportant, but it is their cumulative, discordant unimportance that gives this self-important bustle its comic punch.

In *Nashville,* the sum of the parts is, unfortunately, greater that the whole, but, bit by bit, they are mostly well worth attending to. Even if they do not signify much that is new to us about our society, they do represent a significant advance in Altman's film making. There is something maturer and subtler here that confirms Altman, for all his faults, as Hollywood's most rewarding director. May his faults grow fewer as his rewards keep growing. (p. 42)

John Simon, "The Amazing Shrunken 'Nashville'" (reprinted by permission of Wallace & Sheil Agency, Inc.; copyright © 1975 John Simon), in Esquire, *Vol. 84, No. 3, September, 1975, pp. 34, 38, 40, 42.*

JOEL E. SIEGEL

[*Nashville* is] a bloated, slapdash, simplistic effort, full of hollow attitudinizing about the Emptiness of American Life, an enterprise concocted of equal parts arrogance, condescension, and gall. . . .

Some say you have to be stoned to see Altman's films properly, and I suspect they're right. The director's best movies (*M*A*S*H, California Split*) and his worst (*Thieves Like Us, Brewster McCloud*) are marked by faintly narcotic stylistic similarities—muzzy, soft-edged camerawork, mumbly, overlapping dialogue tracks, limp, somnambulant pacing. Altman has drawn an analogy between how he makes a movie and the way jazzmen improvise. Journalists have bought this one, but the analogy is faulty. True, jazz musicians improvise within the harmonies of a song's structure, but their work remains abstract, consisting of sounds and moods. Altman's work is moody all right, but essentially mindless; language and ideas cannot be manipulated as freely as musical tones. The director's films aren't really thought out or fully imagined. (p. 1)

His screenwriter, Joan Tewkesbury, admits to having spent only a few days in Nashville prior to writing the script and says that Altman knew even less about the place than she did. In the normal run of things, an artist has an experience, discovers that he has something he wants to express on the subject, and then settles down to the job of creation.

Altman and Tewkesbury, in their immense arrogance and ignorance, seem to have decided that Nashville could serve as an easy, opportune symbol for airing their rather sour views on American life. Whereupon they rushed out to make their film without bothering to explore the realities of the world they claim to be depicting. . . .

Despite Altman's often professed concern for "atmosphere," one never gets the sense of being anywhere in Nashville, except inside a mannered, egotistical director's conception. . . . Abstract, formalist movies, like *Letter From an Unknown Woman* and *The Conformist,* can effectively shut out much of the everyday world, but films like *Nashville,* which strive for poetic realism, can't succeed without a detailed awareness of how people actually live and behave. . . .

Altman and Tewkesbury attempt to use the sentimentality and banal patriotism of most country and western music as a metaphor for the jingoistic sloshheadedness they think underlies American political and social life. But because they are ignorant about the music they use to represent their attitudes, their elaborate conceit falls flat.

What's good about the film can be summed up in a short paragraph. Several members of the large cast give impressive performances. . . . (p. 2)

Otherwise, there's little worth remembering. The actors, having been encouraged to create their own characterizations, have drawn upon their collective past—bad old movies, second-rate plays and novels, television time-killers—and what they've come up with is a cornucopia of clichés. (p. 3)

I don't dislike *Nashville* because its view of America is so nihilistic. In fact, some of my feelings about what we are and where we are going are rather similar to Altman's. But the cheap, lovelessly manipulative way he tries to move his audience to those conclusions undermines whatever truths he may have at hand. One wonders, after all, why Altman should have such a grudge against America. (p. 4)

One sure touchstone to a director's sensibility is the way he handles group scenes. Altman's crowds, like those in Eisenstein's movies and other works of totalitarian cinema, react as a single-minded mass, united by a single will. The crowds who alternately worship and torment Barbara Jean don't behave like any assembly of recognizable human beings, but are The Masses, herded about to make easy didactic points. Similarly, when Gwen Welles does her humiliating striptease at the political smoker, all of the pig-faced, middle-aged men leer with the same sordid lust. Not a single man shows a shadow of concern about her degradation.

Nashville, which attempts a serious analysis of the banality of our politics, the shallow materialism of our society and the violence at the core of our national character, fails because its view of people, individually and collectively, is so shallow, so lacking in detail and sympathy. It's like a series of bumper stickers—bright, flashy, paper-thin expressions of attitudes—soon past, soon forgotten. (p. 5)

Joel E. Siegel, "Nashville," in Film Heritage *(copyright 1975 by F. A. Macklin), Vol. 11, No. 1, Fall, 1975, pp. 1-5.*

F. ANTHONY MACKLIN

A Robert Altman film is an experiment in audacity. *Nashville* is about American success—its costs, humiliations, and incredible spirit. Despite some failures in its storytelling, its ambience is tremendous. Altman has used the Mecca of country music to place his episodic film, and he shows what Americans have assumed as their values. In doing so he has created a movie that is provocative, comic, and gaudily melodramatic. . . .

What is so exciting about Altman's movie-making is its many levels. Altman is one of the very few directors whose work deserves more than one experiencing. Mere viewing is not sufficient; in an Altman film, sound is supremely important. He has frustrated audiences previously by having several conversations going on at once. Altman is trying to smash out of the confines of cinematic conventions. (p. 6)

One has to mine an Altman film for its insights; but they truly are there. Colors, like yellow, coordinate throughout the film, and themes, such as the media-crazed world and what it is doing to us, cohere. In almost every scene there are tape recorders, TVs, radios, microphones, and other media paraphernalia. When Opal . . . wanders through a car burial ground and through a lot full of buses creating her ridiculous "poetic" soliloquies, she is startled by one man and is oblivious to another shaving. Humanity means nothing to her, though she doesn't realize it. In all of her grandiose speeches, she is a fool, like so many media people who self-importantly try to influence us.

As always, motifs define Altman's world. One of these is automobiles. Altman finds us caught in a car culture of accidents, automobile graveyards, and auto race courses. . . . Another pivotal motif is flowers. Flowers predominate, but their beauty doesn't help. Barbara Jean's . . . hospital room is full of flowers; a soldier brings a small bouquet; and so does the loyal husband. . . . Bouquets are everywhere, but as nice gestures they are meaningless. And the women and girls are constantly adorned in floral patterns. (pp. 7-8)

Over-all *Nashville* is very human. It makes humiliation of women clear like few films before it have. It is not kind to its men; they are aggressive, ineffectual, and phony. The ending is an example of how Altman views humanity. It is both exhilarating and pessimistic, spiritual and ironic. When the tattered, mysterious gamin Albuquerque picks up the microphone and sings, she is both stirring and not a good singer. Such is the elusive ambivalence that *Nashville* catches.

At the end, can a song break through the lack of communication? For all its spirit, it hardly seems so. We can sing—badly or with grace—but we can't act. Except absurdly, with desperation, or without effect. (p. 10)

F. Anthony Macklin, "'Nashville': America's Voices," in Film Heritage *(copyright 1975 by F. A. Macklin), Vol. 11, No. 1, Fall, 1975, pp. 6-10.*

KERMIT MOYER

[It] is impossible to evaluate Altman's artistic decisions . . . without some sense of the vision which those decisions attempt to clarify. *California Split* is perhaps the most literal, explicit treatment to date of Altman's perennial concern: the relation between risk and belief.

In one way or another, all of Altman's movies are about the necessary risk involved in any attempt to enact an imaginative vision and, thereby, to extend the limits of the "real." The sliding fluidity of reality, its status as a reflector of consciousness, is probably most apparent in his "gothic thriller," *Images*. Altman's premise is that reality is a function of consciousness: if we feel imprisoned, an act of consciousness, a risk of the imagination, may set us free. But such a risk demands belief: therefore his movies are also about the single-minded, committed faith which transcendence necessitates. (pp. 11-12)

[Altman's heroes] are all at work acting out their imaginative versions of themselves, *living* their visions. Their impulse is to impose their imagination upon the intractable context, the convention-bound cultural reality which imprisons them and from which they seek release. Put another way: his heroes try to draw the world into *their* movie in order to break through the deadening limits of the *conventional* movie in which they find themselves. In this sense, Altman's heroes resemble their director. . . .

It has often been noted that in almost all of his films Altman purposely works against the grain of one movie convention or another. . . . The convention against which Altman makes a film becomes the "reality" which he alters through his own imaginative act: he tries to impose his movie upon the movie reality which he challenges; and in altering that "movie reality" he alters too that sense of ourselves which depends upon it. Which is just a way of saying that in Altman's films style and substance coalesce: the improvisational, liberating style *is* the statement.

Altman perceives a world in which imagination (linked to innocence and belief) and convention (linked to cynicism and doubt) perennially battle over the structure of reality. . . . (p. 12)

California Split is a celebration of the gambling instinct. But the instinct Altman celebrates (and evidently tries to live by) must be distinguished from its antithesis, the urge which always seems to accompany it: the compulsion to pocket the money, the desperate need to win all the chips. The true gambling instinct is transcendent: it is the impulse to force reality to follow the imagination instead of the reverse. In the distinction between this impulse and the acquisitive compulsion lies the psychic split between . . . Charlie Waters and . . . Bill Denny. . . .

Charlie . . . believes that he can enact his dreams. In this he resembles Susan Peters, the vulnerable, childlike prostitute. . . . But unlike Charlie, Susan is passive: she accepts whatever comes along in the hope that it will be what she imagines. Because she lacks the will to pursue her dreams, her fantasy life is merely escapist. She reads Lawrence Durrell's *Justine* (a hothouse of exotic imaginings) to avoid the dreariness of her own circumstances. Susan depends upon her partner, Barbara Miller . . . in the same way that Denny depends upon Charlie: to provide her with an imaginative sense of possibility, to help her dream. Barbara guides Susan, but Barbara is herself guided by "the *Guide*" —the television version of reality which only nourishes escapism and numbs the imagination. In other words, the relationship between the two prostitutes reflects the relationship between Charlie and Bill Denny in order to arrive at a contrast between imaginative escape and imaginative action and risk. The movie is full of connections of this sort, links which so extend the movie's theme that the context and the narrative become inseparable, vindicating thematically Altman's stylistic technique of overlap.

Critics have taken to cautioning Altman against improvisational self-indulgence. . . . But Altman has discovered that it is possible to fuse collaborative improvisation and personal, self-conscious vision. His work is like the best of contemporary jazz, especially like the recent work of Miles Davis who often releases the richest talents of his musicians while expressing a mood and a consciousness which is nevertheless deeply and poetically personal, his own. . . . Altman encourages improvisation on his sets because he wants to extend the limits of his own imagination. He also wants to move away from conventional narrative and toward an impressionism which would allow him to meet his audience on a purely emotional level. Here his vision might be felt, experienced, rather than intellectually grasped. This kind of approach obviously poses special problems for the critic interested in Ideas or Tight Narrative Line: he hardly knows where to start with an Altman film, it seems to be all texture. But if we accept the experience Altman offers, we may discover intellectual implications that are as rich and as complex as the emotional and tonal colorations of his famous style. (pp. 15-16)

Kermit Moyer, "'Did You Ever See an Elephant Fly?' Style and Substance in the Films of Robert Altman," in Film Heritage *(copyright 1975 by F. A. Macklin), Vol. 11, No. 1, Fall, 1975, pp. 11-16.*

LEONARD QUART

One feels, and before *Nashville* it seemed a very grave limit, that Altman is in love with surfaces, that style is the essence of his work. And that if his dominant vision is that human life is absurd and fragmented, it is merely a shallow intuition, not deeply felt or thought through. Altman is hip and cynical, but his detachment is of that comfortable variety which often passes for iconoclasm and radicalism in American film. Altman's world is one where dreamers are destroyed (*Brewster McCloud*), friends betray and murder (*The Long Goodbye*), and every relationship is tainted by money (*McCabe and Mrs Miller*). But for all this sense of human corruption, his films gave off little genuine pain. The sum of his perceptions was that since everything is meaningless, you can only survive by being cool, mocking, and uncommitted. (pp. 97-8)

In *Nashville,* Altman can again be faulted for being unwilling or incapable of taking intellectual risks which parallel his formal ones, and for lacking a coherent social and political perspective. The charges cannot be easily dismissed, but this time his intuitions and images convey genuine feeling. This is more than a work of formal display, it is a film which transcends its limits, and is the best and most fully realized of his works. (p. 98)

In this film Altman . . . has moved remarkably beyond his characteristic filmic treatment of women as either dumb or savage. The most sympathetic character in the film is a suburban white gospel singer . . . who enters the sexual orbit of the macho rock singer, but comes out unhurt and even triumphant. She's tough, sensual, sensitive, and conventional. She is, in fact, one of a number of women in the film who seek some measure of freedom beyond the confines of mean or resentful marriages. Part of the spurious restoration of order at the film's end involves the rounding up by the men of their stray and reluctant women. What is unusual for this previously misogynistic director is that sympathy and derision are for a change distributed with some equity between the sexes.

But it's not Altman's gift for psychological nuance that gives the film its distinction. What strikes one from the credits on (these a parody of record cover and music magazine promotion), is the film's sheer energy and sensation. Altman's gift for capturing surfaces doesn't fail him here. He cuts from baton twirlers to political sound trucks, to marching bands, and to country and western performers. The visual movement is dynamic and never lets up—both within a frame and between scenes. . . . One thinks of Whitman's catalogues of America gone amuck: sound tracks overlap and people and events careen about—cars crash, TV Newsmen drone on and planes roar. There is too much to centre on, too many images and sounds, raw energy without meaning or pattern. A fragmented and violent America, an America crammed with life. Altman has beautifully created a metaphor for American excess: a din where everybody is struggling for their own gold record. The idea when baldly stated is of course unoriginal, but the images have considerable impact: here Altman's formal strategies perfectly fit the subject.

Ambitious as that sounds, one gets the feeling that Altman is seeking to do even more; that all the camera movement and images are working towards a final synthesis; that there is a large political statement at the film's core, and the climactic assassination scene is there to act as a final epiphany. But the epiphany doesn't occur. The assassin turns out to be oedipally rather than politically motivated—an inadequate conception in a film which works with primarily social rather than private realities. (pp. 99-100)

Nashville is more than a triumph of style. Altman intuitively understands and successfully dramatizes how bountiful and how destructive American popular culture is, and how appearances beguile and rule Americans. They beguile him too, and prevent him from getting at essences. But in *Nashville,* he does what he does so well that we hardly care. (p. 101)

Leonard Quart, "Altman's America," in London Magazine *(© London Magazine 1975), n.s. Vol. 15, No. 5, December-January, 1975-76, pp. 97-101.*

JOHN SIMON

The two hours' duration [of *Buffalo Bill and the Indians or Sitting Bull's History Lesson*] achieves nothing that could not have been done just as well in 90 minutes, and what sustains us much of the time is not so much lack of boredom as the assumption that so much artful quaintness must have something up its tasseled sleeve. In vain; this film makes me think that the center of Altman is made not of ideas, insights, visions, but of attitudes. And attitudes are not quite good enough. (p. 70)

There are two sides to almost everything: William F. Cody was also a Pony Express rider, Indian scout, hunter, and entrepreneur of remarkable skill, however little you and I may value these talents. . . . Altman's sitting duck of a Buffalo Bill, this all black-and-white—or, rather, all red-and-black—history lesson with its consistently noble Indians and dependably ignoble whites will not wash. Not even if it is presented as madcap satire that is at times ingenious and amusing; there is, after all, more than one way of forking a tongue. (pp. 70, 73)

[It] is not only the improvisational incoherences of the script that are problematical; there is also the notion that *texture* is all that matters, while *structure* can be allowed to shift for itself. It is not that I crave the overtailored plots of yesteryear; I do, however, want to see certain concepts worked out in dramatic terms. Let us call it a progression with intensification rather than mere brute accumulation of incidents. You could chop this movie up into tiny bits, splice them together in any order, and the result would not be appreciably less efficacious.

My point is that in order to deflate a balloon, you must first inflate it. Altman seems to assume that Buffalo Bill and the West are preinflated notions, ripe and ready for the pinprick. But are they? Cummings's famous "Buffalo Bill's Defunct" is a deflationary note that has resounded through numerous works of all kinds; for this film to be effective, some sort of pumping up was needed. Yet Altman begrudges his protagonist so much as his marksmanship; when a hated parakeet gets loose in his bedroom, Bill cannot hit it at almost point-blank range. And, in any case, two hours of unremitting deflation of one solitary subject makes *Buffalo Bill and the Indians* the longest pinprick on record. (p. 73)

I have no wish to talk anyone out of seeing this movie: Altman matters, and his very lapses are fringed with brightness. His quirks, though, have a way of getting the better of him—notably the mania for elaborately overlapping and studiedly blurred sound. I used to think that this was Altman's wrongheaded way of trying to approximate reality. It now looks more like a way of giving apparent significance to triviality—just as conceited people often talk extremely softly to make us strain for their every word. What good is Altman's celebrated eight-track sound if all it conveys is a one-track mind? (pp. 74-5)

John Simon, "Who Is Buffaloing Whom," in New York *Magazine (copyright © 1976 by News Group Publications, Inc.; reprinted with the permission of* New York *Magazine), Vol. 9, No. 27, July 5, 1976, pp. 70, 73-5.*

ANDREW SARRIS

[My] biggest problem with Altman has arisen with his anti-genre derision in "The Long Good-bye" and "Buffalo Bill." I am not saying that Altman or any modern film-maker should revere genre or even narrative. One may bypass it, but it is futile and unseemly to ridicule it. At times Altman evokes late Bergman's skepticism toward all forms of dramatic discourse, but in "Buffalo Bill," particularly, Altman has not devised an adequate substitute for the dramatic discourse. The result is that the grin of the Cheshire cat has frozen into a fashionable grimace of perpetual disenchantment. . . .

What I find lacking in "Buffalo Bill" is any genuine affection for its subject. . . .

Altman's relentlessly roving camera overcomments on the spectacle from such a cold distance that one wonders why anyone ever attended these Wild West Shows. The fault is more in the conception than in the execution. I feel that Altman did what he set out to do. Where he may have miscalculated was with his audience, not politically, since it is always open season these days on America's treatment of the Indians, but emotionally, since audiences around the world are still more interested in the plight of real Indians than in the show-biz image of the Redskin.

Yet though I disapprove of "Buffalo Bill," I thoroughly respect and even grudgingly admire it for its artistic integrity. . . . The ugliness of the film's palette of dull reds, browns, and yellows with a minimum of subdued blues and virtually no greens is undoubtedly part of Altman's strategy of visual alienation, and the mockingly martial music is also an echo of Altman at his most disenchanted. (p. 108)

Andrew Sarris, "Bottom Line Buffalos Altman," in The Village Voice *(reprinted by permission of* The Village Voice; *copyright © The Village Voice, Inc., 1976), Vol. XXI, No. 27, July 5, 1976, pp. 107-09.*

ROBERT J. CARDULLO

[Altman attempts in] his *Nashville* to evoke on screen what he perceives to be the dominant quality of American life today. It is one man's tragicomically exaggerated vision of contemporary American society, and by implication western civilization as a whole, that is the real subject of this film, the timeless universal to be conveyed through the particular vehicle of spatially defined *Nashville*. Altman's method in building and equipping such a vehicle is to be compared with that of character or the writer of comedy. Unlike the dramatic novelist or the tragedian, he is never at one with any of his characters, never at pains to pursue each's fate as he or she comes into being. Their dialogue is anything but profound, they themselves nothing if not ordinary. We do not identify with them as they move linearly from a beginning to an end in time and come to some insight about their lives. The particular actions of the people of *Nashville* are not intended, in this way, to evoke the complete range, the absoluteness, of human experience, and hence to work as Altman's personal, boundless metaphor for or selective aesthetic vision of the character of human life in general. As the polar opposites of "round" introspectionists, these seemingly "flat," self-presenting characters, having sprung full-blown from the mind of their creator, have their fates (or want of them) imposed on them from the start. They exist spatially rather than temporally, much as the figures in a painting. That is, they do not change, are "complete" from the beginning, tangible enough to endure as they are, in the service of Altman's social vision. Their three-dimensionality is sufficiently suggested rather than fully realized, their existence defined more by the presence of people and things, in space, than by their own thoughts, actions, and interactions, in time. These characters do not so much act *upon* one another to produce change in time as act *at* one another to isolate themselves in space. They thus point more to the significance of that space as the artistic extension of Altman's selective social vision than to each other as separate and unique incarnations of his personal, temporal assessment of the human experience.

Appropriately, no one in this film appears alone for very long, if at all. (pp. 313, 315)

Typical or general situation, texture, defines action in *Nashville* and action is designed in turn to bring out the various attributes of characters, which were there at the beginning, or to introduce new characters. Such figures are comparable to those described by Edwin Muir to be "like a familiar landscape, which now and then surprises us when a particular effect of light or shadow alters it, or we see it from a new prospect." . . . (pp. 315-16)

Nashville at its greatest is . . . a film of character, cinematic in style, novelistic in form and idea, tragic in substance, comic in superstructure. Its aim is to expose the discrepancy between appearance—illusion—and reality in America today, to uncover our nation's glaring contradictions. To this end, paradoxically, the film circumscribes time from the start so as to make it inexhaustible and hence unimportant or unreal. (p. 316)

[But] *Nashville* is much more than the sum of its characters. Indeed, it transcends them even as it presents them by framing them largely from the relatively objective distance of the medium and the long shot in the company of one another; at the same time it detaches us from them in some measure by withholding what, in the context of the dramatic film, would be deemed vital information about their characters. We do not feel cheated by this "flat" characterization or that character is being unaccountably obscured, because we know all along as much (or as little) about the characters as they know, or care to know, about each other. Again, these figures exist not so much engrossed in time, *for* each other, as suspended in space, *in the presence of* one another, in the service of Robert Altman's social vision. . . . The people of Nashville are trapped in a vicious circle, frozen in time, as it were. The like and limited offspring of their own creation, they are unable to expend anything but the inflated energies it generates alone. (pp. 316-17)

[Altman should] be lauded for the breadth and pith of *Nashville*'s thematic ambitions as well as for the ingeniousness of their technical execution. To be sure, the film has its weaknesses, the most serious of which is a proclivity to employ strictly visual imagery to convey complex ideas. Still it must be judged a sizeable achievement as is. . . . Technique in *Nashville,* I propose, is a deliberate reflection and projection of the passivity and failure of imagination of its characters in the distance the relatively static camera maintains from events, the seeming randomness of the editing, the apparently casual selection of dialogue to make them intelligible, and the finely disguised writing, composing, and singing of songs by nonprofessionals (the actors themselves). Altman's cinema of distance is fashioned, furthermore, to discourage our total passive, hypnotic, unthinking absorption in events and lives on screen, to goad us into bringing some intelligence and reason to bear on what passes before our eyes. We are made to stand outside this cinema, "estranged" from it, to the extent that its constituent parts call attention to themselves consciously, yet not clamorously, as aesthetic devices and demand integration into a unique artistic universe.

For all the distance it maintains from the object of its social vision-artistic creation, *Nashville,* it must be said, is never cold and condescending. Accordingly, there are no cardboard figures in this film, no vicious caricatures by turns ominously unsettling and comically reassuring. . . . *Nashville* may be finally and most accessibly a coolly, almost deceptively, desperate example of the moral deadness that can infect a society. However, in the dialectic it sets up between distanced camera and animated action, it is perhaps equally an ironically self-deprecatory, self-conscious "I" of this camera juxtaposed against the animal vitality (illusory as it may be) of the aimless "we" on screen. For Altman clearly loves the country-and-western scene for the quasi-primitive vitality of its animal aimlessness. He himself would emulate its unreflective, simple *living* from day to day, but *ipso facto,* as artist and thinker, is unable to. Yet he hates and would transform this same scene for the absence of real inspiration and invention from its motions. In the unresolved tension of its love-hate, his dilemma is at the core of his art. It is the basis for the benign and enduring antagonism between *Nashville*'s form and content, the necessarily unresolved tension of the film's will to gratify even as it edifies. (pp. 318-19)

In a brilliantly reasoned essay which appeared in the Spring, 1975 issue of *The Hudson Review,* Gilberto Perez said that in Dovzhenko's *Earth,* people and things

> are taken out of their spatial context by close-ups; their intrinsic reality, the sense of their independent life, matters more than where they are exactly within a vast space. . . . The spatially discontinuous [or fragmented] shots are linked together by their inner arrangement . . . Dovzhenko prefers to bring out correspondences, connections between things, to juxtapose elements that have an intrinsic similarity. . . . In his effort to establish pattern against the weight of concreteness, to incorporate into a larger design the individual energy that things possess, he gives the film its forward movement. . . .

Perez went on to distinguish between *Earth* as an example of "the cinema of solid objects" and Murnau's *Nosferatu* as its opposite, an example of "the cinema of empty space." He brought up in the process Ortega y Gasset's argument that "close and distant vision are two different ways of seeing. . . . In close vision we look at solid objects; in distant vision we look more at the space between objects, at the air in which objects are submerged."

Like *Nosferatu,* Robert Altman's *Nashville* may be said to be one example of "the cinema of empty space"; like *Earth,* it may be said to eschew portraying its characters and events from the dramatic perspective of time for presenting them from the geometric perspective of space (where it opts to *subjugate* the interweaving and resolution of its stories to the vision inherent in its overall design, however, *Earth* eliminates the flow of narrative almost completely). But, in the uncertain, uneasy distance of *Nosferatu* "what is actually in the world affects us less than what we fear might be there." And, in the sure, restful closeness of *Earth* "what things are in themselves, in their enduring aspect," is more important than the space which surrounds them. In the ambivalent, anticipatory distance of *Nashville,* by contrast, what people are in close relation to their space, how they are simultaneously its products and producers, its pawns and manipulators, is offered up for our scrutiny. (pp. 321-22)

Altman's method is of the film of character, whose real subject is the character of action, of situation or milieu, and whose perspective is objective. To everything on the screen he gives an equal stress. . . . [Unlike Dovzhenko,] his is the evenness of stress of "all in the background," where people and things are often viewed from a distance, in a *mise en scene,* occupying and in turn being enveloped by a space. It is not as if "different things were brought, one after another, into the same space, a kind of constant, a common ground," as in Dovzhenko, but as if different spaces were made, one after another, to be inhabited (and revisited) by the same people, themselves a kind of constant. Just as in *Earth* "what different things have in common is enforced" by their being placed successively within, by their being made to fill, the same frame, so too in *Nashville* is what different spaces have in common enforced by their being made successively to host, to submerge, the same people.

Unlike Dovzhenko's humanistic vision, Altman's is essentially a social one, then, which must needs be take the long, the objective view available from the perch of distance. Thus, rarely is a character seen alone in the space of the film's long shots. This would be to give individual character too much weight at the expense of the company of *Nashville*'s characters. Beyond that, it would be to give space too much weight, too much consequence, at the expense of character per se. Rather, groups of characters are observed in long shot. Unlike the people of *Earth,* the people of *Nashville* cannot "be firmly apprehended for what they are in themselves," in their substance, their essence, and *hence are never viewed in close-up.* They can be apprehended only in relation to the continuous space they inhabit, and to which they have all but sacrificed the intrinsic nobility, grandeur, and vitality of the human spirit. What is left is mere appearance, photographed at a distance, accordingly, so as to give us "the elusive impression, the passing glimpse, the oblique view" of figures of light, animated more from without than within. (pp. 322, 324)

Robert J. Cardullo, "The Space in the Distance: A Study of Altman's 'Nashville'," in Literature/Film Quarterly *(© copyright 1976 Salisbury State College), Vol. 4, No. 4, Fall, 1976, pp. 313-24.*

ANDREW SARRIS

Robert Altman's *3 Women* is such a stimulating achievement in cinematic art that it makes one rethink the whole aesthetic of motion pictures. . . . There is something so utterly unusual about *3 Women* that its like may never materialize again, even from Altman. It seems to be located at a fleeting intersection of two awarenesses—the artist's and society's. It is both a dream and a document, a set of facts and a cluster of myths. But the mixture of ingredients produces a very strange concoction, one difficult to describe in terms of the rhetoric of contemporary criticism. . . .

In all of Altman's films, but most decisively in *Brewster McCloud, Images,* and now *3 Women,* his feelings are filtered through a mystical-aesthetical framework that limits a reviewer's sociological speculation. Since I do not find self-consciousness in an artist, even a film artist, to be a crippling disability, *Brewster McCloud, Images,* and *3 Women* are among my favorite Altman films. It is perhaps my latent, some would say blatant, antipathy to realist aesthetics that makes me react so warmly to what has been widely publicized as a literal "dream" film. (p. 40)

That [Sissy Spacek and Shelley Duvall] are virtually interchangeable, and [their] two characters virtually inseparable, gives *3 Women* a passing resemblance to Ingmar Bergman's *Persona.* Of course, the extraordinarily vivid sensuality of Bibi Andersson and Liv Ullmann provides a visual subtext of erotic entanglement at odds with the self-deprecating eccentricities of Duvall and Spacek. Consequently, Bergman's famous superimposition of one face on another verges on vampirish possession, whereas Altman distances himself from his characters and keeps them distinct from each other.

There are other differences as well, differences that should be stressed in view of the frequent mentions of Bergman's influence on Altman. Ever since *Monika* Bergman has dealt almost exclusively with articulate, attractive, accomplished protagonists with the capacity to serve as spokespersons for the director. Altman's characters, with the possible exception of the doomed McCabe, are down and away from the director's gaze, which mixes irony and compassion in about equal amounts. Perhaps the reason that Altman can allow his players so much freedom to improvise is that they are so completely confined in a formal box that all they actually improvise is the degree and dexterity of their wriggling. From an Aristotelian standpoint Shelley Duvall's Millie Lammoreaux and Sissy Spacek's Pinky Rose are such hopeless nitwits that they are not worthy of all the attention lavished on them. . . . Bergman's characters, regardless of class or sensibility, are afflicted with memory. The past is palpable in their personas. Altman's characters fashion their lives from moment to moment in a perpetual present with no roots in the past, and no regrets for lost innocence. Certainly Altman seems the least nostalgic of all directors, and even when he ventures into the past as in *McCabe* and *Thieves Like Us* he translates supposedly convivial and communal eras into modernist terms of social dislocation. Part of his artistic strategy can be interpreted as a revisionist attitude toward old Hollywood conventions, but part can be attributed also to a very oblique relationship to his own unconscious. In that context, where in Altman's dream of a movie does Altman himself appear? There does not seem to be a character in *3 Women* that corresponds to Altman. Is he then merely the *metteur-en-scene,* a modern equivalent of Pirandello's cynical stage manager in *Six Characters in Search of an Author?*

The production notes quote, presumably with Altman's approval, Carl Gustav Jung's 1928 comment on the subject of dreams: "This whole creation is essentially subjective, and the dream is the theatre where the dreamer is at once scene, actor, prompter, stage manager, author, audience, and critic." . . . I would say that Bergman is more Freudian than Jungian whereas Altman is more Jungian than Freudian. At the moment let us say that we are talking about nothing more than a certain mystical emphasis on the collective unconscious among the Jungians, and a certain skepticism toward the claims of the group on the individual among the Freudians. (pp. 40, 42)

But if I want to convey what *3 Women* really *is* as opposed to what it merely *means,* I could do worse than try to evoke Shelley Duvall's stride as she walks from one social Calvary to another. There is so much spiritual grace in that stride, and so much wisdom in Altman's decision to follow that stride to the ends of his scenario, that one is ennobled simply by witnessing the bonds of compassion between the director and his actress. Nothing else in *3 Women* is quite so overwhelming as the cumulative gallantry under stress of Shelley Duvall's Millie. It makes everything Fellini ever did with Giulietta Masina seem patronizing by comparison. (p. 42)

Andrew Sarris, "Robert Altman Dreams a Movie . . . ," in The Village Voice *(reprinted by permission of* The Village Voice; *copyright © The Village Voice, Inc., 1977), Vol. XXII, No. 15, April 11, 1977, pp. 40, 42.*

JONATHAN ROSENBAUM

Doubling the number of featured players in *Nashville* from twenty-four to forty-eight while shrinking the time scale from three days to one, *A Wedding* offers an extension rather than an expansion of Robert Altman's behavioral repertory. Variations on the same dirty little secrets, social embarrassments, and isolating self-absorptions that illustrate his last ten movies are trotted out once again—articulated as gags or tragicomic mash notes, molded into actors' bits, arranged in complementary or contrasting clusters, orchestrated and choreographed into simultaneous or successive rhythmic patterns, and strategically timed and placed to coincide with unexpected plot or character reversals.

The execution of these pirouettes has never presented critics with much of a problem, for the level of craft is pretty consistent. (Some gags are funnier than others, but all get the same careful/offhand inflection.) What remains a bone of contention is their justification, which shifts more discernibly from film to film. . . .

What's the subject of—and justification for—*A Wedding*? It's hard to say precisely, but it seems perched somewhere between weddings in general . . . and one wedding in particular, i.e., Southern nouveau-riche bride marries groom from established Midwestern aristocracy, a Catholic ceremony followed by a reception and party at the estate of the groom's family. . . . [I] would be quite happy to accept the wedding and party as a motor and catalyst for Altman's interacting pirouettes—if that's all I were being asked to accept.

But something tells me that Altman wants me to accept something more—specifically, a few reverse zooms away from the façade of the church and family mansion accompanied by solemn brass fanfares. Are these shots assertions of a Big Statement or mockeries of such assertions? The question is academic, because they invariably register as both, despite the fact that the referent remains vague. The implication is that Altman has something important to say, even though he can't quite believe it and isn't quite sure what it is.

I'd like to offer Altman an escape clause from the weighty demands that some critics have been placing on him, and propose that style is the subject of, *and* the justification for, most of his work—for better and for worse, and in *A Wedding* most of all. How we come to terms with this is our problem as well as his; a few suggestions are offered below.

If the streets of Altmanville are paved with style and peopled with charming visitors and residents, the urban planning behind the whole complex still has some of the communal formlessness and pathos of condominiums and shopping malls. Families in Altman films nearly always have something makeshift and jerry-built about them, similar to most film crews—temporary arrangements made by restless nomads.

The Corelli family in *A Wedding,* which is supposed to be relatively fixed and stable, comes across as an awkward cipher of dissimilar parts that never quite match up. . . .

As a static entity, this family never really convinces or coheres, perhaps because they appear to be composed in relation to the dynamics of the scattershot plot, which is composed in turn in order to produce pirouettes. . . .

If the Brenners, the bride's trucker family, have slightly more collective coherence, this may be in part a function of their own dislocation, Southern accents included, which bring them closer to Altman's imaginative range. Yet they too seem formed by expediency designed to provoke some of his specialties. (p. 13)

[Consider Hughie], the bride's likable kid brother. When he swallows a lot of pills at the party and explains to a Corelli that they're for his epilepsy, my smirking assumption—already conditioned by the Altman context—is that this is a cover story for uppers or Quaaludes. Much later, after the honeymoon car crashes into a fuel truck and the wedding couple are believed to be dead, an ugly quarrel breaks out between the families, seething with class resentments, until Hughie—passionately echoing my own conditioned sentiments at this point—screams, "Will you all shut up? They're dead!" Then, after tearfully describing the wreckage that he saw, he has an epileptic seizure—in a shot that Altman "tastefully" cuts short. Before I can recover from this, the wedding couple appear, alive; it turns out that the real victims of the accident were the former lovers of each, characters that the film has already conditioned me not to give two hoots about. In algebraic terms, smirk + anti-smirk + false disaster + real disaster = 0. All I'm left with is a nice kid who has epilepsy.

Moving through this charted space like a visitor shoved through a package tour, one is not encouraged or even permitted to settle down; movement itself becomes the purpose of the trip, the nature and sum of this movement the director's signature. Unlimited virtuosity is exercised on a limited terrain, where any possibilities of sustained reflection are thwarted for the sake of glancing cameos and theatrical turnarounds. . . .

Altman reaches for petrified models from other movies: a Corelli suggested by Brando's Corleone in *The Godfather,* addressing a female corpse in a manner recalling Brando's in *Last Tango in Paris;* an adulterous greenhouse rendezvous out of *Rules of the Game;* a car wreck from *Contempt.* One could play the game endlessly. . . . The trouble with such references—which also proliferate in *The Long Goodbye*—is that they're never more than nostalgic touchstones. Like Bogdanovich's and Truffaut's and unlike Godard's and Rivette's, they never add critical insights to the originals, functioning instead as postage-stamp reproductions designed to fill up empty spaces.

"Whatever its sophistication, style has always something crude about it: it is a form with no clear destination, the product of a thrust, not an intention, and, as it were, a vertical and lonely dimension of thought. Its frame of reference is biological or biographical, not historical: it is the writer's 'thing,' his glory and his prison, it is his solitude. Indifferent to society and transparent to it, a closed personal process, it is in no way the product of a choice or of a reflection on Literature. It is the private portion of the ritual, it rises up from the writer's myth-laden depths and unfolds beyond his area of control." . . .

[A] director like Altman [is often oddly] assigned the status of "modernist"—a term that can be made to apply to his work only after the concept has been stripped of its historical meaning, and used as a synonym for *modern, contemporary,* or *alienated/European/jaded/skeptical/self-conscious* (pick one). Precisely because workaday auteurism has chosen to operate without a modernist canon (ignoring the work of Akerman, Duras, Godard, Rainer, Rivette, Snow, Straub/Huillet and others whose strategies depend more on formal decisions), it is understandable why an attempt would be made to enlist someone like Altman as an entertaining replacement. Yet as long as he is perceived and celebrated as a stylist, the effort is foredoomed, for reasons suggested by the passage from Roland Barthes' *Writing Degree Zero* quoted above. And if anything about Altman's work is clarified by *A Wedding*—simultaneously one of his richest and thinnest movies—is that it can't be celebrated or defended any other way. . . .

Good, bad, and indifferent, [the characters of this film] all get dutifully pasted into Altman's family scrapbook, a book that could well be titled, "What We Did at Summer Camp." ("When it's over, it gets real sad," the film's closing line, refers to more than just weddings; it's a campfire farewell.) The sheer unevenness of the items is such that we either have to divvy up the spoils into good and bad piles—which threatens to become tedious—or try to adopt a different way of dealing with all of them.

This instability of response has a lot to do with what keeps Altman's movies interesting, at least as long as we're watching them—one thing that I believe separates his marijuana drifts from the cocaine conceits of his colleagues. It's only after the roller coaster stops that we can evaluate whether the ride was worth taking. Whatever my misgivings, when I think about what most of the rest of the Hollywood carnival wants me to do with my time and money, I'm tempted to brave the tracks once more. At least it beats cotton candy and pinball. (p. 14)

Jonathan Rosenbaum, "An Altman," in Film Comment *(copyright © 1978 by Jonathan Rosenbaum; reprinted by permission of the author), Vol. 14, No. 5, September-October, 1978, pp. 12-14.*

JUDITH M. KASS

Altman likes show-business motifs, which appear regularly in his films, or bits of activity related to shows, and this derives, at least partly, from being comfortable with his performers. Donald Sutherland's and Elliott Gould's behavior in *M*A*S*H* is a show in itself—theatrical, mannered, and even artificial in its heightened, cool relaxation. And there's the spoof of John Schuck's "suicide," a play in itself, complete with music and a grand finale. *Brewster McCloud* takes place at the Houston Astrodome, an arena devoted not only to sports but to shows as well. (p. 19)

Altman's "show" relates to another branch of the arts, painting, which he constantly refers to when talking about his movies. "I look at a film as closer to a painting or a piece of music, it's an impression," says Altman. . . .

Altman's films are all shot in Panavision, which has an aspect ratio shaped like a rectangular painting, and this increases the force of his analogy. The complete control he exercises over the look of his films, as a painter does over his canvases, is another facet of Altman's preoccupation with painting. (p. 21)

All of *Nashville* is a canvas; it was part of Altman's filmic conception that most of the time the screen would be crammed with action and people, giving the impression of a postcard overflowing its borders. *Buffalo Bill* follows the same visual scheme, with its panoply of interrelated events, its swirling movements, all taking place within either the arena or the surrounding tent village.

Just as Altman's films cover the screen from corner to corner, the sound he employs fills the ear as natural, everyday sound does. (p. 22)

Most of Altman's films have had at least one individual who was "insane" or at least obsessed, from the Robert Duvall character in *Countdown,* who's determined to be the first man on the moon, to the person Sissy Spacek plays in *3 Women,* who inhabits another character. (p. 25)

The insanity Altman shows on screen is a social madness; it isn't a private, locked-up-in-a-booby-hatch craziness (with the exception of the Robert Duvall character in *M*A*S*H*). His films relate most directly to the screwball comedies and social justice dramas of the thirties. But madness in the seventies isn't the fey, charming whimsy it was in the thirties. The insanity Altman depicts is sour, deliberate, and streaked with sadism. . . .

Altman takes the form of other movies and bends it into a quirky, mad version of itself to suit the sensibility of the seventies. . . .

Along with the idea of social madness goes the concept of loners with visions, as Bud Cort is in *Brewster McCloud* and Warren Beatty is in *McCabe and Mrs. Miller.* These are men, or boys, stopped at some point in their adolescent development when they still believe that all things are possible. (pp. 26-7)

The worlds depicted in Altman's films are aberrent, self-enclosed microcosms. They look all right from the outside, but they're crazy when you get up close. (p. 2)

Altman likes to take a particular genre and break the form. . . . But it was the *form* that *Nashville* took that was the revelation; it was a kaleidoscope of impressions, vignettes, and thumbnail portraits. The minute the viewer started concentrating on what a character was doing or saying, or where his actions were leading, Altman cut away to another set of characters. He kept firm control of the film, though; *Nashville* may be impressionistic in style, but its realization is concrete. (p. 28)

The structure of any Altman film is deliberately unsettling. Altman takes parallel editing to the point of fracturing his film. This is particularly noticeable in *Buffalo Bill,* with its constant jumps between Bill's activities and Ned Buntline's carping commentary, delivered from the bar, but it was foreshadowed in *M*A*S*H,* which used the operating room as a sort of splicing device to separate the various events but keep them firmly held together, as a form of thematic bridge. (pp. 28-9)

Each character in an Altman film comforts himself by refusing to see the truth around him and nourishes himself with ideas of his own invincibility and ability to overcome whatever obstacles are placed in his path. (p. 30)

Along with this idea of flying in the face of what would normally be considered the accepted wisdom is the notion that Altman's characters are, for the most part, hapless gamblers or romantic, foolish visionaries. To some degree, so is Altman himself, although his movies are, on the surface, cool and distant, with a sense of being rueful observations, rather than committed polemics. Such are the doctors played by Gould and Sutherland in *M*A*S*H* who gamble that they can keep madness at bay with their sophomoric pranks and black humor. Brewster McCloud is the most quixotic dreamer of all Altman's heroes, with his insistence on scaling the Astrodome's heights, gambling that he can do it without falling and that his luck will hold out. (pp. 31-2)

Altman continues to consolidate and enlarge upon his growing popularity as a filmmaker by playing variations upon his greatest virtues: his startling originality, the fact that he never makes the same film twice, and his consistent use of "American" themes. Even *Images,* which is the only motion picture he has made abroad, has as its text the mental and emotional disintegration of an individual. (p. 36)

In spite of the frequently bitter viewpoint he takes in approaching each film, Altman is an optimist. He *hopes* for something better, but, being a realist, he presents his version of the truth, a slightly negative, determinedly ironic, highly idiosyncratic and deeply personal vision of America, a place Altman obviously loves, but which he shows with all its warts left on. He clearly loves making films, and he wants everyone to come to his party. (pp. 37-8)

The Delinquents is the sort of consummately silly movie many directors turn out as a first film. (p. 39)

The Delinquents features a great many raw, underlit interiors, overexposed exterior shots, and erratically moving shadows. It looks the way John Cassavetes's first movie, *Shadows,* would have looked had it been made out of doors. But it tells the same story *Rebel Without a Cause* told two years earlier. It even uses some locations of the same kind: a police station and an abandoned mansion. (pp. 39-40)

The film features a redundant and pointless narration, spoken in tones of darkest foreboding, about the "teenage violence and immaturity" that saps "the moral fiber of our great nation." At the end (the voice is used as if in preachy parentheses) the narrator asks "who's to blame?" for this "crippling disease," and suggests that "church groups" should step in to counsel troubled adolescents and their parents. . . . The results of . . . repressed sexuality, on the evidence of *The Delinquents,* are slashed tires, teenage hangovers, and the hassles one's parents dish out for irresponsible behavior. In fact, *The Delinquents* indicts uncaring, overzealous disciplinarian adults as severely as *Rebel Without a Cause* does, but without the careful motivation the Nicholas Ray/Stewart Stern script develops to explain the outbursts of hoodlumism in that film. One would like to absolve Altman of blame for the use of a poorly written narration for his film, but he and Stern are guilty of using (and overusing) the same device in *The James Dean Story.* (pp. 40-1)

The James Dean Story was an unsuccessful attempt to capitalize on the dead movie star's short-lived screen popularity. It's a rather ordinary compilation film that seeks to add luster to a tradition of dubious film documentaries—the psychobiography. . . . There is no hint, in either the narration or the style in which it was read, that the creators of the film understood what Dean was all about—that he was, as Brando put it, "a lost boy trying to find himself" and doing a bad job of it. (pp. 43-4)

It would have been far more effective to use his tormented screen persona than the shots of a dead seagull washing around in the Pacific, which Stern's narration likens to Dean's unfulfilled dreams. The effect of this kind of silliness is to obscure Dean rather than expose him. The most effective scenes are those among the people in New York who knew him before he made a hit on the stage in André Gide's *The Immoralist* and left for California. (p. 44)

By far the most irritating technique Altman and George employed was that of a "distant figure," an individual of Dean's size and build who is used as a stand-in, in locations from Dean's youth in Fairmount, Indiana. Fairmount is the only place where the filmmakers found cooperative subjects for their prying cameras. (p. 45)

And Stern's narration piles it on with a trowel: Dean possessed "the lonely awareness that growing up is pain," his death meant that "youth mourned itself in the passing of James Dean," and the commentary seeks to explain his passion for motorcycles by claiming that "to test the limits of life he had to approach the borders of death."

There are bits of truth in all this pseudopsychological attitudinizing, but it's hard to sort them out from all the blinding insights that occurred after Dean's death. The film is much better as a portrait of an era—the fifties. Dean belongs to that "silent generation" of "beatniks" who felt nothing but apathy at the Korean War or Joseph McCarthy's anti-Communist hysteria. In the grubby New York of the mid-fifties, when all girls looked like Audrey Hepburn and all boys like Tony Curtis, there was nothing special about the young man who was born James Byron in 1931. What was special was the way those young Hepburns and Curtises worshipped Dean and made him into something he never could have been—an ageless idol, the representation of their youth and the repository of their fantasies. (p. 46)

Judith M. Kass, in her Robert Altman: American Innovator, *Leonard Maltin, General Editor (copyright © 1978 by Leonard Maltin; reprinted by permission of Popular Library, Fawcett Books Group, a unit of the Consumer Publishing Division of CBS Inc.), Popular Library, 1978, 282 p.*

TOM MILNE

Up to a point, at least, Robert Altman's celebration of the celebration of matrimony in *A Wedding* . . . is irresistibly and uncomplicatedly funny. Eavesdropping at precisely the right moment, his camera is invariably well placed to pull a plum out of the surrounding chaos of socially amplified intrigues, obsessions, eccentricities, gaffes, resentments and pretensions. . . . [The] wedding gradually becomes a looking-glass into which one peers, fascinated, at a minor key counterpart to the nine circles of Dante's inferno. . . .

[One] realises, as the film progresses, that the 'naturalism' (comically heightened, of course) is gradually being abandoned for—in the phrase annexed by Jonathan Rosenbaum in defence of *Nashville*—a 'dialectic collage of unreality'. No one wedding could credibly throw out quite so many sins and situations as this one does. Yet Altman keeps on turning the screw, ever more outrageously, until the bones and ligaments of reality snap and, as in *Nashville,* one finds oneself confronted by an almost abstract microcosm which can be interpreted any way one wants. . . .

As in *Nashville,* the socio-political caps left lying around fit very comfortably indeed, with even the wedding guests who fail to show up suggesting the bankruptcy of America's policy of goodwill. The trouble is that, whereas the characters in *Nashville* obstinately maintained lives and wills of their own, often running counter to the allegory and destroying its linear simplicity, here they exist only within, and in terms of, the wedding. *A Wedding,* in other words, is much more simplistic: good fun, but not, like *Nashville,* a kaleidoscopic reappraisal of the American dream.

Tom Milne, "Film Reviews: 'A Wedding'," in Sight and Sound *(copyright © 1978 by The British Film Institute), Vol. 48, No. 1, Winter, 1978-79, p. 57.*

GAVIN MILLAR

[The burden of *A Wedding,* Altman's] very black and very funny new movie is to make us laugh at our romantic, sentimental, pretentious absurdity. We are, in the Altman canon, certainly the oddest creatures on the face of the earth, and he looks at us with astonishment, as if surprised to discover that an animal so ill-equipped for living has managed to get by for so long. One of our chief drawbacks is the yawning abyss between what we think of ourselves and what we are, and it is into this abyss, with ungentlemanly relish, that Altman jumps with all his troops. . . .

Altman believes in pushing his observations on film as close to lifelike experiences as the medium will stand without boring us to tears. So he fills the screen with action and character, floods us with information, breaks up our perception of it into forgettable gobbets, buries important revelations under trivial gossip, and altogether tries to make us do the work, so he says, of making the film.

Of course, there is a deal of double-talk, in the other sense, in all this. While he pretends he is offering us a cheerful chaos, the image of life, his selection processes are ruthlessly imposing: he takes us where he wants, and if we do not see what is there, it is our loss and our failure, not his.

There is a special pleasure for English viewers in seeing an American film so aware of class. The groom's family appear to be grand old Middle West money, the bride's are *nouveau riche* Southern truckers, and the opportunities for display, discretion and solecism are rich, and reaped richly. . . .

Altman scarcely pauses in the dissection process: few stones are left unturned and no opportunity afforded to those who want it, to show that people are all right really. These people are not all right really. They are unhappy, drunk, frightened, lonely, drugged, lying, mad, hopelessly in love, or dead. Some of them, during the course of the film, are all of these things. If you can equate this vision with humour which is not sentimental, but not detached either, you will laugh as much as I did.

Gavin Millar, "Double-talk" (© Gavin Millar, 1979; reprinted by permission of the author and his agents, Judy Daish Associates, Ltd.), in The Listener, *Vol. 101, No. 2593, January 11, 1979, p. 57.*

COLIN L. WESTERBECK, JR.

In all his recent films, including *A Wedding,* Robert Altman has made the kind of satire that delivers a big, round-house right to the whole society. Only a director capable of great economy as a story-teller—Orson Welles is another—can do satire on this epic scale. Just as Welles was able in *Citizen Kane* to describe the entire course of a marriage in a few snippets of conversation at the breakfast table, so Altman can neatly create the personalities of a half dozen characters at a time. Both directors are masters of the vignette. When Altman's wedding party returns from the ceremony to the reception at the house, for instance, Altman just sends everyone off to the bathroom. As people cue up to use the facilities, in that little tension between a formal occasion and everyone's bodily functions, Altman can establish in a gesture or exchange of pleasantries what another director would need a whole scene to get across. (p. 18)

The more people your satire includes, however, the more trouble you are going to have with one person who must necessarily be in it: yourself. If you are sending up the whole world, you somehow have to admit your own place among the victims. . . . After all, what makes *Citizen Kane* great is that Welles played Kane himself. Altman's solution to the problem is not to act in his film, but rather to project onto one of the roles in it a parody of his own role as maker of it. In *A Wedding,* as in *Nashville,* this surrogate figure is the most obnoxious, irredeemable character in the movie, the one whom the satire ridicules most pitilessly. It is the character played in each film by Geraldine Chaplin. (pp. 18-19)

It may even be that this time Altman is a little *too* like his anti-self played by Chaplin. Like Rita [the "wedding coordinator"], Altman gets very caught up in the occasion, the ritual of mating, and practically turns his film into an ark. Every character and every incident have their counterpart. An implication of male homosexuality at one point is matched elsewhere by one of female homosexuality. One latecomer who arrives at the reception on horseback is paired with another who pulls up on a motorcycle. . . . Altman is also like Rita in that he is trying hard—too hard—to keep it all from becoming just an empty ritual. The real significance of ceremonies like weddings having drained away long ago, Rita is the sort of person who now tries to dedicate herself to going through the motions. That's why she's so pathetic.

Altman's films have usually been wonderful because they're one thing in our lives that doesn't just go through the motions. They take cliché people and events—and movie genres—and revive them for us. They breathe new life into them in the very act of poking fun, because these movies are so original, so full of energy. But *A Wedding* might almost make us wonder whether Altman's own, self-invented forms haven't gone a bit dead on him. It's become too easy and automatic for him to do this kind of stuff.

Altman has always had special feelings, special ambitions, for poor, benighted creatures like Rita. In *Three Women,* he showed us what those feelings were, how intent he is on humanizing such characters. But when his aspirations for a character like this fail, the character becomes more odious than ever. He becomes the sort of person you avoid in real life, someone who would try to corner you at a cocktail party and confide in you. He's the type who acts as if you should help him make sense of his life when in fact you can't figure out what the hell he's talking about. You smile uneasily, and look for your chance to escape. Toward the end, our relationship with *A Wedding,* perhaps with Altman himself, gets to be a little like this. (p. 19)

Colin L. Westerbeck, Jr., "Altman's 'A Wedding'," in Commonweal *(copyright © 1979 Commonweal Publishing Co., Inc.; reprinted by permission of Commonweal Publishing Co., Inc.), Vol. CVI, No. 1, January 19, 1979, pp. 18-19.*

ANDREW SARRIS

In the past I have been up on Altman when everyone else was down, and down on Altman when everyone else was up. I have always found it strange that so somber and so pessimistic an artist has managed to be so productive in an industry dedicated mostly to the manufacture of cotton candy.

Part of the answer may be that he was regarded for a long time as a realist and an iconoclast. . . . No one seemed to notice the stylization and absurdism in [his] works. But when Altman went completely abstract in *Brewster McCloud, Images,* and *Three Women,* most reviewers found no outlet for their anti-establishment rhetoric and turned thumbs down on these violent ruptures from all realistic conventions. For my part, I have come to appreciate Altman more and more as a thoroughly eccentric and resourceful artist. His art remains hard edged at a time when much of the cinema is becoming sickening soft.

The Altman films I like least—*The Long Goodbye, Buffalo Bill and the Indians,* and *The Wedding*—are the ones in which he seems to be smirking. Some of his erstwhile admirers are beginning to gossip that he has been taken over by a shifting array of young sycophants and that all his recent films have suffered from script trouble. Yet as I look back over the 14 films he has turned out in the past dozen years, I find an unusually distinctive body of work making up a very personal landscape.

It is this landscape—cold, forbidding, fiercely and uncompromisingly outside of human control—which I recognize in *Quintet,* and everything else followed as a matter of course. Yes, the dialogue is often silly, not as silly as the dialogue in *Convoy,* but silly by most standards. Still, I didn't mind. The dogged endurance of the characters in their icy surroundings was a more eloquent statement of the human condition in cinematic terms than almost any dialogue could have been. Altman's characters endure, as Altman himself endures, not by any shafts of wit but by sudden flashes of intuition and by a visual grasp of the immensity of the unknown.

Andrew Sarris, "Altman at Armageddon," in The Village Voice *(reprinted by permission of* The Village Voice; *copyright © The Village Voice, Inc., 1979), Vol. XXIV, No. 8, February 19, 1979, p. 45.*

MARC GREEN

Robert Altman is like the little girl in the nursery rhyme who had a curl right in the middle of her forehead. When he is good, he is very, very good, but when he is bad—well, did you happen to catch "Quintet"? . . .

In what may be the swiftest rebound in cinematic history, Hollywood's most prolific film-maker has vaulted out of the metaphysical pits to create a wry, engaging, wonderfully perceptive romantic comedy. It is called "A Perfect Couple," and it is far and away Altman's most bracing, most satisfying movie since "Nashville." . . .

Integral to the movie's structure is the use of counterpoint to call our attention to contrasting but parallel elements in the principals' styles of living. And like the contrapuntal technique, the film itself is musical in conception.

Sheila, of course, is into rock; Alex is into the classics. Altman exploits their divergent tastes to create a set of overlapping musical transitions. The songs reflect the technical and thematic concerns of the film, and Altman uses them with dazzling ingenuity. . . .

The contrapuntal musical structure is underscored by a number of recurrent leitmotifs, the best of which involves a second amorous twosome who show up at convenient moments and fortuitously advance the plot. Altman turns these unctuous lovebirds into a delightful running gag, a double-edged device that emphasizes the movie's artifice while making us believe all the more deeply in Alex and Sheila's oddball attraction. The joke culminates in a rather predictable way, but it is hilarious nonetheless. . . .

At least two of the movie's interludes are among the most finely polished gems of screen comedy I've seen in years. The first involves Alex and a nymphomaniacal lady veterinarian . . . who seems to make no libidinous distinctions between her date and her dogs. The second involves a knock-down, drag-out struggle between Alex and another of Sheila's video suitors . . . , which develops into that rarest of comedic commodities—a subtly staged bit of slapstick farce.

For the most part, Altman's attitude toward contemporary courtship is whimsical and tolerant. He pokes fun at the computer dating phenomenon, but he resists the temptation to do it in a glib or facile fashion; his sympathies are clearly on the side of his protagonists. He understands the difficulty we all have breaking out of cocoons, both those that are created for us and those we create for ourselves. And he is refreshingly open-minded about the possibility that modern technology need not be the enemy of romance.

By steadily focusing on the relationship between Alex and Sheila, Altman avoids the sort of narrative diffusiveness that has undermined much of his other work. Still, he is shrewd enough not to turn the story into a thin little two-character study. He populates the screen with his customary gallery of intriguing, eccentric characters.

Marc Green, "'A Perfect Couple' Breathes New Life into Romantic Comedy," in The Chronicle Review *(copyright © 1979 by The Chronicle of Higher Education, Inc.), April 16, 1979, p. 21.*

STANLEY KAUFFMANN

[*A Perfect Couple*] has the usual Altman assets: technical deftness, idiosyncrasy, unexpected subject. But the deftness rattles around in a vacuum, the idiosyncrasy—because unsupported in theme or dynamics—degenerates quickly into egotism, and the unexpected subject is so poorly developed that it quickly becomes sterile. . . .

The story is too strained to support comment. The jokes include: trouble with a car's sun roof in a rainstorm; the woman's taking a swing with a poker at two struggling men and hitting the wrong one; and a silent Gorgeous Couple—a running gag intended as a comment on [Alex and Sheila]—who of course end up badly while the homely pair don't. Beauty is only skin-deep, you see. We hear (spurious) classical music every time we go to the man's home and rock every time we go to hers, just so we can tell one from the other.

Altman's admirers are now advising him to slow down and take stock. Of what?

Stanley Kauffmann, "Alive and Otherwise" (reprinted by permission of Brandt & Brandt Literary Agents, Inc.; copyright © 1979 by Stanley Kauffmann), in The New Republic, *Vol. 180, No. 18, May 5, 1979, pp. 24-5.**

JOHN COLEMAN

A Perfect Couple, which pursues the bitter-sweet progress of a love-affair based on the attraction of opposites, is [Altman's] most conventional entertainment to date, a mild comedy with lots of music and a happy ending. . . .

Somehow, more sheer gusto, a Thirties breeziness, is needed to override our awareness of schematisation. [Paul Dooley and Marta Heflin, who play Alex and Sheila,] play well but without that old black-and-white magic that could have us swallow a dozen unlikelihoods. When, after ups-and-downs, Alex becomes a male groupie ('The people in this bus are my kind of people'), we know it can't last and suspect it would never have happened. He goes home, to discover his beloved younger sister dead, himself disowned by his black-garbed family. So back to the Bowl, with the group *and* the Philharmonic sharing the platform, and big kisses from Sheila over a picnic basket. Inevitably, typical Altman touches keep one intermittently amused, intrigued, waiting about. Once again, we have to work out who's who in Alex's clan and Sheila's gang for ourselves, gradually, and this ensures some complicity. . . . The observation's there, as always, but a sustained gag or device involving an elegant parallel pair, credited as 'The Imperfect Couple' (the end divulges why 'imperfect'), only adds to the sense of an unusually reined-in Altman twitching his figments into a pattern. After the marvellous scatter-effects of films as crowded as *Nashville* or *A Wedding,* it's as if he now lacks the concentration necessary to make his two principals convincing, fully engaging. Here they too frequently seem ciphers defined by their context.

John Coleman, "Mismatch," in New Statesman *(© 1979 The Statesman & Nation Publishing Co. Ltd.), Vol. 98, No. 2535, October 19, 1979, p. 605.**

Ingmar Bergman

1918-

Swedish director, and screenwriter.

Bergman's symbolic dramas deal with internal conflicts and metaphysical crises of human nature. Using a heavily symbolic style, he seeks to discover the mysteries of the universe, pondering matters as various as communication with God and the psychological makeup of women.

Bergman's strict Lutheran upbringing significantly influenced his works. He became fascinated with the external trappings of religion and the beliefs behind the rituals. This is intrinsic to Bergman's work, as is his belief that God is often silent.

At the University of Stockholm Bergman directed several student theatre productions, including some of his own works which already bore signs of his strong religious feelings. His early work for Svenskfilmindustri included editing and scriptwriting. He began his career as a director with *Crisis,* for which he also wrote the script. Several films brought Bergman popular acclaim in Sweden before he achieved international fame with *Smiles of a Summer Night. Summer Interlude* and *The Naked Night,* in particular, foreshadow his artistic skill. Though they differ greatly in content, one savagely bitter, the other poignantly romantic, his structural concepts remain the same.

***Smiles of a Summer Night* shows Bergman's ability to create comedy and effectively portray the age-old theme of the many faces of love. His next film, *The Seventh Seal,* functioned on a theological level. Conveying a contemporary attitude of religious despair, this medieval allegory attempted to resolve some of Bergman's philosophical crises. It is the story of a lonely man's search for God and life's meaning.**

***Wild Strawberries,* often referred to as Bergman's most serene work as well as one of his most successful, explores man's need for love. Isak Borg, the protagonist, is successful commercially, yet a failure emotionally. Like many characters in Bergman films, he is involved in a journey; one that will dramatically change his life. In this film, Bergman claims the route to salvation is through love and communication with others. It is Bergman's most positive view of salvation.**

Bergman's trilogy, composed of *Through a Glass Darkly, Winter Light,* and *The Silence,* deals with the personal experience of God in one's life. Human beings need both God and love, yet are unable to accept either. In all three films, the characters are pitifully incapable of reaching others. The trilogy commences optimistically and ends in the futile statement of *The Silence:* God is indeed silent. After the trilogy, Bergman turned to more personal and interpersonal studies, weaving through the intricacies of the female psyche. *Persona,* the best known of these works, studies the obsessive intimacy of two women and the two consciousnesses that merge as their façades fall away. Bergman's interest in the close-up is particularly effective in this film, fusing together two faces to become one. The films to follow are almost exclusively studies of women. *Hour of the Wolf* and *Shame* are considered, with *Persona,* to comprise a second trilogy dealing with artistic frustration and the artist's failure to deal with reality.

While Bergman's talent is undeniable, several critics have objected to his solemn, trauma-laden films, complaining that characters are unable to act normally. They contend that his fascination with myth and ritual isolates the psychology of his characters. However, most critics agree that as depictions of the search for meaning in life, his films are unequaled. Vernon Young perhaps summarizes general reaction to the magnitude of Bergman's work when he says, "While Bergman appears, at present view, to be characterized, intemperately, by excluding themes that give to all his late films a clothing of monotony—God's silence, man's degradation, love's catastrophe—he is, in fact, when the whole body of his work is passed in review, incredibly various within the limits of his gospel." (See also *Contemporary Authors,* Vols. 81-84.)

ERIC ROHMER

There is certainly naivete in [the allegory used in *The Seventh Seal*], but there is some naivete in every fable. It is the naivete proper to the great periods of art—here the Middle Ages, whose flavor Bergman has captured without any adulterating pedantry and thanks to his incomparable skill in transposing into cinematic terms the motifs that furnish him with the iconography on which he draws his inspiration. The figures and the forms he presents are never flat but seem the fruit of an original creation. His art is so frank, so new that we forget it for the problem it embodies. Rarely has the cinema been able to aim so high and realize so fully its ambitions. (p. 135)

Eric Rohmer, "Avec le septième sceau Ingmar

Bergman nous offre son Faust" (reprinted by permission of the author), in Arts, *April 23-29, 1958 (translated by Kristine Hughie and Birgitta Steene and reprinted as "With 'The Seventh Seal' Ingmar Bergman Offers Us His Faust," in* Focus on "The Seventh Seal," *edited by Birgitta Steene, Prentice-Hall, Inc., 1972, pp. 134-35).*

EUGENE ARCHER

Bergman's essential theme, as expressed in his films, is man's search for knowledge in a hostile universe. The ultimate answer is that there is no answer, but the quest itself provides its own justification. Man must pursue the search alone, since he is as incapable of understanding other men as he is of understanding himself. Society can only handicap man in life's quest for knowledge. Hell is on earth, and life is the process of experiencing it. Maturity comes only from acceptance of these conditions, and from grasping the few comforts that life has to offer. These comforts are in sex, an act of temporary communication which results in procreation as a final justification for existence; in art, which distills the products of man's intellect and emotion into another intangible form of communication and self-expression; and in the imagination, not in any conventional religious form, but as a kind of fatalistic mysticism which offers at least the possibility of an ultimate meaning to the search. None of these comforts provides more than a temporary assuagement of the inevitable solitude of existence, but they are all that life can offer, and as such, they will suffice.

This great theme is evident in all of Bergman's works, from the youthful dramas of adolescent revolt, through a series of brilliant sophisticated comedies, to the mature philosophical films of his most recent period. (p. 3)

Torment [directed by Alf Sjöberg with the screenplay by Bergman], one of the great Swedish films, achieves an intensity which Bergman's own films, less absolute in their conceptions, have never attained, but its theme contains the essence of Bergman's subsequent philosophy. . . . Although the conclusion of *Torment* is enigmatic, suggesting both hope and futility, the youthful protagonist has actually experienced the worst that will ever happen to him, since he will never again be able to respond as intensely as at the age of 17. *Torment* is one of the rare films to achieve catharsis, an effect which Bergman never attempted again. . . .

[Bergman's early films] continue the examination of youthful revolt against society which Bergman began in *Torment,* with the pessimistic conclusion that man can only hope for salvation in retreat, as a social outcast. The realistic seaport drama, *Hamnstad (Seaport),* . . . suggests for the first time that the young lovers, whose need for each other survives their inability to communicate, may find the strength to combat life on its own terms. Bergman's youthful pessimism is climaxed by *Fangelse (Prison),* which depicts modern life as a total hell from which there can be no salvation because man has lost the ability to believe in God. This powerful expressionistic work, influenced by Pirandello and strongly foreshadowing *The Seventh Seal,* is set in a motion-picture studio, and presents life's odyssey as a passage through an artificial corridor populated by inanimate mannequins, in an expression of one of Bergman's favorite conceptions, the relative reality of artistic illusion. (p. 6)

Sommarlick (Summerplay, 1950) is one of Bergman's most personal films, and, for connoisseurs of the director's work, it remains the most satisfying of his early achievements. *Summerplay* introduces a new maturity into Bergman's philosophy and technique. The long flashback to an idyllic summer romance is overshadowed with mystical symbols foreboding disaster, for, in Bergman's philosophy, in the absence of interior knowledge and with only death as a certainty, superstitious omens are fully as valid as scientific facts. . . .

Bergman's early films, strange, exceedingly personal, and deeply provacative, sometimes deriving from the Protestant environment of his own childhood, seem to be groping for a style flexible enough to express his gradually formulating metaphysical conceptions. When he created *Summerplay,* it was clear that Bergman had attained complete maturity as a director, and was capable of expressing anything he chose. His films since 1950 are, without exception, masterful in their evocations of mood and movement, the principal ingredients of cinematic style. (p. 7)

In *Sommaren Med Monika (Summer with Monika),* Bergman returns to the theme of adolescent revolt in the story of a bourgeois boy and a lower-class girl who become lovers through a kind of natural selection and leave the city for a summer idyll in the Swedish north woods. . . . *Monika* is Bergman's most erotic film, a passionate testimonial to the theme that, for intellectual modern man in search of meaning, sex is not enough.

Nor is art enough, as Bergman demonstrates in *Gycklarnas Afton (Sunset of a Clown,* called in England *Sawdust and Tinsel,* in America *The Naked Night).* The artist can exist only by performing before his audience in a mask—the mask of a role to play, a script to follow, of make-up and costume and illusory spotlights to conceal the artist's true identity from the observer. Within this mask, he can achieve the illusion of communication, assuming a kind of universal identity which may bring him greater fulfillment than any other form of action. But by placing his dependence on the mask, the artist confronts a new danger which the layman can more easily avoid, the danger of exposure to his audience without the mask. This, to the artist, is the ultimate horror of existence, to be seen without artifice, in unalterable nakedness, with no retreat from the spotlight. (p. 8)

Smiles of a Summer Night is constructed as an elaborate game of love, with happiness and frustration as the stakes. . . . The quest, as in *The Seventh Seal,* remains a search for meaning, but the object of the search lies with the natural order rather than the spiritual; in the comedy of life, man's primary concern is not religious but sexual. If imaginative salvation offers greater solace to the intellect, physical gratification offers a more tangible reward. (p. 10)

The game entangles and re-matches the sextet, with interference and observation from the upstairs maid and a poetic coachman. The result is a victory for natural order over the social pattern: youth must mate with youth, age with age, like with like. Convention may dominate human emotion and even human will, but in a conflict with nature, nature must triumph. (pp. 10-11)

This victory of nature is as inevitable as the victory of death. Existence may be the tortuous process of searching for a meaning, but life, in the end, imposes its own meaning. Life perpetuates itself, and man, in his quest for knowledge, is powerless in the struggle. . . .

The game, then, must be played at every stage of life, and mature man, trying to savor the three comforts as reward for the completion of his quest, is finally left with none. . . .

Smiles of a Summer Night may be enjoyed as a delightful comedy of manners in the tradition of French boudoir farce, but the film, a typical Bergman creation, is subject to a dual interpretation, and an underlying serious meaning is readily apparent. . . . (p. 11)

Nära Livet (Brink of Life) complements Bergman's symbolic analysis of the theme of death by probing into the mystery of birth, in a powerful realistic drama set in a maternity ward. . . . Bergman handles this material with extreme realism, but his theme is a direct extension of the meanings inherent in *The Seventh Seal.* Birth and death are the ultimate particles of existence, and both are in the realm of a hostile nature which is beyond the grasp of human intellect, yet man, nature's embodiment and justification, continues the search for knowledge which is itself the act of life. . . . (p. 12)

The area of greatest interest in Bergman's films is thematic rather than technical, although Bergman's technique alone would place him among the world's best directors. Bergman consciously subordinates form to content, being more interested in what he is saying than in his method of saying it. The desired result is for an observer to emerge from the film preoccupied with its ideas rather than dazzled with its visual imagery. (p. 13)

Bergman's first film is visually striking, and his fifth, *Seaport,* shows him in command of the medium. By the time of *Summerplay,* his technique is masterful in every respect, and each subsequent film has operated on the highest level of visual imagination. Bergman has continued to experiment with new styles throughout his career. . . .

Such a diversity of stylistic elements might suggest eclecticism, or at best a superficial cinematic erudition, in a director with a less consistently personal viewpoint. There is little danger, however, of a Bergman film ever being mistaken for the work of anyone else. In Bergman's case, the range clearly indicates his interest in all the facets of theatrical expression and his constant desire for expansion and variation in his work. (p. 14)

Bergman seldom lingers over a strong effect, preferring instead to dissolve quickly to a new and contrasting scene. He is abrupt only in order to avoid overstatement, and the effect for the observer is of a series of deeply suggestive words and images, with other images left unseen and words unsaid, to be supplied by the observer's own intellectual reflection. Life goes on, and Bergman's people continue to exist after the camera has ceased to dwell upon them.

This is, finally, the highest form of technique, a method which places its emphasis entirely on content. (p. 15)

Eugene Archer, "The Rack of Life: An Analysis of the Films of the Swedish Writer-Director Ingmar Bergman," in Film Quarterly *(copyright 1959 by The Regents of the University of California; reprinted by permission of the University of California Press), Vol. XII, No. 4, Summer, 1959, pp. 3-16.*

ARLENE CROCE

While Bergman is the darling of the sophisticates, he is nonetheless a cinematic artist of unusual accomplishment, whose works demand a proportionately serious consideration. . . .

The peculiar dualism of Swedish art—what might be called the "noon wine" syndrome—attains in Bergman's films its fullest significance as subjective visual rhetoric. You see in them a characteristic imagery which, with its cold radiance and crystalline gloom, seems continually to convey a perilous balance between the light-dark extremities of human emotion. . . .

He has in fact created a theater of the film, in which landscape itself seems possessed of the power of dramatic suggestion, in which a surgically precise selectivity rules out all ungovernable elements in the course of a film's action. Bergman no longer takes his cameras into the street; the street is horribly empty, the wild fields deserted, the woods ominously still. They are prescient stages for dramas that deal, not in incidentals, but in ultimates. In that sense, all his most personal films are allegories, deeply Swedish in inspiration. (p. 647)

Bergman, although a great tease, is not the oracular prophet some critics have made him out to be. Most of his films are flawed by irresolution as to form and evasiveness as to central meaning. No other filmmaker, with the possible exception of John Ford, is so erratic. But unlike Ford, Bergman is neither an innocent nor a poet (though he often uses poetic devices); nor is he so encumbered by commercial contrivance, and his lapses are therefore the more disturbing. . . . But his erraticism is a clue to the nature of his creative gifts. . . . [It is in] the trilogy formed by "The Seventh Seal," "Wild Strawberries" and "The Magician" [originally entitled "The Face"] that he has begun to put together all the pieces of his great puzzle.

Of the three films, "The Magician" most successfully consolidates Bergman's multiple identities as social critic, moral philosopher, dramatist and fellow-sufferer. Were one to see only this film, without reference to former expositions of similar situations, it would be possible to recognize the extent of Bergman's present intentions and capacities. A concentrated analysis of the limits of perception, it constitutes a corrective to past experiments and a rebuke to ardent exegetes and equally ardent detractors. . . . The artist's hell, in "The Magician," is not only other people, and the various appetites, illusions and dogmas which he must feed, but also his own human vulnerability. To know truth is to know truth to be unknowable. It is this kind of knowledge—which no one will believe—that Bergman's magician suffers from.

Bergman's arrival at the conclusion that truth is unknowable may not, generally speaking, be news; but it is news to Bergman and news to film. . . . It means that the near-chronic inability to resolve a dramatic situation in terms of its sequential logic, which marred "The Seventh Seal," may now be put aside. It is in the final reel, characteristically, that "The Seventh Seal" breaks down. Bergman fails to bring the knight's quandary to a recognizable climax. . . .

Deliberately—and dangerously—cast in the form of a metaphor, ["The Magician"] yet manages to transform its inevitable self-consciousness *as film* into an active expression of the drama's total meaning. It is a film play—a play of shadows, a drama in which the spirit of deception is seen to dominate human affairs: in it the dead wake, the righteous are humbled, seducers are seduced, strong men are made weak. Yet is that what "really" happens? (p. 648)

Bergman employs the more lurid movie conventions, in this case, those of the period thriller. There is the lurching post chaise, the dangling corpse, the thunder crackling in air heavy with diabolical curses. Melodrama thus acquires a new dimension as a heightened metaphor of the way we see. In a magnificent *trompe d'oeil,* Bergman has produced that rare thing, a film whose form blends perfectly with its theme. (pp. 648-49)

There are hopeful signs, also, that Bergman's new grasp of the possibilities of film form may have ended his attempts to make a film poem, at least of the "Wild Strawberries" type. . . .

["Wild Strawberries"] ends with a premonition of life derived from the living past, just as it had begun with a *memento mori* mocking an academic conferral of immortality. Unfortunately, the clarity of these meanings, which gives the film its comparatively distinct outline and finely graded rhythm, is reinforced through a scheme of banal symbolizing. All the perennial figments of the "avant-garde" cinema are elegantly produced—the hearse, the watch without hands, the dream corridor, the enigmatic interrogator, the living corpses, etc. The formal gesture the film makes is mere manner without sympathy or individuality. Poetry is reduced to a facility in mysterioso. . . .

Bergman's reputation in this country is based largely on the brand of faceless philosophical passion he has developed in these late films. In them, his thought has progressed from "Believing in a God who does not exist is like loving someone in the dark who never answers" to "Step by step we proceed into the dark—the movement itself is the only truth." Persistence without certitude, then, is the quintessence of Bergmanism. The difficulty that arises in the quasi-cabalistic atmosphere of the espresso-lounge seminars is in distinguishing Bergmanism from Bergmania.

Bergmania, like Salingeritis, is the scandalous homage paid to a popular artist by idle masters of theses in their pursuit of the age's most viable emblem. This elementary discovery of an artist's terms, the means by which he identifies and condenses life, is then allowed to take on the prepossessing nature of an absolute, the "right" answer and the key to the "rightness" of a whole body of work.

A kind of gay agnosticism is Bergman's preference and one secret of his allure. The other is his eclectic vitality of expression, which preserves him from the mandarin isolation of Bresson (with its attendant commercial neglect) and the chic specializing (with its attendant commercial exploitation) of purveyors like Clouzot or Dassin. No one has more influence over the present generation of young intellectuals who, in every culture, are turning first to film. For them, and for their wide and hopeful audience, Bergman has attained the eminence of a *directeur du conscience.* In the emerging Age of Cinema, he is the first film-maker to have done so. (p. 649)

Arlene Croce, "The Bergman Legend," in Commonweal *(copyright © 1960 Commonweal Publishing Co., Inc.,; reprinted by permission of Commonweal Publishing Co., Inc.), Vol. LXXI, No. 24, March 11, 1960, pp. 647-49.*

WILLIAM S. PECHTER

[*Ansiktet* or *The Magician*] is the film in which Bergman has been able to expose all of his most dominant themes, and the multiplicity of their presence gives the film its complex, yet curiously uncomplicated texture, its finished, definitive character. In *Ansiktet,* the dialectical clangor of faith and reason, which rings through such a film as *The Seventh Seal* and echos resonantly throughout his other work, combines harmoniously with Bergman's preoccupation with the artist and his audience. Vogler, the mesmerist, looks both like a charlatan and a Christ, and this resemblance seems to be at the heart of what Bergman is saying: that the most salient cause of the artist's inevitable failing of his audience is the latter's impossible demand that the artist be also savior, magician and messiah, ingenious imposter and immutable face. It is not a role which the artist desires, but one to which he nevertheless seems inescapably to aspire; and though Vogler may suffer some awful, mute agony at his stigmata, he seems ineluctably to adopt the postures—vainly attempting to be healer instead of entertainer, dumbly mothering the dying actor—of the redeemer. He is doomed to fail in this imposture, and fail, furthermore, as artist in the attempt, in attempting to transcend the natural limits of art. (p. 94)

It is not until Vogler is stripped of his disguises, lost to his defenses and wholly abased in his person, that he is able to achieve the successes proper to his art. But first he must confront his audience without pride or pretension and reveal to it his naked face. . . . (p. 95)

Bergman's flair for verbal wit, his gift for epigram and paradox, seems, here as, occasionally, elsewhere, a bit too brilliant, too facile and merely clever for his own good; too often one feels it to be the substitute for some deeper confrontation. And one comes, finally, even to suspect the strategy of representing the artist as nomadic clown and entertainer as essentially too easy and tractable a simplification and evasion. . . . (p. 97)

A recurrent cliché in Bergman's films is that of an intellectual discussion aborted to the precedence of some natural fact, as in the Squire's rejoinders in *The Seventh Seal,* the students' theological debate in *Wild Strawberries,* and Tubal's interruptions of the dying actor in *Ansiktet.* All ideas are dissolved in some *homme moyen sensuel* "reality," and one cannot but suspect that, although Bergman is willing to use ideas and abstractions, he finally distrusts and even fears them. He can imagine terror, but seems finally unprepared to cope with it; all his final reconciliations amount to a flight from ideas into a suffusion of feeling. And thus, the familiar pieties of Bergman's climactic affirmations: "I'm tired of people, which doesn't prevent my loving them"; "Hell together is better than hell alone."

But the particular genius of the truly charismatic artist—and Bergman certainly is this—is not only to give the right answers but to ask the right questions, and the remarkable thing about Bergman is his ability to sound the temper of his age, to embody and express the spiritual unrest and distress of what he has called "the current dilemma." . . . With Bergman, an existential position, characteristically a gesture of despair, negation, and disaffiliation, and traditionally an opening blow in philosophical inquiry, has become a quasi-religious affirmation, and a final resting place; so what is properly a beginning has become an end. The final kind of relentless excoriation which informs a film like

The Naked Night, Bergman's most pitiless film and also one of his most jejune stylistically, has not been significantly redirected by the time of *Ansiktet,* but has been modified to a simulacrum of faith. (pp. 97-8)

[The conclusion of *Ansiktet,* wrenched bodily from *The Three-penny Opera,*] is a perfect act of artistic strategy; as art it is mere sham. What the unmitigated irony of Brecht's invention forces one to see is the absurdity, wishfulness, and self-deception behind all our happy endings, and by actually manufacturing such a delusion he succeeds in demonstrating its perfect impossibility. But, in *Ansiktet,* the final note is somehow conclusive and triumphant; the irony dissipates itself into mere audacity, and the terrible, irreconcilable spirit of the work has been successfully exorcised. . . .

[Much of Bergman's work seems] especially adduced to put over a point; a fact which may account for the extraordinarily chameleon-like quality of his films, his dazzling stylistic eclecticism. It is not an eclecticism which finally achieves a state of synthesis, as, for example, the synthetic eclecticism of a Shaw or Stravinsky; large portions of Bergman's films seem now to be an exercise in Carl Dreyer, now Dali, Cocteau, Renoir, Germanic expressionism, all fraught with now another studied derivation, and it is only in aggregate, by virtue of the characteristic uses to which such borrowings are directed, that they are recognizably the work of Ingmar Bergman. (p. 99)

It is particularly in the darker side of the world of his films that Bergman seems most willfully to be working against the natural bent of his temperament; . . . a comic temperament. That is why a film such as *The Seventh Seal* fails stylistically, cold, forced, and derivative, a tremendous effort of the will as opposed to the imagination; that is why *Ansiktet* seems, finally, despite its audacity, assurance, and marvelous accomplishment, no more than brilliant sleight of hand, a magic lantern show. Its deepest insight is on the level of irony; but irony unredeemed by passionate conviction and commitment is mere indulgence, and moral frivolity. Bergman has likened himself to a conjurer, with his camera the wonderful apparatus of conjuration and deceit; and perhaps, in his ability to mesmerize us with mere shadows, he is closer to Vogler than we have cared to imagine. . . .

It is only in the brightly lit world, the glitter and glare of his comedies, that Bergman seems to be temperamentally at home, as the dark side of his films seems alien to him; it is only in his comedies that his style loses the ponderous, deliberate quality of his dark films and takes on a quality of lightness and grace. (p. 100)

Ansiktet presents Bergman in an act of exposition, riding on top of his material, and in absolute control of it. This perfect assurance shows itself in the magnificent confidence that is required to bring off the impudent joke of the film's rain to sunshine ending; implied in such trumpery is the sense that you almost have to be great to get away with it, to feel your work so secure as to withstand such facetiousness. It also explains why the work finally rings hollow, while a film like *Wild Strawberries,* even, in its less resonant way, *Smiles of a Summer Night,* reverberates with the kind of infinite suggestiveness of a work servant to vision. . . .

Yet, admitting his limitations, one can nonetheless find Bergman's presence in the contemporary cinema a salutary one. He has been not a director of conscience but of intelligence, and he has opened the eyes of his audience to the fact that the film is a medium respondent to the uses of an artist of high intelligence; that it is susceptible to ideas and to the dialectical conflict incumbent upon them. And he has offered the proof, if we ever really needed it, that intelligence, even great intelligence, is, in itself, not enough. (p. 101)

William S. Pechter, "The Light Is Dark Enough," in The Tulane Drama Review *(copyright, © 1960, The Tulane Drama Review), Vol. 5, No. 2, December, 1960, pp. 94-101.*

CAROLINE BLACKWOOD

Cecil B. de Mille gave the public "Religion and Sex"; Ingmar Bergman has now simply come up with a more esoteric formula, the Supernatural and Sex, decked out with Symbols. The Symbol Blatant and the Symbol Enigmatic provide the two major leavenings to all Bergman's soggy plots. (p. 54)

[It is] very difficult to see that Bergman . . . is covering new realms of reality by constantly resorting to all the old morbid mediaeval metaphors which formed the staple fare of silent German movies of the 'twenties. It is equally hard to see anything very "illuminating" in Bergman monotonously repeating that all knowledge and learning are instruments of the Devil. The only villains in any of his films are always men of science and intellect. Even if his unfortunate intellectual characters do nothing particularly evil, he still makes it clear by their presentation that just their very simple existence is the greatest Evil of all. . . . [In] *The Seventh Seal* Bergman goes so far as to present his most intellectual character in the guise of Death himself. As a thriller-addict after a few specialised clues can easily spot the murderer, so a Bergman-addict need only hear that a character has made a woman pregnant and refused to visit her in the hospital, to spot this man as the egghead.

All Bergman's endless philosophical meanderings always boil down to the same simple moral. Only half-wits and virgins can ever escape disaster. . . . The moronic son in *Smiles of a Summer Night* is impotent with his serving-girl (symbol of Harlotry) and potent only with purity. Bergman naturally favours his uncommon sexual pattern and grants him, what in Bergmanesque terms is the very highest human reward, an unawakened wife. . . .

Bergman's immense current popularity is really a phenomenon in itself. His rabid anti-intellectualism is presumably partially responsible. His message that the fool is wiser than anyone, has an obvious general appeal. He has also, however, a cunning, strategic grasp of currently fashionable trends. He therefore appeases supposedly more sophisticated audiences by serving them up a quasi-modern potpourri of Strindberg, Kafka, and Jung. (p. 55)

Behind all Bergman's stuffy Protestant morality, and behind all his Swedish Modern with his easy reference to Freud, one really senses only all the horrendous mystical superstition of an ancient Scandinavian Goth. One feels all the old Nordic deities (ugliest and gloomiest of the world's divinities) still lurking in the black and insular background of his haunted forests and skies. The god Nor, shaped like an eagle and compulsively nibbling on human carcases, is there flapping the wings which cause winds to moan and desolate tempests to blow through the woods of *The Seventh Seal*. . . .

At the turn of the century the Swedish novelist Söderberg wrote that he believed in only two ultimates, the desire of the flesh and the eternal loneliness of the soul. Ingmar Bergman cannot accept the desire of the flesh as an ultimate; he is, however, obssessed with the loneliness of the soul and his only memorable sequences are always on this theme. The loneliness he presents is not that of *Umberto D,* a man left without friends in a cruel and heartless society, but the self-imposed loneliness of people incapable of either feeling or communicating emotion. (p. 56)

Bergman is never frightened of overstressing his points. Sometimes his repetitiousness has had a certain hypnotic appeal. In *Virgin Spring* it is disastrous. He takes an eternity to merely establish that his Virgin is good. . . . [The virgin's transformation into a sacred spring after her death] is Bergman's message. She was indestructible after all. In her new watery form we have her with us forever.

Bergman started his career as a director of theatre for children; and now can only be called the leading director of children's films for adults. (pp. 56-7)

Caroline Blackwood, "The Mystique of Ingmar Bergman," in Encounter *(© 1961 by Encounter Ltd.), Vol. 16, No. 4, April, 1961, pp. 54-7.*

PETER HARCOURT

[In Bergman's finest work,] there has been a dramatic structure established out of the various elements contained in the films, the minutely observed physical detail generally counterbalancing the more abstract and often rhetorical nature of the central theme.

In *Through a Glass Darkly,* however, all this has changed. As in *So Close to Life,* Bergman has here decided to deny himself all but the most austere imagery, as he has restricted himself to four characters and has taken pains to observe the unity of time. But paradoxically, if this is aesthetically his most austere film, it is thematically his most self-indulgent; for in this barren island world that Bergman has created, there is nothing to offset what one wants to call the abnormality of the film. Here *all* the characters are distressed and inward-turning, and all but the myopic Martin speak in terms of God. (p. 38)

Yet, as its title and opening epigraph imply, the film is supposedly about Christian love. Supposedly, because in *Through a Glass Darkly* love is less experienced than talked about. In the various characters in *Wild Strawberries* (indeed, within the evolution of the central character himself), we could see and thus respond to some of the many possibilities of love from selfish *eros* to Christian *agape,* so that at the end of the film there was really no need of any speech at all between old Borg and Marianne as they reached out and touched one another and thus expressed their new-found sympathy. Whereas at the end of this film, David must explain to his son that love is all-embracing, that in fact God is love, and that even Karin, although she will be away from them imprisoned in her own insanity, will benefit from their love. But the film actually ends in physical separation. . . . Even more than *The Virgin Spring,* and less justifiably, this film ends with the assertion of the validity of faith in love; and it is this verbally assertive quality shared by all the characters, plus the portentousness of the epigraph and music by Bach, which, despite the austerity of the visual images, gives *Through a Glass Darkly* its self-indulgent quality. (pp. 38-9)

If by the end of *Through a Glass Darkly,* we feel with some regret that Bergman has more asserted the value of love than demonstrated it dramatically within the film, nevertheless, in the uniqueness of his imagery and the intimacy with which he observes some of the details of these four people's lives, he succeeds in reminding us that he is still one of the most distinctive and compelling directors in the cinema today. (p. 39)

Peter Harcourt, "Film Reviews: 'Through a Glass Darkly'," in Sight and Sound *(copyright © 1962 by The British Film Institute), Vol. 32, No. 1, Winter, 1962-63, pp. 38-9.*

PETER COWIE

Like all Ingmar Bergman's films, *Through A Glass Darkly* is an intensely personal work. Yet none of his previous films have been so profoundly Scandinavian in their composition or outlook on life. The isolation, the hostile duologues, the psychological malady are all reminiscent of Ibsen and Strindberg. (p. 47)

What distinguishes the film as a whole is its power and atmosphere. These are hackneyed words in the critic's vocabulary, but in *Through A Glass Darkly,* the dark forces of schizophrenia lie menacing behind all the simple scenes and conversations. . . .

I am puzzled by those who call this film depressing. On the contrary it is among the most mature of Bergman's works and ends on a note of conviction. But the characters can only reach this final state of calmness if they have endured the most intense experiences and scrutiny. If one is prepared to enter Bergman's world, to accept his sudden variations of mood, and to accept in their context his conclusions, one will find this film a sombre but stimulating work of art. (p. 48)

Peter Cowie, "'Through a Glass Darkly'" (© copyright Peter Cowie 1963; reprinted with permission), in Films and Filming, *Vol. 9, No. 4, January, 1963, pp. 47-8.*

JOHN RUSSELL TAYLOR

Fängelse [*Prison*] . . . is a highly significant work in many ways. . . . [It] has all the marks of a key work in his career, wildly bundling together any number of themes which are to recur later and, it seems, just had to find expression at this time in some form. Moreover, it is the first of Bergman's films which demonstrates any real desire (or possibly, since we know little of the circumstances in which the early films were made, any real freedom) to experiment with the medium, to use it positively as a means of expression in itself, rather than merely recording with competence but no special aptitude. In *Fängelse* already Bergman is reaching out towards the highly personal style of his later work, integrating the rather faded studio romanticism (derived, apparently, from an enthusiastic study of the works of Carné) which marked his earliest films and the rather hesitant touches of neo-realism in *Hamnstad* [*Port of Call*] into a newer, more complex and, in the first instance, more theatrical style of direction. In *Fängelse,* indeed, the theatrical origin of much in the later films which one would not instantly think of as theatrical, especially where the direction of actors is concerned, is still clearly visible. And in general the main interest of the film now is a by-product of its crudities and awkwardness: it is situated at the vital juncture in Bergman's career when he has found his feet and struck out on his own, but not yet had a chance to cover his tracks: most of what he says, crudely and directly, in the screenplay recurs in an infinitude of transformations and transmutations in later works, elusively difficult to pin down exactly; much of what he does with actors and camera shows in a raw and unformed state the procedures which will underlie his mature practice. (pp. 142-43)

The 'message' of the film, if one seeks a message, is blackly pessismistic: 'L'Enfer, c'est les autres'; 'And this is Hell, nor am I out of it'. There is no God, only the Devil, and the Devil rules: the only possibilities are death and vaguely stoical endurance of an almost insupportable life. It is, in fact, all very neatly epitomized in the only relatively light-hearted, even comic episode: that in which Thomas and Brigitte-Caroline, in the attic of their hideaway, come across some old silent films and a projector, and run a short farce in which the characters, in the midst of frenziedly persecuting each other, are suddenly threatened by a skeleton and vanish. The fact that the message can be so simply and completely epitomized suggests one of the film's weaknesses: it is very much a *film à thèse,* and in its determination to put over its creator's ideas it tends to adopt an almost didactic tone, with things happening, one sometimes cannot help feeling, more to demonstrate a point than from any appreciable dramatic necessity. (p. 144)

The style of direction, too, gives hints of the future, as yet not at all integrated: the scenes involving Brigitte-Caroline and Peter are made in a harsh, realistic style a little reminiscent of *Hamnstad;* the scenes between her and Thomas are given a hazy romantic quality which looks forward to, ultimately, *Sommarlek* [*Summer Interlude* or *Illicit Interlude*]; and Brigitte-Caroline's dream, with its forest of human trees, its mysterious woman in black offering a stone which she says is 'the most valuable thing in the world', and its heavily symbolic play with a doll (representing Brigitte's dead baby) which turns into a fish and is killed by Peter, is conceived in terms of an all-out theatrical expressionism which later will apparently disappear, but actually be completely integrated into Bergman's mature work. (pp. 144-45)

Technically *Sommarlek* is relatively unadventurous, except for a brief and not very successful interlude when some doodles by Marie take on a life of their own and start to move and gesticulate like something from one of Emile Cohl's early animated films; a sort of equivalent to the play with the silent projector in *Fängelse.* It is content to use the normal repertoire of film technique simply and directly, with a strong feeling for sympathetic natural backgrounds and a lavish, perhaps on occasion rather facile, use of visual symbolism derived from nature, both of which characteristics hark back more clearly than anything in Bergman's previous work to the early Swedish cinema of a temperamentally very different director, Victor Sjöstrom. After the uncertainty and sometimes rather wild experiment of Bergman's previous films, it looks very much like an expression of confidence; confidence that his material could, if he wished, stand up on its own without extraneous tricks. Unsuccessful some of his later films might be, but never in quite the way that *Fängelse* or *Törst* failed; at least the later films, when they are wrong, are confidently wrong, not just awkward and fumbling. (pp. 149-50)

[The first work of his maturity is] *Gycklarnas Afton (Sawdust and Tinsel).* The progress in this case is not so much in the material as in the treatment; the view of life put forward in the film is as gloomy and anguished as anything that has gone before, but the style in which it is treated is complex and magisterially confident; for the first time Bergman manages to unite in one film the disparate influences which have appeared in his work—from early Swedish cinema (Sjöström's feeling for landscape, Stiller's flair for bitter erotic comedy), from the French cinema of the 1930s (especially Carné's elegantly artificial studio-bound studies of fate and its workings) and German silent cinema, with its obsession with mirrors and staircases, with hysteria and humiliation. All these combine in a film which is not, perhaps, without its absurd side—it is a little too much like a concoction of absolutely everything the foreign filmgoer might regard as 'typically Swedish' in the cinema—but which still holds together its diverse elements remarkably well and achieves a rich, elaborate, and unmistakably personal style of expression.

Moving for the first time into period settings (the time is somewhere in the early 1900s) Bergman suddenly finds the visual style which, variously modified to suit the subject-matter, is to serve him well throughout his mature career. Whereas before the purely visual side of his films had often lacked any special distinction, and those distinctions it did have had usually been a matter of good isolated ideas rather than any overall quality, in *Gycklarnas Afton* the style all at once becomes rich and strange. Compositions are intricate and bizarre, with much play of reflections, harsh, crisp contrasts of light and shade, and an almost continuous use of deep focus to give the whole thing a powerfully sculptural quality, emphasizing textures and effects of perspective. And this style is used consistently throughout the film, except for a flashback near the beginning, which is set apart from the rest of the film in that it is filmed silent, with a musical accompaniment, as the narrator tells the story, and is photographed in a wan, flat, overexposed fashion to give it the remoteness and insubstantiality of a dream. (pp. 152-53)

With *Smiles of a Summer Night (Sommarnattens Leende)* in 1955 we finally see for the first time, and virtually for the last, all Bergman's diverse talents together in a single film. It is an intricately constructed high comedy for nine characters, whose positions are modified and rearranged with the utmost elegance and precision during the course of a single week-end. (p. 156)

It is difficult if not impossible to explain how exactly this curious *mélange* of comedy and drama, dry wit and poetic fantasy, manages to hold together in the cinema. Essentially, one suspects, it is a matter of conviction: conviction on the creator's part that naturally anything that he thinks of is related to anything else he thinks by the simple fact that it is he who is doing the thinking. The overriding unifying factor here is the sheer force of Bergman's personality; the film is the product throughout of a single idiosyncratic imagination working at full pressure and never for one moment playing safe (anyone else, for instance, faced with Charlotte's outburst to Anna about the ignominy of love, would surely have guyed it a little to fit in with the rest of the comedy, but Bergman shoots it straight and dramatically in harsh close-up, and somehow, inexplicably, it works). (p. 157)

Even though his next film, *The Seventh Seal (Det Sjunde Inseglet),* was responsible more than any other single work for Bergman's international vogue, and was at its first appearance in 1956 generally hailed as a masterpiece, it is difficult now to feel anything like the same degree of enthusiasm for it. In *The Seventh Seal* Bergman turns from marriage and the relations of man and woman and takes up instead the relations of man with God and with death—a theme which has continued ever since at the centre of his work, though sometimes more evidently so than at others. Unfortunately in doing so he does not escape pretentiousness, perhaps because in his eagerness to make a statement of universal validity he has separated himself too far from the clear observation of believable human beings which had always given strength to even his most melodramatic earlier pieces. (p. 158)

Technically the film is impeccable. The black-and-white photography of Gunnar Fischer is constantly striking (it is the sort of film which yields excellent stills, which may or may not be a good thing), with its crisp, clear deep-focus work, its very black blacks and very white whites. The story is told with admirable economy, no detail being wasted or missing its effect. The acting, when acting is called for . . . , does perfectly everything required of it. And yet the film, despite all this and some genuinely enthralling moments, seems somehow too pale and remote, too patently composed as an illustration of its thesis. Its final effect, when all has been said in its favour, is rather lifeless, and lacking as it does the power of a completely realized work of art to sweep aside objections, *The Seventh Seal* strikes one as making implicit claims for itself out of all proportion to its actual achievements. If a film-maker sets out to make a cosmic drama of Life and Death, with a lot of Christian symbolism thrown in, he must expect to be judged by the most rigorous standards, and by such standards *The Seventh Seal* fails. It never finally convinces us, as it obviously intends to, that all its horrors, the rapes, tortures, flagellations, burnings, are valid expressions of a pessimistic world picture only lightly touched with hope; they remain, if not exactly sensational, at least rather pointless, overstating a case that should not need such determined emphasis. (p. 159)

From all points of view *Wild Strawberries* must rank as one of Bergman's best works, showing his complete mastery of the medium, his sheer genius as a director of actors, and some of his most mature and subtle observations of character: it is, as Ravel once said of his musical ideal, 'complexe mais pas compliqué'. (p. 163)

Evidently there must be films among the twenty-six that [Bergman] felt less personally involved with than others, but since *Sommarlek* in 1950 there is not one, major or minor, scripted alone or in collaboration, which does not have the air of being in some way a personal statement. After that, if a film misfires, as for me *The Face* and the first two of the trilogy [*Through a Glass Darkly* and *Winter Light*] do, at least it is a failure on the highest level, judged by the highest standards, while from his greatest successes —*Smiles of a Summer Night, Wild Strawberries*—one can hardly withhold the word masterpiece. Why, then, should any doubts remain about Bergman's right to the vague, ambiguous title of *auteur*? I think because the feeling remains that though at his best he has all the gifts of the outstanding screen-writer and the outstanding screen-director, they are not for the most part inseparably fused, but merely subsist in an uneasy alliance. In *Smiles of a Summer Night* and *Wild Strawberries,* and sometimes elsewhere, sheer force of inspiration fuses them into one complex, indivisible gift, but often in his work one remains conscious of a gap between conception and realization; an attitude, one might say, rather similar to that usual in the theatre, where an author may sometimes direct his own play but no necessary connexion between the two activities is assumed. Too often in Bergman's films one senses the writer doing a good imaginative job on the script, working with complete mastery within the chosen medium, and then the director taking over and setting out to 'do something with' what has been written, to make the most of it, to choose the most telling way of realizing it for the screen.

The fact that writer and director are the same man has little to do with it if there is no essential connexion between their functions; as Bresson has said, 'on an *auteur* worthy of the name a choice is imposed . . . for him, and for him alone, once he has worked out his *decoupage,* each shot he takes can have only one definite angle, one certain length of time'. With Bergman it seldom seems that the choice is *imposed;* one could conceive of a dozen ways, more or less good, of shooting the same material, and the very ease and naturalness with which one finds oneself thinking in these terms indicates the gap which exists between script and finished film. Admittedly Bergman has made some very remarkable films, and will no doubt make more. When they come one will enjoy them and recognize their merits. But a coolness persists in my, and I suspect other filmgoers', relations with Bergman and his work; perhaps because he has, in the last analysis, failed to give himself completely to the film while working in it, we still, however great our admiration for isolated achievements of his, draw back ultimately from giving ourselves completely to him. (pp. 168-69)

John Russell Taylor, "Ingmar Bergman," in his Cinema Eye, Cinema Ear: Some Key Film-Makers of the Sixties *(reprinted by permission of Hill & Wang, a division of Farrar, Straus & Giroux, Inc.; in Canada, by AD Peters & Co., Ltd; copyright © 1964 by John Russell Taylor), Hill & Wang, 1964, pp. 138-69.*

JÖRN DONNER

As an artist in film [Bergman] interprets and transfers his private dreams and imaginings to the celluloid. As an artist he is firmly anchored in a Swedish and European tradition in which Strindberg, Kafka, and Proust were pioneers. And still he has succeeded in convincing, not only a cultured, intellectual world, but also masses of people who perhaps know nothing of the spiritual background of his work. (p. 5)

It is my conviction that B has succeeded in transforming his private perception into a general one, understandable to other people. This is his strength as an artist. It does not . . . become a question of seeking the truth about his private personality, but rather, as much as possible, of hiding it and not talking about it. . . . This is why Ingmar Bergman in this book is designated by the letter B. The person behind the work is a fictitious figure who undoubtedly resembles the private person B. Such resemblances do not interest me. (p. 6)

I find that we are today on our way toward something new, which breaks radically with most in the film's past. We are on the way toward a film art where the personality of the individual artist puts its stamp on the work. The film has learned to write. It is now learning to create form and to compose poetically. In this renewal, B is in the foremost ranks. (p. 7)

B and the other directors who may be regarded as the vanguard of film art give expression to qualities which the pioneering men could not, perhaps did not even wish to, evoke. The intensely personal film art created by a group of artists in different countries undoubtedly has more qualities which separate than which unite. What unites is, to be sure, important enough. It is the chance to realize a deeply personal vision. It can be done in B's way, as a series of questions put to eternity and to mankind. It can be done in the manner of Buñuel, Antonioni, Kurosawa, Renoir, Ford, Rossellini, or Mizoguchi. I have chosen to write about B, not because I consider him a more important artist than those mentioned above, but because certain conditions have made it possible for me to follow his development year by year. Between 1944 and 1962 B wrote and directed thirty pictures. He has therefore almost always been able to realize his personal intentions. One can follow his development from an eclectic yet individual beginning to the maturity he now possesses. He has not let himself be obstructed by commercial considerations—a fate which, for instance, John Ford has often been forced to accept in silence. (p. 9)

B's films have become conversation pieces, something that "everybody" feels he can discuss with authority. The question of whether to accept or reject B becomes for these people first and foremost a question of whether to accept or reject the personal opinions that they believe they find behind his work. Applied to literature, such a point of view would be devastating. Only those who fully shared Strindberg's *opinions* would be able to read him.

Ever since I saw the first of B's films, I have put up a determined but somewhat fluctuating struggle against the thought of accepting them. B's world actually seemed to me to be limited, in a dangerous sense. At times one got the impression that he was a director, at other times that he was an author. It seemed as if some of his characters expressed a dangerous criticism of rationalism. They tended to deny the whole world of social resolution and social action on which the Swedish society of welfare and affluence was, after all, built. His opposition to forces that he regarded as obstructive appeared to be misdirected. The antibourgeois line seemed like a Bohemian flirtation with an impossible freedom. To praise such an artist was perhaps the same as to abandon without resistance the thought that art can exert an influence on society through the individuals who are the recipients of art. In a word, B's world seemed to me one of conformity.

The fact that B nevertheless managed to engage me personally arose from the rich possibilities of choice, the deep analysis of action and thought, that were to be found in his pictures. The perspective in his works varied continually. This richness of fancy could only in part be directly attributed to biographical circumstances. He himself and his critics often stress the fact that he is the son of a man of the church and that his upbringing bore the stamp of the Protestant religion. Those who are not Christians find it difficult to estimate this information correctly—as well as all the other facts that have been told of B's life. It is much more interesting that the Last Judgment which the artist B holds over his head and those of his characters has a general application. Of general application are Knight Antonius Block's questions in *The Seventh Seal* and Professor Isak Borg's dread in *Wild Strawberries*. All this is understandable even for the irreligious. The questions in B's films often deal with man's relationship to eternity, but broaden their scope to include all the painful experience that plagues the man of our time. The dread in B's films relates not only to the petty concerns of a materially thriving society, but dread about the future of man and of life on our threatened planet.

It has been said that the characters in his films seem to live in faulty contact with "the times" as a social and political field of action. (pp. 9-11)

[The] sense of crisis, approaching and full of threat, present and overwhelming, is never distant from B's pictures, even the most idyllic ones. This feeling corresponds to the spiritual unrest that has troubled Swedish society during the last thirty years. . . . A "decline and dissolution of what holds the social unit together" has influenced B's work. He has not been able to solve or to ignore the historic social crisis in which he finds himself. In common with Swedish culture in general, he has taken over only the Christian middle-class aspect of the decline of Hegelianism. The bridges have been destroyed by objective and materialistic dialectics. This concerns primarily art and the intellectuals. (p. 11)

Yet it must be borne in mind that the values B's films aim at are always of a moral nature. The importance of economic and social barriers is underestimated. Still, the social conventions are questioned and examined by the very concentration on moral values. In this respect B becomes a writer of his time just as much as any other. Nevertheless, we can call it a paradox that this poet of the film—exclusive in his selection of dramatic material, marked in an overwhelmingly one-sided way by the intellectual milieu in Sweden, by the spiritual situations of Protestantism—is able to convince great numbers of people. There are greater creators of characters in Swedish literature. Since Strindberg, there has not come forth a poet who intuitively is so attuned to his own time as B. Note, for instance, how in *Winter Light* he lets the dread of the threatening unknown, nuclear warfare, become the film's main dramatic material.

His writing, that of the film, describes and interprets a situation of chaos and insecurity in the Western cultural world, but it also manages to push outside it. The great penetrating thinkers, who stick at nothing in their criticism of the human condition, have found it much more difficult than he to win an audience. They are too nonconformist. We find in B a strange blend of conformity and nonconformity. The battle between these two poles is documented in *Smiles of a Summer Night* and *The Naked Night*. . . . B's analysis of the human condition, of man's attitude toward the great abstract questions, is almost as merciless. But beyond this he is seeking a solution, which may appear romantic and false because it often originates in a defective, purely individual analysis of man's being. But the important thing is that he, thanks to his tremendous ability to narrate on the screen, can make his world clearly visible. He is thereby able to satisfy demands of many different kinds—and arouse dissatisfaction of many different kinds. One might wish for another world for B to depict than the one he shows us. But his skill in showing us his world is not lessened thereby. (pp. 14-15)

With some obvious exceptions, film art for B has seldom been a play with images. It was therefore possible for him to reach the seriousness of prayer, the power of confession. He has permitted his imagination to associate freely. On the basis of personal material and subjective questions, he has staged a series of films which in their compact effect are without parallel in modern motion pictures. This does not mean that they cannot be surpassed, or that other paths are closed.

The play with images is executed by artists who do not feel any responsibility extending beyond the borders of art. But even if the work of art is an answer in itself, action in itself, a rebuttal is needed, a spectator, a protest or an agreement. B feels this responsibility. His development has meant a continuous release from the narrow problems to which his society and his own milieu have given rise.

Like Tolstoy, he has inquired about the meaning of art, whether it has any purpose except to gratify man for a moment. In this endeavor, B has come to ask more questions than he can ever answer. He has posed great, metaphysical questions, about the existence of God and of a judging or delivering authority. Perhaps he has at last found that all this is meaningless so long as man cannot solve the simple problems of living with others, so long as he cannot enjoy the moment which is his life. (pp. 234-35)

Jörn Donner, "Fame and Significance" and "Chamber Plays," in his The Personal Vision of Ingmar Bergman, *translated by Jörn Donner (copyright © 1964 by Indiana University Press; originally published as* Djävulens ansikte: Ingmar Bergmans filmer, *Bokförlaget Aldus-Bonniers, 1962), Indiana University Press, 1964, pp. 3-29, 206-38.*

BIRGITTA STEENE

[There are writers] whose works seem to lend themselves to a thematic interpretation; writers who appear as "hedgehogs" in the literary world, i.e., relate everything to a single central vision, fitting into it, consciously or unconsciously, all experiences and objects. . . . In contemporary Swedish literature we could include in this category Pär Lagerkvist, and, in terms of his major films, Ingmar Bergman, both of whom display in their work a monistic concern with modern man as a metaphysical seeker and whose fictional characters emerge as skeptical pilgrims journeying through a world in which remnants of religiosity fail to appease their questioning minds. Like Pär Lagerkvist, Ingmar Bergman might be said to have assumed the rôle of a modern Bunyan whose unitary inner vision of existential man could run the risk of being called merely epigonic, were it not for the fact that we realize how deeply personal that vision is. (p. 59)

In the four major films that form the nucleus of this essay [*The Seventh Seal, Wild Strawberries, Through A Glass Darkly,* and *Winter Light*] Bergman depicts as his protagonist a man dwelling in a self-contained world, cut off from life around him. Such detachment is not completely self-willed; yet, it becomes a curse for the man and condemns him as a human being. To be cut off from mankind is to be cut off from love, i.e., from God, is in fact to become like Satan. To dramatize what amounts to the emergence of the devil-image into the mind of the central character, Bergman resorts to actions that might be called variations on the myth of the Fall and of the Faust legend. (p. 60)

[*The Seventh Seal*] is an attempt to project on the screen the mythic reality of the medieval church paintings he had observed as a child. . . .

The crusader's mind is not what we associate with the conventional medieval man; he is closer to a modern skeptic whose burning need of faith cannot be fulfilled because he refuses to accept a god who does not give intellectual proof of his existence. (p. 61)

The Seventh Seal sets up a dichotomy, which is to remain a basic one in Bergman's production, between a god who is a silent monster and torturer of man, and a god who is a lover of life. Neither image of God is objectified but exists as fundamental attitudes in Bergman's characters. Hence a man's experiencing of God will, in its wider psychological ramifications, be a reflection on his relationship with other human beings. (p. 62)

Bergman illustrates [the] gradual alienation of man from God by depicting in the crusader a human being at first engaged in a holy enterprise but at last willing to sell his soul to the Devil—could he only find him! For the Devil, he argues with insane logic, must know of God since he only exists in his opposition to God. (p. 64)

Through his quest the crusader has come to deny his wife, and by implication life itself. In a way that seems unknowing, yet deliberate, the crusader has become his own devil, responsible not only for his own but for his bride's loss of joy in living. But his actions are dictated by compulsion rather than temptation. Nowhere do we sense the modern temper of *The Seventh Seal* more strongly than in the realization that moral will has given way to psychological needs —which exclude a possibility of choice. (p. 65)

Only in Mia and Jof does Bergman depict people who know how to live with a god who is *deus caritatis.* It is their voice, but without any direct reference to God, which is heard in Bergman's next film, *Wild Strawberries*. . . . (pp. 65-6)

Although *Wild Strawberries* does not treat any problem of faith, it is conceived as a symbolic pilgrimage, as a form of penance for the central character, Isak Borg. The film is an exploration in the possibility of love and fellowship between human beings. . . .

Isak Borg is Bergman's most clear-cut version of a cinematic Faust. But Bergman lets us know that although Isak's withdrawal from the world is a Faustian search for control over life, it is not caused by a desire for omnipotence but is, in effect, an escape from pain. Isak's isolation is the self-created, secure world of a man who is unable to accept adulthood as a loss of the autonomous world of the child and, in erotic terms, as a loss of separateness. (p. 66)

As in *The Seventh Seal* the psychological implications of the story do not exclude a moral evaluation of the protagonist, but in *Wild Strawberries* they compel Bergman to utilize a structural device that savors of the therapeutic consulting room: the mythic images which torture the dreams of spiritually distraught patients. . . . But of greater importance is the fact that Isak's destiny is not only that of an individual man but to a greater or lesser degree the destiny of all mankind. On one hand the dreams are applicable to Isak's personal problem. But on the other hand, their total impact is that of a moral archetype. (pp. 66-7)

[The nightmare at the beginning of the film] is an expression of Isak's fear of death and also an evaluation of himself: he is beginning to realize that he is a man without identity, without a face.

As he continues his inward search, his fear of death subsides and his dreams become self-explorations, classical examination dreams that could be taken right out of Freud's *Traumdeutung*. . . .(pp. 67-8)

In Bergman's works, travelling is often a release for the conflicts of the soul, and in *Wild Strawberries* Isak's search takes the outer form of a journey through Sweden. (p. 68)

His journey—unlike the crusader's—becomes not so much a journey towards the land of death as an initiation into life, a form of rebirth. Woman plays a key rôle in this transformation, for she is, as the heartbeat in one of Isak's dreams, the living measure of existence. Both Marianne, the daughter-in-law who travels with Isak, and Sara, the hitchhiker, work as catalysts. (pp. 68-9)

Isak Borg not only learns to be a human being but, more specifically, he learns to be a parent confronted by children. He learns to care about his son and daughter-in-law, and he learns to love young Sara who is a child to him. In accepting parenthood, Isak can at last look back on his childhood and youth without bitterness. (p. 69)

The inability to accept adulthood, i.e., parenthood, as a "lesson in love," and the self-absorbed father's lack of communication with his children form the major theme in *Through a Glass Darkly*. . . . (p. 70)

David's search for artistic perfection turns out to be as futile as the crusader's search for God. Both in a sense try to become like God, the one all-creative, the other omniscient. Both are doomed to fail. But David's guilt is more obvious than Antonius Block's, for he not only neglects others, he uses them and in so doing he destroys the life of his child: Bergman hints that David's behavior is the fundamental reason for Karin's defeat in life. (pp. 70-1)

[David, like Isak Borg] is a spectator in life, a curious but uninvolved observer. But David is also conceived as a far more complex and ambiguous character than Isak Borg, for he emerges also as a deputy for Bergman's two gods from *The Seventh Seal*. In a crucial scene up in the attic when Karin has one of her visions, she sees God as an enormous spider at a moment when her father enters the room. Considerably shaken by Karin's experience, David is at last able to reach Minus. He breaks his long silence with his son to tell him that in spite of all the horror, God exists as a power of love: "God is love and love is God." Minus, who has the closing lines of the film, reacts to this message—a starry-eyed look on his face—with the words "Dad spoke to me," which could read "God spoke to me." From the children's point of view the father has become connected, if not identified, with their image of God. David has refused to be a parent to Karin, has refused to give her love and security. In her mind she conceives an image of God that corresponds to that of her father: God becomes a spider feeding upon those that fall in his net, much the same as David in his diary fed upon Karin's illness. For Minus, on the other hand, God is not a silent monster but a sign of forgiveness (Minus is haunted by a feeling of guilt after an incestuous relationship with Karin), just as David is not a threat to him or a severe judge but a parent communicating a message of love.

Yet, God as love remains a message only in *Through A Glass Darkly*, a mere supposition. Perhaps this is all He can be, Bergman seems to say, for those who are to remain in the world. (p. 71)

In *Winter Light* [the] internal world is an absolute spiritual vacuum. Yet, as in Bergman's earlier works this film is not only a study in individual despair but also a study of its repercussions on the surroundings. Man may be an island to himself, but he is still responsible to life on the mainland. (p. 73)

The reason for Märta Lundblad's failure to save Tomas Ericsson seems to lie in her insistence on being a companion in love, a sexual mate. What Tomas is seeking—like all Bergman characters—is parental love, not erotic. Tomas has known his parents only as an authority which has pushed him into his present situation. For this reason, Bergman implies, it is impossible for Tomas to experience God as love; he is unable to disseminate such an image of God because he himself has never experienced love. We see again how the family microcosm in Bergman's world reflects on and encompasses man's whole existence, including his experience of a transcendental or mythic reality. *Winter Light* is constructed as a psychological chain reaction in the failure of parenthood: Tomas' parents fail him→God (as perceived by Tomas) fails him→Tomas fails his congregation (fisherman Persson)→fisherman Persson fails his wife and unborn child.

Tomas Ericsson is torn between a desire to revolt against a hateful God-parent and a need to seek security and proof of love. But the proof must come from the parent. . . . [He] is like Pascal's doubter: he keeps praising God in the hope of convincing himself that God is not all silence. But in doing so, he only perpetuates his own isolation. For Tomas Ericsson, God can only be a personal need, a withdrawal into self, and hence a curse that shuts him off from all life. (pp. 76-7)

Birgitta Steene, "Archetypal Patterns in Four Ingmar Bergman Plays," in Scandinavian Studies, *Vol. 37, No. 1, February, 1965, pp. 58-76.*

TOM MILNE

The easiest way out of dealing with an embarassing white elephant like Bergman's *Now About These Women* . . . is to follow everybody else in sweeping it away under the carpet as a laborious attempt at farce. To do so, however, is to ignore a haunting aftertaste of quiet melancholy which lingers long after the film is gone. It also happens to be enchanting to look at and frequently extremely funny—so much so that it commands a second visit; and this time one penetrates the outer defences to discover why it appears to be limping so heavily. (p. 146)

Bergman takes amiably malicious revenge on his critics. . . . These humiliations, shot with the full barrage of silent comedy techniques to the jazzy accompaniment of "Yes, We Have No Bananas" on the soundtrack, are often deliriously and unexpectedly funny. . . . Yet, even though they make up the bulk of the film, these sequences are merely interludes—they are the dashes in a Morse Code message, meaningless without the dots.

If all that one sees is the dashes, then one is in precisely the same boat as Cornelius, who never actually sees Felix, but remains trapped by the grotesque surface of life in the chateau. . . .

What Bergman is saying, of course, is that art (Felix) must be experienced rather than sought for, explained or understood; and under the surface of the film lies a complex disquisition on the nature of the cruel, deceptive, egotistical, secretive and neccessary thing we call art. Felix, in spite of his arrogance and selfishness, commands the divine quality of harmony, but neither he nor his gift can be pinned down for eternity. . . . This transcience, which Bergman acknowledges as an essential part of genius, is what informs his film with its pervasive melancholy. The only thing, ultimately, that an artist can hope for is to die without having betrayed his art. . . .

"The whole house is crazy," the impresario Jillker advises Cornelius, "You must be adaptable." But Bergman has become so established as the master of spiritual torment or stylish comedy, that his masterly juggling of contradictory moods in this film obviously demands too much in the way of adaptability. No matter: *Now About These Women* will outlive the insults which have been heaped on it. "Genius," as Jillker aptly remarks, "is making a critic change his mind." (p. 147)

Tom Milne, "Film Reviews: 'Now About These Women'," in Sight and Sound *(copyright © 1965 by The British Film Institute), Vol. 34, No. 3, Summer, 1965, pp. 146-47.*

SUSAN SONTAG

[The difficulty in understanding *Persona* is] that Bergman withholds the kind of clear signals for sorting out fantasies from reality offered, for example, by Buñuel in *Belle de Jour*. Buñuel puts in the clues; he wants the viewer to be able to decipher his film. The insufficiency of the clues Bergman has planted must be taken to indicate that he intends the film to remain partly encoded. The viewer can only move toward, but never achieve, certainty about the action. . . . One prime bit of evidence for this thesis is a sequence occurring soon after the two women arrive at the seaside. It's the sequence in which, after we have seen Elizabeth enter Alma's room and stand beside her and stroke her hair, we see Alma, pale, troubled, asking Elizabeth the next morning, "Did you come to my room last night?" and Elizabeth, slightly quizzical, anxious, shaking her head no. Now there seems no reason to doubt Elizabeth's answer. The viewer isn't given any evidence of a malevolent plan on Elizabeth's part to undermine Alma's confidence in her own sanity; nor any evidence for doubting Elizabeth's memory or sanity in the ordinary sense. But if that is the case, two important points have been established early in the film. One is that Alma is hallucinating—and, presumably, will continue doing so. The other is that hallucinations or visions will appear on the screen with the same rhythms, the same look of objective reality as something "real." (pp. 129-30)

Persona is constructed according to a form that resists being reduced to a story—say, the story about the relation (however ambiguous and abstract) between two women named Elizabeth and Alma, a patient and a nurse, a star and an ingenue, *alma* (soul) and *persona* (mask). Such reduction to a story means, in the end, a reduction of Bergman's film to the single dimension of psychology. Not that the psychological dimension isn't there. It is. But to understand *Persona,* the viewer must go beyond the psychological point of view. (p. 130)

This seems clear from the fact that Bergman allows the audience to interpret Elizabeth's mute condition in several ways—as involuntary mental breakdown, and as voluntary moral decision leading either towards self-purification or suicide. But whatever the background of her condition, it is much more in the sheer fact of it than in its causes that Bergman wishes to involve the viewer. In *Persona,* muteness is first of all a fact with a certain psychic and moral weight, a fact which initiates its own kind of casuality upon an 'other'.

Persona makes a remarkable modification of the structure of *The Silence*. In the earlier film, the love-hate relationship between the two sisters projected an unmistakable sexual energy—particularly the feelings of the older sister. . . . In *Persona,* Bergman has achieved a more interesting situation by delicately excising or transcending the possible sexual implications of the tie between the two women. It is a remarkable feat of moral and psychological poise. While maintaining the indeterminacy of the situation (from a psychological point of view), Bergman does not give the impression of evading the issue, and he presents nothing that is psychologically improbable.

The advantages of keeping the psychological aspects of *Persona* indeterminate (while internally credible) are that Bergman can do many other things besides tell a story. Instead of a full-blown story, he presents something that is, in one sense, cruder and, in another, more abstract: a body of material, a subject. (p. 132)

In a work constituted along these principles, the action would appear intermittent, porous, shot through intimations of absence, of what could not be univocally said. This doesn't mean that the narration has forfeited "sense." But it does mean that sense isn't necessarily tied to a determinate plot. Alternatively, there is the possibility of an extended narration composed of events which are not (wholly) explicated but are, nevertheless, possible and may even have taken place. (pp. 132-33)

[One] of the salient features of new narratives is a deliberate, calculated frustration of the desire to know. Did anything happen last year at Marienbad? What did become of the girl in *L'Avventura?* Where is Alma going when she boards a bus toward the close of *Persona?* (p. 133)

The avowal of agnosticism on the artist's part may look like frivolity or contempt for the audience. Antonioni enraged many people by saying that he didn't know himself what happened to the missing girl in *L'Avventura*—whether she had, for instance, committed suicide or run away. But this attitude should be taken with the utmost seriousness. When the artist declares that he "knows" no more than the audience does, he is saying that all the meaning resides in the work itself, that there is "nothing behind" it. (p. 134)

[The] construction of *Persona* is best described in terms of this variation-on-a-theme form. The theme is that of *doubling;* unity and fission, the variations are those that follow from the leading possibilities of that theme (on both a formal and a psychological level) such as duplication, inversion, reciprocal exchange, and repetition. The action cannot be univocally paraphrased. It's correct to speak of *Persona* in terms of the fortunes of two characters named Elizabeth and Alma who are engaged in a desperate duel of identities. But it is equally pertinent to treat *Persona* as relating the duel between two mythical parts of a single self:

the corrupted person who acts (Elizabeth) and the ingenuous soul (Alma) who founders in contact with corruption. (pp. 135-36)

By not just telling a "story" about the psychic ordeal of two women, Bergman is using that ordeal as a constituent element of his main theme. And that theme of doubling appears to be no less a formal idea than a psychological one. As I have already stressed, Bergman has withheld enough information about the story of the two women to make it impossible to determine clearly the main outlines, much less all, of what passes between them. Further, he has introduced a number of reflections about the nature of representation (the status of the image, of the word, of action, of the film medium itself). *Persona* is not just a representation of transactions between the two characters, Alma and Elizabeth, but a meditation on the film which is "about" them.

The most explicit parts of this meditation is the opening and closing sequences, in which Bergman tries to create the film as an object: a finite object, a made object, a fragile, perishable object, and therefore something existing in space as well as time.

Persona begins with darkness. Then two points of light gradually gain in brightness, until we see that they're the two carbons of the arc lamp; after this, a portion of the leader flashes by. Then follows a suite of rapid images, some barely identifiable. . . . (pp. 136-37)

[At the close of the film] there is a complementary montage of fragmented images, ending with the child again reaching caressingly toward the huge blurry blow-up of a woman's face. Then Bergman cuts to the shot of the incandescent arc lamp, showing the reverse of the phenomenon which opens the film. The carbons begin to fade; slowly the light goes out. The film dies, as it were, before our eyes. It dies as an object or a thing does, declaring itself to be used up, and thus virtually independent of the volition of the maker.

Any account which leaves out or dismisses as incidental how *Persona* begins and ends hasn't been talking about the film that Bergman made. Far from being extraneous or pretentious, as many reviewers found it, the so-called frame of *Persona* is, it seems to me, a central statement of the motif of aesthetic self-reflexiveness that runs through the entire film. The element of self-reflexiveness in *Persona* is anything but an arbitrary concern, one superadded to the dramatic action. (p. 138)

[In Alma's monologue about Elizabeth's relationship to her son, which is filmed once showing Alma's face and once showing Elizabeth's face and ends with a composite face, half Elizabeth's and half Alma's,] Bergman is pointing up the paradoxical promise of film—namely, that it always gives the illusion of a voyeuristic access to an untampered reality, a neutral view of things as they are. What is filmed is always, in some sense, a "document." But what contemporary film-makers more and more often show is the process of seeing itself, giving grounds or evidence for several different ways of seeing the same thing, which the viewer may entertain concurrently or successively.

Bergman's use of this idea in *Persona* is strikingly original, but the larger intention is a familiar one. In the ways that Bergman made his film self-reflexive, self-regarding, ultimately self-engorging, we should recognize not a private whim but the expression of a well-established tendency. For it is precisely the energy for this sort of "formalist" concern with the nature and paradoxes of the medium itself which was unleashed when the nineteenth-century formal structures of plot and characters (with their presumption of a much less complex reality than that envisaged by the contemporary consciousness) were demoted. What is commonly patronized as an overexquisite self-consciousness in contemporary art, leading to a species of auto-cannibalism, can be seen—less pejoratively—as the liberation of new energies of thought and sensibility.

This, for me, is the promise behind the familiar thesis that locates the difference between traditional and new cinema in the altered status of the camera. In the aesthetic of traditional films, the camera tried to remain unperceived, to efface itself before the spectacle it was rendering. In contrast, what counts as new cinema can be recognized, as Pasolini has remarked, by the "felt presence of the camera." . . . But Bergman goes beyond Pasolini's criterion, inserting into the viewer's consciousness the felt present of the film as an object. (pp. 139-40)

If the maintenance of personality requires safeguarding the integrity of masks, and the truth about a person always means his unmasking, cracking the mask, then the truth about life as a whole is the shattering of the whole facade—behind which lies an absolute cruelty. . . .

The subject of *Persona* is the violence of the spirit. If the two women violate each other, each can be said to have at least as profoundly violated herself. In the final parallel to this theme, the film itself seems to be violated—to emerge out of and descend back into the chaos of "cinema" and film-as-object. (pp. 141-42)

Susan Sontag, "Bergman's 'Persona'" (1967), in her Styles of Radical Will *(reprinted by permission of Farrar, Straus & Giroux, Inc.; copyright © 1967 by Susan Sontag), Farrar, Straus & Giroux, 1969, pp. 123-45.*

STANLEY KAUFFMANN

Shortly after I saw Ingmar Bergman's *Persona* for the first time, I discovered the writings of R. D. Laing. Laing is a Scottish psychiatrist, blazingly humane, who is trying to understand (among other things) how madness becomes the sanity of the mad. A passage from his book *The Divided Self* might serve as epigraph for *Persona:*

> The unrealness of perceptions and the falsity and meaninglessness of all activity are the necessary consequences of perception and activity being in the command of a false self —a system partially dissociated from the "true" self. . . .

Bergman's film begins with an actress, young and successful, who has suffered these consequences. All activity has become false and meaningless to her. (pp. 13-14)

After the titles, the film slashes ahead with the swiftness that comes not from speed but from a superb power of distillation. Everything is lean, yet everything is rich. This we expect from Bergman. What might not have been expected, and what is highly gratifying, is that he has found an answer in art to what lately has been troubling his art.

In his last three serious films—*Through a Glass Darkly,*

Winter Light, and *The Silence*—Bergman has used increasingly parsimonious means for increasingly subjective exploration. . . . These films were masterfully made, but they seemed introspectively remote rather than dramatized, so much so that they gave the viewer almost a sense of intrusion. I had the growing fear that Bergman, his breathtaking techniques undiminished, his power with actors as full as ever, had become disheartened: by a sense of irrelevance, *his* irrelevance; by the imperative to choose what to communicate, by the hopelessness of choosing, by the hopelessness of finding artistic means after he had chosen. It seemed as if, in refuge, he was keeping a kind of private journal in public. But *Persona* is a successful work of art, and what is especially happy about it is that Bergman, far from abandoning the psychical questions that consume him, has plunged further into them. He has made his film unfold its matter *at* us, instead of hugging it close. (pp. 14-15)

Bergman is no surer than anyone else (he seems to say) as to what illusion is. . . . Bergman's drama is in the attraction of the truth of the "true" inner self (Laing's term) as against the generally prevailing and venerated falsity of the outer world. At the last the nurse pulls free of the actress's state, not because of any indisputable and superior standard of rationality but because of her own irrationality. That, I think, is the essence of the film. If we talk of reason, there is probably as much reason on the mute actress's side, on the side of withdrawal, of inner purgation. What moves the nurse finally is a stubborn *ir*rational will to live—to live in the majority's terms, in terms of the world's continuity. . . .

Persona does not break fresh ground (hardly a requisite of art), but it throws a hot light on certain ideas that make them more painful than ever. The actress's state is so compelling, the nurse's desire to join her is so touching, that we are lashed to this film as to our own psyches (and to our own unacknowledged longings for withdrawal). The bitterness of the "healthy" ending makes this all the more true. (p. 17)

Stanley Kauffmann, "'Persona'" (originally published in New American Review, *January, 1968), in his* Figures of Light: Film Criticism and Comment *(copyright © 1968, 1969, 1970 by Stanley Kauffmann; reprinted by permission of Harper & Row, Publishers, Inc.), Harper, 1971, pp. 13-18.*

RICHARD SCHICKEL

Ingmar Bergman likes to speak of himself as a magician. The film maker, he notes, bases his art on the use of a machine that exploits a weakness in human vision in order to impart the illusion—not the reality—of motion and therefore of life. (p. 175)

I have never been able to definitely decide whether Bergman is, indeed, a consummate magician or merely a mountebank. I change my mind from film to film and even from sequence to sequence in the same film. He is a journalist—not quite a philosopher—of the guilty soul, and the necessity to probe the unconscious states of his characters leads him to a heavily symbolic, sometimes expressionistic, style in which he has created (a) some of the most memorable screen images of our time and (b) some of the most annoyingly obscure and/or pretentious images of the same period. . . . [The] hold he has on me—and, I suspect, on almost everyone else—is based on his attempt, and ours, to resolve the basic tension between the artist and the trickster which exists in his personality and in his work.

It is no wonder that Bergman, so aware that his art—perhaps all art—is based at least partly on trumpery, should be obsessed with the tragedy of the artist figure who suddenly, mysteriously loses the power to cast his magic spells. *Persona,* released a year ago, and his latest film, *Hour of the Wolf,* both deal with this theme and are, in fact, twins more understandable and rewarding considered together instead of separately. (pp. 175-76)

Hour of the Wolf carries [the logic of *Persona*] one step further. The basic situation is the same. (p. 176)

There is, however, one important difference. The companion will not allow herself to be drawn into the artist's insanity, perhaps because she is defending her unborn child, perhaps because she knows the wiles and dangers of her "case" more intimately than the nurse in *Persona* knew hers.

Anyway, the painter . . . cannot fight off his demons. . . . [He] becomes the means of openly stating what was only implicit in the earlier film: that madness undischarged in art or in human relations must be discharged through self-destruction. Somehow or other it will out.

As a kind of journalist Bergman is always an objective observer of such phenomena, and he betrays little overt emotion over this denouement. He accepts self-destruction as coolly (one is tempted to say coldly) as he accepted in *Persona* the destruction of an innocent bystander. He is—as all his films testify—the sort of completely committed, perhaps self-absorbed, artist who has long lived with full awareness that the creative spirit can turn rogue, can destroy with the same passionate intensity that it builds. (pp. 176-77)

I trust his motives in all this. They have, I think, a purity rare among film artists. His methods, on the other hand, are sometimes dubious. In *Persona,* for example, he took very great risks, striving for an elliptical austerity of statement that deliberately puzzled and frankly bored. . . . (p. 177)

In *Hour of the Wolf* Bergman is back to his older, more familiar tricks, mixing memories, visions and external reality in a deliberately confusing, though ultimately decipherable way. (p. 178)

Richard Schickel, "'Hour of Wolf'" (originally published in Life, *April 26, 1968), in his* Second Sight: Notes on Some Movies, 1965-1970 *(copyright © 1972 by, Richard Schickel; reprinted by permission of Simon and Schuster, a Division of Gulf & Western Corporation), Simon and Schuster, 1972, pp. 175-79.*

RICHARD CORLISS and JONATHAN HOOPS

Hour of the Wolf is a story film, with a beginning, a middle, and an end (though, as Godard said in another context, "not necessarily in that order"); it displays specific literary references, as opposed to *Persona*'s general filmic ones; and it confronts the stylistic innovations of certain *nouvelle vague* directors in a way more consistent with what we recognize as good old Bergman. (p. 36)

[Rare] in a Bergman film is the reliance on "outside sources." In *Hour of the Wolf,* the model is Mozart's *The Magic Flute* and, though a specific reference to it during the party seems at first superfluous, we later realize that it is doubly relevant: because the film is a retelling of the *Magic Flute* story, and because, whereas the dramas from

Through a Glass Darkly to *Persona* were "chamber" films . . . *Hour of the Wolf* is frankly operatic. The settings are expansive rather than constrictive; there are many characters, and each is given a verbal aria; the treatment, like most libretti, is melodramatic in the extreme. (p. 38)

As Bergman has reminded us, we spend half our movie-watching time in the dark. A film is made in fragments and edited to form something cohesive. Only in the last decade have many film-makers abandoned the pretension of wholeness; the *nouvelle vague* directors popularized this idea. And only in his last two films has Bergman attempted to relate this to his patented style. If *Persona* was a recognition of the *nouvelle vague, Hour of the Wolf* may be said to be an understanding of it. . . . In this film he has added to his usual reference book the quotes from *The Magic Flute* (and, to a lesser extent, the works of E.T.A. Hoffmann). Although these references are not the irrelevant quotes that Godard, after a morning's browse in Left Bank bookstalls, inserts in the afternoon's footage. Bergman's reliance on them provokes the feeling that he's trying to support, or perhaps camouflage, a weak artistic performance. . . . [To] his personal interests Bergman bends the originally French techniques in a way that is more subdued than that of *Persona* and better suited to those interests.

For instance, *Persona*'s fusion of those two *nouvelle vague* metaphysical mouthfuls, temporal indeterminacy and the narration of possibilities, is reduced in *Hour of the Wolf* to a story with an identifiable chronology, and there is only one sequence, Johan's disappearance soon after his meeting with Veronica, which represents possible variations on a single action. (pp. 38-9)

Bergman has also applied the shuffling of filmic tenses, a technique associated with Alain Resnais, to *Hour of the Wolf.* The present tense is represented by the interviews with Alma, the past by the "story," and the past conditional by Johan's nightmares. The directors differ in the extent to which they use tenses other than the present: Resnais's are usually flashes (whether back, forward or inward), while Bergman's are fleshed out. Resnais's are shots, Bergman's are sequences. Before restricting Bergman to a mere extension of Resnais's innovations, we should recall that Bergman developed a full and integral sequence of tenses in *Wild Strawberries,* released in Paris two years before *Hiroshima Mon Amour*. . . .

[So it] would be demeaning to think of *Hour of the Wolf* as the sum of Resnais's, Godard's, Mozart's and Hoffmann's parts. Bergman elicits most of his best effects from his trademarked bag. (p. 39)

Richard Corliss and Jonathan Hoops, "Film Reviews: 'Hour of the Wolf'," in Film Quarterly *(copyright 1968 by The Regents of the University of California; reprinted by permission of the University of California Press), Vol. XXI, No. 4, Summer, 1968, pp. 33-40.*

BIRGITTA STEENE

[The opening scene of *The Seventh Seal*] is not merely a piece of cinematic exposition; it is a thematic prelude: in the image of the gliding bird seen against a sky which is "a dome of lead," Bergman telescopes the knight's hopeless search for God, who remains distant and silent. (p. 92)

Although the knight's quest is medieval, his skeptic and anxious temper is modern. To help justify such an anachronism Bergman claims that the medieval world depicted in *The Seventh Seal* is basically a historical metaphor for our own world threatened by atomic destruction: "In my film the Crusader returns from the Crusades as the soldier returns from the war today. In the Middle Ages, men lived in terror of the plague. Today they live in fear of the atomic bomb. *The Seventh Seal* is an allegory with a theme that is quite simple: man, his eternal search for God, with death as his only certainty."

Bergman's use of the term "allegory" should be taken in a general rather than medieval sense, being a story in which the spiritual content is set forth in a concrete action and with characters whose movements are realistic but whose basic function is that of abstract symbols. (p. 93)

Philosophically, *The Seventh Seal* departs from medieval allegory in two respects: the metaphysical uncertainty that characterizes Bergman's film has little in common with the *a priori* assumption of an orderly universe, which underlies original allegory; and the central character in the prototypal allegory is not haunted by doubt; his problem is his forgetfulness of God, and God emerges not as an enigma but as a father figure anxious to reach and save His straying child.

The philosophical mood of *The Seventh Seal* is related to the existentialist view that a human life is decided not in intellectual questioning but in the choice of action. (pp. 93-4)

Bergman juxtaposes the knight's intellectual probing and his relationship with Jof and Mia, the visionary artist and the maternal woman, whose son one day will "perform the impossible trick of making a ball stand still in the air" (i.e., like Christ he will transcend nature). The traditional function of the Crusader in medieval art was not as the colonizer of the Holy Land but as the protector of the Holy Family. Bergman's knight performs the same service. But in saving Jof and his family by distracting Death's attention away from them, Antonius Block loses the game—and his life. It is a situation of ironic blasphemy: Man redeems Christ. (p. 95)

The figure of Death stands only on the threshold of the unknown; he is not a messenger, but merely a blind instrument. But he might be considered the focal point in the film . . . *The Seventh Seal* concerns man's reactions in the face of eschatological matters. Almost all the characters can be linked to Death and evaluated according to his influence over them. While Skat and Raval live as though Death did not exist, and Tyan and the flagellants as though nothing else existed, the knight and Jöns carry on a resentful and challenging dialogue with Death. (p. 96)

Jöns is more than the hedonist he appears to be. Like Antonius Block he represents the consciousness of modern man. The knight and his squire complement each other, and depict the skeptic personality facing a world where God is silent: one in futile introspection, the other in gallant action. They do not offer an alternative. All the film seems to say is that some people can live without illusions and still function as useful social beings, while others succumb to their need to believe and lose themselves in a search for God. At one point the knight cries out: "Why can't I kill God within me? Why does He live on in this painful and humiliating way even though I curse Him and want to tear Him out of my heart? Why, in spite of everything, is He a baffling reality that I can't shake off?" In this statement we sense again the modern temper of *The Seventh Seal:* the realization that moral will has given way to psychological needs—which excludes a possibility of choice. Yet, both the knight and Jöns are conceived as moral agents, and in this ambivalence Bergman again establishes his affinity with existentialist philosophy and its tenet that we must live as though we had a free will. The insoluble dilemma dramatized in the fate of Antonius Block also points to one of Ibsen's central themes: the curse (i.e., the moral judgment) that falls upon a man who *must* follow his calling. (pp. 96-7)

Birgitta Steene, "'The Seventh Seal': An Existential Vision," in her Ingmar Bergman *(copyright © 1968 by Twayne Publishers, Inc.; reprinted with the permission of Twayne Publishers, A Division of G. K. Hall & Co., Boston), Twayne, 1968 (and reprinted in* Focus on "The Seventh Seal," *edited by Birgitta Steene, Prentice-Hall, Inc., 1972, pp. 92-9).*

ERNEST CALLENBACH

[In] the disbalances of *Hour of the Wolf,* Bergman was paying some of the immense psychological price that must be exacted for working so near the line between sanity and madness; of all directors, he is the most personally brave in the sense of being willing to work with dangerous psychic material—to dredge, as he himself once said, down into the primitive levels of infancy when we are all frighteningly psychotic.

Shame returns nearer the surface again; it is safer, less daring. . . . There are no "ideas" in *Shame*. Except perhaps for the last shot, the film would make sense without its sound track. Indeed, much of what the characters say does not really make much sense anyway. Bergman has long abandoned the role of the Great Dubber, who used to put into his characters' mouths important thoughts about God, life, and the loneliness of man in an inscrutable universe. His characters now nag fiercely at each other. . . . (p. 33)

Shame is in fact quite remarkable among war films, and takes its place among a tiny honorable handful that may be considered genuinely antiwar. The usual "antiwar" film gains its laurels by including a certain amount of obviously senseless gore and destruction. It may even allege conscious or unconscious villainy on the part of war-makers, like Kubrick's *Paths of Glory*. But the battle scenes prove to have a purposeful choreographic grace and power lacking in the rest of the movie (or indeed in most movies). War may be hell, but it sure does give the camera something to photograph! More subtly, war films almost universally provide an artificial and reassuring orientation to what is happening, both through dramatic devices and dialogue and through the elementary tactics of coherent screen movement (especially having one army move to the right and the other to the left). Whatever the script may say, battles on film thus are given *visual* sense. But *Shame*'s war scenes, like the documentary Vietnam footage in *The Anderson Platoon,* but closer up, never make visual sense. If we found ourselves magically transported, like Keaton's little projectionist, suddenly catapulted into *Shame,* we wouldn't have the faintest idea what to do: which way to run, where to hide. We would be, in other words, in exactly the position of a Vietnamese peasant upon whose village the B-52s, too high for the eye to see, are raining bombs in a carefully computerized random pattern.

Naturally enough, this aspect of the film is enormously depressing, and doubtless it largely accounts for the film not proving popular. . . . (pp. 33-4)

[The] power the ending should have had is somehow diffused. The boat is adrift, its people apparently doomed to starvation. When all possibilities of action in the outside world have been blocked or made senseless, human beings turn inward; they curl and die. The wife can only recount her dreams. This reaction of humanity to the utterly monstrous, the unbearable, is perhaps what Kurtz in *Heart of Darkness* calls "the horror." To Bergman it is the shame of modern man. (p. 34)

Ernest Callenbach, "Reviews: 'Shame'," in Film Quarterly *(copyright 1969 by The Regents of the University of California; reprinted by permission of the University of California Press), Vol. XXIII, No. 1, Fall, 1969, pp. 32-4.*

ROBIN WOOD

Prison is a turgid, tedious film finally invalidated by the tendency to inflate a personal neurosis into a Vision of Life. Its explicit thesis is that life on earth is already Hell, that the devil rules. But all one could deduce from the evidence it presents is that some people are very nasty and some others very ineffectual. (p. 29)

The chief contribution [*Port of Call*] makes is the extension of Bergman's antipathy to parental figures to include the social authorities, presented with consistent hostility.

The limitations of these early films are crippling. It appears to have been impossible for Bergman at this stage to conceive of an acceptable maturity. One can see signs of a tentative awareness of the need to come to some sort of terms with adult life, in the ending of *Port of Call*. . . . (p. 30)

Summer Interlude is the earliest in which one feels in the presence of a great artist, not merely a gifted, or precocious, or ambitious one. The film shows an achieved mastery both in the overall line, the inner movement, and in the minutiae of *mise-en-scène* in which that movement finds local expression. . . .

The importance of *Summer Interlude* in relation to Bergman's early films is immediately evident: it both continues and develops the characteristic preoccupation with youth and the vulnerability of innocence. But here the transition from innocent youth to experienced adulthood is really explored, and with it the possibility of coming to terms with the world of Experience. (p. 32)

The film's most distinctive characteristic is perhaps its feeling for nature. While nature is obviously of great importance in, for example, *The Seventh Seal* and *Wild Strawberries,* I know of no other Bergman film where it is felt as a pervasive influence to the extent it is in *Summer Interlude*. . . . (p. 33)

Summer with Monika is the perfect companion-piece and complement for *Summer Interlude*. . . .

It is a less personal work than *Summer Interlude,* and relatively minor; it never achieves the generalising significance of the earlier film, being in a more restrictive way a study of character and of a particular relationship. (p. 39)

[The] most important thing in the film is the extremely complex and detailed treatment of Monika. She is the direct opposite of the helpless child-women and pure prostitutes of the early work. She entirely lacks purity, but the loss of innocence is felt to be inseparable from her splendid energy, her animal vitality and sensuality. (p. 41)

Sawdust and Tinsel and its immediate successor *A Lesson in Love* both have distinctive flavours unique in strength if not in kind in Bergman's work; and they are at almost opposite poles. *A Lesson in Love* is arguably the warmest and funniest of all Bergman's films, characterized by an overall atmosphere of relaxed good nature. *Sawdust and Tinsel* has a tone of savage bitterness and rage that nowhere else in Bergman's work erupts with such intensity or establishes itself so unequivocally as the central creative impulse. It is discernible elsewhere though, even, very muted, in the occasional tartness that serves to spice the prevailing good humour of *A Lesson in Love*. . . .

Sawdust and Tinsel expresses a view of life one can hardly find balanced or objective. Clearly, in a sense, Bergman 'meant' it; but it must not be taken as absolute. Though it is not as narrow as first impressions and the introductory flashback might suggest its peculiar intensity and narrowness limit *Sawdust and Tinsel,* but they also give it its distinctive character, hence its value as the expression of one aspect of the Bergman world. (p. 49)

[An] intensely *physical* sensitivity informs *Sawdust and Tinsel:* there is a shot near the beginning of bent weeds that a cart wheel passes over and presses down, as the first raindrops splash into an adjacent puddle. No other Bergman film, not even *The Virgin Spring,* which has a more detached presentation, evokes quite such intense and consistent physical empathy in the spectator. . . . (p. 50)

[*Smiles of a Summer Night*] is less a beginning than an end: it has something of the nature of a combined culmination and retrospect, its achieved perfection associating with its consolidating rather than exploratory character. (p. 67)

[Balance] is the keynote of the film: the balancing of irony and sympathy, the balancing of different attitudes. The period setting increases the total effect of a formally conceived summation, enabling Bergman to achieve a stylised, patterned quality. It seems clear that part of the inspiration came from Mozart opera. The formalised effect of the film reminds one at times of Mozart's *ensembles*. (p. 68)

If *Smiles of a Summer Night* has its source in Mozart opera, *Wild Strawberries* is founded on Bach fugue. (p. 72)

Though the parallel is quite close, the form is not forced or externally applied, and there is no question of a schematically detailed working out; indeed, the film could almost equally be seen in terms of a sonata-rondo structure. The sense of a 'musical' structure, at once dense, broad and complex, however, is essential to the total effect, and indeed to the meaning of the film. Above all, one mustn't think of its 'musical' form as something abstract that could be discussed in isolation from the content. (p. 73)

Wild Strawberries represents the culmination and fulfilment of the Christian side of Bergman; the presence of a benevolent deity seems to permeate the film, in form as well as in an overall mellowness of tone that easily assimilates the incidental asperities. Isak became aware of 'an extraordinary logic': Bergman seems to reconcile this hint at predestination with the sort of 'natural' religion upheld by *The Seventh Seal* (which, it should be remembered, preceded *Wild Strawberries*). The 'extraordinary logic' is also the working out of a natural process. The 'musical' organisation, the sense of a quasi-fugal working-out, satisfyingly expresses Isak's sense of a pattern in existence. It is significant that the Bergman film embodying the Christian virtues of love, forgiveness, humility, should be centrally concerned with forgiveness between parents and children. The fact that the film proved for Bergman something of a dead end doesn't invalidate it. Isak Borg's relationship to Bergman himself is obvious enough; but equally obvious is the fact that, unlike certain of these other figures, Isak exists quite independently as a fully realized character in his own right. (p. 80)

The first thing people tend to notice (quite rightly) about *The Virgin Spring* is the convincing reality with which medieval life is created. (p. 101)

Bergman's sensitivity to the nature of material that in some respects lies quite outside the scope of interests revealed in his own screenplays, is evident in his response to the 'ballad' aspects of the film. He uses traditional but highly evocative imagery with great assurance and subtlety. . . .

The opposition of light and dark in the imagery suggests a clear-cut duality in nature, a concept which the film gradually undermines, giving the simple opposition ironic overtones. Nothing is quite as it appears; nothing is unmixedly pure or simply evil. (p. 102)

In the world of *The Virgin Spring,* good and evil are like subterranean streams, potent, determining matters of life and death, but invisible and mysterious. No one is pure. (p. 103)

The treatment of religion in *The Virgin Spring* is perfectly consistent with that in Bergman's films from *The Seventh Seal* to *Winter Light*. Conscious outward shows (the flagellants' procession in *The Seventh Seal;* Märeta's self-mortification and Töre's ritual purification) are worthless, stupid and degrading. Karin's virgin candles and virgin mission only serve to add to her sexual allure. In the world of 'mixed' nature, purification can come only by the fulfilment of evil and the passing beyond it. (p. 104)

[*Through a Glass Darkly*] is an extremely important and extremely unsatisfactory film. To demonstrate its unsatisfactoriness one has only to point to what is beyond question the worst ending in mature Bergman. But it cannot be isolated there. . . . (p. 107)

Karin's emergence as a new 'personal' character is the chief contribution *Through a Glass Darkly* makes to Bergman's development, and its importance can scarcely be exaggerated. It coincides significantly with the relegating of the emotionally impotent characters (the father and, to some extent, Martin, Karin's husband) to a comparatively subordinate role. . . . In *Through a Glass Darkly* [all] concerns take second place to Karin's 'madness', a madness which is also a peculiar clarity of vision. The ice of Bergman's 'frozen' period is shattered at last, and it is Karin who emerges. (p. 108)

One is tempted to see [the] ending as ironic; but nothing in the presentation supports this view. One can only say, in Bergman's defence, that the consistent undermining of the father throughout the film suggests Bergman's lack of confidence in his last words. They are indeed mere words. (p. 109)

Winter Light is an intensely personal film. . . . Yet, without ever violating strict narrative unity, without any suggestion that anything is being imposed on the characters and situations that doesn't grow naturally out of the dramatic data, the film epitomises perhaps the most essential inner movement of western civilization in the last hundred years: the movement away from religious orthodoxy, the discovery of God's 'silence' (or non-existence), the progression into a kind of tentative existentialism. We are far here from the grand but spurious gestures of *The Seventh Seal;* there is nothing picturesque, nothing inorganic, and nothing suspect about *Winter Light.* (p. 112)

The Silence is one of the most difficult films to feel one's way to the heart of: to do so requires an act of courage that testifies to the extraordinary courage of the man who made it. One watches the film almost emotionlessly, as if paralyzed, and comes out feeling that one has experienced very little. Then hours, or even days, later, one comes to realize how deep and disturbing the experience has been; or one finds ways of insulating oneself—it's a 'sick' film, its piling on of miseries and perversions is ridiculous, one was really laughing at it all the time; or alternatively, it's too obscure to be accessible, it doesn't 'communicate'. . . .

[The] film is about the eternal conflict of spiritual and physical; Anna represents body, Ester soul: only through union and harmony could wholeness be achieved, and the two are locked in permanent combat. This sounds—if we withdraw some distance from the detail of the film—temptingly feasible. The temptation should be firmly resisted: to force *The Silence* into this kind of allegory is to simplify and schematize. (p. 123)

The theory of the film as a personal allegory, in which the characters represent different aspects of Bergman's own psyche, is much more cogent, and also much less restricting. One can see it as an image of a shattered personality struggling towards wholeness, or casting off old growth, irreparably stunted and damaged, so that healthy new shoots can emerge. . . .

[The boy Johan tries to observe, assimilate, and adjust to] the mysterious outer world, from which the characters are cut off, but which is felt as a potent menace. . . . The sense of a world *out there,* at least as terrible in its way as the inner world of desire and its frustration, is the more disturbing for remaining undefined: one has an impression of mysterious and terrible forces quite beyond the individual's control. (pp. 127-28)

The effect of the film's final image is dual: we feel the strength and intensity of the boy's determination to understand, and through this the strength of Ester's need to pass on whatever is left of any value in her stunted, wretched existence; but the crescendo of noise on the sound-track seems to obliterate the words that are not, in fact, spoken, reminding us of all the forces and pressures with which the boy's developing consciousness will have to contend. Clearly, we cannot talk here of distinct 'levels': the symbolic significance grows naturally out of the narrative. (p. 129)

We are very far, with Johan, from the idealisation of youth and the corresponding rejection of full adulthood typical of early Bergman. What is emphasized throughout is the enquiring and growing side of the boy's nature—his progress towards a relatively untrammelled adulthood, in fact—which makes of him a figure very different from the doomed young of the early works. And if Bergman is partly identified with him, this is never at the expense of sympathy with the world of adults. (p. 130)

When writing about *The Silence* I suggested that a concept of normality can only exist in relation to a defined social framework. In *Shame* normality is associated with tradition. Love, tenderness, sympathy, the sense of marriage itself, the desire for family, are felt as dependent upon a context of civilised values. (p. 175)

Bergman's maturity is nowhere more evident than in his treatment of Jacobi. In imposing himself upon Eva as a lover, Jacobi uses his position and his knowledge of her situation in a way that is obviously corrupt, knowing that she doesn't love him. Yet his need for Eva cannot possibly be seen as mere lust. She is his link with civilised values, with the possibility of tenderness, integrity and warmth. . . . There is nothing heroic about [Jacobi], but his failure to adjust to the demands for ruthlessness imposed on him by circumstances testifies to his humanity, thereby appearing a strength rather than a weakness. He dies because he cannot cease to be a civilised human being. (p. 180)

Bergman's total mastery of style is confirmed by the fact that he now feels free to allow himself and his actors a certain degree of controlled improvisation. He has reached an ideal fusion of surface detachment and profound emotional impact. It is always the spectator's deepest responses that are touched, beyond any facile direct onslaught. (p. 181)

[*Shame* is] Bergman's masterpiece to date and one of the greatest films of the last decade. It is Bergman's distinction to have established himself as a great, and central, artist in an age peculiarly inimical to great art. His greatest quality is his capacity for development, which is also the drive towards the attainment of human fullness. The journey from *Frenzy* to *Shame* is an extraordinary feat of courage and intelligence. (p. 183)

Robin Wood, in his Ingmar Bergman *(© 1969 by Robin Wood; reprinted by permission of the author), Frederick A. Praeger, Publishers, 1969, 191 p.*

ARTHUR GIBSON

Three persistent and intensifying impressions assail me as I contemplate the consistent whole that is the film series [consisting of seven films: *The Seventh Seal, Wild Strawberries, The Magician, Through a Glass Darkly, Winter Light, The Silence,* and *Persona*].

1. An initial absence gradually evolves into a disturbing and terrifying presence. There gradually emerges that conviction that theists all too often flippantly cast aside in mistaken reverence or dubious pusillanimity: the ultimate religious experience—which is the only truly religious experience—is supremely personal *on both sides:* man is reacting not to a mathematical formula but to a living God, and because this living God is communicating not with a sensitized passive photographic plate but rather with the endless restlessness that is a human person, the dialogue must have the gaps and terrors incident upon all personal communication. (p. 12)

2. Indeed the dynamic of these seven films *begins with man and ends with God.* I see that dynamic sweeping aside restrictive humanism and geometricizing transcendentalism

alike. *Love* is its Alpha and Omega; but what a purifying furnace must not that love traverse between the beginning and the consummation! The trenchant thrust of human longing for certitude and peace and hope for pain is its powering drive; tortuously and deviously that thrust reveals itself as questing, probing, evading, facing, and suffering before it is finally brought to the awful moment of vision. At the beginning, there is a silence that is held to be the proof of God's existence. At the end there is a still more awful silence which reveals itself as the true silence *of* God. The God imagined to be nonexistent because silent reveals his face as precisely the ultimate respecter of human freedom, whose unflinching rendezvous with man is a supremely immanent or incarnational one.

3. *Not only man but also God proceeds through a dynamic evolution* in the course of these films: from an initial serene intransigence to a terminal agonizing involvement. This is what the Incarnation is really all about. And transcendentalistic Monophysitism has most brutally savaged the genuine poetic insight of Christians into the reality of this great event, which here emerges so drastically. These films, taken as an integral whole, reveal the mystery of the Incarnation in an absolutely uncompromising way. No room is left for poetic sentimentality, but no whit of ontological poignancy is lost. Moreover, God looms into these films in two ways, each with its own peculiar dynamic: first, there is the felt absence growing gradually throughout the course of the seven films into a more terribly felt presence; then there is the artistic presence of God in a series of characters who "play" God in the sense of rendering present some portion of his dynamic and problematic in his relation with his creatures. The poet can essay what the theologian must sedulously avoid, the penetration, by poetic language and plastic representation, of the dimension of mystery. If the theologian writes in this vein he lapses into unedifying and unappetizing heresy; but the poet can touch the very nerve of the living God in commerce with his living creatures and expose the stunning love affair so long raging between them. This Bergman does: the dynamic of the ontological absence-presence of God runs exactly parallel to the dynamic of the God-mouthpieces. As these mouthpieces become more and more fleshed out, more and more adequate to the reality, so is the initial gnawing absence gradually replaced and supplanted by a terrifying and challenging presence.

But besides a supreme God-mouthpiece, each film in this series has likewise one character who is the epitome of seeking humanity (and since humanity's seeking is itself ambivalent, part real searching and part rebellious febrile fleeing, so the individual film may have more than one such epitome of humanity). And the line of the dynamic of the human seekers runs exactly counter to the line of the God-mouthpieces: as the God-mouthpieces become progressively more complex and austere, so the epitomes of human seeking becomes progressively simpler and more engaging or more reprehensible.

The radically simplified problematic of the entire series, regarded as a solidary unity, might be stated thus. The initial questioning demands: Is God *there?* And the terminal answer retorts: No, now he is *here!* (pp. 12-14)

The thrust of the film series . . . is the clarification of an initial silence apparently indicative of absence into a terminal silence terribly indicative of presence. What seemed at the outset to be a silence proclaiming God's irrelevance to the human cosmos emerges at the end as a silence proclaiming God's supreme relevance (and even exposure) to human freedom. God is silent not because he is not but because he is *God,* the supreme lover of freedom and thus the supremely silent victim of man's misuse of freedom. (p. 159)

God is luminously present throughout this entire cycle, but the nature of his presence in each film is substantially conditioned by the state of the human protagonists.

Man is most definitely to be taken seriously as a free created moral being, who by his action or sluggishness in action can really affect the future course of his own and the cosmos' destiny. Will man in fact properly respond? That is the unresolved question: and the mastery, the artistic mastery, of Bergman's staging of the final film of the series, with his drastic suppression of the transcendent element and his equally drastic highlighting of the human element, is proof positive of his absolute artistic integrity. For the outcome is still, in our day, really in the balance. God's reality and power do not change; but man is a chameleon even as Alma was so diagnosed by Elizabeth Vogler. Man can alter his stance and his answer from age to age; and man's answering thrust really matters, desperately matters, is indeed crucial. This is no divine comedy; it is a divine-human tragedy in the sense that it can most definitely have a tragic outcome. (pp. 161-62)

The silence of God is a problem at the outset and a tragedy at the end. Initially that silence is a challenge to man and terminally it is the result of man's deliberate rejection. . . .

Every effort to abstract from the intensely personal encounter of God and human creature is intellectualistic cowardice. For at the heart of the created human universe stands freedom; and freedom is the sign of peril, of unpredictability, and of *choice.* (p. 165)

Arthur Gibson, in his The Silence of God: Creative Response to the Films of Ingmar Bergman *(copyright © 1969 by Arthur Gibson; reprinted by permission of Harper & Row, Publishers, Inc.), Harper, 1969, 171 p.*

RICHARD SCHICKEL

With *The Passion of Anna* the art of Ingmar Bergman reaches its pinnacle. Though it is one of his rare color films, it is in every important way his most austere and elliptical work, a thing of silences and enigmas that nevertheless makes very clear the tragic vision of life that possesses its author.

Gone at last are all traces of the baroque symbolism that marked—and often marred—his early work. Gone, too, is the yearning for evidence of the presence of God in the world. Bergman has, I think, accepted His death and, indeed, seems to find that event no longer worthy of comment. His absence is now simply one of the terms of our existence. . . .

[The island to which Bergman has retreated for four consecutive films is], of course, a psychological landscape as well as a physical one, and Bergman has gone there in the same spirit that his people have gone to that stark, spare place—out of revulsion at the meaningless cruelty of the world. There is no escape from it here, as *The Passion of Anna* makes abundantly clear, but it is at least somewhat reduced—to something like a manageable non-institutional human scale. Or so they permit themselves to hope. (p. 314)

We do not care [if the architect follows Anna or not at the end]. It is not important. Any action will, we know, turn out to be without resolving meaning. It will end only in the passage of more time. It is, in its quiet way, a shattering ending, brilliant both in its economy and its clarity. Bergman has, in that concluding sequence, as well as in the rest of the picture, stripped his art bare of all that is non-essential, all that offers any promise of warmth. Such hope as he extends stands outside the frame of the film. (p. 315)

We may leave *The Passion of Anna* more dubious than ever about man's fate, but with our faith in the possibilies of screen art—much tested in recent months—miraculously restored. (p. 316)

Richard Schickel, "'The Passion of Anna'" (originally published in Life, *July 24, 1970), in his* Second Sight: Notes on Some Movies, 1965-1970 *(copyright © 1972 by, Richard Schickel; reprinted by permission of Simon and Schuster, a Division of Gulf & Western Corporation), Simon and Schuster, 1972, pp. 314-16.*

BIRGITTA STEENE

To a great extent Bergman's films from the fifties—*The Seventh Seal, Wild Strawberries, The Magician, Smiles of a Summer Night, The Virgin Spring*—. . . start from the written text, from a *dialogue* meant to convey both thematic meaning and emotional tension. When Professor Borg in *Wild Strawberries* looks into the microscope in one of the dream sequences and sees nothing but his own eye, we are *told* this. (p. 24)

In the fifties, then, Bergman seems to be building up his sequences around a series of verbal episodes or encounters. But at the same time, he appears to be quite aware of his own shortcomings as a writer, and he tries to compensate for this by juxtaposing or reinforcing verbalized sequences with scenes of visual exaggeration. The results are often carefully planned contrasts of shots, executed in spooky darkness or suffused with romantic light; surroundings and weather are used as *Stimmungsmalerei,* as visualizations of a mood. . . . Such externalizations of feelings of peacefulness or terror, where the landscape serves as the artist's tool, might be called a form of film Gothicism. It is often coupled with a certain remoteness in Bergman to his characters, and has thus laid the foundation of the most common charge leveled against him: his lack of human warmth. . . .

Most of Bergman's films fall back on a prototypal literary form: that of a journey or quest. . . . If we compare the journeys in the Gothic films to the travels or suggestion of travels in the later, so-called chamber films of the sixties we find that traveling becomes much more claustrophobic and frustrating and is, in fact, almost completely internalized. It is as though the later films emanate from the state of mind of Professor Borg during his nightmarish dreams in *Wild Strawberries*.

From a literary-formal point of view Bergman moves from an epic pattern and the tangible reality of the Bildungsroman to the world of the stream-of-consciousness novel. From a thematic point of view this implies a much more direct confrontation by Bergman with his personal vision; and from the point of view of cinematic style it leads to a shift from Gothicism to ever greater visual asceticism. (p. 25)

But perhaps the most crucial change that occurs in Bergman's film making in the early sixties is not his discarding of the historical milieu, the flashbacks, the physical travels, the broad perspectives, but his approach to the human figures—with a special emphasis on the close-up. (pp. 25-6)

Whereas his favorite approach to the characters in the Gothic films was to let the camera sneak up on them, so that the person closest to the camera was seen from behind with the director assuming the position of a peeping Tom, Bergman allows the faces of his people in the chamber films to dominate the screen. A shot of the young boy Johan in *The Silence* shows him in a typical Bergman composition, with the human figure up front and a second figure in the background. But Johan's face is turned towards the camera and towards us. . . .

[Such] handlings of the close-up by Bergman are more than technical experiments with camera and audience reaction; first and foremost they are meant to tell us something about his characters. As always in Bergman's case it is futile to approach his close-up style from the viewpoint of cinematic intention; rather, any changes in style must be related, I believe, to central themes, character motivation and other quite "literary" subjects. (p. 27)

In the trilogy (*Through a Glass Darkly, Winter Light, The Silence*), emotions are expressed in facial look, in gesture. . . . The reduced dialogue of the chamber films is not primarily a film maker's attempt to liberate himself from verbal influence, but a questioning, through the cinematic medium, of the trustworthiness of the spoken word. . . .

[We] find a persistent ethical examination of language in these films, which I think should be related to Bergman's religious questioning and his portrayal of the father-child relationship. (p. 28)

[What *Silence*] explores is Johan, the boy, facing a world that has lost touch with the divine—the original title of the film was *God's Silence*—and one in which a traditional, masculine mode of life is being rejected or destroyed. Johan is the only one who encounters all the male figures in the film, from the officers in the opening train sequence (who frighten him) to the old waiter in the hotel, to whom he reacts as though he were a Dickensian bogeyman. Through Johan we see how all the male characters in the hotel are emasculated, deformed (the dwarfs), or killed symbolically. . . . (pp. 30-1)

Although the visual perspective of *The Silence* is Johan's, much of its philosophical focus is on Ester. An alienated believer in verbal communication (she is a translator by profession) she re-enacts the Knight's role in *The Seventh Seal,* for like him she challenges, without much success, an unknown reality through words. (p. 31)

Ester's lesbianism is not as revealing as is her emotional dependence upon Anna. During her initial attack on the train Ester recovers as soon as Anna sends Johan away and devotes herself to her sister. Little by little Ester's search for parental love and support emerges. . . .

Yet, Anna fears Ester whom she looks upon as a moralistic extension of her father. She resents Ester's intellectual achievement and she is indifferent to the written message Ester gives Johan at the end. To Anna silence is comforting, for she can only see and use language as a destructive weapon and connects it with parental authority. (p. 32)

When Anna leaves Ester behind to die, she finally rejects the world of language and fatherly supervision—all "empty principles" as she has told Ester earlier. But Ester does not possess Anna's strength or indifference. She transfers the protective father image to the old waiter. . . . This mumbling and (in the moment of crisis) quite helpless father figure is indeed nothing but a dried-up goblin of a man. . . . The protective father figure, the god-against-fear, is relegated to the realm of death and myth.

With the trilogy, then, it would seem that Bergman brings to a close that gradual shift in man's approach to and experiencing of God, which had obsessed him since *The Seventh Seal;* it is a shift in attitude from an intellectual search for the transcendental to an examination of God as a therapeutic or authoritarian parental figure. (pp. 32-3)

It seems important to recognize that the relevance of language as a basis for film making is no longer a point argued by Bergman on a technical level, but rather is connected with his evolving vision of life. When God dies away, when the father fails or withdraws from his child and leaves it alone, language loses its communicative and healing power. Bergman's exploration of the god-parent-child syndrome takes then, in part, the form of a philosophical testing of language. His conclusion is that conventional language cannot be used by people to convey love. Nor can it be trusted, since it tends to destroy relationships or else lull people into a false sense of security. The perceptive and sensitive individual may at first cling to this verbal reassurance, but he will ultimately be driven to challenge it. (p. 33)

Birgitta Steene, "Images and Words in Ingmar Bergman's Films," in Cinema Journal *(© 1970, Society for Cinema Studies), Vol. X, No. 1, Fall, 1970, pp. 23-33.*

PETER COWIE

The latent power of *The Seventh Seal* stems from an ever-present fear in man's mind; a fear of the unknown. That twentieth-century man lives in the shadow of nuclear catastrophe is not fundamental to the film; but it allows one to share the bewilderment of the knight and his companions. It is this search for knowledge that illuminates all Bergman's mature films. It imposes a pattern on life, which becomes a journey through time and space. The transience of human existence does not depress Bergman so much as the pitiful groping of man to comprehend the world around him.

The Seventh Seal, like *Wild Strawberries, The Face,* and *The Virgin Spring,* ends on a note of optimism, with the Holy Family leading their wagon along the sunlit shore. And to a certain extent the book of Revelation, where the title of the film originates, is for all its violent imagery, a song of consolation. . . . The opening of the seals provides an interval for man to consider his significance on earth. He must realize that he cannot overcome his fear or improve the world unless he chooses the most difficult path. Thus the knight plays chess with Death, risking his entire being for the hope of committing one worthy act before the Apocalypse. Bergman shows that he loses his right to choice of action if he falls under the influence of the church. (p. 101)

Jöns and the other characters in *The Seventh Seal* present the knight with pointers towards a different attitude to life. "Blessed are the pure in heart, for they shall see God," is the most apposite description of Jof and Mia. They are simple folk who escape Death in the end because they never question God's existence or love. "One day is like another," says Mia. "The summer, of course, is better than the winter, because in summer you don't have to be cold. But spring is best of all." Theirs is an implicit faith in the beauty of life which relates them to other Bergman characters such as Sara in *Wild Strawberries* and Simson in *The Face*. (pp. 104-05)

The love that binds Jof and Mia is stronger than the menace of Death. When in the morning sunshine, Mia tells Jof to stop juggling and says, smiling, "I love you," the words are so tender and sincere that Death is no more than an empty mask dangling beside the caravan. . . . [They] are the faultless souls who survive to start a train of hope for humanity again. Bergman has said, "Whenever I am in doubt or uncertainty I take refuge in the vision of a simple and pure love. I find this love in those spontaneous women who . . . are the incarnation of purity." (p. 105)

Perhaps the most intriguing aspect of *The Seventh Seal* is the way Bergman creates an atmosphere in which these afflicted people can perform so persuasively. The film begins on a rocky beach, which is viewed from a lofty angle as the knight awakes with the dawn. There is a marked feeling of desolation and all extraneous sounds are absent from the encounter with Death, giving it an unearthly quality as the landscape darkens. After the initial moves in the game of chess, the knight and his squire ride along the ridge overlooking the sea. Bergman uses a series of dissolves so that the images disintegrate in glaucous sunlight, and the heat becomes almost palpable, as it does in the flashback at the beginning of *Sawdust and Tinsel.* But while the sea summons up resonances of hope, of arrival and departure, the chapel where the Crusaders stop briefly has the aura of a prison. Abstract concepts are translated into hard, tangible symbols throughout *The Seventh Seal,* and the grille that separates Block from his opponent in the confessional bars the knight's progress towards knowledge. (p. 107)

The Seventh Seal, like the moralities, is built on stylization. The characters wear their sentiments on their sleeve. The overriding symbol, Death himself, appears like a motif at a number of crucial psychological stages in the film, culminating in his terrifying confession of ignorance to the knight after he has defeated him in the game of chess. Hope becomes a squirrel bounding on to a tree stump after Skat's death, or a ray of moonlight filling a forest glade as Raval lies dead, or a caravan with its errant, innocent owners trundling along the seashore into the sun. Disillusion becomes the rigid gaze of a girl on the stake; resignation, the tossing of a log on a fire by a listless, lonely wife; horror, the rhythmical banging of beer mugs on an inn table while a man dances for his life. It is this triumphant blend of literary antecedent and visual metaphor that makes *The Seventh Seal* such a profound and ambitious film, unequalled in the Swedish cinema as an exercise in tempered expressionism, less ornate than *Sawdust and Tinsel,* less theatrical than *Miss Julie.* Its theme is universal and yet particularly momentous to the Swedes; the fundamental situation of men faced by death and striving to find some meaning in life is common to the work of Strindberg and Lagerkvist. At this stage Bergman neither denies nor affirms Christian tradition. He probes, he interrogates. (pp. 108-09)

Peter Cowie, "Ingmar Bergman: The Middle Period," in his Sweden 2 *(copyright © 1970 by Peter Cowie), A. S. Barnes & Co., 1970 (and reprinted in* Focus on "The Seventh Seal," *edited by Birgitta Steene, Prentice-Hall, Inc., 1972, pp. 100-09).*

VERNON YOUNG

It must never be overlooked that Bergman is as persistent a showman as he is a moralist. He is of the theatre, and while I should not want to declare that the one talent is all comic and the other—a preoccupation rather than a talent?—is altogether morose, I would suggest that there is a conflict between the two tendencies, between his desire to entertain and his instinct to preach, and that his masterpieces arise when the tendencies are virtually inseparable, when neither dominates the other, as in *The Naked Night, The Magician,* and *The Virgin Spring*. (p. 123)

One of the most fascinating problems of Bergman's development is his perennial return to the schematic disciplines of a primitive or classical mode, even as he is struggling to comply not only with the more fluid, less categorical, more musical medium of film, but also with the relativistic demands of the modern temper. *Sommarlek* was alternately pure movie, subjective, scenic, and time-compounding, and rudimentary classical theatre complete with symbolic attendants and exemplary characters such as crabbed age, hopeful youth, faithful companion, and the Manager as Chorus. *Waiting Women* was a breakaway experiment, not radical but indicative, like *Thirst,* a playing with contrary moods, a test of cinematic control—space, confined or illimitable; time, protracted or foreshortened. But framing it all was a convention, provided by the intrinsically Swedish experience, of the hippodrome of domestic incompatability and the false white nights of summer.

A Summer with Monika resumes this motif with quite another approach than any Bergman had taken in any of the skerry-setting films he had directed before. This is perhaps the least identifiably personal film Bergman has made and I know I am going against judgments indignantly pronounced when I add that I consider it one of his best. Not one of his most profound, for that's another matter; not one of his most revolutionary, yet there is paradox in that thought. Precisely because here he wasn't attempting new dimensions, symbolic extensions, or journeys into the maelstrom of the mind, this film is unique in Bergman's continuity and is an exercise in critical naturalism, lyrically executed and impenitently resolved, with not a whimper nor an accusation on the way. (pp. 123-24)

No film of Bergman expresses more ruthlessly [than *The Naked Night*] the consequence of the formulation by D. H. Lawrence, which I'm sure Bergman never had in mind, that all human relationships are based either on love or on power. When power flows the wrong way between the sexes, catastrophe is inevitable. . . . I do not see, as others have seen, any comfort to be derived from the fact that Albert and Anne are after all still united at the end of the film. This is a fate worse than death, surely, else why would Bergman go to the trouble of creating that macabre prologue and of adroitly plotting each sequel, so that one after the other they move steadily through confirming circumstances toward the self-same direction, with Frost himself as memento and prompter? Albert and Anne become resigned to each other; which must mean that each is resigned to himself. Resignation is not love. (pp. 135-36)

Frost is indubitably the overpowering and most baffling presence in the film. His whole aspect is an equivocation. A mirthless clown—what could be more futile? This is really an ingeniously oblique conception, even if we remember that Picasso had painted lugubrious clowns, for traditionally the clown in literature and drama has been employed intellectually, as a foil to complacency, a critic of absolutes. (p. 137)

[As] obviously unrelated as [*The Seventh Seal* and *Smiles of a Summer Night*] may be otherwise, their raison d'être is decor. *The Seventh Seal* is as artificial, in the best sense, as *Smiles*. Life as theatre and life as allegory; we are saying the same thing. Both demand a style of the impossible while suggesting, in fun or in dread, the borders of the possible. (p. 142)

To my sense [*Smiles of a Summer Night*] is a wholly delightful film; under close scrutiny, however, it is exposed as a precarious act of tightrope-walking. The situations therein are so expertly contrived and carried off, the repartee is so calculatedly brittle, the final adjustments so sensible, that it does pass for heedless comedy, which is to say an anti-heroic mode intended to provide pleasure rather than second thoughts. Yet the more often one sees it, such has been my experience, the plainer it becomes that in it the comic, which is to say the reasonable, point of view is sustained by a tense effort of will. (p. 143)

[There] is certainly little relief in this film from the spirit of masculine self-degradation which Bergman had been exuding in a sort of crescendo, beginning with *Waiting Women* and absent only from *A Summer with Monika*. Egerman, like his predecessors played by Gunnar Bjornstrand, while the most sympathetic male in *Smiles,* is nonetheless written—one might say written off—as the best representative of an inept species. (p. 145)

By a kind of miracle or a kind of superior charlatanry, which in theatre is just what performs miracle, Bergman made this *jeu d'été* imply reaches of mood and space and consequence which are not, to the eye, fully contained in the material. (p. 147)

I should like to restore to *The Seventh Seal* its status of a magical movie, more suggestive than definitive, more lyric than didactic. And the best way I know is to think of it as one might an orchestral suite for a small orchestra, in which certain themes from the motley life of a medieval community, threatened by death in the forest, comprise the various movements, with signature instruments for the principal characters. . . . If you heard a suite of this order, I think you would feel no compulsion to decide whether its composer was agnostic or devout; you would not think to translate the fugue into an ontological argument; you would more than likely miss the implication that those repeated triads symbolize the Trinity and while you might have a favorite movement you would not leave the concert hall asserting you had heard a piece of music which had infallibly pictured the misery of a world deprived of God's mercy. (pp. 159-60)

I think *The Seventh Seal* is a beautiful, harmoniously composed film with indelible pictoral effects but I do not feel that its questions disturb the universe. (p. 160)

The Magician is an incredibly suggestive work; that it is also definitive is as much to my point, and this very suggestiveness has beguiled critical opinion into strange interpretations; equally it has tempted certain critics into suspecting Bergman of trifling with them, of indulging a taste for the occult which he then hopes to endow with a spurious morality. I believe that Bergman has been many times confused, in his several films, as to how best to convey a moral or metaphysical ambiguity; I am of the opinion that in his latest films he has lost the power of discerning what is self-evident to an audience and what is absurd. I am convinced that he has ultimately unclear ideas about the nature of moral catastrophe. And it may well be that there are calculatedly hidden meanings in his later films; but I do not believe that he trades in gratuitous mystification and I do not believe that he manufactures effects which have no meaning to him. Frivolity is surely the last vice with which anyone should charge Bergman.

Above all, *The Magician* is not the film in which to expect irresponsibility, since the conscience of the artist is precisely the burden from which Vogler, the magician, is suffering. (p. 175)

Vogler's fate is left open, as it should be; we have never been quite sure of his identity; it is fitting that we should feel unsure of his future although, for the moment, it looks rosy. There may be undertones, intensities, extremities of feeling in this film which cannot rationally be accounted for, but I sense no fundamental imprecision in the character of the underworld which Bergman was apotheosizing. Obscurity is one thing, mystery another. (p. 176)

The Virgin Spring is the most selfless of his films. . . . [The film script, written by Ulla Isaksson, is] dense, concrete and sensuous, the spirit of the old ballad which is the source of the film captured and retold with the art, common to novelist and filmmaker, of moving through time and space as an eye. (p. 188)

Much for this reason, I would choose it as his masterwork, had I to name a superlative: the most lyrical, the most compassionate, the most lucidly constructed, metre by metre, and the film that most surely enters the heart and mind of the race. . . . (pp. 188-89)

The Seventh Seal is by comparison a charade. For all its talk of plague, desolation, and the fumes of burning flesh it does not draw blood. . . . *The Seventh Seal* has its own subtle gravity and charm but *The Virgin Spring,* while utterly beautiful in its pastoral spaces, cannot be called charming. The actuality before the miracle is an immediate sensation of primal existence, of a world in which you can nose the woodsmoke and the sourness of clothes and the nearness of stinking goats as you eat, and feel the roughness of the table under your hand and the high-country chill which only mead and raw meat, when you can slaughter it, can ward off. (pp. 191-92)

[*The Silence*] is a work I am forced to admire for its infernal compressionism. This is a film that transparently means something other than what you are seeing and this has become a jagged problem for critics who do not care for art as cryptology. I do not myself in numerous instances. . . . I think *The Silence* rewards effort; at its core there is a rancid integrity which compels one's recognition, if not one's affection. (pp. 212-13)

The sisters are Mind and Body. Ester, mind, is sick; she is self-generating; the first Timokan words she learns are for face, herself, and hand, with which she performs onanism. Anna is body, trying to shake off the mind's dominion; her insurrection is chiefly pornographic. Ester is shocked but yet sympathetic with the concupiscence of her other self. With this reading of the central, bisected image everything else in the film falls logically into place, logically, that is to say, as in a poem, not as in a mathematical equation. (p. 214)

The body affronts the mind, the mind fights fear of extinction with reason and brandy; the child of the body wanders in an unpeopled world where the few inhabitants are grotesque and cannot speak to him. Since the total atmosphere is one of *reduction,* it follows that all phenomena will be reduced. (p. 215)

[There] is no doubt that over and above, or below, the appalling accuracy of Bergman's metaphor in terms of the contemporary world, *The Silence* betrays a grindingly personal animus and incidentally a bias of the national temper. When we imagine hell, we extend the worst we already have. Most of us in the Western world would envisage social chaos. Who but a Swede would have a nightmare of body and mind totally irreconcilable, projected into a milieu dwindled to fewer than a dozen people who can't talk to each other, with the sun setting at two P.M.? (p. 216)

One vital force remains and will remain: hate. Despite the omnipresence of love as at least a forlorn hope in the Chamber films and the wistful belief in the power of love which Bergman has professed in interviews, it is hate that provides any dynamic principle to his films of the last decade. (p. 217)

In *Persona,* which is almost as compacted a vehicle as *The Silence* of Bergman's all-and-sundry beliefs, at least three principal themes are mined simultaneously. Any prose attempt to explain these lucidly in A-B-C fashion will inevitably tend to falsify the movie you see, wherein these themes are interlaced, even interlocked, and not separate, linear and exclusively labeled. For one, there is the reality-and-illusion, life-and theatre conflict, enforced and exaggerated in this case by the device of harshly interrupting the action to remind you, as if you needed the reminder, that you are seeing a film. This is an involution by which Bergman was impressed when he made *Prison,* 1949. Second, we are presented with a split-image gambit, exceedingly tricky, the nature of which can only be interpreted with any hope of accuracy if you take the names of the antagonists as your inescapable clue. On this one point, I am dogmatic; beyond this, I have no complacent belief that I have exhaustively interpreted the film. Finally, there is the biographical stratum—for the sake of convenience, I am making a false distinction by so isolating it—which is to say, the portrait of the artist as alternatively victim and cannibal, as evinced by what happens to Elisabeth Vogler, no less than by what happens to Alma the nurse. (p. 226)

The consequences are enjoined in *Persona* whereby the consciousness of art as a fiction (what else can it be?) is utilized, to a maddening degree, as a technique in the narration of the work of art. (p. 227)

In Bergman's film, I find that where his shock-method serves the subject of psychological fission—the fractured, fused, and superimposed faces—it exerts a legitimate fascination; where it is used for the purpose of reminding us that all art is vanity in a cruel world it is trite, it is déjà vu, above all it is a barbarous attack, sadistically motivated, on the nervous system. . . .

The most abusive device here is that violent interruption of the continuity, sufficiently oblique as it is, with snatches of filmmaking (or film-wrecking). (p. 228)

While still asking the nineteenth-century question of Does God exist?, he begins to ask in *The Silence* and *Persona* the question nearer to us of Does Man exist? After the modern ordeal of discovering by what numerous inner and outer determinisms man is governed and of what ignoble stuff he is made when you remove him not so much from religion, itself, that *sine qua non* of Bergman for the secure life, but from the sanctions of a social commonwealth, the guarantees of justice, the intricate, self-preserving defense of manners, the scale of values which, however imperfect and arbitrary, gives his life dignity by lending it aspiration, then what kind of figure does he cut? Lamentably often an hysteric, a modish barbarian, a fractional organism. (p. 237)

Any expectation that *Persona* was more than a skirmish in his inconclusive battle with the duplicity of the artist was certainly frustrated by *The Hour of the Wolf*. This film is almost pure dementia. . . . *The Hour of the Wolf,* chronologically trackable, never rises to the level of any implication you can invent for it, never becomes definition; in it Bergman explores nothing, creates nothing; this is wholly a disintegration product, replying to no serious question; it is theatrically shoddy and built on an ill-bred premise. The tone is that of polemic and self-pity. (p. 238)

The most interesting thing about *The Hour of the Wolf* is its title, the dark promise never fulfilled. Bergman coined a saying with an antique air. "The hour of the wolf is four o'clock in the morning: the hour when most people die and most babies are born". In the Bergman universe nothing is certain but death and babies, tomb and womb, death and birth. (p. 239)

This film reminds one, if in the grossest form, that Bergman's social antenna has an extremely limited range. There is little point in criticizing what an individual artist cannot do until he tries to do it. Believable social intercourse is the most deficient area of Bergman's film world, inevitably, since he is the citizen of a country with a thin texture of social differentiation. . . . Where a classless norm is the ideal, interpersonal subtlety becomes a lost art; realism must find other outlets and abandon a world in which conversation and the right wine count. Bergman today is a symbolist or nothing. (p. 242)

The content of [*A Passion*] is wholly allusive; the images are symbolic deductions from origins invisible, a choir of meanings unheard, an anthology of hints from nearly every motif he has expressed before, a gallery of icons, unidentifiable without a catalogue that names the sources and the conventions which alone give these icons viable significance. (p. 257)

A Passion sums as a total, hopeless ambiguity wherein nothing is finally and endurably explicable: the central vision is one of an eternal reign of inscrutability, deceit, "humiliation," and indifference, with a saving proviso, reduced to code. It is the despondent modern subject. (p. 258)

The moral point of the film, in its peculiar way, is that you cannot read another person without adequate love or knowledge and the point for us, looking at the film, is that you cannot read its story with the slightest claim to certainty if you only look at the succession of shots Bergman has taken. (pp. 258-59)

Bergman's *A Passion,* although it is dedicated to a far different and even more moritfying aim, is incidentally the most audacious answer to [the] universal indifference to meaning which, to my recognition, has been conceived. (p. 266)

What Bergman has done in this film is to abdicate from the conventional conception of time and duration, even more radically than he did in *Persona*. This is *limbo* or, if you like, purgatory. This has all *happened before. It will happen again. Time is spiral.* Andreas and Anna and the others are *reenacting* a convuluted, unending torment, out of the time-space continuum we are prepared to accept. (p. 267)

Let us return to the title. Everything is there. . . . If the filmgoer allows himself to be sidetracked by the secondary meaning of the word passion as a state of strong feeling, associated commonly with anger or with sex, he will get further than ever away from the film. Passion is *passio,* quite simply, to suffer. (p. 273)

The matter of *A Passion* is the drama of the Christian text. As in *Persona,* however, we need not expect to trace every detail consistently with the master theme. There are simply some meanings which emerge unmistakably once you are in the ambience. The moment of the film is the moment of the betrayal and its consequences. The atmosphere is premonitory; signs of cruelty and disaster appear throughout the film. But the pellucid color, the absence of chiarascuro, the offhand, daylight interviews with the actors, the seemingly concrete interplay between Elis and Eva and Andreas and Anna muffle the intimations of doom. (p. 274)

A Passion is an impressive tour de force if you allow that the object of an artist is almost totally to conceal his most authentic meaning and if you are willing to exempt the film from a primary purpose of a work of art, to arouse emotion. (p. 277)

A Passion, insofar as it passes judgment on the human condition, resembles an epistle from one of the Twelve addressed to the elect, carefully coded lest it fall into the hands of a Roman procurator. It is not irrelevant to note that John the Divine received his *Revelation* on an island. But the tone of *A Passion,* when you get down to the tone, is closer to that of St. Paul.

Even so, I have been visited by the suspicion, while writing this book, that Ingmar Bergman is not an authentically religious figure, despite the evidential symbols in his films that accumulate to suggest he is. I would describe him as a retentive personality, in whom belief has been replaced by obsession. (p. 280)

He is the victim and the beneficiary of a traumatic displacement, a shock of disbelief from which he has never recovered in his soul; that shock is responsible for his impetus and for the intense condensation of his art. He cannot now move freely save within the confines of the belief he has tried to repudiate, the symbols it provides, the rejections it assists, the polarities and correlatives of which it is composed. He must retain the belief, if only in a glass darkly, for it is the sole source from which his own creation is supplied; within its conventions he can move. And one has to respect the untiring sagacity with which he has incorporated himself; he has been able to enact his own father, his own erring son, his own wife, God, the devil, and the saints. He has become his own Passion. (p. 281)

To speak in any final way of Bergman's film style is simply to elucidate alternatives and individual preferences. Bergman's art has none of the baroque dynamics to be seen in the films of Max Ophuls, of Orson Welles at his best, of Kurasawa, in Sjöberg's *Miss Julie,* or in Alexandre Astruc's *Le Rideau Cramoisi.* Bergman was not a born filmmaker, as could be said of Eisenstein, Jean Epstein, Walter Ruttmann, Max Ophuls, and certain others. He worked his will with an inherited, popular medium, after a long and erratic apprenticeship. He has disciplined that medium within the range that has served his purpose, a purpose more austere than not, seldom free from theatrical sources; in many instances, of course, the retention of them was calculated. But in any case, and despite *Persona* or *A Passion,* we do not think of Bergman as primarily a virtuoso and innovator but as a poetic moralist. We think of him as a filmmaker of magic with an evangelical point of view—a Druid captured by Lutheranism.

You may be able to name other film artists who surpass Bergman in subtlety, in urbanity, in exuberance, in courtesy of heart, and in scope of social interest; you can choose directors whose styles you favor for their camera inflections, their tempo, their modes of composition, and their rhythms; you will find few who have anything like Bergman's obdurate and sustained integrity; none who has so artfully succeeded in displaying his temperature chart as a map of the world. In his own boreal and phobic way, Bergman has engaged that subterranean crisis of the spirit which we have agreed to call modern. (p. 283)

Vernon Young, in his Cinema Borealis: Ingmar Bergman and the Swedish Ethos *(copyright © 1971 by Vernon Young), David Lewis, 1971, 331 p.*

ART CARDUNER

Living in the same world with Ingmar Bergman is like living in one of those cities which has a perpetual view of majestic snow-capped mountain peaks. Nobody spends his entire day looking at mountains; people go about their daily business for weeks or months on end without ever looking up. But the mountains don't care whether anyone admires them or not—the mountains are THERE, and whether this person or that likes mountains, or doesn't like mountains, or is indifferent to mountains doesn't add to, or detract from, their majesty in any way.

In much the same way, Bergman is THERE. Whether we play his films or don't play his films, whether we see his films or don't see his films, whether we like his films or don't like his films, doesn't matter in the slightest, except to us. We can spend our entire lives in the shadow of a mountain without ever seeing it, until perhaps someone grabs us by the arm and says: "Look! Look at the mountain bathed in the light of the setting sun!" and we experience a few moments of inner radiance before we turn back to the diurnal routines of our existence. But it is in these brief moments of spiritual exaltation that we find, if we are lucky, the real meaning of life—some momentary flash of insight into what the hell it—IT—is all about. (pp. 27-8)

Who in the world today has given us moments like this more than Bergman? . . . In every one of his works, every one of his characters is made up of flesh and blood—only Shakespeare and Dickens have produced a larger and more varied progeny. (pp. 28-9)

Bergman is not, and never will be instinct with the masses; he lacks the common touch, surely a flaw, perhaps a fatal flaw, in his art. Bergman has turned his back on his audience, and the older he gets the more remote he becomes from them. . . . More and more, Bergman not only makes no effort to engage his audience, but deliberately repels them. Why? (p. 30)

[It] is not enough to say he rejects his audience, because this is certainly obvious enough to his audience. The question is, *how* does he reject his audience? What is the machinery that he uses, since we must assume that he can do anything he wants to do? One easy answer is 'obscurity'. Unfortunately, this tells us nothing. (pp. 30-1)

[There] is a kind of obscurity in many of Bergman's films that can't be read. He seems unable, or unwilling, to integrate his symbology. He has a tremendously fertile imagination for creating visual symbols, but he seems to lack the kind of cerebration that carries them through to their logical conclusions. For example, in *The Seventh Seal* he uses a chess game, a great visual symbol, to represent life. In the hands of Bunuel, each piece would represent an archetypal social class, and the relations among them, as individuals and as classes, would be explored with all the infinite nuances of the game itself. But to Bergman, it is just another game, and the only question is winning or not winning. (p. 31)

Hollywood provides something that Bergman doesn't—something that I consider an absolutely essential ingredient in a work or art, and that is a sense of resolution. As human beings, we need resolution, because that's the way our minds work. In respect of our mortality, all things seem to have a beginning and an end. To qualify as art, they must have a fitting end. . . .

Bergman refuses to resolve many of his films. People die, but their souls don't come to rest, so to speak, as they do in *Hamlet,* for example, or in *Ikiru. Smiles of a Summer Night* is certainly resolved with wonderful grace and charm, and without strain or compromise. In *The Seventh Seal,* the resolution is emotionally and intellectually satisfying, and in *Wild Strawberries* we surely can accept that the old man has made his peace with the world. However, most of his films just trail off into space, without giving us any bearings about which way is up. . . .

Another aspect of Bergman that affects me negatively is his almost total lack of concern with the work-a-day world and any psychic or material deprivations arising therefrom. . . . [Nobody] has any fun in Bergman's films, not even in bed. It's a cold, bleak, joyless world, often an island or some barren coast, where mortification of the flesh is exceeded only by mortification of the spirit.

For my own part, I am not sure that this kind of devil-wrestling needs to be quite as grim as Bergman would have us believe. . . . If we are headed for hell in a handbasket anyway, why not go with a bottle of fine wine and a plump whore? (p. 32)

Art Carduner, "'Nobody Has Any Fun in Bergman's Films'," in Film Society Review, *Vol. 7, No. 5, January, 1972, pp. 27-32.*

FRANÇOIS TRUFFAUT

For me, the lesson that Bergman gives us hinges on three points: liberation of dialogue, a radical cleansing of image, and absolute primacy granted to the human face.

Liberation of dialogue. The text of a film is not a piece of literature, but simply honest speech, things said and things not said, confessions and confidences. We could have learned this lesson from Jean Renoir but, strangely, it has been more clearly revealed through a language that is foreign to us and cinematographically pure. And that since *Illicit Interlude,* the film of our holidays, of our twenty years, of our first loves.

Cleansing of image. There are filmmakers who allow chance in their images, the sun, passers-by or bicycles (Rossellini, Lelouch, Huston), and there are those who strive to control every square centimetre of the screen (Eisenstein, Lang, Hitchcock). Bergman began like the first group and then switched allegiances; in his recent films you come across not one passer-by, your attention is not once drawn by a useless object in the decor, nor by a bird in the garden. There is nothing on the white canvas but that which Bergman (anti-pictorial like all real filmmakers) has wanted to put there.

As for the human face, no one has come as near to it as Bergman. In his recent films, there are only mouths that speak, ears that listen, eyes that express curiosity, hunger or panic. . . .

Bergman's most maligned film is called *All These Women* and it is ironic if one realises that the best of his work has consisted precisely in revealing the often-untapped genius in each of a number of women that have chosen the craft of acting. . . . They are neither chicks, nor broads, nor dames, but women, real women. Bergman films the expressions of these women—expressions more and more intense in harshness or in suffering—and the results are admirable films as simple as *bonjour.* But then, is *bonjour* simple for everyone?

François Truffaut, "The Lesson of Ingmar Bergman," in Take One *(copyright © 1972 by Unicorn Publishing Corp.), Vol. 3, No. 10, March–April, 1972, p. 40.*

PAULINE KAEL

Bergman is not a playful dreamer, as we already know from nightmarish films like *The Silence,* which seems to take place in a trance. He apparently thinks in images and links them together to make a film. Sometimes we may feel that we intuit the eroticism or the fears that lie behind the overwhelming moments in a Bergman movie, but he makes no effort to clarify. In a considerable portion of his work, the imagery derives its power from unconscious or not fully understood associations; that's why, when he is asked to explain a scene, he may reply, "It's just my poetry." Bergman doesn't always find ways to integrate this intense poetry with his themes. Even when he attempts to solve the problem by using the theme of a mental breakdown or a spiritual or artistic crisis, his intensity of feeling may explode the story elements, leaving the audience moved but bewildered. (p. 89)

Like Bergman, his countryman Strindberg lacked a sovereign sense of reality, and he experimented with a technique that would allow him to abandon the forms that he, too, kept exploding. In his author's note to the Expressionist *A Dream Play* . . . , Strindberg wrote:

> The author has sought to reproduce the disconnected but apparently logical form of a dream. Anything can happen; everything is possible and probable. Time and space do not exist; on a slight groundwork of reality, imagination spins and weaves new patterns made up of memories, experiences, unfettered fancies, absurdities, and improvisations.
>
> The characters are split, double, and multiply; they evaporate, crystallize, scatter, and converge. But a single consciousness holds sway over them all—that of the dreamer. For him there are no secrets, no incongruities, no scruples, and no law.

That is Bergman's method here. *Cries and Whispers* has oracular power, and many people feel that when something grips them strongly it must be realistic; they may not want to recognize that being led into a dreamworld can move them so much. But I think it's the stylized-dream-play atmosphere of *Cries and Whispers* that has made it possible for Bergman to achieve such strength. The detached imaginary world of the manor house becomes a heightened form of reality—more literal and solid, closer than the actual world. The film is emotionally saturated in female flesh—flesh as temptation and mystery. . . .

In the opening shots, the house is located in a series of autumnal landscapes of a formal park with twisted, writhing trees, and the entire film has a supernal quality. The incomparable cinematographer Sven Nykvist achieves the look of the paintings of the Norwegian Edvard Munch, as if the neurotic and the unconscious had become real enough to be photographed. But, unhappily, the freedom of the dream has sent Bergman back to Expressionism, which he had a heavy fling with in several of his very early films and in *The Naked Night,* some twenty years ago, and he returns to imagery drawn from the *fin de siècle,* when passion and decadence were one. (p. 90)

[The] four women of *Cries and Whispers* are used as obsessive male visions of women. They are women as the Other, women as the mysterious, sensual goddesses of male fantasy. Each sister represents a different aspect of woman, as in Munch's "The Dance of Life," in which a man dances with a woman in red (passion) while a woman in white (innocence) and a woman in black (corruption, death) look on. Bergman divides woman into three and dresses the three sisters for their schematic roles: Harriet Andersson's Agnes is the pure-white sister with innocent thoughts; Liv Ullmann's Maria, with her red-gold hair, wears soft, alluring colors and scarlet-woman dresses with tantalizing plunging necklines; and Ingred Thulin's death-seeking Karin is in dark colors or black. The film itself is predominantly in black and white and red—red draperies, red wine, red carpets and walls, and frequently dissolves into a blank red screen, just as Munch frequently returned to red for his backgrounds, or even to cover a house (as in his famous "Red Virginia Creeper"). The young actress who plays Agnes as a child resembles Munch's wasted, sick young girls, and the film draws upon the positioning and look of Munch's figures, especially in Munch's sickroom scenes and in his studies of the laying out of a corpse. *Cries and Whispers* seems to be part of the art from the age of syphilis, when the erotic was charged with peril—when pleasure was represented by an enticing woman who turned into a grinning figure of death. . . .

The movie is built out of a series of emotionally charged images that express psychic impulses, and Bergman handles them with the fluidity of a master. Yet these images are not discoveries, as they were for Munch, but a vocabulary of shock and panic to draw upon. Munch convinces us that he has captured the inner stress; Bergman doesn't quite convince, though we're impressed and we're held by the smoothness of the dreamy progression of events. The film moves with such eerie slow grace that it almost smothers its own faults and absurdities. I had the divided awareness that almost nothing in it quite works and, at the same time, that the fleshiness of those big bodies up there and the pull of the dream were strong and, in a sense, did make everything work. . . . (p. 91)

[Bergman's] greatest single feat as a movie craftsman is that he can prepare an atmosphere that leads us to accept episodes brimming with hysteria in almost any makeshift context. Here, as Strindberg formulated, the dream context itself makes everything probable; the dreamer leads, the viewer follows. In *Cries and Whispers* Bergman is a wizard at building up a scene to a memorable image and then quickly dissolving into the red that acts as a fixative. The movie is structured as a series of red-outs. We know as we see these images disintegrate before our eyes that we will be taking them home with us. But Bergman doesn't have Strindberg's deviltry and dash; he uses a dreamlike atmosphere but not the language of dreams. (pp. 92-3)

Death dreams that come equipped with ticking clocks and uncanny silences and the racked wheezes of the dying are not really very classy, and Bergman's earnest use of gothic effects seems particularly questionable now, arriving just after Buñuel, in *The Discreet Charm of the Bourgeoisie,* has turned them on and off, switching to the spooky nocturnal as a movie joke. But even when Bergman employs sophisticated versions of primitive gothic-horror devices, he is so serious that his dream play is cued to be some sort of morality play as well. Other chaotic artists (Lorca, for example, in his dream play *If Five Years Pass*) haven't been respected in the same way as Bergman, because their temperaments weren't moralistic. But Bergman has a winning combination here: moral+gothic=medieval. And when medieval devices are used in the atmosphere of bourgeois decadence, adults may become as vulnerable as superstitious children. (p. 93)

Pauline Kael, "Flesh" (originally published in The New Yorker, *January 6, 1973), in her* Reeling *(copyright © 1973 by Pauline Kael; reprinted by permission of Atlantic-Little, Brown and Company in association with the Atlantic Monthly Press), Little, Brown, 1976, pp. 89-94.*

JOAN MELLEN

Bergman employs [women] as spokeswomen to express his personal world-view—a world-view basically defined by the traumatic absence and silence of God, who has coldly abandoned us all to a cruel world. His women characters sometimes serve Bergman to express his agony over our ultimate inability to derive meaning from life except in rare moments of sensual ecstasy, soon contaminated by disgust over the bodily processes in which all experience is rooted. Yet if women occasionally are Bergman's vehicle for locating meaning, it is much more frequently male characters who pursue the ethical issues in his films which are not peculiar to either sex.

What is striking about Bergman's treatment of women is thus not the philosophical role they are called upon to play in his films. It is, rather, his treatment of their characters. Bergman offers a much different explanation for the inability of his female, as opposed to his male, characters to find purpose in a universe without direction. . . . Bergman is far harder on his woman than on his men. They are depicted as if on a lower notch of the evolutionary scale. Although the philosophical quest for an authentic mode of existence can hardly be limited by female as opposed to male hormones, Bergman insists that because of their physiology, women are trapped in dry and empty lives within which they wither as the lines begin to appear on their faces.

If the Knight in *The Seventh Seal* fails to achieve a sentient life because the cold abstractions by which he moves lock him into an ethical opacity, Ester in *The Silence* lives an empty, futile life because she has not accepted the demands of the female body, because she refuses the female sexual role. (p. 2)

Bergman presents us with a double standard. His men move in an ethical realm, his women in a biological one. It is true that his films reveal that these men are frequently found wanting. They contribute little solace or transcendence to a world whose people have lost the capacity to care for each other. But the cause of their moral demise does not rest especially in their male physiology. Bergman's men are distorted human beings, but their intrinsic physical characters and the nature of their flesh are not presented as standing in the way of their redemption. . . .

Bergman's women, on the other hand, are too often creatures whose torment resides in the obligation to submit to the repulsive sexual act. If Bergman's men lack power because there is no ethical imperative rooted outside the individual to which he can respond, his women (like Anna in *The Silence* or Karin in *The Touch*) are powerless before the sway of their lusts. (p. 3)

[One] should not make the mistake of assuming that Bergman endorses this vision of woman as weak, pallid, and locked into her physiology. Yet Bergman's point of view is arbitrary. . . . Absent from Bergman is any sense of how women can surmount and have transcended the norms of the ascetic and rigid late-19th-century philosophical milieu with which he has burdened himself. Far from understanding and showing compassion for the plight of women, Bergman creates female characters who are given the choice only—as in *Cries and Whsipers*—to be a Karin (cold and frigid), or a Maria (mindless and promiscuous), with the secondary alternatives of being an Agnes (inexplicably non-heterosexual and insatiably in Angst) or an Anna (servile and bovine). And Bergman implies through the closed microcosm of human existence he presents that these will forever be our alternatives. (pp. 3-4)

Bergman's intellectual women are vastly less attractive than his spiritually questing men. One is ineluctably brought to the conclusion that for Bergman it is not woman's *role* to quest after meaning. When she does, it is forced, unnatural, and with far less grace, finesse, or hope than with men. . . .

Cries and Whispers presents four women ensnared for the time period covered by the film into obsessive relationships with each other, excluding except in flashback men, children, and parents. It presents an unmistakable culmination of Bergman's sense of how women are inexorably and particularly limited by the physical shells in which their souls have been encased by that absent, unintelligible, godhead who has left us so alone without communication, solace, or release. (p. 5)

All these women suffer deeply. The hurt of all is symbolized by the agony of Agnes, in her torment and struggle. Her lips are bitten, her skin sallow, her hair lank, her teeth yellow, her nostrils distended with pain. She is woman stripped of allure, bared to the repellent essentials of a body in decay.

The women are dressed in white, expressing their unconscious wish to return to the virginal and to exclude men entirely from their lives. All the men in the film—the pompous, self-satisfied doctor, the sardonic, sadistic husband of Karin, and the weak, pallid, plump husband of Maria—are pathetic figures, less physically vibrant than the women. Woman is thus defined at once by being physical and unsatisfiable, a judgment validated by the inadequacy of the men Bergman chooses as their husbands and lovers. (p. 7)

The hatred of women for men is unabated throughout the course of this film. It is as irrevocable and inevitable as life, as the blood red fades to the "normal," pointing to woman's special shame. (p. 8)

Cries and Whispers is broken in half by the reiteration of [the theme of God's silence], which remains as integral to Bergman's work as his sense of the absence of free will afforded by the universe to human beings. It is expressed in his depiction of women as "classical" examples of beings limited by the shape God has given them and powerless to do anything but act in reaction to repellent biological drives. . . .

The last third of the film reveals Bergman's belief that women are not necessarily capable of greater gentleness and feeling than men. It denies that they alone have retained the power to "touch" each other. . . .

Karin's horrid and fought-off emotions are the most deeply felt and are presented as the most authentically derived from experience. At last Karin yields to Maria's embraces only to discover her own awakened needs and feelings unreciprocated at the end of the film. It is only when Karin is physically and sexually aroused by Maria that she responds to her caresses. This summons in her only the return of anxiety, disgust, and self-hatred. Feeling for Bergman, between women as between men and women, has its origin in lust, although rejecting such love as unclean brings only loneliness. (p. 9)

There is a bitter disparity in *Cries and Whispers* between the richness of color, the purity of the white against red, and the absolute degradation visited upon these women, who have been deprived of every saving grace, even the mythical "gentleness" that is said to belong to females but be denied the male. Women are in reality far from being Bergman's "favorite people," as one feminist critic supposed. Bergman exposes himself once again as one of those film-makers most hostile to a vision of women as free, creative, autonomous, self-sufficient, productive, satisfied, or, indeed, gentle. His women, rather, are chained to bodies which leave them little freedom or opportunity to transcend the juices, demonic drives, and subordination peculiar to their gender. Paradoxically, their bodies even deprive them of that sensitivity frequently attributed to women. *Cries and Whispers,* in fact, provides one of the most retrograde portrayals of women on the contemporary screen. (p. 11)

Joan Mellen, "Bergman and Women: 'Cries and Whispers'," in Film Quarterly *(copyright 1973 by The Regents of the University of California; reprinted by permission of the University of California Press), Vol. XXVII, No. 1, Fall, 1973, pp. 2-11.*

PETER HARCOURT

More than any other film artist, Bergman's work is rooted in the past. His early films grew out of the culture that surrounded them and they were invariably concerned with traditional themes. [*Prison, Thirst,* and *To Joy*], all released in 1949, were each in its own way a kind of allegory, a journey through defeat and despair towards some kind of hopefulness at the end. (p. 135)

[In] his early work, one was struck especially by Bergman's imagery, by a recurring pattern of images that seemed to have for him a special force. It would be simplistic, however, to attribute to these recurring images a fixed symbolic significance. While it is true that in his early films Bergman was fond of mirrors, of human hands, certainly of wild strawberries, of the sun and the endless stretch of long summer days, and that dolls, bears, and cannons appear in several of his films, these images by no means always acquire the force and stature of symbols. To generalize about their 'meaning', as some of the French critics have done, is to a large extent to destroy the delicacy of implication that they acquire in his most successful films. At their simplest, Bergman's images are employed to enforce or clarify a given mood or feeling, or sometimes to suggest an idea that in the film is left unsaid. (pp. 139-40)

On the surface, especially when compared with his later and frequently more opaque productions, [*Summer Interlude*] might seem a slight film; yet it achieves an emotional depth and impact largely through the use of a significantly suggestive pattern of imagery. (p. 141)

The fleeting joy of summer is suggested by the call of the cuckoo which opens the film and (as so often in Bergman's early work) by the patch of wild strawberries that the young lovers share together. But when Marie returns to Pike Island for her afternoon reverie, the autumn leaves are blowing about, now crows are calling; and when we see her in her dressing-room at the theatre, we might be further moved to sympathize with her advancing age and vanished happiness if we notice that the pattern on her dressing-gown consists of medlars—an autumn fruit. (pp. 141-42)

At this stage of his career, Bergman was a most traditional, one might even say, a most classical artist. In many ways, his films were playing with conventional themes, themes already thoroughly explored by other Scandinavian artists. His distinction, as I understand it, lies chiefly in the quality of the play.

Bergman is, of course, a master in making us actually participate in the joys and sorrows of his characters. As we watch the film, we too are dazzled by the sun on the water and we feel the bleakness and hostility of Pike Island once the summer has gone. As a film-maker, however, Bergman is far from alone in this ability. One of the problems with the film medium is that we can all too easily become too uncomfortably involved in the action on the screen and so lose the distance necessary to respond to the film as a work of art. In these early Bergman films, I think it is largely the presence of some kind of form or pattern, of some perceptible sequence of imagery, that keeps us from being uncomfortably distressed by what we see.

By having crows answer cuckoos, and medlars follow strawberries, Bergman not only moves us by the strong emotional effect of these sounds and images but he thereby distances the action sufficiently from real life to enable us to be conscious of it as a work of art. To my mind, to complain that such effects are too deliberately done, with the implication that they are too cerebral, as many English-speaking critics did when these films first appeared, to complain in such a way reveals a complete incapacity to feel their force in the film, plus an unwillingness to accept the conventions upon which Bergman's art was based. (pp. 142-43)

Bergman once expressed the wish that his work might have the impersonality of a medieval cathedral. I would argue that, in many ways, his early films do. Somewhat like the pre-Renaissance painters, it is as if Bergman could take his subject matter for granted while he strove to discover new methods of presentation. We are delighted as much with the manner as with the matter of these early films. In these films, we may indeed be at times unbearably moved by the convincingness of the action, but at the same time we experience an exhilaration because, among other things, we can feel the presence of the artist's controlling hand in all the situations that are moving us. By the symmetry, by the beautiful pattern of images, with often the suggestion of a controlling symbol, and by the frequently stylized characterization, we are continually reminded that what we are witnessing is not real life with its irrational muddle and chaos, but the creation of one man's individual mind, reshaping and refining traditional Christian-humanist insights with more than just a touch of Pauline romantic gloom. (pp. 143-44)

Even though these early films are very much cast in the traditional allegorical mode, Bergman takes pains not to present his characters in too schematic a way. They all live in a tangle of responsibilities to one another, as in fact we do in life. The issues may seem simplified, but not (I would argue) falsified. Albert and Anne [of *Sawdust and Tinsel*] are shown to be fond of one another and capable of moods of tenderness, though each is prepared to desert the other if the occasion offers itself. There is also a kind of affection that we feel for even the most pathetic of Bergman's characters. Albert's march through town to ask the help of a travelling theatre director, with the absurb pride he takes in his own pomp and his gaudily provocative Anne, is one of the many touches that help to soften the harsh edges of this grimly conceived film. It also implies a kind of moral value in the processes of life itself.

For instance, not unlike Beckett's *Waiting for Godot, Sawdust and Tinsel* deals with two people who have somehow become dependent on each other 'in this hell together' and who keep waiting for something to happen, something that will free them from their present life and from each other. Of course, like Godot, it never comes. Yet far more than Beckett in his much applauded play, Bergman, even in this gloomy film, realizes that man is still not entirely incapable of compassion, and that from compassion there is hope. If Bergman is fully conscious of the horror and possible vacuity of life, at this stage of his life he is also conscious of its warmth and joy. (pp. 146-47)

I have never been a great admirer of *The Seventh Seal* myself. It is a highly rhetorical film, containing all kinds of extraordinary moments which seem more effective locally than intrinsic parts of the entire film. I have always preferred *Sawdust and Tinsel,* because I feel that the implied pilgrimage of the circus in the earlier film is more subtle and successful than the overtly symbolic crusade in *The Seventh Seal.* Also, *Sawdust and Tinsel* is not weakened by unnecessarily abstract talk. Furthermore, the presentation of Albert and Anne's relationship does still seem representative of the lives of so many people today. But I have come to recognize that *The Seventh Seal* is striving to be a more complex film and, in spite of its weaknesses, it has too its characteristic strengths. (p. 150)

[Death] appears as he does, simultaneously grim and somewhat comical with his white face and black cloak, because this is the way Bergman (and so the Knight) has imagined him from a painting. 'I've been a long time at your side,' says Death when he first appears; and we realize that he is not merely death in time, the end of our actual life, but he also represents the inner death that the Knight, Antonius Block, has been carrying with him ever since he first left his wife and home in search of the absolute, ever since he gave up singing songs to the beauty of his wife's eyes and began to pursue an abstraction. However much Bergman may make us sympathize with the Knight's pursuit, we see that in the film it has been meaningless. His sturdy squire, Jöns, is disgusted with the whole business: 'The crusade was so stupid', he says, 'it would have taken an idealist to have thought of it'. (p. 151)

That some part of us must die before we can truly live, that we must be 'as little children' before we can find real happiness, that the 'Kingdom of Heaven' is either within us or it is nowhere—all these insights form part of our Christian-humanist inheritance and, at this stage of his career, Bergman seemed to be accepting them uncritically. Those of us who admired these early films went to them, not for fresh insights about the nature of life, but to observe the individual working out of traditional themes and attitudes. Watching his films seemed rather like stepping back into a nineteenth-century world. (pp. 153-54)

In *Wild Strawberries,* as in *The Seventh Seal* and with a rather different effect in *Smiles of a Summer Night,* there is a kind of banquet scene, a scene of the pleasure of eating and relaxing together, one might almost say of communion. (p. 159)

[The] travellers all have lunch together. They eat and drink wine together, while Borg is moved to entertain them with stories about his days as a young doctor. Then, while strumming his guitar, the young theological student begins to recite a poem: 'When nature shows such beauty, how radiant must be its source.' When he stops, old Borg carries on: 'I see his traces everywhere, wherever flowers bloom.' When his memory falters, Marianne helps him out. Like the strawberries and milk in *The Seventh Seal,* this poem is passed round the table. They all seem to know it and to appreciate it, even if in different ways. To the theologue, it is a poem about God; to the young atheist, simply a love poem. But the two boys are united in a common feeling for this poem, as indeed they are in their appreciation of the high spirits of the girl. They are thus freed from their 'merely intellectual' disputes.

This scene is magnificent, and, considering the nature of the poem, the sharing of the food and wine together, and what could be called the spiritual theme of the film, it seems to have implications of the most far-reaching kind. If at this time of his life Bergman was still preoccupied with the validity of Christianity in the metaphysical sense of that word, he seems in *Wild Strawberries* to be re-creating in a most sensitive way some of the ritual that has held the church together. This luncheon sequence contrasts sharply in its warmth and affection with the actual communion he was to re-create some five years later for the opening sequence of *Winter Light.* (pp. 159-60)

Bergman's early work, like so much of Scandinavian art, [seems] to stand apart from time. . . . The moral sensibility that [*Wild Strawberries*] contains could have existed any time within the last two hundred years. It is only the cinema that gives it the feeling of being of our era.

Yet this old-fashioned quality is what pleases me most about these early works by Bergman—the sense of a man working in isolation from the rest of Europe, sorting out the validity of his own cultural inheritance. The whole symbolic understructure that we find in Bergman's films seems to come from far away and thus to be much more profound than his merely personal preoccupations. The recurring symbols of the quest, of the forest of darkness, of the life-giving powers of the south and sun might, to the English-speaking world, recall Bunyan, but to the Scandinavians could suggest Ibsen. (pp. 161-62)

The 'new' Bergman really begins with *Through a Glass Darkly*. . . . This was the first of his so-called trilogy, a trilogy completed by *Winter Light* . . . and *The Silence*. . . . His technique through this trilogy and into *Persona* . . . has been to bring us closer to fewer and fewer people, perhaps . . . with the deliberate ambition to 'illuminate the human soul'. One of his methods has been to let his characters speak directly to us, often with no editorial interference or recourse to flashbacks. . . . But such a technique can lead to problems of response and interpretation of a most delicate kind. (pp. 167-68)

[The] lack of certainty about the *truthfulness* of what the characters are saying plus our inability to be certain just where Bergman stands in relation to their words are the twin characteristics that give these films, for all their authority and stylistic asperity, a slightly hysterical, self-indulgent air. The dramatic context of the characters' remarks has often not been clearly enough defined for us to be certain whether we are watching the desperation of dramatically distanced characters (which would mean intellectually comprehended characters), or whether we are being subjected to Bergman's own undistanced and therefore uncomprehended despair. (p. 169)

Since *The Virgin Spring,* up until the re-achieved balance in *A Passion,* it is rather as if the Knight had taken over the making of Bergman's films. By isolating his characters so extremely, he has reduced his moral universe to the utterings of his most desperate characters. There is little sense of any kind of dialectical relationship with a less hopeless world outside, of any possible alternatives. (p. 170)

Were there space in this chapter, both *The Silence* and *Persona* would repay extensive analysis. They are the failed masterpieces of what we should by now be able to call Bergman's Baltic period. They are masterpieces because they courageously, astonishingly, break new ground—certainly for Bergman but also for the cinema itself. But they are failures, in my view, because the thinking behind them is simultaneously schematic yet unclear. It is as if Bergman the thinker has not kept pace with Bergman the artist, as if his new-found artistic authority, which has helped to free him from the allegorical modes of thought that held together his earlier work, has not been accompanied by fresh insights into the nature of human life. Bergman at his best is a most inward director. Essentially, like Fellini's, all his films are about himself. The 'failure' occurs, in my view, when Bergman attempts to persuade us that his films are about more external matters—the validity of art, as in *Persona* or *Hour of the Wolf;* the ravages of war, as in *Shame.* In his earlier work, Bergman tended to pit good against bad, the life-affirming Saras against the life-denying Borgs. Technically this dualism was registered in the dazzling whites of all the exterior sequences in *Wild Strawberries* that contrasted with the dark interiors, say, of Borg's mother's home.

The dualism assumed a different form in *Through a Glass Darkly,* where there is an almost schizophrenic split between things seen and things said. In *The Silence* the dualism between the sisters is so exaggerated that one is tempted to explain them both as different aspects of one woman, as indeed one is forced really to interpret the dualistic structure of *Persona* as well. Interpreting the films this way means that the characters seem incomplete in some way *as characters,* that the dualism is too extreme for its implications to be psychologically convincing. (p. 171)

I don't mean to be positing a critical puritanism, adducing terms like balance, distance and success as the only ones relevant for contemporary art. For even if I am right in my feeling that Bergman's films since *Through a Glass Darkly* have frequently lacked these classic artistic qualities, I in no way mean to dismiss the films or to deny their immense power to disturb. The claim I would like to make for *A Passion,* however, is that it deals with the same problems that have troubled Bergman throughout his career, the problems of loneliness, humiliation, and of the essential isolation of the human spirit. Furthermore, it deals with these problems with all the authority and originality that have characterized his recent work (added to which is his immensely creative use of colour), but at the same time this film *is* balanced and distanced and successful in the most classical of ways. This means, for all its power, it also contains an element of restraint. This means as well, for all its hopelessness, there is an element of affirmation implicit within Bergman's ability to find an aesthetic resolution to all the difficulties posed by the film. *A Passion* is *complete* in a way that I don't feel his recent films have always been, complete and unpretentious in that the problems raised *in* the film are answered *by* the film as well. (p. 176)

The central concern of *A Passion* seems to be with what I have already called the essential isolation of the human spirit. In this way the film is the summation of all of Bergman's work so far. Every detail in it contributes to this concern, even the magnificently staged dinner sequence at the Vergeruses' that shows the characters attempting to break through this isolation (like the ferry sequence in *Shame*). Even here, however, except for the closing four-shot and the moments when we hear them all chattering together, Bergman presents the bulk of the scene through single faces in close-up, separate from each other, each telling his own story. Similarly, the opening talk between Andreas and Johan is presented largely in action/reaction shots. At the very moment that we most feel Andreas's concern for the carter, through the editing Bergman emphasizes their essential separateness.

Related to this concern is the recognition of how unstable our sense of self is, our sense of who we really are. This is why the direct comments of the actors on the characters they are portraying work so well in the film. They not only distance us from the action slightly, in a Brechtian/Godardian way, reminding us that we are after all only watching a film, but they also give us the sense that even the actors cannot fully comprehend the characters they are portraying. (p. 179)

When I write about *A Passion* in this way, so much of what I most admire remains undescribed—the actual texture of the images and the meaningful juxtaposition of scene against scene. . . .

The final sequences form a most masterful conclusion for this most masterly of all Bergman's films. The burning horse that would not die might well stand as emblem for the desperate clinging to life of all the characters in the film, no matter how great their disease or pain. In this way even this image provides a kind of affirmation, the affirmation of blind animal energy within despair. (p. 181)

We believe that when we look more closely at something we see it more clearly, even when we look at another person's identity. The very form of Bergman's film gives the lie to this, certainly the form of the ending. In what is one of the most remarkable shots in the history of the cinema (if I may be allowed this enthusiasm), we move in on Andreas pacing back and forth and then falling to his knees, as the grain swells up and the light increases until the image literally disintegrates before our eyes. Then another stroke on the timpani provides the final punctuation to this most extraordinary film. (p. 182)

Peter Harcourt, "The Troubled Pilgrimage of Ingmar Bergman," in his Six European Directors: Essays on the Meaning of Film Style *(copyright © Peter Harcourt, 1974; reprinted by permission of Penguin Books Ltd), Penguin Books, 1974, pp. 135-82.*

MARSHA KINDER

Scenes from a Marriage is emotional dynamite. That may not be surprising for an Ingmar Bergman movie, but in some important ways this film moves in a new direction. It reaches new depths of psychological realism, and at the same time is actually hopeful. . . . *Scenes from a Marriage* made me feel more hopeful about the human condition—more willing to accept the contradictions in the desires and actions of myself and others, and more willing to believe in the possibilities of growth and change, particularly for women. (p. 48)

Unlike the interior locations in *The Ritual* and *Cries and Whispers,* [the environments in the film] are ordinary and realistic rather than theatrical or symbolic. Yet the rooms inhabited by Marianne and Johan express a great deal about their marriage. Despite the warmth of the earth colors and wood panelling that gloss its surface, their house is dominated by a routine symmetry in the arrangement of chairs, couches, lamps, tables, and flower pots, which is very restrictive. (p. 49)

As in earlier films, Bergman relies heavily on the facial close-up to explore the feelings of his characters, but this technique is handled less self-consciously than usual. Characteristically, a scene starts with a symmetrical medium two-shot. As the conversation becomes more intense and the characters begin to drop their social masks, the camera moves in for a close-up of the individual. The close-ups grow larger as the emotions become more heated. . . . Although the film's style is highly controlled, it is almost invisible; it does not call attention to itself. The only sign of artificiality is the division into six scenes, which is carried over from the original television format (six 50-minute segments, which have been cut down for theatrical distribution to two hours and 48 minutes); yet these divisions function like chapter headings in a psychological novel.

Scenes from a Marriage belongs to a new genre of expanded psychological realism—the four- or five-hour film exploring complex modern relationships, focusing on intense encounters between two or three people, and achieving a depth of characterization previously thought possible only in the novel. (p. 50)

In some ways, *Scenes from a Marriage,* and indeed the entire genre of expanded psychological realism, is related to the soap opera. The basic materials and subject matter are the same, though they are handled very differently. (p. 51)

The primary distinction between *Scenes from a Marriage* and soap opera is the way it affects us emotionally. The film's impact is tremendous. Instead of leading us to forget about our own lives and to get caught up vicariously in the intrigues of others, it throws us back on ourselves and our own experience. . . . We watch Johan and Marianne experience a kind of growth that has never before been captured on film. The portrayal of their marriage is so complex, so subtle, so varied and multi-dimensional that it is bound to trigger personal associations for anyone who has been involved in a long-term relationship. . . . The film implies that if we have the strength to take a relationship as far as it will go, to discard as many false masks as possible, to live through the outbursts of hatred and violence, to confront honestly our full range of feelings, we may discover an emotional capacity that is much deeper and richer than we expect. The doubts are never quieted, the struggle is never over, the confusion is never eliminated, but the imperfect love comforts and survives. (p. 53)

Marsha Kinder, "Reviews: 'Scenes from a Mar-

riage'," in Film Quarterly *(copyright 1974 by The Regents of the University of California; reprinted by permission of the University of California Press), Vol. XXVIII, No. 2, Winter, 1974-75, pp. 48-53.*

JULIAN C. RICE

Bergman defines his principal theme as a concern with the "wholeness inside every human being." This "wholeness" is the basis upon which relationships with other human beings are formed. The fragmenting of wholeness within the self is inextricably bound up with the fragmenting of interpersonal relationships. . . . *Cries and Whispers* mirrors this desire to heal fragmentation between the self and others, and between separated elements in the individual psyche. (pp. 147-48)

Agnes's character is perhaps "incomplete" by literary standards, but here, we know as much about Agnes as is necessary to our understanding of the film's totality—she is dying, and she is, in an important thematic sense, a child.

She is also, in another sense, an artist who works in painting and literature, but primarily in the latter, through her "diary." Agnes is a type recognizable from Bergman's earlier films, the alienated artist, in this case separated from the other characters by her artistic sensitivity and the immediacy of her mortality. It is her feeling of alienation that impels Agnes to write. Her writing, like all artistic endeavor, is the dying child's protest against physical death and the psychological death of infancy, as well as a contradictory effort to accept death and dissolve the confining walls of the isolating ego.

This contradiction arises from the essentially split nature of the psyche. The conscious mind strives for differentiated existence, for physical and psychological survival. But all living entities, including the human psyche, possess a contrary impulse toward unity, ultimately toward dissolution. *Eros* and *Thanatos* do not describe this opposition accurately. The death wish, the sexual drive, and the need to feel and express love are aspects of the unifying impulse, the desire to return to undifferentiated, thoroughly integrated being. Agnes and Anna express this unification impulse most strongly in *Cries and Whispers*. Maria and Karin represent varying intensities of the "adult" impulse to differentiation, which, taken too far, results in the frigid isolation and guilt of Karin.

But every adult has been long banished from the bliss of undifferentiated being. Near the beginning of the film, we learn that Anna's child is dead. The shot of the empty crib fades to a close-up of Agnes holding a white rose and beginning to reminisce about her childhood. In the helpless suffering of her death pangs, Agnes will become, momentarily and redemptively, Anna's child, as the parallelism in the opening sequence clearly foreshadows. The death of Anna's first child deepens the meaning of the death of Agnes, her second child, suggesting the universal death of childhood, a psychological rather than a literal dying. The film presents human beings as crying, dying children, exiled from the perfect contentment of unconsciousness. (pp. 148-49)

[The] image of Agnes on Anna's breast recurs in the film in spite of Agnes's literal death. Bergman implies that the relationship of Agnes and Anna cannot die, and that although God, as a subjectively traumatic concern is dead, the redemptive moments of wholeness remain. As an archetype of the wholeness of integrated being, God remains very much alive in *Cries and Whispers*. Nevertheless, since wholeness is an uncommon and fleeting treasure, Agnes and Anna represent primarily a symbolic ideal, which is only rarely experienced in reality.

The alienation of adult experience and the impediments to redemptive communication are sequentially mirrored in the Maria and Karin flashbacks. Before her flashback begins, Maria is seen in the room she had as a child, surrounded by her dolls. For Maria, other people are usually no more than dolls, subjectively arranged in her life as narcissistic tributaries. Because of her narcissism, which is a negative infantile trait, Maria does not appear strongly to require the feeling of completion supplied by another human being. Rather than the creative, curious childishness of Agnes, Maria's childishness is that of the self-sufficient *id*, an amoral, continual pursuit of pleasure, finding fulfillment primarily in physical gratification. Maria's consciousness is only rudimentarily developed. (p. 151)

While Maria's alienation results from a infantile regression and is essentially a fearful retreat from life, Karin's isolation is the product of her iron-willed repressive pride. And just as Maria's weak husband does not provide the proper counterpoise to her own weakness, Karin's husband is so much like herself that their existence is a perpetual battle for emotional dominance. (p. 152)

In *Cries and Whispers*, several motives for Karin's masochistic act are implied: she is symbolically scourging her sexuality as an act of repression, but, also, as an act of expiation, she is able to express her sexuality only in this masochistic manner. The display to her husband and the triumphant smearing of the blood on her face suggest again the desperate desire to reach someone else and to have her unconscious identity confirmed in the mind of another. Since social convention, guilt, and mutual projective hatred have made it impossible to reach her husband through normal communicative means, this shockingly hostile action expresses both her rage and an attempt to expose her suffering unconsciousness, perhaps to liberate and revive the dying child in herself. (p. 153)

Cries and Whispers is another effort to create a bridge between the alienated self and the other. It is an attempt to create wholeness out of the fragmentations of Ingmar Bergman's previous works and out of the inherent fragmentations of the human psyche. Although the film must end, and the members of the audience, like Karin and Maria, must return to the alienation of their separate lives, something of the shared experience of the film will remain in their minds, helping to overcome the absolute isolation that would exist without this art.

The artist has sought his audience, just as Maria has pursued the Doctor, and as Agnes had called out for Anna. But when the Doctor tried to understand Maria, he could only scrutinize her face in a mirror, seeing in her only what he saw in himself. This despairing view implies that communication is impossible and that fragmentation can never be overcome. In the affair of the Doctor and Maria nothing has been felt and nothing has been communicated. Maria, the Doctor says self-revealingly, sneers too much. But Anna and Agnes do love each other, which implies that the dead "child" in the adult self can be comforted, although it can never really die, and will usually feel alone and isolated. In addition to her identity as the universal crying child in the psyche, Agnes represents art, as an impulse to achieve individuation or psychological completion. The final passage from her diary suggests that wholeness and communication are indeed possible, if only for fleetingly redemptive moments. (p. 157)

Julian C. Rice, "'Cries and Whispers': The Complete Bergman," in The Massachusetts Review *(reprinted from* The Massachusetts Review; *© 1975 The Massachusetts Review, Inc.), Vol. XVI, No. 1, Winter, 1975, pp. 147-58.*

JOHN SIMON

Ingmar Bergman's *Scenes from a Marriage* is not the great film maker's best film, and may not even be the best film of the year. But it is almost certainly one of the most important films ever made, if by importance we understand the possibility of art's influencing people in a positive way—a slight, elusive possibility, perhaps even an impossible one. But one that we must believe in if we are not to give up on art or humanity, either of which strikes me as giving up on life. . . .

Scenes from a Marriage is for our time what *Everyman* was for the Middle Ages. In its simple way, that medieval morality play embodied all the eschatological knowledge the average person needed to live and die by; in a quite similar, though less simple, way, Bergman's film sums up for us all there is to know about love, sex, marriage, divorce—the life of a man and woman together and apart. In that sense, it is perhaps closer in its capaciousness to the great medieval synthesizer, Thomas Aquinas, and can be viewed as a *summa psychologica* and *summa erotica* and, most of all, a *summa matrimonii.* Alongside the great literary tracts on love by writers like Stendhal, Kierkegaard, Ortega y Gasset, we must now place this cinematic treatise on married love—indeed, on basic man-woman relations—by the giant of Swedish and world film making. (p. 12)

Let me deal first with an objection to the film one hears occasionally: that it is too commonplace; that these people are so Everyman and Everywoman that they cease to be specific individuals; that the whole thing is too much of a faceless generalization. I disagree emphatically. . . . But do not let this serve as an excuse for skipping the released version. No, Johan and Marianne are not platitudes; they are encyclopedias. . . .

The fact that we have all known Johans and Mariannes—the fact that we ourselves are, to a greater or lesser extent, Johan and Marianne—only increases their value for us. This would not be so if mere recognition were everything, but something significant has been added: Johan and Marianne are more vividly, juicily, exemplarily what we ourselves are. They represent our flaws and quirks, weaknesses and virtues, more brilliantly and perspicuously than we can. . . .

What Bergman perceives devastatingly clearly is the continual jockeying for power in the most intimate of relationships. But he knows also how unconsciously it all happens, how unaware, these characters are of what they are doing. And so he makes them utter truths that are truer than they realize. . . .

The marvelous thing about *Scenes* is that while showing only two characters in great detail, and a few others only peripherally, it manages to convey a whole bourgeois consumer society—its economics, politics, social structure, feeble idealisms and thriving insecurities—through casual remarks, offhand allusions, the feel of a room, the look of a piece of furniture. (p. 16)

John Simon, "Films: 'Scenes from a Marriage'" (reprinted by permission of Wallace & Sheil Agency, Inc.; copyright © 1975 John Simon), in Esquire, *Vol. LXXX, No. 1, January. 1975, pp. 12, 16.*

REV. ROBERT E. LAUDER

Ingmar Bergman continues to replay brilliantly the same themes. While critics debate various interpretations of his vision, Bergman keeps surpassing his previous accomplishments. His latest opus, a dazzling film production of Mozart's *The Magic Flute,* is a bit different from his usual offering—but just a bit. (p. 55)

What is different of course is the warm, joyous presence of Mozart, which Bergman honors with warm, joyous cinematic images. However, *The Magic Flute* replays many favorite Bergman themes.

All of Bergman's films deal with the meaning of human love in the face of death. Bergman has confessed that when he feels particularly sad he takes courage in the simple love between a man and woman. The simple theme of *The Magic Flute,* that perfect love triumphs, was the theme of Bergman's *The Seventh Seal. . . .* Though in most of his films Bergman's characters rarely encounter each other in love, it is clear that, for the Swedish director, if truth is to be found it will only be found by lovers. . . .

It is particular fitting that in *The Magic Flute* music leads the lovers to salvation. Art finally wins. . . .

Believing that film like music should portray psychic states, Bergman has throughout his career powerfully presented the cries and whispers of the suffering human soul. What makes *The Magic Flute* different from other Bergman films is that, having captured the musical genius of Mozart on film, Bergman seems, at least for the present, to be at peace. (p. 56)

Rev. Robert E. Lauder, "Two Views of 'The Magic Flute'," in America *(© America Press, 1976; all rights reserved), Vol. 134, No. 3, January 24, 1976, pp. 55-6.*

ROBERT E. LAUDER

Ingmar Bergman's most personal work and one of his most profound and provocative efforts, *Face to Face* is probably also the Swedish artist's greatest film. A striking synthesis of his previous work and rich in images and themes, the movie will stimulate analyses reiterating familiar interpretations of Bergman's vision. We can expect *Face to Face* to be discussed in terms of the director's view of women, as an artistic exercise through which Bergman practices self-therapy, as a phenomenology of heterosexual relations and communications, and as a commentary on the silence of God. Though each of these approaches can shed light on Bergman's artistic aims (and each has been helpful with a particular film in the past), none is sufficiently radical to address Bergman's philosophical questions or to encounter his latest work "face to face"—that is, at the profound level at which it was conceived and created. . . .

Of the four interpretive approaches mentioned earlier, Bergman's vision of women will probably receive the most attention. . . . Bergman's primary preoccupation is, however, with humanity rather than specifically with masculinity or feminity. Though some critics may find in Bergman's work a persistent hostility toward women, the truth of the matter is that the filmmaker is involved in a love-hate relationship with women *and* with men—and indeed with himself.

Bergman's love-hate relationship with himself may encourage the suggestion that he is merely using the cinema to work out his own hang-ups. Of this film Bergman has said: "Making *Face to Face* has been the most powerful experience of my life. Working on this picture has meant having to live parts of my life over and over again. For months I was like a piece of celluloid, actually a part of the film." Elements of Bergman's life crop up in the film. . . . But as the film grows more personal, it becomes not private but universal. The film's gibes at psychiatry and psychology indicate that Bergman's preoccupation is at a deeper level than psychological self-analysis.

Though the problem of personal communication looms large in *Face to Face,* Bergman's probing goes beyond both heterosexual and homosexual relations. (p. 936)

Though also inadequate as a key to *Face to Face,* interpretations based on the silence of God are closest to Bergman's deepest questions. The awareness of God's absence is a theme strongly present in every Bergman film, but since *Winter Light* (1962) the Swedish director has focused less directly on the specifically theological. . . . Make no mistake: Bergman's probings are still metaphysical and religious (rather than specifically theological) in the sense that they deal with the most ultimate questions, with what Tillich called "matters of ultimate concern." What does reality mean? What is the significance of human life? Does death make human existence absurd? Whether center stage is occupied by Jenny or a 14th century knight or a Lutheran minister or a married couple or Bergman himself, the director's questions cut to the universal experience of persons. . . .

[*Face to Face*] could serve as a summary of his work. What is new in *Face to Face* is the clear presence of hope. The loving presence of Jacobi and the bond between her grandparents provide Jenny with sufficient insight into reality to enable her to continue living. (p. 937)

For this cinematic exploration of love, in which he examines Jenny's passage through "death" to new life, Bergman has taken his title from a section of Paul's first letter to the Corinthians (I Cor. 13: 12: "For now we see through a glass, darkly, but then face to face"), in which Paul seeks to describe the fulfillment that lovers will experience when they pass through death and encounter Love. With his own interpretation of resurrection and its meaning for human existence, Bergman continues his painfully honest exploration of the mystery of love and death and an odyssey that is the most personal, provocative and profound in contemporary cinema. (p. 938)

Robert E. Lauder, "A Hint of Hope in Bergman's Odyssey," in The Christian Century *(copyright 1976 Christian Century Foundation; reprinted by permission from the October 27, 1976 issue of* The Christian Century), *Vol. XCIII, No. 34, October 27, 1976, pp. 936-38.*

DIANE M. BORDEN

For Bergman, the human face is a register, a kind of antenna that signals and communicates the life of the consciousness. That "life" is a constant existenial search for self, for wholeness and integrity amidst ever present elements of fragmentation and isolation. Throughout the films, characters seek an identity through the "other" in such intimate relationships as patient and nurse, sister and sister, husband and wife. Ego often finds its alter ego in this other. At the core of this convoluted psychology is the key concept of "passion" with both its erotic and religious connotations. For Bergman, the struggle between the flesh and the spirit, between the hidden and known aspects of the psyche, between the self and other, forms the essential crisis, hence passion, of being itself. This baroque psychology, with all its elaborate overlays of nuance and ambivalence, finds its perfect cinematic expression in the facial close-up. (p. 43)

Perhaps in *Persona,* more than in any other film, the genius of Bergman's facial icon seems most pronounced. . . . [Perhaps] the supreme art of facial iconography comes to fruition in the veiled double-door sequence from this film. Surely it must be one of the most numinous in all of film art. . . . Here, Bergman creates facial iconography at its most breathtaking; the aesthetic and psychological dimensions seem perfectly and radiantly realized. Human faces are sculpted into an aesthetic order—and aesthetic objects are humanized.

The facial icon is in itself a technique uniquely Bergmanesque. But it also typifies the general stylistic qualities that characterize Bergman's art. The facial close-up is a "limited" shot, limited not in its potential meaning, but limited by the dimensions Bergman purposely chooses. This limitation of means is symptomatic of Bergman's aesthetic austerity. Nevertheless, within these boundaries . . . resonances of great complexity are created.

The austerity of Bergman's films is primarily descriptive of his aesthetic style. Yet tonally, the films, particularly those of the 1960's and 1970's, in their vision of the human condition are often likewise austere. However, Bergman's world is not necessarily pessimistic; the numinous qualities of some of his facial iconography point out the spiritual elements of human existence. Within a barren, alien world, there does exist a place of grace and beatitude, a possibility of psychological wholeness and "salvation."

Bergman has referred to his work as chamber cinema, and with good reason. If we consider the musical analogy implied in the phrase, we perhaps can better understand the structure and style of his work. Chamber music, in contrast to the symphonic form, sets a limit of instruments and a limit of themes. Its dimension is "small" but its techniques are highly inventive, working as it does in all the varieties of contrapuntal form. Bergman has knowledged his artistic heritage from Bach, so that, like Bach working out the multiple designs of a fugal pattern, Bergman likewise drains a technique, like the facial close-up, of all its aesthetic and thematic possibilities.

We might call Bergman's style then a kind of inventiveness in limitation. This efficiency of means, so striking in the facial icon, is matched by other elements in the films: the limited number of actors, the barren landscape, the simple sets and decor, the few but recurrent images, the terse dialogue, the repeated theme of existential crisis and its concommitant passion. Each film seems a part of a larger piece, as if each production is working out further variations of the master work. That is why, in part, there is such a tight continuity in the overall style and structure of Bergman's opus. And one of the major techniques contributing to this continuity is the facial icon. In it we can recognize Bergman's distinctive cinematic style and genius. (pp. 53-5)

Diane M. Borden, "Bergman's Style and the Facial Icon," in Quarterly Review of Film Studies *(copyright © 1977 by Docent Corporation), Vol. 2, No. 1, February, 1977, pp. 42-55.*

ROBERT BOYERS

[What] Bergman does in this very special and provoking film [*Cries and Whispers*] is to subject to ruthless scrutiny his own extravagant identification with various feminine characters. By coldly exposing them, by forcing them to have at one another and to acquiesce in the process of their own relentless humiliation, Bergman calls into question his own boundless attraction to them. (p. 136)

It is obvious to most of us that a film is more than a series of verbal structures or pictorial images, that it is as well a relation it establishes with viewers; similarly, a body of work, a whole collection of films by a single artist, is more than specific attitudes or ideas taken up in one or more of them. When we think of Bergman we must think necessarily of intonation, the timbre and range of the voice which persists through the changing focus and altogether unstable manipulation of ideas. In Bergman, after all, as with many great artists, vision is not a matter of firm positions or standing or falling on particular ideas. There is a vision, of course, and it has to do with the putting of various questions in a way that suggests they are literally matters of life and death. Not the answers to those questions but the voice that articulates and insists upon their pre-eminence is what constitutes the signature. Just as it is foolish to draw permanent conclusions about Bergman's convictions on the basis of a single film when there are dozens to consider, it is a mistake to probe the complex structure of an ambitious film like *Cries And Whispers* with a simple question: "How does Bergman feel about his women?" There are, believe it or not, more important questions, more important insofar as they more regularly inform the corpus as a whole and more consistently command our attention. With Bergman we are more likely to worry over the problematic relation between feeling and intellect, an issue made fresh and interesting because in the way it's projected it is obviously more than a matter of idle curiosity or a mechanism for thematizing otherwise inchoate materials. We shall be interested as well in the human status of animal need, not as a means of assigning value-points to particular characters or entire sexes, but as a means of understanding the images by which people come to know themselves and imagine their transactions with others. (pp. 136-37)

[In the fifties,] Bergman had found at least some of his standard subjects and was working with a confidence previously unknown to him. Amoung the films to be considered are *Smiles of a Summer Night* and *Wild Strawberries,* surely two enduring favorites. Both contain a variety of male and female types, and both may be said to elaborate a sustained critique of egoism, a malady in which the personality is arrested at the level of excessive pre-occupation with an exclusive aspect of its own development. . . . Each film lovingly develops an alternative to the egoism and the attendant dislocations of function which afflict the egoists. Though one would never guess as much from the writings of Bergman's feminist critics, the corrective to the vision is in each film supplied by the presence of a remarkable, highly intelligent, and highly visible woman character: Desiree in *Smiles,* Marianne in *Wild Strawberries.* (p. 137)

Neither Desiree nor Marianne is soiled by animal needs. If anything, Desiree has an immoderate though never unbecoming sexual appetite which she does nothing to conceal, and Marianne's determination to have a child, to be a mother, is proudly maintained though it compromises her marriage and raises painful questions about her future in general. In fact, no one who sees these films with a discerning eye will imagine that for either woman animal need and its satisfaction is an end in itself, any more than Bergman's need in a film like *Cries And Whispers* is a definitive put-down of women. Always in Bergman the vision of the film as a whole signals the continuing difficulty of large-scale and enduring integration, the difficulty we have in maintaining proportion, in expressing at once what we need, what we think we need, and think we ought to need. Though Desiree is without the paralyzing self-consciousness of Ester in *The Silence,* she knows that some things are more important than others, that confident decisions are likely to be rescinded at any moment for good or bad reasons, and that if there are needs, there is also a reasonably appealing world and intractable others with whom to deal, decently if at all possible. Bergman adores Desiree not because she has especially good ideas or because she is an especially kind or noble person, but because she has some clear notion of what she wants, how to get it, and how far one may legitimately go in pursuit of one's desires; also because she is a beautiful woman whose carriage and demeanor bespeak a clarity of intention and relative harmony of impulse. . . .

I do not think that Bergman has ever created a more admirable character than Marianne in *Wild Strawberries.* With her we move from the limited consideration of animal need to the potential stature of women as autonomous human beings. (p. 138)

In *Wild Strawberries* . . . Bergman develops an attractive character who manages to steer a middle course between, on one hand, the outright narcissism and escapist self-assertion too frequently urged upon women by feminist militants, and a more traditional accommodation to an ongoing 'male' reality. . . . [Though] Bergman has developed as an artist in the course of more than thirty years, he is no less taken with autonomous women than he ever was, and no less likely to note psychological and emotional dangers implicit in too great an insistence upon liberation. Always his films ask not only, 'liberation from what?' but 'liberation to what?' (p. 139)

Bergman's autonomous women do not always succeed in making satisfactory lives for themselves, and there are times when insistence upon one's own truth, or *the* truth, or justice, goes against the grain of one's real interests. In *Through A Glass Darkly* Karin is a defeated and psychotic young woman whose recovery is inhibited by her inability to live with the partial truths that others in her family require. Though her husband loves and cares for her, and puts up with her 'episodes' and delusions, she regularly accuses him of insensitivity, as though if he only tried harder he'd be able to divine the needs which she herself can hardly identify. Bergman admires Karin for her fanatical determination to get at the truth of her feelings and to resist the easy pretenses of others who love her, but he knows that she's not likely to find satisfaction in her refusal to 'let up.' If ultimately the character is "soiled" by her sexual needs the reason has much to do with her failure to integrate sexual need and mundane attachment. . . .

Bergman also admires the psychotic determination of Elisabeth Vogler in *Persona,* . . . but he sees as well the suffering and coldness of spirit required to purchase extreme autonomy. Does Bergman wilfully punish women who resist families, husbands, children, who turn their backs on the biological calling? No more so than he punishes men who are cold and all but indifferent to their functions as integrated human being. (p. 140)

Ms. Mellen [see excerpt above] and others have for long contended that "the personalities of Bergman's women are fixed and pre-conceived; they exist beyond change and development." Surely *Scenes From A Marriage* should put to rest such contentions, though they might as well have been served by the portrait of Sister Alma in *Persona.*

To conclude all this, may we say simply, that Bergman is not guilty as charged with respect to his treatment of women; . . . his films ask to be treated with a grave caution which respects the plurality of his intentions and the scruple with which he examines states of feeling. No literate film-goer can afford to shut himself, or herself, to the rigorous probings of Bergman's camera eye. (p. 141)

Robert Boyers, "Bergman and Women," in Salmagundi *(copyright © 1978 by Skidmore College), No. 4, Winter, 1978, pp. 131-41.*

PHILIP STRICK

It makes sense that [*Serpent's Egg*] takes up the theme by showing a society in wild confusion and dread, where lives are shattered by the arbitrary malice of unknown controllers. . . . The undercurrents stemming from the era of *The Silence* and *Persona* can be charted through all Bergman's later work, forming a familiar geography for the voyages of all his 'island' characters. One looks the more keenly for them in *Serpent's Egg* in view of its origins, despite the new international production environment it represented for Bergman. Here he is, under the banner of De Laurentiis, no less. And as it turns out, the links with a Swedish past are the very reasons why the film doesn't function quite as smoothly as it should, why it leaps too readily into a generalised warning from a specific malaise.

The title is unexplained until the film is nearly ended. Preparing to take a cyanide capsule, Bergman's analyst remarks: 'Anyone who makes the slightest effort can see what's waiting there in the future. It's like a serpent's egg: through the thin membranes you can clearly make out the already perfect reptile.' Spoken in pre-Nazi Germany, the assertion seems unarguable, even startlingly perceptive, assuming we have understood it properly (a complex symbol, the serpent); but if Bergman intends there to be a direct parallel with today something more is called for than the intermingling of *Cabaret, The Damned* and *Mr. Klein* in order to prove the point. . . .

The gaping suicide haunts the film, both spectator and symptom of the later bloodshed, until its broken features are aped by Abel himself, clutching in futility at the tiles of his cell. Bergman has used horrific images before (notably in *The Shame,* with its casual human breakages), but the violence in *Serpent's Egg* is at a new pitch. Similarly, the glimpsed debaucheries of *The Silence* have been updated to the fashionably excessive level of the 1970s. . . .

If this is Germany, it's as seen by a Swedish tourist, for whom the priests are perpetually wrapped in guilt (the tragicomic scene of joint prayer from *Winter Light* is restaged), sheets can conceal living faces as well as dead, and the hour of the wolf, just before dawn, is still a time for the darkest confidences. Newsreels of human suffering, induced by cold chemical curiosity, have also reappeared, examined by Bergman's usual two-in-one team—the dreamer and the pragmatist—who, like their creator, draw conflicting conclusions about the susceptibility of human nature to redirection. 'In ten years,' says Vergerus, 'those people will create a new society unequalled in world history.' Looking at the grey, placid faces drifting slowly down the screen, rightly resembling the victims of the future rather than its masters, one is disinclined to agree. But Bergman has always, it seems, found himself closer to despair than the rest of us.

Philip Strick, "Film Reviews: 'The Serpent's Egg'," in Sight and Sound *(copyright © 1978 by the British Film Institute), Vol. 47, No. 3, Summer, 1978, p. 190.*

GAVIN MILLAR

You must first accept that Ingmar Bergman's characters are involved, not just in moments of crisis, but in lives of the deepest crisis and pain, or the crushing burdens of his plots will simply seem absurd. The two women in *Autumn Sonata* . . . , are what we may now see as archetypal Bergman protagonists. . . .

Some of Bergman's recent films on the theme of how much damage human beings in close contact, through blood and marriage, can do to each other in the name of love, have seemed unfairly grim: challenges to the spectator to suffer as much as to enjoy, and to pay for his increased understanding by a thorough harrowing. In form, they have often seemed, too, no different from a rather intense course of treatment from a mercifully free psychoanalyst. *Autumn Sonata* escapes this criticism chiefly by doing more to enact the relationship as well as talk about it. . . . (p. 492)

Bergman's ability to turn peaceful domestic tableaux into glimpses of the mouth of hell is what distinguishes him at his uncomfortable best, and this is one of those occasions.

There are minor quibbles. So powerful and rich are [the] early enactments of the family history that the later scenes, during which both the women speak (however brilliantly) long monologues about their lives as child and mother, seem anti-climactic.The sheer bewildering pace of revelation slows to the clinical entrail-inspection of the patient on the couch: while what we learn bears out what we have seen, there is no compensatory burst of speed to take us to the tape. It isn't fair of us, but in those early reels Bergman has accustomed us to breathing at such high altitudes that we are still looking round disappointedly for new peaks to conquer. (p. 493)

Gavin Millar, "Painful Prelude" (© Gavin Millar, 1979; reprinted by permission of the author and his agents, Judy Daish Associates, Ltd.) in The Listener, *Vol. 101, No. 2605, April 5, 1979, pp. 492-93.*

GILBERTO PEREZ

The close-up is Ingmar Bergman's stock in trade. No other filmmaker has so relentlessly dwelt on the human face in the attempt to lay bare the soul behind it. His new film, *Autumn Sonata,* is once again pledged to the nuances and intensities of the aggrandized countenance.

Wasn't the close-up, it may be asked, the invention and the glory of the silent film? In an eloquent passage in his *Theory of the Film,* Bela Balazs wrote about the "spiritual dimension" into which silent films would probe with their big close-ups of human faces, the "silent soliloquy" or "mute dialogue" that could be enacted through the sustained enlargement of facial expression. . . . [In] Bergman the close-up is less a matter of a shared language than of his personal utterance. . . . [The] face is not a substitute for the voice but an intensification, or a qualification, of it; and, when the actor is not speaking, the soliloquy of the countenance is now truly a *silent* one. . . .

Ingmar Bergman seems to me fundamentally a latter-day expressionist. I have in mind not only his frequent borrowing (in such films as *The Naked Night, The Magician, Hour of the Wolf, Face to Face)* from the devices of cinematic expressionism that were developed in Weimar Germany, or even the greater spiritual debt he owes to his compatriot Strindberg, the originator of dramatic expressionism. Bergman's close-ups are as much as expressionistic device as the distorted sets in *The Cabinet of Dr. Caligari:* they equally push the medium to an extreme in order to have it express extremities of feeling, and they equally portray a landscape of fear, alienation, anguish. Expressionism portrays fear from the point of view of the frightened, alienation from the point of view of the alienated; it disfigures the world by giving absolute primacy to the distraught individual. If *Caligari* portrays the world as the paranoiac nightmare of a madman, *Scenes from a Marriage* omits the words as immaterial to the troubled husband and wife. The characteristic Bergman close-up is an externalization of despair and a denial of any perspective that may take us outside that despair. . . .

It's hard to escape the conclusion that in these brooding, pared-down films—of which *Autumn Sonata* is the most recent—all confined to very few characters in an elementary situation, Bergman feels he's getting down to the essentials of the human condition. (p. 10)

The conversations between mother and daughter deal mainly with the past, as one would expect, and are punctuated with flashbacks. Done in distant long shot so as to emphasize their remoteness from the present, these flashbacks, though visually elegant, carry little weight dramatically: they are like slides illustrating the voice-over narration rather than autonomous re-enactments. The real drama is in the present as the characters talk about the past, a situation reminiscent of Ibsen. Yet, as Strindberg went beyond Ibsen from the drama of the room (naturalism) to the drama of the mind (expressionism), so also does Strindberg's disciple Bergman—except that Bergman can do without the paraphernalia of stage expressionism and create his drama of the mind by concentrating on the isolated face. It doesn't appreciably matter where, in what concrete situation in the present, the encounter between mother and daughter in *Autumn Sonata* takes place: the real drama is in their heads. . . .

There's a second daughter in *Autumn Sonata,* a spastic cripple confined to bed and reduced to speaking in grunts intelligible only to her sister, the Liv Ullmann character, who nurses her at home. This other daughter's disease is not presented just as an unfortunate fact but as a symbol of the larger malaise—it caps the list of her sister's accusations against the mother, whose selfish withholding of love allegedly cause this too—in one of Ingmar Bergman's unwarranted and irresponsible equations of physical distress with the afflictions of the soul. . . .

The painful condition of a grunting spastic is a lousy symbol for the pain of the human condition and the general inability to communicate with others. Surely Bergman would have done better to omit this second daughter from *Autumn Sonata.* Sometimes, however, an artist's worst mistakes can offer the clearest indication of what's wrong with his fundamental approach. If Bergman can identify the sufferings of a spastic with those of the spirit, it's because he's ready to discount wholly the causes of either in reality, and eager to postulate the experience of suffering as itself the ultimate, inescapable reality. Any attempt to verify the first daughter's charges against the mother by going into the actual past—and examining why, for example, the daughter and her father could find nothing better to do when the mother was away than read her letters over and over—would have been, for Bergman, beside the point. The daughter's charges are not just her version of the story, they are the story: not because they are necessarily the truth but because for Bergman the essential truth is in the close-up view of her anguish. What's wrong with this, in my estimation, is that it merely serves to flaunt the anguish: only by gaining some distance from it can one hope to understand it, let alone cure it. (p. 11)

Gilberto Perez, "Ingmar Bergman: Up Close," in New York Arts Journal *(copyright © 1979 by Richard W. Burgin), No. 13, 1979, pp. 10-11.*

RONALD S. LIBRACH

The largest metaphor in *The Serpent's Egg* is the metaphor of the narrative film itself as a dream—the complete inversion of two levels of "reality." The film opens, for example, with a shot of people's expressionless faces, as they move in slow motion, like the figures in the boat in the dream at the end of *The Shame;* the shot is intercut with the opening credits. The film ends with explicit suddenness, accompanied by the metallic sound of a shutter gate dropping; the screen cuts sharply to black, and there are no closing credits. Throughout the film, there is also a vapor drifting up from the ground, whether it be the cold mist that rises perpetually from the cobblestones or the cigarette smoke which lingers in every cabaret and every bedroom. The narrator identifies this vapor as fear: "Fear," he says, "rises like vapor from the asphalt; it can be sensed like a pungent smell. Everyone bears it with him like a nerve poison—a slow-working poison that is felt only as a quicker or slower pulse or a spasm of nausea." Fear becomes the film's principal theme, the vaporous "slow-working poison" its principal image. . . . (p. 96)

The Serpent's Egg seems to wince occasionally on account of incipient politicalism, which is not, as his critics frequently remind us, Bergman's strongest intellectual suit. If Bergman means to say simply that we must think of the Nazi years as a "nightmare," Hitler a demon hatched from "the serpent's egg" to take upon himself the guilt and fears of the world in what T. S. Eliot has called the apocalyptic "years of *l'entre deux guerres,*" then we would have to assume that his aestheticism and his tax troubles have gotten the better of his sense of history and his human sympathy. But it is far more accurate—and far more reasonable—to read Bergman's decision to situate *The Serpent's Egg* in Berlin during these years as a gesture of historical displacement, much like those he has made before, both in naturalistic films like *The Seventh Seal* and *Smiles of a Summer Night* and in expressionistic pieces like *The Face* and *Cries and Whispers*. Such displacement is a function and privilege of art, and not of politics and history, both of which must assume that the passage of events in time is real and can be analyzed as such; displacement deals not with the causal time-order of "real" events themselves, but rather with the way in which consciousness elaborates these events in its own forms of rhetoric. (pp. 97-8)

[Bergman has] constructed in *The Serpent's Egg* a film which revolves around a male protagonist. Abel Rosenberg eventually comes to live with his sister-in-law. Not unexpectedly, their relationship succumbs to a powerful sexual undertow which is, of course, neither technically "incestuous" nor immoral, since Abel's brother has already committed suicide; but it develops along intensely neurotic lines, nevertheless, and their inability to consummate it—that is, Abel's inability to consummate it, despite Manuela's growing desire to do so—is no doubt the thematic key to their dramatic personalities.

Actually, this character configuration is a variation on a theme which Bergman has played many times before: the woman has become both lover (or would-be lover) and mother-figure, the male both would-be lover and child-figure. Manuela feels compelled to take care of Abel as she had once taken care of his brother, and it is her guilt over her first failure which causes her to insist that they succor one another as if she and Abel, too, were lovers. "You're responsible for someone, and you fail in your duty," she confesses to a priest, "and there you stand, empty-handed and ashamed." Abel, too, suffers from a sense of guilt on account of his brother, but the paradoxical complexity of his guilt makes him a figure emblematic not simply of Abel, but of Cain as well: he is, it would seem, both the surviving brother whom not even death will release from guilt and, ironically, the victimized brother as well—emotionally murdered by the kind of guilt which is shared only by survivors and which can be relieved only by the kind of annihilation which he wills for himself at film's end. What all this guilt frustrates is ultimately sexual impulse and sexual self-knowledge, which is for Bergman . . . the most authentically human means of contact with the other and with oneself. (p. 99)

In *The Serpent's Egg,* Bergman has placed a male at the center of the film, and the issue of the male's sexual self-knowledge thus becomes the film's principal (if not overriding) thematic issue. If the woman's special mode of self-knowledge is a privilege which derives from a sexuality culminating in the certitude of maternity, then the problem of the male's self-knowledge results from the complementary problem—the incontrovertible uncertainty of fatherhood. . . .

The problem, of course, is not simply fatherhood itself, but rather fatherhood as the sign of the male's sexual equality—of his possession of his own sexual powers, of his equal participation in sexual experience, and of his equal access to self-knowledge. Bergman begins by following Strindberg in arguing that it is the irrefragable certitude of maternity which demands an acknowledgment of the woman's sexuality by the male which she need not reciprocate. In a film like *Scenes from a Marriage,* Bergman is concerned to describe the way in which an authentic sexual relationship can elicit the woman's acknowledgment, and it is Abel and Manuela's abject failure in consummating such a relationship which dictates the tragic end of *The Serpent's Egg*. . . .

Abel finally wrenches himself free of Manuela's embrace and admits that he cannot be her lover, both because her maternal supplications have begun to suffocate him and, paradoxically, because he prefers the security which his child's role affords him. (pp. 100-01)

The film's key male figures, Abel Rosenberg and Hans Vergerus, represent opposite ends of any epistemological spectrum which is implied in *The Serpent's Egg,* and neither is able to approximate self-knowledge. Abel . . . prefers the kind of self-effacement for which the dream state is the primordial metaphor, while Vergerus prefers to watch the effects of self-extinction as they work on the object of his body. Except for the nightmares which he induces others to act out for him so that he may commit them to celluloid, Vergerus has no dreams of guilt and fear, and that is why he can purvey terror so confidently. For Vergerus, who looks into a mirror and watches the cyanide work on his own body, fear and death are necessary for the recovery of time and history: the scientist measures such phenomena as guilt and the fear of death according to the way they affect the body; then, by measuring the resulting "changes" in the organism, he assumes confidently the passage of time and the necessity of the future. The difference between Vergerus' clandestine scientific films and the filmed dream which is *The Serpent's Egg* itself is the difference, as Jorge Luis Borges is always telling us, between looking at oneself *in* the mirror and actually passing *through* the mirror itself. To pass through the mirror, as Bachelard puts it, is to create a world in which, as in the dream, the "real" world has been completely *assimiliated* into the "irreal" world of the imagination. When Bergman makes Abel Rosenberg's dream coextensive with the film which he himself has imagined, then he has assimilated the "real" world of his film—pre-Hitlerian Berlin in the 1920's—into the metaphor which he has created for it, and *The Serpent's Egg,* in the truest Borgian sense of the word, is thus a work of "fantasy." (p. 101)

Much like the art of Borges, Bergman's art is the transformation of reality into . . . "an inescapable reality of the mind"—a fantasizing of the nature of consciousness itself, experienced as one experiences a dream, as if it could not be distinguished from reality, and as if it were thus reality itself. (pp. 101-02)

Ronald S. Librach, "Through the Looking-Glass Darkly: 'The Serpent's Egg'," in Film Literature Quarterly, *Vol. 8, No. 2, Spring, 1980, pp. 92-103.*

Bernardo Bertolucci

1940-

Italian poet and filmmaker.

In Bertolucci's films there is constant concern with the bourgeois life-style and its anaesthetic, smothering effect on the characters's potential. Some critics believe this is a response to his own childhood, although Bertolucci himself recalls this time fondly. Raised in the luxuries of an upper middle-class family, Bertolucci was encouraged intellectually. His father was a famous poet and film critic. Accompanying him in his frequent visits to the theater, the young Bertolucci often saw two or three films a day. His first interest, however, was poetry. A collection of his poems, published while he was still an undergraduate, won the Prix Viareggio. But in 1961, when he began to work as an assistant to Pier Paolo Pasolini on *Accattone!*, he stopped writing poetry. In filmmaking he found his primary mode of expression. Now he sees each of his films as a poem, or an attempt at poetry.

Bertolucci made his first feature at the age of twenty. And by the time *Before the Revolution* was released in 1964, his reputation was established. Many critics considered this film a brilliant piece of work from such a young and inexperienced artist. Like most of his later films, it concentrates on the hero's struggle against his middle-class background and his eventual submission to its tenets. Whether they are political, social, or psychological, Bertolucci's films are always lyrical. He has called them poetry, critics have called them choreography. And, indeed, dance imagery abounds. So do lush coloration and visual references to paintings. His work is often called beautiful. Critical response to other aspects has been mixed. He is not favorably received in Italy, by either critics or his fellow filmmakers.

Bertolucci's best known and most controversial film is *Last Tango in Paris*. In an early, laudatory review, Pauline Kael termed the film a landmark in movie history, comparable to the importance of *Le Sacre du Printemps* in music history. Other critics, equally impassioned, have termed the film pornographic for its explicit, often brutal, eroticism.

Probably one of the most important aspects of the film is the manner in which it took form. Much of the script, and therefore the characterization, was improvised. This flexible, organic quality is part of Bertolucci's cinematic vision. In an interview during the filming of *1900*, he said: "All the films I have made seemed desperately autobiographical to me, . . . but the autobiographical dimension has been completely decanted and consumed in the act of becoming film. . . . The film exists for itself." On the same subject, he has also said: "Films are animal events." Some critics and viewers, who respond negatively to the violence and explicitness of his work, would probably agree.

EUGENE ARCHER

["Before the Revolution" is] a poignant love story epitomizing a young man's growth through the dense, chaotic jungle of contemporary civilization. Like many of the best modern films, the drama is difficult, subtle and extraordinarily complex in its imagery.

Mr. Bertolucci, who is nothing if not ambitious, has attempted a symbolic autobiography that is classical in its construction. Fabrizio, the protagonist, is a Stendhal character, residing in Parma and ultimately marrying a bourgeois girl named Clélia. Hs is also an Italian Holden Caulfield, flailing his adolescent limbs and querying intellect against the social structures of 1962.

The title derives from Talleyrand—"Only those who lived before the revolution knew how sweet life could be." In a typical gesture of searching youth, the boy revolts against everything in his surroundings—his respectable middle-class family, his lovely but dull childhood sweetheart, the political climate in his provincial town. He dallies with Communism, with abstract philosophy, with art, and, most meaningfully, with his striking, unhappy young aunt, who falls hopelessly in love while realizing she is only filling an adolescent's temporary need.

It is a moving story on the most immediate level, and the director has given it sweeping connotations. When the boy, unable to cope with the extraordinary young woman, abandons his struggles and lets her drift away, the drama reverberates with evocations of loss. His failure at love symbolizes a death of the past, an angst-ridden sense of futility in any kind of revolutionary striving, whether emotional, political or merely intellectual, amid the defeat of contemporary society.

Viewing life in such romantic terms is the special province of a very young director, but Mr. Bertolucci has approached his story with such deep feeling that its full implications are communicated. This is a young man's film, but it has large social references.

Cinematically, it is also filled with references, to the best modern directors in Italy and France. Knowledgeable viewers can detect strong influences from Roberto Rossellini and Alain Resnais in Mr. Bertolucci's sophisticated style.

Astonishingly, he has managed to assimilate a high degree of filmic and literary erudition into a distinctively personal visual approach. Technically, he displays authoritative control. Here is a new talent of outstanding promise.

Eugene Archer, "'Before the Revolution'," in The New York Times *(© 1964 by The New York Times Company; reprinted by permission), September 25, 1964, p. 32.*

JOHN THOMAS

[If *Before the Revolution* is] a failure, it's a beautiful one; far more exciting than some of the easy successes we applaud and forget each year. [It's often] incoherent, terrifyingly immature, fascinatingly beautiful. . . . [It] has all the faults you'd expect from a very young director, and all the intensity you'd expect from youth. Before the end it falls to pieces, but how lovely the fragments!

Despite some critical opinion to the contrary, I don't think it's at all a film about the boredom and decay of the middle classes, the alienation of Western man, or anything else that will fit some critical pigeonhole. Like most films, it's "about" the people in it. Its theme is hyperintellectualism, the tendency of many bright young people to make ideas a substitute for feelings. . . . Fabrizio's ideas about the world prove inadequate to his understanding of it, for understanding demands the emotional involvement he cannot give. He renounces his aunt not because he is engaged in incest, but because she is too complex for him; he gives up the Communist Party not because of lost illusions, but because his illusions will not allow him to consider the complex problems that underlie the Party's relationship to its members. . . .

It's not just that he lets his friends down, but that he never realizes he has done so. (p. 55)

It's claimed that the film is autobiographical, and if so it would seem that Bertolucci has succeeded only partially in detaching himself from his protagonist; many of the film's faults stem from his rather ambiguous attitude toward Fabrizio. Bertolucci often romanticizes his character to the point of making you believe that his illusions are to be taken seriously. Thus the scene in which Fabrizio renounces the Communist Party, which should be essentially ironic, ends up rather fuzzily realized because Bertolucci does not distance himself sufficiently from the character. And we're likely, all the way through the movie, to take Fabrizio much too seriously.

There are other faults in abundance, mostly related to Bertolucci's extremely self-conscious handling of his images. . . . And the quoting from other movies (is that the Parma opera house or Marienbad?) often distracts annoyingly from the tension of a scene. Too often Bertolucci shatters his best effects with careless decisions and self-indulgence.

What's really remarkable, though, are all the scenes that do work and shouldn't. In particular I think of the sequence in which an aging aristocrat whose land is about to be expropriated bids farewell to the streams and hills of his estate. This sentimental, blatantly romantic business should collapse miserably, but doesn't. For me, at least, it is real and moving. And I can only conclude that this is because Bertolucci deeply believed in what he was saying. . . .

Bertolucci's primary directorial influence has been Godard. His jump cuts, unlike Godard's, often seem gratuitously confusing; and he has the solid determination of the young film-maker never to hold the camera still when he can use his dolly. But all of this engenders an excitement that helps keep the film moving over its frequent rough spots. Like his master, Bertolucci tries something new in every scene; like Godard, often fails; like Godard, sometimes succeeds spectacularly. He seems to me the first of the newer directors really to understand what Godard is doing. . . .

In the end *Before the Revolution* cannot sustain its power, and we recall it as a handful of beautifully realized moments. Certainly a failure, since a controlled emotional impact is necessary to any real work of art. But there's so much in it of beauty that it cannot be dismissed. (p. 56)

John Thomas, "Film Reviews: 'Before the Revolution'," in Film Quarterly *(copyright 1966 by The Regents of the University of California; reprinted by permission of the University of California Press), Vol. XX, No. 1, Fall, 1966, pp. 55-7.*

HENRY HEIFETZ

La Commare Secca, [which has been translated as *The Grim Reaper* but] which means literally "The Dry Housewife" or "Housewife Dry" is a Roman-dialect name for death, and Bernardo Bertolucci's film is basically a treatment of death and of processes and conditions which are a part of its nature: solitude, inevitability, ritual. . . . Compared to *Before the Revolution, La Commare Secca* tries for much less and comes off much better at it, Bertolucci's weaknesses being more evident in the later film.

A weakness which doesn't have to be one at all in the future unless Bertolucci insists on it is simply that, judging by *Before the Revolution* and despite the fact that Bertolucci has written and perhaps still writes poetry, he does not seem to be a good writer. Most of the writing in that film is in a very banal Italian tradition of regional sentimentalism and would-be-elegant sentence-making; and *Before the Revolution* is not the kind of film where weak writing is relatively unimportant, since its basic theme is of the inconsistencies and uncertain relationship of sentiment, action, and statement. Another weakness is a tendency to plunge, all stops loose, into long bravura sequences which are already compromised by a fundamentally sentimental imposition of his theme. In *Before the Revolution,* where the self-deluding sentimentality of youth forms much of the substance of the film, Bertolucci should have either made of that sentimentality a desperate and all-exclusive myth or else treated its separate components with much more sophistication and originality. As it is, too many of the sequences come off as sentimental treatments of sentimentality rather than "inside" presentations. Allied to that tendency is the other major film-making fault of *Before the Revolution:* the question of pace. Scenes are sometimes stretched out to incredible length, with Bertolucci belaboring the same small notion with image after image and seas of words. And yet despite all this, many things in *Before the Revolution* come off well, especially sequences between the boy and his aunt, articulated by Godardian jump cuts—because Bertolucci, letting go with everything he has visually, makes the scene work as something almost extrinsic to the film, a kind of giant, internally well-balanced cameo. (p. 44)

The verbal aspect of *La Commare Secca* presents no problem since, aside from the fact that the language here matters infinitely less than in the very talky *Before the Revolution,* the screenplay stems from Pier Paolo Pasolini who *is* a writer and a good one. . . . Bertolucci's style [in *La Commare Secca*] establishes itself as a passionate romanticism; he uses a restless, widely moving camera, with jump-cuts derived from Godard but without Godard's elegance or his watered emotions, and very different from Pasolini's more painter-like attempts to create myth through simplicity and arrangement. (p. 45)

Henry Heifetz, "'La Commare secca'," in Film Quarterly *(copyright 1966 by The Regents of the University of California; reprinted by permission of the University of California Press), Vol. XX, No. 2, Winter, 1966-67, pp. 44-6.*

BILL NICHOLS

The Conformist, like several other recent films, deals with the complex question of the fascist sensibility. . . . For example, three characteristics of the fascist sensibility that are evident today have figured in films like *Z, Joe, The Confession, Patton, Investigation of a Citizen, The Damned,* and *The Conformist:* the tendency to defend established values and myths as inviolable axioms; the tendency to see ideological and even, sometimes, personal conflicts as irresolvable by compromise and, therefore, to accept and apply violent solutions; and the tendency to use allegiance to institutions of power and authority as a psychic crutch. The result is a preoccupation with a hostile, threatening environment in which the hero, by aligning himself for or against the forces of law and order, achieves a sense of purpose. It is, essentially, the quest for identity played out in political terms. . . .

The overall style and structure of these films are the very means by which the director deals with his responses to this phenomenon. In any case, the director's control of his responses—the degree to which they are assimilated into an aesthetic pattern—becomes a vital test of his work's success. That the director can be a 'dictator' is an old cliche with new implications when his subject matter is related, however peripherally, to the stormy issue of fascism. . . .

[Bertolucci's] artistry seems capable of absorbing the most intense emotions and stylizing them into patterns of consummate aesthetic design that, from a Marxist, world-transforming viewpoint, have a strangely self-enclosed feel about them. . . .

The praise accorded [*The Conformist*] has had an uncommon consistency, suggesting that a major touchstone of the critical sensibility has been courted with deeply resonant overtures. . . . The film elaborates on Freud to show repressed homosexuality not only as the unfortunate, sometimes damaging, price of civilization but also as the breeding ground for fascism. It is a restricted version, and hence less valid, of Reich's assertion that the authoritarian family in the middle-classes of Germany was the breeding ground for Hitler's power. Bertolucci offers us the reassurance that tyrannical oppressors are sick men whose symptoms we can clearly recognize. . . . (p. 19)

Bertolucci also paints the anti-fascist forces in a bad light (literally in the ballet studio embrace and an unflattering shot of the herd-like mob celebrating Mussolini's downfall) and makes the black observation that the 'democratic' front features its own brand of sickness (conformity, decadence and 'charming' sentiments). His Marxist inclinations, in fact, may have contributed more directly to this part of the portrait than to its fascist side. But these insights *seem* peripheral, a brief indication of democratic (or capitalistic) aberrations rather than a full-fledged identification of the abnormal with the totality. (pp. 19-20)

The complement to the film's political sentiment is the lyrical, enveloping style, source of its own pleasure, creator of its own milieu. The deeply satisfying joy of watching the film is something that virtually every critic longs for. Bertolucci's structuring does not force an analogous reading of the film as historical, political commentary. . . . We respond by displacing analysis of the characters and setting from their historical counterparts to the aesthetic structure in which they operate. It is a highly seductive operation and one that undercuts the film's political force. Marcello's alliance with fascism is less a revelatory examination of fascism than a vehicle for putting his latent sexual urges and his desire for physical action onto a collision course. . . .

Bertolucci is basically a lyricist, a film poet whose political thrust is, at best, only oblique. While the film poet can nonetheless be revolutionary, as Dovzhenko was within his historical context, Bertolucci stands closer to a film poet whose work drew only the thinnest sustenance from his political milieu—F. W. Murnau. Murnau, like Cocteau, had little interest in poeticizing the stuff of political struggle. Bertolucci, like both of them, draws from the homosexual sensibility of serene lightness, clear, precise gracefulness and open, innocent awareness of the darker forces that turn more virile, aggressive temperaments to melodramatic confrontations. . . .

Bertolucci's similarity to Murnau goes further than a sharing of poetic sensibility; the actual styles bear close resemblance, especially in the use of light and camera. Like Murnau, Bertolucci uses moving light sources to great advantage. Both the swinging light in the Chinese restaurant and the search lights on the streets of Rome convey a sense of precariousness, of lurching instability that echo the cowardice and uncertainty of allegiance that plague Marcello at these moments. (p. 20)

[But Bertolucci] runs his metaphor along a political axis from repressed homosexuality to compulsive conformism to fascism rather than along the more psychological axis of Murnau (from 'normal' action, usually love, to threatening super-ego or id projected as unnatural or supernatural forces). Why *this* metaphor appeals to Bertolucci . . . seems to have less to do with the essential nature of fascism than with the artist's own sexual preoccupations. And it is this dimension of the film that is most disturbing. The lyricism, the effortless beauty and perfect harmony all transfix us and afford a pleasure that is rare in film or any art. But it also twists the film's political axis around itself so that fascism becomes a universalized, general condition that helps extrapolate repressed energy into the arena of social action. And conversely, Bertolucci's treatment of sexuality suggests that the pleasure is not without a price, that there are levels of guilt and judgment in the film that Bertolucci has not been able to subordinate to his style. (p. 22)

The choice of metaphor is, itself, replete with difficulties. The linking of repressed homosexuality with fascism not only limits the origins of the latter too severely but also implies that homosexuality itself may be more liberating. . . . Making the film may have served a purgative function for Bertolucci himself but the general association of stylistic and decorative opulence with decadence and fascism suggests that there are elements of conflict yet unresolved. The original tightness of the metaphor begins to weaken; sexuality itself, repressed or otherwise, becomes the source of social disease. A position not exactly Marxist.

Bertolucci's virtue lies far more in his artistic discipline than his political acumen. Romantic notions in general and boy-girl romances in particular do not contradict, undercut or belittle the political context. Bertolucci avoids the melodramatic pitfalls that claim many socially conscious films (*The Molly Maguires, La Guerre est finie, Getting Straight* —a few that just begin to indicate the range), crafting a work of considerable polish and remarkable unity. The link between *The Conformist* and the depths and limits of either the homosexual experience or the fascist nightmare, however, is like that of jigsaw piece to puzzle: without the other pieces, its greatest value is in the beauty of its own, unique appearance. (pp. 22-3)

Bill Nichols, "'Il conformista'," in Cinéaste *(copyright © 1971 by Gary Crowdus), Vol. IV, No. 4, Spring, 1971, pp. 19-23.*

RUTH KREITZMAN

From start to finish [*The Conformist*] has been immaculately conceived and constructed. Bertolucci's keen eye for architecture here reaches its most perfect synthesis yet, and each shot is constructed as though traced from a drawing-board. He echoes the Thirties designs of Art Deco, those geometrical shapes and angles, by juxtaposing straight lines, parallels, verticals, diagonals, in vivid patterns, parodied by the camera's oblique angle. He creates his atmosphere of anonymity and conformity with a metaphoric use of colour—greys, browns, cool blues and stark white backgrounds. And he succeeds in conveying that heady decadence of pre-war Europe with a meticulous attention to detail, and even in the very rhythm of the film, which captures the staccato-like movement of a Thirties tango, as performed in a highly stylised sequence in a dance-hall, stunningly shot from above, catching the dizzy, infectious atmosphere. . . .

The significance of *The Conformist* lies not only in its highly individual sense of style, but also in the fact that this individuality is signed with Bertolucci's initial rather than his full name. That is, he has still incorporated personal comments and idiosyncrasies which figure in his earlier films—parodies of Hollywood cinema, parallels with Shakespeare, particularly Caesar and Macbeth, his somewhat extraordinary female types, and a taste for bizarre jokes, but this time with rather less self-indulgence and rather more subtlety. The result combines objective observation with a certain subjective expression, the formula of which hopefully *The Conformist* is but a precedent. (p. 8)

Ruth Kreitzman, "Bernardo Bertolucci: An Italian Young Master," in Film *(reprinted by permission of British Federation of Film Societies), No. 61, Spring, 1971, pp. 4-8.*

RICHARD ROUD

Bernardo Bertolucci has described *The Spider's Strategy* [released in the United States as *The Spider's Stratagem*], one of the two films he completed in 1970, as 'a sort of psychoanalytical therapy, a journey through the realm of preconscious memory.' But even without this hint, and without the knowledge of Bertolucci's recent interest in and exploration of psychoanalysis, it would be evident that both *The Spider's Strategy* and *The Conformist* are linked by more than their 1930s settings and their concern with the problem of Fascism.

Since both films are based on literary works, the surest key to Bertolucci's preoccupations is in the changes he has made in his originals. *The Spider's Strategy* is based on a short story by Borges, *Theme of the Traitor and the Hero*. . . . The Borges story is only a few pages long; and it is in what Bertolucci has added that the true significance of the film lies. In Borges, the discovery of the stratagem is made by Kilpatrick's great-grandson and biographer, some hundred years after the event. In the film it is made by the son of Athos Magnani. . . .

[His] first 'encounter' with the father he never knew takes place on his arrival in Sabbioneta (or Tara, as Bertolucci calls it) when he comes upon his statue in the square. As he circles round it, the image of the father eclipses him and he disappears behind it. This scene is the first clue that the central subject of the film is to be the relationship between father and son, even if one did not know the enormous importance of Bertolucci's relation to his own father: *cf.* his statement in an unpublished interview: 'I first began to want to make films in the desire, the need, to do something different from what my father did. He was a poet, and I wanted to compete with him, but not by doing the same thing. I used to write poetry myself, but I realised that I would lose that battle, so I had to find a different terrain on which to compete.' . . . We can see how far Bertolucci has come along the road of self-knowledge—and the expression of this new awareness—by comparing his treatment of what we will have to call the Oedipal theme in this film and in his earlier *Before the Revolution*. In that film, the hero's father is significantly reduced to one or two appearances. . . .

The discovery by the son in *The Spider's Strategy* that his father was not, after all, an untarnished hero might have been a liberating experience; but somehow it is not. The personality of the father is still too strong: he realises that in Tara he will always be only the son of Athos Magnani. Perhaps for this reason he refuses to divulge the truth. He has still, he thinks, enough strength to run away, to flee the all-devouring father. But when he gets to the railway station, he is caught in the spider's web, caught fast like Oedipus in the snare of the gods: he can never leave Tara. The train is announced as delayed; first by forty minutes, then by two hours. 'Sometimes,' the stationmaster remarks, 'they forget about us altogether.' And as Athos walks over to the tracks, he discovers that they are completely overgrown with weeds: no train will ever pass here again.

But this image of the past overwhelming the present, the landscape taking over man's constructions, is not the first such in the film. Even behind the credits, in the naive paintings of Ligabue, we see images of the jungle, of lions ready to pounce. . . . Shots of maize fields punctuate the film throughout, reminding us of the precarious equilibrium of the town, forever at the mercy of the 'jungle'. . . .

Ontogeny recapitulates phylogeny, we learn at school. And the past of the town, of all towns, of civilisation itself, is shown as being just as tentatively overcome as the son's conquest of his past, his attempt to escape from his heredity, from his father, from his destiny. (p. 61)

But Bertolucci has not simply grafted this Oedipal theme on to a story of Fascism and the idealisation of authority which it represents: there is a more significant and complex relationship between the film's politics and its psychology. . . .

In *The Spider's Strategy,* the father ultimately triumphs: not only does he impose his will on his son, he also reduces that son to being just that—not a man, simply the son of his father. The relationships of the central character in *The Conformist* with his father, and with the various father-figures that dot the film, are still more complex; but they contribute to a better understanding of this subterranean theme which flows so importantly through both pictures, and which was already more obscurely present in Bertolucci's earlier films. (p. 62)

Bertolucci has always attempted to relate psychological problems to a social context, but this film is more successful than either *Before the Revolution* or *Partner* in achieving this integration of Freud and Marx, partly because the relationship between Bertolucci and his hero is less direct, partly because his canvas is broader, more dramatic. The earlier films had their set-pieces, but the Communist picnic or the opera première in *Before the Revolution* had little *dramatic* relevance: their importance was thematic. In this film, every sequence, every lyrical flourish—the blind people's ball and the Parisian dance-hall; the sleeping-car honeymoon and the murderous car chase; the radio station and the Chinese restaurant—is both spectacular and significant. Story line and psychological undercurrents at last come electrifyingly together.

Like *The Spider's Strategy, The Conformist* is an adaptation of a pre-existing literary work. But Bertolucci has cut a good many elements from Moravia's novel, and added more; and once again, it is in these suppressions and additions that one looks for the most reliable evidence of the film's deeper significance. Both novel and film tell somewhat the same story: a young boy is the object of a homosexual assault, which he escapes only by shooting his assailant. The result of this adolescent incident is to imbue the boy with an overpowering thirst for normality. (pp. 62-3)

The last section of both film and novel takes place on the day Mussolini is deposed, the day when Marcello discovers that Lino, the man he thought he had killed all those years ago, is actually still alive. . . . In the novel, [Marcello] and his wife and child are killed by enemy aircraft on the following day as they take refuge in the country. The end of the film is quite different, but this is only one of the key changes Bertolucci has made.

First of all, the book tells the story chronologically; whereas Bertolucci has chosen to frame most of it in the sequence of the murder of Quadri and his wife. Significantly these flashbacks leave out almost all of Marcello's early life. Moravia had provided a somewhat old-fashioned 'psychological case-history' to establish basic aggressions and fears. . . .

In contrast, Bertolucci shows only the attempted seduction of Marcello by the chauffeur Lino; and this comes some twenty minutes into the film as part of Marcello's pre-marital confession and absolution. . . . Most important, he has invented a new character, Italo, who serves as a confidant for Marcello but also plays the more telling role of one among three father-figures. It is he, we are led to believe, who has introduced Marcello to the doctrines of Fascism, and secured his entrée into the upper echelons of the government. Significantly, Italo is blind—like the real father who is mad, and the ex-tutor who is stunted and short-sighted. (p. 63)

The two major changes, apart from the introduction of Italo, come towards the end of the story. In the novel, Marcello's mission is only to identify Quadri to an underling; he himself is to have no part in the killing. In the film, although he is accompanied (indeed chauffeured) by his assistant Manganiello, he is supposed to perform the act himself. When the time comes, however, he is seen to be incapable of action—paralysed, impotent. And just as he got Manganiello to dispose of his mother's lover, so it is Manganiello who actually kills Quadri and his wife. It is as if Marcello's shooting of Lino has rendered him forever incapable of action.

The novel ends, as I have said, with death in an air attack. In the film, Marcello discovers the still living Lino in a Coliseum crowded with squatters and refugees, one of whom Lino is trying to seduce. Marcello's rage when he accuses Lino of Quadri's murder frightens the chauffeur away, and Marcello is left with the handsome young Roman Lino had been trying so hard to seduce. The boy starts to strip down for the night; Marcello, fascinated, stands watching. In the last shot of the film, his glance fixed on the boy's naked body, he blinks. The implication is that the discovery that he had not killed Lino after all, coupled with the shock of the end of Fascism, of his career, have so shaken him that he is at last able to face what has probably always been his true nature. And this ending, along with the other changes, gives a meaning to the film which is quite different from that of the novel.

In a sense, Bertolucci's *Conformist* can be taken as his attempt to overthrow authority in all its forms. There is Marcello's true father reduced to an insane asylum; which, significantly, resembles in its architecture and accessories, and the way they are filmed, both the Fascist Ministry we have seen earlier and the Fascist headquarters in the brothel we are shortly to see. And just as his 'replacement', the mother's chauffeur, is ignominiously sent packing, so Marcello's aggressive taunting of his father is equivalent to a total rejection.

Secondly, there is the father-figure, Italo. In the climactic last scene on the day of defeat, Marcello runs into him in the streets of Rome. And the blind Italo has never, as it were, been blinder. As they walk across the Sant' Angelo bridge, all the trappings of dictatorship—the enormous busts of Mussolini, the larger-than-life imperial eagles—that we saw in the Ministry scenes are being unceremoniously dumped into the Tiber. . . . When Marcello discovers that Lino is not dead, he turns on him; but he also tries to transfer his burden of guilt to Italo. He denounces him to the crowd not only as a Fascist, but as an assassin, as a homosexual. It was Italo who had first expounded the doctrine of normality to Marcello, and the irony inherent in a blind man praising normality was pointed in a scene in which Italo claimed never to be mistaken in detecting normality or its opposite. As he says these words, the camera slyly moves down to show us that the man who never makes a mistake has on shoes of different colours. (pp. 63-4)

The theme of blindness also occurs in the episodes devoted to the short-sighted Quadri, with his shuttered flat in which he reminds Marcello of Plato's myth of the cave. . . . [The] address given for Quadri in Paris, as well as his telephone number, are the actual address and number of none other than Jean-Luc Godard. . . .

What is the significance of this detail? Is it simply a private joke, a pun? I think not, although obviously whatever significance it has is bound to be lost on 99 per cent of the film's audience. Nevertheless let us consider: Godard and Bertolucci have been very close friends and Bertolucci has certainly been influenced by Godard. . . . [However], their friendship has diminished as Bertolucci's political evolution ceased to parallel Godard's. We also know that since Bertolucci signed to make *The Conformist* for 'the enemy' (actually for Paramount), he has had no further communication with Godard. It is also true that both this film and *The Spider's Strategy* mark an almost total liberation from the Godard influence. By equating Quadri with Godard, Bertolucci is perhaps establishing once and for all their separation—one that was forced upon him by Godard's rejection, but which is none the less real and perhaps definitive. . . .

There may be something masochistic about Bertolucci's identification—in this particular instance—of himself with Marcello and of Godard with Quadri; but the important thing is not the very limited similarity of the two, but the act itself. If one can forget for a moment the *character* of Marcello, one can see in his story a metaphor of Bertolucci's liberation from the past; and one can even see in Marcello's final self-revelation a symbol of Bertolucci's separation from his father and from all the father-substitutes. In this context, it is not without significance that his next film is to be a love story between a man and woman who are roughly contemporaries. This may not sound very striking: seventy-five per cent of all films are about exactly that. But not Bertolucci's. Leaving out the first film, with its story by Pasolini (another father-figure, by the way), and which in any case has no protagonist, the Bertolucci heroes have been involved with women much older than themselves (*Before the Revolution, The Spider's Strategy*), or narcissistically with their own double (*Partner*). Even in *The Conformist* Marcello's relations with his wife could hardly be called passionate. So this mass disposal of father-figures is a very important step in Bertolucci's career. (p. 64)

Richard Roud, "Fathers & Sons," in Sight and Sound *(copyright © 1971 by The British Film Institute), Vol. 40, No. 2, Spring, 1971, pp. 60-4.*

ROBERT CHAPPETTA

[The] elaborate, oblique style of *The Spider's Stratagem* works better in its parts than as a whole (which is usually true of Bertolucci's films). Like Pasolini's *Teorema,* which also in its final images goes beyond naturalism into surrealism, its strength lies in its use of metaphoric images rather than in its dramatic power or suspense. (p. 14)

For Bertolucci, the romantic "hero" is more absorbed in giving the appearance of being one than in taking effective action. In a key image of the film, a flashback, the elder Magnani, after having been revealed as an informer, takes his fellow conspirators up to a high place—like Satan tempting Christ—and with his arms outstretched and silhouetted against the sky like a spider's, tells them of his plan to pay with his life for having betrayed them; they will assassinate him at the very performance of *Rigoletto* to which Mussolini was supposed to have come, and as he is well known as an anti-Fascist, the suspicion will fall, not on them, but on the Fascists instead. . . . What is clear is . . . that as the romantic hero is more concerned with giving the appearance of being a hero than anything else, he carries within him the seeds of betrayal. (pp. 15-16)

The heroes of Bertolucci's films are all anti-heroes, which seems to be almost a necessary condition of being *avant-garde*. But the problem is that one can be so insistent on exposing one's central character . . . that there is nothing to expose. Bertolucci might have given us more scenes like the Fascist dance scene in which the father appears with a red kerchief around his neck and a British military jacket, a romantic figure if not a hero. For here at least we sensually enjoy the father's moment of defiance even as we appreciate Bertolucci's ironic comment on it. . . .

Richard Roud, in the Spring 1971 *Sight and Sound,* pointed out the oedipal conflict in the younger Magnani [see excerpt above], but the scenes which express this, like the desecration of the father's statue, come off rather weakly. Repeatedly, Bertolucci executes one of his favorite 360° pan shots around the father's statue, as if to suggest the son is simply revolving around his dead father's image. But the son is played too blankly for the camera work to convey strong feelings of any kind. . . . There is also, I think, a psychological reason the oedipal scenes do not work: a son resolves the oedipal conflict with his father by identifying with him, and since the son and the father are played by the same actor, the sense of oedipal conflict is undercut. The defacement of the father's statue seems less an expression of oedipal conflict than that of dull self-loathing. Rather, the "identity" relationship between father and son is being used as a metaphor for the relationship between the elder Magnani and Mussolini. (pp. 16-17)

Like the elder Magnani, Bertolucci himself delights in reversals and gleefully mocking appearances. . . . Thematically, the most important reversal takes place in the final images, in the surreal ending in which the train is delayed. On one level, the reversal seems a mockery of Mussolini's boast that he finally made the trains run on time. If "literally" true, as a symbol of Fascist efficiency, the boast was illusory. . . . But the final images of the film have a wider resonance than that of the Fascist era. Even before the Fascists took power, Italy's one great painter in the twentieth century, de Chirico, was painting images of stasis: large, empty, and somber railroad stations that seem to mock the monumental grandeur of Italy's past; railroad trains that seem, despite their puffs of smoke, to be going nowhere in the stillness.

The film's final images of stasis are set in the present, however, suggesting that the Fascist past is still present in Italy. The flashback form also suggests this, the past at times being confused with the present. Nor do the actors wear any make-up to differentiate between the characters they play in the past and the same characters in the present. . . . Yet Italy no longer has an authoritarian regime, and if Bertolucci does not have as much freedom as he would like to say things more directly in his films, he does manage to hint at them broadly in his oblique and metaphorical style. And I'm not so sure that the charm of the film, which lies in its ambiguity and playfulness, would have been kept with a more straightforward style in which Bertolucci's themes were delivered as a clear, political message. (pp. 17-18)

The style of *The Spider's Stratagem* . . . counterpoints the content. In a flamboyant, sensual, and theatrical style, Bertolucci is critical of the politics of flamboyance, and of the absorption in sensuality of those who did not oppose it. Though the film is richer by this contradiction, it would have been richer still if Bertolucci had allowed his romantic hero to have been more compelling. (p. 18)

Robert Chappetta, "The Meaning Is Not the Message," in Film Quarterly *(copyright 1972 by The Regents of the University of California; reprinted by permission of the University of California Press), Vol. XXV, No. 4, Summer, 1972, pp. 10-18.*

PAULINE KAEL

The movie breakthrough has finally come. Exploitation films have been supplying mechanized sex—sex as physical stimulant but without any passion or emotional violence. The sex in *Last Tango in Paris* expresses the characters' drives. . . .

Many of us had expected eroticism to come to the movies, and some of us had even guessed that it might come from Bertolucci, because he seemed to have the elegance and the richness and the sensuality to make lushly erotic movies. But I think those of us who had speculated about erotic movies had tended to think of them in terms of Terry Southern's deliriously comic novel on the subject, *Blue Movie;* we had expected *artistic* blue movies, talented directors taking over from the *Shlockmeisters* and making sophisticated voyeuristic fantasies that would be gorgeous fun—a real turn-on. What nobody had talked about was a sex film that would churn up everybody's emotions. Bertolucci shows his masterly elegance in *Last Tango in Paris,* but he also reveals a master's substance. . . .

When his wife commits suicide, Paul, an American living in Paris, tries to get away from his life. He goes to look at an empty flat and meets Jeanne, who is also looking at it. They have sex in an empty room, without knowing anything about each other—not even first names. He rents the flat, and for three days they meet there. (p. 28)

The necessity for isolation from the world is, of course, his, not hers. But his life floods in. He brings into this isolation chamber his sexual anger, his glorying in his prowess, and his need to debase her and himself. He demands total subservience to his sexual wishes; this enslavement is for him the sexual truth, the real thing, sex without phoniness. And she is so erotically sensitized by the rounds of lovemaking that she believes him. (p. 29)

What they go through together in their pressure cooker is an intensified, speeded-up history of the sex relationships of the dominating men and the adoring women who have provided the key sex model of the past few decades—the model that is collapsing. They don't know each other, but their sex isn't "primitive" or "pure"; Paul is the same old Paul, and Jeanne, we gradually see, is also Jeanne, the colonel's daughter. They bring their cultural hangups into sex, so it's the same poisoned sex Strindberg wrote about: a battle of unequally matched partners, asserting whatever dominance they can, seizing any advantage. Inside the flat, his male physical strength and the mythology he has built on it are the primary facts. He pushes his morose, romantic insanity to its limits; he burns through the sickness that his wife's suicide has brought on—the self-doubts, the need to prove himself and torment himself. After three days, his wife is laid out for burial, and he is ready to resume his identity. He gives up the flat: he wants to live normally again, and he wants to love Jeanne as a *person.* But Paul is forty-five, Jeanne is twenty. She lends herself to an orgiastic madness, shares it, and then tries to shake it off—as many another woman has, after a night or a twenty years' night. When they meet in the outside world, Jeanne sees Paul as a washed-up middle-aged man—a man who runs a flophouse.

Much of the movie is American in spirit. . . . Paul (a former actor and journalist who has been living off his French wife) is like a drunk with a literary turn of mind. He bellows his contempt for hypocrisies and orthodoxies; he keeps trying to shove them all back down other people's throats. His profane humor and self-loathing self-centeredness and street "wisdom" are in the style of the American hard-boiled fiction aimed at the masculine-fantasy market, sometimes by writers (often good ones, too) who believe in more than a little of it. Bertolucci has a remarkably unbiased intelligence. Part of the convulsive effect of *Last Tango in Paris* is that we are drawn to Paul's view of society and yet we can't help seeing him as a self-dramatizing, self-pitying clown. (pp. 29-30)

Bertolucci has an extravagant gift for sequences that are like arias, and he has given Brando some scenes that really sing. In one, Paul visits his dead wife's lover . . . , who also lives in the run-down hotel, and the two men, in identical bathrobes (gifts from the dead woman), sit side by side and talk. The scene is miraculously basic—a primal scene that has just been discovered. In another, [Paul] rages at his dead wife, laid out in a bed of flowers, and then, in an excess of tenderness, tries to wipe away the cosmetic mask that defaces her. (p. 32)

The colors in this movie are late-afternoon orange-beige-browns and pink—the pink of flesh drained of blood, corpse pink. They are so delicately modulated . . . that romance and rot are one; the lyric extravagance of the music . . . heightens this effect. Outside the flat, the gray buildings and the noise are certainly modern Paris, and yet the city seems muted. Bertolucci uses a feedback of his own—the feedback of old movies to enrich the imagery and associations. In substance, this is his most American film, yet the shadow of Michel Simon seems to hover over Brando, and the ambience is a tribute to the early crime-of-passion films of Jean Renoir, especially *La Chienne* and *La Bête Humaine.* Léaud, as Tom, the young director, is used as an affectionate takeoff on Godard, and the movie that Tom is shooting about Jeanne, his runaway bride, echoes Jean Vigo's *L'Atalante.* Bertolucci's soft focus recalls the thirties films, with their lyrically kind eye for every variety of passion; Marcel Carné comes to mind, as well as the masters who influenced Bertolucci's technique—von Sternberg (the controlled lighting) and Max Ophuls (the tracking camera). The film is utterly beautiful to look at. The virtuosity of Bertolucci's gliding camera style is such that he can show you the hype of the tango-contest scene (with its own echo of *The Conformist*) by stylizing it (the automaton-dancers do wildly fake head turns) and still make it work. . . . Bertolucci draws upon the movie background of this movie because movies are as active in him as direct experience—perhaps more active, since they may color everything else. Movies are a past we share, and, whether we recognize them or not, the copious associations are at work in the film and we feel them. (p. 33)

I've tried to describe the impact of a film that has made the strongest impression on me in almost twenty years of reviewing. . . . It is a movie you can't get out of your system, and I think it will make some people very angry and disgust others. I don't believe that there's *anyone* whose feelings can be totally resolved about the sex scenes and the social attitudes in this film. For the very young, it could be as antipathetic as *L'Avventura* was at first—more so, because it's closer, more realistic, and more emotionally violent. It could embarrass them, and even frighten them. For adults, it's like seeing pieces of your life, and so, of course, you can't resolve your feelings about it—our feelings about life are never resolved. Besides, the biology that is the basis of the "tango" remains. (p. 34)

Pauline Kael, "Tango" (originally published in The New Yorker, *Vol. XLVIII, No. 36, October 28, 1972), in her* Reeling *(copyright © 1972 by Pauline Kael; reprinted by permission of Little, Brown and Company in association with the Atlantic Monthly Press), Atlantic-Little, Brown, 1976, pp. 27-34.*

STANLEY KAUFFMANN

And after all the advance fuss, what *is* [*Last Tango in Paris*]? Three films. One is new Bertolucci, one is old Bertolucci, and one is old New Wave. The first of these parts is what has been most loudly touted, and, surprisingly enough, this touted part is the best in the picture.

The "new Bertolucci" sections have an unexpected strength and engagement. The good scenes in *Tango,* though never quite free of attitudinizing, strike toward something black and truthful, something deeper than the director's self-licking sleekness in the past (and elsewhere in this film). (p. 173)

[The] *atmosphere* of hot hard sex is there and—for a time—gives these scenes a feeling of collision and relief. Then the tension begins to ebb: as [Paul's] autobiographical musings dribble into the commonplace, as his rue-laden background seems not particularly rueful, and as his bitter iconoclasm—on the subject of the family, for instance—sounds more and more undergraduate. The character, instead of deepening, dissolves into a patchwork of platitudes and actor's improvisations; and the power of the sex scenes dissolves, too. Until then, however, there is a new touch of iron in Bertolucci.

All the rest of the film, including the rest of the [love] story, is poor, and there is a great deal of it outside that story. The old Bertolucci inflicts on us his familiar philosophical doodling with the idea of doubles (the dead wife's lover, who lives in the hotel, has a bathrobe identical with the one she gave [Paul]); the garishly melodramatic (a long scene with [Paul] and his wife's laid-out corpse, in which he reviles her, then breaks down and weeps); and an ultimately stupid obsession with photographic chic (the penultimate scene in a dance hall where a tango contest is going on). (pp. 174-75)

For a time I hoped that Bertolucci was satirizing the New Wave elements [in the Godardian sequences] he was so patently cribbing, but the edge is never turned, we never see *behind.* Apparently Bertolucci is seriously using these ten-year-old references to characterize the youth of the boy friend as against the maturity of [Paul]. . . .

[Paul's] swift psychic regression and [Jeanne's] urgency to kill him are pure theatrical hokum to make that fetus-finish possible. (p. 175)

The chromatic tones of the film are what Bertolucci is pleased to call "uterine," but what I would call corny golden-glow. The depth of his symbolism can be measured by his use of that tango contest as a figure of sexual emptiness and also as a hyper-clear source for the title. (pp. 175-76)

Stanley Kauffmann, "'Last Tango in Paris'" (originally published in The New Republic, *Vol. 168, No. 9, March 3, 1973), in his* Living Images: Film Comment and Criticism *(copyright © 1970, 1971, 1972, 1973, 1974, 1975 by Stanley Kauffmann; reprinted by permission of Harper & Row, Publishers, Inc.), Harper, 1975, pp. 173-76.*

LEO BRAUDY

It is paradoxical that *Last Tango in Paris* should have had [so much critical] attention directed at its parts: are its sexy scenes sexy? are Brando's monologues heartfelt or phoney? is the scene beside his wife's coffin the best or the worst in the film? was it a mistake to show her face or a masterful stroke? Paradoxical because the real subject of *Last Tango* is the elusiveness of objects, images, and characters, the difficulty of making emotional connections, the elements of fraudulence and theatricality in everyone's attempt to create his identity for himself and for the world. In all his films Bertolucci seems drawn to a painter's way of presenting the things of the world—the Vuillard interiors of *The Conformist,* the Magritte-de-Chirico sense of the isolation of open spaces that permeates *Spider's Stratagem,* the empty rooms filled with distorted figures that *Last Tango* draws from the works of Francis Bacon. Such painters convey an intimate, even voyeuristic, sense of the worlds they view at the same time that they emphasize the final mystery of the objects they show us—the bedspreads, the houses, the human bodies. They dramatize the inability of the artist—and Bertolucci's camera—to force these objects to yield their secrets. To take objects out of the film for interpretation . . . , or to disentangle the erotic scenes for praise or blame, ignores their meaning as part of the emotional lives of the characters to make them serve in the intellectual lives of the viewers. To emphasize with Kael "the new realism" of the film or "the terror of actual experience still alive on the screen" ignores Bertolucci's effort to convey the self-consciousness through which real things become reality rather than realism.

Both Jean Renoir and Roberto Rossellini use their films to convey the evasiveness and elusiveness of human character, the illusion of a "real" self, the basic irrelevance of psychological categories to full understanding. Bertolucci in *Last Tango* puts his own particular turn to this theme by using Brando's movie image to energize the inauthentic attempts to be authentic that are essential parts of the character Brando portrays. Everyone in *Last Tango* is cut off from everyone else, and yet each has some vision of the proper way to relate. Paul (Brando) thinks that by divesting himself of his past (another favorite theme of Bertolucci's) he can strengthen his jellied ego. Jeanne (Maria Schneider) thinks she can split herself between the abasements of her relationship to Brando and the worship she gets from Tom (Jean-Pierre Léaud), a young filmmaker who is making a cinéma verité film of her life as a prelude to their marriage. Léaud is Bertolucci's attack on the New Wave implication that all you have to do is follow someone long enough and ask the right questions and you'll understand him. (The sinking life preserver marked "L'Atalante" makes the satire more obvious.)

The "L'Atalante" reference is a false step, for Bertolucci with the manipulation of self-image that his characters go through to shore themselves up in crisis. . . . Bertolucci's characters aren't looking for relation with others, for love, for friendship, or for happiness. They are looking for salvation. And each is continually changing the nature of his particular salvation without telling anyone else. Paul's way is ultimately as cut off as either Jeanne's or Tom's. When she wants him to come without touching he agrees to try. . . . [The scene] may be funny and seem carefree, but it's horrible at the same time—another example of the use of sexual power to avoid emotional connection. Neither Paul, with his obvious attempts to work up feelings he doesn't have, nor Jeanne, with her inability to connect her lives with Paul and Tom, can marry emotion with action, either through violence or tenderness. (p. 267)

[The] true role of the sexuality in *Last Tango* is the way the characters make it up and manipulate it, not its realism, or its implicit statement against censorship. . . . [The film is] preoccupied with characters who desire for themselves and others an impossible purity and self-sufficiency, and who use their sexual natures to confirm and strengthen their separations from each other. . . .

So many recent films—*Last Tango, Cries and Whispers, Chloe in the Afternoon*—make demands on a combination of our intellectual and emotional sympathy as viewers that are not unique but are certainly different in degree from what we are used to in movies. More than any other art, movies are tentative forms for the emotions of the audience, forms that entrap you and relieve you of the self-consciousness of being an audience, of being separate. In films like those I've just mentioned, we are asked to involve ourselves in the partialities of the characters and seek out their mystery in our own uncertainties. This kind of emotional openness to the characters of a film is the first victim of critical overkill and impossibly heightened expectations. The richness of *Last Tango* is to show how human separations occur in the head, no matter how clothed or naked, apart or connected, the body. Its strength is not in its sexual explicitness, its system of symbols, or its scheme of characters, but in the insufficiency of those orders to explain finally what is going on. (p. 268)

Leo Braudy, "Blue Tango," in Partisan Review *(copyright © 1973 by Leo Braudy and Partisan Review, Inc.), Vol. XL, No. 2, 1973, pp. 262-68.*

JULIAN JEBB

The confusion of response which [*Last Tango in Paris*] excites arises, I think, from several sources: the opulent cinematography, Marlon Brando's performance and the sexuality are all accessible, each contributes to the shocking force of the film's impact, but simultaneously they can make one overlook the impenetrable obscurity of some of the imagery. I was sometimes reminded of Auden's early poems, where the force of the ideas and the grace of the language help one to ignore the privacies with which they are spiked. In Auden's case the images and phrases were teases, minute love letters from a subconscious mind to a desired body, perhaps; or snatches of clever dreams given the dignity of poetic utterance. With Bertolucci the subconscious *is* the poetry, and one of his films, *Partner,* which deals with schizophrenia, remains virtually impossible to understand as an idea or even a series of fragmented ideas. There is no co-ordination, and hence no synthesis.

In *Last Tango* there is a quite plain idea—it's very nearly a film with a message: sex as an instrument of power divorced from tenderness or curiosity results in chaos and despair. . . .

[Nearly every sequence is dense with references which are intrusive and puzzling.] To ignore them or to relegate them to some limbo area like 'texture' or 'atmosphere' is to abnegate the right to critical analysis. Yet to dwell on them too much is to reduce a very powerful film to a series of dubious Freudian speculations. But it is necessary to say that after two viewings of the film there is much that I do not understand and believe that no amount of careful scrutiny would help me, because it is Bertolucci's intention to mystify, as much as it is to illuminate and affront. (p. 80)

There is no American 'innocence' about Brando's Paul—he was born damaged and resentful and his solace has lain in his sexual magnetism and prowess. To adapt a memorable phrase of Henry James's, he has no 'visitable past'. This is crucial to the film. Paul's insistence on anonymity in his relationship with Jeanne is no gesture of vacuous narcissism: his belief that 'grunts and groans are better than names' is no less than a statement of his lack of identity and a sick man's desire to incorporate another in his illness. . . .

Unlike his forerunners, Godard and Truffaut, Bertolucci has tended to avoid literary references in his films. Perhaps because of his highly cultivated upbringing as the son of a poet and film critic in Italy he has found such reminders either 'phoney' or otiose. And yet his work is saturated in culture—in history. In *Last Tango* he confronts the decline and fall of America in the last dozen or so years. It is not fanciful, I think, to see Brando's Paul as representing a vision of America's decadence. Here was a country which seemed to pour out more energy and wealth than the world had ever known—the nation where strong puritan will combined with a pioneering spirit of enterprise and improvisation to produce a cornucopia of popular culture. Brando in his early films projected more powerfully and sensitively than any other actor a sense both of the violence and relaxation which lay behind. But neither America nor Brando has aged wisely. The cataclysms of racial and military disorder which have overtaken the country coincide neatly with the decline of Brando's hold over the audience. The Sixties saw him lend his talents to ill-conceived allegories of martyrdom, which often made him look less like the victim of injustice than the willing recipient of punishment.

The genius of Bertolucci is to have harnessed this masochism to a vision. *Last Tango* is an elegy to the European dream of America, and it takes the form of a psychoanalysis in which the patient acts out his fantasies not to an older, wiser man but to Jeanne, a new European, released from all preoccupations except pleasure. . . .

Behind the opening credits are two Francis Bacon portraits —a man and a woman. The male figure sits twisted, a smear of painted flesh; like Paul, one does not imagine that he remembers very many good things. The paint, as in the calmer portrait of the woman, is lavish; the distortions of the features are not necessarily emblematic of pain or horror, but rather to do with what Bacon has called the element of accident which for him is an essential ingredient of a work of art. There may be a clue here to the puzzling combination of symbols and techniques which contribute to the style of *Last Tango in Paris*. The dream of the fall of America seen in the disintegration of one man calls for extraordinary subconscious resources to be applied with the greatest confidence and skill. Hence perhaps the improvisation of Brando's Paul, or parts of it—which and what we are not invited to know. (p. 81)

Julian Jebb, "The Unvisitable Past: Bertolucci's American Dream," in Sight and Sound *(copyright © 1973 by The British Film Institute), Vol. 42, No. 2, Spring, 1973, pp. 80-1.*

NORMAN MAILER

[The separate backgrounds of Jeanne and Paul divide *Last Tango in Paris*] as neatly between biography and fornication as those trick highball glasses which present a drawing of a man or a woman wearing clothes on the outside of the tumbler and nude on the inside. Each time Brando and Schneider leave the room we learn more of their lives beyond the room; each time they come together, we are ready to go further. In addition, as if to enrich his theme for students of film, Bertolucci offers touches from the history of French cinema. The life preserver in *Atalante* appears by way of homage to Vigo, and Jean-Pierre Léaud of *The 400 Blows* is the TV director, the boy now fully grown. Something of the brooding echo of *Le Jour Se Lève* and Arletty is also with us, that somber memory of Jean Gabin wandering along the wet docks in the dawn, waiting for the police to pick him up after he has murdered his beloved. It is as if we are to think not only of this film but of other sexual tragedies French cinema has brought us, until the sight of each gray and silent Paris street is ready to evoke the lost sound of the *Bal musette* and the sad near-silent wash of the Seine. Nowhere as in Paris can doomed lovers succeed in passing sorrow, drop by drop, through the blood of the audience's heart.

Yet as the film progresses with every skill in evidence . . . , as the historic buggeries and reamings are delivered, and the language breaks through barriers not even yet erected—no general of censorship could know the armies of obscenity were so near!—as these shocks multiply, and lust goes up the steps to love, something bizarre happens to the film. It fails to explode. It is a warehouse of dynamite and yet something goes wrong with the blow-up. (p. 4)

The film, for all its power, has turned inside out by the end. We have been asked to follow two serious and more or less desperate lovers as they go through the locks of lust and defecation, through some modern species of homegrown cancer cure, if you will, and have put up with their modern depths—shit on the face of the beloved and find love!—only to discover a peculiar extortion in the aesthetic. . . . [We] never did get into an exploration of the catacombs of love, passion, infancy, sodomy, tenderness, and the breaking of emotional ice, instead only wandered from one onanist's oasis to another. . . .

[In] *Tango,* there is no gathering of forces for the conclusion, no whirling of sexual destinies (in this case, the audience and the actors) into the same funnel of becoming, no flying out of the senses in pursuit of a new vision, no, just the full charge into a blank wall, a masturbator's spasm—came for the wrong reason and on the wrong thought—and one is thrown back, shattered, too ubiquitously electrified, and full of criticism for the immediate past. Now the recollected flaws of the film eat at the pleasure. (p. 7)

[The core of the failure in *Last Tango*] is down in the difficulty of improvisation, in the recognition that improvisation which is anything less than the whole of a film is next to no improvisation. . . . Bertolucci is a superb young director, adventurous, steeped in film culture, blessed with cinematic grace. He gives us a movie with high ambition, considerable risk, and a sense of the past. Yet he plows into the worst trap of improvisation—it is the simple refusal of film makers to come to grips with the implacable logic of the problem. One does not add improvisation to a script which is already written and with an ending that is locked up. . . .

The fundamental demand upon improvisation is that it begin with the film itself, which is to say that the idea for the film and the style of improvisation ought to come out of the same thought. From the beginning, improvisation must live in the premise rather than be added to it. The notion is not easy to grasp, and in fact is elusive. (p. 8)

[Still], Bertolucci has given us a failure worth a hundred films like *The Godfather*. Regardless of all its solos, failed majesties, and off-the-mark horrors, even as a highly imperfect adventure, it is still the best adventure in film to be seen in this pullulating year. (p. 10)

Norman Mailer, "A Transit to Narcissus" (copyright © 1973 Nyrev, Inc.; used by permission of the author and his agents, Scott Meredith Literary Agency, Inc), in The New York Review of Books *(reprinted with permission from* The New York Review of Books; *copyright © 1973 Nyrev, Inc.), Vol. XX, No. 8, May 17, 1973, pp. 3-9.*

MARSHA KINDER and BEVERLE HOUSTON

One way of understanding [*Last Tango in Paris*] is to see it in the context of Bertolucci's earlier works. The central conflicts in *Last Tango* bear close similarities with those in *The Conformist* (1970), *The Spider's Stratagem* (1969), and *Before the Revolution* (1964). In all these films, one of the central characters is a young person trying to escape from his social class and family background, but who inevitably lives out the values from his past. Unconventionality is always associated with left-wing politics. (p. 186)

In *Revolution, Conformist* and *Last Tango,* each of these characters chooses between a conventional marriage and a dangerous love affair associated with childhood. In rejecting the romantic lover (who is neurotic or deviant by society's norms), and entering the marriage, each destroys the potential for growth and, as if to insure that the decision is final, each destroys the loved one. (pp. 186-87)

In all the films the sexual and political conflict is expressed in a brilliant dance sequence where romantic joy and conventional sterility are polarised. In *Before the Revolution* Gina and Fabrizio, who have just become lovers, are celebrating Easter Sunday in the bosom of their bourgeois family. The lovers begin to dance, and finally kiss. The extraordinary eroticism of the scene is achieved by drawing us into their intense feelings, expressed in the music and the subtle detail of their faces, revealed through the lingering close-up. . . . *Spider's Stratagem* presents a dance sequence which is the setting for one of the key flashbacks. The father, at his most heroically romantic moment, mocks the Fascists with his bold moves on the dance floor. In *The Conformist* the contrast is between the tight, controlled machinations of Marcello and his Fascist accomplice and the open, sweeping enchantment of the dance created by the two beautifully clad women. . . . But in *Last Tango* the forces of sterility are represented by the tango dancers, as they snap into ritualised postures and stylised grimaces to compete for a prize dispensed by the bourgeois establishment. It is in this context that Paul offers Jeanne a commitment of an older style, but his behaviour clearly shows that whatever he shares with the past, it is not the deadness. (pp. 187-88)

While all the films share an elaborately textured style, they also imply that style must express the politics of society and emotion in order to transcend an empty formalism. . . .

Although *Last Tango* also has a highly controlled visual surface and many of the same images as *The Conformist*—the elevated train, the frosted glass, the Hotel d'Orsay, the façades of Paris buildings, and images flashing through the windows of a moving train—the style is less self-consciously dazzling. The visuals enhance the romantic tone surrounding Jeanne and Paul rather than deflate or distract from its emotional impact. The stylistic parody is located primarily in the character of Tom the filmmaker. . . .

Tom is constantly translating real life into aesthetic principle. By contrast to the Brando character, Tom is aroused to passion and violence only when Jeanne threatens to withdraw from his movie. Pretending to himself that he is doing *cinéma vérité,* he actually needs to stage and control every movement and speech. He cannot conduct his romance without the help of film allusions. When he proposes to Jeanne, a life preserver marked *L'Atalante* (the name of the Vigo film in which marriage is seen as a trap) is knocked into the water, and promptly sinks. . . .

At worst, Tom offers a modern counterpart to the grotesque tango—a denial of love and spontaneity in the service of a sterile and ritualised art. At best, he offers a possibility for Jeanne that focuses on herself. Though he manipulates her into remembering her past, he gives her the gift of genuine recollections from her childhood. (p. 188)

Despite its close similarities to the other films, *Last Tango in Paris* is a unique artifact—significant in its aesthetic innovation, and almost overwhelming in its emotional intensity. Perhaps the most important reason for this heightened power is the conception and development of the Brando character. Whereas the other films centred on the young men who had to choose between the romantic and the conventional, this film focuses on the exotic, dangerous lover (this time a man). (p. 189)

Bertolucci strengthens the elemental appeal of the Brando character through the style of the film. In contrast to the earlier movies, *Last Tango* is developed through a relatively simple linear narrative, alternating between scenes of Paul and Jeanne in their secret space and shots of their lives in the complex city outside. An element of circularity helps to intensify the experience. Between Jeanne's discovery that Paul has abandoned the apartment and the tango sequence, many scenes from the opening encounter are repeated, but in reversed order. . . .

The fast movement and richly textured surface of the earlier films give way to other visual values. Nearly half of *Last Tango* takes place in the almost empty space of the apartment, which heightens the significance and intensity of what we are allowed to see. Within the apartment, the screen is filled with enormous close-ups of Jeanne and Paul, often bathed in golden light. Like the Francis Bacon paintings in the titles, the characters frequently appear alone in the empty space. . . .

Certain recurring images unite the worlds within and outside the apartment. Throughout the film, doors are opening into new experience or slamming shut in anger. Bertolucci is fascinated by frosted glass, which he uses to soften and romanticise, to distort, and to separate characters and settings. At key moments Jeanne must ride in a cage-like elevator. When she first looks at the apartment, the mood is ominous and the elevator gothic as it ascends out of camera range. . . . In the final scene the desperate chase ends with the dizzying movements of a hand-held camera tracking Paul as he runs up the spiral staircase after Jeanne, who is fleeing from him in the elevator. The great variety of angles and tones makes it difficult to identify which is the real trap—the marriage with Tom or the love affair with Paul. This ambiguity is also visually expressed in the recurring image of the mysterious draped form in the smaller room of the apartment. After Paul has moved out, Jeanne vents her anger by pulling off the drape, discovering that what lies beneath is only a pile of junk. (p. 190)

When the movie's over, two questions haunt us. Why does [Paul] try to move their love outside the room? And, why does she shoot him? Paul's offer of love can be seen in a variety of ways. He is a sadistic chauvinist who wants to extend his control over her in order to possess her entirely. He is a crazy masochist with a record of humiliations who wants to fail again. In pursuing her for the first time, he actually gives up control, perhaps in search of a way to die. . . . He is a courageous idealist, always willing to try again, no matter how many times he's failed, because love is the only thing that makes life meaningful. He is willing to take any risk, because it's the only way of growing. Each identity is true; each is partial. But his vision of love must be lived out with a woman like Jeanne, whose limitations preclude the success of the brave dream.

The final question remains: why does she shoot him? In courageous self-defence, or cowardly evasion? As Jeanne well knows, Paul's preoccupation has been with himself. . . . She also hates her helplessness in the face of his control. When Paul abandons the apartment, she grieves at the loss, but is angry because he has the power to end things and she does not. . . . Because her fantasies are not bound up with Tom's, she can resist his foolish attempts at control. But with Paul, like a trapped animal, she must kill her way out for survival and autonomy.

Her final act can also be seen as fear of risk-taking and involvement, a cowardice that Paul has recognised all along. When he first dictates the rules for their meetings in the room, he asks, 'Are you scared?' and she lies: 'No.' Later he tells her: 'You're always afraid.' When she describes the man she loves, she stresses his mystery and potency, but once outside the room, Paul becomes a vulnerable middle-aged man with a broken-down hotel, instead of a glamorous American sitting on the floor in the middle of a fantasy. She is afraid of the pain and humiliation that have brought him to this point; she's too young to take it on. So, she rejects him, despite her promises to endure anything for his sake. When she sees the reality that he is now presenting, she no longer knows him. Thus, in the end, as she stands bewildered, gun in hand, rehearsing her explanation for the police, the strange phrases that she utters are both true and false: 'I don't know who he is. He followed me on the street. He tried to rape me . . . He's a madman . . . I don't know his name. I don't know . . . I don't know who he is.'

All these interpretations of the final acts have validity in the work of art, combining forces that generate its richness and emotional intensity. But as the film's dark vision implies, they are not equally fruitful in life. Trapped in the conventions and fantasies of their culture, Tom is ridiculous, Paul is dead, and Jeanne is a killer. (p. 191)

Marsha Kinder and Beverle Houston, "Bertolucci and the Dance of Danger," in Sight and Sound *(copyright © 1973 by The British Film Institute), Vol. 42, No. 4, Autumn, 1973, pp. 186-91.*

STANLEY KAUFFMANN

Already [*Partner*] is heavily dated. Cinematically it's redolent of high sixties Godard; politically it's full of late sixties rhetoric and gesture. But for all its imitations, its slavish obedience to mode that poses as bravery, it shows some talent and authenticity.

With Bertolucci's later work, *The Spider's Stratagem, The Conformist,* and much of *Last Tango,* I felt as if I were walking barefoot over rotten fruit. Here I felt it much less; and felt that, despite the clichés, there was some conviction. Although Bertolucci had enlisted in the Godardian ranks and was snapping to attention and executing orders, he was doing it as a zealous partisan. In later pictures he became an interior decorator in cinematic excelsis.

For me, the best whole Bertolucci is still his first film shown here, *Before the Revolution;* his best sequences are the early sex scenes in *Last Tango;* but *Partner* has some genuinely good things in it. Like the very first shot—Clementi in a café, sitting next to a plate-glass window in which we also see his reflection. Our very first glimpse of the film tells us quietly what it's about. (p. 257)

Stanley Kauffmann, "'Partner'" (originally published in The New Republic, *Vol. 170, No. 6, February 9, 1974), in his* Living Images: Film Comment and Criticism *(copyright © 1971, 1972, 1973, 1974 by Stanley Kauffmann; reprinted by permission of Harper & Row, Publishers, Inc.), Harper, 1975, pp. 256-57.*

ROGER GREENSPUN

For part of its basic situation, and for the names given the central characters, [*Before the Revolution*] draws directly upon Stendhal's *The Charterhouse of Parma;* in its mood and tone it draws perhaps as significantly upon Flaubert's *Sentimental Education*. But in its meaning and its particular kind of appreciation for all the life it observes, *Before the Revolution* stands by itself, drawing essentially upon the sensibility and gift for understanding of the man who made it. (pp. 22-3)

Especially in its feeling for the lyric potential of each scene, *Before the Revolution* proceeds not toward one, but through many epiphanies. The film, which in the abstract recounts a series of small failures, becomes for the spectator a succession of glorious high points.

Some of these are minor triumphs: a first romantic meeting between Gina and Fabrizio near the Garibaldi monument in a square in Parma, with the whole sequence photographed from a great enough distance to include the activity of the square, and with the rhythm of the meeting derived from the tempo of a particularly lovely popular song. Some are evocations of the power inherent in a setting: Gina's departure from Parma, through the streets and squares of a city made beautiful by a light spring rain. . . .

Although Bertolucci's film is a love story, it makes use of a strong ideological content, and it quotes, in the manner of many recent films, from other movies, from books, and from folktales. Its purpose, however, is not to present ideology or even, finally, ideas. Rather, it is engaged in the precise and humane activity of discovering in each occurrence, the event; of finding for each human destiny, an answerable image. As in the greatest films of Renoir and Ophuls, it celebrates and commemorates the privileged moments of its personal dramas. It conditions an understanding of the inevitable sadness of private lives with an underlying sense of profound festivity. *Before the Revolution* begins with death, but it ends with a wedding. (p. 23)

Roger Greenspun, "'Before the Revolution'," in Film Comment *(copyright © 1974 by The Film Society of Lincoln Center; all rights reserved), Vol. 10, No. 3, May-June, 1974, pp. 22-3.*

ROBERT ZALLER

At the climactic moment of Bernardo Bertolucci's *Before the Revolution,* the film's hero, Fabrizio, confesses he cannot join the revolution because he suffers from "nostalgia for the present"; Paul in *Last Tango in Paris* closes conversation with: "Everything outside this place is bullshit." This sense of a desperately narrowed world, reduced to near zero both spatially and temporally, is at the heart of Bertolucci's art.

Bertolucci's four major films—*Before the Revolution* . . . , *The Spider's Stratagem* . . . , *The Conformist* . . . , and *Last Tango in Paris* . . .—constitute both a moral autobiography and a critique of late capitalist culture, a culture Bertolucci celebrates, rejects, belongs to, and attempts to transcend in the most bourgeois possible way: by art. Each of the four films is focussed on a single male consciousness adrift in an uncentered world, all middle-class, and all—with the exception of Marcello in *The Conformist*—unattached and unemployed. (p. 807)

The malaise which afflicts both Bertolucci's heroes and the world around them is a decadent but seemingly indestructible capitalism. From the first sweeping shots of Parma which begin *Before the Revolution,* we are contained in a fortress, complete, self-defined, unassailable: the charterhouse is the city itself. Within its walls, Fabrizio conducts his brief, abortive revolt. It consists of the temporary breakoff of his engagement to Clelia, a Della Robbia-like beauty who typifies the vacuous "normality" of middle-class life, and an episodic liaison with his aunt, Gina. Fabrizio's violation of family taboo does not enable him to break free of convention, however, but only sucks him deeper in. (pp. 807-08)

Beneath [its] "manifest content" of events, . . . *The Spider's Stratagem* has the architecture of a dream, and, in its hallucinatory directness, its unnerving symmetries, its abrupt disjunctions and above all the marvelously sustained tonality of enigma and menace which leads with such perfect rightness to the sudden, surrealist ending, it must be considered one of the most successful renderings of subconscious imagery in the history of film. If there is a natural debt to Buñuel, it must be said that Bertolucci's use of dream technique in *The Spider's Stratagem* is far more subtle, and far more deeply integrated into the structure of the whole film, than anything Buñuel had achieved by 1969. (p. 810)

The Spider's Stratagem is a film about the complicity between ruler and ruled on which dictatorship ultimately rests. The Resistance is an illusion because its leader is a double agent; exposed, he pleads not for his own life but for the illusion instead. There may be no resisters; there must be a Resistance. It is a dialectical necessity: every dictatorship calls forth a Resistance; *ergo,* no Resistance, no dictatorship. Is there really a Mussolini at all? Yes, because the Resistance is planning to assassinate him, thereby vouching for his existence. (This is the riddle which Athos Jr. confronts at the railway station. Just as Mussolini's train failed to arrive, so does his: there is no train. But Athos has denied the father too late; the truth no longer sets him free.)

Resistance is the mask with which dictatorship covers its face; which is to say, it is theatre. The assassination of Athos Magnani is staged at the opera: theatre within theatre. In *Before the Revolution,* too, Fabrizio stages his public reconciliation with Clelia at a performance of Verdi's *Macbeth.* In both films, then, opera appears as the theatre *par excellence* of bourgeois illusion. Yet here again, Bertolucci's attitude remains ambivalent. On the one hand, he revels in the opulence and rhetoric of opera; on the other, he treats it as a paradigm of decadence. The operatic becomes, in its broadest sense, that which the Italian is unable to transcend—the seduction of the gorgeous, of pomp, of spectacle, so intimately bound up with the whole Catholic tradition. As Bertolucci has confessed: "I need a certain lushness." (pp. 812-13)

The Spider's Stratagem is, in the final analysis, a monumental fantasy on the primal wish of becoming one's own progenitor, of cheating death by doubling back on one's fate. The result, however, is not immortality but petrification. The abolition of time, the deathward progression of father to son to the son beyond, gives us not the truth of eternity but the lie that time stands still. And the political name of this lie is: Fascism.

The Conformist is at first glance a very different film. Of all Bertolucci's films to date, it is the one most firmly rooted in historical time and place; the superb evocation of Paris in the thirties was an element singled out for praise by almost all reviewers. It is also the one with the most conventionally developed plot, offering suspense and intrigue, a love triangle, and a bloody end. It offers, too as the other films do not, a clear, indeed almost doctrinaire rationale for the protagonist's behavior. (pp. 813-14)

The narrative progress of *The Conformist* is, however, so often broken by surrealist interjection, stylized gesture and action, and thematic refrains from the earlier films, that a surface reading is clearly inadequate. Upon examination it turns out to be, like all of Bertolucci's work, a meditation on the uses of freedom in the prison of time. (p. 814)

Determinism versus free moral choice is the hidden conflict in all Bertolucci's work; there is a war in him between a Freudian conservative and a Marxist radical. This is too simple, of course, because his best work represents a powerful synthesis in which the interaction of sexual, social and political repression is fused in the terms of his art. Bertolucci's problem is that the very intensity of this fusion skirts the pitfall of determinism; the interlock of the system is so coordinated, so airtight on every level, that no escape seems possible. Yet if it *were* airtight, it would be simply co-extensive with reality, and, as such, invisible. To perceive the system as evil, to perceive it as a "system" at all, argues the existence of moral consciousness and therefore moral responsibility. Fabrizio perceives it very well in *Before the Revolution,* and Athos in *The Spider's Stratagem* at the moment when he discovers the truth about his father. This is also the meaning of the myth of the Cave which Quadri tells for Marcello. The Cave is a near-perfect totalitarian system whose citizens are so conditioned they spontaneously put any dissenter to death; yet all anyone has to do to see through the lie on which it rests is to stand on his feet and look up at the light. (p. 818)

[In] *The Conformist,* as in *The Spider's Stratagem,* the basic attraction of Fascism is its arbitrary resolution of the Oedipal conflict. The state assumes a false paternalism that legitimates all behavior obedient to its commands, thus absolving the individual of all responsibility for his acts. The strength of tyranny lies in men's avoidance of freedom; the mystique of its power is the collective consent to illusion.

This implies that Fascism, or indeed any totalitarian system, rests on an ultimate choice, even if that choice is nothing but the refusal to choose. Marcello's choice is his dream [in which, symbolically, he admits his blindness and wants Quadri to cure it], carried over as fantasy during the ride, and stupor and paralysis during the assassination. He negates his free will by remaining deliberately unconscious of his choice, but it is a choice nonetheless. Athos in *The Spider's Stratagem,* on the other hand, is clearly aware of his choice—to expose his father or not—but his consciousness is embedded within the whole dream context of the film. Because we have adjusted to this context, Athos' paralysis of will, his failure to act, seems as natural to us as when, in our own dreams, we see disaster coming but walk right toward it. Marcello puts himself deliberately to sleep in a waking situation, while Athos believes himself wide awake in the midst of a dream. This is why Athos' behavior is credible to us, while Marcello's is merely contemptible. Clearly, the difference is very largely a function of the cinematography itself. *The Spider's Stratagem* is shot in a neutral, nonconnotative style, mostly at eye level, whereas *The Conformist* is often obliquely angled, particularly from above, or busy in corners askew from the principal action. The camera's perspective thus continually antithesizes that of the characters', carrying on a running critique of the action, and implying a different order of reality. The surface realism of the film is also an important element in our judgment. (pp. 818-19)

Coming from the earlier films, one is immediately struck by the absence of a political dimension in *Last Tango*. If this film has any politics at all, it is the anti-politics of anarchism. Paul, the chief protagonist, mentions offhandedly that he was once a "revolutionary," but also a sailor, bartender and . . . actor, as if these occupations were all of equal value or equally of none. The comment of the bourgeois Jeanne is even more ironic: she is a collector of revolutionary antiques, e.g. an executioner's alarm clock.

In the love nest he shares with Jeanne, Paul repudiates the very idea of a society: "Everything outside this place is bullshit." Constituting himself a republic of one, an empire of two, he exorcizes the outside world with blasphemy. (p. 820)

Paul's refusal to "know names" or observe the other rituals of communication thus stems from his own failure to understand Rosa. Working backwards from her inexplicable suicide to the mysterious solitude of her life—the life they ostensibly shared together—Paul is overwhelmed by the futility of even trying to understand. . . . (pp. 820-21)

Paul is on a downward spiral throughout the film. He is still trying to live and cope, but the momentum of his life is carrying him toward destruction. From the opening shot of the film, where Paul cries "Fucking God!" at the elevated train that roars overhead on the Rue Jules Verne, the camera depicts a hunted man. The space he inhabits—a dark, mean universe of hallways, landings, alleys—is ceaselessly narrowed, divided, cut. The split-screen image on which the opening credits are flashed serves as a visual leitmotif for the entire film, and Bertolucci's resourcefulness in using windows, mirrors and doorways to divide the screen and isolate Paul seems endless.

The metaphor of fissure extends to the characters as well. There is constant play on the theme of divided, false or missing identity. Rosa's mother rummages through her things looking for a suicide note that will "explain"; Jeanne searches Paul's pockets for something with his name on it. In the shaving scene, Paul turns to Jeanne with half a face of lather, and she to him with half a face of makeup. Every face becomes a mask, a trap door of identity, behind which the self lurks, impenetrable and incommunicable. Paul violently unmasks others, but insists on remaining hidden himself; he has a dozen punning names for his penis, but none for himself. Stroking Jeanne with the flat of his razor, he offers to write his name on her face: not only a lapidary summation of his approach to interpersonal relations, but of his conviction that revelation entails destruction, either of the other or of oneself.

Yet Paul himself is stymied by the ultimate mask. As he sits by Rosa's coffin, her face is "beatific," and she lies "laughing in a little lake of flowers." He can't stand it: ". . . these goddam leaves in your face. You never wore make-up—all this fucking shit. I'm going to take this off your mouth." . . . Paul rubs off the lipstick and rouge with his own saliva. He touches Rosa's naked cheek, and then "*buries his face in his arms. He cries, his face hidden.*" (Italics mine)

It is at this point that Paul explicitly reveals his own death-wish:

> Rosa, my love . . . forgive me . . . I don't know why you did it. I'd do it too if I knew how. I just don't know. I need to find a way.
> (pp. 824-25)

Suicide is not simple: each death has a different door. "All it took for you to get out was a thirty-five cent razor," Paul says bitterly. There is envy for the act, but contempt for the means. Paul needs a *beau geste;* there is no way to imagine him bleeding to death in a bathtub.

The instrument he finds is Jeanne. Paul closes the apartment. When Jeanne discovers this, she is profoundly antagonized: it is a desertion that reminds her of her father's. Paul now accosts her on the street. He is combed, dressed; everything about him is changed. Breathlessly, he spills out details about himself: "Listen, I'm forty-five. I'm a widower. I've got a little hotel that's kind of a dump. . . ." He does not reveal his identity so much as scuttle it. There is nothing left of the powerful ironic reticence, the mastery and pride. This is a clown with a British accent, a Cagney accent, any voice but his own. And finally there is the most invidious, most ominous role of all: "Just a sip for Daddy." Pursuing Jeanne through the nightmare of the tango contest and the grey indifferent streets of Paris, up the four flights of her mother's apartment, Paul corners her at last, and, donning her father's military cap, mockingly salutes her: "How do you like your hero? Over easy or sunny-side up?"

What Jeanne sees is the madman who was her lover, the stranger who might have been her father, Paul's face and her father's superimposed on an anonymous middle-aged man who has broken into her apartment. Overcome by confusion, horror, and psychic violation, she grabs for her father's gun, the last line of sanity and defense in her life. Paul demands to know her name. "Jeanne," she replies, and pulls the trigger. Paul's prophecy is thus fulfilled: the moment of revelation is the moment of death.

This bare narrative summary can only draw out the main thread of action in these brilliant and hectic final scenes, but, if that were all, they would be little more than a study in clinical psychology. What raises them to the level of a great and fully human art is the razor-fine ambiguity that is sustained to the very end. For Paul is sincere: he really means to win Jeanne. Life and death war within him up to the moment when the colonel's revolver settles all questions. But Paul's will to live is baffled and blind; it affronts where it means to seduce, appalls where it means to assure. Like a man in quicksand, he sinks in deeper with each frantic step he takes. In his last love speech he is finally honest, naked in his need as he had never been in the apartment. Yet this coincides with his fatal gesture of playing the colonel, so that his two appeals climax simultaneously. Which is the image Jeanne ultimately shoots at: the man who pleads for life or the one who begs for death? In either case, Death is the winner; it played a perfect hand.

In purely cinematic terms, *Last Tango* is a remarkable tour de force, running the gamut from soft, deliquescent suspensions in glass to compositions of a formal, almost Bergman-like severity. There are moments of startling invention and beauty: Paris ablaze through the window in the light of late afternoon; the sudden apparition of the night light like a risen moon when Jeanne takes the elevator to the apartment for the first time. The dance theme which . . . figures so prominently in all Bertolucci's work, achieves in *Last Tango* a striking richness and variety. There is not only the tango scene itself, with its devastating comment on the decadence of an entire society, but a host of other quasidance improvisations: the stylized combat between Tom and Jeanne in the subway, Tom's failed dance for Jeanne in the courtyard to the accompaniment of Mozart's Sinfonia Concertante; even the workmen who install furniture in the apartment go through a miniature ballet. Part of this is Bertolucci's own irrepressible animal spirits breaking through, a kind of cavorting; but it is also partly a mind that thinks naturally of expressive movement in terms of dance. Bertolucci is a born choreographer. (pp. 825-26)

Last Tango represents a marked advance in Bertolucci's delineation of character. This is of course most obvious in the case of Paul, who, in Brando's hands, is a many-nuanced figure, a man of compassion as well as violence, pity as well as rage. . . .

But Bertolucci's advance in the handling of female characters in *Last Tango* is also notable. The center of narrative consciousness in his first three films is exclusively masculine; events are perceived through men's eyes only. Paul in *Last Tango* remains the center of gravity, but he is no longer the sole angle of vision. What Jeanne feels and thinks, and, ultimately, how she acts, is as crucial to the film as what Paul does. In the last analysis, however, perhaps the most important personage in *Last Tango* is Rosa. It is her act that seals Paul's fate; it is her hotel, that mysterious honeycombed artifact, that is his tomb. Rosa's presence haunts the film; the conundrum of her life is never solved. Paul's soliloquy beside her coffin is Bertolucci's own ironic homage to the mystery of woman, *i.e.* her impenetrability to man.

In this context we may consider the charge of chauvinism that has been raised against *Last Tango*. Bertolucci has been accused of exalting a *macho* ethic of sexual exploitation and super-potency in Paul. We can do nothing to mitigate the hopeless shallowness of this point of view. (p. 827)

If Paul's view of womankind is less than fully rounded, it is pointless to blame Bertolucci: he is presenting women as such men are doomed to experience them. In an Oedipal-capitalist culture? It is the only one Bertolucci, and the rest of us, have got.

In an essay on revolution and rebellion, Octavio Paz says of Baudelaire: "His rebellion was a nostalgia for childhood and an homage to power: consciousness of separation and a yearning to return to the 'green paradise.'" It is a measure of our dilemma that the remark could equally apply to Bertolucci: we have lived so long with a culture crisis that it has become a tradition instead. This much Bertolucci has already told us: will he seek now for a way out? (p. 828)

Robert Zaller, "Bernardo Bertolucci, or Nostalgia for the Present," in The Massachusetts Review *(reprinted from* The Massachusetts Review; © *1975 The Massachusetts Review, Inc.), Vol. XVI, No. 4, Autumn, 1975, pp. 807-28.*

DANIEL LOPEZ

The premise fundamental to [*The Conformist* and *Last Tango in Paris*] is an indictment of one of society's cornerstones, the bourgeois family, all too apt to suppress manifestations of spontaneous feeling in its members, stifling individuality by forcing it into a uniform limbo of bland conformity. The suppression of natural feelings is not, however, tantamount to their elimination, and thus they are destined to resurface in a distorted guise. For the protagonist of *The Conformist,* Marcello Clerici, an outlet, condoned by his society, is to be found in the potential savagery of Fascism; for the sequestered lovers of *Last Tango in Paris,* Jeanne and Paul, release is sought in a primeval sexual relationship divorced from all temporal and social conditioning. In both instances the influence of the bourgeois family proves itself to be more forceful than all attempts at evading its repressive teachings: neither Marcello, Jeanne nor Paul succeed in integrating their inner reality with an outside world at variance with it. (p. 1)

All three instances of would-be nuclear, bourgeois families in *The Conformist* are made incomplete by the absence, explicit or implicit, of the father. Marcello's father has long since been committed to an asylum for the insane, leaving Marcello and his mother to act out an incipient Oedipal drama of which neither is conscious. Giulia's father, on the other hand, is more definitively absent having died several years previously, leaving behind a daughter and wife whose suffocating effusiveness may well have been instrumental in hastening her husband's demise. Marcello and Giulia, the ill-starred offspring of these two fragmented families, in their turn wed and produce a child who, like her parents, is destined to remain fatherless, if not because of Marcello's incumbent insanity as the film concludes, then by virtue of his no longer latent homosexuality which could not do otherwise than have grave repercussions on the unity of his family. Both Marcello and Giulia demonstrate that once the *pater-familias* fails to fulfill the needs of his progeny, the child will compulsively search for a surrogate figure to replace him. Marcello, moreover, shows himself to be capable of participation in the destruction of this surrogate once it, too, falls short of his expectations just as its prototype, Marcello's father, had done originally. (pp. 2-3)

[Marcello's] insane father, redeemed morally by the presence of an active conscience, has failed in his son's eyes to live up to an ideal of strength and authority, and Marcello is unrelenting in his vindictiveness. The son tries obliquely to destroy still further his father by confronting him remorselessly with the root cause of his guilt. And still true to the Oedipal formula, Marcello also has Alberi eliminated, his father's latest successor in the sexual favors of his mother. (p. 3)

Marcello's attraction towards the Fascist State some years later is then as inevitable as it is absolute. Authoritarian, stern and inflexible, with its compelling aura of purpose, Fascism precludes the necessity on the part of the individual for making decisions; rather the State decides for him in much the same way that a father does for his son. (p. 4)

The three ineffectual father figures in *The Conformist*—Marcello's father, Italo, and Quadri—together with what they represent are counterbalanced and complemented by as many forceful chauffeurs: Lino, Alberi and Manganiello, the latter Clerici's political conscience. They serve to underscore the protagonist's passivity, his incapacity to assume the initiative at decisive moments in his existence. It is Manganiello, Marcello's supposed subordinate, who finally executes the orders for the Quadri assassination, just as earlier he had executed Marcello's orders in disposing of his mother's lover, Alberi. All three men act as contrasts to Clerici, emphasizing his failure to adopt a genuinely assertive role in life due to the refutation of his individuality.

If Anna is drawn towards Quadri by his equanimity and mature years, Giulia is drawn to (and marries) Marcello because she mistakenly identifies his innate reserve and sobriety with a bourgeois ideal of responsible, paternal authority. Nor is he without precedent in her life, for following her own father's death she became a passive victim of the lust of the lawyer Perpuzio, a sexagenarian pillar of bourgeois society given also to blackmail and the penning of anonymous, defamatory letters, as well as having been her seducer. . . . In keeping with her open nature, she divulges to Marcello all details of her six-year affair as they travel by train towards Paris to begin their honeymoon. . . . Marcello proceeds to re-enact Giulia's defloration, deriving vicarious pleasure from envisaging himself as a fatherly figure coercing a pubescent girl. Marcello not only seeks a father substitute himself but fleetingly fulfils that same function when it is tainted with sexual corruption.

The Conformist demonstrates with equal emphasis the political and sexual leanings of its protagonist once all impulses on his part towards individuality have been quashed. *Last Tango in Paris,* while broadly resuming the same theme, illuminates primarily the sexual repercussions of bourgeois repression. As had been suggested by *The Conformist*'s revelling and indulgence in Fascist opulence, Bertolucci's own personal conflicts were not resolved at the film's conclusion. He carries them over into *Last Tango in Paris* so that the concerns which goad its characters are once more the director's personal concerns.

Brando as Paul is at once a father figure and lover to the girl Jeanne. The American expatriate, forty years old and worldly, is like Marcello in that he too is at odds with a bourgeois society that would compel him to be other than what he is. His romantic, unrealizable objective is to release his emotions and instincts outside the conventional and oppressive behavioral patterns sanctioned by society. He fails precisely because he attempts this with the collusion of a girl who is the very embodiment of the bourgeoisie and as such is ultimately incapable of sloughing off its tenets. She submits to his experiment only while he does not encroach upon her world, and while she is still able to regard him as a strong, paternal surrogate. Once he is no longer an enigma to her, once he ceases to be purposeful and in full command, the establisher of the rules of the relationship as much as would be a father, she destroys him as remorselessly (and with infinitely more directness) as Marcello had done with his fallen idols. During one of the most mutually degrading and violent sequences in the film, a rape involving sodomy, Paul forces Jeanne to repudiate verbally the institutions that nurtured her:

> Paul: I'm going to tell you about the family. That holy institution, meant to breed virtue into savages. I want you to repeat it after me.
> Jeanne: No and no!
> Paul: Repeat it!
> His fists dig into her, hurting her.
> Paul: Holy family. Come on, say it. Go on! Holy family, the church of good citizens.
> Jeanne: Church . . . Good citizens (cries).
> Paul loosens his hold.
> Paul: Say it. The children are tortured until they tell their first lie.
> Jeanne: The children . . .
> Paul: Where the will is broken by repression.
> Jeanne: Where the will is broken . . . repression (sobs).
> Paul: Where freedom is assassinated.
> Jeanne: Freedom is . . . (sobs).
> Paul: Is assassinated . . . Freedom is assassinated by egotism . . . family.
> Jeanne: . . . family.

The formula of *The Conformist* remains constant even if the format has changed. (pp. 6-8)

The prompt arrival of Paul's mother-in-law, alone, suggests a possible motive for Rosa's having married such an unlikely candidate for matrimony as Paul: Rosa's father has not made the journey to Paris because he is confined to bed with asthma, rendered impotent as are all fathers representative of the bourgeoisie. Confinement within an asylum or within a sick-room—the difference is minimal. Just as Jeanne sees in Paul a surrogate father, so also Rosa may well have done in the early days of her relationship with him. And although he proves with time to be an imperfect candidate for the role, she nevertheless strives to create a double for him in her lover Marcel by presenting him with a bathrobe and a bottle of whiskey identical to those habitually used by her husband. (pp. 9-10)

If [Jeanne] retreats readily into the apartment on Rue Jules Verne, it is because it enables her return to a childhood wherein she can realize her subconscious incestuous desires. Her very physical appearance attests to this regression which she also shares with Paul. Whereas her hair in the film's opening episodes was pinned demurely back, as her relationship with her lover progresses, she wears it curled girlishly about her face. Jeanne recalls her father as a dashing, alluring hero who taught her how to fire his pistol (an obvious symbol of what for her is a "ha-penis") when she was a child. The discovery among his belongings of the photograph of a comely young Berber girl adds a further dimension of virile prowess to his memory which the presence of his boots, uniform, kepi and gun serves to keep alive in the mind of his wife and daughter. (p. 10)

When her lover within the sanctum of her parents' apartment dons her father's military cap, simultaneously incarnating him and mocking his memory with a cocky grin, Jeanne retaliates by killing him with the colonel's pistol. As Paul lies curled in a fetal position, the logical conclusion to his psychological regression, Jeanne begins to intone her final refutation of him. By failing to recognize and respect the boundary between symbol and reality, between father figure and father proper, Paul triggers off his own destruction.

The underlying motives in Bertolucci's *The Conformist* and *Last Tango in Paris* originate in their fractured bourgeois families with the attitude of the child towards the patriarch. When he disappoints the expectations of his progeny either through some innate weakness in his character, through absence or through death, the child undertakes an unsuccessful search for a surrogate to supplant the relationship for which he yearns. This futile quest draws Marcello in

The Conformist and Jeanne in *Last Tango* into perilous love affairs linked to their respective childhoods. By disclaiming their romantic love, Marcello his for Anna, Jeanne hers for Paul, in favor of a banal marriage, they renounce definitively all possibility of integrating their inner realities with the outside world. As if to make certain that their decision is irreversible, each slays the person he loves. In so doing they destroy all vestiges of their individuality and all potential for subsequent development. (pp. 10-11)

Daniel Lopez, "The Father Figure in 'The Conformist' and in 'Last Tango in Paris'," in Film Heritage *(copyright 1976 by F. A. Macklin), Vol. 11, No. 4, Summer, 1976, pp. 1-11.*

LINDA L. WILLIAMS

Beyond [their] basic theme, the obvious similarities [between Bertolucci's *Before the Revolution* and *The Charterhouse of Parma*,] Stendhal's rich and sprawling novel of courtly intrigue, are few. Only the names of the principal characters, the Parmesan locale, and a shadowy outline of the novel's plot remain, primarily in the love of Gina for her young nephew Fabrizio. Yet, it is Bertolucci's willingness to depart from the most familiar elements of this classic novel—the famous Battle of Waterloo, the melodramatic courtly intrigues, the imprisonment in the tower, and even its Nineteenth Century setting—that allows his film to come so close to its literary source. This particular fidelity does not involve the attempt to *be* Stendhal's novel, but rather, to establish a contemporary and parallel relation to its basic theme. Thus, Bertolucci does not try to render all the novel's twists and turns of plot and subplot, but to render instead its nostalgia for a youthful and joyous way of life that Stendhal saw disappearing from his own modern world. (p. 215)

Since Stendhal's novel is in many ways a celebration of youth tinged with the nostalgia of its loss, Bertolucci has understood that the automatic and indiscriminate nostalgia that almost any period piece elicits in an audience would obscure the real point of the novel's sense of the past. This sense of the past consists of a much more specific nostalgia for moments that have only just gone by. It is a nostalgia for the recent past and for the present as it becomes the past. Thus, Bertolucci's contemporary setting is more than a fashionable "updating" of an old story. It makes the story his own in a very personal way. (p. 216)

The basic conflict in both Stendhal's and Bertolucci's works develops from the insertion of a hero whose values are those of a former time into a more contemporary setting. . . . In both cases the conflicts that arise between the habits of the old era and the demands of the new become the focus of the work. (p. 217)

[Both] novel and film lament a lost idealism that seems to have passed forever. But there is a significant difference between the use of this nostalgia in novel and film. Unlike the novel, the film suggests that this nostalgia, though enormously seductive, can become a trap. . . .

In Bertolucci this nostalgia has become internalized in the self-consciousness of the hero himself. We are constantly aware of the narcissism of a youth who is already melancholy about the passing of his accustomed way of life. Thus, even though both Stendhal's and Bertolucci's heroes are diverted from their youthful, revolutionary visions, Stendhal's Fabrice remains an impassioned and integrated personality uncontaminated by the nostalgia Stendhal's narrator evokes through him, while Bertolucci's Fabrizio is paralyzed by his persistent concern for the past.

This sense of the "pastness" of Stendhal's story is extremely important to the novel's nostalgic tone. Our feeling of distance from the events that are related continually reminds us that these events, though temporarily conjured up by the narrator, belong irretrievably to the past.

Bertolucci's primary problem of adaptation was therefore: how to achieve, in a medium famous for its eternal presentness, this sense of the past, this narrative distance. To do this, he includes several present tense stream of consciousness monologues, much in the manner of Stendhal's famous soliloquys, within the larger framework of a narrative past tense established by written titles and dates that introduce each section of the film. These written titles give the film some of the temporal structure of Stendhal's novel. (p. 219)

More significantly, Bertolucci employs several techniques that approximate the novel's attempt to portray certain moments and events as filtered through the melancholy consciousness of a narrator who knows that these special moments will never recur. In the river lament [narrated by Puck], for example, the freeze frame and voice-over narration combine to achieve this effect. . . . The effect of [the] frozen image and past tense narration is to break up the previous rhythm of the film's succession of images. By virtue of its stillness this frozen composition has already become a part of the past. (pp. 219-20)

Bertolucci's film translates [Stendhal's] narrative tempo into cinematic rhythms. He arrests time in the freeze frame, or, in a more striking technique, repeats a moment of time, often from a slightly different perspective, in an effort to seize upon and commemorate the special nature of the moment. During Fabrizio and Gina's first embrace, for example, a dolly shot that moves from a medium-long shot behind Gina to a medium-close side shot of them both as they begin their embrace is repeated several times, each time coming a little closer to their embrace.

These striking techniques point the way to a freer kind of filmic adaptation of a hallowed literary classic. Bertolucci's film never tries to *be* Stendhal's novel, yet it constantly defines itself in relation to the novel through an independent development of the novel's original theme. Thus, *Before the Revolution* both captures *The Charterhouse of Parma*'s fundamental nostalgia *and* invests this nostalgia with a characteristically modern irony. Because of the greater self-awareness of Bertolucci's hero, because the novel's nostalgia has been internalized in his character, Fabrizio's attachment to the past is tinged not only with the melancholic commemoration that one finds in Stendhal, but with the added irony that this attachment will cut him off from the very experiences that would make his past worth remembering. Thus, the modern Fabrizio's choice of a safe and static bourgeois existence is only superficially seductive. In fact, it is a reductive vision of life's possibilities. Bertolucci's brilliance lies in his ability both to seduce us with the static beauty of bourgeois life and culture, and to criticize subtly the single-minded choice of this mode of life. (pp. 220-21)

Linda L. Williams, "Stendhal and Bertolucci: The Sweetness of Life Before the Revolution," in Literature/Film Quarterly *(© copyright 1976 Sal-*

*isbury State College), Vol. IV, No. 3, Summer, 1976, pp. 215-21.**

GEOFFREY NOWELL-SMITH

At heart *1900* is elegiac, and what it inscribes on its large historical canvas is a lament, in which something akin to a mourning for a lost wholeness plays a dominant role. Consider the temporal unfolding of the film: a world of childhood and unquestioned patriarchy; its interruption by war, class struggle and fascism; and a liberation which is a false dawn. Or the basic dualistic structure: two grandfathers and their two grandchildren (and for one of these grandchildren two 'fathers'), two heroines, two social classes (landowners and peasantry) and two social forces (socialism and fascism)—with the duality becoming more antagonistic as the film proceeds. At the beginning there is harmony; in the centre, conflict; and at the end, uncertainty. If the theme of a 'golden age' is traditional to pastoral, the use alongside it of an explicit mechanism of splitting adds an unexpected psychoanalytic dimension.

The splitting is of a type encountered elsewhere in Bertolucci's films: the choices confronting the young landowner Alfredo . . . , between decadence, submissive conformism and resistance, are very much the same as those between which the young hero of *Before the Revolution* has to decide, while the notion of a hero split into two characters is familiar from *Partner*. The crossing of the pastoral motif with that of the split character is one of the film's most interesting features, and also the most disturbing, since the formal movement towards a 'progressive' resolution is regularly and insistently matched by movements of return. These returns crop up with varying degrees of explicitness and formal efficacy; some are contained within the structure, others are not. But they all tend to contaminate each other, with the result that the film remains in some way or other always bounded by a perspective which cannot cope with the present because everything it shows is a re-projection, however indirect, of the past, whether socio-historical or psychic and individual.

In spite of this tendency towards regression . . . , *1900* is not without its splendours. Above all it has a power to surprise, to show the expected event in an unexpected light. In this sense its eccentricity, and the incorporation of this eccentricity into the staid format of the historical spectacular, proves to be its redemption.

Geoffrey Nowell-Smith, "Film Reviews: '1900'," in Sight and Sound *(copyright © 1978 by The British Film Institute), Vol. 47, No. 2, Spring, 1978, p. 121.*

STANLEY KAUFFMANN

The line of Bernardo Bertolucci's career is beginning to look as wretched as Robert Altman's. Bertolucci, too, began with something more than promise (*Before the Revolution,* even *Partner*). Very soon he began to swamp that promise with self-intoxicating dexterity and egocentric artiness, which is the only kind of artiness actually (*The Spider's Strategy* and *The Conformist*). Then, like Altman, he peaked with a film that was more bulk than weight. (*Last Tango in Paris* can now be seen as Bertolucci's *Nashville.*) Not surprisingly, the same critical pumping stations that later inflated Altman also blew Bertolucci. Then, inevitably, came the shrinking into mannerism and derivation (*1900*), while the laurelers were left holding their oversize laurels. Now comes *Luna,* a picture so ludicrously bad that one is almost tempted to pity Bertolucci. But no, he is a monstrous and disgusting artist, not a failed authentic one, and for the sake of the authentic ones, successful or failed, Bertolucci has to be seen as what he is: a clever, cheap exploiter of everything that comes to his hand, including the talent he began with (like Altman).

I can't even grant that he started *Luna* with a serious idea, even with a serious ambition toward moods and textures for which he had to find an idea. From its first moment, *Luna* feels like self-indulgence, lazy preening while lying on the audience's lap. . . . When the film isn't being portentously symbolic, it's being empty—one or the other. The emptiness of the way that many beautiful locations are used soon becomes exploitation. . . .

What does this big iridescent tumor of a film pretend to be? Underneath the two hours of pomposity is a story that, essentially, is quite old-fashioned, for all its blatantly daring detail. . . .

The theme apparently—not so apparently, in fact—is that the boy has to be surrogate for his father until his father appears, surrogate in both his own life and his mother's. He and Mom are very close. At one point she masturbates him in his moment of need (a mother's work is never done); at another, they come very close to incest, a scene that ends with his head resting on the crotch of her panties. The publicity tells us that originally Bertolucci wanted mother and son to Do It but decided that it would end the picture right there, nothing could follow it. Wrong. He could have finished with a trio, non-operatic, mother, son, and long-lost father. Well, maybe next time. And maybe next time, some glimmer of conviction, of internal imperative for the goings-on. I don't care much for Malle's film about incest, *Murmur of the Heart,* but at least it had an inner rationale. (p. 26)

Stanley Kauffmann, "Moonshine" (reprinted by permission of Brandt & Brandt Literary Agents, Inc.; copyright © 1979 Stanley Kauffmann), in The New Republic, *Vol. 181, No. 16, October 20, 1979, pp. 26-8.*

JOHN SIMON

Luna is a dreadfully poseurish film, whether Caterina, stopping at the gate to the Villa Verdi, improbably apostrophizes the filmmaker's favorite composer, or whether the neurotic homelife of mother and son is shown in the most superficial terms despite all that sensationalistic detail. Human behavior is treated capriciously and mechanistically, so that actions arise not out of psychological necessity or, failing that, some narrative logic, but out of Bertolucci's presumable desire to purge, without in the least clarifying them, his personal problems. We do not learn what the violence and vandalism on screen are really about, and seem to be getting would-be catharsis without confession, coming to terms without coming to grips, *ad astra* (or *ad lunam*) without *per ardua.*

Interestingly, it was a homosexual writer, André Gide, who first capitalized on the *acte gratuit,* and that, significantly, while still pretending to a heterosexual existence. I cannot presume to know exactly what is eating Bertolucci, but scenes like some of those that we get in *1900* and *Luna* must represent the rage of something repressed against a society that appears to demand such repression. This might, of course, be an excellent subject for a movie, but can result only in harmful falsification when it is dealt with evasively, shiftily, dishonestly. (pp. 1636-37)

John Simon, "Operatic Operators," in National Review *(© National Review, Inc., 1979; 150 East 35th St., New York, N.Y. 10016), Vol. XXXI, No. 51, December 21, 1979, pp. 1635-38.**

PHILIP FRENCH

Bertolucci has the reputation of being one of the great intellectuals of European cinema, making films that transpose Stendhal, Borges and Dostoievsky to modern Italy, forever dropping the names of Freud, Marx and Roland Barthes in interviews. In fact his head is full of Verdi and his heart is buried alongside the stars in the pavement of Hollywood Boulevard: and 'La Luna' is a slick conjunction of Italian opera and Warner Brothers woman's weepies of the Crawford-Davis kind. This spongy encounter between movable object and resistible force is stated directly when Joe goes from watching Marilyn Monroe betraying her husband beside the foaming torrents in 'Niagara' straight to the Rome Opera where his mother is grandly emoting beside a fake waterfall as Leonora in a kitschy production of 'Il Trovatore.'

Of course Bertolucci has updated the Hollywood weepie, and he has put in the usual arcane references to his native Parma, his own career, and also apparently his recent experience of psychoanalysis. The identification of the moon with the mother is a personal one and somewhat obscure, though he throws in the honeymoon, real honey, and Verdi's Count di Luna as well; on the other hand the use of knitting wool to symbolise the umbilical cord is rather heavy-handed.

A scene in which Caterina revisits her old singing teacher, an egocentric bully, now sitting paralysed in a wheelchair using a shaft of afternoon sun as if it were a spotlight, is allegedly about the director's own relationship with Visconti. Fortunately it works powerfully enough to prevent us pondering its personal provenance. Other meetings, however, between the boy and a Roman pederast . . . and the mother and a well-heeled Emilian Communist . . . who gives her a lift, remain obscure *divertissements*.

All in all then, though not without its entertainment value, 'La Luna' is a failure that, through its lack of general conviction and narrative drive, has little capacity to shock or disturb.

Philip French, "Incest and Moonshine," in The Observer *(reprinted by permission of The Observer Limited), No. 9828, January 6, 1980, p. 14.*

Robert Bresson

1907-

French director and scriptwriter.

Bresson is best known for austere, stark films which appear to be detached perceptions of humanity. His work has been compared to the flatly expressive style of medieval art. Although his films have little action and often find small audience appeal, they are well received by many critics.

After studying literature and philosophy, Bresson worked as a painter, an experience that greatly influenced his cinematic technique. Rather than allowing the actors to interpret their roles in the film, he prefers to be the creator, or painter, producing a series of related images that cinematically depict his tale. He has written in his *Notes sur le Cinématographe:* "How to hide from oneself the fact that it all winds up on a rectangle of white fabric hung on a wall? (See your film as a surface to cover.)"

In 1934, Bresson made his first film, *Les Affaires publiques,* but no copies exist. He also worked on the scripts of several films, and functioned as René Clair's assistant on *Air Pur* before the outbreak of World War II. During the war, Bresson spent eighteen months as a prisoner of war before returning home in 1941.

Bresson himself marks the beginning of his career with the release of *Les Anges du péché* in 1943. It was a popular success, enabling Bresson to make *Les Dames du Bois de Boulogne,* based on Diderot's *Jacques le Fataliste.* This film, however, was not as well received by the public, and Bresson was unable to find financial backing. Consequently, there is a five-year interval between *Les Dames* and his next film, *Le Journal d'un Curé de Campagne.*

***Le Journal* marks the advent of Bresson's use of non-professional actors, the first sign of emotional overtones in his work, and his steadfast avoidance of anything studiously "cinematic." Sound effects, as well, proved to be a strong symbolic factor to Bresson. *Le Journal,* based on a story by Georges Bernanos, received critical as well as popular acclaim, and won the Cannes Grand Prix for 1951.**

Once again, five years followed before Bresson made *Un Condamné à mort s'est échappé,* regarded by many to be his masterpiece. An intensely barren film, its unique construction stems from Bresson's use of gestures and objects, depicting the essence of the French Resistance.

Bresson's first use of color, in *Une Femme Douce,* allowed him to experiment more with film as an artist's palette. *Une Femme Douce* is Dostoevsky's story transferred to a modern Parisian setting, and some critics feel it suffers from this transposition of time and place. However, it is generally regarded as one of Bresson's finer works.

Bresson considers it important that he be sole creator of his films, and his attitude towards his actors is indicative of this. They are sometimes kept in ignorance of the plot and seldom, if ever, given the chance to improvise or emote. Bresson's films are stripped of superfluous matter, be it plot, dialogue, or props. He wants nothing to detract from the explicit moral message. Catholic philosophy is intrinsic in his work: every character aspires to a level of grace through suffering. Since Bresson does not cater to a popular market, his output is limited, but he continues to produce highly individualized films and retains a faithful following among those who admire his work.

GAVIN LAMBERT

Bresson has . . . remarked that he does not believe "technique," in the accepted sense of the word, exists; he prefers "*L'écriture.*" "An author writes on the screen, expresses himself by means of photographed shots of variable length, and from variable angles. On an author worthy of the name, a choice is imposed, dictated by his calculations or his instinct, never by chance. For him, and for him alone, once he has worked out his découpage, each shot he takes can have only one definite angle, one certain length of time." *Les Anges du Péché* certainly gives this impression, and its mastery is none the less remarkable, especially for a first film. . . . [Though the story written by Jean Giraudoux] has a few of the kind of conventional elements that Bresson was later to reject entirely, already they cannot be accepted on a conventional dramatic level. This is precisely the level that interests Bresson least, and why, no doubt, the film was not popular. For the not always successful plot contrivances are quite obliterated by the film's main purpose, the delineation of a spiritual conflict, exactly analysed, between two young women, against a richly described background of convent life—its ritual, its dedication, its formidable self-discipline and, at times, ruthlessness. (p. 36)

Les Anges du Péché is . . . less spare than its successors because of its almost exotic settings. The convent rooms and corridors, all white-walled, the black and white habits of the sisters luminously patterned against them, inspire a series of exquisite formal groupings. . . . Although the background gives it a pictorial richness that can be admired for itself . . . the emotional force lies completely within the images of faces. (p. 37)

With the movement and the rhythm of the film dictated by its inner development, many of the cinema's devices—above all, editing as a dynamic property—are jettisoned. On the surface the pace of Bresson's films looks inflexible, and yet any external variations would distract from the rigours of the "exploration within." Every film, he has remarked, requires its "uniform"—and, above all, no fancy dress. This uniform becomes, as it were, a garment for the soul. . . .

In the construction of a sound-track, the same classicism: the dialogue in each of these films has a lucid, precise, condensed quality, and in each case is created by a writer of high and meticulous literary skill, Giraudoux, Cocteau, Bernanos. There are no concessions to naturalism, which again would distract. . . . [Natural] sound is used in an arbitrary, succinct manner: usually as a reminder of a world outside the world of the film, momentarily impinging upon it. . . .

The character of Anne-Marie [in *Les Anges du Péché*] expounds Bresson's favourite protagonist, the dedicated, haunted, isolated self-questioning hero or heroine, to whom all human communication seems to become increasingly painful, and whose eye is fixed on a horizon that others cannot see. In his next film, *Les Dames,* this dedication is profane. An attempt at a *tour de force,* it is a film quite without precedent, but in retrospect it appears the least complete of Bresson's films. . . .

Bresson contrives to tell this extraordinary story entirely through the characters as they reveal themselves in a series of encounters mainly pre-arranged by Hélène; everything exists within a powerful, mesmeric vacuum; what the characters do outside their particular situation is never indicated—their social positions emerge elliptically, their friends or acquaintances are never shown except collectively, anonymously at the night club and the wedding—and the action takes place almost entirely within two apartments. . . .

[From the moment Jean leaves Hélène and she vows revenge,] the narrative is dictated by Hélène's obsession. Nothing occurs that does not spring directly from it—she apparently has no qualms, no distractions, no other commitments, and certainly no relaxations; and to heighten the effect of, as it were, a formal distillation of life, a quintessence of a particular essence, the characters are costumed with determined unreality. . . .

All this creates the impressions of ritual figures engrossed in a ritual drama, a kind of human equation, in which nothing is presented on an ordinary, naturalistic level; nothing, that is, until the end, when in the final scene between Jean and Agnès they succeed in emerging intact from Hélène's duplicities and find they can still love and trust each other. . . .

Thus, at the end, one is left with an equation brilliantly, intricately stated and incompletely solved. In the sheer concentration on character, the elimination of all extraneous detail, the film fascinatingly continues and intensifies the method of *Les Anges du Péché*. . . . (p. 38)

[What Bresson has added to Georges Bernanos' *Journal d'un Curé de Campagne*] is, mainly, his own temperament. For the film has a quality of exaltation, of inner revelation about it, not in fact present in Bernanos; the novel's tone is more detached and, at the same time, closer to physical realities. It is profoundly grim. Bresson gives the film a texture more complex, more poetic; everything seen is, so to speak, conveyed through the eyes of a visionary, the exterior world filtered down, real and visible and yet at one remove, the images are two-toned. . . . One has the feeling that Bresson was more personally engaged with his central character and his predicament, for his portraiture of the young priest's agonies, secret doubts and contemplations, . . . produces an intimate and profound concretion of experience. The method goes beyond the analytical, and the camera is admitted to the confines of a soul. The images it captures there take on the aspect of a visual meditation. This soul, this hero, is one of the most remarkable that the cinema has yet given us; for once a character is not externally memorable. . . . Lonely, uncertain, and yet exalted; young, and yet fixed and set; [the character] has a mysterious fervour and dedication that grows more urgent, and more self-contained, as the hostility of a primitive little village asserts itself; it is doomed, and yet will not be forgotten; for it carries its mystery away with it, and it is a mystery which even those of us who do not share, or want to share, would like to understand. *Journal d'un Curé de Campagne* is not, as someone has remarked, a film about religion, but about faith. Though it has (like *Les Anges du Péché* and, in its profane way, *Les Dames du Bois de Boulogne*) the physical and spiritual masochism to be found in so much modern Catholic art, though some of its agonies go beyond ascetism, it also possesses a genuine nobility. That Bresson's inspiration is a Christian and a Catholic one, and that it is the only one seriously at work in the cinema today, is evident; more remarkably, it stems from a pure, elevated and classical tradition. . . . It is joined, in fact, to the tradition of exalted pessimism which, unsparing though it is, derives from affirmation, from intrinsic faith; from love. It is a kind of love the cinema very seldom portrays, bound up as it is with a stringent self-renunciation, a mortified denial of the world and the flesh (and perhaps *Les Dames du Bois de Boulogne* even springs partly from a rejection of a "human" love); it is not the kind of love for many of us; but, hermetically sealed off though it may be, its voice and its particular ecstasy are unmistakable. (p. 39)

Gavin Lambert, "Notes on Robert Bresson," in Sight and Sound *(copyright © 1953 by The British Film Institute), Vol. 23, No. 1, July-September, 1953, pp. 35-9.*

BRIAN DAVIES

[It] is only in the last century that heroes like Stephen Dedalus, Paul Morel, Yury Zhivago and the priest of *Journal d'un Curé de Campagne* have regularly emerged. They are from novels in which the hero is an analysable combination of artistic creation, autobiography and public confessional. The task of deciding whether the author is commentating, revealing or committing becomes almost impossible. This is particularly true of *Journal d'un Curé de Campagne,* written in diary form as a purely first person narrative. . . . Bernanos has foresaken the advantages of distance for the equally great advantages of intimacy. . . . The limitations of the structure of the novel reduces its meaning to ambiguities; Bernanos gives us no indication of the way he feels about the priest.

The film provides an ideal solution to this problem. Bresson chose a most unfilmlike form in which the priest reads for long periods out of his diary, whilst on the screen we merely see him writing in the diary or engaged in some task of housework, or sometimes moving towards the next piece of conversation in the film. None of the direct, personal communion between the priest and the audience was lost; yet at the same time we could stand away from the priest observing him in his day-to-day encounters with people. . . . Bresson has used [the visuals] to reinforce the priest's monologue at all times to provide the atmosphere tone in which the drama is to unfold and to modulate that tone. The relationship between the visuals and the sound track is symptomatic of Bresson's whole approach to the priest's tale. It is the approach of complete simplicity as compared to the relative complexity of Bernanos' priest. . . .

Bresson has used these visual techniques to create the atmosphere of the isolation and disturbance through which his priest is to tell his story. Just as important to note, however, is the way that these visual techniques become part and parcel of the whole change in the nature of the priest's story as it appears in the film. The extreme economy of the visual content with its sparse use of object serves to constantly centre our attention on the drama within the priest. The subjective is made more intense by removing all but the sketched outline of the objective world. Not only are irrelevant objects and lighting removed but the recurrent images of the gate, the cart, and even that of the diary help to create an almost classical unity of place.

As with the visuals, the characters of Bresson's *Journal d'un Curé de Campagne* become subservient to the central and dominating figure of the priest. In the Bernanos novel the characters, although existing for us only through the eyes of the priest, have an existence of their own. The priest's great virtue is his sympathetic understanding of men. Not only is he the victim of the other characters in the novel, he is also their audience. (p. 80)

[Thus, the characters of the novel] are real complete personalities. Some of them are full of intellectualizations but they are not the mere human manifestations of concepts or points of view; even their intellectualizations have the idiosyncratic qualities of true characters. In the film, however, some characters have been dropped altogether and the others have either been unfocused or focused until they are mere caricatures of the personalities which appear in the book. They are reduced to the stature of catalysts for the dramatic unfolding of the priest's story, agents who fashion the priest's destiny. (p. 81)

The film, then, far from being a synthesized préçis of the novel is more like one of those cut up pictures one sees in psychology text-books—some quirk of Gestalt is necessary before we can realize the whole. That one does see the whole is all to Bresson's credit (the fact that it is Bresson's whole and not Bernanos' is incidental) for few of the conversations which make up the film have not been removed from their context in the larger conversations which occurred in the novel.

The priest of the novel was a complex and many sided creature; poet and philosopher, Catholic and heretic, a man, or rather a youth made up of private doubts and public dogma. To the rest of the clergy he is a nuisance and a bungler, to the non-believing intellectuals he is the essence of spiritualism, and to his parish he is a meddling tiddler. At no stage does he become a 'prisoner of saintly agony'. . . .

The idea that the priest is a 'prisoner of saintly agony' is indispensable to the understanding of the film. To achieve this Bresson has completely altered the spirit of the novel at this point. First he reduces the intensity of the chaos into which the priest is thrown after the death of Mme la Comtesse, and secondly he removes much of the primitive and emotional Catholicism from the Curé de Torcy's visit to the priest which culminates in the Curé de Torcy asking the priest to bless him. In the central scene Bresson presents us with a beautiful low angle close up of the gently crying priest; the quietly shaken monologue reveals him as a 'prisoner of saintly agony' and the shot is sustained for several seconds moving then into a slow fade. There may be music but we are unaware of it.

It is about and around this point that Bresson's film has been made, and the reductions in visual content, in the characters and in the priest himself can all be traced back to Bresson's desire to show us the suffering which is inextricably connected with faith. For Bresson the opposite to faith is nihilism, but Bernanos in not happy to leave the situation at this point. For Bernanos faith itself is nothing without justice; and it is 'justice' which is the *raison d'être* of the novel. All the major characters are involved in Bernanos' subtle and searching exploration of the place of justice in Catholicism. . . . It would be gross oversimplification to say that the film is about spiritual suffering and that the novel is about justice, and to leave it at that point. The novel is certainly concerned with spiritual suffering and faith but this theme is entangled amongst many others, and Bernanos is also more concerned with evaluating this spiritual suffering than Bresson; although, as has been said before, the result is ambiguous.

Bresson, then, has entangled the story of spiritual faith and suffering from what was a complex but ultimately unsatisfying novel. His film has stature as a work of art in its own right. But it is no longer sufficient to talk about le Curé de Campagne: one must specify one's priest, for there are two. (p. 82)

Brian Davies, "The Two Priests," in Film Journal *(copyright by Melbourne University Film Society), No. 16, August, 1960, pp. 79-82.*

ISABEL QUIGLY

Bresson is a master of concentration, psychological as well as physical. . . . Prison is the perfect setting for such a director: an intense narrow life with its minute everyday happenings magnified into high drama, the appearance of everything charged with meaning, and the soul—as almost nowhere else—a slide on a microscope. But in the outside world, where others live and other happenings impinge on the central one, this narrow preoccupation becomes too trim, cold and tidy. Bresson, at the expense of life and even of accuracy, *sticks to the point:* the point [of *Pickpocket*] being pickpocketing, or the mentality of a thief. . . .

[Unfortunately,] life isn't like that: or so it struck me, watching this chill analysis of a corner of human aberration. The thief is a young intellectual with superman notions of morality, the deadpan expression of contemporary French film heroes, and a Dostoievskian relationship with a chief of police who has him firmly hooked and occasionally gives the line a twitch, just (it would appear) for fun. . . . The dialogue is chill and tidy too: even in moments of the greatest stress (death, decision, the acknowledgement of love) it sounds like words learnt by rote, which goes with the dream-like quality of everyone's movements, the air of compulsion to act as they do. . . . [Michel is] a literary crook, direct descendant of Raskolnikov, and all he does has the same one-track, joyless and self-conscious determination to be . . . well, consistent seems the main thing.

Bresson's technique is roughly documentary, down to that very stiltedness of dialogue and movement, and the film's most interesting moments are, not surprisingly, those in which we see something new in action: the technical detail of thieving, though surely it can't be as easy as all *that*. . . . When three conspirators go out on a pinching spree, there's an almost balletic movement of frisking, swapping and disposing of the remains. . . . This kind of thing is fascinating to watch, and basically cinematic; it couldn't be shown in any other medium, and even its exaggerations of speed and slickness are cinematic. But it all has to do with *things*—with objects and actions at special, isolated moments, divorced from everything else, 'set pieces.' But life (here I go again) is not a set piece, and to aim for naturalism in so artificial a framework defeats itself. (p. 406)

Isabel Quigly, "To Catch a Thief," in The Spectator *(© 1960 by* The Spectator; *reprinted by permission of* The Spectator), *Vol. 205, No. 6899, September 16, 1960, pp. 406, 408.**

ERIC RHODE

For Michel [of *Pickpocket*] life is like a spy's journey into an alien land. Though every moment is dangerous, the real test of courage is to confront the menace of strangers on the packed trains of the metro. This is the most important part of his day: a weird relationship is set up with the stranger, weird partly because the stranger knows nothing about it and partly because the robbery is not primarily for financial gain (Michel admits his takings aren't often worth the risk) but for erotic satisfaction. Money to Michel is a symbol of sexual rather than economic power; only by rendering the stranger impotent is Michel's anxiety for a moment allayed. The pickpocket can only live as long as he is destroying the anonymous, affluent society about him. (p. 193)

It is in these documentary moments of *Pickpocket* . . . that Bresson shows his mastery as a director. A neurotic world is created without trick photography: menace and boredom are developed partly by the use of the same stations, trains, buses, and even the same extras in different crowds, partly by [L.H.] Burel's subtle camera-work, and partly by Bresson's sense of timing. Bresson suggests, he never states: and this he manages mostly by his cutting. His talent for building shots into sequences, and sequences into a whole film is an exceptional one: in its delicacy and elliptical gravity one feels that Bresson, like Eisenstein, has gone back to a study of Japanese poetry and drama. Yet a fine sensibility alone doesn't make a work of art. The ability to interpret intelligently is required, the ability to make the necessary connections; and this we do not find in *Pickpocket*.

Take for instance the character of Michel. What in fact is the weakness which drives him to "an adventure in theft for which he was not made"? Recent sociological and psycho-analytic knowledge should give us some idea, but Bresson seems indifferent to these findings. (Disturbing overtones in the film suggest he isn't conscious of them at all.) Michel himself is clear only on one point: he isn't a pickpocket for financial gain. Otherwise he is hopelessly confused. . . . Bresson is not interested in the nature of imprisonment: he is only interested in the desire to escape —and this he takes great pains to illustrate. (pp. 193-94)

Yet what is Michel trying to flee from—his neurosis, his selfhood, the human condition? In *Un Condamné à Mort s'est Echappé* (an earlier Bresson with many parallels to *Pickpocket*) a similar theme was treated realistically; enough anyway for it to make sense on a literal level—it was surely clear enough why its protagonist wished to escape from the Gestapo. In *Pickpocket,* however, the far from realistic action compels us to try to work out the nature of the escape.

This would be possible if there were some conflict. Unfortunately, all the characters (including the strangers on the metro) have the same sensitive, histrionic outlook on life as Michel. There is only one noticeable distinction: between the guilty who learn to love (the poor in spirit who shall inherit the earth) and those who lack this kind of understanding. . . . The characters in fact are shaped to *illustrate* Michel's (or Bresson's) sensibility, rather than to *criticise* it; so that the film gives us a picture of a curiously insulated world, on the surface soft and gentle, but beneath inexorably schematic. Its deficiencies are revealing: because there is no difference in planes of awareness, there is no humour; no one takes up a liberal position; and, most disturbingly of all, no one is aware of his motives.

At first one may be impressed by the mystery surrounding these characters, until one realises that they are only mysterious because they are unable to create their own destinies. None of them in fact is free. They remain puppets manipulated by their creator, forced to move along "the strange paths of love"; and the word "paths" in this context signifies tracks already worn and determined. The undergrowths of choice and possibility on either side are ignored. One is tempted to adapt to this film Sartre's words on Mauriac: "M. Bresson has put himself first. He has chosen divine omniscience and omnipotence. But films are made *by* men and *for* men. In the eyes of God, Who cuts through appearances and goes beyond them, there is no film, no art, for art thrives on appearances. God is not an artist. Neither is M. Bresson." (p. 194)

Eric Rhode, "Film Reviews: 'Pickpocket'," in Sight and Sound *(copyright © 1960 by The British Film Institute), Vol. 29, No. 4, Autumn, 1960, pp. 193-94.*

ROBERT VAS

Pickpocket took [Bresson] to an ultimate limit of virtuosity. "You see," he seemed to be saying, "I can apply my vision to *anything*." And after the final fadeout one could only wonder where his cryptic and fastidious extremism would lead him next.

With a master-stroke of self-discipline . . . *The Trial of Joan of Arc* . . . looks for a way back to the essence of that vision. If it didn't sound dangerously like a paradox, one could say that here Bresson discards all the flourishes of his style. . . . Everything is stripped of decoration: the enigmatic faces, the settings of curtains and brick walls, the hole in the dark wall through which hostile eyes peer into the cell. Everything that is profane is only there to serve the sacred: the inner, spiritual drama. Even the blackness of the fadeouts suggests something solemn. To Bresson cinema means a church. And the scenes of Joan's repeated interrogations, composed with a splendour of mathematical precision, rise like the solid pillars sustaining the whole arch of the work. We move along under them as if in some ascetic medieval cathedral, advancing slowly and with echoing footsteps, hesitant and yet drawn on by the spiritual grandeur—irresistibly moving towards the altar, the culmination, the inevitable burning at the stake. (pp. 37-8)

One interrogation succeeds another; the dialogue derives from the curt, accurate sentences of the trial record. An interrogation ends; the door slams behind Joan; the scene fades out. The key clatters in the lock; another interrogation; again the door slams; fadeout. The effect is to give the film a staccato rhythm and also to encourage the spectator to search for the links between the separate scenes. They are all part of the machinery; and it is very much a machinery of an earth which repeatedly proves that it is still not "ready to receive" its saints. . . .

Humanly and philosophically, this is a story filled with tremendous question marks. Joan's tragedy lies in her very agony between faith and doubt. An illiterate genius who puts her faith into her questionable visions and unquestionable truths, she stands there as an outcast, representing an idea the greatness of which she is unable to realise, and standing up for it until her last word—"Jesus"—from among the flames. . . . [One] thing, I feel, cannot be ignored: the tremendous human battle for certainty. And this is where Bresson fails to add the decisive final touch to the crystalline brilliance of his conception.

Is it because Joan's replies to Bishop Cauchon are made much too readily and easily? Or because her decision to sign the recantation—a culmination of the drama of doubts—comes too suddenly, with no real hint of the agonising choice that lies behind it? . . . With a peasant stubbornness, Dreyer's Joan wanted to live; Bresson's Joan doesn't mind dying. When Joan sees the pigeons in Dreyer's film, you feel that she *must* leave something behind, something that would have been worth living for. But Bresson's pigeons flutter their wings above a world not worthy of such a sacrifice. Dreyer's heroine is left painfully alone; Bresson's is made lonely by Bresson.

Such comparisons between the two films are, of course, not really fair: Dreyer's is a *Passion,* Bresson's a *Procès*. But along with the juridical meaning of the word, there is also here a tremendous *human* trial. And Joan, "young, rustic, a woman of action, good-humoured, very pious, very temperate, a sane and shrewd country girl of extraordinary strength of mind and hardihood of body," does not easily lend herself to a merely enigmatic image. It seems that she is to be no more than another instrument put to the service of Bresson's vision. But Joan is no pickpocket. And this is exactly where this seemingly so Bressonian subject loses ground.

The characters of the country priest and the condemned prisoner gave us a key to the philosophical outlook, the spiritual territory covered by these films. The battle between the curé and the countess was fought out in the soul but also on the ground. And in the light of these earlier films, Dreyer's Joan seems a much more Bressonian creation than Bresson's Joan herself. This is why the horrifying crackle of the flames may yield up some abstract intellectual or even spiritual message, but fails to burn, movingly and tragically, a flesh and blood human being and her truth. The cross at the end of *Journal d'un Curé* remains for me the more genuine symbol of that charred stake at which are burnt, one after another, those who have the courage to "hear the voices". (p. 38)

Robert Vas, "Film Reviews: 'The Trial of Joan of Arc'," in Sight and Sound *(copyright © 1962 by The British Film Institute), Vol. 32, No. 1, Winter, 1962-63, pp. 37-8.*

SUSAN SONTAG

In the film, the master of the reflective mode is Robert Bresson. (p. 178)

The reason that Bresson is not generally ranked according to his merits is that the tradition to which his art belongs, the reflective or contemplative, is not well understood. Particularly in England and America, Bresson's films are often described as cold, remote, overintellectualized, geometrical. (p. 179)

[Bresson, like Yasujiro Ozu, has created a rigorous narrative form.] And the form of Bresson's films is designed (like Ozu's) to discipline the emotions at the same time that it arouses them: to induce a certain tranquillity in the spectator, a state of spiritual balance that is itself the subject of the film.

Reflective art is art which, in effect, imposes a certain discipline on the audience—postponing easy gratification. Even boredom can be a permissible means of such discipline. Giving prominence to what is artifice in the work of art is another means. One thinks here of Brecht's idea of theater. Brecht advocated strategies of staging—like having a narrator, putting musicians on stage, interposing filmed scenes—and a technique of acting so that the audience could distance itself, and not become uncritically "involved" in the plot and the fate of the characters. Bresson wishes distance, too. But his aim, I would imagine, is not to keep hot emotions cool so that intelligence can prevail. The emotional distance typical of Bresson's films seems to exist for a different reason altogether: because all identification with characters, deeply conceived, is an impertinence—an affront to the mystery that is human action and the human heart.

But—all claims for intellectual coolness or respect for the mystery of action laid aside—surely Brecht knew, as must Bresson, that such distancing is a source of great emotional power. . . . Ultimately, the greatest source of emotional power in art lies not in any particular subject-matter, however passionate, however universal. It lies in form. The detachment and retarding of the emotions, through the consciousness of form, makes them far stronger and more intense in the end. (pp. 180-81)

For Bresson film is not a plastic but a narrative experience. (p. 181)

[When we hear what is going to happen before we see it] there is a deliberate flouting of one of the traditional modes of narrative involvement: suspense. Again, one thinks of Brecht. To eliminate suspense, at the beginning of a scene

Brecht announces, by means of placards or a narrator, what is to happen. . . . Bresson does the same thing, by jumping the gun with narration. . . . Ideally, there is no suspense in a Bresson film. Thus, in the one film where suspense should normally play a large role, *Un Condamné à Mort s'est Échappé,* the title deliberately—even awkwardly—gives the outcome away: we know Fontaine is going to make it. . . .

[Form] in Bresson's films is anti-dramatic, though strongly linear. Scenes are cut short, and set end to end without obvious emphasis. (p. 183)

Bresson also came to reject the species of involvement created in films by the expressiveness of the acting. Again, one is reminded of Brecht by Bresson's particular way of handling actors, in the exercise of which he has found it preferable to use non-professionals in major roles. . . . His idea is for the actors not to act out their lines, but simply to say them with as little expression as possible. . . . Emotional climaxes are rendered very elliptically. (p. 184)

The reason that Bresson rejects acting reflects his notion of the purity of the art itself. "Acting is for the theater, which is a bastard art," he has said. "The film can be a true art because in it the author takes fragments of reality and arranges them in such a way that their juxtaposition transforms them." Cinema, for Bresson, is a total art, in which acting corrodes. (pp. 184-85)

The nature of drama being conflict, the real drama of Bresson's stories is interior conflict: the fight against oneself. And all the static and formal qualities of his films work to that end. (p. 187)

Notice, though, that the "interior drama" which Bresson seeks to depict does not mean *psychology*. In realistic terms, the motives of Bresson's characters are often hidden, sometimes downright incredible. . . .

But what is central to Bresson and, I think, not to be caviled at, is his evident belief that psychological analysis is superficial. (Reason: it assigns to action a paraphrasable meaning that true art transcends.) He does not intend his characters to be implausible, I'm sure; but he does, I think, intend them to be opaque. Bresson is interested in the forms of spiritual action—in the physics, as it were, rather than in the psychology of souls. Why persons behave as they do is, ultimately, not to be understood. (Psychology, precisely, does claim to understand.) (p. 188)

Such a physics of the soul was the subject of Simone Weil's most remarkable book, *Gravity and Grace*. And the following sentences of Simone Weil's—

> All the natural movements of the soul are controlled by laws analogous to those of physical gravity. Grace is the only exception.
> Grace fills empty spaces, but it can only enter where there is a void to receive it, and it is grace itself which makes this void.
> The imagination is continually at work filling up all the fissures through which grace might pass.

supply the three basic theorems of Bresson's "anthropology." Some souls are heavy, others light; some are liberated or capable of being liberated others not. All one can do is be patient, and as empty as possible. In such a regimen there is no place for the imagination, much less for ideas and opinions. The ideal is neutrality, transparence. This is what is meant when the Vicar of Torcy tells the young priest in *Le Journal d'un Curé de Campagne,* "A priest has no opinions." (pp. 188-89)

[Jean Cocteau has said] that minds and souls today "live without a syntax, that is to say, without a moral system. This moral system has nothing to do with morality proper, and should be built up by each one of us as an inner style, without which no outer style is possible." Cocteau's films may be understood as portraying this inwardness which is the true morality; so may Bresson's. Both are concerned, in their films, with depicting spiritual style. . . . Bresson's Catholicism is a language for rendering a certain vision of human action, rather than a "position" that is stated. . . . The proof of this is that Bresson is able to say the same thing without Catholicism—in his three other films [*Les Dames du Bois de Boulogne, Un Condamné à Mort s'est Échappé,* and *Pickpocket*]. In fact, the most entirely successful of all Bresson's films—*Un Condamné à Mort s'est Échappé*—is one which, while it has a sensitive and intelligent priest in the background (one of the prisoners), bypasses the religious way of posing the problem. The religious vocation supplies one setting for ideas about gravity, lucidity, and martyrdom. But the drastically secular subjects of crime, the revenge of betrayed love, and solitary imprisonment also yield the same themes.

Bresson is really more like Cocteau than appears—an ascetic Cocteau, Cocteau divesting himself of sensuousness, Cocteau without poetry. The aim is the same: to build up an image of spiritual style. But the sensibility, needless to say, is altogether different. Cocteau's is a clear example of the homosexual sensibility that is one of the principal traditions of modern art: both romantic and witty, langorously drawn to physical beauty and yet always decorating itself with stylishness and artifice. Bresson's sensibility is antiromantic and solemn, pledged to ward off the easy pleasures of physical beauty and artifice for a pleasure which is more permanent, more edifying, more sincere.

In the evolution of this sensibility, Bresson's cinematic means become more and more chaste. (pp. 191-92)

While the spiritual style of Cocteau's heroes (who are played, usually, by Jean Marais) tends toward narcissism, the spiritual style of Bresson's heroes is one variety or other of unself-consciousness. . . . Consciousness of self is the "gravity" that burdens the spirit; the surpassing of the consciousness of self is "grace," or spiritual lightness. The climax of Cocteau's films is a voluptuous movement. . . . With the exception of *Les Dames du Bois de Boulogne* (with its final glamorous image, shot from above, of Jean bending over Agnès, who lies on the floor like a great white bird), the end of Bresson's films is counter-voluptuous, reserved.

While Cocteau's art is irresistibly drawn to the logic of dreams, and to the truth of invention over the truth of "real life," Bresson's art moves increasingly away from the story and toward documentary. (pp. 193-94)

Bresson's attempt is to insist on the irrefutability of what he is presenting. Nothing happens by chance; there are no alternatives, no fantasy; everything is inexorable. Whatever is not necessary, whatever is merely anecdotal or decorative, must be left out. Unlike Cocteau, Bresson wishes to pare down—rather than to enlarge—the dramatic and visual resources of the cinema. . . . True, in the last, most ascetic of all his films, Bresson seems to have left out too much, to have overrefined his conception. But a conception as ambitious as this cannot help but have its extremism, and Bresson's "failures" are worth more than most directors' successes. For Bresson, art is the discovery of what is necessary—of that, and nothing more. The power of Bresson's six films lies in the fact that his purity and fastidiousness are not just an assertion about the resources of the cinema, as much of modern painting is mainly a comment in paint about painting. They are at the same time an idea about life, about what Cocteau called "inner style," about the most serious way of being human. (pp. 194-95)

Susan Sontag, "Spiritual Style in the Films of Robert Bresson" (1964), in her Against Interpretation and Other Essays *(reprinted by permission of Farrar, Straus & Giroux, Inc.; copyright © 1961, 1962, 1963, 1964, 1965, 1966 by Susan Sontag), Farrar, Straus & Giroux, 1967, pp. 177-95.*

JOHN RUSSELL TAYLOR

Essentially a quietist in the cinema, Bresson has devoted himself with a quite unworldly dedication to working out and putting on the screen his own vision, entirely without regard for what is going on around him in the cinema and the world at large, and it is this quality of remoteness, the hermetic perfection of the finished films, which many find off-putting. His films are not easy, they do not go out of their way to please or attract; they sometimes seem to be made in complete unconcern over whether anyone will want to see them or not. In this way they achieve a purity which makes even Antonioni seem in comparison rather flashy and vulgar; they may achieve it, however—or so those who do not like them say—only at the risk of deteriorating from the calm detachment of the philosopher to the mere inertia of a dead object. (pp. 115-16)

[Bresson's] most popular films were the middle two [*Le Journal d'un Curé de Campagne* and *Un Condamné à Mort s'est Echappé*], made when he had just achieved full maturity and before he had refined his style to a point beyond which many of his admirers, even, were unwilling to follow him—there is no doubt about the consistency of his development and about his unique significance as the extreme example of a particular view of the film-maker's art put into practice. That view might be briefly characterized as the autocratic view: the director is paramount in every area of the film, and all the others involved—actors, cameraman, editor, recording engineer, composer, etc.—are there only as tools to be used by the director, not as collaborators in any real sense of the term. (p. 116)

Les Dames du Bois de Boulogne is virtually a manifesto of Bresson's belief in the cinema as an interior art. . . . And like most manifestoes *Les Dames du Bois de Boulogne* does not exactly make things easy for unprepared spectators. The story concerns a savage and overbearing passion, but the treatment is formal to the point of being glacial; the picturesque and anecdotal are totally lacking, the narrative being stripped to the bone; and the film progresses consistently by a series of ellipses, wasting nothing, elaborating nothing and calling, at any rate in 1945, for remarkable powers of concentration from its audience. Moreover, the action is all placed in a deliberately remote, artificial world carefully abstracted from all the usual realistic associations on which the viewer might call for help; perfectly hermetic, closed in on itself, the film seems to be made in total disregard of its audience, and this the audience, annoyingly but predictably, tend to resent.

How exactly did Bresson arrive at this extreme position in only two films? Evidently he did it deliberately, to show precisely what he was up to, and having shown it he was able in his next two films to apply the same sort of technique to subjects which allowed audiences an easier way in by starting from something which might by expected to arouse an initial stock reaction of some sort (ascetic, saintly young priest in a hostile parish; young man condemned to death trying to escape). But in *Les Dames du Bois de Boulogne* the subject is deliberately chosen to repel this sort of too-easy sympathy, to place the audience willy-nilly on the outside looking in. Bresson found his subject in Diderot's rambling episodic novel *Jacques le Fataliste*. (pp. 120-21)

[Bresson's modernizing of the story] is the central problem of the film. A lot of argument has raged round the question of Bresson's intentions in thus moving, almost without modification, a completely eighteenth-century plot to a twentieth-century setting. Even critics, like M. Semolué, who recognize that the issue of credibility on a basic documentary level is not vital to the film have tried to make out a case for it in realistic terms, explaining that in the very highest Parisian society eighteenth-century locutions are still employed, eighteenth-century codes still obtain, women wear their hats at table and so on. All of which may or may not be true, but misses the essential point: that the inevitable impression produced by the film on those who are not so enviably *au fait* with the usages of high society—which is to say, nearly everyone—is one of dislocation between the action and its setting. And this obviously is intended: this is the main thing which abstracts the film from too-ready audience involvement and gives it the timelessness of true tragedy. Great care is taken to see that the action broadly makes sense in twentieth-century terms: for the power of rank in the original is substituted the power of money; for the horror of misalliance the horror of being exposed to personal ridicule. But there is no attempt to make the action conform in detail to normal twentieth-century habits of mind; it remains an eighteenth-century plot set down with artful arbitrariness in a setting of two centuries later, so that we are forced to forget all easy ready-made associations (either with 'modern life' or with our accepted notion of the eighteenth century) and respond freshly and immediately to the particular experience the film offers.

This experience is one of such concentration and intensity that the name of Racine immediately springs to mind for comparison. And undoubtedly the comparison is just, perhaps even intended by Bresson, who has frequently quoted Racine in discussing the film. (pp. 122-23)

[The] effect of endistancement by apparent duplication, and [the] use of the spoken word in drama virtually as a commentary on the action, is taken up and developed much further, with many additions, ramifications and apparent contradictions, in Bresson's three subsequent films, all of which actually make use of a fully developed commentary, that anathema of the conventional film theorist. The main objection to a commentary, though, seems to be that it detracts from the visual nature of the film; that it is the film's way to make its points visually, with words as an occasional helpmate, not to be too frequently called upon, and in a story film, at any rate, the use of a continuous commentary is felt to be something like an admission of defeat. What, then, should the purist make of *Le Journal d'un Curé de Campagne,* which not only originates in a novel by Bernanos written in diary form, but actually opens with a shot of a notebook and a hand writing in it, followed almost at once by a voice on the sound-track reading what has been written, and returns almost throughout to the notebook, or the voice, or both?

Before we can answer the question, it is necessary to look more closely at what exactly the commentary does in the film. First, it establishes the film's tone and suggests its structure: it will be quiet, intimate, subjective, . . . and in it events will follow each other naturally, one after the other, as day follows day—carefully-worked-out links of scene with scene which were such a noticeable feature of the previous two films will not be required. Next, it places us in a special, and in some ways a paradoxical, relationship with the protagonist, the young curé of Ambricourt. On the one hand it implies an immediate intimacy, even, one might think, an automatic identification with him, since we are, after all, permitted to see into his mind. But on the other, the device has in practice quite the opposite effect: a barrier, the barrier of what he writes about himself, is put between us and direct imaginative participation in the action. Instead of being presented implicitly with an interpretation of his story which works on us subliminally, we are overtly given his interpretation of what happens and left to judge for ourselves. In the very process of welcoming us into the heart of the story Bresson places us all the more effectively on the outside, seeing it with eyes unfogged by too-easy sentimentality. (pp. 125-26)

The very regularity of the diary's recurrence also has its place in the scheme, giving the film as a whole a rondo-like structure with a refrain, always different yet always immediately recognizable. (p. 126)

In *Le Journal d'un Curé de Campagne* Bresson, given a subject perfectly suited to his special talents, achieved for the first time the ideal realization of his concept of cinematic *écriture;* for once, everything, lighting, composition, setting, sound, all contribute to an infinitely subtle, infinitely complex final effect in such a way that not a shot could be removed or changed without the film losing something—indeed, for me this film remains the most nearly faultless ever made. The way the story is told, with absolute economy and simplicity—nothing too much, and yet none of the ellipses obtruding themselves as virtuoso displays—is model, and the sequence of moods as the Curé moves through his unwelcoming parish and his dark night of the soul towards the moment when he can help another—the Countess—and then see his own way and experience his own vision before dying with the words 'Tout est grâce' on his lips is impeccably managed; perhaps nothing in Bresson's work shows his mastery so completely as the conception and placing of the episode when, at his departure from Ambricourt, the Curé rides pillion on a motor-bike, the one sunny moment in an overcast, drizzling world, and for a short space of time we see him as he might have been in other circumstances, we see how far he is just like all other young men, and how, too, he is fundamentally, irrevocably different. (p. 128)

Curiously for so meticulous a director, Bresson claims to do a lot of improvisation on the set; he usually knows, he says, what he is going to shoot, but not how he is going to shoot it until he starts the day's work. . . . [This technique figures prominently in *Procès de Jeanne d'Arc*], since the text is given rather than written. . . . [It] comes entirely from transcriptions of Joan of Arc's trial, selected, it is true, by Bresson, but not otherwise tampered with. All of Bresson's vision, his 'treatment' of the subject, must be in the precise way he puts it on the screen—the critical fidelity to the originals of *Les Dames du Bois de Boulogne* and *Le Journal d'un Curé de Compagne* carried, if you like, to its logical conclusion by treating historical *faits divers* with fidelity so severe that nothing at all is allowed to come between the event and its literal re-enactment; if Bresson's adaptation of Diderot is a critique of Diderot, his adaptation of Bernanos a critique of Bernanos, taking them apart in order to re-create them in a different medium, so his treatment of the facts in *Procès de Jeanne d'Arc* is a critique of the facts, taking them apart in order to re-create them in their own terms. Nothing is done to explain Joan of Arc, to render her sympathetic or unsympathetic, to colour our view of her; as it is in the spirit of Diderot or Bernanos that we should see things from a certain angle, in a certain light, and Bresson makes sure that we do, so it is, if one can speak so, the 'method' of a piece of literal reporting that we should just see them, in no particular light, from no particular angle, and that is what Bresson allows us here. We must judge the maid not from what we are told about her, but from what she—or the girl playing her—is. (pp. 135-36)

In what, then, resides its quality? It lies, I think, chiefly in its extreme interestingness. It does not involve one, it does not seem in itself to move one (though it is always difficult to keep separate in one's mind the emotions which come from associations and received ideas and those which are excited directly by the object before one). But it is interesting: interesting to hear the exact words which were used; interesting to learn the brutal details of the tortures, the examination of Joan's virginity; interesting, too, to see style pared down to an absolute minimum, where it borders on total non-existence. Bresson's art has always been one of elimination, of seeing what can be left out, what effects can be dispensed with; little by little he has trained himself to do without one resource of the cinema after another, just as before him the Japanese director Ozu gradually eliminated from his films moving-camera work, the dissolve, the fade, and nearly all variations of *cadrage*. It amounts, in a way, to a reduction of the external forms of the cinema in order that the content shall shine through the more clearly, which is all very well except that it ignores the fact that ultimately form and content are the same thing, single and indivisible. If you take away too much of what we for convenience' sake choose to call 'form', you may well find in the end that you have thrown the baby out with the bathwater; that the 'content' you were striving so scrupulously to preserve in all its integrity has somehow disappeared altogether in the process.

Procès de Jeanne d'Arc has, as I say, the interest of any theory carried to an ultimate extreme. (pp. 136-37)

[It] remains an inescapable fact that [Bresson] has made in *Le Journal d'un Curé de Campagne* and *Un Condamné à Mort s'est Échappé* two of the supreme masterpieces of the cinema, and in *Les Dames du Bois de Boulogne* one of the most remarkable of *films maudits*. He has revolutionized our ideas—though not, alas, our practice—of literary adaptation in the cinema, and has been an important technical innovator, particularly in his use of commentary. And all this in a mere six films. Few film-makers can claim as much; none, I think, can claim more. (p. 137)

John Russell Taylor, "Robert Bresson," in his Cinema Eye, Cinema Ear: Some Key Film-Makers of the Sixties *(reprinted by permission of Hill & Wang, a division of Farrar, Straus & Giroux, Inc.; in Canada, by A D Peters & Co Ltd; copyright © 1964 by John Russell Taylor), Hill & Wang, 1964, pp. 115-37.*

RAYMOND DURGNAT

It is easy to see why Bresson has rejected conventional 'realism' [in *Le Journal d'un Curé de Campagne*]—which, in effect, means that the director has to record many inessential and superficial feelings, whims and fluctuations in his characters' experiences. But a man's soul is more sullen, mysterious, withdrawn. In Bresson the monotone and the 'deadpan' represent, not a 'mask', but a revelation of the essential man. His personages seem aloof because they are naked. There is no question of 'expressionism' rather than 'realism'. The physical is spiritualised; the eternal verities permeate the material world. The location photography —'neo-realism'—expresses not just a particular place, a 'mood' (passing emotions) but a spiritual condition of man without God. (p. 31)

[We] see only the essential moment of each scene, a moment which acquires an eerie concentration from . . . isolation and emphasis. Often, paradoxically, the essential moment of each scene is omitted. For example, the 'voice of the diary' tells us that the priest 'makes the gesture of total acceptance', which is presumably stretching himself out on the floor of his bedroom in the posture of the cross; but all we see is the priest hauling himself up by the bedrail, afterwards. And this extraordinary omission provides the clue to Bresson's whole method. What matters is not the gesture itself—which might appeal to the spectator for the wrong reasons (its apparent rhetoric), but the fact of the gesture—the attempted contact with God, the attempted self-discipline, and the fact that the gesture does *not* bring relief. And it is all in his face. . . .

Bresson's film is firmly rooted in the *physical*—in the reflection of cancer in the priest's face—and the cross is an image of its total sacrifice. The spiritual has devoured the flesh. . . . The priest's words have the extra precision, the sharpness, the gratuitousness, which corresponds to a childlike—or Godlike—intuition. He has 'realised', because of his tormenting hypersensitivity, something we vaguely sensed, wondered about, but could not quite *see*. The episode where he *guesses* that Chantal has a letter, and that letter is a suicide letter, is an outstanding example; but the effect is present in many subtler ways. . . .

It is certainly fair to say that the priest's lack of joy is the result, not of sheer goodness, but of a deep-rooted guilt complex. But I can't agree with those critics who seem to assume that if a film's hero is foolish, immature, weak or unsympathetic, this is in some way a point against the film. On the contrary. Saints don't have to be perfect and this film would not only be ludicrous, but quite impossible, if its hero were a pious pantechnicon of all possible virtures. Of course the priest 'morbidly' makes himself more miserable than he 'should'—the episode with Seraphita during his communion class is an example. Yet perhaps his humourlessness here is a response to Seraphita's real feelings—whereas humour would be simply a cowardly way of restoring his own ease of soul. The kernel of the film is: 'How wonderful that we can give others that peace which we ourselves do not possess. O miracle of our empty hands.' . . .

A persistent, but insistent, ellipse is the question of despair and suicide. The word is several times led up to, but never quite uttered. Indeed the dialectic of suicide and sacrifice is one of the 'concealed themes' of the novel, and several times their near-identity is hinted at. . . . The young Curé, a hereditary alcoholic ('Original Sin'?) has nourished himself on bread and wine (the Sacraments?). Yet the symbol of sin and salvation, wine, is the same. And the priest's alcoholism has concealed a cancer—which is, so to speak, a rebellion 'of' the body against the spirit—something malignant and suicidal, foreign to the priest yet within him, like the devil. . . .

Bresson's film is that rare phenomenon, a Christian tragedy, rare precisely because tragedy implies that in this life at least good is pulverised while the evil flourish as the green bay tree; too many Christian moralists seem strangely anxious to assert that good and evil will earn their due reward here and now even if by some mischance there is no life after death. Yet it is because the saint stakes everything on his faith that Christianity has its tragic heroism (and not just the cringing prudence of Pascal's notorious bet). It is essential to the film, as to the novel, that the priest's suffering be maximal, his 'joy' obliterated, and that he reach the limit of experience. Professor Bosanquet once remarked that 'only that optimism is worth its salt which can go all the way with pessimism and arrive at a point beyond it': in Bresson's film the final exaltation is derived neither by mitigating nor by complacently embracing suffering and, here, it seems to me, lies its greatness and humanity. (p. 32)

Raymond Durgnat, "'Diary of a Country Priest'" (© copyright Raymond Durgnat 1966; reprinted with permission), in Films and Filming, *Vol. 13, No. 1, December, 1966, pp. 29-32.*

GILLES JACOB

[The] novelty of [*Au Hasard, Balthazar*] lies less in the wealth of happenings than in the eye, that veiled but disenchanted eye, which Bresson turns on the modern world. The price of progress in this mechanical age is *la civilisation du weekend*. . . . Here Bresson clips the wings from critical comments like "irrelevant to the times," "more and more withdrawn from the world." For if the dancers (us?) in the café sequence seem indifferent to the fiendish destruction which rages round them, the teenage thirst for liberty echoes that of the underdeveloped countries, their need to inflict torture proves that the Algerian tragedy still exists, and their fire-crackers soar into the same sky as space rockets. The moon scudding by so close past the clouds is not just a touch of decorative vanity: it is a reminder that although one must take scientific progress into account, human feelings have not changed. Bresson, at the age of fifty-eight, has dropped his mask. No question here that he is against the need to cause suffering, against brute sensuality, against avarice for money, against avarice of the heart, against self-destructive pride, against the increasing stupidity of man.

The world changes, but not Bresson. *Au Hasard, Balthazar* is his greatest and most Bressonian film. . . . It is great because in the harmonies and dissonances between the characters (Marie in particular) and the donkey, Balthazar, and between successive images, between images and soundtrack, there is a dynamic exchange reaching to the limits of possibility whereby each is enriched, transformed by the contact. Motion and stasis, repetition and fulfilment, transition, resonance of sequence against sequence, reality against fantasy, flesh against spirit, sight against sound: Bresson's style is in perfect working order, a well-oiled machine set to reveal the secret, inner movement he cherishes. (pp. 7-8)

The whole film hangs hesitating in a balance between two poles: between good and evil, richness and poverty, honesty and dishonesty, justice and injustice, love and hatred, novelty and tradition, sacred and profane love, the folly of the modern world and the wisdom of a return to the simple life, to the soft, shadowy hillside landscapes which Bresson has portrayed with the nuanced delicacy of a Corot. . . . A recurring leitmotif in Bresson's work is the breaking of a servitude, or the construction of a liberation. Just as Orsini's failure enabled Fontaine to escape in *Un Condamné à Mort,* so Marie, to break the parallel between her life and that of Balthazar, determines to free herself once and for all from her father's domination and the forces which dispute her soul. . . . The film traces the gradual process by which she is—both literally and figuratively—physically and morally stripped; and no process could correspond more exactly to the whole notion we have of Bresson's aesthetic. . . . In the end, Marie's obsession with domination leaves her equally possessed by a desire to be free. Fleeing one servitude, she chooses another, even more insidious. Can we really be free? Bresson doubts it. (p. 8)

Like Hélène in *Les Dames du Bois de Boulogne,* like Fontaine and Jost in *Un Condamné à Mort,* [Marie] disappears into the night, locked in her own destiny and no longer participating in a contest from which she has disqualified herself. No doubt she will pass from hand to hand like Balthazar, a black knave whose seven masters each represents a deadly sin. But what does it matter? Marie, grown hard and unfeeling, does not arouse sympathy.

Balthazar, on the other hand, does. Submitting to human law, and at times inspired almost by humanity, he is at once witness, judge, conscience, 'hasard'. (pp. 8-9)

Whether metamorphoses or transfigurations, we witness mystical exchanges between Balthazar and Marie, between Balthazar and the others, following the doctrine of transference of sin whereby the innocent atone for the guilty. Seen as a devil by Arnold—a drunk surely viewing the world upside-down?—Balthazar is a modern martyr, a pure example of sacrifice on his road to sainthood. . . .

Allusions and references to the Passion of Christ abound in this hagiography: salt, straw, stable, baptism, the name of one of the Three Kings; the intimation that we are witnessing Balthazar's Agony. . . .

[For discussion, there still] remains Bresson's quarrying of time, different from any other, cutting fragments out of space and time to be reassembled in another space and time: a constant improvisation which forces a sort of virginity of inspiration, the mood of the film a colloquial lyricism and grave tranquillity. . . . There remains, too, a construction so elliptically concise, effect almost always preceding cause, that one can no longer be sure our old keys will open these doors. . . . In a cinema still struggling to find expression, Bresson's work soars like the spire of a cathedral. Yielding nothing, accepting no compromise, he makes his own grace—and his own isolation. After *Balthazar,* we know that only Bresson can make us sense the ineffable, see the invisible, touch the intangible. (p. 9)

Gilles Jacob, "'Au Hasard, Balthazar'," in Sight and Sound *(copyright © 1966 by The British Film Institute), Vol. 36, No. 1, Winter, 1966-67, pp. 7-9.*

ANDRÉ BAZIN

[Bresson's avowal of fidelity to the novel, *Le Journal d'un Curé de Campagne,* conditioned us to look for just that in analyzing the film.] While the characters in the book are presented to the reader in high relief and while their inevitably brief evocation by the pen of the curé of Ambricourt never gives us a feeling of frustration or of any limits being put both to their existence and to our knowledge of their existence, Bresson, in the process of showing them to us, is forever hurrying them out of sight. In place of the powerfully concrete evocations of the novelist, the film offers us an increasingly impoverished image which escapes us because it is hidden from us and is never really developed.

The novel of Bernanos is rich in picturesque evocations, solid, concrete, strikingly visual. (p. 127)

If he had really been faithful to the book, Bresson would have made quite a different film. Determined though he was to add nothing to the original—already a subtle form of betrayal by omission—he might at least have chosen to sacrifice the more literary parts for the many passages of ready-made film material that cried out for visualization. Yet he systematically took the opposite course. When you compare the two, it is the film that is literary while the novel teems with visual material. . . .

Bresson, like Dreyer, is only concerned with the countenance as flesh, which, when not involved in playing a role, is a man's true imprint, the most visible mark of his soul. It is then that the countenance takes on the dignity of a sign. He would have us be concerned here not with the psychology but with the physiology of existence. (p. 133)

There is no development of character. Their inner conflicts, the various phases of their struggle as they wrestle with the Angel of the Lord, are never outwardly revealed. . . .

Eschewing psychological analysis, the film in consequence lies outside the usual dramatic categories. The succession of events is not constructed according to the usual laws of dramaturgy under which the passions work towards a soul-satisfying climax. Events do indeed follow one another according to a necessary order, yet within a framework of accidental happenings. Free acts and coincidences are interwoven. . . . If the word tragedy comes to one's pen, it is in an opposite sense since we can only be dealing here with a tragedy freely willed. (p. 134)

The pattern of the film's unfolding is not that of tragedy in the usual sense, rather in the sense of the medieval Passion Play, or better still, of the Way of the Cross, each sequence being a station along that road. (pp. 134-35)

Death is not the preordained end of our final agony, only its conclusion and a deliverance. Henceforth we shall know to what divine ordinance, to what spiritual rhythm the sufferings and actions of the curé respond. They are the outward representation of his agony. At which point we should indicate the analogies with Christ that abound towards the end of the film, or they may very well go unnoticed. . . .

[But in] no sense is it true to say that the life of the curé of Ambricourt is an imitation of its divine model, rather it is a repetition and a picturing forth of that life. Each bears his own cross and each cross is different, but all are the Cross of the Passion. The sweat on the brow of the curé is a bloody sweat. (p. 135)

It is worth noting that through playing down the psychological elements and keeping the dramatics to a minimum, Bresson is left to face two kinds of pure reality. On the one hand . . . , we have the countenance of the actor denuded of all symbolic expression, sheer epidermis, set in a surrounding devoid of any artifice. On the other hand there is what we must call the "written reality." Indeed, Bresson's faithfulness to the text of Bernanos, his refusal, that is, not only to adapt it but also his paradoxical concern to emphasize its literary character, is part of the same predetermined approach to the direction of his actors and the selection of his settings. Bresson treats the novel as he does his characters. The novel is a cold, hard fact, a reality to be accepted as it stands. . . .

Bresson never condenses the text, he cuts it. Thus what is left over is a part of the original. Like marble from a quarry the words of the film continue to be part of the novel. (p. 136)At first sight the film seems to be somehow made up on the one hand of the abbreviated text of the novel and illustrated, on the other hand, by images that never pretend to replace it. All that is spoken is not seen, yet nothing that is seen but is also spoken. At worst, critical good sense can reproach Bresson with having substituted an illustrated radiophonic montage, no less, for Bernanos' novel.

So it is from this ostensible corruption of the art of cinema that we begin if we are to grasp fully Bresson's originality and boldness. (p. 138)

Bresson disposes once and for all of that commonplace of criticism according to which image and sound should never duplicate one another. The most moving moments in the film are those in which text and image are saying the same thing, each however in its own way. The sound never serves simply to fill out what we see. It strengthens it and multiplies it just as the echo chamber of a violin echoes and multiplies the vibrations of the strings. Yet this metaphor is dialectically inadequate since it is not so much a resonance that the mind perceives as something that does not match, as when a color is not properly superimposed on a drawing. It is here at the edge that the event reveals its true significance. It is because the film is entirely structured on this relationship that, towards the end, the images take on such emotional power. It would be in vain to look for its devastating beauty simply in what is explicit. I doubt if the individual frames in any other film, taken separately, are so deceptive. Their frequent lack of plastic composition, the awkwardness and static quality of the actors completely mislead one as to their value in the overall film. Moreover, this accretion of effectiveness is not due to the editing. The value of an image does not depend on what precedes or follows it. They accumulate, rather, a static energy, like the parallel leaves of a condenser. Between this and the sound track differences of aesthetic potential are set up, the tension of which becomes unbearable. Thus the image-text relationship moves towards its climax, the latter having the advantage. Thus it is that, quite naturally, at the command of an imperious logic, there is nothing more that the image has to communicate except by disappearing. The spectator has been led, step by step, towards that night of the senses the only expression of which is a light on a blank screen.

That is where the so-called silent film and its lofty realism is headed, to the disappearance of the image and its replacement simply by the text of the novel. But here we are experimenting with an irrefutable aesthetic, with a sublime achievement of pure cinema. . . . [The] screen, free of images and handed back to literature, is the triumph of cinematographic realism. The black cross on the white screen, as awkwardly drawn as on the average memorial card, the only trace left by the "assumption" of the image, is a witness to something the reality of which is itself but a sign. (pp. 140-41)

[In *Le Journal,* the] dialectic between fidelity and creation is reducible, in the last analysis, to a dialectic between the cinema and literature. There is no question here of a translation, no matter how faithful or intelligent. Still less is it a question of free inspiration with the intention of making a duplicate. It is a question of building a secondary work with the novel as foundation. In no sense is the film "comparable" to the novel or "worthy" of it. It is a new aesthetic creation, the novel so to speak multiplied by the cinema.

The only procedure in any way comparable of which we have any examples are films of paintings. [Luciano] Emmer or Alain Resnais are similarly faithful to the original, their raw material is the already highly developed work of the painter; the reality with which they are concerned is not the subject of the painting but the painting itself, in the same way as the text of the novel is Bresson's reality. (pp. 141-42)

It is hardly enough to say of this work, once removed, that it is in essence faithful to the original because, to begin with, it *is* the novel. But most of all the resulting work is not, certainly, better (that kind of judgment is meaningless . . .) but "more" than the book. The aesthetic pleasure we derive from Bresson's film, while the acknowledgment for it goes, essentially, to the genius of Bernanos, includes all that the novel has to offer plus, in addition, its refraction in the cinema. (p. 143)

André Bazin, "'Le Journal d'un curé de campagne' and the Stylistics of Robert Bresson," in his What Is Cinema?, *edited and translated by Hugh Gray (copyright © 1967 by the Regents of the University of California; reprinted by permission of the University of California Press), University of California Press, 1967, pp. 125-43.*

TOM MILNE

After the manifold splendours of *Balthazar, Mouchette* seems an altogether thinner experience, exquisite but frail, as though Bresson this time had chosen to tell only the story of Marie without the counterpoint of Balthazar. Unlike the earlier film, which develops as a series of concentric circles spreading from the tethered souls of Marie and Balthazar, *Mouchette* . . . drives straight as an arrow towards its inevitable end in Mouchette's abdication from life. . . .

At the same time, by any other standards than *Balthazar, Mouchette* is a masterpiece: a Bresson film pure and simple with its extraordinary *correspondances* between sound and gesture to evoke the unspoken and the unseen. No one but Bresson, for instance, could have conceived that extraordinary dialogue between hands, veiled eyes and inanimate objects which pinpoints the triangle relationship between Arsene, Louisa and the gamekeeper. . . .

The real importance of *Mouchette,* however, is that it confirms a new departure in Bresson's work which began with *Balthazar.* Always a solitary, the Bresson hero has hitherto lived apart, in a world almost of his creation, isolated not only by circumstance but by his own nature. . . . With Marie and Mouchette, Bresson describes a different kind of solitude: one which exists *within* the world rather than apart from it, and which is resisted rather than courted. (p. 152)

Accordingly, the Bresson landscape has changed. Formerly a reflection of the protagonist's mental state, it is now completely at odds with him (or rather, her). . . . [The] apprehension of the physical world is extraordinarily acute, both visually and aurally. Apparently irrelevant shots—close-ups of glasses on a counter, of the headlamps on a lorry, of the gamekeeper's hands as he talks to Louisa—are given an inexplicable, lowering significance, precisely because the objects seen are autonomous, completely without symbolism. Like the squalor of the village and the beauty of the surrounding countryside, they are simply there, impartial witnesses to rather than actors in Mouchette's tragedy. . . .

This process of exteriorisation, shifting the emphasis from the malleability of the Christian soul to the implacable indifference of the Christian world, leads Bresson not into black pessimism as one might have expected, but to an undefined, almost pantheistic heresy. . . . I doubt whether the image of the Cross could close these two films as it does *Journal d'un Curé de Campagne* and *Procès de Jeanne d'Arc;* but for the first time the epilogue might read, with complete accuracy, 'Tout est grâce.' (p. 153)

Tom Milne, "Film Reviews: 'Mouchette'," in Sight and Sound *(copyright © 1968 by The British Film Institute), Vol. 37, No. 2, Spring, 1968, pp. 152-53.*

ERIC RHODE

[In *A Gentle Creature*] Bresson follows the content, if not the method of [Dostoevsky's story of the same name] closely. It is as though he had listed all its main points, then filmed them with as much clarity as possible so that no one should misunderstand their meaning. A spareness surrounds almost every phrase and gesture, a spareness emphasised by the familiar Bressonian device of using low-tensioned interludes: people walking up and down stairs, opening and closing doors. In the four opening shots he establishes the suicide in an authoritative way: a hand presses down on a door handle; an elderly maid, Anna, watches a table fall on a balcony; a white shawl falls slowly through the air; the girl lies dead on the pavement. . . .

In several ways Bresson's sharpening of Dostoevsky's narrative also deepens it. The ritualised handling of the scenes in the pawnbroker's shop brings out the compulsive element in this work: pawnbroking is like picking pockets. And by a single-minded focus on this act, the monotonous exchange of money for cherished objects becomes momentous. (p. 82)

And yet, as always with this director, clarity of statement does not presume an absence of ambiguity. His plot may have the schematic feel of a French neo-classical tragedy: but what does this schema represent? The authority of his filming, the deliberate progression of each shot, may suggest that he knows where he is taking us to: but where, in fact, is his destination? Like Dostoevsky, he has intuitions about a genuine mystery at the centre of life: but whereas Dostoevsky has to stir up a murky confusion before he can induce the state of mind which allows for religious awe, Bresson has only to scrutinise life under the bright light of reason to break down rationalist assumptions about experience. Like certain theologians, Bresson uses reason to lead us to perceptions, and destinations, that resist being put into words.

Or so it seemed, until a few years ago. Formerly, Bresson used to provide a background of religious allegory to reassure us as he led us through the perplexities of his foreground narrative: his protagonists trod the path to Grace. But at least since *Mouchette* he has given up this guideline. The superficial resemblance of his films to neo-classical tragedy soon reveals itself as deceptive. They are much more like symbolist poems: either their images and rhythms call up an illuminating train of associations and feelings in you, or they don't.

I find *A Gentle Creature* moving, yet there is much to it I cannot account for. Dostoevsky describes his pawnbroker in psychologically convincing terms: his often absurd quirks, his snobberies and inessential scruples, his wish to revenge himself on society because he has been cashiered from the army and cannot face up to this disgrace, are coherent character traits. Bresson simplifies the man to the point of making him into an allegorical cypher. . . .

The girl is even more of a puzzle than her husband. True, we only learn about her through her husband's recollections. But would such a present-day woman . . . fail to find work, or marry an unlikeable man because she fears destitution, or then remain with him when he so manifestly wishes to harm her? . . .

[There] is one complication which Bresson, it could be, failed to allow for. He intimates that the girl has a compassion and a sensuality which the husband does not acknowledge. And Bresson's sympathy, I would think, is with her. Yet, in spite of himself, the style of his filming sides with the husband: when the girl plays jazz records we do not feel that her presence animates the pawnbroker's luxurious yet lifeless apartment; on the contrary, her tastes jar against Bresson's austerity. Eroticism plays only a marginal part in Dostoevsky's story—the narrator has contradictory fantasies that he has saved his wife from prostitution, or that she *is* his prostitute. In the film sexuality takes on a more prominent role. At an art gallery the girl admires a classical painting of a sensual-looking nude. The husband at once manipulates this natural response into the thought that women are instruments of pleasure. Bresson, I surmise, wants to accommodate himself to the instinctive sensuality of his gentle creature, but like the pawnbroker puts a construction on it which inhibits a direct response. It may have to do with his Roman Catholicism and, perhaps, with some half-denied belief that sexuality is sinful. The marriage proposal at the zoo and the reference to the randiness of monkeys, the ray of light touching the nude breast in the bedroom painting: somehow the stress is often wrongly placed.

I keep feeling that Bresson's treatment of the girl is a little like the relationship of some fathers to their teenage daughters. He wants to share her interests and even loves her but, irritably, cannot quite bridge the gap between them.

This ambiguity disturbs—and has nothing to do with Dostoevsky. But it is only one among many perplexities in *A Gentle Creature,* mystifications rather than mysteries. Why is there a staging of a long scene from *Hamlet?* Some commentators believe that Hamlet brings about changes in Denmark only at the cost of damning himself—are we to see the wife's fate as similar? And what are we to make of the shot, seen twice over, of the falling white shawl, which recalls the falling white scarf in Truffaut's *The Bride Wore Black,* and which worries me as sentimental: was some sort of symbolic shorthand intended? . . .

In many ways *A Gentle Creature* is a teasing, uncommunicative film; and yet, by its final shot—of an undertaker's hand screwing down the coffin lid—its slow yet genuine insistence on the nature of loss has made it unforgettable. (p. 83)

Eric Rhode, "Dostoevsky and Bresson," in Sight and Sound *(copyright © 1970 by The British Film Institute), Vol. 39, No. 2, Spring, 1970, pp. 82-3.*

ROY ARMES

Bresson has recreated the novel [*Journal d'un Curé de Campagne*], not simply made an adaptation of it in the conventional manner. He has been concerned to seek out the central core of the book—the spiritual development of the young country priest—and prune all the side issues not directly related to this main theme (but which are nonetheless an essential part of the novel), thereby intensifying the story and giving it the purity of a Racinean tragedy. (p. 128)

The director's personality is to be felt too in the film's tone: all the emotions are muted and there is a lack of violence or passion. . . . This continual understating of the emotions, together with the hero's essentially passive submission to God's will, gives the film its particular rhythm and makes the death of the Curé a real climax. (pp. 129-30)

[Again, in *Un Condamné à mort s'est échappé*] Bresson concentrates on his single theme, the prison escape planned and executed by the hero (here known as Lieutenant Fontaine), and all that is irrelevant to this is omitted. For this reason we learn nothing of the prisoner's antecedents or even the reasons why he is in prison; we can see what sort of a man he is from his actions and this suffices. (p. 130)

The whole film has an evenness of tone that marks it as the product of one man's personality. Fontaine has remarkable similarities with the Curé d'Ambricourt: he is intelligent, withdrawn, in control of himself even in moments of crisis and endowed with considerable force of character which allows him to impose his will on his fellow men and his physical surroundings. Confidently he awaits the success of his plan, and this calm passivity gives the film its rhythm and atmosphere. (p. 131)

Pickpocket takes us more into the ordinary everyday world than before, among the crowds at race meetings, in underground trains and at railway stations. . . . But this is a world where God plays no part, where the hero's life is without spiritual meaning, and in this repect it is the antithesis of the prison world of Fort Montluc in the previous film. The hero's inner life is once more the core of the film and the real drama is the struggle that goes on behind Michel's emotionless face. Bresson has no interest in individual psychology except in so far as it illustrates the workings of the Divine Will and little motivation is offered for the Pickpocket's acts. . . . [His] virtual surrender to justice is Michel's first act of submission and leads directly to his salvation. His love for Jeanne, which is the means of this redemption, introduces a new element into the Bresson world. . . . The love of Michel and Jeanne, though serving as the film's culmination, is muted, with no effusion of emotion shown, and it is typical of the film's treatment of love that their last embrace is through the bars imprisoning Michel. (pp. 132, 134)

[In *Procès de Jeanne d'Arc*] Bresson is faced with a new challenge: in his previous films he had taken life in all its vigour and diversity, and distilled from it a single thread of action; in this film he attempts to breathe life into the historical documents which record the minutes of Joan's trial. For Bresson, with his eternal quest for authenticity, these are the only possible sources for his film and he allows himself to invent nothing. . . . Bresson's fidelity to recorded fact means that he has to do without one element that had been as essential part of the earlier films: the voice of a narrator. Words are as important in *Procès de Jeanne d'Arc* as in the preceding works but their function is different. Whereas previously they had shown an inner struggle and conflict, here they record an outward clash: Joan's verbal duel with Bishop Cauchon. This is perhaps a key to the peculiar coldness of the film. *Journal d'un Curé de Campagne* was near to tragedy in its chronicling of the doubts and hesitations of a terribly vulnerable young priest, but Joan of Arc, as Bresson sees her, has virtually no doubts or regrets at leaving this world; she is content, such is the strength of her faith, to submit herself totally to God's will. The resolute march of a saint to martyrdom may fill us with awe, but we do not feel any personal involvement with her.

Stylistically the film shows Bresson at his most austere. (p. 134)

[*Au Hasard, Balthazar*] not only forged a fresh stylistic approach, it also covered a new range of material with an inclusiveness that the earlier works had lacked. It takes in jazz and teenage dancing, violence and nudity, cruelty and leather-clad motorcyclists while still preserving a Bressonian atmosphere. The director contrives to distance this material by means of a film structure that achieves an effect of de-dramatisation by breaking the action into a succession of tiny elliptical scenes connected in ways that are not immediately apparent. The film has the richness of plot of a Dostoievskian story and an added element of strangeness in that its eponymous hero is a donkey. (p. 136)

The film's distinctive mixture of obscure meaning (the donkey) and quite blatant symbolism (Gérard's leather jacket and motor bike) is held together by Bresson's extraordinary stylistic control. Characteristic Bresson touches such as the use of Schubert's music and the uniform style of gesture and enunciation—this is a film in which dialogue is rare and the silences are most meaningful—are combined in *Au Hasard, Balthazar* with moments of a quite unique unreality: the donkey in a deserted house or amid traffic, amid the sheep on the mountain-side or confronted with the animals in the zoo. The vision which emerges is that of a world of Dostoievskian corruption where evil flourishes and secret vices eat at the hearts of men. In following the course of Balthazar's life we encounter obliquely a whole wealth of worldly experience—the death of a child, pride and the quarrel of friends, pure destructiveness, lust, *amour fou,* avarice, humiliation, crime and death—and Bresson presents us with a world where simple love and laughter vanish with childhood but grace is never absent. . . .

The film *Mouchette,* like the previous work, traces the experience of a whole life-time but obliquely in a succession of fragmentary shots and scenes welded in an almost musical rhythm. The fourteen-year-old heroine does not have to seek humiliation, it comes her way spontaneously. (p. 137)

As in all his mature work, Bresson's personality is imprinted on every foot of *Mouchette.* This domination was achieved at the expense of his actors, as the painter Jean Vimenet (who played the gamekeeper) has pointed out: "None of us was ever aware of what was going on. He would not allow us to look at the script or see the photos taken in the course of shooting . . . He uses people like objects. He leaves absolutely nothing to their imagination: every detail, every gesture, every millimetre of movement of a finger or nose, your nose is in this position, you look in this direction, every indication is given down to the smallest detail by Bresson himself. You have nothing to contribute; you are a robot, you are put in a certain position and you remain like that. At a certain moment you have to turn your head . . ." Vimenet's words make clear how the distinctive acting style of Bresson's work is achieved but do little to illuminate the more mysterious aspects of his art: the ability to remain faithful to a literary source and yet produce a work that is wholly his own, to shoot with non-professional actors on location and yet give his film an air of the supernatural, to insist on total realism at every stage and yet achieve a result that is a marvel of stylisation. (pp. 138-39)

Taken as a whole, Bresson's characters show a unique coherence and constitute a profound investigation into the workings of divine grace in a life lived under the shadow of death. (p. 145)

Roy Armes, "Innovators and Independents," in his French Cinema since 1946: The Great Tradition, Vol. 1 *(copyright © 1966, 1970 by Roy Armes), revised edition, A. S. Barnes & Co., 1970, pp. 126-68.**

CHARLES THOMAS SAMUELS

[*Une Femme Douce*] commences with the [heroine's] suicide. What draws us on, like [her] husband, is the desire to know why. But to know why in Bresson (as is not the case in Dostoevski), we have to watch intently everything that happens because nothing is explained and even the explainer is an item to be fathomed. Many viewers find Bresson cold and remote, but this coldness may be only a reflection of their own passivity. If you can be excited by the search for understanding, you can be excited by Bresson.

So Bresson forces total concentration. . . . Only at the very end of each film does Bresson release us from our hush of contemplation with a shock that sums up what we've seen, as when bubbles emerge from the river in which the heroine of *Mouchette* has drowned herself and a blast of the *Magnificat* admits that death alone is victory for such a life. (p. 312)

The wife is not what her husband thinks her to be, yet when she almost embodies his erroneous image, her integrity is shattered and she can only die. The husband is brutal, not so much when he seeks to possess his hard-eyed wife as when he seeks to make amends for having sought possession. Watching their marriage progress, we feel a growing terror, because opposites merge and solutions turn out to be worse than the problems they solve. . . .

The film's clear point is that tragedy can be comprehended as a process, while still evading our need to fathom motives and fix blame. Therefore, Bresson uses his cinematic means —framing, editing, dialogue, acting—to achieve an even emphasis that precludes abstract summation. Whatever inspires these people can only be inferred from their laconic utterances and meager gestures. But this very meagerness —which we are made to experience—comes as close as anything can to being the source of their solitude. Both Dostoevski's story and Bresson's film light up the distance between two human souls (although Bresson magnifies the distance by giving us a fuller portrayal of the wife). Dostoevski, however, attributes the distance to a fundamental human perversity; Bresson links it to a world without spiritual force. (p. 314)

Many artists would depict a desolation of spirit so profound through more striking dramatization, but Bresson would think this a mistake; he includes in *Une Femme Douce* a scene that illustrates his aesthetic. When the couple see *Hamlet* at the theater, the husband is impressed but the wife doesn't join in his applause. Returning home, she explains why, by running to a volume of Shakespeare to read lines that had been eliminated in the performance only so that the actors could get away with shouting and gesticulation. The lines come from Hamlet's advice to the players (in a French translation) and among them is the veritable motto of Bresson's art:

> in the torrent, the tempest, the whirlwind
> one must always be moderate and acquire
> even a certain gentleness.

Like the wife herself, Bresson shows that gentleness of manner does not deny inner ferocity. For the spectator who can match the film's concentration with his own, Bresson, by rigorously controlling passion, inspires it. (p. 315)

Charles Thomas Samuels, "Bresson's Gentleness," in The American Scholar *(copyright by the Estate of Charles Thomas Samuels; reprinted by permission), Vol. 40, No. 2, Spring, 1971, pp. 309-15.*

PAUL SCHRADER

Bresson's prison cycle [*Diary of a Country Priest, A Man Escaped, Pickpocket,* and *The Trial of Joan of Arc*] provides an excellent opportunity to study the transcendental style in depth for several reasons: one, because the prison metaphor is endemic to certain theological questions; two, because Bresson's statements clear up much of the ambiguity in which critics are often forced to operate; and three, because there are few cultural elements intermingled with transcendental style in his films. (p. 60)

[In] transcendental style the form *must* be the operative element, and for a very simple reason: form is the universal element whereas the subject matter is necessarily parochial, having been determined by the particular culture from which it springs. And if a work of art is to be truly transcendent (above *any* culture), it must rely on its universal elements. (p. 61)

In film, "surface-aesthetics" is the everyday, and is practiced by Bresson. . . . (p. 62)

Bresson's use of the everyday is not derived from a concern for "real life," but from an opposition to the contrived, dramatic events which pass for real life in movies. These emotional constructs—plot, acting, camerawork, editing, music—are "screens." . . . Screens prevent the viewer from seeing through the surface reality to the supernatural; they suppose that the external reality is self-sufficient.

This is why Bresson's work seems so perverse to the uninitiated viewer: Bresson despises what the moviegoer likes best. (pp. 63-4)

Bresson has an antipathy toward plot. . . . The plot "screen" establishes a simple, facile relationship between the viewer and event. . . . The viewer feels that he himself has a direct contact with the workings of life, and that it is in some manner under his control. . . .

In Bresson's films the viewer's feelings have no effect on the outcome. . . . The events are predestined, beyond the viewer's control and beyond—seemingly—Bresson's. (p. 64)

In the everyday Bresson replaces the "screens" with a form. By drawing attention to itself, the everyday stylization annuls the viewer's natural desire to participate vicariously in the action on screen. (p. 69)

The everyday blocks the emotional and intellectual exits, preparing the viewer for the moment when he must face the Unknown. The intractable form of the everyday will not allow the viewer to apply his natural interpretive devices. . . .

One of the dangers of the everyday is that it may become a screen in itself, a style rather than a stylization, an end rather than a means. The everyday eliminates the obvious emotional constructs but tacitly posits a rational one: that the world is predictable, ordered, cold. Disparity undermines the rational construct.

Disparity injects a "human density" into the unfeeling everyday, an unnatural density which grows and grows until, at the moment of decisive action, it reveals itself to be a spiritual density. (p. 70)

[Bresson's] narration does not give the viewer any new information or feelings, but only reiterates what he already knows. The viewer is conditioned to expect "new" information from narration; instead, he gets only a cold reinforcement of the everyday.

When the same thing starts happening two or three times concurrently the viewer knows he is beyond simple day-to-day realism and into the peculiar realism of Robert Bresson. The doubling does not double the viewer's knowledge or emotional reaction, it only doubles his perception of the event. Consequently, there is a schizoid reaction; one, there is the sense of meticulous detail which is a part of the everyday, and two, because the detail is doubled there is an emotional queasiness, a growing suspicion of the seemingly "realistic" rationale behind the everyday. If it is "realism," why is the action doubled, and if it isn't realism, why this obsession with details? (p. 72)

Techniques like doubling cast suspicion on the everyday, and the next step of disparity goes farther: it tries to evoke a "sense" of something Wholly Other within the cold environment, a sense which gradually alienates the main character from his solid position within the everyday. Jean Sémolué [in *Bresson*] has distinguished three levels of such alienation in *Diary of a Country Priest:* (1) sickness: the priest and his body, (2) social solitude: the priest and his parishioners, (3) sacred solitude: the priest and the world of sin. The young priest is unable to relate to any of the elements in his environment; even nature, which does not figure in Sémolué's schema, seems hostile to the suffering priest as he collapses under the gray sky and tall, dark barren trees. At this level Bresson's theme would seem to fit his pseudodocumentary everyday technique: the unending conflict between man and environment is one of the cardinal themes of documentary art.

But the conflict is more complicated than it at first seems. The source of this alienation does not seem to be intrinsic to the priest (his neurosis, misanthropy, or paranoia) or to his environment (antagonistic parishioners, inclement weather), but seems to originate from a greater, external source. The priest is the frail vehicle of an overwhelming passion which in the context of *Diary of a Country Priest* is called the holy agony (*la Sainte Agonie*). (pp. 72-3)

The levels of alienation demonstrated by Sémolué are actually extensions of the holy agony. In fact, what seems to be a rejection by the environment is more accurately a rejection by the priest—and not because he wishes to estrange himself, but because he is the unwilling (at first) instrument of an overwhelming and self-mortifying passion. (p. 73)

On each level the priest's alienation originates in neither the environment nor himself, but in an overpowering, transcendental passion. (p. 75)

[Each Bressonian] protagonist struggles to free himself from his everyday environment, to find a proper metaphor for his passion. This struggle leads Michel to prison, Fontaine to freedom, and the priest and Joan to martyrdom.

The viewer finds himself in a dilemma: the environment suggests documentary realism, yet the central character suggests spiritual passion. This dilemma produces an emotional strain: the viewer wants to empathize with Joan (as he would for any innocent person in agony), yet the everyday structure warns him that his feelings will be of no avail. (pp. 77-8)

The trigger to that emotional release occurs during the final stage of disparity, decisive action, and it serves to freeze the emotional into expression, the disparity into stasis. (p. 78)

The decisive action has a unique effect on the viewer, which may be hypothesized thus: the viewer's feelings have been consistently shunned throughout the film (everyday), yet he still has "strange" undefined feelings (disparity). The decisive action then demands an emotional commitment which the viewer gives instinctively, naturally (he wants to share Hirayama's tears, Michel's love). But having given that commitment, the viewer must now do one of two things: he can reject his feelings and refuse to take the film seriously, or he can accommodate his thinking to his feelings. If he chooses the latter, he will, having been given no emotional constructs by the director, have constructed his own "screen." He creates a translucent, mental screen through which he can cope with both his feelings and the film. . . . Bresson uses the viewer's own natural defenses, his protective mechanism, to cause him, of his own free will, to come to the identical decision Bresson had predetermined for him. (pp. 81-2)

Stasis is the quiescent, frozen, or hieratic scene which succeeds the decisive action and closes the film. It is a still review of the external world intended to suggest the oneness of all things. In *Diary of a Country Priest* it is the shadow of the cross, in *A Man Escaped* it is the long shot of the darkened street with Fontaine and Jost receding in the distance. . . . (p. 82)

This static view represents the "new" world in which the spiritual and the physical can coexist, still in tension and unresolved, but as part of a larger scheme in which all phenomena are more or less expressive of a larger reality—the Transcendent. (p. 83)

The prison metaphor is endemic to Western thought. Western theories, whether theological, psychological, or political, are inevitably couched in terms of freedom and restraint. On the theological level, the prison metaphor is linked to the fundamental body/soul dichotomy, a linkage which is made by the wellsprings of Western thought. . . . (p. 88)

As the body becomes identified with the prison, there is a natural tendency toward self-mortification. The country priest mortifies his body and at the moment of death surrenders himself into the hands of God. In *Pickpocket* the metaphor is reversed; Michel's prison is crime, his freedom is in jail. His is also a self-mortification, but it does not lead to death. (p. 89)

The prison metaphor gains in complexity and depth as Bresson extends it to the theological paradox of predestination and free will. The body/soul conflict is a dichotomy for Bresson: he prefers the soul to the body, even to the point of death; whereas the predestination/free will conflict is a paradox, it cannot be resolved by death but has to be accepted on faith. Predestination/free will is a complex and contradictory concept, and Bresson's prison metaphor adapts to this complexity. (p. 90)

In his films man's "freedom" consists of being a "prisoner of the Lord" rather than a prisoner of the flesh. Joan of Arc seemingly chooses martyrdom of her own free will, yet the film also repeatedly emphasizes that her fate is predetermined. . . . The only tension, as in predestinarianism, is whether or not she will choose her predestined fate. (pp. 90-1)

Bresson's treatment of the prison metaphor justifies his often rather voguish labeling as a "Jansenist." . . .

The mysterious, conciliatory element in the predestination/free will paradox is grace. (p. 91)

In Bresson's films grace allows the protagonist to accept the paradox of predestination and free will. . . . (p. 92)

Bresson's theology, his formulation of the problems of body and soul, predestination and free will, grace and redemption, seems obviously Jansenist, but to infer from this, as some critics have, that his aesthetic and artistic influences were also Jansenist is incorrect. Jansenism, like Calvinism, had little feeling for aesthetics or art in general, and almost none for the "visual arts" in particular. (p. 95)

The Scholastic aesthetic [defined by Jacques Maritain in *Art and Scholasticism*] is . . . appropriate for Bresson's art because it allows a place for the intellectual formulation of ideas within the form. Logic was not opposed to mystery but just another means to appreciate it. The Schoolmen "attempted a task not yet clearly envisaged by their forerunners and ruefully to be abandoned by their successors, the mystics and the nominalists: the task of writing a permanent peace treaty between faith and reason." This aesthetic, which could serve both faith and reason in East and West, can also serve the seemingly contradictory qualities of Bresson's film-making. (p. 97)

Artistically, Bresson's films bear . . . resemblance to Byzantine portraiture, an art form which lived out an aesthetic similar to Scholasticism before there was the need to create an aesthetic. (p. 98)

Bresson uses frontality to create a respectful, noncommitted attitude within the viewer which can result in a stasis very similar to that evoked by a religious icon.

The long forehead, the lean features, the closed lips, the blank stare, the frontal view, the flat light, the uncluttered background, the stationary camera, these identify Bresson's protagonists as objects suitable for veneration. (p. 100)

His techniques of portraiture come from Byzantium, his theology of predestination, free will and grace from Jansenism, his aesthetics from Scholasticism. To each tradition he brings the virtues of the other, and to cinema he brings the virtues of all three. Perhaps this is why no religious denomination has ever embraced Bresson's seemingly religious films; they haven't figured out what sort of heretic he is yet. (p. 105)

Paul Schrader, "Bresson," in his Transcendental Style in Film: Ozu, Bresson, Dreyer *(copyright © 1972 by The Regents of the University of California; reprinted by permission of the University of California Press), University of California Press, 1972, pp. 57-108.*

JONATHAN BAUMBACH

The severity of Bresson's style has earned his films the reputation, depending on whom you read, of being exquisitely or pretentiously boring. In fact, in my sense of it, the opposite is true. There is hardly an uncharged moment in Bresson's meticulous and provocative *mise en scène*. My sense is that certain audiences experience Bresson as boring because his films, while appearing simple, demand so much of the eye. Boredom serves as a means of deflecting pressure.

In *Four Nights of a Dreamer,* it is as if Bresson's influence on Godard had filtered back to him in a kind of circular pollination. A comedy . . . adapted and updated from the Dostoevsky story "White Nights," *Four Nights of a Dreamer* is Bresson's most contemporary film in style and setting. It is also the austere filmmaker's most ungrudgingly beautiful and accessible work. (p. 450)

Whereas in the tragic films, Bresson's isolated, self-imprisoned figures (the curate, the pickpocket, Fontaine, Marie), seeking freedom, make contact at the last extreme with another, *Four Nights of a Dreamer* deals with the romantic charge of hopeless pursuit. Jacques loves Marthe—it is the nature of romantic love, of course—because he is doomed not to have her. The dreamer, committed to loss, pursues only illusory hopes. To make real contact, to love, is to lose the fantasy of loving, which is central to the dreamer's life, the romantic, really masturbatory stuff of his art. Although their romance is dependent on the blindness of mutual self-dramatization, Jacques's loss of Marthe, her rejection of him for her former lover, touches us somehow at the end. Throughout the body of the film, Bresson denies us the least of our illusions about his characters, distances us from them as if a glass door separated our feelings from theirs. Withheld from us unreasonably long, Jacques's pain and isolation—the price he pays for his dreaming—breaks through at the last, releasing us into brief recognition, and the film is over. Jacques retreats into old patterns of survival, does what we've seen him do a number of times before, but for a moment we see him with extraordinary clarity, recognize him as if he were transparent or luminous. (p. 451)

Jonathan Baumbach, "Medium and Message," in Partisan Review *(copyright © 1973 by Partisan Review, Inc.), Vol. XL, No. 3, 1973, pp. 445-54.**

JONATHAN ROSENBAUM

[*Lancelot du Lac* stuns and overwhelms one because of the film's] clarity and simplicity, a precise and irreducible arrangement of sounds and images that is so wholly functional that nothing is permitted to detract from the overall narrative complex, and everything present is *used*. It is a film where the rattle of armour and the neighing of horses are as essential as the faces and bodies of the characters, where indeed each of these elements serves to isolate and define the importance and impact of the others.

The sheer rawness of what is there disconcerts, but it shouldn't lead one to focus unduly on what isn't there, or track down some elusive clue to the Bressonian mystery. To a certain extent, Bresson's films are *about* mystery, but their manner of arriving there is always quite concrete. . . . [It] seems useful to speak here of Bresson's art as one of immanence, not one of transcendence, and one where the inside is always revealed by remaining on the outside. . . .

This is a distinctly modern *Lancelot,* in striking contrast to the relatively 'medieval' atmosphere of Bresson's last two films, both set in contemporary Paris, where the gentle creature often suggested a lonely maiden in a tower waiting to be rescued, and the dreamer resembled a wandering knight in search of a pure love that was equally hopeless. The sense of elongated durations and passing seasons that we associate with the romances of Chrétien de Troyes is more evident in *Balthazar,* or even in John Ford's *The Searchers,* than in the tightly compressed episodes of *Lancelot,* where action and event is all.

The comparison with Ford is hardly gratuitous: *Lancelot* is surely the closest thing we can ever hope to get to a Bressonian Western or adventure film, although it also achieves a tapestry-like stillness in certain scenes that plays against the livelier movements. (p. 129)

Most modern of all, perhaps, are the characters of Guenièvre and Lancelot, although the specific signs of their modernity are not at all easy to pinpoint. The scenes between them seem to adhere rather closely to the courtly tradition, and the spiritual malaise affecting Lancelot—torn between his love for Guenièvre, his vow to God to end their adultery, and his loyalty to Artus—contains no discernible elements that are added to the legend. And yet the absence of any psychology, the elliptical exposition of their feelings, and the degree to which Bresson isolates them from their environments and defines them in relation to each other, all serve to give them unmistakable contemporary reverberations. (pp. 129-30)

[And] of course, there are the voices—neutral and uniform in their apparent lack of expressiveness, but presences charged with meaning and effect in relation to the overall complex of sound and silence, where the lack of overt emotion becomes a sounding brass against which the words themselves are able to resound. (p. 130)

Jonathan Rosenbaum, "Bresson's 'Lancelot du lac'," in Sight and Sound *(copyright © 1974 by The British Film Institute), Vol. 43, No. 3, Summer, 1974, pp. 129-30.*

JOHN GERLACH

[Bresson, in *The Diary of a Country Priest,*] is faithful to the central development of the priest's role, at the same time that he diminishes the significance of the four pairs of characters. The priest is granted three moments of insight, during which he understands the depth of pain suffered by Delbende, Chantal, and the Countess. In each case he acts with certainty, with a nearly hypnotic precision. In the case of Delbende, he is unable to offer comfort, in the cases of Chantal and the Countess, he is energized into compassion and action. But many of the incidents which show the priest's relation to these and other characters are either truncated or omitted. This inherently difficult alteration of the fundamental balance between the study of an individual's soul and the spiritual state of the world around him Bresson manages successfully, primarily by using the resources of film to allow the viewer to discover a design, an order hidden in apparent disorder. Where Bernanos studies priest and parish, Bresson studies priest and Providence, using the mise-en-scène as the vehicle of that discovery. (p. 41)

The movement of figures is typical of Bresson's control of the mise-en-scène. As the priest enters the room of the Countess in the central "medallion" scene, she is poking in the fireplace. Near the end of the scene, to complete the circular design, she throws the medallion containing the picture of her dead son into the same fireplace, misunderstanding the extent of the sacrifice to which the priest has summoned her. . . . Bresson disdains the sentimentality, and instead concentrates on the priest digging in the ashes, a decision which reveals the care and precision of his movements and also gives relief from the extreme tension of the rest of the scene—it is a sudden reminder of being in the unredeemed world, where things take time to be done. . . . (p. 42)

Matching sets of gestures can be far more powerful revelations than contrasts of emotion as treated in more effusive styles of acting. The priest is often contrasted with others by devices such as gestures of the hands and eyes. The gestures themselves are not short-hand symbols for meaning, for often similar gestures have different meanings. When

Louise, the governess who has been having an affair with the Count, is kneeling at Mass, and opens her hands to reveal her face, the hands disclose a guilty expression; in the following shot, as the priest opens wide his hands in a formal gesture to begin the Mass, his face has an impersonal sense of peace; we see not the priest as a person, but the priest, in the best sense of the expression, acting out a role. (p. 43)

[Objects are used in the same fashion as gestures.] Windows at the opening of the film are indistinct blurs of illumination behind the priest, almost halos. If they are to be taken as such, they are meant ironically, for he is timid and unaware of the extent of suffering and darkness he will experience—an innocent only in the sense that he is ignorant. Once he becomes aware that his parish does not want him bringing into the open the evil that is part of its established routine, the amount of light diminishes; he is often illuminated only be a single lamp. Windows stand as frames of his isolation; we look through a window to see him sleeping while his narrative voice tells of his stomach pains and sleeplessness. In the morning he comes to the window in hope of signs of compassion, but finds none. (p. 44)

The use of windows allows us to see the extent of the system of correspondences Bresson has devised and allows us to piece together otherwise puzzling actions. . . . [The window in the interview between the countess and the priest] serves again to reveal a scene which may justly be called the center of the film, the point at which, in the midst of very simple questions, the complexity of the scene is developed. Human intention is thwarted so that design may be fulfilled. The actual force behind these movements is concealed, but the extent of that force is revealed in every corner, in every motion, It is as if the audience were given divine insight, the ability to see transcendental order in what would otherwise, without the restrictions of the frame of the picture that limit our point of view, seem random and mundane.

It is never simple to describe the quality of scenes such as these. Plain descriptions of scenes such as Seraphita delivering the catechism on the Eucharist in a sing-song tone, the priest delivering the speech about the sufferings of Christ to the Countess, and the final image of the Cross, which remains on the screen for more than a minute while a letter describing the priest's death is read, would make Bresson seem sentimental or dogmatic, but the final effect of the film is far different. Each scene is characterized by either perfect restraint or strong, clear emotion, by an efficiency and precision that continually stimulate both perception and participation. The film treats mystery as just that—neither clarifying, nor confusing—only demonstrating. With its dramatic action carried out by constantly meaningful movements, the real energy of the film derives from the viewer's perception of the interaction of each of the elements of the film. (pp. 44-5)

John Gerlach, "'The Diary of a Country Priest': A Total Conversion," in Literature/Film Quarterly *(© copyright 1976 Salisbury State College), Vol. 4, No. 1, Winter, 1976, pp. 39-45.*

TOM MILNE

Even more than in *Mouchette,* Bresson is concerned [in *Le Diable, probablement*] with the system of defences with which modern man shores up the form he has contrived to give to the void: on the one hand, the array of ideologies with which he ensures his spiritual well-being, and on the other, the battery of alarms and devices with which he protects his physical safety. . . .

'What impelled me to make this film is the mess we have made of everything. . . . This immense demolition job in which we shall kill ourselves by trying to go on living. . . .'

Yet it is evident that for Bresson the ecological message conveyed by [the images in his film], familiar or otherwise, is self-evident. Far from preaching to the converted, he is concerned less with the impact of these images and intimations of disaster than with the implications apparent in the ways people respond to that impact. Time was, in Bresson's world, when the tormented soul of the young curé of Ambricourt, even though assailed on all sides by an irredeemably sinful society, could look out from within himself, see that it was good, and contentedly murmur 'All is Grace'. Is this still possible in this most modern of all possible worlds? (p. 16)

[In] casting a cruel, almost Kafkaesque eye on the hands enthusiastically battering at the corridors of power that wend labyrinthinely to a ubiquitous no exit, he does squarely face the essential paradox of the modern dilemma. To survive, you may well have to point the way by blowing up a nuclear reactor station; but if you blow up a nuclear reactor station, how do you survive?

The progressive darkening of Bresson's vision, apparent from *Mouchette* through to the near-nihilism of *Lancelot du Lac,* here comes to its logical conclusion in the line scribbled in Charles' notebook: 'When should I kill myself, if not now?' . . .

For the first time in Bresson's work, someone stands on the brink of the void, seeing nothing there or anywhere, and acknowledging—in direct contradiction to the curé of Ambricourt's declaration of faith—that Nothingness is Grace. Yet Charles is human; accepting the logical consequence of his position, he is still afraid of dying. (p. 17)

[However, *Le Diable, probablement*] would not be a Bresson film were its darkness not lightened somewhere by a ray of some kind, however obscure. Long gone, of course, are the days when Bresson's protagonists found salvation whether they sought it or not. . . .

In a film where the characters are literally assaulted by a barrage of summonses, interdictions and appeals from traffic signals, lift signs and bus indicators, Bresson makes one unusually conscious of places, objects, artefacts. . . . [The] tiny ripples, no bigger than might be caused by rain drops, as Charles frantically empties the gun into the placid river; the quais by the Seine, impartially offering an ambience redolent of peace or despair . . . All suggesting a quality of endurance or permanence that will outlive human frailty.

Diffuse and elusive in their intervention into human concerns . . . , all these elements are brought together in the magnificently strange serenity of the scene where Charles and Valentin, armed with sleeping-bags, record-player and a recording of Monteverdi's *Ego dormio,* spend the night in a deserted church. . . . And in the image of Charles safely tucked into his sleeping-bag under the vaulted roofs, caressed by the Monteverdi lullaby, oblivious of Valentin rifling the poor boxes, of the police entering to investigate

the theft, of everything but his sense of being securely cradled for ever, one knows that he has found, however fleetingly and however undefinably, his own particular mode of salvation. (p. 22)

Tom Milne, "'Le Diable, probablement'," in **Sight and Sound** *(copyright © 1977 by The British Film Institute), Vol. 47, No. 1, Winter, 1977-78, pp. 16-17, 22.*

Tod Browning

1882-1962

American filmmaker and actor.

Browning's horror films are macabre and atmospheric, differing from the stereotype of that genre because of his insight into the characters. Browning began his film career as an assistant to D. W. Griffith on *Intolerance*. Prior to his arrival in Hollywood, Browning had realized a typical boy's dream: he had run away from home and joined a carnival troupe. Through this experience he was exposed to a highly unconventional and unusual way of life. Later he would accurately and compassionately depict the grotesque atmosphere of the sideshow in his film *Freaks*.

In many of his other films, Browning collaborated with Lon Chaney. Understanding Chaney's penchant for parts requiring contortions and bizarre make-up, he devised roles especially for that actor and wrote his scripts around those characters. Most critics consider these films the most successful in the careers of both men.

Still, it may be true that Browning is best remembered as the director of *Dracula*, filmed after Chaney's death and starring Bela Lugosi. Browning's reputation rests not only on the sensationalism of horror films but also on his unique point of view. He portrayed deformed outcasts with understanding and sympathy, giving them unusual dignity and depth of characterization.

MORDAUNT HALL

Although it has strength and undoubtedly sustains the interest, "The Unknown" . . . is anything but a pleasant story. It is gruesome and at times shocking, and the principal character deteriorates from a more or less sympathetic individual to an arch-fiend. The narrative is a sort of mixture of Balzac and Guy de Maupassant with a faint suggestion of O. Henry plus Mr. Browning's colorful side-show background.

Mordaunt Hall, "The Armless Wonder," in The New York Times *(© 1927 by The New York Times Company; reprinted by permission), June 13, 1927, p. 17.*

Metro-Goldwyn-Mayer definitely has on its hands a picture that is out of the ordinary. The difficulty is in telling whether it should be shown at the Rialto—where it opened yesterday—or in, say, the Medical Centre. "Freaks" is no normal program film, but whether it deserves the title of abnormal is a matter of personal opinion. Its first audience apparently could not decide, although there was a good bit of applause.

Based on the life of "these strange people" of the circus sideshow, the picture is excellent at times and horrible, in the strict meaning of the word, at others. There are a few moments of comedy, but these are more than balanced by tragedy. Through long periods the story drags itself along, and there is one of the most profound anti-climaxes of them all to form the ending. Yet, despite this, "Freaks" is not a picture to be easily forgotten.

The reason, of course, is the underlying sense of horror, the love of the macabre that fills the circus sideshows in the first place. Tod Browning, the director, has brought all of it out as fully as possible, trying to prove that the "strange people" are children, that they do not like to be set apart. But they know they are, and in the sideshow is a spirit of mutual protection that holds if you injure one of them you injure all.

"The Circus Side Show," in The New York Times *(© 1932 by The New York Times Company; reprinted by permission), July 9, 1932, p. 7.*

FRANK S. NUGENT

In "The Devil Doll" you will find a St. Bernard, a Great Dane and a circus horse reduced to mouse-like dimensions. By the same magic, Arthur Hohl, Grace Ford and one or two other hapless players are shrunken to fountain-pen length and have a brisk time climbing Christmas trees, staggering under the weight of a jeweled bracelet and sticking tiny daggers into the necks and ankles of Lionel Barrymore's full-sized victims.

Not since "The Lost World," "King Kong" and "The Invisible Man" have the camera wizards enjoyed such a field day. By use of the split screen, glass shots, oversize sets and other trick devices cherished of their kind, they have pieced together a photoplay which is grotesque, slightly horrible and consistently interesting. A freak film, of course, and one which may overburden Junior's imagination, but an entertaining exhibition of photographic hocus-pocus for all that.

Based—and we shall be embarrassed if you ask us how closely—on Abraham Merritt's novel, "Burn, Witch,

Burn," it tells the story of a scientist's discovery of a process by which humans and animals are reduced to a sixth of their normal size and of an escaped convict's use of the pigmies to be revenged upon the three men who conspired to send him to Devil's Island. . . .

[The] picture relies mainly, and with understandable assurance, upon such ingenious bits as Miss Ford's demonstration of Alpine skill in climbing (via a slipper, footstool, bench and drawer handles) to the top of a dressing table; or Mr. Hohl's ludicrous impersonation of a Christmas tree ornament; or the Apache dance with a table-top serving as a ballroom. Tod Browning, who may be remembered for "The Unholy Three," "Dracula" and similar pleasantries, has invested these essentially ridiculous episodes with a menacing, chilling quality which makes it impossible for you to consider them too lightly. That, naturally, is as it should be in a horror film.

Frank S. Nugent, "'The Devil Doll'," in The New York Times *(© 1936 by The New York Times Company; reprinted by permission), August 8, 1936, p. 5.*

RAYMOND DURGNAT

[Despite] its moments of deliberate, grotesque shock, [*Freaks*] is shot through with—not just compassion, but something higher; respect. Tod Browning shows us a dwarf couple first—and for a few seconds the first 'big person' whom we see seems the deformed one.

The film has sufficient humanity to permit itself a tragicomic tone, about the emotional conflicts of the half-man, half-woman, resembling some anatomical apotheosis of the transvestite theme in *Psycho*. There is even some comic relief—it's true that at the press-show on one actually laughed, but the mood is there. When one Siamese twin gets pinched her sister feels it too, which raises interesting speculations as to the in-law's responses to her yokefellow's wedding-night.

Let's make no mistake: an uncompromising film in a censor-free society would have gone nearer the knuckle in evoking, warmly, the psychological consequences of this double-menage, and, in principle, the same criticism applies to other points in the film. It hints at the tragic solitude of some of these freaks, but never deeply evokes it, and in this nonchalance one can perhaps see the cloven hoof of MGM '30s commercialism—at least in intention. But the tragic aspect is a fairly obvious one, and the nonchalance has a grotesqueness of its own; it these freaks are no lonelier than we are, then we perhaps are just as much freaks as they are. After a first viewing, I would hazard a guess that *Freaks* is one of those films which, like so many of Buñuel's, grows at each viewing. At first its very real shock-value seems to mingle with moments which seem shallow, but by the end of the film one begins to catch their mood, a calm, cold combination of guignol and eerily matter-of-fact.

The acting has occasionally dated a little, as in Hercules' and Cleopatra's rowdier moments, otherwise Browning's direction, very different from his *Dracula* Gothicisms, is extremely slick and smooth.

The aftermath to the wedding-breakfast where freaks with flick-knives crawl through mud and rain to despatch the wounded strong man is really obscene yet, paradoxically, the violence of the revenge is an assertion of their human dignity. The 'blackness' of this moral is one more Buñuelesque trait in a film which at every turn evokes the name of Buñuel, in haunting subtlety as well as downright shock. (p. 23)

Raymond Durgnat, "Raymond Durgnat Sees Beauty in Deformity . . ." (© copyright Raymond Durgnat 1963; reprinted with permission), in Films and Filming, *Vol. 9, No. 11, August, 1963, pp. 22-3.*

JOHN THOMAS

Freaks is, in its own way, a minor masterpiece. Certainly it is macabre, and the final sequence in which the freaks stalk and mutilate their victims is enough to scare the hell out of anybody. But the point is that *Freaks* is not really a horror film at all, though it contains some horrifying sequences. The conventional horror film is one of our responses to the nonhuman element in the world, the incomprehensible objective world that threatens to render life meaningless. The movie monster is the embodiment of the nonhuman, the irrational, the inexplicable. It is through his destruction by fire, sunlight, or crucifix that we are purged of our own fear of the nonhuman. We must therefore identify with the victims of the movie monster, and find our release in the monster's ultimate death. In *Freaks* we are asked to identify with the ostensibly nonhuman, to turn against what we normally think of as our "own kind" and to discover in the humanity of the freaks a moral center for the universe. (pp. 59-60)

The crucial scenes in the movie are those which show the daily routine of the freaks, the individual adjustment of the freaks to their handicaps being almost clinically observed. We watch the armless woman drink beer from a glass grasped by a prehensile foot; while the human worm, both armless and legless, lights his own cigarettes with his teeth. . . . It is through these and similar scenes that Browning effects the inversion of values that lies at the heart of the film.

The freaks, as the movie is at pains to point out, live in a world of their own, created by themselves, but open to all of their own kind and to any normal person good enough to accept them. They are very much *in* this world, determined to make the best of it. It is only the nonaccepting attitude of some of the normals which precipitates the crisis that finally turns those normals themselves into freaks.

What, then, are we to make of this as a "horror" film? Can the freaks be seen both as objects of sympathy and as nightmarish incarnations of the nonhuman? Browning does evoke both responses, creating a tension within the viewer which could ruin the movie but which in fact enriches it. The use of the freaks for the creation of macabre effects is skillful enough, but always, until the last scene, mixed with a warm appreciation of their humanity. (p. 60)

Certainly the final sequence in which the freaks hunt down and mutilate Cleopatra and Hercules is as ghoulish as anyone could wish. Amidst a jumble of wrecked circus trailers, lightning splitting sky and sound track, the ground a muddy ooze, the darkness swarms with crawling, hopping shapes, lit grotesquely by momentary flashes, all humanity seemingly erased.

This is our last image of the freaks, and perhaps it may be counted an artistic mistake. If the picture is really an attempt to evoke sympathy, can it end with the freaks transformed into monsters?

It can, and does, because the ground has been so carefully prepared that the audience must, at the end of the film, react against its own revulsion. We are horrified, but we are simultaneously ashamed of our horror; for we remember that these are not monsters at all but people like us, and we know that we have again been betrayed by our own primal fears. Had the picture ended on a more idyllic note we might have been self-satisfied, stuffed with our own tolerant virtue. Instead, we are plunged back into the abyss of our own sick selves, to recall once again that the most fearful inhumanity we can know is our own. With this final scene, then, the double image is complete. (pp. 60-1)

John Thomas, "Film Reviews: 'Freaks'," in Film Quarterly *(copyright 1964 by The Regents of the University of California; reprinted by permission of the University of California Press), Vol. XVII, No. 3, Spring, 1964, pp. 59-61.*

TED ZEHENDER

The Unknown is an important film for several reasons, which I'll consider in a moment, but its plot, unfortunately, isn't one of them. . . . [It] is a variant of the beauty and the beast theme, with the beast this time (Chaney) being a bitter and vengeful knife-thrower in a Madrid circus named Alonzo. He is apparently armless and propels his knives at Nanon, his beautiful partner, by means of his toes. . . .

The skill with which [*The Unknown*] spins a fabric of suspense illustrates the fine technique of director Tod Browning. He never achieved the fame in this field that Alfred Hitchcock has, perhaps because the quality he stresses most in his convoluted plots . . . is irony, and irony leaves the viewer with an unsatisfied and thwarted feeling. Hitchcock eschews it, and occasionally uses humor. Browning never did. (p. 452)

The Unknown is not a horror film, at least not in the sense that *The Hunchback of Notre Dame* and *Phantom of the Opera* are. There's no mutilated or supernatural creature going haywire and wrecking his vengeance on society. *The Unknown* is a *suspense* film, with suspense beginning almost in the first few feet, which show the circus tents flapping wildly in the night wind, and resembling shrouds. The lighting is somber throughout, except in the scenes in which [Nanon] appears, which are all illuminated, so that *light* becomes her leit-motif (her image in Alonzo's eyes).

Many Browning trademarks are in *The Unknown*: the circus is made to seem the sinister outside world in microcosm; man is made to seem a creature bent on its own undoing; and the heart's impulse toward love is made to lead ironically to tragedy.

Browning's camera was a fluid one, remarkably so for the time. Though there are no tracking shots, he packed so much action in front of his lens the camera seems non-stationary, and becomes successively the eyes of the characters. Of Alonzo, as he spies on the girl he secretly desires, and watches her receive the attentions of others; of Nanon, as she peers down from the wagon window, over the shoulder of her father's assassin, and sees the tell-tale thumb; of the dwarf, as he watches in amusement while Alonzo unconsciously smokes a cigarette he holds with his toes, forgetting his hands have been freed from the strait-jacket; of Alonzo again, as he surveys the hospital room where the dreaded operation is to be performed.

The camera reveals some fascinating sights in *The Unknown*. As the dwarf painstakingly unties Alonzo's strait-jacket and we see that the knife-thrower isn't armless at all, we also see how Chaney attained one of his most realistic effects. For the murder scene Browning hemmed the camera in between two towering circus wagons, to add claustrophobia to the victim's fears. The climactic scene in the theatre is brilliantly lit and totally theatrical, with quick cuts from Nanon in a costume made up mostly of white beads, to the increasingly alarmed Malabar, to the galloping horses, to the audience, unaware of what's happening on stage.

Every scene builds upon the preceding one with utmost economy. Nothing is wasted, nothing is superfluous. The pace never falters, and the number of title cards in *The Unknown* is surprisingly small. (p. 453)

Ted Zehender, "Chaney's 'The Unknown'," in Films in Review *(copyright © 1970 by the National Board of Review of Motion Pictures, Inc.), Vol. XXI, No. 7, August-September, 1970, pp. 452-54.*

STUART ROSENTHAL

The adjective most frequently applied to Browning's cinema is "obsessional." Although the work of any *auteur* will repeatedly emphasise specific thoughts and ideas, Browning is so aggressive and unrelenting in his pursuit of certain themes that he appears to be neurotically fixated upon them. He is inevitably attracted to situations of moral and sexual frustration. In this, as well as in his preoccupation with interchangeable guilt, interchangeable personalities and patterns of human repulsion and attraction, he coincides remarkably with Chabrol. What sets Browning apart is his abnormal fascination with the deformed creatures who populate his films—a fascination that is not always entirely intellectual, and one in which he takes extreme delight.

Browning expresses his obsessive content in a manner that may be properly described as compulsive. Certain shots, compositions and montages appear again and again in the Browning *oeuvre* and, however appropriate they are to his ideas, they leave an impression of frank repetition. In fact, he has a limited catalogue of both themes and effects from which he compiles each of his pictures. The overall scope of the entire Browning filmography is not significantly broader than that of any single entry in it. (pp. 8-9)

The typical Browning protagonist is a man who has been reduced to the state of an animal. In almost every instance he displays a physical deformity that reflects the mental mutilation he has suffered at the hands of some element of callous society. . . . [Direct] evidence of the animal affinities of Browning characters can be found in their names: "Tiger," the circus trapper in *Where East Is East,* "Cock Robin," the carnival performer in *The Show,* and the title character in *The Black Bird,* to name a few. As animals they act in response to very simple, innate passions, the strongest of which is a lust for retribution. Their steadfast confidence in their own righteousness and their ascetic dedication to their singular goals contributes to the inexhaustible strength which allows them to triumph over those who have made them outcasts. (pp. 9-11)

Although, in their instinctive behaviour, Browning's heroes are oblivious to the moral contradictions of revenge, they do maintain a latent sense of fairness which influences their dealings with those who have not afflicted them. This is one aspect of Barrymore's willingness to sacrifice his own happiness in *The Devil-Doll* in order to avoid embarrassing his daughter who is ashamed of him. It also accounts for his unwillingness to continue to exploit his "devil dolls" after he has vindicated himself. Chaney trades his own life for that of his daughter in *Where East Is East* and *West of Zanzibar* and risks imprisonment to free the clerk framed by the burglary ring in *The Unholy Three*. The appetite for revenge can be viewed as an extreme of this concern with fairness.

Freaks is the film that is most explicit about the closeness of equitability and retribution. The freaks live by a simple and unequivocable code that one imagines might be the crux of Browning's ideal for society: "Offend one of them and you offend them all." (Browning's other films, however, belie the possibility of practically implementing such an ideal system.) The freaks, as a group, have taken responsibility for the welfare of each individual member. (pp. 12-13)

The solidarity of the freaks is a feature introduced to the story by Browning. It does not occur in "Spurs," the Tod Robbins short story from which *Freaks* is adapted. Browning's handiwork is also evident in the fairness that tempers the implementation of their doctrine. The group does not respond to Cleopatra's disparagement of Frieda, delaying action against Cleopatra and Hercules until it has undeniable proof of their intention to murder Hans. Since this is one of those rare instances in Browning's pictures in which guilt can be indisputably fixed, the freaks can be totally justified in their attack. (p. 14)

In the lower levels of society, to which Browning devoted most of his film-making energies, self-reliance, shrewdness and authority are valuable, highly regarded characteristics. Accordingly, Browning has great respect for men who are in command of their circumstances. This esteem is constant and irrespective of the moral nature of their activities. This serves as one explanation for Browning's attraction to such grossly debased characters as Alonzo in *The Unknown*, Black Mike Silva in *Outside the Law* and Cock Robin in *The Show*. (pp. 17-18)

Having a characterisation in mind, Browning built his films by generating an elaborately interlocking structure of frustration around that individual. Frustration is Browning's dominant theme. It occurs in several distinct patterns, each of which can be recognised in almost every Browning film. These modes of frustration include:

1. *Reality versus Appearance*. The standard criteria by which we form "first impressions" are useless in Browning's universe. Physical beauty and positions of public trust are frequently *façades* for the most reprehensible villains.

2. *Sexual Frustration*. In Browning's films a man's offspring represent extensions of his own sexuality. The father-child relationship is especially sacred. An insult to a son or daughter is also an insult to the parent, and *vice versa*. Under these conditions bastardy is a particularly intolerable state. Sexual frustration is Browning's work may be either experienced first hand or indirectly, through a close relative.

3. *Conflict of Two Opposing Tendencies within an Individual*. This is an internal, identity-related frustration. It may be manifested by the use of alter egos or by the symbolic separation of the pair of qualities into two individuals.

4. *Inability to Assign Guilt*. Any system of justice, especially the Browning hero's revenge drive, is frustrated by situations in which guilt cannot be clearly fixed. In such instances the avenger himself must often sin in order to punish the sins of others. (pp. 23-4)

[As an example of the first form, Browning uses the dichotomy between appearance and reality in *Freaks*, where the bulk of the film] is spent dispelling the viewer's initial revulsion to the title characters. They are shown in the activities of normal life—eating, chatting, playing, working, arranging matrimony and celebrating the birth of a child. The freaks surmount their handicaps by going through sets of bizarre movements. Browning presents these in a matter-of-fact manner rather than as tricks. The involved procedure used by the Human Torso, a man without arms or legs, to light his cigarette is handled as incidental action in a contrived dialogue scene. At the other end of the scale, Browning prevents his audience from pitying the freaks by using their deformities as the basis for a great deal of black humour.

Running countercurrent to the normalisation of the freaks is the bestialising of Cleopatra, the trapeze artist, and of her boyfriend, Hercules the Strongman. In contradistinction to their strange circus colleagues, these two are opportunistic, insensitive, unscrupulous and without allegiance to anyone except themselves. Physical beauty masking perversity is identical to the usual Browning premise of respectability covering corruption. (pp. 24-5)

Browning regularly introduces the theme of secondary or "indirect" sexual frustration through the plot device of a parent who is unaware of the identity of his own child, or the reverse situation. Singapore Joe in *Road to Mandalay* is so ugly that he feels his daughter (who, indeed, abhors that hideous man when he patronises the store in which she clerks) would be ashamed if she were aware of their kinship. The struggle that results when the Admiral, one of Joe's smuggling colleagues, announces his plan to wed her has overtones of a fight to maintain the sexual integrity of the family. (pp. 25, 27)

As Browning approached the peak of his career, the sexual undercurrents of his films became less and less covert. While *Freaks* affords the most explicit expression of the fears that haunt the background of all his pictures, *Dracula* borders upon the surreal as an evocation of repressed sexual horror. . . .

[The] nocturnal blood lust equates to necrophilic passion and the demon appears as a pestilent incubus, preying at night upon sleeping female innocence and turning his victims, through the touch of his fangs, into willing slaves. Dracula was originally billed as "The strangest love story of all."

Though updated from Bram Stoker's novel, the Browning version of Dracula retains the Victorian formality of the original source in the relationships among the normal characters. In this atmosphere the seething, unstoppable evil personified by the Count is a materialisation of Victorian morality's greatest dread. (pp. 33, 35)

Sexual frustration is the very essence of *Freaks*. The central event— the marriage of Hans, the dwarf, to Cleopatra, the statuesque trapeze artiste—is a collision of absolute sexual opposites—the attempted consummation of an impossible union. . . . Cleopatra is seductive, mature, cunning and self-assured in contrast to Hans who looks like a baby and is uncertain of her response to his guilelessly open admiration. In viewing them we are struck primarily by the gross incongruity of the pair, but our reaction to the scene is a product of the two mutually exclusive points of view that are comprised in it. For Hans, a chance at the big lady is a wild goal beyond reach or reason, representing the fulfilment of his most extravagant fantasies. The smug trapeze performer contemptuously regards the midget as an opportunity to enjoy the kind of cruel sexual jest upon which she thrives.

It is here that Browning justifies the disruption of an individual's sexual equanimity as a cause for retaliation. Cleopatra's decision to wed the dwarf for his wealth and then dispose of him is not, in itself, a significant advance in villainy. In the context of the film, her most heinous crime is committed when she teases Hans by provocatively dropping her cape to the floor and then gleefully kneels to allow her victim to replace it upon her shoulders. The decision to commit a murder is merely the natural development of her eagerness to taunt and sexually belittle the dwarf. This kind of exploitation appears more obscene by far than the fairly clean act of homicide. (pp. 35-6)

Contrast the insecurity of the normal-sized leads with the unruffled attitudes of the Freaks. They have accepted their limitations and adapted to them. Even the individuals with radical amputations (which, as elsewhere in Browning, carry strong connotations of castration) have adjusted marvellously to their physical constraints, using arms as legs and mouths as hands. Beyond this, many of the freaks represent reconciliations of prevalent sexual apprehensions. Beside the "half-man, half-woman" there is the comically complaisant attitude toward a kind of miscegenation in the birth of a child to the "human skeleton" and the bearded fat lady. (pp. 36-7)

In the Browning canon *Freaks* is almost allegorical in that it singles out individuals about whose guilt there can be no doubt. Justice is perfectly served because retribution is meted out only for the absolute crime of "attempted murder," but the sentence is such that it appropriately covers the crime of sexual humiliation. Usually, however, there is situational confusion in assigning guilt in Browning's stories. This generates a level of frustration that is directly concerned with the instinctive plane of justice the Browning films seek.

Alonzo, in *The Unknown,* commits what amounts to an act of self-castration. He is driven to that point by Estrellita . . . , who not only leads him into a position in which it is desirable to be without arms but, having brought him there, arbitrarily reverses herself after the damage is irreparable. "Estrellita," a title reads, "wishes God had taken the arms from all men." She is, accordingly, both the film's provoker and the mortal enemy of the kind of physical man Chaney represents—even though she is unaware that Alonzo is exactly the sort she most despises.

In regarding Estrellita's betrayal, it is easy to overlook the fact that Alonzo's guilt is immaterial to his yearning for her. He has murdered a man and thus created a whole new set of circumstances under which armlessness is an asset. He has two reasons, then, for blackmailing the doctor into surgically removing his upper extremities. The first is entirely of his own making while the other results from his victimisation at the hands of his maladjusted female ideal. The implication that Alonzo's affair with Estrellita was a contributing factor in maintaining the tension between him and the circus owner further obfuscates the question of whether the major responsibility for his ultimate solution rests primarily with Alonzo or with Estrellita.

Another facet in this intricate structure of guilt arises from Alonzo's choice of Malabar as the target for retribution. Logically, Alonzo's anger should be directed toward the girl, not the strongman. But in a film in which the sexual tension is almost palpable, it does not seem unreasonable to accept the unification of Estrellita and Malabar as a medium by which the blame may be transferred, or at least redistributed. On symbolic grounds it is fitting that Alonzo should avenge his own castration by attacking a figure of exaggerated masculinity, while the "arm for an arm" punishment, as an illusion of justice, mirrors Alonzo's illusion of the strongman's guilt. In the long view, it is these ambiguous and outrageously twisted threads of guilt and justice that makes *The Unknown* so audacious. (pp. 41-4)

For the most part, Browning's films grip their audience by conditioning it to expect some harrowing event and then holding it at the point of anticipation. The stories are fashioned around the central character and most of our dread springs from fear for or of him. Browning punctuates these formations of psychological suspense with moments of outright shock. His set procedure for generating horror is quickly to throw the audience off balance, overwhelm it with some terrible threat and then cut away abruptly to let the viewer draw his own conclusions. The audience (which has already been put on edge by the film's intrinsic tension) is disconcerted by an unexpected change in camera angle or perspective. These alterations come as a jolt in contrast to the simple three-shot narrative style used for the rest of the film. (p. 46)

The climax of *Freaks* probably achieves the most sustained level of high-pitched terror of any Browning picture. The tension begins to accrue when the ubiquitous aberrations start to appear behind every door, window and wagon wheel, like a force of inevitable doom. The horror builds from there in short, staccato shocks as their macabre bodies pull themselves through the mud between flashes of lightning. Toward the end of the sequence their familiar forms are barely recognisable as they scramble in jerky, energetic movements to carve up their victims.

The technique that Browning used for constructing instants of horror in his silent films was workably carried over into the sound era. It is apparent that Browning conceived horror primarily in visual terms. The track behind the bloodsucking activities in *Dracula* carries only distant street or wildlife sounds and the devil dolls do their work in almost absolute silence. These two films, as well as *Mark of the Vampire,* rely upon a minimum of mood music. (p. 50)

Most of Browning's films stick to the format of melodrama with episodes of horror, but there are at least two in which he carefully develops suspense over an extended period of time.

Nearly one half of *White Tiger* is played out in the secluded cabin where Sylvia, Hawkes and Roy have cloistered themselves following a daring jewellery heist. Each feels that the others are planning a double-cross and Roy suspects Hawkes of being the man who informed on his father. Browning emphasises this mistrust by isolating the characters in separate close-ups as they survey their partners and then, after Longworth's unexpected arrival, separating them into constantly changing groups. . . . Several superstitious omens—a black cat, thirteen pieces of jewellery, a broken mirror—add empirically to the mounting suspense. The claustrophobic cabin contains the action in such a way that the pressure builds to an explosive point. (pp. 51, 53)

In *Dracula,* Browning clarifies some of the early action by means of one of his favourite devices, an animal montage in which a particularly sinister event is intercut with shots of small creatures. As each of Dracula's wives emerges from her tomb a rooting rat disappears behind a ledge or a wasp pulls itself from a tiny coffin-shaped compartment. The metaphor defines the nature of the vampire and conveys the impression of a rewakening of evil and a parasitic search for sustenance. On the other hand, the corresponding sequence in *Mark of the Vampire* uses the inserts to give impetus to an intricately rhythmic passage. As Bela Lugosi and the bat-girl descend the cobweb-covered staircase of the abandoned mansion, their progress is broken into a series of shots, each of which involves continuous movement of either the camera, the players or both. This creates the impression of an easy, unearthly gliding motion. By alternating these with glimpses of bats, rats and insects scurrying about, Browning provides a beat which accents the steady, deliberate progress of the horrific pair. There is no sacrifice of smoothness and the two seem to be, at once, floating and walking. The strange varieties of animals used has a bearing upon establishing the unnatural atmosphere. Spiders and rats are familiar fright symbols, but one is occasionally taken aback by the sight of an armadillo lurking about the crypt. The effect is disorientation and the viewer becomes ill-at-ease because he has entered a universe that is entirely outside his realm of natural experience. (pp. 54-5)

The religious symbolism which turns up periodically in Browning's pictures serves two antagonistic ends. When Dead Legs discovers his dead wife and her child on the pulpit of the cathedral, the solemn surroundings lend a tone of a fanatical irrevocability to his vow to "make Crane and his brat pay." The altar statue of the Virgin and child attests to the innocence of his spouse and baby. At the same time, Chaney's difficult and painful movements upon his belly at the front of the church . . . have the look of a savage parody of a religious supplicant whose faith has been rendered a mockery. God's justice having failed, Dead Legs is about to embark upon his own mission of righteousness.

As Singapore Joe gazes longingly at his daughter through the window of the curio shop, the display of crucifixes testifies of his love for her while paradoxically acting as a barrier between them. The Black Bird/Bishop easily deceives Fifi, Bertie, the police and the locals with his phoney mantle of religious goodness. When Paul Lavond threatens the last of the bankers with a coded note, decipherable by assembling words from the Bible, the "Good Book" suddenly carries a message of effective justice. Religion for the Browning hero is, then, an additional spring of frustration—another defaulted promise.

Browning's overall contribution to the cinema is an insulated one. Many people, to be sure, have emulated the style of *Dracula* and the titles of some of the Chaney films have become legendary. . . . Browning's work acquires its full impact only when considered cumulatively. It is only then that we begin to sense the fanaticism behind the director's pursuit of his themes of justice and frustration and his intense involvement with his monster heroes, and start to develop intuitive feelings about the ferocious vision that gave rise to the audacious *Freaks* and revelled in the fantasised decapitation in *The Show*. Each newly discovered film of this talented monomaniac strengthens our impressions of the rest of his output. Browning, then, is a perfect model of the way an *auteur* approach can enhance our appreciation of the work of selected movie-makers. (pp. 57-8)

Stuart Rosenthal, "Tod Browning," in The Hollywood Professionals: Tod Browning & Don Siegel, *by Stuart Rosenthal and Judith M. Kass (copyright © 1975 by The Tantivy Press London, Great Britain), Tantivy, 1975, pp. 7-59.*

Luis Buñuel

1900-

Spanish director and writer.

Though best known for his surrealistic works, in his films Buñuel encompasses a variety of genres that in turn reflect his compendium of beliefs. Buñuel is a paradox: a religious man who daily thanks God that he is an atheist; a tender man who makes films about sadism; and a realist obsessed with fantasy. Although often obscure and difficult, his work has wide appeal because Buñuel addresses a universal theme: the individual's natural impulses and desires opposed by society and religion.

Buñuel's bourgeois Spanish upbringing is the target of his social criticism and his Jesuit education is partially responsible for his anticlerical attitude. Studies of Freud at the University of Madrid also proved an important influence. Upon graduation Buñuel went to Paris, where he studied at the Academie du Cinéma and assisted Jean Epstein on several films.

In 1928, Buñuel made his first film, collaborating with Salvador Dali. The result, *Un Chien andalou,* is composed of seemingly irrelevant associations, a trademark of surrealist thought. Since Buñuel felt that sleep was the mind's most natural state, his films often have a dreamlike, fragmented quality. Continuity, according to Buñuel, is an example of man's attempt to civilize the irrational by organizing nature. *Un Chien andalou* condemns this effort. More important than the film's intent to condemn, however, is its desire to shock. In fact, Buñuel expected such negative reactions that he went to the opening of the film with his pockets filled with stones. To the contrary, the film won many favorable responses. But his next film prompted explosive denunciations. *L'Age d'Or,* referred to as the only authentic surrealist film ever made, advocated a nonconformist revolution, attacking human reason.

Buñuel broke with surrealism briefly to film a documentary, *Land without Bread,* which graphically depicted the sufferings of an impoverished area of Spain. The chilling objectivity in this film has been likened to the works of Goya, whom Buñuel has long admired.

During the late 1930s, Buñuel worked for the Museum of Modern Art until Dali accused him of atheism and he was released. After dubbing some films in Hollywood, Buñuel traveled to Mexico to make his first film in twenty years. This period is known as Buñuel's rebirth, marked primarily by a brutally realistic style interspersed with touches of surrealism. Though his first films were purely commercial, their revenue permitted Buñuel to direct his successful *Los Olvidados,* a film of social protest. Its violent portrayal of a group of juvenile delinquents left viewers alienated and appalled, yet in awe of Buñuel's skill.

After a brief filmmaking venture in France, he created *Nazarin,* a cinematic definition of his religious philosophy. Unlike his earlier works, it is devoid of ambiguity and confusion. *Nazarin* demonstrates Buñuel's desire to place himself inside the soul of his characters and reflects his belief that an individual must be studied in relation to others.

Buñuel returned to Spain to make *Viridiana.* A restatement of all his previous brutal themes, it was deemed sacrilegious and banned by the Spanish government. The films after *Viridiana* are of an increasingly satiric nature. *Simon of the Desert,* in particular, demonstrates Buñuel's conviction that a pious lifestyle is futile.

One of his most recent films, *The Discreet Charm of the Bourgeoisie,* is considered a hallmark in his career. It is a brilliant satire of bourgeoise conventions, using dream sequences and black humor. Like his other films, *The Discreet Charm* is as confusing and alienating as it is impressive. Probably the best consensus of the general opinion of Buñuel was given by Henry Miller: "They have called Buñuel everything—traitor, anarchist, pervert, defamer, iconoclast. But lunatic they dare not call him."

HENRY MILLER

Buñuel is obsessed by the cruelty, ignorance and superstition which prevail among men. He realizes that there is no hope for man anywhere on this earth unless a clean slate be made of it. He appears on the scene at the moment when civilization is at its nadir. . . .

They have called Buñuel everything—traitor, anarchist, pervert, defamer, iconoclast. But lunatic they dare not call him. True, it is lunacy he portrays in his film, but it is not of his making. This stinking chaos which for a brief hour or so is amalgamated under his magic wand, this is the lunacy of man's achievements after ten thousand years of civilization. (p. 55)

Perhaps it is the baroque element in human life, or rather in the life of civilized man, which gives to Buñuel's works the aspect of cruelty and sadism. Isolated cruelty and sadism, for it is the great virtue of Buñuel that he refuses to be enmeshed in the glittering web of logic and idealism which seeks to mask from us the real nature of man. . . . There is no straddling the issue. Either you are crazy, like the rest of civilized humanity, or you are sane and healthy like Buñuel. And if you are sane and healthy you are an anarchist and you throw bombs. (pp. 57-8)

"L'Age d'Or" is the only film I know of which reveals the possibilities of the cinema! It makes its appeal neither to the intellect nor to the heart; it strikes at the solar plexus. It is like kicking a mad dog in the guts. And though it was a valiant kick in the guts and well aimed it was not enough. (p. 59)

Some people think of the Golden Age as a dream of the past; others think of it as the millennium to come. But the Golden Age is the immanent reality to which all of us, by our daily living, are either contributing or failing to contribute. The world is what we make it each day, or what we fail to make it. If it is lunacy that we have on our hands today, then it is we who are the lunatics. If you accept the fact that it is a crazy world you may perhaps succeed in adapting yourself to it. But those who have a sense of creation are not keen about adapting themselves. We affect one another, whether we wish to or not. Even negatively we affect one another. In writing about Buñuel instead of writing about something else I am aware that I am going to create a certain effect—for most people an unpleasant one, I suspect. But I can no more refrain from writing this way about Buñuel than I can from washing my face tomorrow morning. My past experience of life leads up to this moment and rules it despotically. In asserting the value of Buñuel I am asserting my own values, my own faith in life. (pp. 60-1)

"L'Age d'Or" is no accident, nor is its dismissal from the screen an accident. The world has condemned Luis Buñuel and judged him as unfit. (p. 61)

What I say is only a drop in the bucket, but it may have its consequences. The important thing is that the bucket should not have a hole in it. Well, I believe that such a bucket can be found. I believe that it is just as possible to rally men around a vital reality as it is around the false and the illusory. Luis Buñuel's effect upon me was not lost. And perhaps my words will not be lost either. (p. 62)

Henry Miller, "'The Golden Age'," in his The Cosmological Eye *(copyright 1939 by New Directions Publishing Corporation; all rights reserved; reprinted by permission of New Directions Publishing Corporation), New Directions, 1939, pp. 47-62.*

TONY RICHARDSON

Surrealism is born out of despair; its only power is to hasten the general cataclysm by its own prophetic chaos. Max Ernst said of it, "*In turning topsy-turvy the appearances and relationships of reality, surrealism has been able, with a smile on its lips, to hasten the general crisis of consciousness which must perforce take place in our time.*" No other work of the period expressed this so completely as *L'Age d'Or*. All civilisation is oppression, suffering, frustration; above, the cynical emptiness and callous show of the rich; below, the misery, hunger and incipient revolution of the poor; individuals are ridden with inhibition, anxiety and guilt; beauty is, like Hans Schwitters' haphazard, delicate collages of tram tickets and paper money, the momentary chance of an afternoon's boredom—clouds pass in the mirror as the girl, restless and lonely, waits for Modot's arrival. Bunuel has taken a traditional romantic theme, love thwarted by circumstance, and seen it with "un œil à l'état sauvage", stripped of any sentimental associations; love is a fierce lust with clumsy embraces and frustrated satisfaction. The honesty of his attitude is explosive and cauterising.

Yet it is not despair that finally pervades the film but a savage glee, almost optimistic in destruction. (pp. 125-26)

[Though] the props are still surrealist—the man with "patches" of living flies, the cow on the bed—and the general form loose and episodic, there are indications that Bunuel had exhausted the surrealist approach and had already begun to shape events into drama. Surrealism had become a technique for exposing and analysing reality rather than a means of creating an independent world of fantasy. . . .

[Bunuel records the story of *Land Without Bread,* or *Las Hurdes,*] with a flatness and lack of comment that make it the more alarming. No moral is drawn, no response instructed, no easy attitude given. Bunuel is content, as was Goya in Los Desastres de la Guerra, to let the naked record speak for itself. . . . Though the material is organised with masterly skill, the very conception of "art" here seems irrelevant. It is the most profoundly disturbing film I have ever seen. (p. 126)

In *L'Age d'Or,* Bunuel had begun to create dramatic action; in *Land Without Bread* he had approached reality directly; *Los Olvidados* was the fulfilment of both these developments. . . .

As in all Bunuel's films, the treatment is conceptual. The characters are simplified to whatever aspect or passion Bunuel is creating, and all irrelevant traits are suppressed. The unique force of the film comes from the combination of austerity and strictness in conception with a startling, often ironic, poetry of expression, with its images of donkeys, black hens, doves that can cure fever, cripples, torn meat, pariah dogs, in an almost timeless setting of arid squalor. . . . The prophecies and thunderings of *L'Age d'Or* have become fact, the horrors actual, the vision immensely darkened. . . .

Perhaps only Goya has created horror so acute. Bunuel's vision is too uncompromising to permit any softening of its bestiality; but—and one cannot say this emphatically enough, in view of what many critics have written—he never uses horror inartistically. There is no sensationalism in the handling of violence in this film; terror is balanced by pity, hopelessness by humanity. (p. 127)

[*Robinson Crusoe*] is as remarkable in its fidelity to Defoe as in its transmutation. After establishing the situation in a few sparse images, Bunuel follows Defoe's story-line, through Crusoe's working out of a way of life for himself, the descent of the cannibals, the rescue of Friday, the arrival of the mutineers, his outwitting of them and his final departure from the island. In style, too, Bunuel has matched Defoe's plain, direct prose; the simplicity of *Land Without Bread* is here used for an artistic purpose. Bunuel saw, as did Defoe, that Crusoe's struggle, often clumsy and inept, against conditions on the island, was fascinating on its practical, pedestrian level; he records, simply, the flat, absorbing routine of Crusoe's daily life.

Imaginatively Bunuel pierces further, looking into the heart of the man to see there the desolation and anguish of someone isolated from all human contact. (p. 129)

To see Bunuel in any artistic context, one must look beyond the cinema to the piercing, insolent seers of his own nation, to Goya, El Greco, the Picasso of Guernica. Without honour in his own country, he is a Spaniard first and last. How his vision will alter is difficult to foresee. Perhaps, as with Goya or the Mexican Oroczo, it will become crueller, less supportable; but in all his later films there are signs of a new resolution, a calmer, though not less clear-eyed, wisdom. Pedro can at least turn on Jaibo . . . : Crusoe returns to sanity and fellowship. It is not that Bunuel's view of the world has changed—suffering, struggle, disease and pain are as fierce as ever—but his belief in men seems greater, and, in that belief, prophecy and revolt have given way to understanding and acceptance. (p. 130)

Tony Richardson, "The Films of Luis Bunuel," in Sight and Sound *(copyright © 1954 by The British Film Institute), Vol. 23, No. 3, January-March, 1954, pp. 125-30.*

LINDSAY ANDERSON

The Adventures of Robinson Crusoe is a film by an artist of fresh, still developing talent, a poetic film, with a purity of style that marks it as the statement of a man of integrity, direct, uncompromised. . . . In fact so simple, so inevitable are the images, that you have to imagine what the conventional film treatment of the story would be to appreciate quite how daring—and how masterly—is Bunuel's naked, unadorned presentation of the simple facts. No jolly establishing sequences at Plymouth, no sentimental farewells, no pretty Polly waving a handkerchief from the jetty, not even a smashing storm sequence: just long waves rolling in to a deserted beach, and a man staggering up out of the water. . . .

The first reels of the film are like the best kind of documentary—like *Moana,* with its loving, contented observation of the practical details of living. Then comes the second theme, of solitude. *"I also wanted to tackle the subject of Love . . . that's to say the lack of love or friendship: man without the fellowship of man or woman."* Bunuel emphasises the terrible loneliness of his hero with vivid scenes of hallucination—staged with the utmost economy. (p. 86)

The scenes with Friday are a development of that second theme, of loneliness. . . . The delicate humour with which these scenes are presented, Friday's dignity and naif wisdom, Crusoe's shame, the warmth of their eventual *"grande fraternité humaine"* (Bunuel's words)—all these must surely astonish those who had docketed this director in their minds as a harsh and cruel experimentalist, fascinated exclusively by the violent and the depraved.

But of course there has never been any doubt of Bunuel's great love of life and the living. It has made him angry in the past; in this film it makes him reflective, observant, gentle, stirring but never inflamed. (pp. 86-7)

Lindsay Anderson, "Film Reviews: 'The Adventures of Robinson Crusoe'," in Sight and Sound *(copyright © 1954 by The British Film Institute), Vol. 24, No. 2, October–December, 1954, pp. 86-7.*

BASIL WRIGHT

[*The Criminal Life of Archibaldo de la Cruz*] is in many respects a very remarkable film. It is a *comédie noire* in which the director may have taken himself more seriously than he originally intended. Like all Bunuel's films, it maintains an identity of atmosphere from beginning to end, and in its crucial moments produces the horror which lies behind the farces of life and human behaviour. Viewed in relation to the canon of his work, this film confirms a growing belief that the so-called iconoclasms of *L'Age d'Or,* and the apparently deliberate shock-tactics in many of his films, represent in fact a quite simple outlook on life—the philosophy, in fact, of Luis Bunuel. (p. 87)

I would suspect—no, I believe—that Bunuel is a very simple man who expresses himself according to his beliefs about human beings and their behaviour. He would not accept Gide's Lafcadio, but he would create the same character in his own terms; and the *acte gratuite* would become a piece of Bunuel *reportage*. . . .

[In *Archibaldo*] Bunuel has filmed one of his ideas; and because he has a supremely logical mind, he has stripped his story of everything except those images which truly concern the matter in hand. You may not agree with the original idea—but you are bound to admire the absolute integrity with which it is carried out in movie terms.

It is the screen image which counts; and Bunuel, often unpredictably, is a master of the screen image. All through this film the camera is placed, casually but correctly, in the *obvious* position. . . . Anyone could choose a Bunuel camera-angle, but few could match him in the building-up of a sequence. He uses a sharp knife. He has never handled a bludgeon.

This is what makes *Archibaldo* so fascinating. It expresses one simple story idea. It goes straight ahead, sequence by sequence, and it never loiters or takes a wrong turning. It isn't a deep psychological drama and it isn't a whodunit. It just says, "supposing a small boy grows up to think that he is *literally* a lady-killer—all because his governess is shot dead before his eyes while he is playing an elaborate musical box given him by his rich and doting parents." . . . Well, just supposing. And Bunuel goes right ahead and supposes. That poor chap Archibaldo goes on trying to kill women, and fate and/or coincidence always forestall him. It is pathetic and funny, and in a curious way true; because we are all of us trying all the time to adjust our secret personal life to the life we have to lead, and, however *outré* the plot of this particular film may be, Bunuel's knife is bound to tickle our ribs. (p. 88)

Basil Wright, "Film Reviews: 'The Criminal Life of Archibaldo de la Cruz'," in Sight and Sound *(copyright © 1955 by The British Film Institute), Vol. 25, No. 2, Autumn, 1955, pp. 87-8.*

GAVIN LAMBERT

[The disturbing, overwhelming final episode of *Nazarin*] is in the great tradition of Luis Buñuel, who once said that his aim in making films was to convince people that they don't live in the best of all possible worlds. (And, in parenthesis, that there's no sign of the world getting much better.) He has never dramatized this belief so powerfully, and with such immense sadness, as in the whole of *Nazarin*. (p. 30)

Nazarin loses Christ and finds man. Like Dostoevsky's Prince Muishkin, or his Alyosha ("I am a monk who doesn't believe in God"), he finds him among the derelict, the criminal, and the mad. By implication Buñuel is saying —as he has always said—that this is the way society drives the individual. In all of Buñuel's important work you can find this rich implacable hatred of society—church, conservative governments, bureaucracy, militarism, the bourgeoisie—displayed with a sometimes paranoiac fury. His protagonists seem to snatch their moments of pleasure (usually erotic) in the teeth of official disapproval or hostility. . . . In the end, Buñuel suggests that society is only a legalized mob; beneath the institutional surface lies prejudice and cruelty. . . . [In] *Nazarin* society attacks an innocent, a Fool, because he is just that.

Yet Nazarin, at the end of the film, is no Francisco at the end of *El*, crazily zigzagging across the courtyard of the monastery in which he thinks he's found refuge. . . . Unlike [Francisco], he finds a reality with which to replace an illusion, and the film itself goes beyond protest to reach affirmation. (pp. 30-1)

[The] result has all the impact of an absolute masterpiece, a work of beautiful, explosive force and strangeness. (p. 31)

Gavin Lambert, "Film Reviews: 'Nazarin'," in Film Quarterly *(copyright 1960 by The Regents of the University of California; reprinted by permission of the University of California Press), Vol. XIII, No. 3, Spring, 1960, pp. 30-1.*

EMILIO G. RIERA

Viridiana is a work of genius, and as such has accomplished much more than it set out to. In it Buñuel offers his audience a splendid opportunity for exploring his creative universe and finding enrichment in a fresh point of view, a new outlook on reality. . . .

Buñuel is not a believer to be overlooked. He obviously believes in the miraculous or, rather, in the liberating force of the irrational and in the poetry of instinct. Religion, however, as commonly understood, is paradoxically, merely an attempt to rationalize the miraculous. . . . This is the function of dogma. And of one thing I am certain—Buñuel is utterly free of dogmatism. He likewise instinctively opposes a secular form of rationalism which endows man with the ability to attain absolute knowledge. . . .

On the other hand, Buñuel is not an agnostic. Like any true artist, he explores the furthest stretches of reality, which does not necessarily mean that he refutes the validity of objective, scientific knowledge. . . . Precisely because he extracts the entire substance of his art from the miraculous and the irrational indicates that he is antidogmatic and, therefore, an atheist. . . .

Because Buñuel is an atheist, for that very reason he is not really blasphemous. His attitude is devoid of all diabolism. Not once does this movie-maker deride or insult God, which would be tantamount to acknowledging His existence. Buñuel never discusses God. What he discusses is man's conception of God. (p. 76)

The Buñuelian trinity of eroticism—religion—death, a constant theme in his films is conceivable only within the specific limits of Catholicism and, more concretely, of Spanish Catholicism. *Viridiana* has confirmed what we might have always suspected: Buñuel, the apotheosis of anti-patriotism, has never ceased being profoundly Spanish. . . .

Buñuel's Spanishness explains to a great extent the persistence of the religious theme in his films. Spain has never completely abandoned the Inquisitorial spirit which couples the notion of sin with physical chastisement. Buñuel's films depict carnal flagellation and laceration and how it leads to the wild extremes of abnormal eroticism, masochism and fetishism. . . .

[The elderly Spanish gentleman in *Viridiana*] is representative of the spirit of Spanish Catholicism, which has been nurtured on the pursuit of death, due to the impossibility of attaining the absolute in life. The quest for the absolute is his distinctive trait, as it is Viridiana's, Nazarin's, and as it is likewise prominent in *El* and in *Ensayo de un Crimen*. It is the distinctive trait of poets.

In portraying each of his characters, their confrontation with reality and their personal inadequacy, Buñuel shows in each instance the failure of old Spanish dogmatism. There is here an unmistakable connection with a long literary tradition ("Don Quixote", the picaresque novel, Quevedo and Galdos) and therefore any attempt to regard *Viridiana* as merely a comment on Spain's present-day political and social situation is obviously too facile an interpretation. Actually, the film reflects a perennial picture of Spain (although, I hope, not of its future). . . .

[All] of Buñuel's work reveals a moral position towards a society to which, wittingly or unwittingly, he belongs, and which plays a determining role in his life. *Viridiana's* extraordinary richness and density is a result of its having been filmed in Spain which means that it is not lacking in the essence of Spanishness and concrete significance for Buñuel. (p. 81)

[Unlike] Buñuel's previous films, *Viridiana* has the great advantage in that there can be no confusion between the ambiguity of the physical reality and any ambiguity in its creator's moral position. (p. 82)

Emilio G. Riera, "'Viridiana'," translated by Toby Talbot, in Film Culture *(copyright 1962 by* Film Culture*), No. 24, Spring, 1962, pp. 76, 81-2.*

DAVID ROBINSON

Viridiana still speaks as loud and as clear and with the same voice as *L'Age d'Or*, still asserting sanity and cleanliness in a world whose nature is to be mad and filthy. If there has been a change in the thirty years between [the two films], it is that the Swiftian fury of *L'Age d'Or* has given place to a calmer philosophic clowning, as cool and therefore as deadly as Voltaire. (p. 116)

Viridiana's picture of mankind does not present a very flattering image of God. Buñuel depicts men's viciousness in terms that are no less direct and no more amiable that those of *L'Age d'Or*. If there is a hero at all it is Jorge, who lives positively and (as a good surrealist) according to the dictates of desire. Yet one feels that Buñuel does not prefer him to the others—even to Don Ezekiel, the vicious little clown always good for a laugh and ready to cause trouble, or to the odious man with diseased hands (has he really venereal disease, or is it just the fallacy of the good that disease is the visitation of the wicked?) who repays Viridiana's kindness by abetting her rape.

The film's total effect is invigorating rather than depressing because Buñuel values them all alike as men, and likes them all because they are funny and human. (p. 117)

Other men might be affected to pity by this picture of rot and corruption. But for Buñuel pity implies resignation, and resignation defeat. . . .

Buñuel admits no pity; and no panaceas. Nor does he accept the panaceas that are offered elsewhere. He is set, as he has always been set, against the soporifics of conventional morality and conventional sentimentality. . . .

Viridiana's Christianity is destined to failure. Paradoxically it is her very piety which corrupts corruption. As in *Nazarin,* one feels at the end that there has been an atonement of man to man: Viridiana seems nearer salvation in human contact than in divine service. . . .

The film's rich atmosphere is built out of images which are nothing if not surrealist: Viridiana's sleep-walking, ashes on the bed, dreams of black bulls and so on. Buñuel gives free play to his own private fetishisms. . . .

The real marvel of Buñuel is that he has the technical mastery to fulfil his ideas and his poetry. (p. 118)

With Buñuel, one never feels that technique is something interposed between conception and execution. Problems of *mise en scène* seem to have no more existence for him than do problems of technique in a sketch by Picasso or Goya. (p. 155)

David Robinson, "'Thank God—I Am Still an Atheist': Luis Bunuel and 'Viridiana'," in Sight and Sound *(copyright © 1962 by The British Film Institute), Vol. 31, No. 3, Summer, 1962, pp. 116-18, 155.*

GEOFFREY NOWELL-SMITH

At first sight (and with hindsight too, as the films have reached us in the wrong order), *Nazarin* . . . looks simply like a more ambiguous version of *Viridiana*. (p. 194)

The ambiguity lies in the fact that Buñuel refuses either to approve or condemn his hero, with the result that the film can be read in two different ways. Either we must take in that Nazarin is a fool and his saintliness futile and absurd, or else that his perseverance in the face of adversity is a living proof that faith is its own justification and reward, and the things of the spirit better and stronger than those of the flesh. Taken singly neither of these readings is satisfactory. . . . [If] Nazarin is to be condemned, who is to be saved? If he is wrong, who on earth is right? If he is futile, then what on earth is effective? The Revolution? Possibly, but Buñuel does not say so. In fact he offers no answer at all, even partial. Just a portrait of a sympathetic but otherworldly priest, and a fresco of a brutal but undeniably authentic world. We have no choice, therefore, but to accept both incompatible readings simultaneously, as hypothesis and antithesis, and mediate, for what it's worth, our own synthesis to the problem.

This is the answer, or substitute for an answer, that Brecht provides at the end of *The Good Woman of Setzuan*—"the curtains closed and all the questions open"—and more or less the same as that in *Viridiana,* where at the end Viridiana sits down to play cards with Jorge and Ramona, and the problem is uneasily shelved for the duration. But Brecht did believe that solutions were possible, and Buñuel in *Viridiana* left the audience in no doubt of his hatred for his heroine and all she stood for. In *Nazarin* however the basic moral ambiguity, Nazarin *contra mundum,* is not intended to lead to a solution, but is an end in itself. Buñuel's dialectic is all antithesis here, and his favourite weapon, beside physical shock, is paradox. (pp. 194-95)

Somewhere, I feel, Buñuel does see a solution. But it is an imaginary possibility which impresses itself on the film only by its absence. There could be a world, he implies, in which Beatriz did not have to choose between impotent frustration with a virginal priest and brutalised submission to a possessive husband. This world would be the utopia of the anarchist, but, realisable or not as a utopia, it is certainly not real within the film. Whatever the intellectual possibilities of an alternative, the real world for Buñuel, and the immediate world of his imagination, is a brutal and stupid one. . . .

Because Buñuel's immediate vision covers only what is contained within the circle, and embraces it only in its most crassly material form, the problematic aspect of the film is easily obscured. The spectator is only struck by it after the film has ended, when he tries to piece together what it all actually means, who is right and who is wrong. The weakness of *Nazarin* is that it does require piecing together afterwards. (p. 195)

Geoffrey Nowell-Smith, "Film Reviews: 'Nazarin'," in Sight and Sound *(copyright © 1963 by The British Film Institute), Vol. 32, No. 4, Autumn, 1963, pp. 194-95.*

ANDRÉ BAZIN

The theme [of *Los Olvidados*], on the surface anyway, is the same that, since the appearance of *Chemin de la vie,* has served as a model for all films dealing with juvenile delinquency: misery makes an evil counselor, and redemption comes through love, trust, and hard work. The fundamental optimism of this theme is, first of all, a moral optimism, on the order of Rousseau's, which proposes an innate goodness in man and a paradise of innocence in childhood, laid waste before it is ripe by an adult world. But it is also a social optimism, which suggests that society can repair the evil it has done through reeducation. (p. 195)

With both children and adults, Buñuel avoids making judgments. If adults are more generally wicked, it is because they are more entrenched in misfortune. No doubt the most shocking aspect of this film is that it dares to show the lame and halt without making them pathetic. . . . (p. 197)

It is absurd to reproach Buñuel for having a perverse taste for cruelty. True, he does seem to choose situations for their paroxysms of horror. What more awful sight can be imagined than a child stoning a blind man, unless it be a blind man revenging himself upon a child. . . . But the cruelty is not Buñuel's. He is only revealing the cruelty that exists in the world. If he has chosen the most horrible examples, it is because the real problem is not whether good exists, but how deep into the sphere of misery human life can go. He probes the cruelty of creation itself. (pp. 197-98)

Yet the cruelty in Buñuel's work is entirely objective; it is nothing more than lucidity, nothing less than despair. And though pity is absent from the aesthetics of his films, compassion is a basic ingredient of his work as a whole. . . . Nothing could be more unlike existential pessimism than Buñuel's cruelty. Because it evades nothing, concedes nothing, because it dares with surgical obscenity to make an incision in the corpus of reality, his cruelty can rediscover humanity in all its grandeur, and compel us, by a kind of Pascalian dialectic, to love and admiration. . . . [The] most hideous faces in *Los Olvidados* never fail to be human. The presence of this beauty in horror (and it is not simply the beauty *of* horror), the sublime endurance of human nobility in the midst of decadence, transform that cruelty into acts of love and compassion. And it is for this reason that *Los Olvidados* does not affect us adversely, with either sadistic complacency or false indignation.

It is not possible to avoid touching on the surrealism in Buñuel's films. He is, indeed, one of the rare valuable representatives of this mode. But it would be a mistake to accord it too great a place in his work. His surrealism is a part of the rich and fortunate influence of a totally Spanish tradition. His taste for the horrible, his sense of brutality, his tendency to delve into the utmost extremes of humanity—these are all the heritage of Goya, Zurbaran, Ribera. And above all, it reflects a tragic sense of life, which these painters expressed through the ultimate human degradations: war, sickness, misery and decay. But their cruelty, too, served only as a measure of their trust in mankind itself, and in their art. (pp. 198-200)

André Bazin, "'Los Olvidados'" (originally published in Qu'est-ce que le cinema?: Cinema et sociologie, *Vol. III, Editions du Cerf, 1963), translated by Sallie Iannotti, in* The World of Luis Buñuel: Essays in Criticism, *edited by Joan Mellen (copyright © 1978 by Joan Mellen; reprinted by permission of Oxford University Press, Inc.), Oxford University Press, New York, 1978, pp. 194-200.*

JOHN RUSSELL TAYLOR

Never since *L'Age d'Or* has Buñuel's expression of his beliefs been so intense and concentrated, not even in *Viridiana*, the most complete later expression, since then there is a fully articulated plot to be dealt with and the film is more than twice as long. But one *L'Age d'Or* is enough; no man, not even Buñuel, would need to make two in one lifetime. It offers such riches all at one go that it leaves dozens of fragments of raw material just begging to be taken up again and reworked, as well as numerous ideas to be applied to an infinite number of new situations. The later films, after some twenty years' gap, set out to do precisely this; to build on the firm foundations offered by *L'Age d'Or*.

Buñuel's next film, *Las Hurdes* (1932) also known as *Land Without Bread*, is a perfect illustration. At first sight it would seem the direct opposite of *L'Age d'Or*, a straightforward social documentary about a depressed area in the mountains of Spain marking, one might suppose, a complete break with surrealist fantasy. And yet it is not like that at all. . . . *Las Hurdes* simply offers the reverse of the medal: Buñuel's objective camera-eye applied to the extraordinary gives it the air (all the more disturbing of course) of complete normality; applied to straight actuality, on the other hand, it somehow heightens our awareness to the point where what he sees takes on the colouring of wild surrealist fantasy. The tension in each case between, as it were, the tone of voice and what the voice is saying is exactly the same, and the ultimate effect is astonishingly consistent; not for nothing does Buñuel class *Las Hurdes*, without explanation, or, apparently, a second thought, among 'my surrealist films'. (pp. 89-90)

[*Los Olvidados*] was the first unmistakably 'Buñuel' film since *Las Hurdes*, fully characteristic of his mature vision and showing a quite extraordinary consistency of style and inspiration with the works of his early surrealist heyday.

At one stage, indeed, this was to have been even more evident, since Buñuel intended to include in the film moments of surrealist commentary on the principal story of juvenile delinquents in the slums of Mexico City: the camera, travelling reflectively over a wasteland, would pick out a symphony orchestra playing away in the skeleton of an unfinished building, and then return without lingering to the principal characters, and so on. But ultimately this idea was abandoned, and instead we are given what appears to be a straightforward realistic film, its fantasy carefully limited to a symbolic dream sequence. Appearances, however, are deceptive, as they were with *Las Hurdes:* what Buñuel is really about is the exploration of his private world, under the guise of realism. In *Los Olvidados*, in fact, he has hit at once on precisely the sort of ambivalence which has enabled him subsequently to make his own films quite happily within the commercial system. At one level the film works quite acceptably on the level of an humane social document . . . and that is the level on which it has appealed to a vast public. On another level, though, one can see it as not realistic at all, any more than *Las Hurdes* was realistic; and if this time the effect stops short of an empassioned call to murder, nevertheless the nightmarish, hallucinatory quality of the film is uniquely disturbing.

This result is achieved—though perhaps Buñuel would resent intensely one's saying it—by Buñuel's power to invest the most unexpected things with poetry. Not, of course, poetry in the sense that the appearance of Gabriel Figueroa, Mexico's foremost expert in lush atmospherics, as the film's cameraman might lead one to expect; the photography is throughout bare and stripped of extraneous effects, even in the dream sequence. Rather is it the sort of imagist poetry which comes from an intense heightening of individual sense impressions, so that certain selected objects take on the quality of a fetish, an instrument of ritual significance in the reenactment of some private myth. So in *Los Olvidados* it is with the cockerels which infest the action, heralding doom; with the dove whose soft body caresses the back of an invalid; the raw meat which sets the tone of the dream sequence; the terrible old blind man's stick; the milk which the girl Meche pours over herself to make her skin beautiful. Nothing is ever allowed to be completely and merely what it appears, any more than is the film as a whole. (pp. 92-3)

But as with *Las Hurdes* the apparent ruthless objectivity is only a matter of tone of voice; what is said in this tone of voice is selected with the utmost precision and phrased in such a way as to produce exactly the effect intended by the speaker and no other. Buñuel shines such a hard, unflinching light on external reality that it begins little by little to give itself over to him, to reveal its secrets from the darker, hidden world of instinctive needs or impulses. We look at the reality Buñuel has selected for us so closely and fixedly through his eyes that we begin to lose consciousness of any other criteria: reality takes on something of the feverish intensity of a dream; dreams, when they come, something of the cool matter-of-factness of reality; distinctions begin to blur and dissolve, leaving dream and waking reality alike as projections of Buñuel's own ideas on human life. All is stunted and twisted at the root by society and religion, which organize and limit man in such a way that love without inhibition is impossible, and when the instincts are trammelled in this way they can find expression only in misery, perversion, crime, and death.

As well as being Buñuel's first consistent and successful attempt to accommodate his anarchic, surrealist ideals to the commercial cinema, *Los Olvidados* offers a very fair example of his mature film technique. It is, as far as the use of the camera is concerned, remarkable only in its complete unremarkability. There are no startling 'effects', no beautiful photography, if beauty in photography is conceived only in terms of the arty and artificial, no virtuoso camera movements, no *tours-de-force* of editing. It sounds, therefore, rather as though it must be a dull, conventional film, but not at all. The angle of each shot is chosen and it is framed with an absolutely unerring instinct for conveying the precise nuance intended with the minimum of trouble; the editing style is smooth and free, without any commerce with conventional notions of montage—Buñuel simply cuts from one thing he wants to show to another, with no nonsense about covering and matching or what is and is not academically permissible; if it works he does it, and at least by the time the film is shown it always does. (pp. 94-5)

El is one of the most bitter, and the most frenziedly intense, of all Buñuel's films. His denunciation of Christianity, both directly and indirectly, through the portrait of the 'good Christian' Francisco, has never been so uncompromising, and the transposition of the message of *L'Age d'Or* to a superficially realistic setting if anything increases its power. . . . *El* is also, perhaps necessarily, Buñuel's most elaborate film technically: the overheated mind of Francisco, his inextricable mingling of fantasy and reality, is allowed to work on the spectator in a number of scenes through the use of technical devices usually confined by Buñuel to dream sequences; especially in the church sequence near the end, where we are shown in rapid alternation the priest, choir and congregation as they are and as they appear to Francisco, grimacing and mocking him. But Buñuel's talent for the extremely simple, unobtrusively right has not deserted him either; the sequences of the knitting-needles and the midnight sewing are all the more nightmarish and terrifying for being recorded quite calmly and straightforwardly, even remotely, with something of the documentary quality we noticed in *Las Hurdes*. (pp. 101-02)

Buñuel's prime interest in the cinema seems to lie in what he is saying; he does not start with a literary original and make it cinematic; it is simply that he expresses himself in cinematic terms because he creates films as unselfconsciously as other men write poems or paint pictures. This means that, as in the case of a very different director with whom nevertheless Buñuel has certain affinities, Jean Renoir, there is hardly ever any cinematic effect which forces itself on one's attention and calls for comment, as there is constantly in the work of Welles or Bergman. Effects are achieved instead for the most part with the utmost simplicity; it is simply (in the context that word has an ironic ring) a matter of putting the camera in the right place at the right time. Sometimes, consequently, Buñuel's films, like Renoir's, seem careless from their very ease and informality; he is not, we say, making the most of his material, getting all he can out of it. Ah, but isn't he? Even with his most casual, free-and-easy films like *The Young One*, which looks as if it was made up as Buñuel went along, and probably was, as soon as one comes to consider possible improvements, alternative, better ways of shooting a scene, the complete rightness and inevitability of the way Buñuel has done it is borne forcibly in on one. (pp. 112-13)

[The] highest tribute one can pay to Buñuel's direction is to say that one is hardly ever conscious of it. All the elements are at least competent, and in *Viridiana* . . . they are all . . . outstandingly good. Yet still the parts are subservient to the whole, and it is the overall effect which one takes away, not the excitements of individual elements. (p. 113)

Indeed, one might almost carry the argument a stage further and maintain—except that this would seem to devalue the individual films unduly—that Buñuel's total *oeuvre* is greater than the sum of its parts: certainly each addition to it enlarges and clarifies the significance of what has gone before, while the recurrent motifs, though hardly obscure at first sight, take on further layers of significance when studied as they gradually develop from film to film. Buñuel maintains that he never deliberately 'puts in the symbolism': that he lets his instinct carry him along and often does not know why he has done something until someone else points it out to him (Francisco's zigzag walk at the end of *El*, for example, corresponding to that at the height of his insane frenzy of jealousy, was put in according to Buñuel 'just because I liked the effect'—and yet the significance that emerges from it is ummistakable). But whether consciously or unconsciously, Buñuel forgets nothing. . . . In a study such as this one can only barely indicate something of the unique coherence of Buñuel's work, which is perhaps more completely stamped with its creator's personality than any other in the cinema. Even less can one exemplify its specifically cinematic quality; there is, happily, no substitute for seeing the films, as only that way can the sublime simplicity and case of Buñuel's art be appreciated. (p. 114)

John Russell Taylor, "Luis Buñuel," in his Cinema Eye, Cinema Ear: Some Key Film-Makers of the Sixties *(reprinted by permission of Hill & Wang, a division of Farrar, Straus & Giroux, Inc.; in Canada, by AD Peters & Co Ltd; copyright © 1964 by John Russell Taylor), Hill & Wang, 1964, pp. 82-114.*

STROTHER PURDY

[A] careful look at *Exterminating Angel* reveals it . . . as Bunuel's best film, perhaps, and as a film almost alone in a mode that might be called existential surrealism.

Ever since *Chien Andalou* Bunuel has been expected to put oddly or outrageously juxtaposed images in his films, and not necessarily to have anything in mind beyond an urge to shock, or to express senseless violence, while doing it. . . . In *Exterminating Angel*, on the other hand, the events are generally impossible outside of dreams (truly surreal), but there should be no more presumption that they are therefore meaningless than there should be concerning the events in *Viridiana*, or that events in dreams are meaningless. (p. 29)

[Bunuel put something surreal into his films] because he meant something by it. All the more did he mean something by the central situation and its outcome.

This central situation—the visit of the Exterminating Angel and the pathetic deliverance of his victims—is basically an allegory, just as *Viridiana* and *Chien Andalou* are allegories. Only its greater complexity makes it harder to comprehend than *Viridiana,* for it is both holding the Christian world-allegory up to ridicule, and reworking its terms to present another view, that is existential. It is first the medieval Dance of Death, of which modern examples are Poe's *The Masque of the Red Death* and Bergman's *Seventh Seal* —once Death has appeared, the guests are to die one by one. . . . Death is thus the subject of the film, but several other elements are added, elements that carry it far from Christian allegory. (pp. 30-1)

First is the shipwreck theme, the stranding of a group of characters without food or water, and recording with sardonic relish their interactions in the increasingly desperate fight for survival—these including the erosion of courtesy, male deference to female, social disguises of weakness, aggression, and cruelty—so *The Admirable Crichton, The Lifeboat, The Lord of the Flies,* and so forth. . . .

[Bunuel twists the shipwreck theme here:] the shipwrecked aren't shipwrecked—they are cast away in a drawing room, like the damned in Sartre's *No Exit,* and the doorways to the rest of the house and the city beyond stand open. This is both comic and sinister—what is the force that holds them trapped? (p. 31)

[At the point where the *naufragos* are rescued] where a shallower film, like *Lord of the Flies,* might end, Bunuel is preparing another blow, a final comic absurdity that brings a larger disorientation. When the rescued ones [attend] a solemn high Mass of thanks at the cathedral, they are trapped again! (p. 32)

[What] do the metaphors of surreal time and a plague in the city do to explain the mystery of the invisible barrier—the fatal trap that has no physical existence? Death may come to the city like a plague or a falling out of time, but those who actually die in the film do so neither from infectious disease nor from starvation. Their predicament is not one visited upon them by a supernatural power, but lies within their own natures. It is the existential predicament of loss of will. The open doorway is not blocked by an invisible agency—the sheep trot through it with the same ease the child walks through the gate—but by the individual's incapacity to persist in a determination to pass through. It is a small act, an absurd one to be denied, or to find oneself unable to perform. It is an act we perform without thought, just as we live without thought. If we don't live we die, and the doorway they can't breach brings the guests face to face with death, the Exterminating Angel. Like the Sartrean *nausée,* lack of will is a malaise that can affect a civilization as well as an individual, and be likened to a plague in its spread. (pp. 32-3)

Bunuel, like Eisenstein, employs his most sardonic visual metaphors to mock the church: the doors along one side of the room bear paintings of angels, yet behind them lie death and corruption. One door conceals the lovers' passion and then their suicide, a second the body of the heart attack victim, a third the vases that receive the natural wastes—and as a final touch, several of the ladies have visions as they defecate there. . . .

Exterminating Angel is a film that tries to remind us of the hollowness of our defences against the unexpected, and that the social inventions we employ to lend meaning to life and scare away death are absurd, games like those of the fun-loving hostess. And *Exterminating Angel* tries to indicate, if only negatively, that there is a better way to live. (p. 34)

Strother Purdy, "Existential Surrealism: The Neglected Example of Bunuel's 'The Exterminating Angel'," in Film Heritage *(copyright 1968 by F. A. Macklin), Vol. 3, No. 4, Summer, 1968, pp. 28-34.*

BRIAN MURPHY

For anyone interested in Bunuel, *Simon del Desierto* is essential because this is the one film in which Bunuel takes as his immediate subject that which has played so important a part in the background of all his films: Christianity. . . .

Simon is obviously neither Viridiana nor Nazarin: he is a powerful, fascinating figure, and Bunuel's treatment of him is generally sympathetic. Nevertheless, the film, intellectually a dilemma, is cynical and pessimistic. On the one hand, there is the nihilism of the 20th century which we all know; on the other, there is Simon's world—which is not entirely typical. . . .

One of the most interesting tensions in any Bunuel film is between the elegant, composed construction of the film, so apparently slick and impersonal, and the pervading subjective obsessions. . . .

Precisely what makes *Simon del Desierto* so interesting and important is that the Christian images do not merely float in the background but comprise the very subject of the film. It is as though Bunuel, after privately ridding himself of his own religion, now takes a careful look at the godless world of the 20th century, contrasts it with a simplistic Christian world-view, and is plainly horrified by what he sees. . . .

Bunuel's pessimism is somewhat hollow, rather easy, even a bit theatrical or rhetorical. The pessimism in *Simon del Desierto* comes from the dilemma of an intellectually impossible Christianity versus a spiritually empty, meaningless and mad modern materialism. That there are other possibilities (an intellectually viable Christianity or a responsible humanism, for example) Bunuel never considers.

Even for those who do not much care for Bunuel, *Simon del Desierto* is a powerful statement of an existential no-exit; for those who do like Bunuel, this film is absolutely essential for a complete understanding of the man's thought and work to date. And for anyone who cares about films, *Simon del Desierto* is the work of a master craftsman: it is not only serenely accomplished, it also has some of the tensions and haunting reverberations of great art.

Brian Murphy, "Reviews: 'Simon of the Desert'" (© copyright Brian Murphy 1969; reprinted with permission), in Films and Filming, *Vol. 15, No. 10, July, 1969, p. 39.*

LITA PANIAGUA

Patterned loosely after the picaro novels of the Spanish Renaissance, *The Milky Way* follows two itinerants, amiable, friendly fellows. . . . [They] participate as spectators in periodic episodes illustrating various formalistic squabbles on points of dogma in the life of the Church: the divinity of Christ, the Holy Trinity, the Immaculate Conception, the Eucharist, the Existence of Free Will, the Origin of Evil . . . the whole tiresome bag. It is doubtful if this line of silly medieval chatter could at best be forged into significant thought-provoking questions under the conditions of the world today. In the hands of an aging reforming zealot, they turn into instruments of torture more like the tools of the Inquisition he so roundly condemns. (pp. 28-9)

Characterizations are minimal and rudimentary. The two itinerants emerge less as personalities than as a Greek Chorus of bumblers who give neither emphasis nor counterpoint; the social Establishment types are shown largely as mild-mannered imbeciles; the clergy and the faithful—mostly petit-bourgeois mediocrities—seen consistently as stupid and insensitive, obscurantist and unimaginative, uncharitable when not outright cruel, pettifogging, superstitious, and corruptors of the young.

For symbolism-buffs, *The Milky Way* is at least a good sampler of Bunuel's established fetishistic motifs. . . . And there are also a few incursions into elementary surrealism, as when the father at the school picnic (the children reciting a piping chorus of anathemas) starts at a volley only imagined by the young *clochard*—who had just day-dreamed the firing-squad execution of a Pope; or as in a later scene at the Spanish Inn when an obtuse and sweating priest is shifted constantly back and forth from hallway to bedroom (through a locked door), all the while expounding on the virtues of chastity. Here at least is an echo of Bunuel's best anti-Church work of the past, when he acted like a wicked little boy beating an old witch with her own broom.

But the fine old touch of malice is largely missing here. The film has neither the power and depth of *Viridiana,* nor the ingenious gags and satiric directness of *Simon of the Desert.* Unlike these two films, his best in the genre, *The Milky Way* remains throughout, discursive, banal, pedestrian and uninspired. The problem is partly that the old soldier has fired all his rounds at the wrong target. (p. 30)

Oblivious to all of festering life about him, Bunuel struggles doggedly on, . . . preoccupied with doctrinal trivia. . . . (p. 31)

Lita Paniagua, "'The Milky Way'," in Film Society Review, *Vol. 5, No. 6, February, 1970, pp. 28-31.*

STANLEY KAUFFMANN

[*The Milky Way* is a] parable of Christianity, but it is free of Christ parallels (*Nazarin*), of sterile and protracted allegory (*The Exterminating Angel*), of shallow Evil-as-travail-toward-Good (*El*). The structure of this new film is taut and well-modeled, the interplay between idea and image is delightful, the whole work is funny and bitter and peculiarly devout from beginning to end. (p. 231)

The film is as well made as Buñuel's pictures have often—not always—been. Occasionally he still lets people walk out of shots, leaving us to stare for a second at empty places where the action *was;* and occasionally there is a meaningless emphasis (like a close shot of the wheels of a railroad train arriving in Tours). But for the most part there is discretion, the sense of a mordant eye, and the overall feeling of flow that we get even in lesser films like *Viridiana* and *The Diary of a Chambermaid.* (p. 232)

But the superiority of this film, like that of [*Simon of the Desert*], is not in the filming as such but in the script. . . . It is Buñuel the author, more than the *auteur,* who has made *The Milky Way* the fine work that it is. . . . After one has enumerated the various elements in the script of wit, slyness, compassion, and human bewilderment, there is left the central and controlling vision; and the source of that vision is to me the most interesting and revealing aspect of the film. It is the artistic concept with which Buñuel began his film career, from which he has often divagated, and to which he has recently returned to use with a new depth and power—the concept of Surrealism.

Some years ago Buñuel said:

> It was Surrealism which showed me that life has a moral direction which man cannot but follow. For the first time I understood that man was not free. I already believed in the total liberty of man, but in Surrealism I found a discipline to follow. It was a great lesson in my life. It was also a great step forward into the marvelous and the poetic.

That dialectic between liberty and discipline, resulting in a synthesis that is "marvelous and poetic," has an analogue for Buñuel, I think in the dialectic between God and Church, the synthesis of which is in *Simon* and *The Milky Way.* His vision of religion is a Surrealist one. (p. 233)

Today Buñuel's Surrealist view rests on a more sophisticated and mature base than the juxtaposition of incongruous objects and acts. Dead donkeys on pianos or cows on beds no longer serve as adequate manifests of dream-reality. True, *The Milky Way* scrambles historical periods, refuses to explain how a priest can be inside and outside a bedroom at the same time, and has sweet little schoolgirls fulminating anathema, but these concretized fantasies do not exist merely to shock and stimulate and invigorate our protocols of vision. Underlying them is a *philosophic* vision that is itself Surrealist: a vision that lifts the history of the Church off the ground into one grand condensation and sustains it through an idea of faith that is larger than any pettifogging theological pedantry. Buñuel is no longer interested in extending consciousness through a series of visual puns and oxymorons, however cruelly scintillating, for which the scenario seems almost an afterthought and justification. With *The Milky Way* the process seems reversed. In his old age Buñuel has come back to Surrealism with greater purity, with a deeper perception of liberty through discipline. He has begun this picture with a very clear, almost programmatic dream reality, a surreal *conviction,* and the visual metaphors proceed firmly from it. (p. 234)

Stanley Kauffmann, "'The Milky Way'" (originally published in The New Republic, *Vol. 162, No. 6, February 7, 1970), in his* Figures of Light: Film Criticism and Comment *(copyright © 1968, 1969, 1970 by Stanley Kauffmann; reprinted by permission of Harper & Row, Publishers, Inc.), Harper, 1971, pp. 231-35.*

JOAN MELLEN

[Within] the confines of [*Tristana*'s] rather melodramatic if morally resonant plot, which always borders on the perverse, as do all of the director's films, Buñuel has managed to interweave meanings that go far beyond the Electra theme. Throughout the film, Buñuel comments on the psychological effects of social dependance. (p. 52)

Buñuel's psychology is impeccable. Her mind a *tabula rasa*, it is logical that Tristana would become whatever her surroundings provide, that her psychic impulses would be directed by the will of her domineering guardian. (pp. 52-3)

Sexually, Tristana, after her initiation by Don Lope, becomes the sister of Belle de Jour. . . . Like Belle de Jour, Tristana is a woman whose sexuality has been perverted by a fear of seduction, by an older, forbidding father figure, and who can now respond only to the brutal and the perverse. (p. 53)

It is, of course, perfect justice that Don Lope should fall victim at the end to his own perversion. Tristana responds in the manner he has taught her. "The kinder he is," she says, "the less I love him." She expresses the psychological damage done to women in her culture—the same damage expressed by Belle de Jour, who could be awakened sexually only in a brothel.

Tristana reflects as well Buñuel's preoccupation with the decay of Spain. He explores its obsession with an old order, represented by Don Lope and his cronies who meet every day in a café filled with indolent former aristocrats. It is a world defined by norms and relationships which have outlived their time and have now become dangerous. . . . It conveys the image of a Spain that is already amputated. The crippled Tristana represents in her person the generation to be maimed by the Civil War, embodying as she does the frequent image in Franco's Spain of the amputee. (pp. 53-4)

Don Lope stands . . . for the impotence and historical amnesia of Spain. . . . And Don Lope's impotence is far from innocent. Hypocrisy defines his very sensibility. It is expressed in his self-conscious and superficial rejection of religion as well as in the ridiculousness of his code of honor which decrees that he live by all the ten commandments except those having to do with sex, by which he means seduction. . . .

His morality is thus expressed in limbo, devoid of any real content. It is couched in terms that will not touch upon his life: a duel, a harmless denunciation of priests, the contempt for the degradation of work by a man who is kept all his life by a private income, the rejection of marriage by a man who savors sex more with a mistress, particularly if she is innocent and thirty years younger than he. It is the almost psychotic sense of honor of the hidalgo who would rather starve to death than work, although he must sell everything he owns. In Don Lope's case it is the honor of a man who has debauched a girl destined to live with him as his daughter. (p. 54)

The circular structure of the imagery, the rapid repetition of the images of Tristana's life until we return to the first sequence of the film, reflects the hopelessness Buñuel feels, both toward Spain and toward its victims. Buñuel has relentlessly and brilliantly exposed the destruction of the individual by a corrupt, hypocritical moral code which makes no pretense of improving a society in which class animosities are deepening and brutality is growing. (p. 55)

Joan Mellen, "Reviews: 'Tristana'," in Film Quarterly *(copyright 1970 by The Regents of the University of California; reprinted by permission of the University of California Press), Vol. XXIV, No. 2, Winter, 1970-71, pp. 52-5.*

FRANÇOIS TRUFFAUT

Luis Buñuel is, perhaps, somewhere between Renoir and Bergman. One would gather that Buñuel finds mankind imbecilic but life diverting. All this he tells us very mildly, even a bit indirectly, but it's there in the overall impression we get from his films. Even though he has very little stomach for "messages," Buñuel did manage to make one of those rare, truly antiracist movies, *The Young One* (1960), the only film he has shot in English. It succeeded because of his masterful ability to intertwine sympathetic and unsympathetic characters and to shuffle the cards in his psychological game while he addresses us in perfectly clear, logical language.

The antipsychological Buñuelian scenario functions on the same principle as the hot-and-cold shower—alternating favorable and unfavorable signs, positives and negatives, reason and nonsense. He puts these elements to work on both the action and the characters in his films. Anti-bourgeois, anti-conformist, Buñuel is as sarcastic as Stroheim but he has a lighter touch; his world view is subversive, happily anarchist. (p. 261)

Buñuel is a cheerful pessimist, not given to despair, but he has a skeptical mind. Notice, he never makes films *for*, always *against*, and none of his characters ever appear to be very practical. Buñuel's skepticism extends to all those whom he finds playing too neat a social game, those who live by accepted opinions. (pp. 261-62)

Too many commentators refer to Buñuel as a poet of hallucination who follows the caprices of his fantastic imagination, while in reality he is a brilliant screenwriter very much concerned with dramatic construction. (p. 263)

Let's look at how he constructed . . . *The Criminal Life of Archibaldo de la Cruz (Archibald of the Cross)*, which he made in Mexico in 1955. He was not then universally recognized as a genius, and he was working in a country in which the censors would have prohibited him from showing a murderer who is not only likable but goes unpunished into the bargain. (p. 264)

I'm not familiar with the literary sources of *Archibaldo de la Cruz*, but the cinematic inspirations are clear—Hitchcock's *Shadow of a Doubt* (1948), which tells the story of a man who murders widows . . . set against the musical theme of *The Merry Widow;* a film by Preston Sturges, *Unfaithfully Yours* (1948), in which an orchestra conductor . . . imagines three different ways of killing his wife as he conducts a symphony; and, above all, Chaplin's *Monsieur Verdoux* (1947). The distraught woman whose path Archibaldo keeps crossing is obviously related to the extraordinary Martha Raye (Captain Bonheur's wife) whom Verdoux-Bonheur never quite succeeds in murdering.

But the true interest of *Archibaldo* lies elsewhere—in the ingenuity of its construction, the audacious handling of time, the expertise of the cinematic narrative. If you question the audience at the end of *Archibaldo*—remember, its full title is, mischievously, *The Criminal Life of Archibald of the Cross*—almost everybody will tell you that they've just seen the story of a likable guy who kills women. It is absolutely not true; Archibaldo has killed no one. He's been satisfied simply to wish, after the death of his governess when he was a little boy, for the deaths of the nun who was a nurse in the hospital, the beautiful disturbed woman, the sultry guide, and his unfaithful fiancée. Four of the five women have died in one way or another shortly after Archibaldo has expressed his desire. We have anticipated these deaths as fantasies (flashes forward), and then we've seen certain of them really occur, but only as recounted by Archibaldo in flashback.

In the hands of most film writers, *Archibaldo* would have become a series of sketches, but Buñuel and Eduardo Ugarte were able to intertwine the individual episodes by introducing us to all the female characters early in the story, and then, in the second half of the film, gathering them delicately for their ten-minute scenes to show them as real women.

Archibaldo is one of those rare films so finely constructed, written with such a sense of how to put images on a screen, that reading the screenplay gives only a weak idea of the result, maybe even a completely inaccurate impression. . . . If one simply recounted its scenes literally, it would seem ridiculous. Lubitsch and Buñuel are the masters of the invisible flashback, the flashback that interrupts without breaking the story line and, on the contrary, refreshes it when it threatens to flag. They are also masters at bringing us back to the present without startling us. They both use a two-pronged hook with which they jerk us backward and forward. The hook is almost always a gimmick—comic in Lubitsch's work, dramatic in Buñuel's.

Too many screenplays are conceived for their literary effect, and they end up as novels written in pictures. They are pleasant to read, they make easy promises, and they deliver on them, presuming the director and the actors have as much talent as the writer. I'm not out to criticize the straight story-line movies—of which *Bicycle Thief* is one of the most beautiful examples—but to suggest that the talents of the scenarists who wrote *The Big Sleep, North by Northwest, Heaven Can Wait,* or *Archibaldo de la Cruz* are far greater. The discipline of film has its own rules, which have not yet been fully explored, and it is only through works such as those of Buñuel and the other great director-writers that we will one day realize them fully. (pp. 267-68)

François Truffaut, "Buñuel the Builder" (1971), in his The Films in My Life, *translated by Leonard Mayhew (copyright © 1975 by, Flammarion; translation copyright © 1978 by, Simon and Schuster; reprinted by permission of Simon and Schuster, a Division of Gulf & Western Corporation; originally published as* Les Films de ma vie, *Flammarion, 1975), Simon and Schuster, 1978, pp. 261-68.*

PAULINE KAEL

"The Discreet Charm of the Bourgeoisie" is a cosmic vaudeville show—an Old Master's mischief. . . . Luis Buñuel is no longer savage about the hypocrisy and the inanity of the privileged classes. They don't change, and since they have become a persistent bad joke to him, he has grown almost fond of their follies—the way one can grow fond of the snarls and the silliness of vicious pets. He looks at them now and they're such perfectly amoral little beasts they amuse him; he enjoys their skin-deep proprieties, their faith in appearances, their sublime confidence. At the same time, this Spanish exile-expatriate may have come to a point in life when the hell he has gone through to make movies is receding into the past, like an old obscene story; he is so relaxed about his medium now that he enjoys pinching its nose, pulling its tail. He has become a majestic light prankster—not a bad way for a man full of disgust and pity to age. The movie is slight, but it has a special enchantment: it's a development—more like an emanation—of Buñuel's movies which couldn't have been expected but which seems *right;* that is, the best thing that could have happened. Buñuel's cruelty and mockery were often startlingly funny, but they were also sadistic; that was the power of his work and part of what made his films scandalous. He was diabolically antibourgeois, and he wasn't just anticlerical—he was hilariously, murderously anticlerical. Here his old rages have become buoyant jokes. (Might Swift without his disease have ended up like this?) This movie comes close to serenity, and it's a deep pleasure to see that the unregenerate anarchist-atheist has found his own path to grace. Buñuel has never given in, never embraced the enemy, and maybe that's why the tone of this spontaneous chamber music is so happy. (p. 41)

Pauline Kael, "Anarchist's Laughter" (originally published in The New Yorker, *Vol. XLVIII, No. 38, November 11, 1972), in her* Reeling *(copyright © 1972 by Pauline Kael; reprinted by permission of Little, Brown and Company in association with the Atlantic Monthly Press), Atlantic-Little, Brown, 1976, pp. 41-6.**

CARLOS FUENTES

An obsessive artist, Buñuel cares about what he wants to say; or rather, what he wants to see. A really important director makes only one film; his work is a sum, a totality of perfectly related parts that illuminate each other. In Buñuel's films, from "An Andalusian Dog" to "The Discreet Charm of the Bourgeoisie," the essential unifying factor is sight. His first image is that of a woman's eye slit by a razor and throughout the body of his work there is this pervading sense of sight menaced, sight lost as virginity is lost; sight as a wound that will not heal, wounded sight as an interstice through which dreams and desires can flow. Catherine Deneuve's absent regard in "Belle de Jour" is calculated: She is constantly looking outside the confines of the screen, enlarging the space of the screen, looking at something beyond that isn't there, that probably connects the two halves of her life.

But Buñuel's violent aggressions against sight actually force us back to his particular way of seeing. His world is seen first as a grey, hazy, distant jumble of undetermined things; no other director shoots a scene from quite that neutral, passive distance. Then the eye of the camera suddenly picks out an object that has been there all the time, or a revealing gesture, zooms into them, makes them come violently alive before again retiring to the indifferent point of view.

This particular way of seeing, of making the opaque backdrop shine instantly by selecting an object or gesture, assures the freedom and fluid elegance of a Buñuel film. Sight determines montage; what is seen flows into what is unseen. . . .

Sight and survival, desires and dreams, seeing others in order to see oneself. This parabola of sight is essential to Buñuel's art. Nazarin will not see God unless he sees his fellow men; Viridiana will not see herself unless she sees outside herself and accepts the world. The characters in "The Discreet Charm" can never see themselves or others. They may be funny, but they are already in hell. Elegant humor only cloaks despair.

So in Buñuel sight determines content or, rather, content is a way of looking, content is sight at all possible levels. And this multitude of levels—social, political, psychological, historical, esthetic, philosophic—is not predetermined, but flows from vision. His constant tension is between obsessive opposites: pilgrimage and confinement, solitude and fraternity, sight and blindness, social rules and personal cravings, rational conduct and oneiric behavior. His intimate legacies, often conflicting, are always there: Spain, Catholicism, surrealism, left anarchism. But, above all, what is always present is the liberating thrust that could only come from such a blend of heritages. Certainly no other filmmaker could have so gracefully and violently humanized and brought into the fold of freedom, rebellion and understanding so many figures, so many passions, so many desires that the conventional code judges as monstrous, criminal and worthy of persecution and, even, extermination. . . . Buñuel incriminates all social orders while liberating our awareness of the outcast. . . .

[This] respect for freedom of his characters is translated into respect for the freedom of his audience. As they end, his films remain open, the spectator remains free. (p. 373)

Carlos Fuentes, "Spain, Catholicism, Surrealism, Anarchism: The Discreet Charm of Luis Buñuel," in The New York Times *(© 1973 by the New York Times Company; reprinted by permission), March 11, 1973 (and reprinted in* The New York Times Biographical Edition, *The New York Times Company, 1973, pp. 369-76).*

FREDDY BUACHE

It would be a mistake to try to work out a systematic exegesis of *Un Chien Andalou,* because it is impossible to translate, completely into ordinary language the complexity of this poem—for poem it is, and not a fable or an allegory. On the other hand, it would be equally wrong to see it as the convulsions of two wild imaginations [Buñuel and Salvador Dali]. It *is* open to logical interpretation, and its theme is an extremely serious one. It describes the dramatic collision between desire and the object of that desire in a context that literally bristles with pitfalls. (p. 10)

Man is not free to approach the woman he loves. He carries around with him a whole ramshackle load of moral and social circumstances. He is hamstrung, he is weighed down like a slave who has to carry (to use Buñuel's imagery) pumpkins, priests, and a piano laden with rotting donkeys. Nothing could be more grotesquely further from the truth than to say that the pumpkins evoke cooking and domestic chores, that the smiling priests represent the way the Church tries to trammel love, that the piano is a symbol of bourgeois life, and that the corpses of animals are reminders of the putrefaction that awaits us from the moment we are born and overtakes us when we die. On the other hand, it does not seem to me to be farfetched to interpret the allusive truth of this sequence as a dynamic symbol that reflects everything which a man must take a grip on if he is to approach the woman he desires. She appears to him as something multiple, as a kind of quarry, an enemy, a beautiful animal with mother-of-pearl flesh, a living statue. (pp. 12-13)

L'Age d'Or resorts to the simplest kind of surrealist action —direct insults and a punch in the face. . . . The intertitles that occasionally appear during [the first] part of the film take on, as a result, a very particular meaning (one that goes to explain the tremendous power of Buñuel's art): they create an alienation effect whereby the world and our society are subjected to the impassive examination of an experimenter who apparently knows nothing of them. (p. 14)

But Buñuel's impassivity is feigned: it conceals a burning passion that transforms itself into a diamond or into phosphorus in order better to scratch or to burn everything it touches. *L'Age d'Or* is the most exhaustive catalogue of oppressions ever compiled for the screen. But it is not just a statistical record that can safely be stowed away in some archive, there to enrich the wizened heritage of western culture. This "pavilion of bloody meat" is a quivering, seething, consuming indictment that calls for rebellion and revolution, while at the same time advocating a liberated, totally unrestricted kind of mad love, or *amour fou.* (p. 15)

No other film has ever deciphered the structures of a society better than *L'Age d'Or*; the society in question is our own, even though it may give the false impression of having evolved since 1930. It still camouflages its criminal hypocrisy behind starched dickeys, uniforms and cassocks, behind slogans about the wisdom of the nations of the world and the twin myths of human nature and original sin, and behind Christian morality in general (as interpreted historically—and most ingeniously—by those in power in a bourgeois, capitalist society). Buñuel demonstrates how love is able to destroy established order, and why it is vital for it to do so if there is to be any hope of founding a form of humanism that is truly the measure of man and is stripped clean of idealistic mumbo-jumbo and fallacious freedom. (p. 24)

There is not the slightest trace of a hiatus between *L'Age d'Or* and *Las Hurdes.* Buñuel unceremoniously plunges us "into the icy waters of selfish motivations." (p. 30)

A little boy writes "respect your neighbour's property" on the blackboard in a schoolroom where on one of the walls an engraving has been pinned which shows a bewigged and powdered noblewoman dressed in Eighteenth century clothes—a dramatic confrontation of the two faces of the same class-ridden society. By making visually explicit the relationship between concrete suffering and the abstract universality of an engraving, the film instantly juxtaposes, in a highly revealing situation, the contradictions that are eating away our society. In a flash, it destroys the inevitability of injustice: it is no longer possible to find a reason for it in theological explanations.

Injustice is the product of a human order which through the clever use of parables about Good and Evil makes a travesty of the most basic notions of justice. Buñuel tears away the mask and points an accusing finger at the syphilitic faces and running sores that form part of a world crucified by Christianity. . . . (p. 31)

By getting across the alienation of the Hurdanos without a trace of pathos, Buñuel is in fact postulating that there is but one last hope for them. There is something of all of us in these Hurdanos, victims of themselves and of others. As we, who are chronically overfed, watch these Beckettian creatures in the strangulating syndrome of extreme poverty, we somehow realise that we are their brothers because our human universe, like theirs, is one of scarcity—but on another level. Polluted air and chemically contaminated food are our unripe cherries. What we most lack is time to live. (p. 34)

Like many other great film-makers, Buñuel transforms every subject he touches. More importantly, even when subjected to the pressures of the film industry, he has never betrayed his deepest artistic and personal convictions; he has always seized every opportunity to reaffirm (usually via insinuation rather than in the outright way likely to shock the sensibilities of political and Christian censors) the very same message that emerged with such force from his first films. (pp. 45-6)

L'Age d'Or offers us a vertical cross-section of a society whose hypocrisy stifles love. *El* may be considered as the horizontal cross-section of the same society: Buñuel uses the inverse, negative process, and eliminates the elements of revolt, scandal and insult. But although his attack on established values in *El* may seem more insidious it is nonetheless just as hardhitting as *L'Age d'Or*. (p. 60)

[A summary of *El*'s melodramatic plot] should make it clear that its highlights of jealousy and foot fetichism conceal a subtly constructed piece of psycho-social criticism that unmasks exactly the same oppressive set-up as that . . . in *L'Age d'Or*. But in *El* the motivations for the hero's failure in love are more fully emphasised. . . . Whereas Modot opts for rebellion, Francisco chooses to inflict upon himself a conventional, repressed pattern of behaviour that results, during the sequence, for instance, where he is unable to dictate a letter to Gloria, in a typical manifestation of impotence. Whereas Modot's desire leads him openly to cause scandals and to trample on all established values (to slap wheedling matrons, kick blind men, jeer at pity, insult ministers and put sex before everything), Francisco's urges are caught in a vicious circle, disintegrate, and seethe in the pressure cooker of religious and bourgeois principles. And yet although consistent self-denial results in the gradual stifling of desire, which finally seems to be tamed and completely sublimated in the person of the serene, secluded monk, one should not imagine that this desire has been totally annihilated. For however great the alienation, however powerful the institutional regulations aimed at damping it, love never loses its faculty of suddenly bursting out. This is why the uneasy conscience continually strives to escape the ever-present, ever-watchful threat of love by seeking refuge in mysticism. (pp. 67-8)

[One] has to admit that Buñuel did not "compose" *L'Age d'Or, The Exterminating Angel, Simon of the Desert* or any other of his masterpieces. For he has an innate sense of what is or is not poetic licence. As a director, he has never allowed himself to be governed by the "rules" which are supposed to underlie the grouping of images, the ordering of sequences, and the dovetailing of the editing, according to those cinematic rhetoricians-cum-carpenters who see themselves as teachers but are themselves incapable of planing a plank or knocking in a nail. (p. 79)

Buñuel covers his tracks by mimicking banality. He serves us with a light-hearted farrago of spontaneous invention, serious thinking, ironic winks at the audience, powerfully constructed and original creativity, and a combination of burlesque and tragedy. He slips back and forth from unselfconscious self-discipline to disciplined unselfconsciousness as airily as Picasso. In *Arcibaldo de la Cruz*—probably because Buñuel seems almost to be parodying himself—one can perceive better than in any of his other films how he manages to inject madness into realism, and how a piece of frothy entertainment can be shot through and through with black humour. He does not indulge in any cunning aesthetic devices or spectacular dream sequences, but pads unobtrusively up to his subject in order to be able to sink his teeth into it more devastatingly. (p. 80)

[In *Viridiana*] Buñuel remains faithful to everything he has ever said or stood for, synthesising in a quite startling manner the excessive violence and atrocities of *L'Age d'Or* and *Las Hurdes* with a new, more mature humanism. He is still a rebel who stands by his original principles, but he no longer needs to make his voice heard by having recourse to spectacular provocation. *Viridiana* encapsulates Buñuel's whole *Weltanschauung*. Good and evil are both fallacies that lead to dead ends. All acts are tinged to an equal degree with ambiguity, and nothing will change so long as we still live with our present moral system, i.e. the denial of *amour fou* and the affirmation of mystifying abstract forces. In Buñuel's eyes, there is no point in saving either a dog or a soul so long as the psycho-social set-up encourages the enslavement of dogs and souls—which should not of course stop us saving a dog if ever we can. Such are the concentric parabolae of *Viridiana,* a film that relies less on intellectual argument than on hitting the spectator between the eyes. Once again Buñuel's detractors, the narrow-minded champions of a cinematic language that possesses a semantic specificity, are thoroughly wrong: more clearly than in his other films, the direction is much, much more than the mere visual translation of anecdotal or literary arguments that have been inventively arranged into a shooting script; it creates a magic combination where form and content fuse dialectically at white hot temperature. (pp. 120-21)

[A] free approach, which consists of bringing together the most dissimilar objects and images in the figurative unity of a disturbing combination, is to be found throughout Buñuel's work. But in *La Voie lactée* [*The Milky Way*] it takes on a very particular quality. The director, in the simplest, most casual way, juxtaposes not a monstrance and a pavement, but holy texts, philosophical tirades about God or Christ, and everyday phrases set in a modern context. The fundamental declarations that define dogma answer the heretics' professions of faith, and vice versa.

In the course of this interminable exchange, the truth constantly changes sides. Each protagonist is convinced that he alone is in the right. But the truth as decreed by the ecclesiastical authorities—an unassailable truth because it was engendered by the divine word—inevitably ends up by having recourse to temporal powers in order to impose itself. (pp. 157-58)

Buñuel ruthlessly debunks the whole concept of religious meditation and makes theology look like one enormous hoax clothed in mumbo-jumbo. His documentary description of the heresies brings out all that is unjustifiable in the body of dogma: the sole justification of this dogma is its struggle against a lie which, with a good deal of effrontery, it itself sets up as a lie which should be struggled against.

As the film goes on, Buñuel's demolition of Catholicism becomes more and more devastating: with his derision, irony, humour and geniality he dynamites a spiritual edifice that is little more than a mirage, and demonstrates that when man's nature and condition is looked at in a certain fraternal way dogma is suddenly seen to be the worst heresy of all. (p. 160)

La Voie lactée is basically a comedy. It is a light-hearted film that is sacrilegious without ever aiming to shock in a facile, superficial way; and it calls for a return to conscious atheism and to an individual autonomy that is closely bound up with the desire for collective freedom and with a non-theoretical, concrete struggle against intellectual imperialism. (p. 164)

With *Tristana,* a narrative made up of countless little everyday details, Buñuel once again demonstrates the ambiguity of our values and the relativity of our judgements without ever ramming the fact down our throats. He also shows that no genuine revolt can tolerate any kind of compromise and that no passion can survive without constant nourishment: it must devour us at all times. The trouble is that our condition as human beings tends to make us always want our passion to *last;* we want to make it permanent because we are afraid to lose that nugget of gold which we are constantly trying to track down but of which we never find more than a shadow, that nugget which can only be gained if we take the risk of losing it—in other words, ourselves. We are doomed to senile decay; and all that awaits us at the end of the road is death. Weariness can encourage our cowardice and our thirst for thrift. But nothing can ever be permanently secured. The conquests of passion must not be stockpiled because their capital gain is nil. If the price is to be maintained, only the most courageous course must be taken, which is that of putting them constantly at stake according to a responsibility and a faithfulness of which only we, in the last resort, can be the judges: we alone control the metamorphoses of our existence and we alone are the mystery that throws the arch of dialogue between the invisible and the visible. (p. 185)

Freddy Buache, in his The Cinema of Luis Buñuel, *translated by Peter Graham (translation copyright © 1973 by The Tantivy Press, London, Great Britain), Tantivy, 1973, 207 p.*

PETER P. SCHILLACI

Through forty years of filmmaking, Luis Bunuel has been opening our eyes to see what might otherwise evade our notice. And he is not averse to using a razor slash where it is appropriate. (p. 111)

The personal dimension in each Bunuel film converts the body of his work into a mosaic of the man. (pp. 111-12)

Whatever else he has done, Luis Bunuel has consistently demythologized a vestigially Christian culture, and he has done so since long before theologians announced that God is dead. He has gone from avant-garde visual theatrics to a bland, straightforward directorial style, all the time nourishing the same obsession—to lay to rest all the myths, secular and religious, which diminish man's freedom. (pp. 112-13)

There is no way to "prove" Bunuel's demythologizing role. But the idea can be made plausible and even informative if we can develop it out of his remarkable films, rather than out of a theological context. . . .

[It] is characteristic of Bunuel's work that the contents of its subconscious core of meaning can only be suggested. His images, like fragments of a dream, invite a sensitive reflection on the psyche that produced them. (p. 113)

The life of *Un Chien Andalou* is found, not in [a] catalog of actions and images, but in the shocking and provocative associations it freely creates and breaks. The film confirms Bunuel's contention that cinema is "the superior way of expressing the world of dreams, emotions and instincts." . . . . Characters do not unify the experience. They are all marked by an ambiguous sexuality—effeminate men and mannish women—but they are inconsistent even within these categories. The abrupt and exaggerated eruptions of emotion strike the contemporary viewer as ludicrous, but they are clearly related to the perverse sexuality which rejects any expressive control of the passions. (pp. 118-19)

The dreamlike quality of the film is a function not only of the rejection of waking logic, but of the casual way it presents the most bizarre disjunctions. At times, as in the dying fall of the domineering man, the dream fantasy becomes poetic, beginning in the apartment and ending in the park, where his hand grazes the naked back of a woman in a statuary pose. At other times, the dream becomes a nightmare of nameless fears, pursuits, and frustrations. Throughout, sexual symbols provide what little associational unity exists among the images. They are a catalog of Freudian metaphors, too complex to analyze in detail. (p. 119)

As in the case of Bunuel's first film, [the] action tells us little about *L'Age d'Or*. But if we turn to another level of images, a pattern of relationships emerges. . . . The separation of the lovers is not a mere distraction, but the very premise of the new religious society. The couple represents *amour fou,* the mad, single-minded passion which Bunuel uses to symbolize the natural man, unfettered by time and space, tabu or custom. The Church's frustration of the natural man is its demise. (pp. 121-22)

The ending of the film shows that Bunuel's associational unity is more in control than in his first film. . . . Even the "story" manifests more continuity, as the frustrated love of Lya Lys and Gaston Modot encounters the repressive sexuality of the culture. But in spite of all these elements, discontinuity is still the salient feature of the film. The emotional reversals of the couple are bizarre, played at the height of rage or lust, disorienting the viewer. Hints of sexual perversion abound as warped expressions of the simple love (*amour fou*) which the Church denies. The result is incest, foot fetishism, and such deviate sexuality as the De Sade episode's ultimate degeneracy.

The religious comment of *L'Age d'Or,* if one can summarize it, shows the Church shipwrecked on the hard, unyielding rock of human nature. (pp. 123-24)

[*Un Chien Andalou, L'Age d'Or,* and *Las Hurdes*] are subject to reinterpretation in the light of subsequent Bunuel works, but their consistency with the most important and the most trivial of his large-budget films invites us to reflect on their unity of conception. Bunuel's style had preserved the film version of the surrealist esthetic in a way that no single painting could have done, and yet Bunuel cultivated the form only as a way of looking at reality. His credo was more important than a school of art, and surrealist fantasy was chosen as a way of making his uniquely personal statements effective. The major themes of his lifetime concern had already emerged in their basic outline. The attack on organized religion, the affirmation of a natural humanity seldom given a voice, the fascination with human deformity, perversion, and the capacity for evil—all were there. His iconoclast's hammer was already demolishing statues and idols, churches and institutions that pretended to protect but really destroyed men. The emotions of his films were those of his own life—anger, a lust to live, direct, passionate expression, and a sense of social outrage. With *Las Hurdes,* his social concern took on cosmic overtones that transcended the social, political, or religious. Ultimately, Bunuel's vision is metaphysical and theological. (pp. 128-29)

Exterminating Angel is an extended metaphor, a parable attacking social conventions with vicious, black humor. (p. 142)

The Exterminating Angel is a nightmare we have all experienced in some way, evoking in the viewer a disturbing sense of recognition. It seems obvious that the mansion here is a Freudian place, a set of customs, a life style, a world view into whose structures people are frozen and trapped. The people are high society, but the culture and sophistication (even the courtesy and decency) are apparently only skin deep. . . . [The] extreme sangfroid with which the camera records the horrors makes the film a surreal experience. The evening's conversation has been a barbaric exchange of outrageous insults and allegations, delivered with polite indifference. The disorder of the drawing room soon assaults our senses, its imagined odors seeping under the closet doors to offend us.

Seldom has there been a more savage indictment of "civilization" and its values, and yet, each shock image or sharp word draws a gasp and a stifled laugh typical of black humor's effect. (pp. 143-44)

In *Diary of a Chambermaid,* Bunuel once again surveys the nightmare of decadent class privilege and gross injustice with a calm, almost accepting eye. He raises our hopes that the girl's death will be avenged, and then, as if to say there is no justice, he destroys that hope. . . . The frustration of ideals and the reversal of values are as complete as any achieved by Bunuel in *Un Chien Andalou,* but they appear in the style of his new surrealism, a calm portrayal of absurdities so complete as to become hallucinatory.

Although religious elements abound in *Diary* they are not central to its subject. This may be why Bunuel returned to the Church, a parallel obsession, in *Simon of the Desert.* (pp. 146-47)

Simon of the Desert has a light, comic touch that sets it apart as an amusement. Simon, like Nazarin, seems to have appealed to Bunuel if only for his mad devotion to ideals. This may be why the saint is never ridiculed directly in the film. He preaches lofty ideals to the monks and laymen who approach him, he humbly refuses ordination to the priesthood, he restores hands to a man who lost them for thievery, and he overcomes a variety of bizarre and amusing temptations. However, he is just a bit dotty, and there exists in him something of the coldness which we detected in Nazarin and in Viridiana, a denial of the human. (p. 147)

The film evidences a grudging admiration for Simon's obsession, the religious fetish so calmly accepted by the Church and people of his time. However, most of the humor, if not directed at Simon, is created at his expense. . . . The film's pattern of unblinking acceptance of the miraculous, followed by the man's failure to change anything, ultimately condemns Simon to irrelevancy. (p. 148)

[In *Belle de Jour*] Bunuel has created such ambiguities between fantasy and the real, between dream and actuality, that it is all but impossible to separate these elements. But an effect so carefully planned must be intentional, and so whatever our interpretation of the film may be, it seems clear that Bunuel wishes to remind us that these contrasting realms are really one. (p. 149)

There is, of course, no need to choose, to select what is real and what is unreal, because it is precisely this ambiguity that serves to make the director's point. We see once again how repressed sexuality breeds refined, perverted humanity. As always, however, there is no judgment on persons so afflicted. (p. 150)

The Discreet Charm of the Bourgeoisie may become the parting salvo in a war that began with Bunuel's silent classics and developed in *The Exterminating Angel*—the war on the bourgeoisie. Ten years after this savage attack, the director reverses the plot to play new variations on its savage absurdities. (p. 155)

Not quite a comedy of manners, *The Discreet Charm of the Bourgeoisie* nevertheless evokes recollections of Oscar Wilde, and of Restoration Comedy drawing room farces. It is the unbelievable imperturbability of the protagonists, their supreme self-possession in the midst of social and political disaster, that gives the film its satirical comic thrust. (p. 156)

Bunuel seems to say that the bourgeoisie can take frustrations with equanimity because they know life has never denied them anything for long. Before heroin other forms of business existed, and before that, colonialism and slavery. For the future, one must have confidence, both in one's class, and in its single most precious talent—survival. (p. 157)

Peter P. Schillaci, "Luis Bunuel and the Death of God," in Three European Directors: François Truffaut *by James M. Wall,* Fellini's Film Journey *by Roger Ortmayer,* Luis Bunuel and the Death of God *by Peter P. Schillaci, edited by James M. Wall (copyright © 1973 by William B. Eerdmans Publishing Company; used by permission), Eerdmans, 1973, pp. 111-57.*

PETER HARCOURT

Luis Buñuel . . . is first and foremost a Spaniard and after that a surrealist. His view of life has developed from this primary fact. His inheritance has been Spanish, as his response to life seems largely to have been intuitive. It is only in his more playful moods that he sometimes seems cerebral, content to mock his pet hates from merely the surface of his mind.

A crucial part of this Spanish inheritance was his Jesuit education. Spanish Catholicism, perhaps more extremely than that of any other country, must have brought home to the young Buñuel the surrealist antagonism between the ideals of the spirit and the exigencies of the flesh, as it would undoubtedly have brought home to him the terrifying gap between the rich security of the church and the destitute, precarious state of whole sections of the Spanish people. Yet it is a mistake, I've always felt, to see this influence as negative in any simple way. Not only has Buñuel returned to religious considerations in his films with such regularity that they must be taken as one of the mainsprings of his art, but it seems to me that a large part of what is most positive in his films could have come from this early training as well.

For instance, at the centre of Buñuel's vision is what the surrealists were to call the destructive forces of man, what Freud has categorized as the unmanageable 'id', but what Buñuel would have known from way back as the problem of evil. Related to any form of pessimism, there is always a belief in evil as an abstraction, or at least as an unalterable characteristic of the nature of man. If one simply believes that social injustice is the source of man's problems (as so many fans seem to think Buñuel does), then one can combat this injustice by constructive social action; but if one believes that evil is inherent to the nature of man, then constructive action becomes that much more difficult and one's belief in improvement that much more tenuous. If evil is intrinsic, if the impulse towards destructon is deeply planted in man's nature—as Christianity has always taught and as the Parisian surrealists were excited to reaffirm, as if making a new discovery—then the problem for any civilization is to find some way of containing it. Here too, the church may have helped.

While rejecting the metaphysical consolations of Christianity, Buñuel nevertheless seemed to gain from Spanish Catholicism an urgent recognition of the importance of ritual in combating our more unmanageable desires. . . . Often [such ceremonies] are presented in a bizarre, even a facetious light—like the foot-washing sequence that opens the strange and magnificent *El*—and they are invariably tinged with the suggestion of a repressed sexuality; but sometimes, as in *Viridiana,* the sense of ceremony can lend to what might otherwise be a commonplace scene the feeling of intense personal involvement. (pp. 107-09)

Intertwined with this feeling for ritual, there is also in Buñuel a concern with the peculiarly symbolic associations inherent to inanimate objects, a concern that also must have been encouraged by the iconography of the church. Whether, as in *L'Âge d'or,* it is Modot being distracted from his lovemaking by the foot of a statue of Francisco's valet in *El,* who polishes his bicycle in his bed, in Buñuel these actions take on an additional force from the symbolic role the objects play in the characters' lives.

Finally, when speculating in this way about the relationship of his early environment to his mature view of life, we might be tempted to relate Buñuel's continual concern with human solitude to the fact of his own exile. Almost all his life, in order to work, he has had to live away from Spain; for large sections of it, in order to live, he has had to perform menial roles within the film industry. Although in his private life apparently the gentlest of men, in his films Buñuel has insistently returned to the problems of violence and evil and to the recognition that these passions seem often the result of a man being isolated and made to feel alone. (pp. 109-10)

[In] his films, it would seem to be part of a recognition that, finally, the individual *is* an isolated phenomenon, with only a limited ability to react profitably with another person or to act constructively upon the outside world. Though there is always great gentleness in the films of Buñuel, there is also great destructiveness; and the destructiveness seems, socially, to be the greater force. Power is much more easily organized than gentleness; and in any case, even within any individual manifestation of gentleness, there is also a dammed-up force of destructiveness threatening to break free or to turn in upon itself. (p. 110)

I don't want to appear too solemn about the troubled master; for there certainly is in Buñuel a strong iconoclastic impulse and, as in all great artists, a wry sense of the absurd. But . . . even Buñuel's humour is edged in black despair. More often than not, it is the self-protective humour of a deeply pessimistic person, the humour of a man distressed by his own vision of the universe but who has also a keen eye for the multitude of self-deceptions that, for many of us, make life bearable. (p. 111)

Perhaps it was the defeat of the Republicans in the Spanish Civil War; perhaps it has been Buñuel's hard and (one assumes) lonely life; perhaps it is just the way he sees things that makes his world so without a hope for the eventual triumph of the gentlest impulses in mankind. And even though we might strive to see things differently, Buñuel's vision is not an easy one to disagree with. . . . (pp. 133-34)

Often in Buñuel we experience great tenderness; but almost constantly in his films it meets with defeat. As an emblem of his world, we might remember the deformed Ujo, as if even genuine goodness must be achieved at a terrible price; or we might remember Don Jaime as he writes out his will, the resigned smile on his face as he makes the final dadaist surrender to the powers of darkness, as if his attempt to achieve goodness has been the biggest joke of all. (p. 134)

Peter Harcourt, "Luis Buñuel: Spaniard and Surrealist" (originally published in a different version in Film Quarterly, *Vol. XX, No. 3, Spring, 1967), in his* Six European Directors: Essays on the Meaning of Film Style *(copyright © Peter Harcourt, 1974; reprinted by permission of Penguin Books Ltd), Penguin Books, 1974, pp. 102-34.*

RAYMOND DURGNAT

The spectator who prefers easy butts can easily dismiss . . . [the] commensalist nostalgias [of the dinner guests in *The Discreet Charm of the Bourgeoisie*] as simply some insect-dance, or a deluded and delusive ritual of solidarity, or an essentially egoistic need for reassurance of social acceptability. Yet dinner parties are a residual—and a potentially meaningful—form of potlatch. And, even if it's hopeless, it's only human to attempt to recapture a tribal fraternity by such psychological surrogates as the gang, the clique, the set. Part of the irony is that real needs are denied, and the quest is switched from solidarity to food—seven guests in search of a Host. . . .

The characters certainly eat between meals they miss; and Buñuel has selected only those meals whose bill of fare—or circumstances, or relationships with dream, love, or business—illustrates how a round of dinner parties can do as little to preserve their participants from the emptiness which society has sowed within their hearts as communing with nature could do to redeem the Victorian middle class from its materialism. Nonchalance where concern should be has long been a mainspring of Buñuel's method; certainly, here, passages of dialogue evoke Ionesco, the theater of the absurd, and a livelier, less stylized *Marienbad*. . . .

The affinities of Buñuel and Swift are worth a passing thought. Both are theologians *manqués,* both concerned with the thin line between madness and sanity. As Buñuel's *The Milky Way* is to *A Tale of a Tub, Discreet Charm* is to "Genteel and Ingeniose Conversation." Both are tragicomedies of mediocrity, and it's intriguing to imagine what might happen if the hitch-hikers of Buñuel's theological satire were to encounter the hosts and guests of its profane successor. . . .

The interplay of ambiguities and incongruities, of trivialities and dreams, permits the film its uniquely allusive style. . . . Thus the film ironizes over the paradoxes of a peacetime army (and conscription) continuing twenty-eight years after the "last" war. And it also gratifies our Marxist (*tendance* Groucho) anarchism with images of military chaos for which some sort of mythic correlative exists in *M*A*S*H*.

The hilarious idiocy of everyday chitchat is surely not overplayed, but merely deprived of its ballast (or roughage) of sense. (p. 52)

The Sénéchals . . . represent the bourgeoisie at its most youthful, flexible and engaging. But they take everything for granted, including a lighthearted skepticism, and remain rigidly within its limitations. . . .

The Thévenots . . . are a few years older. Less capricious, more dignified, companionable rather than passionate, they are what the Sénéchals will become. They may seem the most colorless and stable of the group; in fact, they are the champions of the conversational *volte-face,* of inconspicuous disorder, of confusion of appetite. . . .

In status, in style, in age, in cunning and in self-assurance, the Ambassador . . . marks the apex of the little group. He is the least confused and the most violent. (In Buñuel, the two characteristics often go together.) His apparent mixture of paranoia and megalomania fits reality surprisingly well. His friends think he's mad when he levels his rifle at a street vendor's furry toy. But he was right: its seller *was* spying on him. His mental deviousness appears in largely triumphant forms. (p. 53)

The Bishop's filial revenge climaxes a trio of episodes centering on the theme of dead parents. All originate from traditionally monosexual groups (the clergy, the army)—as if, in this debilitated world, the transcendence of the natural order is abandoned, by marital complacency, to conclaves of deprivation and reaction from which, alas, it can't break free. On the one hand, the Surrealist must seek liberation from the pious emotions conventionally associated with the (bourgeois) family and the (Christian) afterlife; the two converge in the idea of God the father, the sacrificed Son, and the Virgin Mother. But, on the other hand, all "primitive" people believe in ghosts, especially those of their ancestors; and the Surrealist may well wish to retain the freedom to "hallucinate" the afterlife of the dead, or some transcendence of separation in time. Similarly, however universal or local the Oedipus complex may be felt to be, the Surrealist will wish to defend both the existence and the legitimacy of incestuous emotions against the taboos under which they labor. Certainly the Oedipal triangle offers a handy schema for the complex weave of desire, taboo, and death. And the three dreams in *Discreet Charm* offer three solutions—or dissolutions—of its Gordian knot.

I. The Bishop who is desexualized always speaks of his parents as a pair. His choice of job, and the outrageous speed with which he adopts a gardener's robes (or at least apron), suggest a childhood identification with an idealized servant. The Bishop's murderous yet glib reaction to disillusionment suggests an only-too-effective sublimation of his own rivalry with his father. Here, a murder by *poisoning* provokes a murder by *shooting*.

II. The Lieutenant's dream shows a far less complete, far more tortuous, pattern of repressions. As a child, he was instructed by his mother's ghost to poison her husband, who, in a duel, has just killed her lover (another lieutenant and the boy's real father). The situation contrasts two conceptions of the family: the husband's (bourgeois-feudal, based on appearances and honor) and the mother's (extralegal, based on love and biology). This *real* family avenges itself but cannot reconstitute itself. And the Lieutenant with the sad, romantic eyes is left, helplessly, dependent on three bourgeois women who don't know what to say to him because the current dissolution of codes makes comment almost impossible. His dream leads nowhere. Here, a killing by *shooting* provokes a murder by *poisoning*.

III. In his dream the Sergeant meets a lost love (who once repulsed him, but now seeks him), and two old friends. In his attachment to his equals and his peers, in a street which is like an indefinite space, the dream comes closest to that image of tentative camaraderie which crowns Buñuel's *Cela s'appelle l'Aurore*. The atmosphere is that of limbo; at any moment we expect the dreamer to be told that his girl, his friends, and he himself are dead. Instead, he leaves her to search for his friends. . . . When the Sergeant returns from a labyrinth of shops-like-a-church (the ecclesiastico-capitalist complex), he is alone, and he is calling, not for his girlfriend, but for his mother, as if a confused repression were underway. . . .

[In] this dream, any father-figure is present in the much less authoritarian guise of "mates." But, coming and going in this maze, they haven't the solidarity of "comrades," and they provoke him to a futile detour. In this dream, all hostility is softened, although the girl's calm confirmation of her earlier indifference may evoke the indifference of the young mother to her son in *Los Olvidados*. Is the Sergeant's absence of reproach exemplary? Or is it a hint of a certain weakness? The equal and opposite excess, on impotent fury with the beloved, leads only to an alternative impasse, the love-hate hallucination of *Wuthering Heights*.

Although the dream can thus be moralized, roughly in terms of the ethic of *Cela s'appelle l'Aurore*, one can't dismiss the more troubling overtones in the evasion of fraternal abrasiveness, of potential rivalries for one woman. While this evasion is of a piece with the dreamer's rank, it also avoids a real crux, just as Surrealist moralizing tended to be romantic rather than realistic, and although it raised the issues it didn't adequately discuss the inevitable conflicts involving *l'amour fou,* revolutionary solidarity, and jealousy vs. fraternity. The Sergeant's rank suggests a lower-class origin. His dream comes nearest to being a nonhierarchical. Perhaps that's why, of the "parental" dreamers, the Sergeant is the least clearly distinguished from his surroundings, and from the mass of soldiers who are his false friends. (p. 55)

[Sequences] of rapid, subtle, dizzying dissonances and incongruities—in effect, twists—give the film that hilarious onirism which is also close to the uncertainties and ambivalences of real *or* feigned attitudes in informal, off-the-cuff, oral culture. The themes of food and drugs modulate into that of poisonings, and the film's subtitles might be "You are what you eat" and "You dream what you aren't."

The threats of violence intimated by the military and then the police are consummated with the appearance of the gangsters. Their leader's dyed hair evokes a certain type of muscular homosexual, or maybe the gangsters of bad French films. The abstraction of these "scorpions" suggests that they stand in for a universal tendency in human nature generally, as well as for something particular to the Ambassador (in whose dream they appear). Maybe they're his "Mr. Hyde": the repressed roots of his violence, and of the narcissism suggested in his dandy style. Their ultra-vulgarity makes them the Ambassador's antithesis, his *nightmare* alter ego; and it's just because they're vulgar and brutal that they succeed where the intelligent, dedicated guerillas failed. (pp. 57-8)

[In the film] the theme-images are far from being merely personal fetishes. Everything suggests that Buñuel, in one way or another, has an exceptionally easy access to (and knows the importance of) hypnogogic mental strata which most of us are too busy, materialistic, or incautious to investigate. Far from taking them to an analyst for "cure", he is particularly attentive to their closeness with "rational" conversation, conscious thought, and perception of social reality. Where we systematically choose the socially relevant remark and forget the others Buñuel's films also follow up the alternatives which (understandably) we don't speak of, but (suicidally) forget—thus progressively obliterating a full reality that might help us replace the living death of hypocrisy by a patient, tolerant, ferocious lucidity. . . .

The general line of *Discreet Charm* wouldn't be incompatible with a story in which international connections involving heroin were replaced by international connections involving oil. If the Ambassador (the film's one anachronistic character) is also its most lucid character, its most duplicitous, its most ferocious, and a foreigner, it's because he's the closest to the "gangster-generals" who, at the right moment, might decide to dispense with diplomacy. Diplomat and gangster are Jekyll-and-Hyde, yin and yang, A.C. and D.C. of a world whose liberalization is, as usual, indefinitely postponed. (p. 59)

Raymond Durgnat, "'The Discreet Charm of the Bourgeoisie'," in Film Comment *(copyright © 1975 by The Film Society of London Center; all rights reserved), Vol. II, No. 3, May-June, 1975, pp. 52-9.*

MARSHA KINDER

Phantom of Liberty is a film about the impossibility of escaping the tyranny of convention in politics, society, and art. . . . Buñuel's anarchistic vision has remained constant. Man persists in denying his animal nature and creating a civilized code of laws and manners that only heightens his absurdity and intensifies his oppression. This theme lies at the center of all Buñuel's work; he never escapes it, and neither do we, his audience.

As in earlier films, the central social ritual is the dinner party, for it offers a prime example of how civilized man copes with his basic animal needs. . . . Using a Swiftian ironic reversal, in *Phantom* Buñuel reminds us that eating and shitting are merely opposite ends of the same biological process and that our culture's decision to glorify the former and forbid all mention of the latter is totally arbitrary. . . . [The] power of convention prevents us from seeing that all aspects of our animal nature must be accepted.

This theme is reinforced by the recurring image of animals placed in an elegant setting. (pp. 20-1)

In *Phantom of Liberty,* Buñuel also explores education, potentially a source of change and freedom. The existing institutions, however, merely reinforce the status quo. (p. 22)

In the incident involving the little girl lost at school, we see that false words, once confirmed by authority and convention, have the power to contradict logic and the direct evidence of our senses. The child, like the horse-drawn cart at the mansion in *L'Age d'or,* is totally invisible because the adults do not expect to see her. Thus, perception and knowledge are almost totally controlled by cultural expectations. Within the school, no attention is paid to the creative potentialities of the child—individuals are named and numbered, they copy dictation and learn by rote. "Speak only when you're spoken to" and "children should be seen and not heard" are the maxims that prevail; unfortunately they lead to the invisibility of the individual child. . . . Ultimately, *Phantom of Liberty* is one gigantic circle of corruption and entrapment. As usual, Buñuel does not tell us how to escape into positive alternatives; but . . . he insists that a courageous and honest confrontation of things as they are is the first step to freedom. If we are to resist the dangers of our society, we must not allow our heads to be buried in the sands of convention.

In *Phantom of Liberty* the struggle against convention is most powerful in the realm of art. . . . Buñuel valiantly tries to rebel against narrative conventions, breaking through to a totally open-ended form capable of frustrating the audience's expectations. Nevertheless, the film is enclosed in a structural circularity and repeats many of the same images, themes, situations, and narrative devices that Buñuel has used before. Despite his playful experimentation, he does not completely escape artistic convention or his own subconscious. Liberty is a phantom even in the creative process.

Previously, Buñuel had explored this idea most fully both in theme and structure in *The Discreet Charm.* Stressing the revolutionary nature of the subconscious, this dream film uses an expansive style opening outward, which defines narrow conventions, linear design, and rational interpretation. . . . In this film, we can never believe what people say, nor can we predict what they will do next. The lines between dream, inset story, and bizarre incident soon break down. (p. 23)

Despite the disruptive narrative structure, in *Discreet Charm* we repeatedly encounter our six bourgeois characters, dressed in their modish clothes, walking down a country road that apparently goes nowhere. . . . These characters are puppets manipulated by Buñuel, the master dreamer, who handles them as easily as the props and settings. Here he uses time to suggest that dreaming is an endless tripping; yet despite the expansive variety of the realities we may encounter along the way, there is always something terrifyingly familiar about the terrain. Despite their resilience and charm, these characters never really escape their anarchistic nature.

In *Phantom of Liberty* Buñuel uses the same kind of expansive, anarchistic structure, but with much greater self-reflexiveness. Personally, he recognizes that although he is an exiled artist, he cannot escape his own national heritage, which he acknowledges in the selection of Goya's paintings, highlighting French imperialism in Spain. (p. 24)

The self-reflexive nature of the film is also expressed in the way Buñuel handles the narrative structure. He seems to combine as many storytelling devices from as many different genres as possible—e.g., the narrative painting, the gothic tale, the inset story, the letter, the dream, the exemplum, the flashback, the omniscient narrator, the horizontal wipe. He creates the illusion that the artist has unlimited powers of invention and that the story has endless possibilities; he can follow any character or story line in any direction according to his will. Or, as in *Discreet Charm,* he can tease us with unfinished business. . . . Like the bourgeois gentleman who exclaims, "I'm fed up with symmetry" as he makes for a spider on his mantle, Buñuel always keeps his narrative off balance and his audience surprised by the unexpected. (pp. 24-5)

Buñuel's artistic freedom, though daring and playful, is . . . constrained. Although he is one of the most truly experimental and anarchistic film-makers who has ever lived, he is also one of the most consistent in expressing the same theme and rebelling against the same conventions. For almost half a century, his career has been one long pursuit of the Phantom of Liberty. (p. 25)

Marsha Kinder, "The Tyranny of Convention in 'The Phantom of Liberty'," in Film Quarterly *(copyright 1975 by The Regents of the University of California; reprinted by permission of the University of California Press), Vol. XXVIII, No. 4, Summer, 1975, pp. 20-5.*

RANDALL CONRAD

The Golden Age [or *L'Age d'Or*] is an attack on repressive society but Bunuel views social repression and individual inhibition as two sides of a single reality. The ambivalent symbolism of *The Golden Age* enables Bunuel to capture a dialectic between the outer prison—"imperial Rome", Christian civilization, bourgeois society—and the inner prison: the guilt which denies pleasure, inhibits instincts and conditions man to conformity. Each side reflects the other; both form an indissoluble whole. It is the whole which is Bunuel's target.

For Bunuel the key to liberation is desire, the mainspring of human activity. The perfect ideological complement to *The Golden Age* is Freud's contemporaneous study, *Civilization and its Discontents*—civilization originated with the sublimation of the sexual urge, a process reflected in the development of the individual. . . .

[The] inhibiting brick and concrete civilization which surrounds us is vulnerable only when our vision is sharpened by passion. During the mock documentary, a row of housefronts along an empty street falls apart in a series of billowing explosions. For the most part in *The Golden Age,* however, the buildings of imperial Rome remain standing—society is impenetrable to all who don't see through it. (p. 3)

The Golden Age constitutes a whole mythology of society and its conflicts, thanks to the double character of its symbols; at the same time, it constitutes an attack upon society, an aggravation of the conflicts.

Furthermore, it is our own society, bourgeois society, which Bunuel attacks. The subversive radicalism of *The Golden Age* has often been identified with Marxism. . . .

The real history of society is irrelevant in *The Golden Age* since its unconscious premises are permanent. The sole dynamic force in *The Golden Age* is sexual desire inasmuch as it negates civilization. In return, the essence of civilization is summed up by its unanimous reaction to one man's erection. . . .

Nowadays *The Golden Age* seems more pertinent to the Freudian critique of civilization than to dialectical materialism; left-wing critics are obliged to perform an exercise of interpretation if they want to reopen a Marxist dialogue with Bunuel's film. Yet in its own time, *The Golden Age* was readily accepted as a politically revolutionary work. (p. 4)

Without being a Marxist film, *The Golden Age* presents strong analogies to a Marxist critique. It insists on the concrete nature of the real world. It tramples upon reactionary ideology—religion, romance, bourgeois rationalism—and it is open to a class conscious and historically conscious reading. (p. 6)

The Golden Age is a surrealist film above all and a Marxist film only by association.

Bunuel's next film, the third and last of his surrealist period, was the short documentary *Land Without Bread*. . . . Using nothing but objective data about one of the most barren regions in Europe and concealing himself in the role of the neutral reporter, Bunuel achieves a reading of reality that is perhaps his purest surrealist work.

It is the very objectivity of *Land Without Bread* which makes it an unbearable experience, a surrealist experience. The element of subjective aggravation is no longer a theme of the film itself (as in *The Golden Age*); it is now the spectator's own consciousness which is aggravated.

Bunuel's achievement in *Land Without Bread* is due as much to his choice of subject—an impoverished area of Spain cut off from society—as to his construction of the film, which proceeds by systematic contradictions of the viewer's logical reactions. . . .

The depiction of labor is an essential theme in *Land Without Bread* but it is not labor as we know it in the civilized world, labor contributing to the furtherance of a developed social system. The labor of the peasants of Las Hurdes is an effort to tame a hostile nature for the first time, an effort which invariably ends in failure and puts their embryonic society back at zero. . . . Bunuel identifies the essential component of the peasants' life as hunger. Not the hunger which can be satisfied and which historically generates political systems (and rebellions against the systems when they no longer meet the primary needs), but a permanent unsatisfied hunger which is identical to life itself. The peasants' famished condition is an objective equivalent to desire in Bunuel's other films. Unlike desire, however, this morbid condition can never be a positive force. . . .

Upon this overall fatalism Bunuel imposes structures which do nothing to relieve the horror but on the contrary create tensions and contradictions in our perception of it that cannot be resolved. (p. 7)

What about help from the outside? The Church is present but its decayed edifices are like the ruins of an ancient colonization which withered long ago. As a bearer of progress the Church is a mockery, for it does nothing for the peasants but mirror the presence of death.

The peasants, however, have one point of contact with modern society, the recently built schoolhouse. The liberal viewer's reflex is to count on this imported education as a potential improvement in the peasants' lives. But the sequence proves only that an education which teaches mathematics to children who are starving is impotent. Worse, the bourgeois education which illustrates the ragged childrens' lesson with a picture of an 18th Century lady in her finery and which teaches them to "respect the property of others" is monstrous. . . .

In miniature the commentary reproduces the contradictions in the bourgeois education it is describing. The humanist consciousness (education is the same everywhere) is vaguely aware that it is out of tune with reality (starvation, rags, bare feet) but never quite renders the discrepancy as an outright contradiction. (p. 8)

Bunuel couches his documentary entirely within the tradition of a socially useless humanism and ethnology, then surreptitiously articulates it upon the premise that that tradition—including documentary film-making—is impotent. The film actually destroys its own premises and, in so doing, it destroys the refuge of humanism.

Made in the midst of violent political upheavals, a sharpening clash between Right and Left in Spain and throughout Europe, *Land Without Bread* strips society of its historical and political aspect and exposes its prehistoric form, when the struggle against nature was the all-consuming task. Yet it insists that *this* society—the primeval horror of which we had almost banished from consciousness—is a part of our civilization. The ultimate horror of Bunuel's film consists in our dissociation, our helplessness, whenever we try to identify the peasants' lives with our own. They are after all men and women like ourselves, going about the daily business of living. Yet their every effort is deflected, by some primal urgency we can scarcely believe, from the goals we would consider normal.

Land Without Bread is nevertheless open to a contemporary political reading—its negation of the 'progressive' options in bourgeois ideology, including liberal politics, make it a radical work. (pp. 8-9)

With *Spain 1937* we are in the forefront of political history, at the opposite extreme from the ahistorical community of *Land Without Bread*. What is more, historical events are conceived and structured according to an ideology that was external to Bunuel's prior films, a Marxist analysis only slightly blurred by the dual rhetoric of 'progressive' politics. (p. 10)

What is difficult to characterize . . . is Bunuel's relationship to the ostensible politics of this film. His cinematic contribution to it generally consists in adding an element of ironic distance or an unexpected turn of perspective to the chronicle of events. While these touches never contradict the political narrative, they do at times veer a bit from the political norms established in the commentary.

Primarily, Bunuel brings a necessary distance to the chaos of events. *Spain 1937* at first seems related to *Land Without Bread* in its dry commentary, which avoids sentimentality and simply relates facts. The objective tone, however, stops short of the applied cruelty of Bunuel's earlier documentary, for it has after all a strictly political task—to publicize the hidden war and win our sympathy and solidarity for the republicans. The understated narration in this case is simply the best means of making both the reality of the war and its political analysis credible to viewers.

Yet Bunuel occasionally contributes another kind of distance, a more facetious irony, with an unexpected cut or image or turn of phrase. Certain discrepancies between word and image give the impression that the editor is at odds with the commentary on some topics and is trying to make the images say something else.

The narrator asserts that the new Popular Front government is a progressive one—"The republic begins to move forward again. Each day brings new progress, opening new perspectives for the Spanish people." Over "new perspectives", however, we are only watching politicians making their way down some official stairway; what is more, the editors have left in one or two jump-cuts, so that the downward progress of the politicians seems endless. (pp. 10-11)

There is a black humor in some of Bunuel's images of the ironies of war. Men and women surprised by an air raid run for shelter while a triple Charlie Chaplin looks on quizzically from some wall posters advertising *Modern Times*. There is black humor, too, in this line about the defense of Madrid at Torija: "The soldiers wept with rage because their swollen and bleeding feet wouldn't let them chase the enemy any further." The same perverse spirit guides Bunuel's construction of parallel sequences contrasting the fascists' annihilation of the Basque country (including "the sanctuaries of Basque freedom") with a sanctuary in which wives and children of nationalists are prisoners of the republicans—"The republic also watches over the lives of its enemy's children." . . .

The music is a surrealist element. Bunuel uses Beethoven. A mincing waltz from the *First Symphony* accompanies the right-wing politicians; the *Egmont Overture* accompanies the rest of the film, including the fascist bombings and the people's counterattacks. Bunuel is undecided whether to use the overture independently, as in *Land Without Bread,* or to assign it a narrower symbolic function—it is often (though not consistently) associated with the aggressors. . . .

Throughout the conflict—and in contrast to the collapsing cities—an impassive nature continues to flourish in the foregrounds and backgrounds of scenes, indifferent to the human tragedy yet inseparable from it. . . .

The collapse of civilization portrayed in *The Golden Age* and *Land Without Bread* materializes in the identical imagery of the actuality footage of *Spain 1937.* But Bunuel subordinates his surrealism to his Marxism. The people are victims, but victors, too. (p. 11)

. . . . .

On the surface Bunuel's politics move back and forth between the positive class consciousness of *Men Call it Dawn* and the anarchist pessimism of *The Young and the Damned* [*Los Olvidados*], between Marxism and the Freudian politics of surrealism. More exactly, Bunuel aims to obtain a permanent dialectic between the two ideologies; at the very least the surrealist basis is overlaid with a deliberate Marxist slant which is Bunuel's caution that his message of revolt will advance revolution, not reaction. . . .

All relationships in *The Young and the Damned* are based

on violence, including those in institutions which are supposed to foster goodness like family and school. Specifically, Bunuel's violent, primary characters are unwitting victims of the oedipal conflicts at work inside their damaged family relations, the source of their violence. (p. 10)

Bunuel . . . displays a consistent preference for melodrama, most obviously in his film's many horror scenes, but also in the film's abundance of coincidence (Jaibo reappears just as Pedro is let out on good behavior) and in the intercutting of different episodes involving different characters so as to afford us a superior dramatic vantage. . . . Melodrama enables us to see the whole picture, heightened. *The Young and the Damned* stands nearly alone even among Bunuel's films in achieving, in the guise of realism, a synthesis of inner and outer realities.

By the same token, however, *The Young and the Damned* is by no means a politically encouraging work. The poor are amoral and vicious, and every character is the plaything of destructive forces as inescapable as destiny in ancient tragedy. What for Bunuel is ultimate realism, perhaps the true test of our compassion for humanity, can also look like reactionary propaganda. (pp. 10-11)

Men Call it Dawn belongs to a politically didactic tradition on the left, the drama of class consciousness expressed through the options of a petty bourgeois character obliged to decide between a life of compromise and a moral stand which in this case is not strictly political but entails a shift of class identity nevertheless. Bunuel virtually puts a cinema of identification in the service of a class typology. It is the petty bourgeois who changes sides: Sandro has no freedom in Bunuel's view. The class spectrum in *Men Call it Dawn* is actually a simple one. It is impossible not to hate the sinister capitalist Sandro kills, while quite to the contrary of *The Young and the Damned,* we sympathize easily with the peasants and workers like Sandro.

Bunuel's placement of Valerio's consuming love in a parallel relationship to his quasi-political gesture in hiding Sandro is intended to complicate as well as heighten the moral choice Valerio makes, beyond the canon acceptable to a positive realism. Valerio is an adulterer and Sandro a murderer. Still, we never doubt they are good men. . . .

Many of Bunuel's films of the early 1950's are domestic comedies or melodramas. Bunuel exploits the archetypes which are the stuff of melodrama; at the same time he abolishes the sentimentality, the cinema of identification that normally conceals the real social content of those archetypes. . . .

Bunuel uses melodramatic coincidence to symbolize a fatality that really is the expression of subconscious impulse. This is reflected at the end of *This Strange Passion* [*El*] when Francisco's paranoia weaves random experience (noises, faces glimpsed) into an obsessive hallucination. It is, precisely, no coincidence that in his delirium Francisco attacks the priest in the very church which has stifled his emotional and sexual happiness in the guise of protecting it. However, one speculates about the subconsciously willed quality of the film's coincidences only in retrospect; what is striking on the screen is their absurdity.

Despite its dark themes, *This Strange Passion* is a work of sustained humor. Bunuel's technique consists of having the actors play the most extreme scenes perfectly seriously with each other, rather than playing to the audience for laughs or pathos. This distancing technique reinforces Bunuel's demonstration by the absurd; it is also at the basis of Bunuel's mock-behaviorism, a curious feeling akin to the clinical detachment with which, one imagines, Marx and Freud made man's irrational behavior the object of scientific study. (p. 11)

In many films Bunuel surreptitiously undermines the normal authority of the family, exposing its perversity, its exclusion of passion, its crippling of children. . . .

In *Tristana,* the quasi-incestuous 'marriage' which Lope creates for his own convenience is a false sexual freedom which oppresses Tristana and finally Lope too. This travesty of a family is Bunuel's symbol for the false consciousness which confines both Lope and Tristana in reactionary sexual, family and class relations while allowing them to believe they are free individuals. . . .

Lope's contradictory class ideology also reflects his false freedom in objective social terms. He calls himself a socialist, yet despises work and lives the life of a propertied, honor-obsessed gentleman in a Spain on the brink of civil war. . . .

The Brute [*El Bruto*] is an unusually class conscious melodrama which approaches the politically didactic model, for it is expressly about a crisis of class allegiance in the hero. (p. 12)

What animates the class conflict in *The Brute* is Bunuel's parallel between Pedro's dawning class consciousness and his archetypal progression from brutality to humanity, to civilization, through his new love. Bunuel is able thus to say two things at once. The capitalist form of society we live in is not civilization at all, but a brutal state preceding it. . . . On the other hand, Bunuel implies through the themes of father-killing and other taboo-breaking that Pedro's violence, while finally revolutionary, inescapably revives the archetypal murder. Revolution itself, without necessarily losing its positive value, is thus assimilated to the irrational rebellion which underlies civilization permanently and generates its conflicts. (pp. 12-13)

Bunuel's survival stories set in jungles or on islands are case studies of civilization's conflicts. Bunuel lifts his characters from their normal immersion in the decadent society to which they were more or less adapted and drops them into a primitive context: they must struggle against an indifferent natural environment and recreate civilization.

A handful of outcasts bound to each other only by bad faith and hostility are forced to keep company as they escape from a riot-torn mining town through an impenetrable rain forest in *Death in This Garden* [*La Mort en ce jardin*]. Once the dubious protection of civilization is left behind, Bunuel reverses the conventional scale of values. . . .

Beyond the surface drama, Bunuel allows us to watch the unspoken dynamics that really move this society in cross-section. We feel—and it is an important clue to the exact nature of Bunuel's pessimism—that the characters *must* play out their destructive games before we can glimpse the possibility (and perhaps no more than that) of genuine relationships. . . .

Bunuel . . . obtains a political perspective upon the survival theme. The refugees all believe that they have no connection with [the society they have decided to leave]. But the religion, venality, and bourgeois ambition which finally undo them originate precisely in this near-fascist society and bind them to it even as they seek freedom.

Bunuel's retelling of a castaway's single-handed reinvention of civilization to keep himself from savagery, *Robinson Crusoe,* contains a more ambitious yet ambivalent effort to integrate the study of civilization with a specific political critique. Crusoe painfully masters nature although he cannot abolish his own solitude. Bunuel contrasts Crusoe's hard-won material success (bread, clothing, etc.) with his spiritual consolation, the Bible. . . .

Bunuel is exploring two things at the same time. On the one hand, Friday stands for a taboo, cannibalism, which Crusoe must overcome anew if his civilization's promise of friendship is to be realized. At the same time Bunuel is out to expose the arbitrariness—the racist imperialism—with which Crusoe's civilization asserts superiority over that of Friday. . . .

The character of Friday must thus do double duty, symbolizing both a pre-civilized way of life which must be domesticated anyhow and a way of life which just happens to be alien to Crusoe and thus reveals Crusoe's unconscious norms. The barbarity of Crusoe's civilization is fully visible when Crusoe winds up teaching the former savage, once his potential enemy, to use firearms to defend themselves against an invasion by plundering, murderous mutineers from Crusoe's own country.

Bunuel's irony in *Robinson Crusoe* is not always adequate to the sometimes contradictory implications of Friday's role, though the general intent can be seen. (p. 14)

Bunuel's ironic twists [in *The Young One*] demonstrate that relative good is accomplished, if at all, only by applying pressure from a position of power, not through moral argument. At the same time the possibility of a breakthrough to truly human relations born of concrete experience is always present. For Bunuel there is a covert dialectic between Miller's budding love for Evvie and his prejudice against the black man. . . . The real meaning of the rapist stereotype, Bunuel implies, is that for Miller Travers represents love and freedom, an unknown tenderness which he fears and which it is easier to repress than to liberate.

Bunuel makes castaways of a group of refined bourgeois in *The Exterminating Angel,* not by lifting them out of their decadent society but by imprisoning them right inside it. . . .

Incarcerated in the midst of their own urbanity, the bourgeois are as cut off from sustenance as the castaways in the midst of nature in *Death in This Garden* and *Robinson Crusoe*. On the other hand, where the castaways must recreate the ways of civilization, the bourgeois drop the cover of sophistication only to reveal plain hostility. Where the castaways must be amoral, violent, murderous in order to lay the basis for civilization, the characters who survive the longest in *The Exterminating Angel* are those whose roles in life are disciplined by professional dedication with an element of resignation: the doctor, the head servant (who "studied with the Jesuits"), and the host himself, who alone among the bourgeois has consciously assimilated the civilized proprieties as a necessity, not a convenience.

Bunuel uses a narrative made of repetition with variation, a mock dialectic which achieves critical perspective by moving freely from the particular to the general, concrete to abstract, reality to myth and back. The bourgeois' collective hallucination becomes the prototype of organized religion when they suddenly find themselves trapped all over again in their church. . . .

Bunuel allows us to glimpse the larger political world—the fascists' demonstration in Cherbourg—only in a fragmentary sequence at the very end of *Diary of a Chambermaid.* He simply thrusts the demonstration upon us; the political references (to Chiappe for example) are actual, but not explained. If Bunuel draws no tighter connection between Celestine's private drama and the political developments, it is because the real theme of *Diary of a Chambermaid* is precisely the disproportion between the private and public dramas. . . .

Bunuel's parallel resolutions and discontinuous political finale abruptly force the 'individual drama' into the context of the social 'relationship.' Bunuel offers no positive image of freedom, political or moral; he demonstrates what freedom is not. *Diary of a Chambermaid* can be taken as a perfectly class conscious demonstration of the proposition that individual freedom is a bourgeois illusion, and worse, an illusion that conceals and perpetuates oppression. It can just as readily be taken as a statement of utter pessimism, a closed universe. . . . It is Bunuel's denunciation of fascism itself which is the ambivalent element in *Diary of a Chambermaid*. It makes the film one of Bunuel's strongest politically, yet at the same time it is a global expression of the pessimism which is after all inherent in Bunuel's vision.

Nazarin and *Diary of a Chambermaid* are not realist cinema, but their style nevertheless gives full weight to the visible, materially determined world. On the other hand, the surrealism of Bunuel's non-narrative films, which give equal weight to fantasy and reality, seriously qualifies any political understanding of the materialist critique we have identified so far. Bunuel realizes his fundamental poetic aim: to create a total mythology encompassing, potentially, the ahole of society, symbolizing its psychological determinants equally with its political ones. . . .

The Phantom of Liberté . . . treats violence and obsession with death as something fundamental, society's reason for existing, paradoxically. The class aspect of that society is identified but not emphasized.

Each scene is originally some commonplace of melodrama, of bourgeois society's self-image, but some discordant element enters the picture, makes nonsense of the conventional content, and uncovers the archetypal meaning of the commonplace, which always has to do with a latent fear of death. . . .

Finally all of civilization in *The Phantom of Liberté* appears as no more than a frantic concerted effort to deny death. Mortality nevertheless leaves its horrid calling card in the psyche of the body. It is the letter the dreamer finds in his pocket upon awakening and it is the cancer which an x-ray reveals in another character's innards. But the doctors whom these two individuals consult refuse to face the final mystery of death. That is not their job; it is not anybody's job; there is no social convention for it, and so death appears, unexpected and disturbing, in everything. . . .

Bunuel insists, whether dialectically or pessimistically, on seeing freedom and life only in terms of oppression and death. Death, as it flits among the unconnected lives in Bunuel's film, may be the only form in which we glimpse the phantom of freedom.

With its unusual effort to treat political and psychological realities as parts of an indissoluble whole, Bunuel's work not only reflects but responds to the struggle between idealism and materialism. Hence the paradoxes which keep Bunuel's art alive and which make it politically challenging to the left it presumably serves. Bunuel is a materialist who nevertheless insists on subjective reality, an idealist who is dialectical, a determinist who exalts the will to freedom. (p. 18)

It is significant that *Grand Casino,* the first of Bunuel's commercial films, opens like several others with a jailbreak. It is no less significant that the hero's escape is accompanied by a sardonic discussion among the cellmates as to whether it's better to break out or stay in. Bunuel rejected the label 'pessimist' at the time of *The Young and the Damned,* yet volunteered it at the time of *The Discreet Charm of the Bourgeoisie*. Ultimately for this 'good pessimist', society is founded on a basis so conflicted that its essential injustice cannot perhaps be eradicated; yet it is nothing other than the constant effort to eradicate it which defines humanity. (p. 51)

Randall Conrad, "'The Minister Bunuel of the Interior Is on the Telephone': The Early Films of Luis Bunuel" and "'A Magnificent and Dangerous Weapon': The Politics of Luis Bunuel's Later Films," in Cinéaste *(copyright © 1976, 1977 by Gary Crowdus), Vol. VII, Nos. 3 & 4, 1976-77, pp. 2-14, 10-18, 51.*

ALLEN THIHER

Buñuel's first film [*Un Chien andalou*] is commonly understood either to be an unadulterated bit of nonsense or a symbol-laden exercise in hermeticism that only the initiated can understand. Neither of these ideas is entirely false, but neither is adequate for a full comprehension of one of the most important films of the avant-garde. (p. 38)

Our initial postulate for understanding *Un Chien andalou* is that surrealist practice is a ludic activity, a form of play, that attempts systematically to subvert the rules of the game, whether it be in the realm of syntax, narration, or iconic representation. *Un Chien andalou* is, then, an anti-game which, by the systematic way it proposes to destroy the rules of earlier cinematic games, transforms itself into a superior form of play. By systematic negation of the rules the surrealist work develops a new set of ludic definitions at the same time it acquires an ironic self-consciousness. Which is to say that Buñuel uses his film to parody, and through parody, to destroy the filmic conventions that two generations of filmmakers had evolved. . . . The film's opening images, which constitute a kind of prologue to the rest of the film, are thus an attack on the passivity with which the spectator accepts the conventional logic of representation—the rules of the game—as well as the passivity that this logic inflicts on the spectator.

The film's first title, "Once upon a time," opens the assault by making an ironic appeal to the conditioned response normally elicited by this kind of narrative signpost. "Once upon a time" notifies us that a certain narrative code is at work, that a sequential narrative order is at hand in which events are subordinated to the simplest form of unfolding chronology. In short, the order to be followed is the linear chronology of epic, myth, and movies. (pp. 39-40)

In thematic terms [the] prologue to *Un Chien andalou* is a prologue to that part of Buñuel's work in which he frequently jeers those "who have eyes and will not see." . . .

The prologue also presents a parodistic sexual metaphor that prefigures the sexual motifs in the rest of the film. One might even say that the severing of the eye is a rape of the spectator's vision, an idea that Buñuel corroborates in a later film, *The Young One,* when he prefaces the girl's rape with the same image of clouds crossing the moon, that traditional symbol of virginity. By forcing us to view unwittingly the razor's penetration of the flesh, Buñuel commits a violent transgression against our own desire to protect our privacy. With seeming impunity Buñuel forces upon the spectator a visual rape that affirms the violent freedom of desire and play over and beyond all categories of good and evil. Like the Marquis de Sade, whom the surrealists placed in their Pantheon of revered heroes, Buñuel uses a razor that cuts in two directions, for his ironic celebration of the absolute freedom of desire also recognizes the primordial violence attached to it. . . .

Buñuel's ironic destruction of the logic of filmic narration and his celebration of violent desire point to what is perhaps of ultimate importance in this prologue and in a good deal of Buñuel's subsequent work. This celebration of violence is a supreme example of black humor. (p. 41)

Having experienced this most direct initiation to black humor, what can the spectator who has opened his eyes now expect? Buñuel offered a key to the rules of the game he and Dali played when he, in a typically laconic fashion, made the following remarks to François Truffaut on the manner in which they made the film: "Dali and I would select gags and objects that would happen to come to mind. And we rejected without mercy everything that might mean something. I have kept this taste for the irrational." The systematic avoidance of meaning—which sets up the formal rules of the game—does not mean that there is no sense to the series of irrationally associated images that follow the prologue. For the destruction of logical meaning is, indeed, a form of sense, conveying, as we have suggested, Buñuel's contempt for the traditional constructs that purport to represent reality. (p. 42)

The parodistic destruction of mimetic devices points to the first level of interpretation of *Un Chien andalou.* And it should be apparent . . . what skepticism one should grant the usual critical approach to the film, which consists in calling the film some kind of dream representation and in then searching for a latent discourse that various symbols give rise to. . . . [Film] can be a mimetic means for representing the world of repressed desire. In addition, the way in which one perceives a film has some features in common with the way in which one perceives a dream. Moreover, film can make use of the irrational associations and transformations that one finds in dreams. These are three distinct points, and if Buñuel chooses to abolish the principle of noncontradiction in his works, this does not mean that he is seeking to represent a dream world, the one realm of our normal experience where the principle of noncontradiction does not hold sway. It would seem more appropriate to say that he frequently borrows from the rhetoric of dream discourse in order to contest the more constrictive rhetoric of traditional narrative discourse. (pp. 46-7)

Once one decides that *Un Chien andalou* is an imitation of dream reality, then it nearly automatically follows that the proper critical approach is to apply the science of the irrational and to interpret the film in psychoanalytic terms. Psychoanalytic concepts offer a useful approach to the film, since they point to a level of symbolic discourse that is present in the film, though not in the latent manner that many critics would have it. For it is our contention that Buñuel and Dali have, in a completely self-conscious fashion, used the symbolism that psychoanalytic discourse utilizes in order to create another level of discourse that they have, in turn, systematically subverted.

A typical psychoanalytic interpretation of *Un Chien andalou* will usually start by positing a general principle of coherence in function of which the symbols are organized, such as, say the portrayal of adolescent sexual development or a symbolic portrayal of themes of sexual frustration. (p. 47)

[Interpretations of the symbols as sexual representatives] indicates the kinds of symbols that one can find in *Un Chien andalou* and the kinds of interpretations they can give rise to. However, the importance of these symbols is not that they express some latent psychic reality, but rather that they are posited in a self-conscious way as the elements of a filmic discourse. There is, of course, an element of parody in this as well as a ludic subversion of this kind of discourse. And it is this self-conscious dimension that marks *Un Chien andalou* as a privileged moment in this history of film, for it is with this surrealist incursion into cinema that filmic discourse becomes subject to the same kind of self-criticism and ironic subversion that the modernist notion of self-consciousness had already subjected literature and painting.

Self-consciousness in modern terms is a reflexive form of creation in which the work is endowed with indices that constantly point to work as an artifact. The work thus contains a perspective on itself, and this perspective, superimposed on the naive perspective of normal vision that wishes to accept the work as an authentic form of representation, creates the double perspective or vision that is the basis for modern irony. Surely, this is one of the marking features of modernism: ironic consciousness of mimesis is raised to the same level of importance as the act of mimesis itself. Surrealism, in its joyful subversion of all fixed forms of representation, goes perhaps one step further in this direction when it finally proposes that this ironic consciousness is the only worthy artistic act that the poet in quest of liberation can undertake.

Buñuel angrily declared that few had understood *Un Chien andalou,* for none had seen that it was a "desperate call for murder." Perhaps by this we might understand the urgency Buñuel felt in attempting to destroy our naive acceptance of film's capacity to order the world through some objective mode of mimesis. For the film is an attempted assassination of that belief. Beyond this attack on discourse, too, we must see *Un Chien andalou* as another manifestation of the surrealist terrorism that, they hoped, would lead to the purging of consciousness. For the surrealist apocalypse would be the eruption of pure consciousness, undivided, rid of all categories, at one with itself as a self-sufficient form of experience. (pp. 48-9)

Allen Thiher, "Surrealism's Enduring Bite: 'Un Chien andalou'," in Literature/Film Quarterly *(© copyright 1977 Salisbury State College), Vol. V, No. 1, Winter, 1977, pp. 38-49.*

RAYMOND DURGNAT

If the inexplicable abounds in Buñuel's work, it is so that his moral arguments are constantly related to the inner world of desires and feelings, related in a way which asserts their irrational existence as categorical imperatives of man's nature. Buñuel is a moralist, but also protests against the rationalist, as well as puritan, attempt to apply moral standards to every impulse and feeling of man.

In his detachment from his own lyricism, Buñuel is more Brechtian than Brecht. He has no need of alienation effects, which in practice delight us aesthetically, thus de-alienating themselves. In his theories, Brecht was a rhetorician, and he pays the price for it. Buñuel needs no alienation effects, because the complexity of his characters and of their predicaments, and the sardonic restraint of his style, force the spectator to careful moral judgements at every turn. (p. 16)

The lack of sympathy for Buñuel's characters, in their absurdity, is often the spectator's response, not the director's. For example many critics thought of Don Jaime (Viridiana's uncle) simply as a morbid fetishist. Buñuel, pointed out that whatever his faults might be, there was a great deal of kindness and nobility in his attitudes. Once one refrains from, in effect, destroying Don Jaime by ridicule, his story takes on a more deeply tragic tone without so immersing the spectator in the tragic that he can't see the tragically derisive too. (pp. 16-17)

Buñuel's films are profoundly dialectical in that every character, every event, is not an assertion of any one point, but is a synthesis between opposing polarities. . . . Excessive simple-mindedness prevails if the spectator feels that because Don Jaime is ridiculous, he isn't tragic, or that, conversely, because the hero of *El* finishes in a tragic predicament, he isn't also funny. The play of contradictions in Buñuel's work is extremely sharp.

Aristotelian logic also underlies the common distortion of works of art by the attribution of excessively cut-and-dried symbolic meanings, although artists work by conglomerates of associations. Nowhere is this associative quality more apparent than in the Buñuelian motif of insects. (p. 17)

Buñuel's own remarks on his 'entomological' interest in people strengthens one's impression that Buñuel characters who have lost their biological integrity as a result of tabus, repressions, and so on, to become mere units in the social ant-heap, often take on insect-like movements. The insect world is a metaphor for all that is tragically derisory in alienated man. . . . Buñuel's motifs are . . . occasions for dissonances, contradictions, ambivalences, for a radically non-hierarchical view of the universe.

This sense of life's disorder explains, too, why Buñuel's films are often visually messy. His characters' rooms or surroundings are often littered with objects: tools, stores, objects of every kind. Formal pleasure is degraded by the impurity of things. The world around is non-symbolic; it is just what it is, a disorder from which man selects what he needs to live with, and whose selected objects also lie around in something of a mess. (p. 18)

So marked is Buñuel's lyrical reticence, and so often does

his lyricism run at cross-purposes to conventional expectation, that Buñuel's films often disappoint the sophisticated spectator when he sees them for the first time. If he likes them it is because, as Jean-Luc Godard observed, a film doesn't have to be consistently exciting to please audiences. All it needs is a few bold ideas or moments which will hold up the duller parts. But even when initially they disappoint, Buñuel's films prove barbed. . . .

His films abound also in *argument*. But we may be misled by this word unless we remember that the logic of Buñuel's films is of course, a dramatic logic. Its content may be moral and philosophical, but its form is dramatic. Fiction is so much a matter of particular people, particular circumstances, particular cases, that the relationship between the particular story and reality in general can never be logically established. Dramatic logic is suggestive rather than exclusive, divergent rather than convergent. It's not 'this *must* follow from that . . . ' but 'had you realised that these apparently distinct factors could be related?' The value of dramatic logic lies not in its irrefutability, but in the insights which it offers, and the lived experience of those insights. By sharing certain experiences with the screen characters, the spectator explores himself and others simultaneously. What he had cursorily dismissed now becomes, not only a theoretical possibility, but in the fullest sense, comprehensible. (p. 20)

Raymond Durgnat, in his Luis Bunuel *(copyright © 1967 by Movie Magazine Limited; copyright © 1977 by Raymond Durgnat; reprinted by permission of the University of California Press), University of California Press, 1977, 176 p.*

DON WILLIS

The archetypal heroes of the comic, or serio-comic, films of Luis Buñuel such as *El* (1952), Nazarin (1958) and *Simon of the Desert* (1965) are pure, in either sense of the word: innocent, simple, homogeneous. They haven't a trace of deceit or hypocrisy and they aren't self-questioning or self-aware. Buñuel doesn't make Nazarin and Simon contradict their moral and religious principles. Instead, he makes them push these to their logical, absurd extreme. Yet the films reveal a dichotomy: the absoluteness of Nazarin, Simon and Francisco, which is their primary strength, is at the same time, in context, their primary weakness, their comic flaw. Buñuel puts his heroes in a multiple perspective which, in effect, defines character as primarily a matter of point of view. . . . The character Francisco [in *El*] is seen to be at once cruel, in his wife's eyes, godlike, in his own eyes, and pathetically comic, in Buñuel's. He is, in effect, a synthesis of perceptions. . . .

Nazarin too is an elemental Buñuel character. A priest in Mexico at the turn of the century, he leads an exemplary, modest, Christ-like existence, despite clerical (and anticlerical) pressure. His example, however, is lost on his era's violent society. Although he believes that, living in it, he is a part of it, Buñuel shows that he's apart *from* it. . . .

Nazarin is mild, likeable, unprepossessing, and has a slight self-consciousness of movement that seems to come from self-effacement. But his subdued and matter-of-fact manner, although it effectively stifles self-importance or self-righteousness, also unfortunately stifles in him the possibility of spontaneity or responsiveness to others. But can he be blamed too badly if, while he's reinforcing the base of his character at one point, it's eroding at another? Nazarin seems to have a natural goodness of spirit which makes him somehow appealing even at his most didactic—perhaps especially then, when one can see a possibility of internal contradiction. (p. 5)

If his spirituality constitutes one form of ignorance, his world's earthiness constitutes another. The exaggeration of both 'true' Christian and heathen/'false' Christian gives the film perfect comic symmetry.

The unpriestliness of other priests in *Nazarin* is played off against Nazarin's strict constructionism, which in turn is played off against peasant superstition/religion. All ground is quicksand. . . .

To Nazarin 'nature' means 'God'; but 'nature', in the film's context, means 'detachment'. . . .

Nazarin's own lack of ego allows him to reduce everyone and everything else to the same level of importance, or unimportance. His principled concern for all merges imperceptibly into unprincipled indifference. Nazarin is genuinely selfless, but equally to the point is that there would be little distinguishable difference if he were genuinely selfish. . . .

[The] missing link between Nazarin's absolute sense of purpose and the world's indifference is the idea of self-realisation. This is the comic-ironic key to the disparity between intention and actuality. . . . [When the thief enlightens Nazarin as to his "Worth . . . in the real world," it] is as if the self-ignorant Buñuel hero had been lifted up out of the narrative and given the opportunity of seeing himself from outside the film. (p. 6)

The primary polarity in *Nazarin* is not faith/lack of faith or even theism/humanism, but passion/detachment. What his society possesses in abundance, Nazarin initially lacks or suppresses. The film might best be characterised as a story of idealistic detachment transformed into idealistic passion. . . .

At the end, Nazarin's comic denial of his emotions is no longer possible. The final psychic picture of him might be: far from detached, now doubting himself and his purpose, but seeing no better one, he presses on. In Nazarin's final fierceness there are overtones of insanity—if not in a clinical then in a practical sense, given his social context—of obsession, damnation as salvation and, perhaps most importantly, of heroism. (p. 7)

Don Willis, "'Nazarin': Buñuel's Comic Hero Revisited," in Sight and Sound *(copyright © 1977 by The British Film Institute), Vol. 47, No. 1, Winter, 1977-78, pp. 5-7.*

DAVID L. OVERBEY

It is the fact, process and results of obsession and desire which are under dissection [in *Cet Obscur Objet du Désir*]. As the title indicates, the object of that desire, while not unimportant, remains obscure, for it may be that within this context the very frustration of desire is desire's true objective. If that is indeed the case, *Cet Obscur Objet du Désir* indicates that Buñuel has begun to despair; his characters here no longer wrestle against the forces of repression and frustration but collaborate and embrace them. . . .

Far from creating a fascinatingly romantic image of desire *á la* Dietrich [as Josef von Sternberg did in *The Devil Is a Woman,* based on the same novel], Buñuel destroys that very idea. . . . [Two actresses who play Conchita] are used interchangeably, arbitrarily, with one often beginning a scene and, after a brief cut away, the other finishing it. The point is not so much that the lover sees the beloved in a multiplicity of guises, as that, once he has 'decided' to desire her, he probably doesn't see her at all. The almost surrealistic melting of one woman into another serves to unnerve us and to make the object of desire even more obscure. In being thus distanced from the object, we are forced to find the lover and his love more than a little ludicrous. . . .

While [Mathieu's fellow travelers] condemn Conchita's emotional and sexual terrorism (she is, after all, an 'object' removed from the first-class carriage), they ignore their own and that of religion, economics, psychology, law, marriage, motherhood, virginity—all of which are subjected to Buñuel's satirical scrutiny. Their reaction to the acts of literal terrorism is a smug complacency and deluded 'understanding', or, that failing, a cry for violent repression. . . .

It is never possible, nor even desirable, to build too exact an intellectual scheme based on individual 'symbols' in Buñuel's films. Obviously, he works less with strictly formulated theories and structures than with almost instinctive images growing naturally from the narrative. Still, it is difficult not to connect recurring patterns of objects between one film and another. That burlap sack which Mathieu carries (similar to one slung over the shoulder of a passing workman glimpsed momentarily midway through the film) reminds one immediately of the burden pulled by the man in *Un Chien Andalou*. A heavy load of social and moral values, perhaps. That one load is comprised of nightgowns and the other of piano, pumpkins, priests and donkeys is beside the point; that exploding sack serves the same function, save that one hinders and the other destroys completely. . . .

[*Cet Obscur Objet du Désir*] is Buñuel's most effective and disturbing film in years. It is more subtle than either *Le Charme Discret de la Bourgeoisie* or *Le Fantôme de la Liberté*. Its humour is less obvious, less accessible, but far more corrosive; its structure more sophisticated in so far as it both creates a hallucinatory world within what seems at first to be a typical melodramatic structure and then itself comments on that world in almost equally hallucinatory terms. *Cet Obscur Objet du Désir* is also Buñuel's most moving film in years. For all his pitiless flaying of every sort of human behaviour, he reveals unsuspected wellsprings of sympathy for the ridiculous characters trapped within the shell of decayed social and moral values. Although the insights of his wit, directed against 'them', are as fresh as ever, this time we are left with a whole world whose evident object of desire when less obscurely seen may well be self-destruction. That final flaming image must, after all, include all of 'us' as well. (p. 8)

David L. Overbey, "'Cet Obscur Objet du desir'," in Sight and Sound *(copyright © 1977 by The British Film Institute), Vol. 47, No. 1, Winter, 1977-78, pp. 7-8.*

ANDRÉ BRETON

The day will soon come when we realise that, in spite of the wear and tear of life that bites like acid into our flesh, the very cornerstone of that violent liberation which reaches out for a better life in the heart of the technological age that corrupts our cities is

LOVE.

(p. 327)

Buñuel has formulated a theory of revolution and love which goes to the very core of human nature; that most tragic of all debates, galvanised by well-meaning cruelty, finds its ultimate expression in that unique instant when a distant yet wholly present voice, so slowly yet so urgently, yells through compressed lips so loudly that it can scarcely be heard:

LOVE . . . LOVE . . . *Love* . . . Love.

. . . All those who are not yet alarmed by what the censorship allows them to read in the newspapers must go and see *L'Age d'or*. It complements the present stock-exchange crisis perfectly, and its impact is all the more direct precisely because it is surrealist . . . The foundations are laid, conventions become dogma, policemen push people around just as they do in everyday life. And, just as in everyday life, accidents occur in bourgeois society while that society pays no attention whatsoever. But such accidents (and it must be noted that in Buñuel's film they remain uncorrupted by plausibility) further debilitate an already-rotting society that tries to prolong its existence artificially by the use of priests and policemen. The final pessimism born within that society as its optimism begins to wane becomes a powerful virus that hastens the process of disintegration. That pessimism takes on the value of negation and is immediately translated into anticlericalism; it thus becomes revolutionary, because the fight against religion is also the fight against the world as it is.

But it is *Love* which brings about the transition from pessimism to action; Love, denounced in the bourgeois demonology as the root of all evil. For Love demands the sacrifice of every other value: status, family and honour. And the failure of Love within the social framework leads to Revolt. This process can be seen in the life and works of the Marquis de Sade, who lived in the *golden age* of absolute monarchy . . . so that it is no coincidence if Buñuel's sacrilegious film contains echoes of the blasphemies which the Divine Marquis hurled through the bars of his jail.

It still remains to be demonstrated that the final outcome of this pessimism will in fact be the struggle and the victory of the proletariat, which will mean the abolition of a society made up of different classes.

In this age of so-called prosperity, the social function of *L'Age d'or* must be to urge the oppressed to satisfy their hunger for destruction and perhaps even to cater for the masochism of the oppressor.

In spite of all the threats to suppress this film, we believe that it will win out in the end and open new horizons in a sky which can never match in beauty that sky it showed us in a mirror. (pp. 327-28)

André Breton, "Manifesto on 'L'Age d'or'," in his What Is Surrealism?: Selected Writings, *edited by Franklin Rosemont (copyright © 1978 by Franklin Rosemont), Monad Press, 1978, pp. 327-28.*

Frank Capra

1897-

American director, screenwriter, and producer.

Capra's optimistic American comedies exalt the "little man" as a figure capable of discovering and healing a corrupt society. His "screwball" comedies, providing simple solutions to complex problems, were popular during the Great Depression.

Born in Sicily, Capra came to the United States at the age of six. After studying at the California Institute of Technology, he was hired to direct "cine-poems" before working as a gagman for Mack Sennett. In 1923 he went to work with Harry Langdon, establishing the actor as a famed simpleton. Capra's association with Columbia pictures began in 1928, with a series of low-budget movies. His interest in social themes as the basis of his unabashedly sentimental films came to the fore in 1932 with *American Madness,* a satirical poke at the banking world. Before beginning the series of New Deal comedies that made him famous, Capra made several films, among them *Platinum Blonde, Ladies of Leisure,* and *The Bitter Tea of General Yen,* displaying an unexpectedly erotic turn to Capra's style.

***It Happened One Night* is Capra's quintessential "screwball" comedy. This simple story attains an aura of glamour that belies its unpretentiousness, because of the film's optimism and high integrity. *Mr. Deeds Goes to Town* and *Mr. Smith Goes to Washington* convey Capra's belief in the innocent man as the American hero who overcomes corruption with honesty and decency.**

While his films have been generally well-received, some critics label Capra's sentimentality "Capra-corn," finding it overly idealistic. *You Can't Take It With You* and *Lost Horizon,* Capra's adaptations of literature for the screen, incorporate his Utopian outlook. His thirties films display strong characterization as well as a sure touch for comical pacing. In 1939 Capra left Columbia and formed his own company, producing *Meet John Doe* and *Arsenic and Old Lace* before the advent of World War II.

During World War II, Capra served as a major in the US Signal Corps and made a series of combat documentaries called *Why We Serve.* These films are now regarded as a serious fusion of documentary style and heroic imagery. The films made after the war are generally conceded to be less successful than those of the thirties. Perhaps an exception is *It's a Wonderful Life,* where the Capra hero does not save the country on his own, but rather is aided by the device of a *deus ex machina.* Even this well-received film had a different mood to it than the engagingly optimistic films of his prewar period, and his attempt to adapt to America's philosophy of the forties was unsuccessful. Both *State of the Union* and *Pocketful of Miracles* are indicative of the weaknesses of Capra's later style. His most recent works are remakes of his own films that seem overly sentimental by today's standards. (See also *Contemporary Authors,* Vols. 61-64.)

ALEXANDER BAKSHY

A superior picture, if only by virtue of its two magnificent scenes of evangelistic mummery in a tabernacle, is "The Miracle Woman". . . . Here, at least, is some excellent and genuine material of life, striking in its unfamiliarity and effectively presented. The director of the film, Frank Capra, can be congratulated on the skilful handling of these scenes; and there is also merit in the story in so far as it attempts to expose the fakery that goes under the name of evangelism. Its romantic motif, however, leaves much to be desired. With all its adumbrations of a blind boy, formerly an aviator, falling in love with the evangelist, and of his rather theatrical penchant for revealing his mind through a ventriloquist dummy, it never succeeds in ringing true and convincing.

Alexander Bakshy, "Films: 'The Miracle Woman'," in The Nation *(copyright 1931 The Nation Associates, Inc.), Vol. 133, No. 3452, September 2, 1931, p. 237.**

MORDAUNT HALL

There are few serious moments in "It Happened One Night," a screen feast . . . , and if there is a welter of improbable incidents these hectic doings serve to generate plenty of laughter. The pseudo suspense is kept on the wing until a few seconds before the picture ends, but it is a foregone conclusion that the producers would never dare to have the characters . . . separated when the curtain falls. . . .

"It Happened One Night" is a good piece of fiction, which, with all its feverish stunts, is blessed with bright dialogue and a good quota of relatively restrained scenes. Although there are such flighty notions as that of having Ellie running away from a marriage ceremony when the guests—and particularly King Westley—had expected to hear her say "I will"; or those depicting Warne volleying vituperation over the telephone at his city editor; there are also more sober sequences wherein Warne and Ellie spread cheer to the audience, notwithstanding their sorry adventures with little or no money.

Mordaunt Hall, "'It Happened One Night'," in The New York Times *(© 1934 by The New York Times Company; reprinted by permission), February 23, 1934, p. 1035.*

OTIS C. FERGUSON

Considering its subject, ["It Happened One Night"] is better than it has any right to be—better acted, better directed, better written. . . . [Everybody] being in love with everybody else in pleasantly conclusive fashion, there enters more confusion as to who loves whom and why than might be expected of a Molière comedy. Barring the incidents of the bus ride, the outlines of the story have a deadly enough familiarity all through anyway. What the picture as a whole shows is that by changing such types as the usual pooh-bah father and city editor into people with some wit and feeling, by consistently preferring the light touch to the heavy, and by casting actors who are thoroughly up to the work of acting, you can make some rather comely and greenish grasses grow where there was only alkali dust before. (p. 364)

Otis C. Ferguson, "Worth Seeing," in The New Republic *(reprinted by permission of* The New Republic; *© 1934 The New Republic, Inc.), Vol. 78, No. 1014, May 9, 1934, pp. 364-65.*

OTIS FERGUSON

[In *Mr. Deeds Goes to Town,* Capra] takes a plot with as few restrictions as possible (it has the necessary sentimental angle and forward motion but is fairly empty of anything else) and proceeds to fill it up with situations and characters from life—working the situations into some direct line with wonderful care both for their speed and clarity as parts and for their associative values, their cumulative effect in the whole story; working over the casting and combined performance of the best actors he can get hold of; making his own show with genius and humble labor from start to finish. His type of comedy differs from that of René Clair in minor respects (with the possible exception of Lubitsch, there have been no others so far who can keep up with him); but the two have in common the same basic drollery, good spirits, and human sympathy, the same quick perception and whatever magic it is that can keep several irons in the fire all the time, and the fire blowing bright. Capra hasn't the hard universal brilliance of Clair at his best (some years ago now) and his prize effects happen in twos rather than in Clair's one-two-three formation; but he is more homey, less apt to make his sentiment slush, closer to the lives of his audience, enlisting more of their belief and sympathy. . . . (pp. 127-28)

And everywhere the picture goes, from the endearing to the absurd, the accompanying business is carried through with perfect zip and relish. . . . The film has some prime examples of the spoken gag ("What's that, who said that?" the boss says, his staff filing out after a terrific dressing down; and the chap says, "Uh, I was saying you got dirty plaster") and it has prime examples of purely visual comedy—precisely timed kicks in the pants, banister glides, headers over garbage cans, etc. It has this and it has that, and I begin to realize about here that it is the kind of thing there is no use talking on about. It is a humdinger and a beauty, but—like anything so conceived and expressed in terms of motion—literally too much for words, more to be seen than heard about. (p. 128)

Otis Ferguson, "Mr. Capra Goes to Town" (originally published in The New Republic, *Vol. 86, No. 1116, April 22, 1936), in* The Film Criticism of Otis Ferguson, *edited by Robert Wilson (© 1971 by Temple University), Temple University Press, 1971, pp. 127-28.*

GRAHAM GREENE

Mr. Deeds is Capra's finest film (it is on quite a different intellectual level from the spirited and delightful *It Happened One Night*), and that means it is a comedy quite unmatched on the screen. For Capra has what Lubitsch, the witty playboy, has not: a sense of responsibility, and what Clair, whimsical, poetic, a little precious and à la mode, has not, a kinship with his audience, a sense of common life, a morality; he has what even Chaplin has not, complete mastery of his medium, and that medium the sound-film, not the film with sound attached to it. Like Lang, he hears all the time just as clearly as he sees and just as selectively. I do not think anyone can watch *Mr. Deeds* for long without being aware of a technician as great as Lang employed on a theme which profoundly moves him: the theme of goodness and simplicity manhandled in a deeply selfish and brutal world. That was the theme of *Fury,* too, but Capra is more fortunate than Lang. Lang expresses the theme in terms of terror, and terror on the screen has always, alas! to be tempered to the shorn lamb; Capra expresses it in terms of pity and ironic tenderness, and no magnate feels the need to cramp his style or alter his conclusion. . . .

[The story] sounds as grim a theme as *Fury;* innocence lynched as effectively at a judicial inquiry as in a burning courthouse, but there is this difference between Lang and Capra; Lang's happy ending was imposed on him, we did not believe in it; Capra's is natural and unforced. He *believes* in the possibility of happiness; he believes, in spite of the controlling racketeers, in human nature. Goodness, simplicity, disinterestedness: these in his hands become fighting qualities. . . . The picture glows with . . . humour and shrewdness, just as Lang's curdles with his horror and disgust. . . . (p. 96)

Graham Greene, " 'Mr. Deeds Goes to Town' " (originally published in The Spectator, *August 28, 1936), in his* The Pleasure-Dome: The Collected Film Criticism 1935-40 *(copyright © 1972 by Graham Greene), Secker & Warburg, 1972, pp. 96-7.*

GRAHAM GREENE

[*Lost Horizon*] is a very long picture, this disappointing successor to *Mr. Deeds,* and a very dull one as soon as the opening scenes are over. . . . Here the Capra-Riskin partnership is at its best, and we are unprepared for the disappointments which follow: the flavourless uplifting dialogue, the crude humour, the pedestrian direction, and the slack makeshift construction. . . .

Of course, the picture isn't quite as bad as that. It does attempt, however clumsily and sentimentally, more than the average film; a social conscience is obscurely at work, but at work far less effectively than in *Mr. Deeds,* and as for the humour—it consists only of Mr. Edward Everett Horton wearing Eastern clothes. The conscious humour that is to say, for the glimpses of English political life give a little much needed relief. . . . But it is in the last sequence that the Capra-Riskin collaboration fails most disastrously. . . . A few newspaper headlines tell us that Conway has reached safety, and it is only at secondhand in a long uncinematic scene in a London club that we learn what we should have seen with our own eyes: Conway's reaction to "civilization." If the long dull ethical sequences had been cut to the bone there would have been plenty of room for the real story: the shock of western crudity and injustice on a man returned from a more gentle and beautiful way of life. (p. 148)

Graham Greene, "'Lost Horizon'" (originally published in The Spectator, *April 23, 1937), in his* The Pleasure-Dome: The Collected Film Criticism 1935-40 *(copyright © 1972 by Graham Greene), Secker & Warburg, 1972, pp. 145, 148.*

GRAHAM GREENE

[*You Can't Take It With You*] is the *Christmas Carol* over again—with its sentimentality and its gusto and its touches of genius: no technical mistakes this time as there were in *Lost Horizon.* The director emerges as a rather muddled and sentimental idealist who feels—vaguely—that something is wrong with the social system. Mr. Deeds started distributing his money, and the hero of *Lost Horizon* settled down in a Thibetan monastery—equipped with all the luxury devices of the best American hotels—and Grandpa Vanderhof persuades, in this new picture, the Wall Street magnate who has made the *coup* of his career and cornered the armaments industry to throw everything up and play the harmonica. This presumably means a crash in Wall Street and the ruin of thousands of small investors, but it is useless trying to analyse the idea behind the Capra films: there *is* no idea that you'd notice, only a sense of dissatisfaction, an urge to escape—on to the open road with the daughter of a millionaire, back to small town simplicity on a safe income, away to remote, secure Shangri-La, into the basement where Mr. Vanderhof's son-in-law makes fireworks with the iceman who came seven years ago with a delivery van and stayed on. A belief, too, in bad rich men and good poor men—though Mr. Vanderhof doesn't, when you come to think of it, seem to lack money. Like the British Empire, he has retired from competition with a full purse.

That is really all there is to the film—a contrast between life on Wall Street and life in the Vanderhof home, where everybody is supposed to lead the life he likes and like the life the others lead. (pp. 203-04)

It sounds awful, but it isn't as awful as all that, for Capra has a touch of genius with a camera: his screen always seems twice as big as other people's, and he cuts as brilliantly as Eisenstein (the climax when the big bad magnate takes up his harmonica is so exhilarating in its movement that you forget its absurdity). Humour and not wit is his line, a humour which shades off into whimsicality, and a kind of popular poetry which is apt to turn wistful. We may groan and blush as he cuts his way remorselessly through all finer values to the fallible human heart, but infallibly he makes his appeal—by that great soft organ with its unreliable goodness and easy melancholy and baseless optimism. The cinema, a popular craft, can hardly be expected to do more. (p. 204)

Graham Greene, " 'You Can't Take It with You' " (originally published in The Spectator, *November 11, 1938), in his* The Pleasure-Dome: The Collected Film Criticism 1935-40 *(copyright © 1972 by Graham Greene), Secker & Warburg, 1972, pp. 203-04.*

OTIS FERGUSON

[*Mr. Smith Goes to Washington*] is a mixture of tough, factual patter about Congressional cloakrooms and pressure groups, and a naïve but shameless hooraw for the American relic—Parson Weems at a flag-raising. It seems just the time for it, just the time of excitement when a barker in good voice could mount the tub, point toward the flag, say ubbuh-ubbah-ubbah and a pluribus union? and the windows would shake. But where all this time is Director Capra?

I'm afraid Mr. Capra began to leave this world at some point during the production of *Mr. Deeds Goes to Town,* his best picture. . . . (p. 273)

Politically, the story is eyewash. The machinery of the Senate and the machinery of how it may be used to advantage are shown better than they ever have been. But the main surviving idea is that one scout leader who knows the Gettysburg Address by heart but wouldn't possibly be hired to mow your lawn can throw passionate faith into the balance and by God we've got a fine free country to live in again.

There are some fine lines and there is a whole magazine of nice types; but the occasional humor is dispersed and the people are embarrassed by just the slugging, unimaginative sort of direction that Capra became famous for avoiding. When the hero is supposed to be made innocent, they write him down an utter fool; when there is supposed to be evil, wickedness triumphs as slick as pushing a button. . . . The only good sequence was the lovely bit where Miss Arthur and friend got very tight by degrees, and by degrees more reckless and tearful, until they weave up to tell little boy blue that somebody swiped his horn. This seems a case of winning by a lapse; it is like the old Capra, and pretty lonesome. (pp. 273-74)

Otis Ferguson, "Mr. Capra Goes Someplace" (originally published in The New Republic, *Vol. 100, No. 1300, November 1, 1939), in* The Film Criticism of Otis Ferguson, *edited by Robert Wilson (© 1971 by Temple University), Temple University Press, 1971, pp. 273-75.*

GRAHAM GREENE

Here is Capra, without the help of Riskin, back to his finest form [in *Mr. Smith Goes to Washington*]—the form of *Mr. Deeds.* It has always been an interesting question, how much Capra owed to his faithful scenario writer. Now it is difficult to believe that Riskin's part was ever very important, for all the familiar qualities are here—the exciting close-ups, the sudden irrelevant humour, the delight—equal to that of the great Russians—in the ordinary human face. (p. 260)

It is a great film, even though it is not a great story. . . . (p. 261)

Graham Greene, "'Mr. Smith Goes to

Washington'" (originally published in The Spectator, *January 5, 1940), in his* The Pleasure-Dome: The Collected Film Criticism 1935-40 *(copyright © 1972 by Graham Greene), Secker & Warburg, 1972, pp. 260-61.*

OTIS FERGUSON

[*Meet John Doe*] is almost a point-for-point replica of *Mr. Smith Goes to Washington,* but some of the old felicity is there again and there are actually comedy sequences in it. I am not holding out too much hope, for today there is nothing Americans so like to be told from the screen as that they are Americans. So why should anybody with a formula and a credit line like skywriting bother with making a swell simple movie as his "production for 1941"? . . . (p. 349)

The message is that since it is all the little men who truly make the big world, they should live together and hang together, doing away with hate and suspicion and bad-neighborliness. Fine. Ringing. Of course there are present among us oppression and injustice and scorn for all unsung heroes whose names are Moe Million. Too bad; an outrage; something should be done. So the lift of the story comes in the doing, in the rallying to a new simple faith, as people and as Americans, through homely things but as a mighty army under the flag. In this story the powers of darkness are able to check the advance, but the victory in defeat is that there will be advance again.

I have no doubt the authors of such theses believe in them, just as it is easy for a songwriter to believe that God should bless America after he has glanced over the recent sheet-music sales. But sifted in with any such half-thought-out hoorah must be the true motivating conviction that the box office is out there and will be terrific. And that is where the thing begins to crack like Parson Weems's Liberty Bell, for in art there is a certain terrible exaction upon those who would carry their show by arousing people to believe, and it is that any such show must be made out of belief, in good faith and pure earnest, in the whole of belief itself. This rhetoric and mortising of sure-fire device of a success today is its sure betrayal by tomorrow—the flag in a game of charades, the mock prayer at a picnic.

As a picture, it does well the things which have proved highlights before: the tender concern over the little fellers with great faith; the underdog finally getting on his hind legs to tell them off; the regeneration of even a hard-boiled newspaper gal; the final blow-off scene with the nation as audience. But it talks too much to no purpose and in the same spot. . . . And one of the saddest things is to find Capra so preoccupied with getting over a message of holy-hokum that he lets in half a dozen of the worst montage transitions—mumming faces, headlines, wheels and whorls—that have been seen in a major effort since the trick first turned stale.

Whether this much of hollowness and prefabrication will spoil the picture for you, I wouldn't know. There are things in it to see. The business of promoting a thesis has distracted Frank Capra's attention from much that he was superb at doing, and he still skips over many of the little fitted pieces which make a story inevitable. But now and then he lingers and you can see the hand of the loving workman bringing out the fine grain—as in the direction of the little crowd around the local mayor when Joe Doe is apprehended, with its naturalness and light spontaneous humor; as in the edge of satire in the management of the radio broadcast; as in the bringing out of homely humorous quirks in John Doe himself; and as always in the timing of a line, its cause and effect, so that it comes out with just force and clarity among the shifting images. (pp. 349-50)

Otis Ferguson, "Democracy at the Box Office" (originally published in The New Republic, *Vol. 104, No. 12, March 24, 1941), in* The Film Criticism of Otis Ferguson, *edited by Robert Wilson (© 1971 by Temple University), Temple University Press, 1971, pp. 349-51.*

JAMES AGEE

One important function of good art or entertainment is to unite and illuminate the heart and the mind, to cause each to learn from, and to enhance, the experience of the other. Bad art and entertainment misinform and disunite them. Much too often ["It's a Wonderful Life"] appeals to the heart at the expense of the mind; at other times it urgently demands of the heart that it treat with contempt the mind's efforts to keep its integrity; at still other times the heart is simply used, on the mind, as a truncheon. ["It's a Wonderful Life"] does all this so proficiently, and with so much genuine warmth, that I wasn't able to get reasonably straight about it for quite a while. I still think it has a good deal of charm and quality, enough natural talent involved in it to make ten pictures ten times as good, and terrific vitality or, rather, vigor—for much of the vitality seems cooked-up and applied rather than innate. (The high-school dance floor coming apart over a swimming pool is a sample of cooking-up that no movie has beaten for a long time.) But I mistrust, for instance, any work which tries to persuade me—or rather, which assumes that I assume—that there is so much good in nearly all the worst of us that all it needs is a proper chance and example, to take complete control. I mistrust even more deeply the assumption, so comfortably stylish these days, that whether people turn out well or ill depends overwhelmingly on outside circumstances and scarcely if at all on their own moral intelligence and courage. Neither idea is explicit in this movie, but the whole story depends on the strong implication and assumption of both. . . .

Yet at its best, which is usually inextricable with its worst, I feel that this movie is a very taking sermon about the feasibility of a kind of Christian semi-socialism, a society founded on affection, kindliness, and trust, and that its chief mistake or sin—an enormous one—is its refusal to face the fact that evil is intrinsic in each individual, and that no man may deliver his brother, or make agreement unto God for him. It interests me, by the way, that in representing a twentieth-century American town Frank Capra uses so little of the twentieth and idealizes so much that seems essentially nineteenth-century, or prior anyhow to the First World War, which really ended that century. Many small towns are, to be sure, "backward" in that generally more likable way, but I have never seen one so Norman-Rockwellish as all that. (p. 193)

James Agee, "Books and the Arts: 'It's a Wonderful Life'," in The Nation *(copyright 1947 The Nation Associates, Inc.), Vol. 164, No. 7, February 15, 1947, pp. 193-94.*

JOSEPH KOSTOLEFSKY

[*A Hole in the Head*] is bound to disappoint some of Frank

Capra's admirers, but they can console themselves, between laughs, by reflecting that if Capra isn't making the kind of pictures he once did, they aren't seeing them as they once did. Much of his earlier work relied on a stereotype of the good little people resisting the bad big people; it belonged to the 'thirties and would seem out of place today (*He Who Must Die* notwithstanding). The goodness, however, remains, and accounts for some sticky passages, most of them centering on Eddie Hodges, a nice youngster but too patently an emblem of vulnerable innocence. He doesn't cry much, but you know he could, and shouldn't have to.

Missing, too, is the kind of ready-made conflict that many of Capra's earlier pictures had in common. (pp. 50-1)

[Unfortunately], the film, or rather its plot, has no direction, and its origins in television and the stage are only too apparent. There is simply too little conflict and much too little motivation for a picture nearly two hours long. The hero isn't willing to be a "little man"; he has plans. . . . The only suspense hinges on whether Tony will realize the folly of his dreams in time to save his hotel from bankruptcy and his son from the living death of adoption by a miserly uncle. This is melodrama without the drama. In the end he keeps the boy, apparently keeps the hotel, gets a girl not only prettier but more sensible than the "wild bird" he's been playing around with, and so infects his brother that they're both convinced that hope is enough. Well. It isn't much, and it doesn't go anywhere, and the laughter-through-tears approach backfires. Leaving what? Mainly laughter.

For this is a funny picture, getting its laughs often and nearly always legitimately. (p. 51)

Joseph Kostolefsky, "Film Reviews: 'A Hole in the Head'," in Film Quarterly *(copyright 1959 by The Regents of the University of California; reprinted by permission of the University of California Press), Vol. XIII, No. 1, Fall, 1959, pp. 50-2.*

JOHN CUTTS

The films of Frank Capra have been a parade of some of the best things yet produced by the American Cinema. And they have been films very American in outlook, humour and feeling. This is not to say, far from it, that his work has been limited in its appeal. Rather that Capra has a definite talent for evoking American dreams and hopes. Since the war, the director has only made a brief handful of pictures . . . , but, even so, his general neglect in post-war critical circles has been shameful. . . . I can't help feeling that his latest film, *Pocketful of Miracles,* is in for a somewhat stormy critical passage.

In the first place, it's such a blithe and cheery piece. A film not above wearing its heart (with a capital H) firmly upon its sleeve. A film unashamedly sentimental, brashly humorous, and determinedly high-spirited. A frolic, a romp, a fairy-tale set against a glitter of neon lights (neon-realism?) —call it what you will. But in short: a completely *open* piece of sunny entertainment. A film to be accepted firmly on its own carefree terms or not accepted at all. . . .

Capra doesn't demand that you believe in [his] Broadway gypsies, nor indeed does he ask you to accept too resolutely his plot. But it's obvious that he hopes that his wild shenanigans will amuse: and this they do very comfortably. . . .

Pocketful of Miracles is far from being perfect: its pace is often slipshod, its dramatic shape is formless, and at two-and-a-quarter hours it's *much, much too long*. All this I readily grant, yet the film is to be enjoyed. It's no earth-shaker, neither is it a revelation.

John Cutts, "New Films: 'Pocketful of Miracles'" (© copyright John Cutts 1962; reprinted with permission), in Films and Filming, *Vol. 8, No. 4, January, 1962, p. 29.*

ISABEL QUIGLY

Strictly for adults of a sort is a fairy-tale you can spot by its title, *Pocketful of Miracles*. . . . The odd thing about it isn't its badness but the fact that, bad as it is, it is made by Frank Capra, that legendary name, and made through and through, produced and directed; and it is tempting to read permanent declensions into what, after all, may be just one of those aberrations that warm-hearted souls are liable to. Capra, champion of the underdog, the simple and the inarticulate, might suddenly—it isn't all that surprising—be carried away into sentimentality by a tale about a tippling old apple-woman and her golden-hearted gangster friends. The surprise is in how far he has gone, how obvious, even how unprofessional it all seems.

Isabel Quigly, "The Gulliver Game," in The Spectator *(© 1962 by* The Spectator; *reprinted by permission of* The Spectator*), Vol. 208, No. 6967, January 5, 1962, p. 18.**

JAMES PRICE

[Whatever] it is that gives the thirties their air of curious innocence also gives Capra, at this distance, a slight but distinct aspect of futility. The hero of *Mr Smith Goes to Washington* consciously embraces a lost cause, but twenty-four years later the nobility of this looks faintly ridiculous and pathetic. In a period insulated at one end by a technical innovation (the sound film) and at the other by the war, Capra suffers the fate of his generation. . . . Capra speaks to us now in accents poignant but somehow muffled. . . .

This is most true of the most perfect of the comedies, the earliest of the films. . . .

[For example, most] of the humours of *It Happened One Night* [rise] out of the contrast between [Peter], tough, self-possessed, uncouth but endearingly honest and straightforward, and [Ellie], tough, self-possessed, extremely at ease yet ready to deceive herself and others about her feelings. (p. 87)

[Peter is] interesting to me as an embodiment of certain native virtues which Capra is holding up for our admiration. Capra is a moralist; and he contrasts [Peter's] independence and absorption with his work with [Ellie's] world of money and idleness. What [Peter] stands for is good: what [Ellie's] aviator stands for is bad. . . .

It is not hard to see how influential the film has been in the later development of the cinema. It may however take a second glance to notice that its success was the result not only of a wily balancing of contrasts, but also of a profound optimism. It is this optimism which gives the film what I can only describe as its quality of euphoric warmth. The sequence at the end of the film, when [Ellie] breaks away from the aviator as they are about to be married, and runs in her wedding dress across the crowded lawn to join [Peter], transports the audience both by the beauty of the images and by the lyrical movement: the talk and the misunderstandings are resolved in one sweeping decisive gesture. Of course, ninety-nine out of a hundred films end with lovers falling into each other's arms; it is part of the common language of popular art. The distinction of this film, I think, lies principally in three things. First, Capra's optimism is of the sort which generalizes, and it asserts itself in the face of unlikely odds. . . .

Secondly, but connected with this, the basis of the comedy is character, and the characters are realized fully enough for the climax when it comes to be both painful and exhilarating for the audience: Capra convinces us, in the terms of his art, that [Ellie] and [Peter] are real people, and their reality is not left behind at the end. And thirdly, his talents (in this instance) are so matched to what he sets out to do, and he works so easily within his own limits, that without any sense of straining for effect he succeeds in giving the film a warmth of feeling and a great fastidiousness of perception. (p. 89)

[*Mr Deeds Goes to Town* and *Mr Smith Goes to Washington*] are more ambitious in content than *It Happened One Night,* but to me they are less successful; not, I think, because he overreaches himself within his own terms but because his analysis of the realities of money and politics seems . . . to be over-simple. . . . Both Smith and Deeds represent a kind of American wholesomeness which (as in the earlier film) Capra proceeds to demonstrate doing battle against impossible odds. They are his personal contribution to the New Deal. (p. 91)

[In spite of surface similarities], *Mr Smith* seems to me to be quite a different film from *Mr Deeds.* In the early days of the Roosevelt era the straightforward solutions were novel and convincing; but by 1939, if this film is a reliable indicator, obdurate problems remained, and the straightforward solutions had a hollow sound to them. The film doesn't recognize alternatives to Jefferson Smith's appeal to constitutional principles (except perhaps obliquely in a reference to representatives of two totalitarian powers watching his performance from the Senate gallery), and this clearly is its serious limitation. It is at once Capra's most overtly patriotic and most desperately sceptical film.

It is also extremely uneven in quality. The scenes in the Senate, including an impressive sequence of Smith's arraignment before a committee (like Deeds he doesn't at first defend himself) have a solidity which I found intensely gripping. But elsewhere it is a little too anxious to get its message across, at the expense of character and narrative flow. . . . (pp. 91, 93)

Mr Deeds is completer, more fully imagined and better written. . . . [Because] it concerns money, *Mr Deeds* is a more obviously Puritan film than the others. Man has a natural dignity which money corrupts and debases. . . .

And yet, for all that, money remains desirable. Deeds becomes fabulously rich and is not corrupted by it; indeed having money makes it possible for him to exercise the supreme Puritan virtue of giving it away. In America all things are possible: a boys' club leader can become a senator, a bashful tuba-player from the Middle West can inherit an empire. The meek shall inherit the earth, say some. But for Capra it is a matter of individuals, and in this sense he is the most unsocialist of preachers. And not merely unsocialist: in his reiteration of optimistic themes, his self-imitation, and above all in his moral and political innocence, there is something of a twentieth-century Pangloss. (p. 93)

James Price, "Capra and the American Dream," in London Magazine *(© London Magazine 1964), Vol. 3, No. 10, January, 1964, pp. 85, 87, 89, 91, 93.*

WILLIAM S. PECHTER

The unique Capra genre has been defined by Richard Griffith, the film historian, as the "fantasy of goodwill," and he has also described its archetypical pattern. "In each film, a messianic innocent, not unlike the classic simpletons of literature . . . pits himself against the forces of entrenched greed. His inexperience defeats him strategically, but his gallant integrity in the face of temptation calls forth the goodwill of the 'little people,' and through their combined protest, he triumphs." This ritual of innocence triumphant did little to ingratiate Capra to an intellectual audience to whom he represented only the triumph of the *Saturday Evening Post.* But though the apparent vein of cheery optimism which informs this ritual's re-enactment *is,* of course, precisely that quality which both endears Capra to his popular audience and alienates an intellectual one, yet, in seeing the films again, this quality seems strangely elusive, forever asserting itself on set occasions, but always dissipating itself finally in a kind of shrill excitement. There are even intimations of something like melancholy constantly lurking beneath the surface glare of happy affirmation. (pp. 125-26)

Compared to Capra's subsequent films, [*Mr. Deeds Goes to Town*] is the most unreservedly "positive" in tone. Longfellow Deeds does, indeed, win out, and innocence triumphs. The rustic poet *cum* tuba confronts the powerful presence of metropolitan venality, and not only effects a personal victory, but manages to impress the cynical—a reminder of their own lost innocence—with his exemplary goodness as well. The memory of innocence lost is a crucially disturbing one in Capra's films, and central to any understanding of them. While the progress from small-town purity to big-city corruption may not, in fact, be part of the audience's personal history, it remains a fact of its acquired cultural legacy. That is, it is part of the inherited myth of an American past—of quiet, shady, tree-lined streets of white wood homes—which is so concretely a part of an American childhood that it persists into adulthood as a psychological fact, with the force of memory. And while the audience is asked to, and indeed must, identify with the innocent hero, it cannot fail to recognize itself, if not quite consciously, more nearly depicted in the images of his antagonists—the cynics, smart guys, hustlers, chiselers, opportunists, exploiters, hypocrites: all the corrupt; all our failed selves; what we have become. We respond finally to the classic Capra hero, whether Mr. Smith or John Doe, the uniquely American Everyman, with a kind of reluctant longing. He is our conscience *manqué,* the image of our childhood selves, reminding us, as we do not wish to be reminded, of the ways and degrees to which we have failed this image; all reaching some comic apotheosis in the figure of . . . Mr. Smith, in Washington, quite literally, a big Boy Scout.

What moderates the merely Sunday school piety of the Capra hero, what keeps his meaning just short of the moralizing "essay" on the page before the murder case in our Sunday supplements, is always some specifically foolish, specifically human trait which becomes the comic correlative of virtue. . . . The virtue of the characters seems inseparable from their absurdity, and, bound up as it is with this absurdity, passes from the ideality of the Sunday moral to the reality of a concrete human embodiment. (pp. 126-27)

It is the formularized happy ending which has always seemed the fatal weakness of Capra's films; the apparent belief that everything will turn out all right in the end serves, finally, only to nullify any serious moral concern. Yet this convention of the happy ending seems, on closer look, to be curiously quarantined in Capra's films, and the observance of it has often been strangely perfunctory. . . . I am not at all sure that Capra rejects the validity of the happy ending, but what one detects, in the abrupt changes of style, is some knowledge, if less than conscious, of the discrepancy between the complex nature of his film's recurring antitheses and the evasive facility of their resolution.

To understand this is to come to a film such as *It's a Wonderful Life* with a fresh eye. For it is in this film that Capra effects the perfect equipose between the antitheses he poses and the apparatus by which he reconciles them; there being, in fact, no recourse in "real life," the end is served by the intervention of a literal *deus ex machina*. And, as George Bailey, the film's hero, jumps into the river to commit suicide as the culmination of his progress of disastrous failures, he is saved . . . by an angel! This is, of course, the perfect, and, in fact, only, alternative for Capra; and the *deus ex machina* serves its classic purpose, from *Iphigenia in Tauris* to *The Threepenny Opera;* namely, to satisfy an understanding of the work on every level. It creates, for those who wish it, the happy ending par excellence, since it had already become apparent, in the previous Capra movies, that the climaxes, by the very extremity of the situations which gave rise to them, were derived *de force majeure*. (pp. 127-28)

It's a Wonderful Life is the kind of work which defies criticism; almost, one might say, defies art. It is one of the funniest and one of the bleakest, as well as being one of the most technically adroit, films ever made; it is a masterpiece, yet rather of that kind peculiar to the film: unconscious masterpieces. (p. 129)

Capra has created for us an anthology of indelible images of predatory greed, political corruption, the cynical manipulation of public opinion, the murderous nature of private enterprise, and the frustration and aridity of small-town American life. There is always a gulf between what Capra wishes to say and what he actually succeeds in saying. He seems obsessed with certain American social myths, but he observes that society itself as a realist. (p. 131)

His films move at a breath-taking clip: dynamic, driving, taut, at their extreme even hysterical; the unrelenting, frantic acceleration of pace seems to be the release of some tremendous accumulation of pressure. The sheer speed and energy seem, finally, less calculated than desperate, as though Capra were aware, on some level, of the tension established between his material and what he attempts to make of it. Desperation—in this quality of Capra's films one sees again the fundamental nature of style as moral action: Capra's desperation is his final honesty. It ruthlessly exposes his own affirmation as pretense, and reveals, recklessly and without defense, dilemma. (pp. 131-32)

Unlike any of Capra's other films, *State of the Union* seems anxious to retreat into its subplot, one of romantic misalliance. And all the hoopla of its finale, as frenetic and noisy as anything Capra has put on the screen, cannot disguise the fact that the hero resigns from politics with the implication being that he is, in fact, *too good* to be involved. In one sense, this is Capra at his most realistic, but also at his least engaged. For the artist, withdrawal from the world—the world as he perceives it—is never achieved without some radical diminution of his art.

Perhaps, having made *It's a Wonderful Life,* there was nothing more Capra had to say. His only fruitful alternative, having achieved a kind of perfection within his own terms, had to be to question the very nature of those terms themselves. Without a realization that the dilemma existed inherently in the terms in which he articulated it, he could, in effect, go no further. It remains only to note that he went no further. (p. 132)

William S. Pechter, "American Madness" (originally published in a different version as "American Madness: Frank Capra's America," in Kulchur, *Vol. 3, No. 2, Winter, 1963), in his* Twenty-Four Times a Second *(copyright © 1960, 1961, 1962, 1963, 1965, 1968, 1969, 1970, 1971 by William S. Pechter; reprinted by permission of the author), Harper & Row, Publishers, Inc., 1971, pp. 123-32.*

ANDREW BERGMAN

Capra's erratic background was reflected in his best films. The seemingly wide-eyed immigrant boy who travelled the traditional path to success in college (carrying trays in the commons, pen and slide rule concealed beneath the white jacket) was obviously one with faith in the classic American route to opportunity and fulfillment. But the Capra who hustled farmers and sold coupons to their wives, the Capra who turned from chemical engineering to the glib sales pitch and "I'm from Hollywood," was more cold-eyed than wide-eyed. Those two Capras—immigrant dreamer and con man—gave a peculiarly attractive and beguiling quality to his best work. He had a perfect pitch for Americana, for depicting what he passed over as American types, and a sheer genius for manipulating those types. Capra's comedy was a wide-eyed and affectionate hustle—the masterwork of an idealist and door-to-door salesman. (pp. 134-35)

Before creating the screwball comedy, Capra seemed comfortable with the shyster mania that prevailed between 1931 and 1933. *Platinum Blonde* . . . showed his initial sympathy with, and attraction to, newspapermen and their racy urban milieu. His hero was an urban Mr. Deeds, an individualist ace reporter with disdain for a world of "phonies." By 1936, the "phonies" would include those very newspapermen. (p. 135)

In the late thirties, Capra evolved the shyster into a vaguely fascistic threat. The urban sharper became the Wall Street giant, communications mogul, munitions kingpin, and reactionary political force embodied in the corpulent and bespectacled figure of Edward Arnold. Capra's emphasis upon the melting of class tensions changed as the decade ended. Class amiability, the end of *It Happened One Night* and *You Can't Take It With You* . . . , became a means. If the mid-thirties witnessed a stress on the resolution of social tensions, Capra, by 1939, fancied that resolution to be an accomplished fact. And so the common decency of all

Americans, rich and poor, got turned, in *Mr. Smith* and *Meet John Doe,* against threats to our most sacred national institutions. Capra was exchanging the symbols and dynamics of the thirties for those of the forties.

To see the Capra films from 1934 to 1941 is to learn more about a nation's image of itself than one has any right to expect. How much did Capra create, and how much did he respond to? His classlessness was an obvious fantasy, but the myth obviously was dear to Americans. He created a tradition in effecting a screwball social peace of *It Happened One Night* and responded to tradition in *Deeds* by neutralizing the shyster world, a world very much Hollywood's creation. Once the thirties had been crossed with the nation's basic institutions intact and relatively unscathed, Capra was free to argue from greater strength; fascism was neither his nor Hollywood's creation.

The way in which Capra manipulated images—city, small town, village hero, profiteer, little man, government, radio—represented genius. He understood enough of what people wanted, after the revelation of the screwball comedies' gigantic success, to help create a consciousness, and to build himself into the system. His fantasy of a social unity entered into the quasi-reality of all mass media. Robert Warshow's remarkable insight that, although Americans rarely experienced gangsterism in their lives, "the experience of the gangster *as an experience of art* is universal to Americans," is extremely relevant to Capra. His America was an experience of art.

That world of Deeds and Smith and Doe had become part of the nation's self-image. No one knew that better than Frank Capra. "I never cease to thrill at an audience seeing a picture," he said. "For two hours you've got 'em. Hitler can't keep 'em that long. You eventually reach more people than Roosevelt does on the radio." By the time he started the *Why We Fight* series, Capra could know that Americans were fighting for, among other things, Frank Capra films. (pp. 147-48)

Andrew Bergman, "Frank Capra and Screwball Comedy, 1931-1941," in his We're in the Money: Depression America and Its Films *(reprinted by permission of New York University Press; copyright © 1971 by New York University), New York University Press, 1971, pp. 132-48.*

JEFFREY RICHARDS

The Pursuit of Happiness is, perhaps, more than any other, the central theme in Capra's work. Happiness is to be found in peace, contentment, enjoyment of life, above all, freedom from the rat race, the individual asserting himself to escape from the oppressive hand of the forces of Organization. This idea was expressed in abstract terms in *Lost Horizon* . . . , a film dismissed by almost all influential film critics as pretentious and absurd. . . . In fact, it is one of the most dazzling pieces of film-making to come out of Hollywood in the '30s. . . . The last memorable image of the film is of Robert, a lone, tiny figure, against a vast expanse of snow, struggling onwards through a blinding storm, trying to find his way back to Shangri-la. This image crystallizes Capra's preoccupation with the Pursuit of Happiness. In *Lost Horizon* the plane's passengers have been carefully chosen to illustrate different aspects of the Rat Race. Robert Conway is a soldier and diplomat (the double-dealing world of diplomacy), Chalmers Bryant is a failed businessman (victim of Big Business), Gloria Stone is a showgirl (the empty glitter of Show Business), and Alexander P. Lovett is a palaeontologist (the aridity of the Intellectual World). All find peace and contentment in Shangri-la, their participation in the Rat Race at an end. (pp. 66-7)

The series of Populist comedy-moralities, which emerged fully formed with *Mr. Deeds*, culminated in *It's a Wonderful Life* . . . and *State of the Union*. . . . With them, it was as if Capra had said the last word on the Populist philosophy. Since then, he has made only four films, and in them he has reverted to his pre-Deeds period (two of the films are actually remakes of early pre-Deeds successes). The detailed philosophic content, and the comment on social, political and economic problems are missing. Gone is the small town background, the Cooper-Stewart innocent. In Capra's later films, his heroes are reversions to the urban figures of the early films (newspapermen in *Here Comes the Groom,* hotel-owner in *A Hole in the Head,* bootlegger in *A Pocketful of Miracles*). The reason for this is easily apparent. Capra has realized that the world has moved on and that the forces of Organization have finally triumphed. The need for unified state control of the war effort set the seal on the victory of the New Deal. Though there was a backlash after the war, with McCarthyism, its anti-intellectual bias, and the triumph of the Republicans under the new folk hero Eisenhower, the heart had gone out of Populism. *It's a Wonderful Life* marks Capra's last, great, triumphant affirmation of faith in individualism. It becomes an allegory of post-war America. Bedford Falls represents the nation, Henry Potter the forces of Organization and George Bailey the spirit of Individualism. In the film, it is George Bailey who triumphs, but in fact it has been Henry Potter. (p. 71)

Jeffrey Richards, "Frank Capra and the Cinema of Populism," in Film Society Review, *Vol. 7, Nos. 7-9, March-May, 1972, pp. 61-71.*

STEPHEN HANDZO

To a remarkable extent, Capra's films caught the mood of America in the Thirties and Forties. When sufficiently little was happening in the world for the masses to be bemused for weeks by the deserved misfortunes of the rich, Capra rebuilt the Depression-bruised male ego with reassurance that, despite unemployment, he was still virile and the master of any situation. . . . *Deeds* and *You Can't Take It With You* combined the folk experience of the Depression (bankruptcy, eviction) born equally of the renewed confidence inspired by the New Deal and the need to dispel the lingering malaise. *Mr. Smith* tempered the muckraking of the earlier Thirties with the vindication of a flawed democracy that was threatened with extinction abroad. *Doe* (visually darker than earlier Capra, and not just because of a different cameraman) caught that moment when, in Roosevelt's phrase, Dr. New Deal gave way to Dr. Win-the-War. . . .

Internally, the Capra films became more pessimistic, though this was not immediately apparent. Only in *Deeds* does the hero win a clear victory by his own efforts. In *Smith*, the end is more absurdist than triumphal, and the popular protests are all beaten down. . . . [In] *Doe* the people's movement is completely discredited. . . . In Capra's later films, the hero is often saved by a directorial decree as dictatorial as it is delirious.

The acquisition of awareness, simultaneously social and sexual, is the subject of *Mr. Deeds, Mr. Smith,* and *John Doe*. In *State of the Union,* awareness includes the hero's own culpability. . . . And, after the confession of *State of the Union*, there was no place left to go. (p. 14)

Stephen Handzo, "Under Capracorn: A Decade of Good Deeds and Wonderful Lives," in Film Comment *(copyright © 1972 Film Comment Publishing Corporation; all rights reserved), Vol. 8, No. 4, November-December, 1972, pp. 8-14.*

JOYCE NELSON

Capra, by utilizing character 'types', references to Populist heroes, and comic-strip forms of editing, has created, in *Mr. Smith Goes to Washington,* a film which, however much it may appear to be exploring complex issues, remains an appeal to child-like wish-fulfillment in its world of hero and villains.

Long before we actually see Jefferson Smith . . . on screen, Capra provides us with the essentials of his character. First, Capra peoples the Taylor Political Machine with rotund, cigar-smoking 'types' easily recognizable as villainous. Smith will contrast both physically and morally with this group. Next, Capra associates him with innocence by having his name be suggested for Senator by the Governor's children: "He put out a big forest fire. . . . He can recite everything George Washington said by heart!" The fact that Smith is leader of the Boy Rangers underscores this innocence. Finally, Capra utilizes a bit of 'divine intervention' by having the coin the Governor tosses to make his decision land on its edge. . . . It is not until the acceptance speech at the small-town banquet that we first see Jefferson Smith, and there the full impact of his Populist features are brought home to us: his name, evoking Thomas Jefferson (a true Populist hero), his stature—tall and lean—suggesting Abe Lincoln, and his awkwardness at 'speech-making' associating him with agrarian values of modesty, honesty and simplicity. (pp. 246-48)

Capra's mistrust of the mass media is substantiated by his having the press humiliate Smith with his homespun bird-calls and ridiculous Indian signs. Since this press conference was set up by Saunders, the film is continuing to shift our identification away from her cynicism to one of real sympathy for Smith. (p. 250)

It is in the action of the filibuster that *Mr. Smith Goes to Washington* seems to most convincingly express its Populism, as differentiated from simple optimistic sentiments. In an interview, Capra has mentioned that "another expression of optimism is movement, life, energy, vibrancy—men going places and doing things, not dropping off in corners." Yet, the whole visualisation of Smith conducting the filibuster is that of a man isolated, backed up against the Chamber wall, standing immobile, while action occurs around him, or more often, entirely away from him. As the Senate Chambers empty, Smith is alone in his mission. Even the people in his home state are first unaware of his stand, and later unable to beat the Taylor Machine through the Boy Rangers' newspaper. By the adoption of the filibuster technique, Smith stops the passage of the entire bill (which is said to be desperately needed by the people) in order to focus on his own smaller portion of it. Obviously, Smith chooses this excessive measure to ensure publicity for his cause, and it is only another individual action—the public confession of Senator Paine/Silver Knight—that can alter the situation. Thus, the film associates oratory, individualism, and public prominence with Jefferson Smith, thereby aligning him with the patriotic figures of the past, first seen in the bus tour montage, as does his choice of reading matter to sustain the filibuster—the Declaration of Independence. (pp. 252-53)

Capra's use of comic-strip elements is at once a source of the film's power to engage its audience as well as its means for avoiding the deeper political and ideological issues it might raise. These qualities in the film may help to explain the antagonism it aroused in contemporary statesmen and the popularity it found commercially. The workings of democracy are obviously more complicated than a game, and its legislators not easily typed as "trained seals" or Silver Knights. (p. 254)

Joyce Nelson, "'Mr. Smith Goes to Washington': Capra, Populism and Comic-Strip Art," in Journal of Popular Film *(copyright © 1974 by Sam L. Grogg, Jr., Michael T. Marsden, and John G. Nachbar), Vol. III, No. 3, 1974. pp. 245-55.*

FRANÇOIS TRUFFAUT

Capra is the last survivor of that great quartet of American comedy; Leo McCarey, Ernst Lubitsch, and Preston Sturges. An Italian, born in Palermo, he brought to Hollywood the secrets of the *commedia dell'arte.* He was a navigator who knew how to steer his characters into the deepest dimensions of desperate human situations (I have often wept during the tragic moments of Capra's comedies) before he reestablished a balance and brought off the miracle that let us leave the theater with a renewed confidence in life.

The growing harshness of social life after the war, the spread of egoism, the obstinate conviction of the rich that they could "take it with them" made his miracles even more improbable. But, in the face of human anguish, doubt, unrest, and the struggle just to manage daily life, Capra was a kind of healer, that is, the enemy of "official" medicine. This good doctor was also a great director.

François Truffaut, "Frank Capra, the Healer" (1974), in his The Films in My Life, *translated by Leonard Mayhew (copyright © 1975 by, Flammarion; translation copyright © 1978 by, Simon and Schuster; reprinted by permission of Simon and Schuster, a Division of Gulf & Western Corporation; originally published as* Les Films de ma vie, *Flammarion, 1975), Simon and Schuster, 1978, p. 69.*

DONALD C. WILLIS

I interpret [the slump of Capra's films in the later thirties] as Capra's initially faltering attempt to assimilate an acute, new, altruistic impulse (which he accounts for, somewhat mystically, in his book) into his highly-refined filmmaking technique. (p. 2)

If *Mr. Deeds Goes to Town, Lost Horizon* and *You Can't Take It With You* happened to become box-office hits, it's almost entirely due to Capra's technical, sugar-coating skills, to his gift for entertaining, to the fact that [his] first "message" movies didn't just awkwardly "say something." There is a discernible gap between the entertaining surfaces of *Mr. Deeds* and *You Can't Take It With You* and their simplistic, preachy cores, and the surfaces were what attracted the public. *Lost Horizon* seems to me defective even on the surface, and its success baffles me. It's only with the end of *Mr. Smith Goes to Washington* that the gap between Capra's need to say something and his technical brilliance begins to close, ultimately to produce *Meet John Doe* and *It's a Wonderful Life*, in which message and technique are one, in which the meaning is the whole film, not just a nugget of wisdom to be extracted from it and examined independently or simply ignored.

Mr. Deeds Goes to Town is primarily important as the blueprint for Capra's idealistic-American-hero films. . . . Capra pits idealism squarely against cynicism, and does it more and more sharply. In *Mr. Deeds, Mr. Smith, John Doe,* and *Wonderful Life,* Capra seemed to be getting progressively closer to what he most wanted to do and say with film. (pp. 2-3)

One difference between those two films, *Mr. Deeds* and *Mr. Smith*, and *Meet John Doe* is that in the latter the accent has shifted, the spotlight is pulled back and up to encompass the simpleton hero and his exploiters. . . .

The difference between *Meet John Doe* and *It's a Wonderful Life* is that both good and evil remain at the end of *Wonderful Life*; one doesn't cancel the other out. (p. 3)

Frank Capra's greatest talent lay in vivifying traditional concepts of brotherhood, of the importance of the individual, of the sacredness of life, and at the same time suggesting why such cherished concepts are inadequate to a full understanding of life. *Meet John Doe* and *It's a Wonderful Life*, in particular, recognize both the indispensability and the limitations of such concepts. Maybe there's a place and a need for blind yea-saying. (p. 4)

What I find so compelling about *Meet John Doe* and *It's a Wonderful Life* is that they take their simple-minded messages of uplift seriously, but in the larger context of a world which requires more than simple, if helpful, formulas, a world which, in fact, seems to require the hero's suicide when those formulas fail. They don't, on the one hand, take their uplifting messages at face value or, on the other, reject them. There's some play between affirmation and negation. Other movies like *Meet John Doe* (e.g., *Ace in the Hole, Face in the Crowd*), on the exploitation of the "common people," are purely cynical, as glibly and efficiently exploiting their subject as their heroes exploit the people. They're exhilarating but incomplete. They have a convincing negative but no positive. Their heroes are just shrewd operators, charlatans, and the fascination of the films lies almost exclusively in the audacity of their heroes' machinations. (pp. 5-6)

[The] main theme of Capra's—the longing for life versus the longing for death, or respite from life—is most urgently expressed in *It's a Wonderful Life*. It doesn't take either easy way out, making its case only for life or only for death. In *Mr. Smith Goes to Washington*, the issues are left hanging, unfinished. In *Mr. Deeds Goes to Town*, the undercurrents of remorse and self-pity are too heavy for the flimsily-constructed vehicle. *Meet John Doe* and *It's a Wonderful Life* are so constructed that suicide at one point seems to be the only answer for the hero. His feelings of bitterness and despair don't seem indulgent or fabricated. (p. 7)

If Capra must be categorized politically, I'd say that, based on his major films, he was apolitical, anti-political, or, based on *Meet John Doe*, a nihilist. . . .

For all their political frenzy, Capra's films are not really definable in political terms. They were made with a vaguely-defined "public" in mind, not a party or an ideology. They break political "rules" and splice ideologies together. It's not for nothing that they're often called "fantasies." . . . (p. 9)

Capra's films (even his failures) generally display a deep dissatisfaction with the status quo, a deep dissatisfaction with life. They say, in effect, that life may or may not be good, but it could definitely be better. . . .

Platitudinizing may mar the surface of most Capra movies, but Capra's dramatic sense wouldn't let it infect the whole (though his dramatic sense failed to detect the laxity of *Lost Horizon,* and the platitudes were stranded in the middle of nothing). The ideals of brotherhood, happiness, and true love aren't taken for granted. They're something to be struggled for, and won (as in *It's a Wonderful Life*) or lost (as with *You Can't Take It With You, Lost Horizon,* or the obviously-wrong, tacked-on ending of *Meet John Doe*), but the usually bitter fight the Capra hero must make to realize them indicates a deep discontent with things as they are. (p. 11)

Donald C. Willis, in his The Films of Frank Capra *(copyright 1974 by Donald C. Willis), The Scarecrow Press, Inc., 1974, 214 p.*

LELAND A. POAGUE

As a general rule, comedy attends to and reflects upon human desires for love, life, and fertility. Comic plots emphasize sequences of reversal and recovery that in turn reflect mythological sequences of death and rebirth. . . .

Elements of the miraculous, the wonderful, and the fantastic are found in all comedies. Shakespeare's comedies abound with fantastic characters and situations. . . .

Capra's films present no exception to this general comic characteristic. Aspects of the improbable, the fantastic, and the unexpected always seem at work in Capra's films, throwing characters off balance, upsetting their sense of equilibrium, deceiving and confusing normally perceptive individuals. Few people, after all, ever find themselves seated beside a runaway heiress on a New York-bound bus. Few people inherit twenty-million dollars. Few Boy Scout leaders suddenly find themselves in the U.S. Senate. Few beggars find themselves hosting the Governor of New York at a penthouse reception.

Hence, the first rule of the comic universe in general and the Capra universe in particular is that normal everyday rules of probability do not always apply. In other words, the everyday rules are "off." Such a suspension of probability allows Capra to put his characters in fantastic situations that require that they rethink their own sense of self and morality, working through the morass of their own emotional and perceptual mistakes towards a renewed awareness of emotional and intellectual reality. (p. 227)

What we see in Capra, then, is actually a latter-day equivalent of the Roman Saturnalia, a period of madcap license in which "all normal business and ceremony [were] put aside for the duration of the holiday, and masters and servants exchanged roles; the slaves sat at table wearing their master's clothes and the *pilleus,* or badge of freedom, and enjoyed the right to abuse their masters, who served them." The rules of everyday human interaction are suspended, and the world is turned upside-down . . . : the low are made great, and the great are brought low, and the final effect is one of "leveling," making all characters undergo the democratic experience of absolute equality under the benevolent providence of the comic spirit. . . . The Vanderhoff household in *You Can't Take It With You* . . . is a good example of such saturnalian equality at work. (p. 228)

[The] second rule of the Capra universe is that the "off" rules are always poised to reassert themselves. As in *Pocketful of Miracles* . . . , we are always aware that the fairy-tales of improbable fortune can return at any moment to the logical fate of everyday life. (pp. 229-30)

Such a balance between wish fulfillment and reality principles is a hallmark of mature comedy. Holiday and everyday only have meaning when placed in opposition. We cannot appreciate the freedom of release unless the bondage of everyday life, with its mundane logic and requirements, remains in our minds. And it is this skill at maintaining the delicate balance between wanting and getting, the probable and the improbable, appealing to our anarchic desires without forgetting our very strong sense of reality and probability, that characterizes Capra's use of the comic form. He is fully aware of human hopes, and yet he is, particularly in the Capra romances, fully cognizant of the ease with which human hopes can lead to disappointment and disaster.

But Capra's mastery of form does not completely account for the great success of his films. Capra's primary concern is with human beings and human emotions. Accordingly, the "reality" of Capra's films depends upon the reality of Capra's characters. Do they act as we would act if we were in their admittedly fantastic shoes? I think the answer to that question is generally an unqualified "yes." Capra creates a sense of emotional necessity: given this situation, these characters would experience these emotions and make these moves. Capra obviously constructs his films to achieve this feeling of emotional verisimilitude, but we never sense the construction. There is a natural "lifelike" flow to Capra's movies, and it is this emotional rhythm that strikes us as realistically accurate. Our reaction as spectators is never "this could never happen to me," but rather "if that did happen to me, that is precisely how I would feel about it, precisely how I would handle it." Therein lies the "truth" of the Capra cinema. His world is self-contained and consistent, yet it arouses and reflects upon actual human emotions.

Thus another key factor in Capra's success is audience identification. His movies are festivities and are about festivities. His characters experience a "rules-off" situation where new emotional and intellectual responses are required, and similarly we as spectators experience a "rules-off" situation where we are free to identify with and feel very deeply about the characters and their struggles. . . .

But our knowledge and hence our experience is often more complete than that of the characters. We are often aware of situational ironies unknown to the characters themselves. For example, in *It Happened One Night* . . . , we know that Ellie and Peter love each other. Accordingly, our sense of anxiety is in fact greater than that of either Ellie or Peter near the film's conclusion when she is about to marry Westley, for we realize how agonizingly narrow yet how unbridgeably wide is the gap between them: if they would only drop their cynical masks for a moment to see each other as we see them, people deeply in love, the properly comic conclusion would be assured and fertility would symbolically triumph. Our sense of frustration is as great as if not greater than that of the characters. (p. 230)

But Capra does not just put us through an emotional ringer. It is not a matter of cheap thrills and Hollywood daydreams. Peter and Ellie count because they represent a properly attentive sort of human concern: were they not so sensitive to each other they would not be so easily hurt. Thus Capra's point, a mature point at that, is that one should remain both sensitive (as we are when we watch the film) and vulnerable (as we are when we watch the film), willing to risk hurt for the sake of legitimate emotional involvement. (p. 231)

To a great extent, then, the Capra cinema is about involvement, the way situations can demand greater degrees of emotional hazard and commitment than we had at first thought possible or necessary. This is true both for Capra's characters and the members of the audience. Capra's moral code is a function of this involvement: life is a swift-running, exhilarating stream, and each person shares the responsibility of insuring that the stream of existence runs ever onward. Capra's cynics and romantics are thus reprehensible because they refuse to immerse themselves in the rhythm of life. They are captured by their dreams or disappointments, and hence they tend to destroy themselves or to destroy others. But life, human life, is too wonderful and precious to be thus destroyed, and the cinema of Frank Capra serves as an aesthetic reminder both of life's mystery and our responsibility as human beings to insure life's continuity. We must maintain an appropriate sense of commitment, sensitive, vulnerable, deeply felt, in our otherwise everyday lives. The Capra universe is a world upside-down, but thus suspended we are given a closer look at the nature of human emotional reality. Such is the poet's task. Such is Frank Capra's accomplishment. (pp. 232, 234)

Leland A. Poague, in his The Cinema of Frank Capra: An Approach to Film Comedy *(© 1973 by Leland A. Poague; © 1975 by A. S. Barnes and Company, Inc.), A. S. Barnes and Company, 1975, 252 p.*

JOHN RAEBURN

American Madness, [Capra's] film about an idealistic banker, is one of the finest American movies to emerge from the early years of the Depression. Very little in Capra's early career as a director suggested he was capable of creating a film as sharp in its social observation and as ambitious in its analysis of American values as this melodrama about robbery, murder, a bank panic, and the conflict between social responsibility and greed. (p. 57)

There is a good deal of "business" in the plot of *American Madness* but basically the film centers on what would become Capra's perennial subject in his best films: the conflict between a resolute individual, full of goodwill toward his fellow men, and the forces of disunity and corruption who would create and exploit social dislocations for their own benefit. (pp. 57-8)

Capra's mastery of his medium is obvious in *American Madness,* as it would be in most of his later films. Form and content are inextricably linked, and meaning derives from the fusion of the two. The tempo of the film, for example, is perfectly synchronized with the action. (p. 58)

Like any superior artist Capra shows rather than tells his audience what it needs to know. The relationship between Cyril Cluett . . . , the chief cashier, and Dude Finley . . . , the gangster to whom he is in debt, is obviously an important one which has to be established early in the film; and Capra reveals it with a visual subtlety and an economy beyond the powers of a less gifted director. . . . [By] purely visual means, Capra establishes not only Finley's disreputability, but also Cluett's indebtedness to him. It is only when the four men are walking together back to Cluett's office that we overhear one of the bank employees say to another, "Isn't that Dude Finley? He's one of the toughest gangsters in town." (p. 59)

[The] dialogue is vivid and colloquial. . . . Capra added to the naturalistic quality of the dialogue by having speakers overlap one another, as they often do in ordinary life; this was an innovation that helped to move the talkies away from the example of the legitimate stage, which early in the history of the sound film was an accepted but imperfect model for it.

It was not only with language, however, that *American Madness* extended the resources of the sound film. Capra also used sound as an important element for creating mood and for underscoring what was being seen on the screen. (pp. 59-60)

[*American Madness*] was a self-consciously topical film, rooted in the social tragedy of its times in a way few other Hollywood movies were. Capra's willingness to confront directly questions of social and cultural value—his artistic ambition, in other words—was one of the reasons his work was, and is, so satisfying. Yet for all its timeliness, the society we see in the movie is not American society of the 1930s, or even the 1920s; it is American society of the mid-nineteenth century, and even at that it is probably mythical. (p. 62)

[There was] a considerable degree of nostalgia in Capra's treatment of Tom Dickson and his bank, certainly not an unusual attitude in a period of extreme social distress. But Capra's nostalgia had a cutting edge that uncovered the reason for the passing of the old system, and it gave to his film a significance that a purely sentimental look at the past would have lacked. If it had not been a comedy, *American Madness* would have been an elegy for individualism; but since it was a comedy it pretended as if individualism were still the dominant ethic, while at the same time it undercut its own primary assumption by demonstrating that Tom Dickson was the last of a dying breed. (p. 63)

Capra was not of course the first to point out that the concentration of capital in ever-expanding corporate enterprises was making the individualistic ethic obsolete, but he was among the few artists—certainly in Hollywood, the very few—who were able to give this perception suitable dramatic form.

Capra's skillful exposition of the clash between the corporate and individualistic ethics would alone have made *American Madness* one of the most interesting films of the 1930s, but there is more to it even than that. Like Mark Twain, an artist whom he often resembles, Capra portrays American culture at its breaking point, but always within the context of a comic vision. . . .

It is in the scenes of the mob panic that Capra portrays most vividly his alarm about the state of American culture in the early years of the Depression. (p. 64)

Individual man, under the pressure of the Depression, was becoming mass man, and mass man was irrational, cruel, and uninterested in the value of community. Capra recently said—referring to *Mr. Deeds Goes to Town,* but the statement is even more appropriate for *American Madness*—that he "was fighting for . . . the preservation of the liberty of the individual against the mass." Tom Dickson is the exemplar of that besieged individual man, and he successfully resists absorption into the herd, and in fact disperses the herd, at least temporarily. But the potential for the mob to form again is still there—is *always* there—and if the conditions are right, it will surely reappear. The comity of American society (at least in Capra's model of it) is based upon the goodwill and the reasonableness of its members; and its encouragement of individually determined standards of conduct is at once its greatest strength and its greatest weakness. (p. 65)

This perception informs much of the action of *American Madness,* but is given specific representation in the figure of Oscar . . . , one of the tellers. Oscar is *l'homme moyen sensuel,* not corrupted like Cyril Cluett, not inspired by a lofty ideal like Tom Dickson; he is also the dramatic depiction of the potential ugliness which a social dislocation can uncover in the average man. He delights in disaster because of the tempting possibilities for self-aggrandizement it gives him. (pp. 65-6)

American Madness was much more than a "fantasy of goodwill." . . . The sense of crisis brought on by the Depression, with all of its implications for the private lives of Americans, permeates the film; and that crisis was far from over in 1932. Capra realized that it took very little in such times to unbalance the delicate equilibrium of American society, and the film never suggests that the period of testing was over. The goodwill was there but so was the implication that the battle would have to be fought again and again. The happy ending of *American Madness,* with Tom Dickson triumphant, only nominally resolved the insistent tension between the individualistic values Capra affirms by his portrait of the benevolent, resolute bank president and the herd instinct of Oscar and the mob which storms the bank; and it is the verve and subtlety with which this tension is made palpable that gives to the film its significance as both a social document and an important work of the imagination. (pp. 66-7)

John Raeburn, "'American Madness' and American Values," in Frank Capra: The Man and His Films, *edited by Richard Glatzer and John Raeburn (copyright © by the University of Michigan, 1975), University of Michigan Press, 1975, pp. 57-67.*

ROBIN WOOD

The most overtly presented of the . . . structural oppositions [in *It's a Wonderful Life*] is that between the two faces of Capitalism, benign and malignant: on the one hand, the Baileys (father and son) and their Building and Loan

Company, its business practice based on a sense of human needs and a belief in human goodness; on the other, Potter . . . , described explicitly as a spider, motivated by greed, egotism and miserliness, with no faith in human nature. Potter belongs to a very deeply rooted tradition. He derives most obviously from Dickens' Scrooge . . .—a Scrooge disturbingly unrepentant and irredeemable—but his more distant antecedents are in the ogres of fairy tales.

The opposition gives us not only two attitudes to money and property but two father-images (Bailey Sr. and Potter), each of whom gives his name to the land (Bailey Park, in small-town Bedford Falls, and Pottersville, the town's dark alternative). Most interestingly, the two figures (American choices, American tendencies) find their vivid ideological extensions in Hollywood genres: the happy, sunny world of small town comedy (Bedford Falls is seen mostly in the daytime), the world of *film noir,* the dark underside of Hollywood ideology. . . .

[Pottersville] is just as "real" (or no more stylized) than Bedford Falls. The iconography of small-town comedy is exchanged, unmistakably, for that of *film noir,* with police sirens, shooting in the streets, darkness, vicious dives, alcoholism, burlesque shows, strip clubs, the glitter and shadows of *noir* lighting. George's mother, embittered and malevolent, runs a seedy boarding-house; the good-time gal/wife-mother opposition, translated into *noir* terms, becomes an opposition of prostitute and repressed spinster-librarian. The towns emerge as equally valid images of America—validated by their generic familiarity. . . .

It's a Wonderful Life manages a convincing and moving affirmation of the values (and value) of bourgeois family life. Yet what is revealed, when disaster releases George's suppressed tensions, is the intensity of his resentment of the family and desire to destroy it—and with it, in significant relationship, his work (his culminating action is furiously to overthrow the drawing-board with his plans for more small-town houses). The film recognizes explicitly that behind every Bedford Falls lurks a Pottersville. . . . What is finally striking about the film's affirmation is the extreme precariousness of its basis; and Potter survives, without remorse, his crime unexposed and unpunished. It may well be Capra's masterpiece, but it is more than that. Like all the greatest American films—fed by a complex generic tradition and, beyond that, by the fears and aspirations of a whole culture—it at once transcends its director and would be inconceivable without him. (p. 49)

Robin Wood, "Ideology, Genre, Auteur," in Film Comment *(copyright © 1977 by The Film Society of Lincoln Center; all rights reserved), Vol. 13, No. 1, January-February, 1977, pp. 46-51.**

JOHN TIBBETTS

The Miracle Woman is perhaps the first American commercial feature film to deal intelligently with the less savory aspects of popular evangelism, showing it as a secularized merchandising of life and hope at the hands of ruthless opportunists. . . .

[The] film carries another implication more specifically pertinent to its immediate cultural and social context: Fallon's message of salvation on earth carries a special significance for the disadvantaged of Depression America. Her adherents, which include tenement families, middle-class citizens, and disabled veterans of the Great War, are a cross-section of those most desperately in need of hope and promise amidst a society plunged into economic chaos. *The Miracle Woman,* like so many other films of the 1929-1934 period, seems preoccupied with examining the nature and methods of those pretending to lead society out of financial, political, and spiritual troubles. Like *Gabriel over the White House, Duck Soup,* and *Diplomaniacs,* to cite just a few examples, it presents an ambiguous, if not overtly troubled portrait of the leaders of the times. Through *The Miracle Woman* we realize that not only were contemporary political and military issues in question, but those of the popular spiritual guides as well. (p. 293)

The film elaborately reveals the rigged aspects of Fallon's Temple. It is packed with shills planted into the audience by Hornsby to come forward to attest to Sister's healing powers. (p. 300)

Miraculously, the fakery in the film operates on a charming and whimsical level also, especially in the scenes between Fallon and her new-found love, the blind John Carson. Putting it bluntly, their courtship is itself one shill after another. (p. 302)

Consistent with her own preachments, her redemption is not one of *religion* so much as it is of *love.* What she really had been lacking all along was, apparently, the love of a man. From the beginning she had been isolated, with only the curt and surly relationship with Hornsby. It was as if her own religion of hoaxes was exacting its own peculiar kind of celibacy. But with John she achieved the traditional fulfillment of frustrations commonly ascribed to be the basis of activism among females of the day. . . .

From the opening sermon to the spectacular fire to the final shot, Capra achieves a carefully balanced variety of tones and textures. The opening and closing shots, for example, are quiet, statically lit, Fallon's garb simple and severe. In between, a more dynamic interplay of light and texture prevails. Her second sermon is a spectacular baroque play of spotlights, flying flower petals, and shimmering, almost transparent white robes halating in the light. (p. 303)

Capra knows that the key to our acceptance of this potentially disagreeable character lies in this variability. He shrewdly manipulates the ambivalence. At the same time she is conning the suckers in the Temple, we are gasping at her transformed beauty. Even before her confession to Carson, she is uncomfortable with her chicanery. . . .

We come away from her with the same kind of confusion felt toward her fictional and real life counterparts like Sister Falconer, Sister Aimee, the Reverend Dylks, and the like. Is she really a fake or not? Every time she tries to tell the truth her listeners, at the beginning and the end, flee from her. Even when she confesses to John, he too refuses to listen. It is striking that the truth always falls upon deaf ears, that only when she speaks her diluted version of the Gospel do her listeners flock to her. They will believe only what they are ready to believe, and in a setting appropriate to that: not the drab severity of a rustic church and the words of a dry, pinched woman, but the glittering panoply of a Temple and the Hallelujah's of an entranced goddess; not denunciations but praises; not damnation but hope. (p. 304)

In her blend of fraud and sincerity, glamor and seduction, Fallon is emblematic of the kind of leader Depression audiences were so willing to respond to. A politics was preferred that, like her religious message, was wiped free of "denominational" affiliations and thereby free to make a basic appeal to everyone. So much the better if the message was itself devoid of specific tenets, principles, and applications—its very ambiguity would strike a response in its auditors. Capra would carry this thematic material into the overtly political arena ten years later with *Meet John Doe,* when Long John Willoughby would appeal to an audience of a world poised upon the brink of another kind of catastrophe. If Florence Fallon could be called a religious figure turned secular prophet, Long John is a secular figure turned Messiah. Both are the agents, however unwillingly, of good works. Ironically, in each case it is the audience that has to reassure the prophet—Carson affirms that to Fallon, and the "John Doe's" plead the same case to Willoughby as he stands on the skyscraper balcony.

It is typical of Capra and the times that the final answer lies with the listeners and not with the prophet. In the case of *The Miracle Woman* Fallon's chief auditor is the blind John Carson—emblematic of the confusion felt by the masses in the early thirties. Because he is blind, he tells Fallon, he is free to invent his own world. Fallon was merely the core around which those fancies were wrapped. That was all that was needed in a leader. And perhaps it was enough. (pp. 306-07)

John Tibbetts, "The Wisdom of the Serpent: Frauds and Miracles in Frank Capra's 'The Miracle Woman'" (copyright © 1979 by John Tibbetts; reprinted by permission of the author), in Journal of Popular Film and Television, *Vol. VII, No. 3, 1979, pp. 293-309.*

Claude Chabrol

1930-

French director, screenwriter, and actor.

Chabrol is generally acknowledged as an important new wave filmmaker. His films are conventionally constructed and his plots are somewhat similar from film to film. Although his work has been compared to that of his idol Alfred Hitchcock, Chabrol marries the master's sense of intrigue with a deep probing into human relationships.

Chabrol worked as a publicity man for Twentieth Century-Fox in Paris, and later became a highly regarded film critic for *Cahiers du Cinéma*. He collaborated with Eric Rohmer on a highly respected study of Hitchcock's films, which was published in 1957. Soon after he began working on *Le Beau Serge*, his first film. This film is considered the forerunner of the new wave, characterized by the use of unknown actors, low budget techniques, and the highly personal attitude of the filmmaker towards his work. Although the critical success of François Truffaut's *Les Quatre Cents Coups* and Alain Resnais's *Hiroshima Mon Amour* brought the movement to fruition, Chabrol's film set the stage for the acceptance of the less-polished, individualistic style of the new wave filmmakers.

Chabrol directed many films during the late fifties and sixties, usually incorporating themes similar to *Le Beau Serge*, often with uneven results. *Les Cousins* concerns a relationship between two dissimilar cousins who are law students, and ends in murder. *Les Biches* involves a *ménage à trois* between two lesbians and a male lover, also culminating in murder. *Les Biches, Le Boucher,* and a number of his other films have starred Stéphane Audran, his second wife, in roles which are typically mysterious and doom-ridden.

Chabrol's work has been for the most part commercial successes. His work was at first linked with the works of Truffaut and Godard, but he has since turned to more conventional techniques. Unlike many of the new wave films, Chabrol's films are not autobiographical. "Telling your own story seems disgusting to me," he has said. Rather, his films are detached studies of characters whose sexual ambiguity and overpowering influences on each other most often lead to violent death.

R. H. TURNER

[In *The Cousins*] Chabrol presents a dispiriting picture of a group of Parisian law students who are deadly serious in their cocky rejection and reversal of the expectations that society has of them. Within the circle which provides them with social warmth they avidly and almost ritualistically seek a hedonistic satisfaction which constantly eludes them. To the bourgeois these young people (like our own beat generation) seem to be absolutely free and irresponsible, and this is an image that they cultivate. To Chabrol it is their lostness, their desperation, their huddling together like children, that are most evident. (p. 42)

Chabrol is strong in feeling for the rules of the game as played by these stranded young adults. Paul's friends pour their energies into devising ever new ways to demonstrate their freedom from the larger society which they have not yet entered. Paul himself is an artist in this respect. In Paris, of all places, what better way of showing contempt for tradition and social solidarity than the affectation of Germanisms? At a wild party in his apartment Paul plays the Siegfried music in hi-fi, dons a Nazi officer's cap, and stalks through the darkened rooms reciting German poetry. This is Chabrol at his best, and it is strange that he has been misunderstood precisely here. Bosley Crowther, writing his *New York Times'* review, could hardly be more wrong in his comment: "The concept of the youth of the nation corrupted by the Nazi image is profound." In its perverse antisocial meaning, Paul's action is about as Nazi as would have been a reading from Proust in Hitler's Germany. The *London Times* critic equally missed the boat by referring to the "pleasant but inappropriate choice of Wagnerian background music." The way in which the music was generated within the film reminded me of Renoir, particularly of his use of the *Danse Macabre* in *La Règle du Jeu*.

Chabrol's moralistic purposes have induced some improbabilities in the motivation. Thus, it was excellent when Florence, the girl with whom Charles fell in love, decided that it would be a change for her to be in love, and she might as well try it; and it was acute to have sophisticated Paul show uneasiness at the apparent success of provincial cousin Charles. It was acute, too, to show Paul and the degenerate Clovis argue Florence out of her experiment. . . . But that Paul should be provoked to the extent of establishing a ménage with Florence is surely convenient for the fable rather than plausible. (pp. 42-3)

The Cousins is imaginatively conceived and well directed. If it lacks punch—the punch of, say, *La Régle du Jeu* or *I Vitelloni*—it is because in it Chabrol is too small a social critic. With rare exceptional moments, in place of richness and intensity Chabrol offers precision and disdain. (p. 43)

R. H. Turner, "'The Cousins'," in Film Quarterly *(copyright 1960 by The Regents of the University of California; reprinted by permission of the University of California Press), Vol. XIV, No. 1, Fall, 1960, pp. 42-3.*

BRIAN DAVIES

Claude Chabrol is a director who has managed to become more estranged from the critics with each film he makes. . . .

It seems to me that Chabrol has been cast aside not so much because of any failing on his own part but because of a reluctance of the critics to respond imaginatively to his films. By no account could his films be held to be high art but at the same time they are serious, skilled, and to a limited extent, successful works. *Leda [A Double Tour]* is Chabrol and [co-screenwriter Paul] Gegauff's (one cannot yet talk of Chabrol without implying Gegauff) most complete statement of their ideas, both of film and of meaning, that they have made. The series from *Le Beau Serge* to *Les Cousins* to *Leda* represents a progression in the disentanglement of Chabrol's ideas and style rather than a regression to the level of chic gesture as has been implied. (p. 78)

The moral of [*Leda's*] fable is simple, and in fact much simpler than *Les Cousins,* the honest and genuine side triumphs finally over the phoney and conniving mother whose respectability is shown to be a sham. Yet two features of the film complicate this simple conclusion. The first of these is the extraordinary emphasis which is made in the film on beauty and beautiful things. . . . The parallel between beauty and moral goodness and ugliness and moral badness is repeatedly stated and reaches its culmination when the son pulls faces at himself in the mirror to make himself appear hideous and then smashes the mirror and strangles Leda.

The reason for this is not immediately easy to grasp, but it probably relates to Chabrol's idea of the hero as aristocrat as opposed to the hero as rebel-crusader which is the traditional guise of the hero in films. (p. 79)

Chabrol himself easily rivals the aesthetic concern of the characters in the film. It is almost pretentiously beautiful in parts. For example, the near grotesque treatment of the lovers' idyll—all dappled leaves and red flowers—shows Chabrol's affinities to the art of *l'objet*. . . . In many ways *Leda* is the best example yet of the "Robbe-Grillet film" in its concern for giving objects the same value as people. . . .

The second facet of the fable is in a way a corollary of this aesthetic obsession. It is Chabrol's concern with the pathetic fallacy, the removal and even the denial of the validity of tragedy. In this attempt he is again akin to the literary work of Robbe-Grillet, and even Samuel Beckett, although he does not find it necessary to work within their attenuated frameworks. It is here that the key to the resistance to his films lies. Nourished as we have been on a steady diet of pathos and tragedy in films (put the adjective "bitter-sweet" before any recent film and it will fit perfectly more often than not) we reject what seems to be a callous lack of humanity in *Leda.* Commitment critics would not even begin to be able to cope and would necessarily find *Leda* to be degenerate. Chabrol is determined to resist the implication of the pathetic; that "more than this is possible" and the "only if" reaction that it engenders. Thus whilst *Leda* could have been written so that the mother was shown in a tragic light Chabrol and Gegauff have not done so. Instead they have shown her as being absolutely evil (not greatly evil but without redeeming features). However, to the end of the film we expect a more sympathetic treatment of the mother from them. . . .

It is not my concern here to question the validity of Chabrol's statements and position. For one thing he has not yet made enough films to justify such an undertaking. Sufficient if I have managed to demonstrate that Chabrol's work is just as serious and worthy of attention as that of any other director currently making film. The difficulty is that his aesthetic and moral position involves the use of subjects which are outside the humanist framework from which most critics view and assess films. (p. 80)

Brian Davies, "Films of the Quarter: 'Leda'," in Film Journal *(copyright by Melbourne University Film Society), No. 20, August, 1962, pp. 78-80.*

RAYMOND DURGNAT

Le Beau Serge was Chabrol's first film, and its immense success on the French Catholic circuit pioneered the New Wave commercially. . . .

The characters generally have more force and dignity than in Chabrol's later films—even though the village flirt says to Francois, 'You have a way of looking at us as if we were all insects'. In the scenes at the village hop one becomes aware of Chabrol picking out little details in a way that is grotesque rather than faithful to the atmosphere the characters would feel, and hints at the laborious eccentricity of the later films, from which I always get the impression of Chabrol hopping about the world like a hungry crow, snapping up fat, squiggly worms in his quick, horny beak, and dangling them in front of the audience, crowing, '*There's* human nature for you'. However, here he approaches his personages with the sympathy and humility which are so woefully lacking after *Les Cousins*. . . .

[Under] the theme of friendship, the film reveals a rather churchmouse view of existence, with undertones about the transference of sin and expiation from one soul to another, and good and evil being inextricably intertwined in every heart. Chabrol himself later denounced this aspect of the film. . . .

Actually, the film is rather more interesting than Chabrol pretends. Its technical brio, its vivid atmosphere, and its sometimes gripping evocation of friendship, make it worth seeing.

Raymond Durgnat, "Raymond Durgnat on the Film That Started the Wave" (© copyright Raymond Durgnat 1963; reprinted with permission), in Films and Filming, *Vol. 9, No. 4, January, 1963, p. 44.*

ISABEL QUIGLY

In those ferocious discussions over Form and Content that shake the film world (well, bits of it) from time to time, in which the lunatic fringe on one side maintains that it doesn't care twopence what a film-maker says so long as he says it beautifully, and on the other that it doesn't care twopence how he says it so long as he's got something to say; and the rest of us, non-lunatics to a man, hover somewhere between the two, feeling craven, the name of Claude Chabrol springs to mind, or at least to my mind, in no time. For if there was ever a skilful film-maker with precious little to say, here, as one thin, vivacious, well-arranged nullity after another has proved, he is. . . .

Individualists like Truffaut, Demy and Godard have gone their own way, each a separate, unallied artist, quickly diverging from any 'norm' there might have been at the beginning of that creative outburst, overpraised like most innovations, which the press rather meaninglessly christened '*nouvelle vague.*' But Chabrol remains what everyone suspected the whole bunch of them to be, a sort of amalgam of them all, with his alarming, representative figures of Youth (which parody everyone's most gruesome views on the subject), his overheated situations, his whole presentation of life as being at the same time souped-up and squalid, and, of course, his intense, myopic view of human affairs. Obviously Pope had a prophetic view of the cinema when he said:

> Why has not man a microscopic eye?
> For this plain reason, man is not a fly,

and a director like Chabrol is the classic example of the industrious, self-important fly, crawling over the face of the universe and exclaiming at the tree-like quality of a single bristle.

Ophelia is not exactly a modern version of *Hamlet,* but a variation on the theme of *Hamlet,* with (of course) a film within the film instead of the play within the play (and the director lecturing his cast about the duties and limitations of film-actors, just as Hamlet did the players), a chat with a jolly gravedigger, and, in case we may have missed the parallels, posters for Olivier's film of *Hamlet* which is showing at the hero's local cinema. . . .

It is all pretty inept, false and absurd, and yet Chabrol has the skill—even if it is an empty skill—to keep the screen satisfactorily, sometimes touchingly, sometimes beautifully, filled for much of the time he uses it, and this has so little to do with what he is trying to say that it's maddening.

Isabel Quigly, "Less than Kind," in The Spectator *(© 1963 by* The Spectator; *reprinted by permission of* The Spectator), *Vol. 211, No. 7057, September 27, 1963, p. 388.*

ROBERT GIARD

If the cinema of Claude Chabrol is anything, it is glib. What could be more glib than that scene in *The Third Lover* [*L'Oeil du Malin*] in which the betrayed husband examines some photographs serving as evidence of his wife's infidelity. The shots constitute a gradual progression from indifferent medium shot, the subject squarely and objectively centered within the frame, to oppressively intimate close-up. This is disarmingly glib. . . .

The flexible, functional beauty of this example is modestly intellectual as well as frankly sensational in its appeal. Here is the cinema of basic literacy; Chabrol employs an articulate and correct grammar of film-making. Such exactness of intention and effect immediately recalls Hitchcock, whose name, along with that of Minnelli, invariably arises in a discussion of Chabrol.

Minnelli's influence is most apparent when Chabrol is working in color and "in period," responding to both as he does with a marked sensitivity, as in *Landru.* An almost excessive concern for the niceties of *mise en scène*—witness the pivotal representational use of violently contrasting décor in *Un Double Tour*—would at first suggest that both directors see the world from the point of view of an interior decorator. Such a perception would not be too far from the truth.

This Minnelli strain is not very emphatic in *The Third Lover.* However, the film does to some extent fall in line with the lush American cinema tradition of "the musical without music," especially as propounded by MGM and exemplified by Minnelli. *The Third Lover* features enough choreographic fluidity, a well-groomed artifice, and an accumulative attention to production values, on however modest a black and white scale, to qualify it as an entertainment package boasting a certain amount of elegance. Finally, the whole possesses a peculiarly theatrical perfection, the telling, undeniable air of the well-rehearsed. No action is allowed to expand in a leisurely fashion; everything transpires at an aggressive, assured, and, finally, stylized clip. The show, in short, is "well-paced." . . .

No far cry from Minnelli's cinema of chic is Hitchcock's cinema of shock; both lean heavily on sensation. *The Third Lover* more than pays its respects to Hitchcock. Aside from the perversely adapted romance-mystery formula, there is the technical dexterity. . . . (p. 53)

Chabrol's kinship with Hitchcock extends beyond . . . stylistic and visual similarities to certain psychological and moral foci. One motif recurrent in the Hitchcock canon—the transference of guilt—plays an important role in *The Third Lover.* Here this theme functions as but a single aspect of the film's overall stress on the narrator's voyeuristic absorption in the lives of his two married friends. Charrier's specific guilt results from an abnormally intense reaction against the husband as second lover and identification with the husband as cuckold. He shares as well an actual instrumentality in the discovery of the adultery and the consequent crime of passion.

Chabrol like Hitchcock then is engrossed in the devastating power of everyday evildoing, evil often originating from exceedingly petty, if vaguely pathological, motivations. . . .

Even more fundamental is a low estimation of humanity which Chabrol and Hitchcock share. Theirs is often a sobering art. They find man prone to perversity, and they find that this perversity snowballs into crime—or, as Chabrol so frequently reminds us in this film and in others, into a state of total warfare and destruction, threatening all life and all decency. (p. 54)

Robert Giard, "'The Third Lover' by Claude Chabrol," in Film Culture *(copyright 1963 by* Film Culture), *No. 31, Winter, 1963-64, pp. 53-4.*

RICHARD DAVIS

Very few of us are really interested in an end of term or end of course thesis which is what [*Bluebeard,* or *Landru*] appears. There is no point of contact between the audience and what is going on on the screen, and unless, as in certain specific cases the intellectual purpose of a film is so valid and significant that it will survive on its own rarified level, any anti-emotional film, by its deliberate withdrawal, will fail. An art of the people should stay of the people.

Chabrol has so heavily stylised his treatment of the Bluebeard story that form comes to impose a disproportionate tyranny over content. The shapelessness advocated by the young enthusiastic practitioners of the New Wave in France, and still typified faithfully in Godard, has here caused a reaction so fundamental that reality has little or no place in the stately proceedings. Also, Chabrol's passion for detail—he shows every one of Landru's victims, where Chaplin, for instance, would have shown three or four only—becomes irritating and distracting. . . .

This version of the story is bound to be compared with Chaplin's *Verdoux*: the basic principles underlying the creator's philosophy are the same, and for this reason the two works demand comparison, much to the latter's detriment. (p. 32)

Richard Davis, "The New Films: 'Bluebeard'" (© copyright Richard Davis 1965; reprinted with permission), in Films and Filming, *Vol. 11, No. 5, February, 1965, pp. 32-3.*

ROY ARMES

Claude Chabrol is assured of a place in any study of the new French cinema, for he was the first of the Cahiers group to make a feature film and as a producer gave Godard, Rivette and Rohmer valuable assistance on their first efforts, but there is less certainty as to the actual merits of his work as a director.

Until his recent spy films Chabrol had concerned himself principally with personal relationships. His early films depict the close, almost homosexual, relationship of two young men, and a constant theme is the precariousness of love, which, indeed, is treated as almost purely illusory in several works: *L'Oeil du Malin,* where the apparently successful marriage is undermined by a tissue of lies, and *Landru,* the hero of which makes his living by robbing and killing gullible women who believe his flattering words of love. Chabrol's attitude to his characters is one of unmitigated coldness, partly because of his belief that people in general are stupid and that their fascination lies precisely in this stupidity: "Foolishness is infinitely more fascinating than intelligence, infinitely more profound. Intelligence has limits whilst foolishness has none." Typical in this respect is his attitude to the shopgirls of *Les Bonnes Femmes:* "I wanted to make a film about stupid people that was very vulgar and deeply stupid . . . When we wrote the film, the people were, for Gégauff, fools. It was a film about fools." Chabrol's detachment does allow him to manipulate his characters like puppets, but precludes him from arousing any deep emotion. He is unable to portray romance with any lyricism and the love scenes in *A Double Tour,* for instance, are utterly lacking in grace or passion. Chabrol's best love scene is undoubtedly that between Jacqueline and her motorcyclist in *Les Bonnes Femmes* and this, significantly enough, is a mere prelude to murder.

Despite a tendency towards documentary, apparent in the distributed versions of *Le Beau Serge* and *Les Bonnes Femmes* and even more marked, it would seem, in their original scripts, Chabrol's work reveals only a restricted grasp of the problem of fitting characters into a convincing social environment. His repeated attempts at portraying bourgeois households are singularly unsubtle and carry little conviction, so that only a limited impact is made by those outsiders (Laszlo in *A Double Tour* or Yvan in *Ophélia*) who are intent on attacking middle-class behaviour and values. Caricature is not limited, however, to the handling of the bourgeoisie. Even *Le Beau Serge* contained a quaint rustic sub-plot, involving the vamp (Bernadette Lafont) and her stepfather, that tended to obscure the central issues, and in the subsequent works this element of the grotesque has increased until all the characters in *Ophélia,* except perhaps the heroine, are mentally unbalanced. This development is linked with Chabrol's basically unserious attitude to film-making: explaining the differences between the original script for *Ophélia* and the completed film Chabrol said: "I pushed it more towards having fun." Fun, in Chabrol's sense, involves the inclusion of long eating scenes and dotting the films with absurdly overacted minor characters. (pp. 47-9)

If one wishes to pin down the essence of Chabrol's style, one cannot do better than consider the short episode *La Muette* which he made in 1964 for the film *Paris Vu Par* . . . Not only is this a highly professional piece of work, based on an interesting notion (the possibilities of opting out of family life by means of earplugs) and showing a sheer technical skill which the subsequent spy films have confirmed, it also incorporates all Chabrol's obsessional quirks: a grotesque caricature of bourgeois life, interminable eating scenes, a married couple whose only communication is by shouts and quarrels, a sexy maid, a startling and gratuitous ending of violent death and, significantly enough, the director himself lustily overacting and pulling rude faces at his wife . . . and at the audience itself. (p. 49)

Roy Armes, "Claude Chabrol," in his French Cinema since 1946: The Personal Style, *Vol. II (copyright © 1966 by Roy Armes), A. S. Barnes & Co., 1966, pp. 43-9.*

GORDON GOW

Chabrol, detached but perceptive, takes one of his coolest looks at the instability of human nature in *Les Biches,* a film which could have been made as an emotional drama but which Chabrol prefers to treat as a suave and objective tragedy with disquieting undercurrents. While the flow of the work is exceptionally smooth, provoking the mind rather than the nerve-ends, and is therefore unusual enough to be set apart from conventional cinema, it still has allegiance to filmic precepts. (pp. 40-1)

For neither of the women [Frédérique and Why] is sympathy invited: to neither is compassion denied. But the aspect is clinical, the visuals serene and uninvolved. The locale shifts early from Paris to St Tropez, bland in winter sunshine. . . . And the formality of technique is subtle, amounting to one of the cinema's nearest approximations to ballet. The movements of figures, individually and also in relationship to one another, are immediately significant in the prologue on the bridge, and are to remain of greatest importance in the style of the entire movie. Placement and pattern, the smooth participation of the camera in the moving design, the geometric highlighting of central figures at a party, which is also decorated sparely and aptly by a male couple who have battened upon Frédérique for money and a species of affection and who serve their transient turn as court jesters: these are affiliations with the dance, all assimilated quite naturally into the medium of cinema, and crystallised eventually in a pas de trois. (p. 41)

[The hapless trio in *Les Biches*] are creatures perplexed by the indeterminate naggings of their passions; and the droll conclusion, in which deception is cultivated as a final bid for 'comfort', deprives the spectator of any other balm than the smile of self-protection. It is one of Chabrol's major efforts, just a bit too slow within the first half-hour perhaps, but after that quite holding and admirable. (p. 42)

Gordon Gow, "The New Films: 'Les Biches'" (© copyright Gordon Gow 1969; reprinted with permission), in Films and Filming, *Vol. 15, No. 6, March, 1969, pp. 40-2.*

MICHAEL McKEGNEY

The placid surface of *Les Biches* should blind no one to the spirit that moves within—slightly unbalanced, corrosive, morally alert—unless we are to be as deceived by appearances as one of Chabrol's characters. (p. 17)

Chabrol successfully evokes the stifling quality of daily life during the winter season in St. Tropez, with its outdoor games and flower markets which only add to the boredom and suffocation. The film becomes increasingly more claustrophobic as the characters cut themselves off from reality to inhabit a dream world. The growing sense of social disorientation from the second episode, "Frederique," to the third, "Why," reflects the ascent to power of the film's most deranged character. . . .

Whereas for Sternberg political activity seems to be a sublimation for sexual activity, sexual relationships in Chabrol's films seem to come under the heading of political discipline, an arbitrary exercise of authority insecurely imposed upon an essentially chaotic world. Thus Frederique sees her house as a king of empire, to which she brings people primarily in order to control them, and from which she dismisses them when they seem to get beyond her control. (p. 18)

With characteristic Chabrolian irony, the traditional roles of master and servant are consistently reversed in *Les Biches,* and at several points in the first half of the film Frederique exercises command over Why on the psychological level by serving her on the social level. (p. 19)

The entire film can be seen as an abstract demonstration of the psychological structure of Hitchcock's films, although *Les Biches* is fundamentally anti-psychological and even (unthinkable for Hitchcock!) anti-dramatic. Chabrol makes explicit the poetic patterns which in Hitchcock would remain concealed within a self-contained narrative. In his perverse character relationships as well as his dialectically satiric-moral sensibility, Chabrol is the true disciple. (p. 22)

For Chabrol as for Hitchcock, the line between the normal and the abnormal is never as it seems. There is always something of a Why or a Norman locked inside those characters who have successfully managed to repress it for the sake of social survival. As Norman says to Marion Crane: "We all go a little mad sometimes." To confront the abyss within oneself may save or destroy, but in Hitchcock we feel that free will has at least some role to play in the outcome of the struggle, and in this respect Chabrol characteristically tends to diverge from the Master's way. *Les Biches* is extremely deterministic in tone; so much so as to risk becoming unhealthy in its point of view. . . . (p. 23)

If the relationships are inspired by Hitchcockian psychology, Chabrol places them within the context of a biological view of life which is distinctively his own. . . . *Les Biches* is Chabrol's most explicit development to date of the idea that "civilized" life still operates very much according to the law of the jungle, and its characters can be traced to their origins in the brilliant zoo sequence of *Les Bonnes Femmes*. "We're playing animals. Want to join?" one of the painters says to Why before proceeding with his partner in a game of psychological torture. . . . (p. 24)

As is not surprising in a film by Chabrol, for whom the flora in any given scene may possess as much dramatic life as the human fauna, Why's attainment of power over Frederique and Paul is most clearly signalled by a gorgeous bouquet of flowers she picks for them one morning, photographed from such an angle that it completely dominates their breakfast table, enveloping them in the shot as if to stifle them. Thus we are poetically prepared for Frederique's behavior during the epilogue—exhausted, empty, lifeless. The systematic examination of its material in terms of biological phenomena paradoxically transforms *Les Biches* into one of Chabrol's least naturalistic films.

Like that of Renoir in *Toni,* Chabrol's view of human life in the context of nature is harsh but compassionate. Psychological ugliness is never ignored, but always transcended. When Paul and Why walk through the woods and pause in the moonlight for their first kiss, on one level each is callously using the other as pawn in a game against Frederique, but our awareness of their destructive motivation only makes the scene more deeply moving and beautiful. Chabrol never settles for cheap irony, nor does he indulge in the sentimentality with which a misanthrope so often masks his true feelings (as, for example, Truffaut does in *Stolen Kisses*).

Les Biches is an extraordinarily beautiful film to look at. Its style is no pointless embellishment, moreover, but the logical outgrowth of content. An action involving characters who shed their "skins" to acquire new ones is expressed in a *mise en scene* which dwells lovingly upon the surface appearances of people and other objects—"un cinema epidermique," as Bernard Eisenschitz characterized it. . . . [Chabrol's] visual fascination with surfaces suggests a confusion of the normal distinction between essence and appearance, a confusion at the heart of the kind of sickness which afflicts Chabrol's characters.

Even the most extravagant stylistic gestures in the film can be justified as invariably revealing some otherwise invisible level of meaning in the situation depicted. Thus when Frederique becomes intoxicated during a visit to Paul's housing project, her condition is conveyed through an extraordinary shot employing simultaneously a backward track, forward zoom, and three shifts of focus! This vertiginous effect is an extreme example, but it is characteristic of the unsettling style through which Chabrol communicates the precariousness of mental and moral stability in life. As the film progresses, its disturbing formal patterns are gradually intensified. The angles become more oblique, the compositions more unbalanced; shots increasingly tend to begin with the camera already in motion and to end before it comes to a point of rest. Thus the audience is forced to identify with Why's psychic disorientation, even to the moment when her final plunge into madness is announced by a seductive movement of the camera through an open window toward the inviting chaos of a blue night streaked with blood-red sunset.

Far from being the mere repetition of previous accomplishments which some critics have suggested, *Les Biches* is one of Chabrol's most adventurous and daring films. If some of the decadence of *Leda* is still observed, the later film must surely be accounted superior in its structure and selectivity of detail. Never before has Chabrol so completely eschewed the clinical details of psychology, so that his characters fulfill their dramatic and aesthetic functions with an unprecedented degree of abstract purity. . . .

In its extreme stylistic abstraction, the film itself bears striking resemblance to the does Why compulsively draws on the sidewalks and bridges of Paris. *Les Biches* is Chabrol's Portrait of the Artist as Madman. (pp. 24-6)

Michael McKegney, "Chabrol's Zoo Story," in Film Heritage *(copyright 1969 by F. A. Macklin), Vol. 4, No. 4, Summer, 1969, pp. 17-26.*

GAVIN MILLAR

Nearly a year ago, just after he had finished *La Femme Infidèle* . . . , Claude Chabrol said in a television interview that he always made films about the bourgeoisie because that was the class he knew best. And the reason for that was simple: "I am one of them," he went on, "I am one myself—*but I don't like them.*"

He's talking about a class of Frenchmen we should judge as somewhere between comfortably-off and rich. He's fascinated by their high degree of social organisation. . . . [On] the whole Chabrol seems inclined to view [the organisation] as a defence against the unexpected, against indignity, and against passion. In this aspect, *La Femme Infidèle,* set as it is in a mansion in Versailles, inescapably presents a picture of an *ancien régime*. It is as though Chabrol had decided that the barriers that crashed in 1789 were the most superficial ones: economic, political, social. Beneath them the emotional rites which sustained the *haute bourgeoisie*—refined or calcified according to your taste—clicked on unperturbed, even in the arriviste. *La Femme Infidèle* is about the irruption into this ritual not so much of passion itself, as of the evidence of passion, the awareness of passion, above all the threatening acknowledgment of passion. . . .

The marks of ritual are beautifully recorded. The long, slow left-to-right pans bringing the car to the side of the house and Desvallées across its frontage, the patient and smooth attention of the camera as Desvallées and his wife take tea on the lawn, look at snapshots, enjoy the sunshine. . . .

What's even more impressive is the manner in which Chabrol controls the pace. A great deal of the film passes in watching movement, not always purposeless, but often inconsequential. The interest lies in the degree of haste, the familiarity of the movement, its utility or pointlessness. Desvallées is steady-paced, his small purposes served by careful, economic movement, the camera following him with unemotional, unironic attention as he proceeds from telephone to cigarette packet to car-parking disc to record player. Hélène is more languid, more mysterious, her secret purposes hinted at by long slow tracks-in which close her off from her surroundings, isolating her narcissism, her passion or her grief. With Pegala [her lover] gone, she shuts herself in her bedroom and, standing at the foot of the bed, lowers herself backwards on to it, her limbs dead, the only sound a wordless gasp of hurt which the camera has to lean over her to hear. (p. 209)

When Desvallées kills [Pegala] we are at first as astonished as the murderer is by the revelation of that secret strength, not merely physical. But we recognise that the core of subterranean violence is not only held in check, but husbanded, by a skin of civilisation which perhaps generations of Desvallées had worked hard to preserve. . . . Desvallées' violence is suddenly shocking because it is in contrast to his habitual economy of effort, and the power of the sequence in which he disposes of the body is proportionate to that economy. For here he turns himself with great efficiency into a work-machine and, mopping blood, wrapping, dragging, heaving, driving the body of Pegala, he is sustained as always by the rituals of habit and the pull towards normality which govern his life. . . .

What has Chabrol demonstrated? That despite appearances—everything in Chabrol is despite those—the heights and depths of emotion can be visited and returned from safely?—or encompassed and assimilated?—or encountered and avoided?—paradoxically by cleaving to just these restrictive forms of life? Chabrol doesn't like the bourgeoisie, but we doubt whether he is more fascinated or repelled by this artificial skin of behaviour. Are the heights scaled, as it were, or skirted, after all? Doesn't he admire, despite himself, the sophistication of this fighting unit, and their ability to survive? When Desvallées confesses to Hélène, 'Je t'aime comme un fou,' is he preserving an invaluable relationship or (the bourgeois sin) a priceless possession? At any rate this sure-footed, finely acted and spellbinding film is not ruffled, but deepened, by that ambivalence. (pp. 209-10)

Gavin Millar, "Film Reviews: 'La Femme Infidele'," in Sight and Sound *(copyright © 1969 by The British Film Institute), Vol. 38, No. 4, Autumn, 1969, pp. 209-10.*

MARGOT S. KERNAN

Chabrol has found a rich mine of material in what he calls the "little themes," and [in *La Femme Infidèle*] he is working within a very narrow range, both visually and emotionally. However, within these limits, few directors are more skillful at using a sensuous cinematic style to suggest a world of minimal feelings and reified relationships. (pp. 56-7)

Chabrol establishes his characters as ambulatory objets d'art in luxurious settings. Everything is pretty. . . . [Hélène] harmonizes so well with the decor of her drawing room—her pale grey eyeshadow echoing the soft tones of the carved wood paneling, her earrings catching the light and sparkling like the television commercials her husband . . . is so fond of watching—that we see her primarily as an object in a perfectly arranged background.

In fact, the idea of *nature morte* seems to inform the imagery throughout the film. Objects are arranged in patterns that convey a sense of still life and suspended animation. In an early scene in the dining room when Hélène and Charles eat pears with a knife and fork and discuss some forged paintings which he had inadvertently bought, the image is dominated by a beautiful Renoir-esque arrangement of fruit in an elegant porcelain basket. Even the murder is shown as a series of formal acts composed within a frame, and the scene where Charles disposes of the body of his victim becomes imprinted on our mind because of the patterns the bubbles make on the blank green surface of the pond. (p. 57)

Chabrol's characters contact their environment as it reflects them—or sometimes as it encloses them—and mirrors and reflecting surfaces invest his films with a pervasive sense of the narcissism of his subjects. . . .

Chabrol's preoccupation with surfaces serves to establish his characters' isolation from each other and formal composition within the frame tends to define these characters as objects. And to sharpen our perception of this, from time to time Chabrol introduces characters who are gross or grotesque in their action. . . . In comparison to the bland exteriors of the main characters, these jackanapes people provide a bizarre inverted mirror of behavior, almost as if they were in fact venting and miming the panic feelings that the main characters are unable to express.

In this context of narcissism and manipulation, sex becomes a ploy and a means of domination—and this is the way we see the relationships between Hélène, Victor, and Charles. We are never shown anything really erotic happening between either husband and wife or wife and lover. Hélène prepares for bed with her husband and walks seductively around in her nightgown but he puts Mozart on the phonograph and stares up at the ceiling. (pp. 57-8)

When Charles finally does kill his rival we sense that it is only because a prize possession has been taken away from him. In fact, it is the sight of a cigarette lighter in Victor's bedroom which he had earlier given Hélène for an anniversary present that seems to trigger the act. The murder becomes a gesture of reclaiming objects that another had snatched away, and the murder weapon is an Egyptian stone head that looks remarkably like Hélène.

Because Chabrol defines his characters by means of the spaces and things that surround them, our understanding of them is ultimately limited. His lavish and seductive physical style does not function as mere ornament—in his films style *is* the subject matter. Warhol is another example of a filmmaker who uses this kind of style-content fusion. And as with Warhol, when resonance and nuance replace energy and force we have trouble becoming emotionally involved. On the other hand, there is something beautifully entertaining about a film which shows people as arrangements of light-reflecting surfaces, especially since other directors often make these same types into messengers for serious thoughts about the destructive bourgeoisie. Chabrol makes murder into a "little theme" by using a style which shows nothing more than meets the eye. Decor vincit omnia. (p. 58)

Margot S. Kernan, "Reviews: 'La femme infidèle'," in Film Quarterly *(copyright 1970 by The Regents of The University of California; reprinted by permission of the University of California Press), Vol. XXIII, No. 4, Summer, 1970, pp. 56-8.*

ROBIN WOOD and MICHAEL WALKER

An artist lives in his art; that is, his art is characterised by the impulses, sympathies and recoils which determine his nature as a human being. Yet equally, for the artist who loses faith, art can become a perverse refuge: an enclosed, private world within which he spins fantasies of his own defeat. . . . Unlike 'ivory tower' artists, who exclude pain, 'private world' artists . . . indulge in it masochistically; but, to almost an equal extent, have ceased to explore, to seek out new *positive* values by which to live.

Chabrol's work has shown a constant tension between these opposing ways of living in his art. Since the rather laboured, and subsequently disowned, Catholic affirmation of *Le Beau Serge,* his great problem as an artist has been the difficulty of affirming belief in anything. Rejecting the bourgeois world for its materialism, pretensions and repressiveness, but finding the various alternatives to this world either self-destructive (the 'student' milieu of *Les Cousins*) or completely arid (the Paris of *Les Bonnes Femmes*), Chabrol could have reached the impasse of the 'private world' artists. The degree to which he has transcended this possibility, and the balance of conflicting impulses in his work—hatred and tenderness, disgust and generosity, cynicism and belief—are central to the concern of this book. . . .

Chabrol's relation to Hitchcock provides a useful starting-point for an examination of his work. It is a very complex relation, manifesting itself in many forms and on many levels. At times it is quite superficial, an obviously deliberate borrowing or *hommage,* as in the on-stage murder of Stéphane Audran in *Le Tigre aime la chair fraîche,* which recalls the Albert Hall sequence of *The Man Who Knew Too Much.* (p. 6)

Chabrol does not, however, encourage audience identification as unambiguously as the Hitchcock of, say, *Vertigo* and *Psycho.* Hitchcock involves us with his protagonists to the extent that we *live* the film with them emotionally, and then abruptly, through some sudden shock, shatters this identification so that we are forced to construct a new, more complex relationship to the action. Chabrol at times constructs and shoots his films so that they appear to be setting up precisely an identification of this kind, but counterbalances this effect by arousing greater sympathy for the watched than for the watcher. (p. 7)

[For Chabrol] to be influenced by Hitchcock is the most natural thing in the world, because their art shows such great affinities of outlook. The themes that Rohmer and Chabrol find in Hitchcock's films [in their book *Hitchcock*] —grouped around the central concept of 'exchange' or interchangeability—are explored and developed more rigorously (because, surely, more *consciously*) in Chabrol's. (p. 8)

When *Le Beau Serge* first appeared, it looked like an attempt at developing a French neorealist school, with Chabrol shooting entirely on location, using the real inhabitants of a real village, showing a consistent concern to represent the surface details of the environment and the people's lives with the greatest possible fidelity. . . . Yet, beneath the film's deceptively 'documentary' surface, Chabrol's formal and thematic preoccupations are as strong in *Le Beau Serge* as in any subsequent works. The film is as germinal to Chabrol's oeuvre as *A bout de souffle* to Godard's: if it looks back to the Hitchcock book, it as surely looks ahead to the 'exchange' films of Chabrol's present phase, *Les Biches, La Femme Infidèle, Que la bête meure.* The 'formal' and 'thematic' preoccupations are not to be thought of as separable. As with Hitchcock's two Charlies, the François/Serge parallels offer far more than formal symmetry: not only the film's structure, but its meaning, derive from them. Chabrol and Rohmer see as a recurring motif in Hitchcock the 'exchange of guilt'. . . . [This is] significant in relation to Chabrol's work, where the sense of *inherent* evil is so strong.

In *Le Beau Serge,* however, we are concerned less with an exchange of guilt than with an exchange of salvation. The parallels between the two men suggest that they are to some degree interchangeable: François could have been Serge and vice versa. At first François appears the morally superior character, Serge the lost. . . . But as the film progresses, we realise that François's efforts to save Serge are really efforts to save himself: he once wanted to be a priest; he has ceased even to 'practise'; beyond that, he has lost all sense of aim in life, and his disease is (as its 'reflection' in Serge's alcoholism suggests) to be seen as more than an unhappy chance. He needs above all to give validity to his role of 'example', as a means to self-justification. (pp. 11-13)

Chabrol . . . presents us with an interesting moral problem [in *Le Beau Serge*]: if, engaged upon an action one knows quite rationally and objectively to be good, one is suddenly led to suspect one's own motives for performing it, does one then go on or retract? (p. 13)

Characters who crave excitement in his films, or aspire to anything beyond their known and habitual environment, always get cruelly punished for it. . . . The psychological implication is that the ultimate terror is of the Id. Characters who embody the drives of the Id are frequent in Hitchcock's films, and almost invariably corrupt, perverted, frighteningly evil (though often insidiously charming at the same time). (p. 14)

It is easy to pass from this to Chabrol; his is also, and in the same sense, a cinema of fear. Consider the series of Id-figures in Chabrol's early work: Glomaud in *Le Beau Serge,* Clovis in *Les Cousins,* André the motor-cyclist in *Les Bonnes Femmes.* They lack the corrupt charm of their equivalents in Hitchcock, but the relationship is clear enough. . . .

Retrospectively, however, it is André who seems more of a Chabrol Id-figure, as, in a less dangerous sense, is Laszlo Kovacs in *A Double Tour.* This is confirmed by the appearance of *Que la bête meure* and *Le Boucher.* Paul in the former is a much more powerful development of Laszlo, and Popaul in the latter a much more human development of André. It is significant that overt Hitchcockian touches are, in these films, undetectable: even the affinities between the two directors cease to mean very much. The later films are purely Chabrol, and the development of his personal vision is crystallised in *Le Boucher.* . . .

Chabrol's awareness of powerful determinant forces, uncontrollable because below the level of the conscious mind, makes him perhaps the most Freudian of all important directors. His films revert repeatedly to the idea of the impossibility of 'reading' appearances: of reading the thoughts, emotions, motives behind the masks. More than this, there is the sense (which reaches a peak in *Les Biches*) that the characters themselves know little of what is going on behind their own masks. (p. 15)

Though certainly not the opposite of robust, Chabrol's films are denied the particular kind of robustness that characterises Hitchcock's. If he shares Hitchcock's distrust of the Id and its energies, it is impossible for him to share Hitchcock's acceptance of the bourgeois world. . . .

This raises the question of what Chabrol does believe in—not in terms of ideas, creed or philosophy, but in the practical terms of exploring the possibilities of life in the world the films depict. . . .

If one puts together Chabrol's first five films, one has a composite portrait of contemporary France (by extension, contemporary western society) as he sees it. . . . The most striking characteristic of the world of Chabrol's films is that it is essentially perverted, poisoned at its sources of energy, with corruption spreading through all its strata. The deranged and murderous motorcyclist of *Les Bonnes Femmes* is the central figure, not only of that film, but of all Chabrol's early work. (p. 16)

[Chabrol's overall] development can be traced through a single motif: the family. Only four of Chabrol's features are strictly centred on the family group: *A Double Tour, Ophélia, La Femme Infidèle* and *Que la bête meure;* but there is also, in the middle of his 'commercial' period, *La Muette* [a section of *Paris Vu Par*] . . . so these 'family' films virtually span his whole career to date. Besides them, there are films where the family motif appears peripherally (for instance, the ludicrous and pretentious bourgeois families of Henri—same name, same actor—in *Les Bonnes Femmes* and *Les Godelureaux*) or in disguise: the shopgirls of *Les Bonnes Femmes* resemble each other sufficiently in general characteristics to be considered sisters, with the proprietor and cashier as grotesque parent-figures. There are also films in which envy, and the resulting desire to destroy what can't be possessed (one of the most frequently recurring emotions in Chabrol's work) is directed specifically against a relationship from which the envier feels excluded, a reaction explainable less as sexual jealousy than as a frustrated desire to be accepted into a family group. One sees this in Charles in the later part of *Les Cousins;* it is more striking in Albin in *L'Oeil du malin;* it can be felt partly to motivate the enigmatic Why in the later scenes of *Les Biches.*

The motif, then, is constant; what has changed is Chabrol's attitude. In most of the early films, the family is conceived in entirely negative terms, relationships within it being almost exclusively destructive. (p. 17)

The pivotal film is *La Muette,* which takes on an importance out of proportion to its length. In 'meaning' it belongs very clearly with the earlier films: again the family is presented as entirely destructive. But there are two particular points of interest. The first is that Chabrol himself not only wrote and directed the film, but plays the role of the father, with his own wife Stéphane Audran as the mother. It would be absurd, as well as libellous in the extreme, to suggest that in these coarse, brutal, materialistic, mutually destructive grotesques we are being treated to a glimpse into the home-life of the Chabrols. Yet, if Chabrol has consistently savaged the bourgeois world, it is equally evident that he belongs to it and can't convincingly imagine any alternatives. (p. 18)

The second point about *La Muette* is that it is the first Chabrol film (since the somewhat dubious and rhetorical ending of *Le Beau Serge*) in which a child takes on a central importance. . . . The emotional force of the film, generated partly by the abrupt movement from grotesque comedy to equally grotesque horror (the mother's fatal accident on the staircase), derives primarily from our sense of an environment that destroys its own potentialities for growth.

The family group of *La Muette*—father, mother, son—is repeated and transmuted in *La Femme Infidèle.* . . . The tone [of *La Femme Infidèle* and *Que la bête meure*] is mellow, tender, almost serene, qualified by a sense of desolation. Both films affirm unity as a supreme value, though, ironically, through its loss: the husband and wife in *La Femme Infidèle,* the father in *Que la bête meure,* become dignified and ennobled by their strengthened sense of family. (pp. 18-19)

This new positive emphasis on marriage and family has led Chabrol to a much more tolerant attitude to the bourgeois world that such institutions support and are supported by. It is still a highly critical attitude: no one could suppose that he is upholding the world of *La Femme Infidèle* as the best of all possible ones. But he no longer feels the need to caricature it; or, more precisely, the elements of caricature have been displaced from the centre to the peripheries of his films. . . .

In common with Chabrol's new feeling for the potentialities in the traditional social institutions of marriage and family, they are a testament to his deepening sense of humanity. Inevitably, too, Chabrol has become more melancholy. The final tone of [*La Femme Infidèle, Que la bête meure,* and *Le Boucher*] is a poignant fusion of serenity and desolation. The savage derider of the bourgeoisie has become its elegiac poet. (p. 19)

Robin Wood and Michael Walker, in their Claude Chabrol *(© 1970 by Robin Wood and Michael Walker; reprinted by permission of Robin Wood), Frederick A. Praeger, Publishers, 1970, 144 p.*

TOM MILNE

[*La Rupture*] is based on a thriller by Charlotte Armstrong about a woman, blameless in her marriage, whose small son is injured in a fight with her husband, and who subsequently has to fight like a tigress against the forces massed against her when her wealthy father-in-law tries to gain legal custody of the child. The French title, *Le Jour des Parques,* plays happily on the similarity between 'Pâques' (Easter) and 'Parques' (The Parcae, or Fates).

So, remembering the fascination Destiny holds for Chabrol —whether simply present, as in Lang, or intervening, as in Hitchcock—one sits up, nose aquiver with recognition, as the camera zooms in with awestruck slowness to the black door of a private *pension* which stands serenely white in its own tree-shaded grounds and where Hélène . . . has taken a room to be near her child in hospital. For here, unmistakably in the three parched old ladies who rule the salon with their inquisitive stares and their tarot cards, are the Fatal Sisters.

Or so it only seems, since Chabrol, like Blake, now sees beyond the disc of fire to glimpse the dazzling mystery it conceals; and the three old ladies are as much a red herring as the quotation from Racine which serves both as an epigraph and as a critical lifebuoy. Fate is indeed present in the film, actively intervening to preserve the innocent heroine from the wolves that would prey on her, but in a mysterious, evanescent form that even the three old ladies, inquisitively alert to every nuance of gossip and behaviour, cannot comprehend. It is there, magically, in the involuntary gesture of benediction made by an itinerant balloon-seller with his stick as he bends over to talk to the despairing Hélène in the park. It is there, too, even more gravely and luminously, in the ghostly hand which hovers almost invisibly over the tramlines—a reflection, presumably, of the unseen driver at the helm—as she retraces the marvellous tram-ride of Murnau's *Sunrise* to pour out her anguished love story to a sympathetic lawyer.

Actually, the Racine quotation ('Mais quelle épaisse nuit tout à coup m'environne?') is not quite so arbitrary as Chabrol would suggest. Not only because it evokes the tigerish passions of Racine heroines, but because it reminds one (the line is from *Andromaque,* and is spoken by Orestes when he learns that Hermione has killed herself) that *La Rupture* is first and foremost a love story, and one which has its roots in melodrama as unashamedly as any Racine tragedy. Gone, therefore, is the serpentine elegance of *Les Biches,* the calm stasis of *La Femme Infidèle,* the geometrical urgency of *Que la Bête Meure,* to be replaced by an abrupt, staccato style in which one is constantly caught off guard by *la rupture.* (pp. 7-8)

[In a] magnificently imagined sequence on the tram, with awakening conscience enclosed by twin paretheses of concern, Chabrol not only justifies his quotation from *Sunrise,* but shows with the naked, unguarded simplicity of Blake in his *Songs of Innocence and Experience,* how the angels rally to the defence of the innocent: 'When wolves and tygers howl for prey / They pitying stand and weep / Seeking to drive their thirst away / And keep them from the sheep / But if they rush dreadful / The angels most heedful / Receive each mild spirit / New worlds to inherit.' (p. 8)

The film ends as it began, in melodrama transcended. The husband, a zombie by his own definition, hurls his mother downstairs out of the way (echoes of *La Muette*). . . . And Hélène, drugged in the last twist of the plot against her, rushes out to the park with the three old ladies flapping joyously after to prevent her from floating away, and begs God the balloon-seller to free her guardian angels. He does so, grumbling 'Who's going to pay me?' 'I'm going to see my son,' cries Hélène; and the last shot shows the balloons —celebrating her resurrection, or *le jour de Pâques*— drifting away, at home in the sky. Love itself, as in *Sunrise,* is perfect; only society can spoil it.

'It portrays the world as it will be in ten years time if . . .' said Chabrol of *La Rupture* when it was in production. 'A really black film.' True, but also a dazzlingly tender one which confirms the emotion, moving beyond reach of the printed word in its utter simplicity. . . . (p. 9)

Tom Milne, "Songs of Innocence," in Sight and Sound *(copyright © 1970 by The British Film Institute), Vol. 40, No. 1, Winter, 1970-71, pp. 7-9.*

ROBERT GIARD

This Man Must Die (Que la Bête Meure) may be Chabrol's *Iliad.* It is, at least according to the description of that work given by the film's protagonist as he helps Philippe with his homework—Philippe, adolescent son of the man whom he intends to kill for the death of his own young son in a hit-and-run accident. He offers *The Iliad* as an example of a work which is conventional, even banal, in its story, but unconventional, even "poetic," in its details. That, he announces, makes for art. These very words are a fair description of Chabrol's own film. . . . The broad lines of the action follow the conventions of a conventional genre: the detective story.

However, Chabrol is nodding a bit half-heartedly in the

direction of these conventions. Any hard-core devotee of the detective story who goes to this film anticipating the customary delights of the genre will come away feeling, to some degree at any rate, disappointed and cheated. Chabrol is after other game. Yes, it is a detective story and, yes, it is about one man looking for another; but the emphasis is not on the plot details of seeking and finding. The emphasis is on why a man looks, what it feels like always and only to be looking, and what it means at last to find. And yes, as the opening shot gently coming into focus reminds us, it is, very importantly, about a child.

Chabrol is cooly cavalier about the niceties of plot and character. He and the hero relinquish the mechanics of discovery to chance, sheer chance—with happy, if unlikely results. Charles is unexpectedly put on the trail of [Hélène], a television actress, who was in the death car, may even have been driving it. They are introduced; he says he is working on a script; they see a great deal of each other. There is a deft and curiously artificial scene in which the platitudes of conventional courtship are parodied by the characters. . . . [Chabrol's] object is to get you beyond the mechanics of plot and character towards where he is really headed. He couldn't be less bothered with these matters of a smooth surface; so he handles them as just that, mere surface—thin and stylish. What he exhibits is the civilized outer shell of his two characters. (pp. 26-7)

[What is being played out is a] story of the pleasure to be found in the contemplation of vengeance. This detective format is heavily laced with Chabrol's own deft observation of the social habits and physical accoutrements of the French middle class—a comedy of manners in its own right —especially at table.

Chabrol, a lover of Hitchcock, is attracted to the thriller. Throughout his career he has regularly employed the shape of the mystery or detective genre as a superstructure on which to pin his particular idiosyncracies. Often an artist will consciously exploit some known genre or story in order to play against it his own less conventional intentions. The combination generates a certain tension which is part of the aesthetic pleasure of the work. In *This Man Must Die* there is just such a tension between the instantly recognizable mechanics the traditional genre evokes and the highly personal stylistic and emotional preoccupations of the director.

But there is one problem: the artifices of a genre have a life and an energy of their own, apart from the more subtle purposes of the director. These mechanics march inexorably and autonomously along, making their own particular insistent demands on plot and character. Chabrol's detective story is the occasion for the appearance of two recognizable kinds of lawmen—recognizable, that is, not from life, but from other experiences within the genre: one bureaucratic, remote, and ominous in his dark glasses; the other personal, tactful, and appreciative. There are moments when Chabrol allows these mechanics to take over in order to move us on ahead to a point that interests him. For example, when the odds are against Charles' getting a first clue to the identity of his man, he—and Chabrol—entrust themselves to sheer chance—with expedient results when Charles' car gets stuck on a muddy stretch of road. Scenes required by conventions can be curiously flat and mechanical, comically deadpan. Charles' perfunctory courtship of Hélène Lanson is the most conspicuous example. The characterizations are subservient, not to our conventional expectations of three-dimensionality, but to the specific thematic concerns of Chabrol. Charles is a cypher beyond the ruling passions of his life. As for Hélène, those scenes in which Charles is getting to know her are telescoped. He tells us that she is intelligent, charming, etc., but we are given no persuasive indications that this is so. What dominates in her portrait and eventually involves the viewer and Charles in her story is that nervous vulnerability which has already led her, like Charles, to a break-down after the accident. (pp. 29-30)

Where Chabrol really runs into trouble with his conventions is in the last part of the film, after the television announcement of the murder. That is because these final scenes are taken up with cat-and-mouse, whodunnit, reversals stuff. The drive of the film has been Charles' obsession and that was consummated as he witnessed the sickly ritual of slow death on the television screen. The subsequent conversation with the sympathetic local police chief still exists in the aura of Charles' enormous satisfaction, and, as such is delicious—a quiet celebration of revenge. But what about the rest? Chabrol doesn't seem to be quite certain on what note he should conclude his film. What has been the main business of the film as stated in these final scenes? Are they the resolution of a genre plot? There is even a faint and seemingly deliberate ambiguity as to who really did commit the murder. Structural ironies? A man kills another man's son and in turn is murdered by his own son who has taken the other man for a substitute father. Philosophical questions? Something's funny because the beast of "Ecclesiastes," from which the title is drawn as well as the lyrics to the Brahms song on the soundtrack, is not a monster but one with man, the mortal animal. Meanwhile the film has worked, not with ideas of mortality, despite its heavy atmosphere of bereavement, but rather with images of a monstrous man—the costume-party bear in the home movies threatening the children: Paul in all his rambunctious animality.

Are those last moments merely lyrical gratuities? The Homeric embellishments Charles spoke of? Why then are they suffused with intention by the letter which Charles is leaving with Hélène? Finally, do they constitute the resolution of some journey of character? (p. 30)

If this detective story is the convention, what are the details which are the poetry of Chabrol's *Iliad*? What is the film really about that places it squarely in the Chabrol canon? . . . [The] long elegy which is the first part of the film [is] best represented by the tracking shot as the camera passes by but turns towards Charles clutching the toy bear. This sideways movement occurs at several of the most exciting points in the film. . . . On a smaller scale, there are the obliquely angled tracking shots across table and desks in various scenes as he makes entries into his diary. Sometimes there will be a deliberately obscuring object: a lamp, for example. In characteristic Chabrol fashion a scene at table becomes the vehicle for many things other than eating. Charles, a gourmet of sorts, is celebrating his victory with fine food. While taking evident delight in what is set before him, he calmly tells Hélène who he is and that his intention at the beginning had been to use her. The camera pans from his contained triumph, expressed only by his almost total absorption in his food, past an arbitrarily striking vase of yellow daffodils, to Hélène, always vulnerable, now crumbling. She fumbles with her cigarette and weeps. Meanwhile, the camera has been cutting to the chef who is performing the masterful operation of dismembering a duck and serving it up. The tension between the controlled ceremony of eating on the one hand and Hélène's uncontrolled emotion on the other hand, between the precise classical surface and the groping undercurrent of pain is characteristic of the entire film. These shafts of revelation penetrating the limpid surface of Chabrol's film are the Homeric details which are unique and personal and for which the conventions of the detective film provide a framework. Charles recounts for Philippe a scene in *The Iliad* in which a warrior is pierced by a spear through the neck. The spear comes out through his mouth, and the warrior bites a cold metal tongue. Chabrol's spear-head tongue is a strangely menacing rotating overhead shot of two fried eggs sizzling gorgeously and monumentally in a frying pan. (pp. 30-1)

Robert Giard, "'This Man Must Die': Chabrol's 'Iliad'," in Film Heritage *(copyright 1971 by F. A. Macklin), Vol. 6, No. 3, Spring, 1971, pp. 26-31.*

JOHN BELTON

Claude Chabrol's *Le Boucher* explores the possibility (or impossibility) of love in a morally fatalistic universe. Working within the conventional context of a suspense thriller, the director creates a world limited by its characters' own perceptions and a love relationship restricted by the imperfect nature of that world.

Nevertheless, Chabrol's sympathetic direction of the story permits his characters a range of emotional expression—although inarticulated and tragically unrealized—that makes their frustrated love affair strangely beautiful. The director develops this love relationship on two levels: first, through the use of genre to define the ambivalent nature of their love and, second, through an infusion of uniquely Chabrolian moral elements to investigate the impossibility of his characters' redemption through love.

Le Boucher's use of a suppressed thriller format and its repeated references to Hitchcock continue a New Wave tradition of filmic film criticism. But Chabrol's formalism is never forced; he uses Hitchcockian elements because they belong, naturally, to the genre. And he uses a thriller structure because it best describes the relationship between his two central characters. In this respect, *Le Boucher* is more than a film about film, for Chabrol's characters have a real life of their own; they have a relationship outside of the superficial one given them by the conventional aspects of the story. . . .

If Chabrol's films have had any flaw in the past, it has been their overly schematic formalism—like the use of the Hamlet motif in *Ophelia* which is ultimately too powerful an analogy for Chabrol's own melodrama to overcome. But in *Le Boucher,* the formalistic aspects of the plot (thriller convention) actually serve the thematic interests of the film's love story. What's most important in *Le Boucher,* as with Yvan in *Ophelia* and Jacqueline in *Les Bonnes Femmes,* is that the central character *imposes* a romanticized thriller perception upon her relationship and, *by willing it so,* forces her affair (and the film) to its tragic conclusion. . . . (p. 46)

The exploration of the limits of love within a limited universe has been one of the chief concerns of Chabrol's cinematic career. *Le Boucher* is the most subtle, most concise, most gentle, and perhaps most beautiful realization of this uniquely Chabrolian motif. The central characters, Popaul and Helene, have, as we are shown in the opening wedding scene, an intangible bond between them; the two-shot framing and the cutting from the bride and the groom to them reinforces their spiritual union. But they also lack something; Chabrol's anonymous introduction of them and their apparent uneasiness together (e.g. Popual's awkward entrance into her classroom with a leg of lamb instead of flowers, like a lover, or an apple, like a student) make their relationship seem somewhat limited. There is a mysterious gulf between them, and it is this lack, this absence, which dooms their relationship.

The cigarette lighter that represents their love relationship paradoxically ties them together and tears them apart. As an object it symbolizes the divergent forces within each which limit their ability to love one another. When Helene first presents the lighter to Popaul, right after she has turned down his awkward sexual proposal, it represents a surrogate relationship, but a relationship nevertheless. Later, when she finds the lighter by a murdered girl's body and hides it from the police, the lighter, originally a symbol of her love for him, becomes a symbol of the new state of their relationship, or her tacit complicity with him and his guilt. It not only implicates her literally and psychologically (her rebuff of his advances?) in the murder through a Hitchcockian transference of guilt, but also widens the invisible gap that holds them apart.

As Chabrol's brilliant treatment of the subsequent scenes suggests, it's not really important whether the lighter belongs to Popaul or not. What is important is that Helene *believes* that it does. In a sense, then, it is the limitations of each character's perceptions that limit their relationship. As Hamlet says, in lines as characteristic of Chabrol as Shakespeare, "there is nothing good or bad but thinking makes it so." (pp. 46-7)

Why should Chabrol point out a disharmony between perceived guilt and real guilt when both of them ultimately point to the same truth? Because he sees a fundamental imperfection in the universe which allows no possibility of the absolute truth and the perceived truth coming together, *even when they are the same. . . .* Thus, it is not Popaul's real guilt that keeps the two apart, but an imperfection in perception, an imperfection in the world, a state of Original Sin. In this light, then, Chabrol's distinction between absolute truth and perceived truth is analogous to the relationship between real sin and venial sin, which Catholic dogma paradoxically distinguishes between *and* equates.

In *Le Boucher,* Chabrol creates a universe in which there is no possibility of redemption or salvation for his characters. He represents evil, for the most part, as an absence, as something unseen but, nevertheless, deeply felt. (p. 48)

Le Boucher moves from public to private. The film begins with long sweeping pans, suggestive of a visual openness. . . . All these shots present the characters in a smooth temporal and spatial continuum and help to define their seemingly impenetrable surfaces as their sole reality. But the second half of the film is quite different. Chabrol begins to cut intensively during the last schoolhouse scene and the editing seems to destroy this initial continuity of surface. . . . Chabrol's cutting gives this section of the film a sense of conflict and of personal emotional turmoil which the long takes and public tracking shots in the first half lacked.

The last scene of the film, in terms of editing, is a sort of enigmatic compromise. Chabrol's cuts in and out on the same axis (from medium to long to longer shot), which give an illusive sense of a syncopated tracking shot . . . , break the continuity of time and space that a single track or zoom would create. As a result, the editing adds a highly-charged emotional element to the scene in that it both traps Helene in a sadly melancholic setting (long shots) and suggests, in its discontinuity, her emotional isolation in that setting.

In many ways, this last scene represents the purification of the absence that has haunted the film from its first scene. Spatially, it leaves Helene with no architectural stability to cling to, no protective environment. Where, at first, the solid presence of the village seems to give Helene moral strength, to make her almost invulnerable, now its absence leaves her defenceless and alone. The absence of emotion in her face, a purification of the inarticulation of her emotion throughout the film, transforms it into a mysteriously inscrutable mask, concealing the depth of her emotion. The camera movement which draws away from her at the end becomes a cosmic statement on a character unable to transcend her limitations, and leaves us with a sense that we have been seeing, through Chabrol's vision, not a limited view of the universe, but a view of a limited universe. (p. 50)

John Belton, "'Le Boucher': The Limited Universe" (©, 1972, by Spectator International, Inc.; copyright reassigned to the Author's estate; ©, 1980, by the Kilimanjaro Corporation), in Cinema, *Vol. 7, No. 2, Spring, 1972, pp. 46-8, 50.*

DIANE JACOBS

At first glance Henry James' "Bench Of Desolation" seems an odd choice of subject matter for a Claude Chabrol film. A rather low-keyed short story pivoting around a fastidious rare-book shop owner, "Bench Of Desolation" is a far cry from such recent Chabrol oeuvres as *Wedding in Blood* and *Nada*. Nevertheless, *Bench of Desolation* is the finest short film I've seen in years, and I suspect that its success, like that of Chabrol's "Hitchcockian" works, is directly related to an aesthetic tension—in this case the tension between the auteur's sensibility and the author's craft. . . .

[Chabrol] has always been fascinated with the darker aspects of complacency (most often bourgeois complacency) and the ambivalences of apparent good versus evil; thus his sympathy with James is as natural as his intuitive empathy for Lang.

Both James and Chabrol are concerned with the idiosyncrasies of the particular, and the discrepancies in their thematic preoccupations are reflected more in style than in substance. While the former tends to implode and distill, the latter is inclined to dazzle and externalize. In *Bench of Desolation*, we are treated to the best of both worlds. . . .

The sensibilities of James and Chabrol coalesce most beautifully at the end of the film when Dodd is once again seated on his bench of desolation—this time with a transformed Kate. In deference to James, Chabrol has eschewed his habitual outward manifestations of passion—the *deus ex machina* violence that arises in all his other works to finish off plot, theme, and usually at least one major character as well. Nonetheless, when we watch the camera pull back to reveal Kate's body entangling Dodd, we are aware that she has killed Nan as sure as any Chabrol lover ever killed his or her rival. More important, in accepting Kate's succor, the apparently victimized Dodd has become a posthumous collaborator in his wife's death, the recipient in Chabrol's habitual transfer of guilt.

Diane Jacobs, "Claude Chabrol's 'The Bench of Desolation': Implosions Externalized," in Take One *(copyright © 1973 by Unicorn Publishing Corp.), Vol. 4, No. 6, July-August, 1973, p. 26.*

DAVID L. OVERBEY

If Chabrol is to be believed, *Les Noces Rouges* . . . is the last film of his Balzacian *comédie humaine* of French society in the middle twentieth century. In this new film, written by Chabrol without the active help of his usual scenarist Paul Gegauff, the bourgeoisie are less charming, less discreet, less intelligent, and far more corrupt than Chabrol has ever before shown them. . . .

The shape of Chabrol's plot is a classic triangle-murder, owing as much to the tradition of James M. Cain's *The Postman Always Rings Twice* as to press stories about the similar murders in Bourganeuf. . . .

The characters and story, of course, no matter what their ultimate source, are pure Chabrol. His tone and manner are the aciform irony we have come to expect, tempered in (can it be said once again?) the hell of a Langian trap and the revelational—if not redemptive—Hitchcockian confessional. . . .

[When Pierre and Lucienne have a love affair because of their loveless marriages, we are not] being offered a romantic solution to provincial frustrations. Just as Chabrol parodied the romantic cinema with his swooping tracking shots in the lovers' walk through the poppy fields as long ago as *La Double Tour,* in *Les Noces Rouges* he so controls the love scenes of Pierre and Lucienne that they are as hilarious as they are erotic. (p. 234)

In *Les Noces Rouges,* as in every film Chabrol has made in the series, which can be extended back as far as *Le Beau Serge,* there is a Paul. This time, however, there is no Hélène or Charles. Chabrol has said that Hélène is partially a creature of myth, and that 'Charles will never kill Paul.' Charles was the character who was incapable of final corruption, who was often an idealist and dreamer. In *Les Noces Rouges,* as in the underrated *Doctor Popaul,* it would seem that Paul can be killed by a changed Charles character. The dreamers and the dream, as well as the Hélène of romantic myth, are no more. So it is that Chabrol ends his rich series of bourgeois melodramas. A new sort of system? A new basis for human relationships? Why, they never even dreamed of that! (pp. 234-35)

David L. Overbey, "Film Reviews: 'Les Noces Rouges'," in Sight and Sound *(copyright © 1973 by The British Film Institute), Vol. 42, No. 4, Autumn, 1973, pp. 234-35.*

TOM MILNE

In a blue silk dressing-gown royally patterned in gold, the Minister of the Interior sits in his salon watching television. Just for a moment, as his private secretary hurries in to inform him that a terrorist group has kidnapped the American ambassador in Paris, he and his lady, her white hair piled high in a discreet pompadour, are waxwork echoes of Louis XVI and Marie-Antoinette learning that the mob is at the gates. Seconds later, as a helicopter lands in front of the chateau to whisk the Minister off to deal with the crisis, floodlights illuminate the façade of the building as though it were a *monument historique* for public delectation.

This superb gloss—the irony, of course, is that nothing in the state's machiavellian handling of the situation will bear public scrutiny—is almost the only flourish Chabrol has brought to *Nada*. . . , a hallucinatingly faithful adaptation, scripted by the author himself, of Jean-Patrick Manchette's *Série Noire* thriller. Gone are the serpentine camera movements and brooding half-lights of intention and responsibility one has come to associate with Chabrol. Instead, working brilliantly as a straightforward thriller, the film is shot in a direct head-on style taken from the book where everything is on the surface, and the transference of guilt is to the spectator forced to take sides by the events themselves. . . .

[Chabrol's] terrorists are a confused, ramshackle bunch. . . . Their vague, undefined motivations—frustration, despair, curiosity, camaraderie—are pulled shakily together by an equally vague symbol of meaningfulness: the Spaniard. . . , picturesquely attired in black from beard to broad-brimmed hat, who infuses them with the long-dead spirit of the anarchists. . . .

All the more explosive for their ideological uncertainty, the NADA group are presented without complaisance. . . .

[The] film undermines reactions by demonstrating that, however wrongheadedly, however reprehensibly, the NADA group are on the side of life against an insidious, creeping rigor mortis. In spite of the monstrosity of the situation, normality reasserts itself at the hide-out with disarming, unforced innocence: the alcoholic dozing in the sun, huddled like a puppy in a nest of straw; the touchingly fumbling, disappointed affair between the veteran and the girl; the sense of friendship, complicity, pride in the new day they may be making. Against this, and against the proud banner of loyalty still flying at the end between the Spaniard and the philosopher (who has opted out for reasons of conscience), are set the cold, calculating machinations of the forces of order. . . .

Nada is a tough film, all the more so in that it refuses to pledge its heart unequivocally to the Left.

Tom Milne, "Film Reviews: 'Nada'," in Sight and Sound *(copyright © 1974 by The British Film Institute), Vol. 43, No. 2, Spring, 1974, p. 119.*

JOHN SIMON

To the French, the drama of adultery is what the Western is to Americans. And no Frenchman in recent times has churned out more of these dramas than Claude Chabrol, whose specialty is adultery seasoned with murder. Chabrol is an interesting case: a charter member of the New Wave, he is, in terms of camera movement, framing of shots, and subtle sense of how to play on the viewer's sensibility, the equal of his idol, Hitchcock. He falls short only of the true artists: the Welles of *Citizen Kane,* and the great European and Japanese masters. In his finest film, *La Femme Infidèle,* Chabrol may have achieved that intensity of perception, sympathy for human joy and suffering, and economy of expression without histrionics that are three of the hallmarks of art. But for all his basic elegance, Chabrol has made some remarkably trashy films.

His characters often behave with an absurdity or perversity that is artistically unacceptable and even clinically inconceivable. It surpasses mere stupidity but falls short of genuine pathology, coming off instead as deliberate, meaningless authorial manipulation, producing on the audience numbness rather than shock. Along with this dehumanization of his characters, Chabrol goes in for plot developments and endings that are worse than simpleminded—almost imbecile. People who have managed to function with appreciable ingenuity suddenly commit inordinate errors or become profoundly untidy; are unmasked by their most primitive opponents, or voluntarily turn themselves in for no good reason. . . .

If criminals collapsed as easily as they do in Chabrol's new *Wedding in Blood,* very few would have the nerve to commit a crime in the first place. The adulterous killers of this film are caught out so easily that one cannot avoid the impression that Chabrol's real concern was only with the ironic concluding close-up of their hands fatally united by manacles, and that it hardly mattered to him how to bring this about. His deus ex machina is the woman's pretty, staring-eyed daughter, whose behavior is generally puzzling, but whose final maneuver is not so much beyond as beneath credibility.

Yet *Wedding in Blood* is still among Chabrol's better films, despite, or because of, its simplemindedness: at least it avoids the elaborately excogitated absurdities of some of the others. Actually, what makes the film interesting, over and above the sheer technical expertise, is its evocation of physical passion. Its hero and heroine . . . are sometimes grotesquely, sometimes shatteringly, in the grips of a fleshly craving for each other such as has seldom if ever been conveyed on screen. . . .

Too bad, however, that all this is not at the service of a more imaginative plot or more fully developed characters. Outside their exemplary passion for each other, these two beings are not accorded much of a personality, and the fact that their respective spouses are so gross or so dreary makes for a sadly unequal contest. . . . [The fluidity of the camera is] truly impressive, except in one of those overfanciful circular pans that have become Chabrol's personal signature, like Hitchcock's walk-ons. A beautiful film, then, with no baroque effects, but, ultimately, empty.

John Simon, "Films: 'Wedding in Blood'" (reprinted by permission of Wallace & Sheil Agency, Inc.; copyright © 1974 John Simon), in Esquire, *Vol. LXXXII, No. 2, August, 1974, p. 10.*

PENELOPE GILLIATT

Passions that exist only in infirm half forms are a theme of ["Juste Avant la Nuit"]. Charles's fatal game with Laura is one of danger without adventurousness and of sex without eroticism. His very story is one of calamity without tragedy. The only thing moving about it is the pity of the fact that perhaps, in his catastrophic link with Laura, he was outmatched. . . .

In "Juste Avant la Nuit," the suggestion is that the hero is in a state of madness because he believes that he has savaged the natural order and that the natural order can be reinstated only by his own extinction. The more Charles repents, the more he enforces the death he importunes. He chooses to solicit his wife to murder him, but it is really a case of suicide: at the end, he can hear as clearly as we can the sound of the exorbitant number of drops of laudanum falling into the glass, administered by a wife who is less his accomplice than his hireling. He is thus doubly guilty, according to the count of this ambiguously religious film: guilty of causing his wife to murder, and guilty of killing himself. Then Chabrol's extremely pagan sense of humor comes into play, and the end of the film shows Hélène on a windy beach reading a letter from François in which he admires his friend for his courage in committing suicide and finishes with an invocation to God. As the film sees it, Charles's plight is his liking for a state of disruption. It is a liking that he recognizes to be satanic but is powerless to do anything about. . . .

The prankish cynicism of Chabrol may be one of the masks that he uses as a means of provoking conjecture about virtue: including the matter of his own virtue, which he treats skittishly and with a braying laugh that quite possibly hides prayer, as Hamlet's does. "Juste Avant la Nuit" could be taken to be a wittily knowing essay on sadomasochism. But it seems to me to be much more concerned with doubt. A psychoanalytic interpretation belittles the work. . . . (p. 51)

Chabrol's notion of justice is distinct and barbarous. An idiotic act like Charles's, he thinks, can be rectified only by an idiotic conclusion. Charles's death is idiotic in the antique sense of uncultivated, and also in the eighteenth-century sense of clownish. It lays itself open to being misunderstood even by his best friend. Both lack of cultivation and clownishness are recurring strains in Chabrol's characters, and he would not regard either of them as being antithetical to the heroic. Charles's will to destruction, it seems, comes from a fear of mediocrity. . . . [His] clownish last gesture, in which even his suicide is a piece of stage management, seems meant by Chabrol to be the act of one of aesthetics' long line of holy fools. In Charles are concealed the nobility and distress of the simpleton in literary tradition. (p. 52)

Penelope Gilliatt, "Chabrol's Holy Idiots," in The New Yorker *(© 1975 by The New Yorker Magazine, Inc.), Vol. Ll, No. 24, August 4, 1975, pp. 51-2.*

JOHN RUSSELL TAYLOR

Of all the filmmakers who emerged in the first flush of the French *nouvelle vague* during the mid-1950's, none has remained more of a problem to critics than Claude Chabrol: mainly because there seems to be no problem. All the rest who belonged to the group of writers on film gathered around the intellectual magazine *Cahiers du Cinéma* and its inspirer and spiritual leader, André Bazin, were immediately recognizable as, in conventional critical terms, "serious" filmmakers. . . . But Chabrol, after what seemed like a decent if relatively conservative start in the same direction with *Le Beau Serge* and *Les Cousins,* drifted off into films that were taken as eccentric, baroque, marginal, camp, and then, horror of horrors, downright and unashamedly commercial. (p. 8)

Then came *Les Biches,* and a hasty reevaluation process began. A revival of talent was postulated, or a change of heart, or the triumph of Chabrol's better artistic nature over the temptations of commercial success, or a last, late chance to make something "worthwhile" bravely taken by Chabrol to release himself from the commercial grind which maybe (for we could have misjudged him) he had accepted only as a painful necessity preventing him from doing better things. Yet, if we look back over Chabrol's career to date, all these formulations seem simplistic, because the films he has made do not *feel* like that: of all the New Wave directors, Chabrol seems to have been the most consistent in his style, his choice of subject matter, his attitude toward his medium. None of these has been in itself fashionable, though from time to time they have lent themselves to the production of something that could fit in with fashionable prejudices of the moment. But faced with Chabrol's by now considerable body of work, it is difficult to believe that he has really cared whether he was fashionable or unfashionable. . . . (pp. 8-9)

There are few directors whose films are more difficult to explain or evoke on paper, if only because so much of the overall effect turns on Chabrol's sheer hedonistic relish for the medium. Obvious enjoyment of a craft or an art (or both) is one of the hardest things to convey in words, and one tends to fall back on a flat statement that it is there, hoping one's readers will accept this, or make allowances by referring written statements constantly back to their own experience of the work under discussion. . . . But even when the film is unsuccessful, uncommunicative, perverse on account of its private nature, there is something lovable about a director who can still, within the bosom of the commercial cinema, approach his medium in this grandly throwaway fashion.

And Chabrol is above all, I think, a lovable director. . . . "Lovable" may seem a strange word to apply to a filmmaker who has concentrated almost exclusively on crime and violent, often perverse passions in his films; who is consciously and unconsciously the most prominent and gifted cinematic disciple of that splendid old monster Hitchcock. And yet the quality immediately apparent in Chabrol's most ruthless films is a certain irrepressible jollity and good nature; his view of life is, I believe, essentially comic, even if sometimes bitingly, one might say cruelly, comic. . . . But solemnity and seriousness are not the same thing; and within Chabrol's comic vision of things lurks an attitude just as serious as and decidedly more realistic than that of many whose seriousness is more obtrusively worn on their sleeve. (pp. 9-10)

Even today, it is hard to come to any cut-and-dried conclusion about Chabrol. Part of the problem is that he seems so easy to pin down. His world is so small and limited; he deals with the same situations over and over again, from slightly different angles; even the names of his characters recur—Hélène, Charles, and Paul forever locked in a triangle, forever reenacting the same drama, beginning with *Les Cousins,* which set the pattern and introduced us to the first Charles and the first Paul (*L'Oeil du Malin* gave us the first Hélène). Nearly all his films have a dinner-table scene; murder is involved at some point; detectives usually come in twos and Chabrol does not take them too seriously; most *femmes* are *infidèles;* and evil and its embodiments we can be sure exist.

Beyond that, one can see two distinct phases in his style, separated by his commercial period. The films from *Les*

Cousins to *Landru* are visually ornate, baroque in their treatment of surface and texture, their penchant for extravagant effects of lighting and color. . . . [Since] *Les Biches* his films have been cool, limpid, simple in style almost to the point of self-denial. All these things are true of Chabrol. And yet the man himself, and the exact nature of his talent, remains elusive. Is he Christian or atheist, social critic or bourgeois conformist? Does he condemn his beasts implicitly, or is his obsession with them, his consistent attempts to get us to see their point of view, symptomatic of some deeper fascination . . . ? (pp. 41-2)

Chabrol is a puzzle, finally, because where others of his generation and background have devoted themselves assiduously and sometimes in a self-deflating way to art, Chabrol has given most of his attention to the elaboration of entertainment. (p. 42)

And yet, after all, though he can fit in with commerce and make, even at his most uncommercial, films that seem to present few surface difficulties to the spectator, no matter how complex the human truths they embody, his main concern outside the admitted potboilers is much more hermetic-seeming than that of most of his more evidently highbrow colleagues and contemporaries. His obsessions are thoroughly private and personal, and he has pursued them from film to film with a concentration and dedication seldom matched elsewhere in the modern cinema. (p. 43)

John Russell Taylor, "Claude Chabrol," in his Directors and Directions: Cinema for the Seventies *(reprinted by permission of Hill & Wang, a division of Farrar, Straus & Giroux, Inc.; in Canada, by A D Peters & Co Ltd; copyright © 1975 by John Russell Taylor), Hill and Wang, 1975, pp. 8-43.*

RAINER WERNER FASSBINDER

Chabrol has not crystallised himself. On the contrary. Otherwise, in his later works, he would have developed more creatively François' perception at the end of *Le Beau Serge* that one must lend a helping hand. And thereby—honourably—he would probably have become a great film-maker. Now, with hindsight, the end of *Le Beau Serge* stands out as an artificially imposed, constipated Christian attitude. And Chabrol has not become a great film-maker—even though he has made many beautiful and successful films and even a few great ones.

Chabrol's viewpoint is not that of the entomologist, as is often claimed, but that of a child who keeps a collection of insects in a glass case and observes with alternating amazement, fear and delight the marvellous behaviour patterns of his tiny creatures. . . . His standpoint, in fact, varies. He doesn't investigate. Otherwise he could, and must, discover grounds for the brutality of existence and have more to say about it. Apart from the fact that there has to be a number of creatures who are less colourful than the others, less iridescent, in fact an overwhelming majority of colourless little creatures who provide the basis for the existence of the more beautiful ones. These, however, the child disregards; he does not investigate but merely glances at them, dazzled as he is by the glittering, strange ones. This prevents him from grasping the drawbacks of his preferred creatures. (p. 205)

Chabrol asks no questions, as his later films show; he advocates marriage. And marriage is first and foremost an establishment institution. Chabrol is opposed to the hypocrisy in marriage, opposed to the claims of ownership instead of being against marriage in itself. It is all cheap, both the feelings and the needs. No questions about the real needs and the real feelings. No indication that the needs one thinks one has are really only those expected of one.

In itself, everything seems to be in order. The disorders that arise for Chabrol are irrational, not inevitable deviations as they actually must be in such a system of society. Richard Marcoux (in *A Double Tour*), a badly brought-up son and murderer, does not become a murderer because of his upbringing but because he is weak-minded. And that is Chabrol's lie, a lie which prevents the spectator from taking the fairy-tale for reality. . . .

Chabrol must have become aware of the blind alley he'd landed in with *A Double Tour* and from which he was to extricate himself so perfectly later—when he made *Les Bonnes Femmes*. And had trouble with it. *Les Bonnes Femmes* is the only Chabrol film which deals almost entirely with real people and not shadows. At last Chabrol reveals a trace of tenderness for his characters—a tenderness later only manifested towards isolated characters. . . . Here, he enters with his characters into the most hateful and repugnant situations but he stays with them; the child has put his hand inside the glass case with the insects. Naturally he gets bitten. Thereafter, he won't be so quick to put his hand inside to deliver his creatures. At any rate, he hasn't done so up to date. True, he has fished out some particularly glittering insects and cautiously stroked them. But he's gone no further. . . .

Les Bonnes Femmes is a revolutionary film, for it provokes genuine anger against a system that leaves people so demoralised. It is a film which makes it quite clear that something must be done. . . .

In Chabrol, France has no critic, no twentieth-century Balzac (the role in which these films indicate he would like to see himself); but France does have an embryo cynic in Chabrol, a cynic with enormous nostalgia for the naïve, for lost identity. And from this remarkable juxtaposition spring films like *Marie Chantal contre Dr. Kha, La Ligne de Démarcation* and *La Route de Corinthe*. Apparently naïve films with naïve heroes. That is tolerable with the detective films, *Marie Chantal* and *La Route de Corinthe,* because the detective film is a naïve genre, but it becomes farcical when it aspires to reality as in *La Ligne de Démarcation*. (p. 206)

Le Scandale, although made before *La Route de Corinthe,* led him into the fourth period of creativity which is generally associated with the name of Chabrol. One could say, as a generalisation, that from now on Chabrol aims to knock bourgeois values. The question is: is he knocking them in order to overcome them or to maintain them? I think the latter is more likely. Agreed, Chabrol is somewhat saddened that things are no longer so clear and orderly; sad that mankind is so bad. It is still not the conditions and the system which makes people the way they are that interests Chabrol but the result—as long as it is picturesque enough. And that is really inhuman.

Chabrol's films in this latest period are inhuman because they are fatalistic, cynical, and contemptuous of mankind. Exceptions prove the rule. Remarkably, in contrast to the earlier periods, it is the stories of *Les Biches* and *La Rup-*

ture which, being non-realistically proposed from the outset, one can tolerate. And *Le Boucher* is a great film in which Chabrol consistently, and for the first time, develops a story dealing with real people. Alas, the only time. The only film where he doesn't pummel the audience into accepting senseless proceedings as inevitable. Otherwise, he knocks the public over the head and does so with such perfect form that one can hardly resist. That's why it's so dangerous. In itself, this universe seems all right. But it has nothing to do with the lives of those who pay for films at the box-office; it makes no connection with them, apart from *Les Biches* and *La Rupture*.

Both these films, remote though they are, are still to some extent accessible, and it doesn't matter that there are no people there, only shadows. Shadows with an elusive glamour whose tale will be well told. Chabrol controls his narrative art to perfection—even though the films become ever more slovenly in their form. . . . And two downright bad films: *Dr. Popaul* and *Nada*. Here we have complete fascism. Quite clearly. But it was always lurking there and had to come out one day. (p. 252)

Rainer Werner Fassbinder, "Insects in a Glass Case: Random Thoughts on Claude Chabrol" (originally published as "Schatten freilich und Kein Mitleid," in Reihe Film 5: Claude Chabrol, *edited by Peter W. Jansen and Wolfram Schütte, Carl Hanser Verlag, 1975), translated by Derek Prouse, in* Sight and Sound *(copyright © 1976 by The British Film Institute), Vol. 45, No. 4, Autumn, 1976, pp. 205-06, 252.*

DOUGLAS McVAY

Several episodes [in *Les Innocents aux Mains Sales*] of legal skirmishing and police detective-work are at once verbosely expository and tiresomely facetious. Chabrol's direction occasionally lapses into repetitive cross-cutting during dialogue exchanges, or alternatively into gratuitous visual and aural excess for moments of eroticism or melodrama. These flaws prevent the film from being ranked among his supreme achievements in the vein of bourgeois sexuality, emotional conflict and physical violence.

Yet *Les Innocents aux Mains Sales* still possesses many sequences and flashes of great skill, beauty and power: and it remains essential viewing for anybody who believes Chabrol to be one of the three best movie-makers currently working in France. Like Hitchcock in *Shadow of a Doubt* and Resnais in *Stavisky,* Chabrol in this picture expresses his subject-matter (duplicity) in a series of duplicated effects. . . .

The resolution of *Les Innocents* like those of all Chabrol's better films, operates on more than one level. The numerous plot twists, typical of the whodunit genre, give rise to deeper and more affecting shifts of emotional allegiance amongst the protagonists. Thus the sadistic raping of the wife by the husband turns from an explosion of mutual hatred into a recognition of mutual love, crystallised in his words to her, "I will trust you, if you will trust me: and I will forgive you, if you will forgive me", accompanied by their gradual stretching out and clasping of hands as they lie together on the floor. . . . The concluding sequence, likewise, provides us with the second of two "resurrections". This finale is so ambiguous that it fails to round off the film with the meticulous psychological and dramatic rightness, the sense of rigorously worked-out Q.E.D., which distinguishes the finest of Chabrol's works.

Douglas McVay, "Films: 'Innocents with Dirty Hands," in Film *(reprinted by permission of British Federation of Film Societies), No. 33, January, 1976, p. 8.*

RICHARD COMBS

The last of Chabrol's films from the early Seventies to straggle into this country, *Docteur Popaul* arrives with a dauntingly unprepossessing reputation as a coarse misogynist jest. Coarse it certainly is, with its abrupt fluctuations between love triangle melodrama, soft-core sex farce and slapstick self-parody—and with a hero whose moral development seems to be from heartless cad to bewildered buffoon. . . .

The exact nature of the Chabrolian spoof, however, is rather easier to identify from the perspective of *La Décade Prodigieuse* and *Innocents aux Mains Sales* than it would have been in the context of *Le Boucher* and *Juste avant la Nuit*; its strategies roughly adumbrate the later films (particularly *Innocents*), removing moral complexities from bourgeois revenge-and-guilt plots . . . and trying them out for size on characters who will either distend and toy with them with Wellesian presumption or kick them about with the raffish conceit of a Belmondo. A comic book motif is tossed into a couple of early shots of *Docteur Popaul,* to cue the way we should see its hero; his vaunted preference for ugly women because only they have "moral beauty" remains as narcissistic a mannerism as the way he combs back his hair. . . . [Chabrol's closely worked moral patterns] are resoundingly overturned by *Docteur Popaul*—the bull in Chabrol's china shop; to such an extent, in fact, that the Providence which reliably helps Popaul out of every jam has little to do with Lang and begins to look, self-mockingly, like the nastiest Hollywood convention. . . . (p. 27)

[What] most limits Chabrol here is his failure to come up with any kind of formal strategy for holding all the jokes and narrative shifts together (certainly nothing like the wicked toying with the story-telling processes themselves that underlies *La Décade* and *Innocents*). He seems instead to have stuck to his original thriller material, with all its twists and surprises, despite an equally evident compulsion to send it up; the result, particularly in the final scenes, is an indigestible conflation of plot and camp parody. But for all its uncertainties and excesses, *Docteur Popaul* remains a genuine and quite appealing Chabrol oddity, and not the ignominious flaunting of the director's vulgarity for which it has been taken and roundly condemned. (p. 28)

Richard Combs, "'Docteur Popaul' ('Scoundrel in White')," in Monthly Film Bulletin *(copyright © The British Film Institute, 1976), Vol. 43, No. 505, February, 1976, pp. 27-8.*

JAMES MONACO

Chabrol owes a debt to Hitchcock, but there are significant differences between their universes. Chabrol himself in recent interviews has not missed an opportunity to suggest that Fritz Lang's films might be more important referents than Hitchcock's, and with good reason, I think. Central to the classic Hitchcock film is a sense of the tension in the relationship between pursuer and pursued—an element which is not all that important in Chabrol's films, and which he often avoids completely, as in *Juste avant la nuit (Just Before Nightfall)*. Hitchcock's films develop a political sense because the detective so often represents the state and because the pursued is often innocent. But everyone is always guilty in Chabrol's films. This is a darker, more Langian guilt than we ever see in Hitchcock where in fact most characters are innocent. Chabrol's people, like Lang's suffer psychological guilt even when the law overlooks their transgressions, while Hitchcock's people don't—even when they are rightly accused. (pp. 256-57)

However, to concentrate on the moral dimensions of Chabrol's world—whether religious, Hitchcockian, or Langian—is a bit misleading; for Chabrol is more concerned with the structure of his films than with the metaphysics of his characters. . . . This—not metaphysics—is Chabrol's most important debt to Hitchcock: a sense of the curious relationship between filmmaker and audience and an understanding of the psychological power of the medium. We may criticize Chabrol's films for their insipid politics, for their cavalier attitude towards their characters, but when he is at his best Chabrol has no peers as a manipulator of the medium. (p. 257)

The elements of Chabrol's "decameron" [the ten films produced between 1968-1973] are easily identified: the materials are thoroughly bourgeois, as is the ambiance. One of the central questions in Chabrol criticism is whether or not (as Robin Wood has put it [see Wood and Michael Walker excerpt above]) "the savage derider of the bourgeoisie has become its elegiac poet." This is not such an easy question to answer as might at first seem. Chabrol reveals a considerable ambivalence towards the bourgeois universe, as we shall see, but it should be emphasized that the subtlety of his films demands a corresponding sense of irony in his audiences. Even when Chabrol is most rhapsodically bourgeois there is still a distancing which gives the films a critical dimension. The problem arises when we place more emphasis on character than Chabrol does and therefore identify with (or infer that Chabrol identifies with) the good businessmen and carefully coiffed and perfumed matrons who people his landscape.

More important, I think, than the bourgeois subject matter of the films is what Chabrol does with it. These are all strongly materialist films in which the qualities of light and texture, the "meanings" of landscape and color, and the way the camera captures, conveys, and modifies these materials take precedence over the données of plot and character. Chabrol is acutely aware of the function of location within a film, and much of his energy during shooting is devoted to capturing the particular qualities of the locale. (p. 258)

In the context of these finely observed backgrounds, Chabrol's characters find themselves absorbed, not in the melodramatic events which usually constitute the fabric of a thriller, but in the mundane rituals of everyday life. It has become almost a joke, for example, that meals are an obsession with Chabrol. . . . The family, as a political concept, is extended in several of the films to embrace the village—a larger matrix out of which arises, as in *Le Boucher,* occasional aberrant violence. Chabrol's films seldom come to a distinct period; the reason is that the plane of focus is this larger unit (the family or the village), which continues even after the particular story ends. There is an ironic tension between the environment and the passion which is basic to a Chabrol film.

Chabrol organizes all of these structural elements in three dimensions. First, there is the basic excuse of the genre: the *policier* provides the framework within which these elements can be set; the murders are the catalysts which help in our analysis of the structures. Second, Chabrol sets up an elaborate network of conventions—some of which come from the genre, many of which are his alone—which formalize and de-dramatize the proceedings. There is, for example, a recurrent pattern of exchanges of responsibility between characters throughout the films, which some critics have interpreted as signifying Catholic theories of guilt transference. The dialectic between city and country first established in *Le Beau Serge* (and mirrored in *Les Cousins*) is probably the most striking example of this. . . . Last, and most important, is the subtle emphasis on point of view which marks Chabrol's films. As we have indicated earlier, mise-en-scène almost always takes precedence over psychology—and the strength of the mise-en-scène forces our consciousness that these events and characters are seen from a precise point of view. This dimension is more abstract than the previous two and not so easily apprehended, but it just may be the key to understanding Claude Chabrol's movies. On the one hand, it is a sign of the formalism of the films; on the other, if we don't have a sense of this filmmaker's irony, not a few of his films degenerate into maudlin exercises in melodrama: this irony is the ultimate rationale for his devotion to "little themes." If we can't sense it, then most of his films have only formal interest for us. (pp. 259-60)

The ten films Chabrol made between 1968 and 1973 are an unusual achievement. They are simpler in design than the films he made a decade earlier, and that simplicity gives them a sharper focus. With the exception of *Nada (The Nada Gang),* the last one, each of them concentrates on the finely tuned sensibilities of the bourgeois characters Chabrol knows best. Whereas the earlier films had been populated for the most part by young people, this group deals almost exclusively with middle-aged characters. *Nada* is a blow for independence from that middle-aged, middle-class milieu; but this time Chabrol is a stranger in the city of youth.

There is less psychologizing now, but paradoxically a greater depth of character. There is a much more controlled formalism, but—again paradoxically—less distance felt between us and the characters. Our sense of these changes is communicated through the increasingly masterful mise-en-scène, now more restrained, almost rigid at times. What strikes us first about these films is their stunning craftsmanship. There isn't one that doesn't offer at least three or four sequences that are breathtaking tours de force. It's a curious fact that the parts of Chabrol's films are often more impressive than the wholes—and conversely, each of his films has more meaning when seen in context with its neighbors than it does when it stands alone.

This loosely linked series began in 1968 with *Les Biches (The Does, The Girlfriends),* a film which . . . has a structure that is congruent with both *Les Cousins* and *Les Godelureaux:* the classic triangle of sexual jealousy. *Les Biches,* however, has a symmetry which was lacking in the earlier films. It is still a story of initiation, of an innocent corrupted, but Chabrol now gives equal weight to each side of the figure. . . . The genius of the film lies in this highly subtle symmetry, a system of balances which gives it an illusive shimmer. (pp. 269-70)

As in all Chabrol's best films the closely worked details of the relationships are the key. It is through them that he achieves the aura of violent, fatal complicity which links all his characters and which makes the films, finally, not case histories of aberrant *others*, but memories of ourselves. The murder plots, more and more obviously, are cinematic conventions which serve mainly to heighten strong, wide currents of passion—emotions which envelop and represent repressed bourgeois society. The trip towards the politics of *Nada* is a long one, but *Nada* is always the destination on the horizon. (p. 271)

[*Nada*] is Chabrol's first venture outside the safe confines of the charmed bourgeois lifestyle. It elicits a complex response, for the salient characteristic of the film is its ambivalent tone. The irony with which Chabrol treats the bourgeois power structure is lethal, as we might expect, but the attitude the film takes towards the varied crew of militants who comprise the Nada group is at times self-conscious and tendentious. Chabrol is not nearly so familiar with these people as he is with their natural enemies. And he seems to find it necessary to excuse the serious nature of his subject by injecting the exaggerated flavor of a cheap thriller, mainly through the soundtrack (loud, insistent "chase" music and military themes) but also in the mise-en-scène. *Nada* reveals very little of the visual sophistication we have come to expect from Chabrol. It is filmed in a straightforward style which betrays his uneasiness with the subject matter. (p. 282)

Existentially, the actions of the Nada group justify themselves. The point is that the question of terrorism is a serious dilemma for the left; it has not yet been resolved, it never was resolved in earlier eras, it probably won't be resolved in our own. By rephrasing it Chabrol answers the question, but avoids the dilemma. The solution is semantic, not practical. . . . We could, nevertheless, read into *Nada* an understanding of the excruciating nature of that dilemma were it not for the ambivalent mise-en-scène of the scenes with the Nada group. With the bourgeoisie Chabrol is more at home, as in the scenes devoted to the actions of the Minister of the Interior (who sleeps under a glowing portrait of Pompidou and enters the fray in his own personal helicopter as his wife waves goodbye from the steps of their floodlit chateau), and to the chief of police and the various operatives of intelligence and counterintelligence who are at war with each other while they are battling Nada. . . . There is considerable humor in these scenes, which contrast sharply with the scenes of the group alone.

It is doubtful that Chabrol will ever be able to get any closer to the people of Nada; but with all its problems the film is a refreshing attempt to move out of the constricting circles of bourgeois guilt into psychological as well as political liberation. (pp. 283-84)

[His current] furious schedule of production is a sign of Chabrol's most important contribution to the New Wave. Truffaut may have investigated genres with greater intelligence. Godard condemned them in order to begin again. Resnais and Rivette have worked slowly, exploring the crucial dimension of time. Rohmer has made the connection between cinema and literature. But only Claude Chabrol has thrown himself completely into the role of entertainer-filmmaker which, when it was played by the great American directors of the thirties and forties, first inspired the group as a whole. (pp. 284-85)

James Monaco, "Chabrol," in his The New Wave: Truffaut, Godard, Chabrol, Rohmer, Rivette *(copyright © 1976 by James Monaco; reprinted by permission of Oxford University Press, Inc.), Oxford University Press, New York, 1976, pp. 253-85.*

GAVIN MILLAR

No one would pretend that *Blood Relatives* is vintage Chabrol, nor that it is a profound meditation on sexual relations and the family, sexual taboos and society. But Chabrol has more ability than anyone, within the framework of the thriller, to provoke the odd reflection in his audience, and strangely enough the ironical gaze he directs at our assumptions about what the decent thing is, and who's doing it, is what stays with you afterwards, more than the rather tame unravellings of the thriller plot. (pp. 512-13)

[The] central weakness is the inexperienced lovers, the flashbacks to whose affair seem interminably dull. That apart, there are all Chabrol's other skills to relish: the bloody handprints on a glass door; his and Jean Rabier's use of the camera to create suspense or suspicion; his flair for witty detail. . . . (p. 513)

Gavin Millar, "Family Love" (© Gavin Millar, 1978; reprinted by permission of the author and his agents, Judy Daish Associates, Ltd.), in The Listener, *Vol. 100, No. 2582, October 19, 1978, pp. 512-13.*

TIM PULLEINE

The tone of the opening [of Chabrol's *Violette Nozière*], detailing Violette's stealthy nocturnal departure from the scene of the crime, is that of a thriller, mesmerisingly Hitchcockian in its camera style (and possibly one may detect a specific echo of the start of *I Confess*, a film Chabrol especially admired). Flashbacks ensue, summoning up Violette's double life between the claustrophobic pseudo-gentility of her parents' working-class apartment and the ritual exhibitionism of the bar-room hangers-on in the Quartier Latin, and between the dowdily well-scrubbed schoolgirl of her parents' wishes and the carmine-lipped voluptuary of her forays into amateur prostitution with a succession of callow students.

Intriguing as these revelations are, however, the inconsequentiality of their assembly is far removed from the thriller's rigorous patterning of events, and the film's unbalancing oddity of construction is emphasised by the fact that the flashbacks continue at random beyond the point—rather more than halfway through the movie—at which they meet up with the initial action. Not only this, but the obsessive doubling back within the time scale is echoed by a secondary chain of memory flashes, arbitrary and unexplained, to episodes (possibly imaginary) in Violette's childhood. . . .

Together with this shifting formal structure, though, a Langian strain of determinism can unmistakably be discerned in the film. This is evinced in the motifs of railings and stairs, particularly the stair well in the Nozières' apartment building, in the architectural stress on enclosure . . . , and in the recurrence, when the action does briefly move outdoors, of grey skies and gaunt, leafless trees. . . .

To this extent, Violette, enmeshed in a net of social contradictions, becomes a heroine fit for a latterday Zola, a correspondence coincidentally heightened by the fact that her father is an engine driver, as well as by the theme of hereditary syphilis. Violette has persuaded her parents that they are responsible for the venereal disease she has contracted, and the poison is administered [to them by Violette] in the guise of medication. . . .

Chabrol's avoidance—disconcerting as it may be—of a traditionally well made form comes both to reflect the pettiness of the world in which Violette outwardly lives and to adumbrate an inner world which asserts itself in irrational impulses, like the extraordinary moment (worthy of Buñuel) when immediately after seeing her parents collapse from the poison, Violette voraciously hacks herself a slice of meat from the family's supper roast, impulses whose unknowability goes deeper than any legalistic unravelling.

And this mysteriousness seems finally to fuse with the film's contemplation of a vanished past, its evocation of the 30s in terms of the exotic ephemera—jazz bands, cocktails —which at once represent for the conservative establishment of the time the harbingers of a corrupt future, for Violette an escape into modernity, and for us, the present-day audience, a comforting retreat into nostalgia. The movie's world is ornate but almost disembodied. . . .

In the movie's closing moments, after an unmoved Violette has told her cell-mate that she is confident of never going to the guillotine, the camera closes in on her enigmatic half-smile as a voice-over retails the remaining facts: commutation of sentence, release in 1945, a marriage to the son of a prison official which produced five children, a pardon in 1963, shortly before her death. As the close-up of Violette fades to black (there is no end title) a kind of transference seems to be achieved: we shall never be able to understand the past which formed her, yet she can comprehend the compromises that lie ahead. (p. 126)

Tim Pulleine, "Film Reviews: 'Violette Nozière'," in Sight and Sound *(copyright © 1979 by The British Film Institute), Vol. 48, No. 2, Spring, 1979, pp. 125-26.*

(Sir) Charles (Spencer) Chaplin

1889-1977

English director, actor, producer, screenwriter, and musical composer.

Chaplin is widely heralded as the first genius of the cinema. He will be forever remembered for the creation of one of the most popular characters in the history of film—the little tramp. "Charlie"'s tottering gait and expressive face distinguished the character that many imitated but few equaled. Audiences saw the tramp as a symbol of humanity—a man becoming involved in dangerous situations, only to escape each time and still retain a warm love of friends and foes alike.

Chaplin was born in the slums of London to parents who were entertainers. Charlie and his brother were sent to an orphanage at an early age, where there was little food and severe punishment for any wrongdoing. The fact that the tramp character was sympathetic to the poor and underprivileged appears to stem directly from Chaplin's childhood.

Chaplin was introduced to the stage while very young, and joined the Fred Karno vaudeville troupe in 1906. On a tour to the United States in 1913, Chaplin was discovered by Mack Sennett, who signed him to a contract with Keystone Studios, despite Chaplin's worry that he would fail in films as a mime. He made thirty-five films within a year for Keystone. *Kid Auto Races at Venice* was the first film in which the "little tramp" appeared, and the character soon became widely popular.

When Chaplin switched to Essanay in 1915, he was allowed to direct all fourteen of his films, and the slapstick became less frenzied, with the tramp's sentimentality becoming more apparent. *The Tramp,* made during this period, is viewed as Chaplin's first masterpiece. His now standard character took on many roles—the mischievous boy, the frustrated lover, the underdog—in order to unify the theme of the individual crushed by the pressure of society.

In 1919 Chaplin, along with D. W. Griffith, Mary Pickford, and Douglas Fairbanks, formed United Artists, and distributed his own films for the rest of his career. He wrote and directed *A Woman of Paris,* showing his great abilities as a director in a serious work. Chaplin had always had ambitions to star in a serious film, but did not get the chance until much later. In *The Gold Rush, The Circus,* and *City Lights,* Chaplin began to voice his increasing dissatisfaction with the modern world and its inventions. In fact, he refused to use sound, except for music, in *City Lights,* even though it had become a very popular addition to films. *Modern Times* was also mostly silent, and continued to satirize modern machines, but was also vicious in its portrayal of society.

The Great Dictator marked the decline of Chaplin's popularity. His divorces had made him more and more susceptible to ridicule and scandal, and the political commentary in the film further outraged many critics and fans. *The Great Dictator* was his first film in which sound was used throughout, and it was Chaplin's speeches that angered people the most. His concluding speech was thought to be Communist dogma, but Chaplin had intended it as a plea for freedom and peace. Chaplin played two roles in the film, and his tramp character was clearly overshadowed by Hynkel, the Hitlerian dictator. It seems not coincidental that Chaplin's popularity declined when he began to speak in philosophical jargon. *The Great Dictator* marked the last appearance of the "little tramp" on the screen.

Chaplin was labeled a Communist when, in 1942, after a paternity suit and another divorce, he urged American friendship with Russia. *Monsieur Verdoux* was widely picketed and withdrawn soon after its release. Most critics seemed to view the film as a "bad joke," others as a brilliant satire on capitalism. *Limelight* saw Chaplin at his most philosophically vocal, so much so that many critics wished he had never abandoned silent films. A most serious film, it deals with an aging clown on the decline, and appeared to parallel Chaplin's own life. When on his way to England to promote the film in 1952, the U.S. government branded Chaplin as a Communist sympathizer, and informed him that he probably would not be allowed back into the country. Chaplin settled in Switzerland, where he continued to live until his death. He returned once to the U.S., in 1972, to accept a special Academy Award and was triumphantly welcomed.

Chaplin is seen by many critics as an egotist who was successful only insofar as the tramp was successful. Others see him as a comic genius, writing scripts which paralleled his own early life, and making films in which his philosophical views were portrayed more effectively through mime than through the verbose lectures of his later films. His creation went beyond class boundaries, and it was the tramp's overtly "human" character that film audiences took to heart. His comedy continues to delight audiences today, and his lasting fame as a film pioneer and comedian is secure. (See also *Contemporary Authors,* Vols. 81-84; obituary, Vols. 73-76.)

MINNIE MADDERN FISKE

It will surprise numbers of well-meaning Americans to learn that a constantly increasing body of cultured, artistic people are beginning to regard the young English buffoon, Charles Chaplin, as an extraordinary artist, as well as a comic genius. To these Americans one may dare only to whisper that it is dangerous to condemn a great national figure thoughtlessly. First, let us realize that at the age of twenty-six Charles Chaplin . . . has made the whole world laugh. This proves that his work possesses a quality more vital than mere clowning. . . . To the writer Charles Chaplin appears as a great comic artist, possessing inspirational powers and a technique as unfaltering as Rejane's. If it be treason to Art to say this, then let those exalted persons who allow culture to be defined only upon their own terms make the most of it.

Apart from the qualified critics, many thoughtful persons are beginning to analyze the Chaplin performances with a serious desire to discover his secret for making irresistible entertainment out of more or less worthless material. They seek the elusive quality that leavens the lump of the usually pointless burlesques in which he takes part. The critic knows his secret. It is the old, familiar secret of inexhaustible imagination, governed by the unfailing precision of a perfect technique.

Chaplin is vulgar. At the present stage of his career he is frankly a buffoon, and buffoonery is and always has been tinctured with the vulgar. . . . When a great buffoon like Chaplin is engaged in making people laugh at the broad and obvious facts of life, he is continually so near the line that separates good taste from bad taste that it is too much to expect him never to stray for a moment on the wrong side of the line. If, in the name of so-called refinement, we are going to obliterate Chaplin and set him down as not worth considering, we must wipe all buffoonery off the slate and lay down the absolute rule that it is not a legitimate part of public entertainment.

Further, we must remember that the medium of Charles Chaplin's expression is entirely new. He has had only two years to develop his particular phase of the moving picture art. . . .

Anyone who has seen the primitive and meaningless comic scenes in which Chaplin began his career will see the difficulties under which his art was at first forced to express itself. Undoubtedly he will fare better in the future. It is said that his newest travesty . . . shows that with a really intelligent scenario to aid him he can be supremely comic and at the same time free from vulgarity. Those of us who believe that Charles Chaplin is essentially a great comic artist look forward to fine achievements. We think that we know, perhaps better than he knows himself, what he is capable of accomplishing, and we are confident that he will attain the artistic stature to which it seems he is entitled.

Minnie Maddern Fiske, "The Art of Charles Chaplin," in Harper's *(copyright © 1916 by* Harper's Magazine; *all rights reserved; reprinted from the May 6, 1916 issue by special permission), Vol. LXII, No. 3098, May 6, 1916, p. 494.*

MAX REINHARDT

According to recent press reports from Berlin *The Circus* has been hailed both as a supreme screen comedy and as a philosophic contribution of the highest significance. Some critics profess to see a philosophy in every scene. (p. 6)

Fortunately we have passed beyond that stage. We can enjoy Chaplin and let who will philosophize. There was a time, just before and after *The Gold Rush,* when we too used the heavy approach. There was much talk of the underlying pathos, the tragedy of frustration and other phrases invented by self-conscious critics who were afraid of laughing at Chaplin for his own sake. Echoes of this higher criticism seem to have reached Chaplin himself and to have cramped his spontaneity for a while, if we are to judge from some of the scenes in *The Gold Rush* where the pathos was laid on a little too thickly.

Chaplin has recovered from that phase and so have we. . . . [Whatever] Chaplin's philosophy may be, it has been present from the beginning in every one of his comedies and does not have to be hauled out on every occasion. Chaplin himself has been artistically most discreet about it, no doubt hiding much of its edge and its implications because he is a keen enough showman to know that too many philosophies are bound to spoil the laughter laden pudding of which he is the unchallenged chef. (pp. 6-7)

[It] is well to bear in mind that Chaplin's enormous success is due entirely to his personality and the sheer force of his acting ability. To the technique of the motion picture, its development as an art in terms of pure cinema, Chaplin has contributed little except here and there in *The Woman of Paris.* As a matter of fact his technique is old-fashioned, photographic rather than cinematic. . . . In one respect the old-fashioned technique celebrates a triumph. We refer to the final scene where Chaplin, having married off the bareback rider whom he loves to his rival, sits in the desolate circle of his despair and chews the cud of fate. That is indeed a marvellous scene which should never have been spoiled by the subsequent close-up. Shot in the middle distance, with the hazy outline of a town behind it, this scene has a symbolic and (we might as well admit it) a philosophic significance scarcely equalled in the annals of the screen. (p. 7)

Max Reinhardt, "Screen Visions: 'The Circus'," in National Board of Review Magazine *(copyright, 1928), Vol. III, No. 2, February, 1928, pp. 6-7.*

G. W. STONIER

I do not think that [Chaplin] is a great genius or that in a hundred years' time his films, if they still exist, will excite the amusement they do to-day; but of this I am certain, that no other living person, writer or actor, exhibits as truly the particular element of city life which we call Cockney.

In this sense he is in the long tradition of English humour, starting with Chaucer and ending in the last century with Dickens and the music-halls. . . . His material is of the slightest, his tricks are the commonplace of every vaudeville comedian, he has created only one character, and that a theatrical one; yet he is as much above the Robeys and Fratellinis as Bach is above the usual village organist. None of his films, not even *The Gold Rush* or *The Circus,* can be properly judged by a standard which is purely artistic. That is not to say that Mr. Chaplin is not an artist, for he undoubtedly is, in his treatment, for instance, of pathos, and in the direction of his latest films; but all those positive qualities, which made him popular fifteen years ago, are as remote from any literary or artistic standard as a music-hall performance or a holiday fair.

G. W. Stonier, "Charlie Chaplin," in New Statesman *(© 1928 The Statesman Publishing Co. Ltd.), Vol. XXI, No. 778, March 24, 1928, p. 763.*

ALEXANDER BAKSHY

The sad ending of [*The Circus*] is significant. The tragic mask is increasingly apparent in the comic make-up of the waif whom the world has so tenderly taken to its heart. The irresponsible harlequin is receding. The tendency may or may not enrich Mr Chaplin's art. But if it is true that each new film reveals an ever growing maturity of thought, one would welcome similar progress in the "direction." *The Circus* is neat and competent but here as previously, its author has failed fully to rise to the opportunity placed before him by the extraordinarily fantastic world of the character he has created. The great screen genius of our time should not be afraid to find for the play as a whole, the fully expressive visual form he has found for himself. (p. 414)

Alexander Bakshy, "A Knight-Errant," in The Dial *(copyright, 1928, by The Dial Publishing Company, Inc.; reprinted by permission of J. S. Watson, Jr. and Scofield Thayer), Vol. 84, May, 1928, pp. 413-14.*

BARNET G. BRAVER-MANN

[The] grotesque figure we call "Charlie" has carried into cinema one of the oldest and most characteristic traditions of pure theatre, that of the *Commedia dell'Arte*. Chaplin is in direct line from the mimes of Roman comedy, the players of the Italian *Commedia dell'Arte* of the sixteenth and seventeenth centuries, and the English pantomime of the eighteenth century.... Like [the] players of other times Chaplin has built certain elementary frailties and foibles of human nature into the framework of a conventional figure known as Charlie, whose shabby costume furnishes the needed mask. (p. 23)

The influence of tradition appears most strongly in the highly individual way in which he makes his own pictures and in the use to which he puts his gift for improvisation when on the set....

Chaplin builds his films altogether on what he calls "feeling," that is, he begins, let us say, with Charlie, and studies the emotional values that his own creation will yield in various situations. The Harlequin of the films knows intuitively that the secret of comic effect lies in the relation between emotion and laughter.... Chaplin proves himself not only a rare clown but a practical psychologist when he makes his working basis for a film the result of an amazing thinking-through of all the possible emotional responses which are peculiar to an individual character. (p. 24)

Chaplin always tries for expression of strong elemental emotion in his films on the basis that since the majority of people are swayed by their emotions the entertainment values are certain to be satisfactory, if the emphasis in scene or in sequence is upon *the right emotion*. His aims are to attack rapidly all the emotions of the spectator, using gradations of movement to suggest sorrow, gaiety, pensiveness. But he never begins with the story. He begins always with the emotional in relation to the reactions peculiar to the characters chosen....

Once a character or situation becomes gripping in quality of interest, then Chaplin seeks to apply all the artistry he can summon in the terms of cinema as a medium. He neither over-acts nor indulges in that unexpressive restraint typical of feeble playing.... (p. 25)

When Chaplin is playing and directing on the set he utilizes everything, introducing all sorts of things to keep the action going. There is no let-down in his work. It is a continual flow of motion and situation which makes the spectator feel that he is looking into the mind of Charlie Chaplin....

[Alas], it is his inability to think and work in terms of montage which visually and technically keeps Chaplin's films in the theatre tradition and prevents them from becoming truly cinematic in character. At times one regrets the many montage opportunities passed by in his films—opportunities that would have greatly heightened the fine feeling and situation in Charlie's productions....

The Woman of Paris, the only film that he directed without playing in it himself, had a charming flow in its visual continuity. Although it is the most systematically planned picture of any that he has made, even here he had no organized script but simply a plan in the back of his head. He works best on the inspiration of the moment; and in this seemingly formless fashion he has made some of the best scenes in his films, as for example, the last scene in *The Pilgrim* and the wire-walking stunt in *The Circus*. (p. 26)

Charlie is Falstaffian in vigor of conception, universal in his appeal to healthy, cleansing laughter, and fascinating both as a survival and a continuation of a great theatrical tradition. Moreover, he is intimately a part of the culture of this age—something in which audiences a hundred years from now may behold a reflection of the times the great clown of early cinema interpreted through his unique creation. (p. 54)

Barnet G. Braver-Mann, "Charlie: A Close Up of the Greatest of Comedians as Director," in Theatre Guild Magazine *(copyright 1930, by Theatre Guild Magazine, Inc.), Vol. VII, No. 12, September, 1930, pp. 23-6, 54.*

GILBERT SELDES

["City Lights"] is a completely organized and a completely created whole which exists for itself without question and without comparison. The immediate effect of the picture is that it is funnier than many things [Chaplin] has done and infinitely inventive; the second effect is that it is magnificently organized, deeply thought out and felt, and communicated with an unflagging energy and a masterly technique. Chaplin is the only artist whose pictures always give the impression of being created before your eyes, with this extraordinary result, that when you see them you cannot believe that they have ever been shown before, and that when you see them a second time you are constantly surprised and elated by their perfection.

Chaplin's "secret" is so plain that it seems an absurdity to state it; nevertheless, it is a quality which occurs only once or twice in a generation. He creates illusions out of the actual material in his hand. Whatever he touches becomes the image of something else, an image associated with emotions. In "City Lights," these creative impulses are almost always turned to laughter and the danger is always that we will be so affected as not really to see what is happening.

There is one scene in which Chaplin is being entertained by a drunken millionaire, who pours a glass of brandy for each and then tilts the bottle so that it floods into the gap in Charlie's trousers. This is extraordinarily funny, but the underlining, which is the foundation of creative comedy, is Charlie's misconception of where the flood is coming from and his desperate endeavors to prevent his host from tilting the tiny cordial glass out of which, against all reason, he thinks the liquor is flowing. In the brief moments of this scene Charlie creates for us the character of the embarrassed guest trying to cover the *faux pas* of his host. (p. 46)

Throughout the picture [a] sequence of created moods broken by comedy continues. There is a moment of indescribable beauty at the very beginning when Charlie becomes aware of the fact that the flower girl is blind—an episode as tricky and as dangerous as could be imagined, done with an absolute purity of emotion, at the end of which the flower girl, filling a pot at a fountain, throws the dirty water aside—and into Charlie's face. The slapstick is perfect, but it rises legitimately out of the pathos of the girl's blindless. . . .

There has been some question about the end of the picture. The blind girl has always assumed that her benefactor was a rich and rather grand person. When he comes out from jail, Charlie meets her, by accident, with extreme reluctance. He tells her nothing, but the further accident of their hands meeting, forces her to recognize him, and it is on this recognition that the picture ends. It is not one of those endings which constitute a new beginning. It is infinitely sad and altogether appropriate. For in this picture Mr. Chaplin has not for a moment suggested that our laughter hide our tears; only that at the end of our laughter there will be nothing but tears for the gayest of us. He has with his beautiful serenity calmly broken our hearts, and we are endlessly grateful to him for having done so. (p. 47)

Gilbert Seldes, "A Chaplin Masterpiece," in The New Republic *(reprinted by permission of* The New Republic; *© 1931 The New Republic, Inc.), Vol. 66, No. 847, February 25, 1931, pp. 46-7.*

WILLIAM HUNTER

Historically this remarkable film [*Public Opinion (A Woman of Paris*] is as important as *The Cabinet of Doctor Caligari* and *Potemkin*. It was in its time a remarkable technical film. But its technique was concealed; it was rather an "emotional" than a "scientific" technique, an instrument for bitter comment rather than for the conscious construction of a filmic scene. [Chaplin's] technical gifts have been given to the cinema almost, as it were, unconsciously.

What is certainly more important than the accomplished technique of *Public Opinion* is the expression of an individual attitude. Such of the technique as is capable of transference has been assimilated by other directors, and if the film (as it does) remains, after nine years, of value, it is for intrinsic and personal rather than for technical reasons. Chaplin has a very remarkable personality, and in [*Public Opinion*] he has communicated a valuable experience with a considerable success. His instinctive knowledge of technique is used, not to construct "a work of art," but to enable him to say what he has to say as fully as possible. He has a deep and original knowledge of human experience. Not from a technical, but from any point of view of ultimate importance, *Public Opinion* must be placed in the same category as [Pabst's] *Joyless Street,* [Pabst's *The Love of*] *Jeanne Ney,* and [Pudovkin's] *Mother*. Like them, it is a symbolism of life, and a record of experience, as lived vitally by the creators of these films. (pp. 42-3)

City Lights is, in my opinion, [Chaplin's] finest film, and in this he often seems deliberately to disregard technique. The emotional and technical commonplaces of the pre-war cinema are reintroduced with a superb disregard of mechanical advance. The cinematic technique doesn't matter; there is no brilliant virtuosity . . . , no camera angles, no cross cutting, and the camera rarely moves. His decision as to the length of time a shot shall remain on the screen is far more instinctive than consciously scientific. The personality of Chaplin on the screen and the experience of Chaplin behind the cameras, giving life and vitality and point to the pantomime, are all that matter. (p. 43)

In all [his] films there is an attitude to life, and a tragic attitude embedded in comedy. There is an extraordinary and terrible cruelty in the trapeze scene in *The Circus,* and *City Lights* is the bitterest and saddest of all the Chaplin films. Only a man with a deep experience of human motives and behaviour could have made such a film, only a gifted artist could have communicated so successfully such an experience. At his best he introduces an element of fatality into his films; a sense of imminent and inevitable disaster, against which it is futile to struggle, a despairing realisation of the bitterness and cruelty of life; but a realisation against which one nevertheless struggles. For his concern with the under dog and the spiritual values which may lie behind failure is not pessimistic. His attitude is not a beaten attitude. (pp. 43-4)

Chaplin's films frequently contain the grossest sentimentality; but this, like his disregard of technical virtuosity, seems often to be a triumph rather than the disaster it might so easily be. He is the Dickens of the films. But never, even at his worst, is he so embarrassing as Dickens can be. . . . Of his later films, only *The Gold Rush* ends happily; the other two end inconclusively, trembling on the verge of sentimentality, but never, I think, quite tumbling over. The end of *The Circus,* for instance, is such a blending of attitudes, such superb, incredible gesturing, that for me at least it is a complete success. In this respect he is nearest the edge in his latest film, *City Lights*. But the communication of such genuine and deep feeling is rare in the cinema. Sentimentality is false; but here the helplessness, the tragedy which is implied in such a banal ending, is, rather, a complete success, his most profound realisation. His latest film is the most successful reconciliation of the most varied impulses and attitudes. (p. 44)

William Hunter," Charles Chaplin: 'Public Opinion', 1923, 'City Lights', 1931," in his Scrutiny of Cinema, *Wishart & Co, 1932 (and reprinted by Arno Press, 1972), pp. 42-5.*

WINSTON CHURCHILL

Between [Charlie Chaplin and Charles Dickens] there is, I think, an essential similarity. Both knew hardness in childhood. Both made their misfortunes steppingstones to success. They developed along different lines, chose different mediums of expression, but both quarried in the same rich mine of common life and found there treasure of laughter and drama for the delight of all mankind. (p. 24)

[An] indomitable spirit is an integral part of the make-up of the screen Charlie Chaplin. His portrayal of the underdog is definitely American rather than British. The English workingman has courage in plenty, but those whom prolonged unemployment has forced on the road are nowadays usually broken and despairing. The Chaplin tramp has a quality of defiance and disdain.

But the American scene as a whole has influenced Chaplin —its variety, its color, its animation, its strange and spectacular contrasts. And the States did more than this for the little English actor; they provided the opportunity for which, without knowing it, he had been waiting. They introduced him to the ideal medium for his genius, the motion picture. (p. 37)

Winston Churchill, "Everybody's Language," in Collier's *(copyright, © 1935, by The Crowell Publishing Co.), Vol. 96, No. 17, October 26, 1935, pp. 24, 37-8.*

OTIS FERGUSON

Modern Times is about the last thing they should have called the Chaplin picture, which has had one of the most amazing build-ups of interest and advance speculation on record. . . . [It is] a silent film, with pantomime, printed dialogue, and such sound effects as were formerly supplied by the pit band and would now be done by dubbing, except for Chaplin's song at the end. . . .

Part of this old-time atmosphere can be credited to the sets. The factory layout is elaborate and stylized, but not in the modern way or with the modern vividness of light and shadow; . . . the costumes are generally previous; and as to faces and types, Chaplin has kept a lot of old friends with him, types from days when a heavy was a heavy. . . . (p. 117)

But such matters would not call for discussion if all together they did not set up a definite mood, a disturbing sense of the quaint. Chaplin himself is not dated, never will be; he is a reservoir of humor, master of an infinite array of dodges, agile in both mind and body; he is not only a character but a complex character, with the perfect ability to make evident all the shades of his odd and charming feelings; not only a touching character, but a first-class buffoon and I guess the master of our time in dumb show. But this does not make him a first-class picture maker. He may personally surmount his period, but as director-producer he can't carry his whole show with him, and I'll take bets that if he keeps on refusing to learn any more than he learned when the movies themselves were just learning, each successive picture he makes will seem, on release, to fall short of what went before. The general reaction to [*Modern Times*] anyway is the wonder that these primitive formulas can be so genuinely comic and endearing.

There has been a furor here and there in the press about the social content of *Modern Times*, and this could be skipped easily if Chaplin himself were not somehow confused . . . over its worth as corrective comment. Well, the truth is that Chaplin is a comedian; he may start off with an idea, but almost directly he is back to type again, the happy hobo and blithe unregenerate, a little sad, a little droll. (p. 118)

Otis Ferguson, "Hallelujah, Bum Again" (originally published in The New Republic, *Vol. 86, No. 1107, February 19, 1936), in* The Film Criticism of Otis Ferguson, *edited by Robert Wilson (© 1971 by Temple University), Temple University Press, 1971, pp. 117-19.*

LOUIS ZUKOFSKY

A long time ago, Charlie [Chaplin] achieved a perspicuity of style, or a readiness for being imparted. . . . Charlie had let go in a make-up and dance raising American acting to a world position, soon to offer comparisons with the histrionic poetry of the Japanese Noh.

There were differences. Instead of allowing him to say in concise Japanese verse, 'I am going on a journey down the road, it will lead me past' etc., and poising him graciously on the property, celluloid permitted him only movement and silence. The result was the composition of action on the screen: his back ambled off into the open. Drama was brought into the actual air. (p. 51)

Charlie's devices and "types" live with material thoughtfulness and thus historical meaning. It was some years ago that people began to see satire in Charlie, as distinguished from comedy to which rhetorics have tagged one definition or another and decided it ends well. . . . Charlie the actor never revealing his natural self is also Charlie in the set, an intelligence working itself out in the concrete. So that a new idea in a new Chaplin film is not merely a notion, a general sense of today, or an understanding of politics, art, life or whatever, but inventive existence interacting with other existence in all its ramifications: sight, hearing, muscular movement, coordination of all the senses acting on the surrounding world and rendering it laughably intelligent. (pp. 53-4)

A herd of sheep, driven, and their appointment is the pen or the slaughterhouse. Evaluated in this opening shot of *Modern Times*, taken from above, in the sportsmanship of the montage—the cinematic equivalent of material thoughtfulness—, are the backs of sheep bulging. They urge each other out of the picture. The satire of nerves and their obverse—events—follow. People fill a subway entrance and crowd the screen; then, a street; and the inside of the factory in which they work at the conveyor belt appears. The rest is the active sentience of continuity which includes a simple but strong plot, so effective it can be seen again and need not be told since as story it is like everyday's newspaper. Useful as a frame of reference it includes a multitude of things, material as well as fantastic things made possible: the screen action holding together in the timing, the sound devices, and the light. The elements of opposition in these cinematic effects and their emotional absorption into relations of the story further the historical validity of the screen by inventing out of the actual world of the spectator. (pp. 54-5)

Tears, said a master of the Noh, are justly not wrung out of one. In Chaplin, they remain finally in the satire and the movement. His direction, encompassing his acting, sees all around as well as arouses. The *sportsmanship* of the montage has been referred to in passing. The phrase reduces itself to the fact that nothing is fair on the screen unless shown in a relation (or a strained relation) that has the amplitude of insight impelled by the physical, to be found in actual events themselves. (p. 55)

Perhaps the one scene in *Modern Times* that will not bear seeing again is Charlie skating alone, blindfolded, over the unfenced mezzanine, while the girl looks on in terror. The feeling is that Charlie is not doing so well here as he did in *The Rink*. And it is significant in that the cinema is not a one-man show, or the tired symbolism (if that was intended?) of man always skating over the edge. Charlie cannot, in 1936, go back to a dance that he *did,* or to a sentimental spectator's idea of what his dancing might be, but must continue to develop the cinema. (pp. 56-7)

What distinguishes Charlie from film technicians of lesser calibre is that he is usually not taking his career as a standstill for a display of personal sensitivity, charm, or whatever. (p. 57)

In a shot in *Modern Times,* placing the romanticism of *going out to find work* against the rest of today's situation, Charlie is extravagantly and pathetically heroic when the beam of a crumbling shack falls on his head. To yoke oneself to the world of the facts and to keep a pace is of an altogether different order of decision than trying to swim in one's poverty. Finally and despite odds, Charlie and the girl decide to go off together in the film, and their arms bend up at the elbows, their fists are clenched, too powerfully fast for the spectator to speculate what Mr. Chaplin means. If the spectator is intent on the film and not on his own thought, what can the action of the shot mean but what it *does*—i.e. *performs.* (p. 58)

Louis Zukofsky, "'Modern Times'" (1936; originally published in Kulchur, *No. 4, 1961), in his* Prepositions: The Collected Critical Essays of Louis Zukofsky *(copyright © 1967 by Louis Zukofsky; reprinted by permission of Celia Zukofsky), Rapp & Carroll Ltd, 1967, pp. 51-8.*

LEWIS JACOBS

To think of Charlie Chaplin is to think of the movies. Yet this unique actor, director, and producer has added little to movie technique or movie form. He has been not a technician but a pantomimist, a commentator, a satirist, a social critic. His artistic problems have not been cinematic; they have been personal, always being solved by feeling. His importance lies not in what he has contributed to film art, but in what he has contributed to humanity. If he is negligible as a movie craftsman, if he has evolved no new formal aspects to enrich the medium, he has created many moments to enrich society. Chaplin will always be known for his social outlook, his insight into human nature, his pantomimic skill, his ingenious development of the incident, and his evocation of a mood. It is these qualities rather than any plastic contributions which have made him significant as a screen artist. (p. 226)

Since his first screen appearance in 1913, Charles Chaplin has made history. As a whole, his career during twenty-five years has been marked by ripening ability and a steadily rising reputation. Until 1918 his pictures were experiments in technique and style, containing all the external characteristics that Chaplin was later to synthesize, and revealing his growing awareness of aims. His films during the following years were mature, rich in insight and understanding. In recent years, since the advent of the talkies, he has used his genius humorously and pathetically to reveal the sores of modern life. Intensely conscious of modern social conditions, he employs his artistry on behalf of the underprivileged, speaking out for the individual against all forms of oppression. His social conscience has been the inspiration that has transformed his outmoded silent-screen technique and kept his work contemporary and meaningful. (p. 229)

Chaplin's Keystone films were, in the main, rapid-fire farces, as can be seen from their titles. They were not built around Chaplin's personality but rather employed his talents to carry out the usual [Mack] Sennett pattern. Incident followed upon incident swiftly, so that Chaplin's individual pantomime and subtlety were sacrificed for pace and action. These elements Chaplin was later to incorporate in his own films, but he adapted them to his personality and individual style. (p. 231)

Chaplin is David confronting the Goliath who makes life miserable for the weak until he is resolutely challenged. Battered, pursued, frustrated, lovesick, through his quick-wittedness and nimbleness Chaplin finally emerges from the conflict victorious—and alone. The sparks that fly from his many engagements are touched with deep humor, tender pathos, bitter satire, any of which he can achieve by the use of any prop at hand—an escalator, a mannikin, a violin, a carpet, or a clock. Gems of Chapliniana, [the Mutual pictures] reveal his increasing social awareness. The self-consciousness and groping that marked his Sennett and Essanay films are gone; he now has self-assurance and a ripened purpose. (pp. 234-35)

After 1918 his movies are fewer and longer, ever growing in complexity and profundity but springing from essentially the same sources that became apparent in his earlier years.

No longer concerned with mastering a technique, Chaplin now was free to develop his unique characterizations and subtle witticisms further, giving comedy emotional depth and satirical significance in his criticism of conventions, dogmas, and injustices in society. (p. 236)

The Idle Class (1921), *Pay Day* (1922), and *The Pilgrim* (1923) were thrusts at social inequalities. Sympathetic toward the working man, they tried to show that spiritual good is more likely to be found in a convict than in those who make convicts what they are. All three films were adroit expositions of Chaplin's credo, although they were not propagandistic in the common sense of the term and did not essentially differ from the points of view of his previous films.

After *The Pilgrim* Chaplin suddenly surprised everyone by directing a dramatic film in which he did not star. It is upon this film, *A Woman of Paris* (1923), that his reputation as a great director has often been wrongly based. In direction the film was neither brilliant nor remarkable, though many claimed it to be both. Its style was elementary; it had none of the remarkable camera work of the German school, then at its best, nor any unusual insight regarding movie continuity. The film's interest lay in psychological portraiture, in its honesty in depicting character, environment, and human relationships. What mattered most in the film was the motivation of the characters' actions—the petty quarrels and jealousies, the thinking processes. "I treated the subject," Chaplin said, "in the simplest possible manner." (pp. 240-41)

Chaplin stands out as perhaps the one unforgettable actor of the screen, the symbol of human struggle against regimentation and, now more than ever, for the rights of the individual.

Beginning as a slap-about comedian he has made himself a symbol of the spirit of the common man, readily recognized wherever mankind gathers—a humble and pathetic figure in search of beauty, the butt of jests, harassed by poverty, the law, and social forces that he can neither understand nor resist. He is the contemporary Don Quixote, venturing forth in a bewildering word to set things right single-handed, to take up the gauntlet for chivalry, honesty, beauty, and truth. (p. 247)

Lewis Jacobs, "Charles Chaplin: Individualist," in his The Rise of the American Film: A Critical History *(copyright 1939 by Lewis Jacobs; reprinted by permission of the author), Harcourt Brace Jovanovich, Inc., 1939, pp. 226-47.*

OTIS FERGUSON

The Great Dictator opens on some pretty dated nonsense in the war zone and the kind of lighting and movie action they used in *Shoulder Arms*. What's new is the acting, the new and different character, a mixture of sharp mimicry and the devices of absurdity. And as we might have expected from the wonderful double-talk song in *Modern Times,* Chaplin is as acute and perfect verbally as he is in pantomime: he has the splenetic and krauty fustian of the German orator as exactly as Hitler himself. . . .

[When a scene is funny] it is funny as always, in the shop, on the street, around the chimney pots, with some of the oldest Chaplin favorites still peeping through. But it is also tragic because a people is being persecuted; these Jews are straight characters, not the old cartoons; and the laughter chokes suddenly and is reluctant to start again. Chaplin likes to pull out all the stops on sentimental passages, but this thing is too near and meaningful. It isn't that a comedian should be denied indignation and kept clowning forever; it is that old thing in all art of the demands of unity, of a complete and sustained mood or tone. He was always a funny figure against the rude world, but the gulf between a kick in the pants and a pogrom is something even his talent for the humorous-pathetic will not cross. And his unrelieved six-minute exhortation to the downtrodden of the world, look up, stand up, etc., is not only a bad case of overwriting but dramatically and even inspirationally futile. (p. 315)

Otis Ferguson, "Less Time for Comedy" (originally published in The New Republic, *Vol. 103, No. 19, November 4, 1940), in* The Film Criticism of Otis Ferguson, *edited by Robert Wilson (© 1971 by Temple University), Temple University Press, 1971, pp. 314-16.*

BASIL WRIGHT

[*The Great Dictator*], which is neither more or less episodic and shapeless than *Modern Times,* is at times unwontedly serious in its direction, weighted down, as it were, by its suspended advance towards Chaplin's final apologia. At such moments his failure fully to master the sound medium becomes painfully noticeable. The scenes are long; the composition stilted; the dialogue banal. Their object—for the most part—is to emphasise the misery of the Jews under the Nazi *régime;* but they are too dully sentimental to do more than bore.

It is only with Chaplin himself that we can feel and understand the cruelties and stupidities. As the little Ghetto barber, plunged after many years of amnesia into a vile world of stormtroopers and spies, his audacious application of pails of whitewash to the thugs says all, for the time being, that we need. The barber, indeed, is the old Charlie—though a little alarming at first because he talks, and we are not used to that. . . .

There remains for consideration the finale. This will no doubt be a matter of considerable controversy, for in it Chaplin directly takes up the position of spokesman for humanity. . . . Those who are embarrassed and possibly enraged by being asked to consider the New Testament in relation to the realities of life will be embarrassed and possibly enraged by being asked to do so by Chaplin. They will at any rate have the excuse that the speech is not well written and that Chaplin clearly has difficulty in expressing himself. But nevertheless he speaks with such sincerity that the speech is true and moving; and perhaps his difficulities of expression are of special effectiveness, for they are difficulties which also pertain to the "little men and women" all over the world of whom Chaplin is the most visible living champion.

The Great Dictator may be an uneven film both in mood and construction, and it is certainly too long. But it has an undeniable greatness. . . .

Basil Wright, "The Cinema: 'The Great Dictator'," in The Spectator *(© 1940 by* The Spectator; *reprinted by permission of* The Spectator), *Vol. 165, No. 5868, December 13, 1940, p. 636.*

NORTHROP FRYE

Since Mark Twain, no anarchist of the full nineteenth-century size has emerged except Charlie Chaplin. But the hero of the Chaplin films, with his quixotic gallantry and courtesy, his pity for the weak, his apologetic and ridiculous isolation from society and the amount of damage he does against his own very good will to that society makes this Yankee cussedness an ideal worthy of respect. For all its plethora of revolutionary symbols, *Modern Times* is not a socialist picture but an anarchist one: an allegory of the impartial destructiveness of humor. . . . We are left with a feeling that the man who is really part of his social group is only half a man, and we are taken back to the primitive belief, far older than Isaiah or Plato but accepted by both, that the lunatic is especially favored of God. . . .

This, of course, is not fully intelligible without some reference to religion, and it is in this that *The Great Dictator* shows its chief advance on *Modern Times*. To the Nazi the Jew sums up everything he hates: he is of a different race, he is urban, he is intellectual, he is often undersized, he has a sense of humor and tolerance. For these reasons he is also the perfect Chaplin hero: besides, a contempt for this big-happy-family racialism is the first principle of American anarchism. Imagine *Huckleberry Finn* without Jim or *Moby Dick* without Queequeg, and you can soon see why Chaplin had to be a Jew. But the picture itself is not Jewish, but Christian to a startling degree. The parallel between the dictator who gains the world but loses his soul and the Jewish barber on the one hand, and Caesar and a Jewish carpenter on the other, is very unobtrusive but it is there. Chaplin knows well enough what the Jew Freud and the Christian Pope Pius agree on, that anti-Semitism is a preparation for, and a disguised form of, anti-Christianity. But his conception of Christianity is one conditioned by his American anarchism. What attracts him about Christianity is that something in it that seems eternally unable to get along with the world, the uneasy recurrence, through centuries of compromise and corruption, of the feeling that the world and the devil are the same thing. Hence the complement to his Jewish barber is a dictator who is also an antichrist. (p. 149)

Northrop Frye, "The Great Charlie," in The Canadian Forum, *Vol. XXI, No. 247, August, 1941, pp. 148-50.*

JAMES AGEE

I could write many pages . . . about the richness and quality of [*Monsieur Verdoux*] as a work of art, in fact, of genius; and as many more trying, hopelessly, to determine how Chaplin's intellect, instinct, intuition, creative intelligence, and pure experience as a master artist and as a showman, serve and at times disserve one another: for intellectually and in every other kind of self-exhaustion this seems incomparably his most ambitious film. And since the film is provocative of so much that cannot be examined as fun, I wish I might also use the many thousands of words I would require to do it adequate honor, purely as fun. And all the more because I love and revere the film as deeply as any I have seen, and believe that it is high among the great works of this century, I wish I might discuss at proper length its weaknesses as a work of art and of moral understanding. I have reluctantly chosen, instead, to suggest a single aspect of its meaning, which seems to me particularly important. And this itself, I fear, I may have reduced beyond usefulness. (p. 256)

Chaplin's theme, the greatest and the most appropriate to its time that he has yet undertaken, is the bare problem of surviving at all in such a world as this. . . . [He] has set aside the tramp, whose charming lessons in survival are too wishful for his purposes, for his first image of the Responsible Man, and of modern civilization. . . . The tramp is the free soul intact in its gallantry, innocence, eagerness for love, ridiculousness, and sorrow; we recognize in him much that is dear to us in ourselves. Verdoux is so much nearer and darker that we can hardly bear to recognize ourselves in him. He is the committed, dedicated soul, and this soul is not intact: we watch its death agonies. And this tragic process is only the more dreadful because it is depicted not gravely but briskly, with a cold savage gaiety; the self-destroying soul is rarely aware of its own predicament. (pp. 256-57)

The problem of survival: the Responsible Man. Chaplin develops his terrible theme chiefly as a metaphor for business. But the film is also powerful as a metaphor for war: the Verdoux home as an embattled nation, the wife and child as the home front, Verdoux as expeditionary force, hero in the holiest of causes, and war criminal. But it is even more remarkable and fascinating as a study of the relationship between ends and means, a metaphor for the modern personality—that is, a typical "responsible" personality reacting to contemporary pressures according to the logic of contemporary ethics.

In the terms of this metaphor the basic cast is small. Verdoux, his wife, and their son are differing aspects of a single personality. Verdoux is the master, the intelligence and the deep unconscious; he has estranged his soul and his future. He has made the assumptions on which modern civilization rests. That is, that in order to preserve intact in such a world as this those aspects of the personality which are best and dearest to one, it is necessary to exercise all that is worst in one; and that it is impossible to do this effectively if one communicates honestly with one's best. Accordingly the personality which, until the world struck that living down, lived in poverty and docility, but happily, is broken and segregated. The wife and child are shut away in a home which is at once a shrine and a jail; and there, immobilized, and cut off from the truth, they virtually cease to exist as living objects of love; they become an ever more rigid dream. For when the worst and the best in the personality are thus segregated, and the worst is thus utilized in the nominal service of the best, it is inevitably the good which is exploited; the evil, which thinks of itself as faithful slave, is treacherous master; and evil, being active and knowledgeable, grows; and good, rendered motionless and denied knowledge, wither. (p. 257)

[Why] does Verdoux become a murderer? One good answer is: why not? Verdoux is a business realist; in terms of that realism the only difference between free enterprise in murder and free enterprise in the sale of elastic stockings is the difference in legal liability and in net income. And if the film is regarded as a metaphor for war, we may blush to ask Verdoux *why;* or if it is regarded as a metaphor for the destruction of the soul, murder is almost too mild a vocation. Yet we may still ask why, and wonder why Chaplin's only direct statement, most of which are made through Verdoux, are so remarkably inadequate. Verdoux, to be sure, is grandly in character in holding "society" accountable and in absolving the individual; but is this all that Chaplin knows? If so, he is as surely a victim and dupe of evil as Verdoux of the civilization he excoriates, and all that goes deeper in the film is achieved intuitively, as if in a kind of waking dream. If he knows better, then he is gravely at fault, as artist and moralist, in making clear no more than he does, still worse in tossing the mass-audience so cynical and misleading a sop; and one of the purest and most courageous works I know of is, at its climax, pure and courageous only against the enemy, not in the face of the truth. For the answers to why and how criminality can be avoided, we can look inward more profitably than at the film; for all that is suggested in the film is operant in each of us. If Chaplin had illuminated these bottom causes more brightly than we can see them in ourselves, *Verdoux* would be a still greater work of art than it is. But in proposing so richly suggestive an image of process and effect in the world and in the personality, and in proposing it so beautifully, the film, with all its faults, is one of the few indespensable works of our time.

It even contains and implies the beginning of the answer. Good and evil are inextricable, Verdoux insists. But his fatal mistake was in trying to keep them apart. If the film is regarded as a metaphor for the personality, and though that metaphor, as a metaphor for the personality as the family as business as war as civilization as murder, then this is certain: if the man and wife had honored their marriage with more than their child, the murders would never have been committed, the paralysis would never have imposed itself or would have been dissolved, and the wife and child would never have been shut into that exquisite tabernacle of a closed garden, but all three would have lived as one in that poverty for which the wife was forlorn, in the intactness of soul and the irresponsibility of that anarchic and immortal lily of the field, the tramp, the most humane and most nearly complete among the religious figures our time has evolved; whom for once in his life Chaplin set aside, to give his century its truest portrait of the upright citizen. (pp. 261-62)

James Agee, "'Monsieur Verdoux'–II" (originally published in The Nation, *Vol. 164, No. 24, June*

14, 1947), in his Agee on Film, Vol. 1 *(copyright © 1941, 1942, 1943, 1944, 1945, 1946, 1947, 1948, 1949, 1950, 1958 by The James Agee Trust), Grosset & Dunlap, 1969, pp. 256-59.*

JEAN RENOIR

It is agreed, some will say, that [in *Monsieur Verdoux*] Chaplin has created a highly personal work, and we admit that he has undergone a natural artistic transformation. We only feel that he has done all this in a wrong direction. And they add that the greatest crime of *Monsieur Verdoux* was the killing-off of the beloved little vagabond who had been such a charmer. His creator should not only have kept him alive but depended on him in his search for a new form of expression. I cannot share this opinion.

In giving up the rundown shoes, the old derby hat and willowy cane of the raggedy little guy whose pathetic hangdog look used to melt our hearts, Chaplin has gone deliberately into a world that is more dangerous, because it is closer to the one we live in. His new character, with neatly-pressed trousers, impeccably-knotted tie, well-dressed and no longer able to appeal to our pity, does not belong in those good old situations, outlined in strong broad strokes, where the rich trample the poor in so obvious a manner that even the most childish audience can immediately grasp the moral of the story. Before, we could imagine that the adventures of the little tramp took place in some world that belonged exclusively to the movies, that they were a sort of fairy tale.

With *Monsieur Verdoux,* such misapprehension is no longer possible. This one really takes place in our time, and the problems faced on the screen are really our own. By thus giving up a formula which afforded him full security, and undertaking squarely the critique of the society in which he himself lives, a dangerous job if ever there was one, the author raises our craft to the level of the great classical expressions of the human mind, and strengthens our hope of being able to look upon it more and more as an art. (pp. 2-3)

Jean Renoir, "Chaplin among the Immortals," translated by Harold Salemson, in The Screen Writer *(copyright 1947 by The Screen Writers' Guild, Inc.), Vol. 3, No. 2, July, 1947, pp. 1-4.*

AL CAPP

All comedy is based on man's delight in man's inhumanity to man. I know that is so, because I have made forty million people laugh more or less every day for sixteen years, and this has been the basis of all the comedy I have created. I think it is the basis of all comedy.

But I had forgotten, until I saw Chaplin again, that comedy can become sublime when it makes men sorrow at man's inhumanity to man by making men pity themselves.

When the history of art in our time is written, and when the ideological passions of our time are laughable curios, the great artist that our time has produced will be recognized as Charlie Chaplin. (pp. 25-6)

In the Chaplin films you will find thousands of miraculously funny gags (and no matter how much they've been copied, his originals have still a pure, bright freshness). You will find scores of unique characters, each warmly funny because, no matter how wildly they're drawn, they're based on real, instantly recognizable types. You'll find a treasure-trove of hilarious and intricate comedy situations—you'll find everything that comedy is made of. But the most important thing you'll find is this: that for all his dazzling succession of gags, characters, and situations, Charlie Chaplin told again and again, with infinite variation, one story—the story of man's inhumanity to man. And that is a very funny story. (p. 26)

Chaplin, more than any other comic of our time, understood his fellow man's pitiful and cruel mixture of insecurity and inhumanity.

A few years ago, Chaplin was shown around a great automobile factory. Its owners were mighty proud of their new gadgets. They were proud because their new gadgets were time-saving. Chaplin was horrified because they were also man-killing.

The superiority of gadget to man, the slavery of man to gadget, was to him a hilarious perversion of the only same reason *for* the gadget—namely, to make man's life easier.

So Chaplin made a picture called *Modern Times*. . . .

[People] howled at *Modern Times,* and industry howled *to* Chaplin. It was un-American, said they, to make people laugh at the inhumanity of gadget to man. Gadgets, they claimed, were a blessing to man. It had been okay for the comic to make people laugh at a vaguely inhuman society that generally kicked 'em around, but it was unfair, and unsporting really, to make people laugh at a specific system of dignified industrial "efficiency" that robbed them of their dignity as human beings. . . .

No confused, despondent lover ever saw a Chaplin picture who didn't come away feeling considerably cheered up. Cheered up because, no matter how inept in his lovemaking he had been, he had seen someone even more inept; no matter that the fair object of his affections had been unresponsive, the girl Chaplin courted had been downright contemptuous. Chaplin understood that the surest way to delight a world of lovers who suffered because they weren't loved enough was to show them a lover who wasn't loved at all. . . .

The more secure a man feels, the more ready he is to laugh. So Chaplin—the instant he appeared—gave us all a feeling of security. Certainly none of us, no matter how badly off we were, were as badly off as this bundle of rags. . . .

And that's what a comedian is for, isn't he? To make people feel fine? (p. 29)

Al Capp, "The Comedy of Charlie Chaplin," in The Atlantic Monthly *(copyright © 1950, by The Atlantic Monthly Company, Boston, Mass.; reprinted with permission), Vol. 185, No. 2, February, 1950, pp. 25-9.*

THEODORE HUFF

Chaplin's first picture in five years has for its theme "the glamor of the limelight—from which age must pass as youth enters." . . . However *Limelight* is garnished with a little Freud, some ballet, a few aphorisms about life, and a certain artiness. . . .

In accord with Chaplin's tendency of recent years, there is little comedy in *Limelight.* One of Chaplin's lines in this picture is: "Life isn't a gag any more. From now on I'm a retired humorist." There is scarcely a trace of the gags, satire, fantasy, caricature and slapstick of his earlier work. (p. 466)

Limelight is filled with autobiographical overtones. Although there is something in it of Chaplin's father, a music hall entertainer of the nineties, much more of the story and of the dialogue derives from Chaplin's position today. He was stung to the quick by the financial failure of *Monsieur Verdoux,* the only one of his 77 films which did not make money. (p. 468)

[Because] of his egocentricity, he never really immerses himself in the story. There is a pervading narcissism, and not infrequent vanity. . . .

It would be pleasant, at this point in Chaplin's career, to state that *Limelight* is his greatest film. Unfortunately, it is not. . . . *Limelight* seems to have been designed to please audiences, instead of merely Chaplin himself, as of yore. Chaplin long ago became too refined to be able to do his old comedy, and, as he says in *Limelight*: "What a sad business is being funny!"

In spite of the shortcomings I enumerated, there is a strange glow to *Limelight*. . . . [There] does emerge once more that something so characteristic of Chaplin, that humanity which has warmed millions all over the world for nearly forty years. (p. 470)

Theodore Huff, "Film Reviews: 'Limelight'," in Films in Review *(copyright © 1952 by the National Board of Review of Motion Pictures, Inc.), Vol. III, No. 8, October, 1952, pp. 466-70.*

GAVIN LAMBERT

Thirty years ago Chaplin had encompassed tragi-comedy with a purity of form and feeling unique in the cinema, and from a historical point of view the qualities of *Limelight* are beautifully logical; what is less logical, perhaps, is the intense success with which they have been realised. At 63 Chaplin has executed an imaginative portrait of the artist as an old man and shown his creative powers to be at their height. The cinema is apt to exhaust its great talents early, but *Limelight* has all the vitality and sureness of Chaplin's best work, and it touches some new moments of experience. (p. 123)

The poetic unity of *Limelight* is a deep, calm, fatal emanation of sadness. . . . (p. 124)

The directness of sentiment in *Limelight* has found its detractors, as direct sentiment always does; nothing exposes an artist more. It is easy enough to write about today's Chaplin as "sententious" . . . , as "self-pitying" . . . or "self-infatuated". . . , but these charges seem to reflect a temperamental dislike of the film's approach rather than to refute it. They miss the essential thing, the passion which is the motive and the justification of *Limelight.* Nothing could be truer to itself; the difference is in the identification point. Charlie the tramp, the anarchist, was everyone's symbol, and Chaplin since *The Great Dictator* has ceased to be that. In his last three films he has become articulate, and become a particular person. The fact that *The Great Dictator* and *Monsieur Verdoux* did not make the transition completely, that they were manifestly imperfect films, may account for the unwillingness of many to appreciate what Chaplin was trying to do. Because Chaplin tells the story of *Limelight,* as of most of the other films, in simple and superficially old-fashioned terms, it has been assumed that the emotions which go with it are old-fashioned. . . . But to condemn this only reflects the naive fallacy that any age is artistically self-contained, and that true "contemporary" art must discard all traditional methods. The revolutionary artist is not the only valid one; what counts on the personal level is the artist's own imagination and technique, whether stimulated by tradition or repelled by it. (pp. 124-25)

Within the story itself there is no slapstick, but a certain amount of traditional comedy and, in the dialogue, of irony; the actual world of the clown is separated into the music-hall acts. In this way *Limelight* has far more unity than *Verdoux,* which veered from farce to sentiment, satire to caricature, and lost, I think, the singleness of purpose its subject demanded. *Limelight* shows Chaplin the actor and Chaplin the film-maker equally prominent. He uses dialogue and sound with as much mastery as he brought to silent film-making at the peak of his career in *City Lights.* As a director, Chaplin's talent has often been under-rated; his best films have always been carefully constructed, the simplicity of their continuity is disciplined, and his use of the camera for recording physical action no less remarkable in its way than that of [Erich von] Stroheim or [Georg] Pabst. . . . Of the major films, only in *Modern Times, The Dictator* and *Verdoux*—which will, I believe, seem in perspective the most transitional of his career, the gradual elimination of Charlie being a rather intellectual process and reflecting, especially in the sometimes shrill bitterness of *Verdoux,* the lack of emotional shelter which he found in *Limelight*—is the style considerably less satisfying. (p. 125)

The comedy in *Limelight* continues the line of sophistication drawn in parts of *Verdoux.* We are made conscious of two conventions; of the old-fashioned London music-hall, and of Chaplin's own pantomime style, a deviation from it. The final sequence with Buster Keaton, classically abstracted as ever, is probably the "straightest" comedy turn in the film, with its gags impeccably accumulated both in the action and the use of the camera. Yet even here Chaplin's demonic fiddler, a sort of Mephisto Waltz parody, suggests a diversion. The difference seems to be that Charlie's humour was the humour of a figure who had become a universal symbol, and that in *Limelight,* in keeping with the rest, the comedy is the comedy of character. (p. 126)

Gavin Lambert, "The Elegant Melancholy of Twilight: Impressions of 'Limelight'," in Sight and Sound *(copyright © 1953 by The British Film Institute), Vol. 22, No. 3, January-March, 1953, pp. 123-27.*

J. L. TALLENAY

"Limelight's" scenario unquestionably sounds melodramatic. Various critics have expressed the opinion that it is poorly done. Its very construction involves instances of ineptness: the entire first part of the film is broken up by long monologues on the part of Calvero, and the dramatic action takes too long to get under way. Finally although it is fictitious the film has a number of sequences that sound a personal and autobiographical note which may strike some people as discordant.

But despite these seeming weaknesses, and perhaps even because of them, "Limelight" is a major work of extraordinary richness and unprecedented originality.

Its primary originality is precisely in the personal tone which Chaplin has adopted. Never before has the motion picture reached a similar degree of intensity in the dialogue between the author and his audience. Not that "Limelight" is a confidential work addressed only to the initiate. For here again Chaplin has succeeded in addressing himself to different levels, different strata, of the public. . . .

The word 'dignity' which recurs in this picture as a *leitmotiv* would seem to supply the key: a comic figure, no matter how much he is weighed down with honors, senses that his dignity as a man is constantly threatened by the very laughter he is able to create. To illustrate his universal theme of the sadness deep within a man who makes the public laugh, Chaplin, himself universally honored, has had to choose a character whose external failure and misery convey this inner disorder. That is one of the explanations of the character of Calvero, together with the unmistakable reticence which prevented Chaplin from revealing such intimate personal sentiments in his own name. . . .

[There] exist two types of confessions: those which express a man's peculiar individuality and those which attain the heights of universality, mirroring what is true of all men. The tragedy which Chaplin evokes in "Limelight" is of the latter sort. Beyond the inner drama of a clown named Calvero, beyond that of the comic figure, Chaplin, he conveys the deep loneliness and uneasiness of every man who has yielded himself up to the public. (p. 452)

Chaplin embarks on a veritable meditation on his calling, on men and on life. Attempts of this sort are hardly current now in movies; here again Chaplin is an innovator and his novel conception requires a construction quite at variance with most current scenarios, for which the essential element is suspense.

The soliloquies of the first part of the picture are indispensable to the understanding and the balance of the picture as a whole; they go against the conventions of film making, to which a creative artist such as Chaplin does not feel bound. "Limelight," like all Chaplin's pictures, shows a fine disdain for the recognized technical and artistic rules for cutting, montage and *mise en scene*. (pp. 452-53)

J. L. Tallenay, "The Tragic Vision of Charles Chaplin," in Commonweal *(copyright © 1953 Commonweal Publishing Co., Inc.; reprinted by permission of Commonweal Publishing Co., Inc.), Vol. LVII, No. 18, February 6, 1953, pp. 451-53.*

PARKER TYLER

I think that [*Limelight*] is to be considered a *mea culpa:* an expression by the comedian that is more than art or entertainment; in brief, a moral credo that was designed to set everyone straight about its creator's positive and enduring convictions as a member of human society. It would be foolish to pretend such an assumption is irrelevant; that a work of art or a piece of entertainment is that and no more, has no moral value, and is not to be construed as an expression of private opinion, and so on. There are myriad signs that *Monsieur Verdoux,* like its predecessor *The Great Dictator,* not merely carried a view of contemporary life intended seriously in the moral sense but also was Chaplin's personal platform as a contemporary thinker. (p. 75)

In *The Great Dictator,* Chaplin dissolved the traditional Tramp into two strictly contemporary phases of social personality: Hitler's parody, Hynkel, was bohemian, irresponsible, hallucinated, malevolent, and generally unhappy and frustrated; the Barber was gentle, humble, gay, loving, loved, and well acquainted with decent human values. If we reflect upon the long film repertory of the Tramp from the year when his original arrived on American soil, 1913, we may observe that as a personality he has exhibited, from time to time, all those qualities belonging respectively to the "twins" of *The Great Dictator!* . . .

What happened, then, to induce Chaplin to convert the Tramp into a split-personality? Historic events "happened"; Hitler "happened." And what happened to make Monsieur Verdoux, in effect, more like the Dictator-half than like the Barber-half? The Second World War, and its dark international heritage, "happened." At least, these are the self-evident explanations from Chaplin's viewpoint, and they are chronologically consistent with the appearances of the film-works. (p. 76)

What may be termed . . . the "economic necessity" for Chaplin's changing the Tramp's personality becomes quite clear. To the comic artist's imagination, the significant thing became not the *subjective* impossibility of having a permanent job, which was the Tramp's case, but the *objective* impossibility of having one, which was the Barber's case. . . . The Second World War had vindicated the structure of the social-political plot in which the Tramp's heir found himself in *The Great Dictator,* yet it failed to justify the moral hope contained in the oratorical plea tagging that film: the plea in which all the Tramp's good and constructive qualities were presented frankly as propaganda for the democratic faith. It was as though the Tramp in 1940 publicly pleaded for the heart of his human reality—and forthwith was snubbed by the universal social destiny: a frightful war.

Monsieur Verdoux, as a result of this reasoning, appears an entirely lucid if treacherous heir of the Tramp in Chaplin's imaginative world. (p. 77)

When Chaplin . . . wished to make a kind of peripety, a "moral" reversal, in his art by coming back to the human goodness and charm of the tramp, it was artistically and morally *inevitable* that it should take the form of his imaginary hero's pure and genuine, and radically selfless, love. We have arrived at the theme of *Limelight.* (p. 78)

I believe that nobody who knows Chaplin's film history can see *Limelight* without being aware how much it is the artist's moral testament. (p. 79)

The point is now how exact is the parallel between his private life and the imaginary story of the screen; obviously, the parallel is most inexact. But the literal parallel is not the one that is relevant here. When, at the end of *Limelight,* the injured Calvero, following his last performance, dies in the wings while watching his lovely protegée achieve a dancing triumph on stage, what appears to us is the very symbolism which has been especially accented in this situation. The hero's "job" is the professional comic art and only old age has withered his greatness in it. A ballet presented earlier in the film has made it clear that the girl dancer is a symbol of resurrection and external beauty. Thus, in terms of the traditional love legend, the female ideal now appears as the professional spirit of beauty, its Muse. Essentially, in Chaplin's art, woman was the inspiration of sentiment to transcend all real circumstance and create a pure imaginative domain. Art is what gives this visionary domain concreteness. (pp. 79-80)

Parker Tyler, "Chaplin: The Myth of the Immigrant," in The Western Review *(copyright 1953 by* The Western Review*), Vol. 18, No. 1, Autumn, 1953, pp. 74-80.*

VERNON YOUNG

Limelight cruelly exposes the limitations of Chaplin as producer, for it is everything, most of the time, a movie *shouldn't* be: overwritten, underdirected, slowly paced, monotonously photographed, fumblingly cut—and oh so *dreary*, far beyond any justification from the milieu, a penury of the soul. . . . The first ten minutes, roughly, are good Chaplin, relatively pure cinema. . . . Up to this point, or shortly thereafter, the situation is managed with a fine balance of tragic and comic, dramatic and ludicrous, theatrical and cinematic. But from here on, Chaplin abandons all effort to keep his invention within these disciplined commutations of method. The whole gorgeous potentiality breaks down, washes away in a welter of tears, archness, smut, coincidental meetings, Pagliacci closeups, and in *talk, talk, talk*. For interminable stretches he either sets his camera while two or three actors play out a scene virtually face front, with no cuts to benefit either their comfort or the scene's modulations, or he simply moves in to a close shot from middle distance. These are almost the limits of his *motion*. When, during a ballet sequence, he suddenly gives us four overhead shots in as many minutes, the change of perspective is so unprepared for as to seem completely out of key.

Chaplin should have long ago—as far back as *Modern Times*, for instance—placed his idiosyncratic genius for pantomime and his occasionally seminal ideas at the disposal of a sympathetic director who might have created a context in which they were neither dissipated nor overdeployed. But this is to imagine a totally different personality for an artist who has increasingly become his own worst enemy from the deluded notion that it is not enough for him to be an ingenious comic—he must also be an entrepreneur with a message about faith, hope, and charity who can yet afford to ignore the finer details of everything but his own performance. (pp. 31-2)

Vernon Young, "Inside Chaplin" (1954), in his On Film: Unpopular Essays on a Popular Art *(copyright © 1972 by Vernon Young), Quadrangle Books, 1972, pp. 31-3.*

PENELOPE HOUSTON

The lapses of genius are always interesting, sometimes baffling, and inevitably sad. The important thing is that they don't, in the long run. greatly matter. Genius means, as often as not, an infinite capacity for taking risks: and with an artist like Chaplin, who has played for high stakes and never been concerned to hedge his bets, there is no possibility of failure in any small way. His new film. *A King in New York*, is for me as much of a failure as *Monsieur Verdoux* and *Limelight* were successes. Those were flawed masterpieces; this seems a failure that occasionally—but only occasionally—touches the edge of brilliance. And it is a film that appears at once important and of little lasting account; immensely revealing and discussable, as any work of Chaplin's must be, and at the same time a picture by which one would no more consider judging its creator than one would judge Shaw by one of his very late plays. This is not to suggest that *A King in New York* looks like the work of an ageing man, something to be written off as coming out of the dim twilight of an artist. It has a good deal more to it than that. If it stands apart from Chaplin's other work, it is because here the artist's comment on his times reflects not the sureness of knowledge but the uncertainty of betrayal. (p. 78)

After the great defiant statements of *Monsieur Verdoux*, the twilight wisdom of *Limelight*, the actual words of *A King in New York* seem muffled and indistinct. Very early in his career, Chaplin made his major discovery as an artist: that great truths are mostly very simple. Since he took to speech, his danger has always appeared to lie in assuming that the converse also applies. The true, great satire on McCarthyism that Chaplin might have given us would not have been content with pointing out that committees can easily be made to look foolish and that people who stand in the way of a machine are likely to get hurt. There is also the state of mind, the climate in which the excrescence flourishes. Missing it, the film misses more than that; the great weapon of laughter misfires; the McCarthyist committee is drenched, but not lampooned.

Chaplin's laughter has always been that of humanity. In *A King in New York*, it runs thinly and at times almost sourly. . . .

If one finds oneself withholding laughter, it is perhaps because Chaplin so often invites us to laugh not with but at Shahdov. Elements of Charlie have survived into the other characters he has played: the loneliness of Verdoux, the immense pathos of Calvero, carried on Charlie's great role of tragic comedian. Others may find King Shahdov a figure of pathos; and in the scenes with the boy, the practical, protective tenderness, one gets glimpses of the wonderful sadness of *Limelight*. But on the whole, the spruce, debonair king, surveying the world from a hotel room he is unable to pay for, pursuing his vague plans for improving conditions through the peaceful use of atomic energy, remains enigmatic. We laugh at his embarrassments, but they are those of a stranger.

This impression of remoteness persists through the film's technical shortcomings. It is a pity, for instance, that Berkeley Square should form such an instantly recognisable background to one scene; that the mob of angry revolutionaries attacking the king's palace in the opening episode should resemble nothing so much as an English shopping crowd besieging the counters on the first day of the sales. These things would not, I think, have mattered in any previous Chaplin film. He has often been charged with making his films badly, which as a rule has meant simply that he has not been concerned with technical effect. Everything that he wanted to express has found expression, and if style means the correct relationship between ends and means, then Chaplin has been in every sense a film-maker of style. If this relationship no longer seems to exist in *A King in New York*, then one must look beyond mere technical deficiencies for the reasons.

I have tried in this review to indicate what I think these to be: distance, withdrawal, uncertainty, a wasting of satirical ammunition on insignificant targets and a hesitancy before the big theme. Where *Limelight* seemed like a homecoming, a return to the scenes and places out of which Chaplin's art developed, *A King in New York* has about it the remoteness of exile. (p. 79)

Penelope Houston, "A Review: 'A King in New York'," in Sight and Sound *(copyright © 1957 by The British Film Institute), Vol. 27, No. 2, Autumn, 1957, pp. 78-9.*

FRANÇOIS TRUFFAUT

I don't see any great difference between the first and the second parts of *A King in New York.* I didn't expect to laugh. We all read the newspapers, and I was well aware of Chaplin's misfortunes in America. I knew what his new film was about and I knew how profoundly sad his preceding films were. We could have known that *A King in New York* would be the saddest of all, also the most personal. The man who made *The Gold Rush* can, if he wants to, make his public laugh or cry at will; he knows all the tricks; he's an ace, that's sure. If we neither cry nor laugh at *A King in New York,* it's because Chaplin made up his mind to touch our heads instead of our hearts. The awful gentleness of this film makes me think of [Resnais's] *Nuit et Brouillard,* which also rejected the simplemindedness of the propagandist or the hater. (pp. 58-9)

The film doesn't broaden out or force itself on the viewer. There are no scenes that are amusing or ironic or bitter. It is a rapid and dry demonstration of a single point, almost like a documentary. The shots of New York and the two images of airplanes that Chaplin inserts are like a montage of documents. *A King in New York* is not comparable to a novel or a poem; it is more like an article, a few pages from a journal called "Charlie Chaplin comments freely on political reality." (p. 59)

If *A King in New York* is not amusing, it's because Joe McCarthy's America represents a depressing world. It's an autobiographical film and there's no complacency about it. If it's a sadder slice of life than the ones that went before it, it's because Chaplin understands that the most agonizing problem of the time is not poverty or mistakes in the name of progress, but an organized attack on freedom in a world of informants.

"The work of art," Jean Genêt says somewhere, "must resolve the drama, not merely present it." Charlie Chaplin resolves the drama. It's a gift of great lucidity. (p. 60)

François Truffaut, "Charlie Chaplin: 'A King in New York'" (1957), in his The Films in My Life, *translated by Leonard Mayhew (copyright © 1975 by, Flammarion; translation copyright © 1978 by Simon & Schuster; reprinted by permission of Simon & Schuster, a Division of Gulf & Western Corporation; originally published as* Les films de ma vie, *Flammarion, 1975), Simon & Schuster, 1978, pp. 57-60.*

ERNEST CALLENBACH

The Gold Rush, certainly, is one of Chaplin's achieved masterpieces of silent comedy, the work of a great artist of sentiment and pathos. (pp. 31-2)

The story-line (*The Gold Rush* was made after *A Woman of Paris*) has become firm and rich. And if the film has none of the flabbergasting imagination of a Keaton . . . it nonetheless creates a comic world as viable as any, and with a great deal of genuine poetry to it. (p. 32)

The key elements in the vision?—The search for love, above all; this time found in the person of a girl harder and less "good" than the usual Chaplin heroine. . . . The existence of good and evil, too; the Big Jims and Black Larsens of the world exterior to the tramp's person, who struggle violently, often for objectives the tramp has no hope of reaching through struggle, and can only attain through luck or guile. . . . It is worth noting that in Chaplin films as a whole evil is portrayed rather convincingly and in detail: greed and poverty, guile and deception; but the goodness of the tramp rests upon charm and pathos much of the time, or, as in *City Lights,* is dramatized mawkishly. —Most of all, the vision shows the world as a series of traps and dangers: physical peril, hunger, trickery that will not always be reversed. It is a world, like those of all great artists, having the power to haunt us afterwards, physically: we *see* that world in our mind's eye, more real than the supposedly real world of most "realistic" films, with a timelessness that every "serious" film-maker, beset with problems of costume, slang, and manners, must sometimes wildly envy. The wonderful shabbiness of dress and settings in *The Gold Rush* seems beyond our art directors today. The grime and disrepair seen now in the beautiful soft grays of a good print have disappeared from the screens but not from our minds; and they still remind us of poverty, sadness, and the essential human condition—the last because, no matter how materially fat and sassy we become, we sense all too well on other levels that moths still corrupt and thieves break in and steal—and villains wield sticks and what is old must be made to serve. (p. 35)

It is because of the intensity of this vision, of course, that films like *The Gold Rush* will last and last, when today's bloated extravaganzas have crumbled to dust in the vaults. Even in the heartless and mechanical world of the cinema, art tells. . . .

It is an art of charm or sympathy of character, ingenuity, timing, grace: an athletic and kinesthetic kind of beauty that can be very moving. . . .

Chaplin has often been referred to as the greatest artist the screen has yet produced. Whether this is true I personally doubt: he never reached the tough unity and compression of *Le Jour Se Lève,* the finesse of *Rashomon,* the searing intensity of *Los Olvidados,* and in a sense one must judge every artist by the highest point he has reached. Nearer home, I would maintain that Keaton surpassed Chaplin with *The Navigator* and *The General,* both works of astonishing virtuosity and purity of aesthetic motive, and moreover of great technical brilliance.

But Chaplin's work as a whole clearly stands out far and above Keaton's as it stands out above everyone else's: he is the undeniable Hero of the cinema, who has shown beyond doubt what can be done with this new medium. (p. 36)

The question in reëvaluating Chaplin today centers around the problem of his sentimentality. This is in reality a complex social as well as artistic problem. . . . [The] object of much of film art is to produce an emotional involvement with events portrayed which will be strong enough to seem overwhelming and "real" but without asking ridiculously much, as does sentimental melodrama or overt political propaganda. In the long cultural run, evaluations of artistic success in this balancing act are bound to shift—sometimes drastically, so that Pope after a time seems chilly, and Shelley overblown, though their immense technical skill cannot be brought into doubt. It is from our own peculiar position on this sort of social sand, therefore, that we must judge any artist who, like Chaplin, is good enough to bother thinking of in terms longer than a decade or so.

Of *The Gold Rush* we may say, I think, that it is Chaplin near or at the peak of his powers. He had mastered feature-length construction; he had peeled away from the tramp almost all of the mere silliness inherited from the music halls. . . . *The Gold Rush* has the simple, lasting appeals of a well-defined constellation of characters, an overwhelmingly sympathetic hero, a satisfying pattern of frustrations followed by surprising and deserved success. It is a remarkable film, though it is not "life". . . . (p. 37)

Ernest Callenbach, "Classics Revisited: 'The Gold Rush'," in Film Quarterly *(copyright 1959 by The Regents of the University of California; reprinted by permission of the University of California Press), Vol. XIII, No. 1, Fall, 1959, pp. 31-7.*

DWIGHT MACDONALD

[MacDonald quotes from a review which he wrote in 1956:]

> *Monsieur Verdoux* is really two films, one a sentimental melodrama, the other a comedy in the old Chaplin style that burlesques the melodrama. What makes it confusing is that Chaplin shifts gears between the two without apparently knowing he is doing so. . . . It is unsettling to see an actor brilliantly taking off the conventional rhetoric of his trade one moment and the next employing it seriously, especially since Chaplin's serious rhetoric expresses a vain and foolish concept of himself—as the tragic man-of-the-world, disenchanted, elegant, sensitive, the gallant protector of the weak who, to make the bogus diamond shine all the more brilliantly, are usually crippled or blind. In the film after *Verdoux,* the disastrous *Limelight,* this mawkish exhibitionism goes right over the edge. . . . (p. 18)
>
> There is even a third film here, that bursts into the last part with shattering banality, a 'message' drama. . . . It was a sad day for Chaplin when the intellectuals convinced him he was the Tragic Clown, the Little Man. From a parodist, he graduated into a philosopher, but since his epistemology was all instinctive, even physical . . . it didn't help him in his new role. The nature of reality, which he understood intuitively as a mime, became opaque to him when he tried to think about it, and where he once danced lightly he now stumbles into bathos and sentimentality.

Rereading the above, after seeing *Verdoux* again last year, I think it on the whole accurate. (p. 24)

Chaplin's direction is no better than his script. . . . Neither realistic nor stylized, *Verdoux* is amateurish without freshness, Hollywoodish without technique. It comes to life only when Chaplin is on stage, and even then only when he is parodying his boulevardier and not in the longer stretches when he is trying to impress us as a philosopher. . . . As Chaplin's script is only a device to show him off . . . so his direction reduces all the other performers to stooges. . . . His directorial eye finds nothing interesting in the inanimate world either, which is also reduced to a conventional background for his own performance. I can recall few films in which there was so little to *see.* Since it is a movie, Chaplin thinks he has to show us realistic interiors and real landscapes and cityscapes, but they are botched in so routinely, with so little sense of what they look like, that they might as well be those painted backdrops of a park or a street, bordered with local advertisements, in front of which vaudevillians used to do their turns. (pp. 26, 28)

Dwight Macdonald, "On Chaplin, Verdoux and Agee" (copyright © 1965, Esquire Publishing Inc.; used by courtesy of the magazine), in Esquire, *Vol. LXIII, No. 4, April, 1965, pp. 18-34.*

ROGER EBERT

Walking away from the camera, down a dirt road, his cane bobbing behind him, Charlie Chaplin is not a comedian but a clown. Emmett Kelly was the same kind of clown, smiling through a painted-on frown.

In Chaplin's films, the frown is painted on with a camera, and the audiences have to supply the smile themselves. Chaplin's deadly seriousness makes it clear that he does not understand why the joke should be on him. . . .

The difference between Chaplin and the other great screen comics was that Chaplin played a clown. The others, by and large, played comedians, with a few exceptions such as Lahr, Keaton, and possibly Jerry Lewis.

Comedians and clowns aim in opposite directions. Comedians live in imaginary worlds that look just like our own. In "The Apartment", for example, Jack Lemmon inhabited a flat as realistic as it was unlikely.

Clowns, on the other hand, live in real worlds which consist of a few props. No worlds are more real than the clown-worlds of "Waiting for Godot" or Chaplin's early shorts.

Comedians use fantasy to make the real world seem funny. Clowns use reality to make our fantasies seem ridiculous.

Chaplin was also the only one in his world who believed in its conventional morality. He believed honor should be defended. He believed customers in restaurants should be polite. He believed little flower girls, especially if they are beautiful and virtuous, will be treated kindly by the world. In short, he was naïve.

It's almost as if everyone in Chaplin's world was a W. C. Fields, and everyone in Fields's world was a Chaplin. Fields took great relish in beating down the naïve idealists ("Out of my way, you fools," he once snarled at a flock of chickens). But Chaplin never did quite learn how to handle the cynics. And that was the point of his art.

Roger Ebert, "Of Comedians, Clowns and the Cinema," in The Chicago Sun-Times *(reprinted with permission of* Chicago Sun-Times*), March 26, 1967.*

DAVID BORDWELL

The recent reappearance of Chaplin's *The Circus* [1928] provides an example of a rich film which has been overshadowed by its predecessor (*The Gold Rush*, 1925) and its successor (*City Lights*, 1931). True, *The Circus* lacks the superb economy of *The Gold Rush* and it does not plumb to the depths of pathos of *City Lights*. But its virtues are rather special, and, I think, ones which we, forty years later, are in a special position to notice. For *The Circus* is one of the few films in which Chaplin's nineteenth-century sensibility deals symbolically with art and despair in a truly twentieth-century way.

It is a commonplace that the conemporary cinema has begun to comment on art as well as life; in *Lola Montes, 8½, Persona,* and *Blow-Up,* we see directors exploring the nature of cinema itself. In the light of this tendency, *The Circus* seems highly modern.

Perhaps Chaplin's most objective analysis of his screen *persona,* it uses the circus as a metaphor for both Film and Existence. Like Bergman in *Sunset of a Clown,* Chaplin fills his circus with symbols that suggest both the depths of art and the bleakness of life.

From the star on the hoop that fills the iris in the very first shot to the crumpled-up star Charlie kicks away in the last shot, the film traces patterns of circularity. On the plot level, this pattern is enacted in the rhythm of changes in Fortune—the essence of comedy. . . . Bad fortune—a twist —good fortune—a twist—bad fortune—ad infinitum: but always, as in all comedy, survival. The recurring scenes—the nightly performances, the ringmaster's blustering—find their place in the rhythm we know must be completed by the circus' eventual departure for a new town.

On the level of symbolism, circularity visually pervades the film. Merna's hoop, the wedding ring Charlie buys, and the controlling symbol of the circus ring itself: we are witnessing the ceaseless cycle of futile love. At the end, the image is almost too powerful: Charlie is imprisoned by the circle in the dirt, trapped in the cycle of life. As he had strolled into the film facing away from us, so he leaves by walking off into the distance, as if the entire film were only a short pause along his way. The road will never end.

This idea of ongoing life, which comedy typically projects, is modulated by the idea of performance—an image from the world of art; in Chaplin's case, cinema. *The Circus* analyzes the nature of audience-attitudes toward comedy and contrasts Chaplin's art with another variety of screen comedy. (p. 40)

On the screen, we see an audience thirsty for fun (like ourselves) enjoying Charlie's performance, but we are also privy, as they are not, to the clown's private grief. The moment both aspects crystallize—the audience screams, "Where's the Funny Man?" and a title, *The Funny Man,* takes us to a sleeping tramp curled up in a chariot—we are forced to analyze our own response to the public side of Chaplin's art. Might he not be reminding us—at the time of his much-publicized Lita Grey divorce—of the ultimate loneliness of the artist's private life?

Similarly, Chaplin brings in another comedy style to highlight the uniqueness of his own. The Keystone-Kops chase that opens the film soon tapers off into Chaplin's more intimate comedy of glances, gestures, and feelings. . . . In Sennett, slapstick is a catharsis of repressed dislike; in *The Circus*, it is kindness veering out of control. (pp. 40-1)

David Bordwell, "Film Favorites: On 'The Circus'," in Film Comment *(copyright © 1970 Film Comment Publishing Corporation; all rights reserved), Vol. 6, No. 3, Fall, 1970, pp. 40-1.*

ANDRÉ BAZIN

It is easy to foresee what people will find to criticize in *Monsieur Verdoux*. There is a fairly complete list of them in an article in *La Revue des Temps Modernes* which goes about as far as anything could in misrepresentation. The author of the critique expresses herself as profoundly disappointed by Chaplin's work because to her it seems ideologically, psychologically, and aesthetically incoherent. "Monsieur Verdoux's crimes are dictated neither by a need for self-defense nor in order to repair injustices, nor by a deep ambition, nor by the desire to improve anything in the world around him. It is a sad thing to have expended so much energy and proved absolutely nothing, to have succeeded in producing neither a comedy nor a film with social implications, and to have beclouded the most important issues." (p. 103)

If *Verdoux* has a "meaning," why look for it in terms of some moral, political, or social ideology or other, or even in reference to psychological categories that we are in the habit of seeing as revealed in the characters of our theater or our novels, when it is so easy to discover it in Charlie?

The critic quoted above attacks Chaplin's performance, accusing him of failing to escape altogether from the comic format of his former character, of hesitating, not choosing one way or another, between the realistic interpretation that the role of Verdoux demands and the conventions of a "Charlie." The fact is that in this instance realism would add up to illusion. Charlie is always there as if superimposed on Verdoux, because Verdoux *is* Charlie. It is important that at the right moment the public should recognize him without any shadow of a doubt; and this wonderful moment arrives in the final shot when Verdoux, alias Charlie, goes off in shirtsleeves between the executioners. Verdoux, or Charlie disguised as his opposite! There is no feature of the former character that is not turned inside out like the fingers of a glove. (pp. 105-06)

Monsieur Verdoux is Chaplin's New Testament. The Old ended with *The Gold Rush* and *The Circus*. Between the two, the Chaplin myth seems to be confused, troubled, uncertain. He is still trying to rely on gags and comic bits which, however, grow fewer and fewer. *The Great Dictator* is significant from this point of view. Although badly constructed, mixed up, oddly assorted, it did have one brilliant and fortuitous justification, a settling of accounts with Hitler. . . . (p. 110)

What is admirable about Monsieur Verdoux is that his activities have a much deeper significance than those of Charlie in *The Gold Rush* although they are of a completely opposite kind. Actually, from the first Keystone shorts to *The Gold Rush* and *The Circus* Charlie's character has passed through a moral and psychological evolution. (p. 111)

[With *The Gold Rush*] Charlie is at the end of a process of evolution that justifies our coming to the conclusion that it does not represent his work at its best. As far as I am concerned, I would rather have the rich equivocation of *The Pilgrim* in which his art has not yet troubled about, or become enfeebled by, a concern for psychological and moral values. In any event, *The Gold Rush* is the most forceful apology for the character and most clearly calls for us to revolt against Charlie's fate.

The Saint Verdoux of today is the dialectical answer to

Saint Charlie of *The Kid, The Circus,* and *The Gold Rush.* But in my view the indictment of Charlie's enemies and the vindication provided by the character are all the more convincing because they are not based on any psychological proof. We go along with Verdoux, we are *for* Verdoux. But how can our sympathy be based on our moral estimate of him? On that level the spectator too could only condemn Verdoux's cynicism. Yet we take him as he is. It is the character that we love, not his qualities or his defects. The audience's sympathy for Verdoux is focused on the myth, not on what he stands for morally. (p. 112)

Even under the guise of Verdoux-Bluebeard, Charlie follows and perfects his personal myth of the woman. . . . There is no need to have recourse to the latest subtleties of psychoanalysis to see quite evidently that Chaplin, by way of Charlie, pursues symbolically one and the same feminine myth. Between the tender and gentle Edna Purviance, the blind girl of *City Lights,* and Verdoux's frail invalid there is no noticeable difference except that Verdoux is married to the last named. Like Charlie, they are all unhappy human beings, ill adjusted to society, physical or moral invalids of society and morality. . . . If we correctly interpret the symbolism of these female characters then the whole of Charlie's work would be the ever-renewed search for the woman capable of reconciling him to society and by the same token to himself. . . . Love alone can prompt his desire, albeit blundering and comic for other reasons, not only to adapt himself to society but one might even say to accept a moral way of living and a psychological individualism. (pp. 114-15)

For the first time in Monsieur Verdoux, we see Charlie after his marriage to Edna Purviance. Maybe because he has rounded the cape of love that, at least according to the logic of the myth, Charlie can change himself into Verdoux, or perhaps, if you prefer, Verdoux simply had to be married to Edna Purviance. In any case, although he is not all that reconciled to society, he at least knows how to make use of it. (pp. 115-16)

Chaplin does not build the substance of his narrative on the basis of a skeletal scenario, of an abstract dramatic structure, even the very substantial one of tragedy. . . . [His films] are only sequences of quasi-autonomous scenes, each of which is content to exploit a situation to the full. Think back to what you can remember of Charlie, and dozens of scenes will come to mind as clear cut as the picture of the character himself; . . . all are sufficient unto themselves, . . . so that one might almost extrapolate them from one film to another. . . . Even in the best-made of his films the so-called structural qualities are the most extrinsic to them, the last by which we would determine their excellence. Of course it would have been better if Chaplin had known how to reconcile the dramatic development of a story with the development of the situations of which it is composed, even better still, if this useful ordering of succession and interrelation conveyed a more hidden order in the conceiving and developing of a gag, and, most of all, that mysterious economy which gives the scenes, however short, their spiritual density, their specific gravity as myth and as comedy. The only serious formal criticisms that can be leveled against a Chaplin film concern its unity of style, the unfortunate variations in tone, the conflicts in the symbolism implicit in the situations. From this point of view the quality of Chaplin's films since *The Gold Rush* has definitely fallen off. (pp. 118-19)

As a rule, this falling off in quality in Chaplin's next to last films is attributed to a parasitic ideology. As we know, Chaplin has some pretensions to being a social philosopher, and no injustice is done to the artist to find his ideas, though appealing, also an encumbrance. Clearly *Easy Street,* or for that matter *The Gold Rush,* do not set out to prove anything, while there is no mistaking the purpose or theses of *Modern Times, The Great Dictator,* and *Monsieur Verdoux.* We could willingly do without these; but it remains to determine if they are as important as has been alleged. (p. 119)

We must not conclude . . . that [*Monsieur Verdoux*] has no formal structure, no narrative architecture, and that the direction consists in nothing more than setting up situations. Just the opposite, in fact. To recall what film direction owes not only to *A Woman of Paris* but to Charlie's work as a whole is to repeat a truism. *Monsieur Verdoux* shows its originality precisely in achieving a kind of synthesis between the celebrated psychological film directed by Chaplin and the films in which Charlie appears. Whereby we clearly see that the technique of ellipsis and allusion which was the definitive aesthetic revelation of *A Woman of Paris* somehow naturally befits the character. Chaplin's method of direction consists in carrying Charlie's performance over into the camerawork, the shooting script, and the editing. But Chaplin's ellipsis, whether applied to space or time, is not really concerned with what we call the scenario. It only affects the narrative at the scene level in immediate relation to the actor within the structure of the situation. It would be impossible to think of a closer dependence of content and form, or, better, a more perfect fusion of the two. Ellipsis gives definition to the aesthetic crystallization of Chaplin's work. But in this connection, *Monsieur Verdoux* is undoubtedly the most completely crystallized film of all. (pp. 121-22)

What could mislead us about the formal qualities of *Monsieur Verdoux* and make us consider it less well made than, for example, *The Gold Rush* (whereas it is certainly more perfectly made) is a natural confusion in the spectator between the comic density of the film and the myth. Whenever one thinks of Charlie, he is inseparable from the comic routines with which he won over the public. Since *The Gold Rush,* there has been a sharp decline in the wealth of Chaplin's comic imagination. There is more inventiveness, there are more gags in three hundred feet of *The Pilgrim* than in all of his last four films. There is certainly no room here for congratulation. On the other hand, neither should we harbor any resentment against Chaplin, nor interpret the fact as necessarily indicating an aesthetic impoverishment. Rather, everything takes place in *Monsieur Verdoux* as if this undeniable draining of his comic genius was the price to be paid for, or perhaps the cause of, an increased refinement of the myth. (pp. 122-23)

. . . . .

[What] would *Limelight* mean to an imaginary spectator who had never heard of Chaplin or of Charlie? Probably the question is meaningless because it contains a contradiction in terms—and this contradiction immediately gives us the measure of the film. There are certainly more people on earth who have never heard of Napoleon or Hitler or Churchill or Stalin, than of Charlie. *The Great Dictator* was not possible, indeed had no meaning, except insofar as Chaplin was sure that the myth of Charlie was more powerful and more real than that of Hitler, that their physical resemblance worked in his favor, and that Charlie would thereby drain his double of his blood, leaving only skin and bone. For it is crucial to grasp that the basis of the film was not the exploitation by Chaplin of his likeness to the man of Berchtesgaden; on the contrary, it was based on the unwitting imitation of Charlie by Hitler. To unmask the dictator, Chaplin had only to remind the world of his copyright in the moustache.

This is something that must be thoroughly understood before one starts thinking about *Limelight*. It is impossible to separate the story of Calvero from the Chaplin myth. I do not mean in the elementary and primary sense that one can discern in the story some obvious autobiographical elements—"a portrait of the artist by himself," as one English critic put it; but in a more basic sense, namely of a self-criticism of the myth by its author. *Verdoux* was already meant to do this: the killer of widows was Charlie disguised as his social opposite number. In *Limelight* the machinery is much more complex, to the decisive degree that we are not concerned with Charlie but with Chaplin himself. Verdoux, in a sense, represented the dialectical triumph of the character of Charlie and by the same token the end of him. *Limelight* treats by implication the relations between an actor and character he plays. (p. 125)

While *Limelight* is a direct evocation of Chaplin's childhood, this evocation is subordinated to the theme of the actor's relation with the character he plays. The true subject of the film remains: Can Charlie die? Can Charlie grow old? Instead of handling this two-fold and touching inquiry like a question to be answered, Chaplin exorcises it through a story of the lost fame and old age of a man who resembles him like a brother. (p. 126)

The film was just a sublime bad dream, but a dream as true as reality, one that allowed us to measure our love for him in his most beautiful role: the death of a clown called Charlie. Who in the world since theater began, what playwright or actor, has ever reached that supreme and paradoxical position in his art of being in himself the object of his tragedy? Doubtless many authors have put themselves more or less into their works, but without the knowledge of the public and hence without the elements of drama. (p. 127)

. . . . .

It was easy at the outset to see how much in *Limelight* would disturb people who had gone in the anticipation of seeing "a Charlie Chaplin film"—which retained, even more than *Monsieur Verdoux*, some element of comedy. Nor was the melodramatic aspect of the story calculated to please people, because it was based on illusion. *Limelight* is a pseudo melodrama. Where melodrama is primarily defined by the absence of ambiguity in the characters, here Calvero is ambiguity itself; and whereas, from a dramatic point of view, melodrama requires that one should be able to forsee the outcome of the plot, *Limelight* is precisely a film in which what happens is never exactly what one might expect—its scenario is brim full of inventiveness as any ever written. (p. 129)

Chaplin is not trying to deviate from the conventions of melodrama as Cocteau did in *Les Parents terribles*—on the contrary, no one has taken himself more seriously. It is simply that situations which start out as conventional are exploited with complete freedom, and without any concern for their traditional meaning. In short, there is nothing in *Limelight* which on the face of it could guarantee it wide public acceptance unless through a misunderstanding. (p. 130)

Almost everybody praises the second half, but many deplore the *longueurs* and the talkiness of the first half. However, if one were truly responsive to the last 24 minutes of the film, in retrospect one could not imagine a different opening. It becomes apparent that even the boredom one might experience enters mysteriously into the harmony of the over-all work. In any case, what do we mean here by the word boredom? I have seen *Limelight* three times and I admit I was bored three times, not always in the same places. Also, I never wished for any shortening of this period of boredom. It was rather a relaxing of attention that left my mind half free to wander—a daydreaming about the images. There were also many occasions on which the feeling of length left me during the screening. The film, objectively speaking a long one . . . , and slow, caused a lot of people, myself included, to lose their sense of time. I see that this phenomenon and the special nature of my periodical boredom have a common cause, namely that the structure of *Limelight* is really more musical than dramatic. I find this confirmed by the English pressbook of the film, three quarters of which is devoted to the music of *Limelight* [and] to the importance that Chaplin attached to it. . . . (p. 132)

Since *Modern Times*, the last of his films to come directly out of the primitive genre of Mack Sennett and the last of his virtually silent films, Chaplin has never stopped moving forward into the unknown, rediscovering the cinema in relation to himself. Alongside *Limelight*, all other films, even those we most admire, seem cut and dried and conventional. Although they may express their author's views, although they may have a personal style, they are only original in part; they conform to some film usages, they are defined by current conventions, even when they contravene them. *Limelight* is like no other film, above all like no other Chaplin film. (p. 139)

André Bazin, "The Myth of 'Monsieur Verdoux'," "'Limelight', or the Death of Molière," and "The Grandeur of 'Limelight'," in his What Is Cinema? Vol. II, *edited and translated by Hugh Gray (copyright © 1971 by the Regents of the University of California; reprinted by permission of the University of California Press), University of California Press, 1971, pp. 102-39.*

RICHARD SCHICKEL

Nearly everyone who has cared about Chaplin's art has been convinced that in The Tramp or The Little Fellow, to use the terms invariably employed in discussing Chaplin's great creation, we had a very direct expression of the artist's personality—"so simple and unaffected" despite the onslaught of previously unimagined celebrity. Certainly Chaplin has wanted us to believe that. . . . Surely what is best and wisest in him can be found in The Tramp. (p. 13)

There are lots of ways to put it; he found poetry in the ordinary, he transcended reality, he extended the range of pantomime to previously unimagined dimensions. Yet none of them quite explain his phenomenal appeal. Chaplin has never been generous in acknowledging influences, but some critics have noticed a correlation between his work and that of Max Linder, who had earlier brought something of the European comic tradition to the screen through his Pathé shorts. Edmund Wilson has emphasized how much Chaplin owed to the classic turns of the English music halls. And despite his protests it is clear that Chaplin learned a great deal from Sennett, especially about pacing and the use of the chase as a climax.

In short, he summarized much that had gone before, linking the art of screen comedy to a much older tradition. This was very significant to those intellectuals who began to take the movies seriously in the teens and twenties of this century. . . . Through all the long years when most of them were exercising their contempt for movies in general, Chaplin was always cited as the medium's one unquestioned, unquestionable artist, the individualist amid the corporate herd, a man clinging to his peculiar vision while everyone else went hooting off in pursuit of momentary fads. . . .

Yet this fact remains: Chaplin never again achieved the perfection of those first years. The little films of The Little Fellow were, in effect, solo ballets. As such, they had no more need of plot, of subsidiary characterizations, of great themes than one of Nijinsky's variations did. Despite the reams of appreciative analysis written about the early films, the pleasure we derived from them was essentially kinesthetic and therefore non- (and even perhaps anti-) intellectual. One could go on watching them for a lifetime. Indeed, one has.

But popular arts like the movies are cruel in their demand for novelty. And so are the intellectuals who have taken such arts for their province. No matter what they *thought* they thought, there was in their endless nattering over Chaplin an implicit demand for "development," for big ideas and statements. No doubt Chaplin made the same demands on himself. Beginning with "The Kid" in 1920 he began to inject larger and larger doses of pure sentiment into his work. No less than Griffith's, his was essentially a Victorian sensibility and he turned naturally to a rather cloying sweetness when he was forced, by the public demand for feature-length films, to extend his works.

There were other problems as well. As Edmund Wilson accurately noticed in 1925, "His gift is primarily the actor's, not the director's or the artist's. All the photographic, the plastic development of the movies, which is at present making such remarkable advances, seems not to interest Chaplin. His pictures are still in this respect nearly as raw as "Tilly's Punctured Romance" or any other primitive comedy." He added, presciently, that Chaplin "is jealous of his independence . . . he is very unlikely to allow himself to be written for, directed or even advised." (p. 47)

The coming of sound, naturally, was a threatening problem, solved in "City Lights" and "Modern Times" by the simple expedient of ignoring the microphone and filling the track with music, sound effects, and an occasional burst of gibberish. But dramatic as Chaplin's confrontation was with a technological advance he disliked, and exciting as his triumph over it was (no other screen artist dared so radical a strategy), I do not think it was fear of movies that talked which stayed Chaplin's hand. . . .

[Every] stylistic and technical change which has come to the movies since the end of World War I has implicitly interfered with his (and our) contemplation of his screen self. Length, of course, implies the necessity for sub-plots and the presence of other actors in significant roles. Very distracting. The growth in movie "plasticity" that Wilson spoke of was similarly likely to disrupt our concentration on the nuances of his art. And, of course, talk was perceived to be fatally interruptive. (p. 48)

[There is something disturbing] in the late films. For what we see surfacing in them is something that we may well have been aware of right from the start, yet dismissed as unworthy of us.

That, of course, is the increasingly shrill egoism of the artist, a quality transcending mere self-consciousness, and preventing those of us who were not part of the first, uncomplicated love affair between Chaplin and the public from surrendering to his insistent demand for a continuance of that affair in the old simple terms. (p. 49)

Richard Schickel, "Hail Chaplin—The Early Chaplin," in The New York Times Magazine *(© 1972 by The New York Times Company; reprinted by permission), April 2, 1972, pp. 12-13, 47-9.*

STANLEY KAUFFMANN

[*A King in New York*] is produced in typical Chaplin style—tackily. The lighting, photography, settings and editing are banal and cheap. The music is music-hall. The concern for accuracy is so small that, in what is supposed to be New York, the doors to a theater orchestra are labeled "Stalls," an elevator is labeled "Lift," and in a street scene we see the office of a famous London bookmaker. The direction is, as always, Chaplin-centered and theater-oriented. Most of the actors seem hardly to have been directed at all, and the predominant motions of the film are of actors' entrances and exits, rather than any intrinsic cinematic mode. (p. 247)

The script, by Chaplin, seems a series of ad hoc inventions with only the vaguest general plan. Whenever the phone rings or the door-buzzer sounds in Shadhov's hotel suite, which is the story's "basic" set you know that the sagging plot is going to get another boost. . . . The script has . . . effective satire on film violence, wide screens and TV commercialism. The one consistency in this adventitious collection of bits is that most of the seeming disasters turn out to be advantageous. Shadhov is trapped by a hidden camera into making a TV spectacle of himself, and it transforms him into a celebrity. He "blows" a TV whiskey commercial by coughing, and it makes him a comedy hit. The implication—that nothing is too ridiculous for American success if only it's sufficiently "exposed"—is much better satire than any of the political stuff. And into the midst of all this topical satire Chaplin thrusts his inevitable Dickensian strand—the lonely misunderstood schoolboy. (pp. 247-48)

If this film were by and with anyone else—a stupidly impossible conjecture—it would simply be bad. But being Chaplin's, it has many fascinations even in its faults. It's the last film he will ever make—he subsequently directed the unfortunate *Countess from Hong Kong* (1966) but appeared only briefly in it—and it's one that makes ultraclear what happened to his latter-day career. As political satire it's feeble, as cultural satire it's moderately keen, as self-revelation by Chaplin, it's an essential work.

First, it shows most vividly how schizoid the later Chaplin had become. In all Chaplin films up to *The Great Dictator* there was only one Chaplin, the Tramp. In the anti-Nazi film he played two roles which at least were tonally related; the real split came at the end when he launched into the long, controversial speech. There the "serious" Chaplin divorced himself from the clown, as if in fear that the clown whose very persona had won him his claims to seriousness, was no longer serious enough—or not explicitly serious. . . . In *A King in New York* the schism between comedy and seriousness is not only deepened but takes on another color. Shadhov represents not only Chaplin's politically and socially conscious self but Chaplin himself as King—the King that the Tramp had made him! . . . True, strands of the Tramp-persona are intermittently woven through the King-persona. . . . But the integrated character of the great films is gone, split into a comedy person and the (very literally) self-conscious creator of that comedy.

This schism derives from the schism in film history: the advent of sound. The classy Chaplin, the speechmaking Chaplin, the intellectual parvenu, would have been inconceivable in silent films. He was worried by sound, and he resisted speech in the first two films he made in the sound era, *City Lights* and *Modern Times*—his last two great works. When he succumbed to speech, it took over and hag-rode him; he overcompensated for his earlier resistance. He split his world-worshipped character in two and made the "serious" half a vehicle for talk; but sound also affected the comedy self, usually adversely. The moment here when he is fingerprinted by the Immigration Department at the airport as he talks about his joy at being in free America would have been funnier in dumbshow with subtitles, without the limitations of Chaplin's limited voice and the *fact* of the words. Shadhov recites "To be or not to be" as a party entertainment—misquoting it, incidentally—but it's neither funny nor an effective instance of the classic clown-as-Hamlet idea which Chaplin wants us to admire.

So, under or above all, *A King in New York* shows how the coming of sound was a curse to Chaplin; how its freedoms dissipated his strengths; how his attempts to exploit it intellectually and ideologically played to his weaknesses, not his strengths; how, in short, he was much more grievously hurt by history in art than by history in politics. (pp. 248-49)

Stanley Kauffmann, "'A King in New York'" (originally published in The New Republic, *Vol. 169, No. 24, December 15, 1973), in his* Living Images: Film Comment and Criticism *(copyright © 1971, 1972, 1973, 1974 by Stanley Kauffmann; reprinted by permission of Harper & Row, Publishers, Inc.), Harper, 1975, pp. 246-49.*

COLIN L. WESTERBECK, JR.

At their funniest [*Monsieur Verdoux* (1947), *Limelight* (1952), and *A King in New York* (1957)] hark back to the sort of antics in Charlie's early work. The brightest moment in any of them is a mime recital in *Limelight* at which Charlie's accompanist is Buster Keaton! Yet even in *Limelight* there is a pall hanging over the most comically intended moments. . . .

[At] the mime recital in *Limelight,* we have the uncomfortable feeling Charlie is putting his whole reputation as a laugh-getter on the line. This is the effect of preceding scenes where Calvero plays to an empty house in his nightmare and is hooted off the stage in reality. At the recital it's as if we're being challenged to laugh, and our laughter is therefore nervous. We see Calvero's performance from the viewpoint of the music-hall audience in the film; and like any audience put in that one's position, we laugh out of politeness, half fearing someone will be humiliated if we don't laugh. Implicit on Charlie's part is an attempt to recapture the comedic style of his youth, as if it were an innocence whose loss were now being regretted terribly. . . .

[That] innocence was indeed irretrievably lost by the time of these three late films. What makes them a separate, isolated part of Charlie's career is the fact that they forsake the Tramp character he'd played in every film since his second Mack Sennett comedy. The figure who emerged so late from the Tramp's cocoon is an elegant boulevardier—the deposed monarch in *A King in New York,* the dapper has-been in *Limelight,* the suave and fastidious bluebeard in *Monsieur Verdoux.* In a sense this fellow isn't so different from the Tramp. He's the Tramp dignified by a bit of success, the person the Tramp aspired to be. Or maybe he's the Tramp grown worldly-wise at last, for in the progression of the films up to these last three we can almost see the new man emerging. . . .

The Circus and *City Lights* still exemplify the sort of timeless romantic farce Charlie had been perfecting ever since he outgrew slapstick. But in *Modern Times* and *The Great Dictator* the Tramp is suddenly thrown into the very thick of contemporary history. (p. 463)

Maybe Charlie found it impossible to play the Tramp anymore because he had come to feel that the ways in which the little fellow is society's victim are no longer funny. Though he had never before apologized for his sense of humor, he did say after World War II that he regretted making *The Great Dictator*. After his own persecution here during the fifties, he may well have thought he had become the Tramp—the lonely outcast, shunned and excluded by his own society—a bit too painfully to make jokes about it. . . .

[The] main reason Charlie could no longer play the Tramp has to have been that, even in his own mind, he no longer was the Tramp. The Tramp's is a popular art; and like all popular art, it relies on a lack of self-consciousness in the artist. It is other-directed. It reflects the lives of the millions of people in Charlie's audience who enjoy the Tramp because they can identify with him. But the aging boulevardier in the three late films is a self-reflective figure, even a self-pitying one at times. He is much more like the serious sort of modern artist—the poet or painter—who is unpopular and from whom audiences feel alienated. . . . By the time he made *Monsieur Verdoux, Limelight* and *A King in New York,* Charlie's original genius as a screen comedian had indeed become moribund. (p. 464)

Colin L. Westerbeck, Jr., "The Late Charlie Chaplin," in Commonweal *(copyright © 1974 Commonweal Publishing Co., Inc.; reprinted by permission of Commonweal Publishing Co., Inc.), Vol. XCIX, No. 18, February 8, 1974, pp. 463-64.*

RONALD TUCH

It is possible to propose . . . that [Maya Deren's] *Meshes of the Afternoon* finds its central derivations from a film made by Chaplin in 1916. . . . *1 A.M.*, a momentary departure from Chaplin's preoccupations with the Tramp, contains a wide range of formal characteristics which influence *Meshes,* not only directly but by an indirection through

Dada and surrealism. Dada, the aesthetic movement which generated surrealism, which engendered the comic and irrational strategies of surrealist cinema, is, of course, most intimately affiliated with American comedy, with Sennett and Keaton and Chaplin. The leap from Chaplin's *1 A.M.* to Dada to [Buñuel's] *Un Chien Andalou* to *Meshes of the Afternoon* covers, quite obviously, a whole range of aesthetic variables which constitute the history of film itself, but it is here possible to substantiate formal affinities between two diverse works, possible to determine derivations, by way of a simple inventory of respective designs. Such an inventory, however, does not propose that Deren consciously modeled *Meshes* on *1 A.M.*, but rather, that a certain historical-aesthetic process generated various formal "genes" which can be objectively detected in seemingly unrelated specimens.

1. The titles of both films suggest a specific time of day—a time in which normal activities are suspended and ordinary things suddenly assume an unfamiliar hostile visage. Chaplin, the tuxedoed gentleman, returns home at 1 a.m. drunk and finds that he cannot get into his house because he has lost his key. Once in the house the furniture poses for him a belligerent challenge. He tries, in his drunkeness, to maintain his balance against these imposing forces. . . . (pp. 17-18)

In *Meshes of the Afternoon* we find an elaboration of these conceits. The young girl, near the opening, tries to enter a house but loses her key. It is afternoon and, as in *1 A.M.*, the ordinary suddenly generates confusion. . . .

2. In both films we find the trance state as the central psychological condition which motivates the action. Charlie the drunk is not unlike the young girl disenfranchised from reality—both wander through an "imposing landscape," animated by aggressive objects. . . .

3. Deren's concern with the aesthetic affinities between dance and film has a certain germinal historical basis in Chaplin's work. In Chaplin's choreographed comedy we find an assertive aesthetic proclamation that film form is generated to a large extent by the physical and spatial logic of dance.

4. Both films are essentially solo performances. . . .

5. *1. A.M.* presents no narrative order but is simply an exposition of choreographed incidents between Chaplin and his furniture. It is precisely this spontaneous and illogical transition from one point to another, here and in American early comedies in general, which appealed to the dadaists and which is projected as a more elaborate strategy in surrealism and the American avant-garde films. (p. 18)

Ronald Tuch, "Chaplin and the American Avant Garde," in Film Library Quarterly *(© copyright, Film Library Information Council, 1974), Vol. 7, No. 2, 1974, pp. 17-18.*

ERIC BENTLEY

There are things to find fault with in *Monsieur Verdoux,* but I should say that there is something heartening even in Charlie Chaplin's faults, because they are faults of excess, not of deficiency. If some scenes in *Verdoux* are puzzling, is it not because they might mean several things, not that they might mean nothing? In the revolutionary act of making the screen say something, Chaplin has made it say too much. There is more material in his latest film than he is able to manage—which is to say, more than any living dramatic artist could manage. (p. 161)

Chaplin takes the familiar moral dichotomy between the private life and the public, which in modern life has taken form as the dichotomy between the solid citizen's respectable Christian home and his dirty Machiavellian dealings in business, and he broadens the moral contrasts until they are expressible in terms of his own art, which is, if you like, slapstick. The strong contrast between the kind of treatment the material suggests and the kind of treatment it actually meets with at Chaplin's hands is likely to baffle the solemn modern spectator, whose imagination has been deadened by naturalism. For Chaplin's purposes, however, the broader the contrast, the better. Like the classic comedians, he thrives on the contrast, (pp. 162-63)

Chaplin is broken, but about his boss, the stockholder and speculator, polygamist and murderer, Henri Verdoux. The aspiration after a refined life, after courtesy and elegance, which the clowning always stood for has no longer any spontaneity. The hollow appearance of such an aspiration is brought into being for strictly business reasons by Henri Verdoux. (p. 166)

We watch the comic gags with admiration, but also with horror because their usual meaning has been shockingly inverted. That the clown lays the table for two when he is quite alone is funny, but in *Monsieur Verdoux* we know that he has removed his partner by cold-blooded murder; it makes a difference. At every turn, devices that were quite lighthearted in early Chaplin movies become macabre in *Monsieur Verdoux*. . . .

The general context effects a general inversion of meaning, and in addition Chaplin sometimes inserts particular inversions. The Pursuit of Charlie—an archetypal pattern of movie comedy—is ruthlessly inverted in the night-club scene where Chaplin shows his old skill in leaping first to this side, then to that while his pursuer rushes past. But the gymnastics are little more than futile virtuosity: Verdoux only wants time to say good-by to the Girl. The Pursuit of Charlie cannot take place, because Charlie is not running away. (p. 167)

Pursuit and flight or mock pursuit and mock flight: such cultural commonplaces, such comic turns and gags, are the bricks from which Chaplin constructs his edifice—and it is an edifice, not just a pile of bricks. To change the metaphor: *Monsieur Verdoux* is a network of continuities and cross-references. Some of these are matters of detail (but then every detail in a Chaplin movie is a studied effect). (pp. 167-68)

It is by stage properties—or at any rate by objects in the environment—that continuity is indicated in the two major affairs of Verdoux. In the courtship of Mme Grosnay roses are the leitmotiv. Verdoux is carrying a rose when he first meets Mme Grosnay. He gives her the bunch of roses that we have seen him cut. He courts her exclusively with roses until she capitulates. The leitmotiv in the courtship of Annabella is water. As a sea captain, Verdoux-Bonheur lives by water; Annabella enters upon speculations that, if successful, will make her ruler of the waves—"that's all," as she puts it. Finally Verdoux resolves that Annabella shall die by water. But Annabella has the capitalist virtue of luck, and it is Verdoux who goes overboard.

I am not saying that all the groupings and parallels in *Monsieur Verdoux* are equally successful. Chaplin makes the parallel between Verdoux and the Girl a little too sentimental. She had had a wounded husband. He has a crippled wife. She is up against it; he has been up against it. Both are given a cat to be kind to. The music played for the sparing of the Girl is the music associated with the Verdoux home. And so on.

I am not praising Chaplin for the sheer number of parallels, but for the degree of expressiveness achieved by most of them. To conceive of the parallels was something, no doubt; but it is in the individual "frame," the particular movement, that Chaplin's genius is manifest. (pp. 169-70)

It is simply not true . . . that Chaplin is only an actor. What he does in *Verdoux* in the creation of characters shows an amazing creative talent. With the exception of two roles that are not very well acted—The Girl and the Flower-seller—every role in the film has a significant and well-defined identity, and, moreover, is sharply etched in the classic manner of dramatic characterization. for here at least one can agree with Professor E. E. Stoll: the playwright doesn't have to put together detailed psychological portraits of complete human beings: he has quickly to bring into relief the relevant trait. This is exactly what Chaplin does with a whole gallery of people in *Monsieur Verdoux*. . . . Chaplin understands that comic characters more often exist in pairs than alone. Each of the principal women was obviously chosen to make the most interesting pairing with Verdoux, a kind of contrast that is redoubled by the fact that he is a different man with each wife. Chaplin understands also the specially cinematic way of portraying character. The cinema, need one say, is a visual art, and we find from *Monsieur Verdoux* that Chaplin has something of the talent of a great caricaturist. (pp. 171-72)

As one who writes a good deal about theater, about comedy, I should like to record that, had I never seen Charles Chaplin, I should never have known what the possibilities of comic performance are—what the full realization of comic action is. I am much addicted to playgoing. I have seen Jonson and Molière competently and even expertly performed. But I wonder if the competence and expertness of a hundred different productions taught me more about the way comedy works than the film *Monsieur Verdoux*. I can now imagine what sort of performance a Jonson or Molière play would require before it could fully exist. (p. 172)

Eric Bentley, "'Monsieur Verdoux' and Theater" (originally published in a slightly different form as "'Monsieur Verdoux' As 'Theatre'," in The Kenyon Review, *Vol. 10, Winter, 1948), in his* In Search of Theater *(reprinted by permission of Atheneum Publishers; copyright 1953 by Eric R. Bentley), Atheneum, 1975, pp. 161-73.*

STANLEY KAUFFMANN

[Before *The Gold Rush,* Chaplin] made very few films that took the Tramp out of contemporary city or country life. Tramps are, after all, a by-product of industry, urban or rural. Evidently (we can deduce after the event), Chaplin's unconscious saw at once, in those stereoscopic pictures, the advantages of the novelty of putting the Tramp into a context that, so to speak, had no direct relation to Trampdom, the possibilities for the "epic" that he was seeking. And, presumably, he saw the power in putting the image of the Tramp, whose black moustache is the center of the figure's color gradations, against predominantly white backgrounds. All in all, it was a chance to simultaneously vary and heighten what he had done up to now. (p. 299)

[*The Gold Rush*] is the "epic" that Chaplin was looking for. (p. 300)

[A] title announces "A Lone Prospector," and we see a narrow mountain path on the edge of a steep drop. I always laugh at once, not just because I know Chaplin is coming and the path is dangerous, but because—separated from the opening only by one title—the scenery is so patently phony compared with the reality of the Pass. Thus, early in the film, Chaplin sets a pattern that weaves throughout, the real world posed against the theater of that world, unblinking reality as the ground for a comic abstract of that reality. It's dangerous to mix modes like that, of course, unless you are able, as Chaplin is, to make the return to each mode instantly credible and supportive of the other.

Then in he comes, dancing along with a pack on his back. This first sequence shows the touch that made him great. As he skips and skids along the narrow path, a gigantic bear appears behind him and follows him. A lesser comic would have turned and seen the bear, and possibly would have got a lot of laughs out of panic on the slippery path. But the bear disappears into a cave just before Charlie stops to turn around and see how far he has come. *We* know the danger he has escaped, he doesn't. This is not only funnier, it is also serious: it exemplifies two of the Tramp's most important qualities—innocence and an unwitting faith in the power of that innocence.

Later, when he and Big Jim are trapped and starving in the cabin, the other man, delirious with hunger, imagines that Charlie is a gigantic chicken. . . . The delirium is funny, but Chaplin says he got the idea from the tragic story of the Donner party, the emigrants who were lost in the Nevada mountains in the winter of 1846 and resorted to cannibalism. Grimness as a source of comedy! On this point Chaplin himself said: "In the creation of comedy, it is paradoxical that tragedy stimulates the spirit of ridicule, because ridicule, I suppose, is an attitude of defiance: we must laugh in the face of our helplessness against the forces of nature—or go insane." (pp. 300-01)

All through Chaplin's body of work, hunger is a recurrent subject of comedy. . . . Hunger is an inevitable subject for a Tramp, particularly one whose creator had a childhood in surroundings of wretched poverty. Three times a day, life puts the Tramp at the mercy of "the forces of nature," and three times a day Chaplin has the option of transmuting those forces into laughter so that the Tramp will not "go insane." But there is an extraordinary aspect to this theme in *The Gold Rush.* Usually in Chaplin's films the pinch of hunger comes from a social stringency: no money. Here in the cabin, money is irrelevant. Chaplin takes the theme that has always had a social-political resonance for him, isolates it into the Thing Itself, and makes it funnier than ever.

The harmonics of the picture—light tone against dark, light tone arising *out* of dark and vice versa—is enriched by his first entrance into the dance hall in the boom town. Chaplin, the director, avoids the conventional sequence: showing us the bustling saloon and then showing us the Tramp looking at it—which would mean looking at the camera. He shoots past the Tramp, from behind, to the saloon interior. Charlie is in outline; the brightness is beyond him. He watches from the edge, and we watch from an edge ever farther behind him. Yet because he is seen from slightly below eye level, there is something strong, almost heroic, in the pathos, and, simultaneously, there is something comic in his silhouette. It is the classic, quintessential Chaplin shot. (pp. 301-02)

[The] dream dinner, we should also note, exemplifies another theme that runs through Chaplin's work, the mirror image of the hunger theme discussed earlier. Instead of hunger, we get here the other extreme, the feast, the laden table, which has an effect in Chaplin films like the effect of feasts in Dickens. . . . Plentiful food means not gluttony, but love: an atmosphere of community, conviviality, and affection. One of the most touching moments in *The Kid* is the huge breakfast that the Kid prepares for himself and his "father," the Tramp. In *The Gold Rush* the golden brown turkey is the Tramp's contribution to an atmosphere in which human beings can be human. Chaplin's idea of a low and dehumanized state is not hunger, but the insult to the full table. In *Modern Times,* the Tramp is strapped to an automatic feeding machine, with food enough but without feeling. It debases a daily joy.

I describe one more scene in *The Gold Rush,* although it is hard to limit oneself, as an example of Chaplin's comic invention. When Charlie and Big Jim wake up in the lonely cabin to which they have returned in their search for Jim's lost claim, they don't realize, of course, that during the night the cabin was blown to a new location: the very edge of a cliff. They can't see out the frost-covered windows. As the cabin begins to shift on the precipice, Charlie decides to have a look at the trouble. He opens the back door—and swings out into immense space, hanging onto the doorknob. (If I had to vote for the single funniest sight gag in films, I'd probably choose this moment.) (pp. 303-04)

Like so much in Chaplin's films, and in farce generally, this cabin sequence is built on danger, scary but seen from safety. It is the quantum of the banana peel greatly multiplied: we know what it would feel like if it were happening to us, but we also know that it isn't. Comedy, of all kinds, depends on perception and superiority. In high comedy, which usually deals with social criticism, we can recognize the hypocrisy or vanity or whatever it may be, acknowledge secretly that we share it, and laugh with relief that it is being pilloried in someone else. In farce, the materials are often physical, often the dangers of daily life that surround us all the time, even when crossing the street. The *farceur* makes injury and possible death simultaneously real and unreal. We know that the Tramp and Big Jim will not be killed in the cabin—it simply could not happen in this kind of picture; yet we feel the danger in our viscera. We are frightened at the same time that we enjoy the skill of the artists who have nullified death. Farce characters—important ones—never get killed. They contrive for us a superiority over mortality, even as they make us laugh at their struggles to escape it.

To this comic heritage of danger combined with subconscious assurance of safety, Chaplin adds a unique touch: grace. All through his career, it is manifest: as in the dangerous skating sequences of *The Rink* and *Modern times.* (pp. 304-05)

[The ending of *The Gold Rush* differs from some of Chaplin's other films] only in that we *see* Charlie rich. Essential though the wealth is thematically, this was not the image that Chaplin wanted to leave before our eyes, so he devised a way for the rich Charlie to put on his Tramp clothes once again. This persona, resumed, gives Georgia, the prostitute, a chance to prove the genuineness of her feelings, and it gives Chaplin a chance to score a last point. The Tramp had to be dragged away from Georgia by Big Jim, had to be dragged to wealth; now the wealth brings the lovers together again on the ship. Money and happiness, Chaplin seems to say, are at the whim of two powers: Fate and authors.

But an even subtler complexity runs through the film, through most of his major films. The element that persists, through the comedy and through the pathos that makes the comedy beloved, is a sense of mystery. Who *is* the Tramp? What is the secret of his unique effect on us? (p. 305)

I propose no supernatural answer, that he is a divine messenger in ragged clothes, a fool of God. I do suggest that part of the genius of Chaplin, part of his superiority to all other film comics except Buster Keaton, is his ability to make us believe in a comic character whose standards are better than our own, just as his body in motion is more beautiful than our bodies. I suggest that one of the reasons we have loved him all these decades—and young people seem to feel that *they* have loved him for decades, too—is that he has not concentrated on merely making us laugh, he has shown us the funniness in a hero-clown, an unsententious agent of exemplary values. He is not dully angelic; he sometimes pulls off con games, though usually to a good end or to flout oppressive authority. But in the main he compensates for the shortcomings, social and physical, of our lives and beings. In his magical movement and in his code, even in his cunning, he is what we feel we ought to be. (p. 306)

***Stanley Kauffmann,* " 'The Gold Rush' "** *(originally published in a different form as "Landmarks of Film History: Chaplin's 'The Gold Rush'," in* Horizon, *Vol. XV, No. 3, Summer, 1973), in his* Living Images: Film Comment and Criticism *(copyright © 1971, 1972, 1973, 1974 by Stanley Kauffmann; reprinted by permission of Harper & Row, Publishers, Inc.), Harper, 1975, pp. 298-306.*

Michael Cimino

1943?-

American director and screenwriter.

Cimino is best known for *The Deer Hunter,* his analysis of the Vietnam War and its effects on the men who fought in it. This film is more a character study than an action war film, with many of the scenes taking place as either a prelude or an aftermath to war.

Cimino received a Master of Fine Arts degree from Yale University in 1963. He directed documentaries and television commercials in New York following graduation, moving to Hollywood in 1971. His first film credit, as cowriter of *Silent Running,* was followed by an assignment rewriting the screenplay for *Magnum Force.* In 1974 he wrote and directed *Thunderbolt and Lightfoot.*

The actual facts of Cimino's background are cloudy. In an interview with Leticia Kent for *The New York Times,* Cimino claimed he was thirty-five years old and that he had been assigned to a Special Forces Medical Unit in Texas. After his Army discharge, Cimino stated he learned moviemaking with a documentary filmmaker. However, Tom Buckley of *Harper's Magazine,* upon researching Cimino's background, found several discrepancies. He is closer to forty years old than to thirty-five and did not, according to sources Buckley found, spend two years in the armed forces. Nor was he ever, as he claimed, a Green Beret. These differences in allegation would appear irrelevant were it not for the fact that they are closely mirrored in *The Deer Hunter.*

While the artistic merit of *The Deer Hunter* is generally recognized, many critics have condemned its view of Vietnam, finding it manipulative and accusing it of portraying an adolescent perception of the war. Others, however, applaud its celebration of the "new patriotism" and its view of Vietnam as a historical tragedy rather than a political event. *The Deer Hunter* has received as much publicity for its controversial topic as for its aesthetic worth, and most objections about the film stem from ideological conflict rather than a negative assessment of cinematic skill.

If it is true that the sinner has a desire to be caught and punished, [*Thunderbolt and Lightfoot*] suggests that Hollywood is unable to handle its new-found freedom and is determined to sin so grossly that even its best friends will deliver the industry over to the ire of censors. . . . [This] sex-saturated film . . . degrades everyone and everything it touches, including the genre of the caper film, which serves as the vehicle for this voyeuristic appeal to youthful preoccupation with sex, cars and violence. This is not hard-core sex . . . or serious sex. . . , but adolescent sex that touches, smirks and runs. (pp. 570-71)

"Current Cinema: 'Thunderbolt and Lightfoot'," in The Christian Century *(copyright 1974 Christian Century Foundation; reprinted by permission from the May 22, 1974 issue of* The Christian Century*), Vol. XCI, No. 20, May 22, 1974, pp. 570-71.*

JAY COCKS

The best thing . . . about *Thunderbolt and Lightfoot* is its quality of going over familiar territory and coming up with things never quite expected. This is Director-Writer Michael Cimino's first film, and he demonstrates a scrupulously controlled style that lends sinew even to such usually dreary scenes as the preparations for the robbery and strategies of escape.

In his feeling for the almost reflexive defenses of masculine camaraderie and for its excesses, with his eye and grudging affection for Western lowlife, Cimino has an obvious affinity for the work of Sam Peckinpah. What really animates *Thunderbolt and Lightfoot,* though, and makes it distinctive is its shellbursts of lunatic comedy. . . . This movie adeptly creates the sort of antic cartoon world where crooks case the getaway route in ice cream carts, disarm a security guard by dressing in drag, and break into a bank vault by the simple expedient of blasting it with an enormous anti-tank gun.

The movie is shaky when the friendship between Thunderbolt and Lightfoot is sentimentalized, and at the end, when invention gives in to a mawkish resolution. . . . Cimino himself renders most of the movie with enough cunning to make it one of the most ebullient and eccentric diversions around.

Jay Cocks, "Ebullient Heist," in Time *(reprinted by permission from* Time, The Weekly Newsmagazine; *copyright Time Inc. 1974), Vol. 103, No. 23, June 10, 1974, p. 83.*

PETER CARGIN

[In *Thunderbolt and Lightfoot,* we] are treated to the usual fascist touches which first emerged in *Dirty Harry,* with nearly everyone being degraded for cheap laughs, women are really very simple objects to be endured and nearly everything made as nasty as possible.

The second part of the film turns to the staging of a similar robbery to that carried out a few years earlier by the same team. The preparations for the robbery are rather casually depicted and the robbery of the money from an armoured bank vault seems almost too good to be true, a couple of people tied up and the safe blasted open with small artillery. . . . Of course, it is not so much how they carry out the robbery that is of interest to the spectator but how they don't eventually get away with it.

Peter Cargin, "Film Reviews: 'Thunderbolt and Lightfoot'," in Film *(reprinted by permission of British Federation of Film Societies), n.s. No. 17, August, 1974, p. 20.*

ANDREW SARRIS

[*The Deer Hunter,* a] three-hour saga of three Russian-American Pennsylvania steelworkers in and out of Vietnam, turns out to be massively vague, tediously elliptical, and mysteriously hysterical. The script . . . does not contain a single witty, sharp, or revelatory line of dialogue. As if to compensate for this verbal aridity, the players are encouraged to indulge in interminable wet-eyed sensitivity sessions. . . . *The Deer Hunter* thus reflects in its operatic inarticulateness certain tendencies in the supposedly ambitious American films of the past decade, while at the same time it slips in a disturbing subtext for which Cimino alone must held accountable.

Frankly, I suspect that this film has less to do with Vietnam or even male bonding than it has to do with a particularly devious expression of homosexual panic. . . . In a sense, *The Deer Hunter* has thrust the subject upon me by failing to be convincing on the psychological, sociological, or historical surfaces of its narrative. All that is left is Cimino's personal mythology, and therefore a description of *The Deer Hunter* is in order before we commence with the diagnosis. . . .

There is no feeling of an oppressed proletariat in Cimino's vision of industrial labor. At most there is an intimation of boredom, from which male camaraderie after working hours functions as a boisterous release. Michael and Nick and Steven and Stan and a few other of their buddies surge into a barroom where the Steelers-Eagles games is playing on TV, and there is some palaver about betting on the points. But there is no knowingness or conviction in the way the scene is handled. No one really seems to care whether the Steelers win or lose. The banter is all too self-consciously fleeting and perfunctory, and the atmosphere is already too hot-house actorish for cold beer.

The film spends a whole hour at the Russian Orthodox wedding of Steven and Angela without telling us anything interesting about either the characters or the community. . . .

Because the viewer's mind may start idling during this first hour, the fact that only three young men, all apparently volunteers, are leaving for Vietnam and that one has just been married may seem statistically improbable. But despite all the American flags in view, the spectacle is never condescending or contemptuous. To his credit, Cimino never looks down on his characters or their milieu. The problem is that much of his material emerges as shapeless and undeveloped and, hence, boring.

When Michael and his merry ethnics set off for a deer hunt, the scene seems to be set at last for some sort of classy metaphor for machismo. At the very least one would hope for some inventive interplay among the hitherto opaque characters. All that is provided, however, is a desultory disagreement between Michael and Stan over the borrowing of boots, and a prolonged solo pose by De Niro [who plays Michael] as the Noble Hunter in a setting so idiotically idyllic that one would not be surprised to see Bambi bounding out of the brush. De Niro dispatches his deer in a solitude of such splendor that it would seem the other members of the hunt are just along for the ride. There is some mystical mumbo-jumbo about De Niro's needing only one bullet for the kill. Cimino's tone here is that of a humorless animated cartoon rather than of a nuanced novel.

Vietnam engulfs the screen in the first of Cimino's jolting ellipses, but it is not the Vietnam of American self-flagellation that we have come to know from previous movies in the cycle. Cimino actually shows the VC committing atrocities against both Vietnamese civilians and American prisoners of war. (p. 67)

For Cimino, the VC are brutal simply because war is brutal, and because life itself is brutal. The ideological issues seem to count for little in what explodes on the screen as the ultimate test of one's courage and manhood. . . .

If the Russian roulette episodes are found metaphors they satisfy the irreducibly realistic requirements of the cinema, but if they are merely fictional metaphors they degenerate into immoral and irresponsible fantasies of the artist. . . .

[The] fact that Michael's last name is Vronsky may mean that he is graced or afflicted with a Tolstoyan largeness of spirit. He thinks nothing of intervening boldly in other people's lives. After he discovers that Steven has lost both legs he blithely drags the resisting paraplegic home to his traumatized wife and child. At times Michael so reeks of disinterested do-goodness that he makes the Jon Voight character in *Coming Home* look like a used-car salesman. And he becomes almost completely magical when he strolls casually through Saigon in civilian clothes in search of his self-destructive buddy on the very night the city is falling.

Far from achieving Tolstoyan heights, however, Cimino fails even to attain a Scorsesian or Coppolian level. The structure of the film is so rickety, and the details so incongruous, that whatever feelings were intended finally peter out in a half-hearted chorus of "God Bless America," again, mercifully free of derision or condescension but hardly transfigured into national poetry. (p. 68)

Andrew Sarris, "Is the Metaphor the Message?" in The Village Voice *(reprinted by permission of* The Village Voice; *copyright © The Village Voice, Inc., 1978), Vol. XXIII, No. 51, December 18, 1978, pp. 67-8.*

ARTHUR SCHLESINGER, JR.

The Deer Hunter is a self-appointed American epic. Its scale is large, its ambition vast. It seeks to invest a sweep of American experience with mythic significance. It is designed to overwhelm.

Its subject is the Vietnam War. Consciously or not, it approaches Vietnam in terms of ancient American themes. The very title recalls *The Deerslayer* of Cooper, and *Deerslayer* recalls D. H. Lawrence's famous comment: "You have there the myth of the essential white America. All the other stuff, the love, the democracy, the floundering into lust, is a sort of byplay. The essential American soul is hard, isolate, stoic, and a killer. It has never yet melted."

Deerslayer embodied the hunter myth that the white man's encounter with the wilderness had given peculiar force in America. This myth reached its literary culmination in the greatest hunt of all, in *Moby Dick,* and it has been utilized by Faulkner, Hemingway, and Mailer in our own time. Lawrence's account of the American as hunter is perhaps incomplete. For the American soul, at least in the national mythology, does melt. . . .

The seeds of many American tragedies, [as Richard Slotkin concludes in *Regeneration Through Violence: The Mythology of the American Frontier, 1600-1860*], "are planted in the captive-and-hunter myth, the myth of regeneration through violence." (p. 50)

[A] new captivity, a new hunt, and a new ceremony of exorcism repeat the myth scenario. Michael Cimino, the director and co-author of the story on which the screenplay was based, has, deliberately or inadvertently, adopted salient elements of the old mythology. I cannot say, however, that he has successfully fused them into an organic whole. There is too much confused symbolism—not only the hunter and captivity myths, but Russian roulette and the blast furnaces—and too little integration and characterization.

The pervading defect is in the writing. It is not enough to say that Pennsylvania steelworkers cannot be expected to talk like characters out of a novel by Henry James. . . .

The language in *The Deer Hunter* is boring and banal. . . . [The] characters are badly undernourished. . . . Cimino's deer hunter remains unrevealed to the end. . . .

Where Cimino succeeds brilliantly is in his panorama of war—refugees along the jungle road, *Walpurgisnacht* on the Saigon strip, panic and hysteria in the last days of Saigon. These scenes fulfill the film's epic pretensions. But in the end an epic should leave a sense of purpose, not of confusion. . . . *The Deer Hunter,* for all its merits, substitutes portentousness (the choral singing behind the deer hunt) for pattern, noise for observation, obscurantism for dramatic coherence. A failure, yet an exciting failure. (p. 51)

Arthur Schlesinger, Jr., "Deer Hunter, Man Slayer," in Saturday Review *(copyright © 1979 by* Saturday Review; *all rights reserved; reprinted by permission), Vol. VI, No. 4, February 17, 1979, pp. 50-1.*

TED WHITEHEAD

Here we go on another trip around those old American obsessions—the primacy of courage, the worship of nature, the inflation of male friendship into a love surpassing the love of women. Writers as varied as Mark Twain and Fenimore Cooper, Walt Whitman and Jack London, have contributed to the development of this cowboy ethic, which finds its clearest expression in Hemingway. . . . The disappointing thing about *The Deer Hunter* is that it starts as if it's going to be a critique of [the cowboy loner ethic popularized by Hemingway] and then proceeds in wild confusion both to glorify and dilute it. . . .

The three buddies are bound for Vietnam but before leaving they join some companions for a final hunting trip in the mountains. By now Mike is taking shape as the stereotype Hemingway Hero: he's revered by the others (whom he refers to as 'assholes') but has only one really intimate friend, Nick. He's not much good with women, and in fact is loyally repressing his love for Nick's woman. . . .

[The] merits of the film are apolitical: the joyous recreation of a homogeneous community (no blacks in view), the animistic vision of valley and mountain, the alternation of Nietzschean rhapsody and Slav gloom, and the intensity of the roulette confrontations. The style swings constantly from German Expressionism to Russian Epic, reminding us that the Americans have almost nothing in common with the English. . . .

To this English eye the film is a naive romantic fantasy of male self-sufficiency, compromised by the attempt to hitch this to the communal good. At his best the Hemingway hero had no interest in family or society, which is why he is so popular in the suburbs now. What we get here is Hemingway plus vodka and patriotism.

Ted Whitehead, "Loners," in The Spectator *(© 1979 by* The Spectator; *reprinted by permission of* The Spectator), *Vol. 242, No. 7860, March 3, 1979, p. 26.*

GAVIN MILLAR

The Deer Hunter is not run of the mill. It is made with great seriousness and dedication. . . . So much about *The Deer Hunter* is impressive: it is said that strong men are carried, nightly, weeping from the cinema, to say nothing (I suppose) of weak women.

I can see how people are invited to be moved, but without diminishing my admiration for the film's skills . . . or making itself dislikeable, the film failed to move me. There is something about it—a solemnity, a lack of humour, a lack of warmth, a deviousness even, or, more fairly, a lack of self-awareness—that seems to result in not telling us as much of the truth about human beings as it purports to.

What it is pretending to tell us is that a code of values exists, embracing courage, resourcefulness, strength, ruthlessness even, in the interests of survival, and that this code is principally exemplified by brotherhood. But what it effectively asserts is that there is a bond, deep and strong and true, between men that, beyond other loyalties—to religion, country, family, honesty even—binds them together and is a paramount code of values in itself.

This is a less interesting message partly because it is disguised or unacknowledged, and partly because it is more questionable, and therefore, less can develop from it. In a word, it is built on some kind of self-deceit. If people are moved by the film, it may be that they are moved less by the revelation of human inadequacy and bewildered strength than by the simple, battering terror of the awful events, with which it is always possible, but rarely therapeutic, to move ourselves.

When Michael goes to rescue Nick from the fleshpots and charnel-houses of Saigon, we are invited to care less about the fact that a country—two or three countries—have been torn to shreds than that the knight is not going to be able to rescue the damsel-in-distress. It scarcely matters that the damsel is a man: the buddy-buddy genre is well-established and needs no apology. What matters is that it is here appropriated to serve a thesis of truly national, in other words, historical and philosophical and social, scope; and worse, that it is felt to be adequate on its own to that task. There is something more dissatisfying beyond that: that *The Deer Hunter* proposes a terrible lesson about war which should, we feel, distil a mood of sober humility; whereas the exultant, hysterical drive in the blood of the film is towards an overwhelming mystique of brotherhood that is not merely chauvinistic (which wouldn't matter so much), but, in the long run, self-congratulatory. (p. 356)

Gavin Millar, "War and Peace" (© Gavin Millar, 1979; reprinted by permission of the author and his agents, Judy Daish Associates, Ltd.), in The Listener, *Vol. 101, No. 2601, March 8, 1979, pp. 355-56.*

JOHN PILGER

The Deer Hunter is technically slick, and perhaps its documentary and *verité* effects are even brilliant; *something* must have prompted usually discriminating critics to opt for unction and naïvete.

And, I suppose, for those who have forgotten what Vietnam was really about, or would wish to forget, or are too young to remember, or are truly naive, the slickness is persuasive; the wedding guests, the blood gushes, the bullets thud and the rotors of helicopters make the sound that is forever embedded in my brain, from years of attending the reality. Otherwise, the symbolism is leaden (one shot for the proud stag etc.), the *schmaltz* elongated and the sadism utterly gratuitious: the kind of sadism that packs 'em in.

There are times when, even by the film's own standards, the slick runs precariously thin. . . .

The Deer Hunter is harmless enough unless you happen to be a gook, Commie or otherwise, or of a generation too young to remember genocidal 'free fire zones' and towns and villages that 'had to be destroyed to save them'.

That the same cynical mythmaking is now being applied to Vietnam (there'll be *Deer Hunter 2,* I bet) induces more melancholy than anger in those like myself, who saw whole Vietnamese communities used as guinea pigs for the testing of a range of 'anti-personnel' military technology, and who saw demoralised, brutalised, often mutinous and doped American teenagers lying in their own blood and shit, for the purposes of some pointless, sacrificial siege staged in the cause of nothing, except the gratification of inept brass in their air-conditioned bubbles.

There is not a passing hint in *The Deer Hunter* that Vietnam was, above all, a war of rampant technology against human beings. There are, however, heavenly violins. . . .

Michael Cimino is being hailed in America as the champion of the 'new patriotism'. . . .

Cimino is an expert salesman. He sold *The Deer Hunter* without a script. Originally, it was to be the recollections of a group of former GIs, but what helped to convince the major backers that they were on to a winner were the orgiastic Russian roulette scenes that recur throughout the film and leave an audience with the impression that the Vietnamese gamble on human life as casually as the British gamble on the pools. . . .

[Much] of Cimino's picture is given over to this 'meaningful horror', which he insists happened and which is meant to be somehow redemptive. (p. 352)

The timing of *The Deer Hunter* is perfect. The 'new patriotism' and the mood of the national redemption decree that it is time the American conscience was salved and the Vietnamese 'punished' for defeating and humiliating the greatest power on earth. . . .

[A song sung by American-fathered children in a Saigon orphanage runs:] 'The war is gone . . . planes come no more . . . do not weep for those just born . . . the human being is evergreen'. If you see *The Deer Hunter,* you may like to remember these words. (p. 353)

John Pilger, "Why 'The Deer Hunter' Is a Lie," in New Statesman *(© 1979 The Statesman & Nation Publishing Co. Ltd.), Vol. 97, No. 2504, March 16, 1979, pp. 352-53.*

RICHARD WEST

It might be said . . . that Michael Cimino, who wrote and directed *The Deer Hunter,* had chosen an off-beat locale for the part of his film set in America. But what of his treatment of Vietnam? Naturally it can and has been argued that *The Deer Hunter* is not a film *about* Vietnam, and that those parts portraying the war (less than a third of the three-hour total) were introduced only to show how this experience marked three young Americans. After all, to invent a grand comparison, the battle scenes in *War and Peace* are of interest not in themselves but in the way they affect Prince André and Pierre.

But the Vietnam war was much more than just a series of battles. . . . Vietnam, both during and after the war, has been too unpleasant for most Americans to contemplate, which is why it has so far failed to produce any great work of imagination, whether novel, poem, painting or film. (p. 10)

[A plot] summary should convey the excitement and shock of *The Deer Hunter.* But is it true of the Vietnam war, either historically or poetically? It is true that the American forces frequently bombed and burned out villages where they suspected that the enemy were taking shelter. But why should the Vietcong then murder the very peasants who might be presumed to be on their side? . . .

Michael Cimino may say Russian roulette has only symbolic significance—though for the life of me I cannot see what this is. No symbolism, however, can justify the representation of all the Vietnamese in this film (and also the one Frenchman) as fiendish torturers and killers. This perpetuates and even exaggerates the worst propaganda produced while the war was still on. . . . [*The Deer Hunter*] is a travesty of the war and an insult to those who fought in it. (p. 11)

Richard West, "Vietnam and 'The Deer Hunter'," in The Spectator *(© 1979 by* The Spectator; *reprinted by permission of* The Spectator), *Vol. 242, No. 7962, March 17, 1979, pp. 10-11.*

ARTHUR LUBOW

The Deer Hunter is the first postwar Vietnam epic, a film that tries to say it all. . . . Into three hours of well-written, artfully edited, superlatively acted color film, director Michael Cimino has packed an extraordinary emotional wallop, making *The Deer Hunter* the most memorable American saga since Coppola's *Godfather II.* Like Coppola, who chose the Mafia as a microcosm of America, Cimino uses Vietnam to try to explain far more that one particular war. The white-faced, silent audiences leaving the theater tremble from a sense of knowledge they think that they understand not just Vietnam but some larger truths about America.

Like most great war stories, *The Deer Hunter* is a Bildungsroman tracking the passage of young men to maturity. Cimino's ambition is impressive. (pp. 95-6)

The movie is structured as a symphonic song cycle. From a number-one single it moves to a Slavic dance at the wedding, a requiem at the hunt, a Chopin Prelude at a bar; and then, in an abrupt, brilliant cut to the rice paddies of Vietnam, the only music is artillery blasts and duets for AK-47s and M-16s. The songs resume in the Saigon bars. . . . The film's coda is a moving, ambiguous rendition of "God Bless America," sung by Nick's friends in the bar after the funeral.

Music belongs in a Vietnam movie. For soldiers, pop music was a common cultural reference, and the radio was a link to "the World"—GI slang for America. . . . Propped up against the events recounted in *The Deer Hunter,* pop songs acquire the poignancy of old photographs. They are historical relics, cultural artifacts that have survived intact. Although not intrinsically connected to the war, they have soaked up its blood, sweat, and tears, and swelled with meaning, simply by being there.

The innovative pop music of the sixties grew out of the drug-conscious, pacifist, anti-establishment counterculture. And yet, curiously, no such songs are sung in *The Deer Hunter:* no Beatles, Stones, Bob Dylan, Joni Mitchell, Neil Young. . . . In a three-hour 1979 movie that hopes to record what the Vietnam War did to America, this omission is puzzling. There are other oversights: we notice that while blacks constituted nearly a third of U.S. combat troops at the start of the war, all the Americans in *The Deer Hunter* are white. Take another look, and we see that although heroin is an important element in the film's scrutiny of the seamy side of Saigon, Cimino takes no notice of dope-smoking among American GIs, or among Americans at home. He never acknowledges that this was the first American army that fought a war stoned, the first college generation that matriculated high. Subtract antiwar sentiment, black self-assertion, and marijuana from a film about the impact of Vietnam, and what remains?

The traditional war story. *The Deer Hunter,* like most of the new wave of Vietnam culture, focuses on the camaraderie among soldiers and the intensity of life under fire. When each moment could be your last, each moment takes on a new power. (p. 96)

In *The Deer Hunter,* the Vietcong are sadistic killers and the Americans heroic saviors. Like any big lie, this is such a fantastic distortion that, when presented with assurance, it appears plausible. It isn't even *presented* in *The Deer Hunter;* it is assumed. . . .

[The] legacy of bitterness, among those who fought the war and those who fought against it, is the central issue for anyone who hopes to depict how the Vietnam War affected Americans. . . . It can be addressed in many ways, but it must be addressed. Cimino ducks it.

No one in *The Deer Hunter* is demoralized by the traitorous home front. No one is disillusioned by the strange logic of a war in which a country is destroyed in order to save it from its own inhabitants. For Cimino, the Vietnam War is horrible in the way all war is horrible. That vision leads him to choose the movie's terrifying metaphor, the image he uses to convey the hideousness of Vietnam—Russian roulette. . . .

There is something unsettling about Cimino's image. Every other postwar movie about Vietnam has employed a central moral metaphor. . . . The metaphor in *The Deer Hunter* is amoral; it is also by far the most shocking.

Russian roulette. It embodies the random, senseless violence of war. We can feel much more of war's impact in a gun barrel against the skull than we can in the countless color photos that we have deadened ourselves against. As an emotional metaphor, Russian roulette works. It's beside the point that these casinos did not exist, and that Vietcong soldiers did not use that form of torture. Or is it? It's beside the point, yes; but it's not far from it. The use of a metaphor that seems to be descriptive of Vietnam but is not is symptomatic of a movie that appears to be about Vietnam but is not. By shooting a film not about a particular war but about War—seeking to capture not the meaning of America's involvement in Vietnam but rather the grander truths of friendship, strength of will, and the American character—Cimino becomes trapped by the mythical web he spins. If at this point, after the loss of our men, our money, and our pride, all we have learned is that war is hell, we have salvaged pitifully little from the wreckage. (p. 97)

Arthur Lubow, "Natty Bumppo Goes to War," in The Atlantic Monthly *(copyright © 1979, by The Atlantic Monthly Company, Boston, Mass.; reprinted with permission), Vol. 243, No. 4, April, 1979, pp. 95-8.*

TOM BUCKLEY

There is no story [in *The Deer Hunter*], only a succession of unconnected episodes strung together for what seems like an interminable three hours and four minutes. Cimino has refused to be trammeled by dramatic convention. Problems of motivation, plausibility, relationship, even chronology, are ignored. There is no development or illumination of character. Instead of dialogue there are grunts and obscenities.

Cimino has said he was not, after all, *trying* to make a realistic film. The implication is that he could do so if he wanted to, but that would be like setting Picasso to painting a barn. *The Deer Hunter,* he has said, is surrealistic, a dreamscape. He is wrong. His characters, their milieu, his version of the Vietnam war, all suffer from the same defect. They are neither real nor surreal—merely pretentious and false.

[*The Deer Hunter*] doesn't hold the mirror up to nature. It holds it up to Cimino. (p. 85)

[The early scenes in the bar, at the wedding, and of the hunt] run for more than an hour and they provide little more than negative inferences. The dominant impressions one gets are that Mike, Nick, Steve, and the three others who make up their circle prefer the company of one another to that of women, and that they are the only six men in the United States who have never talked about the Vietnam war. (pp. 85-6)

In fact, as presented by Cimino, these relatively prosperous, strongly unionized steelworkers of western Pennsylvania are revenants of the 1930s. Their houses are little better than shacks, enveloped in the acrid smoke of the mill. They don't read the papers or look at television except for sports events, they haven't traveled and are without curiosity about the land beyond the Alleghenies. . . .

[One scene] reveals Cimino's undeniable accomplishment in *The Deer Hunter.* In a medium that has been soaked in depictions of cruelty and violent death since its earliest days, he has hit upon a novel and, it must be said, particularly repulsive method of presenting torture and murder. One by one the prisoners are pulled up into the hut by a grinning giant. While their implacably cruel captors, most of whom are played by Thais, perhaps on the theory that all Orientals look alike, giggle and bet heavily on the outcome, they are forced to play Russian roulette with the survivor of the previous coup. Those who refuse are beaten and confined in a cage submerged in the river, there to be nibbled by rats and eventually to drown. On the other hand, there doesn't seem to be any reward for playing and winning—that is, pulling the trigger on an empty chamber. You apparently continue against other opponents until you lose. . . .

It is a brilliant scene, acted with ferocious intensity, directed and edited in staccato flashes, and all the more exciting because it comes after so much tedium. But the effects that Cimino learned in the [Clint] Eastwood school of violence must be pushed to the limit because they occur in a dramatic vacuum. (p. 86)

[The final scene would be] a remarkable conclusion if there were ironic intent, but there isn't. The political and moral issues of the Vietnam war, for ten years and more this country's overriding concern, are entirely ignored. By implication, at any rate, the truth is turned inside out. The North Vietnamese and the Vietcong become the murderers and torturers and the Americans their gallant victims.

Cimino's ignorance of what the war was about, symbolically and actually, as reflected in *The Deer Hunter,* is incomplete and perverse to the point of being megalomaniacal. He had no technical adviser and no one who even served in Vietnam on his production staff. It is as though he believed that the power of his genius could radically alter the outlines of a real event in which millions of Americans took part and that is still fresh in the memory of the nation.

The Deer Hunter is a version of comradeship in the factory and the battlefield as it might have been rendered by Luchino Visconti, the late filmmaker, or Helmut Newton, the fashion photographer, both of them experts in the lush presentation of perversity.

Intense male friendships have always existed in wartime, of course, but for several reasons the Spartan virtues seemed rare in Vietnam. . . .

The Deer Hunter does not examine cruelty, it exploits it. Cimino, in a small way, seems to be as insulated from reality as the Marquis de Sade in his cell. To invent forms of cruelty—the Russian roulette game—where so much suffering actually occurred seems doubly perverse. (p. 88)

Tom Buckley, "Hollywood's War," in Harper's *(copyright © 1979 by Tom Buckley; reprinted by permission of International Creative Management), Vol. 258, No. 1547, April, 1979, pp. 84-6, 88.*

GLORIA EMERSON

[*The Deer Hunter* is] a sick and manipulative film—remarkable only for its adolescent perceptions and wild self-indulgence—that is impressing many people as the truth, the real version of what the war was like in Vietnam. Cimino has done what no one else has succeeded in doing: he has rejected the immense suffering of the Vietnamese in the South, of the Vietnamese in the North, of the Americans who fought there, in favor of a story that suits his own longings and his own fantasies about men. Do not enrich him further by going to see *The Deer Hunter.*

In our desperation to explain our defeat in Vietnam, and to be comfortable with it, many people need a film like *The Deer Hunter* which shows the Americans in Vietnam as gallant, good, noble fellows pitted against the despicable, giggling and inhuman Asian monsters who do not, of course, value human life. It is the most racist film I have ever seen. The story of three friends, steelworkers from a small town in Pennsylvania, who are captured and forced to play Russian roulette by the Viet Cong, and who are each destroyed by the war, *The Deer Hunter* makes a mockery of the real pain, the real losses and the real nightmares of the survivors in all the armies. The film is the creation of a shrewd monster, a man of tremendous energy, ambition and staggering ignorance.

Using Russian roulette as his metaphor, Cimino is not bothered by the fact that this odious form of enforced suicide was not practiced by the Vietnamese and the Chinese who gambled, yes, but with cards or by playing mah-jongg. It is a stupid and offensive metaphor in terms of the American infantrymen in Vietnam who did not casually risk their lives.

The Deer Hunter sells us a version of the war, of American goodness, that we can comfortably swallow between our sobs. In the darkness of the movie houses, no one need feel guilty or ashamed of that long, long war. The hero, as played by Robert De Niro, is a strange man, almost a cartoon of a Hemingway figure, and his first name is Michael. It is Cimino's name and *The Deer Hunter* is his fantasy. (p. 540)

[If] only one sentence could be used as an indictment of Cimino's film—in which we see so much blood spurting across the screen during Russian roulette games—it is [Tom] Buckley [see excerpt above] who provides it. "*The Deer Hunter* does not examine cruelty, it exploits it," he said. And it is this which makes it an unforgivable film. (p. 541)

Gloria Emerson, "Oscars for Our Sins," in The Nation *(copyright 1979 The Nation Associates, Inc.), Vol. 228, No. 18, May 12, 1979, pp. 540-41.*

STANLEY KAUFFMANN

Early in the 1960s I joined the protests against US involvement in Vietnam, kept protesting as that involvement grew, and kept on after the withdrawal of US troops while money and supplies continued to flow to Vietnam. I mention my actions, which were no more than what thousands of others did, only to "place" myself on the subject. And to me, the torture sequence in *The Deer Hunter*—the Viet Cong forcing their US prisoners to play Russian roulette—did not seem intrinsically incredible: because neither I nor anyone I knew objected to the Vietnam War on the ground that the

North was angelic. We knew fairly early of the tortures and murders done by South Vietnamese and US forces, but we also knew of tortures and murders done by the North Vietnamese. The issue for us was US intervention—its effects there and at home—not the moral superiority of North over South Vietnam. Thus when I saw this 15-to-20 minute torture sequence in the middle of this three-hour film, I took it as given. I had no knowledge as to whether the Russian-roulette routine had ever actually been practiced (and much has since been made by ex-correspondents of the fact that they never heard of it there), but I accepted it as symbolic, for two reasons.

First, the Viet Cong were quite capable of barbarism and the killing of prisoners. Does anyone doubt that? Second, the sequence fits the film, thematically and metaphorically. *The Deer Hunter* is *not* about Vietnam: it's about three steelworkers, bonded in maleness, who work and drink and hunt together, who enlist together as paratroopers, who are captured and tortured together, who escape together, and who then—which is usually omitted in comment—move on to the longest part of their story, the differing resolutions of that experience with their futures. They do not see the war as other, embittered, horrified or numbed soldiers saw it, or as I saw it, or for that matter, as Jane Fonda saw it: they see *their* war. The Russian roulette was the obvious extension of the "one shot" credo by which these former hunters had lived; enlistment in war and survival of torture were the testings *in extremis* of their maleness. I was so convinced of this—and still am, after seeing the film again—that I suggested the alternative ironic title Games People Play.

So I was surprised that some intelligent people—I disregard the loudmouthed opportunists—have seen the film otherwise. The Vietnam experience, in all its ramifications, was a wound from which this country may never recover, worse in some ways than either of the World Wars; perceptive people are understandably sensitive about it. Still their reaction here seems odd: the objection seems to be not so much that the VC are shown as vicious, but that the ARVN and US forces are not *also* shown as vicious, maybe more so. This seems to me an inhibiting, almost juvenile critical equation: if we show bad actions by people with whom we sympathize, we must at least balance them with bad actions by people with whom we don't sympathize. Did these critics also object to *Slaughterhouse-Five,* novel and film, because it showed the Allied fire-bombing of Dresden but did not show the German bombing of Coventry? (p. 22)

I submit that, if we are going to be moved to thought and action by *The Deer Hunter,* it ought to be by the implications of its true subject: the limitations for our society of the traditions of male mystique, the hobbling by sentimentality of a community that, after all the horror, still wants the beeriness of "God Bless America" instead of a moral rigor and growth that might help this country.

None of the above is to say the *The Deer Hunter* is a first-class film, as such. It is not. Although the direction is generally good and the acting is always fine, the script flounders increasingly as it goes on, particularly in the third and longest section. The extraordinary acting is what holds the film together when the script straggles. Still, it ought to be slated for its real faults, not for adduced ones. Anyway, with further irony, *The Deer Hunter* is a much better piece of work, in artistic wholeness and thematic cogency, than *Coming Home,* that flabby and compromised picture on the Vietnam War made by people whose political views are, apparently, close to my own. (p. 23)

Stanley Kauffmann, "The Hunting of the Hunters" (reprinted by permission of Brandt & Brandt Literary Agents, Inc.; copyright © 1979 by Stanley Kauffmann), in The New Republic, *Vol. 180, No. 21, May 26, 1979, pp. 22-3.*

MARSHALL DELANEY

[Cimino's] attitude toward the material is the source of *The Deer Hunter*'s great success and at the same time the reason it has been a subject of controversy ever since it appeared in December. Cimino shrewdly refuses to be drawn into a discussion of the war; against all temptation he avoids any trace of sententiousness. He presents the war not as a political event with political implications but as a great historic tragedy that fell upon the American people—rather like some gigantic earthquake that leaves tens of thousands of dead behind it. This is not how politicians and newspapers see the war, but it is how the America that Cimino is interested in—the non-political, working-class America that lives outside the debates of politicians and newspapers, the America for which Washington is almost as foreign as Saigon—actually experienced the Vietnam era. Something happened, and then stopped happening. There was never a time when these people, so far as they knew, could keep it from happening or change the way it happened. . . . Cimino's film is a portrait of the unexamined life lived by people who do not know any other way of living and would be astonished if one were described to them.

These people, these victims—Cimino seems to say—deserve their poet, too, and he has named himself to that office. He looks deeply into the themes and rituals of their lives, particularly into the theme of intensely physical male comradeship. . . . There are times when *The Deer Hunter* seems to be an illustration of Leslie A. Fiedler's seminal book, *Love and Death in the American Novel,* which depicts American life as a series of homo-erotic male bondings. Cimino makes every turn of his drama heighten the intensity of these male feelings. Even the endless wedding scene focuses on what the men are doing, feeling, saying to each other—as if the women were there mainly for decoration. (p. 48)

It is . . . an attempt—largely successful—to suggest some of the ways some Americans live and reflect in their lives the great movements of history. . . . Those who hate *The Deer Hunter* because it refuses to deal with American guilt in the war are missing Cimino's point. *The Deer Hunter* is not a documentary; it's a nightmare. In Cimino's hands the facts of the war are arbitrarily re-arranged, just as we re-arrange the details of life in a nightmare. (pp. 48-9)

The Deer Hunter accomplishes what the best dramatic art does: it takes us somewhere we have never been before and brings us back enlarged and broadened. (p. 49)

Marshall Delaney [pseudonym of Robert Fulford], "From Inside the American Nightmare," in Saturday Night *(copyright © 1979 by* Saturday Night*), Vol. 94, No. 5, June, 1979, pp. 48-9.*

Shirley Clarke

1925-

American filmmaker, dancer, actress, and videotape artist.

Realism, stark and electrifying, marks Clarke's cinematic style. Her early work centers on her preoccupation with dance. But it was cinéma vérité films such as *Portrait of Jason* which gained her recognition as a talented documentary filmmaker.

Her techniques are extremely pure. In *Jason,* she filmed a running monologue delivered by a black homosexual. It is a revealing film due partly to Jason's candor, partly to Clarke's direction. Her use of real time lapses and the revealing particulars of Jason's unconventional life style, combined with an immobile camera, give the film its unrelenting realism. When commissioned to make a film on poverty for UNICEF, she created *A Scary Time.* It was so frightening that it was never used by the organization. Even when Clarke turned to fictional sources, she has maintained her loyalty to realism. For *The Cool World,* her cast was comprised of children from the streets who created their own dialogue. The filming was done inside a tenement building which had been condemned. With the same commitment to reality, when Clarke's film *The Connection* was censored, she fought for the inclusion of words she thought were crucial to the depiction of drug addicts. She won a Supreme Court case and opened the way for freer use of language in films.

Since then, Clarke has moved on to videotape because she enjoys the immediacy of that medium and the relative convenience that allows taping under almost any circumstances. She does such an inordinate amount of taping, that she has said of her work: "My life is one long electrical cord."

HENRY BREITROSE

Shirley Clarke was originally a dancer. Before making films she took the precaution of learning a great deal about film technique; but she remains an instinctual film-maker, whose feeling for movement generally seems to have carried over into her feeling for the camera.

The theme of *Bridges-Go-Round*—as far as words can describe it—is the bridges that link Manhattan to Brooklyn, Queens, the Bronx, and the New Jersey shore. In actuality, the bridges become plastic materials for a highly abstract subjective study in structures and movements. The images were printed "bi-packed"—running sandwiched together through the printer—in order to give them equal intensity. They are manipulated in a complex but extremely arresting way: the great steel girders, the taut cables, the towers and railings and roadways and abutments seem almost to dance. An exciting sense of color works with Mrs. Clarke's lively rhythmic sense. . . .

On its simplest level *Skyscraper* is the chronicle of a building, 666 Fifth Avenue, from the time its site is cleared . . . to its ultimate employment as a forty-odd-floor stack of offices. But the film is also a comment on the contrast between the nobility and quietly unconscious heroism of the actual construction workers and the shallow, highly polished routinism for which their labor provides a home. (p. 57)

As in *Bridges,* there is an astonishing lyric quality, even when dealing with mechanical processes. Not only are the shots edited dynamically . . . but the changes in tempo, the pauses, accelerations, retards, and even visual glissandos—such as a shot looking up an elevator shaft as the elevator ascends—work with a remarkably complex correctness and grace. (p. 58)

Henry Breitrose, "Films of Shirley Clarke," in Film Quarterly *(copyright 1960 by The Regents of the University of California; reprinted by permission of the University of California Press), Vol. XIII, No. 4, Summer, 1960, pp. 57-8.*

GIDEON BACHMANN

The Connection appears to be one of those legendary "firsts" like *Citizen Kane* or *Breathless,* which not only excel filmically, but also set standards for other film work. In short, *The Connection* is *important.* There is no doubt that in many ways this will be a pace-setting film, from the points of view of form, impact, and method of production. (pp. 13-14)

The Connection [breaks] long-established movie axioms. For one thing, the camera plays a part in the film itself, and thus a new kind of audience identification is created, which borders on audience *participation;* the camera represents the viewer. This, in fact, is part of the intention of its appearance: the actors . . . are confronted by its peering presence, and begin to act for it, so that their reality is geared to the intrusion of the spectator. This is as close as film has ever come to providing the creative "feedback" which live performances often cause as a result of the interaction between actor and audience. . . .

The importance of *The Connection* is not so much in the manner in which it was made or in its final quality. It is important primarily because it *was* made, and because it was made with a clear consciousness of audience participation. This is really a most important point, and one which ties in with the work of film-makers in Italy (Antonioni), Japan (Kurasawa), France (Godard), and Poland (Wajda), who are all working toward the establishment of a new, expressive cinematic syntax, the basic element of which is greater allowance for public intelligence and discrimination. All the films made by these people, and *The Connection* perhaps most of all, are antifilmic in the sense that they do not *explain* but *present,* and that only to the extent that nature presents itself to the artist to be moulded in his vision. (p. 14)

Gideon Bachmann, "Shirley Clarke," in Film Quarterly *(copyright 1961 by The Regents of the University of California; reprinted by permission of the University of California Press), Vol. XIV, No. 3, Spring, 1961, pp. 13-14.*

PENELOPE GILLIATT

[*The Connection*] is one of the rare stage pieces that is improved in its screen version.

This often means, as the junkies beadily note, nothing more than that the director has been visually flashy, eliminated the lines that can be better expressed in the cinema by the way someone shrugs or behaves when he is alone, and perhaps realised the potentialities of film to the extent of adding a car crash to the action. Shirley Clarke, the young American who made *The Connection,* has done something more crucial: though she adheres closely to the original text and never stirs outside the junkies' pad, she has altered the relation of the audience to what is going on, which in *The Connection* is peculiarly important.

In the stage version, the play hangs on the Pirandellian device of an "author" who is planted in the audience, complaining intermittently that his work is being ruined by junkie actors. . . . In Gelber's screenplay the character of the author is eliminated: part of his function is appropriated by the "director", Jim Dunn, but because he is on the screen with the others he is absorbed into the fiction. The opposition is no longer between actors and author, pretending to be sparring at a rehearsal, but between actors and spectators, which is what Gelber always intended. . . . [In] the cinema the correct, discomfiting question becomes one about our own motives in wanting to spy on drug addicts. In the theatre the audience often felt embarrassed; in the cinema it feels accused.

This is partly due to the rewriting, but mostly to Shirley Clarke's brilliant insistence that the camera is the instrument of our own curiosity. . . .

[In *The Connection,*] the camera is always a palpable object. The junkies glare at it, are amused by it and turn away from the lights as blindly as they do from the director's questions. Apart from the sequences when the shooting is taken over by Jim Dunn with a hand-held camera, the operator is an unseen but powerful presence, occasionally speaking monosyllabically from behind the camera and always severely doubtful of his boss's propriety in thinking to make art of such sorry goings-on. The spectator's identification with this character, called J. J. Burden—a variant on Jaybird, the author-character of the stage version—becomes, in time, complete and perturbing, for his silences emit a pretty square and unbudging personality.

After films like *Hiroshima, mon Amour,* and *Moderato Cantabile,* and *Une Aussi Longue Absence,* we have grown used to the notion that films can be driven forward not by a plot but simply by the way the characters react upon one another. *The Connection* goes further: not only is it without action, but it is also very nearly without interaction, for like all addicts the characters are effectively sealed off from human communication. Their talk is idle self-colloquy: they expect nothing of one another, do only what is absolutely necessary, and would scorn, as true hipsters, the idea of selling themselves as characters or even justifying their addiction. "That's the way it is. Man, that's the way it really is," becomes a recurring phrase in the play; and apart from some desultory speculation about why heroin should have been made illegal, they ask no questions. . . . *The Connection* is a study of men with scepticism but no curiosity, great insight coupled with total inertia: they are, in the most precise sense, anti-social. (p. 145)

One can pick a few holes in the play, particularly for its unremitting scorn of its characters, and its respect for a coolness that is sometimes downright moribundity. There are moments, too, when *The Connection* romanticises the anti-romantic. Against this one has to put an admirably unsensational attitude to dope, a matching refusal to supply theatrical kicks, an impeccable ear for the hipster's *patois,* and a black, abrupt humour. For Shirley Clarke's direction there can be nothing but praise: with *Shadows,* this is a film with more creative flair than any that has come out of America for years. (p. 146)

Penelope Gilliatt, "'The Connection'," in Sight and Sound *(copyright © 1961 by The British Film Institute), Vol. 30, No. 3, Summer, 1961, pp. 145-46.*

RAYMOND DURGNAT

At first I thought [*The Connection*] was pretending to watch its own gestation so that we should feel like we're in the actual pad, man. But this pseudo-Pirandellism is self-defeating. The screen is a place of the mind and the spectator is present "in" any film from the moment he starts caring what will happen next. All aesthetic hoopdedoo meant to convince us we are not in a cinema only reminds us we are; and the equivalent of a play which admits it is a play in a theatre, is a film which admits it is a film in a cinema, that is, *either* a filmed interview, *or* (in this case) a film about an intelligent director making the honest film which we see. A film about another film creates no more illusion of reality than a film about a stageshow, and only cramps and flattens the inner subject. This film's unusually pedantic pretence of "actuality" only focuses our attention on the quality of pretence—the long takes, the beautiful compositions-in-depth, the clever stage management (all unhip virtues) and too many clangers, e.g. the jazzmen go straight from absolute silence to really groovy stuff without so much as tuning-up, while the cameraman for some mysterious and therefore obtrusive motive never cuts however often the director yells "Cut".

So possibly *The Connection* is also about the disconnection between "them" and "us"—you're either an addict or an outsider and never the twain shall meet; all you can get is teasing glimpses. But the film cheapens this issue of non-communication because Dunn is a hopelessly petulant 'stooge', a young male Aunt Sally representing the earnestness of modern Art. As all the non-junkies are as eccentric as the junkies one guesses this is really a farce, that is, a compassionate *anti-tragedy* about both the addicts and the others. This hipster's in-joke doesn't really facilitate *our* connection. . . .

It is truest when the people as people prevail over their function as rebellious 'props'. We catch the peculiar combination of lethargy and impatience of waiting for a fix, and (by a rigidly non-subjective, exterior attitude) a sense of the childlike yet grotesquely desperate abandon as the junkies get 'high'. Some of the group shots evoke an inertia compared to which Hamm and Clov are Keystone Cops, and a loneliness by comparison to which the finale of *The Chairs* is community hymn-singing. . . .

The Connection needles but we don't get high. Still, it usefully widens the loopholes in our ignorance, and so is worth seeing. In the bigger leagues it is a small success.

Raymond Durgnat, "'The Connection'" (© copyright Raymond Durgnat 1962; reprinted with permission), in Films and Filming, *Vol. 8, No. 4, January, 1962, p. 31.*

ARLENE CROCE

The extent to which we can believe in the actuality of events, and not merely in their verisimilitude, is certainly the test of *The Connection*. If it doesn't impress us as an honestly played-out psycho-drama in which crucial revelations are at stake, it becomes an ingenious hoax to which our sympathies attach only at a level of execution and performance. . . . Because the cinema is now passing through its Pirandello phase, *The Connection* is being cited as an example of what movies can do to baffle our perceptions creatively. It is not a good one.

The Connection, unfortunately, doesn't fool you as a living record. In fact, for the first few minutes you think it isn't going to work at all. By mid-film, however, it has succeeded in posing a visual paradox that anyone who understands how movies are made can appreciate; and of course the more you understand the more there is to appreciate. But the paradox of a *staged* documentary is surely a thin one for a movie. If most of the criticisms one can make of the film can also be made of the play, it is because *The Connection* remains theater. Gelber's film script maintains exactly the same pact with reality that was formed in his play. The result is that the film is less effective than the play, less immediate, and less immediately emotional and strange. What ought to have taken us to the heart of the Kracauerian dilemma takes us instead around and around in a maze of technical wonders. (pp. 43-4)

[Because] the entire action of the play is cast into or against conventions of stage time and stage place, it is only like changing the frame around a picture. The effects are not phony, but they are not the effects of a real film either. . . . I am not now speaking of content, or even technique, because if technique is camera-handling, lighting, cutting and sound manipulation, Mrs. Clarke knows all about it. My point is that these films are uncreated. They do not occupy space in time. That is really the only rule for the "well-made film" that *The Connection* should have observed, and it is a rule I think Mrs. Clarke has that gift for, which is very like the gift of a dancer, but she does not show it here. (p. 44)

If *The Connection* is to succeed as a human and not a mental experience, it must persuade us that we are involved in the consequences of an act committed in the real world—not the world of realism, but the world we re-enter when we leave the movie theater. I am making the terrible suggestion that Mr. Gelber and Mrs. Clarke, if they are really serious about experimenting with the way it "really" is, should have come into the film themselves. If they had done so, and followed out their own emotions with truth and unforced logic, we should have had a film that was a film. I will hazard that it would have been a film with very different philosophical conclusions from the play, and perhaps not like the play at all. The very least it could have been is something completely undreamed of. The most that can be said of it now, and it is being said with shameless enthusiasm on all sides, is: "It's not *really* real." (p. 45)

Arlene Croce, "Film Reviews: 'The Connection': . . . Con," in Film Quarterly *(copyright 1962 by The Regents of the University of California; reprinted by permission of the University of California Press), Vol. XV, No. 4, Summer, 1962, pp. 42-5.*

GORDON HICHENS

[*The Cool World*'s] merits and demerits belong, ultimately, to Clarke. Hers is the coldness, the story-line of half-events half-happenings, and the stroboscopic blur and shaky pans masquerading as technical virtuosity. She really must make a bold plunge into expressionism and outrageous satire, for a cold director can pull these off, as she demonstrates in her powerful opening to *The Cool World*. Alas, the film soon breaks down exactly where she hopes to succeed, i.e., in making us care about characters as people. Clarke's self-effacement in deferring to the intuition of actors is unnatural for her, and she'd do better to engage us through the use of characters as illustrations of her own ideas and attitudes. In this way, she can establish through the use of symbol and startling juxtapositon—for both of which she shows a penchant—her own strong biases and feelings. These are, after all, the stuff of art, to which she aspires. (p. 53)

Gordon Hichens, "Film Reviews: 'Cool World'," in Film Comment *(copyright © 1964 by Lorien Productions, Inc.; all rights reserved), Vol. II, No. 2, Spring, 1964, pp. 52-3.*

ALBERT JOHNSON

For all its brusque cutting, disjointed narrative, and frustrating half-glances at its characters, [*The Cool World*] is the most important film document about Negro life in Harlem to have been made so far. It is a steadfast perusal of a group of adolescents, members of a gang calling themselves the "Royal Pythons"; but Clarke is as interested in the streets, buildings, backyards, and faces of Harlem as she is in her misguided young hero, Duke Custis. . . . With the aid of two extremely perceptive cameramen, Baird Bryant and Leroy McLucas, the director manages to seize upon those details that make *The Cool World* a work of visual poetry, and in sound, a tone poem of the slums. There is little humor in the film, although an early sequence, in which an anguished high-school teacher leads his unruly class of Negro boys through the Wall Street district, has a wild, improbable sort of inanity about it. Most of one's attention is drawn to the routine of the gang as they quarrel, fight, and disperse in Harlem's pattern of violence and moral corruption. (pp. 172-73)

In the novel form, *The Cool World* was easier to tell; in the film version, every character is so vivid that each one struggles (because we are able to see him in many varying and fascinating situations) to have his story told. The film is so totally alive with the desperation of the dark, of being black and ignored, that Duke is often the least interesting person in the story. (p. 173)

It is amazing that Shirley Clarke was able to compress as much into the film as she did, because it is fairly bursting with questions to unresolved problems and unresolved people. The cry of displacement is sounded by Duke's grandmother. . . . His mother . . . , a deeply disillusioned, hip scuffler, knows too well that Harlem usually gets to be "too much" for its men to endure; they run away to a less stultifying oblivion. Most denizens of Harlem are not overtly aware of their isolation, because when one is born into a ghetto, it becomes a refuge, and disturbingly enough, a comfortable retreat from the vast anonymity of white life "downtown." (pp. 173-74)

In *The Cool World,* the white world is rejected: its codes and standards, its well-meaning visitor, its curious stares from Sunday bus riders, its storekeepers, its landlords, its *everything* is rejected. Harlem's dependence upon the white world around it is not explored in this film, adding to the peculiar incompleteness of the story. For example, there had been some episodes in the book (and, I believe, in the initial cut of the film) describing the boys' hustling of white homosexuals in Central Park for spending money; and one of the boys, Chester, became the kept lover of a wealthy patron in a swank Manhattan penthouse. However, probably because of the taboo subject matter and contemporary concern with "the image" of racial characterizations, these aspects of the narrative were eliminated. (p. 175)

The struggle for self-improvement is made to appear a hopeless one for these Harlemites. When Duke stops in a playground to talk to Hardy, a neighborhood basketball player, it becomes clear that Hardy's skills are aimed toward athletic success that will surpass all similar accomplishments by "those half-assed little grey boys": At the basis of every motivation in *The Cool World,* there is an undercurrent of antiwhite anger. The "coolness" that *must* be maintained is an emotional control, repressed in turmoil, camouflaging the Negro's realization that the white world, no matter how "uncool," is one in which he *needs* a place; a desirable world with which he is not yet able to cope.

Shirley Clarke's contributions to the American cinema are honest, extremely personal works, and *The Connection*'s portraits of Negroes in the narcotics underworld and *The Cool World*'s violent Negro juveniles illustrate the background of that urban demoralization which ultimately destroys whatever might possibly flower in American Negro culture. To Negro audiences, these lessons and images are not new; the works of Richard Wright and Ann Petry, for instance, long ago dramatized the ghetto-as-battleground in American literature. But to white audiences, wherever *The Cool World* is shown, the beautifully observed vignettes of Negroes living calmly in an unnatural habitat—the baking, narrow streets and tenements, the sidewalk conversations, the gambling, a tight-suited girl waiting for a bus—these are etchings of cinematic truthfulness. Naturally, there are jazz trumpets in the air; after all the decades of history-with-myth, the linkage of dark people and jazz music is inescapable, an accepted cultural cliché. But Shirley Clarke is very much aware of all these matters and in Harlem the muses do hum the blues. (pp. 175-76)

Albert Johnson, "The Negro in American Films: Some Recent Works," in Film Quarterly *(copyright 1965 by The Regents of the University of California; reprinted by permission of the University of California Press), Vol. XVIII, No. 4, 1965 (and reprinted in* Black Films and Film-Makers: A Comprehensive Anthology from Stereotype to Superhero, *edited by Lindsay Patterson, Dodd, Mead and Company, 1975, pp. 153-81).**

VINCENT CANBY

Thanks to the responsiveness of the subject, and the cold simplicity with which Miss Clarke handles the camera, ["Portrait of Jason"] is a good deal more than an unusually frank interview with a homosexual who, at one point, exults: "I'm bona fide freaksville!"

The truth is, of course, that he isn't.

The portrait of Jason that takes shape from the bits and pieces of remembered orgies, profitless hustles and traumatic family confrontations is that of a black, sardonic Candide, who dreams one day of becoming a nightclub performer.

Jason camps in a rather muscular imitation of Mae West, recalls his mother in what was apparently a not particularly poverty ridden home in Newark . . . and relives the disgust his father . . . felt for a son who liked to skip rope. In these moments the film says more about the need for personal identity—not only in black-and-white America, but also in the world at large—than do any number of pretentious fiction films. . . .

"Portrait of Jason" is a curious and fascinating example of cinema verité, all the ramifications of which cannot be immediately known. As the life of Jason Holliday (né Aaron Paine 33 years ago) is the film, so now has the film become a part of that life—an extraordinary recognition and, perhaps, even a kind of reward for having survived.

Vincent Canby, "'Portrait of Jason'," in The New York Times *(© 1967 by The New York Times Company; reprinted by permission), September 30, 1967, p. 26.*

CHARLES HARTMAN

Perhaps the closest that cinema has yet approached the province of Genet, [*Portrait of Jason*] is an incredible peeling away of a man's soul layer by layer—his defenses, his pretensions, his lies and, ultimately, his truths. The film is an attempt not so much to find the core of the man as to see the whole structure in its internal relationships, to see the man with all that jumbled baggage that one calls personality. . . . It is obviously a film of sociological and psychological relevance beyond its immediate subject, but it is entertaining as well, because Clarke has found in Jason the natural actor. (p. 27)

Charles Hartman, "The New and Independent Film Maker," in Film Society Review, *November, 1967, pp. 27-9, 31.**

ERNEST CALLENBACH

In *Portrait of Jason,* a man talks to the camera for almost an hour and a half; yet the film is intensely interesting. We hear some other voices besides his—an old friend named Carl, who berates him toward the end from offscreen, and a female voice (Shirley Clarke's) laconically directing the proceedings. The camera tracks Jason around from couch to chair, to hearth, from a fixed position; it zooms in and out on Jason's face; sometimes, when it goes out of focus, moments of soft, abstract image mask a hiatus in camera time (during which, we learn, the camera magazine was changed). Otherwise, it is almost as if we were looking at the Empire State Building with Andy Warhol: we are made to stare, in real camera time, at a real event. Its reality, however, soon proves questionable in every sense except the optical. For Jason is a performer; even his name is adopted. The first role he adopts is the genial, cynical black hustler, conning the white world; and we enjoy and admire the deftness and humor of his stories about a checkered past as houseboy, male prostitute, drifter. . . . There are, however, glimpses of other levels, when Jason stops smiling and sips a drink, looks for an instant at the camera without talking, or confesses (not for the first time) some ingratiating sin. As the evening wears on, such instants become more intriguing. We begin to watch for the revelation of "the real Jason," for the camera to show us the secret that lies behind his chronic, complex, ironic, and comically self-destructive role-playing. . . . Toward the end, goaded by Carl, he becomes tearful, self-critical. Is this the real Jason? No, the film forces us to realize; we are no further beneath the surface than with the entertaining hipster of the opening. The role is the man. We now know, in a rough outline such as a psychiatrist might get from a good first session . . . , what Jason knows or will reveal about himself. . . . This involuted film portrait, thus, may not be a film in the sense usually attached to the term, but it is certainly an immensely curious psychological and social document. We find ourselves, with such novelties, still further from an answer to Bazin's question, What Is Cinema? *Jason* proves that cinema may be, among other things, compelling even if used as a simple recording device for a single person. The lens may be an explicit stand-in for the viewer; and Jason, or any of us, can speak to it and be dispassionately observed. The responses given by such a celluloid oracle may be shocking or inscrutable, like those of its ancient precursors; but men will consult it nonetheless. (pp. 75-7)

Ernest Callenbach, "Short Notices: 'Portrait of Jason'," in Film Quarterly *(copyright 1968 by The Regents of the University of California; reprinted by permission of the University of California Press), Vol. XXII, No. 1, Fall, 1968, pp. 75-7.*

TONY RAYNS

Far from being the luridly cautionary tale that [a] narrative outline perhaps suggests, *The Cool World* works primarily as a flow of everyday incident, in much the same way as Shirley Clarke's earlier feature, *The Connection;* for every calculated 'dramatic' scene there are at least three others that draw their interest from the commonplaces of life in the Harlem ghetto. The film's dramatic focus, of course, is on Duke as central character: both the turns of the plot and the generalities are filtered through his growing self-consciousness of his position, explored in a series of introspective voice-overs. But these interior monologues . . . are only one element in an exceptionally well-thought soundtrack—the method might best be described as an extension of Kerouac's narration for *Pull My Daisy*—which 'orchestrates' Duke's voice and Mal Waldron's mournful jazz score with direct and post-synched sound into consistently rich, fluid aural textures. This uncommonly active *use* of sound [is a major strength]. . . . [The] script makes occasional forays into redundant social comment through overt irony (as police manhandle Duke into their car a radio commentator enthuses about the plan for astronauts to plant the American flag on the moon) or crude schematisation (Douglas Thurston is introduced all too pointedly as a black who has acquiesced in the white system, unlike his diametrically opposite brother, a resolutely delinquent junkie); and some of the dialogue—notably monologues on loneliness by Duke's mother and Miss Dewpont—carries a poetic charge out of key with the prevalent authentic street slang. In the event, none of these misjudgments damages the film at all seriously, and several are accommodated in such a way as to work to the film's advantage. . . . With the film's good and poor qualities . . . in miraculous balance, the element that registers most powerfully is the sheer energy of the characters, their capacities for delicacy and anger alike. Ms. Clarke's subsequent *Portrait of Jason* reveals that she became as suspicious of the kind of artifice that drives *The Cool World* as most of her contemporaries. But *The Cool World* was made at a time when the American independent and underground film-makers saw themselves as presenting a viable alternative to Hollywood, rather than (as now) working within an entirely different aesthetic. And among the 'alternatives' of the day, from *Guns of the Trees* to *Echoes of Silence, The Cool World* now stands as the film most controlled and inventive in its methods, and most spiritedly committed in its vision. (p. 45)

Tony Rayns, "'The Cool World'," in Monthly Film Bulletin *(copyright © The British Film Institute, 1974), Vol. 41, No. 482, March, 1974, pp. 44-5.*

Jean Cocteau

1889-1963

French director, poet, dramatist, novelist, scriptwriter, and painter.

Cocteau is a distinguished filmmaker noted for his blending of myth and reality in films of visual beauty. His involvement with the artistic avant-garde of his time is evidenced in innovative contributions to many artistic genres, many of which bore an influence on his filmmaking.

Born near Paris into a family of lawyers, Cocteau early showed literary and artistic promise, publishing his first volume of poetry, *La Lampe d'Aladin*, at the age of seventeen. His circle at that time included Marcel Proust and Léon Daudet. Through their influence, Cocteau became enthralled with the ballet, an interest which led to a friendship with Serge Diaghilev, Russian ballet impresario and director of the Ballet Russe de Monte Carlo. It was Diaghilev who inspired in Cocteau the philosophy he embraced throughout his artistic career: to shock and surprise his audience.

Towards the end of World War I, Cocteau entered the circle of the creative avant-garde, which included Pablo Picasso and composer Eric Satie, with whom Cocteau created the ballet *Parade*. Though a failure at the time of its creation, it is now regarded as one of the twentieth century's most innovative ballets. Another valuable influence on Cocteau's creative career was the young writer Raymond Radiguet. Radiguet steered Cocteau away from the avant-gardists and told him to "lean on nothing . . . and develop an attitude that consists of not appearing original." The death of Radiguet devastated Cocteau, and he turned to opium, an addiction that plagued him all of his life.

It was not until the early 1930s that Cocteau began working with cinema. His first film, *Le Sang d'un poète* (*The Blood of a Poet*), imitates Cocteau's ever-present image of the Poet and the Dream. Cocteau wanted his audience to pass through the celluloid barrier into his film world, and enjoy the experience of creator and dreamer.

Cocteau's films served as a sort of personal journey reflecting his obsessions and fantasies as well as his delight in cinematic devices. *La Belle et la bête* (*Beauty and the Beast*) allowed Cocteau to unleash his fantasies of decorating cinema as an objet d'art. He employed classical legend in works such as *Orphée* (*Orpheus*), a film he made based on one of his own plays. While several of his films are adaptations of his plays, the three films which have established his filmmaking reputation are *Le Sang d'un poète*, *Orphée*, and *Le Testament d'Orphée*. Deeply original and personal, they are concerned with the role of the artist and his source of inspiration.

Cocteau found in the cinema a means superior to all other media in depicting his poetic view of death and the fantastic. Critics feel, however, that the intensity of his artistic vision sometimes makes his films difficult and obscure. However, Cocteau is regarded as a filmmaker of unique gifts, an artist striving to make real his original conception of film: "A film is not a dream that is told but one we all dream together." (See also *CLC*, Vols. 1 and 8, *Contemporary Authors*, Vols. 25-28, and *Contemporary Authors Permanent*, Vol. 2.)

C. G. WALLIS

Cocteau's *Le Sang d'un Poète* is one of the authentic classics of the cinema, in the small group that includes *Caligari, The Ten Days that Shook the World,* some René Clair, and some Chaplin. It is perhaps Cocteau's own magnum opus, even if we compare it with *Thomas L'Imposteur, La Machine Infernale,* or *Les Chevaliers de la Table Ronde*. And among the works of the '30's—a decade fairly arid in poetry and myth—it is one of the few landmarks, like *Murder in the Cathedral* and *Finnegans Wake*. I make these simple unanalytic statements of praise, because certain people at present disparage the poet Cocteau as a faker, a master of aesthetic sleight of hand and nothing more, and *Le Sang d'un Poète* itself as a pretty piece of legerdemain or at best as a myth purely private in its reference. (p. 24)

[That] I am right in calling [*Le Sang d'un Poète*] an allegory is evidenced extrinsically by Cocteau's preface, in which he tells the spectator that all poetry is a coat of arms whose symbols can be deciphered only after the expenditure of blood, and that he is dedicating the allegories of *Le Sang d'un Poète* to Pisanello, Paolo Uccello, Piera della Francesca, as painters of arms and blazons. Internal evidence is given by the prologue and epilogue of the falling tower, whose masonry has crumbled before the story proper commences yet whose collapse is completed only after the end of the story proper, so that the temporal expanse of the total action is comprised within the instant or brief interim elapsing between the two shots of the tower, that is to say, the total action is timeless or without duration and is therefore an allegory of eternal objects rather than a story of particular things. Furthermore, within the story proper the datelessness of the action is emphasized by the mixtures of period and costume, i.e., the studied anachronism in dress signifies that the action is not merely instantaneous or without duration but is not localized at any one point of time. Moreover, the machinery of events which obey laws other than those of the natural world, viz., the transsubstantiation of a charcoal mouth to a living, of a woman into a statue; the agility and levitation of bodies, in entering a mirror or flying to the ceiling; the disproportion between cause and effect, as the quick wasting away of the bronze statue beneath the snowballs; or the coexistence in one subject of contrary states, as life and death—all this serves to compose a world of miracles, that is to say, one where the system of causes transcends its phenomenal effects, or where the phenomena are merely the iconography for various relations among ideas. (pp. 25-6)

[Let] me make some cursory generalizations about the structure and content of the film—sticking fairly close to the literal level—before proceeding with a more detailed analysis. The falling tower serves formally as a symbol of a beginning and an end; and, in content, it introduces the theme of destruction in general and even, since the cause of the collapse of the tower is not shown, that of self-destruction. Now within the action proper, it should be noted that the relation of person to person or even thing to thing is usually that of victim to victor or agent to patient and that the crises in the action are often reversals of this relation. . . . [It] is evident that the separate incidents usually compose a unification of some or other contraries; and hence the whole film at first glance has a right to be considered, in the Coleridgean categories, as a work of the Imagination rather than of Fancy, even short of the exegesis of its iconography. (pp. 31-2)

[The film is divided, by subtitles, into four parts: *La Main Blessée ou la Cicatrice de Poète, Les Murs Ont-Ils des Oreilles?, La Bataille des Boules de Neige,* and *La Carte Volée*]. (p. 32)

The plot of *La Main Blessée* is essentially the destruction of an image or icon, viz., the erasure of the sketch, followed by the reception of a wound, viz., the mouth in the hand; and that of *La Bataille des Boules de Neige* is similar, viz., the crumbling away of the statue beneath the snowballs and the mortal blow sped from the hand of Dargelos. . . . The vivification of the statue by the wounding mouth in *La Main Blessée,* I do not count as a separate theme: for the original mouth is miraculous and unknown in its causation; consequently its appearances and transmutations will, in poetic probability, be many; while the mortal blow, as such, is one and final, and natural and determinate in origin. The plot of *Les Murs Ont-Ils des Oreilles?* is, I think, that of the journey through an unfamiliar medium, viz., the subterranean world behind the mirror, leading to a false suicide (at the instigation of a woman) and the false transformation of a man into a statue. . . . Similarly, in *La Carte Volée* the pilgrimage of the dead boy's guardian (he wears an apparatus for flying and swimming trunks and has a limp: hence walking on the earth is an unfamiliar mode of locomotion for him) leads to the true suicide of the hero, followed by the woman's turning into a mythical statue—which constitute a real glory as opposed to the false glory in *Les Murs Ont-Ils des Oreilles?* In brief, the theme of each might be epigrammatized as: the wound, the suicide, and the statue. (pp. 33-4)

The allegory of *Le Sang d'un Poète* (which Cocteau had once announced as *La Vie d'un Poète*) might be described, for the purposes of this essay, as "the pilgrimage of a poet." The linear story tells of a progress from being a Naive Poet, through various intermediate rôles, to being a depersonalized poet. *La Main Blessée ou la Cicatrice de Poète* tells of the progress from Naive Poetry to archaeology. . . . [The young man] is a Naive Poet because he is making a series of simple likenesses or improvisations. What, if any, relation there is between the mark of the wound and his gift as an artist, we do not know. His naiveté becomes sophisticated when he discovers that poetry is magical. . . . But the magical power of poetry is still limited by its nature as an imitation, and consequently it is an incomplete reality which it achieves, viz., a mouth and not a whole person or even face, that is to say, it is a monster. It is significant that he does not become conscious of this magical power, until there is a visitor or messenger from the outside world. . . . His discovery of the mouth in his hand is his recognition that, while the magical effect may reside in the poem, the magical power is in the poet himself. It becomes further evident that this power is in the poet himself. It becomes further evident that this power is daemonic, like another substance within him; for it is both rational, i.e., it talks to him, and erotic, i.e., it kisses. That is to say, the poet's pleasure in making poetry is both intellectual and symbolically sexual. For a short while he lives in communion with this power. But since he does not understand it (for its existence appears to him to be uncaused and miraculous) he still tries to deny it in some way. His transfer of the mouth to the pre-existent statue, I take to be a symbol of a compromise which he tries to effect, viz., he no longer tries to deny universally that poetry has daemonic and magical properties, but seeks to impute them to the art of the past, of which he becomes the interpreter or archaeologist himself. (pp. 34-6)

[The] poet in *Les Murs Ont-Ils des Oreilles?* finds himself a prisoner with the statue in a windowless, doorless room whose only aperture is a mirror. The mirror, let us say, signifies contemporary art (for art "holds the mirror up to life") as opposed to the art of the past, which was unrealistic (for the statue had no arms) and daemonic. . . . The allegory portrays only his relation to the theatre; for the four episodes in L'Hotel des Folies Dramatiques compose a comedy of the theatre in general and of the contemporary theatre in particular, at which he is a mere spectator as he peeps through the key-holes. . . . The four scenes through the key-holes signify four properties of dramatic poetry, represented comically or satirically, in respect to the contemporary drama: the first, viz., the fall, unfall, and fall again of the peon before the firing squad, signifies the reversal or peripety, which was the mainstay of the classical tragic plot but which in a debauched contemporary theatre is like a camera trick; the second, viz., the opium pipe and the Chinese eye, may signify seriously the property of mystery, which is inherent in all poetry, i.e., its inexhaustibility by rational analysis, so that the poem remains still looking back at reason, as the Chinese eye at the spectator; or comically, that the theatre is a spiritual opium, although as an imitation of life it may still be found to be looking back at you; third, viz., the flying lesson, the quality of sublimity, which in the contemporary theatre quickly passes into the ridiculous; and fourthly, the figure on the sofa and the false suicide, the confusion between a poetic imitation and reality—a confusion which may arise through the very nature of the theatre itself. . . . The moment of the suicide is the dilettante's attempt to imitate within his own life an artificial action; for it is at the *command* of the other figure that he aims the revolver and pulls the trigger; moreover, the semi-hypnotic and sudden manner in which he obeys also suggests that it is out of unreasoned imitativeness and not from reasoned choice that he commits the act. Furthermore, the generic act of imitating a stage drama is fabled as a suicide, because it is the imitation of an imitation and therefore the negation of his natural living. Hence the suicide must be a false suicide, because it is impossible to die a *natural* death merely by imitating an artificial action. . . . [In] attempting to persuade himself universally that the daemonic, magical power of poetry is non-existent and to deny the seat of this power in himself, he finds that he has transformed himself into something as lifeless and immobile as a conventional statue in a public square. This statue is really a false ego, which is formed out of the total suppression of the poetic daemon, and is consequently a statue within the soul of the poet, just as the partial inhibition of the poetic daemon, in transferring the living mouth from the hand to the plaster-of-Paris face, resulted in the daemonizing of an external object, our archaeological or poetic heritage.

Consequently *La Bataille des Boules de Neige* should be interpreted, I think, as a flashback: the recollection of the childhood incident in which the hero received his original wound—a wound in the heart which in his later forgetfulness appeared transformed into a scar on his shoulder. The wound was unrequited love—the death of the heart and of the child within himself. . . . This recollection of his childhood further destroys the statufaction of his ego which was caused by his ignorance of the relation between the developed daemonism of poetry and himself. In his imagination the figure of Dargelos has taken the place of the statue, because the ego is the repository of the privations of love. Consequently the loss of the love of Dargelos is the primary privation; and hence the ego-formation represented by the statue, which was caused by the final self-deprivation of poetic power (symbolized by smashing the statue of the woman) is dissolved on recognizing Dargelos, who returns a deadly snowball in answer to love, as the source of the primary wound. That is to say, as the smashed statue is to the statufied poet and as the slain child is to Dargelos, so is the daemonic power of poetizing to the poet manqué and the boyhood love to its unrequital. (pp. 36-9)

In *La Carte Volée* the hero is no longer statufied, i.e., he is no longer dominated by the false ego formed by his denial of the poetic daemon, but the possibilities of action still open to him are still limited by the ego formed by his original loss of love as a boy. He is now trying to be a man, viz., by making love to a woman—like all poets, before the eyes of a fashionable world which does not understand what is happening. But since the child in himself is lying there slain, his own heart dead, love can only be a game, conventional and nonspontaneous, played by means of mere symbols and outward forms. . . . [The] hero, as cut off from the sources of life represented by the boy, is himself nil in relation to the woman. Hence he can no longer be a complete man at all, but can only be man qua poet pure and simple, that is to say, his recognition of this reduction in humanity must be his symbolic suicide as a man. Similarly, the woman does not actually change into the statue, but her place is taken by the statue or muse . . . ; for now the only possible fructifying relationship is between the poet and his muse or between the sculptor and his statue; the relation between man and woman has vanished. . . . The woman has now become transformed into the mythical formal schematism of a bust, and the temporally unfolded action is seen to lead to the idea of the "deathly boredom of immortality." The poet has attained his salvation; but it is the salvation of artifice, like Yeats's Byzantium, and neither natural nor divine, but constructed by a man after a laborious and heart-destroying discipline. (pp. 39-40)

Looking at *Le Sang d'un Poète* superficially, it is obvious that its aesthetic power resides in its special combination of simplicity of elements, enigma of intention, and a pervading sense of an underlying rationality. But as, in ethics, the principle of virtue may be formulated as: Act according as your maxim may be made universal; similarly in poetics, the principle of classicism might be stated as: Unify your content with such formalities as are universal in scope. For the actual plot of *Le Sang d'un Poète* is narrow in its significance. (In fact, it is paradoxical for a hero to be a poet. For a hero is some one who acts or suffers. But the poet as poet does not act or suffer but is the maker of fictions about those who act or suffer. Cocteau resolves this paradox by making poetizing the inevitable outcome of a sequence of actions and sufferings, like the death or calamity which was often the outcome of an ancient tragedy.) But the scope of the plot is universalized by defining its content in terms as powerful as the relation of victim to victor, of agent to patient (which is metaphysically the fundamental relation in all human action, whether the action be conceived as social or as occurring within the soul of one individual) and by unifying its plot-structure by the formal device of the reversal, which, as Aristotle argues, has a most powerful psychological effect, and which, as a mode of unifying poetic contraries in a time-scheme, distinguishes (in Coleridge's sense) a work of the Imagination from one of Fancy. (pp. 41-2)

C. G. Wallis, "'The Blood of a Poet'," in The Kenyon Review *(copyright 1944 by Kenyon College; reprinted by permission of* The Kenyon Review*), Vol. VI, No. 1, Winter, 1944, pp. 24-42.*

BOSLEY CROWTHER

["Beauty and the Beast"] is an eminent model of cinema achievement in the realm of poetic fantasy.

This should be understood, however: the achievement is on a definitely adult plane and the beauties of Cocteau's conception will be most appreciated by sophisticated minds. It is not the sort of picture that will send the children into transports of delight, unless they are quite precocious youngsters of the new progressive school.

For Cocteau has taken the old story . . . and has used it as a pattern for weaving a priceless fabric of subtle images. In the style of his "Blood of a Poet," though less abstract and recondite, it is a fabric of gorgeous visual metaphors, of undulating movements and rhythmic pace, of hypnotic sounds and music, of casually congealing ideas.

Freudian or metaphysician, you can take from it what you will. The concepts are so ingenious that they're probably apt to any rationale. From the long corridor of candelabra, held out from the walls by living arms, through which the wondering visitor enters the palace of the Beast, to the glittering temple of Diana, wherein the mystery of the Beast is revealed, the visual progression of the fable into a dream-world casts its unpredictable spell.

The dialogue, in French, is spare and simple . . . and the music of Georges Auric accompanies the dreamy, fitful moods. The settings are likewise expressive. . . .

Studied or not for philosophy, this is a sensuously fascinating film, a fanciful poem in movement given full articulation on the screen.

Bosley Crowther, "'Beauty and the Beast'," in The New York Times *(© 1947 by The New York Times Company; reprinted by permission), December 24, 1947, p. 12.*

BOSLEY CROWTHER

It sometimes helps if a reviewer has a faint idea of what a film he is reviewing is supposed to be about. That is, at least, some information which he can pass along. But we can't even shoot you that knowledge on Jean Cocteau's "Eagle With Two Heads." Unfortunately, Mr. Cocteau neglected to make it clear.

Apparently his drama . . . has something to do with a romance between a melancholy queen and an initially rebellious subject who resembles her long-dead spouse. From the rapturous and reckless embracing . . . we gathered this general impression. Something is cooking. That is plain. . . .

But how all these elements dovetail (if they do) and what they're supposed to prove are never transmitted to the audience in the excess of posturing and talk. Slightly intriguing situations which pop up along the way are lost in murky miasmas of fancy but pointless dialogue. And evident pretensions toward symbolism get all tangled up in wooden words.

Too bad—because plenty of money and taste have plainly been spent on a handsome physical production. Hapsburg splendor is in the regal sets and the costumes . . . are lovely and flattering. But they all add up to nothing.

Bosley Crowther, "'Eagle with Two Heads'," in The New York Times *(© 1948 by The New York Times Company; reprinted by permission), December 30, 1948, p. 24.*

A. H. WEILER

As an artist who has been known to exercise a fertile imagination, Jean Cocteau is disappointingly unimaginative in "The Storm Within." . . .

M. Cocteau, who herein is inspecting the amours of a singularly unstable family, merely has come up with a series of tempestuous harangues, hysterical outbursts, nebulous soul-searchings and petty plots signifying nothing especially new about either sacred or profane love. And, despite a generally proficient cast, "The Storm Within" is, anomalously, a static drama, which talks a great deal about emotions while projecting little of same. . . .

"The Storm Within" is only a tempest in a teapot.

A. H. Weiler, "'The Storm Within'," in The New York Times *(© 1950 by The New York Times Company; reprinted by permission), April 24, 1950, p. 21.*

BOSLEY CROWTHER

Perhaps the most tell-tale tip-off to the nature of the "Orpheus" of Jean Cocteau . . . is thoughtfully offered by the author in a signed statement in the program: "When I make a film," says M. Cocteau, "it is a slumber and I dream."

That is as fair a forewarning as any that we can provide to the curious conceits of fancy that you may expect in this film. For plainly the writer-director has let his imagination roam through a drama of images that resemble the vagrant phantasms of sleep. And while the famed legend of Orpheus provides the framework of a plot and the pictorial character is concrete, the context is utterly abstract.

Indeed, at one point in this crisscross of phantoms and images, which clearly defy interpretation along any logical line, the author permits one character to drop this significant remark: "You try too hard to understand and that is a mistake."

A mistake it is, beyond question—for, in telling a modern-dress tale of a young poet by the name of Orpheus who becomes strangely enamoured of Death and almost (but not quite) loses his pretty blond wife, Eurydice, M. Cocteau has so coagulated his picture with fantasies and stunts that a serious attempt to seek some meaning in all of them might drive one mad.

There is a chic and sophisticated lady who rides around in a Rolls-Royce car and ominously hangs over Orpheus. She seems quite simple. She is Death. Only she isn't all Death exactly. She is the Death of Orpheus. But she is also the personal Death of Cegeste, another poet. A little confused. There are also two mad motorcyclists who recklessly knock people down. They are quite clearly Death's agents. We can fathom them. But how about this fellow, Heurtebise, who drives the Rolls-Royce car? He is some sort of in-betweener. What is his place in Cocteau's realm?

And then there are all those mirrors through which people nonchalantly pass—that is, if they're properly departed or are wearing the magical rubber gloves. They are easy. As someone mentions, "Mirrors are the doors through which Death comes and goes." But what is the symbolism? And how about that stupid radio? Why does it drone monotonous numbers and speeches as though in code? You can say it again, M. Cocteau: "It is not necessary to understand; it is necessary to believe."

No doubt the true believers (whoever they are) will get much from this film, for it is produced with remarkable authority and photographed magnificently, thus enhancing the pictorial richness of its symbols and images. . . .

But for this corner's taste, the style of Cocteau, while valid, perhaps, does not embrace sufficient intellectual comprehension to justify so much film, and the visual here lacks the fascination of the same author's "Beauty and the Beast." Somnambulistic symbolism may be art for art's sake. Maybe not. This writer finds it slightly tiresome. It's more Morpheus than Orpheus by us.

Bosley Crowther, "'Orpheus'," in The New York Times *(© 1950 by The New York Times Company; reprinted by permission), November 30, 1950, p. 42.*

JEAN R. DEBRIX

Orpheus simultaneously presents two aspects of the poetic process: that of the poet—Cocteau; and that of an ideal poetic instrument—the cinema. . . .

The central theme of *Orpheus* is poetry's all-pervading power.

For Cocteau, as for every poet, poetry is the only truth, the only way of life, the only means of approaching essential reality. All else is the gross and perishable imaginings of earth-bound men. (p. 18)

Cocteau has poured into *Orpheus* all his obsessions; his preoccupation with mirrors (narcissism); his weakness for cruel and unmotivated practical jokes (poets cannot help being *enfants terribles*); his awe for the "holy"; his complete familiarity with all aspects of the dream, trance states and second sight (Cocteau experimented with almost every drug); and, finally, his penchant for mystification—an infantilism that has persisted to the threshold of old age.

To dazzle, to intimidate, to reveal marvels of all kinds, to invent new and unheard of universes, to evoke specters and phantoms, Prince Charmings or what have you—all this fascinates Cocteau. As he himself says, he wishes to appeal only to the child who lingers deep within each of us. For Cocteau, as for so many others like him, the lost paradise of childhood is the only kingdom over which every man may hope to reign. (p. 19)

Everything in *Orpheus* is symbolic. The principal symbols can be analyzed as follows:

1. ORPHEUS. The poet is a man as other men, but feels an imperative need, unknown to ordinary men, to extend the horizons of human perception, to explore and illumine human destiny, and to possess himself of new, hitherto unimagined realities. . . .

2. EURYDICE. She is our literal, earthy, day-to-day life—that humdrum daily life men must continuously strive to enrich and extend, and which the poet must abandon ruthlessly from time to time so that he may be free to run after even the wildest chimeras.

3. THE PRINCESS. According to Cocteau, each of us has in our secret hearts an image of Death, of *our* Princess, who irresistibly allures and fascinates us. In the film the Princess is a double symbol—of Death, and of this truism: each man must die many times (*within* himself) before he can know himself truly and before he can become his true, un-self-deceived self. . . .

4. THE MIRRORS. Although mirrors, as symbols, belong to Cocteau's private mythology, they are, of course, part of that folk-lore of psychology which is universal. In a mirror one perceives one's own decay. Hence, in the depths of a mirror slumber the riddles of life and death. . . .

5. THE RADIOPHONIC MESSAGES. These phenomena constitute a somewhat puerile symbol for creative intuition. Cocteau believes there are certain human beings who possess a genius for pure invention, such as the poet and the mathematician. They bring to the rest of us news of realities which they have discovered and we did not suspect, and upon which mankind builds its future. (p. 20)

6. THE "ZONE". It is the region in which the Princess (Death) has her dwelling, from which she emerges to abduct her victims, and to which she carries them. It is a no-man's land, a hideous limbo strewn with rubble and garbage, and resembles the weird, distressful areas that encircle every city. (p. 21)

In *Orpheus* Cocteau has used the cinema to create a poetic, supernatural universe. The cinema can triumph over both space and time, can ignore our normal chronology, can dispense with distance, disregard the limitations of mere human beings. What is more, it can transform our world before our very eyes, can alter the appearance of reality, create fanciful realities, and make us believe in all of these metamorphoses. (pp. 21-2)

[There] can be no doubt that for two hours this universe of Cocteau's *does* exist for us and that we leave it with the feeling of having been there.

In order to materialize his imaginary world, which has its own laws and its own ways of coordinating the unrelated, Cocteau uses many subtle and amusing cinematic tricks, among which the following are the most outstanding:

1. SLOW MOTION. When Orpheus and Death's chauffeur, Heurtebise, cross over the "zone" which leads to the world "beyond," their gestures and movements are slowed down so that they appear to be moving in a dream. They glide along, moved only by invisible winds, like ectoplasmic emanations from a spiritist medium. The effect suggests the disintegration of personality that takes place in trance states and day dreams.

2. REVERSED OR CONTRARY MOTION. When Death, after transporting the mortal remains of Cégeste to her villa and depositing them there, wishes to awaken him to the reality of his new existence, she causes him to raise himself miraculously from the ground and resume a vertical position without the slightest effort. (pp. 22-3)

3. NEGATIVE IMAGES WITH REVERSED LIGHTS AND SHADOWS. When Death's limousine reaches the world "beyond," the landscape takes on a strange and mysterious coloring—the sky is black, the trees white. . . .

4. THE MIRROR. Passing through mirrors is done either by double exposure, or by means of horizontal shots taken with a foreground of water.

Today few films utilize these tricks. . . .

But at the same time we must reproach Cocteau for failing to create a more satisfying and convincing film. However much *Orpheus* may excite our admiration by the beauty and nobility of its theme, by its expansion of our mental horizons, and by its cinematic techniques, it is a disappointment because of weaknesses and obscurities in its plot. Although the story Cocteau unfolds, in an atmosphere of supernaturalism tinctured with gangster-film vulgarity, is dedicated to the exaltation of the poet and his mission, it is unconvincing, puerile, without motivation, frequently ridiculous, and sometimes incomprehensible. Its outmoded surrealism belongs to a past decade.

Poetry today demands new and different forms and symbols. It can find them in a new art of the cinema. (p. 23)

Jean R. Debrix, "Cocteau's 'Orpheus' Analyzed: Its Chief Virtue Is What It Tried to Do," translated by Edith Morgan King, in Films in Review *(copyright © 1951 by the National Board of Review of Motion Pictures, Inc.), Vol. II, No. 6, June-July, 1951, pp. 18-23.*

C. A. LEJEUNE

I cannot pretend to know what [*Orpheus*] all means, and I

have a lurking suspicion that Cocteau doesn't know either, but I do know that it sent me out of the theatre quivering with excitement, and more provocatively engaged than I have been by any film for seasons. Cocteau, of course, has two prevailing ideas, that run like coloured thread through all his work: the idea of a poet as an extra-sensory medium, and the idea of a hungry marriage between life and death. He twists these two ideas together in *Orpheus,* as he did in a tentative way in *L'Aigle a Deux Têtes,* and has produced a picture that is bewildering, stimulating, sometimes touching and sometimes quite hateful, but always a provocation to the mind and eye. (pp. 185-86)

Since the author believes that all flights of high fantasy must be touched off from a firm earthhold, his film, astonishing in its camera tricks and devices of pure cinema magic, is grounded here and there in moments of contemporary realism. The ferryman Charon becomes a smart chauffeur: the messengers of death are goggled motor-cyclists: code messages are tapped out by a secret radio: a trial in the shades is conducted along the lines of a war crimes tribunal.

All these things, plus the fact that it is hardly possible to *act* Death, Death's servants, or Death's victims, . . . make *Orpheus* a trifle confusing to the spectator. But it is an experience that is very well worth trying. I am not quite sure, in my own heart, whether the film is healthy: some tiny thing suggests to me that it is a work less inspired by wisdom than by the splendid, fleeting, unco-ordinated ideas that flash across one's mind in a moment of perilous exhilaration. Nevertheless, exhilaration is such a rare quality in the cinema that I cannot help but welcome it, and entreat that you will look at this thing openheartedly, with a mind and eye equally alert. (p. 186)

C. A. Lejeune, in her review of "Orphée," in Shots in the Dark: A Collection of Reviewers' Opinions of Some of the Leading Films Released between January 1949 and February 1951, *Edgar Ansley, General Editor, Allan Wingate Ltd, 1951, pp. 185-86.*

NEAL OXENHANDLER

What Cocteau has attempted to do in his films is to convey, through the cinematic medium, the conception of poetry which exists in his purely literary works. Let me begin then by briefly characterizing this conception of poetry.

For Cocteau poetry is not primarily a dramatic representation of experience as in Racine, Baudelaire, Rimbaud. He is definitely in the tradition of "pure" poets for whom poetry is an end in itself and for whom morality is essentially an esthetic function. He insists in his poetry on purely verbal and syntactical manipulations. (p. 14)

Cocteau is not fundamentally interested in dramatic action; nor is he interested in ideas. His concern is less philosophical than that of other pure poets such as Mallarmé, Valéry or Giraudoux. He manipulates language like a kaleidoscope, creating new and surprising combinations, enjoying the illusion that poetry can change the face of reality.

Poetry has also a self-revelatory role for Cocteau, but it is a limited one. He reveals shifting states of consciousness rather than some fundamental human drama expressed in symbolic polarities. The drama is only revealed implicitly, by what the poetry leaves out, and by a study of the *dramatis personae* of his plays and novels. These characters are distinguished by their lack of involvement and for their ability to use language as a means of resisting any form of concrete solicitation to a course of action. The great human drama of Cocteau's plays and novels is never expressed. It is a drama of flight and negation, brilliantly disguised, yet masking a tragic human failure.

The movies offered Cocteau an ideal medium. To begin with, of course, he was not only a writer but also a pictorial artist. His sense of caricature and his feeling for the literary rather than the more painterly aspects of art were ideal equipment for a *cinéaste*. . . .

This is partly due to the fact that Cocteau thinks in images more directly than in words. . . .

Cocteau seems to feel freer in attributing sexuality to the actors in his films than to the characters of his books. It is his own emotions that he must inject into the characters of a book or play; working directly with the actor he seems to feel less fear that he will be held responsible for the emotions represented.

These observations are, I believe, sustained by the strong sexual overtones of all his films and primarily by *Le Sang d'un poète*.

There have been innumerable and contradictory exegeses of this film, including one which sees it as the history of Christianity. Cocteau himself has repeatedly refused to explain the film. (p. 15)

Le Sang d'un poète has no more unity than Cocteau's verse. Unity in the sense in which Mr. Wallis would find it in Cocteau [see excerpt above] is something that this poet is not especially concerned with. Instead of the traditional unity of an unfolding plot he achieves a kind of unity through the use of parallel themes. . . .

These themes run all the way through the film but the form of the film is such that a truly dramatic development is impossible. We pass from image to image in a kind of "qualitative progression" which does not attempt to produce anything like the classical dramatic structure of Purpose, Passion and Perception. What we are given is a series of astonishing and unforgettable images which to a large extent justify the conception of poetry here implied.

Cocteau has generously insisted on the role played by his technicians in the making of a film. They provide him with the mechanical resources that he modifies in his own ingenious way. . . . (p. 16)

The images of Cocteau's films defy the laws of nature. Props are always used suggestively with a hint that they themselves are part of the intimate life of the actors. The camera always finds the unexpected angle from which the event is illuminated in a new and true perspective. The image does not merely pass across the screen; it unfolds, using the full space of the screen, living organically with its background and every other object represented, painted in the infinite range of colors from white to black. . . .

Yet, in his later films, Cocteau has specifically chosen to dramatize a myth or to tell a story. In what sense then does this theory of "discontinuous poetry" still hold true for *La Belle et la Bête* [*Beauty and the Beast*] and for *Orphée*?

La Belle et la Bête is a fairy-tale fantasy. What is more natural than that it should be told in a fantastic way? This is a point which has unfortunately not occurred to the producers of most of our films. How can the Bible stories or the wanderings of Ulysses or *Moby Dick* be filmed as if they had been written by Ibsen? Each image of *La Belle et la Bête* is framed for the viewer as the fable itself is framed in enchantment and wonder and lore. The camera-work in this beautiful film situates it in that area of imagination where we half believe the impossible, where metaphor is normal speech and miracle is a deeper truth than nature. (p. 17)

What exactly is the nature of the fantasy which is dramatized in *La Belle et la Bête*? A monster of abnormality wins a beautiful maiden. Cocteau's work is full of such monsters who eventually discover their own monstrosity. Self-knowledge he considers the height of moral beauty; hence it is not surprising that the monster, at the close of the film, becomes physically beautiful. Real beauty, in other words, is moral beauty and moral beauty is self-knowledge. This psychological process must of course be dramatized on the screen by a symbolic outward transformation.

This fable suggests to us, I think, the yearning of a man who has always secretly felt himself an exile from society and dramatizes his triumphant acceptance by society. At the same time it places this triumph in the impossible realm of fantasy. That is, Cocteau does not believe that the world will ever accept his personal morality; and perhaps he is right, for the world equates morality less with knowledge than with right action. (It might also be pointed out that the kind of self-knowledge that Cocteau proposes has a definitely Gidean ring—discovery and acceptance of one's total psychological diversity through the undifferentiated experience of life.)

The poetry of discontinuous images in this film is a product of a theory of lyric poetry which, as I have said, uses poetry as a means of evasion of responsibility. Poetry is a flight from and a substitute for action. But the theme of the film is itself an evasion of the real world and the facts of existence. It shows us the realization of a child's fantasy of reality. (p. 18)

Orphée, which is Cocteau's third poetic film, revives once more the theme of *Le Sang d'un poète*. Again we have a poet searching for the meaning of his vocation in the midst of love and death. The poet is more in love with Death . . . than with his wife, Eurydice; again it is implied that poetry brings us into contact with another world and that this other world is somehow more significant than the routine and responsibility of everyday life. (pp. 18-19)

Because *Orphée* is based explicitly on a myth it has more dramatic unity than *Le Sang d'un poète;* it is less of a poem and more of a plot. The question to be raised in regard to *Orphée* is this: does the story of Orpheus require such a special and distorted vision? Granted that we want to see this story as myth, are all the concomitants of motorcycles, mirrors, radios, etc., necessary to the mythic perspective?

Orphée is the poet and we have seen what Cocteau's special conception of the poet involves. The poet is a man who frees himself from the world by making images, by entering into an oneiric world where the freedom of language is equivalent to the freedom of action.

Most of the images of *Le Sang d'un poète* suggest confinement and enclosure—a room, a hotel corridor or the confinement of death. There is confinement in *Orphée* too, but there is also freedom. There are many more exterior shots, more movement. The poetry has become oriented, it has orchestrated itself upon a theme. That theme is, paradoxically, the absence of theme in life, the recognition of the dangers of involvement and the determination to flee them in the hall of mirrors which is pure poetry. The difference in the two films, the principle difference, is this recognition, this undoubtedly unconscious orientation by Cocteau towards his ultimate principle. We can call it "freedom" or "purity" as he does or by one of the less flattering terms used by his critics—"bad faith" or "sleight of hand" or "mystification." But here again, as in *La Belle et la Bête,* it must be conceded that the technique of the film is essential to its truth. Mirrors and motorcycles are its version of pure poetry. (p. 19)

The ultimate assessment of Cocteau's work is extremely difficult; perhaps it is enough that his films give a sharp and special pleasure, they can be and are seen over and over again. For they are poetry and that they be the ultimate in poetry is too much to ask. There have been few artists able to adapt the films to the expression of their own most intimate vision; and fewer still are able to narrow the gap between the profound intellectual concerns of literature and the filmy world of the screen. (pp. 19-20)

Neal Oxenhandler, "Poetry in Three Films of Jean Cocteau," in Yale French Studies *(copyright* © Yale French Studies *1956), No. 17, 1956, pp. 14-20.*

WILLIAM WHITEBAIT

Cocteau has been an innovator, a fashionable one, whose artificialities have always made him open to ridicule; and now that he's getting on, abuse yaps at his heels. But that's not to say that he has not been truly a poet and also that less definable thing a fascinator. His understanding of poetry has always had more than a touch of Chan Canasta. He dazzles with a few absurd props; he brings it off; how does he do it? We have been lured as by some perfect sleight of hand or feat on the high wire. An impossible lightness, a transparent charm, together with the situation to curdle one's blood, have set him apart from contemporaries: and so far as publicity goes, he has no more dined off it than Epstein. His last film, then, should ideally have completed the flourish from *Sang d'un Poète* to the present; and that includes at least two masterpieces, *Les Parents Terribles* and *Orphée*. The fact that it does not, that it's rather a post-script, an entertainment of galvanic old age, is the more pity. Peter Pan's black-sheep brother must spin odd fantasies about death and immortality.

There are in *Le Testament d'Orphée* . . . some inspired moments and for the first time, thinking no doubt of posterity and of Picasso's personal appearances, the Master himself plays the leading role of the Poet. He is out of time, appears, disappears, gets killed more than once, and lopes away on his young-old shanks to another day. Distinguished figure, but little more. Is he arraigned before Minerva and another, condemned of innocence and of battering his head against the world's walls? Does an adopted son lure him among gipsies? Does he stalk about quays and the crypts of Les Baux, where black horseheaded guards await him? The twists and turns, under the shadowing of death, are ingenious, disturbing. A torn-up flower is brought back to wholeness; but too many such reversal tricks have made us languid. In a notable scene the spear pierces him through: we know, only too well, he will prance again. It is Cocteau doing his act, even if it is his last act.

William Whitebait, "Aftermaths," in New Statesman *(© 1960 The Statesman & Nation Publishing Co. Ltd.), Vol. LIX, No. 1523, May 21, 1960, p. 753.**

PETER JOHN DYER

[The early scene between the old man and the black centaur] from *Le Testament d'Orphée* . . . communicates something of the sense of purpose and finality underlying the whole film. It is, in fact, Cocteau's swan-song, and completes a thirty-year-long obsessional cycle, from the manifesto of *Le Sang d'un Poète* and the actual execution of *Orphée* to the explication of *Le Testament d'Orphée*, with a shape and symmetry unique in the cinema. . . .

Though this labyrinth of dream associations, latent memories, myth and materialism (Cocteau's paintings and his film *Orphée*, as well as many of his friends, make appearances) is closest to *Le Sang d'un Poète* in pattern, it is considerably more successful. Familiarity and time have lent clarity to some of the symbols; others are disarmingly obvious—as Cocteau approaches Minerva, the disembodied voice of an air stewardess instructs him to fasten his safety-belt, and when a few seconds later he "dies", we hear the roar of jets. The stylistic problems involved in the use of the same subjective approach as the earlier film have also been largely by-passed. The material has been shaped into a considerable degree of dramatic unity . . . ; and though the spiritual strip-tease method of revelation remains very much a matter of personal taste and sympathy (not everyone, after all, longs to meet an *homme-cheval* on a lonely road), Cocteau now displays his fetishes with a wit and candour and darts of self-parody which are positively enchanting. (p. 143)

[The] impression one carries away from *Le Testament d'Orphée* is one of generosity, gaiety and lightness: the lightness of autumn leaves, the gaiety of an absurdly youthful old man, and the generosity of an artist who has at last found peace and contentment in the company of those who love him. (p. 144)

Peter John Dyer, "Film Reviews: 'Le Testament d'Orphée'," in Sight and Sound *(copyright © 1960 by The British Film Institute), Vol. 29, No. 3, Summer, 1960, pp. 143-44.*

ROGER MANVELL

[In *Le Testament d'Orphee* Cocteau] observes the continuity of a dream and not the logical pattern of a drama. [The film] therefore proceeds broadly from image to image and from symbol to symbol in its presentation of Cocteau's poetic concept of existence, and like his other personal films it is a most powerful demonstration of the cinema's technical capacity to project the world of the image created by the fluent but captive imagination of a poet, who claims to be pressing passionately against the cell-walls of the mind for the release his spirit demands.

Cocteau the poet confronts the creatures of his personal mythology in settings which occur not because they exist solidly in time and space (the bare studio stage, the cliff path above the sea, the crumbling but still colossal ruins), but because the atmosphere they successively create is appropriate to the symbolic action taking place within them. "The secret of poetry," says Cocteau, "is to take things from the places in which habit has set them and reveal them from a different angle as though we see them for the first time." He also states that the film itself is not a projection of a dream; it is "realist in so far as it depicts, with exactitude, the personal world of the artist." It gives, as he said once of *Orphee*, reality to the unreal. . . .

Cocteau's own work as a painter appears now and then in the background, and, as witnesses of friendship, Cocteau's more famous admirers, including Picasso and Yul Brynner, appear momentarily in the film. There is always the touch of showmanship in Cocteau's work, but, as he says, he resorts to the cinema in order to make contact with the world.

Whether Cocteau's images and symbols seem valid or not is a matter for each individual who sees the film to decide; for those to whom mythology no longer embodies imagery which remains relevant to mankind, *Le Testament d'Orphee* will no doubt appear little but dream-like decorations created in a mood of human decadence. But Cocteau's eye and ear are so well tuned to realising images corresponding to psychological states that he has in this and his other personal films revealed a form which extends the cinema still further into the virtually unexplored field of imagery and symbolism.

Roger Manvell, "New Films: 'Le Testament d'Orphee'" (© copyright Roger Manvell 1960; reprinted with permission), in Films and Filming, *Vol. 6, No. 10, July, 1960, p. 21.*

BOSLEY CROWTHER

It is hard to think of anybody (with the evident exception of Jean Cocteau) who, however egotistical he might be, would have the nerve to make a full-length film about himself. But M. Cocteau has done it. He has made a film all about Jean Cocteau in his "Testament of Orpheus". . . .

That is to say, he has made a picture about his own spiritual-esthetic search through a surrealist world of phantoms and symbols for the favor of the goddess of wisdom, Pallas Athene. . . .

[This] remarkable old show-off, who has done enough good things in his time to excuse a splurge of arrant narcissism in his declining years, has made a film that, for all its high pretension to being a symbolization of the poet's quest . . . , is really just a glorified home movie that should appeal mainly to the poet's admirers and friends.

Indeed, it is almost essential that one not only admire M. Cocteau but also be thoroughly familiar with his "Orpheus" . . . in order to get the least glimmer of what goes. For this "Testament of Orpheus" is in the nature of an explanation of (or possibly an excuse for) that previous film, constructed with so many references to it, as well as to various paintings and murals of the versatile artist, that one would be lost coming into it cold. . . .

This is all the clarification of the picture you are going to get from this critical source. M. Cocteau is much too far-out for our figuring.

[The] total "testament" is so completely and complexly intellectualized that its meaning is totally clear, we'll warrant, only to M. Cocteau. Nor does the graphic content of the picture so stimulate and fascinate the mind that it generates an emotional reaction. . . .

Bosley Crowther, "'Testament of Orpheus'," in The New York Times *(© 1962 by The New York Times Company; reprinted by permission), April 10, 1962, p. 48.*

ROY ARMES

The legend [dramatized in *La Belle et la Bête*] is handled in a variety of styles. The home life of Belle's family is parodied and is often broadly farcical in tone (as, for instance, in the use of cackling ducks to accompany the shots of Belle's two sisters). By contrast, the departure of Belle for the Beast's castle and her entry there are stylised, Cocteau employing slow motion photography to obtain a dreamlike effect. The fairytale world of the Beast's castle is given great solidity for Cocteau aimed at giving a "realism of the unreal" and it is arguable that in fact the setting has been given too much weight: there is a degree of ponderousness about the film which Georges Auric's music serves only to emphasise. In evoking the magical qualities of the castle Cocteau has made strangely little use of the film's trick shot possibilities; the living faces of the statuary and the disembodied human arms that act as the Beast's servants are essentially theatrical devices. One of the great difficulties facing Cocteau was that of making the oversimplified and unpersonalised figures of a fairytale into characters capable of sustaining interest in a film lasting some ninety minutes. The solution found for the minor characters was caricature and an often humorous approach. As far as the two principal characters are concerned, the make-up of . . . the Beast emphasises his bestial nature in a number of ways, as do such scenes as that of the Beast drinking and that where he scents game. But Belle remains a rather dull figure. . . . The film does, however, constantly open up odd perspectives—particularly through the ambiguities of Belle's attitude to the Beast. . . . (pp. 59-60)

[*Les Parents Terribles*] is a tragi-comedy of tangled family relationships, filled with melodramatic confrontations, incorporating deliberately shocking elements (incest and suicide) and a plot of vaudeville complexity. Cocteau has himself admirably defined his objectives in this film: "I had set out to do three things: firstly, record the acting of an incomparable cast; secondly, walk among them and look them straight in the face, instead of contemplating them at a distance on the stage; thirdly, peep through the keyhole and catch my wild beasts unawares with my tele-lens." (pp. 60-1)

Realising that his characters are monsters, inconceivable outside the closed walls of their apartment, Cocteau has limited himself to just two settings—the family home and Madeleine's flat. The combination of close-ups and non-naturalistic acting emphasises the intense theatricality which is so essential to the work. The exact sequence of speeches (with only a few tiny cuts) and the three act structure are also preserved from the play and nothing is done to make the plot more realistic. The film opens with a shot of a curtain rising to reveal the actors, and the plot follows a highly artificial pattern, opening and closing in the family apartment, beginning with a fake suicide and ending with a real one, and containing a succession of dramatic revelations and "coups de théâtre". (p. 61)

Orphée is a film set apart from the works of its time and inevitably its production involved numerous difficulties. It is an intensely personal work and its creator has described it as the orchestration of a theme which twenty years before, in *Le Sang d'un Poète*, he had played with one finger. The poet Orphée reflects Cocteau himself in many ways, adored by the public and hated by his fellow poets, even being admonished with the words: "Etonnez-Nous." Cocteau claims to have avoided symbolism and as with Resnais's *L'Année Dernière à Marienbad* it is doubtless naive to seek too exact an interpretation. The film embodies Cocteau's personal mythology and conception of the poet as an exceptional being who has a unique and intimate relationship with death. Eternally self-preoccupied, Cocteau regarded the myth of Orpheus as *his* myth, for he felt himself to be a man with one foot in life and the other in death. For him the conflict of life and death is not a contrast of light and darkness but a matter of degrees of greyness and twilight merging into one another. The boundaries between the two are never drawn with exactitude—the Princess comes to watch Orphée asleep and the poet moves from this world to the next without pain or anguish. For a work dealing so largely with death *Orphée* is remarkably idyllic in tone. There is no sense of terror here, for death is a beautiful princess who can return the poet's love. There is no sign of physical struggle or decay, for Orphée remains handsome in death and his love for the Princess is never expressed on a physical level. Nor has death any irrevocability or awesomeness: the dead can be revived and the servants of death are often bungling and inefficient.

It is on the level of its mythology that *Orphée* must be judged. In his handling of the film medium Cocteau remains an amateur in the best sense of the word. The film is not without its defects: the transitions of mood are not always adequately handled (the farcical comedy of Eurydice's return from the Zone sits oddly in the film), the integration of Aglaonice and the Bacchantes into the modernisation of the myth is poor, and the whole handling of Eurydice's pregnancy is very weak in its use of dialogue clichés and facile symbolism. But despite these blemishes *Orphée* is a most remarkable and independent work. . . . (p. 63)

[*La Testament d'Orphée*] is in many ways a summing up of [Cocteau's] whole career. . . . [He reveals in this film] to the greatest extent his delight in the conjuring possibilities of the cinema, the ability to move freely through time and space, or to perform (by means of reverse projection) such impossible feats as making a picture appear by rubbing it out or reassembling a shattered flower or creating a photograph from the flames. While the mythology of the film is sometimes obscure, there is no mistaking the poet's serenity and good nature, here emphasised by his own slightly awkward performance. (pp. 64-5)

Characteristic of Jean Cocteau's work, in the film and in the theatre, is the fusion of contrasting, even opposing elements. We find in his films a unique combination of the real and the unreal, seriousness and farce, personal obsession and antique myth. One of the reasons why Cocteau succeeded in creating an acceptable and absorbing fantasy world was his ability to make myth and reality intermingle. (p. 66)

Contrast and change are the recurring features of Cocteau's films. Never is one allowed to adopt a single way of looking or remain in one mood. In *La Belle et la Bête*, for instance, he adds farce and beauty, tragedy and trickery to the original ingredients of bestiality and love. Cocteau followed the same principle in his treatment of the music Georges Auric has composed for his films. He rejects the conventional approach: "Nothing seems to me more vulgar than musical synchronisation in films. It is a further pleonasm. . . . The only synchronisation that I like is accidental synchronisation, the effectiveness of which has been proved to me by innumerable examples." (p. 67)

It is doubtless futile to attempt a rational interpretation of the symbolism in Cocteau's films. His whole approach defies logical analysis and much of his imagery is based on personal symbolism and private associations. This is a closed world to which one must surrender totally or not at all. If one is not to regard his whole work as a mere charade one must accept Cocteau's conception of the poet as a supreme being, living outside time and in proximity to death. To be moved one must accept too Cocteau's eternal self-preoccupation and his idyllic conception of life. Though death is the central theme of all his major films there is no sense of conflict or suffering. . . . Death in Cocteau's world has no finality: the poet in *Le Sang d'un Poète* commits suicide twice, Orphée is returned to life and humdrum happiness after being shot, Cocteau in *Le Testament d'Orphée* is raised from the dead after being slain by Minerva. All this is possible because the world of Cocteau is that of the dream. He has spoken of the importance of dreams in his life: "I begin to live intensely only when asleep and dreaming. My dreams are detailed and terribly realistic." Cocteau's films, for all their unevenness and reticence, are the cinema's most sustained attempt at capturing the reality of this unreal world. (pp. 67-8)

Roy Armes, "Jean Cocteau," in his French Cinema since 1946: The Great Tradition, Vol. I *(copyright © 1966 by Roy Armes), A. S. Barnes & Co., 1966, pp. 58-68.*

GEORGE AMBERG

Though unadmitted, *The Testament of Orpheus* has far greater ambitions and implications than its modest format indicates. And in this resides its particular significance. (p. 23)

Testament is too deliberate and lucid a work to be dismissed as an old man's self-indulgent gratification—as many critics chose to do. Wanting or capricious though it may be, *Testament* is neither pointless nor irrational and, least of all, senile. To the extent that this controversial film fails, as it ultimately does, it is for nobler reasons than pretentiousness, incompetence or declining power. . . .

[It] is not only one of the great confessional documents of our time but probably *the* most original and audacious. The question remains, however, whether it has a chance to survive on its inherent merit, with the answer depending on the position one adopts toward the film as primarily a work of art or a poet's self-portrait. Of course, it is both at once, with the aesthetic and the private, the subjective and the objective so intimately intermingled that the poet himself got caught in the trap of ambivalences. In the Preface to the book edition of *The Testament of Orpheus,* Cocteau remarks that the filmis "possibly the first attempt of a transmutation of verbs into actions; of an organization of actions in the place of an organization of words, in a poem; of a syntax of images instead of a story accompanied by language." . . . Why does the poet, from the vantage point of his advanced age, make the claim of novelty for his last work rather than for *Orpheus,* the prototype of the poetic film and the model of an "organization of actions?" Why does the creator of *Blood of a Poet* consider this retrospective and nostalgic treatment of his favorite subject a first attempt, whereas it is so obviously intended to be the last and final one? Why does he disregard *The Eternal Return* and *Beauty and the Beast,* two films that are respectively visual embodiments of the poetic myth and the poetic fable rather than "stories accompanied by language?" If *Testament* is taken as lightly as it appears or pretends to be, these questions are confounding. There is good reason to believe, though, that Cocteau is guilty of a canny deception in that this seemingly slender work actually masks a confessional document of great personal import.

Testament is ostensibly nothing but a candid and informal autobiography, composed of loosely connected incidents literally referring to the author's past, his work, his friends and associates, as well as to things and places remembered. He wants his readers and viewers to believe that he produced the film as an unpremeditated venture, "without expecting anything else from it but the deep pleasure derived from making it." . . . The ease and candor he professes, however, only thinly disguise the urgency of his true endeavor, which is to establish *the authentic public image* by which he hopes to be remembered. That, essentially, is the legacy contained in this cinematic treatment, its "resurrectional" message and purpose, which is furthermore confirmed by the "phenixological" poem that precedes the printed scenario. Cocteau might well have proclaimed, with Camus' *Caligula,* "I do not have to make a work of art; I live it." Only, in this case, it implies less hubris than total self-obsession. (p. 24)

In 1932, Cocteau delivered an address in which he opens up new vistas of the poetic cinema: "With the film, death is killed, literature is killed, poetry is made to live a direct life. Imagine what the cinema of the future might be." At this point, it is important to appreciate that *Testament* is not a poetic film in any conventional sense, its subject notwithstanding. More accurately, it amounts almost to a lecture-demonstration, with the poet candidly explaining what it means to be a poet, why he is perennially on trial and "condemned to live," why he is fated to die "invisibly" as well as assured to be resurrected. Even more specifically, *Testament* tells us not only what it means to be a poet but what it means to be the poet Jean Cocteau. As a source of information, the film is probably more self-revealing than any other of his literary or cinematic works, and quite possibly beyond its author's actual intentions. While portraying the poet Cocteau, the film author Cocteau refrains, even more rigorously than in *Orpheus,* from dwelling on lyrical mood or evocative imagery. No sooner has he created a poetic atmosphere, or established a fictional illusion, than he destroys or subverts it. . . . If Pirandello created characters in search of an author, Cocteau may be said to have created an author in search of a character. . . . Cocteau's own method . . . consists in exposing one illusion as a deception while simultaneously authenticating another, equally artificial one. He resembles a prestidigitator pretending to reveal his trick in order to divert the spectator's attention from the decisive one he wants to bring off. In *Orpheus,* the realistic and illusory spheres are clearly separated, each one representing its own valid realm of existence; in *Testament,* they are so inextricably interwoven that the poet loses control and, consequently, the viewer loses his rational bearings. (p. 25)

There would be no doubt in Cocteau's own mind that *Testament* is a poetic film, by the same token as *Blood of a Poet,* which he claimed to be "completely indifferent to what the world considers *poetic.*" Cocteau, it must be remembered, conceived of poetry not so much as a medium of spontaneous or intuitive expression than as of a means of revealing "the design and detail of images emerging from the profound night of the human body." They are called upon to represent at once internal and external reality, neither of which admits or recognizes its limitations. These poetic images, the poet insists, "have no recourses to either dreams or symbols"; rather, they represent different stages of consciousness, an assumption the poet would presumably refute. It is evident again that poetry, for Cocteau, is functional and instrumental. *Testament,* like *Blood of a Poet* thirty years previously, provides "a vehicle for poetry which may or may not serve its purpose." This reservation exonerates the poet conveniently of all poetic conventions and obligations, allowing him ample leeway for alternating freely between extremes: exact realism or pure fantasy, direct representation or allegorical transformation. "Still, this contempt for the rules does not go without a contempt for the danger that excites a great many souls." Surely the poet is aware that he is skating on perilously thin premises. . . . [The] two films are not only thematically related; they also pursue similar ends. But while premises and objectives are identical, the execution is radically dissimilar. It is not a facile play of words, but relevant to the nature of the works, to suggest that Cocteau's description of *Blood of a Poet,* as "a realistic documentary of unreal events," may be reversed to read an unrealistic documentary of real events for *Testament.* The distinctive quality of *Blood of a Poet* resided in the discovery of visual equivalents for traditional verbal poetry. It unwinds on the screen "like a band of allegories." The unique quality of *Testament* is neither cine-poetry nor, certainly, its consciously manipulated artistry (which tends to be precious), but its implicit self-revelation which is genuine—in fact intense and anxious. . . .

In *Testament* it is virtually impossible to distinguish between symbols, allegories and metaphors because of their constant interaction. There is, however, the unmistakable symbol of the Hibiscus flower which the poet carries through the whole film, which he calls the film's "true star". . . . As is so often the case, and consistent with Cocteau's stated principles, his treatment is rather too literal and explicit to be called symbolic. His pictorial style, in spite of its imagination and elaboration, is essentially descriptive. For instance, when Cocteau encounters himself in one of *Testament*'s key episodes, he observes uneasily that the other self pretends not to see him, while his companion comments that "he probably goes whence you came and you go whence he comes." He is seeking himself, finding himself and disavowing himself all at once in one brief scene which is both admirably suggestive and thoroughly cinematic. At this instant it becomes evident that the *film* itself, the tangible image on the screen, is the point of encounter, of the meeting or the clash of illusion with illusion as well as of illusion with reality. It is noteworthy that the encounter does not occur in either a conceptual or a metaphysical point, as it might in verbal poetry, but in a concrete point in time and space. . . .

Cocteau submits that "*The Testament of Orpheus* is nothing but a machine to fabricate meanings [*significations*]." Does he mean to suggest that nothing is to be taken literally, in fact that nothing is what it seems to be? If so, it would follow that Cocteau does not signify Cocteau, or Picasso not Picasso, which is patently absurd and surely not what the author has in mind. The assumption is, of course, that he is in complete control of the machine, hence also of the meanings he intends to fabricate. *Testament* proves his thesis wrong. As an artist, a maker of images, Cocteau relies on the fact that every image, including his own, is other than the original to which it refers. And yet, while every object is physically changed when transformed from one mode of existence into another, it becomes not automatically endowed with transcendent meaning, or indeed any meaning. This is Cocteau's error and the origin of a critical ambiguity in the film's concept. Minerva, the Idol, the Sphinx function on one level of meaning; the Princess and Heurtebise on another; Cégeste on yet another; Oedipus intrudes from the dramatic stage; Picasso and Aznavour are private visitors, while Cocteau himself remains altogether himself. The result is not a new poetic order but confusion and disorientation. (p. 26)

We should be wary, though, of judging anything in *Testament* as arbitrary or irrelevant, since the object and intent of the work are not lost out of Cocteau's sight for one single instant. . . . In *Cocteau On Film,* he confesses that "a film, whatever it may be, is always its director's portrait." That this portrait is not a metaphorical term for personal style, but a likeness of its creator, is affirmed in *Testament.* As Cocteau attempts to draw the Hibiscus flower, it keeps assuming the traits of his own face. . . . It is fitting to quote a statement from *Blood of the Poet* . . . : "I shall not conceal from you the fact that I have used tricks to make poetry visible and audible." In spite of this assertion, however, it is not so much poetry he makes visible as himself. His posthumous concern is blatantly evident. Lest there remain any doubt whatever, he even makes us, and his personal friends, witness his death and resurrection. He states, and elaborately stages, what Yeats put simply: "The tree must die before it can be made into a cross." All the evidence points to one inescapable conclusion: if everything we witness and observe contributes to the emerging self-portrait, the meaning of *Testament* becomes unequivocally clear. It fits the words of Jean Genet—"a true image born of a false spectacle." (pp. 26-7)

George Amberg, "The Testament of Jean Cocteau," in Film Comment *(copyright © 1971 Film Comment Publishing Corporation; all rights reserved), Vol. 7, No. 4, Winter, 1971-72, pp. 23-7.*

Francis Ford Coppola

1933-

American director, producer, and scriptwriter.

Along with George Lucas and Steven Spielberg, among others, Coppola established the reputation of the textbook filmmakers. He is also a producer and the head of Omni Zoetrope (formerly American Zoetrope), a studio he started in 1969 to help young filmmakers produce their work.

Trained in film at the University of California at Los Angeles, Coppola worked with Roger Corman as an assistant director and writer. Corman offered him his first opportunity to direct on *Dementia 13*. But *Dementia 13* was not well received and his next film, *You're a Big Boy Now,* was overshadowed by Mike Nichols's *The Graduate,* released at the same time as Coppola's film. In retrospect, many critics find *You're a Big Boy Now* a fresh, zany look at the disillusionment and the joys of growing up.

In 1968, Coppola directed his first—and perhaps his last—musical. His version of *Finian's Rainbow* was released, amidst a barrage of negative reviews. All during production, Coppola was plagued by the problems of an inexperienced filmmaker attempting to create a large-scale musical. Warner Brothers, however, dealt the death blow. The studio, sure of the film's success, expanded the 35mm print to 70mm to give it the aura of a grandiose musical. In the process, however, Fred Astaire's feet were cut off the bottom of the screen. When his next film, *The Rain People,* received a lukewarm critical reception, Coppola's future looked questionable.

The brilliant success of Coppola's adaptation of Mario Puzo's novel *The Godfather* established Coppola in the film world. While *Part I* was in production, Coppola fought for three things: Marlon Brando for the part of Don Corleone, Al Pacino for the part of Michael Corleone, and the adaptation of the film as a period piece rather than setting it in the present. Because of these aspects of the film, among others, Coppola transformed what some considered a strictly sensational novel into an epic of family loyalty within the world of organized crime.

Coppola's most recent project, *Apocalypse Now,* has become as notorious as it is famous. Stories of the difficulties of production and the skyrocketing costs have given the film an aura of unbridled extravagance. For many critics, this has detracted from the film and jaded their perception of it. In *The Movie Brats* Michael Pye and Lynda Myles have said of Coppola: "[There is] a fatal flaw that eats at Coppola's filmmaking. He makes appropriate noises to hearten his liberal constituency . . . and then concentrates on performance, style, and rhythm. His skills do not present the message he says he intends." The critical response to *Apocalypse Now* echoes this view. Most critics find it lush, overwhelmingly beautiful, spectacular . . . and empty. (See also *Contemporary Authors,* Vols. 77-80.)

ALLEN EYLES

The horror story is heavily red-herringed and none too credible, and [*The Haunted and the Hunted, or Dementia 13*] doesn't escape looking a bit of a quickie. But the director, Francis Coppola, has confidently assembled the film and given it a sharp sense of atmosphere. It lacks polish but its ideas are right.

Allen Eyles, "The New Films: 'The Haunted and the Hunted'" (© copyright Allen Eyles 1965; reprinted with permission), in Films and Filming, *Vol. 11, No. 6, March, 1965, p. 35.*

STEPHEN FARBER

[In *You're a Big Boy Now*] Coppola shows a fine feeling for New York's grimy excitement, especially in a sequence in which his young hero peeps in and out of porny book stores and amusement parlors on 42nd Street; the *cinéma-vérité* casualness, bouncy editing, and Lovin' Spoonful music nicely render the city's exuberance without skimming its sordidness. The story, what little there is, concerns a boy's effort to break the complicated parental bonds (his ambivalent feelings toward his father are suggested by his chronic inability to decide what to call him) and discover sex. It is not the freshest idea in the world, but Coppola has enlivened it with amusing details. . . . Coppola's invention and energy run down about halfway through the movie, and he tries to recover with an arch, frantic slapstick chase. (The rediscovery of Mack Sennett has been one of the most disastrous influences on comedy of the last few years.) In addition, most of the movie, even the funny parts, looks cute rather than true; Coppola seems to have had a good time making it without being really committed to it. There are a few scenes which are much more urgent—those with a tough and vicious dancer named Barbara Darling, especially a brilliant discotheque scene whose psychedelic light effects exaggerate Barbara's body movements to gargantuan, overpowering twitches, and a chilling seduction scene in which she arouses the hero almost to orgasm and then crawls into bed and tells him to go away. In these scenes Coppola makes the aphrodisiac function of rock music clearer than ever, and he creates a truly intense, only superficially comic mood of sexual nightmare that, unlike the rest of the movie, cannot be dismissed as merely larky. These moments are enough to confirm that Coppola is a director worth watching. . . .

Stephen Farber, "Entertainments: 'You're a Big Boy Now'," in Film Quarterly *(copyright 1967 by The Regents of the University of California; reprinted by permission of the University of California Press), Vol. XX, No. 4, Summer, 1967, p. 80.*

RENATA ADLER

There is something awfully depressing about seeing "Finian's Rainbow" this year this way. . . .

It is not just that the musical is dated. Something lovely and nostalgic could have been made out of old Missitucky for the generation that grew up on "Finian's Rainbow" and "Brigadoon." It is that it has been done listlessly and even tastelessly, with quick updatings of Negro personalities to match what people who have lived in Beverly Hills too long must imagine modern black sensibilities are. The cast is full of children who act as artificially and insincerely as the whole enterprise, directed by Francis Ford Coppola, would suggest. . . .

[The whole story] has just gone dim, as though nobody had troubled with it—hoping only to sell it to television as a family musical and get it over with.

Renata Adler, "'Finian's Rainbow'," in The New York Times *(© 1968 by The New York Times Company; reprinted by permission), October 10, 1968, p. 59.*

TOM MILNE

Anyone who refused to abandon himself to the pleasure pure and simple of such films as *French Cancan* or *Silk Stockings* had better give *Finian's Rainbow* . . . a miss. Like Renoir with his rosily moonlit Butte de Montmartre, or Mamoulian with his Paris which loves lovers, Francis Ford Coppola has created a dream world, half-fact, half-fantasy, and all enchantment: a rural paradise reached by way of the Brooklyn Bridge, Mount Rushmore and the Mississippi riverboats, but unquestionably at the end of the rainbow in a never-never America where true love and simple faith conquer all obstacles.

Schmaltz? . . . [The] point is that *Finian's Rainbow* is all of a piece, and like all the best musicals, transmits its feelings not by words or even deeds, but by movement. And the *movement* of the film is pure exhilaration, without trace of schmaltz or whimsy. . . .

Movement, in fact, is quintessential to *Finian's Rainbow* (which is as it should be), not only in the musical numbers but in the whole structure of the film. Somehow Coppola manages to give the impression that his characters are not merely involved by ones, twos and threes in individual songs and dances, but are all caught up in one vast, informal musical number which is the film itself. His secret seems to lie partly in the way he choreographs the action beyond the limits of the frame, and partly in the impeccable rhythms of his curiously fragmented technique. (p. 43)

[There is] effortless choreographic flow and overall rhythm that hasn't been seen in the cinema since *Summer Holiday* and *Silk Stockings*—and allows one to hope that Coppola can and will take over the Mamoulian mantle. . . .

Finian's Rainbow is a stunning piece of cinema. I loved every minute of it. (p. 44)

Tom Milne, "Film Reviews: 'Finian's Rainbow'," in Sight and Sound *(copyright © 1968 by The British Film Institute), Vol. 38, No. 1, Winter, 1968-69, pp. 43-4.*

STEPHEN FARBER

[It] cannot be quite coincidental that *The Rain People* . . . concerns a journey across America. . . . This film, like *Midnight Cowboy* and *Easy Rider*, certainly depends for part of its meaning on American myths of freedom on the open road, our traditional belief in the journey away from civilization as a source of refreshment and renewal. The very first traveling shot of the countryside has an exhilarating sweep and romanticism; the land itself tempts us to believe that Natalie will find on her journey the insight into herself that will redeem her future. But *The Rain People* sees the general and the mythical *through* the individual. Although it contains a genuine responsiveness to some of the beauties and horrors of today's Midwest, it never claims to present a major statement about contemporary America.

Interestingly enough, one of the movie's failures is that it is *not* specific enough about contemporary society. Because it never ties its heroine to her period, the film loses its grip on her. We never learn enough about Natalie's background, the New York milieu that oppresses her. It is important to know, for example, whether she's an educated, intellectual woman or simply an average American housewife. . . . What is she running from exactly? What is she running *towards?* We don't expect her to have well-defined answers, but we do expect to get some idea of what qualities in her are frustrated by marriage, family, suburbia, what she hopes to find on her own. . . . By cutting her free from her time and her specialized milieu and making her a "universal" character, Coppola loses the intensity of her dilemma, fails to dramatize the tension between her maternal, domestic instincts and her more personal needs.

But Coppola's own ambivalence toward this woman cuts very deep and is probably ultimately responsible for his omission of the requisite background material. (pp. 13-14)

The real confusion in the film is not in Natalie, but in Coppola's *attitude* toward Natalie; his vision of her wavers between passionate sympathy and terrified hostility and revulsion—an oscillation that is apparent simply in the *visual* treatment of the character. . . . Coppola's feelings are out of control. He is frightened of Natalie's excesses, of her potential destructiveness, and as the film goes on, he judges her more and more harshly for abandoning her marital responsibilities. He seems to want to say that a woman's natural role is her domestic role, and that if she tries to deny her "nature," she will hurt herself and other people. So it becomes understandable why he never explores Natalie's background or the alternative to domestic life that she is seeking; if he got too close to her, it might complicate and undermine his moral position. Fortunately, the schizophrenia of the film—Coppola's irrespressible responsiveness to Natalie—keeps it from turning pat or unpleasantly moralistic. (pp. 14-15)

Coppola offers the kind of qualification to the frontier myth that *Easy Rider* and *Midnight Cowboy* dwell on—the land itself is no longer pure, it is blighted by poverty, greed, desperation, hate. But his most searching criticism of the myth is his questioning of the *value* of freedom. To some extent one has to respect Coppola's skepticism about Natalie's unexamined faith in the westward journey as elixir. The grotesque scenes of Natalie putting on her make-up can perhaps be understood as Coppola's bitter parody of sexual and emotional freedom. "Freedom" can really be callous, cruel, destructive. And the lyrical shots of the countryside thus take on an especially ironic meaning in this film; we have to test our thrilled response to these romantic images against our growing realization that the dream of freedom—even if contemporary America would allow its fulfilment—is itself inadequate, for it denies other, richer possibilities and responsibilities in human relationships. Coppola has not quite successfully dramatized the full complexity of that theme, but his attempt is a fundamental criticism of American myths. . . . (p. 15)

In *You're A Big Boy Now,* there were traces of intensely personal material in the handling of the man-hating bitch Barbara Darling, and in the recurring images of sex as an engulfing experience and women as devourers—images charged with highly ambivalent feelings. But that personal material was almost lost in a superficial, tricky, and familiar film about an adolescent breaking free. In *The Rain People* Coppola's ambivalence toward women has taken the center of the screen, and he has explored his conflicting feelings in much greater depth, until finally the exploration becomes too painful, and Coppola drops his heroine for a series of safer, more manageable, still moderately interesting subordinate character sketches. (p. 16)

Stephen Farber, "End of the Road?" in Film Quarterly *(copyright 1969 by The Regents of the University of California), Vol. XXIII, No. 2, Winter, 1969-70, pp. 3-16.**

PAULINE KAEL

If ever there was a great example of how the best popular movies come out of a merger of commerce and art, *The Godfather* is it. The movie starts from a trash novel that is generally considered gripping and compulsively readable, though (maybe because movies more than satisfy my appetite for trash) I found it unreadable. . . . Francis Ford Coppola, who directed the film, and wrote the script with Puzo, has stayed very close to the book's greased-lightning sensationalism and yet has made a movie with the spaciousness and strength that popular novels such as Dickens' used to have. . . . Puzo's shameless turn-on probably left Coppola looser than if he had been dealing with a better book; he could not have been cramped by worries about how best to convey its style. . . . He has salvaged Puzo's energy and lent the narrative dignity. Given the circumstances and the rush to complete the film and bring it to market, Coppola has not only done his best but pushed himself farther than he may realize. The movie is on the heroic scale of earlier pictures on broad themes, such as *On the Waterfront, From Here to Eternity,* and *The Nun's Story*. It offers a wide, startlingly vivid view of a Mafia dynasty. The abundance is from the book; the quality of feeling is Coppola's.

The beginning is set late in the summer of 1945; the film's roots, however, are in the gangster films of the early thirties. . . . We see the ethnic subculture, based on a split between the men's conception of their responsibilities—all that they keep dark—and the sunny false Eden in which they try to shelter the women and children. The thirties films indicated some of this, but *The Godfather* gets into it at the primary level; the willingness to be basic and the attempt to understand the basic, to look at it without the usual preconceptions, are what give this picture its epic strength.

The visual scheme is based on the most obvious life-and-death contrasts; the men meet and conduct their business in deep-toned, shuttered rooms, lighted by lamps even in the daytime, and the story moves back and forth between this hidden, nocturnal world and the sunshine that they share with the women and children. . . . The dark-and-light contrast is so operatic and so openly symbolic that it perfectly expresses the basic nature of the material. The contrast is integral to the Catholic background of the characters: innocence versus knowledge—knowledge in this sense being the same as guilt. . . . The killing, connived at in the darkness, is the secret horror, and it surfaces in one bloody outburst after another. It surfaces so often that after a while it doesn't surprise us, and the recognition that the killing is an integral part of business policy takes us a long way from the fantasy outlaws of old movies. These gangsters don't satisfy our adventurous fantasies of disobeying the law; they're not defiant, they're furtive and submissive. They are required to be more obedient than we are; they live by taking orders. There is no one on the screen we can identify with—unless we take a fancy to the pearly teeth of one shark in a pool of sharks.

Even when the plot strands go slack about two-thirds of the way through, and the passage of a few years leaves us in doubt whether certain actions have been concluded or postponed, the picture doesn't become softheaded. The direction is tenaciously intelligent. Coppola holds on and pulls it all together. (pp. 420-22)

The people dress in character and live in character—with just the gewgaws that seem right for them. The period details are there . . . but Coppola doesn't turn the viewer into a guided tourist, told what to see. . . . *The Godfather* keeps so much in front of us all the time that we're never bored (though the picture runs just two minutes short of three hours)—we keep taking things in. This is a heritage from Jean Renoir—this uncoercive, "open" approach to the movie frame. Like Renoir, Coppola lets the spectator roam around in the images, lets a movie breathe, and this is extremely difficult in a period film, in which every detail must be carefully planted. But the details never look planted: you're a few minutes into the movie before you're fully conscious that it's set in the past. (pp. 424-25)

When a film has as much novelistic detail as this one, the problem might seem to be almost insuperable. Yet, full as it is, *The Godfather* goes by evenly, so we don't feel rushed, or restless, either; there's classic grandeur to the narrative flow. But Coppola's attitudes are specifically modern—more so than in many films with a more jagged surface. Renoir's openness is an expression of an almost pagan love of people and landscape; his style is an embrace. Coppola's openness is a reflection of an exploratory sense of complexity; he doesn't feel the need to comment on what he shows us, and he doesn't want to reduce the meanings in a shot by pushing us this way or that. The assumption behind this film is that complexity will engage the audience.

These gangsters *like* their life style, while we—seeing it from the outside—are appalled. If the movie gangster once did represent, as Robert Warshow suggested in the late forties, "what we want to be and what we are afraid we may become," if he expressed "that part of the American psyche which rejects the qualities and the demands of modern life, which rejects 'Americanism' itself," that was the attitude of another era. In *The Godfather* we see organized crime as an obscene symbolic extension of free enterprise and government policy, an extension of the worst in America—its feudal ruthlessness. Organized crime is not a rejection of Americanism, it's what we fear Americanism to be. It's our nightmare of the American system. . . . *The Godfather* is popular melodrama, but it expresses a new tragic realism. (pp. 425-26)

Pauline Kael, "Alchemy" (originally published in The New Yorker, *Vol. XLVIII, No. 4, March 18, 1972), in her* Deeper Into Movies *(copyright © 1972 by Pauline Kael; reprinted by permission of Little, Brown and Company in association with the Atlantic Monthly Press), Atlantic-Little, Brown, 1973, pp. 420-26.*

STANLEY KAUFFMANN

Hurricane Marlon is sweeping the country, and I wish it were more than hot air. A tornado of praise—cover stories and huzzahs—blasts out the news that Brando is giving a marvelous performance as Don Corleone in *The Godfather*. . . .

But from his opening line, with his back toward us, Brando betrays that he hasn't even got the man's voice under control. (p. 104)

Like star, like film. The keynote is inflation. Because the picture has so much of the commonplace, it escapes being called commonplace. In no important way is it any better than *The Brotherhood* (1968), on the same subject. (The word Mafia is never mentioned, but it doesn't need to be.) *The Godfather* was made from a big best-seller, a lot of money was spent on it, and it runs over three hours. Therefore it's significant.

We're getting the usual flood of comments that the Mafia is only mirror-image corporate capitalism. (All the killings in the film are said to be "business, not personal.") These high-school analogies ignore, among other things, the origins of the Mafia and its blood-bonds of loyalty, which have nothing to do with capitalism. Almost every one in *The Godfather* is either a murderer or an accessory, so its moral center depends on inner consistency and on implicit contrast with non-murdering citizens around it. As the picture winds on and on, episode after episode, its only real change is the Mafia's shift from "nice" gambling and prostitution to take on "dirty" narcotics. (Time, the late 1940's.) Well, I suppose everything's going to hell, even the morality of the Mafia, but the picture certainly takes a long, long time to get there. (p. 105)

Stanley Kauffmann, "'The Godfather'" (originally published in The New Republic, *Vol. 166, No. 14, April 1, 1972), in his* Living Images: Film Comment and Criticism *(copyright © 1971, 1972, 1973, 1974 by Stanley Kauffmann; reprinted by permission of Harper & Row, Publishers, Inc.), Harper, 1975, pp. 104-05.*

ROBERT HATCH

Among other things, *The Godfather* is a strongly nostalgic film. Its period is post-World War II, but its flavor is of at least a decade earlier—it is a "big" picture, a Hollywood extravaganza of the sort that used to bring out the truck-mounted searchlights on opening night and the stars fluttering from autograph book to autograph book. . . .

But that said, the success of *The Godfather* is deplorable, if you believe that popular entertainment both reflects and modifies social morale. In a sentence, the picture forces you to take sides, to form allegiances, in a situation that is totally without moral substance. . . .

The authors of this film would say that they do not pander to vice, and I would agree at least that they do not intend to. They describe the society of Sicilian crime in America in the bleakest possible terms. . . .

In this respect, *The Godfather* is probably more scrupulous than the classic gangster films of the Muni, Raft, Cagney era. But it is also more persuasively internalized than I remember those movies to have been. It is not a view of crime but a view from deep within crime. . . . There is no one in the picture to provide a bench mark of normality. . . . Nor is this the theatre of ideas. . . . Coppola has created a work that is extraordinary for the thick, sickish luxury of its texture and weak in narrative organization. (p. 442)

Michael is the character that best exemplifies the moral queasiness of the whole venture. . . . What the film overlooks, or at least studiously refrains from showing, in Michael's metamorphosis from modest war hero to reptilian gang chief, is that there is a purpose behind all the plotting and killing: it is to determine which gang of Sicilians shall have the right to suck the life out of an unsuspecting public. The film is mad, but at the end, so is the audience. (p. 444)

Robert Hatch, "Films," in The Nation *(copyright 1972 The Nation Associates, Inc.), Vol. 214, No. 14, April 3, 1972, pp. 442-45.*

WILLIAM S. PECHTER

The Godfather is an incontrovertible demonstration of the continued vitality and artistic power of two things in films whose resources had increasingly been thought to be exhausted: of densely plotted, linear narrative, and of naturalism—social observation and the accumulation of authenticating detail—as a method. And it possesses, moreover, that special excitement and authority available to a film which is both a work of artistic seriousness and one of truly popular appeal, a mass entertainment made without pandering or condescension.

The Godfather is all these things and more, with such immense skill and assurance that I feel almost impatient with my own inability to enjoy it more, to escape some nagging dissatisfaction. The basis of that dissatisfaction is perhaps best expressed by the compliment which has been paid to the film by one of its many admirers: that it is the "*Gone with the Wind* of gangster films." . . . But it is in its attempt at definitiveness in relation to its antecedents in a genre—as a gangster film among other gangster films—that my reservations about *The Godfather* chiefly lie. And despite all the novelty of its variations on familiar material, it is primarily as a genre movie that I see it. . . . (p. 88)

At least, I'm far from prepared, as one who has watched (and shared) the responses of an audience as it assents to the killings by the Corleone family in *The Godfather,* to say that the appeal of the gangster in popular art has become one in which sadism no longer plays an important part. . . .

The effect of stressing that the Corleones are in business, but limiting our view of their business to the expansion and consolidation of their power by their liquidation of the opposition, is to create probably the most consistent depiction of business-*as*-murder since *Monsieur Verdoux.* But despite this, and despite the film's sporadic gestures toward extending its trope of business-as-murder into the political sphere—the allusions to the Kennedys, to Lyndon Johnson (a meeting of rival mobs commenced with a sentiment about "reasoning together"), the remark by Michael, Don Corleone's heir, to his fiancée that she is being naive in saying the power of the Corleones is to be distinguished from that of Senators and Presidents because the latter do not kill people—it is not primarily in their aspect of businessmen that we see the gangsters in *The Godfather.* Rather—and one sees here the inadvertent felicity of the notorious expunging of all mention of the word "Mafia" in the film—it is as members of a "family": as godfather, father, grandparent, son, and brother. (p. 89)

What is this family whose claims override all others in *The Godfather?* It is, for one thing, a patriarchy, and the story the film has to tell is basically not Don Corleone's but Michael's: a story of his initiation into the family by an act of murder, of the succession of the youngest, most assimilated son to the patriarchal powers and responsibilities and the ethnic mystique of his father. . . . But is *The Godfather* an unambiguous celebration of this family? For a time, while its members are barricaded together from their enemies under the interim reign of Michael's brother, Sonny, there is, even in the sweaty, suffocating togetherness of their confinement, a real sense of *Gemütlichkeit.* But Sonny is a false godfather: hot-headed, bellicose, given to acting impetuously on his feelings without letting the family's interests temper his personal pride; he is, in the classic generic mold, an overreacher. . . . Under Don Corleone and, later, under Michael, what we are aware of instead is a large house whose dark interiors convey no sense of spaciousness, a feudal deference to rank and the lordly granting of dispensations, the suppression of dissent (so as not to give aid and comfort to the family's enemies), and a foundation of blasphemous hypocrisy. . . . (pp. 89-90)

Coppola at one time described his work on *The Godfather* as a commercial chore, distinguishable from his direction of a "personal" film like *The Rain People,* and yet, when one thinks back to *The Rain People*'s ambiguous sense of family life as something whose responsibilities, however burdensome, could not be simply left behind, it almost seems that *The Godfather* is a film the director was fated to make. . . .

What *The Godfather* does is to literalize this similarity: the gang's chieftain is no longer *like* a patriarch, he *is* a patriarch; the gang no longer resembles a family but has become one, and not just one more fragmented family among others but virtually the realization of that ideal of the nuclear, fortresslike family. . . . But is this image of *gangsters* as the fulfillment and embodiment of our discarded ideals—as the family next door in the 40's—a *celebration* of the values of which those ideals consist? I think it is rather more like a criticism of them, but a criticism of a peculiarly bland and muffled kind, a criticism to be found less in the content of the film than in the phenomenon of our response to it: in our ability to accept gangsters as embodiments of such values. *Within* the film, the ambiguity of its celebration of family life is never violated. . . . [The] effect of domesticating the genre in this way is less to subject familial values to a criticism than to strip the gangster of his mythic dimension and his tragic meaning for us: to convert him into only one more of those "good husbands and fathers" so familiar to us from the crimes of bureaucrats and obedient soldiers. . . . But at its best . . . the effect of the gangster genre was to press us to a recognition of the source in us of the gangster's disturbing hold on our imaginations. What are we that in this outsize, driven figure and his terrible excesses we can see an image, however extravagant and distorted, of ourselves? (p. 90)

William S. Pechter, "Keeping Up with the Corleones" (copyright © 1972 by William S. Pechter; reprinted by permission of the author), in Commentary, *Vol. 54, No. 1, July, 1972, pp. 88-90 (and to be reprinted in his* Movies plus One, *Horizon Press, 1981).*

STEPHEN FARBER

In *The Godfather* Coppola has almost reconciled the artistic and commercial impulses in his work. It is a spectacular that isn't vulgar or overblown or contemptuous of the audience; on the contrary, it seems smaller than it is—always thoughtful, often intimate, with a depth of feeling in its portrait of Italian family life that must grow from understanding and firsthand experience. Coppola has not sacrificed the quiet perception that he brought to *The Rain People,* but this time he has a strong narrative line to give the film dramatic momentum.

Considering the limitations of the material, it is remarkable how much social commentary Coppola manages to introduce. . . .

The Corleones would in fact be difficult to distinguish from many respectable immigrant families. Their goals of material success are certainly estimable; the godfather is a perfect example of the American self-made man. The film plays up the contrast between the ruthless business ethics of the mafiosi, and the warmth and banality of their home lives. . . .

[One] reason for the enduring power of the Mafia is that families like the Corleones operate under a more primitive code of justice and retribution than American society allows; they invest their work with Old World passion. . . . The Mafia brings a barbaric ferocity into American life, and satisfies the repressed but universal lust for revenge.

Here . . . the commentary on American history is provocative. The immigrant generation that struggled for a footing in America may have been ruthless and materialistic, but they tried to bring a measure of personal feeling into everything they did. (p. 218)

An intriguing sub-theme is the sexual bias built into American society. The film constantly emphasises the priority given to men in the Corleone family. 'May their first child be a masculine child,' a well-wisher tells Don Corleone on the day of his daughter's wedding. . . . The Sicilian sequence helps to locate the origins of this sexual prejudice in the Old World ideals of womanhood, a glorified conception of woman as a goddess who is automatically removed from mundane affairs—and therefore not really taken seriously.

It is tempting to elaborate on this theme in view of Coppola's other films, which seem very concerned—if ambivalent—about the question of the oppression and emancipation of women. The final image of *The Godfather* underscores Coppola's concern. When Michael's wife Kay asks him if he had anything to do with the murder of his sister's husband, he lies to her, comforting her with the patronising affection one would show a child. . . . That haunting conclusion exemplifies the film's ability to enrich its melodrama with a full-scale commentary on the failures of a generation. (pp. 218-19)

The film represents a union of Coppola's technical gifts with his understanding of actors. Visually it is a stunning work. Gordon Willis' slightly washed-out colour photography instantly evokes the 1940s, and Nino Rota's music adds to the nostalgic mood—particularly in the Hollywood sequence, a witty allusion to a dreamlike style of movieland glamour that has all but disappeared. . . .

[Coppola] almost transforms *The Godfather* into a major film—almost, but not quite. The plot is so elaborate and methodical that it prevents some elements in the film—the transformation of Michael, and the evolution of a new-style bureaucratic Mafia—from being fully explored. We seize at hints in between the obligatory scenes that push the plot forward. Particularly in the middle of the film, there are long sections that work entirely on the level of narrative suspense and surprise, and on a second viewing anyway, these sections lag. *The Godfather* does not quite fuse its divergent elements; it remains brilliant in pieces, always engrossing, but not fully satisfying. (p. 219)

Stephen Farber, "Coppola and 'The Godfather'," in Sight and Sound *(copyright © 1972 by The British Film Institute), Vol. 41, No. 4, Autumn, 1972, pp. 217-23.*

RICHARD SCHICKEL

[Mr. Coppola has neither a personal statement to make in *You're a Big Boy Now* nor a personal style in which to make it.] His story is a compendium of clichés partially disguised in fancy dress, and his style is an anthology of what used to be new among the avant-garde pussycats—tricks and gimmicks that have now been so thoroughly absorbed into film language that you can see them any night on the television commercials. (pp. 98-9)

To give this mess movement, Mr. Coppola relies very heavily on shots of people running through the streets. . . . Sometimes people run around for no reason at all—they just run, run, run to demonstrate what free spirits some of the younger characters would be if the world were not so much with them. What they are running from or through or (in misguided moments) to are lots of crazy shots of the garish and vulgar sights of the Broadway area, of that discotheque and of the nightmarish lair Miss Hartman (as the beloved sicky) is made to inhabit and where, of course, Bernard suffers a dreadful sexual failure (it shouldn't really bother him—Don Juan himself would have been put off by the room's décor and her manner). All of this symbolizes decadence, while Bernard symbolizes healthy life, and the message of the contrast between him and his surroundings comes through loud, clear and repeatedly. Bad values, bad values—our Bernard has been growing up absurd, in his own little way is fighting a society that would rob him of his youthful innocence but replace it with nothing of value.

For the sake of argument let us concede that this viewpoint may have some validity if not, any more, much news value. The trouble is that it is only an abstraction, the merest and indeed the most conventional starting point for the true comic spirit to work from. What an artist would do is particularize it in terms of characters and situations which might give us a new, or at least arresting, vision of the ancient seriocomic battle of the generations. Instead, Mr. Coppola gives us only grossly exaggerated caricatures acting out the clichés of a psychological casebook, against backgrounds containing only the most conventionalized symbols of evil and innocence, joy and anguish. (pp. 99-100)

Mr. Coppola is a young man standing in front of a distorting mirror, trying on both the old and new intellectual clothing of his culture while trying out at the same time the imperfectly observed manners and gestures of the adult world. Somehow he has managed to convince himself that the occasionally bizarre combinations that sometimes result from this activity are, taken together, a creative act and not just self-indulgence.

It makes one very tired, as self-admiring brattiness always does. (p. 100)

Richard Schickel, "'You're a Big Boy Now'" (originally published in Life, *March 24, 1967), in his* Second Sight: Notes on Some Movies, 1965-70 *(copyright © 1972 by, Richard Schickel; reprinted by permission of Simon and Schuster, a Division of Gulf & Western Corporation), Simon and Schuster, 1972, pp. 98-101.*

JONATHAN P. LATIMER

The world of *The Godfather* is one is in which the cruelties, the excesses, the vices of the "family" are legitimized, and, in almost every case, imbued with the sanction of moral necessity. Rather than subverting the common morality, this film supports all the traditional sanctions of our society; honor, love, support of family, and worldly success through competition. The film is so constructed that we are not even allowed to consider the true nature of the Corleone's business. (p. 205)

And, most important, there are no victims! We are never allowed to see the real human cost of the family business. We see no prostitutes, no junkies, no victims of extortion, or robbery; none of the actual human effects of the decisions and actions taken by these families. It is like watching the Viet Nam War from the Pentagon; it is all a simple bookkeeping operation.

And that is the first clue to the appeal of *The Godfather*. What we recognize, what appeals, is the fact that the film creates a kind of metaphor for life in the United States today. And, what sets it apart from other films is the fact that it not only depicts, but it also offers explanations for what have seemed to be such irrational acts in the last few years. It provides a backdrop of necessity for almost any act of mayhem, so long as you are true to your own. That nice young soldier, Michael, introduced at the opening of the film, is driven by events to become the new Godfather. He doesn't really enjoy the work, but it has to be done. Every act he plans or commits is a response to some previous violence committed against him or his loved ones. Isn't this the way we would (and some do) choose to think about Viet Nam? Isn't the way these movie Mafia families deal with one another analogous to our own international relations?

Let me sketch the world of *The Godfather*. The family is only seen in their walled compound, a kind of fortress shielding the idyllic family life within. This world inside is ruled by a wise and, above all, honorable lord who protects and cares for his subjects. Outside this "happy kingdom" is a much different world, threatening, competitive, mean and ugly. This is the world in which the Corleone men must fight and compete. The Corleone women, such as we are allowed to see, do not venture into this world.

The major forces with which the Corleone men contend in this outside world are other, similar, families competing for the same "markets." We see "acceptable" mayhem between members of these families. These acts are "acceptable" because a state of "war" exists, and these men are soldiers doing their duty. They are defending their homes and holdings in the classic western tradition, a modern version of "the Code of the West." (pp. 205-06)

Occasionally, we are given a glimpse of a larger "real" world, a society with laws and mores, but this world's intrusion only seems to justify the Corleone's way of life. . . . [We] see Michael slapped around by a police officer. That officer, a Captain, turns out to be the most odious personality in the entire movie, and he is very satisfyingly disposed of by Michael, who is absolved, of course, by the motivating slap.

The police Captain is noteworthy because he performs several functions simultaneously. Aside from moving the plot along, by forcing Michael to flee to Sicily, his corruption is emblematic of the very evil Don Vito Corleone is fighting. He is a man without honor, the bought betrayer, evil of evils. And we are led to feel that his murder is justified, even though we should know that no murder can be. (p. 206)

The parallels between the world of the Corleones and a world picture widely held in grassroots America seem obvious. Fortress America, rich and powerful, surrounded by covetous neighbors alternately fights and negotiates with the powerful ones, exploits the weaker. Because America is strong, its use of strength with other nations is justified. We are the "happy kingdom." The council of bosses is analogous to a summit conference and the police and the FBI is a kind of world force, the U.N. perhaps, to be used or ignored as called for by the situation. But, underlying all, is the firm belief that there *are* easy answers, that intensifying bombing will stop a war, that cutting welfare payments will cure poverty. This belief, coupled with the ideal that individual action can right the world or alter history, is the basis of the appeal of this film. And, although intentionality is not an issue in this paper, it is one of grave concern.

I would hypothesize that a work of popular art provides a metaphor for our problems and dilemmas and then solves those metaphorical problems. In that way it provides for our need for explanations of the way things are, and simultaneously gives us solutions to those problems, a way out. The success of *The Godfather* rests primarily on its success in accomplishing both of these ends. (pp. 206-07)

Popular art tends to harden and support values already held by the audience and, in the case of *The Godfather*, to justify any act that will maintain these values. The audience comes away from that movie feeling vindicated. (p. 207)

Jonathan P. Latimer, "'The Godfather': Metaphor and Microcosm," in Journal of Popular Film *(copyright © 1973 by Sam L. Grogg, Jr., Michael T. Marsden, and John G. Nachbar), Vol. II, No. 2, 1973, pp. 204-08.*

DAVID DENBY

The Conversation is remarkably ambitious and serious—a Hitchcockian thriller, a first-rate psychological portrait of a distinctive modern villain (a professional eavesdropper) and a bitter attack on American business values, all in one movie. I feel that Coppola has partially botched the thriller, but the film is a triumph none the less—gritty, complex, idiosyncratic. . . .

The Conversation, which is about a man rather like Watergate bugger James McCord, profits from the great American national uproar over privacy and illegal surveillance. But Coppola claims that he began writing the screenplay for *The Conversation* in 1966, years before such things became national issues, so let us call his timeliness prescient rather than lucky. Timeliness isn't necessarily a sign of triviality in an artist; it may be a sign of good instinct, an ability to connect personal concern with national obsession. I think Coppola may become this sort of non-exploitative 'public' artist, a kind of cinematic Dickens (all proportions kept).

There's no doubt that he develops his protagonist, Harry Caul . . . , with a Dickensian richness of eccentricity, an extension of spiritual condition into physical metaphor. The conception is audacious and aggressively paradoxical. . . . We soon realise that Harry suffers from an extreme desolation of the spirit, a nearly pathological loneliness and guilt; his insistence on 'privacy' is just a way of keeping people at a distance. Repressed, awkward, terrified of his own powers and feelings, he cannot bear the demands people make on him, *any* demands. (p. 131)

Coppola's paradox grows in power and wit as its logic becomes clear. Poor Harry is so fearful, so given over to obsession, that he begins spying on himself. Before entering his mistress's door he hides outside, 'casing' the apartment; since it's clear that she has not been unfaithful, who is he casing but himself, a man caught red-handed in the act of visiting his mistress? . . .

Against his will, Harry has become part of a murder plot; when he discovers that his own apartment has been bugged by the plotters, he rips it to pieces, tearing up the walls, the floor, the furniture in a fruitless search for the microphone. The insane logic of Harry's obsession has thus been fulfilled: the bugger gets bugged, the man with only his privacy to protect destroys his possessions and winds up guarding literally nothing—an empty space, a cavity sealed with locks. The American mania for 'home security' here reaches its comic apotheosis. Our last view of Harry is very sad: he sits alone in the wreckage playing a saxophone along with a jazz record—halfway into life, halfway out. We're left with little doubt that the stasis is permanent. (p. 132)

Indeed, Harry Caul would like to operate as efficiently and impersonally as any other professional. He would like to think of his victims as anonymous 'targets', to lose himself in the delightful technical intricacies of robbing them without regard for what he is stealing or what they might feel about it.

The movie is an angry, funny attack on this sort of thinking, which Coppola sees as a natural product of American business values and our eternal boyish enthusiasm for technology as an end in itself. Stealing privacy has become part of the American way of life, and to make the point clear Coppola sends Harry to a San Francisco convention of security experts and equipment manufacturers, at which evil, destructive but undeniably ingenious little spying gadgets are hawked and sold like kitchen appliances or motorboats. . . . In *The Godfather,* also, the most extreme and fantastic behaviour was shown to emerge from a setting of normality—family life. Coppola seems to relish the more bizarre American contradictions, the clash between context and substance, between the style of an act (banal) and its meaning (horrifying).

Although he is drawn to extreme behaviour, Coppola's style of representation remains straightforwardly realistic. That's why his films may not at first appear to be the work of an artist. His attitudes and personality emerge not so much from the camera style as from the behaviour on screen. For instance, he has a genius for shallow, noisy, self-propelling types—the American as untrammelled egotist, powerful and infantile at the same time. He appears to love their theatrical energy and flash, and his sense of how such people reveal themselves in social situations is so accurate that he can do very funny, outrageous scenes without a trace of caricature. (Much of *The Godfather,* of course, was extremely funny.)

In *The Conversation,* Coppola has a savagely good time with Harry's surveillance colleagues. Boastful, frenetic, absurdly aggressive, these American go-getters can't stop competing for a moment, not even at a party, and so they begin showing off and playing dirty tricks on one another. . . . The surveillance experts are hideously funny and also tragic; looking at them it's hard for an American not to think of soldiers testing weapons in Vietnam and other examples of professionals run amuck. By immersing himself in a particular, idiosyncratic corner, accurately perceived, Coppola has made contact with a major strain in American life, a malaise that persists through generations. His unresolved love-hate relationship with the characters makes the bitterness of his criticism acceptable; if he entirely hated them, the film would have collapsed into diatribe, and we would have rejected his attitudes out of hand.

In a long, fascinating sequence, Harry reconstructs on tape the lovers' conversation as they walk slowly around a crowded San Francisco square. . . . As Harry mixes the separate tracks together, perfecting the aural image, we actually see the conversation; and it occurs to us that Harry is reconstructing and perfecting life—or at least a simulacrum of it. Of course film-making is also a reconstruction of life, and it's tempting to view *The Conversation*'s attack on irresponsible professionalism as also an implied attack on certain kinds of irresponsible filmmaking—empty, technically perfect work in which beautiful images are the director's only achievement; art without feeling or bite. (pp. 132-33)

Did Coppola intend *The Conversation* as a critical commentary on *Blow-Up,* a way of showing how that kind of story could be done? (He started work on the screenplay the year *Blow-Up* was completed.) The similarity is suggestive; both films centre on technological voyeurism and irresponsibility, and Harry's work with the tape parallels the famous sequence in which the fashion photographer discovers a murder by repeatedly cropping and blowing up a photograph. . . .

Coppola has rescued the story from 'art'. He places his alienated man in a recognisable American business/social world, and the details and mood seem intuitively right, making emotional contact in a way that Antonioni's awkward, vaguely metaphorical use of swinging London commonplaces did not. Moreover, Coppola is far too *interested* in Harry to allow this sad technological wizard to become an example of modern man's inability to feel or communicate or any rot like that. Contradictory, stubbornly eccentric, intensively imagined as a particular kind of human futility, Harry could never inspire any such banal interpretation. . . . [He] is anything but emotionally dead (that cliché of 'advanced' film-making)—he's inarticulate because he feels too much and too incoherently, immobile because every possible road of conduct becomes an imagined disaster. Participating in life is an agony for such a man; therefore whether he acts or fails to act, we are drawn to him emotionally.

Unfortunately, after all the suspense build-up, the repeated playing of the tape, etc., Coppola never satisfies our curiosity about the mystery itself. Limited to what Harry knows, we never quite understand what is going on, and some of this confusion could have been avoided with a little extra exposition. . . . Murder mysteries are often full of . . . loopholes, but we generally don't notice them—the pacing is too fast. *The Conversation*'s slow, repetitive, accumulative method forces us to review what we know, like a detective building a case, and the narrative sloppiness becomes irritating. Worst of all, the surprise denouement, in which the victims and murderers get reversed and Harry realizes that he has been used even more viciously than he had thought, occurs so quickly and casually that we can hardly take it in. I sympathise with Coppola's dilemma. A confrontation between Harry and the young couple might have straightened things out easily enough, but by presenting Harry with an actual physical threat (as Hitchcock did to his voyeur in *Rear Window*) Coppola would have turned *The Conversation* into a more conventional melodrama. He sticks to the internal and psychological threat, thereby losing a part of his audience at the end—an honourable failure. (p. 133)

David Denby, "Stolen Privacy: Coppola's 'The Conversation'," in Sight and Sound *(copyright © 1974 by The British Film Institute), Vol. 43, No. 3, Summer, 1974, pp. 131-33.*

WILLIAM S. PECHTER

[*The Conversation* calls strongly to mind] Antonioni's 1966 film, *Blow-Up.* Though this is most obvious in the actual "blow-up" (i.e., tape-deciphering) sequence itself, the resemblance extends from the painterly look of the film (some of the shots in Harry's apartment have an almost Vermeer-like quality of sculptured light) to such small details as the appearance of a mime in the opening sequence who seems to constitute a quite pointed reference to the mimes whose appearances bracket the action of the Antonioni film. Indeed, the resemblance extends even to the overall design of the two films: in both, a protagonist, through some means of mechanical reproduction, uncovers a mystery, and in both an ambiguous mystery-thriller plot is used to get at something beyond the thriller's conventions.

It's here, however, that the flaws of the Coppola film begin to reveal themselves. For whatever one may justly say about *Blow-Up*'s superficiality, in it, the mystery plot is perfectly geared to the film's meaning. (p. 63)

But this relation of plot to theme has gone askew in *The Conversation*. I'm not referring merely to minor implausibilities along the way. . . . Rather, it is the resolution of the mystery itself that seems to work against the movie. For it turns out, in the plot's final twist, that the conversation Harry records is taking place not between the potential victims of a murder but between its planners—and Harry's attempts at intercession fail to prevent it.

"I thought I was writing a film about privacy," Coppola has said, "but I was also making a film about responsibility." To the extent that *The Conversation* is a film about the invasion of privacy, a statement against bugging (and it is only partly this), it's one whose plot could be used (indeed, could more easily be used) to *justify* bugging, in that Harry's surveillance uncovers a plan to commit a murder which thus could conceivably have been prevented. . . . And to the extent that the film is about the taking of moral responsibility for one's actions (which it also is in part), it ends with Harry attempting for the first time to do just that, and failing; and, moreover, being, in effect, punished for attempting in a final too-easy irony of the bugger bugged, himself being spied on by those whose crime he has discovered. Perhaps because Coppola is on some level aware of these contradictions, the mystery plot is allowed to sputter out in a welter of ambiguities, not in the sense of *Blow-Up*'s but rather those of a *Marienbad*-like confusion of images which may or may not be real, some (or all) of which may exist, that is, only in Harry's imagination. . . . Ambiguity serves here not so much for resonance as for camouflage: to create a deliberate vagueness. (pp. 63-4)

I may seem, then, to be saying *The Conversation* is a failure, and yet the wonder is, for all that's wrong with it, just how impressive a work it remains: impressive in its very seriousness (a seriousness I value more than all of *Blow-Up*'s cleverness), but also for its intensity of feeling and for the many parts of it which rise above the mystery plot's defects to attain a haunting life of their own. And despite its faults, it leaves one more impressed than before with the qualities of its director. For if a wholly definable personality has yet to emerge from Coppola's films as, for better or worse, one can be seen in the work of a Peckinpah or Altman, some features are nevertheless beginning to grow more clear. . . . *The Conversation* seems, among other things, a deliberate attempt to turn away from the florid, operatic style of *The Godfather,* to create a kind of chamber work, which is perfectly valid except insofar as Coppola may believe the later film's unyieldingly somber mood and textural spareness are in themselves the mark of its superiority. Though I have reservations about *The Godfather,* as about all of Coppola's films, those reservations have nothing to do with that richness in portraiture and storytelling which has earned the film its popularity, and which really gives it more in common with *The Rain People* than that earlier, more "personal" work has with *The Conversation. . . .*

But if *The Conversation* began in ideas about "privacy" and "responsibility," it ends in Harry Caul, neither an abstraction nor a figure from the headlines but a singular human being tormented by his own private demons. Which is to say the film *is* about responsibility, not in any legalistic Watergate sense, but in *The Rain People*'s sense of our interconnectedness, and about a character, as much as the wife in *The Rain People,* in flight from that responsibility—from the burden of human contact and its attendant pain. And as in *The Rain People,* Coppola is able to depict such a character with a kind of cold, clear, unsentimental sympathy, without either condescension or moralizing: the kind of moralizing one sees in the Antonioni of *Blow-Up*. . . . For all its flaws and its sharing with Coppola's other films the sense of having been made by an artist who hasn't yet wholly discovered his ideal materials, *The Conversation* stirs with an emergent life. The photographer-protagonist in *Blow-Up* is complete and perfect, but he's merely a construct, a conceit. Harry Caul may not be fully formed or quite understood, but he is a creation, and his squalid anguish is sometimes genuinely lived through. (p. 64)

William S. Pechter, "Coppola's Progress," in Commentary *(reprinted by permission; all rights reserved), Vol. 58, No. 1, July, 1974, pp. 61-4.*

FRED KAPLAN

[Much of *The Conversation*] is very well-made. . . . There is, of course, no James Bond glamour, and yet Coppola also manages not to show off his sense of realism in any ostentatious manner. It is understated, subtle and at times probing.

But when he starts in with the whodunit nonsense, the whole film begins to fall apart. Replacing the cool intellectual detachment, there emerges a frenetic paranoia wildly hopping about. . . .

In the most crucial spots, in fact, *The Conversation* is muddle-headed, phony and cheap. Muddle-headed because although Coppola appears, at times, to say that Harry Caul is responsible for his actions and their consequences, we see, at the conclusion, that his bugging did not lead to a murder but in fact might have prevented one—moral substance subordinated to pyrotechnical shenanigans. Phony because Harry, who is shown to be so paranoid that he won't tell his loved and loving girlfriend a single fact about himself, nonetheless allows a party whore whom he scarcely knows to bed down with him in his office, all of the tapes and his valuable equipment a few steps away—plot convenience outbidding character development. Cheap because the ending strikes one as being a sleazy trick and exposes as nonsense any thoughts up until then that the film might have any political cogency—again, mindless form taking precedence over thoughtful content.

Indeed, toward the end of the film, things become so blurry that it's difficult to tell what is really happening and what is merely a product of Harry's paranoid imagination. Not even Coppola seems to know—nor, as he has indicated in at least one interview, does he care. Still, it makes little difference: reality, fantasy, or some literary shade of 'ambiguity'—nothing adds up to anything interesting, whatever the view.

The point is that these flaws—and many others that could be cited—are not mere foibles that can be mentally tucked away and forgotten about. It is these plot inconsistencies, lapses of logic, stupid 'surprise' twists, and pointless confusions, these ineptitudes and dishonesties, in short, that characterize the mentality that went into this film's making. They reveal that Coppola has no real social, political, or any other sort of point in mind (at least not anything of consistency), while at the same time posing as if he ever so profoundly does.

Fred Kaplan, "Film Reviews: 'The Conversation'," in Cinéaste *(copyright © 1974 by Gary Crowdus), Vol. VI, No. 3, 1974, p. 32.*

PAULINE KAEL

The daring of ["The Godfather, Part II"] is that it enlarges the scope and deepens the meaning of the first film; "The Godfather" was the greatest gangster picture ever made, and had metaphorical overtones that took it far beyond the gangster genre. In Part II, the wider themes are no longer merely implied. The second film shows the consequences of the actions in the first; it's all one movie, in two great big pieces, and it comes together in your head while you watch. Coppola might almost have a pact with the audience; we're already so engrossed in the Corleones that now he can go on to give us a more interior view of the characters at the same time that he shows their spreading social influence. The completed work is an epic about the seeds of destruction that the immigrants brought to the new land, with Sicilians, Wasps, and Jews separate socially but joined together in crime and political bribery. This is a bicentennial picture that doesn't insult the intelligence. It's an epic vision of the corruption of America. (p. 63)

Structurally, the completed work [of both Godfather films] is nothing less than the rise and decay of an American dynasty of unofficial rulers. Vito rises and becomes a respected man while his son Michael, the young king, rots before our eyes, and there is something about actually seeing the generations of a family in counterpoint that is emotionally overpowering. It's as if the movie satisfied an impossible yet basic human desire to see what our parents were like before we were born and to see what they did that affected what we became—not to hear about it, or to read about it, as we can in novels, but actually to see it. It really is like the past recaptured. . . . The whole picture is informed with such a complex sense of the intermingling of good and evil—and of the inability to foresee the effects of our love upon our children—that it may be the most passionately felt epic ever made in this country.

Throughout the three hours and twenty minutes of Part II, there are so many moments of epiphany—mysterious, reverberant images, such as the small Vito singing in his cell —that one scarcely has the emotional resources to deal with the experience of this film. . . . You need these moments as you need the terrible climaxes in a Tolstoy novel. A great novelist does not spare our feelings (as the historical romancer does); he intensifies them, and so does Coppola. On the screen, the speed of the climaxes and their vividness make them almost unbearably wounding. (pp. 63-4)

Many people who saw "The Godfather" developed a romantic identification with the Corleones; they longed for the feeling of protection that Don Vito conferred on his loving family. Now that the full story has been told, you'd have to have an insensitivity bordering on moral idiocy to think that the Corleones live a wonderful life, which you'd like to be part of.

The violence in this film never doesn't bother us—it's never just a kick. For a movie director, Coppola has an unusual interest in ideas and in the texture of feeling and thought. This wasn't always apparent in the first film, because the melodramatic suspense was so strong that one's motor responses demanded the resolution of tension. . . . But this time Coppola controls our emotional responses so that the horror seeps through everything and no action provides a melodramatic release. Within a scene Coppola is controlled and unhurried, yet he has a gift for igniting narrative, and the exploding effects keep accumulating. About midway, I began to feel that the film was expanding in my head like a soft bullet. (p. 64)

Pauline Kael, "Fathers and Sons," in The New Yorker *(© 1974 by The New Yorker Magazine, Inc.), Vol. L, No. 44, December 23, 1974, pp. 63-6.*

JOHN SIMON

[*The Godfather, Part II*] strikes me as better than its predecessor, though this is lukewarm praise at best. . . .

Better an honest gangster than a crooked politician, [*The Godfather, Part II*] is saying, as if those were the only possible choices.

Repellent as these stances are, they at least occupy the mind that tries to oppose them. There was nothing to think about in *The Godfather* except when, of what sort, and how big the next bloodletting will be. Here there is less bloodshed, more scheming and counter-scheming, which is more interesting. (p. 31)

However, the final argument in favor of Part II is that it is better made, of sounder workmanship. Coppola is getting to be a more competent director: A scene here is allowed more leisure and breathing space, is less like a guided missile trained with dumb, mechanical determinism to explode on a specific target. Thus the characterizations of Hyman Roth, the Jewish gangster . . . , and Pentangeli, an aging Mafia *capo* losing his grip . . . , create a dense, credible atmosphere rather than just advance the plot. (p. 32)

True, he does fall back on the tricks of Part I: beginning with a gay festivity with troubling undertones, and ending with a rapid pileup of major murders and suicides followed by Michael's dark, lonely, supremacy. But, somehow, the hand is steadier here, the sensationalism kept at bay. . . . (pp. 32, 47)

[The] film moves along for its two hundred minutes without actually boring us. The moral defects are undeniable and repugnant—no amount of canting comparisons of the Mafia to the Roman Empire or tributes from Michael Corleone to Fidel Castro's revolution can alter that—but the movie is well put together and steadily watchable. One could ask for more, but nowadays one is likely to get much less. (p. 47)

John Simon, "Films: 'The Godfather, Part II'" (reprinted by permission of Wallace & Sheil

Agency, Inc.; copyright © 1975 John Simon), in Esquire, *Vol. LXXXIII, No. 3, March, 1975, pp. 31-2, 47.*

JOHN YATES

The Godfather, Parts I and II, are at their deepest level a brilliant revelation of the family, how it worked through the generations, and how it now falls apart. In *Part I* Coppola and his actors create a real, living, breathing world. Coppola presents his world with what Pauline Kael calls an open camera; everything is shown, the detail is absolutely convincing, and it is convincing because the viewer is allowed to take it all in naturally, without comment by the director. Watching the movie, you know that this is how life is. The director reveals, he does not preach.

Coppola reveals a family, in that first grand scene of *Part I,* engaged in the most familial of rituals, a daughter's wedding. The scene is a picture of tradition, and not merely Italian tradition, but the tradition of the West. The man of respect in the community gathers his neighbors around him, to observe the relinquishing of the care of his daughter to another man, her husband. Implicit in this act is the key to the Western family, the subservience of the woman to the man. The woman bears and tends the children in the home, and the man is strong for his family, to protect them and his home from a hostile world. This is how things work in *Part I;* all the action takes place in this framework.

Even the violence and brutality of Don Corleone's criminal empire fit within this family framework. To call an organization that deals in murder and revenge a "family" is not hypocritical at all. Indeed, it evokes the very origin of the family, that primordial time when anybody or anything that threatened a man's home was beaten to death with a rock. Don Corleone's family is a throwback to that violent time when the family existed primarily for mutual protection. (pp. 158-59)

Don Corleone dies in the sun, in his garden, with his grandson thinking it's all a part of the game. It is. The game goes on, the rules are in force, Anthony will become a man in the same rich, brutal family tradition in which his grandfather, and his grandfather's grandfather, became men.

Before Anthony takes his first communion, the game is over. The world of the wedding party in *Part I* is, in the Tahoe party at the opening of *Part II,* in chaos. Throughout *Part II* there is a terrible sense of things falling apart. Murders, executed with cruel efficiency in *Part I,* are clumsily botched in *Part II.* Panic sweeps the city of Havana as the government collapses before the rebels. . . .

The most distressing and fundamental sign of change in *Part II* is evident in the women of the family. Connie neglects her children and hops from husband to husband. Fredo's wife gets drunk and falls all over other men, humiliating her husband and his family. These crimes are most disturbing because they are crimes against the institution of the family, committed by those on whose obedience the family depends. If women leave the home, the very reason for the family is gone, there is nothing left for the men to protect, the bottom has fallen out. (p. 161)

Michael's father would fare no better in this new world than Michael does, and that is Michael's tragedy. For Michael, it is clear that the most important thing, the only thing, is to establish what his father would have done in a situation and follow that lead. . . . His success at following his father's lead, and the devastating inadequacy of Vito's example as a model for action in Michael's generation, is clearly established by the jumps between the two men's stories.

The scene switches back and forth repeatedly from a family scene in Vito's young manhood to a family scene in Michael's time. (pp. 161-62)

Technically Michael stands up well against his father's example as head of the family. (p. 162)

Connie acknowledges this in her return to the family at her mother's death. "You were just being strong for all of us the way Papa was," she tells Michael. By now, however, Michael knows that his strength is his family's doom. He knows how hard it is in his time to emulate his father. "It's not easy to be a son, Fredo," he says in the banana daquiri scene in Havana, and there is real empathy in that statement. He and Fredo, as sons in the family, must follow their father. Fredo fails, Michael succeeds, but both are destroyed. Michael, unlike Fredo, suffers the terrible fate of awareness. He must watch himself die without being able to do a thing about it. "He was being strong," he says of his father, "strong for his family. But," he asks his mother, "by being strong—could he lose it?" The old woman doesn't understand. She tells him he will have other children. "No," Michael pleads, "I meant lose his family." "But you can never lose your family," she answers from another universe.

"Times are changing."

These are conservative movies that Coppola has made, conservative in the noblest sense. They apologize for nothing in the past, and hide nothing. Nor do they pretend that the past could or should have survived. But they mourn its passing. (pp. 162-63)

John Yates, "Godfather Saga: The Death of the Family," in Journal of Popular Film *(copyright © 1975 by Sam L. Grogg, Jr., Michael T. Marsden, and John G. Nachbar), Vol. IV, No. 2, 1975, pp. 157-63.*

DAVID DENBY

[The Corleones were portrayed—at least in the first half of *The Godfather*]—as a model of health, yes, as happy monsters whose violent behavior emerged from a high appetite for life as much as from the family's peculiar way of doing business. The ambivalence was morally audacious for a popular movie, and it's a mark of Coppola's skill that he got almost everyone to accept it. By the time Michael Corleone shoots his father's enemies in the restaurant scene, Coppola had most of us where he wanted us; the hair-raising use of conventional narrative techniques secured our acquiescence and complicity. With an awed laugh, directed at ourselves as much as the screen, we accepted the notion that Michael's violence was an act of family piety, a way of accepting his father, his family past, his natural destiny.

Those few who didn't accept it, who were alarmed by the mixture of graciousness and murder, complained of sentimentality. For the anti-sentimentalists there was too much happiness in the Corleone family and too much pictorial beauty in the movie. Despite the disingenuous strategy of *The Godfather* that I mentioned earlier, the charge of sentimentality makes no sense to me. It ignores the entire second half of the movie, where Michael Corleone gradually becomes an isolated and ruthless killer, up to the remarkable moment when he looks his wife straight in the eye and lies, shutting her out forever. As for the ingratiating visual quality of the film, a grainy, intentionally sordid photographic style would actually have been the more conventional option for a gangster movie. Instead, Coppola emphasized the beauty of the gangsters' lives in both Sicily and America, increasing our sense of moral squalor and violation: they lived in beauty and acted vilely. . . . During the shimmering, slightly overexposed Sicilian sequences we are meant to feel the corruption gathering in the lemon and green ripeness of the countryside. Sicily, that eternally fouled paradise! The rottenness became an emanation of its heat and sun. This may not impress historians or political scientists very much, but it's the most expressive kind of movie shorthand. The dark brown and red American interiors, a setting for secrets and plots, carried associations of the corrupted stained-leather atmosphere, the phony distinguished style, of boardrooms, manor libraries, and clubs. Like so much of the best popular art, *The Godfather* was almost seductively easy and pleasurable, but its pleasurableness functioned for the audience as a variety of knowledge—we were provoked by the satisfaction the movie gave us into new forms of understanding.

The Godfather II is also extraordinarily beautiful, but it's a much slower, heavier, more obviously ironic film, without the paralyzing energy, audacious wit, or imperious command of the audience. Admirers have found a quality of new "depth," but to me it feels like new weight. . . . My complaint is that it draws on Part One with rather dismaying reverence and over-explicitness, dulling the interest—through sheer attenuation—of ideas that were clear and forceful in the earlier film's closing scenes: the increasing isolation of the Americanized Mafioso, Michael Corleone, and the persistence of Sicilian patterns of "honor" through the generations. In Part One the cultural mix of Sicily and America produced some episodes that were funny and bizarrely "right" (the men plotting tribal vengeance over a take-home dinner) and also a convincing denouement. In Part Two, however, the intercutting of America in the sixties with earlier periods in Sicily and Little Italy produces the effect of a pattern sustained by will power and heavy labor after its logic has collapsed. Now that Michael's so completely an American it's no longer unequivocally "right" that he act with Sicilian thoroughness and cruelty at the end, murdering his own brother. . . . The results are hollow, mechanical on a grand scale, and incomprehensible. They try to place the "sociological" view of Italian-American crime in historical perspective, ranging from Fanucci, the florid turn-of-the-century neighborhood extortionist in white suit and erotic moustaches, to Michael Corleone, grey-suited, corporation-cold, ruthlessly presiding over the fouling of contemporary America with WASP and Jew as equal partner. This is beguiling as social history but extremely vague as information on the details of criminal activity in any period. After six hours and twenty minutes of film I still haven't understood how a single one of these gangsters actually operates. (pp. 114-16)

A movie epic needs an eccentric character as its focus or else it solemnly tells us what we already know. Unfortunately, as Michael Corleone grows older he becomes another of those familiar, semi-mythological American bastards, an obscenely rich and completely lonely man of great power. . . . The final scenes, with Michael brooding over his darkened blue lake while memories of the family he's decimated torture his mind, resound with the hollow certainty of an irony too easily achieved. In Part One Coppola escaped from those moralists who wanted the Corleones to be *unhappy,* but now he's succumbed.

Still, despite all one's dissatisfactions, Coppola appears to be a uniquely central and powerful American talent. His feeling for American surfaces—the glancing intimations of social status in gesture, tone of voice, decor, clothes—is as precise as any director's in American film history. Perhaps one has to cite John O'Hara for the proper comparison, but Coppola is more playful. His showpiece big party scene near the beginning of Part Two, an obvious contrast with Part One's wedding celebration, depends on observation so acute it becomes a form of malicious wit. The Corleones have charged into the American center by the late fifties, and they've paid the price in blandness: their lakeside bash is a ceremonial drag, more like a TV variety show than a party; the hearty Italian street music has been replaced by a suave-sounding dance band and a blond cherub's chorus, the natural gaiety by a desperate desire to have fun. Having moved the base of their operations from Long Island to Lake Tahoe, they've fallen in with western WASPs, or at least the dissolute remainders of a WASP ruling class. . . . Coppola's unusual curiosity about such things as fatherhood, marriage, power, spiritual anguish, etc., sets him apart from the run of Hollywood directors as a central interpreter of American experience, a man taking the big risks, working outside the limits of traditional genres. The lack of eccentricity or repeating obsession, the avoidance of obvious visual metaphor or radical foreshortening of narrative may deceive some viewers into declaring there's no artist behind the perfectly achieved images, the marvelous amplitude and evenness of flow, but that would be a mistake induced by the influence of the auteur theory on educated taste. Those looking for "personality"—the flourishes of "signature"—may be too distracted to feel the power of Coppola's work. His personality (sad word) emerges in the way he chooses to reveal his characters. . . . To expose the murderous falsity of appearances without betraying the appearances themselves remains one of the principal tasks of realism and one of the things movies do most successfully. Coppola's work, at its best, sustains the highest traditions of realism. Despite everything that can be marked off against him, there's every reason to expect Coppola to be a principal exponent of American themes in the movies of the next two decades. (pp. 116-18)

David Denby, "The Two Godfathers," in Partisan Review *(copyright © 1976 by Partisan Review, Inc.), Vol. XLIII, No. 1, 1976, pp. 113-18.*

JAMES W. PALMER

Francis Ford Coppola's *The Conversation* is a perplexing film about a wiretapper named Harry Caul who becomes involved in a murder. Harry is less a character in the traditional sense than he is a symbol or cipher for modern man immersed in a technological society that undermines human values and thwarts human needs. As a technician in this dehumanizing environment, Harry seems unwilling or unable to relate to people or to take the moral action necessary to change his life or even save the lives of others. Hired by the director of an unnamed corporation, Harry tapes a conversation between the director's wife and her lover. Although this conversation forces Harry to see the terrifying consequences of his work, he remains isolated, alienated, and in a sense unborn because of his inability to make moral choices. (p. 26)

Understanding this complex film is somewhat easier when one recognizes the significance of Harry Caul's name because it is a key to his character and to the visual style and themes of *The Conversation*. . . . A caul is a "thin membrane enveloping the foetus, which covers the head of some newly born children: an omen of good fortune with powerful magical properties; it protects sailors from drowning, presumably because it was thought to keep the foetus from drowning in the womb." (pp. 26-7)

[But] "caul" is only ironically a good omen for the withdrawn and incommunicative Harry. We can see his ever present plastic raincoat as the veil or caul that he uses to protect himself against the world; it is his prophylactic against human contact. . . .

The caul, the membrane enveloping of the head of a child, is the most frequently recurring image in the film. Harry is seen dimly through screens, translucent glass, plastic curtains, or less frequently through bars and grillwork. This visual motif presents Harry as a trapped, caged man who is difficult to penetrate, to understand, to get close to. The caul protects the unborn foetus, but Harry subverts the use of the caul by making it a shield against life and the moral responsibility that comes with maturity. (p. 27)

The film is, in fact, a study of Harry's abortive struggle to get himself born as a moral man. It begins, ironically, on Harry's birthday. Harry's obsessive need for privacy arises partly out of his inability to face the world where moral choices are inevitable and have consequences. Clearly terrified that his own privacy could be invaded and that he might find himself getting involved with anyone, Harry erects elaborate defenses against his "birth." Such protective strategies insure his loneliness, but are otherwise ineffective. (p. 28)

Harry does not prevent the director's murder, but manages to take the hotel room adjacent to the murder room. Crouched behind the toilet and toilet paper, Harry taps into the next room and listens to an ongoing argument between the director, his wife, and her lover. Frightened by what he hears, Harry drops his equipment and begins pacing his hotel room like a trapped animal. We see him slumped in a chair and looking blankly at the wall and the wallpaper mural depicting the San Francisco Bay. Coppola shows us several shots of the wallpaper scene from Harry's point of view. As an American skilled in escaping, evading and avoiding himself, Harry has, like the pioneers before him, run out of the territory ahead. Starting in New York where his work led to several murders, Harry has made the historical trek from East to West, and now at the edge of the Pacific he may have to confront the consequences of his actions. But once Harry goes out on his balcony and sees a bloody hand pressed against the glass door of the adjoining room, he retreats back into his room where he draws the curtains, turns on the TV set, and, in an action that visually parodies his surname, pulls the bedclothes over his head like a caul. Harry falls asleep and wakes to the blaring TV set where the prehistoric Fred Flintstone, in a kind of parody of Harry's anxieties, is impatiently pacing a room, waiting for his wife to give birth.

Awake or asleep, Harry cannot escape from his Catholic sense of guilt or his incipient moral concerns. In a dream, Harry has previously envisioned the murder he anticipates will be committed in the hotel room, but because of the misinterpretation of his tape, he has the murder-victim roles reversed. A final definition of caul is pertinent here, as cauls are valued not only as protection against drowning, but can also "confer powers of second sight on their owners." The film suggests that Harry may be clairvoyant, although his clairvoyance is faulty because he believes so strongly in the power, reliability, and certainty of the rational, scientific "truths" of his technology. (pp. 29-30)

Whatever the intentional or unintentional frustrations we feel at the end of the film, the last scenes are consistent in focusing on Harry's character and in completing the visual motif of the caul. Harry's revision of the murder involves the recurring image of the caul. First, we glimpse in the hotel room the young man, the lover, in a clear plastic rainsuit, reminiscent of Harry's raincoat, which the young man wears presumably to keep the director's blood off of his clothes. Second, as Harry envisions the act of murder itself, the young man throws a large, clear plastic sheet over the director's head just before the stabbing; thus the caul has become part of the modus operandi of the murderer. The final shot of this sequence, one we saw briefly at the beginning of Harry's revision, is that of the bloody body of the director laid out on the hotel bed and completely covered by the plastic sheet like an aborted foetus in its sac. Whether this scene accurately portrays the murder is beside the point. The caul images are most appropriate in Harry's version of the murder because the cauls further convey his feeling of guilt and complicity in the crime.

Harry's surname, Caul, is skillfully translated into visual motifs that help us understand Harry as a lonely, withdrawn and paranoiac American. His desire to control reality through his technology is Harry's way of arranging the world so that he does not have to experience it. Like an artist, Harry wants to construct his own world. Harry's assistant even calls the taping of the couple "a work of art." When we first see Harry sitting down to his keyboard of recorders, he synchronizes his tapes like a concert pianist about to perform. Harry's one creative outlet, his one personal act of expression is his saxophone playing. Even here he plays it safe by joining in a jam session in his apartment with his phonograph, and by pausing at the right moments to accept the recorded applause.

The film ends with Harry systematically tearing up his wiretapped apartment, smashing a statue of the Virgin Mary (a bit of intrusive symbolism here) to assure himself that the icon is not hiding an electronic bug. The angry and frightened Harry never learns how or where his place is bugged. This last scene of destruction and desolation is reminiscent of the chilling conclusion to Coppola's *The Godfather, Part II*. Harry, like Michael Corleone, is alone in a room and in a world where everyone is a potential enemy. Harry has failed to control his experience or protect his privacy; even more important, he has aborted his own moral and emotional life. His surname has come to symbolize his arrested development. Like Randall Jarrell's ball-turret gunner, Harry can say, "From my mother's sleep I fell into the State / And I hunched in its belly till my wet fur froze." (pp. 30-1)

James W. Palmer, "'The Conversation': Coppola's Biography of an Unborn Man," in Film Heri-

tage (copyright 1976 by F. A. Macklin), Vol. 12, No. 1, Fall, 1976, pp. 26-32.

STANLEY J. SOLOMON

Coppola's insight into the [crime film] genre reveals itself in his handling of the film's structure, which features a gallery of criminal types with wit, charm, courage, and heroic stature (who never change or develop)—an achievement that can only by accomplished by limiting the film's sphere of life to the criminal element. Coppola certainly understood that if the world of crime obtruded into the realm of society's ordinary activities—if, for instance, the general citizenry were shot at—ordinary moral concerns would dominate our relationship to the figures in the film. But *The Godfather* is populated only by criminals and their relatives or by people corrupt enough to belong to their world. . . . *The Godfather*'s power struggles and economic and social conflicts take place in the world of the gutter, but like most films depicting microcosms, the film also operates in the abstract realm, where the believers confront the pagans, and the upholders of order and government clash with the rebels who wish to destroy a hierarchical establishment that has brought a long reign of peace. (pp. 194-95)

The actual criminal business carried on by the Don and his successor Michael is typically vague. Late in the film the family decides to get out of the "olive oil" business and buy a Las Vegas hotel. We are surprised by their ever having been in olive oil, but the gambling operation is simply the genre's traditional enterprise of gangsters. Don Corleone, in fact, tries to keep them out of narcotics, but some accommodation has to be made to the new spirit of commercial enterprise rising in the national organization of crime families. Michael pledges to his girlfriend that in five years virtually all of the Corleone enterprises will be legal—and many critics view the film as a kind of businessman's allegory of American private capitalism. Yet the business operations remain unspecified; the board meetings are really just Sicilian-style family outings, not really for generating corporate strategies. What is symbolized, perhaps, is the nature of corporate competition. The family wars resemble nineteenth-century cutthroat commercial practices energetically pursued by the great "robber barons" of American industry and finance, who engaged in similar violence, but without machine guns. The Corleones are depicted as just on the verge of moving onto that level of American myth. No wonder the film engendered a sequel bringing the family's story up to date as a fulfillment of one aspect of the American Dream. (pp. 197-98)

Stanley J. Solomon, "The Life of Crime," in his Beyond Formula: American Film Genres *(© 1976 by Harcourt Brace Jovanovich, Inc.; reprinted by permission of the publisher), Harcourt, 1976, pp. 157-98.**

ROBERT K. JOHNSON

The first of the seven films [Coppola] has directed, *Dementia 13,* is not a horror-film classic nor an embarrassment. It has some thoroughly effective sequences, and it has some bland or belabored scenes. Basically, the photography is adequate; the acting, pedestrian; and the dialogue, functional. The film is only of any special interest because it is the first full-length film that Coppola directed.

With regard to what have been called his "personal" films, *You're A Big Boy Now, The Rain People,* and *The Conversation,* the first is by far the best. The pace of both *The Rain People* and *The Conversation* is too slow. The stylistic shuttlings in *The Conversation* are a mistake. *The Rain People* is done in only one style, a semidocumentary style (aided by flashbacks), but it does not help the film very much. The plots of both pictures are weak. The main characters in *The Rain People* are exceptionally interesting, but they are not fully developed. In *The Conversation,* the main character, though interesting in the early scenes, is delineated even less successfully.

You're A Big Boy Now, all in all, holds up well. Coppola was no more technically innovative in this film than he was in his other two personal films. But the influence (stronger perhaps than Coppola has acknowledged) of Richard Lester and others was salutary. It encouraged Coppola to employ a fast pace, which fit the material perfectly. There was enough looseness in the script to allow Coppola to incorporate "bits of business" (especially in the chase scenes) that emerged during the on-location filming. Yet, as was not the case with his other two personal films, Coppola finished the screenplay for this film before the shooting began; and this might well account, in part, for the superior quality of *You're A Big Boy Now.* It includes an almost endless stream of clever "touches," touches that create very interesting nuances in characters that at first appear to be strictly stereotypes.

Of the bigger productions that Coppola directed, *Finian's Rainbow* is a failure. Most of the music holds up nicely, but it already had for a good number of years before the movie was made. (pp. 176-77)

But the two *Godfather* films are decisive successes. As a profound metaphorical study of the United States or a keen realistic study of the Mafia, the first *Godfather* fails. Nonetheless, it builds on the material in the novel with extraordinary skill. The long opening sequence, the wedding reception, holds our attention completely. And from the time Michael becomes centrally involved in the family's affairs (after his father is shot and hospitalized) to the last scene, the film is almost continuously riveting. It is an outstanding gangster film. (p. 177)

[Despite] its flaws, [*The Godfather, Part II*] graphically presents the descent into hell—or at least into hollowness—of its main contemporary character, Michael. It dramatizes the early life of Michael's father, Vito Corleone, a time in which Vito leads his family to prosperity. But it also implies that the climb to prosperity created problems that Michael, when he becomes the head of the family, copes with successfully in terms of wealth and power, but unsuccessfully in terms of the unity and happiness of the Corleone family. We see, finally, the disintegration of the family. Michael at the end is all-powerful, and all alone.

Except for *The Godfather, Part II,* none of Coppola's work would encourage one to predict that Coppola will someday be seriously compared with such filmmakers as Ingmar Bergman or Federico Fellini. (pp. 177-78)

On the other hand, this still-young artist's work compares quite favorably with the work produced by Mike Nichols, Arthur Penn, Sam Peckinpah, Peter Bogdanovich, Haskell Wexler, Martin Scorsese, and many others. There is a maturity of attitude governing the violence in the second *Godfather* film in particular that is depressingly absent in ***Bonnie and Clyde, Bullitt,*** and the films made by Sam Peckinpah and Martin Scorsese. For all its faults, *The Conversation* probes the contemporary scene in a deeper way than *Joe* or *Medium Cool* do. *The Rain People,* though not a success, is a far more honest "road picture" than *Easy Rider* and almost every other film of that genre. While full of fun, *You're A Big Boy Now* has a poignant, serious point that raises it above the slicker comedies of Mike Nichols and Peter Bogdanovich. (p. 178)

Coppola's moral awareness is clearly present in many of his films, beginning with *You're A Big Boy Now.* There are rich moral-social overtones in *The Rain People.* Coppola's musings about responsibility and about particular problems confronting the American woman (problems the women's liberation movement later focused on) serve as the foundation for this film. Then one comes to *The Conversation,* in which Coppola's valid moral observations are blunted by the flaws in the film. In *The Godfather, Part II,* however, the moral dimension blends beautifully with the other major elements in the movie. Though faulty and muddled at times, the moral outlook Coppola has brought to most of his films is one of the things that set him apart from many of his Hollywood contemporaries.

Another reason that Coppola deserves to be singled out for special credit concerns his adventurous probings of the possibility of emphasizing character more than plot in a medium that very much lends itself to enhancing plot more than character. Films thrive on completely stereotyped characters because such characters need no "explaining"—hence, do not cause any "delay" in the presentation of plenty of plot. So, too, the writer-director is pressured to present only that kind of stereotyped character—the cowboy, the detective, the racing car driver—who is frequently in motion.

Coppola, at his best, is an exceptionally fine creator of film characters. A host of only semi-stereotyped memorable characters appear in *You're A Big Boy Now.* All the main characters, and just about all of the minor ones, in *The Rain People* are unique and thoroughly interesting. Although Harry Caul in *The Conversation* proved too uptight, too elusive to allow Coppola to make him into a successful character delineation, Caul is still original and worth pondering. Coppola's portrait of General Patton is excellent. It also offers, in Patton's opening monologue, Coppola's successful attempt to present a character in an innovative way. In the two *Godfather* films, numerous characters break through the mere stereotypic. (pp. 178-79)

[Coppola] has been slow in bringing a steadily mature vision to his film efforts. It is, in fact, still too early to tell whether he has yet achieved such a vision. He has also depended too much on his ability to improvise and to ad-lib while making a movie; what evidence we have indicates that he does a better job when at least a great deal of the work is carefully thought out before he steps onto the set.

But, as a director, he is an exceptionally knowledgeable craftsman. As a writer, he has adapted and co-authored several fine screenplays. In *The Godfather, Part II* he did his best job thus far in presenting a vivid, meaningful story and many gripping, rich characterizations in one film. And, because that film is such a recent effort, it is certainly not foolish to hope for more such high-quality work from him. (p. 180)

Robert K. Johnson, in his Francis Ford Coppola *(copyright © 1977 by Twayne Publishers, Inc.; reprinted with the permission of Twayne Publishers, A Division of G. K. Hall & Co., Boston), Twayne, 1977, 199 p.*

DAVID DENBY

Apocalypse Now is about Americans in Vietnam, and its themes are the perversion of the natural by the technological and the eerily sensuous beauty of war, in which the nightmarish all too easily becomes commonplace.

The images are not intended to be totally subjective or surreal; they are meant to illustrate the very real stages of demoralization—the rituals of defilement—that marked America's self-destruction in Vietnam. *Apocalypse Now* feels like one of those doom-laden pieces by the Grateful Dead that go on forever in a spreading luxuriousness of panic and dismay, leaving a residue of anxiety in your stomach while making you high at the same time. It's a two-and-a-half-hour acid-rock opera all in the same mood of ominously drifting horror, and finally it's just too pretentious. Like those sixties hipsters who boasted of their terrifying drug trips, Coppola is something of a show-off. He's eager to prove to us that he can handle any sort of weirdness or nihilism and make a work of art out of dread. Yes, there are passages of horrifying beauty in *Apocalypse Now,* but it's a heavy, self-important work, redundant and undramatic—more like a bad trip than art. (p. 87)

David Denby, "Hollow Movie," in New York Magazine *(copyright © 1979 by News Group Publications, Inc.; reprinted with the permission of* New York *Magazine), Vol. 12, No. 33, August 27, 1979, pp. 87-9.*

ANDREW SARRIS

[For] all of Coppola's emotional involvement in [*Apocalypse Now*], it is a remarkably cold film. Coppola undoubtedly felt strongly about the Vietnamese War, but the vehicle for his feelings is constructed in such a way that none of the characters can project them. Hence, the characters tend to be either animated cartoons (*vide* Robert Duvall's Lieutenant Colonel Kilgore) or ciphers (Brando's shadowy Kurtz). . . .

[If] two-thirds of the film are great, and one-third problematical, is not *Apocalypse Now* superior to most other movies? Of course it is. Certainly it is better than *Alien* or *Moonraker* or *The Amityville Horror* or *Meatballs* or *The In-Laws* or *Dracula,* to mention some of the current blockbusters. We must keep everything in perspective. Coppola is a major American director, whose work is mandatory viewing for every serious cineaste.

Is *Apocalypse Now,* then, better than *The Deer Hunter*? That is a tougher question. . . . In a sense, the films are almost dialectically antithetical. Where *Apocalypse Now* is cerebral, cold, and chic left, *The Deer Hunter* is visceral, hot, and gauche right. *Apocalypse Now* revels in the asexuality of drug-addicted hallucinations, while *The Deer Hunter* revels in a brand of macho-homoeroticism. Finally, *Apocalypse Now* tends to be macrocosmic whereas *The Deer Hunter* tends to be microcosmic. It follows that *The Deer Hunter* is an infinitely juicier entertainment than *Apocalypse Now*. . . .

Now I am, if anything, less impressed by *Apocalypse* than I was at Cannes. Even the visual pyrotechnics of the first two-thirds now leave me cold. For me the great glory of the cinema is not its affinity for motion and light, but its affinity for life in the matrix of time and space. What I wish to see on the screen is the process of human development and interaction. As it is, there is no growth or enlightenment in *Apocalypse Now*. It is as if the whole film took place within five minutes of an LSD trip. Some people are into instant emotion and profundity. I am not. I prefer to watch the whole process as it develops within narrative and dramatic structures.

Andrew Sarris, "Heart of Coldness," in The Village Voice *(reprinted by permission of* The Village Voice; *copyright © News Group Publications, Inc., 1979), Vol. XXIV, No. 35, August 27, 1979, p. 45.**

VERONICA GENG

Viewed as a conventional updating of Joseph Conrad's "Heart of Darkness" . . . "Apocalypse Now" looks like not much more than a cannibalization. For better and for worse, the movie confirms the idea that a work of art consists of local particulars. To use somebody else's work of art as a skeleton, you first have to turn it into a skeleton. Where "Apocalypse Now" is least successful (the last half hour), it seems to have been made by people who have read Conrad with their teeth. Where it is amazingly successful (the first two hours), it takes least from Conrad—or, rather, it takes subtly and delicately, for form and inspiration. . . . The movie is inconclusive not in the sense that it is meaningless but in the sense that it refuses to interpret itself as it goes along. Coppola at his best does not let us remove ourselves one safe step from what is happening on the screen to the *meaning* of what is happening on the screen. Coppola has the "weakness"—as "Heart of Darkness" ironically calls it—of Marlow: "the weakness of many tellers of tales who seem so often unaware of what their audience would best like to hear." . . .

I don't know what "Apocalypse Now" is in its entirety (and I am not sure Coppola does), but for most of the way it is the blackest comedy I have ever seen on the screen, taking its spirit and tone not from Conrad but from—this is the shortest way to say it—Michael Herr.

Herr's reporting from Vietnam (collected in his book "Dispatches") shows us a war that justifies Baudelaire's statement "The comic is one of the clearest Satanic signs of man": people living through Vietnam as pulp adventure fantasy, as movie, as stoned humor, as a collage that Herr once saw in a helicopter gunner's house, on a wall near a poster of Lenny Bruce—a map of the western United States with Vietnam reversed and fitted over California. . . .

Herr also wrote the movie's narration. . . . Willard [the narrator] talks in the easy ironies, the sin-city similes, the weary, laconic, why-am-I-even-bothering-to-tell-you language of the pulp private eye. "I hardly said a word to my wife until I said yes to a divorce. . . . I'm here a week now, waiting for a mission, getting softer. . . . Everyone gets everything he wants. I wanted a mission. And for my sins they gave me one. Brought it up to me like room service. . . ." . . . Our first look at Willard is the classic opening of the private-eye movie: his face seen upside down, a cigarette stuck to his lip, under a rotating ceiling fan (all this superimposed on a dreamlike scene of helicopters brushing across the screen, a row of palm trees suddenly bursting into flame), and then the camera moving in tight closeup over his books, snapshots, bottle of brandy, cigarettes, Zippo, and, finally, obligatory revolver on the rumpled bedsheets. This guy is not Marlow. He is a parody—maybe a self-created one—of Philip Marlowe, Raymond Chandler's L.A. private eye. (p. 70)

With the first of its war scenes, "Apocalypse Now" becomes a horror comedy. It is what "Dr. Strangelove" might have been after the bomb fell, except that the comedy is not exaggerated and detached from suffering in a way that tells us we may safely laugh; it is realistic, and it exists simultaneously with realistic horror rendered with the physical brilliance and amplitude of "2001." The horror is not drained off, as it is by the easy absurdism of "The Deer Hunter," into a symbolic game; and the comedy is not drained off, as it is by the wordplay of "Catch-22," into a cute craziness. (p. 71)

Willard is not Marlow: his narration does not have a deep historical perspective, and it is spoken in a psychological state as numbed as the one he is in on the screen. He is not even Marlowe: he is not above the garish evil that surrounds him. Where Willard is pitiless, "Apocalypse Now" is not. The men on the boat, whom we get to know . . . , keep the movie from spiralling off into the impersonal, and we suffer for everyone in it. Though this is a matter of instinct, it seems to me that "Apocalypse Now" earns every second of its display of evil, because it has coherence, truthfulness, and conviction—up to a point.

The point is Kurtz. By the time Willard reaches Kurtz, Coppola has not made a movie version of "Heart of Darkness;" he has made his own movie—one in a class with Lina Wertmüller's "Seven Beauties," not just in its somewhat different use of comedy and horror but in its refusal to go for generalizations instead of particulars. Kurtz, the biggest, fattest temptation to generalization in English literature, has no more place in Coppola's movie than Raskolnikov or Othello. Yet he is the only character Coppola takes literally—right down to his name—from Conrad. Maybe Coppola thought he could show us not just evil but Evil. Maybe he could not think of any other reason to send Willard upriver. Most likely, he just fell in love with the romantic idea of Kurtz, Kurtz, Kurtz of the voice, the "bewildering," "illuminating," "exalted," "contemptible" voice.

Veronica Geng, "'Mistah Kurtz—He Dead'," in The New Yorker *(© 1979 by The New Yorker Magazine, Inc.), Vol. LV, No. 29, September 3, 1979, pp. 70-2.*

MICHAEL WOOD

[*Apocalypse Now*] ends in a welter of bathos that has to be seen to be believed, and that weighs down the whole work with its mournful freight of clutching, unappeasable ambition. But the film holds together well enough until it reaches its final muddle, and it has scenes and moments unequaled in recent European or American movies. Indeed, it has one long sequence so right and so powerful that it actually causes the confusion of the end, since it leaves Coppola with nothing to say. He cannot discover the promised "heart of darkness" in the murk of his conclusion, because he stumbled across it much earlier—earlier in the finished film and in the shooting—on a bright, noisy beach strewn with soldiers and helicopters, sheets of flame lighting up the background, as a plausible imitation of napalm devoured the jungle. He went on looking—writing, directing, editing —for the horror he had already found. . . .

What has happened? For more than half its length *Apocalypse Now* comes off as a well-conceived and only slightly rambling film, designed to represent the lure of Vietnam for Americans. Vietnam, for Captain Willard, is a nightmare that cannot be forgotten, admirably rendered in an opening sequence which mingles helicopter blades with rotating ceiling fans, the noises of the jungle with the noises of technology, and Willard's state of mind with the state of that ravaged Asian country. . . . But for Kurtz, Vietnam does more. . . . He mounted successful, unauthorized operations, but finally, it seems, fell in love with his own ruthlessness, and lost all sense of boundaries.

He represents what Mary McCarthy once called the metaphysical element in the American involvement in Vietnam. Not the unwillingness to admit defeat, and not the doctrinal attachment to our system of production and consumption which McCarthy herself identified as metaphysical, but the enormous charm of the inexhaustible enemy, an endless, heartless darkness where a madman could go looking for victory, never finding it, and never having to give up the search.

The trouble is, Coppola has already invented a commanding character who represents all this better than Kurtz does. Lieutenant-Colonel Kilgore . . . is in charge of a cavalry regiment which has traded in its horses for helicopters. He wears an old-fashioned cavalry hat, as if he were in a western, and a dashing yellow foulard. He is a good officer, and cares for his men. (p. 17)

Kilgore makes a remark which has already been much quoted. "I love the smell of napalm in the morning." But what he says a moment later is less brittle, and more interesting. He describes an earlier napalm strike, which left no bodies, only a smell. "That gasoline smell," he says, musing. "It smells like. . . ." He hesitates, looking for a comparison. Then he finds it, and the glint in [Kilgore's] eyes here, and the firm, friendly smile on his amiable face suggest realms of craziness beyond anything Brando's antics can muster, ". . . like victory." He nods, pleased with his formulation: just what he meant to say.

What Coppola has pictured here is the casual everyday lunacy of the war in Vietnam, and the unearthly, overwhelming power of American hardware. . . .

But Coppola doesn't know when to stop, and he lets Willard continue into trouble, just as he lets Kurtz continue into bathos. "It wasn't just insanity and murder," Willard says, "there was enough of that to go around for everybody." And with that phrase, the trap closes and the luminous moment has gone. Coppola has let himself in for a search for something *worse* than insanity and murder. What he might have done, perhaps, is to suggest that Kilgore's lively craziness is quite different from a guilty, overwhelmed insanity which knows itself, and had Kurtz represent that. But he doesn't. Kurtz instead becomes the name for a hyperbole that can't be had, a bulky ghost lost in a forest of symbols, floundering among suggestions of romantic evil and primordial lusts.

There *is* something there, a sense of a condition beyond our power to name it, and when Willard, on his way to kill Kurtz, emerges red-eyed and mud-stained from a swamp, like a creature from an ancient, prehuman world, we glimpse, briefly, the film's other subject: the absolutely unimaginable, caught by miracle in a camera. But this is not a political subject, it has nothing to do with Vietnam, and Coppola in any case can only hint at it, a faint touch of the authentic in a pile of maudlin fakery. Insanity and murder ought to be more than enough even for the most ambitious of moviemakers. They take up more than enough of our history and they were enough for Coppola, before he himself caught the smell of ever-receding victory. (p. 18)

Michael Wood, "Bangs and Whimpers," in The New York Review of Books *(reprinted with permission from* The New York Review of Books; *copyright © 1979 Nyrev, Inc.), Vol. XXVI, No. 15, October 11, 1979, pp. 17-18.*

JOHN TESSITORE

Toward the end of Francis Coppola's "Apocalypse Now," the camera casually, almost randomly, roams across a disheveled hut, passing a small number of scattered books lying in such a way as to suggest recent usage. One of these books is Sir James Frazer's "The Golden Bough." It is no accident. Indeed, this book holds the key to understanding the conclusion of the film that has baffled—and annoyed—most critics and will very likely be unsettling a number of moviegoers now that "Apocalypse Now" is entering general distribution. . . .

If, as most critics have done, we look to Joseph Conrad's "Heart of Darkness" for the answer, we will be . . . disappointed. True, the film does rely upon Conrad's novella for its characters and plot structure, but still it does not explain Mr. Coppola's ending: In the book, Marlow, a young ship's captain, is hired by a rubber firm to guide a boatload of greedy Europeans (Conrad calls them "pilgrims") up the Congo River to the conpany's central outpost, a camp run by an agent named Kurtz. Marlow discovers that this Kurtz has undergone a transformation during his many years of isolation, that the man of culture and ideas had become something primitive and barbaric, a veritable god among the natives. . . . But Marlow has not come to kill Kurtz; on the contrary, he does all in his power to retrieve the sickly agent back to England. In the Conrad novel, Kurtz's death is, in a sense, anticlimactic, resulting at least ostensibly from fever. Obviously "Heart of Darkness" has taken Mr. Coppola just so far; to follow the film to its conclusion we must turn to "The Golden Bough." . . .

[The evidence becomes strong] when in the following paragraph Frazer writes: *"The mystic kings of Fire and Water in Cambodia are not allowed to die a natural death. Hence, when one of them is seriously ill and the elders think that he cannot recover, they stab him to death,"* (emphasis mine).

It is from Frazer and not Conrad that Mr. Coppola has borrowed the location, Cambodia, and the mode of death, stabbing. Perhaps more subtle, but no less telling, is the notion of Mr. Coppola's Kurtz as king of "Fire and Water"—Frazer's symbols which the director exploits and builds upon from the film's very first frame. Fire plays almost no role at all in "Heart of Darkness," whereas in "Apocalypse Now" it operates on several levels—firepower, napalm, burning villages.

Lastly, there is the issue of Kurtz's illness. In both Conrad and Coppola, Kurtz is physically ill; but only with the latter does this invoke the necessity of death (Willard tells us that Kurtz himself, his followers, the very woods wanted him to die), whereas in Conrad the villagers are outraged by the prospect of their loss. Ironically, the Kurtz of "Apocalypse Now" is considered "seriously ill" not only by his devoted followers but by the society that has produced him; for as the General and his staff say repeatedly over luncheon, Kurtz is "definitely insane." They too want Kurtz killed, and Mr. Coppola has thus nicely linked together two seemingly disparate cultures, the so-called civilized and barbaric, in a manner not unlike Conrad's, while arriving at an anthropological conclusion in perfect harmony with Frazer's own. . . .

Of course, it can be argued that Mr. Coppola has failed to cinemagraphically convey the all-important operative myth. One who is familiar with Frazer would know that the death of the man-god springs not from malice but, as with the film's Montagnards, "from their profound veneration for him and from their anxiety to preserve him, or rather the divine spirit by which he is animated, in the most perfect state of efficiency."

But Mr. Coppola has not chosen to share this with his audience, even though it thoroughly explains why, when Willard emerges from the scene of regicide, he is greeted not, as one might expect, with fury, but with adoration. Willard is "the most perfect state of efficiency" to house the sickly king's divine spirit—he is white, he is crafty, he is strong. Willard is the one "whose life the fertility of men, of cattle, and of vegetation [note how the pagan fertility festival perfectly parallels the ascension of the young king] is believed to depend, and who are put to death, whether in single combat or otherwise, in order that the divine spirit may be transmitted to their successor in full vigour, uncontaminated by the weakness and decay of sickness or old age."

To understand "Apocalypse Now," specifically its long final scene, we must see that it rests upon not one work but two: the one for its plot structure, the other for its mythic structure. Where "Heart of Darkness" leaves off, "The Golden Bough" picks up. It is, in fact, a rather textbook formula, and this may explain why Mr. Coppola chose not to give away the full figure in the carpet. By not doing so, however, he has created a Sphinx that is neither man nor beast, and one that poses a riddle to all who come before it.

John Tessitore, "The Literary Roots of 'Apocalypse Now'," in The New York Times, *Section 2 (© 1979 by The New York Times Company; reprinted by permission), October 21, 1979, p. 21.*

JAMES MONACO

The *Godfather* is arguably the most important American film of the 1970s (especially if both parts are considered together) not only because it struck a deep, mythic chord in most Americans, but also because it demonstrated clearly that a highly popular film need not be superficial, that art and commerce need not be antithetical. (pp. 339-40)

Coppola is by no means a *film*maker, the way Cassavetes and Altman are. He makes movies, and thus we tend not to pay attention to his mise en scène. We shouldn't. He obviously wants us to concentrate on the mythic dimensions of his movies, not their cinematography and montage, not even their acting. Nevertheless, as a cinéaste Coppola can hold his own against any rivals. He takes real chances, artistically, and he succeeds. Gordon Willis's cinematography for both [*Godfather*] films manages to capture both the harsh light of southern Italy and the brown shadows of the American forties in direct contradiction to the sort of high-key lighting we would ordinarily expect in a film meant to attract massive audiences. Visually, both films really are private and personal.

This quality extends to the mise en scène. Coppola has a special distaste for closeups, preferring to set his actors in broad visual contexts for the most part. This too causes him to sacrifice some immediately visceral power for more atmospheric, intelligent ends. (pp. 343-44)

Coppola also showed an unparalleled attention to detail in the practical mise en scène of the *Godfather* films. It wasn't necessary. He would have got by with less. A few of us recognize the rightness of a car with wooden bumpers in 1945. (p. 345)

Meticulous attention to period detail is, at the least, nostalgic. Coppola makes something more of it here. He re-creates times and places that many of us half remember. In the process he helps us to integrate the experience of our own pasts.

Similarly, a significant, if minor, reason for the films' success with audiences is their evocation of the forties and fifties. Coppola knows that what the world knows as tomato sauce Americans with Italian backgrounds call "gravy," and that the first thing you do upon entering the kitchen is to dip a piece of bread in the slowly simmering pot, as Sonny does when he goes to see his mother to break the news that Pop has been shot.

These thousands of details eventually add up to a powerful and affecting authenticity which measurably moves audiences, even if it doesn't call attention to itself. This profound—even reverent—reconstruction of a common past, together with an understanding of the inherent dilemmas of American family life that approaches tragic dimensions, and a political perspective that thoroughly dissects the myth of the American Dream and demonstrates with painful clarity that "we are all undesirables," makes *The Godfather* (both parts—all seven hours of it) the most significant American film since *Citizen Kane*. Charles Foster Kane and Vito Andolini Corleone, separated by thirty years, are brothers. Together they explain a great deal about this country—more than most books, more than most songs. They are the best evidence of the extraordinary power of the medium of film.

If Francis Coppola never made another film save *The Godfather,* his place in the history of American film would be assured. (pp. 345-46)

James Monaco, "Who's Talking? Cassavetes, Altman, and Coppola," in his American Film Now: The People, the Power, the Money, the Movies *(copyright © 1979 by James Monaco; reprinted by arrangement with The New American Library, Inc., New York, New York), The New American Library, 1979, pp. 295-348.**

MICHAEL DEMPSEY

Apocalypse Now seeks less to meditate on the war and more to plunge us as viscerally into it as any movie possibly can. Structurally, it is a river movie the way *Easy Rider* is a road movie, a succession of events and set-pieces. The characters are quite simple; apart from Willard and Kurtz, hardly any register for more than a sequence. . . .

The shot of the chopper in the tree quotes from a similar image in *Aguirre, Wrath of God,* a boat high above the river which looks like a mirage to the conquistadors. Visually—with its concentration on the immensity of the jungle, the strangeness and the intermittence of riverbank existence, the textures of the water, pristine vistas of pellucid sky through which warplanes streak and bomb, and a pervasive sense of blinding, stoned nightmare—*Apocalypse Now* draws on Herzog and probably on *Deliverance* as well. The results are nothing less than awesome—the movie frequently has the menancing visual clarity and the morbid luminescence of a De Chirico deserted plaza—and, besides all this, the film is very funny, too. . . .

Coppola states that his goal was 'a film experience that would give its audience a sense of the horror, the madness, the sensuousness, and the moral dilemma of the Vietnam war.' The first three he has captured as no one else ever has. However, what Coppola means by 'moral dilemma' is not especially clear, since, like the other recent movies about Vietnam, *Apocalypse Now* says nothing about why America got involved in the war. (p. 6)

[The images and sounds of *Apocalypse Now* seek to] capture the nature of American grandiosity, a pervasive sense of limitless power being wielded by cracked-open minds which have lost their compass, which have become caught up in a collective madness for its own sake. This is what Willard's journey reveals, just as Marlow's equivalent journey gradually brings to light the rapacities of colonialism. *Apocalypse Now* wants to make us experience these monstrosities, these distortions, as directly as film is capable of doing, leaving us to make of them what we will afterwards. (pp. 6-7)

The genuinely thorny matter of *Apocalypse Now* is the relationship between Kurtz and Willard. This becomes glaringly apparent in the way that the final segment of the picture shifts drastically from amphetamine action to portentous soliloquy as its prime stylistic motif. Kurtz is the principal speaker. He muses over an ethereal memory of his Midwestern homeland, quotes T. S. Eliot on the decline of the West, recounts a grotesque anecdote. . . . [We] never see Kurtz's men in action or any sign of their rapine other than the corpses and the heads strewn around his headquarters.

To a certain extent, this strategy is understandable. If Coppola showed Kurtz and his men running amok or even detailed the results of their activities, he would probably dilute the idea that what Willard experiences on the river is even worse than the crimes attributed to Kurtz. . . .

But Kurtz does hew to Conrad's characterisation; Willard, on the other hand, has been strangely reconceived. Conrad's Marlow is a stolid, sane, plodding man despite a life spent in tropical regions. So it is believable that he would feel the lure of Kurtz and his legend; they are so foreign to his nature that they can tease his imagination and as a result gradually draw him into a confrontation with everything that he has suppressed in order to become stolid, sane, plodding. But Willard is emotionally and mentally unbalanced almost from frame one. . . . Willard is an undercover assassin for the American military who has already experienced Kurtzian madness, unlike Marlow. This makes it a trickier matter to accept the fascination which he, like Marlow, is supposed to feel the closer he gets to Kurtz and the more he hears about his legend.

Reading a classified dossier, Willard learns that one of Kurtz's primary offences in the eyes of the American high command was the unauthorised assassinations of some Vietnamese officials whom he considered Viet Cong double agents. These killings sound like just the sort of assignment which Willard has carried out; in the narration, he even speaks of having felt the last breaths of his own victims against his face. Perhaps we are supposed to surmise from this hint that Willard feels a sense of obscure kinship with Kurtz. Both have thrown off civilised restraints; both have committed brutal crimes. But Kurtz has gone infinitely further, and his reputed kingdom of horror tantalises Willard, makes him yearn to divine its profoundest secrets, especially what it feels like to shed all restraints. Within the film's frame of reference, this seems like the only possible catalyst for Willard's interest in Kurtz. Yet *Apocalypse Now* never articulates it. Why not? (p. 7)

One way of possibly teasing out an answer is looking back at his other films, in which two recurring figures are prominent: Godfathers and Loners. The first category includes, besides Kurtz, the crazed matriarch of *Dementia 13,* General George Patton in the Franklin Schaffner-George C. Scott film (which Coppola first scripted), Vito Corleone in *The Godfather,* and Michael Corleone in *The Godfather, Part II.* Along with Willard, Harry Caul, the surveillance man of *The Conversation,* and Natalie Ravenna, the runaway housewife of *The Rain People,* are Coppola's prime examples of Loners. Both figures are intimately connected with families, which are frequently tribes of killers (the Corleone mafia family, Kurtz's army). The Godfathers rule these families almost as if they were demigods. The Loners try to deny family ties (Harry Caul), flee them (Natalie Ravenna), take them over (Michael Corleone), or annihilate them (Willard). . . .

In *Apocalypse Now,* Kurtz suggests a Godfather at bay, swollen with power yet unable to satisfy his deepest longings. Orson Welles' abortive version of *Heart of Darkness* evidently would have drawn parallels not only between Kurtz and Hitler but between Kurtz and Welles himself. Comparably, Coppola has said, 'I found that many of the ideas and images with which I was working as a film director began to coincide with the realities of my own life, and that I, like Captain Willard, was moving up a river in a faraway jungle, looking for answers and hoping for some kind of catharsis.' Even allowing for a certain amount of hubris, this sounds odd, for it is Kurtz, rather than Willard, who suggests a self-portrait. And catharsis of what?

Coppola has not only made movies about Godfathers; he has also become one. For years, he has been seeking to make himself Promethean, both as an artist and as a mogul. . . . Analogies between his ambitions and Kurtz's reveries spring readily to mind; Coppola, too, has his extended family and would be king, though a benevolent one. . . .

[The] grandiosity of Coppola is a matter of colossal fantasies of art, fantasies which only a particular kind of film director can possibly hope to challenge. One imagines a film-maker like Coppola supposing that, with such power and wealth as he commands, vistas of artistic magnificence ought to lie within his grasp. Certainly, the scale of *Apocalypse Now* suggests an all-out assault on Greatness, Meaning, Art.

Yet art proves to be elusive, with or without the capital A, just as victory did to the nearly unbridled military might of America during the Vietnam war. The beached, inert figure of Kurtz bears witness to this frustration; like Coppola, he has gone the limit in trying to attain not just ecstasy but permanent ecstasy, yet it remains mockingly out of reach. This same intimation, that existence is fundamentally hollow and ultimately disappointing, afflicts all the major Coppola characters, and the sombreness of his cinematic vision bears further witness to it. When (in a departure from Conrad) Willard the Loner kills Kurtz the Godfather, we are meant to understand it as a mercy killing which releases Kurtz from unbearable loneliness and despair. Perhaps, symbolically, Coppola the Godfather is dying at the hands of Coppola the Loner, who might be his younger self from the days when he was merely an artist. (pp. 8-9)

Michael Dempsey, "'Apocalypse Now'," in Sight and Sound *(copyright © 1979 by The British Film Institute), Vol. 49, No. 1, Winter, 1979-80, pp. 5-10.*

Maya Deren

1908-1961

Russian-born American filmmaker, dancer, film critic, and actress.

An important figure in American avant-garde filmmaking of the forties, Deren created the trend and the marketplace for avant-garde films. She wrote extensively about her own work and film theory in general. In 1959 she wrote an article defining what she considered truly independent films: films made by one person. In this article, she praises amateur filmmakers and what they stand for: "[That] very word—from the Latin 'amateur'—'lover' means one who does something for the love of the thing rather than for economic reasons or necessity." Her profound respect for independent films inspired her own work and she became involved in promoting the work of others. To this end, she established the Creative Film Foundation to give financial aid to filmmakers.

Deren's early films were surrealistic and fantastic, constructed to portray a dream rather than tell a story. Abandoning this somewhat narrative style, unstructured as it was, in favor of purely physical expression in free form, she made films such as *Meditation on Violence*. Her work is difficult and obscure and the reaction to her films is sometimes negative.

Deren has been called the "Mother of Underground Film." She was a leader in certain areas; for instance, she legitimatized the use of 16mm film as an artistic medium. In 1946 she rented the Provincetown Playhouse to show her films. It was the first time that a public theater screened privately produced 16mm films. A large crowd gathered for the showing, prompting police to investigate. When asked if the crowd was planning a demonstration, one participant answered, "No, it's a revolution in filmmaking."

JAMES AGEE

"Meshes of the Afternoon" and "At Land" can be roughly classified as "dream" films and also approach, as Parker Tyler has said, "a type of personal expression in cinema analogous to the lyric poem." . . . There are many satisfactions of mood and implication and image in the movies, of kinds which are the unique property of the movie camera, and which are hardly even hinted in studio productions. Yet I cannot feel that there is anything really original about them—that they do anything important, for instance, which was not done, and done to an ill-deserved death, by some of the European avant-gardists, and especially by the surrealists of the 1920's. At worst, in fact, they are solemnly, arrogantly, distressingly pretentious and arty. Nevertheless, I think they are to be seen, and that there is a good deal in them to be liked, enjoyed, and respected. I don't at all agree with Miss Deren that "reality," in its conventional camera sense, cannot be turned into a work of art without being turned also into a fantasia of the unconscious; but if you have to believe that in order to try to do it—which I doubt—then I am glad that she does. For I certainly believe that it is worth doing; and I know of nobody else in films, just now, who is paying any more attention to that great universe of movie possibility than to make safely conducted little tours of the border villages. (p. 270)

James Agee, "Films: 'Meshes of the Afternoon' and 'At Land'," in The Nation *(copyright 1946 The Nation Associates, Inc.), Vol. 162, No. 9, March 2, 1946, pp. 269-70.*

MANNY FARBER

[Miss Deren's] movies, which she once called "Abandoned Films" and now calls "Films in the Classicist Tradition," are Freudian-toned, lesbianish, freezing, arty, eclectic, conventional and safe. Utilizing real environments and people, they show people who look mesmerized or often ghostly moving through situations that have been contrived to have some Freudian meaning. You are always conscious of a mechanical-mindedness because of the pretense and self-consciousness of the acting, the labored arrangement of objects and people, and Miss Deren's fascination for trick effects with acting, composing and camera. The bleakness of these brief films comes out in the hard, stolid treatment of subject matter. Whether she is filming a perfect stretch of Long Island beach or a mugging esthete, her touch is totally lacking in sensuousness, humor and love, and she seems to petrify the subject until it takes on the character of a museum piece. The lack of sparkle is largely due to a dead eye for photography—she has no feeling for light and dark and is as unable to spot a cliché as a Tin Pan Alley hack. . . .

"At Land," which is fairly typical of the substance of her movies, starts at a lonely postcard-pretty beach where the waves operate in reverse and leave in their receding wash a dead girl in a sarong (Miss Deren)—all of which may be meant to symbolize a birth fantasy. (p. 555)

This opening stretch of "At Land" gives an indication of how trite and funereal these movies are. The first scene of a clear day at the beach, of breakers washing over a corpse, is such a cliché you feel that you're seeing it for the hundredth time, and when the girl stares up the stand of beechwood you are reminded of arty beach photographs and annoyed by the pansyish composing and lighting. . . . With thousands of people from the Fifty-seventh Street art world simulating gayety at a banquet table and Miss Deren crawling the length of the table as though she were paying off an election bet, it is hard to believe that there is not one exciting detail in the whole episode. Instead, there is a seedy, dreary air about the affair because of the barren hall, the bleak lighting and the fact that the guests seem so uncomfortable and unhappy. (p. 556)

Manny Farber, "Maya Deren's Films," in The New Republic *(reprinted by permission of* The New Republic; *© 1946 The New Republic, Inc.), Vol. 115, No. 17, October 28, 1946, pp. 555-56.*

MAYA DEREN

It is the privilege of an individual to say, privately, of a work of art: "I don't like it" ; but it is the public responsibility of a professional critic to indicate why it isn't art. Mr. Farber [see excerpt above] has reviewed my films in a piece remarkable for its substitution of emotionally charged invective for considered analysis. Since the former is by far the most economical form of expression, he is able to imply in one sentence more than I can answer in one page. The issue here is that of responsible criticism. My objection is not that Mr. Farber does not like the films and/or me, but that he does not explain or justify his appraisal of them. Instead, he creates a "review" out of extraneous information, misleading half-truths, snidely derogatory personal references and a Farberian version of Freudianism.

Although he is skilled enough to make both a "corpse" and a "birth-fantasy" out of the same image, he has not grasped the primary fact that Freudianism is a method of interpretation and is not a quality of the person or object interpreted. The films cannot be "Freudian-toned," as he called them. Only an analyst can be Freudian, as Mr. Farber has chosen to be, in defiance of my printed program notes which specify that the objects and events are *not* intended as symbols "to be interpreted according to some exterior system of psychology" but are "images whose value and meaning are defined and confined by their actual function in the context as a whole." And by what ethical acrobatics does he simultaneously criticize me for the very "Freudianism" which he imposes upon the films against my will.

Only one of the four films is even remotely concerned with sex. Certainly none of them is homosexual (unless, in his anxiety, Mr. Farber understands homosexuality whenever two members of the same sex appear on the screen at the same time). As a matter of fact, Mr. Farber is singular in his capacity to create out of the films (as if they were Rorschach tests for him) such an excess and gamut of sexual implications. . . . And what of his effort to imply narcissism to me by stressing my personal performance in the first two films, when he knew it to be a matter of expediency, and omitting the last two films, in which coöperative friends replace me in the principal roles? Or of neglecting the last two films entirely, which would ordinarily have been considered the most indicative of future direction in a young artist, and which he said, privately, that he liked best. The issue here is clearly one of critical responsibility, quite apart from the merit of the films as art.

Maya Deren, in her letter to the Editor, in The New Republic *(reprinted by permission of* The New Republic; *© 1946 The New Republic, Inc.), Vol. 115, No. 19, November 11, 1946, p. 630.*

MEPHISTO

[*Image in the Snow*] is a combination of poetry, music and cinematography which envisions the march through life, through the city streets, and finally through a cemetery, of a young man in search of spiritual understanding and peace. Miss Deren's photography, Mr. [William] Maas's poetry, and Mr. [Ben] Weber's music complement each other so closely and are so completely interwoven as to produce a single work of art in which no one element is dominant. In combination with Miss Deren's simple, yet daring and frequently unorthodox photographic techniques, this collaboration produces a startling mobile fresco in three dimensions, which engrosses the attention despite the fact that no conventional story apparatus is present. . . .

[In *Meshes of the Afternoon, A Study in Choreography for Camera, At Land, Ritual in Transfigured Time,* and *Meditation on Violence*] the photographer, largely without the aid of music or sound of any kind, has been preoccupied with choreographic problems in relation to photography, and each of these short films is a kind of dance. There is no question of simply taking motion pictures of dancers in action. The picture itself, in various remarkable ways, becomes part of the choreography, whether by camera movement, contrasts of blacks and whites, timing, rhythmic film sequences, repetitions, or whatever means the producer has found the camera to be capable of.

Miss Deren always seeks integration, even total identification, between subject and picturization, so that, in the end product, one does not and could not exist without the other. There is a vitality in this fusion of arts that may represent the real and the ultimate function of the motion picture as an artistic medium. Miss Deren has gone farther in the exploration of its possibilities, and from sounder esthetic premises, than anyone else I know.

Mephisto, "Mephisto's Musings," in Musical America *(all rights reserved), Vol. 73, No. 7, May, 1953, p. 9.**

MAYA DEREN

My films might be called metaphysical, referring to their thematic content. It has required milleniums of torturous evolution for nature to produce the intricate miracle which is man's mind. It is this which distinguishes him from all other living creatures, for he not only reacts to matter but can meditate upon its meaning. This metaphysical action of the mind has as much reality and importance as the material and physical activities of his body. My films are concerned with meanings—ideas and concepts—not with matter.

My films might be called poetic, referring to the attitude towards these meanings. If philosophy is concerned with understanding the meaning of reality, then poetry—and art in general—is a celebration, a singing of values and meanings. I refer also to the structure of the films—a logic of ideas and qualities, rather than of causes and events.

My films might be called choreographic, referring to the

design and stylization of movement which confers ritual dimension upon functional motion—just as simple speech is made into song when affirmation of intensification on a higher level is intended.

My films might be called experimental, referring to the use of the medium itself. In these films, the camera is not an observant, recording eye in the customary fashion. The full dynamics and expressive potentials of the total medium are ardently dedicated to creating the most accurate metaphor for the meaning.

In setting out to communicate principles, rather than to relay particulars, and in creating a metaphor which is true to the idea rather than to the history of experience of any one of several individuals, I am addressing myself not to any particular group but to a special area and definite faculty in every or any man—to that part of him which creates myths, invents divinities, and ponders, for no practical purpose whatsoever, on the nature of things. (pp. 162-63)

Maya Deren, "A Statement of Principles," in Film Culture *(copyright 1961 by* Film Culture*), No. 22, Summer, 1961, pp. 161-63.*

RUDOLF ARNHEIM

[Maya Deren] insisted that the true magic of the photograph in motion is more than a reshuffling of raw material, more than a masquerade. And she, who could be energetic to the point of violence when she fought for her ideas, had the sensitive fingers and eyes of a surgeon, when it came to shaping her photographic visions without hurting the tissues of the physical surface.

What does she show us? What was she after? She was one of the artists and thinkers who speak of the great paradox of our time; who say that, although our civilization has come closest to penetrating the secrets of inorganic and organic matter, we are less familiar with the world of tangible things than any human tribe has ever been. And, thus, in Maya Deren's films, the familiar world captures us by its pervasive strangeness. The white hands press against a window pane that is not there. The human body drifts through weightless space. Geographic distances give way to new visible connections. There is no practical plot to these films. When two faces look at each other, two minds call on each other. When an actor or dancer walks across the screen, he travels the path of his life's journey. The staircase turns in symbolic space, and a seated woman winds the thread of a hank of wool fatefully.

Do these pictures show us more than the alienation of the familiar? Are they simply the ghosts of a world that has died on us? I would not undertake to make the happenings in these films explicit through words. Nor do I believe that they were verbally explicit in Maya's own thoughts, articulate though she was. What we can assert is that the sequences of her images are logical. They are neither arbitrary nor absurd. They follow the letter of a law we never studied on paper; but, guided by our eyes, our minds conform willingly. (pp. 85-6)

Rudolf Arnheim, "To Maya Deren," in Film Culture *(copyright 1962 by* Film Culture*), No. 24, Spring, 1962 (and reprinted in* Film Culture Reader, *edited by P. Adams Sitney, Praeger Publishers, 1970, pp. 84-6).*

TONY RAYNS

The Chinese martial arts clearly offered [Maya Deren] exactly what she was looking for, not just in their balletic grace but also in their implicit union of philosophical and physical essences. Accordingly, *Meditation on Violence* shows a martial arts performance in virtual isolation, and is shot and edited in a way that 'expresses' the film-maker's reading of the performer's actions. It is apparently structured as a cycle: the half-naked performer is first seen practising so-called 'Wu-Tang' movements (a 'soft', interiorised style of boxing), then abruptly switching to 'Shao-Lin' movements (which are 'harder', less physically harmonious and more aggressive), and then escalating into 'Shao-Lin' swordplay. For the latter sequence only, the performer appears in exotic robes and is seen in the open air; the swordplay climaxes with a series of slow-motion leaps and a protracted freeze-frame. The film then retraces its steps through the cycle, ending as it began. (Although only the most hawk-eyed viewer would spot it, the movements in the second half of the film are in fact shown in reverse motion.) . . . Deren's intention that the film be perceived as a single continuous movement is partially realised through her skill in cutting always on a physical motion, creating elisions rather than jumps. But her grander metaphysical pretensions in the project . . . are muffled and largely obscure in the actual film . . . , partly because of Deren's own reluctance to admit the limitations of her effects. What does emerge is a sense of the critical relationship between theory and practice, evident in the contrast between the graceful 'Wu-Tang' sequences and the relatively graceless 'outgoing' movements in the 'Shao-Lin' sequences. And the fact that the film is both unequal to Deren's ambitions and misleading as a 'study' of the martial arts does not ultimately diminish its interest—which is that few, if any, other directors were thinking of film form in comparable terms in 1948. Deren's significance as a theorist continues to outweigh her shortcomings as a film-maker.

Tony Rayns, "Short Films: 'Meditation on Violence'," in Monthly Film Bulletin *(copyright © The British Film Institute, 1976), Vol. 43, No. 505, February, 1976, p. 40.*

THOMAS MAYER

Meshes of the Afternoon marks the revival of independent film in America after the experiments of the 1920's and early 1930's died out during the Depression. A modest, simple film of less than 20-minutes in length, it combines elements which arise in several of Deren's later films: elements such as the use of ritualistic figures, a rich combination of interiors and exteriors, and a fluid use of the camera —including the intelligent use of subjective camera angles before they became the rage in the late 1940's in Hollywood filmmaking. (p. 8)

Meshes of the Afternoon is a fascinating and monumental short film which never fails to astound those who see it for the first time. Even today the film appears fresh and inventive, unlike most *avant-garde* films of the Forties. Some of the credit for the inventiveness of this film must go to [her collaborator] Alexander Hammid. . . .

At Land retains some of the influence of Alexander Hammid, but is radically different from *Meshes of the Afternoon.* Though somewhat less polished than *Meshes,* it is also a seminal film in the American *avant-garde* in use of imagery, disjointed montage to relate disparate locations, and innovative design.

A Study in Choreography for Camera (1945), Maya Deren's third film, has influenced nearly every dance film made since, although this study is a mere three minutes long. In it, a dancer . . . begins a stretching-out movement in an outdoor setting, and ends the step in a room. Through the montage, the dancer appears to dance through discontinuous spaces (rooms, a woods, a museum courtyard) with continuous movements. *A Study in Choreography for Camera* has a beauty and grace rare in a film of such short duration and, even today, provides a fresh look at the possibilities of filming dance. (p. 9)

[*Meditation on Violence*] suffers from Deren's personal over-intellectualized concept—not sufficiently borne out in the film itself. It is one of her most ambitious films, and her biggest failure. It shows a Chinese . . . performing three modes of traditional Chinese boxing, from Wu-Tang, Shao-lin, and Shao-lin with a sword—freezing the frame in the middle of the film—then reversing the motion back through Shao-lin with sword, to Shao-lin, to Wu-tang. The interest of the concept not withstanding, the film rapidly becomes tedious to watch. . . .

The Very Eye of Night [which is totally in negative] concerns the Sleeper, who enters a new universe and is pulled into a *pas de trois* of "Self, Sleeper, and Venus", as Ms. Deren puts it in her writing. Unfortunately, while the film is a fascinating experiment in presenting dance on film—in its own way, as important a film as Norman McLaren's *Pas de Deux*—it is impossible to follow what happens in the film without reference to the filmmaker's writings. And again, as with *Meditation on Violence*, her concepts about *The Very Eye of Night* are far more interesting and complex than the film which resulted.

The dancers appear as white figures surrounded by black, portraying gods as parts of constellations in the heavens. The film experiments with shifting perspective, conflict of scale, and abundant use of superimpositions to give a layered effect of the dancers floating in space. . . .

In 1973, twelve years after her death, her third husband, Teiji Ito, and Cherel Ito, his wife, announced plans to edit the many hours of film and wire recordings Deren had made, into a film which would preserve as much as possible the intention of the original film, while keeping it to a manageable and commercially viable length.

An excellent introduction to the subject of the Voudoun religion of Haiti, [*Divine Horsemen: The Living Gods of Haiti*] incorporates Deren's footage in a skillful and constantly fascinating way. . . .

Thomas Mayer, "The Legend of Maya Deren: Champion of American Independent Film," in Film News *(© Rohama Lee, d/b/a Film News Company), Vol. 36, No. 4, September-October, 1979, pp. 8-10.*

Carl Theodor Dreyer

1889-1968

Danish director and screenwriter.

Dreyer stands as one of the seminal figures in the evolution of film. His output spans the most formative decades of cinema, from silent movies to sound and subsequent innovations. Before he became a filmmaker Dreyer worked as a journalist for several Copenhagen newspapers. Later he fell back on this profession during the sometimes lengthy intervals between his cinematic projects. He was next employed by Nordisk Films Kompagni, where he adapted novels for film and acquired experience in the mechanics of the art form. In 1920 Dreyer made his first film, *The President,* a competent melodrama which early illustrates the director's characteristic use of the close-up. The innovator of the close-up device, D. W. Griffith, influenced Dreyer's second film, *Leaves from Satan's Book,* which contains structural echoes of *Intolerance*. More closely related to Dreyer's later style of intimate character portraits was *The Parson's Widow*. Influenced by the work of Swedish directors Mauritz Stiller and Victor Sjöström, *The Parson's Widow* is generally acknowledged as the first artistic success among his early silent pictures.

Dreyer's last silent film, recognized as a late masterpiece of the era, was *The Passion of Joan of Arc*. Distinctive for its preponderant use of the close-up, this work is an unusual one for Dreyer because, rather than being adapted from literature, the story has as its basis actual transcripts from the famous trial. *The Passion of Joan of Arc* also introduces the thematic core of spiritual concerns central to Dreyer's mature artistic vision. *Vampyr* further points to a supernatural realm and more particularly examines the ordeal of those who exist on its brink. *Day of Wrath* revived the subject of religious persecution seen previously in the ordeal of Joan of Arc, now dramatized through the tragedy of seventeenth-century witch trials.

Dreyer is noted for his generous and compassionate portrayals of the spiritually alienated, a recurring role exemplified by the seemingly mad Johannes in *The Word*. His emphasis on unorthodox forms of mysticism has sometimes caused Dreyer to be stereotyped as a visionary Dane; but his emphasis, as many critics and Dreyer himself have indicated, is more directly on the inner spiritual world of individuals than on any external cosmic design. Dreyer has said that "the artist must describe inner, not outer life," and he used the transcendental primarily as a vehicle to achieve symbolic heights in his themes and characterizations.

Dreyer's last film, *Gertrud,* made after a creative hiatus of ten years, is more conventional in its background than the ones preceding it. However, the film continues the director's basic thematic interest in his characters's interior lives. Widely criticized as a monotonously paced affront to its audiences when initially released, *Gertrud* has since been reevaluated as a masterpiece of nuance, a status that only a few early critics claimed for it. Other Dreyer films have also received belated acceptance. Because Dreyer sought to realize highly individual themes and effects, his work is not easily compared to that of other filmmakers: it is difficult to categorize within cinematic trends and movements. It is this very individualism, however, which places Dreyer among the masters of cinema.

HARRY ALAN POTAMKIN

[*The Passion of Jeanne d'Arc* is a] profound and truly passionate motion picture. (p. 7)

There is no extraneous detail in the film. Not once does a detail fail to directly relate and contribute to the subject-matter. At one point, Jeanne sees the grave-digger pull up a skull. Unnecessary? Obvious? There is a swift succession, almost staccato in its brevity, of a field of flowers. The previous detail becomes inevitable, poignant. In fact, the entire film has that virtue, that at any moment the detail on the screen validates what preceded it. This is rhythm, this is art. The beautiful flight of birds, as Jeanne is perishing, the mother suckling her child—the former might be a sentimentalism, the latter a sur-realistic simplicism; but by the severe control of the director, they become terrible convictions of the world that would let one who loved free flight perish bound, and one who herself would suckle life burn at the stake. Creation against desolation! (p. 8)

[In the film there is no] specious prettiness, but hardiness, man in his physical variousness, man in his spiritual diversity serving the same master—Interest. The Interest of State, the Interest of Church, the Interest of God. . . .

The Passion of Jeanne d'Arc is an historical film, but not a costume film; an historical film that is contemporaneous in its universal references. *The Passion of Jeanne d'Arc* is a religious film, but not a sanctimonious film. Life, it urges, is transcendent. It is a transcendent film. (p. 9)

Harry Alan Potamkin, "'The Passion of Jeanne d'Arc'," in National Board of Review Magazine *(copyright, 1929), Vol. IV, No. 1, January, 1929, pp. 7-9.*

JOHN HUTCHENS

The Maid of Orleans has come singularly and movingly to life in Carl Th. Dreyer's film, *The Passion of Joan of Arc.* (p. 373)

The legends and fancies built about Joan in the last five centuries are so many and diversely colored, so blighted by fanaticism or fervor or chilling "analysis", that most of them have led either too tricky or too mystic a path back to that gray day of the murder at Rouen. To its vast credit, the scenario wrought by Mr. Dreyer and Joseph Delteil does nothing of the sort. Instead, with the absorbing directness of a piece of excellent trial reporting, it has hurdled the boundaries and by-the-way distractions of some centuries of legend, has gone back to understand what happened to Joan, and why. And such are its qualities, as suddenly refreshing and clarifying as those of good painting, that from it she now emerges a still simple child, heartbreaking alike in her helplessness and her courage.

Under Mr. Dreyer's direction, her story is told entirely as a series of individual studies,—of Joan herself and those who judged her, and the telling of it is a sharp and unsparing performance, the first of its kind the screen has seen. In each study is the completeness of a single portrait, such that the composition of *The Passion of Joan of Arc* is that of a gallery stirred to life and given flow and beauty by movement. Save for a few moments at the end of the film, the spectator stands no more chance of escaping that ring of mediaeval cunning and cruelty than does Joan herself: in one face after another you see her doom awaiting her with the inevitability of all great tragedy, here made more tragic still by occasional flashes of useless sympathy. In the selection and photography of this overpowering milieu, Mr. Dreyer knew his technique and handled it with all competence. If occasionally the medium seems insistently used, it must be realized that, while the "close-up" is usually reserved only for dramatic crises, there could be in the depiction of Joan's last few days no faltering of emotional pitch, no moment when a helpless audience would not have been torn between foreboding, indignation, passionate sympathy and an equally deep sense of futility. (pp. 373-74)

John Hutchens, "'The Passion of Joan of Arc'," in Theatre Arts Monthly *(copyright, 1929, by Theatre Arts, Inc.), Vol. XIII, No. 5, May, 1929, pp. 373-74.*

WILLIAM TROY

[What makes Dreyer's "Passion of Joan of Arc" still an exciting cinema experience] is the directorial enterprise which dared recreate one of the great European stories in terms of the new art. The picture belongs to the last days of the silent era; it was the culmination of the close-up school of direction, the last and most serious attempt to reduce the complex cinema art to the narrowly stylized art of pantomime. Against a blank white background Dreyer casts his heads of priests, soldiers, inquisitors, and by an abstraction of everything but the facial expressions registered by each of them in the course of the situation, seeks to communicate something purer and more essential than could be communicated by words or action. . . . [The] picture must be considered one of the minor masterpieces of the screen. (p. 364)

William Troy, "Time and Space," in The Nation *(copyright 1933 The Nation Associates, Inc.), Vol. 137, No. 3560, September 27, 1933, pp. 363-64.*

BOSLEY CROWTHER

["Day of Wrath" is] a curious study of the power of evil. . . . And again it manifests the stark integrity and the solid character of Dreyer's style—his absolute perfection of the image, his interest in faces and his heavy restraint.

Indeed, the visual richness of this picture and its brilliant instrumentation of the human face cause one to wish very strongly that the drama were more insistent than it is. But, unfortunately, in telling a story of love and hate in a Danish parish house back in the middle ages, Dreyer has kept his idea so obscure and the action so slow and monotonous that the general audience will find it a bore. . . .

[In] spite of the fine, tasteful production and the photogenic excellence of all the cast, the drama lacks any compulsion. "Day of Wrath" is handsome but dull. . . .

Bosley Crowther, "'Day of Wrath'," in The New York Times *(© 1948 by The New York Times Company; reprinted by permission), April 26, 1948, p. 27.*

JAMES AGEE

[Of] the movies made during the past twenty years I think [*Day of Wrath*] is unquestionably one of the dozen or so best worth seeing. (p. 303)

Movies seldom contain any material, except by inadvertence or head-on outrage, which can interest the morally curious; this one contains a good deal, and none of it is inadvertent or outrageous. I particularly respect the film's interest in the deeply entangled interproductiveness of good and evil among several people and within single people; its steep, Lutheran kind of probity—that is, its absolute recognition of the responsibility of the individual, regardless of extenuating or compulsive circumstances; its compassion; and its detachment. . . .

Carl Dreyer has done a very hard job beautifully. He has not only preserved an amount of psychological and moral complexity which isn't popularly supposed to be possible in movies; he has also made them very clear visually, as a rule by very simple means. (p. 304)

Dreyer's lighting, and pace, and sound—including his use of dialogue—I wholly respect. My impression is that, short of absurdity, he wants to work close to their respective absolutes of darkness, stasis, and silence, and never to deviate from these absolutes beyond the minimum that is justified. I don't think this is the only good way to work or necessarily the best; but I suspect for instance that Gluck, and Beethoven, in some of their finest music, were acutely aware of silence. I'm not implying that Dreyer has done anything here to approach their work; I do mean that the style he has worked out for this film has a severe, noble purity which very little else in movies or, so far as I know, in contemporary art can approach, or even tries to. By one seeing, anyhow, I don't think there is a single excess in word or lighting or motion, or a single excessive stopping-down of any of these. Dreyer appears to know and to care more about faces than about anything else; it seems to me a sound preference; and since he is served at worst by very good actors and faces and at best by wonderful ones, the finest things in this film are his close-ups. They are held longer than anyone else except Chaplin could dare or afford to hold them; and as a rule they convey the kind of intricate subtlety, mental and spiritual, which one can ordinarily expect to find only in certain kinds of writing.

In these long close-ups, as in much else that he does, Dreyer goes against most of the "rules" that are laid down, even by good people, for making genuine and good motion pictures. In a sense I have to admit that he is far out at the edge rather than close to the center of all that I think might be most productive and original. But there is only one rule for movies that I finally care about: that the film interest the eyes, and do its job through the eyes. Few movie-makers do that, few even of those who are generally well esteemed. Dreyer has never failed to, and I cannot imagine that he ever will. For that reason alone, even if I did not also respect him as one of the few moralists, and classicists, and incorruptible artists, in movies, I would regard him as a master and this film as a quiet masterpiece. (pp. 304-05)

James Agee, "Films," in The Nation *(copyright 1948 The Nation Associates, Inc.), Vol. 166, No. 21, May 22, 1948 (and reprinted in his* Agee on Film, Vol. 1, *Grosset & Dunlap, 1967, pp. 303-05).*

RICHARD ROWLAND

[Dreyer's aim in *The Passion of Joan of Arc* is close] to that of the early Flemish painters whose painstaking realism is as full of compassion as it is unrelenting in its mirroring of nature. One thinks of Breughel's stubble-chinned "Old Shepherd," or the brutally unmistakable humanity of Bosch's "Crowning with Thorns" . . . ; like theirs, Dreyer's art stems from a conviction, both disillusioned and confident, that whatever coarseness or cruelty may characterize them, men are what matter in this world; now you, the spectator, are the dead center of that world, involved in mankind with a painful, inescapable, and somehow ennobling intensity.

One scene in *Joan of Arc* underlines this with curious power. The court has decided that Joan is ill (else how could she defy the Church and claim to have seen naked angels?) and may possibly be cured if she is bled. No detail of the bleeding is spared us; the audience writhes as the cut is made and the black vital stream spurts into the bowl. But, curiously, in the end the effect is neither unpleasant nor clinical. One feels the river pulsing in one's own veins; one remembers mortality, and immediately, as its corollary, vitality. This is the sort of physicality that Dreyer's films have, but it springs not at all from Swiftian disgust. He never lets us forget the shell of flesh which we inhabit, but he never forgets the mystery of the personality that fills the shell—the quality to which Swift's outrage at natural functions never let him penetrate. The love scenes in *Day of Wrath* are brilliant in their ability to suggest, without representing, the tumult of lust. The dappled sunlight agitating the faces of the lovers suggests overpoweringly what is made more specific by the image of the plunging horses later. The lovers' experience is general and universal, but it is also individual, and it is the individuality that is ultimately of interest to Dreyer. The physicality serves, as it were, to draw us into the film, but the real subject is the ceaseless struggle that individuality wages against the enclosing world. (pp. 55-6)

Day of Wrath is a study in witchcraft, and yet there is no historical analysis of the cause and effect of the phenomenon. Here is a witch; what does that mean? Dreyer tells us. It means, specifically, to be a lonely and frightened girl longing for tenderness and companionship, uncertain of her own worth and strength, a quiet girl with sly slant eyes which suggest her lusting after the flesh and an external repose which is her only strength against the jealousy of her mother-in-law and the frozen righteousness of her pastor husband. Was she a witch? It is a question that is almost impertinent. Dreyer on the whole avoids the supernatural although the subjects of both films invite supernatural treatment. Only when the pastor hurries home in the storm does the extravagance with which nature conforms to humanity, in the storm-swept skies and the black threatening trees, suggest a decisively supernatural element in the story. And in fact the scene seems in many ways a mistake. For the girl has discovered that she is a witch, and the audience is not interested in supernatural corroboration.

The Passion of Joan of Arc, in the same way, avoids the question of Joan's voices. Was she a saint? This, too, is an irrelevancy. She was Joan; she heard these voices; she was *such* a person. And in the end we know her as a girl strong chiefly in her simplicity, confused and frightened and uncomprehending of what has happened to her but determined to abide by what she believes in. And the face which seemed so plain as we first saw her has grown to have a beauty quite beyond expression or convention.

In these pictures no judgment is expressed. The ugly churchmen who doom Joan are mixed and muddled in their motives; they are not wrong; we can spare pity from Joan for them. The bored and silly witch, the cruelly possessive mother, the troubled ineffectual pastor, are all seen with the same detached compassion as is Joan of Arc. One subject of *Day of Wrath* is the inarticulate isolation of all souls. Partly we feel this because the dialogue is so sparse, not only because the central characters are taciturn, but because each of the characters finds himself cut off by private desires and ambitions; we see these people as we see the pastor's young wife through the web she has spun, a tapestry of the temptation, where a stiff and formal Eve offers the apple to Adam, and behind which the wife's eyes burn in witchery.

The effect depends almost entirely upon the close-ups which magnify and isolate the personalities. Joan, for all her humility, her plainness, her obvious ignorance, has an almost Homeric stature. The characters in *Day of Wrath* are in no possible sense "larger than life," yet they crowd the imagination because we have seen them in their terrible isolation and with an appalling completeness, in the flesh and in the spirit. And this is what such loving cinema techniques were designed for; the humanist (and Dreyer is one) can use them to reveal the darks and lights of humanity with unrelenting art; the antihumanist (as Eisenstein proves to be, at heart) can use them only to oversimplify men into the cogs of a vast and mindless machine. Dreyer's humans are independent, and are frightened and frightening because of that independence. Even the unrelieved grimness of *Day of Wrath* has a certain lift because it is such a tangled web of responsibilities. And *The Passion of Joan of Arc* . . . remains an exalted portrait of the splendid solitude of a pure and determined woman; we do not know whether she is a saint, but we know what it is like to burn at the stake and why it could be thought worth doing. By so much has our experience been enlarged. There are few films of which we could say more. (pp. 58-60)

Richard Rowland, "Carl Dreyer's World," in Hollywood Quarterly *(reprinted by permission of the University of California Press), Vol. V, No. 1, Fall, 1950, pp. 53-60.*

HARRY SCHEIN

[All Dreyer's films] deal with man on the outer borders of his being. I believe that the land beyond this border is really of no interest to Dreyer. It makes no difference to him whether there is a heaven or a hell, occult light or biological darkness, a triumph of reason, faith, or tyranny. It is the border situation itself that is of interest.

Nowhere has Dreyer's humanistic pathos found more cogent expression than in *The Day of Wrath,* that jewel of his works, that jewel of the film art. *The Day of Wrath* is not based on an "impossible" idea, and perhaps for that very reason is less aesthetic and more direct in its appeal than are Dreyer's other films. . . . Appearing during the war, it stood *for* reason and *against* faith and superstition. And yet, the same motif as in *The Word* is woven into it: man facing the border of man's being.

When one sees Dreyer in this perspective, it is easier to understand why [*The Word (Ordet)*] is so superior to Kaj Munk's drama. Yet this film labors under an important handicap—in its basic idea, in use of the original dialogue, and in the rigid form of the play. It is apparent, however, that Dreyer has conquered not only the theme on its own plane but the form as well. In *The Word,* Dreyer has once again rendered possible the impossible. One "has faith" in the miracle; one sees "theatrical film" as great film.

Dreyer's form is difficult, analytically, to grasp. It is all so directly concerned with the inner essence, with artlessness and naked reality. His tempo has always been slow; but this very slowness has a function which it fills with unerring precision. He tries to activate the viewer negatively—to escape the customary sweeping the audience off their feet through a strongly accelerated tempo, through whole series of sensations. This active stimulation, so unique in film production, is, however, not forced into the picture through fulsome promises or temptations, but through puritanical simplicity. It is concentrated around the graphic line, the creative lighting, the musical structure, and, most of all, through the purity and naked simplicity of the action itself. Not only are the skies, ocean, and grass of the Danish sand-dune landscape shown archaically pure; but the same is true of every single feature of the film, each being so obviously self-evident that any alternative would seem unreasonable.

The sound technique in this film is supreme. Nature's sounds are heard constantly behind the dialogue. Coastal winds sound their accompaniments throughout the entire film; household noises, the ticking of the clock, the doctor's shears, the sounds of the farm animals—all are noted and reproduced with a subtle refinement that serves as a constant reminder of the reality present in the background of the spiritual drama. (pp. 259-60)

The Word belongs to the very few films which leave the happy impression of a great gift. One is grateful, agitated, overwhelmed by an exaltation which only art but almost never film can provide. (p. 261)

Harry Schein, "Mankind on the Border," in The Quarterly of Film, Radio, and Television *(copyright, 1955, 1956 by The Regents of the University of California; reprinted by permission of the University of California Press), Vol. X, No. 3, Spring, 1956, pp. 257-61.*

JOHN CUTTS

Very few [horror] films can stand serious analysis, but one which does is Carl Theodor Dreyer's *Vampyr.*

Vampyr (also known as *The Strange Adventures of David Gray*) is the story of a haunted world. A story of the dark and of the evil that dwells there. A morality play in which good and bad do vigorous battle for the soul of an innocent. *Vampyr* is also the work of one of the few genuine stylists the cinema has yet produced. (p. 17)

[If] there is one thing which really comes over in *Vampyr* it is atmosphere: the malignant, decaying atmosphere of a community dominated by evil. . . .

Vampyr is an odd, difficult film to respond to completely, so many things are left in mid-air, so many things are not so much mysterious as just plain baffling, but providing you are prepared to accept the film on its own particular terms of reference, it can grip like a grappling-hook. For the first half-hour, the film is all vague suggestion, every little piece of mysterious action rising from the subtle derangement of the normal. The carefully phrased preface starting the film on a note of distinct intrigue—"*There exist certain beings whose very lives seem bound by invisible chains to the supernatural . . . David Gray's personality was thus mysterious*"—and after which one becomes interested in seeing the extent of David Gray's "mysterious personality" (that he subsequently turns out to be something of a weed, does, I admit, distinctly disappoint!). . . .

[The] early scenes are but a prelude to the main action, which begins with the moment when David Gray leaves the sanctuary of the inn and steps out into the haunted night.

What follows . . . is beautifully managed; the photography, background music, and direction, skilfully evoking an atmosphere of the truly macabre. Particularly effective is a long tracking shot along the wall upon which the phantoms perform their eternally damned dance. The gay little waltz theme accompanying the scene contrasting with the grey melancholy of the image to produce an almost lyrical effect.

But in a film full of striking scenes, perhaps the most memorable is the sequence in which Leone, weak and gradually wasting away through the vampire's continued attacks upon her, is watching her young sister, Gisele, walk about the bedroom of her sickbed. The scene is shot and played in tight close-up: the movement of Gisele about the room causes Leone to stir from her half-sleep and she watches her young sister with a weak smile of affection. Then Leone's eyes begin to light up as she begins to see in Gisele a future victim for blood-sucking. Leone's eyes are now ablaze, with demoniac hunger and her whole face begins to twist in hungry calculation; her lips curling to reveal sharp, cruel teeth. Then as the blood-lust reaches its peak of longing, human revulsion sets in, and the animal figure suddenly slumps into a weak and dying girl.

This terrifying scene . . . contains in a way, the complete essence of *Vampyr*—the struggle against overwhelming evil for the purity of the soul. This conflict between good and evil appears in all of Dreyer's important work. But never, to my mind, is it more powerfully stated and felt than in this brief, but thoroughly alarming scene. . . .

The climax to *Vampyr* is constructed with almost mathematical precision, yet oddly enough, the total effect is poetic rather than rigidly precise. . . .

Vampyr is strange, haunting and beautiful. More than just another film, it is an experience. (p. 43)

John Cutts, "Great Films of the Century: 'Vampyr'" (© copyright John Cutts 1960; reprinted with permission), in Films and Filming, *Vol. 7, No. 3, December, 1960, pp. 17-19, 43.*

KEN KELMAN

The President was Dreyer's first film, not the least pleasing visually, but the least personal. Still, there are many anticipations of what is to follow. The setting of romantic episodes in a rowboat on a lake—beautifully photographed—is a device later used more elaborately in *Day of Wrath.* The intercutting of the hero being honored with his daughter preparing to escape prison is quite in the straightforward style of all such passages in later Dreyer. And the concept of honor and duty versus nature and love; along with that of the hypocrisy which results from attempting to both save face and have heart; can already be detected in this rather conventional melodrama of a respectable father who betrays his trust out of compassion for his disreputable daughter.

Leaves from Satan's Book follows the theme of betrayal throughout the ages, in four separate stories, a procedure (un)inspired by Griffith's in *Intolerance.* The prime betrayal however is that of a most promising title by a tedious movie. (p. 1)

Little remains to comment on, except suggestions throughout of the Dreyeresque themes of desire in conflict with duty and masked by hypocrisy . . . , and natural love opposed to ideals. . . . The irony of the function of evil is superficially treated in the frame story of Satan's reluctant career of tempting man on earth; a concept expressed at its fullest in *Ordet.* But apart from isolated gorgeous shots, it is hard to conceive of *Leaves* being Dreyer.

The Parson's Widow is most refreshing, the best of the early films, funny, touching, the real revelation. . . . Of all the pre-*Passion* pictures, it is the only one where the major later themes are found with some definition. Here we have the first clear confrontation in Dreyer of the forces of life and death. For the two young lovers life is just a gambol, until the boy wins the job of parson with a joyous, vital, affirmative sermon, as opposed to the torpid, gloomy talks of his rivals. The parson's ancient widow goes with his position, though; and when the youth drunkenly accepts both, we have the first instance in Dreyer of the opposition and suffocation of youth by age, which later becomes a recurrent motif; as well as a fully developed case of socially imposed duty conflicting with natural love. . . . [In] this third film of Dreyer age yields gracefully, graciously to death, and leaves life to youth. Later solutions will not be so simple, but the matter is already stated unmistakeably. (pp. 1-2)

The splendid *Parson's Widow* makes its immediate successors all the more disappointing. *Love One Another* is Dreyer's most complicated movie plotwise. . . . It does seem that the narrative technique is flawed, though, since the images themselves fail so often to give even a trace of what is going on. The struggle of love in a repressive society is central here as in later work; and the brutality of the mob scenes anticipates that in *The Passion of Joan,* as well as the violence in *Vampyr* and *Day of Wrath.* . . .

[There] is to the naked eye not much formal interest or plastic beauty in *Mikael.* . . .

[With] the old artist trying to hold onto his young male model Mikael we recognize a constant theme of Dreyer, that of youth up against age. (p. 2)

Master of the House is probably the master's least remarkable feature film. . . . The imagery never possesses the power or glory which even in Dreyer's poorer works shows in random redeeming shots. The story is not only melodramatic, but predictable and ordinary; though the situation of repressive, dogmatic authority crushing love and life may be faintly related to themes in other films. (pp. 2-3)

[*The Bride of Glomdale* is] a pleasant undistinguished romance. The use of wheatfields for love scenes is later found in *Day of Wrath;* and the story of young lovers forbidden by parents to marry has some similarity to *Ordet.* The lack of emotional charge in *The Bride* is plainly indicated by the fact that the climax is a suspense sequence where the hero is being swept toward a waterfall; an episode of purely superficial excitement obviously suggested by the perils of Gish in Griffith's *Way Down East,* but not cut nearly as well. . . .

[With] *The Passion of Joan of Arc,* there occurs a most striking change in both the film-maker's style and his intensity of thematic concentration. A few potent shots in previous movies hardly promise the unique and brilliant imagery which here bursts forth frame after frame. Chiefly striking earlier were lushy lit views of lakes and trees; now there is almost no nature, but empty sky; and mostly stark interiors, with all picturesqueness sacrificed for all intensity's sake. . . . The basic pictorial principle of *Joan* is that the eye should be undistracted from the passion itself. . . .

This passion charges ideas already familiar from earlier films. The frictions between freedom and authority; between love (here, of God) and repressive custom; between youth (Joan states at the start that she is nineteen) and age (all the clerics except the few who side with her are e d tinctly old, if not ancient); between duty (to her ideals) and love (of life); and ultimately and essentially, between life (for which Joan struggles) and death (which her opponents impose); all existed before, but never before struck fire. (p. 3)

Vampyr transpires in no real world at all. Characters are not psychologically observed, but serve as functions of mysterious forces. The shaggy doctor-villain, who pulls sinister strings to control trance-bound victims, is altogether in the tradition of Caligari. There is a plot, but its elements lack casual relation. Toward the end, even chronology is violated when the hero inexplicably repeats a previous scene, with only the coherency of dream. The darkest subject is thus treated in the most bizarre manner, for evil . . . is a distortion of nature for Dreyer.

An early image, of a reaper and his scythe in silhouette, graphically established *Vampyr*'s preoccupations. The death-scented smoke from *Joan of Arc* seeps into this film as a thick mist pervading the whole landscape. There is not a sunny frame in the whole movie. . . . But youth and love do survive and escape age and death, the land of the old, the old Count, the old servants, the old doctor and old vampire who drain the life-blood of the young (as the old doctor bled and weakened Joan).

And death again, as it did for Joan, has its salubrious side. It is a deliverance for the Count and the bedridden girl, animated as they are by evil spirits. On the other bony hand, it is unnatural and horrible for the hero David Gray, as he is borne, alive and healthy, but trancefixed, in a coffin toward his grave.

So Dreyer's old themes operate in a very new way in *Vampyr*. (pp. 3-4)

The conclusion, with good triumphant and evil destroyed, would be more comforting were it the integral function of a complete process; and not the fluke of a fanciful providence and literal deus ex machina. But the happy end is just a fragment of a figment of fantasy, and the afterimage of the whole is disturbing, a dark taste in the eye.

But not so black as *Day of Wrath*'s. Insofar as *Vampyr* is a horror and/or fantasy film, it constitutes escapist entertainment. Insofar as it is what Parker Tyler calls "trance film" the horror is definitely imagined rather than grounded in any real world. Such colorful buffers and morbid distractions as *Vampyr* does offer give way in *Day of Wrath* to relentless investigation. (p. 5)

In this film more than ever, then, Dreyer opposes death to life. Before, the lethal stake was, at least on one level, a deliverance for Joan, and for the victims of *Vampyr;* but here it means stark destruction to the old witch who raves in no ecstasy but terror. Yet the smothering vapor, of *Joan*'s burning, of *Vampyr*'s woods, of the final rustic tryst of Anne and Martin, does mistify this agonizing scene so the smoke becomes incense, as the choir sings angelically. (p. 6)

[*Ordet* is] quite different from any other Dreyer film. While *The Passion of Joan* proceeds by abstraction and intensification of a historical world, *Vampyr* by variations on a dream world, and *Day of Wrath* by conjuring up the spirit of a dead world, *Ordet* is the re-creation of our own world. (p. 7)

[As] *The Passion of Joan* was a trial of faith (and of the deliverance Joan believes in); and *Day of Wrath* a trial of magic (and of the faith it destroys, between Martin and Anne); so the whole of *Ordet* is a trial of faith and its miracles. (p. 8)

Ken Kelman, "Dreyer," in Film Culture *(copyright 1964 by* Film Culture*), No. 35, Winter, 1964-65, pp. 1-9.*

KIRK BOND

[It is difficult if not impossible to assess Dreyer's] later films without knowing the earlier films. One might go further. All or nearly all of the later films are in one way or another symbolic, and we can even say that the key to them lies in the early work. . . .

I divide the films, perhaps arbitrarily, into two main groups. In the first group I put his five earliest films: *The President, Leaves From Satan's Book, The Parson's Widow, Love One Another,* and *Once Upon a Time*. In the second group are most of the rest: *Michael, The Master of the House, The Bride of Glomdale, Vampyr, Day of Wrath,* and *Ordet*. . . .

The compelling point in this division is that in the best of the films of the first group—and *only* in those—can we see Dreyer as a finished artist, a master serenely working in complete command of his medium. All the rest—and this applies to *Joan* as well—are at least technically weakened by some ultimate lack of creative stylistic quality. . . .

Each of the later films (except *Glomdale,* which is the one really weak Dreyer film) is a film with less or with uncertain style, but it is a film of symbolism. The idea takes precedence, and perhaps *malgré lui* Dreyer found himself using less than perfect forms to express the idea he had in mind. Deliberately or by the hand of fate something was sacrificed to get the idea out. Perhaps it could not have been otherwise.

If we had only three early films—*The President, Love One Another,* and *Once Upon a Time*—just these three—I would gladly say that Dreyer was a great master. (p. 26)

I cannot think of more than two or three first films that compare with *The President*. Perhaps none quite equals it in maturity and finished style. *Strike* is more ebullient, *Citizen Kane* is more ambitious, but neither has the polish of *The President*. *Pather Panchali* comes closest possibly. But I still think Dreyer's film has the edge.

The story is not remarkable. It is essentially a typical nineteenth-century melodrama. . . . What matters is what Dreyer does with this material.

Here at a single stroke Dreyer creates a new filmic world like no other we have ever known. He owes much, obviously, to Griffith. There is the Griffith cutting, the Griffith imagery, the Griffith handling of people. But Griffith is only a beginning.

The most immediately apparent, most obvious quality that one sees at a first viewing is the amazing decor and the use Dreyer makes of it. (p. 27)

There are the bare wooden floors, gleaming like polished ivory. There is a simple kitchen scene of white walls, white steps, bare floors—it might come out of the work of a Sienese master. There is a Griffith-like scene of the couple on a small wooden bridge in a landscape. But the combination of the bright white boards of the bridge and the surrounding shrubbery give us again the haunting semi-abstract quality of all this Dreyer decor. . . .

It has the effect of the torches in the religious procession in *El Dorado,* but if L'Herbier is more delicate, Dreyer is more overwhelming. The scene is close, at the least, to Lang's tremendous shot of the burning hall of the Huns in *Kriemhild's Revenge*.

I have the feeling in this film especially of something more than real, of something that never was on land or sea. It is not fantasy in the conventional sense. It is reality, but reality filtered through some strange glass that makes the simplest scene at once human and natural and yet unearthly. . . .

Dreyer's next two films do not seem to me at all comparable to this. . . . [*Satan's Book*] seems inordinately heavy and stiff, though of course showing the same feeling for stylized decor. (p. 28)

The Parson's Widow presents other problems. Personally I do not find much in it. To me it is no more than a pleasant, minor Swedish film with little to mark it as Dreyer. (pp. 28-9)

The one important thing in the film is the theme itself, and I can best explain that when I come to the symbolic films. It is more or less the theme that dominates Dreyer's later films, but here still simply a dramatic theme, not a symbolic theme, and so of little importance in this elementary form. . . .

With *Love One Another* we are back in the world of the master. It is very different from *The President*. It is on a broader scale, with politics, religion, and history all playing parts. It does not have the special decor of *The President*—it is on a much more realistic plane. But by the same token it leads us in another direction. It reminds us of Pabst, and then as we watch it suddenly seems to take us to the Russians. And still it is Dreyer. No one else could have made it. (p. 29)

Everything about [*Once Upon a Time*] is fantastic, incredible. The one thing it most certainly is *not* is a "simple fairy tale." It is at once a legend on the grand scale of *The Nibelungen,* a whimsical, tongue-in-cheek comedy in the Lubitsch manner . . . , and a story so close to the Griffith of *Isn't Life Wonderful* . . . that we feel Griffith must have seen the film. At one extreme there is a scene that has all of the stately epic beauty of the Italian *Odyssey,* at the other extreme there are shots that could come right out of *The Virgin Spring*. It is, even in its present small, dismantled form, a veritable history of film, and to anyone with a feeling for creative film it is an overpowering experience. (p. 31)

[The] film is to a point symbolic. First there is the high comedy of the rococo world, then the visual grandeur of the forest (and the sea if we count the serenade interlude), then the simplicity of the Middle Ages. We go backward in time to find a new life, a new world.

But at this rate we are on the verge of the later Dreyer, the Dreyer of the symbolic films, the Dreyer who is, in film after film, talking about a new life, as are, I believe, Bergman, Antonioni, and Resnais. . . .

With *Michael* we come to the first of the symbolic films. And it seems essential to consider at the outset the main theme. . . .

This theme I call the Death of the Master. It is in fact a retelling of the story of The Golden Bough: the story of the death of the god. The Master, like the god, grows old, impotent, and dies, to be succeeded by a new, young master who continues the life and work of the race. (p. 32)

[*The Master of the House*] is a curious, rather moving film that follows a theme dear to the hearts of nineteenth-century writers from Dickens on—the theme of the revoltingly harsh creature who in the end reforms and becomes a human being. Beautifully acted, beautifully photographed, beautifully salted with homely little touches of everyday life in a simple, middle-class apartment, it is delightful without being coy, warm without being suffocating. I do wonder, though, whether it is much of a film. (pp. 33-4)

[*The Bride of Glomdale*] has a few nice landscapes, but on the whole it is a weak film, presumably shot to order, a heavy-handed Romeo and Juliet sort of thing that is none the better for having some very obvious Griffith cutting injected into the *Way Down East* climax on the river. . . .

To say that *Vampyr* is the most confusing of the Dreyer films would be an understatement. It might well be the most confusing of all films. (p. 34)

My own feelings toward it are mixed. I like it—perhaps I should say I am fascinated by it, which is not necessarily the same thing. But I do not feel it is really a major film. It is—as is not very commonly realized—made up of two parts. It has on the one hand a succession of magnificent visual passages in a style virtually unique. But then after these purple passages it turns to a style that is hardly more than commonplace.

And I do not feel that it is an ordinary instance of alternating high and low key work. The two elements are too different, the change from exciting visual imagery to rather routine imagery is too great.

In any event I do not feel that even the purple passages are wholly satisfactory. One may ask, I think, what has Dreyer done with them? They seem to me to be fine things in themselves, but not parts of a creative whole. . . .

Still, who can resist the appeal of the great things that Dreyer has poured into it? . . . The film may come apart as a film, but in its ruins there are flashes of lightning.

As for symbolism it obviously follows the theme of the Master to a degree. (p. 35)

[*Day of Wrath* is] almost a new version of *The Parson's Widow,* albeit with great changes of detail and approach. It is somber not light, and much of the story is new, but still there is the basic situation of the old Master and the young couple, one of them married to the Master.

As a film its most interesting aspect is its use of the same brilliant style, involving bold lighting and (for the hard, precise Dreyer) a reovlutionary soft photography, which we also find in *Vampyr*. But here it is considerably toned down. On the other hand the film as a whole is unified, and so succeeds as a whole better than *Vampyr*. . . .

[*Ordet*] is not an easy film. In some ways it can be criticized as a rather unsuccessful film. But I suppose that on the whole, with all its superficially literal quality and its very leisurely pace, it is the finest of Dreyer's symbolic films after *Joan*. . . .

It is a fascinating film, one which sticks in the mind, from the haunting voice of Johannes to the innumerable little bits of daily life that flow about the main events. Slow perhaps, it is still definitely creative.

But above all is its symbolism. . . . Dreyer's film is far more than religious. Here is a sort of culmination of the thread of symbolic truth that Dreyer had been following ever since *Michael,* a generation earlier. Not that Dreyer is particularly clear about it. But he has said more here, and he seems to have reached more definite conclusions. (p. 36)

In style [*Joan*] is certainly impressive. Much more than any of the three preceding films it has a firm style, and a style that is indubitably Dreyer. Here Dreyer has gathered together the decor, the imagery, the cutting, the serene purity of his early masterpieces and has produced a splendid symphony that remains unequaled, unapproached. (pp. 37-8)

It seems clear that the symbolism of the film is at least distantly related to the main theme of the Master. It is the Passion story, and of course there is the death and the gain for the world. Dreyer might well be pardoned for stretching his theme to take in the old story of Joan of Arc.

Yet I wonder. Dreyer specifically emphasizes the *passion* of Joan—in virtually every shot of her, her eyes are filled with tears. She is a far cry from the Shavian heroine of *St. Joan,* much less the brilliant, headstrong girl I see as the historical Joan.

I cannot help feeling that this is a personal confession. After the debacle of *Once Upon a Time,* after the surely less than satisfactory *Michael* and *The Master of the House,* after the unfortunate *Glomdale,* it would not seem unfitting. It is not something to dwell on. But we can make our own impersonal comment. It would be irony of the purest hue if that film which was a cry from the depths against the world were blandly, eagerly accepted by that same world as a "great work of art." (p. 38)

Kirk Bond, "The World of Carl Dreyer," in Film Quarterly *(copyright 1965 by The Regents of the University of California; reprinted by permission of the University of California Press), Vol. XIX, No. 1, Fall, 1965, pp. 26-38.*

ELSA GRESS WRIGHT

Dreyer himself has subtitled *Gertrud* "a period piece," and a period piece it is, rendered nostalgically and with tender irony. It is also, in his intention, a tentative effort in the direction of the tragic film poetry which he believes will come about, when the truly cinematic tragic style has been formulated. The question is, however, whether he himself is not the tragic film poet he is waiting for. The style he has developed, and, with modifications dictated by his choice of milieu and theme has used in *Gertrud,* is certainly so close to film tragedy that probably only he himself could see any distance to the goal. It is an Apollonian kind of tragedy, in the vein of Euripides, the first "modern" tragic poet, but austere, almost Doric, in style. By creating it, Dreyer has refuted the words of his compatriot and contemporary, Isak Dinesen, to the effect that tragedy is no longer possible in modern times. Tragedy, he proves, is not only possible, but possible in the most modern of contemporary media. (p. 39)

Elsa Gress Wright, "Film Reviews: 'Gertrud'," in Film Quarterly *(copyright 1966 by The Regents of the University of California; reprinted by permission of the University of California Press), Vol. XIX, No. 3, Spring, 1966, pp. 36-40.*

STANLEY KAUFFMANN

[In "Gertrud"] Mr. Dreyer's theme—the suffering of a woman who finds that men do not devote themselves entirely to love, that they also concern themselves with their careers—can just as easily be seen as feminine egotism instead of male egotism. But this whole subject of Love as Life can hardly be taken seriously today. The script seems a pallid post-Ibsen revolt against the idea of woman as chattel or toy. . . . The spiritual hierarchy of the sexes in "Gertrud" seems as dated as the costumes.

But Mr. Dreyer takes this [Hjalmar] Soderberg play seriously—one index that he is out of touch. Worse, his technique is the least fluently cinematic of any work of his that I know.

Its slowness will not surprise those familiar with Dreyer. His tempos have always been deliberate. But here his camera movement and his editing defy the minimal drama in the script. . . .

But in his best films there has always been an underlying human concern that sustained us through any longueurs of execution. Here, under the slow, posed pictures, there is nothing but the dated theme described above.

The man whose intense love for men informed so many well-wrought films will probably never be forgotten as long as films are remembered. Whether or not one likes all of his works, there is in his life and person a quality that can be called angelic. "Gertrud," however, is the work—not of a fallen angel—but of a very old one.

Stanley Kauffmann, "'Gertrud'," in The New York Times *(© 1966 by The New York Times Company; reprinted by permission), June 3, 1966, p. 33.*

DON SKOLLER

[*Gertrud* tends] toward abstraction, and its method, as Dreyer wrote in 1955, is simplification. It is this simplification that, not "dug"—not grasped from head to toe—becomes the boredom or the anachronism of which [Stanley] Kauffmann [see excerpt above] and his sympathizers complain. But the boredom, one feels, is the tension that the unremitting purity of Dreyer's film creates. It is not an objective boredom; it is not the depiction of boredom by being boring; it is a simplification and selectivity that leaves the viewer with nothing to become distracted by, that provides him with the opportunity to make contact with only the truths of a situation, of himself, so that suddenly the gnawing of his own spirit becomes perceptible. *Gertrud* is one of the coolest works of art ever made, but its arctic white is really an incandescence.

Much of the reaction to *Gertrud* parallels reaction to Chekov—"nothing ever happens" to "The Three Sisters." But when you stop to inventory *Gertrud* you find an incredible richness of detail and event. (pp. 72-3)

We meet [Gertrud] on the day that her husband is to become a cabinet minister. This same day, she is about to consummate an affair with a young composer. Also, her first lover, a poet and national hero, is returning after years abroad. That's all. Not much to work with? Too much—. It could get easily out of hand. But Dreyer uses it all as a matrix, a narrative pre-text, almost, to present graphically the values within the situation.

Most of *Gertrud*'s scenes occur within rooms, rooms that have been simplified so that the tone of the life within each room vibrates from the screen in delicately shaded and balanced lightings and modelings. . . .

[In] *Gertrud* the evocation of texture and the tone of situation are sure and right to an uncannily consistent degree. . . .

To learn what Dreyer is saying, and more significantly, the way he is saying it, we must continue to develop the non-eventfulness of his film: After an opening scene in which two principals are posed in what is almost a series of extend freeze-frame dissolves—a technique that gives the film a *Marienbad* flavor and that communicates an undercurrent of spiritual torpor or paralysis—the film moves through

Gertrud's meeting with her young composer to the banquet honoring the returning poet, Gabriel Lidman. This scene has an air of wit that is thereafter present in the film (it is clear in earlier scenes, if the film is seen again) and this wit becomes the primary action of the sequence. (p. 73)

Can texture and tone become primary elements in a film? Can this be a mode of the cinematic? And if it is, can it be done in any way other than at a savoring pace? If, as Dreyer has done, the images fall upon the screen with an inner subtlety and variation of texture and tone that make each frame an imitation of living tissue, would the larger, macro-movements of camera and montage be appropriate? Or would they be antagonistic?

The point is that the life that Dreyer gives to his films is radically different from the more current zap stylists. There is validity in jump-cutting and swish-panning and zooming, of getting effects from acute movement within and of the frame. But does this mean that filmic textures and tones are invalid? Throughout *Gertrud,* Dreyer seems to say and eloquently—"What is happening before your eyes is happening to living, pulsing matter, something that is part of a universal flame that burns low and almost invisibly but with crucial intensity." It is this that Dreyer materializes.

Unless this is grasped, the plot of *Gertrud* becomes lost. Because the plot is presented through the lighting and toning to a degree never before encountered. If one were to abstract the plot-line in terms of the development of the central character, Gertrud herself, it might be said that she undergoes a journey to memory. Please don't judge the "artiness" of that phrase too quickly. It is based upon tangibles of the picture. Throughout *Gertrud,* flashbacks occur. They take place in Gertrud's mind, and in high-key lighting of about the level of the "taken-by-force" moment in *Marienbad.* (p. 74)

[These] are recollections, moments of pure spirit within the mind of the heroine: one feels that she lived those moments in the first place only to capture them for memory. They are moments of detachment. By the end of the film she has attained an isolation that allows this detachment to exist completely in the present; or perhaps a better way of saying it is that she has completely detached herself from the world of affairs in order to permit this inner spirit to suffuse her daily living. And this is rendered completely, wordlessly—except for the accessories that Kauffmann chooses to focus upon—through the texture and tone of the lighting.

Dreyer does not, as Kauffman implies, present *Gertrud* as a victory of spirit over matter, any more than he has ever been inclined to clear-cut, black-and-white victories and defeats, goodnesses and evils. Dreyer shows us the price that Gertrud pays. The last image of the film, after Nygren has departed in long-shot with a pathetic, dream-like gesture of the hand, is the closing and closed door and wall outside of Gertrud's room, sealing her in behind a monolithic, grossly and dumbly materialistic facade of grey. (pp. 74-5)

Don Skoller, "To Rescue 'Gertrud'," in Film Comment *(copyright © 1966 by the Film Comment Foundation; all rights reserved), Vol. IV, No. 1, Fall, 1966, pp. 70-6.*

PAUL SCHRADER

Dreyer was not an unwavering formalist; he did not define a single style throughout his career. . . .

Each of Dreyer's individual film "styles" is, to be more accurate, a synthesis between three basic and opposing styles at work in his films. In his study of Dreyer, Claude Perrin notes two of these opposing forces. "In order to define Dreyer's aesthetic," he writes, "one must confront two opposing artistic schools: the *Kammerspiel* and expressionism." Perrin goes on to demonstrate how the tension between these "schools" underlies all of Dreyer's work. This tension, to be sure, is integral to Dreyer's films, but, it seems to me, it is unable to account for that peculiar, "spiritual" quality Perrin and others ascribe to his work. A "fundamental opposition" between Kammerspiel and expressionism was a consistent stylistic feature of the early German cinema, as Lotte Eisner points out; yet none of the German films evoke a world of transcendent values in the way Dreyer's films do. There is, I suggest, another force—transcendental style—which interacts with both Kammerspiel and expressionism in Dreyer's films, and brings them each a certain spiritual weight which they do not innately possess. Of the three "styles," Kammerspiel is the artistic raw material of Dreyer's films; expressionism and transcendental style act upon and distort that material, turning it to their own ends. (p. 113)

The interplay of these forces, styles, or schools in Dreyer's films may be schematized thus: (1) some films are straightforward, relatively unhampered Kammerspiel, such as *Mikael* (1924), *Master of the House (Du Skal Aere Din Hustru,* 1925*), Two People (Tva Manniskor,* 1945*), Gertrud* (1965); (2) in one film, *Vampire (Vampyr,* 1932*),* expressionism predominates over Kammerspiel and transcendental style; (3) in another, *The Word (Ordet,* 1955*),* transcendental style predominates over Kammerspiel and expressionism; (4) in others, most importantly *The Passion of Joan of Arc (La Passion de Jeanne d'Arc,* 1928*)* and *Day of Wrath (Vredans Dag,* 1943*),* expressionism and transcendental style vie for control of the Kammerspiel. (p. 114)

In each of Dreyer's films one can detect elements of Kammerspiele: intimate family drama, fixed interior settings, unembellished sets, long takes emphasizing staging, the use to gesture and facial expression to convey psychological states, plain language, and a thoroughgoing sobriety. *Master of the House,* for example, contains almost all these elements; its enclosed interiors, its measured pacing, its emphasis on revelatory gesture, all place it within the Kammerspiele tradition. (p. 115)

Vampyr is Dreyer's only exclusively expressionistic film. The expressionism seems to have run away with the Kammerspiel; there is little tension between the two. Both the subject matter (vampires, afterlife) and the techniques (chiaroscuro, exaggerated gesture, nonrealistic sets, rampant fantasy sequences) of *Vampyr* exhibit a confident appreciation of the strengths of expressionism and a calculated use of its methods. (p. 117)

Like expressionism, transcendental style in Dreyer's films stems from the Kammerspiel and opposes it. But it also opposes expressionism and its right to control the Kammerspiel. (p. 118)

Dreyer's films often feature a character totally estranged from his environment: Joan of Arc, Marthe, the witch in *Day of Wrath,* John, God's fool in *Ordet.* As in Bresson's films these characters have no human metaphorical contact with reality, and their effect on the audience is similarly schizoid. To a large degree this disparity is caused by the tension between Kammerspiel (naturalistic settings) and expressionism (contrived camera composition and angle). Such a stylistic tension explains the protagonist's psychological dilemma, but it does not explain that other tension of which Dreyer speaks: "It is that latent tension, that smoldering discomfort behind the minister's family's everyday life that I have so urgently been trying to bring forward." This disparity (the Other within the physical) is the disparity of transcendental style. Dreyer not only creates disparity in the conventional psychological sense by contrasting Kammerspiel and expressionism, but he also creates disparity in the manner of transcendental style by designing a character like John in *Ordet* who has no psychological (interior or exterior) cause for his estranging passion, a character who is truly the "fool of God." (pp. 119-20)

Dreyer's lack of commitment to the transcendental style becomes most apparent in his failure to achieve stasis. Some of Dreyer's statements ("We hope that film will set ajar for us a door into other worlds") as well as his partial use of everyday and disparity indicate that he genuinely desired to create transcendental art, although the nonstasis endings of his films, as we shall see, suggest other intentions. Whatever Dreyer's true intentions were (and I tend to think they were mixed), he was never able to achieve stasis, the final test of transcendental art, to the extent that Ozu and Bresson did because, it seems to me, he never relied on the transcendental style to the extent that they did. When the final moment of would-be stasis occurred, Dreyer had hedged his bets, leaving elements of Kammerspiel untouched and intertwining expressionism with transcendental style, thereby offering the viewer alternative explanations, spiritual and psychological, for the decisive action.

Like many artists with spiritual intentions Dreyer uses the "frozen image," but it is crucial to ask what he is freezing. Is he freezing the commitment which comes after the decisive action, or is he freezing the disparity itself, creating an endless syndrome of earthly struggle?

Because Dreyer increasingly used elements of transcendental style in his films, one may suggest that he was progressing toward a thesis-antithesis-synthesis/Kammerspiel-expressionism-transcendental style evolution. Although a late Dreyer Kammerspiel film (*Gertrud*) has more of the ascetic elements of transcendental style than an early one (*Master of the House*), Dreyer, as far as one can ascertain, rejected complete stasis to the very end of his career. (pp. 120-21)

Paul Schrader, "Dreyer," in his Transcendental Style in Film: Ozu, Bresson, Dreyer *(copyright © 1972 by The Regents of the University of California; reprinted by permission of the University of California Press), University of California Press, 1972, pp. 109-48.*

ROBIN WOOD

The Passion of Joan of Arc and *Vampyr,* though on opposite sides of the great sound barrier, are separated by less time than any films Dreyer made subsequently. The difference in subject matter is reflected in great differences of style, *Joan* all clear outlines and strong, sculptural compositions, *Vampyr* all shadows, haze, and movement. Yet they stand out from all the other feature films of Dreyer I have seen by virtue of the subjectivity with which the action is presented. This is more obvious in the case of *Vampyr,* in which virtually everything is shown through the consciousness (and often through the eyes) of the protagonist David Gray, to the point where one is tempted to see the whole film as an interior drama enacting itself within the psyche of a single individual. It becomes impossible to distinguish between what we, as audience, are shown and what David Gray sees: as a defined character, he has scarcely more existence than Lila Crane . . . in the second half of Hitchcock's *Psycho.* (p. 12)

Dreyer, in *Vampyr,* very consciously plays up the myth's potential for religious allegory but minimizes the sexual implications. They are not, however, altogether absent, and the form they take is interesting in relation to a general characteristic of Dreyer's work: it is strong on female sexuality, weak on male. The chief vampire-figure of *Vampyr* is strikingly androgynous in appearance: we take her at times for a man. She appears to batten exclusively on young girls. (p. 13)

To place *Vampyr* beside *Joan of Arc* is immediately to suggest that his treatment of the theme of persecution is, to say the least, complex. Each film offers, within itself, clear-cut oppositions, yet in certain respects the two are inverse mirror-reflections. Joan embodies an instinctual, mystical faith; she is persecuted by rationalists who deny the promptings of instinct. But in *Vampyr* it is the shadow people who represent suppressed instinctual life, and here *they* are the persecutors. And when one looks ahead from *Vampyr* to *Day of Wrath,* one finds striking anticipations of that film in the figure of Marguerite Chopin. In her costume and her masculine appearance she resembles the repressive church dignitaries; in her femaleness and ultimate vulnerability she resembles the helpless old woman they burn as a witch. Marguerite's role is unambiguous in the context of *Vampyr,* but it takes on ambiguities in relation to Dreyer's whole *oeuvre,* uniting in one person the recurrent figures of victim and victimizer.

If *Day of Wrath (Vredens Dag . . .)* is Dreyer's richest work it is because it expresses most fully the ambiguities inherent in his vision of the world, the conflicting attitudes to nature (in the widest sense of the word): is "nature" the instinctual faith of *Joan* or the menacing and destructive underworld of *Vampyr*? In *Day of Wrath* the two attitudes fuse into a view of life that sees good and evil as not merely coexisting but inseparable and at times indistinguishable. In this way it can be seen as the synthesis resolving the dialectical progression of its forerunners. . . .

The function of the subjective presentation in *Joan* and *Vampyr* was to encourage in the spectator a sense of participating in the working out of an inevitable process. In his last three features Dreyer places us outside the consciousness of his protagonists to encourage us to analyze rather than participate; but the overall movement, the sense of inevitable process, remains constant—and this is nowhere truer than in *Day of Wrath.* The archetypal theme of the working out of a curse offered Dreyer the ideal material for the expression of his view of life, the process being conceived as at once metaphysical and psychological, predestined yet achieved through human interaction. Few films more powerfully convey the complexity of causes that go to produce an effect—the idea that responsibility for an outcome is not to be simply assigned, but is made up of a dense network of interrelated motives, wills, actions. In this, as in the intensely imagined, meticulously observed medievel setting that reminds us again of how obsessed Scandinavian culture is with its remote but potent past, *Day of Wrath* strikingly anticipates *The Virgin Spring*. (pp. 14-15)

The resolution of *Day of Wrath* already reveals a severity that, whatever its spiritual justification, could be felt to lack humanity. Dreyer's apparent endorsement of Anne's acceptance of her doom cannot but seem somewhat monstrous to anyone viewing it from outside the confines of Puritanical Christianity. This severity becomes the keynote of [*Ordet (The Word)* and *Gertrud*], which, for those less than completely compelled by Dreyer's authority, hover perpetually —dare one say it?—on the brink of the unintentionally risible. *Day of Wrath* is a film with plenty of blood flowing in its veins; in *Ordet* the arteries are noticeably stiffening, and *Gertrud* appears dangerously close to petrifaction. It is a striking paradox that *Ordet*, a film ostensibly upholding life-affirming religion and celebrating the mystery of resurrection-in-the-flesh, should impress itself stylistically as above all a denial of life.

In one respect *Ordet* is the perfect complement of *Day of Warth*. It is another film about the interconnectedness of all things, and whereas in the earlier film Anne's death seemed demanded as the outcome of, and eventual release from, an intricate web of interlocking tensions, in *Ordet* everything moves toward the equally "necessary" climactic miracle of Inger's resurrection. The style of the film can be seen as a refinement of that of *Day of Wrath*. (p. 16)

The subject matter of *Gertrud* draws attention to an aspect of Dreyer's work I have hitherto only touched on: his feminism. Throughout his career one finds women at the center of his films, and this tendency has an interesting corollary: the frequent—sometimes implicit, in *Gertrud* explicit—denigration of the male. . . .

Dreyer's feminism is not restricted to *Joan of Arc:* both *Day of Wrath* and *Ordet* have women at their centers, the male characters—especially in the former—coming off rather badly. *Gertrud*, very much a work of old age, is the logical outcome of this trend. Attempts to see it as a film *against* Gertrud—in my view, the only way to save it—are doomed to failure. There are those who see Gertrud as a noble and beautiful figure, accepting at face value her refusal to compromise, her demand for all-or-nothing; to me she is a monster, and Dreyer's celebration of her an act of perversity. Gertrud's attitude to human relationships and consequently Dreyer's, as the film uncompromisingly endorses her is essentially antilife and suffocating: she demands not merely that she be of central importance in a man's life but that everything, including his work and creativity, be subordinated to her. Denied such homage, she prefers an old age of sterile solitude.

I cannot help seeing a connection between this abasement of the male principle and the film's stylistic stultification: given that its director was, after all, a man! In stylistic terms it is the most repressed of all Dreyer's films. Give and take the modifications demanded by subject matter, there seems to be a correlation in his work between psychological freedom and camera movement: to survey his feature films from *Vampyr* to *Gertrud* is to witness a systematic denial of the spontaneous and intuitive, a triumph of the perverse will over healthy instinct. In a sense, the male in Dreyer gets its own back by turning Gertrud herself, inadvertently, into a cross between vampire and zombie. . . . (pp. 16-17)

This sense of the progressive repression of life in Dreyer's films suggests another way of accounting for the parallels between his work and Hitchcock's. Both directors view the world with suspicion and distrust, and a part of their creative impulse is the desire to dominate it. Both directors show great fear of suppressed instinctual forces. Hitchcock confronts those forces more openly, acknowledging their fascination. . . . Dreyer, always an intensely conscious artist who takes himself very seriously indeed, can never allow himself such freedom—hence the increasing sense of repression in his films. The expression of spontaneous, vital impulse in a Dreyer movie is usually punished: the only people who dance with gaiety are the shadows of the damned in *Vampyr;* the heroine of *Day of Wrath*, rebelling against her monstrously unnatural existence, ends by acknowledging the justice of her execution at the stake; the dynamic motorbike ride of *They Reached the Ferry* ends with two coffins poled to the land of the dead.

A further explanation becomes possible of why, in comparison with Bergman, there is relatively little development in Dreyer's work. For the development one discerns is of a very worrying kind, and "development" hardly seems the right word: a progressive stylistic tightening and rigidifying, a movement away from freedom and fluency. As one moves from *Vampyr*, his freest film, perhaps the one film in which spontaneous or subconscious impulse is allowed real freedom, through *Day of Wrath* to *Ordet* and *Gertrud*, one moves into an increasingly arid world where it becomes harder and harder to breathe. . . . In Dreyer free expression is progressively stifled and development, in the true sense, becomes impossible. One sees more clearly, perhaps, why the sustaining of religious faith was as essential for Dreyer as its casting off has been for Bergman. Dreyer's God is a god of "Thou shalt not," and his cinema, for all its extraordinary distinction, is essentially death-oriented. (p. 17)

Robin Wood, "Carl Dreyer," in Film Comment *(copyright © 1974 by Film Comment Publishing Corporation; all rights reserved), Vol. 10, No. 2, March-April, 1974, pp. 10-17.*

DAI VAUGHAN

What kind of experiences shock the soul? What manner of abstraction is required for these spiritual experiences to be presented on film? Taking the Christian terms 'soul' and 'spirit' at their given values, I think these are questions which may usefully be kept in mind in any attempt to understand Dreyer. (p. 156)

Dreyer's *Passion of Joan of Arc* is concerned exclusively with the trial and martyrdom; and the crucial moment occurs in the scene leading up to Joan's retraction of her confession of heresy. As she watches a prison guard casually sweeping up the straw crown which has become, for her as for us, the symbol of her torments, she makes the decision which will lead her inevitably to the stake. Just as Dame Margaret [in *The Parson's Widow*] chooses between her past love as innocent and her past love as guilty, so Joan, in this scene, makes the final choice between herself as the tool of the Devil and herself as the agent of God. (p. 157)

[There is an] almost total neglect of the political background to the trial. Early in the film there is an incident where Houppeville, having expressed the belief that Joan is a saint, is escorted from the court by English soldiers; but the effect of this is merely to stress that there can be no hope of recourse to compromise, no appeal to the Pope. It is a circular system in which the judges have judged themselves competent to judge, and Joan must either confess to being a heretic or die as one. Similarly, at the end of the film, the crowd is stirred to rebellion by the spectacle of Joan's martyrdom. But this happens after Joan is dead (so that from one point of view it may be considered a monstrous irony); and there is no implication whatever that an assessment of the possible consequences of martyrdom played any part in her decision. The sequence simply confirms our conviction that Joan's choice was honourable by reminding us that the way we resolve our innermost doubts does have consequences in the real world, and that these consequences may be neither foreseen by us nor ever known to us.

Another element which tends to insulate Dreyer's Joan from the complexities of events outside the courtroom is the hinted parallelism with the story of Christ, a story familiar in outlines worn smooth by repetition. This parallelism is suggested not only in the film's title—The *Passion* of Joan of Arc—but by the crown of straw, resembling the crown of thorns, with which the soldiers mock her, placing an arrow in her hand and genuflecting before her; by her being spat upon by a judge; by her being garbed in a special robe before execution; and by the sign over her stake which bears four initials signifying, 'Heretic, Relapsed, Apostate, Idolatress', and which inevitably recalls the 'I.N.R.I.' over the cross.

Joan of Arc is commonly considered an extreme example of Dreyer's technique of 'abstraction', in the simple solidity of its sets and its isolation of the human face against bare backgrounds. Certainly the costumes, whilst not appearing anachronistic, seem to place the action outside any specific historical period, so that few people even notice that one of the priests is wearing a modern pair of spectacles. But it seems to me that the technique, rather than being a purely cinematic imposition, is the outward expression of a more fundamental abstraction in which the circumstantial elements of the story are eliminated until we are left, not with a spurious symbolism, but with the human essence of the drama. (pp. 157-58)

Let us now ask the question: what exactly is Joan doing in the scene where she resolves to retract her recantation, and where she makes her final decision between the alternatives—of repudiating the voices which she believes to come from God or of accepting excommunication from the Church which, equally, she believes to represent God's will on earth? She is not exercising moral judgment, since it is between two mutually exclusive criteria of moral judgment that she must decide. She is not deliberating, since deliberation is the attempt to define what one is (or wants) and to act accordingly, whereas Joan can define what she is (and has been) only by the action she is now called upon to take. She is moved to her retraction not by an image of her triumphs at arms, nor of the world she loves, but of her suffering; and by the amplication that it has been meaningless. We in the audience, unless we are Christians, will have no prior views about the provenance of Joan's 'voices'; and the film has purported to offer no evidence. Neither have we been given any information on which to assess the justice of her political ends. But we do know that only by dying for her cause and her convictions can Joan constitute these as having been worth dying for. (p. 159)

Day of Wrath is a film about love—love not merely as erotic attraction between two people but as that commitment of faith without which it can never be more than the concurrence of transient emotions. Here . . . we have a situation where our present actions alter the significance of our past, since faith once broken has never been faith at all. (p. 160)

The prevalence of women as central characters in Dreyer's work has frequently been remarked. In this we may see a further expression of his principle of abstraction. Since women have, until recently, been permitted to play little direct part in the affairs of the world, they are subject to fewer of the formalised codes of conduct which, for a man, can govern his choice—or enable him to evade it by acting 'in character'—in almost any conceivable situation. Such an idea is frequently employed in comedy, and its comprehension by the audience relied upon, where a husband, standing on his dignity, is embarrassed by his wife's refusal to obey the unwritten rules. This, at any rate, seems to offer a more helpful explanation than the appeal to some 'eternal' feminine principle by those who seek in psychological theory merely the excuse to replace one demonology by another. (p. 161)

Dreyer characteristically directs our attention to the anguish of choice by posing the alternatives in terms unacceptable to us, so that our sympathy will not be refracted through our prior commitment. . . . It may be argued that this is a defect, in that his concern for human authenticity is such as to preclude any concern with what people are to be authentic about. True, he seems to combine a hatred of authority with a distrust of any means by which men might group together to overthrow it. At the end of the French episode in *Leaves from Satan's Book,* Satan gleefully accuses his victim of having betrayed three women, but says nothing of his having betrayed the Revolution into the bargain. On the other hand, it is difficult to see how Dreyer's distinctive merits could have been combined with those he may be said to lack.

It may be said that we have no use for a story which hinges upon a miracle. But there is a sense in which we all believe in miracles. We should never do anything if we believed the world to be frozen in immutability—if we did not have faith in the unforeseeable, in the possibility of change in people, in institutions, in ourselves, change in the very quality of reality, public or private, in the quality of consciousness. By his process of abstraction, Dreyer focuses attention on those moments which reveal our need for, and the demands of, such faith. These are the experiences which shock the soul. (p. 162)

Dai Vaughan, "Carl Dreyer and the Theme of Choice," in Sight and Sound *(copyright © 1974 by The British Film Institute), Vol. 43, No. 3, Summer, 1974, pp. 156-62.*

VLADA PETRIC

Regrettably, most critics try to explain Dreyer's cinematic style by analysing and interpreting solely the literary component of his films, that is, his manuscripts. For example, the recent article by Dai Vaughan [see excerpt above], typifies such attempts at the philosophic interpretation of Dreyer's films as if his work existed in the form of literature and not in the form of cinema. This approach stems from the writer's presumption that Dreyer's 'technique [read: cinematic style] is the outward expression of a more fundamental abstraction in which the circumstantial elements of the story [sic!] are eliminated until we are left, not with a spurious symbolism, but with the human essence of the drama.'

One can hardly accept this separation of the form (technique) and content (story), particularly in the case of Dreyer, who insisted on the 'amalgamation' of all film's components, because 'only when *all* the artistic elements of a film have been welded together so firmly that no single unit can be left out or changed without damaging the whole, only then can film be compared to a piece of architectural art; films which do not satisfy this demand are like those conventional, uninspired houses that one passes by without even noticing.' Since Dreyer's films undoubtedly are not 'conventional, uninspired houses', and because interest in their structure has been growing, it is the theorist's duty to discover how the components are welded together, how the amalgamation of the filmic devices and the literary/dramatic continuity results in the cinematic abstraction which is a *sine qua non* for the film's authentic style.

It is difficult to substantiate the view that the spiritual value of Dreyer's films emerges from the plot or 'the human essence of the drama', rather than from the amalgamation of *all* the given components, including (I repeat: including) the narrative and dramatic constituents, into a cinematic whole which can be experienced only (I repeat: only) by viewing the projected images. . . . In contrast to Dreyer's emphasis on the visual aspect, Dai Vaughan pays 'little attention to Dreyer's technique', contending that it 'has in any case been amply and well analysed by others', although I am curious to know where. Vaughan goes so far as to claim that Dreyer's technique 'serves primarily to intensify our involvement in the reality of the situation.' Such a literary approach to Dreyer reveals a misunderstanding of his creative method and is in contradiction with his theoretical concept, which proclaims that 'many different components, such as the effect of rhythm and composition, the mutual tension of colour, interaction of light and shadow, the gliding rhythm of the camera, combined with the director's conception of his material, decide his style.' Dreyer emphasises that although technique for him is 'a means and not a goal', yet 'the goal has been to give the spectator a *richer* experience.' Conversely, without the technique the spectator would not be able to have such a rich experience in the process of viewing films.

Hence, Dreyer's concept is consistent and clear when it maintains that 'spiritual content' as well as 'inner life' can become active in a film only through a cinematic integration which gives the film-maker 'the chance of replacing objective reality with his own subjective interpretation.' Integration is the means by which the filmmaker achieves a stylistic unity, and the closest road to achieve abstraction in cinema is the 'road of simplification' which 'transforms the idea into symbol.' Again, Dreyer has in mind *cinematic* simplification, while he insists that 'this abstraction through simplification' takes place 'in the actual rooms of a film.' The actual rooms of a film are, in fact, sequences tied into an overall cinematic structure which only *as a whole* can reach the necessary degree of abstraction, to help the film-maker to get 'outside of the fence with which naturalism has surrounded this medium.' To achieve this the director must 'use his mind to transfer what *his eyes can see into a vision* [my italics].' Here again the final goal of abstraction is identified with a vision inspired by what the film-maker sees with his eyes, not what he reads. (pp. 108-09)

With this in mind, it is useful to analyse his masterpiece, *Ordet,* about which Dai Vaughan drew conclusions but by merely comparing Kaj Munk's play with Dreyer's published script, being unable to view the film itself. It is hard to believe that someone would risk seriously tackling the question of 'whether this film can take on meaning only within the assumption of Christian belief', and discussing the ideational implication of the film's ending, without *experiencing* its imagery. To Vaughan, the fact that Dreyer dramatically changed Munk's ending and 'set the action entirely within the *context* of religious belief by abstracting from it those elements which, in a day-to-day world, might hold that belief to question,' seems evidence that Dreyer successfully accomplished abstraction in *Ordet*. But purification and simplification of the literary text is merely the initial step towards the final goal. Dreyer describes it as the method of 'cinematisation' of literary works: 'If a Kaj Munk is to be converted into film, then the goal must be to transform the work into a wholly cinematic entity. And my approach to working with Kaj Munk's *The Word* has, therefore, always been and still is: first to possess oneself of Kaj Munk and then forget him.'

The ending of *Ordet* is a particularly good example of the cinematisation of a dramatic text, and one of the most beautiful achievements in cinematic abstraction. Inspired both by the play and by his own experience, Dreyer achieved something which has rarely occurred in this medium: 'transformation of an idea into a symbol' (Dreyer's term), while maintaining 'cinematic authenticity' (my term) on the screen. The term cinematic authenticity implies the 'delicate balance' ([Maya] Deren's term) between 'remodelled reality' (Dreyer's term) and the 'independent life of reality' (Deren's term) which the film viewer needs 'to recognise and believe in' (Dreyer's term). (p. 109)

Evidently, the components [of *Ordet*] were carefully chosen by Dreyer and are consistently simplified, i.e., deprived of all decorative features which do not reveal the 'spiritual content of the work'. Therefore, every subtle movement of the camera, every gesture of the actors, every change of lighting, every distortion of angle or introduction of sound effect becomes significant, and assumes a deeper meaning. In general, the cinematic structure of *Ordet* is a brilliant example of a presentation of a transcendental idea by the simplest, most austere cinematic devices, which are constantly kept in balance with the 'director's conception of his material'.

There are many films which deal with the theme of death and the philosophical aspect of human existence, but few succeed in expressing the spiritual meaning of life and death in a manner that is not available to any other medium, and which can be perceived only through the process of the direct viewing of a film. Only this direct perceptual experience of Dreyer's *images* permits the audience fully to understand his concept of abstraction, which provides the 'fourth dimension' in cinema. . . .

The idea of resurrection is one of the most evasive and most difficult to be realised in terms of cinema. Yet it is often exploited in horror movies or conventional religious spectacles. Almost regularly, the screen presentation of a man's resurrection turns into a mechanical optical effect; all that these tricks amount to is the trivial illustration of a fable aimed at triggering the viewer's fascination with the supernatural. Dreyer both avoided these clichés and succeeded in describing 'inner life' of the human desire to possess a god-like power; man's irreconcilability with the state of death, or, conversely, his acceptance of death as the beginning of a new, spiritual life. This ideational 'message', or, to use Dreyer's term, 'spiritual mood', is generated in *Ordet* by the work in its totality. The cinematic stylistics of Dreyer's method are best exemplified in the film's last sequence. The highly transcendental, philosophical meaning of the film is expressed in a highly cinematic manner, and therefore, one does not experience the same mood from merely reading Dreyer's adaptation of Munk's play. The basic ideological message is, of course, similar, but the experience of the 'spiritual mood' is essentially different. It is also dissimilar in its cinematic impact from Gustav Molander's film *Ordet* . . . , based on the same play and—though more faithful to the original—structured in a disparate cinematic manner.

The purification and simplification of Munk's dramatic text, which Dreyer radically condensed in his manuscript, was not only continued but fully elaborated in the studio by the means of cinema. This becomes evident when one compares the published script with the actual shot-by-shot breakdown of the film. The script contains only dialogue with a very few indications of the characters' psychology and a very general description of the action designed to help the actors understand the situation and the relations among the characters. Out of this literary/dramatic material, Dreyer created a cinematic vision whose hypnotic impact cannot be appreciated without actually projecting the film on to the screen. . . .

In *Ordet,* the genuine impact of overtone emerges from the dynamic counterpoint between all the partial rhythmic lines which lead to an overall rhythmic vibration and the metaphoric meaning of the film. After the finale, the sensitive spectator becomes aware that his strong impression and unique experience result from an amalgamation of all the film's components into cinematic abstraction which reveals and strengthens the spiritual content of Dreyer's masterpiece. (p. 112)

Vlada Petric, "Dreyer's Concept of Abstraction," in Sight and Sound *(copyright © 1975 by The British Film Institute), Vol. 44, No. 2, Spring, 1975, pp. 108-12.*

JONATHAN ROSENBAUM

[*De Naede Faergen (They Caught the Ferry)* is an] adept Hitchcockian exercise. Devoted almost exclusively to the tension and exhilaration of speeding down a country road, it is one more demonstration that Dreyer's art, principally praised for its spiritual qualities, in fact rests on its concrete realisation of material experience. Despite its effective cautionary ending, the general thrust of this short is to convey the excitement of speed along with its dangers—a significant object-lesson for spectators who equate the director with slowness.

Jonathan Rosenbaum, "Short Films: 'De naede faergen' ('They Caught the Ferry')," in Monthly Film Bulletin *(copyright © The British Film Institute, 1976), Vol. 43, No. 512, September, 1976, p. 204.*

ANDRÉ TÉCHINÉ

[There] is no film-maker more rudimentary than Dreyer. Unqualified to lay down the law or to pressurise in any way, Dreyer makes talking pictures considered and reconsidered strictly subject to the means he employs or, if you prefer, the elements on which they are founded.

Each new film is not approached as an isolated venture having only distant resemblances to past experiences, but as a voyage of discovery constantly penetrating deeper, an investigation that constantly becomes more exacting. Dreyer exhausts the resources of his own vocabulary, working his material until all resistance is overcome and he contrives to mould the scant and stubborn forces with which he set out and to which he limits himself. For what Dreyer accepts, or to be more precise acquires, is a refusal to resort to the appurtenances, details, incidental hurdles, external flourishes and irrelevant variations, the whole gamut of effects offered by an expedient rhetoric.

So manifest an absence of elegance and virtuosity may lead one to think that Dreyer's range is seriously lacking in scope. But this poverty purely and simply indicates the only riches possible in Dreyer's view: those of discovery and of creation. Instead of taking up and integrating the successive modifications sustained by an aggregate of signs considered in an evolutive perspective, Dreyer sets up his own independent system and steadfastly sticks to it, permitting no borrowings. If he is commonly assumed to be outdated as a film-maker, it is because each of his films demonstrates his insistence on marking out a distinctive cinematic policy that remains resolutely aloof from other concurrent discoveries. This does not mean that influences are non-existent (that of Griffith is even acknowledged). Nor does it mean that Dreyer has established a language all on his own. He remains dependent upon the cinema, but does not acknowledge its evolution or take it into consideration except where the change is radical (for instance, the passage from silents to sound). In that case, faced by a different means of expression, he adopts and moulds it to his own use. 'A reorganisation and a simplification are necessary. One can, if you like, say that it's a question of purification because all elements not engaged in the central idea are suppressed. One concentrates and one compresses.' This strict reduction is effected with the object of commanding increasingly precisely a specific articulation. It sets up a sort of univocal, indeed autonomous, field of action. A divestment as ruthless as this infallibly throws into relief its configuration, lays it bare in other words, reveals its mechanism. There is a scheme, a sort of architecture exhibiting, contrary to an apparent complexity (as is the case with Lang, for instance), an extreme simplification. This simplification enables one to pick out the elements Dreyer has at his disposal and which he contents himself with developing. It is hardly the result of an omission—from any lack of consideration, that is—but on the contrary of a structuring in the most artisanal sense of the term; of an accretion, in other words, a selective montage. Dreyer learns his art by experience, staking out his path to restrict it more surely and reinforce it even more strongly than before. (pp. 72-3)

Dreyer proposes precise forms only in so far as they conjure imprecisions. When he films a figure sitting in an armchair, one sees 'the moon, the sea, the forest', as one of the characters says while looking at Gertrud. Reverie is sparked off by a gesture or a look, as though conducted by music and propagating itself against an inner background stripped to the point of abstraction. 'My only desire is to show the world of the imagination,' Dreyer says. In this respect *Vampyr* accumulated in the course of its progress every imaginable opening independently of any coherence. The level, however, may seem somewhat incidental in this sombrely surreal story. This melodic oneirism requires a rigid framework before it can come into being and venture its modulations. *Two People,* on the other hand, stifles the rhythmic fluidity beneath a framework whose density encroaches too much. But in either extreme the equilibrium has nothing to do with careful proportionment, compromises, precautions. Dreyer is not a stylist. He uses the cinema, or rather invents his cinema in order to imagine life through feminine characters bruised in their passions and disappointed in their dreams (Anne in *Day of Wrath,* Inger in *Ordet,* Marianne in *Two People,* and Gertrud). (pp. 74-5)

Rudimentary, solitary, timeless, Dreyer owes nothing to anyone and seems to owe nothing to the cinema itself. (p. 75)

André Téchiné, in an essay in Cahiers du cinéma, *No. 170 (translated by Tom Milne and reprinted as "The Nordic Archaism of Dreyer," in* Dreyer *by Mark Nash, British Film Institute, 1977, pp. 72-5).*

Federico Fellini

1921-

Italian director, screenwriter, artist, and actor.

Fellini's films are an intense mixture of fantasy and reality. He often appears to be a naive bystander observing the carnival of life. His films are deeply personal; for example, his wife plays herself in *Juliet of the Spirits,* the story of their marriage. While many critics find his films imaginative and perceptive, others accuse him of egotism and self-indulgence. But even though the quality of his work is disputed from film to film, his exuberance is undeniable; he revels in the eccentric, the colorful, and the bizarre, but he does not mock the characters he depicts. Rather, he seeks to understand them.

Born in Rimini, Italy, Fellini moved to Florence at the age of seventeen. Already he had acquired traits that reappear in his work: a love of the sea and antipathy toward the Catholic hierarchy. In Florence, he worked as a street artist until he was offered a position in a vaudeville show. He became a gag writer, then progressed to scriptwriting. An assistantship with Roberto Rossellini on *Open City* exposed him to neorealism, the cinematic movement that used non-professional actors and worked on location, thus bringing about an effect of verism. Fellini's first directing effort, with Alberto Lattuada, was *Variety Lights*. Though critics deemed it a failure, its revenue enabled him to direct his first solo film, *The White Sheik*. Its strict adherence to neorealistic style gave little indication, however, of Fellini's creative prowess.

***I Vitelloni* is regarded as a transitional work that retains various neorealistic elements of *The White Sheik* while foreshadowing the broader thematic aspects of *La Strada,* the film which brought Fellini international renown. Fellini used a carnival metaphor in *La Strada* for his theme, a lonely person's search for love. Some view it as Fellini's first acknowledgement of Christian belief, seeing *La Strada*'s structure as a pilgrimage. Others interpret it in more secular terms. In their opinion, Fellini is merely sympathetic towards all humankind.**

***La Dolce Vita* caused an uproar in Italy due to its condemnation of Rome's upper class. Some critics misunderstood its mockery and felt Fellini was glorifying, rather than lampooning Roman society and its morals. Not surprisingly, it most upset the very people it attacked.**

***8½* marks a new stylistic development and is considered his most poetic film. Though the story of a filmmaker, *8½* is actually the story of a man in the process of finding himself artistically and personally. It, too, is subject to more complex interpretations that examine Fellini's concern with aging and religious ambivalence.**

The films following *8½* have been more intimate, interspersed with fantasy and reality. Some, such as *Satyricon,* are blatantly flamboyant, and it is in this film that his obsession with the grotesque and bizarre is most evident. His most recent film, *Orchestra Rehearsal,* received mixed critical reviews due to his controversial treatment of an orchestra rehearsal as a metaphor for the cyclical nature of life.

Although many critics have accused Fellini of immorality and conceit, his uniquely personal means of depicting life has resulted in innovative cinematic expression. Indeed, flaws are considered part of his personal statement. Fellini brushes aside accusations of egotism with "If I made a movie about a filet of sole, it would be about me." (See also *Contemporary Authors,* Vols. 65-68.)

BOSLEY CROWTHER

The first film of Federico Fellini, a highly touted young Italian director, to be shown publicly in these parts is a 4-year-old item called "The White Sheik." . . . In fairness to Signor Fellini, we will not speculate on his talents until we see a few more of his films.

For the truth is that this little item, which significantly has to do with the naive and farcical adventures of a hick honeymoon couple in Rome, is surprisingly broad and ingenuous, in the manner of early silent comedies. And, except for a few clever touches, it is devoid of the robust fun of the antique form. . . .

We won't count this against Signor Fellini. This one was just a practice swing.

Bosley Crowther, "'The White Sheik'," in The New York Times *(© 1956 by The New York Times Company; reprinted by permission), April 26, 1956, p. 37.*

EDOUARD DE LAUROT

In its internal consistency, *La Strada* is more than a remarkable example of personal style. We may then ask: What is Fellini's image of the world we live in, his conception of man and the ethic he advances? Men are separated by astral distances and do not realize their unity in the human condition. Obstinately and gropingly they quest for understanding and belonging: everyone needs someone. . . .

Undeniably, man's highest quest is to give meaning to his existence in the world. But neither pure matter (here, a pebble) nor man as a pure existent have being, or else this quest, expressed through man's conscious action, would be superfluous. In Fellini's Pantheism, however, the meaning of things and people is pre-existent to man's conscious actions; it is offered from above, metaphysically, by a spiritual agent. Meaning precedes existence. Therefore, there is no need—and no place, even—for man to create his own meaning through action of his free will, by imposing human significances upon things. . . .

Aside from metaphysical doctrine, we also find in *La Strada* Catholic mythology: the Franciscan world inhabited by saints, beggars and simpletons, the weak and the oppressed who alone possess the secret of happiness and salvation—a world antipodal to that where "wealth is a sign of God's grace" and salvation is sought through efficiency. . . .

The temptation to create myths is known to all artists. But to believe in myths is to believe in the immutability of human nature, to believe that man is in the hands of ineluctable destinies. Beyond its poetic appeal, the secret of the "ineffably touching" quality in *La Strada* can be summed up by a phrase of Descartes: "All our failings come from the fact that we were once children." *La Strada*'s philosophy is for those who have secretly remained children; for those too who, not having been previously exposed to the mithridatic effects of "angelism," will be quietly drugged by its magic. . . .

Whether we should accept *La Strada*'s message is a matter of taste—and depth. But while a great work of art cannot be created out of slight substance, an exquisite one can. Fellini has given the screen a poem of bitter and tender beauty. Between the triumphant chant of Man in the revolutionary epic and the morbid howling of egos in the psychological drama, Gelsomina will be heard intoning the plaint of a soul and offering up an inarticulate plea for mercy. (p. 14)

Edouard de Laurot, "'La Strada'—A Poem on Saintly Folly," in Film Culture *(copyright 1956 by* Film Culture*), Vol. 2, No. 1, 1956, pp. 11-14.*

EUGENE ARCHER

Avoiding the studied poetic imagery of [*La Strada*], *Vitelloni* is at once a subtler and a more perceptive work. The protagonists, no longer alienated from the conventions of civilization, are now isolated within the social organism. Existing under the watchful observation of family and friends, these *vitelloni,* too young to have fought in the war but old enough to have suffered its consequences, are trapped in a wasteland of their own devising.

The young wastrels chosen to represent the modern generation in *Vitelloni* are carefully differentiated as illustrations of Fellini's ambitious theme. . . . These young men, their thinking molded erratically by Hemingway, Nietzsche, and the Hollywood Myth, dream of big-game hunting in Africa with Esther Williams, but settle for a drunken evening at the local pool hall. (pp. 24-5)

Fellini is incisive in mocking the empty pretensions of these youths, and employs a series of trenchant symbolic images to illustrate this contemporary wasteland. . . .

The distinction of *Vitelloni,* however, lies beyond the symbolism, in Fellini's understanding of his characters, and his unusual sympathy for their problems. The rich comedy of this film is intensified by the compassion of the director's approach. There have been many faithless lovers on the screen, but the childish Fausto, whose delighted pleasure in a successful attempt of seduction turns immediately to overwhelming remorse over the tears of his betrayed bride, is a unique and memorable characterization. . . . In a way of life seemingly marked by unexpected variations of conduct, the final pattern is constant. Fellini's subtle technique underlines this meaning, for this technically unconventional film ends within the confines of a rigid artistic frame. Leaving the other *vitelloni* to continue along their fixed and unregenerate path, Moraldo, the observer, makes his final agonizing decision, and exits from the scene. As his train slowly moves away to an unknown destination, the child who represents the new generation steps tentatively onto the railroad track, and, balancing precariously along this symbol of the open road, returns to the game of life. (p. 25)

Eugene Archer, "'Vitelloni'," in Film Culture *(copyright 1956 by* Film Culture*), Vol. 2, No. 4, 1956, pp. 24-5.*

ANDREW SARRIS

By casting the diminutive, clown-visaged, essentially sexless Giulietta Masina as his prostitute [in *Le Notti di Cabiria*], Fellini has automatically divorced himself from the currently fashionable exploitation of lurid themes. His treatment is neither sensual nor sentimental. By depicting Cabiria's spirited recovery from her ludicrous betrayal, Fellini indicates his concern with the indestructibility of his heroine, and by implication, of the human spirit generally. We sense that Cabiria's dunking in the stream is not her first setback, and Fellini quickly insures that it shall not be her last. (p. 19)

God enters Cabiria's life in the guise of a miracle-seeking procession to a shrine of the Virgin Mary. Here Fellini divides his attention between Cabiria, who prays for the intangible miracle of a new life, and a crippled procurer and dope-peddler, who has come to have his limbs healed. In a brilliantly composed and edited passage, Cabiria and the procurer alternately struggle through a milling, hysterical crowd of pentitents to reach the altar. At the edge of one overhead shot, an elaborate loudspeaker subtly mocks the spontaneity of the occasion. The forward motion of the scene relentlessly accelerates until the procurer throws away his crutches and collapses, writhing and threshing briefly on the floor before Fellini tastefully fades out the scene.

Fellini's treatment of this episode is crucial to an understanding of his general position. Although he does not believe in the more obvious manifestations of the miraculous (he was the author of Rossellini's controversial work, *The Miracle*), Fellini does not indulge in De Sica's sly anti-clericalism. The problem for Fellini is one of individual faith rather than social responsibility. The emotional power of the religious spectacle he creates suggests that God is sanctioned by man's need for faith, possibly even that God was created by man to supply hope for a better life. Fellini never spells out his personal commitments, but he seems to accept the Church as part of the furniture of his environment. There are indications in *Cabiria* as well as *La Strada* that Fellini is more kindly disposed to the humanistic influences within the Church than to its authoritarian dogmas. A mendicant friar whom Cabiria meets on a lonely road has a greater impact on her soul than all the elaborate machinery of the miracle festival. However, like Cabiria and Gelsomina and the nun in *La Strada* who shares Gelsomina's sense of rootlessness, the friar is something of an outcast in the eyes of the Church. To accept the universality of these people as Fellini apparently does, it is necessary to consider the notion that in some sense we are all outcasts in our moments of loneliness and in the individual paths we follow to our salvation. In any event, by stressing the pugnaticy and indestructibility of Cabiria, Fellini comes closer to creating a viable symbol of humanity than does De Sica with his whining protagonist in *The Bicycle Thief.* (pp. 19-20)

In *Cabiria* one sees the familiar landmarks of the anarchic sub-world of Fellini's imagination. Empty fields, roads, and streets set off by solitary travelers and distant buildings convey an image of the world as a lonely desert peopled by insubstantial De Chirico figures vainly striding towards mathematically improbable intersections of humanity. In such a world, social theories are meaningless since society itself seems to exist beyond the horizon of any given individual. Personal relationships, however tenuous, achieve an exaggerated intensity, and the mystiques of romantic illusion and religious faith become the indispensable components of existence. This would be a forbiddingly dismal view of life if Fellini did not provide compensations with a rich sense of humor and a perceptive eye for colorful detail. Fellini does not merely assert that life is worth living under the worst circumstances: he demonstrates the strange joys which flourish in the midst of loneliness and suffering. Without this demonstration, *Cabiria* would be an unbearably sadistic experience.

Fellini's work since *The White Sheik* has been a continuous adventure in symbolism within the framework of unusually complex plots. Yet, Fellini's technique does not lend itself to what we are accustomed to in the way of symbolic imagery. He does not give surfaces or objects any special gloss or lighting to emphasize their significance. There are never any meaningful shadows in a Fellini film, nor any unusual contrasts between sunlight and darkness. His shots, day or night, fall into a neutral zone of grayness. (p. 20)

It is odd to think of Fellini following in the footsteps of the neorealists, but it would be an error to consider his work completely apart from their influence. Indeed, it is the realism in Fellini's technique that enriches his symbols. He does not prettify reality although he tends to control it somewhat more than his predecessors. He does not shrink from dirt or grime or the garish ugliness of stage make-up. Indeed, like most neorealists, Fellini seems more at ease with settings of poverty and moderate means than with citadels of luxury. His cheap, noisy music hall in *Cabiria* seems more authentic than the plush, unusually quiet night club. Cabiria's drab house seems less of a caricature than the actor's incredibly palatial villa. It is not a question of visual reality, but one of camera treatment. Fellini looks at the poorer settings objectively, picking out their most characteristic elements. However, the luxurious settings are viewed satirically and only their most ridiculous features are emphasized.

Similarly, in *Cabiria* at least, the upper class people—the actor and his mistress—are seen mechanically from the viewpoint of a lowly wide-eyed prostitute. Fellini's unwillingness to study a wider range of social strata does not imply an inability to do so. Still, with all its merits, *Cabiria* may represent the point at which Fellini's concern with the stragglers of society begins to yield diminishing returns. Somehow *Cabiria* does not have the feel of greatness that *Vitelloni* communicates. In *Vitelloni* every character counts for something and every incident advances toward a common truth. *Cabiria* is too much of a one-woman show with Giulietta Masina's heroine achieving a sublime illumination while all the other characters linger in the darkness of deception and irresolution. Like *La Strada,* Fellini's other near-masterpiece, *Cabiria* has some of the limitations of an acting vehicle that sometimes loses its way on the road of life and forks out into the by-path of a virtuoso performance. (p. 21)

Andrew Sarris, "'Cabiria'," in Film Culture *(copyright 1958 by* Film Culture*), Vol. IV, No. 1, January, 1958, pp. 18-21.*

NORMAN N. HOLLAND

La Dolce Vita amazes indeed the very faculty of eyes and ears. Eyes and ears are not just the targets, though, but recurring symbols for what author-director Fellini has on his mind. (p. 425)

The music of the film parodies itself, and the point of Fellini's images of sound seems to be that they fail. It was, of all people, Robinson Crusoe (though he was surely not the first) who pointed out that sound and language are the means of which human beings can achieve more than an animal relation with each other. Sound and language in *La Dolce Vita,* however, seem always to fail to create such a relationship. (p. 426)

La Dolce Vita seems more tied to reality than Fellini's earlier work, but only "seems." It really has that same strange hankering after myth as his other films. His script for *The Miracle* reached essentially toward the traditional mating in the fields of sun-god and mortal woman. *The White Sheik* with its horseplay on different kinds of hats balanced the impotent male of church and marriage against the absurdly sexual male of the *fumetti* (visual images again). *I Vitelloni* constitutes a parody of the whole male pantheon, while, in *Le notti di Cabiria,* a tawdry and pathetic image of Venus renews herself in water after venal Adonises have chosen and abused her. *La Strada* is the clearest of them all, a classic agon between *eiron* and *alazon* over a (more or less) mute woman that could have come straight out of Cornford's *Origins of Attic Comedy. La Dolce Vita* has the same theme and mythic dimension as the others, men overpowered physically, morally, or psychologically by the gorgon-like image of woman. (p. 427)

In this matriarchal world, men become mere consorts, lover-kings, ridiculous, impotent. . . .

Throughout the film, from the vulgarized Christ at the opening to the transvestite dance of the homosexuals at the end, man seems weak and helpless. Throughout, women lead men—Maddalena leads Marcello to the prostitute's apartment; Sylvia bounds up the steps of St. Peter's leaving behind clusters of exhausted Romans, and the haunted-castle sequence ends with the old *principessa*-matriarch leading the shamefaced "men" of the tribe off to Mass. Throughout, men seem awed, overcome by women, often trying to make themselves into women, sinking down into women. The men seem unable to get places; they have to clamber, grope, fly, break into places women seem to sink into effortlessly. (p. 429)

The film, then, uses its two central images, sight and sound, to set off men against women. The women are goddesses, mythical, unreal *belles dames sans merci,* the sight of whom bewitches men into a kingdom of improvisation and illusion. Man is impotent, helpless, Marcello's dying father or Steiner, with his sounds and language, frozen, turned into stone by the fixity of his life. (Indeed, sacred to Cybele was a small meteoric stone *acus,* supposed to have fallen from the heavens.) Marcello, Everyman, is caught between these two alternatives, male and female, his mistress vainly seeking to play the role of goddess and petrify him into matrimony.

These themes all come together in the final dreary episode, the despairingly hedonistic party that follows Marcello's appearance at the scene of Steiner's suicide. (p. 430)

As with any important work, *La Dolce Vita* defines its own art. Fellini's concern about turning people into images finds its expression in what might be called the rotogravure style of the film. Fellini had both sets and costumes of *La Dolce Vita* designed to photograph in exaggerated blacks and whites, so that everything in the film would have the hard, contrasty look of a flash photo. The film itself seems almost to be composed as a series of stills rather than as a moving picture. Fellini's sense of the new, the unexpected, his theme of improvisation, finds its expression in the episodic structure (here, as in *Vitelloni,* this episodic quality seems a weakness of the film; only in *La Strada,* it seems to me, did Fellini overcome this his besetting vice). Fellini's brilliant use of dissolves also suggests a kind of impulse or improvisation (the best example being the opening dissolve where the gilt image of Christ suddenly, startlingly becomes a gilt Siamese dancer). This sense of improvisation, by the way, is not inappropriate for perhaps the only major director in the world who likes working on a chaotic set, who insists a script can only be an outline and "writes" his pictures by improvising on the set. . . .

The good, grey *Times* insists on a Fellini "taking the temperature of a sick world," and that is no doubt true, but it is also a Fellini preoccupied with dehumanizing people, making them into things (*Cabiria*) or heroes (*La Strada*) or gods (*The White Sheik*), but in every case, dehumanizing them, making them into images—not an unnatural preoccupation for a man whose work in life is to turn people into celluloid. (p. 431)

Norman N. Holland, "The Follies Fellini" (copyright © 1961 by Norman N. Holland; reprinted by permission), in The Hudson Review, *Vol. XIV, No. 3, Autumn, 1961, pp. 425-31.*

RAYMOND DURGNAT

Fellini's *La Dolce Vita* is a great bas-relief of the day-dreams and the ideals of an age—the rootless hedonism, the sensationalised religion, the spiritual nostalgias and an erotism which is blatant and obsessive because it is rootless. . . .

If ever erotism and social context were inseparable, it is in *La Dolce Vita.* The film itself is massive yet disjointed, its structure recalls the tumbled slabs of a Roman temple. One feels Fellini chose the images that he fancied; because he is a poet, and, more important, a poet who does not disdain to use images which have common currency, these images are solid and relevant. Still, their import has to be felt rather than restricted by a literal exegisis (art always suggests more than it says), which is why everybody can understand it except most critics. (p. 17)

Raymond Durgnat, "Some Mad Love and the Sweet Life" (© copyright Raymond Durgnat 1962; reprinted with permission), in Films and Filming, *Vol. 8, No. 6, March, 1962, pp. 16-18, 41.**

JOHN J. NAVONE

In his art Fellini reflects an Italy facing harsh and complicated realities yet fortified with the traditional wisdom of the centuries. He offers an image of hope, an image of a magic land which has rejuvenated itself throughout history more than any in the world. . . .

Though his vision includes sin, Fellini is too Christian for despair, too convinced, even in the face of the worst human perversity, that God is love and cares for us through those ministering angels which find their way into every Fellini film. . . .

Significantly, Fellini reflects the Italian character in his view of poverty: the absolute lack of a future without any corresponding despair seems alien to the Anglo-Saxon character. In "The Nights of Cabiria," Fellini takes it all in stride: it manages to assimilate the whole burden of poverty, misery, and shame without surprise or emphasis. (p. 640)

Simpatico, the one characteristic an Italian must find before he can approve of another, would be almost an understatement in Fellini's case. Yet, despite Fellini's bounce, there is always a sense of the *lacrimae rerum,* as is exemplified in "La Strada," Fellini's magnificent conception of the road of life down which, no matter how fast one runs, one cannot escape the Hound of Heaven. Using extraordinarily poetic cinema but always clinging to realism, Fellini mixes fun and sadness, gaiety and sorrow, beauty and bestiality in a work that breathes the incomparable humanity of the Italian spirit. . . .

For him friendships are not interludes in our travels, but rather our travels are interludes in the comradeship and joy of our friendships. In a world where so many live as if friendships—the communication of ideas, ideals, dreams, hopes, joys and experiences—were mere incidents or side issues to the main problems of human existence, Fellini proclaims that reality is quite otherwise: we live our lives for our friendships; they are the goals, not the means. This is the true wisdom of Christian Italy which grounds the contemporary significance of Federico Fellini. Communication with others, the striking of a human spark, is Fellini's truest joy. (p. 641)

John J. Navone, "Age of Transition: Fellini's la dolce italia," in Commonweal *(copyright © 1963 Commonweal Publishing Co., Inc.; reprinted by permission of Commonweal Publishing Co., Inc.), Vol. LXXVII, No. 25, March 15, 1963, pp. 639-41.*

DWIGHT MACDONALD

Like Baroque art, of which it is a belated golden ray, "8½" is complicated but not obscure. It is more Handel than Beethoven—objective and classical in spirit as against the romantic subjectivism we are accustomed to. It's all there, right on the surface, like a Veronese or a Tiepolo. . . .

[In] "8½" Fellini borrows from everybody, just like Shakespeare. Borrowing on this scale is creative: "8½" is an epitome of the history of the art. His borrowings are also creative because they are returned with his fingerprints all over them. The childhood episodes are Bergmanesque chiaroscuro, as the great scene on the beach when La Saraghina dances for the schoolboys, which echoes, right down to the brutal beat of the music, an even greater beach scene, that between the soldiers and the clown's wife at the beginning of *Naked Night:* but this is a Latin Bergman, sensuous and dramatic and in no way profound. (p. 152)

Dwight Macdonald, "Fellini's Masterpiece" (copyright © 1964 by Dwight Macdonald; reprinted by permission of the author), in Esquire, *Vol. LXI, No. I, January, 1964, pp. 149-52.*

JOHN C. COCKS, JR.

What we are seeing [in *Il Bidone*] is Fellini in a kind of Stylistic transition, and a search, too, for an adequate expression of the director's highly personalized vision of, as he has said, "the terrible difficulty people have in talking to each other—the old problem of communication, the desperate anguish to be *with,* the desire to have a real, authentic relationship with another person." *Il Bidone* . . . is the second part of what Fellini has called "my trilogy of solitude" and the religious theme which so permeates all his work is easy to trace through these three films: in *La Strada,* the anguish of Zampano on the dark beach; Augusto's ritual death on the hillside in *Il Bidone;* and [in *Le Notte di Cabiria*] Cabiria's symbolic resurrection, a sweeping re-affirmation of life. But this film is the weakest of the three; Fellini quite obviously knows what he wants to say, but he seems in *Il Bidone* unsure about exactly how to say it. (p. 55)

Around [an] essentially simple tale is woven the sur-neo-realistic fabric of Fellini's own dream world which manifests itself in images of the seashore, of empty landscapes and fairgrounds, of lonely piazzas with a fountain bubbling, of empty streets, of big, expensive cars, of bizarre night-clubs and loud parties, of alienation and, ultimately, of life without resolution. . . . But there are scenes too which come close to disaster, which approach, tease and barely escape sheer bathos. Augusto's first meeting with his daughter is at once too pat and too abrupt to be entirely believable. . . . (pp. 55-6)

Social reality (the scene in the slum with the trio passing themselves off as government representatives of the new housing project), spiritual reality (the conflict between Augusto and the peasant girl . . .), metaphysical reality (Crawford's walk home, alone, New Year's morning across an empty piazza with two whores casually accosting him as he moves along the rainy street), all have been touched upon, but it is not until [the final scene when Augusto is stoned] that Fellini finally manages to probe any deeper than his brilliant surface. And by now it is almost too late. (p. 56)

Admittedly *Il Bidone* seems to be more underkeyed than the other two sections of the trilogy, but these several glaring abridgements only make it seem clumsy and uncertain.

Il Bidone remains an interesting addition to the Fellini canon and a flawed but vital second part of the trilogy. What we see in it perhaps most of all is the disquieting, almost painful struggle of one of the major film poets of our time to make a statement about which he seems uncomfortable, from which he seems almost at time to retreat. (p. 57)

John C. Cocks, Jr., "Film Reviews: 'Il Bidone'," in Film Quarterly *(copyright 1964 by The Regents of the University of California; reprinted by permission of the University of California Press), Vol. XVIII, No. 1, Fall, 1964, pp. 55-7.*

JOHN RUSSELL TAYLOR

[*Luci del Varieta* is the first real Fellini film.] It is so, obviously, in the subject-matter: the faded underside of show-business, the gaudy, tawdry, improvised world of one-night stands and not knowing where the next meal is coming from. Here Fellini is speaking from his own experience of people he has known. . . . What makes it a film which no one but Fellini could have invented (both conceived, that is, and put on the screen) may perhaps best be illustrated not by generalities but by studying two particular sequences: the party at the castle and the wanderings of Kecco, the comedian-manager, after he leaves his new star Liliane one night in the city. Each is developed according to a ravelling and unravelling process which is to become characteristic of the key sequences in Fellini's work: from a simple beginning, through a complex action in which the main characters and their problems become swallowed up, or nearly, and then a gradual disentanglement which leaves them alone at the crisis of their troubles before they and those around them are scattered—to a new and probably joyless day, I nearly said, taking it for granted that all these scenes take place at night, and their aftermath in those bleak, cheerless dawns which punctuate Fellini's films with confirmation of the old despair. (p. 19)

As might be supposed in a private world so coherent as Fellini's, there are certain backgrounds—and, naturally, the characters and situations they so intimately complement—which recur again and again, and so acquire, beyond their general effectiveness in colouring our vision of what takes place in front of them, the quasi-independent significance of a constant symbol. Once one starts trying to pin them down in this way, though, it is all too tempting to force everything into the pattern, and clearly Fellini's mind does not work that way. (p. 20)

[This can be illustrated by a consideration of] the sea, which dominates much of *Lo Sciecco Bianco* and plays a significant part in all his other feature films except *Il Bidone,* where its marked absence is equally significant. In *Lo Sciecco Bianco* it might be taken to symbolize romantic adventure: the young bourgeois bride runs off from her conventional tourist's honeymoon in Rome and encounters her favourite dream, the 'white sheik' who stars in a silly photo-romance she follows, on the sunny sands by a glistening sea. In other films it appears much more gloomily as perhaps the reminder of impossible dreams, unrealized possibilities (the grey uninviting sea of *I Vitelloni,* the bland sea from which the monstrous fish is drawn in *La Dolce Vita*), and Fellini commits himself no further than to say that for him in general the sea is a comforting mystery, conveying the idea of permanence, of eternity, of the primal element. But, he adds, of course it takes colour in any given situation from the character and attitude of those who see it: again the inescapable union of foreground and background, of people and things in Fellini's work, which makes such terms as 'objective' and 'subjective' quite irrelevant to the central phenomenon and totally incapable of indicating its nature. The sea is a real sea; the sea is also a sort of extension of the characters' moods and attitudes, a mirror to which their natures are held up; a stage further, and both characters and location are embodiments, or rather the single unified embodiment, of their creator's moods and attitudes—those of the little God who within his own world can make everything be as he would have it be. (p. 21)

There is something almost womblike about a Fellini film; Fellini does not so much sympathize with his characters—often he clearly doesn't approve of them at all—as envelop them, and however uncomfortable they may be in the world he has made for them there is always the comfort, for the spectator, of knowing that they are watched over and in some way protected—perhaps because they are fragments of Fellini himself, or of the past which has made him, and so he cannot bear to see them totally lost. It is the consciousness, basically, in Fellini and in us, that by salvaging these fragments and embodying them in works of art that he has saved them, that *temps perdu* has become *temps retrouvé*. (pp. 22-3)

All this, of course, even if it conveys a little of the overall effect a Fellini film has, is impossibly vague unless one can explain also to some extent how he does it: it is one thing to say that Fellini *is* all his characters and all his places, quite another to show how this identification is made a reality on film. Perhaps the best place to start doing so is with his [second] film, and for many still his masterpiece, *I Vitelloni*. (p. 23)

[What] is Fellini's attitude to his film vitelloni? There has been much argument, and in the abstract, judging solely from the script, a number of solutions are possible. The film might, for instance, be a light social satire about wild boys with a happy ending when the two principals reform and opt respectively for happy fatherhood and a new constructive life somewhere else. It might be a grim picture of a lost generation, cut adrift in the modern world from their roots in a settled faith and a stable social order. It might be a denunciation of the decadent petty *bourgeoisie*. A case, of sorts, could be made out for any of these views from the script, but the film itself rejects them all. To begin with, it is clear at once from the way the actors are directed that though none of the characters is exactly a shining hero, they are certainly not either double-dyed villains, but merely contradictory, likeable, insufficient human beings. Nor can the 'happy ending' of the ringleader, Fausto, with his wife and their child be taken at its face value: his last appearance, playing childishly with his new son under the troubled gaze of his wife, makes it clear that the child is just another new toy, and that nothing has really changed. And as for the view of the film as a moralistic tract for the times, one can set against it scene after scene in which the camera is very much with the characters, involving us willy-nilly on their side, inviting us irresistibly to sympathize with them instead of shake our heads.

The first way that this is done is by a very flexible, subjective attitude to time. The time of the film is the vitelloni's time, not ours. It can expand suddenly for an improvised dance in the street, an impromptu game with the stones or, stretched out beyond endurance, it can crucify its victims in an aching void before the aimless, endless fury of an icy, windswept sea. Equally it can contract as the camera weaves and dodges and turns in an ecstasy of swift motion at the climactic ball sequence which swallows them all and then at length spews them out into the empty, unwelcoming streets. We are with them; this is the way not so much that it was as that it felt. And as the film progresses it becomes heavier, as the characters become heavier with the weight of ills unremedied and chances missed. . . . (pp. 23-4)

[There is a] magical tenderness which irradiates Fellini's evocation of this life no longer wholly innocent but yet rejecting the fruits of experience and the adult responsibilities that come with them. It is an intensely romantic view, of course, and the physical appearance of the film is similarly romanticized: the real streets taking on the aspect of deserted baroque stage sets; the delicate, diffused greys of the railway and Moraldo's morning departure; the harshly etched scene on the shore; the almost expressionist lighting of the theatre sequences; the hysterical, nearly indecipherable eddies of movement which rip and swirl over the screen during the showily impressionistic ball scene. Indeed the vitelloni, whose real background one half appreciates to be drab and ordinary, live through Fellini's eyes in a world full of unexpected, inexplicable beauties. . . . (p. 25)

The technical means by which Fellini achieves his effects, here as elsewhere in his work, are in principle very simple, though the application of the simple principles is often extremely complex. Fellini's films are built round a number of long, sustained scenes worked out in the characters' own good time: not only are we encouraged to adjust our timetense to that of the characters, but we are forcibly compelled to, since there is no escape in constant changes of locale, artful intercutting of separate sequences or anything like that: once we embark on a key sequence we are with it obsessively through to the end. Fellini loves to begin his scene with a long shot establishing at once the place, the number of people involved and their spatial (and generally by implication emotional) relationship with each other and their surroundings. This done (as in the scene on the seashore, or the aftermath of the ball) he can move in to a closer examination of his actors. . . . [The] face, one sometimes suspects, is for him the ultimate in symbolic landscape, the object which is at once a thing-in-itself and a token of something more. (pp. 25-6)

[While] proclaiming himself a realist and indeed making [*La Strada*], save for the employment of professional actors, in a way of which even the earliest, most doctrinaire theorists of neo-realism would have to approve, Fellini has produced something which has more genuine validity on practically any level one can think of than that of straightforward realistic observation of things as they are. And in doing so, of course, he has shown up the fallacy of doctrinaire neo-realism very clearly: its failure to accept that film realism is entirely in the eye of the beholder. We may say that Rossellini's early films are more objective—and therefore more 'realistic'—than Fellini's, and mean something by it; but what we mean is that when his camera is turned on a scene it is likely to be recorded with the emphases falling where they would normally fall for most of us, and with the ordinary and typical receiving more attention than the atypical and extraordinary. When Fellini looks at the same scene, though, with equally 'realistic' intentions, it is precisely the extraordinary, unexpected, and unpredictable which catches his eye.

When, for example, at one point in *La Strada* Gelsomina is sitting alone and dejected by the side of the road a solitary, riderless horse suddenly traverses the screen the effect is positively surrealistic: totally arbitrary, yet giving an instant visual reinforcement to the mood of the scene. The lost horse might well be a figment of Gelsomina's imagination, an image of her own state. But it is also a real horse, and its appearance here at this time is not impossible, only mildly peculiar. There may, for all we know, have actually been a stray horse there at the time of shooting which was seized on and pressed into service, in the same way that the three musicians whom elsewhere she falls in behind as they march along playing cheerfully to the empty countryside were, in fact, itinerant musicians who turned up in just this way. But what has struck Fellini about the horse and the musicians is their peculiarity and oddity, their—terrible word to the neo-realist—picturesqueness, their ability to embody the mental states of the protagonist, rather than their value as documents of any sort. All Fellini's films filter and select—and therefore colour and distort—external realities in this way, but the process is so much clearer, so stripped of ambiguity in *La Strada* that it can at once be recognized and accepted for what it is.

Up to *I Vitelloni,* or even *Un' Agenzia Matrimoniale,* . . . it would have been quite possible, if increasingly odd, to continue regarding Fellini as a realist with a special gift for social satire, but *La Strada* makes it clear (or should have made it clear, though by *La Dolce Vita* many seemed to have forgotten the lesson) that he is nothing of the sort and never has been: his forte, even when his films have nearly all the trappings of external reality in their expected places, is symbolic fantasy of almost baroque elaboration and artificiality (the word, in this context, had no hint of denigration). Looking back from the viewpoint of *La Strada* at the earlier films we have been considering, indeed, we are likely to find that the perspective changes everything, and that brilliant though the touches of observation are (whatever else one may say about Fellini's films, every frame of them is undeniably bursting with life) it is the non-realistic side which now comes uppermost in the mind, so that even the most obviously comic and 'social' in its outlook, *Lo Sciecco Bianco,* comes in retrospect to look like a variation on the plot of *La Strada,* played for laughs and with the male and female roles reversed. (pp. 29-30)

[The] later films, while not deserting Fellini's basic source of inspiration in his own experience, become increasingly complex in their handling of their resources, the interplay between 'real' reality and imaginative reality becomes increasingly involved and elusive. (p. 30)

[At] its inception *La Dolce Vita* had in it the makings of a summary of Fellini so far, a complete statement of his mature views on all the recurrent themes in his work. And so, perhaps too readily, it has been taken to be by many critics, a savage denunciation of the world as he sees it now, bringing his spiritual autobiobraphy on film up to date with a gesture of despair because the visionary gleam of his childhood (which shone most brightly in *La Strada*) has now faded for ever. This seems to me a dangerously partial view of what the film actually says, and an evident distortion of Fellini's interests and intentions in making it. . . . [It] is highly doubtful if Fellini ever sets out to make a film of ideas, putting forward a certain interpretation of society and human personality: these may emerge, though invariably defined exclusively in terms of the single, special case (his films are more like novels or fairy-tales than allegories), but embodying them never seems to be the first impulse towards creation. (p. 39)

[We] appreciate the film. To begin with, we should accept the immediate impact of the film on our senses, which is not at all that of a reasoned argument against a way of life and its representatives. Rather, it is as a series of vast decorative compositions on the same basic theme, like, say, Doré's illustrations to Dante's *Inferno.* They trace a sort of intellectual rake's progress downwards in seven giant steps, represented by seven confused, dreamlike nights and seven terrible dawns stripping away whatever illusions the nights have left. One of the compositions, that involving the mistress of Marcello, the central character, and his curious philosopher friend Steiner, is fragmented to provide a sort of continuity, but when put together the pieces of this fit into the same pattern as all the rest, which is precisely the scene structure which we have noticed as the basic shape throughout Fellini's work, the principals starting alone, being drawn into a more and more intricate pattern of action as the night draws on, and then unwound, left alone to face their own personal problems, and scattered as day breaks. (p. 40)

Fellini's *Inferno* leaves us looking sadly across the stream at Paradise; a paradise of sorts is assumed to exist, somewhere else, back in time or removed in space, but whichever it is, and whatever the precise nature of this paradise may be we are not told. However, the very fact of its existence, and the way that its existence is expressed, serves to discountenance the view that *La Dolce Vita* is a complete picture of Fellini's imaginative world at the present stage in his career. It is, rather, an exhaustive exploration of one side of that world: the dark side which we have previously encountered with some admixture, particularly in *I Vitelloni* and *Il Bidone.* (p. 42)

Fellini's habitual selection of reality could hardly go further: here all is monstrous, misshapen, overgrown, the settings, the clothes of the characters, the faces, startlingly beautiful or shockingly grotesque, but never ordinary. All these elements are found in life, everything that appears in the film may well have been seen somewhere in the streets or clubs of Rome, but this unremitting concentration on the peculiar, the exceptional, the larger-than-life gives the film, within its superficially realistic coating, a feverish, expressionistic quality which takes it in effect farther away from reality than anything Fellini had previously done, even *La Strada.* 'This town is not Rome—it is *my* Rome,' says Fellini, 'a town which has its external appearance in common with Rome because that is the place I live in and know best, but is really a creation of my own imagination.' . . . Fellini's Rome corresponds no more and no less to the world we normally live in than his time—the long, hectic nights, the almost non-existent day—corresponds with ours; that is to say, it has imaginative validity as a nightmare image of modern life, but hardly any literal validity as documentary picture of things as they prosaically are.

I must apologize for labouring this point, which ought to be obvious, but the film has been so much misunderstood as a piece of savage social criticism, an inside picture of Roman high life by a man who knows (and praised or blamed according to the critic's assessment of its efficacy in these fields) that I can only suppose it is not so obvious after all. The very look of the film, surely, ought to put such commentators on their guard: the bizarre locations; the intricately baroque chiaroscuro effects of light and shade in the night scenes, often not even vaguely explained in realistic terms; the highly artificial composition of many of the shots, the complete antithesis of unvarnished actuality; the bold use of symbolic trappings like the deceptive echo-chamber from which Marcello makes his proposal to Maddalena; the occasional excursions into complete unreality like the instantaneous and in this instance overtly subjective dawn over the fountain of Trevi. And yet, and yet. . . .

La Dolce Vita, then, remains a monument, and a very imposing one, to Fellini's doubts and fears. Life here is hell, and no one escapes from it, like Moraldo, or learns from it, even in extremes, like Zampano and Augusto, or even manages somehow to pass through it unscathed, like Cabiria. Relentlessly the film gathers force, as one after another every escape route Marcello might consider is closed in his face, and instance piles on instance; it works not by logical argument, but sheer agglomeration of circumstances, each one weighing the protagonist down further. But there is always one character, the girl on the beach, free from all this, living in a different world, and it is towards this world, with its clear, pearly grey light (visually very much the world of *La Strada*), that our attention is turned in the closing sequence. (pp. 43-4)

[*8½* seems] to be the ultimate summary and personal confession that *La Dolce Vita* was rather prematurely taken to be. (p. 45)

The hero of his film . . . is a film director with all the means of making a film at his disposal and no film to make. Or at least, he has a lot of ideas for a film, but they will not crystallize into a coherent script; essentially because, though he does not at first realize it, he is trying through the film to work out the problems of his own life, and so cannot make sense of the film's pattern until he has made sense of his own life as well. The action of the film takes place at a weird and dreamlike Edwardian spa (one occasionally suspects parody of *L' Année Dernière à Marienbad* lurking at the back of Fellini's mind) where Guido, the director, is taking a cure, scouting locations, and generally trying to sort things out while a gargantuan set of a rocket-base rises inexorably on a near-by lot and the whole machinery of a mammoth production little by little engulfs him. Throughout the film we, and he, flit backwards and forwards between dream and reality, sometimes seeing bits of the film he means to make as they form in his mind, sometimes the dreams which come to him while he sleeps, and sometimes the discussions with his producer, his unhelpful script collaborator and others in which ideas are considered, modified, or rejected. Indeed the film, finally, proves to have a structure rather like Gide's *Les Faux Monnayeurs,* being at once a film about making a film, and the film which in the process is made, and containing in addition a complete auto-critique, in that the harshest things which can be said against it—that it is pretentious, empty; that Fellini has nothing to say and does not alter that fact simply by openly admitting it to be true—are already said, by the director himself or by the critical intellectual he works with. (p. 46)

Guido has in the end to face the fact that even suicide, of which he dreams as the climax to a disastrous press conference, is not possible for him, and that he must just settle down to live with his own contradictions; not to seek the one, 'true', uncomplicated him, but to accept instead that all the different aspects of his character are necessarily and inescapably part of him for the rest of his life. His only answer is the classic artist's answer: to try again to make sense in his art of what in his life remains ever unsatisfactory and elusive. In his life he may be hopelessly incapable of coming to terms with the world around him, but in his own world of cinema, where he is a little god, he can order things as he thinks they should be. . . . (p. 49)

The material of *8½* evidently, and deliberately, recalls at many points that of Fellini's earlier films. Favourite images recur: the sea, suggesting freedom and infinity, the empty square at night as a setting for self-examination. So do Fellini's two principal types of women, the thin, angular, exacting wife and the plump, warm, complacent mistress, as well as the unseizable, mysterious innocent who passes momentarily across the scene, like the boy in *I Vitelloni* and the girl on the beach in *La Dolce Vita*. . . . The list could be continued almost indefinitely; *8½* is rather like a poet's notebook, which can only exert its full fascination for someone already well acquainted with the author's previous work and his whole imaginative world.

But that is only one aspect of the film. It remains part of the film, to the extent that it perhaps never quite achieves total independence as a self-sufficient work of art (one wonders what someone who had never seen a Fellini film before would make of it). But if the comparison with a poet's notebook suggests that the film is unpolished, unfinished, a succession of parts which never add up to a whole, this is quite unfair. In construction the film is Fellini's most intricate and in some ways his most masterly; the pieces, apparently so different and incompatible one with another, ultimately fall into place with fantastic precision and inevitability. Above all, it is a triumph of style; a new, fuller, wider-ranging Fellini style which finally leaves realism, in any sense that a neo-realist would recognize, far, far behind. . . . Fellini has evolved an ornate, extravagant visual style to match the fantasy of his plot. Not only do the dream sequences veer towards the expressionistic in their nightmarish exaggeration—never have we been drawn more deeply by the camera into the centre of Fellini's world; never have we been forced more ruthlessly to live by the characters' time rather than our own—but the 'real' scenes are often equally dreamlike, as in *Le Tentazioni del Dottor Antonio,* so that the edges of dream and reality are constantly blurring for us, as they are for Guido. When we start with a blanched, ghostly panorama of the springs themselves, with dozens of mysterious figures in black standing out in hallucinatory relief, many of them extremely strange and grotesque, are we in a dream or in life? In life, as it turns out, but by the time we can be really sure the significance of the distinction is liable to escape us. In *8½* Fellini clearly shows himself to be what we have always at least half suspected him of being, a baroque fantasist whose private world has nothing more than a few accidents of apparent time and place in common with any 'real' world which we may obstinately persist in supposing we know and can recognize. (pp. 49-51)

As a film-writer, as a creator of plots and characters, Fellini is remarkably gifted, but by no means unique: where his real greatness lies is the complete certainty with which he builds up his films not by a series of careful translations and transformations from a purely verbal origin, but by a process of co-ordination, bringing together and into focus sights and sounds, the character he sketches on a menu-card and the place he knew as a child, the hut on the Via Veneto and the face on the Spanish Steps, the fold of a dress and the manner of speech of a tawdry vaudevillian or a sleek aristocrat, into one complex, coherent, indivisible film. If any creator expresses himself in film first, last and always, it is Fellini; his films may sometimes appall the nicer sensibilities with their unashamed sentimentality, their occasional self-indulgence, their complete lack of inhibition, but these, if faults they are, are the necessary faults of his virtues. Above all with his films, even the most complex, one has the feeling of instantaneous creation, an undivided and joyful process from first conception to finished result. If that is not the mark of a great film-creator I don't know what is. (p. 51)

John Russell Taylor, "Federico Fellini," in his Cinema Eye, Cinema Ear: Some Key Film-Makers of the Sixties *(reprinted by permission of Hill & Wang, a division of Farrar, Straus & Giroux, Inc.; in Canada, by A D Peters & Co Ltd; copyright © 1964 by John Russell Taylor), Hill & Wang, 1964, pp. 15-51.*

ROBERT BRUSTEIN

[*Juliet of the Spirits*] is specious and hollow, in addition to being very boring; and its failures bring into focus what has been bothering me about Fellini's more celebrated successes: they are indebted less to true perception than to carnival showmanship. . . .

In *La Dolce Vita* Fellini revealed himself to be deeply attracted by the very things he was pretending to ridicule or expose (upper-class orgies, intellectual parties, Catholic ritual and pageantry, Anika Ekberg's chest); and in "8½" he dropped the mask of impersonality entirely, initiating some superficial explorations of the unconscious which, for all their disarming self-irony and technical dazzle, seemed to me little more than a cinematic acting out of his own autoerotic fantasies, resolved by an outrageously dishonest conclusion. In *Juliet of the Spirits,* Fellini's artistic flashiness and moral ambiguity are even more conspicuous; and while the fantasies he invents are now supposed to belong to a middle-aged housewife, they are still more appropriate to a Hollywood producer with a gaudy mind, or a pubescent male weaned on girlie magazines. (p. 22)

The film is well-photographed, and some of its ideas are interesting as a series of visual balances—the conflict between sex and religion, for example, is illustrated by a contrast between a bevy of blowsy whores with smeared lipstick and exposed breasts, and a somber procession of hooded, faceless nuns in black habits. Still for all the obvious expertise, the conflict itself has no more depth than a secularized morality play; while the development of the action despite the manipulation of dream images, owes less to Strindberg than to soap opera. I am well aware that narrative line is of little importance in this film, but it is still disturbing to find what little plot there is so predictable and sentimental; and the climax, dependent as it is on Giulietta's defiance of a mother who is of marginal importance in the action, is simply arbitrary and contrived.

The film has even less validity as a study of character, for the female protagonist is convincing neither as a woman nor as a human being. . . . Giulietta is simply a sponge, soaking up visual experience, a passive witness to expert cinematography, whose responses and attitudes are commonplace in the extreme. . . . (p. 23)

Fellini's use of color . . . while vivid and daring at first glance, is ultimately too garish to serve his purposes. . . . [His] strategic error is to superimpose fantasy on romance; but there is not sufficient difference between the two styles, and he compounds his error by his choice of background music—a tinny ragtime score, dominated by saxophone and piano, which marks every action that should be real and convincing as a piece of romantic nostalgia. In short, where Fellini could once be trusted implicitly, his choices have not become eccentric, doubtful, and random, and one begins to suspect that he will sacrifice anything—form, character, coherence itself—for the sake of a sensational image or an ingenious effect. (pp. 23-4)

At the present moment, Fellini is using his camera as an expensive toy, and his love of luxury is accounting for a lot of fakery and sham. Unless he can learn to control his excesses, his films, I suspect, will continue to deteriorate until they become mere stimulants for the jaded appetites of precisely that world that he travesties and mocks. (p. 24)

Robert Brustein, "La Dolce Spumoni" (reprinted by permission of the author), in The New York Review of Books, *Vol. V, No. 10, December 23, 1965, pp. 22-4.*

ANNE PAOLUCCI

Fellini's imagination is inexhaustible. He rarely uses scripts, but follows his own inspiration from moment to moment to decide what sequence to adopt, working out the details, *via facendo,* as he goes along.

What emerges is the full and varied complexity of modern life. The existential *noia,* the lethargy of man face to face with his reconstituted *tabula rasa,* is but a single moment, a small corner of that life. Fellini does not dissipate his artistic energies in the desperate task of trying to extract meaning out of a meaningless existence. The existential theme is there, not as a philosophical axiom, but as a subtle epiphany which illuminates the vast canvas at key moments. The naive prostitute, the pimp, the aristocratic dandies, the corrupt society women, the humanitarian writer, the shrewd peasant, the pathetic yet laughter-provoking idiot, the suicide, the insensitive cruel children, the everyday saints, the callous men and women who know how and where to pick their ripe pleasures, the bigots who pray for the salvation of others; the secularism of priests who have lost sight of their divine mission, the self-effacing beauty of the pure-hearted—all are depicted with human compassion and understanding in what T. S. Eliot has described as the dramatic objectivity of the "third voice of poetry."

In the end, Fellini too shows the false values of the world to be self-destructive. There is perhaps a greater feeling of despair in his films than in Antonioni's, because the loss can be measured against an articulate reality. The realization of the meaning of love, in *La Strada,* is felt to be hopeless precisely because it rises from a powerful contrast between the man's rough indifference and the girl's inexpressible sympathy; the abandonment in *La Dolce Vita* is felt all the more keenly in the insistence with which Fellini draws the nostalgic yearning of the hero to lose himself in some all-consuming faith; in *Nights of Cabiria,* simple childlike trust though crushed by petty interests and deceit seems somehow to rise above its humiliation. Fellini's stories strike deep in the human soul; his characters cast a haunting spell over us. We are painfully aware of hard truths in the midst of commonplaces, of noble spirits touching, for a moment, spiritual depravity and illuminating with sudden insight ordinary, everyday events. The procession in *La Strada,* like Dante's pageant at the top of Purgatory, is recognizable in all its details, but the final effect is strange and nightmarish; the all-night orgy in *La Dolce Vita* is, in its isolated moments, perfectly clear, but the surrealistic Matelda-like encounter at the end, jolts us into perplexity; the scene between the prostitute and the magician in *Nights of Cabiria* seems perfectly commonplace as we see it unfold, but inserts itself into our troubled consciousness later. (pp. 563-64)

In *8½* we see the drama of life with all its confusion of values, its pain, its sordid pleasures, its human mistakes, the short-lived joys which haunt the memory but can never be recaptured. The innocent love of the past and the rote-like lust of the present are shown side by side in an expressive juxtaposition that is grim and sad and beautiful all at once. (p. 564)

Anne Paolucci, "The Italian Film: Antonioni, Fellini, Bolognini," in The Massachusetts Review *(reprinted from* The Massachusetts Review; *© 1966 The Massachusetts Review, Inc.), Vol. VII, No. 3, Summer, 1966, pp. 556-67.**

FORREST WILLIAMS

[Taken by themselves the] reels of dazzling visual images [in *Giulietta degli Spiriti*] may well come to seem gratuitous and even tiresome. A terribly earnest and pathetically ingenuous wife makes her psychological journey through facts and hallucinations in sequences of astonishing exoticism. The scenes are often not so much in color as coloristic, and the settings, both actual and hallucinated—with no particularly insistent demarcation—are not so much extravagant as extravaganza-ed. Virtually every shot has a contrived air, to the spent and twitching point of mannerism. Hence the frequent characterization of the film as "baroque." But the dialogue, precisely by being just as "frou-frou," just as *"spumone,"* as the visual style, does something other than provide information and develop a story. Dialogue turns out to be a way of life in Giulietta's milieu, or more exactly, a way of *escape* from a genuine life of action for the people who surround her. (p. 22)

Fellini's strategy for accomplishing this mutual reinforcement of dialogue and image is not to emphasize to any abnormal degree *what* things are said, but to emphasize more than usual the *ways* in which they are said. . . . When the visual exoticism is thus taken in conjunction with the unremitting dialogue, it ceases to look gratuitously mannered or exaggerated; for together they are the warp and the woof of a major theme of Fellini's work: the incessant conflict between the comparative concreteness of Giulietta's responses, however ingenuous and even hallucinatory they may sometimes be, and the triviality of her milieu. . . .

Another theme of the film, as has been frequently noted, is the conflict in Giulietta between the sentimentalized asceticism of her convent childhood and the sexual libertinism of the Italian bourgeoisie—which includes her own repressed, bourgeois fantasies. But Fellini has set this erotic disturbance in a context of deafening glibness that gives to the personal dilemma of Giulietta a larger and unusual social setting. Words themselves, if you like, are one of the chief problems of Giulietta's life with her "grand openings" husband and well-heeled friends. . . .

The role of dialogue as a false mode of behavior, as *a substitute for action,* rather than as a means of effective communication of ideas and feelings, is thus firmly established from the outset, and returns again and again throughout the narrative. (p. 23)

The film is . . . about, not only infidelity, eroticism, and childhood repression, but a profound and far less explored evil, personal and social, having nothing directly to do with sex as such. Dante, I suggest, would have placed Giulietta's entourage, with his famed sense for the really relevant fault, not in the upper circles among the lustful, but deep in the malbowges, where are punished abusers of words, sinners against one of the highest of human faculties.

The dialogue thus provides, it would seem, the social context of the film at least as strikingly and satirically as do the visible settings. Fellini has produced an auditory Inferno which exactly parallels the visual phantasmagoria, and his Giulietta emerges as a kind of sacred fool in a perfectly hellish world of talk, talk, talk. (p. 24)

Forrest Williams, "Fellini's Voices," in Film Quarterly *(copyright 1968 by The Regents of the University of California; reprinted by permission of the University of California Press), Vol. XXI, No. 4, Spring, 1968, pp. 21-5.*

STANLEY KAUFFMANN

Go to see *Spirits of the Dead* about an hour after it begins. It's a three-part film—three Poe horror stories made by three different directors. The first two are silly bores, by the justly disregarded Roger Vadim and the greatly overrated Louis Malle. The third is by Federico Fellini. And his horror story is joyous.

Joyous, not because Fellini has no sense of the macabre—after all, his story ends with decapitation—but because he revels in making films and because his darting invention never stops playing around and through the picture, so that even this film of terror plunges us into a sort of Satanic champagne. Fellini's career easily divides into two periods: the first, in which his cinematic mind serves his humanist concerns; the second, in which his humanist concerns are the base for stylist exultation. (*La Dolce Vita* is the transitional film between the two periods.) This short film is very much a matter of execution, not content; although I don't suppose there is a "new" visual concept in it, Fellini's familiar ideas are still exciting.

Toby Dammit, liberally adapted from Poe's "Never Bet the Devil Your Head," is about a sodden English film star (Terence Stamp) as he arrives in Rome to make a Western that will allegorize the myth of Redemption. Stamp, as we can see and the others cannot, is haunted by the devil in the figure of a sly little girl who bounces a white ball. (p. 196)

Sparkling as it is, *Toby Dammit* is not as good as Fellini's previous short film, *The Temptation of Dr. Antonio* in *Boccaccio '70. Dr. Antonio* was a simple antimoralistic morality tale, but its very simplicity made the complex style tickle. The new script is a solo for Stamp, with various accompaniments, but it never much engages us as a morality drama and Stamp has little chance to do more than look damned, which he certainly does. But from the first moments of his arrival in Rome (echoing Anita Ekberg's arrival in *La Dolce Vita*) on through a TV interview that made one TV interviewer (myself) wriggle with its truth, to a sort of Italian Oscar-award ceremony, the switch is turned, the motors are humming, Fellini is flying. And if a director is going to concentrate on flash, as he does here, short films are better than long ones, for an obvious reason. I wish the script of *Toby Dammit* were more diabolical, but Fellini's deviltry is almost enough. (p. 197)

One point about Fellini's lighting is specially interesting. In his recent films the lighting has been much more theatrical than realistic: low angles, profiles cut out of the dark, the frequent recurrence of silhouettes, and the changes of light during a shot. In *Toby Dammit* an additional theatricality is clear. Often, but especially in the TV interview and in the award ceremony, scenes are lighted like stages and are surrounded by dark, the location in the world is treated like a setting in a theater, and we get the feeling that these lives—by implication, our lives—are being enacted before an unseen audience. Before whom? Perhaps Fellini has remained more of a Catholic than he likes to admit. (pp. 197-98)

Stanley Kauffmann, "'Spirits of the Dead'" (originally published in The New Republic, *September 27, 1969), in his* Figures of Light: Film Criticism and Comment *(copyright © 1968, 1969, 1970 by Stanley Kauffmann; reprinted by permission of Harper & Row, Publishers, Inc.), Harper, 1971, pp. 196-98.*

PAULINE KAEL

The idea that sticks out in every direction from "Fellini Satyricon" is that man without a belief in God is a lecherous beast. I think it's a really bad movie—a terrible movie—but Fellini has such intuitive rapport with the superstitious child in the adult viewer that I imagine it will be a considerable success. . . . Fellini is not a sanctimonious manipulator . . . ; he makes fantasy extravaganzas out of tabloid sensationalism, but he appears to do it from emotional conviction, or, perhaps more exactly, from a master entertainer's feeling for the daydreams of the audience. He seems to draw upon something in himself that many people respond to as being profound, possibly because it has been long buried in them. When he brings it out, they think he is a great artist.

Fellini's pagans are freaks—bloated or deformed, or just simulated freaks with painted faces and protruding tongues. . . . The freak show of "Fellini Satyricon" is a grotesque interpretation of paganism, yet I think many people in the audience will accept it without question. . . . Fellini's popular strength probably comes from primitive elements such as these in a modern style that enables audiences to respond as if the content were highly sophisticated. (p. 134)

Like a naughty Christian child, Fellini thinks it's a ball to be a pagan, but a naughty ball, a *bad* one, which can't really be enjoyed. . . . In "Fellini Satyricon" the party scenes are no longer orgiastic climaxes. Fellini uses Petronius and other classic sources as the basis for a movie that is one long orgy of eating, drinking, cruelty, and copulation, and he goes all the way with his infatuation with transvestism, nymphomania, homosexuality, monsters.

"Fellini Satyricon" is *all* phantasmagoria, and though from time to time one may register a face or a set or an episode, for most of the film one has the feeling of a camera following people walking along walls. The fresco effect becomes monotonous and rather oppressive. It's almost as if the movie were a theatrically staged panorama, set on a treadmill. . . . Fellini never does involve us: we seem to be at a stoned circus, where the performers go on and on whether we care or not. And though there's a story, we anticipate the end a dozen times—a clear sign that his episodic structuring has failed. Afterward, one recalls astonishingly little; there are many episodes and anecdotes, but, for a work that is visual if it is anything, it leaves disappointingly few visual impressions. . . . It's a tired movie; during much of it, we seem to be moving past clumsily arranged groups and looking at people exhibiting their grossness or their abnormalities and sticking their tongues out at us. . . . Fellini's early films had a forlorn atmosphere, and there were bits of melancholy still drifting through "La Dolce Vita" and "8½;" if the people were lost, at least their sorrow gave them poetic suggestions of depth. There was little depth in "Juliet of the Spirits," and there is none in this "Satyricon." Perhaps Fellini thinks Christ had to come before people could have souls, but, lacking emotional depth, the movie is so transient that elaborate episodes like Trimalchio's banquet barely leave a trace in the memory.

Somewhere along the line—I think it happened in "La Dolce Vita"—Fellini gave in to the luxurious basking in sin that has always had such extraordinary public appeal. . . . And, though he doesn't appear in them, he became the star of his movies, which are presented as emanations of his imagination, his genius; he functioned as if the creative process had no relation to experience, to thought, or to other art. As this process has developed, the actors, and the characters, in his movies have become less and less important, so at "Fellini Satyricon" one hardly notices the familiar people in it—it's all a masquerade anyway. . . . I feel that what has come over Fellini is a movie director's megalomania, which has not gone so far with anyone else, and that part of the basis for his reputation is that his narcissistic conception of his role is exactly what celebrity worshippers have always thought a movie director to be. . . . People coming out of "La Dolce Vita" and "8½" could be heard asking, "Where do you suppose he found them?"—as if he were a magician of a zookeeper who had turned up fabulous specimens. This increasingly strange human zoo into which he thrusts us is what people refer to when they say that there is a Fellini world. (pp. 134, 137-39)

Fellini's work has an eerie, spellbinding quality for some people which must be not unlike the powerful effect the first movies were said to have. Perhaps the opulence and the dreamlike movement of his films and the grotesques who populate them are what some people want from the movies—a return to frightening fairy tales. I don't think "Fellini Satyricon" is effective even on this level, because I don't find the Pop decadence beautiful. . . . I should say that emotionally his "Satyricon" is just about the opposite of "free;" emotionally, it's a hip version of "The Sign of the Cross." There's a certain amount of confusion in it about what's going on and where, so some people may take it "psychedelically" and swallow it whole. . . . Maybe if Fellini personally didn't impress people so much as a virtuoso they'd become as conscious of the emotional and intellectual shoddiness they're responding to in *his* films. The usual refrain is "With Fellini, I'm so captivated by the images I don't ask what it means." But suppose it's not the "beauty" of the images they're reacting to so much as that step-by-step intuitive linkage between Fellini's emotions and their own almost forgotten ones? I'm sure there are people who will say that it doesn't matter if Fellini's movies are based on shallow thinking, or even ignorance, because he uses popular superstitions for a poetic vision, and makes art out of them. The large question in all this is: *Can* movie art be made out of shallow thinking and superstitions? The answer may, I think, be no. But even if it's yes, I don't think Fellini transformed anything in "Fellini Satyricon." (pp. 139-40)

Pauline Kael, "Fellini's Mondo Trasho," in The New Yorker *(© 1970 by The New Yorker Magazine, Inc.), Vol. XLVI, No. 4, March 14, 1970, pp. 134, 137-140.*

STANLEY KAUFFMANN

Fellini's life has been spent in the service of both reality and nonreality, largely because he knows, as one of the few film masters who also understand theatricality, that theater without artifice is a fake ideal and a naïf's idea of truth.

His movie dream of Petronius [*Fellini Satyricon*] is another work of truth and artifice. . . . [*Fellini Satyricon*] is elegiac, joyless, resigned. There are many scenes of revel and of sex in it; there is very little gusto.

Another burden from which Fellini has to be freed is our expectation of method. He has taught us to expect lightning play in his editing, swift referential humor and counterpoint, drama and dialectic by deft junctures of material, and he has used this method even in his recent short film *Toby Dammit* (a part of *Spirits of the Dead*). There is some splintery referential editing in *Satyricon,* but the principal method is immersion in texture and color, steady progression through the "feel" of a scene, rather than any lightning mosaics or kaleidoscopic flow. (pp. 250-51)

[What] is there—in the picture itself—that indicates why this man, who has made only contemporary films that were psychologically pertinent even when stylistically extravagant, has abandoned pertinence for extravagance: has chosen a subject that freed him of pertinence and allowed him to concentrate on the extravagance? . . .

[There is] a connection, at the very base, between this *Satyricon* and Antonioni's *Zabriskie Point.* Both are the works of mature artists that reflect the contemporary artist's relation to the world as material for art. Experience is not less than it was, it is too much more: our culture's expanded consciousness (within) and amplified communication (without) overwhelm and enervate some artists and produce, finally, a bankruptcy, rather than a surfeit, because of a sense of incompetence to deal with that enlarged experience.

Still, artists must work or wither. Antonioni's solution . . . was an emigration to a different place and a different generation. Fellini's emigration was to the past: where his sense of futility and oppression was relieved of the necessity of point and *could express itself as a function of film making itself*. . . . It is difficult—at least for me—to imagine Fellini making this film unless, in a way, he was forced to. *Satyricon* is a step past *8½*, which was about a director looking for a film to make and (despite the desperate ending) failing to find one. *Satyricon* is the film that Guido, the hero of *8½*, might have made. (p. 253)

It does indeed deal with the monstrous and impure; its moral tone is funereal. It might better have been called *Fellini Inferno,* rather than his *Satyricon.* But the inferno, I believe, is the sum of the conditions of life, and *his* life in particular, that forced him to make the film at all.

So the film depends for its being entirely on the way it is made. There are of course recognizable Fellini hallmarks: the silent opening (as in *8½*), the big fish (*La Dolce Vita*), the abrupt ending (like the freeze frame at the end of *I Vitelloni*), the earth mother whore (from several pictures). But it is the first Fellini feature film that has, in the post-Renaissance sense, no characters. There are only persons, some of whom are on screen more than others. The film has no cumulative story, let alone drama. There is not even a cumulation of adventures, in the picaresque manner; many of the sequences are simply scenes observed. *Satyricon* depends entirely on its look, and, unlike *8½*, which finally lives through its style, there are few afferents to bind us to the style, to make us care about it in anything more than a graphic arts, "gallery" way—a way that is directly opposed to theatrical experience. (p. 254)

Stanley Kauffmann, "'Fellini Satyricon'" (originally published in The New Republic, *April 11, 1970), in his* Figures of Light: Film Criticism and Comment *(copyright © 1968, 1969, 1970 by Stanley Kauffmann; reprinted by permission of Harper & Row, Publishers, Inc.), Harper, 1971, pp. 250-54.*

JOHN RUSSELL TAYLOR

[*Satyricon*] starts where *Giulietta degli Spiriti* left off, moving wholly into a world of dreams and visions, bigger and more bizarre even than the highly-coloured fantasies of Giulietta in full flight. The result should be impossible, utterly indigestible, but paradoxically it is not: one adjusts rapidly to accepting the extreme ornateness of the action (what is going on in front of the camera much more than how the camera records it) as a sort of norm, so that effects which even in *Giulietta* would have drawn attention to themselves as extraordinary and exceptional here seem hardly more remarkable in themselves than a dead metaphor in everyday speech. . . .

Charm and grace are not particularly Fellinian qualities, and the last thing he ever is is a sophisticate. In a way this is his greatest strength. In all his films, though particularly of course those from *La Dolce Vita* on, it is the sheer spate of ideas that pours from him and on to the screen, like a force of nature, which silences criticism if anything can. Of discretion, good taste, or anything namby-pamby like that, he knows and cares nothing.

Especially in *Satyricon.* For the light and good humour of Petronius he substitutes something dark, menacing, lit at best with flames of hellish fire from some John Martin vision of cosmic disaster in the ancient world. Hardly any of Fellini's *Satyricon* is actually funny; it is instead a sort of nightmare vision of a civilisation on its last legs, over-rich, over-ripe, decorating its surfaces with a neurotic elaboration because form has come to be the only consideration, and what the form should express counts for nothing. . . .

8½ is a work which shows Fellini's creative imagination working at maximum intensity. Its greatest effect lies in a paradox of which, one suspects, Fellini was hardly aware while he was making it: that while it is about the mind at the end of its tether, the imagination exhausted and impotent, the film he has made on this subject is full of imagination exuberantly and fruitfully at play. *Giulietta* is a work of fancy rather than imagination, if we may try to preserve the Coleridgian distinction: lighter, slighter, less deeply involved or involving, it frolics pleasurably with and on parts of Fellini's regular mental furniture. What *Satyricon* does is to return yet again to these materials, but now using them in such a way that they contain a built-in criticism of themselves. The spate of invention is still there, but it is no longer joyful. Its effect in *Giulietta* is sometimes smothering, suffocating, where one senses it was not meant to be. Here, even as one is battered and weighed down by the sheer accumulation of detail, one can recognise it as part of Fellini's intention that one should be. (p. 217)

[The] film does, though sometimes by a very narrow margin, function as a work of art, recreating effects rather than reproducing them. It even achieves that most difficult of feats, conveying boredom without actually boring. . . . We are not touched by the characters, we do not care at all about their fate . . . , the characters are simply part of the overall pattern, and it is the pattern which works on us if anything does.

As with all Fellini's later, more confessional films, I suspect that *Satyricon* is a film you have to succumb to completely, live along with for more than two hours and accept the discomforts as well as the insights involved in seeing things as Fellini sees them, if it is to work at all. But for those who can let it work on them, Fellini's journey to the end of night is a chastening and, surprisingly enough, an elevating experience. (p. 218)

John Russell Taylor, "Film Reviews: Fellini 'Satyricon'," in Sight and Sound *(copyright © 1970 by The British Film Institute), Vol. 39, No. 4, Autumn, 1970, pp. 217-18.*

WILLIAM S. PECHTER

La Dolce Vita is not so much long as redundant. Scene duplicates scene; and scene after scene is protracted long after its every point has been unmistakably made. The trouble would seem to be that the film is *conceived* on a grand scale, but *imagined* only within rather narrow limitations. Fellini almost invariably extends all his scenes beyond every interest save the visual. . . . [A] negative compensation in all of this is in the proof it offers that the film is definitely *more* than a visual medium. (pp. 39-40)

There is nothing more beautiful or more terrible in *La Dolce Vita* than what is suggested by, and contained by implication in, its opening. It is a metaphor charged with meaning that the rest of the film strives in vain to equal.

Fellini seems unable, but is more likely unwilling, to accept this. . . . [When he] goes after the Big One, he brings back the bulk of *La Dolce Vita* and *La Strada*. Where, as in that earlier film, all else gives way to allegory and abstraction, there must at least, by way of justification, be some compensating profundity and complexity of ideas. In *La Strada*, we are deprived of all the density of life and lifelike art, and, in its place, served up one simple, huge abstraction; you know it: Love. And in *La Dolce Vita:* Innocence. *Reductio ad abstractum;* the operative word is *reduction.* (p. 42)

Fellini *is* a fine artist; he might be a great one. *La Dolce Vita* is, I think, a failure, but not, I believe, a disreputable one. Fellini has failed before, but never disreputably. Of how many other artists can we say as much? (p. 43)

William S. Pechter, "Two Movies and Their Critics" (originally published in a different version in The Kenyon Review, *Vol. XXIV, No. 2, Spring, 1962), in his* Twenty-Four Times a Second *(copyright © 1960, 1961, 1962, 1963, 1965, 1968, 1969, 1970, 1971 by William S. Pechter; reprinted by permission of the author), Harper & Row, Publishers, Inc., 1971, pp. 37-50.**

PAULINE KAEL

Urban chaos is used as spectacle in *Fellini's Roma,* an ambivalent celebration of decay. The opulent rotting city of the film is indeed his own, with extras painted up as voracious citizens, and mock excavations, and a high-camp ecclesiastical fashion show that is also meant to be some sort of glittering, satirical comment on the old aristocracy, though it's hard to know exactly what the point is. *Roma* is an imperial gesture at documentary—a document about the city of Fellini's imagination, an autobiographical fantasy in which he plays ringmaster to the Roman circus. . . . The usual critical encomium "No one but Fellini could have made this movie" is certainly appropriate. . . . [Who] but Fellini would construct in a studio parts of the motorway circling Rome, in order to stage a traffic jam that would be a miracle of lashing rains and stalled cars under darkly beautiful skies? And in the middle of it there is another false movie crew, pretending to be shooting what we see—the camera high above the congestion, with silky while plastic flapping around it, as if protecting a mikado. The conceits are becoming so ornate they're getting spooky. (pp. 25-6)

This ringmaster feels no need to relate to the circus people. Fellini is an unparalleled extrovert, even for a profession rich in extroversion; he is so extroverted he has abandoned interest in characters and is interested only in his own projections. He is at the center of the movie, played as a young man fresh from the provinces by a toothsome, lusciously handsome actor . . . , and then by himself, speaking in English—most of it dubbed—in this version. He interacts with no one; he is the only star, our guide, and, like many another guide, he often miscalculates our reactions, especially to his arch, mirthless anticlerical jokes. The ambience is least oppressive when he stages a forties vaudeville show—a return to the world of his early movies. Here his nostalgic caricatures aren't so cruelly limiting, and the performers briefly take over. Emotionally, Fellini obviously lives in the past; the modern scenes have no emotional tone and no precise observation—not even any new caricatures. One modern sequence—a sci-fi treatment of subway digs and the uncovering of a Roman villa, with frescoes that disappear as soon as the air from outside hits them—is so clumsily staged that we may become embarrassed for the Maestro, and particularly by the Sears, Roebuck quality of the frescoes. The tragedy of their disappearance is a blessing. The new elements in this film are the psychedelic use of sound—din, actually—to empty our heads and intensify our sensory impressions, and the semi-abstraction of several of the modern sequences: the torrents of rain falling on the movie company caught in traffic, the wind in the subway excavations, a horde of black-leather-jacketed, death-symbolizing motorcyclists speeding to an unknown destination, and so on. Some of these images are magisterial and marvelous, like a series of stormy Turners. If one could turn off the assaulting noise—a lethal mix of car horns and motors and gothic storms—these passages might be mysteriously exciting, though they go on too long. But whenever there's dialogue, or *thought,* the movie is fatuous. . . . Fellini appears to see himself as official greeter for the apocalypse; his uxorious welcoming smile is an emblem of emptiness. (pp. 26-7)

Pauline Kael, "The Irish Inheritance" (originally published in The New Yorker, *October 21, 1972), in her* Reeling *(copyright © 1972, 1973, 1974, 1975, 1976 by Pauline Kael; reprinted by permission of Little, Brown and Company in association with the Atlantic Monthly Press), Atlantic-Little, Brown, 1976, pp. 21-7.**

ROGER GREENSPUN

'Fellini's Roma' is perhaps three-quarters Fellini and one quarter Rome; a very good proportion for a movie. Although an appreciation of the city informs every part of the movie, Rome is not so much the subject as the occasion for a film that is not quite fiction and surely not fact, but rather the celebration of an imaginative collaboration full of love and awe, suspicion, admiration, exasperation and a measure of well qualified respect. It is also, for me, the most enjoyable Fellini in a dozen years, the most surprising, the most exuberant, the most beautiful, the most extravagantly theatrical. . . . The director's mind, whether you like it or not, is one of the most important phenomena of contemporary filmmaking and 'Roma' gives it a kind of freedom I have seen in no other Fellini movie. Its capacities for pleasure and terror, for sympathy and irony, are all perfectly met in 'Roma.'

Roger Greenspun, "The New Movies: 'Fellini's Roma'," in The New York Times, *Section 2 (© 1972 by The New York Times Company; reprinted by permission), October 22, 1972, p. 7.*

STANLEY KAUFFMANN

[Fellini's *Roma* is] another quasi-documentary: of what the city meant to him as a provincial youth, how it seemed when he arrived, what it seems to him today.

Not a bad commission for a picture, and anyone who has never seen a Fellini film might be struck by the fertility and easy skill of this one. Unfortunately not many of us have the requisite ignorance of Fellini. We keep seeing remakes here of what he has done before. The scenes of youthful longing are varied only slightly from those in *The Clowns,* which even then were not as good as in *I Vitelloni.* The burst of outdoor communal eating in Rome is only a domesticated modern version of the feasts in *Satyricon.* Fellini's "typage" (Eisenstein's term)—the ability to select unusual faces that are self-explaining, that serve their functions without dossier—used to be a kind of wonderful caricature; here the method caricatures itself because it is so repetitious and because there is no main substance to which it can contribute. The brothel scenes are the nadir in this matter; the use of raddled faces of cheap whores is always the last infirmity of a social commentator's art. Besides, after La Saraghina in *8½,* Fellini has said everything he has to say on the subject—which is precisely his problem on most subjects.

He hasn't even enough resource and observation to fulfill his own commission for this film. Desperate for material, he tacks on a long parodic ecclesiastical fashion show near the end, saying that he and his camera crew are going to visit an old lonely princess who lives in a huge palazzo. The fashion show is her dream. Why *her* dream in this picture?—except that it gives Fellini one more chance for clerical mockery, complete with drifting mist, and dramatically shifting lights? Besides, why would a pious woman have dreamed this satirical dream?

He pads the picture with some rainy-day traffic sequences—blurred auto lights in the mist, for heaven's sake, from Fellini! (Together with a brief recap of the traffic jam from the beginning of *8½.*) And things are so low with him that the only way he can think to finish is to follow a bunch of nighttime motorcyclists as they vroom through the city. (p. 149)

Stanley Kauffmann, "Fellini's 'Roma'" (originally published in The New Republic, *Vol. 167, No. 17, November 4, 1972), in his* Living Images: Film Comment and Criticism *(copyright © 1971, 1972, 1973, 1974 by Stanley Kauffmann; reprinted by permission of Harper & Row, Publishers, Inc.), Harper, 1975, pp. 148-50.*

GIDEON BACHMANN

[The traffic sequence in *Roma*] is one of those ever-more-rare sequences in Fellini's work which treat a simple, daily matter in an abstracted, symbolic way, but still so beguilingly realistic as to become prototypes of the matter portrayed.

This ability to make one see that which one should really have seen all along but somehow hasn't seen, has been Fellini's major force. Because of it, his films have a haunting quality between realism and stylization even when they are (or rather, were) about everyday things. . . .

[The mixture of reality and fantasy] is still the thing Fellini does best. In fact, sometimes the suspicion grows that he may be on the road to losing the capacity for distinguishing the difference.

Thus for those to whom a certain tie to reality is not one of cinema's essentials, this must appear to be Fellini's best film since *8½.* It is certainly the most formally cohesive. And if self-expression at the expense of engagement is a choice you are willing to make, Fellini provides marvellous alibis for renouncing social and political concerns. . . .

[His] self-deprecation, or the surface appearance of it, has become a major confessional tool: the film is permeated by breast-beating cameos of people who berate him. (p. 37)

But there is no absolution and the self-criticism falls flat, because what he makes Romans say about him is not invented: it is what they actually say about him, and with good reason. They don't trust him, and they are right not to. This is no longer the real Rome. His reality-fantasy pendulum has swung all the way. This is a Rome of dreams and illusions. He is doing what he set out to do when he said: "Reality doesn't exist. The artist invents it."

On the other hand, it is an admitted subjectivity. It would be wrong to tag as simple presumptuousness Fellini's habit of calling his films by his own name or by opus number (*8½*, *Fellini Satyricon* and now *Fellini Roma* are the original Italian titles; *Juliet* is his wife's name). Foreign, more modest renaming may not do them justice, because in fact these titles accurately describe the contents of the films.

Unfortunately, they also raise our hopes, inasmuch as we expect to encounter a personality of some universal meaning, or at least a continually changing one, a character, as it were, who walks with the times.

In *Roma*, his most avowedly autobiographical work to date, Fellini does in fact seem to try to do that. But the result can only be defined as sad. . . .

The whole film is in fact overlaid with [a] vague underarm odor. (p. 38)

Add to this the strictly additive style of cutting, the musical underscoring for effect, fabulous decor often wasted by careless camera use, the lack of dramatic development, of character exploration, of viewer identification elements, of subtlety, of social consciousness, of storyline, involvement or even just plain compassion, and you begin to realize that the antiquity aspect, the faint mustiness, permeates not just the subject matter but the form of the work as well. It is the nostalgic odor of an aging talent.

But in all honesty, the space of a review does not allow one to do justice to a work which in essence is like the top tip of an iceberg. . . .

[Finally] one finds oneself with a certain compassion towards this man who in his time has well-nigh revolutionized film language, and who for a period was perhaps a dying craft's major exponent. That is why the adjective that springs to mind is *sad;* nothing really critical, really destructive, because somehow one is left with the feeling that to attack Fellini on a serious level, to demand responsibility or realism, becomes irrelevant in face of his patent inability to go beyond himself. (p. 39)

Gideon Bachmann, "Reviews: 'Fellini Roma'," in Film Quarterly *(copyright 1972 by The Regents of the University of California; reprinted by permission of the University of California Press), Vol. XXVI, No. 2, Winter, 1972-73, pp. 37-9.*

ROY ARMES

Fellini is totally autobiographical but unproblematic: like those Renaissance painters who filled the walls and ceilings of innumerable villas and palaces with exuberant portraits of their mistresses and friends, barely disguised as figures of classical or biblical allegory.

Such reflections are brought to the fore by Fellini's latest film, *Roma*, which presents a dual portrait of the city and the *cinéaste*. The confrontation of these two runs as a unifying thread throughout the film. All great baroque art is a cry of defiance against death, and Rome, seen as a dying city eaten away from within, provokes Fellini to some of the most dazzling sequences of his career. The opening is deceptively idyllic: Rome as it is seen from the provinces. . . . Above all, it is a paradoxical mixture of past dignity and present temptation. . . . Fellini's handling of these sequences—recreating his Cinecittà epic as well as his Fascist newsreel . . . is an important clue to his stylistic methods in the later portions of the film, where even the most apparently direct passages of *cinéma-vérité* are in fact staged reconstructions.

Roma is a film without a story in the conventional sense, but it does move in a roughly chronological fashion from these memories of the distant past towards a vision of the present and premonitions of a possible future. But within this pattern it is the contrasts set up that are most important and give the film its impact. (p. 119)

Fellini captures with incredible precision the extravert side of Italian life, that of existence conceived as a show. Even the neo-realists failed to convey so powerfully the profound deception underlying this vivid surface. In their dimensions these scenes are no less impressive than the orgies of the *Fellini-Satyricon* in which the very vivacity of the participants carried such an undertone of death and decay. In *Roma* too one senses something of the same despair, for this is Rome on the brink of the futile Fascist adventure into war. The noise is there to cover a void, the eating is an excuse for ignoring the world outside. This is the Rome of Fellini's early experience. . . . (p. 120)

With a meticulous attention to detail . . . Fellini conveys his vision of the urban environment. This is far blacker, for the highway leads, as darkness falls, to a nightmare picture dominated by an accident that has left dead calves scattered over the road and a truck in flames and then to police brutality in an assault on youthful demonstrators. Parallel to this chaos above ground is the other contemporary piece which again begins disarmingly as *cinéma-vérité*. (p. 121)

Roma is a film of total maturity. Gone is the sentimentality of *La strada*, the pretension of *La dolce vita*, the self-conscious intellectualizing of '8½'. Instead we find a filmmaker with full confidence in his own powers and an amused eye for his own foibles and those of his gallery of grotesques. His vision is pessimistic—pleasure is a prelude to death, the church and state are farcical or brutal, the present erodes the past without mercy or humanity—yet there is a great exhilaration in Fellini's virtuosity. Like '8½' (where a critic shouts at Fellini-Mastroianni 'He has nothing to say!') *Roma* contains within itself the cliché judgements we might be tempted to use. If we find it too long, there is Anna Magnani saying 'Go home, Federico, it's late.' If we are tempted to literary allusion, there is the bespectacled intellectual rebuffed for his perpetual evocations of Proust. *Roma* is clearly Federico Fellini's masterpiece to date. Continually playing on our acceptance of the reality of his images and delighting us with startling innovations, Fellini displays to the full his supreme talents as storyteller and master of spectacle. (p. 122)

Roy Armes, "Rome, from Rimini," in London Magazine *1973), Vol. 12, No. 6, February-March, 1973, pp. 116-22.*

WILLIAM J. FREE

Federico Fellini, discussing his film *I Clowns* in the French periodical *L'Arc*, attributes the disappearance of the clown to the sense of absurdity and disorder which pervades modern life. "The clown," he says, "was always the caricature of a well-established, ordered, peaceful society. But today all is temporary, disordered, grotesque. Who can still laugh at clowns? Hippies, politicians, the man in the street, all the world plays the clown, now."

Fellini's explanation of the disappearance of clowns is appealing in its simplicity and stimulating in its suggestiveness, but it is hardly an adequate accounting for either the phenomenon of clowns or for the film which his remarks intend to illuminate. . . . [The] clown represents the modern world most of our literature describes—absurd, grotesque, meaningless, chaotic, suited only for the blackest of comedies or the most ironic of tragedies.

Yet Fellini is also right when he says that the clown has all but disappeared. . . . Paradoxically, the absurd clown may be an alien in the age of absurdity.

This paradox, central to Fellini's lifelong involvement with the clown, goes deep into his own work and into modern art. Baudelaire said that one of the artist's tasks is to expose those qualities of life lacking in his age so that it might recover a sense of wholeness. To this purpose, he must be alienated from his society to gain perspective. No one would seriously contend that the sense of the grotesque is lacking in the twentieth century. (pp. 214-15)

Fellini's world is no less grotesque than that of his contemporaries. But, unlike most modern artists, he does not see a dialectic of despair. He administers no doses. His reaction to the absurd world is joyous, his laughter optimistic. (p. 215)

I will concentrate on his film *I Clowns* because it seems central to an understanding of his other works and because its apparent simplicity has misled many reviewers and viewers to misunderstand its form and tone. But before discussing the film, I shall trace the outline of a theory of the grotesque within which I think Fellini is working and which provides an alternative to the language of the grotesque as dark absurdity which dominates much of the art of our century.

The word *grotesque* originally designated a style of decorative art which flourished at the beginning of the Christian era and which came by the Renaissance to suggest, as Wolfgang Keyser states, "not only something playfully gay and carelessly fantastic, but also something ominous and sinister in the face of a world totally different from the familiar one—a world in which the reality of inanimate things is no longer separated from those of plants, animals, and human beings, and where the laws of statics, symmetry, and proportion are no longer valid." (p. 216)

But the grotesque was not a single vision. It had two faces, the fanciful and the sinister, perhaps best represented visually by the works of Pieter Brueghel and Hieronymus Bosch.

The grotesqueness of Brueghel's paintings comes about chiefly through two techniques, the amassing of detail and the distortion of the human face and figure. . . .

This irreverent attitude toward subject, combined with the distortion of perspective and the caricature of faces, gives Brueghel's canvases a comically grotesque look which conveys the artist's joy at contemplating the hurly-burly confusion of life which swallows up any attempt of history to impose meaning on it.

Bosch, on the other hand, presents a terrifying grotesque which expresses demonic forces through the mixing of distorted human, animal, and vegetable forms. (p. 217)

The circus has captivated Fellini's imagination throughout his life, and from this fascination has come much of the reckless abandon and comic optimism which characterize both his fictional world and his method as a director. "Clowns," he says, "are the ambassadors of my profession. In my childhood they were the premiere image of disrespect." *I Clowns* champions the need for disrespect in a solemn and all-too-respectable world.

Fellini has talked a great deal about *I Clowns* and has, consequently, planted many mistaken expectations. Most of the comments concern a White Clown-Auguste game which Fellini likes to play with contemporary figures: "The white clown is the symbol of authority. He is your mother, or your teacher, or the nun who was always right. . . . the *augusto* is yourself, doing all the things you'd like to do: making faces, shouting, rolling on the ground, throwing water at people." (p. 219)

[The] Clown-Auguste contrast does not necessarily imply as neat a psychological dialectic as Fellini's statements indicate, a fact that Fellini's own use of clown figures attests to. . . . The Clown and the Auguste are a contrasting pair. This contrast, to operate successfully, needs some sense of the normal against which the grotesque image appears aberrant. In caricature, the norm is our perceptual experience with the human face; we perceive the caricature as a distortion of recognizable features, but a distortion still. In the contrast of Clown and Auguste, the same perceptual structure operates. Clown becomes the norm against which Auguste is a comic contrast. (p. 220)

Auguste has in a sense taken over the traditional role of the Clown as bungling and bewildered country bumpkin and the Clown, descendant of the mild-mannered Pierrot and the English rustic, has assumed a new identity as haughty, elegant, and somewhat effeminate. However, this seems to be a functional contrast for the purposes of the comedy, not the kind of psychological sheep and goats game which Fellini the thinker made of it.

The second irrelevancy comes from the assumption that Fellini the artist set out to make a documentary illustrating the Clown-Auguste contrast, a mistake which most reviewers seem to make. The mistake is understandable. (pp. 220-21)

Through [the relationships between the two sets of clowns] Fellini develops a set of interlocking themes which are central to his concerns as an artist.

Fellini's first theme is the ambiguity of the clown and the average man in our time. (p. 221)

The structure of the [opening] episode, and of the film, involves a complex set of multiple Clown-Auguste relationships (understood as just such a functional contrast as described above). The villagers of Fellini's youth and the clowns of the circus ring which open the film exist in a shifting Clown-Auguste contrast. In one sense, the villagers provide the norm of human conduct which the clowns parody. But in another sense the clowns are a norm by which we recognize the grotesqueness of the villagers. . . .

Beyond both levels, functioning as the eye of "reality," is Fellini. The villagers are stylized and grotesque in their own right. The village of Fellini's youth resembles a film version of an Italian village, a parody of the world created at Cinecittà, and even of Fellini's own films. (p. 222)

But the most obviously and broadly comic parody is the pool room scene. . . .

At this point we become acutely aware of a third clown, Fellini himself, manipulating the act in the ring and emerging as the ultimate grotesque of the performance, the creator who rebels against absurdity by creating the ultimately absurd performance in which he himself is the star clown; for, if, as is frequently contended, the face of reality in the modern world is grotesque and absurd, and if that grotesqueness stems from man's alienation from himself, to rebel against the grotesqueness of reality is to attempt to create a unified and meaningful self. But the nature of the world makes such an attempt the act of a clown.

A second theme of the film records Fellini's quest for the clown—an abortive attempt to find reality and to film it. From the blank expressions of the camera man and sound man to the fumbling incompetence of the script girl Maya, the film crew is as clownly a collection of bumpkins as was ever assembled. Fellini also indulges in a luxurious series of self-parodies. (p. 223)

The parody also has its serious side. Fellini is a fool to attempt such a film. Seeking reality (the clown), he finds only old men, memories, faded photographs, and legends. No one cares any more. People have forgotten how to laugh. The question keeps recurring: why make a film about clowns? The circus no longer exists; the clown deserves to die. . . .

The third theme of the film presents the consequences of that conclusion. If the clown is dead, Fellini will resurrect him in a bizarre and fantastically imagined funeral played in the circus ring. Here is the creator at his most arrogant and clownish. . . .

But three ideas undercut and finally destroy the funeral. First, there is age. (p. 224)

Secondly, there is the continued comic reminder that Fellini's clownish crew is making a film. This comes particularly in two bits of comedy. In one, an elaborate piece of special effects machinery repeatedly fails to work, to the growing irritation of the clowns, and then explodes unexpectedly, setting fire to the equipment around it. The structure of this action duplicates that of Grock's famous violin bow act. It parallels another fire set by the clowns in the ring to bring on the traditional clown fire company. In this way, the reality of film making and the fictional action being filmed are intermixed. The machine becomes the Auguste.

The second bit of comedy comes at the height of the mayhem. We cut to a shot of Fellini and a reporter sitting behind the lights. The reporter asks Fellini, what is the meaning of all this? Before Fellini can answer, a bucket thrown from the ring where it is part of the clown show falls over his head. Another falls over the reporter, silencing them both. The author of the spectacle is thus mocked by his own creation. The idea of "meaning" in the sense of an explication of the comic action into ideas is ridiculed.

But the most serious undercutting comes from the idea of death itself. (pp. 224-25)

The white clown in tails clearly represents death and order. He is the driver of the hearse, and in that role he has urged the funeral to its completion and has become the dignified foil of much of the clowning, particularly that of the horses. . . .

Fellini concludes the film by reproducing [the elderly] clown's act and in the process summarizes the film. (p. 225)

This ending is clearly reminiscent of the conclusion of *8½* in which Guido, having decided to try again to make order of his life and to make another film, assembles the people from his past, who are also characters in the film he is to make, in a circus ring, and leads them through a dance around the ring and out, leaving only the uniformed child version of himself in the spotlight to exit into the darkness playing a piccolo. Both scenes appear almost as codas. Both are grotesques verging on sentimentality. Both record the triumph of the creative imagination over the absurdity of the world.

In each of four feature films—*8½*, *Juliet of the Spirits*, *Satyricon*, *I Clowns*—Fellini has shown us characters almost destroyed by the grotesqueness of their times but at the end saved by acceptance or exuberance. . . .

In these films, I think, Fellini has widened the dimensions of the grotesque vision in contemporary art. He has rebelled against the darkness which is so pervasive that it is the established view of life for the modern artist. (p. 226)

Fellini's films function like Brueghel's paintings. Reality and the grotesque become completely merged in the illogicality and detail of the work of art, so that rather than being frightening or apocalyptic, as are the works of Bosch and most twentieth century artists, the grotesque seems natural and acceptable. Acceptance is essential to a true comic vision. In *I Clowns* Fellini accepts the comic grotesqueness of his own obsession with clowns in a world in which the clown is dead and the grotesqueness of the artist's attempt to create a meaningful vision amid a grotesque and humorless reality. In the process of laughing at his own and the world's absurdity, he accomplishes the creative task which he has accepted as impossible. At the end of the film, the clown becomes apotheosized in a world beyond reality. (p. 227)

William J. Free, "Fellini's 'I Clowns' and the Grotesque," in Journal of Modern Literature *(© Temple University 1973), Vol. 3, No. 2, April, 1973, pp. 214-27.*

ROGER ORTMAYER

In another age Fellini would have been a Botticelli or a Bosch rather than a Leonardo. His vision is comic and surreal rather than realist. (p. 71)

Fellini is a thoroughly filmic artist. He is often put down as being a romantic. But, as with objective and subjective, the description is irrelevant. (p. 73)

Fellini's inability to stick to a predetermined course, his constant improvisation, his delight in coincidence is no more irrational than their opposites. It is irrational only if rationality is equated with the rules of logic the rationalists invented. Fellini's mind is one of the most alert and perceptive of the twentieth century—that he will often start a film or a scene with a sketch rather than with words is simply his way of conceptualizing and planning his work. He thinks visually. Does that make him irrational? Only if rationality is limited to the vocabulary of those who insist that meaning must be put into words, surely one of the most irrational claims ever to bedevil the human scene. (pp. 73-4)

La Strada is a mysterious film, mysterious in the religious sense. In viewing the film one is in "seeingfeelhearing." One knows, but has difficulty making the knowing rationalization. Taken in isolation, incidents and scenes may be outrageously sentimental, incongruous, even contrived. The artist makes them right and proper.

La Strada is love and indifference and gentleness and violence. It is not about persons who are violent or gentle, but is about the incarnation, the real appearance, of the destroyer . . . and of holy innocence. . . . (pp. 76-7)

[Gelsomina's] ingenuousness, spontaneity, affinity with nature is a delicately subtle communion and difficult to communicate. But whenever it seems that we are going to be pushed into the kind of difficult emotional feeling we have when in the presence of the mentally handicapped, we find that instead of being embarrassed we can relate to the complete guilelessness of Gelsomina. She is not only authentically a whole person, she is more alive, more really a person, than we can ever be without holding under cover our inner selves. (p. 78)

Both Juliet and Giorgio [in *Juliet of the Spirits*] are victimized by their false, unsustainable attachments and expectations, although the focus is on the woman. Fellini does not moralize. He is too strong as an artist to give us a documentary on marriage; he provides us with illuminations. And they come through the eye, not by being told to us in words.

Like Gelsomina in *La Strada,* Juliet is a natural person, surrounded by extravagant situations, persons, and events. (p. 82)

Giorgio is guilt-filled, knowing he has been false to his wife. But where does the real falseness lie? In his relations with another woman? Or in his expectations of a marriage which are themselves false? Can a marriage "succeed" if the precognitions are illusory? And are cognitions themselves destructive? Is marriage more a matter of living than of definitions? What mean the ties of marriage (recalling that this is pre-Vatican II Italy, where marriage bonds are legally and religiously indissoluble)?

The focus, however, is on the woman. And she has to come to her own reality, really be her natural self, rather than a woman distorted by living according to false expectations. (pp. 82-3)

Juliet's liberation is not simple, not linear. The exorcism of dividing spirits will not come through unrestrained escape, nor anarchy. She has to free herself of false status and conventions. . . .

She had to break such false ties to being—but can she be free of time? The clock keeps ticking, the cheeks sag, the heels click down a corridor like the seconds on a clock.

She cannot escape time, those clicks keep going. But she will be a free person, in possession of herself. Part of the falseness she has been trying to live with is regarding time as the enemy. Rather time *is,* and Juliet *is,* and to be is to join the procession of free creatures. (p. 84)

Fellini does not use color symbolically. That is, certain colors do not stand for certain objects, situations, persons, etc. As we shall note, such is usually the case with Fellini's imagery. It is seldom symbolic in such a mechanical sense. Color is, however, apt to his imagery. In fact, color becomes imagery.

An aspect of the revolutionary character of modern art has been this change in the way in which the painter uses color. Traditionally it had been used as attempted verism. (pp. 85-6)

The color in *Juliet* is sensational. By that I do not mean that Fellini sought to produce some kind of public excitement. Rather, the color is used as art, to heighten perceptivity. Seeing the film, one feels more keenly, more exquisitely, than he could otherwise. The film is a full sense apprehension. It is sensate. (p. 87)

Fellini has said that to do *Satyricon* was to do away with the Renaissance inventions of antiquity, or the nineteenth century's, or our own. They were all invented Romes, unhistorical histories. He wanted the Rome without Christ; the Rome where tickets were sold to the amphitheaters to watch people die, the Rome without any of the touches of compassion and love which are what Christ is.

Color is both an affliction and a tension. Different hues drain each other off, saturate with brightness, diminish and gain strength. (p. 88)

Photographers identify film speed, etc., and their relation to the light available in terms of "temperature." The color reactions provoke sensations of "warm" and "cold." Such "temperature readings" are apt for both *Juliet* and *Satyricon.* Withdrawal, centering, aggression, expanding, contracting—all help us to see the alienation and integration in these movies. Dominant in *Satyricon* is alienation; in *Juliet,* integration.

To insist that in *Satyricon* Fellini's mixture of hues is dynamic, full of tension, while the use of more primary colors strengthens the quality of wholeness in *Juliet,* is not to point to instances of color symbolism. What must not be done is to interpret the colors allegorically. (p. 89)

In *Juliet of the Spirits* the Venus shell and Eve and the serpent flash by, venerable images of the goddess of love and of erotic temptation. Religious images abound in most Fellini films. Such figures are there because in their presence the recognition of the scene is established. That is, when he deals with erotic love he also plays with Venus images. Such usage, however, should not be transferred to the multitude of Fellini images. . . .

This is the main trouble with symbolic theory. Symbols have meaning because of the preconceptions to which they are attached. . . .

This, however, is not Fellini's world. He demands an involvement in life, not an abstraction from it. (p. 93)

It is necessary to see *8½* (as well as *La Dolce Vita, Juliet, Satyricon*) several times to get real enjoyment from it. The overlaps and focus are varied and shift in clusters rather than line continuities. We are used to the continuities of narrative film, which makes it difficult to deal with the different rhythm of *8½.* It is something like music which changes beat in the middle of the piece, abandons key signatures, and then adopts them again. (p. 94)

Fellini always surprises us. Images jostle each other and us, and we realize that in dealing with them different possibilities and levels are possible. Some will be discarded. Some are exciting entries. But in any case we are asked to go along the journey, and our joining the pilgrims makes of the journey something else than it could otherwise have been. (p. 97)

Fellini's films often deal with the church by odd mixtures of satire, irony, and love. Probably there is no other way for a modern Italian artist to do it. His patronage, unlike Michangelo's, has nothing to do with the church except tangentially—that is, it might try to censor the film. Yet wherever he has gone he has been fronted with its images and persons. And these images are in themselves so powerful, so varied, so wonderfully visual that they have inevitably had an impact on his own sense of reality. (p. 102)

Satyricon is the most religiously potent of them all. Fellini attempts an amazing *tour de force,* namely an answer to the question, What is a world like without Christ? Fellini invents another world, elusive as colors through stained glass, bloody as an abattoir, sterile as a moonscape, ambiguous as the Delphic oracle, decipherable as a medieval palimpsest.

Satyricon has a story to tell, but the narrative line is fragmentary, disconnected. In literary terms it is a bit like the picaresque, but it is filmic rather than literary. It is dreamlike strange in color and incident, and yet it mysteriously hangs together. . . .

Fellini felt he needed to destroy our myths of antiquity, the "clean" ancient world of serene temples and classic statuary. Could such an image possibly be compatible with people paying their way into Madison Square Garden to eat nuts and joke with one another as they watched people die? (p. 105)

Roger Ortmayer, "Fellini's Film Journey," in Three European Directors: François Truffaut *by James M. Wall,* Fellini's Film Journey *by Roger Ortmayer,* Luis Buñuel and the Death of God *by Peter P. Schillaci, edited by James M. Wall (copyright © 1973 by William B. Eerdmans Publishing Company; used by permission), Eerdmans, 1973, pp. 71-105.*

JOHN RUSSELL TAYLOR

Compared with [Fellini's] other recent films, *Amarcord* is simple and classic to the point of self-denial. It resolves itself into a succession of scenes from provincial life, strung loosely round the experiences of Bobo, the representative of Fellini in the film, during the summer of 1935, aged about 15-16. In a sense, the film consists of nothing but set-pieces, but hardly anything is played up to the pitch of frenzy which usually seizes a Fellini film somewhere along the way. This seems to be very much Fellini playing it cool, toning down the extravagances, trying, heaven help us, to make a tasteful film. (p. 244)

But who really wants a tasteful, restrained Fellini? Inevitably, the bits of the film one remembers are those which come closest to the old reprobate Fellini we love or loathe according to taste. (pp. 244-45)

Even these sequences, though, are disappointingly played down. It is as though there is something slightly faded and tired about the whole film, some indefinable lack of vitality which leaves it all looking a bit dusty and distant. . . .

Strangest of all, and the only sustained passage where the film comes up with the old Fellini magic, is the sequence in which most of the town's population goes out at night in small boats to wait—but for what? The Rex, a super-liner which eventually moves majestically past like Leviathan, risen at last from the deep, or a mysterious creature from another planet. Its apparition has the effect of a sort of religious experience, with tears in the crowded congregation and all: the feeling is very close to that of the climactic appearance of the Pope in *Roma's* fashion parade. For just a few moments, Fellini catches us by attacking where he is strongest, at gut-level. We don't know exactly why we are moved, awed or whatever, but we are. Sad that in the rest of *Amarcord* we know all too clearly why we are not. (p. 245)

John Russell Taylor, "Film Reviews: 'Amarcord'," in Sight and Sound *(copyright © 1974 by The British Film Institute), Vol. 43, No. 4, Autumn, 1974, pp. 244-45.*

TIMOTHY HYMAN

8½ demonstrated how a film could be about a temperament: the events it dealt with were interior events, and its most important episodes happened outside time, in fantasy, dream and vision. In *8½*, Fellini renounced the political or social emphasis of neo-realism, and the new relation between the artist and the outer world that resulted has since become fundamental to much Italian cinema. Guido, groping blindly from within toward his millennial vision, is the blueprint for a new kind of film director, whose ideology originates not in any analysis of society, but in the artist's own constitution.

Everyone would perhaps agree that each one of us has a fundamental and recurrent 'pattern', to which his experience largely conforms. I take *8½* to be the description of one such pattern, the mapping-out or 'anatomising' of a particular constitution. In every way, Guido's pattern defines the film; both its structure, since in the course of the film Guido works through one complete cycle of experience; and its subject, because Guido's predicament is shown to be caused by a conflict between his pattern and his conscious self.

8½ is about an inner process which takes place in Guido on several levels, his reaching for artistic potency, for intellectual consistency and for spiritual purity. But Fellini shows Guido's development as occurring, not through his conscious will or intellect, but rather as springing directly from some interior bodily rhythm, to which Guido remains almost passive. . . .

The riddling title, *Fellini 8½*, goes far to clarify the film's problem; it points, beyond the opus number, to a fusion of the film's conflicting polarities, not only Life and Art, but physical and abstract, person and pattern—that is to the 'solution', the state of integration momentarily achieved at the end of the film.

Film is the ideal vehicle for the kind of experience Fellini wants to convey here—the sense that every event is subordinate to a prevailing inner rhythm. . . . [Watching] *8½*, one is peculiarly aware of film as a 'total art', harnessing enormous and diverse powers so as to bring the spectator into the fullest possible relation with the director's most personal experience. (p. 172)

Of all Fellini's films, *8½* is the one in which the cathartic intention—the use of the 'white magic' of cinema to 'liberate the spectator'—is most explicit. (pp. 172-73)

Correspondingly, the language in *8½* has an urgency unique in Fellini's work. In *La Strada* or *La Dolce Vita* the script, in *Giulietta* and his subsequent films the sets and costumes, have the central role, which here belongs to the exclusively cinematic means of sequential juxtaposition and rhythm. . . . The syntax of the film becomes the embodiment of Fellini's doctrine: that our experience is cyclic, that pleasure comes out of pain, true out of false, comedy out of tragedy.

The cyclic structure of Guido's experience is announced at the outset of *8½*, in the Crisis, Liberation and Fall, archetypally enacted in Guido's dream. . . .

This pattern, of crisis, liberation and fall, is the key to Guido's behaviour. Just as the necessity of waiting on liberation forces on him his indecisive and conditional manner of action, so the mysteriousness and unreasonableness of his experience enforces his ambiguous ideological stance. He is caught in a machine, yet his moments of liberation seem evidence of a *deus ex machina*. . . .

[The] pattern of *8½* is that of melancholy; the ambiguous commerce between archetypal and real is typical of that state; and Fellini has himself described the mood of *8½* as 'melancholy, almost funereal, but also resolutely comic.' . . . There is a 'double potentiality in melancholy, for Good or for Evil.'

Now it seems to me that this double potentiality provides the structure of *8½*: we are made to see Guido first as a sick man, then as a visionary artist. Guido's crisis, his inability to begin his film, results from his own interpretation of his experience as being fundamentally diseased, false: doubting its validity, he cannot express or reflect it in his art. . . . Fellini's theme can be summed up, that liberation consists in our acceptance of the interdependence of contrary states within our experience; only his failure to accept distinguishes the impotent from the creative individual.

First, as a sick man. Fellini makes us not only observe Guido's descent, but also participate in it. The pattern of crisis endlessly repeated soon becomes as alienating for the spectator as it is for Guido. And that initial ambiguity of dimension, of our entering in the middle of the traffic jam of Guido's dream, which we assumed to be reality, persists. (p. 173)

The white episodes continue to well up, like coherent messages from the unconscious, and with their slower rhythm and narrative unity, each offers a momentary respite against a present world where consciousness is staccato and fragmented. Each presents Guido with some variant of a visionary reality. (pp. 173-74)

Guido's film is an allegory of his own predicament. His wish to commit his will to the Church, or to his marriage, or to ideal love, is a wish to escape to so many 'new planets', to be liberated once and for all from the wheel of his temperament. This wish is what has defined him, and the making of the film itself is the last remaining hope of its fulfilment; so that his abandonment of it at the press conference really does constitute his personal extinction, the 'suicide' shown us.

Then, as visionary artist. For it is only here, when Guido, in losing each of his alternatives, has been stripped of his ego, that the real protagonist of the film, not the personality of Guido but the fatality of his temperament, is able to assert itself. These final minutes entirely alter our view of what has gone before. Unfurling out of Guido's extinction, the emergence of the vision unifies the film's interior oscillation into a single cathartic motion of crisis transformed to liberation. It is as though the movement of the whole film were to trace out this transformation as a kind of graphological curve; to define the rhythm by which sickness becomes vision. . . .

The vision is an affirmation of the temperament, as a creative centre beyond the personality. . . .

Once the vision has reaffirmed Guido's integrity, we see that his sliding from dimension to dimension may have been not evasion or confusion, but the necessary completion of a journey towards a view of life that must include several distinct worlds, a 'multiverse'. . . .

At the beginning of *8½*, Guido has his seed, his idea of a film; but it is only when he has accepted its extinction that the flowering, the vision which is the true film he has to make, is able to appear. And in this affirmation Fellini's monumental fresco imagery at last finds a content fitting to its epic scale. . . .

8½ is pivotal in Fellini's work. What had remained implicit in the earlier films, a core of the personality, a certain rhythm of experience, here becomes explicit. . . .

It is a reversal common to much Italian cinema, the transition from neo-realism to what might be called 'neo-symbolism'. The critic in *8½* is the voice of neo-realism, who regards the subjectivity of Guido's script as evidence that 'Cinema is fifty years behind the other arts.' (p. 174)

What we have to accept meanwhile is the lack of any glimmer, in a work like *Satyricon,* of wholesome reality. It exists solely, as Fellini says, to 'realise his fantasy'; the inner world is presented not, as in *8½*, as part of a process, but as though it were sufficient in itself. . . .

Yet while *8½* defines the moment of perfect balance in Italian cinema, the subsequent descent into self, into archetypal realms, has resulted in a kind of profundity. The obvious parallel is with Mannerism; it arouses the same ambiguous responses, and it may, like Mannerism, become more fascinating to future generations, less starved of an art of above ground, and less nostalgic for the achievements of the High Renaissance of cinema that the years of *8½* now seem to represent. (p. 175)

Timothy Hyman, "'8½' as an Anatomy of Melancholy," in Sight and Sound *(copyright © 1974 by The British Film Institute), Vol. 43, No. 3, Summer, 1974, pp. 172-75.*

JOHN SIMON

[The] worst thing about "Amarcord" and its immediate predecessors is that the chief joke is human ugliness. Whether it is obese women displaying their behinds on bicycles, a ridiculous-looking uncle (another one) making himself more obviously repugnant by sporting a hairnet, a female Goliath using her naked bosom as a weapon, a family dinner scene in which almost all the faces, even those of the youngsters, are profoundly unprepossessing, . . . the joke is always on humanity, and almost always on the easiest, cheapest, and, finally, most witless level.

There is no denying that witty satire thrives on savaging mankind, but where in "Amarcord" is there witty satire? Alternatively, where is compassion? Even the figure of the whore, whom Fellini used to depict with almost excessive, often sentimental, sympathy, has become a ghoulish, nymphomaniacal madwoman, wallowing in a crude parody of autoeroticism. . . . [The] best Fellini can look forward to is equaling the dismal record of Ken Russell.

And to think that this once great artist is still only 54; an age at which one hasn't even earned the right to the excuse of senility. (pp. 17, 19)

John Simon, "The Tragic Deterioration of Fellini's Genius," in The New York Times, *Section 2 (© 1974 by The New York Times Company; reprinted by permission), November 24, 1974, pp. 17, 19.*

VINCENT CANBY

Amarcord is a haunting, funny, beautiful work that makes most other recent movies, with the exception of Ingmar Bergman's *Scenes from a Marriage,* look as drab as winter fields without snow. . . .

[The film] is his memory of a year in the life of Rimini, or a town much like it, and for Fellini memory has a lot in common with dream. It needn't be what literally happened but what he wanted to believe, or perhaps what time has forced him to believe. (p. 264)

Amarcord has the circus's pace, drive, good spirits, fascination with costume and masquerade (sometimes grotesque), and abundance of events. The characters tumble onto the screen one after another, as if there weren't going to be enough time to get through all the acts. . . .

One of Fellini's greatest gifts is his ability to communicate a sense of wonder, which has the effect of making us all feel much younger than we have any right to. Fellini's is a very special, personal kind of cinema, and in *Amarcord* he is in the top of his form. (p. 265)

Vincent Canby, "Funny, Marvelous Fellini 'Amarcord'," in The New York Times *(© 1974 by The New York Times Company; reprinted by permission), September 20, 1974 (and reprinted in* The National Society of Film Critics on Movie Comedy, *edited by Stuart Byron and Elisabeth Weis, Grossman Publishers, 1977, pp. 264-65).*

PETER HARCOURT

In essence, the whole of Fellini can be found in [the first] sequence from *La Strada* [which ends with Gelsomina following the circus band after leaving Zampano]. His thematic centre is here. To begin with, reinforced by the title itself, there is the sense of life as a journey, as a constant tearing away from things known and a plunging into the unfamiliar. Unlike Bergman, however, whose allegoric wanderings are generally from place to place . . . in Fellini, there is seldom any sense of direction or eventual goal. The form of his films tends to be circular, the characters usually ending where they began.

This restlessness of movement can work in different ways. Occasionally, as with the nuns in *La Strada,* there is the feeling that we must give up things dear to us before we get too fond of them; but more frequently there is the feeling that only by moving on, by probing and searching, can we ever come to know the purpose of life. Fellini's fondness for processions is obviously related to this. Indeed, it sometimes seems as if the celebration of movement such as we witness in processions may by itself provide the purpose, as if in terrestrial terms there may be, in fact, no goal.

Of course, Fellini would reject such intellectual speculations. For Fellini is an intuitive in his response to life, a great muddleheaded irrationalist with very strong feelings and no clear thought. He lives life from the senses, yet his intelligence has informed him that the senses can deceive. Hence the intellectual indecisions, the apparently inexhaustible interviews with all their self-contradictions. Yet hence too all the passionate affirmations of his films up until their acme in *8½*. It is as if Fellini recognizes that 'truth' must lie somewhere, though locked up in subjectivity, but he is unable to seize it with the merely rational surface of his mind. Hence all the turbulence, all the restless energy, the endless travelling along streets and long corridors. (pp. 186-87)

But in this sequence from *La Strada,* there are also some examples of the twin experiences that, as Fellini understood it at this stage of his career, this directionless journey through life must entail—experiences of the freshness and unexpectedness of innocence which are immediately followed by the experience of something dreadful that in a world freed from the devil is now without a name. On the one hand, we have the presence of Gelsomina herself and of the somewhat querulous Il Matto who appears from on high; but more characteristically we have the fleeting image of [the] little boy in the cloak passing along the corridor that charms us so gratuitously. For it is also a part of Fellini's irrationality that childhood innocence should so often play such a formally gratuitous role in his films, that children should simply appear and then disappear—providing us with a momentary pleasure and perhaps renewing our faith in the wonder of existence but remaining essentially apart from the troubled business of life in Fellini's adult world. (p. 188)

In all of Fellini's films, there are these disturbing images, moments of disillusion that serve to challenge simple faith. There is the sinister homosexual who so disappoints Leopoldo in *I Vitelloni,* as there had been the more-than-disappointing flesh-and-blood reality of the White Sheik before. But in *I Vitelloni* more powerfully and more like Osvaldo is the woman in the cinema who so easily tempts Fausto and who is again encountered one day on the beach. Within the subterranean depths of Fellini's imagination, she serves as a link between Osvaldo and La Saraghina and simply appears at odd moments as a threat to the flesh. Also in *I Vitelloni* there is the married man in the dark glasses who tempts Olga away. He too is first encountered on the beach. But most ominous of all is the shot of his dark car just before they drive away: it is almost hidden by the early-morning shadows in the street while the light glares out above it threateningly, like a scar. (pp. 189-90)

Excluding for the moment La Saraghina, who is a more complex incarnation of this kind of nameless threat, simultaneously described as evil yet *felt* to be beautiful, and excluding for the moment the whole of *Satyricon,* which, on one level, seems a surrender to this frightening aspect of life, in *La Dolce Vita* we have a summary of this sort of effect in that strange blob of a fish that pollutes the stretch of beach at the end of the film and forms the imaginative counterpole to the young Paola waving to Marcello across the protective inlet of the sea. It is as if something deep in Fellini recognizes that in childhood and childlike responses to existence, there is beauty and affirmation of a frequently troubling kind, troubling because unconscious of the terrible threats and temptations that can lurk in the unknowable depths of adult life; and in the way that so frequently these polar elements seem more an accompaniment to the main theme than a formally intrinsic part of his film, it is as if at this stage of his development, Fellini cannot consciously work out the exact relationship between these two extremes or even find a settled place for them within the narrative structure of his films. Constantly he creates situations for which he can find no earthly solution, and his characters encounter difficulties beyond their means to control. For the end of *La Dolce Vita,* it is as if the gods themselves must be evoked to bring about the closing affirmation. Failing to communicate anything helpful to Marcello, the little Umbrian angel looks straight at the camera, and at us. What do we make of it all? What do we feel about innocence by the end? (p. 190)

One of the difficulties that Fellini's films pose for more rational minds—indeed, we could even say, one of the limitations of Fellini's particular kind of cinematic art—is that he has too often been too careless about the surface credibility of his films, confusing and alienating all but the most sympathetic of his viewers as the conventions of his films have seemed so strange. Yet at their best, in the early days, they are strange only to the expectations of literary narrative and of psychological realism. Fellini's conventions are not at all strange to the language of painting, which, beneath the narrative surface of his films, is the language that he used most frequently to employ.

There is in all real films—in all films that have the lasting interest that characterizes a work of art—what I have found it convenient to call a subliminal level, a level largely of images plus the complex associations of scarcely perceived sounds. Although we are often not really conscious of these vital ingredients, especially on a first viewing, we can nevertheless be immensely moved by their power to affect us. Indeed, it is generally these elements that give a film its atmosphere or mood.

If there are in Fellini certain constantly recurring themes or motifs, there are also certain constantly recurring images and effects that, when responded to, can make an extraordinary impression upon us and which are cumulative in their power. For these images to be discussed at all, criticism has to lean away from the comfortably confident tone of literary-cum-film analysis and draw upon the tentativeness of art appreciation. For the central fact about art criticism is the elusiveness of the total power of the image when talked about in words and of the greater subjectivity of the way paintings speak to us, moving towards music, which is the most subjectively elusive of all. (pp. 191-92)

[If] we contemplate the effect of the foreground shadow in . . . *The Rose Tower* [by the contemporary Italian painter Giorgio de Chirico], and remember that the entire proposal scene between Oscar and Cabiria is similarly played in shadow with the landscape and buildings luminous behind, we might feel that by the very light itself, both de Chirico and Fellini, working independently in their quite different ways, have employed these foreground shadows to lend a worried aspect to the scene and yet to suggest that there is something worthwhile in the distance, something worth achieving beyond.

In fact, de Chirico, perhaps because as an Italian he too has been particularly sensitive to Italian space and Italian light, can be used again and again to illuminate by analogy the images in Fellini. (pp. 192-93)

In Fellini, the town square is never felt to be the social centre of a community. De Chirico too seemed to be sensitive to the empty feeling of such places at unused times of day—indeed, to the very irrelevance of such vast structures to the little intimacies of human life. And so in de Chirico, we find a number of such paintings that depict huge buildings and exaggerated shadows, where the tiny figures serve both to emphasize the hugeness of the structures (as do the miniature trains that we frequently see puffing away on the horizon) and to give a feeling that the little human things don't really belong in such a space. Sometimes this feeling is further emphasized by the presence of some stray object in the foreground, some object made bizarre by being torn from the context of its function. . . .

So in *I Vitelloni,* in the much-admired beach sequence—admired for its sensitive observation of these five men imprisoned in their own apathy and defeated by the feeling that there is nothing they can do—Fellini emphasizes their own feeling of irrelevance and functionlessness by the many apparently useless structures that we see sticking up out of the sand. Skeletons of summer changing-huts and odd inexplicable bits of wire frequently dominate the scene and create the feeling of something strange with an almost surrealist intensity. Everywhere throughout the film as throughout every Fellini film there is the recurring presence of the bizarre. (p. 193)

In fact, this recognition of the bizarre is at the centre of Fellini's world, the physical parallel of his response to the irrational, the source both of his humour and of his sense of dread. For if humour is uppermost in most films by Fellini, beneath the comic observation of the discrepancies of human life there is always this feeling of something beyond our control, something not fully known to our rational selves—like that grotesque fish at the end of *La Dolce Vita,* like Osvaldo in that guarded-over room, like the frightening labyrinthine journeys in *Satyricon,* or the grotesque distortions of *The Clowns.* (p. 194)

So far in this account of Fellini, I have been concerned only with the thematic consistency of his work and with the peculiar force of his imagery. Taken all together, his films create a world that is uniquely and personally his own. Even the films that follow *8½,* though less intimate, still manage to enact Fellini's vision of the universe. All this, although true, tends to ignore the great differences between his individual films, differences of surface characteristics but also finally of quality as well. For much as I respond with pleasure to nearly everything that he has produced, I recognize that if Fellini is a man of immense inventiveness, he is also a director of uncertain control over the many elements that his mind, with apparently so little effort, can with such energy invent. Also, if Fellini is a man who has created for us an immensely personal view of life on the screen, I recognize that it is just that—an immensely personal view of life which is frequently egotistic, self-indulgent, sentimental, and wilfully irrational, courting mystery at every corner and asking from us as much compassion for all these difficulties as he has bestowed upon them himself. (pp. 195-96)

If it is true that there is nothing in Fellini's films that we can properly call thought, there is nevertheless evidence of an intelligence of a totally different kind. Everywhere in his films there is the presence of a mind that responds to life itself on a subliminal level, that is acutely conscious of the natural metaphors to be found in the trappings of day-to-day life and which struggles to find a structure both flexible and persuasive enough to contain them within his films. (p. 196)

Throughout this account of certain aspects of Fellini, . . . I am trying to do basically one thing: I am anxious to explain the form of [the] director's films in terms of the *view of life* that has necessitated it. . . . However, before looking at *8½*, the film that I consider to be Fellini's most *complete* achievement, I'd like to glance at some of his less successful works and at the view of life that all his films embody; for with Fellini, . . . any breakdown in the form of his films is inextricably tied to inadequacies within the view of life at the base of them.

In many ways, Fellini's view of life is that of a child—a simple creature of nature, a kind of self-regarding mystic. When we think of art in more social terms, Fellini's self-obsessions can be worrying. Yet surely society is still robust enough to be enriched by the products of its artistic egotists—Federico Fellini, Hector Berlioz, Benvenuto Cellini, a distinguished genealogy of men who have created in extravagantly personal ways. These men, with their insistence on the inner life of man, have made their own contribution to our increased self-understanding. At their best, they have pursued their self-bound concerns with such energy and completeness that their explorations of their purely private problems have managed to illuminate the problems of us all. (pp. 198-99)

[While] I can find little to admire in his sketch for *Boccaccio 70,* I can see in much of the poster-raising sequence, hilarious in its way and absurd in its chaos, a kind of rehearsal for the press conference in *8½*, where both the hilarity and the chaos have a tougher context to contain them. But it is the essential tastelessness of the central conception of the Boccaccio episode that has always made me doubt that particular piece of film and wonder what it might presage.

In the image of the little puritan who has such grotesque fantasies, there is possibly something funny (though not to my taste) but there is also a contradiction between Fellini's most undeniable gift and his intentions in this film. Whether we like him or not, at his best Fellini has certainly succeeded in creating for us images that convey the innermost recesses of his own teeming mind. But what about the mind of another person essentially different from himself: could he explore that with the same kind of intimacy? I should never have thought so; and yet this is what he was offering to do in this film. He would appear to be trying to convey to us how another person thinks and feels, which is perhaps what makes the film so unsubtle in the effects that it achieves, so lacking in compassion, finally so lacking in taste. (pp. 199-200)

[*The Clowns*] contains elements of self-parody of a most inescapable kind. There is one moment during which all the clowns are running round and round the circus ring in a frenzy of purposeless movement as if in deliberate mockery of the finest moments in *La Strada, Le Notti di Cabiria,* and *8½*. 'Mr. Fellini, what is the message of this sequence?' asks an onlooker (in words to that effect). Whereupon a pail is suddenly thrown over his inquiring head, as immediately afterwards over Fellini's. Obviously, Fellini is mocking both himself and his interpreters. We shouldn't even try to understand!

When an artist is driven to mock his own achievement, it may imply an artistic crisis. At the same time, such self-mockery may be merely a playful response to the role thrust upon Fellini of superstar; or, more seriously, it may be an attempt to exorcize once and for all his own clichés (as Bergman did in *The Face*), as if to prepare himself for new things to come. Moving backwards to *Satyricon,* perhaps that film could be seen as an exorcism of this kind—as an attempt at last to probe the fears that have haunted his earlier work but which have never been confronted head on. (pp. 202-03)

[In *Satyricon*] the fears seem largely sexual. Sexual love has always been somewhat oddly handled by Fellini, as if it were something that he himself didn't understand fully. 'You cannot tell a proper love story!' one of the 'nieces' associated with the production team giggled outrageously to the Guido/Fellini figure in *8½*, leaping up and down in the bed; and in all his films Fellini has been attracted to the androgynous figure of the clown. (p. 203)

It is as if Fellini, in all his films, equates innocence of the body with purity of soul. He gives to all his children, his simpletons and clowns a sensitivity that seems lacking in his adult world. . . . In *Satyricon* however, with the exception of the children in the patrician's scene . . . , there are no children in this film at all. As a result of this, given Fellini's private store of metaphor, there is little sense of hope. There is also little sense of any alternatives, little sense of a life that is not whole-heartedly opportunistic and grotesque. 'Friendship lasts as long as it is useful,' says Ascyltus in his opening soliloquy; 'at least that's what I think'. And there is little in the film to give us the sense of characters behaving in any other way, especially as regards their sexual lives. With the exception of the patrician and his family, they are studs and whores all.

What does Fellini intend by this? The acceptance of so many of the homosexual elements obviously derives from Petronius himself; but one can never explain too much in films as personal as Fellini's by reference to his sources. Why did he pick this and not that? This remains the critical question. Similarly, he surely doesn't intend the film to be a realistic treatment of the mores of an ancient society, painstaking though much of his research into the authenticity of surface details in the film actually has been. Nor is it simply an allegory of our own times, as *La Dolce Vita* was erroneously assumed to be. The film is a mixture of all these things, and certainly not so obviously a personal statement by Fellini as his other films have been. Yet the perfunctory nature of the narrative and the paper-thinness of the characters, alongside the urgency with which some of the scenes are actually handled, would seem to be our clue for decoding the film, for locating Fellini's own centre of interest. Again and again he returns to scenes of banquets or arenas, and again and again these scenes become the settings for some kind of sexual humiliation. (pp. 203-04)

There is a slightly sinister Gioconda smile that Fellini's characters have assumed over the years. It was there in Gelsomina in *La Strada,* apparently harmless then, part of her slightly simpleton nature. Indeed, Fellini's simpletons have often assumed that smile, as have his homosexuals; but it wasn't until *Giulietta* that, both in the figure of the maid and more especially in the vision of Giulietta's young school friend who killed herself for love, this enigmatic smile began to seem menacing. (pp. 204-05)

In the *Satyricon,* this Gioconda smile is most evident on the face of the pathic Giton, but curiously, bafflingly, it is also painted on to the faces of the patrician's children as they prepare to take their leave. It also appears on the lean and sensual sphinx-like face of Tryphaena, both when Encolpius first spies her at Trimalchio's banquet, and most forcefully and most sinisterly when she sees her husband's head cut off and flung into the sea—a very strange moment in the film indeed and a most inexplicable and unexplained response. Yet it is a striking moment in the film, an image that stays with us, as does the preceding sequence when the crew on Lichas's ship hoist a dead whale (or something like it) up out of the sea—all in striking silhouette as if in early morning, after the male marriage between Encolpius and the brutal Lichas. Like that big blob of fish that is thrown up on the beach towards the end of *La Dolce Vita,* the whale, as inexplicable in terms of plot as Tryphaena's smile, gives us a strong sense of something revolting at the bottom of all this debauchery. It is as if Fellini feels, deep inside himself, that something disastrous will follow the surrender to physical love. So too, after Encolpius's and Giton's night of love together—another remarkably tender moment in the film—the entire building crumbles and stones its inhabitants to death.

In this surrealist world where, through the images, the tensions of sex seem related to pain and disorder, it seems right that the font of wisdom should lie in the hermaphrodite—a strange albino creature, with a small boy's penis and a young woman's breasts. Yet when the two protagonists steal their treasure away from the old man that guards him, the hermaphrodite cannot survive the full sunlight of the world outside. In yet another compelling sequence in the film, the screen itself is bleached to white and the hermaphrodite withers and dies. So compact a resolution to the sexual problem cannot exist in the outside world, this episode might seem to imply. We seem cursed and doomed to suffer the humiliations of desire. . . . (p. 205)

The most human (and hence most moral) moment occurs to one side of the central story—the gentle freeing of his slaves and the parting from his children of a noble patrician who then slits his wrists as he is having a farewell supper with his wife, a moment that I understand is based on the end of Petronius's own life. This scene stands out in the film for its quietness and for its single appeal to our old-fashioned natural human sympathies. In *Satyricon,* it is as if the little surrealist moments that troubled and deepened the surface narrative of Fellini's earlier films have assumed the centre of the stage while the more human elements have been pushed to one side.

While *Satyricon* is the film by Fellini that troubles me most, personally, I have been struck by the complete insensitivity with which the film has been received. If in his work since *8½* Fellini seems to be stumbling, even his stumbles seem full of interest and possess an undeniable authority. Besides, who knows where they may lead?

However, to tie together the various perceptions that seem to characterize Fellini's world, we have to backtrack and take a considered look at *8½*—the film that, in my view, most succeeds in resolving the dilemmas and balancing the paradoxes of Fellini's most personal, most fantastic universe. *8½* is the summation of Fellini's work to that date, and, for me personally, is one of the greatest films of all time. (p. 206)

[If *8½*] is incomparably the finest film that Fellini has ever created, it is largely because, along with Fellini's characteristic sensitivity to sounds and images, the film contains within it a subtle dialectic. (p. 207)

All the old ingredients are there in this film: the acutely accurate observation of surface behaviour which characterized *I Vitelloni* plus the response to both the semi-mystical and the bizarre that was so evident in *La Strada.* We still have the same sense of life as a quest, as endless movement with uncertain direction, as we still have the twin polarities in this film, principally of Claudia and La Saraghina, here seeming to imply a split between the subtler imaginations of the spirit and the coarser attractions of the flesh. But in this film things aren't quite that simple. Both figures in their different ways are presented as somewhat motherly and it is only the church that keeps insisting that La Saraghina is evil. Innocence and evil are no longer separate categories locked away on opposite sides in the wings of the film. But along with these familiar themes and effects, the film puts forward a structure of argument and self-criticism that recasts all these elements in a decidedly clearer light.

This structure can conveniently be examined by looking closely at the final reels. Guido is reaching the point of no return during the auditions while he watches with extreme discomfort the various imperfect approximations to the creatures who have meant so much to him in his private life. Daumier, his intellectual friend, scriptwriter, and adviser, is being particularly tiresome and unhelpful; so, in his imagination, Guido simply has him hanged. Luisa is growing increasingly impatient at the way that she, as his wife, is being made use of in this projected film and she stalks out of the theatre-studio. Then Claudia arrives.

We have seen her as part of Guido's fantasies several times before in the film—sometimes as nurse or mother, bringing him his elixir at the spa or turning down his bed, sometimes as the incarnation of his ideal mistress figure, freed from the physical vulgarities of his actual mistress, Carla. As his ideal mistress, Claudia has her black hair loose about her shoulders while she lies in bed stroking herself, smiling lovingly and talking about her desire to look after him and to create order—really less like a mistress than an ideal wife. But this is the first time in the film, twenty minutes before the end, that she actually appears on the level of present time as the possible star of this impossible film. They go off for a drive together, she at the wheel although she explains that she doesn't know the way.

Guido muses about his incapacities as a man and artist, about his inability to stick to any one thing, to select anything, to reject, to choose. And even here the structure is nicely balanced if we look closely. 'Could you choose one thing and be faithful to it?' he asks in some despair as the light in the darkened car narrows around him revealing only his eyes. While she simply smiles, as if reassuringly, and with a Fellini-like evasiveness replies: 'I don't know the road.'

They turn off into what looks like a deserted village square, the most de Chirico-like image in this film yet actually one of the few natural sets, close by some springs. (We never see the water although we hear it on the soundtrack.) There, in sudden silence, we now see the imagined Claudia as nurse-and-mother in an upstairs window, luminous in her white frock, at first holding a lamp in her hand and then descending the stairs to lay a table in this deserted village square. Then natural sound again as Claudia asks: 'What happens next?' Fellini/Anselmi is talking about the role of the woman-goddess in his film who must be both child and woman (as Sylvia was seen to be by Marcello in *La Dolce Vita*). They get out of the car, she expressing displeasure at the cold bareness of the place, he replying that he likes it enormously. Then he tries to explain that there will in fact be no role for her in the film because 'no woman can save a man' and because 'I don't want to film another lie'. Meanwhile she keeps intercutting her own interpretation of his difficulty. Three times she says 'because you don't know how to love . . . because you don't know how to love . . . because you don't know how to love.' But at his further announcement that there will also be no film, two cars tear into the square announcing a new idea to launch the film, and the swirling chaos of the press conference begins.

Partly here, but even more in the following episode, Fellini depicts the helpless quandary to which all his contradictory impulses seem to have led him. Everyone makes demands upon him and asks for explanations which he cannot give, while a harsh American face looms up into the screen taking obvious delight in the apparent fact that 'He has nothing to say.' Fleeting images of both Claudia and Luisa in her bridal gown appear, distracting him momentarily from the troubles around him; but when someone slips a revolver in his pocket, he climbs under the table and in a fashion that recalls the young Guido running away from the prospect of a bath, he crawls along the ground and shoots himself. 'What an incurable romantic!' he exclaims before the end. Then a glimpse of his mother standing by the sea; then the shot; and then silence except for the wind.

Here the epilogue to the film begins, the recapitulation of its argument, which is in essence a recapitulation of the complete works of Fellini. The huge rocket-launching apparatus is being dismantled, that useless structure which is the culmination of all the structures that we have seen throughout his films. It is apparently of no use. Daumier is talking incessantly about the wisdom of abandoning the picture: '. . . the world abounds in superfluity . . . it's better to destroy than to create what's inessential . . .' Throughout the film, it is as if Daumier stands for Fellini's more rational self, the self that has taken cognizance of all the critical attacks that have been made on his self-indulgent and irrational universe but which . . . Fellini feels to be destructive. At the same time, he recognizes that this rational analytical voice is not the only one in his life. At the very moment that Daumier is discoursing on the futility of unnecessary creation, the ring-master appears—that androgynous clown-like figure who has played such an important part in all of Fellini's work and seems to stand for something like creation for its own sake, for pure activity without thought or purpose. '*Aspetti,*' he smiles; 'wait a minute! We're ready to begin . . . All my best wishes . . .' It is as if Fellini cannot free himself from the conviction that in spite of all the reasonable criticisms that can justifiably be brought against him as against life itself, there is something deep within him that remains more affirmative and that exists beyond thought, that *must* go on creating simply for the sake of creation, as clowns or aerialists must continue to perform their intricate though meaningless routines.

Then another vision: first Claudia, then La Saraghina, then his parents appear before him—all dressed in white and all floating along noiselessly by the side of the sea accompanied only by the wind. And then most importantly, Luisa appears, her eyes slightly lowered as if in embarrassment or shame. If the critical voice of Daumier represents part of the toughness of the structure of this film, then the resentful, mistrustful, yet possibly forgiving presence of Luisa represents the other part that tugs against Fellini's natural tendency to make things a little too easy for himself. Guido is here experiencing a vision of love for all the creatures he has ever known and is trying to communicate the beauty and simplicity of this feeling to Luisa, even while recognizing his own unworthiness: 'Luisa, I do not know, I seek, I have not found . . . Only with this in mind can I look at you without shame . . . Accept me as I am.' And Luisa, while seeming to recognize the possible self-deception and self-dramatization of these remarks, nevertheless out of female kindness strives to accept him all the same: 'I don't know if that's true, but I can try.' So once again in Fellini, though in a far subtler form, we have salvation by grace. Man, although unworthy, can still be saved.

From this confession and acceptance, this exchange of imperfect terrestrial love, the characteristic Fellini miracle follows, the miracle of self-renewal that enables life to go on. Like the three circus musicians that appear at the comparable moment in *La Strada,* here a similar little troop come into view. With the characteristic horizontal stripes again very much in evidence, they march into the circus ring to receive instructions from Guido, the megaphone of authority having been thrust into his hands by the always smiling, always helpful magician/ringmaster, this embodiment of the impulse towards life without demanding why. Then, from the top of this vast structure, itself miraculously reassembled, down the equally vast staircase—like the White Sheik from the sky—all the people we have seen in this film parade into the ring and join hands and dance in a circle about its rim. (pp. 207-11)

So we have this final image of the circus ring with the little band still playing at its centre, the circus that has meant so much to Fellini all his life and has played such a large part in his films. And so too we have the mystic circle of eternity, ancient symbol of the Christian church incorporated by Dante. And so too we have the final consummate image of movement without direction, dancing round and round for ever in an infinity of shared acceptance. (p. 211)

Peter Harcourt, "The Secret Life of Federico Fellini" (originally published in a different form in Film Quarterly, *Spring, 1966), in his* Six European Directors: Essays on the Meaning of Film Style *(copyright © Peter Harcourt, 1974; reprinted by permission of Penguin Books Ltd), Penguin Books Ltd, 1974, pp. 183-211.*

LESTER J. KEYSER

Fellini's avowed purpose in *Amarcord* is very straightforward: "I simply wanted to create a portrait of a little Northern Italian town for a couple of hours. A town with its fantasy, its cynicism, its superstitions, its confusions, its fetes, and the passing of seasons." The film, however, is much more complex than a simple reverie or unvarnished history. No one remembers quite like Fellini, as we all know, so the film is really a quite personal and idiosyncratic vision of social history.

Fellini's loving portrait of his little town lacks a unifying plot; *Amarcord* is an impressionist mood piece that generally outlines the seasons of the year and the stages in life. There are births and deaths, weddings and orgies, holidays and holydays, parades and movies, motorcycles and peacocks. Yet beneath the frivolity and sentimentality, under the gentle satire and savage grotesques, lies a rich perception of the appeal of fascism. . . . To visit Fellini's home town in the thirties, to know the families there, to share Titta's relationship with his teachers, his mother, the town prostitutes, his schoolmates, and his church may finally be the only way to understand fascism. The very emotional, and seemingly harmless, attachments and taboos Fellini so lovingly delineates grew into a mass movement, a fanatical movement where inflamed emotion replaced reason. (p. 25)

Intellectually it's sometimes hard to tie social forces like fascism, militarism, sexual repression, and religion together; cinematically, Fellini draws the connection with ease. Youths who hear of saints crying when they masturbate can easily fantasize about fascist figureheads lauding them and their virgin brides. The glories and ceremonies of the ancient Church of Rome can quickly shade into the glorious rebirth of the Roman Empire under fascism. The majesty of sacramental liturgy can also be paralleled by the exhibitionism of military ceremony. Religion, nationalism, and repression thus go hand in hand in forming an authoritarian personality. (pp. 25, 27)

Light and dark, the best and worst, are strangely mixed in life and in Fellini's films. Fellini's touch is a gentle one, however, and to view too much of *Amarcord* as a structural vision of the roots of fascism would be to belie the other obvious charms of the movie: the peacock in the snow, the madman in a tree, the overendowed tobacconist, and Fu Manchu on his motorcycle. The thirties were not, Fellini intimates, a black era populated only by dark forces, for even his most earnest fascists do little more than use castor oil for their third degree. Instead of ominous symphonies, Fellini offers us what he calls "little music," a pleasant interlude "to be heard without needing to serve the chorus of eroticism and violence." (p. 27)

Lester J. Keyser, "Three Faces of Evil: Fascism in Recent Movies," in Journal of Popular Film *(copyright © 1975 by Sam L. Grogg, Jr., Michael T. Marsden, and John G. Nachbar), Vol. IV, No. 1, 1975, pp. 21-31.**

FOSTER HIRSCH

Amarcord may be the director's warmest, most subdued film (who goes to Fellini for warmth and good nature?), but it is also his safest. I miss the grand flourishes, the master showmanship, the epic heightening, that I've come to expect from Fellini. *Amarcord* lacks the vigor and drive, the joyous high spirits and sense of release that have been for me the chief pleasures of Fellini's work. . . .

Amarcord is a trimming away, a paring down, rather than a return to the style of his earliest films. . . . Fellini has always shown impatience with strict realism. Rather than objectively recording the surfaces of Italian life, he always worked from personal predilections that hardened into obsessions. (p. 50)

Amarcord, like all of Fellini's work, far from being a "return" or a "departure," is a blend of the real and the fanciful—it's a distinctly stylized version of Italian life. This time, though, Fellini has avoided a circus atmosphere; the film isn't the collection of breathtaking tableaux that is, for me, the essential Fellini. He has deliberately simplified his canvas, but he hasn't substituted anything in place of the intoxications of his previous work. . . .

Fellini doesn't impose himself on the material to the degree he has in his most recent films, but he hasn't found anyone else to guide us through the film's fragmented panorama. The point of view is shifting, confused. (p. 51)

Fellini keeps us away from all his characters. His main family, who are the anchor and focus for the anecdotes, are simply stage Italians, comic opera buffoons who conform to facile preconceptions about what Italians are like: they're hot-tempered, warm-hearted, they gesture extravagantly. We're encouraged to laugh at their squabbles, and then, when the mother dies unexpectedly, we're to be moved by their vulnerability. The pathos is unearned.

The townspeople consist of the usual Fellini dramatis personae, only the types this time are less vivid and exact. (pp. 51-2)

As a treatment of adolescence, the film is ordinary. Sexual initiation is mined for conventional comedy. As a chronicle of a town, the film is surprisingly flavorless. . . .

The composition is deliberately unstructured, nonpictorial, but it's also unimpressive—there's nothing to hold on to. The finale completely lacks the sense of communion or the joyous resolution or the formal beauty which have marked every one of the director's previous endings. Easy, likable, filled with flashes of charm, *Amarcord* is Fellini's thinnest performance. (p. 52)

Foster Hirsch, "Reviews: 'Amarcord'," in Film Quarterly *(copyright 1975 by The Regents of the University of California; reprinted by permission of the University of California Press), Vol. XXIX, No. 1, Fall, 1975, pp. 50-2.*

LOUIS D. GIANNETTI

What we see [in *Amarcord*] is not a year from the lives of several citizens of Rimini during the Fascist period, but Fellini's poetically stylized remembrance of things past. Like Proust, Fellini organizes his experiences subjectively, as in a dream, where "insignificant" details loom overwhelmingly, and "important" facts are either ignored, or casually noted then cast aside as emotionally irrelevant. . . . In keeping with the impure nature of the film, Fellini the documentarist fuses with Fellini the lyrical poet. . . .

Like many of the director's later films, *Amarcord* is unified by a dense substructure of leitmotifs. Perhaps the most obvious of these are seasonal. The film opens and closes with the coming of spring. Each season is typified by a characteristic sky element, which is related to the themes of aspiration and transience. . . .

Related to this seasonal structure is a sense of progression in the episodes in terms of the age of the protagonists. Roughly speaking, the film moves from youth to maturity to death to rebirth. (p. 156)

Most of the characters feel trapped by their mundane lives in this provincial town (hence, the "bitter" implications of the title). Despite their almost universal earthiness, they aspire to a more spiritual state. They yearn for escape and grasp at any symbol, however flimsy, of release from their prosaic existence. In addition to the sky elements, an important leitmotif of escape deals with vehicles. Throughout the movie, a mysterious motorcyclist whips in and out of the town square, an image of excitement, glamor, and liberation. . . .

Perhaps the most moving episode dealing with this motif is the arrival of the "Rex," a mammoth luxury ship which briefly passes through the ocean waters a few miles beyond the town's beaches. Like many of the sequences in the movie, this one begins comically and ends in poignance; it commences as a public spectacle and concludes on a note of private anguish. The opening takes place in the daytime, which Fellini characteristically associates with comedy and earthy vulgarity, and ends late at night, which is generally associated with solitude, spirituality, and aspiration. (p. 157)

Like many of Fellini's films, *Amarcord* is dialectic, and contrasts boisterous public events with poignant private dreams. A prominent motif in the film deals with community rituals, where the loneliness and isolation of individuals are temporarily assuaged: the opening bonfire to banish winter and welcome the spring, the Fascist rally, the meeting of the "Rex," the funeral service and procession, Gradisca's wedding. The private dreams in the film are generally associated with romantic fantasies, usually in some sexual form. But like most of the characters' aspirations, these fantasies are essentially masturbatory. . . .

[Reality], with its cruel impurities, reduces these romantic fantasies to mockeries. It inflicts humiliating compromises on the dreamers. (p. 158)

Just as Fellini seems incapable of offering us a picture of spirituality uncorrupted by vulgarity, so is he temperamentally incapable of showing us a portrait of evil "uncorrupted" by humanity. The episodes dealing with the Fascists are a good example of Fellini's "impure" vision. The Fascists are not the terrifying and inexorable figures portrayed in De Sica's *The Garden of the Finzi-Continis,* but clowns and buffoonish bullies. They too aspire to some "higher state," with their banners proclaiming the mystical fusion of "God, Country, and Family," and their ludicrous Cult of the Athlete. We may shudder at their hollow clichés about the "Glorious Empire," their simpleminded rhetoric about being "immortal," yet at the same time, we smile a little at their ragged pageants, their strutting, their childish theatricality. Even the sinister scene at Fascist Headquarters is "corrupted" by a certain clownish humanity. (p. 159)

The tone shifts in the film are audacious, a perfect demonstration, in fact, of Fellini's dialectical sensibility at work. The concluding scene of the Fascist sequence is a good case in point. At Party Headquarters, Aurelio is forced to drink two glasses of castor oil, the traditional form of humiliation employed by the bullies of the Party. . . . The scene shifts to [Miranda's and Aurelio's] kitchen, where Miranda is gently washing Aurelio in a large tub of water. His naked back to the camera, he hangs his head in shame while the haggard and sweat-soaked Miranda quietly gives vent to her fears. We can almost feel the steam and smell the excrement, yet the tone of the scene is one of exquisite tenderness. It is, in fact, the purest example of love in the film. . . . What an extraordinary poet this Fellini is: a fuser of images, one who's outrageous enough to portray a Fascist chieftain as a whining, mock-martyred Jewish Mother, and to offer his most moving love scene amidst the smell and smear of shit!

Fellini's use of multiple narration is another example of his ability to fuse apparently contradictory elements. Of course multiple narration is hardly new in the cinema—one thinks immediately of *Citizen Kane* and *Rashomon.* But Fellini's use of the technique is characteristically impure. It's not used as a schematic device whereby the filmmaker is able to reveal information that would otherwise be awkward to convey, as in the films of Welles and Kurosawa. In *Amarcord* a limited point of view is not so rigorously maintained. . . . Fellini relates events from various isolated points of view, but the form of the narration isn't dictated by any rigorous sense of inevitability. There's an element of arbitrariness, of randomness even, in Fellini's use of multiple narration.

In keeping with the mosaic structure of the movie, Fellini *demonstrates* rather than states the theme of the film: that despite the isolation and individual differences of the narrators, despite their solitary ruminations, they are all bound by a common romantic yearning. Superficially, the narrators in the film barely know each other socially, let alone spiritually, yet like isolated pieces of glass in a mosaic, they are part of a larger unity, a unity that is not apparent except to Fellini from a distance. Just as we can perceive the overall design of a mosaic by stepping back, so Fellini steps back in time and sees a similar coherence in what was once merely an undifferentiated jumble of isolated events, feelings, characters, and images.

Most narrators are used as endistancing devices: we are at one remove from a given event. The storyteller is a kind of filter, often a distorting filter, which prevents us from observing an event directly or objectively. In *Amarcord,* Fellini uses a kind of multiple filtration, a characteristically impure technique which totally obliterates the "objectivity" of an event, yet paradoxically fuses the fragments into a higher imaginative unity. (pp. 159-61)

[Movie] allusions abound in *Amarcord.* The theatre owner is called "Ronald Coleman" because of his presumed resemblance to that "elegant" actor. We see film posters announcing coming attractions, which include not only the romantic Norma Shearer, but also the clowns, Laurel and Hardy. Gradisca is teased about her great love for Gary Cooper, and is jokingly called "Greta Garbo" by one of the boys. These movie allusions represent another example of the escape motif in the film: the townspeople love the cinema, which provides them with romantic fantasies that permit them to escape their everyday existence. . . . Fellini believes that life often imitates art. But the differences between the two are too complex to be glibly separated: like life itself, *Amarcord* is an amalgam of both life and art. (p. 161)

Like all dialectics, Fellini's is ultimately concerned with a synthesis, with a fusion of opposites. In their everyday lives, Titta, Pinwheel, Gradisca, the lawyer, and the others lived isolated existences, yet they shared a common yearning, a unity that Fellini was able to perceive only with the endistancement of time. Perhaps this is the ultimate triumph of *Amarcord:* that it recognizes and dramatizes the bitter isolation of its characters, while cherishing their spiritual unity. Fellini manages to portray himself through his characters, and, in retrospect, he is able to see his characters in himself. And it's no small measure of his genius that he also succeeds in permitting us to see ourselves in him/them, and him/them in ourselves. (p. 162)

Louis D. Giannetti, "'Amarcord': The Impure Art of Federico Fellini," in Western Humanities Review *(copyright, 1976, University of Utah), Vol. XXX, No. 2, Spring, 1976, pp. 153-62.*

JOHN SIMON

Time and again I have written that after *8½*, a deeply flawed but suggestive satire and, in a scene or two, even affecting film, Federico Fellini was a burnt-out case. There were signs of decline even before that, but few major filmmakers have, after two or three great films and as many estimable ones, gone on to a series of abominations comparable to what Fellini has spewed out since *8½*. This, for me, includes even his one subsequent success, *Amarcord,* which I found a gross, witless, ham-fisted rehash of earlier Fellini movies, especially the incomparable *I Vittelloni.* Whoever puts these two films side by side without perceiving the later work as a lumpish travesty of the earlier is, in my view, tasteless, mindless, or blind.

Now Fellini has become almost too obliging: As if to prove me right so palpably that even the tasteless, mindless, and blind can get it, he has dropped *Casanova* like a ten-pound weight on our toes. . . . Particularly offensive and depressing is that Fellini has taken a fascinating protagonist and very rich story only to make them as hollow and aimless as he himself must have become. If this artistic fiasco were not accompanied by boundless arrogance in Fellini's behavior and recorded utterances, one could feel profoundly sorry for the man; as it is, one can only feel revulsion. (p. 57)

What in God's name does this tell us about Casanova? Or even about Fellini, except what we already know: that he is obsessed with dwarfs and giantesses, who appear, singly or together, in almost every one of his later films. And then what? . . .

[What] about this antisex business? Yes, the couples are always shown copulating with most of their clothes on; they are shot as if they were in separate rooms while making love to each other; and some or all of them seem to be on a kind of trampoline during the act. This makes for the sort of bouncing that, along with bestial panting, grotesquely distended and rolling eyes, and hideously contorted mouths, might well put an impressionable soul watching it off sex altogether. But why? Is Fellini in the pay of some ultrapuritanical hellfire sect? Has he gone mad with repressed sexuality or overindulged lust? Or has he become impotent and determined to spoil what he can no longer enjoy for everyone else as well? Whatever the purpose—assuming there is one—the result is more unstructured, repetitious, witless, and ugly than most moviegoers can endure, except perhaps as some extreme form of penance. You do not go to *Casanova* when you see this film; you go to Canossa. . . .

Fellini continues, with a few exceptions, to seek out some of the most freakish and nauseating actors and amateurs and to stuff his films with them. For this sort of thing, his genius remains unabated, which may come in handy when he flunks out of movies: It should get him a job running a circus and freak show. (p. 59)

John Simon, "'Casanova': Dead Film in a Dead Language," in New York *Magazine (copyright © 1977 by News Group Publications, Inc.; reprinted with the permission of* New York *Magazine), Vol. 10, No. 8, February 21, 1977, pp. 57-9.*

ANDREW SARRIS

Federico Fellini has been given a blank check by his American admirers ever since *8½* in 1962. Now, finally, in 1977 *Fellini's Casanova* is being returned for lack of fun(ds). . . . A joyless, sexless, often pointless caricature of Casanova is hardly the current notion of making whoopee, and a running time of two hours and 45 minutes makes this puritanical pill even harder to swallow. . . .

[In] the desperate world of filmmaking every artist must double as a con man, and Fellini has made fewer compromises with his personal vision than most of his contemporaries have. That may be the problem: He has made so few compromises that he has virtually ceased to communicate. For more than a decade he has been encouraged to exploit his personality, and his facility with satire and pathos, until now both his personality and his undeniable talent seem to have been depleted. Even his sense of humor seems to have deserted him. . . .

I am prepared to concede that I grossly underrated *8½* when it first came out, and that I utterly failed to comprehend its impact on the American cultural scene. The movie itself was a commercial failure, but all sorts of people seem to have seen it and been moved by it. . . . More than even Bergman or Godard, the name of Fellini provoked cries of, "Maestro!" And I am sure that the adulation can be attributed more to *8½* than to *Vitelloni* or *La Strada*—and not to *8½* as a whole, but rather to its wow ending in which all the people in Fellini's past dance around in a compliant circle as the companions of his artistic imagination. There is something in this quintessentially Fellinian image that struck a reassuring note in the sensibilities of American urban intellectuals with their messy private lives and public egos. Here Fellini was preaching a lyrical forgiveness and redemption in the name of artistic expression, and, better still, he was being forgiven by all the people he had used for his own pleasure, simply for incorporating them in his remorseful film fantasies.

Somehow the Fellini legend reached a point at which it would have seemed degrading for the director to make mere movies. Few of his fans seemed to suspect that *8½* reflected a creative crisis in Fellini's existence. Instead, *8½* came to represent a Pirandellian plateau from which the director could descend only at his own peril. . . .

Where, then, does *Fellini's Casanova* leave us? In years to come it may seem even more inexplicable than it does now. The continuity is so ragged and so gratuitous that the present film seems to have been hacked out of a much longer version with all the vital thematic connections severed. . . . There is no particular insight into—nor even much information about—either Casanova or the 18th century. There is no eroticism or sensuality, and no good conversation. One must see the film, though more for Fellini's sake than Casanova's. . . . Yet I can't help feeling that Fellini has been wrestling with his own demons for so long that he has lost sight of the real world with its changing tastes and obsessions. It is as if history ended for Fellini sometime in the early '60s, and his own mental odyssey began. . . . Fellini's very precisely visualized fear and loathing of femaleness in the universe through a symbolic rendering of vaginal labyrinths now seems too parochial a response to the turbulent shifting of relationships between men and women. . . . Fellini has no need to demonstrate the range of his talent. One can only regret that midway through his career he chose to film essays rather than make movies. To put it more bluntly, *Fellini's Casanova* could have used some of the crass showmanship of Nadia Gray's striptease in *La Dolce Vita*.

Andrew Sarris, "'Fellini's Casanova': A Failure in Communication," in The Village Voice *(reprinted by permission of* The Village Voice; *copyright © The Village Voice, Inc., 1977), Vol. XXII, No. 9, February 28, 1977, p. 39.*

FRANK BURKE

If we were to single out one quality that distinguishes Fellini's career-long imaginative evolution, it would be the drive for individuation, the search for ever more authentic ways of rendering growth in his world. Even his early movies—films of increasing alienation—reveal growing pressure for individuation within his imagination and his characters. (His characters individuate themselves *from,* rather than *through,* their world; hence their ultimate alienation.) And as Fellini's imagination refines its capacity to create unique and singular creatures, it also evolves beyond stories of individuation-through-alienation to stories of individuation-through-integration: the stories of unitive individuality which inform his movies from *The Nights of Cabiria* through *Fellini's Roma*. (p. 68)

[The] evolution from accommodation to breakout within Fellini's first three films seems to usher his imagination into a realm of near-total alienation which becomes visible in his next two feature films, *La Strada* . . . and *Il Bidone* or *The Swindle* . . . , which are both of them creatures of extreme dissociation and estrangement. (p. 70)

[While] Fellini's imagination becomes seemingly more alienated, and increasingly sophisticated in its capacity to envision alienation, as it moves from *Variety Lights* through *Il Bidone,* it becomes at the same time immensely more sophisticated in its capacity to envision individuals. The process of its evolution is, in effect, a process of individuation. . . .

In rendering the attempted . . . reintegration of a main character and his world, Fellini's imagination begins to evolve a vision of individuation-through-integration which supplants the vision of alienated individuality that prevails in the earlier films. And in moving from *Cabiria* to *8½* Fellini also profoundly alters his relationship to his art. He evolves beyond the relative detachment from his films that had characterized his work prior to *8½*, and develops the much more intimate interrelationship between his imagination and his movies that is evident in his films from *8½* to the present. (p. 71)

The Nights of Cabiria is the least autobiographical of the three features following *Bidone,* centering as it does on a prostitute as the main character. Nevertheless, it does return Fellini's imagination to the familiar world of Rome, a world present only sporadically in *Bidone*. In *Cabiria,* Fellini images a process of breakout, alienation, and reintegration which carries his imagination through and beyond the estrangement that gave birth to the two preceding movies. . . . Cabiria ushers Fellini's imagination back from the hillside, or brink, of total estrangement where, in *Il Bidone,* Augusto surrenders his moral and physical existence, and reunites it with a world of human connection whose presence and energy are essential to imaginative vision and growth. The evidence that Cabiria has indeed effected a creative connection between Fellini's imagination and its world lies in the film's final shot, in which Cabiria looks vibrantly and acceptingly into the camera eye—binding lover and loved, creator and created, in rich and total harmony.

In *La Dolce Vita* . . . we have precisely the same kind of pattern as in *Cabiria*. (p. 72)

[Like Cabiria, Marcello] concludes his odyssey to disillusionment with reintegration of sorts; for as the movie ends, he is being led back into the community of revelers with whom he has just spent the night. It is clear, however, from his behavior during the night's festivities—dedicated to celebrating the annulment of a marriage—that Marcello's reintegration is not affirmative, as was Cabiria's. . . .

Of vital importance, however, to the film and to the evolution of Fellini's imagination is the fact that *La Dolce Vita* does not conclude with the false reintegration of Marcello and his world. . . . Like the marriage of the camera eye and Cabiria, the wedding of the camera and Paola constitutes the marriage of Fellini's imagination with its own feminine powers, an act of total integration wherein the imagination encounters the visible manifestation of its own capacity for love, connection, and wholeness—its own capacity to transcend alienation.

What has happened in the course of *La Dolce Vita* is that Marcello, having annulled everything in his world (including himself), has annulled all the alienation and distance that pervade it. He has annulled the unauthentic process of reintegration he has undergone; he has annulled the failure or death of love in his world; and he has annulled mediation, the principal deterrent to love in that world. (As a reporter, he functions as the film's prime example of mediation.) In so doing, he clears the way for an entirely new world and mode of relationship, the world and relationship of love implicit in the final shots of the movie. So, while reintegration doesn't work for him, it clearly works for Fellini's imagination. (p. 73)

Having discovered in his three preceding films both reintegration and the annulment of distance as viable stories, Fellini employs both in *8½*. . . .

In *8½*, Guido's greatest challenge in the course of his growth toward integration is to eliminate the distance that separates him from his world, and consequently from his art. The film's major motif is that of directing; Guido's function as a movie director is the focal point of his principal weakness—his inclination to direct his life from outside rather than to connect intimately and completely with the life process. (p. 74)

In the course of his moral and imaginative evolution, Guido in effect resolves the problems of the protagonists of each of Fellini's three prior films. The problem of feminine individuation encountered by Cabiria is resolved through Guido's growing integration of and marriage to the feminine powers within him (embodied by all the women in his life, including the dream woman or anima personified by Claudia Cardinale). This process of integration and marriage culminates with his total acceptance of the principal females in his life: Luisa, Carla, and, in the film's final scene, his mother. The problem of detachment represented by Marcello is resolved through Guido's gradual abandonment of his impulse to direct, an impulse which mediates his relationship to his world. The problem of censorious, critical distance as expressed by Dr. Antonio is resolved by Guido's mock hanging of the critic and script consultant Daumier, and by his assimilation of Daumier's critical impulses as the power of creative conscience. And the problem of connection encountered by the camera eye, the *real* protagonist of Fellini's earlier movies and the embodiment of Fellini's imagination, is resolved through Guido's attainment of creative vision in the film's closing moments. In engaging Fellini's camera-eye imagination in the perception and cocreation of the harmonic dance that concludes *8½*, Guido enables that imagination to marry the visible evidence of its own powers of love and creativity as it had done in uniting its vision to that of Cabiria, Paola, and Cupid at the ends of Fellini's three preceding films. (pp. 74-5)

Another major act in Fellini's career, begun in *Dr. Antonio,* is also completed in *Juliet of the Spirits*—the movement from black and white to color. This is not just a cinematographic movement, but a moral-aesthetic one as well, rooted in the fact that black and white movies offer a radically different vision of life and its possibilities than do color films. . . .

A color movie . . . particularly one in which color is used as lavishly as it is in *Juliet of the Spirits,* offers a world that is pluralistic rather than dualistic. It assaults one with its infinite variety of concrete, individual entities, no one of which exists in a strictly polar relationship to another, no one of which asserts its priority over any other, and no one of which demands choice-and-rejection as a mode of relating to it. (p. 76)

In *Juliet of the Spirits* Fellini makes his first authentic color film. Not only does he make *Juliet* in color of his own moral/aesthetic volition . . . ; he also completes in *Juliet* what Guido began to evolve at the end of *8½*: a "Love for Everybody" *morality* of color. . . .

At the end of *Juliet of the Spirits,* having struggled successfully to attain integration and having made peace with her "spirits," Juliet breaks out. She leaves behind the boxlike house that has been both image and source of her imprisonment, and walks out into the world a liberated creature in a liberated universe. Fellini's imagination has achieved a breakout or breakthrough, as it did at the end of *I Vitelloni.* (p. 77)

With the evolution in [*Fellini: A Director's Notebook*] of a new, more open way of dealing with human images, Fellini enters a new phase of film-making which will last through *Amarcord,* in which none of his major figures will be stars, and most will be people with little or no acting experience, whose personal rather than professional powers have ignited his imagination. This shift constitutes a movement by Fellini from character to human image—from a theatrical, symbolic, and relatively static notion of players-in-their-roles to a much more dynamic phenomenon of vital, concrete images creating their own reality in a world of cinematic motion and change. (p. 79)

For two short and often overlooked movies, *Toby Dammit* and *Director's Notebook* did a great deal for Fellini, enabling him to (1) move beyond his post-*Juliet* crisis; (2) eliminate the actor and move to the center of his own work; (3) leave behind characterization for what might be called "image-generation" as a mode of creating human images; and (4) move beyond stories of personal, psychological individuation to stories about the refinement of his own movie-making. The fruit of all this is *Fellini-Satyricon* . . . , which capitalizes on the first three achievements of the two previous films and propels Fellini's imagination beyond the fourth. . . .

But perhaps the most interesting thing about *Fellini-Satyricon* is the fact that it moves Fellini beyond the consideration of his own art to the consideration of art itself. Here Fellini addresses himself to individuation as not a personal or movie-making phenomenon but rather an as aesthetic one. *Fellini-Satyricon* is primarily a rendering of the way art generates art and life transforms itself into art. The generation of art from art is pointed to in the movie's title, which suggests the evolution of Fellini's film art from the literary art of Petronius. (p. 80)

Living in a world of boundless aesthetic energy, indicated by all the theatrical art, poetry, music, painting, and literary and mythic narrative that surround him, Encolpio himself is less a person than an aesthetic force. He certainly is not a human "character" in a traditional theatrical (dramatic) or humanist sense—a creature with *person*-ality or "essence" possessed of stable and definable qualities which give him depth, substance, and a consistent, predictable mode of behavior. (pp. 80-1)

Like *Fellini-Satyricon, The Clowns* . . . is a work of aesthetic individuation. Taking the art of the clown as its point of departure, it not only generates movie art, but also resurrects the seemingly dead art of the clown as the movie draws to a close. It employs the art of the clown (particularly the White Clown-Auguste relationship which is the film's central structuring device) to organize personal experience and to enhance the growth of Fellini himself. But more than that, its ultimate end is to provide aesthetic form to experience and growth, to turn life into art. (p. 81)

Having moved from stories of personal growth through stories about the growth of his own art to stories of the growth of art itself, Fellini then creates in *Fellini's Roma* . . . a movie which incorporates all these aspects of individuation and includes yet another, the historical. *Roma* is, first of all, a story of Fellini's growth. . . . Second, *Roma* is a film about the growth of Fellini's art, as is clear from his emphasis on his attempts to make a movie. Third, it is a film about the evolution of art itself, with its incorporation and use of sculpture, architecture, Roman painting, the theater, photographic slides, the music hall, and movies. Finally, it is a film which, within the context of these other growth processes, examines in all its richness the cultural, religious, and political history of Rome. (pp. 81-2)

By weaving all this into a single film of individuation, Fellini has made by far his most imaginatively sophisticated, complexly integrated work of art. (Its complexity, as might be expected, earned it total lack of comprehension at the hands of critics, who saw it as either a travelogue or a meaningless work of Fellinian self-indulgence.) By focusing on Rome as a vital microcosm of himself and his world, an image of his personal and cultural heritage and creative power, Fellini has been able to weave the individuation of Western civilization into his own personal growth toward wholeness. (p. 82)

[At the end of *Fellini's Roma*] Fellini emerges as both child and potent partner of the creative life forces, seemingly prepared to encounter the future and transform it into visions of creative change.

Unfortunately the future has, in a sense, not yet come for Fellini. After the incredible act of integration he performed in *Roma,* after "putting it all together" and then breaking out, he has entered yet another period of alienation. Instead of encountering a future pregnant with creative possibility, he has, with *Amarcord* . . . and *Fellini's Casanova* . . . , moved back into the past. . . . *Amarcord,* for all its charm and magic, is about people who never grow up; *Casanova* is about a figure whose dissociation from his own powers of love (his "feminine" powers) is so radical that those powers ultimately atrophy to a state of total mechanical (f)rigidity.

Because *Amarcord* and *Casanova* do not deal with Fellini's capacity to work toward individuation and integration, they seem to signal the end of his journey toward wholeness, a journey which began with *8½*, and culminated brilliantly in *Roma*. . . . It might be best, however, to view them more as detours on his journey than as signals of its end. (pp. 82-3)

Frank Burke, "Fellini's Drive for Individuation," in Southwest Review *(© 1979 by Southern Methodist University Press), Vol. 64, No. 1, Winter, 1979, pp. 68-85.*

HARLAN KENNEDY

[Can] one ever have too much of Federico Fellini's special brand of excess? The maestro, after one of his customary long silences, has come out with all cameras firing. . . .

[For his film *Provo d'orchestra*] Fellini had the majestically simple idea of using a rehearsing orchestra as a symbol of social order and hierarchy. And of their fragility. No sooner does discipline break down in the orchestra—when its members stage a sudden, headstrong rebellion against their autocratic conductor—than Heaven itself seems to thunder in anger by pulling down the walls of the ancient Italian church in which they are rehearsing. Order is restored amid the dust and debris, but is it the same as before? The conductor seems to have gradually changed his brand of Italian autocracy for a more sinister Teutonic version, and as the screen darkens at the end of the film, a führerlike voice starts to bark forth in fluent German.

The natural heir to anarchy, the movie suggests, is despotism. Fellini's film describes the same teasing trajectory as many of those trompe l'oeil episodes from *Roma:* What begins as an apparently documentary slice of Roman life imperceptibly changes course and metamorphoses into a full-blown surrealist allegory. *Provo d'orchestra* plays with the audience's uncertainty and adds the Chinese-box, film-within-a-film complexity of a television crew filming the orchestra as well. Only gradually, like a slow-motion jack-in-the-box, does Fellini reveal the dramatic trick he is playing on us. The film's throwaway humor and eye-blink editing are a marvel. . . . (p. 66)

Harlan Kennedy, "Berlin: I. The Festival," in American Film *(reprinted with permission from the May issue of* American Film *magazine; © 1979, The American Film Institute, J. F. Kennedy Center, Washington, DC 20566), Vol. IV, No. 7, May, 1979, pp. 64-6.**

ROBERT HATCH

Federico Fellini, whose habit it is to offend the sensibilities of his fellow Italians, is at it again in a film with the precisely accurate title, *Orchestra Rehearsal,* and an explanatory subtitle, "The Decline of the West in C# Major." Beginning with *La Dolce Vita,* Fellini has made a series of films dealing with moral and social decadence; here he turns allegorically to political chaos and violence. (p. 221)

The message is clear enough, if perhaps a little simplistic: shape up, do your jobs, show some responsibility toward the society of which you are a part—in short, discipline yourselves, for if you don't, someone will come along to discipline you. In the present Italian context, it seems cogent advice, nor would I deny that it has wider application. But somehow the bite does not seem very sharp.

One problem, I think, is that Fellini has chosen an unfortunate model for his parable. Orchestra musicians, by and large, are a rebellious breed. For the most part, they are gifted and many of them slaved for years to achieve virtuoso careers that narrowly escaped their grasps. They are highly individualistic, fiercely proud of their skills, and yet they are forced to submit to the will of a conductor whom they have not chosen and of whose ability they are often scornful. . . .

So *Orchestra Rehearsal* might readily be understood, at least until the closing scene, as an instrumentalist's dream of sweet vengeance on the bête noir of his trade. And this interpretation would be encouraged by the fact that the cast, with the exception of the conductor . . . , is composed not of actors but of musicians. Being amateurs, they appear self-conscious, they are aware of the camera, they tend to preen and giggle, there seems to be more pretense than passion in their rages. This is how they might behave among themselves to demonstrate how a visiting celebrity could be given his comeuppance, if they cared to bell that cat. For all the cracking of walls and intrusion of wrecking ball, the atmosphere of the film is more that of a comic charade than of a solemn admonition, and the notion of an orchestra kicking over the traces is not sufficiently fantastic to make a strong metaphorical point. (p. 222)

Robert Hatch, "Films: 'Orchestra Rehearsal'," in The Nation *(copyright 1979 The Nation Associates, Inc.), Vol. 229, No. 7, September 15, 1979, pp. 221-22.*

JOHN SIMON

For the first few minutes of *Orchestra Rehearsal* it is as if the early, good Fellini had miraculously risen from the ashes of his self-indulgent, self-parodying, overblown and vacuous later works. A decrepit music copyist sets the scene for a symphonic rehearsal in a trecento oratory where several buried popes and bishops seem somehow to make the acoustics perfect, and where a TV crew is about to film the rehearsal. The atmosphere is vintage Fellini: the old fellow, an amateur actor and typical Fellinian oddball, is comfortably crotchety and eccentrically sensible; the oratory looks austerely authentic. . . .

The films's interest . . . dies quickly, because the point—the contrast between an orderly but dead past and rebellious contemporary confusion—is soon made unpleasantly obvious. As each arriving musician praises or patronizes his particular instrument to the invisible television interviewer (Fellini's voice), and does so in blatantly anthropomorphic terms; as, moreover, each player speaks with a different regional or snobbish accent, the suggestiveness of symbolism promptly yields to the predictability and constriction of allegory. To cap it all, the conductor is a dictatorial German, and the union delegate who causes considerable mischief, a Sardinian-like Berlinguer, the president of Italy's CP. When the orchestra members hurl mud or excrement at the portraits of the great classical composers, clamor for the death of the conductor, and set up a giant metronome in his place, then proceed to smash everything, we are submerged in Fellini's bitterness about present-day Italy after the Moro slaying, and though we may share his disgust, we yearn for a form more dramatic than the parable. . . . The old order is gone, and every new system leads to one kind of tyranny or another, Fellini is saying. Agreed; I just wish he were not saying it quite so schematically.

John Simon, "Simplistic Complexities," in National Review *(© National Review, Inc., 1979; 150 East 35th St., New York, N.Y. 10016), Vol. XXXI, No. 43, October 26, 1979, p. 1377.*

John Ford

1895-1973

(Born Sean Aloysius O'Fearna) American director, screenwriter, producer, and actor.

Ford is regarded as the master of the western film and an American cinema titan whose career spans the entire history of the film. Several characteristics distinguish Ford's work: among them a single strong situation, unity of time and space, and vivid characterization.

Ford's career began in 1913 when he moved from Maine to Hollywood, where his brother worked for Universal Studios. He changed his name to John, and began work as a prop boy and bit actor. He appeared in *Birth of a Nation,* and was influenced by its director, D. W. Griffith. These influences would surface in Ford's films, particularly in his attention to detail.

***The Tornado,* made in 1917, marked Ford's debut as a writer/director. A series starring the actor Harry Carey brought Ford critical approval, and the ensuing contract with Fox enabled him to make *The Iron Horse,* a story of the American transcontinental railroad. This film established him as a leading director. Themes that were to recur in later works appeared in *The Iron Horse:* the spirit of the pioneers and the strong bond of familial ties. Ford's films of the thirties signalled the advent of his collaboration with Dudley Nichols, who wrote for some of Ford's most admired films.**

The success of *The Lost Patrol,* a saga of a British cavalry patrol, allowed Ford to fulfill a project he had long wanted to do: directing his version of Liam O'Flaherty's *The Informer.* Nineteen thirty-nine was Ford's most prolific year, during which he produced *Stagecoach, Young Mr. Lincoln, Drums Along the Mohawk,* and *The Grapes of Wrath.* These films exemplify Ford's affection for the family and the legends of America.

When World War II broke out, Ford made several documentaries for the U.S. Marines, winning an Oscar for *The Battle of Midway,* the first U.S. war documentary. However, with the release of *They Were Expendable* in 1945, many critics questioned Ford's nostalgic attitude. Of the film, which dealt with the U.S. defeat in the Philippines, Andrew Sarris has written: "What could have seemed more perverse than Ford's celebration of gallant defeat in the aftermath of glorious victory?" Ford's popularity was reaffirmed with a string of Westerns, including *She Wore a Yellow Ribbon* and *My Darling Clementine.* His love of Ireland surfaced in *The Quiet Man,* a sensitive tale of an Irish-American returning to his motherland. The film is generally believed to be one of Ford's more significant works.

Most critics agree that Ford's work for the last twenty-five years of his life was not as important as that which preceded it. His films of the fifties were regarded as old-fashioned and unsophisticated. *The Man Who Shot Liberty Valance* served as the finest example of Ford's work in the sixties, and a nostalgic view of things past. His output diminished after this film, although he directed a documentary on Vietnam in 1971. His last film, *Seven Women,* while altering Ford's traditional view of women as subservient creatures, did not receive critical acclaim. Many critics found it indicative of Ford's failure to have a hold on the American public's interests.

Opponents of Ford have labeled him a bigot, claiming his philosophy is a mask for ignorance and bias; that he glorifies a nonexistent world. However, Ford's lengthy cinematic career and diversity of achievement is a milestone in the film world. Ford himself said of his work, "The secret is to make films that please the public and that also allow the director to reveal his personality." (See also *Contemporary Authors,* obituary, Vols. 45-48.)

[The Iron Horse," an] ambitious production, dwelt trenchantly upon the indomitable energy, resourcefulness and courage of those who spanned the continent with steel. . . .

In this picture is shown with true dramatic emphasis the welding together of two great points with steel. . . .

Yet with all their discomforts amid the great risk, it is shown, and truthfully, in this picture that these pioneers had a keen sense of humor. They were sports, and as sports they had to settle disputes even among themselves. For no chapter of history in a film can be told without a heroine, a hero and a villain, and the chances are that this is a more or less accurate description.

As scene after scene passes in shadows and lights upon the screen one cannot help thinking of that remarkable production, "The Covered Wagon," to which "The Iron Horse" is a sort of sequel. . . .

John Ford, the director of this film, has done his share of the work with thoroughness and with pleasing imagination. There are certain stretches in the production that are long and at times tedious, but this is due to the cutting and is a fault which can be remedied. . . .

This is an instructive and inspiring film. . . .

"The Railroad Pioneers," in The New York Times *(© 1924 by The New York Times Company; reprinted by permission), August 29, 1924, p. 6.*

LOUISE WALLACE HACKNEY

[While] cinematic quality is one of the most important tests, if not the most important, that can be applied to a moving picture, the increasing filming of well known novels has made it necessary that such a picture be judged also by the fidelity and intelligence with which the spirit of the novel is presented. Unfortunately, too often of late, the novel picturized has been used only as a springboard for the imagination, or lack of it, of the producer, and bears little relation to the original except in title and the names of the characters.

A pleasing exception is the . . . production of *Arrowsmith*, by the recent Nobel Prize winner, Sinclair Lewis. While from the limitation of time, many parts of the novel have had to be omitted, the picture has been unified and given significance by emphasizing the theme of a scientist's devotion to his work. It is an adequate and satisfying translation of the written word into the speech of the screen. (p. 10)

There are times when the rapidity of the sequences are almost too fast for easy comprehension and mar an otherwise unusually well done picture. . . . A laboratory is not usually a place of beauty to the layman, but Mr. Ford gives us many beautiful shots that linger in the memory. The scenes in the West Indies, a place that always lends itself to picturesque presentation, while beautiful and arresting, are never allowed to overbalance the others. . . .

It is one of the few pictures of the year that presages the time when our American scenes will receive the interpretative handling that distinguishes the best European films. (p. 11)

Louise Wallace Hackney, "Exceptional Photoplays: 'Arrowsmith'," in National Board of Review Magazine *(copyright, 1932), Vol. VII, No. 1, January, 1932, pp. 10-11.*

OTIS FERGUSON

The picture that John Ford has made out of Liam O'-Flaherty's "Informer" opens a lot of new possibilities for Hollywood, tackles something that is really fine, and manages several memorable scenes. But because it deals with the sort of thing that must be handled adequately if it is to go over, its persistent inadequacies make it more disappointing than many pictures with less to recommend them.

The story gets off to a beautiful start, riding along on the unfamiliar color and excitement of the period when the Terror was in Ireland, tightening on the country and walking through its streets in armed squads. And it carries well through the early part of that evening when Frankie McPhillip . . . came in from the hills, to slip home in the fog and be sold to his death. . . . For dramatic vigor and beauty of composition there have been few sequences to compare with the one that ends with the camera looking from behind Frankie down into the court where the Tans look up with their machine gun.

So far, the atmosphere and the sense of a tragic character have been well built. But shortly after Gypo has stumbled out with his blood money, there begins a train of happenings many of which hang fire altogether. . . . [Heather Angel, the rebel leader, and the chief aide] all play inevitably into the story, and are abetted by the director, who must needs drive every nail down three inches below the surface: hence whole organic stretches are made flabby or (as is the case with the last episode in church, the intercession of Katy) actually distressing. What is more, there is constant reliance on symbolic fade-ins and ghostly voices, on an elaborately cued and infirm musical score, and on the device of squeezing the last drop of meaning or sentiment out of a ten-minute sequence by hanging onto it for a quarter of an hour. It hardly seems that the man responsible for these cheap shifts could be the one who schemed the earlier episodes, the extended revelry of the middle parts and the final trial scene. (p. 76)

Otis Ferguson, "Two Films," in The New Republic *(reprinted by permission of* The New Republic; *© 1935 The New Republic, Inc.), Vol. 83, No. 1069, May 29, 1935, pp. 75-6.**

JAMES SHELLEY HAMILTON

[The] movies have rarely tried to look at modern Ireland with modern eyes, in spite of the riches of dramatic material to be found there. . . .

Which is one reason *The Informer* comes with such novelty and vitality. Another is that Liam O'Flaherty's novels have little in them of the stuff from which ordinary movies are made. . . . His books would be a stiff dose for the ordinary audience if they were put on the screen in the key he wrote them in.

Dudley Nichols and John Ford have struck a somewhat gentler strain from the harp of old Erin. One with his scenario, the other with his directing, they have made of *The Informer* something that popular sympathy can more conventionally respond to. They have romanticized the motive for Gypo Nolan's turning informer, making him do it for a girl —as if hunger were not an effective enough reason. All the women in the story have been stereotyped into lay figures used to suggest the usual heart interests of commonplace fiction, and do not count very much. But these little compromises have left intact what is essential to the tragedy of a man who was the victim of his own character. (p. 8)

There is a grim splendor to it, both as a tragedy and as a motion picture. Fundamentally it is honest in intention and sincere in execution. The man's character is truly understood and truly portrayed, with the inevitability coming from its own nature that great tragedy always has to have. The film illustrates powerfully the old dictum that character is destiny. . . .

The writer of the scenario dealt honestly and ably with the O'Flaherty character, and encompassed it in a framework that follows the best motion picture technique. John Ford has directed it with a fine eye for picture effect, both atmospherically and dramatically. Occasionally he slips into old movie ruts that seem outworn—fade-ins to supply deficiencies in the audience's imagination, for instance, that must seem quaint and unnecessary at best to any alert audience of today. But subtle and powerfully suggestive is the way he has paralleled the blind twistings of Gypo's inner nature with an exterior presentment of dark foggy streets peopled with dim figures and dimmer shadows, with the action erupting into some place of light and noise whenever Gypo emerges into positive activity. . . .

Pictures like this come rarely, and it will make an interesting test of how justified people are who insist that audiences are eager for better films than producers provide. (p. 9)

James Shelley Hamilton, "Exceptional Photoplays: 'The Informer'," in National Board of Review Magazine *(copyright, 1935), Vol. X, No. 6, June, 1935, pp. 8-9.*

FRANK S. NUGENT

In one superbly expansive gesture, which we . . . can call "Stagecoach," John Ford has swept aside ten years of artifice and talkie compromise and has made a motion picture that sings a song of camera. It moves, and how beautifully it moves, across the plains of Arizona, skirting the sky-reaching mesas of Monument Valley, beneath the piled-up cloud banks which every photographer dreams about, and through all the old-fashioned, but never really outdated, periods of prairie travel in the scalp-raising Seventies, when Geronimo's Apaches were on the warpath. Here, in a sentence, is a movie of the grand old school, a genuine rib-thumper and a beautiful sight to see.

Mr. Ford is not one of your subtle directors, suspending sequences on the wink of an eye or the precisely calculated gleam of a candle in a mirror. He prefers the broadest canvas, the brightest colors, the widest brush and the boldest possible strokes. He hews to the straight narrative line with the well-reasoned confidence of a man who has seen that narrative succeed before. He takes no shadings from his characters: either they play it straight or they don't play at all. He likes his language simple and he doesn't want too much of it. When his Redskins bite the dust, he expects to hear the thud and see the dirt spurt up. Above all, he likes to have things happen out in the open, where his camera can keep them in view. . . .

[Onward] rolls the stage, nobly sped by its six stout-hearted bays, and out there, somewhere behind the buttes and crags, Geronimo is lurking with his savage band, the United States Cavalry is biding its time to charge to the rescue and the Ringo Kid is impatiently awaiting his cue to stalk down the frontier-town street and blast it out with the three Plummer boys. But foreknowledge doesn't cheat Mr. Ford of his thrills. His attitude, if it spoke its mind, would be: "All right, you know what's coming, but have you ever seen it done like this?" And once you've swallowed your heart again, you'll have to say: "No, sir! Not like this!" . . .

This is one stagecoach that's powered by a Ford.

Frank S. Nugent, "'Stagecoach'," in The New York Times *(© 1939 by The New York Times Company; reprinted by permission), March 3, 1939, p. 21.*

PHILIP T. HARTUNG

"Young Mr. Lincoln" might better be called "Incident in the Life of Lincoln." . . . The 1832 episodes in New Salem are sketchily done; if Ann Rutledge meant very much to young Abe, one would never know it from this version. In fact most of the standard biographical scenes are avoided and emphasis is placed on character, with repeated inferences and hints of the future. Mary Todd smirks at Abe possessively. Stephen A. Douglas decides he must respect him. Abe reminisces, tells many stories and plays "Dixie" on a Jews-harp. Lack of excitement, understatement and John Ford's careful and extremely slow direction give Young Mr. Lincoln" an air of actuality. . . .

Although "Young Mr. Lincoln" is nicely done, it does not have the depth, poetry or historical importance of the Robert Sherwood play. (p. 218)

Philip T. Hartung, "Springfield to Titipu to Green City," in Commonweal *(copyright © 1939 Commonweal Publishing Co., Inc.; reprinted by permission of Commonweal Publishing Co., Inc.), Vol. XXX, No. 8, June 16, 1939, p. 218.**

OTIS FERGUSON

Drums Along the Mohawk is a candy-colored period bit, nice in general but nothing to break your neck getting to. Life in upstate New York during the Revolution. Since John Ford directed it, it is well above the average historical picture, but not up to Mr. Ford's best. There are too many type situations and too many types—ugh-ugh-Indian, hell's-fire army widow, little feller with big jug, etc. And except for the skirmishes, the action is pretty slow.

But when the skirmishes happen there is plenty of fun. It is good to have a lot of Indians milling around in a picture shooting arrows and everything, and now that sound has been added to catch the unearthly rumpus they make, the effect is complete—the audience practically saves that fort with the arms of its seats. . . . There are touching things too, and instruction and blood. Perhaps if you can manage to break it only a little bit, you may wish to break your neck getting to see the film after all. (p. 277)

Otis Ferguson, "French and Indians" (originally published in The New Republic, *Vol. CI, No. 1303, November 22, 1939), in* The Film Criticism of Otis Ferguson, *edited by Robert Wilson (© 1971 by Temple University), Temple University Press, 1971, pp. 275-77.**

OTIS FERGUSON

The Grapes of Wrath is the most mature picture story that has ever been made, in feeling, in purpose, and in the use of the medium. You can drag out classics (it is often safer not to go back and see them) and you can roll off names in different tongues and times. But this is a best that has no very near comparison to date.

I still don't know how they did it, though its possibility has been latent in Hollywood for years. The story of the Joad family, with its implied story of a migration of thousands of families, is told straight, and told with the sternest care for cause and effect and the condition of society. . . . (p. 282)

Everything is there as it should be: people dispossessed and shoved around and miserably in want, the fruitgrowers and their armed thugs and snide dodges, men clubbed and the strike broken but the spirit of it living, carrying on in the people. . . . (pp. 282-83)

To get minor flaws out of the way, there was possibly too much of the partial lighting of faces that was in general so effective . . . ; the starving kids were too plump and glossy; a few of the intercut devices of transition, with road signs, overlaps, etc., were a little trick. But that's all. . . .

[Ford] has deliberately forced his subject out into the open, and carries more of his story in long shots than most directors would dare, giving the whole picture a feeling of space and large movement. He works all the way from distances to those tight compositions of two faces, half in the dark: in the tent or the back of the truck or the cab in front (one very striking effect here, in the three set faces seen faintly in the windshield, nothing directly visible but the hand on the wheel). With nothing but the drone of the motor in low, the camera manages the whole story of the Okie camp as it moves down shack after shack, face after face, silent, hostile, and defeated. (p. 283)

Otis Ferguson, "Show for the People" (originally published in The New Republic, *Vol. 102, No. 7, February 12, 1940), in* The Film Criticism of Otis Ferguson, *edited by Robert Wilson (© 1971 by Temple University), Temple University Press, 1971, pp. 282-85.**

BOSLEY CROWTHER

The majesty of plain people and the beauty which shines in the souls of simple, honest folk are seldom made the topics of extensive discourse upon the screen. Human character in its purer, humbler aspects is not generally considered enough. Yet out of the homely virtues of a group of Welsh mining folk—and out of the modest lives of a few sturdy leaders in their midst—Darryl Zanuck, John Ford and their associates at Twentieth Century-Fox have fashioned a motion picture of great poetic charm and dignity, a picture rich in visual fabrication and in the vigor of its imagery, and one which may truly be regarded as an outstanding film of the year. "How Green Was My Valley" is its title. . . .

Persons who have read the haunting novel by Richard Llewellyn from which the story is derived will comprehend at its mention the deeply affecting quality of this film. For Mr. Ford has endeavored with eminent success to give graphic substance to the gentle humor and melancholy pathos, the loveliness and aching sentiment of the original. . . . In purely pictorial terms, "How Green Was My Valley" is a stunning masterpiece.

If, then, it fails to achieve a clear dramatic definition and never quite comes across with forceful, compelling impact this must be charged to the fact that the spirit of the original is too faithfully preserved. . . . [Mr. Llewellyn's] was a story told in reverie, episodically, running through a period of years.

And that is the form of the screen play which Phillip Dunne has prepared. . . . [It] is, by implication, the story of a good people's doom, the story of how the black coal wrung so perilously from the fair earth darkens the lives of those who dig it and befouls the verdant valley in which they live.

And that is the weakness of this picture. For in spite of its brilliant detail and its exquisite feeling for plain, affectionate people, it never forms a concrete pattern of their lives. Opportunities for dramatic intensity, such as that in which Huw saves his mother's life, are deliberately thrown away. And the obvious climactic episode, in which Huw's father is killed in the mine, is nothing more than a tragic incident which brings the story to a close. Apparently the intention was to have the film follow the formless flow of life. But an audience finds it hard to keep attentive to jerky episodes for the space of two hours.

Bosley Crowther, "'How Green Was My Valley'," in The New York Times *(© 1941 by The New York Times Company; reprinted by permission), October 29, 1941, p. 27.*

MANNY FARBER

John Ford's slow-poke cowboy epic, "My Darling Clementine," is a dazzling example of how to ruin some wonderful Western history with pompous movie making. . . . Given almost equal billing with the Earps in this version of old Tombstone are cloudscapes which are as saccharine as postcard art. Typical of director Ford's unimaginative, conforming tourist sensibility is the setting he uses—dead, flat country with Picassoesque rock formations jutting dramatically here and there—that has happened in Westerns ever since Art Acord was a baby. "Clementine" is in the new tradition of cowboy films: instead of hell-for-leather action there is concentration on civic-mindedness, gags, folk art. This one goes in for slow, heavy, character-defining shots. (pp. 836, 838)

Manny Farber, "Portrait of the Artist," in The New Republic *(reprinted by permission of* The New Republic; *© 1946 The New Republic, Inc.), Vol. 115, No. 22, December 16, 1946, pp. 836, 838.**

BOSLEY CROWTHER

In whatever whisps of foliage are left on Director John Ford's head, he wears a yellow ribbon—and, in the spirit of that rousing soldier song, he wears it with pride and affection for the old United States Cavalry. This you can see as plain as daylight and beyond the shadow of a bullet-scarred redoubt in Mr. Ford's grand "She Wore a Yellow Ribbon." . . .

For in this big Technicolored Western Mr. Ford has superbly achieved a vast and composite illustration of all the legends of the frontier cavalryman. He has got the bold and dashing courage, the stout masculine sentiment, the grandeur of rear-guard heroism and the brash bravado of the barrack-room brawl. And, best of all, he has got the brilliant color and vivid detail of those legendary troops as they ranged through the silent "Indian country" and across the magnificent Western plains. . . .

[The] nimble scriptwriters, Frank Nugent and Laurence Stallings, scribbled diligently right alongside the bold director—or maybe one jump ahead—in the course of the headlong production of this obviously runaway film. And since they were snatching freely from a James Warner Bellah yarn, they scooped up some heterogeneous details with which the director could work.

And Mr. Ford has employed them to what is usually termed the best effect. His action is crisp and electric. His pictures are bold and beautiful. No one could make a troop of soldiers riding across the western plains look more exciting and romantic than this great director does. No one could get more emotion out of a thundering cavalry charge or an old soldier's farewell departure from the ranks of his comrades than he. . . .

Bulwarked with gay and spirited music and keyed to the colors of the plains, "She Wore a Yellow Ribbon" is a dilly of a cavalry picture. Yeehooooo!

Bosley Crowther, "'She Wore a Yellow Ribbon,' at Capitol, Stars John Wayne As a Cavalry Captain," in The New York Times *(© 1949 by The New York Times Company; reprinted by permission), November 18, 1949, p. 35.*

LINDSAY ANDERSON

Ford has always found his true image of reality in this

world, not in the deliberately fashioned symbolism of a literary invention; his symbols arise naturally out of the ordinary, the everyday; it is by familiar places, traditions and themes that his imagination is most happily stimulated. There is a sort of strain, apt to evidence itself in pretentiousness of style, about his attempts with material outside his personal experience or sympathy. (p. 9)

[Ford's most successful films] manage with remarkable success to revive the manners and appearances of past times. Designed with obvious care, they show a keen pleasure in their period appurtenances, in dresses and uniforms, furniture and decoration. Delighting in dances and communal celebrations of a long-forgotten style, there is a sense about them of regret for ways of living at once simpler and more colorful than those of today.

This implied lack of concern with contemporary issues is evident also in Ford's present-day films. *They Were Expendable* is hardly, in the modern sense, a film about war, but rather a film about a species now almost extinct—the professional, dedicated warrior. . . .

The films all start with the advantage of a good story. Further, they are the work of expert writers . . .—experienced story-tellers with no pretentious ambitions to transcend the natural bounds of their subjects. As a result their scripts leave Ford free to tell the stories at his leisure, to enrich and enliven them through his own humane inspiration. (p. 10)

[It] is evident in the whole approach, in the texture of the films: in odd, unscripted actions and gestures; in the robust humor which runs through them all, simple and genial, of character rather than incident; in the consistent dignity (rising at times to grandeur) with which the human figure is presented. (pp. 10-11)

Where . . . integrity is not preserved, where Ford's true sympathy is not with his material, or the material itself is counterfeit, . . . visual opulence can become overblown. This objection may be made to *The Informer*—a brilliant but sometimes showy exercise in the sort of expressionism one has come to associate rather with the German cinema, with its use of heavy-contrast lighting, studied grouping, and deliberate non-realism. Equally it is possible to criticize the last section of *The Long Voyage Home,* where the visual pretentiousness stems directly from the script; portions of *Tobacco Road,* in which Ford's tendency to idealize is not really in tune with the writing; or all *The Fugitive,* where Figueroa has been given unfortunate license to reinforce Nichols' vulgarity with his own. But when the material is genuine, and Ford's response to it a spontaneous one, his technique is characterized by its extreme simplicity. Seldom indulging in the sophistications of camera movement, his films proceed in a series of visual statements—they are as sparing in their use of natural sound as of dialogue. Rich in phrasing, simple in structure, it is a style which expresses a sure, affirmative response to life—the equivalent to that Biblical prose which, today, it takes greatness of spirit to sustain. (p. 14)

With the collapse of its popular traditions, Western art has become increasingly sophisticated and eclectic; the popular themes are in general left to be exploited, and degraded, by the opportunists. Ford's films, in this context, seem hardly to belong to our time at all. His art is not intellectual; his impulse is intuitive, not analytical. Unsophisticated and direct, his work can be enjoyed by anyone, regardless of cultural level, who has retained his sensitivity and subscribes to values primarily humane. He applies himself to traditional themes, and is happiest when his story is set in the settled society of another era—typically, Ford's is a man's world, one in which woman's function is largely domestic, to build the home and bear children, to sympathize and support. Relationships in these films are never complex (which does not mean that they are not subtle). Ford's heroes do not analyze themselves into negation; uncomplicated and instinctive, they realize themselves in action; and they win. Even the defeated heroes of *They Were Expendable* are indomitable in disaster, and Ford ends his film with a positive symbol, a presage of the ultimate victory. (pp. 14-15)

Ford's art is inspired by an optimistic faith in man's nature, a reverence for the human creature which is evident always in choice of subject and manner of treatment; but this is combined with a firm emphasis on discipline, an implicit stress on moral and social duties which may properly be described as classical, and which are matched by the sympathetic decorum of style. The poetry which, at their most intense, the films attain, approximates more closely to the Johnsonian "grandeur of generality" than to the romantic's glorification of the particular. (pp. 15-16)

Lindsay Anderson, "John Ford: His Work Is a Portrayal of the Righteous Man," in Films in Review *(copyright © 1951 by the National Board of Review of Motion Pictures, Inc.), Vol. II, No. 2, February, 1951, pp. 5-16.*

LINDSAY ANDERSON

Wagonmaster is the nearest any director has come to an *avant-garde* Western. To use this word of a film by Ford may sound strange; take it, though, not as implying an experiment in any new -ism, but in the sense in which it is perhaps more frequently used, of an absolute, self-delighting liberty on the artist's part. . . . Ford's handling of [the plot] shows clearly enough that his interest is aroused less by those which propel and shape the narrative (these are apt to be perfunctory) than by the characters and events which give colour to his favourite themes; the dogged persistence of his heroes, the moral beauty of their lives of enterprise and creation. Unconcerned with novelty, he is quite content to draw, for incident and characterisation, on his earlier films. . . . In *Wagonmaster* Ford has composed, with the simplicity of greatness, another of his poems to the pioneering spirit. It is a tragic reflection on the progress of the cinema that modern audiences, unused to the exercise of the poetic sense, expecting only the cruder impact of a conventional plot, gape and are unhappy when Ford rests his Olympian camera on one of these magnificent prospects, as the wagons trundle on their way and a few voices join together in a revivalist hymn or one of the traditional ballads of the West. (p. 333)

Lindsay Anderson, "Retrospective Reviews: 'Wagonmaster' and 'Two Flags West'," in Sight and Sound *(copyright © 1950 by The British Film Institute), n.s. Vol. 19, No. 8, December, 1950, pp. 333-34.*

ABRAHAM KAPLAN

[*The Long Voyage Home*] is neither a war movie nor an adventure sea story. It belongs, rather, to that great class of works of art which deal with the eternal human quest—the *Odyssey,* the Holy Grail romances, *Moby Dick,* Kafka's *Castle,* perhaps *The Old Man and the Sea.* In all of them man is presented as traveling some long, weary road in order to attain a supremely desired objective. The various specific elements in the film are interpretable as expressive of this theme. They delineate the human condition—not just in the merchant marine, or in a century of war and revolution, or in any other particular social circumstances. The symbol, to be sure, is specific, but not what it symbolizes: man's situation in this world and in relation to other men.

The film begins with the explicit statement that it is a saga of the changing sea and the unchanging men upon it. In aesthetic substance, the sea is the whole external world, the forces of nature with which man must cope; just as the authority of the police and the captain is expressive of all the social constraints within which man's life moves, regardless of the particular features of his society.

Smitty is not permitted to jump ship, and shore leave is denied to every one. Does this not have the expressive content of the "no discharge in war" of Ecclesiastes—no escape from our humanity, from the constraints which the external world inevitably imposes on our private ones? And when the cargo is safely landed, the men find that they have nowhere to go but back to the ship, to sign up again. Is this not poignantly moving, not in the petty "realism" of how empty the satisfactions society allows men of their class and station, but in the more profoundly realistic sense that there is no other life than the present one, no place to live it but where we are? "Earth's the right place for love," the poet says: "I don't know where it's likely to go better." There *is* only the ship and the voyage.

And at the end of the film you know that although some of the men have gone home at last—Yank, Drisc, Smitty, and Ole—there is nothing for the others to do but resume the voyage, and it is the same voyage, and the voyage will go on and on, always with different men; perhaps the ship itself will change, but nothing essential in the situation will change. There will still be the struggle with the external world, there will still be the constraints imposed by authority, and there will still be the heartaches, frustrations, and also the recurrent gratifications which are just enough to give man the strength and courage to go forward.

This is not to say that every work of art is an allegory, that *The Long Voyage Home* is a kind of secular *Pilgrim's Progress.* It is not a question of allegory, or even of conscious and explicit symbolism. It is a matter only of expressiveness rather than restrictive representation, of giving to the arts the full richness of their meaning. (pp. 381-83)

Abraham Kaplan, "Realism in the Film: A Philosopher's Viewpoint" (originally a lecture delivered at the University of California at Los Angeles; reprinted by permission of the University of California Press), in The Quarterly of Film, Radio, and Television, *Vol. VII, No. 4, Summer, 1953, pp. 370-84.**

GERALD COCKSHOTT

Towards the end of 1947 in the second number of *Sequence* there appeared a study of some of the films of the Hollywood director John Ford. Although the author did not so much as mention Ford's amusing and accomplished comedy *Passport to Fame* . . . and though he referred to Ford as a "great" director, this was on the whole a fair survey. In subsequent numbers of *Sequence* Ford's films were criticised, certainly, but in terms that suggest that Homer had nodded. . . . It was not that the writers in *Sequence* were blind to the faults in Ford's films: it was rather that, good or bad, these were treated not as the ephemeral entertainments of a commercial director but as lofty communications from a great artist who sometimes had lapses. By the time the *Sequence* office had moved over to the B.F.I. the tone of lyrical adulation had become more marked. "In *Wagonmaster,*" we were told [see Anderson, *Shots in the Dark,* excerpt above], "Ford has composed, with the simplicity of greatness, another of his poems to the pioneering spirit. It is a tragic reflection on the progress of the cinema that modern audiences, unused to the exercise of the poetic sense, expecting only the cruder impact of a conventional plot, gape and are unhappy when Ford rests his Olympian camera on one of these magnificent prospects," etc. Ford, you see, is a poet. It is "tragic" that an audience may not appreciate one of his pictures, and we spectators are taken to task for our insensitiveness. He photographs his films with an "Olympian camera" (whatever that may be). Later still *The Quiet Man* is accorded a review twice as long as that given to *Rashomon* and is finally summed up by the critic as "Shakespearean."

Thus one may trace the development of a cult—from an article that errs on the side of youthful enthusiasm, through reviews which hint that Ford's failures represent a falling-off from some lofty artistic peak that he has previously scaled, to the woolly language of unrestrained hyperbole. (p. 8)

What is immediately striking about many of Ford's films is the over-consciously "beautiful" photography, one element in the composite art of the film for which the cameraman surely deserves a good deal of the credit. But granted that Ford himself has an eye for pictorial composition, are his films distinguished in any other way? . . . With Ford every shot is beautifully composed, but I am not sure that he takes much trouble to select what is most essential to the unfolding of the story. And he certainly has no ear. I cannot recall a single example in any of the films by Ford that I have seen of sound used with imagination. Often it is not even used well: though there have been exceptions, with him a superfluity of banal, heavily scored incidental music seems to be the rule—and if Ford is to be given credit for the excellence of the photography in his films, perhaps it is not unreasonable to blame him for the banality of the music.

And what about the script? What do these beautiful images all add up to? No doubt this director has not always been given a free hand in his choice of subjects, though when a picture is labelled "A John Ford Production" one may perhaps assume that he has not merely been ordered to do what he could with fifth-rate material. If Ford has had freedom of choice, one can only conclude that his taste is uncultivated and adolescent. Time and again he has returned to the sheriff, the bad man and the Red Indians. . . . Even those members of the audience who are easily entertained and expect no more from a director than that he shall tell a plain unvarnished tale with clarity and force are not going to be wholly satisfied with Ford. The narrative line in some of his films has been hopelessly muddled. Who would offer to make a lucid summary of the action in *They Were*

Expendable, My Darling Clementine, or *She Wore a Yellow Ribbon?*

I have devoted some space to pointing out what to most readers must have been obvious: that Ford is a director who seems to prefer the novelette (even when making a film about a world war), who has sometimes shown himself incapable of coherent narration even on the modest level of the wild west adventure story, who is not particularly subtle in his selection of visuals, and who is painfully insensitive in his use of sound. In fact he lays himself open to serious strictures with practically every film. . . . With Ford, . . . what is cheap and sentimental on the printed page is even worse on the screen, where vulgarity and mawkishness are laid on with a trowel. Yet this director, who is not even among the best of the Hollywood film-makers, is ranked by implication with Dreyer, Lubitsch and Clair, his work being treated with a solemnity out of all proportion to its merits, in periodicals that we had hoped would become a forum for serious writing on the film. (pp. 9-10)

[Although] the cult has its comedy value, I do not think it should be treated simply as a joke. . . . When a director who has rarely produced anything comparable with even a moderately adult novel is persistently regarded, by a vocal minority, as a great artist, it is time that voices were raised in protest. As a hardworking Hollywood director Ford is no doubt worthy of respect. Some of his films (*Passport to Fame,* in particular) have given a good deal of pleasure to a wider public than the American teenagers whom he so obviously aims to please. But no valid purpose is served by pretending that his work has much importance in the history of the film as an art. . . . (pp. 10, 31)

Gerald Cockshott, "The Curious Cult of John Ford," in Film *(reprinted by permission of British Federation of Film Societies), No. 2, December, 1954, pp. 8-10, 31.*

PENELOPE HOUSTON

There may be no wholly new subjects left for the Western, but there are still a few blank spaces to be filled in on the screen's gigantic map of the West. Ford's latest film, *Sergeant Rutledge* . . . stumbles on one of them: the history of the Negro regiment, the 9th Cavalry, formed soon after the Civil War to join in the last frontier battles with the Indians. To the Negroes, in 1881, the White House is still "the place where Mr. Lincoln lives"; slavery is a living memory; loyalty to the regiment, if we are to believe Ford, has become a fierce, fighting expression of racial pride.

It is a theme which carries echoes and reverberations, a subject too intriguing in its own right to be smothered beneath our own modern reactions to questions of race prejudice and so made the material for an up-to-date polemic. What did these men think of the cause they were fighting for; of their officers; of those bleak Arizona battlefields where they engaged the Indian war-parties? But these are not the questions Ford raises in his film. His immediate dramatic theme is the court-martial of Sergeant Rutledge. . . .

There is a perfunctoriness about the whole film, in the maddeningly casual, take it as you find it manner of latter-day Ford. The script, by Willis Goldbeck and James Warner Bellah, allows witnesses to give evidence of events at which they were not present; the trial meanders backwards and forwards. . . . As so often with Ford, the comedy, at the outset entertaining, gets out of hand. At the back of the courtroom's fan-waving audience of station wives are a group of men out for a lynching, brandishing their home-made nooses. But Ford is too genial about the whole business to leave much scope for tension. In the action scenes, the Negro soldiers are easily absorbed into his own passionate loyalty to the cavalryman—any cavalryman—in his blue jacket. He poses them heroically against the skyline; he ensures that they die bravely; he lets them grin and swagger. He seems to like them almost as much as he likes the Irish. But, while Ford's Irish now need no explaining, the casual approach here discloses too little.

Yet, of course, there are moments when everything is working for the director: the opening, with the bustling arrival at the cavalry post and the quick, firm establishment of the scene. . . . Ford's knowledge of how to place and manoeuvre an action scene seldom deserts him. His escapes into man-to-man sentimentality, his taste for bad jokes, his utterly careless attitude to some of his players (the store scene, introducing the murdered girl, is atrociously played), are inseparable from his qualities as a film-maker. Ford still writes the poetry of heroes; it is the prose of *Sergeant Rutledge* that he has neglected.

Penelope Houston, "'Sergeant Rutledge' and 'The Unforgiven'," in Sight and Sound *(copyright © 1960 by The British Film Institute), Vol. 29, No. 3, Summer, 1960, p. 142.*

ANDREW SARRIS

The Man Who Shot Liberty Valance is a political western, a psychological murder mystery and John Ford's confrontation of the past; personal, professional and historical. The title itself suggests a multiplicity of functions. "The man who" marks the traditional peroration of American nominating conventions and has been used in the titles of more than fifty American films. In addition to evoking past time, "shot" may imply a duel, a murder or an assassination. "Liberty Valance" suggests an element of symbolic ambiguity. This is all *a priori.* After the film has unfolded, the title is reconstituted as bitter irony. The man who apparently shot Liberty Valance is not the man who really shot Liberty Valance. Appearance and reality? Legend and fact? There is that and more although it takes at least two viewings of the film to confirm Ford's intentions. . . .

The remarkable austerity of the production is immediately evident. The absence of extras and the lack of a persuasive atmosphere forces the spectator to concentrate on the archetypes of the characters. Ford is well past the stage of the reconstructed documentaries (*My Darling Clementine*) and the visually expressive epics (*She Wore a Yellow Ribbon*). His poetry has been stripped of the poetic touches which once fluttered across the meanings and feelings of his art. Discarding all the artifices of surface realism, Ford has attained the abstract purity of Renoir. (p. 13)

It is hardly surprising that the plot essence of the flashback is less important than the evocations of its characters. Whatever one thinks of the *auteur* theory, the individual films of John Ford are inextricably linked in an awesome network of meanings and associations. (p. 14)

In accepting the inevitability of the present while mourning the past, Ford is a conservative rather than a reactionary. What he wishes to conserve are the memories of old values even if they have to be magnified into legends. The legends with which Ford is most deeply involved, however, are the legends of honorable failure, of otherwise forgotten men and women who rode away from glory toward self-sacrifice. . . .

Although *The Man Who Shot Liberty Valance* achieves greatness as a unified work of art with the emotional and intellectual resonance of a personal testament, there are enough shoulder-nudging "beauties" in the direction to impress the most fastidious seekers of "mere" technique. . . . The vital thrust of Ford's actors within the classic frames of his functional montage suggests that life need not be devoid of form and that form need not be gained at the expense of spontaneity. Along with *Lola Montez* and *Citizen Kane, The Man Who Shot Liberty Valance* must be ranked as one of the enduring masterpieces of that cinema which has chosen to focus on the mystical processes of time. (p. 15)

Andrew Sarris, "Cactus Rosebud or 'The Man Who Shot Liberty Valance'," in Film Culture *(copyright 1962 by* Film Culture*), No. 25, Summer, 1962, pp. 13-15.*

ERNEST CALLENBACH

"Liberty" Valance is a pathologically vicious, whip-wielding outlaw; the man whose reputation came from shooting him didn't do it; the reign of law in The Territory is established by a cold-blooded murder.

Such are the dominant ironies in this rather sinister little fable, constructed in an offhand but mildly entertaining manner by the old master, John Ford. . . .

Nothing of [the story] quite holds together if taken seriously; the direction of actors is loose and indulgent, and the dialogue is witless. Also there is a persistent nastiness of underlying tone; the film has too much of a *parti pris* for the personality and power of Wayne to attain a balanced structure—we know from the outset that only Wayne's gun can preserve Stewart from the whip of Liberty. If the film had been made in France, we would point out its "crypto-fascist" tendencies: that it ignores the actual power basis of organized society in favor of a romanticized version glorified by Wayne, and that by isolating The Territory it makes a foolish individualist allegory out of a mighty social drama. (p. 42)

As with most of the Westerns I've seen on TV, however, the trouble is that the genre materials have been manipulated to death. Only the twists of plot retain a certain puzzle quality. One may here, for instance, note a neat thematic parallel between *High Noon* and *Liberty Valance*—in both, a central figure who espouses order, law, and peacefulness learns that plain violence is sometimes necessary. . . . But the stock materials are terribly worn by now, and we cease to take morality or amorality plays seriously if they do not have some human novelty and reality, some structuring artistic force. *Ride the High Country* rose above the routine Westerns it resembles in many respects because it had solid and fairly complex characterization, a vividly realized sense of interpersonal atmosphere, and a serious Faustian theme; the shooting and editing had drive, economy, cogency. *Liberty Valance* is by comparison very laxly made. Its flashback construction is a distraction, . . . its bows to racial "equality" in the person of Wayne's helper Pompey are embarrassing; its shameless repetitions of the cowardice gag with the marshal are tiresome. Worst of all, its over-all sugary tone belies the sinister line of the story. I suppose some will try to make the case that this disparateness only illustrates how consummate an *auteur* Ford is; to my mind it destroys the film. (p. 43)

Ernest Callenbach, "'The Man Who Shot Liberty Valance' and 'Donovan's Reef'," in Film Quarterly *(copyright 1963 by The Regents of the University of California; reprinted by permission of the University of California Press), Vol. XVII, No. 2, Winter, 1963-64, pp. 42-4.*

BOSLEY CROWTHER

In "Cheyenne Autumn," . . . John Ford, that old master of the Western, has come up with an epic frontier film. It is a beautiful and powerful motion picture that stunningly combines a profound and passionate story of mistreatment of American Indians with some of the most magnificent and energetic cavalry-and-Indian lore ever put upon the screen.

It is based on an actual event—a footnote to history. . . .

But it is more than a footnote in this picture, which Mr. Ford has endowed with the kind of atmospheric authenticity and dramatic vitality that he so brilliantly achieves, when in top form. It is a stark and eye-opening symbolization of a shameful tendency that has prevailed in our national life—the tendency to be unjust and heartless to weaker peoples who get in the way of manifest destiny. . . .

Mr. Ford has spread a rumbling, throbbing drama of the stoicism and self-sufficiency of the Indian who is an alien in his own country, of the meanness and perfidy of the whites and of the compassion and heroism of some good people who try to see that justice is done. . . .

There is poetry in the graphic comprehension—in a scene of the Indians at dawn, wrapped in their Government blankets, their chiefs standing stalwart and strong; in scenes of the cavalry wheeling and thrashing in skirmishes with the tribe. And there is tragic and epic grandeur in the enactment of the whole exodus theme.

Along toward the middle of the picture there comes an odd and disconcerting break which initially makes one wonder whether Mr. Ford has suddenly and frivolously abandoned the Cheyennes. In a switch to a barroom in Dodge City, he embarks on a lengthy, comic phase in the spirit of "The Man Who Shot Liberty Valance," one of his less brilliant films. . . .

Although richly and roaringly comic, it seems entirely superfluous—until one senses that Mr. Ford is subtly mocking a familiar attitude in Western films. He is actually injecting a satiric estimation of the usual callous way the pathos and plight of the Indians are tossed off in favor of sheer clichés.

However, it must be acknowledged that the picture does not rise again to its early integrity and authenticity after this episode. . . .

Even so, "Cheyenne Autumn" is a strong film, grandly directed. . . .

Bosley Crowther, "'Cheyenne Autumn'," in The New York Times *(© 1964 by The New York Times Company; reprinted by permission), December 24, 1964, p. 8.*

PETER WOLLEN

[Wyatt Earp, Ethan Edwards, and Tom Doniphon] all act within the recognisable Ford world, governed by a set of oppositions, but their *loci* within that world are very different. The relevant pairs of opposites overlap; different pairs are foregrounded in different movies. The most relevant are garden versus wilderness, ploughshare versus sabre, settler versus nomad, European versus Indian, civilised versus savage, book versus gun, married versus unmarried, East versus West. (p. 94)

The master antinomy in Ford's films is that between the wilderness and the garden. As Henry Nash Smith has demonstrated, in his magisterial book *Virgin Land,* the contrast between the image of America as a desert and as a garden is one which has dominated American thought and literature, recurring in countless novels, tracts, political speeches and magazine stories. In Ford's films it is crystallised in a number of striking images. *The Man Who Shot Liberty Valance,* for instance, contains the image of the cactus rose, which encapsulates the antinomy between desert and garden which pervades the whole film. . . .

Earp, in *My Darling Clementine,* is structurally the most simple of the three protagonists I have mentioned: his progress is an uncomplicated passage from nature to culture, from the wilderness left in the past to the garden anticipated in the future. Ethan Edwards, in *The Searchers,* is more complex. He must be defined not in terms of past versus future or wilderness versus garden compounded in himself, but in relation to two other protagonists: Scar, the Indian chief, and the family of homesteaders. . . . Edwards is ambiguous; the antinomies invade the personality of the protagonist himself. The oppositions tear Edwards in two; he is a tragic hero. (p. 96)

Ethan Edwards's wandering is, like that of many other Ford protagonists, a quest, a search. A number of Ford films are built round the theme of the quest for the Promised Land, an American re-enactment of the Biblical exodus, the journey through the desert to the land of milk and honey, the New Jerusalem. This theme in built on the combination of the two pairs: wilderness versus garden and nomad versus settler; the first pair precedes the second in time. (p. 97)

The Man Who Shot Liberty Valance has many similarities with *The Searchers.* We may note three: the wilderness becomes a garden—this is made quite explicit, for Senator Stoddart has wrung from Washington the funds necessary to build a dam which will irrigate the desert and bring real roses, not cactus roses; Tom Doniphon shoots Liberty Valance as Ethan Edwards scalped Scar; a log-home is burned to the ground. But the differences are equally clear: the log-home is burned after the death of Liberty Valance; it is destroyed by Doniphon himself; it is his own home. The burning marks the realisation that he will never enter the Promised Land, that to him it means nothing; that he has doomed himself to be a creature of the past, insignificant in the world of the future. By shooting Liberty Valance he has destroyed the only world in which he himself can exist, the world of the gun rather than the book; it is as though Ethan Edwards had perceived that by scalping Scar, he was in reality committing suicide. (pp. 97, 101)

Ransom Stoddart represents rational-legal authority, Tom Doniphon represents charismatic authority. Doniphon abandons his charisma and cedes it, under what amount to false pretences, to Stoddart. In this way charismatic and rational-legal authority are combined in the person of Stoddart and stability thus assured. . . . [The] character of Chihuahua, Doc Holliday's girl in *My Darling Clementine,* is split into two: Miss Lafleur and Lelani, the native princess. One represents the saloon entertainer, the other the non-American in opposition to the respectable Bostonians, Amelia Sarah Dedham and Clementine Carter. In a broad sense, this is a part of a general movement which can be detected in Ford's work to equate the Irish, Indians and Polynesians as traditional communities, set in the past, counterposed to the march forward to the American future, as it has turned out in reality, but assimilating the values of the American future as it was once dreamed. (p. 101)

Peter Wollen, "The Auteur Theory," in his Signs and Meaning in the Cinema *(copyright © 1969 by Peter Wollen), Indiana University Press, 1969, pp. 74-115.**

JOSEPH McBRIDE and MICHAEL WILMINGTON

Time has proven *Young Mr. Lincoln* one of John Ford's finest works. Ford takes the legend of the youthful Lincoln —his rustic humor, his love for Ann Rutledge, his craftiness as a lawyer—and weaves it into a simple elegaic tapestry, alive with nuance. It is a magical film, deriving its strength and charm from what Sergei Eisenstein described as its "stylized daguerrotype manner that is in unison with the moral character of Lincoln's sentences" and from its genesis in a "womb of national and popular spirit." As Ford, in 1939, began to immerse himself in the landscape of the American past, he became preoccupied with the tortures and consolations of memory. The vague melancholia which plays around the edges of the luminous images of *Stagecoach, Young Mr. Lincoln,* and *Drums Along the Mohawk* reflects a Sisyphean desire to push past an unbreachable boundary—the boundary of time.

The cherishing of a momentary image, immutable in its delicacy and precision of framing, begins to assume obsessive proportions as shot after shot rolls inexorably away. It is as if the very perfection of the image is the cause of its transience. Nostalgia is not an adequate word to describe the feeling called up by such an image; it is something more urgent, more desperate, almost like the feverish sense of being trapped in a maze. The populist optimism which suffuses the pioneer films of 1939 begins to be weighed down by a regret for the loss of possibilities, the loss of primitive simplicity, and in particular, the loss of family.

Ford is both an iconographer and an iconoclast. After setting up a precise, harmonious composition, he likes to get the actors going before they are completely familiar with their lines, creating a freshness and rambunctiousness which stands in curious contrast with the rigor of the framing. This is more than a directorial trick; it is a vital part of his outlook. He loves to seek out the common aspects of legendary characters and the heroic aspects of unknown characters. . . . His viewpoint is based on the recognition that while great events revolve around the smallest moments of individual decision, those very decisions are a response to inevitable social and historical forces. (p. 13)

Ford neither embalms Lincoln with reverence nor turns him coyly into a "folk hero." This Lincoln is a rustic but never a buffoon; despite his immaturity, all of his actions possess a natural dignity. Ford humanizes him with a kind of affectionate mock derision. But Lincoln is also a self-conscious comic and entertainer; the film's Stephen Douglas . . . says of him, "Lincoln is a story-teller. Like all such actors, he revels in boisterous applause." . . .

Ford chooses to explore the mundane moments in which his universal qualities are closest to the surface. It was Lincoln's equanimity and sense of understatement, after all, which allowed him to triumph over the more flamboyant politicians. To Ford, he is a fascinating mixture of the idealist and the charlatan, and the portrait combines a Northerner's skepticism with a Southerner's idolatry. (p. 15)

Joseph McBride and Michael Wilmington, "'Young Mr. Lincoln'," in Film Heritage *(copyright 1971 by F. A. Macklin), Vol. 6, No. 4, Summer, 1971, pp. 13-18, 32.*

ROBIN WOOD

One way of defining the relationship of Ford's late films to his previous work would be to compare *The Man Who Shot Liberty Valance* with *My Darling Clementine.* One's immediate reaction to the juxtaposition may at first seem paradoxical: that the later film is more complex but less rich. In fact, the sense that *Clementine* is the less complex work proves on reflection to be illusory: the impression derives simply from the fact that its complexities are experienced as resolvable in a constructive way, the different positive values embodied in East and West, in civilization and wilderness, felt to be ultimately reconcilable and mutually fertilizing. There is, it is true, as in all of Ford's westerns a pervading note of nostalgia to be taken into account. But the tone of the opening and close of *Liberty Valance* is more than nostalgic: it is overtly elegiac.

It is, however, the long central section of *Liberty Valance* that most invites comparison with *Clementine,* and the difference of tone here is very marked. It is partly determined by the movement away from location shooting to studio work in the later film, and partly by the characterization: both tend strongly towards stylization. The sense of community is certainly there in *Liberty Valance*—in the restaurant, the school-room scene, the political meeting—but it is sketched rather than lovingly created. It is not that there is an absence of detail; what is lacking in the later film and present in the earlier is something much less tangible, something perhaps only describable in loose terms such as "aura" but palpably *there* in *Clementine*. . . . The characterization in the later film is very much broader, two-dimensional, verging in several cases on the comic-grotesque. . . . It is difficult to make these distinctions without suggesting that *Liberty Valance* is the inferior film, and this is not my aim (I think both reach a level of achievement where discriminations of the A-is-better-than-B kind become merely petty and academic). All I want is to establish here, as starting point, the different natures of the two films, and to suggest that there is more than one possible explanation. (p. 8)

Ford's westerns have always implicitly acknowledged that American civilization was built on the subjugation of the Indians; it is his attitude to that fact that changes. It is obvious that Indians in westerns are not just a people but a concept; they have a basic mythic meaning on which individual directors ring many changes but which remains an underlying constant. As savages, they represent the wild, the untamed, the disruptive, the vital forces that remain largely unassimilable into any civilization man has so far elaborated: in psychological terms, the forces of the id. (p. 11)

Central to Ford's work is the belief in the value of tradition. This is clearly what attracts him so much to the cavalry—*his* cavalry, for, despite the authenticity of material details of dress, ritual, etc., it is obviously a highly personal creation. In the trilogy, the cavalry becomes Ford's answer to mortality and transience. Individuals come and go, but the continuity of tradition is unbroken, the individual gaining a kind of immortality through the loss of his individuality and assimilation into the tradition. The emphasis is on continuity rather than development: indeed, the moral objection to the end of *Fort Apache* is that it deliberately and perversely eschews the possibility of development by insisting that nothing in the tradition must change. (p. 13)

In Ford's presentation of a growing civilization in *Clementine* and a "permanent" civilization in the cavalry films, nostalgia plays a key role. It is a paradox of the cavalry films, in fact, that "the army" is regarded as at once unchanging and in the past—it isn't the modern army. Ford's respect for the past works on various levels, in his casting as much as in the lovingly detailed re-creation of time and place. . . .

It is easy to argue that, in *Clementine, Wagonmaster* and the cavalry trilogy, Ford is primarily concerned with constructing a value system, only secondarily with depicting various stages in American civilization. Yet the two impulses are so closely interwoven as to be really inseparable. For his vision to retain its vitality, it was necessary for him to feel at least a possible continuity between the civilization depicted in his films and that of contemporary America. Already in the Forties this must have been difficult; by the Sixties it had clearly become impossible. What can Ford possibly be expected to make of contemporary American society—whether one calls it disintegrating or permissive—where no values are certain or constant, all traditions questioned and most rejected, all continuity disrupted, and where the army is a dirty word? Yet how could he possibly remain unaffected by it, unless his art became finally petrified and sterile? What is lost in *Liberty Valance* that was triumphantly present in *Clementine* is faith; hence the film's elegiac tone, and the sad, and very saddening, lack of conviction in the subsequent films.

Returning at last to *Cheyenne Autumn,* we can now clearly see the effect on Ford's structure of values of the reversal-patterns: it is, quite simply, undermined, and falls in ruins. The change in Ford's attitude to American civilization can be vividly illuminated by juxtaposing his two Wyatt Earps and the communities for which they are spokesmen. . . . An obvious weakness in *Cheyenne Autumn* is Ford's failure to define a coherent response to Deborah. . . . One can explain his failure with the character in terms of a clash between his original concept and the conventional noble heroine. The problem is that Deborah most of the time seems silly and ineffectual, with her ludicrous inculcation of the alphabet, but the spectator is never sure that she is meant to be, so that the foolishness comes to seem in Ford as much as in the character. Deborah's ineffectuality is the more disappointing in that there are signs near the beginning of the film that she was partly meant to embody values that would effectively challenge those invested in the cavalry, and especially the Fordian nostalgia: she tells Widmark in the schoolhouse scene that he thinks only about the past, but she thinks of the future. Nothing in the film really fulfills the promise of radical questioning implicit in that moment.

Centrally revealing in the film is the incident involving Sergeant Wichowsky . . . and his decision not to re-enlist. . . . No reason is given for his change of mind: perhaps none in necessary: there is simply nothing else for the man to do. And this is precisely Ford's position. The cavalry values have become shallow and worn: nowhere in the film is the treatment of the cavalry warmed and enriched with the loving commitment that characterized the trilogy. Yet, although Ford sees this well enough, like Wichowsky he can only "rejoin" them. (p. 14)

Ford's values are not really reversed; they are just disastrously weakened. His commitment to the cavalry is a commitment to the establishment; when he tries to place the Cheyenne at the center of his value-system, he merely turns them into an alternative establishment, but without the richness and complexity of the cavalry world of the earlier films. The conception remains obstinately paternalist, the Indians' stiff and boring nobility thinly concealing Ford's condescension. . . . *Cheyenne Autumn* is a film without any really convincing positive center that yet never quite dares take the plunge into despair.

For all its failures, *Cheyenne Autumn* is a sufficiently rich and substantial film for some sort of positive case to be made out for it. . . . *Donovan's Reef* is formally a mess: it quite lacks *Hatari!*'s relaxed but unifying rhythm. Its narrative line is hopelessly broken-backed, Amelia Dedham's capitulation to the Ailakaowa way of life being so rapid (and so perfunctorily chartered) that by half-way through the film there seems absolutely no reason why she should not simply be Told All, and the resulting plot-maneuvers to eke out the narrative before the final denouement become tedious and irritating in the extreme. This may seem a superficial objection—an apparently weak narrative line, after all, may serve (as in *Hatari!*) merely as a pretext for a series of thematic variations. But there is a difference between the almost unnoticeable narrative of *Hatari!* and the positive annoyance of that in *Donovan's Reef,* and the slipshod impression the film makes on this level seems to me symptomatic of a more general slovenliness and unconcern. (pp. 15-16)

Donovan's Reef is only interesting if one ignores the film and concentrates on its abstractable motifs; it can be defended only by a method that precludes any close reading of what is actually on the screen.

The tiresome and protracted buffoonery of *Donovan's Reef*, far from embodying any acceptable system of values, merely conceals an old man's disillusionment at the failure of his ideals to find fulfillment. The sadness inherent in Ford's situation reaches partial expression in *Seven Women,* which is why that film is so much less irritating. . . . [If] the film is Ford's acknowledgement of the disintegration of everything he had believed in, it is all done at several removes. He has fled not only to the other end of the world but to (for him) eccentric and partly uncongenial subject-matter. . . . The result is at best an accomplished minor work, though that is perhaps a generous estimate of a film that only intermittently transcends the schematic conventionalities of its script. There are numerous incidental felicities of *mise-en-scène,* but of the kind that suggest an old master skillfully applying his "touches" rather than an artist passionately involved in his material. (pp. 16-17)

My chief impression of *Seven Women* is of hollowness. The essence of the film is a thinly concealed nihilism. . . . [On] the whole Ford's sense of positive human value seems greatly enfeebled.

It would be ungenerous to end on such a note. My primary aim is not to offer gratuitous insult to the failed late works of one of the cinema's great masters, but to right an injustice; for it seems to me that sentimentally to hail films like *Donovan's Reef* and *Seven Women* as masterpieces is insulting to Ford's real achievement. That achievement depended on a commitment to ideals which the society Ford lives in has signally failed to fulfill. But that invalidates neither the ideals nor the films. One shouldn't expect Ford to be able to cope with the kind of radical reorientation the failure of those ideals within American society demanded. The late films, certainly, have their poignance, but it is the product of their failure, not of their strength. (p. 17)

Robin Wood, "Shall We Gather at the River?: The Late Films of John Ford," in Film Comment *(copyright © 1971 Film Comment Publishing Corporation; all rights reserved), Vol. 7, No. 3, Fall, 1971, pp. 8-17.*

JOHN BAXTER

On all levels of Ford's work, Catholic dogma, philosophy and imagery play an important role. At the most basic, religious morality affects his choice of plots; speaking of sexual subjects, he remarked "they would be against my nature, my religion and my natural inclinations." A powerful religious conscience is apparent in his selection of the moral lessons for which his films are always vehicles. All of these reflect Catholic thinking. He supports the concept of a "just war" in favour of the American liberal view best synopsised as "War is hell, but . . . ," assigns to large social groups a collective piety, implies in all deaths the existence of an afterlife, accentuated by his habit of bringing back the dead, either in concluding flashbacks, or by implication in the form of portraits, themselves imitative of religious images; the quasi-devotional offering of flowers before portraits of women is common in his films, yet another aspect of his veneration of the Virgin Mary. (pp. 32-3)

As echoes of the Holy Family, the Trinity and the eternal Church enrich many of Ford's most moving films, so subsidiary Catholic themes like the parable of the Prodigal Son distinguish his more personal works, those films that, over the years, he has chosen as his favourites. Many share the theme of a man who breaks away from his community and beliefs, experiences a crisis of faith, returns to the fold and is welcomed back. That the community and beliefs are often spiritual, and the welcome death is immaterial, since it is made clear throughout Ford's films that a death for one's principles guarantees immortality. . . . This key theme, and the larger issue of martyrdom for a cause, is examined most ambitiously in two of Ford's least seen and discussed films, *Mary of Scotland* . . . and *The Fugitive*. . . . (p. 59)

Nevertheless, Ford's vision unites them, making each film a work of arresting if occasionally obscure quality, deserving closer attention. Only Ford, who likes both, seems to have any genuine appreciation of their merit. (p. 60)

[Both] films end with the same symbol of resurrection; as Mary mounts the scaffold, the camera tilts off her exalted face to the stormy sky and the thunder of her lover's pipers while, as the priest dies in front of a firing squad, his wooden cross in his hand as Mary's gold one gleams on her breast, the fact of his assumption into heaven is conveyed by the same shots of the sky and the action of his killer crossing himself in an image of absolution. Between these two moments, both have fought a losing battle with their destinies, resisting the pain and death they know has been prepared for them, but succumbing finally to the moral necessity of fate. In fighting to stay alive, they sacrifice their integrity. . . . (p. 60)

Deaths in both films are given a powerfully heightened significance. (p. 65)

Mary of Scotland, though superbly engineered by Ford and his collaborators, is essentially a studio production in which Ford's usual imagery has insufficient room to expand, but *The Fugitive,* by contrast, is one of his most personal and deeply significant works, its examination of religious conscience making it fit to be compared with the greatest European films on this theme. Far from being the "dishonest" work of *Sequence*'s estimation, *The Fugitive* if often painfully frank and open in its dealing with a subject obviously close to Ford's emotions; its faults, and one does not deny their existence, stem from the director's characteristic inability to function as a detached stylist when his feelings are engaged. The use of Ford's language of religious symbolism is, one admits, often too obvious for true stylistic balance; contrasts between characters are drawn on many occasions with a lack of subtlety that reduces some scenes to a grotesque level of melodrama, and Fonda lacks the detail in his character that might have made him less a symbol and more a man. But if one balances against these the richness of the conception, the depth of feeling in almost every gesture and scene, the insight Ford so clearly conveys into the nature of belief and the higher motivations of spirituality, they seem minor, ruffles on the surface of an otherwise smooth and confident work. (p. 67)

Among his films on the destruction of communities, *The Last Hurrah* . . . represents Ford's furthest excursion into the modern world, whose homogenous and unstructured society he plainly despises. [It] is ostensibly the story of one man's fight to keep alive some of the civic virtues of an earlier age, a fight he is doomed to lose. . . . [It is long, episodic and like *They Were Expendable,*] more fabric than story. . . . The useful device of Skeffington calling in his newsman nephew Adam Caulfield . . . to observe the campaign, which he fears will be the last of its kind, allows Ford to interpolate long passages in which the mayor reexamines his background, the community that has sustained him through a long political career and the social values he now sees about to be crushed by the soulless automation of Twentieth century life. (pp. 154-55)

Ford shows the mayor drawn to a dead and forgotten past, and his contemplation of the dark and silent alleys of the tenement suggests a world from which its inhabitants have retreated, leaving only Skeffington as a last lonely watchman. (p. 158)

In Skeffington, Ford sees the essential emptiness of a life devoted to tradition, in which mere age is an assurance of value. The inflexibility of the Plymouth Club begins to find its reflection in the mayor's actions as the film progresses, implying that he is destroyed not, as in Edwin O'Conner's novel, by the combined power of technology and new techniques of persuasion, but by his own irrelevance to the society he leads. His lack of understanding, his manipulation of the community for what he conceives to be its own good is suggested in an early shot where the mayor, respecting a tradition he has established, receives suppliant voters in the luxurious foyer of the mayoral mansion, sun flooding in through the open door as he greets with heavy political hospitality his first client. The contrast between his poor background and this piece of stage management interrupts our admiration of Skeffington, Man of the People, and hints at a later rightful collapse.

Skeffington is not, like Lincoln or MacArthur, a charismatic figure embodying the virtues of his society, nor a hero who inspires the community in time of danger and goes to his death peaceful in the knowledge that it has been saved, but rather a last dinosaur left behind by history, a casualty of the dead areas between great movements in which Ford often chooses to place his stories of communities in decline. (pp. 160-61)

Donovan's Reef, Ford's last important film, eclipses the later *Seven Women* which, although both assured and provocative in its analysis of contrasts between professed religious and social feeling and the more real convictions sometimes held by apparent outsiders, relates essentially in theme to Ford's late Thirties and Forties period of soul-searching and realignment of religious convictions. So central are the issues of *Donovan's Reef* to Ford's dilemma as an artist that it is difficult not to see it as his final testament, and its analysis of morality as the most profound summation of a preoccupation that has dominated his films. Conventional categorisation is less and less appropriate to Ford as his career progresses in skill and authority, and his last films, in which he is most in command of his subjects and less concerned than ever with the superficialities of entertainment, transcend descriptions like "comedy" and "Western" to approach the heart of his essential interest, the relationship of men to each other, and to God. (pp. 172-73)

John Baxter, in his The Cinema of John Ford *(copyright © 1971 by John Baxter), A. S. Barnes & Co., 1971, 176 p.*

THOMAS H. PAULY

[In *The Grapes of Wrath* the] emphasis falls upon the sentimental aspect of the conditions confronting the Joads. At the outset this takes the character of the loss of a home which deprives the family of its essential connection with the land. Tom's initial return assumes the character of a search for a place of refuge from the suffering and hostility he has been forced to endure in prison and on his truck ride. That everything has changed is made clear by his encounter with Casy, but the full impact of this upheaval is registered only when he beholds the vacant, crumbling house in which he was raised and hears Muley's distracted tale of how his reverence for the land has been desecrated. . . .

In dramatizing the intense suffering these people experience, [Muley's] lines serve the more important function of locating its source. The former agrarian way of life predicated upon man's intimate attachment to the land has given way to an economy of industrialization with its efficiency, practicality and inhumanity. For Tom and his fellow farmers, there is no possibility of retaliation. The fury that drives Muley to take up a gun produces only frustration and helpless dejection because there is no enemy to shoot. The man on the caterpillar turns out to be his neighbor who is trapped by the same problem of survival. The machines that level their homes, like the foreclosures which are delivered in dark, sinister automobiles, cannot be associated with particular individuals; they are the weapons of a system devoid of both personality and humanity. (p. 206)

However great may be their need for food and money, keeping the family together, Ma Joad makes clear, is the most pressing concern. She sees that nourishment involves the spirit as well and in the face of the increasingly depersonalized world confronting her, the shared concerns of the family offer the only remaining source of humanity. These become the basic issues by which the audience measures the significance of the ensuing trip to California. As Ford dramatizes them, the policemen who harass the Joads, the strawbosses who dictate to them, the thugs who break up the dances and union gatherings are, like the handbills that bring them to California, products of a sinister conspiracy beyond human control. (pp. 206-07)

The Grapes of Wrath, however, is more than a mere drama of defeat. The futility of individualism and the breakdown of the family furnish, in the end, a distinct source of optimism. Having witnessed the miserable living conditions in which the Joads have futilely struggled to endure—the filthy tent in the clapboard road camp, the concentration of starving people in Hooverville, the gloomy squalor of the cabin at the Keene ranch—the audience is now introduced to a utopia of cooperative socialism which has been as scrupulously sanitized of communism as it is of filth. In contrast to the derogatory view expressed earlier in the movie, working with the government is shown to offer a more valid prospect of salvation than fighting against the prevailing conditions; at the Wheat Patch camp the spirit of Tom's involvement with Casy is realised without the self-defeating violence and killing. . . .

Even the language has been changed to accord with this new society; one finds here not a shelter, a house or a home, but a "sanitary unit." Though this community has been conceived to accord with the depersonalized society outside its gates, it has also incorporated a basic respect for human dignity. It is a world characterized by its Saturday dance with its democratic acceptance, its well-controlled exclusion of the forces of anarchy, its ritualistic incorporation of the outdated family into a healthy new society. . . . (p. 208)

The Grapes of Wrath is a fine movie, but it is considerably flawed. (p. 209)

Thomas H. Pauly, "'Gone With the Wind' and 'The Grapes of Wrath' As Hollywood Histories of the Depression," in Journal of Popular Film *(copyright © 1974 by Sam L. Grogg, Jr., Michael T. Marsden, and John G. Nachbar), Vol. III, No. 3, 1974, pp. 203-18.**

FRANÇOIS TRUFFAUT

Ford was an artist who never said the word "art," a poet who never mentioned "poetry."

What I love in his work is that he always gives priority to characters. For a long time when I was a journalist, I criticized his conceptions of women—I thought they were too nineteenth century—but when I became a director, I realized that because of him a splendid actress like Maureen O'Hara had been able to play some of the best female roles in American cinema between 1941 and 1957.

John Ford might be awarded (the same goes for Howard Hawks) the prize for "invisible direction." The camera work of these two great storytellers is never apparent to the eye. There are very few camera movements, only enough to follow a character, and the majority of shots are fixed and always taken at the same distance. It's a style that creates a suppleness and fluidity that can be compared to Maupassant or Turgenev.

With a kind of royal leisure, John Ford knew how to make the public laugh . . . or cry. The only thing he didn't know how to do was to bore them.

François Truffaut, "God Bless John Ford" (1974), in his The Films in My Life, *translated by Leonard Mayhew (copyright © 1975 by, Flammarion; translation copyright © 1978 by, Simon & Schuster; reprinted by permission of Simon & Schuster, a Division of Gulf & Western Corporation; originally published as* Les Films de ma vie, *Flammarion, 1975), Simon & Schuster, 1978, p. 63.*

JOSEPH McBRIDE and MICHAEL WILMINGTON

Stagecoach revolutionized the Western. Nowadays it is fashionable to speak of it as 'the Western which created the clichés,' but *Stagecoach* did not create clichés nor even sustain them. It defined Western archetypes and created a new frame of reference rich in irony and sophistication. . . .

The effect of the film has been mixed. On the one hand, the self-consciousness it brought to the form has enabled the Western to continually transform itself, chameleon-like, to pressures in the society which produces it. Before *Stagecoach,* the Western seemed to be dying; after *Stagecoach,* it became the one permanently popular film genre. (p. 53)

What makes *Stagecoach* so durable, however, is not its historical significance but the vividness with which it creates a dream landscape from the American past and peoples it with simple and striking characters who, despite their reincarnation in countless 'A' and 'B' Westerns, still retain a believable ambivalence and depth. . . . [What] seemed to delight Ford most in *Stagecoach* was the possibility of glorifying disrepute by plunging a group of pariahs into danger and having the most apparently abject of them emerge as heroes. (p. 54)

[Like] all good fables, *Stagecoach* has a universal application. It is the idea of the noble outlaw, the 'good bad man' represented most concretely by . . . the Ringo Kid, which provides the film's centre. Outlaws (and outcasts in general) have always fascinated Ford not so much for their rebellion as for the subtle ways they are linked to the society which scorns them. They act *for* society in ways society cannot see, and they understand society better than society understands itself. Their rebellion (even at its most complex level, that of Ethan in *The Searchers*) is as much a matter of circumstance as of temperament. (p. 55)

The ending is a paean to primitivism, but it is important to realize that the film is endorsing primitivism as an *ideal* rather than as a viable reality. . . . *Stagecoach* leaves the question of American imperialism, the Cavalry vs. the Indians, tantalizingly unresolved. The Indians are totally one-dimensional here, but Ford's attitude to the role of the Cavalry, which will undergo complex metamorphoses in his later work as his interest in the Indians grows, is strangely ambiguous. . . . (p. 56)

Both the challenge and the salvation are metaphorical. What was it, after all, that threw the outcasts together but the rupture of order in their own lives? The war-ravaged desert through which the stage passes (the curtains on the windows for ever whipping in the wind) becomes a metaphor for the instability of this archetypal primitive community, thrown together of necessity and chance and forced to rediscover the meaning of society. (pp. 58, 60)

[The exchange between the doctor and the sheriff] adds the perfect note of irony to the film's portrait of society. The primitive couple's flight into the freedom of the wilderness is seen through the eyes of society's watchdogs, the lawman and the doctor-poet. It is as if they are watching their own dream being realized at a distance—a dream whose beauty lies in its contrivance and improbability. This is Ford's vision of primitivism and the American past. We can feel it, watch it and cherish it, but we cannot quite touch or recapture it. (p. 62)

It is characteristic of Ford that *They Were Expendable* did not attempt to offer an upbeat, jingoistic view of the war, but dwelt instead on its most hopeless moments—the crushing defeat in the Philippines after the bombing of Pearl Harbor. It was at this point, this 'tragic moment', that the human meaning of the war could be most clearly and deeply felt. (p. 75)

They Were Expendable is probably unique for a war film of the period in that it contains not a shred of enemy-baiting. In fact, we never even *see* an enemy soldier or sailor. This can be attributed in part to Ford's professionalism—the warrior's instinctive respect for his enemy's ability—and partly to his respect for the integrity of separate cultures. . . . [What] the invisibility of enemy troops gives *They Were Expendable,* most of all, is a pervasive sense of fatalism. (pp. 79-80)

Ford's use of the family as a metaphor for national solidarity governs all the relationships in *They Were Expendable*. The squadron is representative of the national 'family', Brickley the stern but understanding father, and Ryan the prodigal son. Ford places great emphasis on the touching callowness of the ensigns—most memorably in the shot of a very young sailor drinking a glass of milk as the men toast their retiring doctor—and on the paternal overtones of Brickley's authority. (p. 82)

Ford shows the squadron as a group of ghostly shadows on the ground as Brickley leaves his command post and, eyes shadowed by the brim of his hat, gives his last order: 'You older men . . . take care of the kids.' (pp. 83, 85)

[There is an] explicit point of contact between [*Fort Apache* and *Liberty Valance*] which has gone unnoticed; it occurs at the exact moment of climax in Thursday's tragedy. Conferring with his officers on what to do about Cochise's flight from the reservation, Thursday murmurs to himself, 'The Man Who Brought Cochise Back'. Ford underscores the legendary and megalomaniac implications of the phrase by having Collingwood remove his pipe from his mouth and stare at Thursday in shock, realizing that from then on the commander will be working for his own posterior glory at the expense of his men's lives. It is instructive, in this context of individualism vs. community, to contrast Ford's handling of the massacre itself—the group bunched tightly together waiting for the Indians, and dying as one in long-shot under a cloud of dust from the Indians' charge—with the massacres in two other superb films about the Custer legend, Arthur Penn's *Little Big Man* and Raoul Walsh's *They Died With Their Boots On,* both of which show the troopers deployed at distances from each other, dying not *en masse* but one by one, as individuals. (pp. 106, 108)

What makes the ending so complex and powerful, and so difficult to reduce to a simple statement, is that Ford, . . . forces the audience's collaboration. He does this by . . . forcing us to see through York's lie, and perhaps most disturbing of all, by forcing us to realize that we are sympathizing with men who are following a suicidal course. Ford has not only exposed the danger of Thursday's play-acting at legend, he has given that play-acting the same glorification—in his romantic, 'magnificent' depiction of Thursday's Charge—that he ridicules through the reporter's naïve description of the painting. And, daringly, he repeats the glorification moments after ridiculing it: he has York stand at a window eulogizing the Cavalry while an image of marching men is romantically superimposed on the glass. (p. 108)

The remarkable achievement of *Fort Apache* is that it enables us to see with Brechtian clarity that an insane system may be perpetuated by noble men, and indeed, that it *needs* noble and dedicated men to perpetuate itself. Whether this will shock or intrigue a viewer probably depends upon his devotion, or lack of it, to an ideological system. It is comforting to think that evil is done by beasts, monsters or 'pigs', but profoundly disturbing to realize that it is done by human beings. (p. 109)

The Rising of the Moon and *The Last Hurrah* look at the same subject from different sides of the Atlantic: the dwindling away of Irish communal traditions in the face of modern social pressures. The latter film, which deals with the Irish immigrant community in Boston, has hard, bright, sculptural lighting, as if it were all taking place in a mausoleum, and is climaxed with the most grandly protracted deathbed scene since Dickens (a full eighteen minutes of screen time). *The Rising of the Moon* is jovially melancholic, for the Ould Sod is within touching range. On the face of it, the three stories which make up the film seem arbitrarily selected to illustrate different 'humours' in the Irish character. . . . [However], *The Rising of the Moon* reveals a rigorous, almost schematic orderliness. It deals with what could be called the national consciousness of the Irish people (more precisely, the people of the Irish Republic), evolving a concept of folk heroism by means of a subterranean chain of logic running through the three stories. Ford's better-known Irish films, *The Informer* and *The Quiet Man,* both present the land through a single character's perspective; here, Ireland itself is the hero, a mass hero gradually revealed through successive incarnation in a series of individuals. It is the dream-world of *The Quiet Man* brought into the waking air, an *insider's* view of the national mystique. The soft pastels of the earlier film give way to the sharp, argumentative clarity of black-and-white.

All three of the apparently dissimilar stories centre on the Irish people's anarchic tendency to resist any kind of externally applied order. (pp. 125-26)

[After being accused of making illegal liquor,] Dan's self-defence at the impromptu 'trial' before the magistrate—conducted over cups in his own home—is a long, eloquent harangue, similar in spirit to O'Casey's words, about the ancient and honourable art of liquor-making, which is 'not what it used to be'. Old Dan is speaking for Ford. . . . (p. 128)

[*The Sun Shines Bright*] is simultaneously a work of nostalgic Americana, a raucous comedy, a caustic social protest and a Christian parable. And Charles Winninger's Judge William Pittman Priest is probably Ford's idealized self-image—humble, sagacious, comic, melancholic. Billy Priest, the old clown who sneaks drinks at a temperance rally and has to take a dose of 'medicine' to 'get my heart started' in moments of crisis; Billy Priest, who leads the funeral procession of a prostitute on election day; Billy Priest, who leaves his Confederate encampment to escort a 'captured' Yankee flag back to the GAR Hall; Billy Priest, the indomitable rebel who defies a town gone mad from lynch fever; this *is* John Ford. (p. 136)

Like Mark Twain, Ford is sufficiently sure of his touch to be able to ridicule the sources of racial discrimination even while brushing round the edges of stereotypes. He could never *ignore* a man's origins or the colour of his skin because, as a social commentator, he must acknowledge that these are among the basic data of American culture. Ethnic humour is never divisive in Ford, but always a sign of sanity and fellow-feeling, a refusal to evade distinguishing characteristics in the name of a spurious and enfeebling homogeneity. (p. 137)

The Sun Shines Bright is like a *précis* of the Judge's life, a testing and a summary of his ideas in a series of events which dovetail into each other with the uncanny symmetry of a dream. But the film finally seems less concerned with the Judge himself than with the community's reaction to him. (pp. 138-39)

The Sun Shines Bright is closest in spirit among Ford's works to *Wagon Master,* because like Elder Wiggs, the Judge proselytizes Christian values through *secular* communal activity, as the name 'Judge Priest' indicates. The fact that there does not appear to be a priest or a minister in Fairfield underscores the importance Ford places on personalized religion. . . . The moral vision Ford gives us in *The Sun Shines Bright* is that of a child, a magical, exaggerated, innocent vision in which a lynch mob, after being rebuffed like a gang of unruly schoolboys, undergoes such a complete transformation that it reappears at the end of the film marching behind a banner reading 'He Saved Us From Ourselves'. (pp. 140-41)

For all its sense of communal life, the film contains none of the traditional family unity which gave *How Green Was My Valley* its sense of order. The Judge is a widower (this is not made clear in the film, though it may have been in a cut scene, but the most poignant moment in *Judge Priest* was the character's address to his dead wife's portrait); the general's family is chaotically scattered; and the prostitutes are a constant Fordian testament to maternal longing. The absence of nuclear family life is actually the impetus for the film's religious spirit, its gathering of all the characters, however old, eccentric, wretched or abandoned, under the mantle of 'children of God'. The prostitutes, the old soldiers and, especially, the blacks, form communal 'families' based on a childlike sense of protectiveness, and the Judge (who is still 'Little Billy' to the old general) reconstitutes the benevolent paternalism of the fabled Old South by bringing them all together. Pointedly, it is the superannuated and socially disreputable communities within the disorganized community of Fairfield which are its real source of unity and strength. (p. 142)

By any standard of historical accuracy, Ford's view of the Old South is rosy and unreal, and by contemporary standards, his solution to the racial problem is drastically limited by its overtone of paternalist condescension. The beauty of *The Sun Shines Bright* is in its innocence; the film is not a piece of historical documentation but one man's fervent creation of a simpler, kindlier and more gentlemanly America than ever existed. (p. 147)

The Searchers has that clear yet intangible quality which characterises an artist's masterpiece—the sense that [Ford] has gone beyond his customary limits, submitted his deepest tenets to the test, and dared to exceed even what we might have expected of him. Its hero, Ethan Edwards . . . , is a volatile synthesis of all the paradoxes which Ford had been finding in his Western hero since *Stagecoach.* A nomad tortured by his desire for a home. An outlaw and a military hero. A cavalier and a cutthroat. Ethan embarks on a five-year odyssey across the frontier after his brother's family is murdered and his niece taken captive by the Comanches. Like Homer's Ulysses, he journeys through a perilous and bewitching landscape.

Even more than in Ford's earlier Westerns, the land is felt as a living, governing presence. . . . The demons which drive [Ethan] onward, almost against his will, seem to emanate from the 'devilish and grinning' land. The killing of the family, an action horrifyingly abrupt, brutal, and gratuitous, is only the first in a long chain of bizarre events which bedevil Ethan and, finally, drive him mad. Within the classical symmetry of the story—the film begins with a door opening on Ethan riding in from the desert and ends with the door closing on him as he returns to the desert—Ford follows a subjective thread. (pp. 147-48)

[The film is] a crystallisation of the fears, obsessions and contradictions which had been boiling up under the surface of Ford's work since his return from World War II. . . . Ethan is both hero and anti-hero, a man radically estranged from his society and yet driven to act in its name. His strengths and failings, like the promise and danger of the land around him, are inextricable. *The Searchers* is, on the surface, a highly romantic subject—a knightly quest—but the knight's motives are impure, and as the search progresses, Ford begins to undercut his morality.

Ethan starts out seeking the return of his nieces, Debbie and Lucy, but after he finds Lucy's mutilated corpse and realizes that Debbie is being made into an Indian squaw, he becomes nihilistic, seeking only revenge. When he finally catches up with Debbie, he tries to kill her. And the search itself would have been a failure had not Old Mose Harper (a Shakespearean fool . . .) accidently found Debbie after Ethan had spent years losing her trail. Ethan loses her again, and Mose finds her again.

It is this grotesquerie, and the anarchid humour that accompanies it, which the contemporary reviewers found incomprehensible. But Ford's sense of humour is one of his strongest trumps. In his greatest works, the plot line oscillates freely between the tragic and the ridiculous, with the comic elements providing a continuous commentary on the meaning of the drama. The comedy, broad and idiosyncratic and self-conscious as it may seem, is the rough prose to the exalted visual verse. Just as Ford's few actual comedies have had notably grim undertones (such as *The Quiet Man,* which is about the romantic fantasies of a guilt-ridden boxer), his tragedies always have undertones of giddiness. . . . His view of drama embraces the conviction that what is most noble, most poignant and most terrifying in life is frequently a hair's breadth away from howling absurdity. What makes films such as *The Searchers* and *Seven Women* great is the striking manner in which they reconcile the noble with the absurd, the way in which their seemingly straightforward situations are shaped to encompass the maddest perversities and still retain a sense of order. When Ford fails, his sense of humour is usually the first casualty. . . .

The first images of *The Searchers* are the invocation of a myth. . . . Ethan rides slowly, silently, inexorably toward the little homestead, Ford cutting again and again from him to the waiting family; the intercutting gives a feeling of magnetic attraction. . . . As Ethan goes to kiss his brother's wife, Ford gives us, for the first time, a full shot of the home, harmonious with the landscape. The home is a shrine of civilisation in the wilderness, a shrine almost as ridiculous as it is sacred, for we see only one other pioneer home in the entire film. The communal impulse around which the generative principles of Ford's universe are organised is centred precariously around these tiny dwellings. The two pioneer families are infinitely precious and infinitely vulnerable.

Ethan is a descendant of Fenimore Cooper's Leatherstocking, whose character, according to Henry Nash Smith in his classic study of the Western myth, *Virgin Land,* is based on a 'theoretical hostility to civilisation'. Ford is usually considered a conservative, but despite his nostalgia for traditional values, the term is somewhat misleading. Like Cooper, he is impatient with the artificial harmony of organised society, as his fascination with the West and with all varieties of nomads, outlaws, outcasts and warriors makes abundantly clear. There is a strong streak of anarchy in his Irish temperament. His characters are typically refugees from constricting societies (Europe, urbanised America) in which once-vital traditions have hardened into inflexible dogmas. The traditions he celebrates are the tribal traditions of honour, justice and fidelity, and all of these come together in the image of the family, the purest form of society.

Ford's heroes, whether they are outlaws (Harry Carey in his early silents, the bandits in *Three Bad Men* and *Three Godfathers,* Ringo in *Stagecoach*) or lawmen (Wyatt Earp in *My Darling Clementine,* the soldiers in the Cavalry films), all have a primitive awe for the family. (This, to Ford, is beyond reason. When a French interviewer asked why the 'theme of family' is so important in his work, he replied, 'You have a mother, don't you?') Some of these men seek revenge for the murder of members of their own families; others sacrifice themselves for orphans; the cavalrymen act to keep the plains secure for the pioneer homesteads. All, to some degree, are also loners and outcasts: their role as the defender of primitive society forces them to live in the wilderness with its enemies, the Indians. But of all Ford's Western heroes, only Ethan turns his violence *against* his family—against Debbie, who could just as well be his own daughter—and that is what makes him such a profound and unsettling figure. (pp. 148, 150)

As the search progresses, it becomes increasingly difficult to appreciate the difference between Ethan's heroism and the villainy of Scar, his Indian nemesis. Ethan hates Indians —is he envious of their freedom? Certainly Scar and Ethan are the only characters who fully understand each other, because their motives are so similar. We learn eventually that the massacre, which seemed at first totally wilful, was performed in revenge for the death of Scar's own children. 'Two sons killed by white men,' he tells Ethan. 'For each son, I take many scalps.' The pattern of primitive revenge is endless; Ethan will eventually take Scar's scalp. . . . There is a very strange scene early in the pursuit when Ethan shoots out the eyes of an Indian corpse so that, according to Comanche belief, the dead man will never enter the spirit-land and will have to 'wander forever between the winds'. Seemingly a blind act of vindictiveness—or a gesture of contempt toward an alien culture—the act in fact has undertones of kinship. Ethan himself is doomed to wander forever between the winds. He takes on the nature of a primitive in desperate recognition of his own failure to find a place in civilised society. (pp. 151-52)

What lures him out of the wilderness is a home impulse—his love for Martha—but it is also an anarchic impulse, for his presence threatens the stability of the family. Ethan's attachment to his sister-in-law is futile, and any overt action would be unthinkable, the shattering of a taboo. (p. 152)

When the massacre occurs (the very day after Ethan's arrival), it has the disturbing feeling of an acting-out of his suppressed desires—destruction of the family and sexual violation of Martha. With the links between Scar and Ethan in mind, it becomes easy to see why Ford, much to the consternation of certain critics, cast a white man in the Indian role. Scar is not so much a character as a crazy mirror of Ethan's desires.

The Searchers stands midway between the 'classical' or psychologically primitive Western and what could be called the 'neoclassical' Western (more commonly, if rather crudely, known as the 'psychological' Western). It was not, of course, the first Western to criticise the basic assumption of the genre—that the solitude of the hero, because it is an instinctive revulsion against the hypocrisy of civilised society, is *a priori* a good thing. In the decade before *The Searchers* appeared, a whole rash of Westerns were made in which the hero's solitude was presented as socially unjust (*High Noon*), wasteful (*The Gunfighter*), callous (*The Naked Spur*), insane (*Red River*), or impossibly pure (*Shane*). Little as Ford is usually influenced by film trends, he could hardly have escaped coming to terms with the radical questions posed by this departure. Shortly before he began shooting *The Searchers,* Ford described it as 'a kind of psychological epic'. The terms are contradictory, certainly, but contradictions are what the film is about. (pp. 152-53)

[The] 'anti-Westerns', particularly *Red River,* jarred Ford into a new area of thinking by suggesting an alternative course for the working-out of the hero's impulses. In the classic *Stagecoach* and *My Darling Clementine,* Ford seemed to be endorsing an uneasy equation between force and morality by portraying revenge as socially beneficial and morally pure. The revenge transformed the community by cleansing it of its internal pressures—which were also the hero's pressures—and it won the hero the community's respect because he had done a necessary deed of which they, because of their civilised stultification, were incapable. When Ringo and Wyatt Earp take leave of Lordsburg and Tombstone at the end, it is of their own volition. Though they are still men of the wilderness, their desires and ideals are close to those of civilised men.

Now what is Ford, of all directors, to do with a hero like Ethan? ***Red River*** may have a parallel plot, but it is really about something altogether different, the maturing of the relationship between Dunson and Matthew. *The Searchers* is about Ethan's relationship to society, and the film's abruptly shifting moods and moral emphases are determined by the imbalances in that relationship. Since Ethan, for instance, finds it impossible to enter society through marriage, all the marriages the film portrays are, in varying degrees, grotesque. Either the female dominates the male (the Edwardses, the Jorgensons), or the female is held in literal bondage to the male (Scar and his wives) or the partners are wildly incongruous (Laurie Jorgenson and the goonish cowboy she turns to in Martin's absence; Martin and Look, the chubby Indian wife he inadvertently buys at a trading post).

Fundamentally alone though Ethan is, all of his dilemmas are shared by the community around him. When Brad Jorgenson learns, as Ethan did, that his lover (Lucy Edwards) has been raped and killed, he rushes madly off to be slain by the Indians, who are lurking in the darkness like the unseen, ungovernable forces of the libido. Martin, who is more restrained and civilised than Ethan, nevertheless resembles Ethan enough to suggest that his continual fleeing into the wilderness, away from Laurie's advances, holds a clue to what drove Ethan and Martha apart in the first place: a fundamental reluctance to become domesticated. Just as Laurie turns to the dull, dependable cowboy in despair of taming Martin, so it must have been that Martha turned to Ethan's dull brother for stability. (pp. 154-55)

Even after Martin becomes, in effect, the hero by attempting to restrain Ethan's nihilism, he is merely following the principles with which the search began. And despite Martin's actions, it is finally Ethan who makes the decision about whether to kill Debbie or bring her home. Gestures against Ethan tend to remain only gestures; minor characters are continually frustrated in their attempts to change his course. Toward the end, Martin cries, 'I hope you die!' and Ethan responds with his characteristic assertion of invulnerability: 'That'll be the day.'

The one white character who is able to give Ethan pause is Clayton, who keeps his schizoid roles of minister and Texas Ranger in a subtle, if disturbing, balance. . . . The most pragmatic of Ford's characters, he is a representative of the civilised order who has won his position by restraining an innate primitivism. He averts his eyes on witnessing Martha's infidelity. . . in acknowledgment of the tissue of discreet lies and tactful evasions which enables a struggling society to stabilise itself.

The difference between Clayton and Ethan is succinctly expressed in their first meeting since the end of the war, when Clayton asks Ethan why he didn't show up for the surrender. 'I don't *believe* in surrenders,' says Ethan, adding sarcastically, 'No—I still got *my* sabre, Reverend. Didn't turn it into no ploughshare, neither.' Ethan, the eternal rebel, carried his rebellion to the point of madness. Clayton compromises, and this is what makes him a leader. The two men are several times seen tossing things back and forth—a canteen, a coin, a gun—in wary gestures of mutual forbearance. Although they never come to blows, they are close to it several times. What holds Ethan back is the same fundamental indecision which holds him back from Scar. To make a decisive move against either one would imply a commitment to either civilisation or primitivism, and Ethan's dilemma is that he can't make the choice. (pp. 156-57)

When Scar dies, it is Martin, the half-breed, who kills him. In transferring the actual heroic deeds, the killing of Scar and the finding of Debbie, to Martin and to Mose, the fool, Ford is destroying the myth of the heroic loner. If Ethan's search is motivated by a desire to preserve the community, then the community, even against its will, must participate in the action. It would never have taken place if the outsider had not initiated it, but it is fundamentally a communal action. If the pragmatists (Clayton, the Jorgensons, Martha) are needed to stabilise society, the visionaries (Ethan, Martin, Mose) are needed to motivate it and define its goals. All, whether they realise it or not, are part of society, a fact which Ford visually underscores with his repeated shots through the doorways of homes. But the film is, as Ford has said, the 'tragedy of a loner': Ethan must reject a society he can neither accept nor understand, and the society must reject him, since he belongs to neither the white nor the Indian world.

Martin belongs to both, which is why he is able to accept both Debbie's miscegenation with Scar and Laurie's desire for a home. Until the search is consummated, however, he is unable to accept Laurie and civilisation, for her perspective is just as distorted as Ethan's. Resplendent in the virginal white of her wedding dress, she urges that Ethan be allowed to kill Debbie because 'Martha would want him to'. Martin has told Laurie that Ethan is 'a man that can go crazy-wild, and I intend to be there to stop him in case he does,' but it is chillingly clear that Ethan's craziness is only quantitatively different from that of civilisation in general. Even the United States Cavalry, which Ford had eulogised in his 1940s Westerns, have by-passed their role as trucekeepers and become vindictive white supremacists. . . . Immediately after Ethan begins slaughtering buffalo so that the Indians will starve, a cavalry bugle merges with his gunshots. Ford gives the cavalry his traditional romantic trappings—jaunty marching lines, 'Garry Owen' on the soundtrack—but he undercuts their romanticism, as he does Ethan's.

The cavalry has frozen into an inflexible role: they make their entrance against a background of snow; they gallop through a river whose natural current has turned to ice; and —pre-dating *Little Big Man* by fourteen years—we are taken into an Indian village whose inhabitants they have massacred. Like Scar and Ethan, the cavalrymen have been trapped in a social tragedy whose terms have been established long before their arrival. The innocent Indians they slaughter, like the family slaughtered by Scar, have become pathetic pawns in a cycle of retribution which will end only when one race exterminates the other. (pp. 157-59)

Miscegenation, next to war itself, is probably the most dramatic form of collision between cultures, and by exploring a community's reaction to miscegenation, Ford is testing its degree of internal tension. The dark man, red or black, occupies a peculiar position in the American mythos: he is both a cultural bogey and a secretly worshipped talisman of the libidinous desires which the white man's culture takes pains to sublimate. The Western genre in both literature and film, which usually replaces the black man with the red man, is particularly expressive of the American psychical dilemma; Leslie Fiedler's celebrated thesis about American culture, which was received with scandalised disbelief at the time of its propagation, is rooted about equally in the writings of Cooper and the New England Puritans. . . . As Ford, starting with *The Sun Shines Bright* in 1953, began to probe deeper and deeper into the causes of social dissolution, racial conflict began to assume almost obsessive proportions in his stories, providing the dramatic centre of *The Searchers, Sergeant Rutledge, Two Rode Together, Cheyenne Autumn, Seven Women* and even the comic *Donovan's Reef.* LeMay's novel lingers over the grisly details of the murders and rapes committed by the Indians on the frontier women. Ford's treatment of the massacre, by contrast, is marked by a devastating elision. The Gothic shot of Scar's shadow falling on Debbie in the graveyard and the fade-out on his blowing the horn are far more suggestive than an actual depiction of the massacre would have been. Our minds work much as Ethan's works when, in the next scene, he stares at the burning home with a fixed expression of horror. He is contemplating the unthinkable.

The emotion Ford emphasises in the moments before the massacre is the women's fear, conveyed through the camera's compulsive pull into a huge close-up of Lucy screaming (a very uncharacteristic shot for Ford and, as such, a doubly brutal shock) and through Martha's anxiety for Debbie. When Ethan, toward the middle of the film, finds a group of white women driven mad by their years among the Indians (one of them croons distractedly to a doll), he reacts with revulsion, and the camera pulls in to a large close-up of *his* face. He has become possessed by the same fear which possessed the women in the home.... It is revealing that the arch-racist Ethan finds Martin's 'marriage' to Look, the Indian woman, amusing rather than frightening. It has nothing to do with white culture. If a white man impregnates a dark woman, he is planting his seed in an alien culture; but if a dark man impregnates a white woman he is, in the eyes of the primitive white, violating her. The scene in which Ethan finds the mad white women is so disturbing that the spectator may momentarily wonder whether Ford is not succumbing to the same fear of miscegenation and trying to convey it to us with the subjective camera movement toward Ethan. But our first glimpse of Debbie as a woman makes it clear that the fear has a purely neurotic base. Like Martin , she has accepted her dual heritage; resigned to her role as Scar's wife ('These are my people'), she nevertheless remembers her childhood ('I remember . . . from always . . .'). Miscegenation has not destroyed her identity but deepened it. (pp. 159-60, 162)

[During Ethan's climactic encounter with Debbie, it] is not *just* the physical contact that prevents Ethan from killing the last of his family; there is also a sense of the profound memories which are flooding into his consciousness as he touches her. The lifting gesture, which seems almost involuntary, recalls the moment inside the home long ago when he lifted the child Debbie into his arms. Gone now is the hatred caused by his knowledge that she has slept with the man who violated his lover; gone are the years when she only existed for him as Scar's squaw. The proximity of his scalping of Scar is vital. When Ethan rises after the scalping, we do not see the corpse. We see only his face, and it is a face almost identical to the one which looked upon the burning home, a face purged of all passion. When Ethan chases Debbie, it is more out of reflex (this is the moment he has been steeling himself to for years) than from any real hatred or desire to kill her. He has been freed from his memories of Martha by a deeper, tribal memory.

At the end, the symbolic acknowledgment of white and red heritages takes place as Martin accepts Laurie and the family embraces Debbie still wearing her Indian clothes, on the doorstep of their home. And it is then that Ethan, who seemed on the verge of entering the Jorgensons' doorway (the future), steps aside to let the young couple pass him by and turns away to 'wander forever between the winds' like his Indian nemesis. Scar and Ethan, blood-brothers in their commitment to primitive justice, have sacrificed themselves to make civilisation possible. This is the meaning of the door opening and closing on the wilderness. It is the story of America. (pp. 162-63)

What makes Ford's work in the 1960s so moving is his courage in trying to come to terms with problems he had tended to simplify or evade in the past; a desire to cut through long-accepted dogmas and traditions to find out 'what really happened'. One need only compare Hallie in *Liberty Valance* with her earlier counterpart, Ann Rutledge in *Young Mr Lincoln,* to see how disillusioned Ford was becoming with the woman's traditional role as catalyst for the man's ambitions. (pp. 198-99)

If there is one characteristic common to all Ford's heroines, it is this: they suffer. Their children leave home, their husbands are killed, their homes are burned. If they are single, they struggle to keep their men from leaving or neglecting them; if they are prostitutes, they are humiliated; if they are queens, they are beheaded. (p. 199)

To emphasize the unnaturalness of the group's isolation in *Seven Women,* Ford shoots the film in a hermetically sealed studio set with only a few glimpses of the world outside that the women are trying to ignore. The perverse thing about these missionaries is that, in their lust for purity, they have constructed a sanctuary which all but invites attack. Just as Ethan's odyssey in *The Searchers* becomes a parody of a heroic quest, the mission in *Seven Women* becomes a parody of civilization: the ideals which gave it birth have turned into a stale, joyless repetition of form which collapses in its first confrontation with the world it is supposed to contain. (p. 200)

The character of Dr D. R. Cartwright . . . embodies everything Ford believed in: candour, compassion, moral commitment, defiance of hypocrisy, sacrifice. She is also completely alone, utterly rootless, far more radically estranged from society than Ethan or Tom Doniphon. The fact that she is a woman makes her solitude, for Ford, all the more terrible and all the more heroic. *Seven Women* superficially seems to turn its back on the ideals of community and tradition which had always animated his work, but it is precisely our sense of the *loss* of these values which makes the doctor's sacrifice so important; this sense of loss coupled with her rekindling and passing on of communal values in the last part of the film.

What *Seven Women* ultimately affirms is the necessity of individual integrity in the face of nihilism. (p. 201)

Joseph McBride and Michael Wilmington, in their John Ford *(copyright © 1974 by Secker & Warburg), Martin Secker & Warburg Limited, 1974 (and reprinted by Da Capo Press, Inc., 1975, 239 p.).*

JOHN P. FRAYNE

Ford's strength lay in the treatment of powerful, simple themes—the value of friendship, the loyalty to a cause, the virtues of honor, courage, fortitude. Ford's characters must meet a standard of appropriateness—of knowing when and how to get drunk, and when to sober up; of holding one's own at a poker game in the dance hall; and of dancing a waltz at a Sunday morning church-raising. There are strong conflicts in his films, but some of his characters seem to know what is right. Ford honors old soldiers of either side, but they have to have fought to gain his respect. His escapism is into a simplistic past—he seems to have had little compassion for the contemporary form of escapism into apathy.

His westerns present the standard racist view of the American West. Except for his late *Cheyenne Autumn,* the Indian is the enemy, whether noble warrior or drunken savage. Mexican Americans form a picturesque chorus; their accents and strange foods and customs provide comic relief. But Ford's films exhibit such a warm-hearted affection for human vices and foibles that one tries to minimize the ideological shortcomings of his westerns. In *The Man Who Shot Liberty Valance,* a newspaper editor says, "Between the fact and the legend, print the legend." Ford's movies are about the legend. His vision of the American West may be faulted on historical grounds, but man needs legends, and there is much fundamental human truth in his films. During the last decade the 7th Cavalry has stopped arriving in the nick of time. Perhaps we should enjoy all the more those films of Ford's in which, after much suffering and adversity, at the end the trumpet sounded the charge. (pp. 23-4)

John P. Frayne, "'Stagecoach'," in The Journal of Aesthetic Education *(© 1975 by The Board of Trustees of the University of Illinois), Vol. 9, No. 2, April, 1975, pp. 18-31.*

Werner Herzog

1942-

German director and screenwriter.

Herzog is one of the leading figures to emerge from a creative revival in German cinema during the past decade. His films express his fascination with the uncommon and the freakish, seeking to make central in art what is usually eccentric in life and society, claiming artistic rights to a marginal territory. An insane soldier in South America, rioting dwarfs in the Canary Islands, and a man brought up in the confinement of a cellar in Germany are some of the characters and locales defining Herzog's dark cinematic world. "I make films to rid myself of them, like ridding myself of a nightmare," states Herzog.

Herzog's use of far-flung locations in his films, including Crete, the Sahara Desert, and Guadalupe, is patterned very much after his own life. At fourteen he left home and set out for Albania, reaching Greece and later visiting the Sudan. Herzog also traveled to the United States, where he worked in a steel factory, rode in a rodeo, and attended the University of Pittsburgh. At this time he made his first film shorts, one of which features a rooster as the central character. His first full-length film, *Signs of Life*, introduces situations of madness and isolation which would come to be enduring thematic concerns. This film and the later *Woyzeck* are based upon works by nineteenth-century German authors, and Herzog himself has been described by critics as a nineteenth-century romantic for the turbulence of his cinematic subjects. A further connection to the past is evident in Herzog's best-known work, *Every Man for Himself and God Against All, or The Mystery of Kaspar Hauser*, which derives from a true historical incident in the early nineteenth century. *Aguirre, the Wrath of God* takes place in the historical context of a still earlier era but nonetheless shares in the mood of desperation and turmoil common to Herzog's films.

Herzog turned to the history of cinema for the subject of one of his most recent efforts, *Nosferatu, the Vampyre*. The film is a tribute to F. W. Murnau's expressionist masterpiece of the same title, and this supernatural story of a deathless evil harmonizes particularly well with Herzog's work thus far. From hypnotizing his actors for *Heart of Glass* to featuring a deaf and blind woman in *Land of Silence and Darkness*, Herzog consistently pursues new ways of probing the extremes of human experience. Though Herzog's films are occasionally censured for depicting abnormal subjects considered irrelevant to the mainstream of life, more often the German filmmaker is commended for presenting the unfamiliar and the bizarre with compelling relevancy. (See also *Contemporary Authors*, Vols. 89-92)

A. H. WEILER

["Signs of Life"] is true to its title and its theme of destructive boredom that only climactically forces its principals into explosive action. But as an apparent parable set in a peaceful Grecian backwash of World War II it is almost metaphysically obscure as allegory, even though its characterizations and intentions are as honest as its impressively authentic pastoral backgrounds.

Using the Dodecanese island of Cos, Werner Herzog . . . proves to be strikingly effective as a director if not altogether convincing as an allegorist. These are indeed mere placid signs of life he has captured in a dozing microcosm of whitewashed houses, lapping waves on a pebbled shore, a moldering bastion, broken ancient Greek statuary, meadows, mountains and listless people, young and old, bathed in enervating heat and sunlight.

Against this area touched but not struck by war, he has focused on three German soldiers (and the Greek wife of one of them) who go about the daily stultifying business of guarding a repository of ammunition in a crumbling fortress. The essence of their mounting ennui is dissected in a series of seemingly unconnected scenes. . . .

Mr. Herzog has failed to make his harried hero's case or his parable believable. Otherwise, his "Signs of Life" provides vivid signs of considerable talent and promise.

A. H. Weiler, "'Signs of Life'," in The New York Times *(© 1968 by The New York Times Company; reprinted by permission), September 26, 1968, p. 60.*

TONY RAYNS

Werner Herzog's [*Fata Morgana*] takes the *reductio ad absurdum* narrative patterns of his other films to their logical conclusion by dispensing with narrative altogether. . . . Individually, many of the shots have a great formal beauty;

and the visual juxtaposition of elements from both Western and indigenous cultures (huge aircraft touching down and cadavers of animals decaying where they dropped; distant oil flares and decrepit shanty housing) yields frequent surrealist shocks in line with André Breton's most polemic requirements. Herzog makes no attempt to structure this material through montage; the film has no visual rhythm, and no cut infers any direct meaning. Rather, he adopts a mock-heroic form that divides the film into three sections: The Creation, Paradise, and The Golden Age. Each is accompanied by an occasional voice-over narration, which alters its stance as the film proceeds from aloof omnipotence to bitter engagement. Just as Stroszek in *Lebenszeichen* [*Signs of Life*] disappears from the film at the midpoint, his paroxysm visible only through its effects, so here the entire film is 'effects', visual evidence to the aftermath of some previous action. The first section, composed chiefly of mirage-like stares into the desert void and racing aerial shots of the landscape slipping past, is accompanied by an account of the Creation (supposedly drawn from ancient Persian myth, but probably as spurious as the narrator's log in *Aguirre, Wrath of God*); the described actions of the ancient gods find a bathetic analogue in the telephoto shots through extreme heat-haze of jets coming to earth. In the second section, introducing the tourists along with the natives eking out their horrifyingly deprived lives, another narrator offers bizarre, nihilistic axioms: "In Paradise, you call hello without ever seeing anyone . . . you quarrel to avoid having friends . . . man is born dead". And in the final section, where Herzog's surrealist sensibility blooms full in images of an ageing duo performing antique popular songs on piano and drums while other humans lapse into mania, obsession or simple oblivion, a third narrator turns to outright gallows sarcasm: "In the Golden Age, man and wife live in harmony . . . now, for example, they appear before the camera lens, death in their eyes, a smile on their lips". Herzog concludes his film where he began, facing the desert squarely. His mirage, the *fata morgana*, is a vision entirely consistent with his other work but seen *in extremis* because abstracted from conventional perception. The desert becomes a terminal beach, littered with civilisation's debris, its vestigial signs of life rapidly fading. The few survivors are those who were always outcasts, left clinging to the debris to make their mark on the desert, and those who once produced the debris, now reduced to self-conscious aberrations and the most vacuous of rituals. They, of course are the only gods in the film, and though fleeting moments suggest that they were once savage or dark gods, Herzog really sees them only as failures, fascinating for their ludicrousness and the precariousness of their existence. His vision, as ever, is clear and true, free of compassion, regret and dogma alike; his recourse in the face of the horror and enormity is again to humour, neither cruel nor indulgent, but merely sane.

Tony Rayns, "Feature Films: 'Fata Morgana'," in Monthly Film Bulletin *(copyright © The British Film Institute, 1974), Vol. 41, No. 480, January, 1974, p. 6.*

RICHARD COMBS

Where [Herzog's] later films have located the history of man in a terrain and on a time scale all their own (the terminal ward of *Even Dwarfs Started Small,* the desert myths of *Fata Morgana*), *Lebenszeichen* . . . extracts a similar meditation from a specific historical situation and a not unfamiliar plot format. Wounded in Crete during the Second World War, good soldier Stroszek is removed from the fighting and left to heal in the sultry, dulling climate of a non-combat zone. In the 'time out of war' situation, his physical wound becomes an opening on the frightening illogic of his situation, the absurdity of not just the war but of all the artefacts of human existence which stand petrified around him. Herzog gives peculiar weight to the initial 'accident' of the wounding of Stroszek: "It occurred during a lull in the fighting, in a village held by the Germans", the narrator comments, and a long, swooping camera track through deserted, sun-baked streets makes an abrupt turn and comes upon two uniformed bodies, flicking away instantly to stare idly down another empty street, before returning briefly to the evidence of this glancing intrusion of death. Having been brought so close, and so inappropriately, to extinction, Stroszek's convalescence is clouded by a growing, oppressive sense that existence itself may be no more than an absurd accident; the signs of life are drenched with associations—all the family possessions which Stroszek finds so touching in the house where he and Nora have been billeted; the pieces of ancient statuary used by later generations to patch up the walls of the fortress—but like the inscriptions over which Becker patiently toils, they are now devoid of meaning. In the brief histories it gives of the three guardians of a useless treasure, *Lebenszeichen* provides a catalogue of casual dislocations: all three are peculiarly unsuited to their present profession, and to most of the activities they have engaged in all their lives. . . . Eventually collapsing in terror in the face of the tiny circlings of existence (the routine of the pointless duty; the colony of flies that are bottled within the gypsy's tiny wooden owl in order to produce its minute, puzzling movements; the forest of windmills that finally provoke a breakdown), Stroszek struggles to launch a grandly romantic rebellion, which Herzog films lyrically as if it were the last gasp of an individual no longer able to live as a man and unable to become a god. In a lushly mesmerising atmosphere of suffocating heat and chattering insects, where all history might be drying up at the roots, Herzog's first film is a limpidly clear meditation on life shrivelling under a self-imposed oppression; and in its championing of a failed rebellion, an anticipation of the darker scenes of *Aguirre, Wrath of God.* (pp. 9-10)

Richard Combs, "Feature Films: 'Signs of Life'," in Monthly Film Bulletin *(copyright © The British Film Institute, 1974), Vol. 41, No. 480, January, 1974, pp. 9-10.*

TONY RAYNS

All Werner Herzog's fictions evince a fascination with the mechanisms of human madness—especially those engendered by the will to power—and yet the uniquely disturbing quality of his movies seems to spring less from this consistent theme than from a central ambivalence. Like one who at once observes and participates, Herzog balances between two positions, offering both lucid analyses of chaotic situations (undertaken in a spirit not unlike that of scientific research) *and* hallucinatory, seductive visions that plunge his audience into active experience of the irrational.

The analytic strain is, of course, a modernist trait; it yields the entomological metaphors of *Signs of Life,* the dislocations of physical scale in *Even Dwarfs Started Small,* and the entirety of *Fata Morgana* as a catalogue of the debris left in the wake of a 'drama' already played out, the latter establishing an improbable rapport between Herzog and certain contemporary avant-garde film-makers. The strain of irrationality, though, draws on a very much older tradition; it conjures the dark undertow of the German Romantics, immanent in many of Casper David Friedrich's landscapes and explicit in a novella like Eichendorff's archetypal *Aus dem Leben eines Taugenichts,* where the 'hero' is forever on the point of succumbing to mysterious forces that he senses in the forests and lakes around him. In Herzog's case, the point is the balance itself; it might alternatively be characterised as the ability to infect 'realism' with expressionism and vice versa, without any overriding commitment to either mode. . . .

[*Aguirre, Wrath of God*] is something of a departure for Herzog. . . . Herzog has used it to engage—for the first time—in a specific historical reconstruction, although the action, like the diary on which it purports to be based, is his own invention. (p. 56)

The factors that superficially distinguish *Aguirre* from Herzog's earlier movies in fact serve to throw his consistent qualities into sharper relief. As in *Even Dwarfs Started Small,* the exposition is both functional and extremely concentrated: each scene and each detail is toned down to its salient features. On this level, the film effectively pre-empts analysis by analysing itself as it proceeds, admitting no ambiguity. Yet at the same time, Herzog's flair for charged, explosive imagery has never had freer rein, and the film is rich in oneiric moments of the kind that spark Stroszek's paroxysm in *Signs of Life*. The extraordinarily beautiful opening scene illustrates the ambivalance. In long shot, the image of the conquistadors descending the Andes pass brims with poetic resonances: the men are situated between the peaks and the valleys, between conquered land and unexplored forests, between 'heaven' and 'earth', shrouded in mists. In close-up, the procession picking its way down the narrow path is presented and defined with specific accuracy; all the leading characters are introduced, the social hierarchy is sketched (the slave porters in chains, the women carried in chairs) and the twin poles of the expedition's ideology are signified through the loads it carries (a large Madonna figure, and an even larger cannon). Neither 'reading' of the action contradicts the other; they are rather mutually illuminating.

Later the distinction between the literal and the figurative (or perhaps the factual and the speculative) becomes less palpable; by the final sequence, it has disappeared entirely. In the last shot, Herzog's camera races along the river to Aguirre's raft and circles it twice before fading out. The effect is to circumscribe Aguirre's fantasy, localising it to the tattered, infested remains of his raft, isolating him from the land he dreams of owning; but the circling motion further signifies that the quest has reached its goal, that there can be no further to go. Just as the dwarfs' abortive revolution found its climax at the sight of a helpless camel, so here the quest for a new world and all its riches finds its apotheosis and its cipher in an image of 'magnificent' dementia.

Herzog never falters on his way to this complex but uncompromising conclusion. As ever, he eschews the easy formulations of political or moral dogma, and avoids sentiment and rancour alike. By now it's clear that Herzog is incapable of dishonesties of this kind; like Buñuel or Franju, he will obviously remain true to himself whatever his subject. The clarity and truth of his method, and the value of his tension between rationality and its opposite, are summarised to perfection in a speech by one of the slaves, Runo Rimac ('He who peaks'), dubbed 'Balthasar' by his captors, when he tells Aguirre's uncomprehending daughter that he pities her and her companions, for he knows that there is no way out of 'their' jungle. (p. 57)

Tony Rayns, "Film Reviews: 'Aguirre, Wrath of God'," in Sight and Sound *(copyright © 1974 by The British Film Institute), Vol. 44, No. 1, Winter, 1974-75, pp. 56-7.*

RICHARD COMBS

As a well-formed narrative, in fact moving along at times like Hollywood costume drama with a message to deliver about vaulting ambition, *Aguirre, Wrath of God* has all the beguiling simplicity of Werner Herzog's first feature, *Lebenszeichen.* Both are situated in clear historical periods (and in the general context of an invader being gradually driven mad by an aggravated 'cultural shock'—a social and metaphysical displacement), both concern individuals who decide that to cease obeying orders is the key to personal exaltation and to reversing history altogether, and in both, the events that are set in motion by this decision finally wear away the narrative *and* the hero, obliterating the individual as surely as they fulfil his ambition of wiping the historical slate clean. An obvious difference between the two lies in Herzog's viewpoint on these respective rebellions: Stroszek in the earlier film is allowed to go romantically, all-embracingly mad, with the long final shot reproducing his view of a world receding in the dust and distance; Aguirre is an openly satirised over-reacher, a Shakespearean villain whose thirst for fame and power tips him into a solipsistic madness, a ridiculous puppet . . . jerked on the strings of his overweening ambition, and finally doomed to drift on the same raft as his more evidently venal companions. Aguirre burns himself out attempting to extend the conquistadors' physical conquest of Peru to the mythical paradise of El Dorado, and the last shot of *Wrath of God* reveals Herzog working backwards, to mordant effect, through the descriptions of the Creation in *Fata Morgana,* with a skimming aerial camera approximating the approach of the gods to the benighted desert, to the very first shot of *Lebenszeichen,* with the army truck carrying the wounded hero away from the action meandering in the distance, like some closely observed bug, over tortuous mountain roads. Here the camera swoops and circles like a curious divinity around the strange apparition of Aguirre's raft, its human crew wholly wiped out and now aswarm with hordes of tiny monkeys, while the 'Wrath of God' himself still stands addressing to the sky his plans for a further "great treachery" in the overthrow of all the realms of New Spain. His figure is frozen in a rigid pose—an imminent fossil of this absurd, illusionist enterprise. The confrontation of the Spaniards with the alien, Amazonian landscape also represents something of a merging of the lyrical detail of *Lebenszeichen*—the bric-à-brac of past civilisations basking in the sun, as forlorn and meaningless as the hero keeping guard over a useless ammunition dump—and the more blackly humorous and surrealist imagery of the wreckage-studded desert of *Fata Morgana.* Like the Western Zoologists in the latter film who paw clumsily at the local wild-life, Aguirre at one point holds up for his daughter's inspection, as a kind of love token, a minute baby sloth ("It sleeps its whole life away . . ."); the turning point in Stroszek's madness, the vista of windmills that finally cracks his tolerance of the infinite multiplication of the signs of life, has its equivalent here in the scene where the soldiers set about plundering a deserted Indian village, only to be horrified and put to flight—despite their need for food—by the rotting evidences of cannibalism. Much of the satiric effect of *Wrath of God* derives from the way it slides in and out of various movie conventions—this, after all, is the tale of an epic journey, the historically fabricated account of a 'lost expedition' whose conveniently surviving trace is the diary of one of its members. It is also a social drama on *Ship of Fools* lines, with life on Aguirre's raft a tiny microcosm of the political world—the inevitable cycle of insurrection, consolidation and repression. (p. 4)

Richard Combs, "Feature Films: 'Aguirre, Wrath of God'," in Monthly Film Bulletin *(copyright © The British Film Institute, 1975), Vol. 42, No. 492, January, 1975, pp. 3-4.*

DEREK ELLEY

[In *Aguirre, Wrath of God*] Herzog paints his most ambitious canvas. . . . No blockbuster this, however, despite some imposing set-pieces Herzog's manageable cast is fairly small and it is not long before the paranoid Aguirre dominates proceedings and script alike. (p. 38)

Herzog is at pains throughout to show the reality of the expedition behind the glamorous legend: cannons trundling through muddy swamps, raging rivers to be crossed, sudden death from darts or arrows from the Indians following on the river bank. The metaphor of the journey itself for Aguirre's breakdown is obviously but painlessly applied, and Herzog's film, not at all to its detriment, can be compared with the similar *Deliverance* of John Boorman. In both the main characters soon take to the river, but where Boorman concentrated more on the suspense of the situation, Herzog assuages the viewer with the savage beauty of the landscape, inserting sudden jabs of violence and paranoia like so many pinpricks.

There is an intangible quality to the film, moreover, which never allows the viewer to become too relaxed. The dialogue, if it may truthfully be described as such, is more in the form of spoken recitative, the characters mouthing rather than conversing, and its stylised, declamatory feel works well with the fantastical side of the expedition. For, despite Herzog's constant reminder of Sixteenth-century realities, there is an abiding sense of the other-worldly throughout the film—a dreamy quality underlined by native pipe-playing and hallucinations made concrete. . . . The presence of the two women on the journey also affords a contrast between their pristine beauty and calm, and the filth and fatigue of Aguirre and his crew. Although Herzog's film is about one man's paranoia, it is a fantasia on that theme rather than a closely-documented record. If anything, it is *too* cool, *too* detached, to make any emotional impact. . . . A film which can be admired from afar and relished for its memorable moments, most particularly the final shot of a lone Aguirre ranting on the raft as hordes of monkeys clamber over the timbers—as potent a visualisation of madness as one might wish for (pp. 38-9)

Derek Elley, "'Aguirre, Wrath of God'" (© copyright Derek Elley 1975; reprinted with permission), in Films and Filming, *Vol. 21, No. 5, February, 1975, pp. 38-9.*

DAVID L. OVERBEY

Although [*Every Man for Himself and God Against All*] begins with an aria from Mozart's *The Magic Flute* asking 'Is love the answer?' and ends in the same aria with 'Yes, love is the answer,' this musical parenthesis cannot be denied a certain irony. 'Love' is, after all, the non-ironic solution given in several films which at first glance seem to parallel *Every Man for Himself*. In both Truffaut's *L'Enfant Sauvage* and Penn's *The Miracle Worker,* it is assumed that 'love and patience' will bring salvation to the deprived children. Perhaps it is because they are children, however, that their salvation through education is never questioned. Both films end with the sentimental device of an educational 'break-through'—as if learning to say 'lait' and 'wawa' were enough. In neither film is the society, or the reality of that society as embodied in its language, ever really questioned.

It can hardly be an accident that, while both the wild child and Helen Keller learn to ask first for what is contained in their cups, Herzog's Kaspar learns the word 'empty' first when his cup is drained. This is not to suggest that it would have been better to leave Truffaut's boy in the darkness of his forest or Helen in her blindness, any more than Herzog would suggest that Kaspar's narrow cell was superior to the world he found outside; but simply that there is more to these tales than the assimilation of the beliefs of a middle-class society which leaves scant room for individual visions of reality, or for human dignity that has little to do with table manners. As Herzog's description of the story suggests, it is the very act of conformity which deforms the soul. . . .

A series of obligatory scenes condensing several years of Kaspar's education mark the consecutive stages of his comprehension that the people around him are not the inhabitants of Paradise. At first he is taught language, although he never speaks with the fluency which would indicate his full acceptance of the medium by which a hostile reality is described. These early scenes are shared either by Kaspar and children or by Kaspar and birds, beings with whom Kaspar shares his uncorrupted vision. Later, Kaspar is 'taught' the way the world is seen to work by his keepers and hosts. Examined by several ministers who insist that he confess to having had a 'natural' idea of God while in his cellar, he, in his honesty, cannot. While filled with righteous anger, the men of God 'charitably' allow him to repeat a prayer with them; if he cannot share their reality, he can at least learn the ritual which sustains it. During his examination by a professor of logic, Kaspar works out a problem in his own way, but the solution is rejected because 'it is not a logical answer.'

If religion and abstract logic are thus shown as empty systems in which the answers precede the questions, there remains that reasoned order of the world which begins with the 'objective' observation of phenomena. The key sequence, then, to Kaspar's 'education' comes with the lessons in natural history in which his benefactor Daumer uses apples for illustration. At the end of a long session, Kaspar suggests that they stop for the day 'as the apples must be tired.' Laughing at this 'misconception', Daumer explains that apples have no consciousness, and to prove his point tells Kaspar he will roll an apple on the ground and that it will stop when it hits the boot of his friend. Instead, the apple bumps over an uneven place in the path and jumps over the boot. 'Smart apple!' exclaims Kaspar. One is amused, of course. . . . But is one amused at Kaspar's naïve inability to grasp our usual division of the world into subject and object, or at Daumer (and ourselves?) in his inability to grasp Kaspar's reality?

Here one is confronted with Herzog's method: a cool, neutral observation of characters and events. If Truffaut and Penn insist on our identification with the teachers, and therefore their assumptions about the world, Herzog stays aloof from such an easy response to such a complex situation. (p. 74)

We must remember Herzog's own statement ('I am not a philosopher. I have no system to illustrate'), and we must take it seriously. At only one point does Herzog move away from observation to the self-conscious creation of an abstract construct within the film, and it is this sequence which is at once the film's weakest and the one which sheds most light on Herzog's usual method. Kaspar is made to 'earn his keep' by appearing in a sideshow with other 'freaks' for the edifying amusement of the townsfolk. As Kaspar has already 'progressed' beyond the catatonic state in which the townsfolk first saw him, he 'acts' for his employers by dressing in his earlier costume and reverting to his earlier state. In so far as Kaspar is later unable to 'act' successfully the role of educated ape for his adoptive father, Lord Stanhope, and his aristocratic friends at a coming-out party at which Kaspar is the debutant, his appearance at the country fair is re-enacted to make an abstract point about the exploitation of innocence.

That the scene is in the film to illustrate an abstract concept is further underscored by the presence of 'The Little King', the dwarf . . . from *Even Dwarfs Started Small,* and an actor playing Hombrecito, the Indian flute player from *Aguirre,* two characters of dignity who share the freakshow spotlight with Kaspar. The scene makes its abstract point, as well as conceptually summarising Herzog's earlier work. This philosophical interlude, however, breaks up into a mad chase across the surrounding country as the 'freaks' attempt to escape, and we are once again in the world of sensation and Herzog's neutrally observed reality. Although the scene is in no way bad, or destructive of the ultimate reality which Herzog has created, it does momentarily run against the texture of the film and jolt the viewer to another level.

The beckoning landscape into which the sideshow attractions seek to escape is of prime importance to Herzog, who maintains that his first conception of a film is in terms of seeing a landscape. . . . The town of Dinkelsbühl, with its surrounding farmlands, fields and small woods in midsummer, is not only appropriate historically . . . , but exactly appropriate in emotional and intellectual atmosphere. The farms, like the rooms of the town's houses, are modestly rich and smugly well-ordered, allowing the townsfolk and farmers to sink comfortably into their unquestioned notions of the way the world should work. At the same time the glittering, ordered space, as seen from nearby hilltops, allows one to partake of some of the same sensations as Kaspar when he is first taken from his cell. Even the rippling fields of grey-green grass and the streams shadowed by overhanging trees with which the film begins prompt an ambivalent response that combines the possibilities of well-being with an undertone of the sinister. In this landscape a man might live fully, or might well be thrown from paradise by an inability to adapt to its dappled patterns. (pp. 74-5)

[The] glowing centre of the film is Bruno S as Kaspar. . . . Herzog has been able to tap Bruno's private world to nourish the inner life and exterior manner of Kaspar. His presence in the film gives unshakeable strength to the director's belief that, history aside, the story of Kaspar does not have to end in the death of spontaneity, and that in spite of all, the human spirit can not only endure but triumph. (p. 75)

David L. Overbey, "Every Man for Himself," in Sight and Sound *(copyright © 1975 by The British Film Institute), Vol. 44, No. 2, Spring, 1975, pp. 73-5.*

PAULINE KAEL

[In "The Mystery of Kaspar Hauser"] Werner Herzog has achieved a visionary, overcast style. The higgledy-piggledy pink and blue roofs of the town of Dinkelsbühl . . . suggest the world of a German primitive painter, or of an awkward, self-taught puppeteer who has gone a little haywire. The gentle farmlands have something ominous hovering in the atmosphere, and even normal domestic scenes are airless and oppressive. The estrangement is poignant. Herzog's images look off-balance, crooked, as if the cameraman were wincing; there are distances, large vistas, but the perspectives aren't inviting. The universe is enclosed in an invisible hand. Caught in that grip, nobody seems warmblooded; everyone is alone, immobilized, slightly stiff. Herzog holds shots for a second or two longer than one is used to, so that a character is left with a reaction on his face when what he's reacting to is gone. You're aware of every shot, because each one suggests a visual or emotional displacement. Even the children, who are Kaspar's first teachers, are unnaturally lacklustre. You're looking at a drained, dissociated world—a godforsaken world. The hand that holds it belongs to that black figure with the truncheon. (pp. 142-43)

Kaspar seems conceived sculpturally—man being formed out of clay. Rooting in the muck in his dungeon, he shows no fear of his guardian, and he doesn't suffer any visible pain when he's beaten: he doesn't cower, he doesn't cry out. It's not until he walks upright and has experienced the freedom of mingling with flowers and birds that he learns to suffer. . . . Kaspar is the only one who hasn't lost his innocent responses to the world about him, who hasn't been blighted by society. He's still got his soul. The film becomes "The Passion of Kaspar Hauser." (pp. 143-44)

Herzog says that society puts you through the pain in order to deform you, and he makes it absolutely impossible for you to identify with anyone but Kaspar.

Incidents are devised to show how society attempts to degrade him. . . . Kaspar is a holy innocent whose wisdom stumps [society's] dummies. (Throughout, Herzog's assumption is that philosophers don't raise the questions that Kaspar does, though they are precisely the questions that philosophers have worried over endlessly.) Typically, Herzog sets up what might be a dramatic situation and then just lets it sit there, flat on; and it can be effective in its formality. He's worst when his purposes are clearly decipherable (as with [a] logician, or in an even more specious scene involving Kaspar's belief that apples have feelings), because then he's pointing up the idiocy of those who can't understand Kaspar. (pp. 144, 147)

Personalizing the unknown in the form of [a] black-caped

murderer, Herzog creates a fable of a demonic universe—"Every Man for Himself and God Against All"—which is just the reverse of the faith that the churchmen want Kaspar to accept. It's Christianity turned upside down, and given a bitter, malignant tinge, but Herzog has found in Kaspar Hauser a new, uncorrupted Christ figure. And then had him martyred all over again. . . . [If this film] succeeds at all with audiences the reason will be, I think, that it presents a sentimental view of man's natural state. One of the oldest audience-pleasing gimmicks in mass culture is to show the simpleton outwitting the learned. Herzog has given this gimmick a metaphysical framework that could make it appeal to present-day moviegoers who want to believe that the spacy innocents have the answers.

There's something of a contradiction involved in using modern film technology to argue against learning in favor of an innocent response to nature; a filmmaker is not exactly a hewer of wood. Werner Herzog comes as close as he can, though. . . . His technique owes little to previous commercial films; it doesn't owe very much to previous films of any sort. And there are penalties for working as a self-conscious artist in movies, as there are in the theatre. . . . A movie or a play has a duration, and a director who has never served a commercial apprenticeship may rhythm his work in ways that seem punishing to an audience. Herzog's pacing may be masterly in terms of his cool, objective, controlled style, but the hour and fifty minutes of this film is a trial for anyone of a restless disposition or an agnostic temperament. You fight to keep your eyes open. Buñuel's best work draws upon irrational sources of humor; Herzog is anti-rational, in an almost self-satisfied way. In Buñuel's world, everyone is alive; there's a raucous, lewd energy in the characters. Herzog's people are unanimated; life is dormant in them. And though one could not fault this in a painter's vision, in a filmmaker's it is numbing to an audience.

A pretty fair case can be made for the idea that a little corruption is good for the soul: it humanizes you. Werner Herzog is an artist before he's a human being, and we may experience his dedication to art as a form of priggishness. Bergman may be obsessive, he may be frightfully high-toned, but he's a man of the theatre. . . . Herzog has just about everything to be a great film artist but this alchemical element: there's no theatre in his soul. As with Robert Bresson, we can admire Herzog's work abstractly, intellectually, but we may find it perversely academic. . . . [In] Herzog's dedication to film art he denies us the simple pleasures of story involvement, of suspense, of interest in the people on the screen, of sexuality. His goodness saps our strength. (pp. 147-49)

Pauline Kael, "Metaphysical Tarzan," in The New Yorker *(© 1975 by The New Yorker Magazine, Inc.), Vol. LI, No. 35, October 20, 1975, pp. 142-44, 147-49.*

JAY COCKS

[*Every Man for Himself and God Against All*] is a casebook of insensitivity. Every character is vigorously and grossly caricatured. The short supply of ideas is presented with all the insight of a caption in Ripley's *Believe It or Not!*

Herzog . . . is a sort of social anthropologist *manqué* who has been prominent in the perennially fizzling resurgence of the West German cinema. It has been suggested that in *Every Man* Herzog is struggling to create a new metaphor for the state of modern Germany. This is one of those facile, coverall apologies, like saying an Italian film is a thinly disguised attack on the Roman Catholic Church, or a novel about contemporary Ireland reflects the agonies of civil war. It cannot save the movie from indistinction. . . .

Herzog's previous work . . . includes a film entirely populated by dwarfs. These works were also defended as metaphors for modern Germany. Some fresh excuses are needed.

Jay Cocks, "Grave New World," in Time *(reprinted by permission from* Time, The Weekly Newsmagazine; *copyright Time Inc. 1975), Vol. 106, No. 18, November 3, 1975, p. 74.*

PENELOPE GILLIATT

["Stroszek"] is a brilliant, poetic film about a man's clutch on a difficult existence. Stroszek's story shows us the bitterness of exile, and the rewards of concentration on singular tasks misapprehended by the common run. He could strike only those in step as a man of folly. And, in Scheitz, Herzog has created one of the most fragile and sweet-natured characters to be seen in any contemporary European movie: a man of infinite mental fortitude and physical frailty, who could be blown away like a skeletal leaf. Herzog has made a funny, very serious film about a tonic sort of nobility practiced in territory as foreign to his characters' cast of mind as the world is to the premature baby's. (pp. 74,77)

Penelope Gilliatt, "The Current Cinema: 'Stroszek'," in The New Yorker *(© 1977 by The New Yorker Magazine, Inc.), Vol. LIII, No. 23, July 25, 1977, pp. 74, 77-9.**

ROBERT HATCH

Werner Herzog is belligerently romantic in an age subservient to plausibility. Whereas other directors build their fictions, however extreme or grotesque, with the mortar of cause and effect, he invokes his tales with a magic wand. I think, though, that he does so because he is not only romantic but impatient. He sees a truth, is eager to share it and cannot pause to touch each base along the way. Thus in *Stroszek* . . . he needs to get his quite moneyless people from Germany to America. So he sends Eva, a street whore, down to the warehouse district of Berlin where, in five quick tricks, she gets the plane fares from some Turkish "guest workers," as the Germans call them. Never mind that Turks on temporary visas cannot pay that kind of money for their pleasure—Herzog is moving as briskly as possible in the direction he wants to go. And it should be noted that his magic wand is tipped with acid, not a star.

He calls [this] picture a ballad; it could as well be termed a pilgrimage. . . . Just who Stroszek is may be the subject of the film, and it may be that we never quite know. Clearly, he is a "natural," but not in the sense that he is touched in the head (though he may also be that); rather that he moves in ways of his own devising, unmoved by outward circumstance. Live and let live is Bruno's far from original philosophy, but he pursues it with a doggedness that is at least unusual, given that he is entirely incapable of enforcing his golden rule. . . .

In its final reels, *Stroszek* begins to jump its sprockets, its peculiar romanticism spinning into phantasmagoria, as

Bruno robs a barber shop (a very quick, very funny Western holdup), buys a frozen turkey, "borrows" the garage tow truck and sets off for the hills. . . .

Moral? None at all, I would say; the film is intended to open your eyes, and you are expected to draw the conclusions. However, of observation there is plenty. Herzog has filmed an America that many Americans have never seen, but that all of them should recognize. It is the land where everyone is equal and the devil take the hindmost. Where your credit is as good as your signature, and the auctioneer will sell you up the day your payments stop. It is a place where friendliness is next to godliness and bad luck is deemed the best of jokes. If you believe in magic, America is the place for you, but you are a fool if you trust your fairy godmother. Thus Herzog brings manner and matter together in *Stroszek,* probably his best work to date. (p. 157)

Robert Hatch, "Films: 'Stroszek'," in The Nation *(copyright 1977 The Nation Associates, Inc.), Vol. 225, No. 5, August 20-27, 1977, pp. 157-58.**

STANLEY KAUFFMANN

[Werner Herzog's *Stroszek*] continues one of his favorite themes: craziness in and of our world. . . . Stroszek is a young man, not quite competent mentally, who is battered by today's Germany and who emigrates to the US with two other battered people—a young whore and a very old man—looking for refuge with the old man's American nephew in Wisconsin.

The picture splits in more than setting. The German half is a broodingly taut, if somewhat trite account of the bullying of the helpless Stroszek by two burly pimps because he has befriended their abused whore. Herzog handles this section easily, taciturnly. But strain runs through the American section. The ease is gone, and what we get is a collection of grotesque souvenirs. As with Wim Wenders' *Alice in the Cities,* the tourist's notebook is figuratively out, for crudeness and rudeness. . . .

Also, in the American section Herzog relies a lot on improvisation and "stolen" footage, and much of it is clumsy. Worst, he manufactures the debacle at the end. Everything seems to be going OK in Wisconsin, then suddenly—just because Herzog needs it—everything goes wrong. He ends with very heavy symbolism: Stroszek circling aimlessly on a cable car while some conditioned chickens in an amusement arcade react repeatedly to repeated stimuli. This corn is far beneath the best of Herzog.

Stroszek has touches of that best. For instance, Stroszek, in middle distance, his back to us, watches his American trailer-home being hauled away in the background because payments are overdue. He is stationary: the house he has been living in simply slides laterally out of the frame. It's a Keaton touch. (p. 25)

Stanley Kauffmann, "Films: Watching on the Rhine" (reprinted by permission of Brandt & Brandt Literary Agents, Inc.; copyright © 1977 by Stanley Kauffmann) in The New Republic, *Vol. 177, Nos. 8 & 9, August 20 & 27, 1977, pp. 24-5.**

COLIN L. WESTERBECK, JR.

Werner Herzog should be thought of as a kind of seer, perhaps even something of a mystic. Only then does the nonsense begin to make sense in his films. Those films are a peculiar combination of an impulse both to comprehend all of life and at the same time to respect its incomprehensibility. The result is films that are like parables. The only way Herzog can embrace life fully enough is to deal with it in a symbolic and anagogical way instead of a literal one. Rather than the explanation of a particular situation, his films are revelations of the general. The colony of dwarfs in *Even Dwarfs Started Small* or the African desert in *Fata Morgana* are microcosms of all creation. They suggest everything while specifying little. In almost all of Herzog's films to date, in fact, the characters behave, like figures of myth, by the laws of the imagination alone. They behave only in accordance with the laws of Herzog's own imagination, which is an all-consuming, singular and very private one. . . .

[By contrast, *Stroszek*] seems the most naturalistic [film] he has made. . . . As is suggested by the use of the actors' names for the characters they play . . . Herzog intends his film to seem, ambiguously, a document as well as a fable. Yet at the same time, *Stroszek* is only a document in the same peculiar sense that *Fata Morgana* is. At heart it is still predominantly an attempt to mystify and mythologize all life. It's an attempt once again to comprehend the incomprehensible.

As in past films, so here, Herzog attempts almost physically to comprehend as much of human civilization as possible. He does this by seeing in Stroszek's immigration a continuity between European and American cultures. Soon after Stroszek's arrival, the parallel between the Germany he has left behind and the America to which he has come is implied by an incident he witnesses. Two farmers engaged in a legal battle over a strip of land ride on their enormous diesel tractors armed with rifles and stare provokingly at each other across the disputed ground. Thus does rural Wisconsin become, like the institution in *Even Dwarfs,* the microcosm of a nation—an East and West Germany in miniature.

Even before Stroszek leaves Germany the parallel with America and the impossibility of escaping his problems there seems inevitable. From his cellmate in the opening scenes to the pimps who terrorize him, half the people Stroszek knows in Germany wear Western hats and cowboy clothes like the Wisconsinites (indeed, like Stroszek himself, after he has been in America a time). In Germany Stroszek goes to a doctor who once treated him and now consoles him in his new troubles with a tour of the hospital nursery. Holding up a tiny, wrinkled baby the doctors asks philosophically who can tell which such infant will be a great man. And in America Herr Scheitz, who looks almost like the infant, begins to have delusions that he is a great man, the discoverer of animal magnetism. So does the immigration to America become, in effect, the passage from infancy to senility—life's pilgrimage not to the promised land, but to ruination.

At times Stroszek's fate is, like the desert life portrayed in *Fata Morgana,* accompanied by a kind of solemn rhetoric. At one point, for instance, Stroszek tries to explain to Eva his feeling that America does to the spirit what Germany does to the physical and political man. Were we to take it seriously, such an insight into his own situation would at the least be out of character for poor Stroszek. But I don't believe Herzog intends us to take it seriously any more than we did the voice-over narrative in *Fata Morgana*. . . . In his film, both story and dialogue are similar gestures—an attempt to get as close as possible to what can never be entered or known directly. Like the over-arching symbolism of Herzog's plots, any rhetorical wisdom those plots may contain is only an effort to surround a truth which exists, by its nature, in silence.

In *Land of Silence and of Darkness* . . . , in fact, Herzog made a documentary about a woman both blind and deaf. The fascination she had for him was not so much her extraordinary ability to understand the world outside herself, but rather our inability to enter and understand the world *inside* her. In *Stroszek* Herzog again deals with a character who lives, increasingly, after he immigrates to America, in a land of silence and of darkness. What really binds together the episodes of Stroszek's life more than anything else is the failure of language. The more different ways of talking about human experience are introduced into the film, the less sense language makes to Stroszek. The immigration to America makes us especially aware of this since Stroszek speaks no English. When he, Eva and Herr Scheitz arrive in Wisconsin, Scheitz's cousin greets them with a sign reading "Willkommen" on one side and "Welcome" on the other. But Stroszek's experiences in Germany don't translate in such easy, hospitable ways. (pp. 624-25)

In Germany Stroszek earns money as a street singer, and at one point we hear a performance he gives where he narrates and interpolates each verse of his song before he sings it. This anticipates beautifully the duality of his experience in Europe and America and the double failure of language for him. Ultimately the myth Herzog would create here is a very pessimistic one. All the efforts to comprehend the incomprehensible leave us, in the end, with a pretty empty universe. At the end of this film, after he has lost his home, his Eva and his friend Scheitz, Stroszek leaves a truck he has stolen circling by itself in a parking lot and goes off to commit suicide. That driverless truck going round and round is an image Herzog has employed before. It's a horrific image of the attempt to encompass somehow a void which we cannot know in any other way. (p. 625)

Colin L. Westerbeck, Jr., "The Failure of Language," in Commonweal *(copyright © 1977 Commonweal Publishing Co., Inc.; reprinted by permission of Commonweal Publishing Co., Inc.), Vol. CIV, No. 20, September 30, 1977, pp. 624-25.*

JANET MASLIN

[*La Soufrière*] is one of Werner Herzog's most exquisite efforts, a perfect distillation of his talents. . . . [The] film is a serene, strangely clear-headed documentary about the end of the world. . . .

"Heart of Glass" [is] a feature by Mr. Herzog that is far less successful. Mr. Herzog hypnotized his entire cast to film a parable about a medieval town that has thrived by producing ruby-colored glass, until the only man who knows the formula dies. . . .

In its own way, "Heart of Glass" is as much about the end of the world as is "La Soufrière," but ["Heart of Glass"] is much less accessible, and often obscure. The actors' trance is contagious, and the film has some genuinely mesmerizing moments, as when the town seer, whose words have made little sense, suddenly begins to predict an alarmingly familiar future in which "no man will like another man." Mr. Herzog seems not to be working with real actors, but rather with apparitions.

At times, the script reads like a collection of nonsequiturs. "Do you want our people to eat oatmeal bread again, that gives them headaches?" asks one character. "Rats will bite your earlobes," someone swears. Even the film's meticulousness—every trace of red anywhere, even on a goose's head, is clearly planned—is not entirely decipherable.

The elusiveness of "Heart of Glass" makes it something of a disappointment. But it is too mysteriously lovely to be regarded as a failure.

Janet Maslin, "One by Werner Herzog Soars, but 2nd Doesn't," in The New York Times *(© 1977 by The New York Times Company; reprinted by permission), October 1, 1977, p. 10.*

JAN DAWSON

Herzog's power as a film-maker has always been primarily a visionary one. Nature, untamed and sometimes even uncharted, has provided the cosmic hot-house in which his awesome visions have best flowered; 'civilisation', where he has treated it, has appeared as an arrogant illusion, a Babel-tower of foolish human ambition; and his heroes, victims of and outcasts from that civilised social norm, have lived their deformed and misshaped lives in some pale, Platonic shadow of the State of Nature. Which state, though awesomely aspiring, is hardly a cheering one. It proclaims the transience, the nothingness of human endeavours, and the greater glory of a universe which yields its secrets only to those who submit to the attraction of its fatal, all-engulfing embrace.

Linking nearly all Herzog's films is a thirst for death, but for death as a pure and transcendental force, a moment of fusion with a superior nature. It is this thirst, and this purity, which elevate the woodcarver Steiner's death-defying ski jumps from the materially competitive to the incalculably mystical. But where the self-sought death is the apotheosis to which all his films advance, Herzog treats as the ultimate irony and indignity death at human hands. Feeling away the foggy layers of intellectual confusion, one finds, at the glassy heart of all his films, gratuitousness as the single value he consistently celebrates: in his state of nature, motivation is the one cardinal sin.

At any rate, it seems an act of perfect consequence that Herzog, on learning that the volcano La Soufrière was about to erupt and that one local inhabitant had refused to join in the evacuation from the island of Guadeloupe, should promptly have set off to film the eruption. . . . [In *La Soufrière,* death] is, literally, in the air, and the message of the sulphurous exhalations drifting in beautiful, lethal clouds across the mountainside is modulated in Herzog's distinctively unaccented commentary, whose litanical chant is further echoed in the film's more overtly religious music.

In the event, *La Soufrière* proves, in Herzog's own words, to be a record of 'an inevitable catastrophe which didn't happen.' His disappointment, balancing his fear, contributes to the film's air of other-worldliness, ultimately reinforcing its strength, its sheer gratuitousness. The deserted town, its streets patrolled by dogs too hungry to bark, serves as a mute monument to the folly of human ambition;

the unapproachable crevice on the mountain-top becomes a magnetic force, drawing the film crew towards its noxious embrace; the last inhabitant proves to be not one man but three, all of them blacks, all of them so exploited by a greedy civilisation that they have nothing to live for and hence no fear of dying.

It is here that the disquieting moral ambivalence of all Herzog's work comes most sharply into focus: the old man, stretched out with his cat to die on the grassy mountainside, is offered at once as an object for emulation and for indignation. By staying *gratuitously,* he becomes not a martyr but a hero; but for the earlier generation (on the neighbouring island of Martinique) which stayed for something, namely an election, Herzog reserves his finest irony. The moral is labyrinthine and confused, but the vision is hypnotic, powerful and persuasive. Even the presence of the film crew, honestly recorded, proves barely intrusive, since they attempt, not to modify the situation, but rather to succumb to its inevitable force.

Stroszek . . . , on the other hand, attempts to leap from the sublime to the ridiculous. Of all Herzog's films it appears the one most calculated to please. It places humanity rather than nature in the centre of the screen, and sets its humans down in mean city streets and arid wastelands whose muddy monotony is relieved only by mobile homes (perhaps the ultimate metaphor for the transience of human constructions) and pre-fabricated out-buildings. The closest the film comes to a moment of exaltation is when its three naive misfits contemplate the view from the Empire State. Some thousand miles of flat lands later, after acres of junk food, jerry-building and clapped out automobiles, one of the three reaches another high point, a mountain on an Indian reservation in Wisconsin—the mountainside is cluttered, not only by a funicular railway that takes the sightseer in pointless circles, but also by an amusement arcade filled with dancing chickens and musical ducks, and by craft shops where the natives sell the mass-produced versions of their traditional wares. In the parking lot at the base, a lone Cherokee stands watch in full warrior costume.

Stroszek is, both literally and figuratively, a film about prostitution; and in its recourse to facile irony and no less facile sentimentality it comes perilously close to partaking of what it denounces (Henry James—of course—had a phrase for it: 'the age of trash triumphant'). The film begins in Berlin, where Bruno S. . . . , on his release from prison, forms an unlikely alliance with a streetwalker called Eva who is being brutalised by her pimp. The opening scenes might belong in a Fassbinder melodrama, were it not for Herzog's determination to compel us into an affection for his characters that is inevitably patronising. For these big-hearted victims (Bruno, the girl and an elderly neighbour) are set up to represent the little people, and their colourful eccentricity is that of the Gallic courtyard comedy. If Bruno's speech and appearance are as startling as they were in *Kaspar Hauser,* Herzog has none the less diminished the credibility of his victim hero by giving him a girlfriend, companions, a concerned neighbour; and by having him uncynical enough about man's inhumanity to believe that America may still be the promised land.

Yet although the film's ideas might best be described as elementary, and although it frequently treats its characters with a condescending cuteness, *Stroszek* works as powerful argument on the level of its images. The 60-foot trailer, the lone Indian, the dancing chicken, the funicular, provide an effective emblematic critique of our trashy society. They also have a persuasiveness that the fictional characters lack. The metaphysical, this time, takes a back seat to the social and the ephemeral. Herzog's transatlantic fable proves a worldly *divertissement,* after which one can only hope he will, like Moses, go back up the mountain. (pp. 57-8)

Jan Dawson, "Herzog's Magic Mountain," in Sight and Sound *(copyright © 1977 by The British Film Institute), Vol. 47, No. 1, Winter, 1977-78, pp. 57-8.*

KAREN JAEHNE

Stroszek is neatly divided between the old world of Berlin shadows and the new world, lying under one mammoth shadow. When Bruno S. is released from prison, he seems to be just rounding the track of another relay race. 'It all moves in circles,' he shouts, above the mild admonitions of a functionary at the prison. Bruno's cry has the prophetic tone of all his proclamatory acting in Herzog's films. The movement within the film then fulfils Bruno's worst fears: from prison to freedom and back again has until now been the pattern, and when Berlin's working class district, Kreuzberg, proves to be a static ghetto of static violence, Bruno tries to widen the circle to extend to the shores of American freedom. The circle then becomes a motif of absurdity, which can be traced from the clawing dance of the glassy-eyed chicken to the machine that carries Bruno in circles even after his death. This feigned movement is an image of America running in circles, where the potential for violence is brilliantly depicted by two farmers on their tractors, shotguns in hand, ploughing a disputed piece of land. (p. 101)

Herzog projects his obsession with Fate in this film into an American darkness that will eventually absorb Bruno. In Berlin, Bruno lives in a sort of pact of destiny with the darkness and seems to have no great expectations. . . .

Bruno is the kind of hero whose very alienation would be his saving grace, if he were not to get mixed up with Woman. In a role-reversal, Eva tries to 'take him away from all this'—the brutality that her own invasion of his world has caused—and they emigrate to Railroad Flats (Wisconsin, Plainsfield), where railroads have been replaced by trucks. Eva gets a job serving in a truck-stop and quickly adapts to easy-going American ways, trying to beat the payments on their colour TV and mobile home as a part-time hooker. Herr Scheitz develops a marvellous theory about measuring animal magnetism in people with a geiger counter. The Americans he encounters don't understand him, of course, and if they did, they wouldn't believe it. Nothing changes in Bruno's destiny; there is no solace in transition, for he only moves from his private corner of darkness to an entire land plunged into darkness. (p. 102)

Bruno and Herr Scheitz plunge into the American Way of Life—as they understand it—and rob a cash register of $22, spending it across the street on a cold turkey. This subtle bit of Americana escapes some German audiences, but is a hilarious symbolic variation on Herzog's obsession with fowl and simultaneously incorporates what it means to break a habit 'cold turkey'. Bruno's habit has been to bend with the wind, literally depicted in Berlin when he bent over his piano, forced by Eva's former pimps to wear a bell on his head. The pimps' violence had also been linked to the influence of American standards, in a cut to the street where they stand next to a shiny American car. The contradictions of the American Dream must inevitably be resolved by prostitution: to achieve the goal of 'something for nothing', one has to sell oneself or someone else. But Herzog's America is not full of prostitutes and criminals typical of New German Cinema films. Indeed, his Americans have no excess of dignity, and their casual attitude is a veil for more insidious purposes. Even the act of prostitution is draped in seduction when we are shown how it all operates at the truck stop. . . . It seems that in America money is slipped back and forth, under the guise of friendliness. Perhaps the sleaziest scene in Herzog's film is that with the debt collector from the bank, a scene worthy of Altman, as the slick young man blushes at the sight of Eva's pile of bills: 'We usually only accept credit cards.' He is thoroughly convincing.

It is the wheeling and dealing that separates Bruno and Eva, for she can do it in an offhand manner, as was evident back in Berlin's back-alley, while Bruno has nothing to sell. Increasingly, he is equated with the American Indian, first through his fellow worker and ultimately when he seeks refuge and dies on the Indian Reservation in North Carolina. The immigrant and invader is embodied in Eva and her decision to migrate with the truckers on their long-distance runs to Canada. Bruno takes off in the other direction and drives until he comes to a Reservation where the Indians have turned to exploitation, selling their very ethnicity, and where a chicken and rabbits dance and make music for a coin stuck in their cage. Here Bruno takes his last free ride in America.

This American attitude towards life is captured in the way Herzog uses animals as a motif, parallel to human development. 'What kind of land is it that takes Bruno's [pet bird] Beo away from him?' This line . . . expresses Bruno's first loss in America. The customs authorities can no more appreciate Bruno's attachment to Beo than he can understand their reasons for depriving him of his pet. The same gap of understanding provides comic relief when Herr Scheitz attempts to measure the animal magnetism of two dead deer and explain his ideas to two indifferent hunters. The life of animals is a measure of the general indifference to life which Bruno meets in Railroad Flats, where his boss is obsessed with a recent murder. Where the Cherokees parade as Indians, animals parade as machines in a sensational attraction that is surely the most absurd element in Herzog's work: the last sequence cuts back and forth from the glassy eye of the chicken dancing in circles to the burned-out tow-truck running down in circles and Bruno caught dead on the circling ski-lift, in a fulfilment of his prediction, "It all moves in circles." (p. 102)

Karen Jaehne, "The American Fiend," in Sight and Sound *(copyright © 1978 by The British Film Institute), Vol. 47, No. 2, Spring, 1978, pp. 101-02.*

PHILIP STRICK

[Herzog's *Nosferatu—The Vampyre*] is concerned not with Bram Stoker but with F. W. Murnau. . . . (p. 127)

From Murnau's images, Herzog creates his own: the magnificent staging of the plague ship taking aboard its deadly cargo, and the helicopter shot of its course across a placid sea; . . . the brief, astounding glimpse, straight out of *Aguirre*, of a raft laden with coffins being swept down a torrential river. Finally, *Nosferatu* shows the plague-carrier galloping across sand-flats on his endless, lethal journey, his continuity praised by a reverential choir on the soundtrack: Herzog finds both image and concept equally glorious.

It's a conclusion that confirms the reason behind the remake—the reprise is not of Murnau but of Herzog. Dracula is an outsider like Kaspar Hauser, Stroszek and Aguirre, a death-seeker amid the troops of somnambulists. Invading Holland with his conquistadorial rats, he bears a priceless gift, as promised by all true prophets—the knowledge of how *not* to die. There's just one catch: eternal life, secured through the sharing of blood, has its disadvantages. [The voice of Klaus Kinski (Dracula)] conveys them superbly by its despairing weariness. 'Can you imagine,' he murmurs hopelessly, 'what it's like to endure centuries of experiencing the same futile things?' . . . Such is the continuing fatalism of Werner Herzog, continuing to revolve in an elegant solitude. (pp. 127-28)

Philip Strick, "Film Reviews: 'Nosferatu—The Vampyre'," in Sight and Sound *(copyright © 1979 by The British Film Institute), Vol. 48, No. 2, Spring, 1979, pp. 127-28.*

HARLAN KENNEDY

[*Nosferatu*] is perhaps the most circumspect, least red-blooded Dracula movie ever made. Herzog's visionary madness needs room to whirl and gesticulate, but here he has straitjacketed himself in his respect for Murnau's 1922 vampire classic. The film is like a silent movie with the titles missing. Individual scenes are full of magic, but there is nothing to propel the story forward.

Herzog scatters the film early on with promising thematic motifs and images, especially when Bruno Ganz's Transylvania-bound hero approaches the Land of Silence and Darkness in which Nosferatu lives, and when the still canals of the Nordic town he has left are exchanged for rushing rivers and sounding cataracts. But once the action returns to "Wismar" on the Baltic, the languid, azure-hued beauty of the film's surface and a lack of aim or urgency in the editing rob the story of surprise and momentum.

Klaus Kinski as Nosferatu looks magnificent—bald, bony head, bat-wing ears, rat teeth. And he speaks with a fetching, Peter Lorre-like purr. But until Isabelle Adjani's climactic death, there is little bloodletting. What the film surely needed was at least one moment of terror early on, in which the vampire's awesome powers are seen in action rather than taken on trust. (p. 65)

Harlan Kennedy, "Berlin: I. The Festival," in American Film *(reprinted with permission from the May issue of* American Film *Magazine; © 1979, The American Film Institute, J. F. Kennedy Center, Washington, D.C. 20566), Vol. IV, No. 7, May, 1979, pp. 64-6.*

JAN-CHRISTOPHER HORAK

Herzog's images are reflections of his inner landscapes. Like those Expressionist filmmakers whose legacy he has inherited, he is possessed by dreams so powerful, they can only be exorcised through cinematic creation. *The Mystery of Kaspar Hauser, Or Every Man for Himself and God*

Against All, Herzog's mysterious film of a nineteenth-century wild child, can then be seen as a meditation on its subject through a conscious awareness of the classic German film of the Weimar Republic. . . . (p. 223)

[The] sense of the physicality of nature, of its material reality, and of man's position within it, yet apart from it, seems central to Herzog's personal universe. In previous films such as *Signs of Life,* or *Aguirre,* the landscape is a dangerous force, threatening by the very nature of its cosmic indifference to man. In *Kaspar Hauser,* and even more so in *Heart of Glass* . . . , the landscape exudes an aura of warmth and tranquility. With *Heart of Glass* this feeling almost takes on mystical aspects, when an imprisoned soothsayer, cut off from the landscape that is his meditational life blood, is unable to see his visions. Yet to mistake Herzog for a transcendentalist would be to infer a spirituality *Kaspar Hauser* in no way implies. (p. 226)

Kaspar's physical connection with nature is . . . continually reinforced, e.g. when he feeds various blackbirds, or when Kaspar rows on a quiet lake. The images always have a great depth of field to them, connecting Kaspar to the natural environment. Later he writes his name in the soil by planting watercress and cries bitterly when an unknown culprit destroys his creation. . . . Kaspar's tragedy is that he remains a solitary among men, even after he is released from the black nothingness of his cell. Tieck's "monsterous emptiness and horrid chaos" . . . has an especially depressing effect on Kaspar, whose consciousness now awakened realizes "the hole was better than outside." Kaspar talks of "birth being a painful blow." At one point, shortly after he learns to talk, he cries while holding a baby, and says to the farmer's wife, who has become his foster mother: "Mother, I feel so very distant."

I am reminded of Camus' dictum in *The Myth of Sisyphus,* that the absurd is first perceived emotionally. Clearly, the isolation Kaspar feels is a result of his intuitive grasp of the irrationality of existence. At one point Kaspar runs out of a church service, saying he can't stand the terrible screaming of the congregation whose hymn to God can still be heard. Camus, too, talks of man's fundamental isolation from other human beings and his perception of the inhuman essence people often exude. Kaspar says "humans are like wolves." These ideas, then, seem to connect very directly to Kaspar's perceptions. His dream of the masses wandering up the mountain of death seems in fact to be a direct translation into visual terms of Camus' Sisyphus Myth.

Moreover, Herzog's heroes from the insane Stroszek in *Signs of Life,* to the anarchistic colony of dwarfs in *Even Dwarfs Started Small,* to the power-mad Spanish conquistador in *Aguirre,* to the little ex-con in *Stroszek* . . . , are, in their hopeless, often insane revolt against circumstance, battling an absurd universe which seems directly connected to Camus' existential vision. Kaspar, a madman by bourgeois standards, maintains his freedom through passive noncompliance. Madness and revolution, despite the knowledge that failure is inevitable, become acts of liberation in Herzog's films, just as Sisyphus' damnation is his liberation. (pp. 226-27)

[Unlike] Camus' hero in *The Stranger,* knowledge of the absurdity of existence does not paralyze Kaspar emotionally. Kaspar, like the expressionist man still capable of direct feeling, "wears his heart on his chest." . . . Society has not yet socialized him to the point where he represses his emotional self. Without regard to who or what happens to be around him, Kaspar freely confesses his dreams and fears. Only the necessity of language to express himself seems to imprison him. Slowly, deliberately pronouncing every word for fear he may not make himself clear, Kaspar painfully articulates each of his utterances. This seriousness of purpose carries over into his concentrated, earnest attempts to understand those around him. Kaspar seems incapable of shielding himself with personal bias and thereby exudes an honesty lacking in others.

Kaspar's relationship to music, as well as the film's treatment of music as a whole, underlines his intense emotionality. When the blind Florian—like Kaspar, a societal cripple under Herr Daumer's patronage—plays piano, out of key and without rhythm, Kaspar remarks: "the music feels me strongly in my breast." (This use of the passive voice is typical for Kaspar's speech.) Later Kaspar learns to play the piano himself, and is asked to perform at a fashionable party given by a rich, effeminate nobleman, the Earl of Stanhope, under whose tutelage Kaspar is to continue his education. Kaspar plays Mozart like Florian, full of emotion, but technically unskilled to say nothing of incompetent. The party guests of course become uncomfortable and even impatient with such uncouth behavior, and their false and affected interest only makes their emotional sterility all the more obvious. These aristocrats, with their powdered noses and small-minded aesthetic of good taste, are incapable of appreciating the love Kaspar brings to his attempted music-making.

Mozart, in one damaged form or another, is heard throughout the film. . . . For those who listen carefully, it becomes apparent that Herzog picks up the aria [from *The Magic Flute*] at the end of the film, at the very point he fades out in the beginning. . . . Thus, the aria acts as a frame for the film, and functions as Herzog's declaration of love for his subject. This symmetry is reinforced at the exact midpoint of the film, where Herzog plays all seven and a half minutes of Albinoni's exquisite orchestral fragment "Adagio for Strings and Organ." We see Kaspar writing his autobiography, as he narrates the story of his destroyed watercress garden. The simple emotional beauty of the strings answers Kasper's hopeless wish, that creating music "be like breathing." Intuitively Kasper stumbles upon the ultimate goal of all musicians.

As mentioned above, a "young Mozart" also makes an appearance, and again the theme of music as emotion is picked up. The boy, a child prodigy who loved Mozart's music with a passion, now stares into a hole in the ground, "because the whiteness of the page blinded him." He is paralyzed by the difficulty of translating emotion into aesthetic form and so retreats into a mindless void. Ironically, Kaspar, having emerged from the nothingness of his hole, overcomes his paralysis and writes prodigiously in his diaries.

Kaspar's paralysis, as he stands immobile in the town square, or later in the exact same position in front of the magistrate's door, is, like that of the young Mozart's, the result of his utter passivity. Kaspar is taught to walk by his Caligari, who manipulates Kaspar's legs by kicking them, one in front of the other. Without language, without thought, his body is doomed to puppet-like manipulations. When a swordsman swings a blade in front of Kaspar's face, he does not even blink, because he has not yet learned to fear bodily harm. As the film progresses, and Kaspar is socialized through language, he also learns to control his body, and his movements appear more naturalistic. Yet there is still an unnatural slowness, a stiffness, a passiveness in Kaspar's movements recalling German Expressionist cinema. One thinks of Conrad Veidt's Caesare in *Caligari,* and Fritz Kortner's cowering postman in *Backstairs.* But while expressionist acting "uses stylization to create a stereotype" . . . , Herzog's actor, Bruno S., uses his body to underscore his otherness.

The secondary characters, on the other hand, are more stereotypical, and it has been argued that the roles of these players are nothing but a series of shallow caricatures: self-righteous priests, pedantic university professors, drunken peasants, callous noblemen, and petty bureaucrats. Never projecting more than a one-dimensional image, most of these characters are, to be sure, exceedingly unsympathetic. Even the farmer and his wife, or Herr Daumer and his elderly housekeeper, Kaspar's guardians and staunchest allies, are more typical than individual. . . . [*Kaspar Hauser's* characters] may exist only in so far as they contribute to defining the central character. Thus, Kaspar's imperfect piano playing is contrasted to Lord Stanhope's ever so refined narration of a trip to Greece. Dressed in a slimy green suit, he spews forth one tired, romantic cliché after another, as his guests politely oh and ah, and Kaspar turns ill from the parlor heat. Then there is the little town clerk, who records every detail of Kaspar's short life with anal accuracy. When the books on Kaspar have been closed after the autopsy, the clerk is absolutely certain the mystery has been solved through his diligence: "a beautiful protocol, an exact protocol." If town councilors are beasts as E.T.A. Hoffmann feared . . . , then Herzog's town clerk is a species of rodent. (pp. 228-30)

Using the diminuitive form, . . . Kaspar anthromorphizes with child-like tenderness almost everything around him, whether animate or inanimate. Kaspar's very first word is "Ross" (archaic German: "horse"), the name he gives a toy Trojan horse he rolls with endless fascination back and forth in his cell. . . . [Unlike] the Expressionists, Kaspar does not find these objects with a life of their own dangerous, but accepts them as quite normal. In Herzog's *Even Dwarfs Started Small* these demonic overtones are more obvious: "That is a world in which objects have become independent and monstrous. Not the dwarfs are the monsters, but a door handle or a chair, which has grown out of proportion." But for Kaspar objects are less threatening than human beings, and he has no sense "of doors that become gaping maws and shrieking gullets." . . . (pp. 230-31)

This sense of living in an animate, constantly fluctuating environment carries over into Kaspar's attitude towards dreams. At one point Kaspar says to his mentor, Herr Daumer, "Mich hat getraümt" (I was dreamt). Daumer congratulates Kaspar for finally differentiating between dream and reality, instead of relating dreams as facts. Yet Kaspar's use of the passive voice still indicates his continuing belief in dreams as a kind of reality. The passive voice implies that the dreams come to him externally and are thus no different from the perceptions made during waking hours. That he did not dream until he was born into the physical world also adds to Kaspar's confusion. At the same time, Kaspar dreams of places he's never been, e.g. the Caucasus village or Sahara desert. Kaspar's dream of the mountain of death, on the other hand, mirrors the exterior reality of his near fatal wounds. . . .

But it is Kaspar's last dream of a caravan wandering in the Sahara, which may hold the key to Herzog's film. The caravan stops when the leaders see mountains in front of them, and fear their compasses have failed them. The blind Berber leading the caravan gets off his camel, tastes the sand, and proclaims the mountains to be a mirage. The caravan moves on and realizes the truth of the blind man's vision, but Kaspar never learns whether they reach the city they were looking for. Here reality, as observed by the camel drivers, is discovered to be a mirage, a dream, a joke played on them by the desert winds, while the perception of the blind Berber corresponds to the actual order of things. It seems clear that for Herzog empirical reality is only an illusion of another kind. . . . (p. 231)

But the problem is more complex, involving as it were a bias against rational, dualistic forms of thinking. For Herzog, neither scientific method, nor a theory of logic, nor objective rationalizations, can reveal any systematic order to the universe. The universe is unknowable, as Camus would have argued. Herzog's ending reinforces the anti-scientific bias: during an autopsy, the learned doctors discover Kaspar's brain to be oversized, and thus find, they believe, a pat solution for the anti-social behavior he has displayed. Again, Herzog's attack on science has its roots in Camusian existentialism. One need only remember Camus' approval in *The Rebel* of Bakunin's tirade against the tyranny of science. Interestingly, Camus' parable, "All Cretans are liars," in *The Myth of Sisyphus* is reworked by Herzog in *Kaspar Hauser:* a university professor of logic visits Kaspar to see if he is capable of rational, deductive thinking. To test Kaspar he gives him a problem of logic. . . . Kaspar's answer uses such simple logic, given the specific circumstances of the problem, that it annihilates any pretense to analytic thought. To find humanity at the very edge of madness, of physical and mental deformation, as Herzog does in all his work, is to assert the humanity in all men. Kaspar, like almost all of Herzog's subjects, looks at the world from a different perspective. And, like all of those who see through different eyes, Kaspar is doomed to be an outcast, whose presence in middle-class society invariably causes consternation.

Society, intolerant of otherness, of physical defects, and of uncontrollable psyches, denies these damaged individuals their humanity through bureaucratic institutionalization, persecution, and simple neglect. Yet Herzog's criticism of bourgeois values is basically apolitical. Like Camus—and in contrast Sartre—Herzog does not connect the attitudes of Kaspar's adversaries to class structure, although the clerics, clerks, and academics Kaspar comes into contact with are of the same class. The implication, that his otherness, like the class-bound otherness of the poor, is a financial burden to the bourgeoisie best ignored, is never followed through.

Rather, *The Mystery of Kaspar Hauser* is structured as a series of individual confrontations between Kaspar and the representatives of a normal, bourgeois culture: priests (religion), town clerks (government), professors (education), nobility (capital). . . . Like a Christ figure, or St. Joan, Kaspar tacitly accepts his suffering by remaining passive in the face of maltreatment. The very passiveness of these martyrs, their refusal to actively conform to the norms society requires, however, becomes their revolt against those norms. Their uncompromising goodness, their lack of malice even towards their persecutors, on the other hand, becomes a visionary example for man's redemption. Just as the blind Berber brings salvation through his disability, so does Kaspar through his otherness force us to reconsider the values on which society is predicated.

Ironically, then, this godless passion play, in which every man is for himself, and the universe against all, leaves us, like the work of Albert Camus, with an anarchistic, albeit humanistic visions of man. Like the caravan trekking over the barren sands towards an unseen goal, life becomes an act of faith in Herzog's films. *Heart of Glass* in fact ends with a group of men rowing out into an unchartered ocean, not knowing whether they will fall off the edge. Man's only hope is that through creation—Kaspar writes an autobiography, Herzog makes his films—hope is maintained. Despite the chaos, despite the irrationality of existence, man must persevere. (pp. 231-33)

Jan-Christopher Horak, "Werner Herzog's Écran Absurde," in Literature/Film Quarterly *(© copyright 1979 Salisbury State College), Vol. VII, No. 3, Special Issue, 1979, pp. 223-34.*

DAVID OVERBY

Herzog has claimed that he wanted [*Woyzeck*] to look as primitive as the main character, but the film looks not so much simple and primitive as badly made. The images have an inexpensive flat quality, and the editing of the film often ruins what magic there is in the images. The murder sequence in which Woyzeck stabs his prostitute mistress is filmed in extreme slow motion and is hypnotic at first. Unfortunately Herzog rather pointlessly cuts away for a moment to a dance hall, and when he returns to the murder the emotions first engendered have melted away. *Woyzeck* suffers from the same problems as *Nosferatu:* lack of life, a lack of atmosphere and far too many rather pretentious speeches (one delivered straight into the camera) about death and eternity. There is by now little doubt that Herzog is a major talent, but after the last few films there would also seem to be little doubt that he has hit a dry period. It may well be that literary adaptations and "stars" get in the way of Herzog's unique vision. (p. 34)

David Overby, "'Unclean, Unclean': A Report from Cannes," in Take One *(copyright © 1979 by Unicorn Publishing Corp.), Vol. 7, No. 8, August, 1979, pp. 33-35,42.**

ANDREW SARRIS

Woyzeck contains two or three epiphanies involving . . . [Woyzeck and Marie], and two or three epiphanies is more than you get from all but a handful of film artists in the world. As in *Aguirre, Wrath of God,* the epiphanies come at the beginning and the end. The problem, as always with Herzog, is in the middle where he is unable to create a cinematically dynamic narrative. Indeed, Herzog is as fragmentary in his ways as Georg Büchner, author of *Woyzeck* was in his. Moreover, Herzog displays little feeling for fiction, for archetype, for a representation of the world with its normal constituents. Herzog is instead the eccentric par excellence, searching out what differs most radically and most violently from the norm in order to express a more exalted level of consciousness.

Andrew Sarris, "Films in Focus: 'Woyzeck'," in The Village Voice *(reprinted by permission of* The Village Voice; *copyright © News Group Publications, Inc., 1979), Vol. 24, No. 35, August 27, 1979, p. 45.**

RICHARD COMBS

Herzog has perhaps been assumed (not least by Herzog himself) to be such an original that he doesn't need to be referred to any tradition. And it may be perverse proof of that to find both *Nosferatu* and *Woyzeck* awkwardly digesting their given material, and Herzog with more determination than conviction adapting himself to alien dramatic traditions (in what might be seen as an attempt, ironically, to find himself a specifically Germanic home). Whether or not, by switching to adaptations, Herzog has exhausted his 'originality' is another question, but it was probably only a matter of time before this dauntless conquistador should run out of new territories to explore, new landscapes in which to set man (the ridiculous) before nature (the sublime). Herzog, arguably, was already heading up a dead end with *Stroszek,* in which the child of nature suffers the familiar indignities of the road movie hero. [*Nosferatu* and *Woyzeck*] have at least restored the cosmic level to his irony, which never bothered to suggest that such inspired fools as Aguirre, Woodcarver Steiner or Kaspar Hauser should be pitied for their social maladjustment.

That the old Herzog is alive and well might be assumed from the provisional way he has treated his pre-existing texts. It hardly seems relevant to consider whether the films are successful adaptations—the texts are simply manmade landscapes which Herzog rifles for his favourite manmade contradictions: between social roles and transcendental aspirations; between life's 'little' deaths and a profounder death-wish that amounts to life everlasting; between prescribed circles and some limitless trajectory. Herzog's implicit assertion here that he belongs to certain traditions (Murnau and expressionism; Büchner and the first tragedy of common man) might be construed as an attempt to run for cover—rather in the way his short film *La Soufrière,* having failed to show nature cataclysmically cancelling man, makes do with comments on the social disgrace of the people who live on the side of a volcano. But far from becoming 'home' to him, the texts seem to be locations as exotic as the Amazon jungle or the African desert, substitutes for a new physical direction; and if not entirely satisfactory as such, they do allow some room for manoeuvre.

One can assume that Herzog is respectful of Murnau because his *Nosferatu* literally duplicated so many images from the original. That he wants—or is able—to remake Murnau's classic is doubtful, because his own identification with the extraordinary, the supernatural, keeps running counter to the story's insistence on the tragedy of a being who can never die, therefore never love, never live in the present. What Herzog does is to make his own contrary film inside the original, elevating Jonathan Harker from functionary to dual protagonist, so that at the very moment Dracula is released from eternal life by lingering with Lucy beyond first cock-crow, Jonathan is released from the bourgeois present . . . to become the new emissary of the undead.

A less schizophrenic work, *Woyzeck* . . . is in many ways a faithful adaptation of George Büchner's strange fragmentary play. . . . Herzog has deleted and compressed some material but invented nothing, and one might assume that he found Büchner's terse, gnomic dialogue, his non-linear construction and his yoking of a cosmic and a social sense of injustice adaptable enough to his own declamatory, disjunctive style. There is also a characteristic Herzog tension in Büchner: the contradiction between his 'new' naturalism (a proletarian hero, first driven crazy and then to murder by an unjust society) and his 'new' expressionism (the brief, elliptical scenes) that made the play unperformable for so long.

Herzog even draws imagery from Büchner that is strongly reminiscent of previous Herzog. The fair which the soldier Woyzeck . . . attends with his common-law wife Marie . . . features a demonstration of the 'human' understanding of animals and the low evolutionary standing of some humans (i.e. soldiers) that recalls the exhibition of freaks in *Kaspar Hauser*. Büchner's archetypes of the bourgeois order, the Doctor and the Captain, who prod experimentally at Woyzeck, and push him towards his final madness by teasing him about Marie's infidelity with the Drum Major, are also dotty rationalists in the Herzog tradition. The stream beside which Woyzeck kills Marie, and in which he tries to wash away his sin, is conjured at the very beginning of the film as an idyllic setting for the placid, strangely toy-like garrison town (Herzog's treatment of man and nature taking him by a more direct route than the conventions of expressionism back to Murnau). *Woyzeck*'s most severe limitation, in fact, might not be its given literary qualities but the extent to which it has allowed Herzog to remake something like *Kasper Hauser*. Woyzeck is explained here even less than he is in the original: he is an obscurely obsessed mooncalf, tortured by cosmic visions as much as he is victimised by military discipline and the economic need that drives him to take part in the Doctor's experiments. Büchner's references to silence, darkness, blindness, and his apocalyptic biblical parables, are also typical of Herzog, but remain tensely contained in the text, unreleased in the imagery. (pp. 259-60)

[In *Woyzeck,* Herzog] has, more successfully than in *Nosferatu,* accommodated his own personality to the original author; and if it is less than exploratory, the film works finally as a canny holding measure. (p. 260)

Richard Combs, "Film Reviews: 'Woyzeck'," in Sight and Sound *(copyright © 1979 by The British Film Institute), Vol. 48, No. 4, Autumn, 1979, pp. 259-60.*

DONALD BARTHELME

In "Nosferatu," Herzog has desexualized the [vampire] story, in two ways: first by a stress on the classic 1922 Murnau version which gives his own film an air of pious re-creation, and, second, by a bothersome uncertainty of tone. The film is very much of a piece with his "Woyzeck" . . . , as if he had set out to make a pair of salon paintings to be placed at either end of some vast museum gallery. Herzog makes abundant references not only to Murnau but to his own previous films. A shot of coffins on a raft immediately recalls the voyaging raft in "Aguirre, the Wrath of God." . . . (pp. 183-84)

The problem [in "Nosferatu"] is that Herzog was unable to bring new life to his much-handled material. I assume he thought he had a viable approach in conceiving of the film as being "after," as it's phrased, Murnau. He's better at creating new myth; at this, he has few peers. (p. 184)

Donald Barthelme, "The Current Cinema: 'Nosferatu'," in The New Yorker *(© 1979 by The New Yorker Magazine, Inc.), Vol. LV, No. 35, October 15, 1979, pp. 182-84.**

DAVID DENBY

Werner Herzog's *Nosferatu* is extraordinarily beautiful and also creepy beyond belief. Like F. W. Murnau, . . . the young German director has made not a conventional horror film (there are no shocks) but an anguished poem of death. The colors are nightmare blue-black, the mood sepulchral and hushed. Herzog sustains long stretches of imagery that work on the imagination and the emotions through vile suggestion rather than explicit enactment. . . . As always, Herzog holds his actors in static, sculptured poses; his narrative tempo is as poky as ever, his landscapes as placidly sinister. Only this time there's a most explicit reason for everything to be drained of life. Having passed into the realm of myth, Herzog, for once, seems like a realist filmmaker. (p. 89)

David Denby, "Movies: In Praise of Older Women," in New York *Magazine (copyright © 1979 by News Group Publications, Inc.; reprinted with the permission of* New York *Magazine), Vol. 12, No. 41, October 22, 1979, pp. 86, 88-9.**

STANLEY KAUFFMANN

Herzog clearly feels a special affinity with early 19th-century Germany, the period in which Caspar David Friedrich was the preeminent painter, the period of *Kaspar Hauser,* of *Woyzeck,* of *Nosferatu*. The pellucid air, the dainty neatness of the households, the serenity overlying the anguished idealism, all these engage Herzog's eye and mind. Those qualities and [Jonathan Harker's] encounter with gypsies on his way through wild mountains are the best directorial elements in [*Nosferatu*]. Herzog seems more at ease with them than with the supposedly macabre sequences in Dracula's castle. . . .

But to detail this picture's accomplishments is finally a sorry business because they all come to so little. We're being told by some that this is not a horror film. Well, then, what is it? Not even good acting like most performances here, not even direction as good as the best moments, can exalt *Nosferatu*. Its Christian parable is wonky; its psychosexual implications are factitious; its social symbolism is thin. Worse, none of these possible subtexts coheres because none is genuinely intended. At the last *Nosferatu* is only a tale to make the flesh creep, if it can—a superior eerie entertainment. (p. 22)

Stanley Kauffmann, "Films: Foreigners" (reprinted by permission of Brandt & Brandt Literary Agents, Inc.; copyright © 1979 by Stanley Kauffmann), in The New Republic, *Vol. 181, No. 7, October 27, 1979, pp. 22-3.**

ROBERT ASAHINA

Herzog's *Nosferatu* is an esthetic triumph. A feeling of subtle horror practically oozes from the screen—a remarkable achievement, considering that the director managed it with techniques and imagery (the soft-focus pastels) not normally associated with horror films. Yet if this film may be a feast for the eyes, it is dreary for the mind. No amount of directorial prestidigitation can disguise the bareness of the material. One wishes that Herzog had chosen a more worthy vehicle for his talents. (p. 24)

Robert Asahina, "Novels into Films," in The New Leader *(© 1979 by the American Labor Conference on International Affairs, Inc.), Vol. LXII, No. 21, November 5, 1979, pp. 23-4.**

LAWRENCE O'TOOLE

In visual terms, Herzog's movies define the boundaries of the exquisite; there's an eggshell delicacy to them. He will hold an image long enough for the senses to accommodate it, but not so long that you can indulge yourself with too much free-association. The image is withdrawn at the point where it has made the sufficient impact it has set out to make. It is, as it were, given gallery display; but, as it were, taken away at the critical point. It's not the image that matters so much (though in the conventional sense Herzog's imagery is more often than not stunning) as *seeing* the image. . . .

Herzog lets you see the thing in its essence, but there is also the dramatic context of the narrative to give it meaning and resonance. Given the not unjust reputation of minimalist and conceptual art, it would probably be wise not to attach the label "minimalist" to Herzog's work. Also, he is as much a miniaturist as he is a minimalist, focusing on the small detail to give it added texture and more bulk. (p. 38)

Life may be pointless, according to Herzog's movies, but it isn't necessarily meaningless. Knowing futility is self-awareness, and there's a tranquility in *knowing*. There is also a stasis in that state of being. And there are moments that have, or at least suggest, a great ecstasy. (p. 39)

Lawrence O'Toole, "The Great Ecstasy of Filmmaker Herzog" (copyright © 1979 by Lawrence O'Toole; reprinted by permission of the author), in Film Comment, *Vol. 15, No. 6, November-December, 1979, pp. 34-9.*

GILBERTO PEREZ

[In *Nosferatu–The Vampyre*] Herzog tells the story with a certain irony (most salient in the deliberately archaizing mode of some of the performances) but without any intention of parody: he is asking us to take it in all seriousness. True, his source of inspiration was not Bram Stoker's *Dracula* but the first film rendering of it, F. W. Murnau's silent *Nosferatu*, the one occasion in which Stoker's tale yielded a great work of art. . . . Herzog is paying his respects to an old film he particularly admires, and attempting to reinstate the story to the kind of validity Murnau was able to give it. (p. 14)

Despite the recreation of the vampire's makeup, and the adherence to some significant changes the old film made in the plot of the novel, Herzog's conception of Nosferatu diverges notable from Murnau's. Herzog shows us his Nosferatu very often in close-up, or with the camera close enough to him for his striking face to become the center of attention, in a marked departure from Murnau's technique which reflects a basic difference in theme. For Herzog's closer look serves his endeavor to humanize the vampire, changing him from Murnau's sovereign fiend into a figure of more lifelike dimensions, and inviting our sympathy in his behalf. . . . Murnau's Nosferatu comes to seem pathetic in the end; but Herzog's Nosferatu seems pathetic from the beginning.

We first encounter the vampire, in Herzog as in Murnau as in Stoker, when Jonathan Harker, on his journey to Transylvania, encounters him in his castle; but Herzog's Count, unlike the others, looks nervous in that first appearance. He breathes heavily as he stares at Harker eating his supper; he makes an embarrassed excuse for sucking the blood in Harker's thumb when Harker accidentally cuts it with a knife, and he awkwardly proceeds to suck that blood anyway after Harker resists the suggestion that this would be therapeutic. Herzog's Count doesn't relish his blood-sucking, but can't help doing it: it's his curse, or his neurosis. In the young wife's bedroom at the end, he lifts up her nightgown, groping for a more conventional sexual interaction, and she has to direct him toward her neck, which is what vampires are supposed to be interested in. Unlike Murnau's, Herzog's Nosferatu doesn't disappear after the plague breaks out in the Nordic town, and well before the end he turns up in the young wife's bedroom and tells her that death isn't the worst thing, that life without love is worse. Herzog even shows us the woman and Harker, the husband she so loves, from the point of view of the vampire spying on their domesticity. . . . [In] Herzog we are expected to sympathize with the vampire's need for love, and so we are given his perspective from the outside looking in at the couple's home. Instead of personifying the threat of death, this Nosferatu laments the fact that he is unable to die, and must keep on doing the same futile things he has been doing for centuries; he seeks in the woman a redemption from his plight. One result of this changed conception is that, whereas Murnau's Nosferatu is the most frightening of vampires, Herzog's hardly scares us at all—though perhaps he wasn't intended to.

In portraying a more human vampire, it may seem inappropriate to have adopted, and to display in prominent close-up, Nosferatu's macabre makeup, the least naturalistic of any Dracula. Yet Herzog, one gathers, wants us to regard his Count's grotesque appearance not so much as the embodiment of evil but as if it were the manifestation of some kind of disease, like the elephant man's, and hence as another reason we should feel compassion for the vampire. Not only does this Nosferatu need love, he is a monster utterly lacking in the vampiric sex appeal of the standard Dracula. The Dracula story, however, doesn't mix very well with the story of Beauty and the Beast. Dracula is as fundamentally evil as the Beast is fundamentally good, and Herzog's vampire, being responsible, either by himself or with the help of his attendant rats, for the death of innumerable people, is no less evil than any other. It's of course possible to see the evildoer as afflicted by a disease, driven by forces he cannot control, and to that extent to feel sorry for him: that was how Herzog presented the maniacal conquistador in *Aguirre, the Wrath of God.* His Nosferatu is like another version of Aguirre. . . . But I think Herzog was misguided to have attempted such a presentation in the realm of the fantastic tale: only if we are made to confront evil as an actual human possibility, unbelievable yet incontrovertible, can we be expected to harbor mixed feelings about it. (pp. 14-15)

If in his other films Herzog has often seemed bent on reconstructing the exaggerations of the old German expressionists with material taken from life, in *Nosferatu* he has taken material from an old expressionist film and treated it as if it were part of life, as if we could accept vampirism as another human aberration.

And the new film, it must be added, exaggerates much more than the old one, what with the vampire's grotesqueness magnified in the frequent close-ups, the few rats in the original multiplied into the hundreds and dwelt on at length, many more shots of many more coffins in the streets of the pestilential town. Herzog exaggerates much more but to much diminished effect: all those additional coffins, for example, fail to add up to anything like the indelible impact of Murnau's shot from the young wife's window. . . . Of course Herzog has at his command technical resources undreamed of at the time of the original, but his style is much coarser, his structural sense much weaker than Murnau's. Among the several shots he replicates from Murnau is one of the most impressive in the original . . . : that showing the arrival in the Nordic town of the ship carrying Nosferatu and the plague. Herzog does a good job of recreating the plastic qualities of the shot: the town in the background, the line of the waterside close to the left edge of the screen and nearly parallel to it, in the middle water and mainly an empty space which is gradually, inexorably, filled by the ship as it makes its slow entrance into frame from the right. In Murnau the shot has a powerful effect in conveying the feeling that the ship, and its lethal cargo, are gaining dominance over the town; but not in Herzog. Why not, since the images are closely similar? Because in Murnau the shot comes as the culmination of a carefully developed rhythm, as a stopping point after a succession of brief, briskly cut shots, whereas in Herzog the shot follows a leisurely helicopter shot circling the ship at sea, a shot which seems complete in itself rather than leading forward to the next one.

Herzog is being modest in so attempting to recreate Murnau—too modest, as some of the reviewers have observed, since he is more successful when creating images of his own. Indeed, the best sequence in his film is one without precedent in Murnau, that in which several people make merry in the town square amid the devastation, celebrating the fact that they are alive for another day, that the plague hasn't claimed them yet. But Herzog is also being immodest in presuming that he can rescue Count Dracula from his debased mythology and match the qualities of the original *Nosferatu*. Although he has come up with a new rendering of the vampire, and one which accords with his own preoccupations, Dracula as the malformed outcast carries little conviction. The failure of this new film, moreover, points up the questionable nature of Herzog's general pursuit of the grotesque, of a view of life granting such centrality to the outlandish as to include the bloody Count among the odd specimens of our common humanity. (p. 15)

Gilberto Perez, "Herzog's 'Nosferatu'," in New York Arts Journal *(copyright © 1979 by Richard W. Burgin), No. 16, 1979, pp. 14-15.*

COLIN L. WESTERBECK, JR.

It is to rescue Dracula from the defilements of high camp that Werner Herzog has . . . made his own *Nosferatu*. Herzog wants to restore Murnau's film to its rightful place in movie history, so he has remade the Murnau version scene by scene. . . . This is not to say that Herzog has no ideas of his own. Where his film departs from Murnau's, it is in the direction of naturalizing, even humanizing, the Dracula character. (p. 17)

At the same time that he is trying to revive the Dracula legend, Herzog is trying to make us sense its lost power. We should be able to understand, he is suggesting, how compelling a figure Dracula was in a world where death could take such an inexplicable and irresistible form as the plague. Dracula answered a human need which we may have yet, but no longer recognize.

Herzog has naturalized Murnau's Dracula in other ways, too. The over-use of special effects and trick photography in Dracula films came after Murnau, who employed them only to a limited extent. Herzog makes almost no use of them. As a consequence his Dracula seems, though always a creature separate and distinct from human beings, still subject to the world in which they live. He is not the mere ghost that Murnau's film sometimes makes him. (pp. 17-18)

At moments . . . Herzog succeeds in making Dracula a richly paradoxical creature. On the one hand, Herzog's film restores the immutable otherness of Dracula as Murnau conceived him. He is no longer the chameleon character of the Hollywood tradition, the oily, familiar villain in a Victorian melodrama. On the other hand, he is not quite the ethereal being that Murnau made him either. He is in his strangeness a more pathetic figure. He is world-weary. We understand his premonition that, because he will live on in a modern world with an insufficient sense of evil, he will outlive his own glory.

The beauty of Herzog's film is that it makes no apology for Dracula. It isn't embarrassed by him. It doesn't cringe when the figure he cuts becomes a ridiculous and laughable one. Unlike other recent filmmakers, Herzog feels no need to make a spoof out of the Dracula legend, to show his modern superiority to it. His treatment of it is "innocent," as he himself has said. The result is that he has made the best Dracula film since Murnau, and maybe the best ever. (p. 18)

Colin L. Westerbeck, Jr., "An 'Innocent' Dracula: Myth Rather Than Melodrama," in Commonweal *(copyright © 1980 Commonweal Publishing Co., Inc.; reprinted by permission of Commonweal Publishing Co., Inc.), Vol. CVII, No. 1, January 18, 1980, pp. 16-18.*

(Sir) Alfred Hitchcock

1899-1980

British director.

Hitchcock's name is synonymous with the sophisticated, graceful thriller. His films demonstrate a consistent view that transforms the ordinary into the exotic. An outstanding technician, Hitchcock uses the camera to advance his story and mood, introducing dialogue only when it is absolutely necessary. His plots shun conventional terror gimmicks, centering instead on common anxieties and human weaknesses.

Hitchcock's first job in the cinema was as a designer of title cards for silent films. Subsequently, he rose to script writer, art director, and assistant director. In 1925, Hitchcock directed his first feature, *The Pleasure Garden*. However, *The Lodger* was the first film to display his inimitable style. Motifs to reappear included his interest in cinematic effects, the "transference of guilt" whereby an innocent character is accused unjustly of a crime, and the inevitable appearance of Hitchcock himself. *Blackmail,* Hitchcock's first sound feature, brought him international fame and led a string of spy thrillers, culminating in *The Lady Vanishes* and *The Thirty Nine Steps*. Products of his peak creative period, they demonstrate a developing talent for manipulating audience reaction by suspense. At the same time, there surfaced his macabre humor as a means of increasing anxiety.

In 1939, David O. Selznick lured Hitchcock to Hollywood. Hitchcock's first Hollywood film, *Rebecca,* dealt with another recurring Hitchcock motif: a woman haunted by the memory of another. As an indication of his American work, *Rebecca* introduced a new psychological aspect which took several directions. One, the insinuation of unfounded suspicion, is developed in later films, including *Suspicion* and *Shadow of a Doubt*. Later work demonstrated his interest in psychodrama. Such films as *Vertigo* and *Marnie* explore the depths of a female psyche, while causing the audience to alternately embrace and disdain the heroine.

Hitchcock's British chase films of the 1930s reemerged in much altered form in the 1950s. Many critics find these films his finest works, since they provide an ideal setting for Hitchcock's fascination with technical challenges. In particular, these films allowed him an opportunity to place endangered protagonists in settings symbolizing order, such as Mount Rushmore, in *North by Northwest*. By disturbing that which is traditionally stable, Hitchcock brings out his theme of a world in disorder, increasingly penetrated by evil.

While encompassing a wide variety of thematic materials, Hitchcock eschewed the "whodunnit" genre by studying the evil inherent in what one already sees. The mass appeal of his films occasionally led reviewers to treat them as popular entertainment instead of cinematic art. However, their appeal to the French new wave filmmakers has inspired many viewers to reevaluate Hitchcock's work in terms of his visual narrative and technical ingenuity.

[*The Thirty-Nine Steps*] neatly converts its essential implausibility into an asset by stressing the difficulties which confront its hero when he tries to tell outsiders about the predicament he is in. (p. 44)

In the last two years, by making a specialty of melodrama, the English cinema industry sometimes appears to have taken its motto from the words of a song popular in the U.S. a year ago, "Here Come the British with a Bang, Bang." *The Thirty-Nine Steps* is the most effective demonstration to date of Director Alfred Hitchcock's method of artful understatement and its success, which has already been sensational abroad, should be a lesson to his Hollywood imitators. (pp. 44-5)

"Cinema: 'The Thirty-Nine Steps'," in Time *(reprinted by permission from* Time, The Weekly Newsmagazine; *copyright Time, Inc. 1935), Vol. XXVI, No. 13, September 23, 1935, pp. 44-5.*

OTIS FERGUSON

"The Lady Vanishes" is a typical work of that genius in the art of motion pictures, Alfred Hitchcock, the overstuffed and delightful gentleman from London. But Hitchcock chooses to use his genius where it will do the least harm to the most effect, and so while everything he does has such speed and clarity it's a pleasure to sit there over and over and watch him work, he works frankly in surface motion. There is human interest and sympathy because his people are always right; but the action is violent, the need for it somehow unreal, and emotion does not mature. . . .

The story is almost unimportant: boy and girl find lady, have to shoot their way out, saving the nation and getting married. But it's just the thing for Hitchcock, who has more fun with the people on that train than a barrel of monkeys—the fun more liberally interjected than usual into throttled guitar players, false compartments, drugs, guns and evil.

It's as much comedy as straight plot, in fact, and some of the exploration of the English mind is as neat as you'll see, done with relish and droll good humor, planted not only in dialogue and perfect delivery but in the concept of type and situation. . . .

Hitchcock is a one-man show, getting every detail straight in his head and the way he wants it before the first camera starts rolling. He is almost an academy, too, because no one can study the deceptive effortlessness with which one thing leads to another without learning where the true beauty of this medium is to be mined.

Otis Ferguson, "War and Other Pieces," in The New Republic *(reprinted by permission of* The New Republic; *© 1938 The New Republic, Inc.), Vol. 86, No. 1245, October 19, 1938, p. 307.*

FRANZ HOELLERING

Precise and without pretensions, ["The Lady Vanishes"] is the best spy thriller in a long time: growing suspense from beginning to end, no empty threats, no sticky romantics, no stupid explanation, no misleading clues—every minute is used to advance the plot, which has an almost mathematical logic. Of course, a whole arsenal of old tricks is employed, but with authority and irony. By this quantity is changed into quality. About the excellent use of the comic relief provided by two English sport enthusiasts one could write an essay. Besides being an excellent story, presented with technical perfection, the picture vividly conveys the ruthless, machine-like methods of an organization which has the features of a modern totalitarian system. Our compliments to Mr. Hitchcock: the thriller addict leaves this film not only highly satisfied but with no pricks of conscience at having been taken in again by trash.

Franz Hoellering, "Films: 'The Lady Vanishes'," in The Nation *(copyright 1939 The Nation Associates, Inc.), Vol. 148, No. 2, January 7, 1939, p. 45.*

THOMAS BURTON

"Rebecca," the novel by Daphne du Maurier, for all its great popularity, limped badly and never really came completely to life. . . . But in the motion picture version all this is brushed aside by the understanding and literary style of a greater craftsman than Miss du Maurier.

Alfred Hitchcock has made of "Rebecca" one of those perfect things—one of those masterpieces that we remember, like his other perfect cinema entertainments "The Thirty-nine Steps" and "The Lady Vanishes." The novel is all there. . . . Hitchcock touches [the young girl] with a spark of genius and she moves in terror—flits before you a live, living person whom you pity and with whom you share some obscure dread. You become extremely susceptible to her fears. And Lord! but this Hitchcock has a sense of humor. There is no one making motion pictures today who can touch him for sly wit, fancy touch, or good rib-loosening laughter. . . . There is a delicate, instinctively alert intelligence in every scene. . . .

Like the simple poems of A. E. Housman, this story gives you the feeling that you are face to face with a master, yet to analyze the why of it is hard. The simple direct statement tricks you into thinking it is done with ease—yet behind every statement is the great skill and cunning of its creator.

Thomas Burton, "Books into Pictures," in The Saturday Review of Literature *(copyright © 1940 by* Saturday Review; *all rights reserved; reprinted by permission), Vol. XXII, No. 7, June 8, 1940, p. 21.*

JOHN MOSHER

"Suspicion" may just mean Joan Fontaine and Cary Grant to a big majority, but the select should be advised at once that it is also a screen version of Francis Iles' "Before the Fact." This eclectic minority may seethe at the treatment accorded one of the beautiful murder stories of the day. . . . As Mr. Hitchcock didn't rewrite the story, I suppose, but only directed what material was given him, he wouldn't seem much to be blamed.

Though there has been an insistent effort to make this novel of embezzlement and murder a cozy screen tale of domestic life in prewar England, with all the trouble really a notion in the wife's meandering mind and marital love a pretty boon abloom at the end, Mr. Hitchcock again and again manages to suggest the true Iles spirit and make of his smiling Cary Grant a plausible poisoner, a wavy-haired killer. For my part, I can't see that the wife who is so ready to believe the worst of her mate is such a lovely spirit. Just because her husband turns out to be bad about money, it doesn't mean he's a murderer, as any heiress knows.

The polish of the piece is a pleasure.

John Mosher, "Freshening Up Cary Grant," in The New Yorker *(© 1941 by The New Yorker Magazine, Inc.), Vol. XVII, No. 41, November 22, 1941, p. 98.*

MANNY FARBER

"Shadow of A Doubt" has a good deal of the peculiar, almost revolting emotion movie director Alfred Hitchcock tries to capture by suggesting that the most ordinary circumstance may turn up something sinister—the census takers at your door may be part of a widespread plot, the next time you cross the street somebody may push you in front of a truck. Hitchcock threatens your very possible world with the impossible so often in this movie that at the end, in addition to the emotion mentioned, you are not sure of anything. . . .

Unfortunately, Mr. Hitchcock's people here tend to resemble figures on a Saturday Evening Post cover or actors in a stock-company production of Tarkington. Not that they are made silly or have to say silly things; but rather that the treatment of the family and friends is corny and superficial, lacking insight and seriousness. They are homespun, clean, gentle people, but they do nothing, say nothing and inflict nothing that is telling. . . .

Hitchcock shows here that sensationalism is not necessary to every part of a movie if the details of ordinary activity are examined for their fullest suggestiveness. His most expressive moments are the sudden switches in emotion in midstride of an activity: the abrupt change in the pace of a walk or the tone of a voice, the sudden hurrying of people into position. As a result he is producing movies of high quality. As for his famous horror and suspense, they are here, and better than in any other of his American movies so far.

Manny Farber, "Hitchcock in Stride," in The New Republic *(reprinted by permission of* The

New Republic; (© *1943 The New Republic, Inc.), Vol. 108, No. 6, February 8, 1943, p. 182.*

DAVID LARDNER

One of the most remarkable of a number of remarkable things about "Lifeboat," written by John Steinbeck and Jo Swerling and directed by Alfred Hitchcock, is that the characters in it are not reformed or even radically changed by their experience, which consists of being torpedoed and compelled to endure considerable hardship in a lifeboat before they are rescued. I'm afraid that in less competent, and in fact most, film-producing hands, this experience would have been represented as a rather salutary one and at least some of the people involved would have begun mending their ways by the end of the picture. I don't say that perilous circumstances do not sometimes lead people to resolve to lead better lives if God or somebody will only get them out of this mess, or that on rare occasions such bargains are not kept, but I agree with Mr. Steinbeck and Mr. Swerling and Mr. Hitchcock that the average reaction of average people to rescue from extreme danger is a vast relief coupled with a determination to be as comfortable as possible for as long as possible.

This is not to say that in this picture the characters' forced confinement in each other's company or their hunger or their thirst is represented as having no probable lasting effect on them. It's plain that they learn a lot about each other and about the meaning of real privation, and in the end, though they're the same people they were at the beginning, they're better informed. (p. 56)

Mr. Hitchcock has chosen to keep the camera in the lifeboat too. He has done all his shooting from inside the boat and has never once backed off to show the boat itself in relation to its surroundings (ocean). That way he has lost a chance to do some effective contrast stuff and missed out on some of a camera's capabilities but he has unquestionably furthered the mood he was after. He and the writers are to be commended, also, for not over-elaborating. They have not made this the longest or severest trip in an open boat on record but have been content with what you might call an average shipwreck. Although those in the audience who have been torpedoed themselves may miss some of the experiences they recall, there are sure to be others there for them to recognize. Realism is rampant in the picture. In making it, some of the cast must have got very wet. (p. 57)

David Lardner, "Shipshape," in The New Yorker *(© 1944 by The New Yorker Magazine, Inc.), Vol. XIX, No. 48, January 15, 1944, pp. 56-7.*

JOHN McCARTEN

As a study of psychoanalytic procedure, "Spellbound," the latest creation of Old Master Hitchcock, wouldn't merit a footnote in Freud. But when the film stops trying to be esoteric and abandons arcane mumbling for good, rousing melodrama, it moves along in the manner to which Hitchcock has accustomed us. I don't think anybody could take seriously the proposition, advanced in "Spellbound," that an amnesia victim could install himself with no trouble whatever as a substitute for the head of a high-class sanitarium. . . . (p. 69)

Few amnesia victims of our time have held on to anonymity quite as grimly as Mr. Peck, and since his tenacity is spread over almost two hours, the film needs plenty of Hitchcock prodding to keep it from bogging down into lethargy. Fortunately, the English expert hasn't forgotten any of his tricks. He still has a nice regard for supplementary characters, and he uses everything from eerie train whistles to grand orchestral crescendos to maintain excitement at a shrill pitch. He manages his camera, as usual, with vast dexterity, and unless you're emotionally gelid, I think a good many of the shots will have you twitching. . . . Mr. Hitchcock has also included some dream sequences confected by Salvador Dali which seem pretty similar to those dreams of yesterday that the Surrealist scattered around Bonwit Teller's windows. (pp. 69-70)

John McCarten, "Hitchcock, with Freud's Help," in The New Yorker *(© 1945 by The New Yorker Magazine, Inc.), Vol. XXI, No. 38, November 3, 1945, pp. 69-70.*

JAMES AGEE

"Spellbound," Alfred Hitchcock's surprisingly disappointing thriller about psychoanalysis, is worth seeing, but hardly more. . . . I felt that the makers of the film had succeeded in using practically none of the movie possibilities of a psychoanalytic story, even those of the simplest melodrama; and that an elaborate, none-too-interesting murder mystery, though stoutly moored to the unconscious, merely cheapened and got in the way of any possible psychological interest. To quite an extent the psychological pretensions cluttered up the murder mystery too. . . . There are some frightening shots of the kinds of striated whiteness which mysteriously terrifies the patient—the mark of forktines on a table cloth, for instance; the remembrance of the initial trauma is excitingly managed; and in one crisis of mental dereliction, in which the camera flicks its eye forlornly around a bathroom, you get a little of the unlimited, cryptic terror which can reside in mere objects. But these are practically the only suggestions of the hair-raising movie this had every right and obligation to be. As for the dream designed by Salvador Dali, it is as frankly irrelevant to dream reality, and so to criticism for its lack of reality in that direct sense, as Markova is for not growing a four-foot larynx for "Swan Lake." The trouble is that this decision in favor of unreality was mistaken in the first place. In the second, the dream is none too good in its own terms. . . . "Spellbound" is just so much of the Id as could be safely displayed in a Bergdorf Goodman window.

James Agee, "Films: 'Spellbound'," in The Nation *(copyright 1945 The Nation Associates, Inc.), Vol. 161, No. 19, November 10, 1945, p. 506.*

MANNY FARBER

"Spellbound" is a soupy, synthetic movie that will probably hold your attention. For one thing it deals, as few movies have, with the analysis of a man . . . who is said to be suffering from paranoia, schizophrenia and a guilt complex. What is more, it reveals the basic situation in psychoanalysis wherein the patient lies on a couch and says whatever comes into his mind, regardless of the consequences. It is also fairly accurate about some of the questions an analyst asks, some of the things a patient says, and both their reactions. The attitude is always youthful and wide-eyed and the movie as slow-motion and unbelievable as a story in the *Woman's Home Companion*. The plot . . . is worked out with excessive care to give each step some degree of logic, but it is a logic you never believe in and you don't feel that its director . . . does either. Hitchcock's methods of creating tension, fear and obsessive fascination in a character for some threatening or alluring object, have become very mechanical, but he still produces those elements better than most directors. Also he still makes a tight, streamlined mystery. . . .

The mixture of analysis and murder doesn't come to much, especially for analysis. . . . There is an almost imperceptible amount of characterization of the hero—he has the quality of being less a person than a limp object. One reason for this is that only one brief instant of his past and little of his present are shown. When he comes into the picture he appears completely misplaced and he always seems to be suffering from the fact of being there. . . . Throughout, Hitchcock and his script-writer, Ben Hecht, imply that the hero is both completely capable and completely incapable of murder. Confusion doesn't seem to be their aim so much as the fact that every time they imply the worst in their hero they are able to build a melodramatic situation.

It is my belief that the analysis, which takes about three hours and is performed literally on the run from the police, on a Pullman, in a New York hotel room and during a ski jump, was just getting started as the picture ended.

By this time the talent and intelligence that Hitchcock showed in his English movies have been diluted to the point where he no longer seems very talented or intelligent. . . . The average Hitchcock shot today is usually without an effective, provocative or original detail; the photography is an all-soft, warm, harmonious kind in which backgrounds are blurred out; his real efforts at expression now seem extraneous, utterly pretentious and often have a wooden-soldier articulation.

Manny Farber, "Dream Manors," in The New Republic *(reprinted by permission of* The New Republic; *© 1945 The New Republic, Inc.), Vol. 113, No. 23, December 3, 1945, p. 477.*

ROBERT HATCH

Alfred Hitchcock might be grateful to us all if we would forget "The Lady Vanishes" and "The Thirty-Nine Steps." We pay him the compliment of believing that in his chosen field of melodrama he is a craftsman and stylist, and as a result we raise the passing mark. The later, or Hollywood, Hitchcock might be willing to trade us his reputation for a little charity, and that's the deal we may eventually make.

It would not be easy, however, to indulge him in the case of "Rope," for he seems to offer it as vintage Hitchcock. . . . [It] develops a portentous theme—one that goes far beyond cops and robbers, spies and crown jewels to examine good and evil and to hint of very dark corners in the human soul. It purports to be serious, so we must take it seriously.

Before getting into the question of "Rope's" thesis, I must protest twice against Hitchcock's mechanics. The first objection is that in a story involving a "perfect" murder (*i.e.*, a tidy one) you may not pretend that the assassin would neglect so obvious a chore as disposing of the victim's hat. The second is that very wealthy New Yorkers are not obliged to put up with large electric signs that overlook their drawing rooms and blaze garish, intermittent light into the eyes of the occupants. Even in his enthusiasm for atmosphere, Hitchcock must observe such things as zoning laws or forfeit that super-realism of detail that has always been his special trick. (pp. 29-30)

The film is full of talk about the moral law, superior and inferior beings, the sensuous pleasures of murder, rare books and chamber music. But it is all virtually pointless because open-and-shut nuttiness makes poor subject matter for ethical hair splitting. Raskolnikov pretty well disposed of the genius theory of justifiable blood-letting, and no one has to pause for a moment over the confusions of a couple of obvious psychopaths.

Despite Hitchcock's virtuosity in keeping the action moving and varied in the confines of one stage set (it is difficult to understand why a picture director should want to perform this unnecessarily confining trick), "Rope" is more fidgety than thrilling. . . .

I don't doubt that something very like "Rope" has happened, just as I don't doubt that there are a number of people around who confuse themselves with the Avenging Angel. But neither disordered state in itself makes very rewarding fiction. (p. 30)

Robert Hatch, "Murder for Profit," in The New Republic *(reprinted by permission of* The New Republic; *© 1948 The New Republic, Inc.), Vol. 119, No. 11, September 13, 1948, pp. 29-30.*

RICHARD WINNINGTON

When, nearly ten years ago, Alfred Hitchcock broke away from his Daphne du Maurier phase with *Shadow of a Doubt*, there were premature congratulations. He was first in with the real location melodrama, and it looked as if he might have returned to his older and more entertaining style. The succeeding Hitchcock films, popular, adept and replete with useless trick effects, have been, however, peculiarly depressing in that their hollowness has derived from Hitchcock himself, and not—as in the cases of some other expatriate directors—from Hollywood. . . .

Strangers on a Train . . . to some extent restores the situation and recalls the old virtuoso of the art of suspense. Here again fear and paranoia are let loose in the open against normal backgrounds, and the tension mounts and writhes through humdrum human activity to its bizarre, sensational climax. (p. 21)

Strangers on a Train confirms Hitchcock's utter dependence on his script—in this case the best he has had for years—and a basic superficiality which prevents him from developing the psychological conflicts his characters do no more than suggest. His power of observation and his flair for surprise, counter-poising of the realistic against the bizarre, are still in evidence, but beyond a wider (and effective) use of close-ups he makes no innovations or advances. But in spite of its many and obvious lapses the film will certainly be classed as one of the successes of the year. And rightly. (p. 22)

Richard Winnington, "Reviews: 'Strangers on a Train'," in Sight and Sound *(copyright © 1951 by The British Film Institute), Vol. 21, No. 1, August-September, 1951, pp. 21-2.*

DERWENT MAY

Gracelessness is the word one wants to describe the overall quality of Alfred Hitchcock's latest film, *Rear Window;* and no word could be sadder. For what are the qualities that we associate with classic Hitchcock if not, precisely, the elegance of proportion, the ease and sureness of manner? Here, however, the unevenness runs from beginning to end, the intermittent brilliances and delicacies serve only to emphasise it.

Rear Window has a situation which promises intricacy and then fails to provide it. (p. 89)

The thriller . . . leans back for long stretches on a rather half-hearted plot of love and character: Jefferies doubting until this happens whether his society girl-friend is adaptable enough to enjoy being married to him. . . .

Dial M for Murder is excellent; but it remains predominantly a success for the playwright, Frederick Knott. This story of a murderer whose plan misfires but who gives it a new lease of life by some brilliantly fast and then some sustained thinking, is only an exciting piece of algebra, all human reverberations ruthlessly deadened; however it is ingeniously written . . . and Hitchcock has moved about very sure-footedly on what continues to be for the most part just a stage. (p. 90)

Derwent May, "'Rear Window' and 'Dial M for Murder'," in Sight and Sound *(copyright © 1954 by The British Film Institute), Vol. 24, No. 2, October-December, 1954, pp. 89-90.*

FRANÇOIS TRUFFAUT

I am convinced that [*Rear Window*] is one of the most important of all the seventeen Hitchcock has made in Hollywood, one of those rare films without imperfection or weakness, which concedes nothing. For example, it is clear that the entire film revolves around the idea of marriage. When Kelly goes into the suspect's apartment, the proof she is looking for is the murdered woman's wedding ring; Kelly puts it on her own finger as Stewart follows her movements through his binoculars from the other side of the courtyard. But there is nothing at the end that indicates that they will marry. *Rear Window* goes beyond pessimism; it is really a cruel film. Stewart fixes his glasses on his neighbors only to catch them in moments of failure, in ridiculous postures, when they appear grotesque or even hateful.

The film's construction is very like a musical composition: several themes are intermingled and are in perfect counterpoint to each other—marriage, suicide, degradation, and death—and they are all bathed in a refined eroticism (the sound recording of lovemaking is extraordinarily precise and realistic). Hitchcock's impassiveness and "objectivity" are more apparent than real. In the plot treatment, the direction, sets, acting, details, and especially an unusual tone that includes realism, poetry, macabre humor and pure fairy tale, there is a vision of the world that verges on misanthropy.

Rear Window is a film about indiscretion, about intimacy violated and taken by surprise at its most wretched moments; a film about the impossibility of happiness, about dirty linen that gets washed in the courtyard; a film about moral solitude, an extraordinary symphony of daily life and ruined dreams.

There has been a lot of talk about Hitchcock's sadism. I think the truth is more complex, and that *Rear Window* is the first film in which he has given himself away such a degree. For the hero of *Shadow of a Doubt*, the world was a pigsty. But in *Rear Window* I think it is Hitchcock who is expressing himself through his character. I ought not to be accused of reading things into it, since the honest subjectivity of *Rear Window* breaks through each shot, and all the more so because the tone (always serious in Hitchcock's films) is geared as usual to its interest as a spectacle, that is, its commercial appeal. It's really a matter of the moral attitude of a director who looks at the world with the exaggerated severity of a sensual puritan. (pp. 78-9)

To clarify *Rear Window*, I'd suggest this parable: The courtyard is the world, the reporter/photographer is the filmmaker, the binoculars stand for the camera and its lenses. And Hitchcock? He is the man we love to be hated by. (p. 79)

François Truffaut, "Alfred Hitchcock: 'Rear Window'" (1954), in his The Films in My Life, *translated by Leonard Mayhew (copyright © 1975 by, Flammarion; translation copyright © 1978 by, Simon and Schuster; reprinted by permission of Simon and Schuster, a Division of Gulf & Western Corporation; originally published as* Les films de ma vie, *Flammarion, 1975), Simon and Schuster, 1978, pp. 77-9.*

ANDREW SARRIS

[Both *To Catch a Thief* and *The Trouble With Harry*] drag along from scene to scene without much inner motivation.

Of the two films, *To Catch a Thief* is much more successful because of its superior cast and brighter sense of fun. . . . *The Trouble With Harry* is the more ambitious film of the two, and consequently, the nobler failure. It doesn't come off because even the little touches are done badly.

The chief interest of both productions is their conscious ridicule of chases and corpses, two of the staples of melodrama. Hitchcock has always had a sense of comic counterpoint in his melodramas, but, never before, has he attempted to invert his melodramas into parodies of themselves. It is in this inversion, this gateway to high comedy, that Hitchcock reveals his major flaws.

Part of the trouble with Hitchcock is that he has seldom demonstrated a sense of milieu as opposed to an instinct for locale. He has been everywhere and nowhere. . . .

A director of bits and parts can never become a fist-rate comedy director. Comedy, or for that matter, serious drama, requires a continuity and development of character and idea. The longer Hitchcock remains with the tricks, twists, gimmicks, and charged props of melodrama, the less likely he is to ever graduate from a minor genre to a major theme. And that is not to say that Hitchcock does not deserve a great deal of credit for his restless spirit and his endless experiments with the tools of his art.

Andrew Sarris, "The Trouble with Hitchcock," in Film Culture *(copyright 1955 by* Film Culture*), Vol. 1, Nos. 5 & 6, Winter, 1955, p. 31.*

PENELOPE HOUSTON

[*The Trouble with Harry*] opens with a characteristic flourish, an incisive transition from tranquility to violence. . . . Unlike *The Ladykillers*, which broke wholly with reality, or Bunuel's *Criminal Life of Archibaldo de la Cruz*, with its ambiguous terrors. *The Trouble with Harry* establishes a setting neither entirely fantasticated nor disturbingly close to the real. (pp. 30-1)

Relaxed and deliberate, *The Trouble with Harry* spins out its single joke—the calm acceptance of the fact of violence that is the basis of *comedie noire*—with an alert regard for the possibilities of a situation. . . . Although the corpse is kept persistently in the foreground, the film blandly skirts the macabre, Harry exists merely as an inapposite feature in an idyllic pastoral scene. Quietly concentrated, the film's humour is largely a matter of a balance precariously sustained: the blazing splendour of the landscape sets off the grim little joke of a plot: the characters are normal people who in unguarded moments reveal fantastic preoccupations. In its insolent determination to explore the limits of good taste, the comedy is poised on a knife edge.

The authentic gaiety that lightens this gallows humour comes somewhat unexpectedly from the latter-day Hitchcock. . . .

The Trouble with Harry is personal and idiosyncratic, a film with the somewhat specialised appeal of a John Collier short story or a Charles Addams cartoon. *The Man Who Knew too Much* is a thriller off the Hitchcock assembly line, a 1956 model with a setting on the fashionable tourist circuit (Marrakesh) and a smooth chromium finish. What it lacks, simply, is an engine powerful enough to set the whole apparatus in motion. . . .

Momentarily, Hitchcock still brings off the shock of surprise. . . . But where the earlier film went like a bullet, the remake weightily ambles. *The Man Who Knew too Much* is a thriller of the most straightforward kind, an affair of pursuit and movement; and for Hitchcock, it is now apparent, the chase itself has lost its excitement. (p. 31)

Penelope Houston, "A Hitchcock Double," in Sight and Sound *(copyright © 1956 by The British Film Institute), Vol. 26, No. 1, Summer, 1956, pp. 30-1.*

PENELOPE HOUSTON

A good deal of Alfred Hitchcock's interest in film-making seems these days to consist in setting himself technical problems for the satisfaction of overcoming them. . . .

In *The Wrong Man* . . . Hitchcock has filmed his first true story, a precise and documented account of a case of mistaken identity. The problem here is to achieve a particular atmosphere of factual suspense, a spider's web entanglement of circumstantial detail enmeshing the bewildered and passive victim. . . .

After [a] gripping and splendidly circumstantial opening, the film's extreme slowness becomes an increasing dramatic liability. . . . The dramatic thread [breaks] somewhere in the middle of the film, and Hitchcock can no longer effectively tighten the screw of suspense.

In some of [the] later scenes, one even begins to wonder whether Hitchcock has not come slightly under the spell of those French intellectual critics who are always reading deeply symbolic interpretations into his work, finding a fatal mystical fascination in *I Confess* or *Under Capricorn*. The master has given them some additional ammunition here.

It is action that the second half of *The Wrong Man* lacks and with this director nothing else ever seems entirely to work.

Penelope Houston, "Film Reviews: 'The Wrong Man'," in Sight and Sound *(copyright © 1957 by The British Film Institute), Vol. 26, No. 4, Spring, 1957, p. 211.*

JAMES AGEE

Notorious lacks many of the qualities which made the best of Alfred Hitchcock's movies so good, but it has more than enough good qualities of its own. Hitchcock has always been as good at domestic psychology as at thrillers, and many times here he makes a moment in a party, or a lovers' quarrel, or a mere interior shrewdly exciting in ways that few people in films seem to know. . . . [He is] resourceful, and exceptional, in his manufacture of expressive little air pockets of dead silence. He has a strong sense of the importance of the real place and the real atmosphere. . . . There is perhaps no telling how much of all this should be credited to Ben Hecht's screen play; but it seems safe to credit a good deal of the sharpest movie sense, and of a cool kind of insight and control which suggests a good French novelist, to Hitchcock. (pp. 98-9)

James Agee, "'Notorious'," in his Agee on Film, Vol. 1 *(copyright © 1958 by the James Agee Trust; reprinted by permission of Grosset & Dunlap, Inc.), Grosset & Dunlap, 1958 (and reprinted in* Focus on Hitchcock, *edited by Albert J. LaValley, Prentice-Hall, Inc., 1972, pp. 98-9).*

ERNEST CALLENBACH

Hitchcock is said to be very pleased with [*Psycho*], and well he might be. In it he has abandoned the commercial geniality of his recent work and turned to out-and-out horror and psychopathology. The film begins with a drab, matter-of-fact scene in a hotel bedroom. . . . It imperceptibly shifts to a level of macabre pathology, unbearable suspense, and particularly gory death. In it, indeed, Hitchcock's necrophiliac voyeurism comes to some kind of horrifying climax. . . . So well is the picture made, moreover, that it can lead audiences to do something they hardly ever do any more—cry out to the characters, in hopes of dissuading them from going to the doom that has been cleverly established as awaiting them. (p. 47)

To allow the personae involved to become human beings would destroy everything, in the usual Hitchcock film. *Psycho* is better: the people are acceptable, at any rate; there is no need to make excuses for them. Still, it is the film *itself* that grips one—in these times, a remarkable achievement, and a hint that "realism" in the cinema is perhaps not so important as people think. *Psycho* is full of jokes, twists, pieces of nastiness that one would think gratuitous in any other film-maker. Hitchcock forces one to realize that these things are *the point*. . . .

Psycho is surely the sickest film ever made. It is also one of the most technically exciting films of recent years, . . . perhaps an omen. . . . (p. 48)

Ernest Callenbach, "Film Reviews: 'Psycho'," in Film Quarterly *(copyright 1960 by The Regents of the University of California; reprinted by permission of the University of California Press), Vol. XIV, No. 1, Fall, 1960, pp. 47-9.*

CHARLES HIGHAM

At heart, [Alfred Hitchcock is] a practical joker, a cunning and sophisticated cynic amused at the French critical vogue for his work, contemptuous of the audience which he treats as the collective victim of a Pavlovian experiment, perennially fascinated by his own ability to exploit the cinema's resources. His narcissism and its concomitant coldness have damaged those films whose themes have called for warmly sympathetic treatment: *The Ring, I Confess,* and *The Wrong Man* are obvious examples of stories which, demanding humanism, have been treated with a heartless artificiality.

The mechanics of creating terror and amusement in an audience are all Hitchcock properly understands. The portrayal of physical or intellectual passion is beyond him, and he has never directed a sexual encounter with the slightest perceptiveness. (pp. 3-4)

I believe that an understanding of Hitchcock's *oeuvre* can only be reached when it is seen in the hard, unwavering light of . . . commercial-minded philistinism. He remains at heart a cheerful London showman with a tough contempt for the world he has made his oyster. . . . He has simply taken the most dynamic popular art form of the twentieth century, toyed with it, and dared to explode some of the central myths it has established.

Where he has been most skilful of all is in his grasp of what can move the masses without fail. His pitiless mockery of human susceptibilities springs from a belief in the essential absurdity of those susceptibilities. (p. 4)

[In] *Psycho* . . . the plunging of a knife blade into a woman's nude body in a shower is deliberately made to represent the thrustings of the sexual act, so as to unleash the repressed libidinous sadism of large numbers of spectators. In nearly every case, the effect has come off so strikingly that even the most detached critic is bound to be engaged. Hitchcock's mastery of the medium is never more sharply expressed than in those sequences where he wants to make us release our repressions vicariously as he has released his cinematically.

The skill with which he has engineered the mechanism of his films has varied sharply from work to work, but in those films dominated by morbidity, physical disgust, and terror his gifts have usually been in striking display. . . .

The love scenes Hitchcock so elaborately shoots, usually set in "high life" for the hicks to goggle at, are invariably sexless, antiseptic, and rather nauseatingly cold. . . . He is more at home with people who show no visible evidence of sexuality at all: notably an array of dead, middle-aged Englishmen and Americans who come on and off the chalk-line in successive films to commit murders or shudder obediently in moments of disaster. And the perverted also fascinate him: one recalls the Lesbian housekeeper Mrs. Danvers in *Rebecca,* caressing the transparent nightdresses of her dead mistress. . . . (p. 5)

The numb hero and heroine, the sexless but useful character players, and the parade of sexually twisted oddballs in Hitchcock's films are, more often than not, engaged in a chase, and it is in the chase that he has found his central dynamic. To ensure universality, he has seized on monuments everyone can recognize and to set his characters in motion across them. . . . (pp. 5-6)

Sometimes the chase is the director's own: he is trying to discover the way people die, or the way they react to danger. The observation, the degree of understanding, is adolescent, but the chasing after facts about modes of behavior is adult, similar to a novelist's insatiable curiousity. (p. 6)

Sometimes [Hitchcock's silent style] is so elaborate, so exhibitionistic, that it destroys, rather than enhances, the dramatic content. In *The Ring* . . . , a story about the infidelity of a boxer's wife, the theme would have excited another writer-director to provide a moving study of human fallibility. Hitchcock simply used the plot-line to excuse a stunning display of technical virtuosity. The technique is the opposite of, say, Pabst's: the camera is used to play with, not explore in depth, the characters and their relationships. The whole film is a heartless *jeu d'esprit*. . . . (pp. 6-7)

The Lodger . . . remains the best of Hitchcock's silent films. Its reputation, thoroughly deserved, has remained intact because in it the soulless mechanism works perfectly, the detachment and coldness suit the subject—a straight murder story—and the setting, London, lends itself perfectly to bizarre stylization. (p. 7)

What Hitchcock manages [in *Vertigo*] (as often before) is a total suspension of disbelief in the impossible goings-on before one's eyes. Surrendered to, the film invades one's consciousness with rules of its own: this is one of those films . . . which completely creates a decadent, artificial world unrelated in any way to the real one. It has taken the French, not bound by the rule of thumb that judges a film by its verisimilitude, to see that the unreality of *Vertigo,* its free play with time and space, makes it a genuinely experimental film. . . . *Vertigo* is one of the peaks of Hitchcock's career, a film in which his coldness, his detachment, have found their perfect subject. (pp. 14-15)

He has now, after almost 40 years in cinema, got the power to do almost exactly what he likes, to scrawl his signature on the world's lavatory walls without restraint. He's still a child, pulling wings off flies, playing with the cinema like a toy. But there is no other director whose *jeux d'esprit* can be shared with equal pleasure by the masses and specialists alike. (p. 16)

Charles Higham, "Hitchcock's World," in Film Quarterly *(copyright 1962 by The Regents of the University of California; reprinted by permission of the University of California Press), Vol. XVI, No. 2, Winter, 1962-63, pp. 3-16.*

PETER BOGDANOVICH

The Birds could be called a hybrid of *Shadow of a Doubt* and *Psycho*. It combines the former's character-exploration with the latter's shock-effects, and emerges as one of Alfred Hitchcock's most striking and formidable achievements. On any level, a masterpiece. . . .

The Birds is a modern fable about the complacency of Man and the uncertainty of his position in the universe. Life is going carelessly by, but out of nowhere comes a dreadful enemy—one that no amount of reasoning can put down. Without explanation, seemingly without reason, the enemy strikes and persists until it has won. Man is powerless under its force; his struggles, however valiant (and Hitchcock feels that people show great bravery during times of crisis) are futile. *The Birds* is a fearful parable of the twentieth century. . . .

Hitchcock calls the movie a fantasy, but it is not approached that way; reality is the keynote. . . . This is part of the film's brilliance: it is happening and so you believe it. Such is the strength of Hitchcock's genius.

There are sequences in *The Birds* that will literally leave you limp. (p. 69)

Reviewers say it all the time: it's indescribable. But this movie is. The savage impact, the staggering effects, the uncompromising intensity, the depth, the artistry. Let's stop calling Hitchcock a wry trickster, a great craftsman, an enterprising entertainer, the master of suspense. He's all that too. But, mainly, he is a consummate artist. (p. 70)

Peter Bogdanovich, "'The Birds'," in Film Culture *(copyright 1963 by* Film Culture*), No. 28, Spring, 1963, pp. 69-70.*

ERNEST CALLENBACH

[*The Birds*] is disappointing. The film has been made, it seems to me, on two mistaken assumptions. One is that a frightening film can be made in naturalistic color, and the other is that an attack by birds carries the emotional impact of a really horrific situation. . . .

No doubt Hitchcock's reasoning was that the pastoral loveliness of Bodega Bay, rendered in soft color, would make us feel more attachment to the scene when it is abruptly threatened by thousands of attacking gulls and crows: so beautiful a little town, to have such a thing happen in it! Yet the effect is precisely the reverse: it reduces the scene to postcard dimensions, so that we care less rather than more, because it is only picturesque. The ratty motel in *Psycho,* by contrast, was a setting apt for the most extreme horrors; in itself it was a ratty motel only, yet quickly. . . . the film slid into an area of real emotional impact. *The Birds* never does. . . . [The] film has too many obvious loopholes. . . . [Nagging] mundane questions arise, obviously, because the film is unable to tap in, as a skillful thriller does, on unconscious fears. . . . A flock of attacking birds may be surprising, since we all have a somewhat rosy picture of the gentleness of birds, but they remain just a lot of attacking birds; they are natural, external forces to be combatted somehow or other, or fled from; they do not share the potentially supernatural mysteries and terrors of those things which are human or inhuman. (p. 44)

Whereas *Psycho* is a sickening slide into ever more terrifying events, until the ridiculous psychiatry sets in at the end, *The Birds* uses up its excitement early, then tries to rise to what is only an anticlimax—the escape of the four individuals in the sports car. (p. 45)

Ernest Callenbach, "Film Reviews: 'The Birds'," in Film Quarterly *(copyright 1963 by The Regents of the University of California; reprinted by permission of the University of California Press), Vol. XVI, No. 4, Summer, 1963, pp. 44-6.*

PENELOPE HOUSTON

What interests Hitchcock? Not precisely character: he creates it, and his flair for casting sustains it, but it is character directed to the ends of a limited dramatic situation, star personality cut to size, Not, certainly, professional crime, the mechanics of a bank robbery or the operations of a spy ring. Professionalism hints at routine, and Hitchcock's is the art of the unexpected—a celebration of that jarring moment when, walking in the dark down a staircase which you know every foot of the way, you suddenly hit bottom one step too soon. When Hitchcock talks of his own technique, it is often in terms of a deliberate avoidance of cliché. (p. 161)

What *does,* then, interest this bland, smooth man? The quirkish, English Hitchcock and the American Hitchcock who deals in the twists and turns of the mind are not perhaps as far apart as they seem. Humour at one end, monomania at the other, are alike in disturbing equilibrium and order. Hitchcock is fascinated, one deduces, by the way unreason keeps breaking in, by the ease with which system can be overturned. But it's the dark of the mind rather than of the soul that concerns him: his own position is that of the rational man for whom the world is a place of sublime and alluring unreason. A smashed cup, however, gives him more to work with than a smashed city; and a weakness of *The Birds* . . . is that it seems to be reaching out, however half-heartedly, towards some kind of larger significance. . . .

[Two] things become evident. Firstly that the crows and gulls, however well trained, must have been the very devil of a nuisance. . . .

Secondly, the bird—people relationship remains precarious and tenuous. Admirers have made resolute efforts to forge links by pointing out that the mother weakens under fire while the girl stands up to it, and someone has even claimed that Annie, the school-teacher, gets pecked to death because she hasn't been properly attuned to life. (This seems a bit hard on Annie, but no matter.) I would strongly suspect that Hitchcock, a realist in most things, has got precisely the measure of his problem. . . .

A little obscurity, however, does wonders for a contemporary film. If *The Birds* is really intended as a doomsday fantasy, one can only say that it's a lamentably inadequate one. But why not try the birds as the Bomb; or as creatures from the subconscious; or start from the other end, with Tippi Hedren as a witch? One could work up a pretty theory on any of these lines, if only one could suppress a conviction that Hitchcock's intention was an altogether simpler one. . . . And a director who has told us so often that his interest lies in the way of doing things, not in the moral of a story, invites us to take him at his own valuation. One stumbling block finally stands in the way of abstractions, metaphysical or otherwise Hitchcock's own intense concern for the concrete, and a sneaking suspicion that the best critic of Hitchcock is Hitch himself. (p. 164)

Penelope Houston, "Figure in the Carpet," in Sight and Sound *(copyright © 1963 by The British Film Institute), Vol. 32, No. 4, Autumn, 1963, pp. 159-64.*

JOHN RUSSELL TAYLOR

Hitchcock's career to date falls neatly into four phases: the silent period (nine films); the 1930s in Britain (fourteen films); the 1940s in America and Britain (thirteen features and two shorts); and the period since then, beginning with *Strangers on a Train* (twelve films). To indulge in drastic oversimplification, these phases represent respectively: apprenticeship; the perfection of a style; appreciation of the limitations of that style and an erratic quest for a new style; and final maturity. (p. 171)

Even for *The Lodger* allowances have to be made; to enjoy it fully requires an exercise of deliberate 'thinking-back', to see it in the context of the British cinema of the time. . . . In itself the film is clearly something of a declaration of independence: deliberately showy in style, it leaves no one in any doubt that its maker is a director to reckon with, even to the extent of being over-rich and weighed down with set-pieces of technical bravura. . . . (p. 172)

For all that the film has perhaps, retrospectively, been overrated; it is all rather too self-conscious, too determined to impress, and therefore finally less fresh and appealing than *The Ring,* arguably Hitchcock's best silent film, since there at least the technique is all properly functional and the aim unpretentious. (p. 173)

[By] the time we get to his third sound film, *Murder* . . . he is completely in control of the medium. *Murder,* in fact, is his first fully mature and characteristic film, full of little tricks and ingenuities, of disturbing overtones of all sorts; of the mixture of cheerful brutality, sexual innuendo, and black humour which makes up so much of 'characteristic Hitchcock'. . . . Already, too, the subject-matter, starting from a basically banal story-line, is developed to imply much that is normally far outside the range of the thriller (even now, and much more so then); the implications of homosexuality in the case of the real murderer are carefully placed for anyone with an eye to see. . . . (pp. 173-74)

It is difficult to go all the way with those critics—Eric Rohmer and Claude Chabrol, for instance—who regard [*Rich and Strange*] as one of Hitchcock's masterpieces: it is too muddled in execution, too extreme in its fluctuations of tone, for that. But it is interesting as one of his most immediately personal, 'felt' films; one suspects that in it, unselfconsciously and even perhaps a trifle naïvely, the young Hitchcock was wearing his heart on his sleeve, and when the reaction of critics and public was thoroughly unfavourable he decided to set up securer defences the next time. Hence, perhaps, his decision to throw himself instead into the series of thrillers which are the chief glory of his period in the early British sound cinema—films in which ideas close to his heart could be touched on more safely, under the guise of popular entertainment, than when left to speak out for themselves in films like *Rich and Strange*. (p. 175)

In making the six great thrillers [*The Man Who Knew Too Much, The Thirty-Nine Steps, The Secret Agent, Sabotage, Young and Innocent,* and *The Lady Vanishes*] Hitchcock had achieved perfection in the genre and had become typed to it. Everyone knew what to expect from him and tended to resent it if they got anything else. But the genre is limited and the dangers of self-repetition or falling back on an increasingly sterile search for new ways of extracting thrills and surprises from the same small round of basic situations are all too clear. Evidently they were clear to Hitchcock and he did what he had to: he got away to entirely new surroundings and started again. The next ten years or so, despite regular (though not quite invariable) commercial successes and some outstanding individual films, among them one (*Shadow of a Doubt*) which Hitchcock still names as his favourite of all his films, is mainly, on the artistic level, a record of trials, false starts, and disappointments, but from the experience he emerged with a new maturity and a new vitality which have made him, and kept him, one of the most dynamic forces in the cinema today. (pp. 181-82)

[*Shadow of a Doubt*] is a very curious, complex film, on the one hand in many ways Hitchcock's most scrupulously realistic, almost documentary in the care and precision with which its small town background is established . . . , and on the other in construction it is one of his most intricate and artificial, with shot answering shot and idea answering idea down to the smallest detail (what François Truffaut analysed as a regular principle of duplication and reflection; what Chabrol and Rohmer call visual rhymes). (p. 184)

It gains particularly over the other films of this period in two respects. The first is the extreme neatness and ruthless logic of the script's development, with everything in its place in a perfectly ordered, morally ambivalent world where everything goes by twos—Chabrol and Rohmer detail two scenes in a church, two scenes in a garage, two visits of the police to the house, two meals, two attempted murders, and a number of identical shots of the two Charlies, uncle and niece: two close-ups of the back, two travelling shots from in front, two shots from below, and so on. The second is in the use of locations, which lets air into the airless world of Hollywood studio realism, where all too often in other films Hitchcock's special talents seem to suffocate and droop. (pp. 184-85)

Stunningly proficient, [*Spellbound* and *Notorious*] are both very fair entertainments and if, to my mind, the better of them, *Notorious,* still fails to reach the highest class of Hitchcock, it is only by a certain deadness in the execution, a fatal heaviness which makes it, for all its brilliance, just a tiny bit boring. (p. 185)

Notorious, though usually bracketed with *Spellbound* . . . , is a far better and very different film. It is the film, in fact, which comes nearest to justifying the wilder claims of the *Cahiers du Cinéma* critics, especially when we remember that Hitchcock himself, exceptionally, takes responsibility for the original story. It is an intricate and subtle love story set in the familiar surroundings of spy adventure but showing just how far Hitchcock has travelled since *The Lady Vanishes*. This time the spy intrigue counts for little, the relationship between the principal characters for almost everything. (pp. 185-86)

The whole story, in fact, is whichever way you look at it based on the importance of an explicit avowal, a confession if you like, as liberating factor: the action turns entirely on the unwillingness of either party to say the necessary word. Moreover, the theme is developed with extraordinary concentration; there are no irrelevant extravagances of any sort (even the famous travelling shot which sweeps down from the top of the grand staircase and finally comes to rest in a close-up of a key in the heroine's hand can hardly be described as irrelevant, though in its context undeniably a little showy) and the big scenes—the bravura display of physical passion near the beginning, the scene in which the heroine realizes that she is being poisoned—are all managed with the utmost directness and simplicity. *Notorious* is also perhaps the most visually ravishing of all Hitchcock's films, certainly of all those in black-and-white. . . . In fact, virtually the only thing to be urged against the film is its ponderousness and claustrophobia—a quality often justified by the story but sometimes, as in the scenes on the hotel balcony against a very hazy back-projection of Rio de Janeiro, certainly not. (p. 187)

Rebecca, Lifeboat, Spellbound, Notorious, Rope, Under Capricorn: these are the characteristic Hitchcock films of the 1940s, and there is no escaping the fact that they suggest a spectacular decline in his talents as a director. The increasing heaviness of the direction, the general humourlessness, the pretentiousness of many of the subjects, the tendency of glossy impersonality to take the place of individual invention, the evident loss of the zest and gusto which used to characterize even Hitchcock's feeblest works before: these damage all of them, including the best (*Notorious*), and give rise to the gravest doubts about Hitchcock's future. Admittedly to set against them there is one unexpected, idiosyncratic masterpiece, *Shadows of a Doubt,* which is exempt from all these criticisms and at the same time quite different from the pre-war British Hitchcock, but in 1950 that was seven years and seven films away, and Hitchcock's latest, an attempt to return to the straightforward thriller entertainment in *Stage Fright,* was hardly more encouraging than his preceding heavyweight flops.

Then suddenly and quite unexpectedly, another masterpiece, *Strangers on a Train,* and the new, dazzling, mature Hitchcock of the 1950s was upon us before we knew it. (pp. 189-90)

In *Strangers on a Train* at last we are back in the open air. With a story after his own heart . . . , Hitchcock makes full use of outdoor locations . . . and succeeds in making his interiors and studio scenes match them closely in life and verisimilitude. The effect is instantaneous: the *mise en scène* loses the ponderousness of the last few years and becomes light and adventurous, full of little inventions . . . and elaborate set-pieces. . . . Seldom if ever had Hitchcock's sheer technique been more dazzling, but, significantly, this time it was not technique in a void, as in suspense-machines like *Saboteur* and *Stage Fright,* but technique used to create an atmosphere, advance a coherent narrative and put before us believable characters. . . . (p. 191)

Since *Strangers on a Train* Hitchcock's unmatched expertise has never deserted him (even the despised remake of *The Man Who Knew Too Much* is unshakeably adroit), and in his full maturity and confidence he has been ready to tackle almost anything. The sheer variety of his films in this period is staggering: from the macabre comedy of *The Trouble With Harry* and the romantic comedy of *To Catch a Thief,* through the light-hearted thriller-entertainment of *North by Northwest* and the neat mechanics of *Dial M for Murder* to the unsettling ambiguities of *Rear Window* and *Strangers on a Train* and the rigours of *The Wrong Man,* all are encompassed with equal ease and success. And, more astonishing still, they all come out unmistakably as 'Hitchcock films'; one is never tempted even for a moment to wonder if they could be the work of a technically brilliant but quite impersonally eclectic talent. . . . Themes and attitudes recur constantly in his films, tying them into a web of references and reflecting, evidently, Hitchcock's own interests and preoccupations, though not, I think, anything like a coherent personal philosophy. It is rather a question of mental furniture, 'keepings', to use Hopkins's word for it, which somehow crops up in everything that passes through Hitchcock's hands. If Hitchcock does not have 'a style', in the way that, say, Ophuls or Minelli does, so that a few feet extracted from any film would be constantly recognizable by a certain way of moving the camera, of lighting, of composition, he has nevertheless something much less self-conscious: a personal *écriture* which comes, like Buñuel's, simply from trusting to his personality to colour all his work (or, perhaps, from not considering such matters at all, but just unselfconsciously following his own bent wherever it may take him). Like Buñuel, Hitchcock achieves his style by an inspired absence of style; of him perhaps more unarguably than of anyone else in the cinema can it be said quite simply 'le style, c'est l'homme'. (pp. 198-99)

John Russell Taylor, "Alfred Hitchcock," in his Cinema Eye, Cinema Ear: Some Key Film-Makers of the Sixties *(reprinted by permission of Hill & Wang, a division of Farrar, Straus & Giroux, Inc.; in Canada, by A D Peters & Co Ltd; copyright © 1964 by John Russell Taylor), Hill & Wang, 1964, pp. 170-99.*

FRANÇOIS TRUFFAUT with HELEN G. SCOTT

To stay with the audience, Hitchcock set out to win it over by reawakening all the strong emotions of childhood. In his work the viewer can recapture the tensions and thrills of the games of hide-and-seek or blindman's bluff and the terror of those nights when, by a trick of the imagination, a forgotten toy on the dresser gradually acquires a mysterious and threatening shape. . . .

[This] brings us to suspense, which, even among those who acknowledge Hitchcock's mastery of it, is commonly regarded as a minor form of the spectacle, whereas actually it is *the* spectacle in itself.

Suspense is simply the dramatization of a film's narrative material, or, if you will, the most intense presentation possible of dramatic situations. (p. 9)

[Although] Hitchcock's art is precisely the ability to impose the "arbitrary," this sometimes leads the die-hards to complain about implausibility. While Hitchcock maintains that he is not concerned with plausibility, the truth is that he is rarely implausible. What he does, in effect, is to hinge the plot around a striking coincidence, which provides him with the master situation. His treatment from then on consists in feeding a maximum of tension and plausibility into the drama, pulling the strings ever tighter as he builds up toward a paroxysm. Then he suddenly lets go, allowing the story to unwind swiftly.

In general the suspense sequences of a film are its "privileged moments," those highlights that linger on in the viewer's memory. But Hitchcock wants each and every scene to be a "privileged moment". . . .

It is this determination to compel the audience's uninterrupted attention, to create and then to keep up the emotion, to sustain the tension throughout, that makes Hitchcock's pictures so completely personal and all but inimitable. For it is not only on the crucial passages of the story that he exercises his authority; his single-mindedness of purpose is also reflected in the exposition, the transitions, and all the sequences, which in most films are generally inconsequential.

Even an episode that merely serves to bridge two key sequences will never be commonplace, for Hitchcock loathes the "ordinary." (p. 10)

The art of creating suspense is also the art of involving the audience, so that the viewer is actually a participant in the film. In this area of the spectacle, film-making is not a dual interplay between the director and his picture, but a three-way game in which the audience, too, is required to play. . . .

To reproach Hitchcock for specializing in suspense is to accuse him of being the least boring of film-makers; it is also tantamount to blaming a lover who instead of concentrating on his own pleasure insists on sharing it with his partner. The nature of Hitchcock's cinema is to absorb the audience . . . completely. . . . (p. 11)

One of the charges frequently leveled at Hitchcock is that the simplification inherent in his emphasis on clarity limits his cinematic range to almost childlike ideas. To my mind, nothing could be further from the truth; on the contrary, because of his unique ability to film the thoughts of his characters and make them perceptible without resorting to dialogue, he is, to my way of thinking, a realistic director. (pp. 11-12)

Hitchcock is almost unique in being able to film directly, that is, without resorting to explanatory dialogue, such intimate emotions as suspicion, jealousy, desire, and envy. And herein lies a paradox: the director who, through the simplicity and clarity of his work, is the most accessible to a universal audience is also the director who excels at filming the most complex and subtle relationships between human beings. (p. 12)

If Hitchcock, to my way of thinking, outranks the rest, it is because he is the most complete filmmaker of all. He is not merely an expert at some specific aspect of cinema, but an all-round specialist, who excels at every image, each shot, and every scene. . . .

The suspense sequences are by no means the only cues to Hitchcock's authorship. His style can be recognized in a scene involving conversation between two people, in his unique way of handling the looks they exchange, and of punctuating their dialogue with silent pauses, by the simplified gestures, and even by the dramatic quality of the frame. . . .

If I apply the term "complete" to Hitchcock's work, it is because I find in it both research and innovation, a sense of the concrete and a sense of the abstract, intense drama as well as a subtle brand of humor. His films are at once commercial and experimental. . . . (p. 13)

While the cinema of Hitchcock is not necessarily exalting, it invariably enriches us, if only through the terrifying lucidity with which it denounces man's desecrations of beauty and purity. (p. 15)

François Truffaut with Helen G. Scott, in their introduction to their Hitchcock, *translated by François Truffaut (translation copyright © 1967 by François Truffaut; reprinted by permission of Simon and Schuster, a Division of Gulf & Western Corporation; originally published as* Le Cinéma Selon Hitchcock, *Robert Laffont, 1966), Simon & Schuster, 1967, pp. 7-15.*

LEO BRAUDY

Hitchcock cares little about the minor springs of plot—what he calls the "MacGuffin," the gimmick—because he is dealing with more inclusive rhythms. "To me, the narrator, they're of no importance." And this narrative sense, Hitchcock asserts . . . , is the most important part of his directional method. (pp. 22-3)

Hitchcock's films frequently approach the problem of detachment and involvement through separate but complementary treatments that night almost be called "genres." In "comedies" like *The Lady Vanishes, North by Northwest,* or *Torn Curtain,* the central characters are a romantic couple, with whom the audience automatically sympathizes. They serve as audience surrogates in a series of adventures that turn out happily. The axe is never far away from the neck in these comedies, but all conflict is finally dissipated by the end of the film, frequently by near fairy-tale or romance means. . . .

Hitchcock manipulates our desire to sympathize and identify. He plays malevolently on the audience assumption that the character we sympathize with most, whose point of view we share, is the same character who is morally right in the story the movie tells. He gleefully defeats our expectation that our moral sympathies and our aesthetic sympathies remain fixed throughout the movie.

Hitchcock begins this manipulation at the very beginning of *Psycho.* He forces the audience, although we may not realize it immediately, to face the most sinister connotations of our audience role—our participation in the watching and observing that shades quickly into voyeurism. (p. 24)

Norman's psychosis is the MacGuffin of *Psycho;* its special nature is irrelevant. Hitchcock concentrates instead on problems of presentation and point of view, the uncertain line between the normal audience and the psychotic character, and the actually hazy areas of moral judgment. Throughout the movie we are placed in situations that challenge our conventionalized aesthetic and moral responses. Hitchcock's attack on the reflex use of conventional pieties is basically an attack on the desire of the audience to deny responsibility and assert complete detachment. The viewer who wants such placidity and irresponsibility is mocked by the pseudo-documentary beginning of the movie. If he chooses, he has another trapdoor available at the end—in the explanation of the psychologist.

Because Norman has murdered both his mother and her lover, we don't have the conventional out of psychiatric exoneration from guilt. But the psychologist does offer us a way to escape responsibility by even more acceptable means: he sets up a screen of jargon to "explain" Norman. For the viewer who has learned anything from *Psycho* he must be dismissed. The visual clues are all present: he is greasy and all-knowing; he lectures and gestures with false expansiveness. But it is his explanations that are really insufficient. And one wonders if any categories would be sufficient. Like the moral tags dispensed by the Chorus at the end of *Oedipus Tyrannos,* the bland wisdom of the psychologist bears little relation to the complex human reality that has been our experience in the rest of the movie. . . . Through Hitchcock's manipulation of point of view and moral sympathy, we have entered the shell of his personality and discovered the rooted violence and perverse sexuality that may be in our own natures. Our desire to save Norman is a desire to save ourselves. But we have been walled off from the comfortable and reasonable and "technical" explanations of the psychologist. The impact that *Psycho* has upon us shows how deeply we've been implicated. (p. 27)

Leo Braudy, "Hitchcock, Truffaut, and the Irresponsible Audience," in Film Quarterly *(copyright 1968 by The Regents of the University of Cali-*

fornia; reprinted by permission of the University of California Press), Vol. XXI, No. 4, Summer, 1968, pp. 21-7.

JOSEPH McBRIDE

What Hitchcock has done in *Topaz* is exciting to anyone who believes that an artist's work has coherence, a progression, and a deepening of fundamental themes. (p. 17)

In Hitchcock's curious and largely unsuccessful *Torn Curtain,* a statement of some kind about modern political morality seemed to be competing with the personal story for significance. Hitchcock is not a socially-oriented director, though certain social motifs (especially fear of the police) trace back to the beginnings of his career. His movies almost invariably center around a man-woman relationship; whatever outward plot there is usually is no more than a counterpoint or a poetic extension of the basic theme.

Spies are a graphic metaphor for anarchy, for the underworld of organized society in which conventional morality becomes chaotic. Hitchcock's dread of psycho-sexual anarchy is always held in check by the highly schematized logic of his visual style—by his sense of irony. Spies and more individual voyeurs are a predominant impulse in his work because voyeurism, with its connotations of impotence and its threat to sexual and emotional trust, undermines the stability of a heterosexual relationship. (pp. 18-19)

Fear of impotence and fear of authority go hand-in-glove throughout Hitchcock's films; the fact that he gives many of his heroes dominating mothers confirms the relation. In *Notorious,* Hitchcock centers on a destructive voyeurism ordered by the father-land in opposition to the universal Nazi chaos. It is significant of earlier Hitchcock, however, that the social background is merely a pretext for the hero's actions and is ignored when the personal problems reach a crisis. (p. 19)

In *Topaz,* Hitchcock reflects the freezing inhumanity of abstract power systems as well as an old man's sad regrets about romanticism. He extends the idea of voyeurism from the hero vs. spies pattern into a dizzying web of cross-references among the acts of a complex of people and governments. (pp. 19-20)

Though Hitchcock's vital concern is with the love relationships, the social background is given unusual, though not totally unprecedented, prominence. What emerges in the way of committed political statement, however, is very simple, and typical of Hitchcock throughout his career—anti-Fascism. Hitchcock has no sympathy for mass action beyond that of a man and woman: in fact he fears it. The thin line between Communism and Fascism is broken immediately, in the frightening images of tanks and artillery intercut with marching Russian masses under the credits. The French Communist's invoking "the final solution" confirms the paradox. (pp. 21-2)

Finally, a crucial point, the nature of the new Hitchcock hero. There is his insistence on social responsibility. . . . Patriotism gets short shrift in all of his films, especially in *Topaz,* because it . . . places its characters on the brink of world annihilation. In *The Birds,* the menace is totally irrational, a whim of nature. But the nihilistic political machinations in *Topaz,* which amount in the end to a monumental, unresolved, impotent truce with oblivion, are humanly-inspired.

In his last few films, Hitchcock seems to have been making a deliberate attempt to come to terms with the particular horror of modern society, with the banality of evil, not its romanticism. (p. 22)

Though the undercurrent of chaos in his films would seem to suggest it, Hitchcock is not precisely a determinist. The Jesuitical lucidity of his style is his defense against an irrationality he can never hope to resolve. His feelings are expressed not through the hazardous fluidity of an actor's presence, but through the orderly schematization of cause and effect. Hitchcock motivates his characters in his editing. And if, like the Jesuits, he is accused of casuistry, he will make no further argument. Hitchcock has never pretended that people can explain their suffering. (p. 23)

Joseph McBride, "'Topaz'," in Film Heritage *(copyright 1969 by F. A. Macklin), Vol. 5, No. 2, Winter, 1969-70, pp. 17-23.*

CHARLES THOMAS SAMUELS

Although Alfred Hitchcock is the most primitive of major directors, he belongs in their company. Those who emphasize his primitivism also dismiss his achievement, but his achievement is fundamental to the art of cinema—more specifically, to the art of using cinematic means for audience manipulation. (p. 295)

Most of Hitchcock's ideas about the real world are indistinguishable from the commonest pieties—which, of course, helps to explain his unique popular appeal. To begin with, he is discomforted by intellectuals. (pp. 295-96)

Occasionally in all of his films and always in the best of them, Hitchcock is the master of evocation. Intellectual emptiness and spurious realism are preconditions for his effects. Since Hitchcock depicts a world in which anything can happen, and therefore everything is a threat, distinctions and priorities are forbidden.

Like Poe, the writer he most resembles, Hitchcock is obsessed by a small stock of situations which we can mistake for themes; but, as in Poe's case, these "themes" are only emotional stimuli born from the primitive stage of indiscriminate terror. Both men are sensationalists, but Hitchcock has the advantage of working in a medium that thrives on sensations which it can transmit with irresistible completeness. Sometimes Poe appears to be unveiling a metaphysical terror behind a physical threat, but since words can only point, and since Poe wielded one of the clumsiest pointers in English literature, he had to fall back on insinuation, validated by an aesthetic that argued for vagueness. Hitchcock's vocabulary is the very world from which he wants us to shrink, its items an inexhaustible stock of palpable terrors.

Yet Hitchcock never merely exhibits the sources of dread. As countless horror films and Hitchcock imitations prove, the naked ugliness is likely to excite only laughter. Not by accident do Hitchcock's excursions into direct brutality—*Psycho* and *The Birds*—contain his most elaborate contrivances, his most artful examples of aesthetic distance.

The secret of Hitchcock's terror lies not in the objects he employs but in the timing with which he presents them. He understands, as Poe understood, that emotion, which, imperious when it peaks, cannot be long sustained but may be extended through counterpoint. Like other romantics harassed by the essentially cognitive nature of language, Poe always yearned to transform himself into a musician—which, with a tin ear, he eventually became. For Hitchcock, no such transformation is required, since inherent resemblances between music and film have only to be exploited. . . . [By] choosing precisely what we may see and hear at any given moment, by altering the amount of information and by varying the tempo at which it is conveyed, Hitchcock can play upon each spectator's emotions in much the same way that a piece of music plays upon his hands and feet. (p. 297)

The key to *Psycho* is less Sigmund Freud than Richard Strauss. That is why most of Hitchcock's best films are devoid of meaning, peopled by mere containers of stress, and set against backgrounds chosen simply because their innocuousness counterpoints terror. Primitive in insight, Hitchcock is a sophisticated man revelling in pure form, whose films are ends in themselves and so can please both the plebes who want thrills and the cognoscenti thrilled by such an arrogant display of craftsmanship. That is why, like music, Hitchcock films are always most striking at the beginning and the end (introduction and coda), and why he sustains interest only when there are enough crescendos to provide rhythm, paralyzing reason and achieving kinesthesia. (p. 298)

North by Northwest is a prime example of contentless virtuosity. It is also notable for showing, with peculiar clarity, the function of Hitchcock's cynicism. Matching his display that no object is innocent is his belief that no person is. The ubiquity of guilt and of corruption in Hitchcock's world, however, contrary to the view of solemn critics, are rarely moral observations but usually emotional cues. Since no one is very good in the typical Hitchcock movie, we needn't take sides and can root for naked skill. (p. 301)

Hitchcock's cynicism makes an advantage of his moral indifference by freeing him and his audience to admire pure aggression, including the aggression of film form. But his fear that nothing is what it seems (of which the skepticism about moral distinctions is only one consequence) sometimes approaches the status of serious belief, and then we see, most dramatically, the special underpinnings of his work. . . . (p. 302)

Shadow of a Doubt is erratically written (its collaborators running from Sally Benson to Thornton Wilder), but it almost succeeds in making a serious comment. Thus we get the first important example in Hitchcock of visual symbolism. . . . But Hitchcock ruins this subtle equation, not only through blatant details in the script (uncle and niece share first names and telepathic powers), but by his final submission to conventions of melodrama. Since these necessitate someone to root for, Hitchcock must ultimately dissolve the equation whose irony sustains the film. In totally amoral movies like *North by Northwest* rooting for the hero implies no disruptive judgment; in *Shadow of a Doubt* it is profoundly illogical.

Nevertheless, *Shadow of a Doubt* helps us measure the extent to which Hitchcock's art is based on his assumption that normality is merely a thin veneer covering a lust for thrills. Like the niece, we tolerate thrills just until they threaten permanently to taint our self-image, so Hitchcock obligingly neutralizes the threat with last-minute melodrama. But his concern for us is specious, only a reflection of his concern for the box office. (pp. 302-03)

Strangers on a Train is a happy instance of an impulse suddenly finding its proper form. Throughout his work, Hitchcock had used, strictly for emotive purposes, the device of one character's being accused of another's crime. Patricia Highsmith's novel, while itself a pretentious, even brazen affair, has the virtue of making this device accord perfectly with Hitchcock's most fundamental attitude: that everyone is latently a killer. (p. 303)

For sheer invention, unfailing pertinence of every frame, and occasional suggestions of deeper purpose, *Strangers on a Train* is Hitchcock's masterpiece. . . .

As a craftsman, Hitchcock ranks with the best. He has taught essential lessons to directors with greater aspirations because he has realized one of the potentials of film form. . . . What Hitchcock has supremely understood is that the line between perception and feeling can be manipulated by the director, can be sustained or broken, quickened or retarded so that the spectator feels only what the filmmaker intends. Moreover, he has understood that no other medium can simulate action with most of life's reality but none of its limitations. As a result, Hitchcock has produced a new experience, a new kind of art. It is low but powerful; it does not exploit the full range of his medium, but it takes to the limit one of the things that film can do more fully than any other art. In Robert Warshow's phrase, film is the "immediate experience." No director knows that better than Hitchcock. (p. 304)

Charles Thomas Samuels, "Hitchcock" (copyright by the Estate of Charles Thomas Samuels; reprinted by permission), in The American Scholar, *Vol. 39, No. 2, Spring, 1970, pp. 295-304.*

GEORGE KAPLAN

Marnie is the culmination of Hitchcock's concept of cinema as an artificially fabricated construct; it is also among the films in which one senses him most emotionally engaged. The paradox is only apparent: it is in the nature of Hitchcock's art that it is most intense when it leaves daily reality, the "normal," behind to explore unnatural relationships and extreme mental states, especially the obsessive compulsive, in a kind of abstraction only cursorily disguised as naturalism. (p. 48)

The camera, almost invariably objective, moves to exclude some characters from the frame and include others: there is a continual sense of a world out there beyond the confines of the screen, of other lives coexisting simultaneously, a world too vital and complex for the camera to contain. At the same time, although every artist in film guides the spectator's eye (and the mind behind the eye), the objectivity of presentation and the sense of a world rich in varied potentialities allow us a certain freedom of response, leave room for the flexible play of individual moral judgment.

In Hitchcock's films, I have the sense that such tendencies exist only in so far as they can't be suppressed—in so far, that is, as they are inherent in the nature of cinema, and of the camera as a recording instrument. Hitchcock's images contain nothing superfluous, and, for the most part, only the barest minimum of what is necessary: we see what he has decided we *must* see. . . . Everything is conceived and executed in accordance with the experience Hitchcock has ordained that we are to receive. It's an extraordinary, audacious concept of cinema, and I don't think Hitchcock has ever entirely realized it. (p. 49)

I would posit two levels on which Hitchcock is involved in his art. The first is very conscious, and is bound up with his preoccupation with audience response and the concept of pure cinema. From the creative viewpoint, it is highly abstract, and closely connected with Hitchcock's practiced showmanship on the one hand and his pride in the technical mastery of his craft on the other. The second level is much more obscure, very private, partly unconscious—and from it derives the genuine power and intensity of Hitchcock's cinema. The two levels are neither separable nor unified, the second frequently masquerades as the first, with Hitchcock converting his thematic obsessions into deliberate attempts to give the audience experiences. (p. 50)

The Birds ought to have been Hitchcock's greatest film. It is seriously flawed—more than any other of his works—by the split between levels. One feels that here Hitchcock came very close to total seriousness, which would involve either the integration of the two levels or the rejection of the first and conscious acceptance of the second. (p. 51)

There seems to me one other major area to which Hitchcock's interest intuitively gravitates, and the pull is very strong. It is an aspect of his art barely hinted at in the British films, and the fact that it only reached free expression in Hollywood accounts for the decisive superiority of the American half of his career. . . . It can best be suggested by pointing to the most striking and haunting of the man-woman relationships in his films, and pondering their common elements. . . . All are characterized by some form of romantic passion (in *Shadow of a Doubt*—the earliest and least fully representative—hero-worship on one side and nostalgia for lost innocence on the other), rather than any realized sense of possible marital stability.

Beyond that there is perhaps no single element common to all, but several that recur and combine in various permutations: (1) the sense of the woman as mysterious, perhaps treacherous, perhaps unreal—the embodiment of a dream or an illusion (in *Shadow of a Doubt* the roles are partly reversed); (2) extreme distrust, arising from a variety of causes but usually closely related to (1); (3) a strong sense of instability and precariousness, arising from inner tensions, outside dangers, or both; (4) attempts on the part of the man to dominate or control the woman; (5) the emotional coloring, if not the fact evoked by the Oscar Wilde phrase of which Hitchcock is so fond: "Each man kills the thing he loves." (p. 52)

It seems as if the very precariousness of these relationships is indispensable to the maintaining of Hitchcock's interest. . . . [The] reason why *Vertigo* is so decisively Hitchcock's masterpiece is surely that there, and there alone, he pursues the tragic implications of this very romantic and inherently pessimistic view of life to their logical conclusion.

This theme—or complex of elements—is altogether lacking from *Frenzy*. If one places that film beside *Vertigo*, the limitedness of Hitchcock's response to life and to human relationships is strikingly illuminated in *Vertigo* he allows free rein to the tragic-romantic side of his vision, the yearning after a higher reality that may be illusory and is almost certainly unattainable in life: in *Frenzy* he looks at things as (from his viewpoint) they are. (p. 52)

[The cynicism in *Frenzy*] is expressed in the whole treatment of human relationships and human potentialities. The marriage bureau (its achievements typified by the couple we see leaving it) emerges as a central image. . . . No-one in the film is allowed much stature, or even dignity, except in the most superficial "British" sense. . . .

If one searches for some kind of affirmation, the best one can come up with is the relationship between Inspector Oxford and his wife. One can certainly agree with Hermie Wallack that Hitchcock treats this with "great affection"; the two gourmet dinner scenes are the most endearing in the film. But when *that* emerges as a human norm, is one not forced to reflect that something, somewhere, has gone seriously wrong? The Oxfords would seem to represent, for Hitchcock, the workable alternative to those disturbing romantic relationships best summed up by *Vertigo* a relationship built on the negative virtues of patience and forbearance, and the suppression of everything else. . . .

In *Frenzy* Hitchcock tries to go one better than *Psycho:* this time two successive heroines-apparent get horridly murdered just as our sympathies (in so far as they are aroused at all) are gravitating towards them, leaving us with a problem of re-adjustment. *Psycho* survives in the murder of Marion Crane because of our interest in and concern for Norman Bates; but when the Anna Massey character disappears from *Frenzy* there isn't much left, unless we are satisfied by a somewhat arid recapitulation of Hitchcockian themes. . . .

Anna Massey seems to me clearly the most attractive character of *Frenzy*—plucky, loyal, forthright. I know that a dead body is just so much useless matter and it's no use getting sentimental about it; nonetheless, my sensibility revolts violently against *Frenzy*'s already-celebrated potato-sack scene. It sums up for me everything in Hitchcock that is morally most suspect. It's not just the callousness with which he treats the character, but the callousness with which he treats his audience, by cynically violating our sensibilities. . . .

The dangers of pure cinema and its techniques of audience manipulation have never been more apparent. And don't tell me, oh brother and sister critics, that I shouldn't confuse cinema and life, and write about characters as though they were real people—because when you ceased to engage with movies at this old-fashioned human level, at that same moment you lost all touch with the way in which the audiences for whom the films were made experience them. You invalidated your critical position at the very moment when you thought you had purged it of impurities.

Doubtless this overstates the case against *Frenzy*, by isolating certain aspects at the expense of others. It has the distinction of which even the worst works of a great artist are likely to partake. For Hitchcock is, at his best, a great artist. . . . [However, his] work is too far removed from any healthy concept of normality, or from any sense of *potential* norms, to have the kind of Shakespearean centrality [Robin] Wood suggests. *Marnie* is not, even remotely, *The Winter's Tale;* leave that to late Mizoguchi. The profoundly disturbing intensity of Hitchcock at his best—though remarkable in its way—is of another, and lesser, order. (p. 53)

George Kaplan, "Alfred Hitchcock: Lost in the Wood," in Film Comment *(copyright © 1972 Film Comment Publishing Corporation; all rights reserved), Vol. 8, No. 4, November-December, 1972, pp. 46-53.*

MAURICE YACOWAR

I Confess is no soap bubble, but a profoundly circumspect investigation of the interrelation of good and evil, the vulnerability of virtue in the Manichean scheme of things, and the competitive tension between man's laws and God's. (p. 19)

Christian myth permeates the film. Villette is the serpent in Eden. He has two gardens, one where he first discovers Logan with Ruth, and one in town, which he hires Keller to tend. Ruth first meets Villette at sacramental occasions: her marriage to Pierre and Michael's ordination to the priesthood. Keller is a more human agent of evil, the Cain figure, a man without a country, driven by his evil compulsions to kill the things most dear to him, his wife and his best friend, Logan. There is even the obligatory apple in the film, eaten ostentatiously by a fat woman in front of Otto and Alma when Logan is mobbed outside the courtroom. (p. 20)

In contrasting the order of nature and the order of grace, man's two legal systems, Hitchcock draws sometimes outrageous parallels between them. Detective Larue . . . pursues the truth with the ugly diligence of an avenging angel. . . .

The legal system is treated as a parody of the religious. The Crown Prosecutor . . . is a happy-go-lucky playboy sort who is seen balancing a glass of water backwards on his forehead at a party—an emblem for the delicate equilibrium Hitchcock conceives justice to be. . . . Of course the parody is serious. One must choose which justice he will serve, man's or God's, for as the film demonstrates, the two are not always compatible. (p. 22)

Two kinds of privacy bind Logan to his silence. He is silent on questions about his relationship with Ruth to preserve her honour and he is silent on the knowledge given him in confession. Similarly Ruth's silence on questions about her affair leaves the listener increasingly suspicious about what she seems to be concealing. In contrast to the lying and bitter garrulousness of Keller, the redundant suspicions of the judge and foreman, and the excessive confessions of Ruth, however, Father Logan's silence is dignified.

The shooting style has been called austere. It may be more austere than the baroque, Catholic landscape of Quebec City, with its steep streets, plethora of "direction" (one-way) signs, and Stations of the Cross, but it is far more lively. (pp. 22-3)

The film opens and closes with shots of a Gothic castle against a horror-movie sky. The church, society, and the individual mind have the murky foundation of that castle. . . .

The characters tend to triangular arrangement in the shots. . . . Other triangles are completed off camera, by the character's semi-presence via telephone. . . . [A] two-man composition on the screen is really a two-character representation of a three-character situation. . . .

The trinitarian structure is continued in the pattern of confessions throughout the film. Keller prefers an atypical religious confession over confessing to the police. . . . (p. 23)

A final confession perhaps lies in the title of the film. The "I confess" could be the Catholic Hitchcock facing his maker with appropriate penitence for having squandered his devotions upon the sensations and delights of the secular life.

But in this film Hitchcock is The Maker. . . .

Hitchcock plays God in *I Confess,* sublimely aloof from the worries, regulations, rigidities, and tensions of the foolish mortals below. (p. 24)

Maurice Yacowar, "Hitchcock's 'I Confess'," in Film Heritage *(copyright 1972 by F. A. Macklin), Vol. 8, No. 2, Winter, 1972-73, pp. 19-24.*

JOSEPH SGAMMATO

When we speak of [Hitchcock's] camera, of course, we are speaking of an amalgam of director and audience: the director's eye and the eye of the beholder welded into a single screen image. The nosy, rubbernecking camera of the opening montage of *Frenzy* is an admission from Hitchcock that he is a thrill-seeker at heart (his is the most prominent of the gaping faces on the screen) and a reminder to his movie audience that they are no better: a serio-comic blending of 'I confess' and 'J'accuse'. It is fair warning of what is to follow: not only further titillations of the peek-a-boo variety but constant reminders of the voyeuristic impulses which are all too willingly being aroused within us by the Master of Prurient Suspense, the patron saint of Peeping Toms and moviegoers. (p. 134)

Much of the vitality of *Frenzy* results from this implied relationship between director and audience. Hitchcock plays with our anticipations, showing us sometimes too little, sometimes too much of what we expect to see, but in every case drawing our somewhat ruffled attention to the expectations themselves. . . .

What distinguishes Hitchcock's films from others which serve the audience in the same way is that Hitchcock is aware of the secret gratifications moviegoing affords and incorporates this awareness into the forms themselves of his films. (p. 135)

If we are to verbalise the 'meaning' of *Frenzy* we must look to the politics of cinema, to the mutual dependences of film-makers and filmgoers for our vocabulary, for this is what *Frenzy* is 'about'. To pursue other trails will lead us to dead ends. To be sure, the film is filled with the familiar signposts of Freudian sexuality: dominating women, mother complexes, diagnoses of impotence as well as frigidity, high-flown talk of the 'pleasure principle' and the 'connection between religious and sexual mania', and so on. . . .

This is not to say that one should pay no attention to these signposts, but that one should not force oneself to pay attention to them, forgetting that the pleasure of the journey is itself the goal of a Hitchcock film. . . . If *Frenzy* is about sexual mania it has precious little to say about it, if these old chestnuts are the sum total of its insights.

The fact is that Hitchcock's films have never been rewarding on the 'theme and structure' level. The usual avenues of interpretation—the development of plot and character to express theme—are closed in Hitchcock's case. His films have structure, but not theme; form, but not 'meaning'. Hitchcock has a great deal to show to his audiences, but nothing to say. This fact has occasioned many critical difficulties, and two familiar errors. On the one hand are those who think that since Hitchcock's films have nothing to say, he is not a major artist, while on the other are those who think that since Hitchcock is a major artist, his films must be saying something. (p. 136)

Frenzy is not about a sex killer; it's about looking at a sex killer. Its manner is its matter.

This is not merely the inevitable distinction between film and other art forms, such as literature. There *are* some directors whose films can be discussed in terms of characters as well as actors, plot developments as well as camera movements, symbolism and themes instead of the immediate effect on the audience, but Hitchcock isn't one of them. . . . Hitchcock is thoroughly a Movie Man, a Cinematiser. The materials out of which his films are wrought are those of movie-making and movie-going.

Hitchcock's heroes, for example, are characteristically handsome, innocent, vacant, constantly forced to run about for reasons they can't fathom, ignorant of the large design in which they figure, totally unaware of the forces which are controlling their behaviour: they are like actors. Hitchcock's villains are more suave than handsome, dignified, urbane, unruffled, never forced to run about, not at all naïve, totally aware of what's going on and in fact in perfect control of the actions of the others: they are like directors. Hitchcock's camera does not record subjects: it creates them. How the camera looks, from what angle and for how long, how it turns away or lingers, how it moves or stays still, in so far as this determines what ends up on the screen, and therefore in the mind of the audience, is itself the subject.

Perhaps it would be clearer to say that the real subject of Hitchcock's films is the fluctuating rhythm of the middle-class imagination, the picture-making power inside the mind of each member of his audience, to which his camera approximates. Hitchcock's films are the concretised naughtiness of the imagination, which refuses to dwell on the images which Reason dictates as the soundest, best, and in closest correspondence with reality, but which summons up irrational images (as Don Quixote did) because they are more fun. His films cinematise that part of all of us which prefers hell to heaven. His is a cinema 'governed purely by the pleasure principle', to quote one of *Frenzy*'s characters. But it is also a cinema which incorporates an awareness of what it is doing into the doing itself: it transforms our imaginations into just the parade of images we want privately to see, but always with the humorous detachment of one who is on to our little secrets. . . .

If *Frenzy* resists interpretation except in these terms (which are, to a large extent, the familiar ones of French and American *auteur* critics), it is because Hitchcock's films have nothing to do with our cognitive life. They have their source and inspiration in the imaginative life, and it is to the imagination that they return. (p. 137)

Joseph Sgammato, "The Discreet Qualms of the Bourgeoisie: Hitchcock's 'Frenzy'," in Sight and Sound *(copyright © 1973 by The British Film Institute), Vol. 42, No. 3, Summer, 1973, pp. 134-37.*

HARRY RINGEL

Like his painter in *Blackmail* . . . Alfred Hitchcock employs pointedly nonverbal methods—and not the expositional theatrics so common to most early sound films—as brushstrokes to bring life to his murderess's dilemma. . . . [In] *Blackmail* ". . . sounds are linked to movements, as if they were the natural consummation of gestures which have the same musical quality. . . . Everything is thus regulated and impersonal; not a movement of the muscles, not the rolling of an eye but seem to belong to a kind of reflective mathematics which controls everything, and by means of which everything happens." The quote belongs to Antonin Artaud: contemporary of the young Hitchcock, and a peripheral member of the French surrealist clique. Its ideal—the fierce, absolute segregation of the visual and the aural from the verbal tradition of the occidental theater—might just as well have been Hitchcock's; for in its exclusively cinematic use of the language of film, *Blackmail* asserts, as did surrealism, that no such threat from theater need ever have existed. (p. 17)

Hitchcock, sharing the surrealists' interest in nonaction, has always specialized in reflecting his protagonists' inactive sides: the perversely detailed bedroom Norman Bates (*Psycho*) has shared with his mother, for example; or how Bob Rusk (*Frenzy*) relaxes after committing a murder. Similarly, the crime itself in *Blackmail* does not concern Hitchcock so much as the effect of the deed upon its perpetrator. . . .

In what proves to be *Blackmail*'s most absorbing section, Hitchcock focuses upon the face of a woman just turned killer. His actress, without speaking, becomes Artaud's athlete of the heart: her purpose, the communication of ". . . a mental alchemy which makes a gesture a state of mind . . . a state prior to language which can choose its own: music, gestures, movements, words." . . .

Like the surrealists, the Hitchcock of *Blackmail* inverts this reality, equating a fevered state of perception with actuality. The murderess's reaction to what she has done is not depicted mimetically; instead, after the murder *Blackmail* ceases to be a suspense story and becomes a dream. (p. 18)

Like the most artfully placed brushstrokes, then, *Blackmail*'s most effective details apparently have little to do with what is actually occurring on the screen. Yet the greater their apparent distance from the subject, the greater is the sense of reality they convey. Like surrealism, the Hitchcock technique in *Blackmail* does more than approximate mere mood. Linked figuratively to the action, these superficially incongruous sights and sounds reproduce the flow of a life temporarily bogged down in the compulsive repetitions of obsession.

For Hitchcock and the surrealists, the logical extension of such obsession was the personalization of one's immediate environment. . . .

Blackmail's murderess is isolated by her guilt. Simple objects, displayed at ostensibly insignficant moments, establish haunting objective correlatives when reseen. The dead man's portrait of a Pagliacci clown becomes a ridiculing Puck, sneering disdainfully at her predicament. (p. 19)

One can choose to view *Blackmail,* like a Jarry play or Chirico painting, as an abstract comment on the morals of its middle-class audience; but from *The Lodger* to *Frenzy,* Hitchcock has touched upon politics and religion solely as extensions of the most intimate conflicts within the self. Only on these terms will he approach problems of public morality, much less collective involvement. . . .

Hitchcock's use of surrealist techniques in *Blackmail* presages its later employment in some of his most memorable sequences. . . . Time has modified the fervor of *Blackmail*'s experimentation; what remains is Hitchcock's notion of the subjective itself as phenomenon, even more visible now through a surrealist backdrop which Hitchcock has been molding to his own purpose since the beginning of his career. (p. 20)

[The] Hitchcock technique, at its best, does more than simply match moods: it approximates the very look and feel of the thought process itself. In *Frenzy,* we need not be told that Bob Rusk has come to rape Mrs. Blaney; the camera, tracking in a slow arc around her, does the stalking for us. . . . Similarly, the very meaning of such an improbable film as *The Birds* lies not only in the directorial challenge inherent in creating the necessary illusion, but in conveying this illusion as it would logically be perceived. Hitchcock's perpetual concern with matters of form in his interviews is no mere camouflage: one cannot portray the subjective more accurately than to show what it literally looks like.

Hitchcock's interest in such formal challenges has sustained him over a half century of filmmaking. He has lasted by pausing for wind. Indeed, moods maintained from beginning to end in any one Hitchcock film are rare. Thus, *Blackmail,* drawing heavily upon surrealist themes and techniques, may represent Hitchcock's first important step in his journey toward the subjective; but it drags, nonetheless. (p. 22)

Harry Ringel, "'Blackmail': The Opening of Hitchcock's Surrealist Eye," in Film Heritage *(copyright 1974 by F. A. Macklin), Vol. 9, No. 2, February 4, 1974, pp. 17-23.*

GORDON GOW

[*North by Northwest*] is arguably as good an indication as can be found of Alfred Hitchcock's ability to match his sense of humour to his lively suspense tactics. Strictly speaking, according to those who claim to know such things, the title is a compass point that doesn't exist. It is our cue to disregard any measure of 'reality' in the film. 'Realism' is there, of course; but not, overtly at any rate, 'reality'. Further nudges towards levity are given by the leading character, Roger O Thornhill . . . , who emphasises that his initials spell 'rot', and that his central 'O' stands for nothing. There is, however, a nuance to that 'nothing': the plot is one of mistaken identity, Thornhill being considered by the villains to be a spy who is actually as non-existent as the compass point to which symbolically he eventually travels; and therefore when this false identity is thrust upon him, Thornhill is nothing indeed.

All of which goes to suggest that Hitchcock's intention was purely to divert us by letting his fancy take idiosyncratic flight. Nevertheless we must not overlook the significance of the relationship between the film's tricky title and Prince Hamlet's famous account of his own mental condition. Happily, most of us can distinguish hawks from handsaws. Likewise, although we seldom stop smiling while Hitchcock's *jeu d'esprit* progresses, we can acknowledge a political comment of sorts in the fact that government intelligence agencies, such as the one depicted and satirised in the film, have their real counterparts which are thought in certain cases to be ruthless in their methods.

Psychologically there is valid comment, too—comment upon the resilience of human nature under duress, as heightened in the case of Roger O Thornhill, a man whose smooth lifestyle as an advertising executive in New York City is abruptly changed, as if the ground had been whipped out from under him. One might even associate Thornhill's 'nine-lives' staying power with the religious belief that man is never given a burden which is greater than he can bear: a comforting idea of course, although it is frequently given the lie by life and the news.

North by Northwest has gained the status of a cult film, hardly on account of such political and psychological meaning but primarily because it is a fun thriller. It turns screws as cleverly as it splits faces into broad grins: while our palms sweat, we chuckle. (p. 51)

My enthusiasm for *North by Northwest* is just about boundless. . . . [All] in all it is so damned good. (p. 54)

Gordon Gow, "Cult Movies: 'North by Northwest'" (© copyright Gordon Gow 1974; reprinted with permission), in Films and Filming, *Vol. 21, No. 1, October, 1974, pp. 51-4.*

GABRIEL MILLER

Frenzy is Hitchcock's most pessimistic film. It is a portrait of a fallen world, a modern wasteland where moral values have entirely disappeared, the landscape has been defaced and polluted, and man (always, for Hitchcock, a very imperfect thing) has been beaten down and dehumanized so thoroughly that no redeeming qualities are left. (p. 1)

Frenzy develops around a thematic structure common to many of Hitchcock's films: the hero (man or woman; in this case a man) gets caught up, usually by accident, in a series of irrational events from which he must extricate himself. What he experiences in doing so generally has a therapeutic effect on him; by the end of his adventures, the hero often has gained a new sense of human responsibility and commitment. (p. 2)

It seems that over the years Hitchcock's belief in the possibilities of man to save himself and his world have diminished. His later films have revealed a tendency that leads eventually to the total pessimism of *Frenzy*. The ending of *The Birds,* while we do see a new Melanie Daniels . . . is tenuous. She has changed, and there is the possibility of marriage with Mitch Brenner . . . , but there is a catch. We see them driving off to San Francisco, but the final shot is of the birds, a reminder of the irrational and precarious nature of our existence. Perhaps they won't make it to San Francisco; perhaps the birds are stronger than man's ability to remake his world. *Topaz* brings us even closer to the final theme. It is a picture of political chaos, which results in many deaths. The world is saved from nuclear destruction, but the final scene of a man tossing into the garbage can a newspaper announcing that the Cuban missile crisis has been averted demonstrates Hitchcock's concern over man's growing indifference to life. In *Frenzy* Hitchcock pulls no stops in giving us a portrait of total decay. Civilization seems to have died, and, with it, man's spirit. (p. 10)

Gabriel Miller, "Hitchcock's Wasteland Vision: An Examination of 'Frenzy'," in Film Heritage *(copyright 1976 by F. A. Macklin), Vol. 11, No. 3, Spring, 1976, pp. 1-10.*

JOHN SIMON

Though less pretentious and preposterous than *Torn Curtain* and *Topaz,* less ludicrous than *Marnie,* and less offensive than *Frenzy,* [*Family Plot*] is still late Hitchcock, and not very good. (p. 84)

There are moments of inventiveness, here and there. When a woman tries to escape from a man in a cemetery whose paths are laid out like lines in a Mondrian painting (Hitchcock's own simile), there is something amusingly nutty about the pair's puny convergences and divergences, when mere cutting across a lawn could put an end to it all. . . . Let no one tell me that Hitchcock is not expressing once again his deep-rooted dislike of women, which first struck me in his treatment of the Madeleine Carroll character in *The 39 Steps,* and which reached its unappetizing apogee in a couple of scenes in *Frenzy.* Yet I could forgive the anti-feminism, but not the contrivance and overextension.

And speaking of miraculous rescue, do you know what breaks the impetus of that car hurtling toward disaster? A large wooden cross, of a kind unlikely in this landscape. And when are the miscreants apprehended? When their victim is a bishop, kidnapped from a cathedral during a religious service. And how is the heroine alerted to the danger that threatens her? By a telltale glimpse of the bishop's cope in a place where it shouldn't be. And what is the name of the chief malefactor? Adamson, the son of Adam and inheritor of his curse. And so on. French film critics and their disciples have long indulged in tracking down Catholic symbolism, hints of salvation through faith, in Hitchcock's work. What if the director denies such unconscious symbolism—might it not be unconscious, and all the more ingrained? In any case, *Family Plot,* with its deceptive cenotaph that may itself be religiously construed, should provide a happy symbol-hunting ground.

What it does not provide, along with suspense, is interesting clues. (pp. 84-5)

John Simon, "Old Man Out," in New York *Magazine (copyright © 1976 by News Group Publications, Inc.; reprinted with the permission of* New York *Magazine), Vol. 9, No. 16, April 19, 1976, pp. 84-6.*

ROGER GREENSPUN

Ultimately, *Family Plot* may be more fun to think about than to see—or at least, to see for the fourth time. There are moments of quite stunning intensity. . . . But some of the principle action sequences seem relatively lax and unfocused, and I suspect that *Family Plot* figures only half-heartedly as an adventure film. Indeed, it mistrusts adventure, as the best Hitchcock movies often do. Its central position is that a healthy respect for love and money offers better guidance through this vale of tears than does the secret shudder down the spine of life lived recklessly for beauty and thrills. That's practical philosophy. Like Bresson, like Ozu, Hitchcock constructs a cinema of philosophic principles.

In this respect, *Family Plot,* which some have praised for its hilarity, may just be Hitchcock's most serious movie—or one of his most serious, or anything but his funniest and most erotic. It deals in private human relations on several levels. . . .

There is nothing too original in the notion that the Hitchcock movie titles carry a glamour all their own, and that with a few exceptions they are as witty as anything that gets into the films. Sometimes they *do* get into the films, virtually sum up the films on several levels at once. . . .

"Plot" vs. "pattern." You can feel the release from ominous solemnity. You can appreciate the pun, and knowing enough about Hitchcock, you can guess the pun will count. But it must be understood that the habit of mind involved in using a pun also counts, and that it reflects not only upon graveyard matters and the convolutions of a story, but also upon the idea of the "family," which is really the key to the film. (p. 21)

[There] are some chills, and there is a serious theme as well. Old Julia may not be the murderess she is in Victor Canning's novel; but she committed a crime years before, when she removed her wayward sister's son. . . .

The colors that dominate in *Family Plot*—deep red, white, black, occasionally green—create a continuing moral interplay of the most powerful intimations of death, life, purity, and passion behind the semi-social comedy up front. Similarly, the cross references between Blanche and Fran, and between Blanche/George and Fran/Arthur, do more than just establish a comparison by contrast. They help extend a context in which everything somehow connects. Not so much for the specifics of connection as for the *idea* of connection, an idea that when necessary can raise the energies of a zany missing-persons plot into near sublimity.

I doubt that such potential makes *Family Plot* a masterpiece, or even a near miss. . . . The central comedy-fright sequence, the uncontrollable automobile, fails sufficiently to scare (me, at least) or to amuse, and the suspense tricks associated with it seem derivative almost to the point of embarrassment. Enough of those things together depress a movie. . . . The revelation of *Family Plot* within this context is not its excellence but its benevolence, a benevolence that even its cardboard villain. . . . has trouble dissociating himself from. . . . As the film works out from mystery into certainty and from darkness into light, it discovers prospects for casual good feeling that through the memories of generations extend even beyond the grave. (p. 22)

Roger Greenspun, "Plots and Patterns," in Film Comment *(copyright © 1976 by The Film Society of Lincoln Center; all rights reserved), Vol. 12, No. 3, May-June, 1976, pp. 20-2.*

ROBIN WOOD

To trace the creative drives behind Hitchcock's films to sources in psychopathology (possible, after all, to some degree with *any* artist) does not necessarily invalidate the emphasis placed in my book on their therapeutic impulses: indeed, it could logically be felt to strengthen this emphasis by giving the therapeutic impulses a particular focus or motivation. I still feel that the Hitchcock films I most admire are centred on a movement towards health via therapy and catharsis. I have, however, become much more keenly aware of a need to insist on sharp discriminations—a need to stress the limitations of Hitchcock's art and to distinguish the work (a small proportion of the total *oeuvre*) that succeeds in transcending them.

The limitations are of two kinds, though perhaps not entirely unconnected. There is, first, the somewhat equivocal relationship between Hitchcock the artist and Hitchcock the showman-entertainer. Obviously, the two can never be cleanly separated, nor would it be desirable that they could be, as their inter-relationship is in many ways crucial to the robustness of Hitchcock's work. One can, nevertheless, set up fairly obvious polar opposites: the intensely involved personal art of *Vertigo,* say, as against the businessman who lends his name to anthologies of largely trivial horror stories or the comic fat man who introduces the Hitchcock half-hour on television. Between the two, however, lie areas where the relationship becomes problematic. What concerns me here is the way in which some of Hitchcock's finest work is flawed by compromises that, in an artist free of "commercial" constraints, would appear neurotic, the result of a reluctance to allow certain disturbing implications to be fully explored, but which Hitchcock encourages us (sometimes, in interviews, explicitly) to regard as the result of external pressures, fears of alienating his audiences (the two motivations are not, of course, incompatible). (p. 20)

The second limitation is more damaging: I would define it as the relative weakness in Hitchcock's art of the normative impulse. That great art strives—however implicitly—towards the realisation of norms seems to me axiomatic, though the principle I am stating is frequently misunderstood or misrepresented. It is not a matter of whether a work is "optimistic" or "pessimistic", and certainly not a denial of the validity of a tragic vision of life. It is a matter of the nature of the creative impulse, which, to flourish, must be rooted in a sense of at least a *potential* normality to be striven for, values by which to live. "Normality" here must not be understood in terms of the re-affirmation of established values, least of all the norms of bourgeois society. . . .

It is not really paradoxical that Hitchcock's art is usually at its most creative when his material permits or encourages the most complete immersion in the abnormal. If creativity is, almost by definition, a striving towards norms, this implies a process, a *moving through*. The problem with Hitchcock is that the movement seems almost always blocked. His work typically equates "normality" with a bourgeois life in whose values the creative side of him totally disbelieves but to which it can provide no alternative. (p. 21)

Why should we take Hitchcock seriously?

It is a pity the question has to be raised: if the cinema were truly regarded as an autonomous art, not as a mere adjunct of the novel or the drama—if we were able to *see* films instead of mentally reducing them to literature—it would be unnecessary. (p. 29)

[What] can one adduce, positively, once all the false preconceptions have been cleared away, to encourage the doubters to believe that Hitchcock deserves serious consideration as an artist? . . .

First, then, one might point to the *unity* of Hitchcock's work, and the nature of that unity. I mean of course something much deeper than the fact that he frequently reverts to mystery-thrillers for his material; I also mean something broader and more complex than the fact that certain themes —such as the celebrated "exchange of guilt"—turn up again and again, although that is a part of it. Not only in theme—in style, method, moral attitude, assumptions about the nature of life—Hitchcock's mature films reveal, on inspection, a consistent development, deepening and clarification. . . .

The thematic material of Hitchcock's films is much richer than is commonly recognised. True, he never invents his own plots, but adapts the work of others. . . . (p. 36)

The mystery-thriller element is, in fact, never central in Hitchcock's best films; which is not to deny its importance. We could put it this way: "suspense" belongs more to the method of the films than to their themes (insofar as any distinction is possible, such distinctions applied to organic works being necessarily artificial). Look carefully at almost any recent Hitchcock film and you will see that its core, the axis around which it is constructed, is invariably a man-woman relationship: it is never a matter of some arbitrary "love interest," but of essential subject-matter. . . .

It is true that one can find a profound theme underlying almost anything if one is predisposed to search it out sufficiently diligently; what distinguishes a work of art is that this theme should be seen, on reflection, to inform the whole—not only the "content" (if there is such a thing as distinct from treatment; for what is the content of a film but sounds and images, and where else can we look for its style?), but the method. (p. 37)

More practically, perhaps, in answer to my opening question, one can point to the disturbing quality of so many Hitchcock films. It is one of the functions of art to disturb: to penetrate and undermine our complacencies and set notions, and bring about a consequent readjustment in our attitude to life. Many refer to this quality in Hitchcock but few try to account for it: how often has one heard that a certain film is "very clever" but "leaves a nasty taste in the mouth" (*Shadow of a Doubt, Rope, Strangers on a Train, Rear Window* . . .). This "nasty taste" phenomenon has, I believe, two main causes. One is Hitchcock's complex and disconcerting moral sense, in which good and evil are seen to be so interwoven as to be virtually inseparable, and which insists on the existence of evil impulses in all of us. The other is his ability to make us aware, perhaps not quite at a conscious level (it depends on the spectator), of the impurity of our own desires. The two usually operate, of course, in conjunction.

This disturbing quality is frequently associated with the Hitchcockian "suspense," and it is this which I would like to consider next. It is very rarely a simple thing, very rarely "mere" suspense; but it is not easy to define, since it has many functions and takes many forms. (p. 38)

The theme [of] the necessity for trust above all, whatever the risks is the theme of one of Hitchcock's early, and not entirely satisfactory, Hollywood films, *Suspicion.* I pass to this now because it offers a convenient focal point for disentangling two threads which run through Hitchcock's later work and, while they do not in themselves *explain* his films, offer a means of access to them. (pp. 40-1)

First, what I call the *therapeutic* theme, whereby a character is cured of some weakness or obsession by indulging it and living through the consequences. Joan Fontaine falls in love with and marries Cary Grant. He is soon revealed as a liar and she comes to suspect that he is a murderer—eventually, that he is trying to murder *her.* The suspicions poison their marriage, making any open communication between them impossible. Only when they are eventually forced into the open is the fallacy exposed and, in the film's very last shot, a new start made. (p. 41)

The second thread is the extension of this "therapy" to the spectator, by means of encouraging the audience to identify. The outlook of the Joan Fontaine character is a very common one, certainly not restricted to colonels' daughters. From the time of her marriage onwards, we are restricted to the one consciousness: we know only what she knows, see only what she sees: we share her suspicions and learn from experience with her. With her, we find the Cary Grant character attractive: he is so romantic and dashing, so careless of mundane cares and restraints. But with her, we are gradually dismayed by his excesses: the reckless abandon with other people's money—and other people's feelings—comes to appear very unpleasant. So we become ashamed of having found him so attractive: if he were a complete blackguard, now, we would be exonerated, merely the victims of deceit, and we would be revenged on him when his downfall came. As Joan Fontaine's fingers arrange those letters into the word "murder", the camera places us in her position: they are *our* hands. The film endorses the man's attitude to life no more than the woman's: if the limitations of her inhibited, sheltered respectability are chastised, so is their inevitable complement—the attraction towards total irresponsibility. And always it is our own impulses that are involved, not only the characters'. (pp. 41-2)

Vertigo seems to me Hitchcock's masterpiece to date, and one of the four or five most profound and beautiful films the cinema has yet given us. (p. 77)

The objection has frequently been made that the plot hinges on a wild improbability: not so much that a man who has seen the woman he loves fall from a height should not stay to make sure she is dead, as that the murderer should count on his not doing so. But if one is going to approach the film in this way, a moment's thought will make it clear that the whole plot is quite fantastic—no one would ever set about murdering his wife in *that* way. . . . As in Shakespeare's plays, in fact, the organisation of *Vertigo* is thematic; plot, characterisation, psychology, all are strictly subordinated to thematic development. (pp. 77-8)

In one way Hitchcock is throughout the first half of *Vertigo* using his audience's escapist expectations, the fact that they go the cinema in order to see a "hero," with whom they can identify, involved in romantic wish-fulfillments: hence at this climactic moment dream and romantic cliché merge. But, at a deeper level, the sea as the culmination of this part of the film has another significance: if the sequoia trees are "the oldest living thing," the sea is older still, beating eternally against the rocks, eroding, wearing down; and it is against such sea-associations that the two embrace on the cliff-edge, a tiny, precarious moment placed against eternity. But this is perhaps merely to suggest why the cliché itself still has emotional validity. (p. 84)

Vertigo seems to me of all Hitchcock's films the one nearest to perfection. Indeed, its profundity is inseparable from the perfection of form: it is a perfect organism, each character, each sequence, each image, illuminating every other. Form and technique here becomes the perfect expression of concerns both deep and universal. Hitchcock uses audience-involvement as an essential aspect of the film's significance. Together with its deeply disturbing attitude to life goes a strong feeling for the value of human relationships. To object that the characters' motives are not explained in terms of individual psychology is like demanding a psychological explanation of the sources of evil in Macbeth: Hitchcock is concerned with impulses that lie deeper than individual psychology, that are inherent in the human condition. . . . In complexity and subtlety, in emotional depth, in its power to disturb, in the centrality of its concerns, *Vertigo* can as well as any film be taken to represent the cinema's claims to be treated with the respect accorded to the longer-established art forms. (p. 95)

Psycho begins with the normal and draws us steadily deeper and deeper into the abnormal; it opens by making us aware of time, and ends (except for the releasing final image) with a situation in which time (i.e. development) has ceased to exist. (p. 106)

With [Marion], we lose all power of rational control, and discover how easily a "normal" person can lapse into a condition usually associated with neurosis. Like her we resent, with fear and impatience, everything (the policeman, the car salesman) that impedes or interferes with her obsessive flight, despite the fact that only interference can help her. . . . (pp. 108-09)

The confrontation of Marion and Norman Bates . . . is in some ways the core of the film: the parallel made between them provides the continuity that underlies the brutal disruption when Marion is murdered. It is part of the essence of the film to make us feel the continuity between the normal and the abnormal: between the compulsive behaviour of Marion and the psychotic behaviour of Normal Bates. . . . Norman tells her, "We're all in our private trap. We scratch and claw, but only at the air, only at each other, and for all of it we never budge an inch": he is defining the psychotic state, the condition of permanent anguish whence development becomes impossible, a psychological hell. . . .

It is not merely its incomparable physical impact that makes the showerbath murder probably the most horrific incident in any fiction film. The *meaninglessness* of it (from Marion's point of view) completely undermines our recently restored sense of security. The murder is as irrational and as useless as the theft of the money. It also constitutes an alienation effect so shattering that (at a first viewing of the film) we scarcely recover from it. Never—not even in *Vertigo*—has identification been broken off so brutally. At the time, so engrossed are we in Marion, so secure in her potential salvation, that we can scarcely believe it is happening; when it is over, and she is dead, we are left shocked, with nothing to cling to, the apparent centre of the film entirely dissolved. (p. 109)

Psycho is Hitchcock's ultimate achievement to date in the technique of audience-participation. In a sense, the spectator becomes the chief protagonist, uniting in himself all the characters. . . . Each stage in the descent adds to the tension within us: we want to know, and we dread knowing, we want the investigators to find the truth and put an end to the horrors, yet we have involved ourselves in those horrors through our identification with Norman. (p. 110)

Lila's exploration of the house is an exploration of Norman's psychotic personality. The whole sequence, with its discoveries in bedroom, attic and cellar, has clear Freudian overtones. The Victorian *décor,* crammed with invention, intensifies the atmosphere of sexual repression. (p. 110)

Our discovery of the truth, of course, partly changes our attitude to what has gone before. It adds, for example, many complexities to our understanding of the shower murder, which we see now as primarily a sexual act, a violent substitute for the rape that Norman dare not carry out, and secondarily as the trapped being's desire to destroy a woman who has achieved the freedom he will never achieve. . . . (pp. 111-12)

No film conveys—to those not afraid to expose themselves fully to it—a greater sense of desolation, yet it does so from an exceptionally mature and secure emotional viewpoint. And an essential part of this viewpoint is the detached sardonic humour. It enables the film to contemplate the ultimate horrors without hysteria, with a poised, almost serene detachment. (p. 114)

Robin Wood, in his Hitchcock's Films *(copyright © 1966, 1969, 1977 by Robin Wood), A. S. Barnes and Co., Inc., 1977, 174 p.*

ANDREW SARRIS

Hitchcock provides only one of many possible approaches to cinema. He is not and never has been a raw realist. To enjoy Hitchcock's films, one must accept the fact that he reprocesses reality into pliable cinematic images. His is, therefore, more a cinema of signs than of essences. He has never been interested in sensuality for its own sake. His vision of life is more Freudian than Jungian, in that he does not allow any possibility of heroic regeneration. Fear is far more common than courage, and helplessness more prevalent than courage. His theory of character could be faulted on Aristotelian grounds if there were any claims made for Hitchcock as a cinematic tragedian, but there are not and have never been. His most frequently employed mode of expression is a dark and morbid variety of comedy, which he himself has invented. (p. 46)

Andrew Sarris, "The Hitchcock Heritage," in The Village Voice *(reprinted by permission of* The Village Voice; *copyright © News Group Publications, Inc., 1979), Vol. XXIV, No. 14, April 2, 1979, pp. 45-6.*

ERIC ROHMER and CLAUDE CHABROL

With *Rebecca,* the "Hitchcock touch," which has previously been merely a distinguishing feature, becomes a vision of the world. Spontaneity submits to a system. This is a critical moment for an artist, for he must not develop tics, a pedagogical fury. Hitchcock was to avoid these traps. From now on, the two poles of his future work—because we can now talk of a body of *work*—are clear. One is fascination, moral captation—in other words, depersonalization, schism: in psychoanalytic terms, schizophrenia; in philosophic terms, amoralism; in Baudelairean terms, the assumption of evil, damnation. The other pole is its opposite: knowledge—or, more exactly, reknowledge—of self, unity of being, acceptance, confession, absolute communion. (p. 58)

Alfred Hitchcock's stories come from a great variety of sources, but very early on, he began to alter them in his own way, setting to work on the double job of purifying and enriching them. First he trims the basic idea to bring out a pure relation of force between the characters. Once this has been established, he draws from it, like so many consequences of this relationship, each of the events of the plot. Generally speaking, this deduction operates on two parallel levels, the physical and the moral, and establishes a relation of symbol to idea. (pp. 106-07)

The handcuff scene in *The Thirty-Nine Steps* is a humorous expression of the idea of solidarity, one of the aspects of the "exchange." Little by little the system was to become more coherent, and for each given work the "finds" gushed from the same vein. The films became more homogeneous, and the formulas governing their construction could be more and more easily isolated. It is these formulas that we must return to if we want to study Hitchcock's symbolism; it is these formulas that we must keep our eyes on if we venture to use the dangerous word "metaphysics." . . . [It] is in the form that we must look for the depth of the work and that form is heavy with a latent metaphysic. It is therefore important to consider Hitchcock's work in the same way we would that of an esoteric painter or poet. The fact that the key to the system is not always in the lock, that the doors themselves are skillfully camouflaged, is no reason to insist that there is nothing inside. (p. 107)

[It] is in form that basic essence resides, just as skin, according to biologists, is the original and therefore essential part of an organism. The weak point in *Spellbound* was that the character is depicted as a clinical "case." Psychoanalysis was the prima donna of the film, and esthetics followed along as best it could. [In *Strangers on a Train*], on the contrary, the object that haunts Bruno is not presented to us in its strangeness, but in what it shares with the most ordinary and harmless of our tendencies. And this is done through the intermediary of form.

The attraction of murder, a taste for scheming, sexual perversion, and sick pride are taints presented under the aspects of Figure and Number, depicted in a way that is sufficiently abstract and universal for us to recognize a difference of degree rather than of kind between the obsessions of the protagonist and our own obsessions. Bruno's criminal attitude is only a debased form of an attitude basic to all human beings. In his sickness we can distinguish—corrupted, perverted, but given a kind of esthetic dignity—the very archetype of all our desires. (p. 110)

Hitchcock's art, thrown into particularly sharp relief by this film, is to make us participate—by means of the fascination exercised over each of us by a figure that is almost geometrically refined—in the vertigo of the characters; and beyond this vertigo we discover the essence of the moral idea. The current that goes from the symbol to the idea always passes through the condenser of emotion. (pp. 110, 112)

[Though] Hitchcock is a practicing Catholic he has nothing of the mystic or the ardent proselyte about him. His works are of a profane nature, and though they often deal with questions relating to God, their protagonists are not gripped by an anxiety that is properly speaking religious.

And yet there is not one of Hitchcock's films that is not more or less marked by Christian ideas and symbols. . . .

These signs may justifiably be seen as the workings of chance, but this is in no way irreconcilable—quite the contrary—with Christian dogma. As for the devil, it is not difficult to recognize him. . . .

[A] simultaneous presence of Good and Evil in the same person does not, however, constitute the mainspring of the drama, as it does in classical tragedy. Though Hitchcock's protagonists participate simultaneously in guilt and in innocence, it is impossible to discern the exact point at which these two extreme poles are balanced. Each of these two forces, the positive and the negative, seems to grow not inversely but proportionately; the guilt of the innocent will increase in proportion to his absolute innocence and vice versa. Or at least, if this strange state of equilibrium is never actually reached, we are made to glimpse it as a possibility, an asymptote against which all our good or evil resolutions will come up, and which defines the constitutive —or let us rather say the *original*—flaw in our natures. (p. 113)

If ever the word metaphysic could fearlessly be used about a Hitchcock film, it would certainly be about [*Rear Window*]. But this isn't only a reflexive, critical work in the Kantian sense of the word. This theory of spectacle implies a theory of space, and that in turn implies a moral idea which necessarily—apodictically, as is said in philosophy—derives from it. With one masterly stroke, Hitchcock has here designed the key construct of his entire work, and every one of his other blueprints is probably a corollary, an individual example of this "matrix-figure." We are at the intersecting point of all the material and moral dominants of Hitchcockian mythology, at the heart of a problem whose elegant solution has yet to be found. (p. 124)

The thread of deduction, followed to the end, leads the photographer to extremes. The passion to know, or more exactly to see, will end by suffocating all other feelings. The highest pleasure of this "voyeur" will coincide with the apex of his fear. His punishment will be that his own fiancée, a few yards away, but separated by the space of the courtyard, will be surprised in the suspect's apartment. But no matter how profound this motif, it is only one of the fibers of a sheaf. Parallel to this line, which could be called that of *indiscretion,* run at least two other major themes.

The first is that of *solitude*. This idea is made concrete on the one hand by the photographer's inability to move from his wheelchair, and on the other by the group of well-separated rabbit hutches that are the apartments he can see from his window. Realistic, indeed caricatural, this latter motif provides an opportunity to paint several of the types of fauna flourishing in Greenwich Village in particular and a big city in general. . . . As is true of Edgar Allan Poe's stories, this work is constructed on the implicit base of a philosophy of *Ideas*. Here, the idea—even if it be only the pure idea of Space, Time, or Desire—precedes existence and substance.

But this allegory of knowledge is enriched by the intrusion of a third anecdotal element, the love story of the photographer and his fiancée. . . . It is enriched by a moral symbol—one might even say a *theological* symbol. As will be true in *The Wrong Man*—and much more than was true in *I Confess*—this is a Hitchcock work whose significance cannot be grasped without precise reference to Christian dogma. (pp. 125-26)

Neither the reporter nor his fiancée want to see that paradise which they insist on believing lost and which is nevertheless very close to them, as is indicated—among other signs—by the bouquet that transforms the invalid's room into a flower garden: there are fugitive moments in life when poetry can blossom even in a sewer. . . . Hitchcock is not a censor of the flesh but of the desire whose constitutive vice is to feed on itself and forget the love which must serve as its base. The world he denounces is, on the contrary, the hypocritical world of Victorian society. (pp. 126-27)

All these themes mutually serve as counterpoints, and as is only right in a work so rigorously elaborated, there comes a moment in which they crystalize in a single perfect accord: the death of the little dog. . . . [In] this world of appearances, of inauthenticity, the most atrocious tragedy takes on the mask of the ridiculous. The dog is the gimcrack repetition of that "innocent" who, as in *Sabotage* or the merry-go-round scene in *Strangers on a Train,* might have been a child: as it happens, the dog-owning couple is childless.

The important thing is that because of the woman's words, once the reaction gets underway, each of these people will drink the cup of his egoism down to the lees. (p. 127)

This film is one of those that best illustrates the cardinal virtue of Hitchcockian morality: *exigence*. We can never be hard enough on ourselves—such is its lesson. Evil hides not only under the appearance of Good, but in our most casual and innocent acts, those we think have no ethical significance, those which in principle involve no responsibility. The criminals in this universe are attractively portrayed only so that they can better denounce the Pilates, which in one way or another we all are. . . .

Hitchcock may be a moralist, but there is nothing of the moralizer about him. As we have said, this is not his concern. His role is only to illuminate the situation and let everybody draw his own conclusions. And then too, this guilt which he is so skillful in bringing to the surface is perhaps less of a moral than of a metaphysical order. (p. 128)

Even if *The Wrong Man* were only a faithful account of an item on the police blotter, it would be enough to justify our admiration. A man is arrested in another's place and because he is innocent has a certain distance on what he is undergoing, even if he is therefore undergoing it more intensely. Hitchcock, who enjoys dragging his characters through the mud of contempt, finds the most efficacious form for the expression of this contempt. (p. 146)

This is a documentary without embellishments, even though the camera that shows it to us is never impassive but always descriptive, narrative, as Hitchcock's camera always is. And this veristic detail only helps to buttress the strength of the symbol. We not only clearly discover the Idea, but—if it can be put that way—we feel it. The idea is an extremely complex one, the components of which we can successively identify as: that of the fundamental *abjectness* of a human being, who once deprived of his freedom is no more than an object among other objects; that of *misfortune,* which is simultaneously unjust and merited, like that of Job (everything seems to conspire against our musician); and that of *guilt,* as fundamental as the guilt that serves as the theme of Kafka's *The Trial*. (pp. 146-48)

Therefore, in this film the extraordinary is not, as in the previous works, merely a motor force, a pretext for dazzling developments. It is shown for what it is, and becomes the very object of the study. (p. 148)

Was there really a miracle? We are given no reason to deny it; but unlike what happens in Carl Dreyer's *Ordet,* and despite the clear prejudices of the narrator, a certain freedom of judgment is left us. Certainly Hitchcock has no intention of ridiculing this idea of Providence, which we have encountered elsewhere along the way. On the contrary, what the auteur denounces is the weak surrender to change (significantly enough, our wrong man plays the horses in his spare time). What he excoriates more severely still are those two theological sins of presumption and despair. (pp. 148-49)

The conclusion is obviously ambiguous, but this is no

hedge: the ambiguity is in things themselves. It is characteristic of Hitchcock to show us both sides of the coin. His work moves between two poles which, like extremes, can meet. . . .

As for the form, its basic postulate is perhaps more difficult to isolate in this case, but it is no less rigorous than in the works of so-called pure virtuosity. The "matrix-figure," as is only right, will be that of the *wall.* (p. 149)

Hitchcock is one of the greatest *inventors of form* in the entire history of cinema. Perhaps only Murnau and Eisenstein can sustain comparison with him when it comes to form. Our effort will not have been in vain if we have been able to demonstrate how an entire moral universe has been elaborated on the basis of this form and by its very rigor. In Hitchcock's work form does not embellish content, it creates it. All of Hitchcock can be summed up in this formula. *This is what we wanted to demonstrate.* (p. 152)

Eric Rohmer and Claude Chabrol, in their Hitchcock, the First Forty-four Films, *translated by Stanley Hochman (copyright © 1979 by Frederick Ungar Publishing Co., Inc.; originally published as* Hitchcock, *S.A. Editions Universitaires, 1957), Ungar, 1979, 178 p.*

VINCENT CANBY

Though Hitchcock's work remained out of the reach of fads, except to the extent to which he cast currently popular actors in his films, he absorbed as natural and fitting all of the technical changes of the decades through which he proceeded with his natural caution, like someone crossing a mine field, not because he was afraid of being blown up but because of his aversion to disorder of any sort. . . .

Though Hitchcock pretended to consider himself a prude as movies became increasingly gamey, I suspect that the sex in his films will never look prudish. Hitchcock was a romantic. He loved sexual euphemism—the sudden burst of fireworks in "To Catch a Thief," the train barrelling into a tunnel in "North by Northwest." In the service of lesser filmmakers, such euphemisms look prudish. Not in Hitchcock's movies. . . .

All of his films are sexually aware. That's very different from being sexually explicit, which is often the mask of profound ignorance. (p. 1)

To shock us, Hitchcock devoted himself largely to three kinds of films—the international spy thriller ("Saboteur," "Foreign Correspondent," "Notorious," "North by Northwest," etc.), the film about ordinary, down-home folks suddenly caught in a real horror story ("Shadow of a Doubt," "Strangers on a Train," etc.), and the film about elegant but recognizable people confronting some outrageously anti-social behavior ("Rear Window," "To Catch a Thief," etc.).

No Hitchcock film can be so neatly classified, though. He was always shifting things around. . . .

There are no psychotics in either "Family Plot" or "The Birds." The quality they share with all of his greatest work is the way they manage to implicate everyone who watches them. This, I suppose, is what suspense is. . . .

The difference between a Hitchcock film and a Hitchcockian film is, more often than not, Hitchcock's civilized irony, the courtly, discreet way he persuades us to watch the grisly shower-murder in "Psycho," which prompts us to laugh even as we gasp. . . .

Hitchcock refused to squander his talents on other people's visions. In his old age he continued to make the kind of suspense films he might have made decades earlier, though the style had become simplified, compacted, refined. If he had been a novelist, one would be able to note the almost complete absence of adjectives and adverbs in his later novels. Hitchcock's vocabulary became such that he seldom had to modify anything. The nouns and the verbs he chose said everything.

Irony: To say one thing and mean another. In a Hitchcock film irony is the director's showing us one thing that has, for us in the audience, a dozen meanings not anywhere visible in the film frame. Hitchcock could load the audience with such information that, in "Shadow of a Doubt," a few bars from "The Merry Widow Waltz" become a death knell. We all know too much to be able to watch the film passively. The agony is exquisite. . . .

Like the reading of good prose, the watching of a Hitchcock film has the effect of clearing the cobwebs out of our minds. His films prompt us to see, and to associate what we see with what we've already seen or haven't been allowed to see.

Could it possibly be that one of the reasons for Hitchcock's continued popularity is not that his films are "easy," which is to say obvious and simple-minded, but because they are complex? They require the audience's participation. They make us work, and we like it.

Subversive genius, Hitchcock. . . .

His life—his obsessions, his phobias, his interests, his dreams—was in his films, all right, but it was not his style to call attention to it. His movies say all he has to say. (p. 19)

Vincent Canby, "Alfred Hitchcock Was the Poet of Civilized Suspense," *in* The New York Times, *Section 2 (© 1980 by The New York Times Company; reprinted by permission), May 11, 1980, pp. 1, 19.*

Elia Kazan

1909-

(Born Elia Kazanjoglou) American theatrical director, film director, actor, and author.

Kazan is well-respected as a consistently competent director of actors. Such films as *On the Waterfront* also depict Kazan's interest in individual sagas of the American lifestyle, specifically, those which parallel his own.

Kazan's professional career began in 1932 when he joined Lee Strasberg's Group Theater. Starting out as an actor, he quickly rose to the position of director and his later films reflect this experience and Strasberg's influence. During the thirties, Kazan developed an interest in radical politics and joined the Communist Party. It was not until the 1940s that he finally realized his ambition to direct a film. A short subject, *Pie in the Sky,* was Kazan's first cinematic effort, to be followed by several documentaries.

***A Tree Grows in Brooklyn,* Kazan's first feature film, received critical acclaim and provided him with a graceful transition from stage to screen. Kazan's first films generally reflect postwar discretion in their handling of controversial topics. *Gentleman's Agreement* and *Pinky,* in particular, were intended as indictments of anti-Semitism and racism, but emerge rather as sentimental and naïve, in the opinion of many critics.**

In the late 1940s, Kazan instituted the Actor's Studio. In his work there, he developed the talents of young actors and actresses, most notably James Dean and Marlon Brando. Their respective roles in *East of Eden* and *A Streetcar Named Desire* exemplify Kazan's typical concentration on the characters in his films.

In 1952 Kazan testified before the House Un-American Activities Committee, naming his ex-Party comrades, an action that upset many of his former companions when he signed a lucrative Hollywood contract soon afterwards. *On the Waterfront* is often viewed as Kazan's defense of his testimony.

Shortly after this, Kazan became introspective, and the films following are partially autobiographical. *America, America* and *The Arrangement* are both based on his own writings, and are more concerned with human motivations than with social injustice. Kazan went into semi-retirement in the 1970s. After this he directed only two films: *The Visitors,* a drama of disturbed Vietnam veterans written by his son Chris, and *The Last Tycoon,* a poorly received version of F. Scott Fitzgerald's unfinished novel. While Kazan's ability to direct actors is undisputed, debate still remains as to whether he is an equally significant talent as a filmmaker. (See also *CLC,* Vol. 6, and *Contemporary Authors,* Vols. 21-24, rev. ed.)

BOSLEY CROWTHER

The warm and compassionate story of a slum-pent family in Brooklyn's Williamsburg which was told with such rich and genuine feeling in "A Tree Grows in Brooklyn," by Betty Smith, has received pictorial embodiment to a remarkably harmonious degree. . . . If some of the ripe descriptive detail of the original is missing, that is due to the time limitations of the picture. The essential substance has been maintained and presented in a manner which carries tremendous emotional punch.

For the producers have very bravely shunned the more felicitous course of making their film a humorous abstract of neighborhood folklore and folkways and have got to the core of the story which Miss Smith plainly tore from her own heart. That is the rare and tender story of a valiant and sensitive little girl reaching hopefully for spiritual fulfillment in a wretchedly meager home. It is the story of the wondrous love she gathered from a father who was a cheerful ne'er-do-well and of the painful peace she made with her brave mother after the adored father had died.

Where Miss Smith impinged her printed pages on a vast complex of human love and hope rooted wistfully in tenement surroundings, the camera has envisioned on the screen the outward and visible evidence of this inward and spiritual grace. . . .

[As] well as the pathetic attachment between father and daughter, the film transmits a deeply affecting conception of the mother, . . . whose life was a constant struggle against the family's only adversary, poverty. . . .

Elia Kazan has directed this picture, his first, with an easy naturalness that has brought out all the tone of real experience in a vastly affecting film.

Bosley Crowther, "'A Tree Grows in Brooklyn," in The New York Times *(© 1945 by The New York Times Company; reprinted by permission), March 1, 1945, p. 25.*

C. A. LEJEUNE

[*Pinky*] is an adroit attempt to beat a highly controversial subject in a discreetly uncontroversial way; to flatter the public by giving them the types and situations they have always liked, while persuading them that this time such appreciation is only possible from persons of courageous outlook and advanced social consciousness.

Pinky is not really a "daring" film, except in so far as it admits that there is a colour question at all. It seems to me a fair film: it does not, I imagine, unreasonably distort either side of the picture. It is very smoothly directed. . . . But it is not, I repeat, *daring*. Compared with a really audacious film like *Henry V* or *Hamlet*, it has about as much daring as a cheese-mite. It is careful to affront no particular section of the public, to draw no particular conclusion, to outrage no particular code of cinema ethics, to challenge no particular box-office convention. (p. 107)

C. A. Lejeune, in her review of "Pinky," in Shots in the Dark: A Collection of Reviewers' Opinions of Some of the Leading Films Released between January 1949 and February 1951, *Edgar Anstey, General Editor, Allan Wingate Ltd., 1951, pp. 106-07.*

DILYS POWELL

Pinky belongs to a group of American films with a new attitude to racial questions. (p. 107)

[It] is a film about principles; but principles conveyed by emotional means—and rightly so conveyed; for colour prejudice, whatever elements of reason it may embrace or conceal, is in essence an emotional force, and will be defeated only by a stronger emotional force. *Pinky* is an extremely moving piece of work; moving in its acting, its direction and its writing. It is a good film, in fact, not because it has a praiseworthy subject . . . but because it speaks to us with understanding, pity and indignation of the suffering, the courageous human figure. (p. 108)

Dilys Powell, in her review of "Pinky," in Shots in the Dark: A Collection of Reviewers' Opinions of Some of the Leading Films Released between January 1949 and February 1951, *Edgar Anstey, General Editor, Allan Wingate Ltd., 1951, pp. 107-09.*

KAREL REISZ

Kazan's film of [*A Streetcar Named Desire*] gives one of the first opportunities to see what can be done with [harsh, class-conscious realism] in the cinema. . . .

Behind [the protagonists's] personal drama there develops the conflict of values which Tennessee Williams has explored elsewhere: the clash between the young and the old; the sordidly real and the magically bogus; between the precarious dignity of Stanley's primitive sensual nature and Blanche's equally vulnerable refinement. (p. 170)

The style does not transplant readily to the screen. Tennessee Williams' script . . . changes little of the original. All the usual objections to stage adaptations apply; there is too much talk, too little broad action, and the contrived unnecessary excursions into exterior sets merely break up the narrative's rhythm—the brief scene with Stanley at the factory seems particularly arbitrary. Over and above this, there is a discrepancy between the director's handling and the quality of the writing, which somehow throws all the larger effects out of gear. Staged with the minute attention to details of movement and gesture that one expects from Kazan, the creation of the images is surprisingly unadventurous. Most of the action is caught between medium and close shot—roughly from bosom upwards—and gives much too passive a record for scenes conceived on the large dramatic scale. In the absence of a real visual style, the camera, getting in among the players, merely destroys that automatic sense of one remove one inevitably experiences in the theatre, and achieves a literal, fussy and sweaty realism which jars against the stylised dialogue. . . .

The recurring metaphor of the blind Mexican flower-woman, so apt on the stage, appears as an unconvincingly planted intrusion. The constantly jangling "blue piano" has, for some mysterious reason, been replaced by an orchestra. The isolated attempts to summon Blanche's emotions through a disembodied voice from the past are made too briefly to establish an acceptable convention—and, besides, anchor emotions which were more effective as allusions. There seems to be no instance where the play's effects have been enhanced, and the ambiguous new ending, which allows Stella to leave Stanley, gives a senselessly destructive twist. (p. 171)

Karel Reisz, "Film Reviews: 'A Streetcar Named Desire'," in Sight and Sound *(copyright © 1952 by The British Film Institute), Vol. 21, No. 4, April-June, 1952, pp. 170-71.*

KAREL REISZ

That even the most talented and successful directors are, with varying frequency, obliged to accept subjects in which they can have little real interest is, it seems, part of the scheme of film-making almost everywhere; it happens, perhaps, most often in Hollywood—as most things do—and might as well be accepted. . . .

Elia Kazan has been relatively lucky in this respect; his Hollywood assignments so far have nearly all been interesting, and his latest, *Man on a Tightrope* . . . , has, on the face of it, all the ingredients of a good, topical adventure story. A circus owner in present-day Czechoslovakia decides, when the communist authorities come to restrict his activities—the clown's act must be given political content—to escape into Germany. Because of its unexpectedness, the plan works, and the whole circus, elephants, Chinese jugglers and all, rolls its way over a frontier bridge into Germany.

An adventure of this kind may, of course, deal by implication with serious issues. What is not permissible is a long series of discussions of moral problems, interleaved with bursts of action and written in elaborately "literary" dialogue—in this case the issue is between the commissar's and the "non-political" man's view of life. . . . [The] characters have hardly lifted the flaps of their circus tents before they are deep in the middle of simple truths—freedom, intolerance, man's responsibility to man are all soon and smoothly disposed of. The plot's physical manoeuvres are less carefully worked out; in particular a final twist to the story whereby the commissar allows the circus to proceed on its route just to see what happens, is utterly unconvincing.

Kazan brings to this material the qualities one has now come to expect from him: a brilliant and ultimately boring surface efficiency. He succeeds in some cases in getting remarkable performances from his players, but in a way that makes one feel he is "good with actors" rather than that he has a real, a direct response to character. And as a storyteller he now snatches at his climaxes too fiercely (*cf. Panic in the Streets*), overloading everything with layers of indiscriminate atmospheric detail that stifle tension. There seems more than ever something much more genuinely personal about his earlier films, *A Tree Grows in Brooklyn, Boomerang,* when compared with this inflated virtuosity.

Karel Reisz, "Film Reviews: 'Man on a Tightrope'," in Sight and Sound *(copyright © 1953 by The British Film Institute), Vol. 23, No. 1, July-September, 1953, p. 32.*

A. H. WEILER

A small but obviously dedicated group of realists has forged artistry, anger and some horrible truths into "On the Waterfront," as violent and indelible a film record of man's inhumanity to man as has come to light this year. And, while this explosive indictment of the vultures and the meek prey of the docksides . . . occasionally is only surface dramatization and an oversimplification of the personalities and evils of our waterfront, it is, nevertheless, an uncommonly powerful, exciting and imaginative use of the screen by gifted professionals.

Although journalism and television already have made the brutal feudalism of the wharves a part of current history, "On the Waterfront" adds a graphic dimension to these sordid pages. . . .

[Elia Kazan has] limned a bestial and venal boss longshoreman; the "shape-up" by which only his obedient, mulct, vassals can earn a day's pay; the hard and strange code that demands that these sullen men die rather than talk about these injustices and a crime commission that helps bring some light into their dark lives.

Perhaps these annals of crime are too labyrinthine to be fully and incisively captured by cameras. Suffice it to say, however, that while Mr. Kazan and [screenwriter Budd] Schulberg have not dug as deeply as they might, they have chosen a proper and highly effective cast and setting for their grim adventure. . . .

Despite its happy ending; its preachments and a somewhat slick approach to some of the facets of dockside strife and tribulations, "On the Waterfront" is moviemaking of a rare and high order.

A. H. Weiler, "'On the Waterfront'," in The New York Times *(© 1954 by The New York Times Company; reprinted by permission), July 29, 1954, p. 18.*

PENELOPE HOUSTON

Elia Kazan's *On the Waterfront* . . . is a significant, almost a definitive, example of a type of film which traditionally finds Hollywood at its most expert: the melodrama with a stiffening of serious ideas, the journalistic exposé of crime and corruption. Its subject harks back to the racket-smashing thrillers of the 'thirties; its style—location shooting, conscientious concern with surface realism—belongs to the present decade; its pretensions, the attempt to build authentic drama out of an investigation of waterfront gangsterism, are characteristic not only of the director but of a whole school of Hollywood thought. . . .

Budd Schulberg has written a script which is vigorous, credible, at times (in the scenes between Terry and the girl) authentically touching, and which, though it has its over-conventional elements in the characterisation of Friendly and of the priest, never falls into the familiar, specious habit of "dignifying" its working class characters by making them speak in pseudo-Biblical language.

The script, in fact, contains the basis for a sharply observed journalistic investigation of a man's slow realisation of the truth about his environment. . . .

Kazan, however, not content to let the story develop its own impetus, tends to over-inflate the simplest situation, to build up an atmosphere of artificial tension and urgency. Abetted by Leonard Bernstein's score, which undoubtedly contributes forcefully to the mood of the film, he has gone all out for the raucous, aggressive, showy effect. The virtuosity of Kazan's handling, the skill with which he sets a scene of violence, are not in doubt; one does, however, question the validity of his methods and of his approach. (p. 85)

During recent years, Hollywood "realism" has developed its own immediately recognisable conventions and attitudes. A now familiar technique of handling actors demands those mannerisms—Karl Malden's check in mid-speech, for instance—always just a little too studied for naturalism. . . .

In *On the Waterfront,* there is a scene in which Terry has to tell the girl of his part in her brother's murder: as they speak, their voices are drowned by a bellowing ship's siren. If the picture were presented as no more than melodrama, the trick would seem acceptable enough; but in building up his subject as he has, Kazan has foregone his right to evade so crucial a stage in this particular relationship. In a sense, the incident may be taken to sum up the film: excitement is whipped up, attitudes are struck, but the incidental detail blots out the human situation and—though it is not for want of trying—the transition from melodrama to drama is never made. (p. 86)

Penelope Houston, "Film Reviews: 'On the Waterfront'," in Sight and Sound *(copyright © 1954 by The British Film Institute), Vol. 24, No. 2, December, 1954, pp. 85-6.*

LINDSAY ANDERSON

It has been remarked that the success this year of three films like *From Here to Eternity, The Caine Mutiny* and *On the Waterfront* is a hopeful sign, demonstrating that inflationary techniques are not essential to the seduction of mass audiences. All we need are good films. . . . *On the Waterfront* is a bad film. Unfortunately, bad films are important too. This one is important because of its special kind of badness, and because of the enormous degree of acceptance it has won. . . .

The film, in fact, has been accepted at its face value; or, more correctly perhaps, at its *sensation* value—as if it were a strong drink or an electric shock—and liked to a greater or lesser degree, according to individual taste. . . .

Yet a preliminary title to the film is quite specific in its claims. The story will show how *"self-appointed tyrants can be defeated by right-thinking people in a vital democracy."* We are entitled, even invited, then, to examine closely the social implications of what we are shown.

The first thing revealed is the virtual absence of at least half the elements necessary to make the situation convincing. A social problem of this kind needs to be placed in a context, shown with a certain fullness, in the round. Rackets like Johnny Friendly's do not spring up out of the ground; they are not the productions of one wicked man. (p. 128)

[It] may be objected that the makers of *On the Waterfront* have purposely chosen to dramatise the problem through one particular case: the moral awakening of Terry Malloy. There is nothing to be said against such an approach, so long as its limits are clearly defined. The vital question then arises: what exactly does Terry awake to? Over her first beer-and-chaser, Edie is not slow to remind him that no man is an island; but after this promising start, the subject is dropped. Terry finds his dignity—that is to say, he develops a capacity for individual action; but what he does, he does for himself, to avenge his brother's murder, and for the *beaux yeux* of Edie. All of which has little relevance to the duties of "right-thinking people in a vital democracy." In fact, *On the Waterfront* is essentially an extremely artful conjuring trick; underneath its brilliant technical surface, essential conclusions are evaded and replaced by a personal drama whose implications are entirely different. (p. 129)

The dishonesty of method becomes clear when we compare *On the Waterfront* with one of America's really great social films. *The Grapes of Wrath* provided its adaptors with a similarly radical subject, where a general social (or political) problem is approached through the sufferings of a handful of selected individuals. Also, as a film *The Grapes of Wrath* owes its greatness to its affirmation of human dignity (as *On the Waterfront* seeks to do), rather than to any factual indictment of the society in which its disasters take place. But it does this without evasions. . . . [While] Ford's images of human dignity have faith in them to make them true, Kazan's ingenious lip-service reduces all aspiration to a platitude. (pp. 129-30)

If we praise a film like *On the Waterfront* for the "mastery" (etc., etc.) of its direction, we are attaching considerable over-importance to skill on a very superficial, not to say dubious level. . . . This is hysterical film-making, every incident whipped up by tricks to a quite spurious dramatic intensity: music to shock and scare, effects that boom, dialogue incomprehensibly shouted or mumbled in a theatrical affectation of realism, looming close-ups that seek to impose their mood on us by sheer size, jazzed-up cutting and compositions meaninglessly bold. A style, in short, of horrid vulgarity; to which the notion of *decorum* is unknown; using every possible device to batter and bemuse. (p. 130)

Lindsay Anderson, "The Last Sequence of 'On the Waterfront'," in Sight and Sound *(copyright © 1955 by The British Film Institute), Vol. 24, No. 3, January-March, 1955, pp. 127-30.*

BOSLEY CROWTHER

Only a small part of John Steinbeck's "East of Eden" has been used in the motion picture version of it that Elia Kazan has done, and it is questionable whether that part contains the best of the book. . . .

Compressed in a script by Paul Osborn, which reduces the mother to little more than a black shrouded figure of a madam of a sporting-house in a California town, this quarter-part of the novel is boiled down to a mere review of the coincidental way in which the conflict between the father and son is resolved.

Yet Mr. Kazan has at it, . . . with such elaborate pictorial build-up and such virtuosity on his actors' part that he gets across the illusion of a drama more pregnant than it is.

In one respect, it is brilliant. The use that Mr. Kazan has made of CinemaScope and color in capturing expanse and mood in his California settings is almost beyond compare. His views of verdant farmlands in the famous Salinas "salad bowl," sharply focused to the horizon in the sunshine, are fairly fragrant with atmosphere. The strain of troubled people against such backgrounds has a clear and enhanced irony.

Some of Mr. Kazan's interiors—especially his final scene in the bedroom of the father, where the old man is dying of a stroke—have a moodiness, too, that moves the viewer with their strongly emotional overtones. The director gets more into this picture with the scenery than with the characters.

For the stubborn fact is that the people who move about in this film are not sufficiently well established to give point to the anguish through which they go, and the demonstrations of their torment are perceptibly stylized and grotesque. . . .

In short, there is energy and intensity but little clarity and emotion in this film. It is like a great, green iceberg: mammoth and imposing but very cold.

Bosley Crowther, "'East of Eden'," in The New York Times *(© 1955 by The New York Times Company; reprinted by permission), March 10, 1955, p. 33.*

ROBERT HUGHES

On the Waterfront is "political," Lindsay Anderson claims [see excerpt above], in a way comparable to *The Grapes of Wrath*. I would put the whole emphasis differently. Whatever its origins, the film comes to us and should be judged primarily as personal drama. Implications there are, of course—but apparently not the ones Mr. Anderson wants.

There are two sides in the film, one characterised by a thorough-going viciousness, the other given a Christian shading. To which sides does Terry owe loyalty? The question is central to the action, and we get the answer in the last sequence. One value dominates the waterfront: loyalty. It is the moral criterion of docker and thug, a mechanism continually at work. . . .

Politically, the film could perhaps end with Terry's testimony, but as personal drama it demands the final sequences. Isolating them, Lindsay Anderson finds them "implicitly Fascist" and, at the last, "pointless." But the enquiry does not leave Terry on the other side; he finds himself in a no-man's-land. If he refuses to regard himself as a betrayer, others do. . . .

Certainly the conclusion, which Lindsay Anderson dislikes, offers no facile solution. Kazan is honest enough not to pretend that the waterfront situation has magically changed. The dockers' victory is by no means total. Grim authority still exists over them, but they have asserted themselves in a limited fashion. . . .

Friendly's sponsor apparently goes scot-free; another Friendly may arise. To ask for more than this is to cry for a moon of social perfection, for some ideal political "five." (p. 215)

Robert Hughes, "'On the Waterfront': A De-

fence," in Sight and Sound *(copyright © 1955 by The British Film Institute), Vol. 24, No. 4, Spring, 1955, pp. 214-15.*

ANDREW GEORGE SARRIS

[In *East of Eden*] Kazan has done more than master the static temptations of Cinemascope. For the first time in his film career, he has harnessed his violent technique to the emotional content of his material.

As a consequence, *East of Eden* is the deepest film Kazan has ever made and, in many respects, the best. The shock effects in *East of Eden* are even more jarring than those of *On the Waterfront* because they occur within the feelings of his characters rather than without. Also, there is none of the superimposed melodrama in *Eden* that we find in *Waterfront* just as there are no easy melodramatic solutions. . . .

Where Steinbeck had reinforced his biblical parable with a well-observed social background, [the screenwriter Paul Osborn] and Kazan have stripped away social details to concentrate on the feelings of the characters.

Unfortunately, *East of Eden* fails to develop its characters through meaningful dialogue. Kazan seems interested mainly in the visual aspects of an idea; the intellectual weakness of his films seems to follow from this. There are many moments when the screen cries out for articulation and explanation and Kazan responds only with a quick movement on a swing, a line mumbled in passing, an intense shrug of a shoulder. The many stylized mannerisms and movements that replace cogent dialogue are part of the Kazan-Strasberg, Actor's Lab, East of Hollywood trend in motion pictures. . . .

East of Eden has serious structural flaws. Events are introduced too obviously and often without any narrative logic. The incidents and atmosphere of the film's historical setting, the anti-German hysteria, the mechanics of war-profiteering, the moral problems of a draft board are too sketchily indicated and too obviously tacked on to the central plot. Puzzling shifts in feeling in the main characters are unexplained.

Whatever unity *East of Eden* possesses is an emotional unity of character and familial situation. To appreciate this unity, one must identify with the situation; one must feel its emotions. In addition, one must accept Kazan's short hand, his elliptical style that never fully explains or resolves any situation with language. . . . [However,] its importance transcends its flaws.

Andrew George Sarris, "Reviews of Current Films: 'East of Eden'," in Film Culture *(copyright 1955 by* Film Culture*), Vol. 1, No. 3, May-June, 1955, p. 24.*

DEREK PROUSE

Somewhere about the middle of *East of Eden* . . . there is a scene when the boy Caleb, . . . visits his mother whom he has discovered to be the proprietress of a brothel, in the hope of borrowing money for a business venture. This scene . . . is handled with such meaningful economy, and seems the result of such cogent understanding, that it contrasts sharply with the empty show of so much of the rest of the film, and the unhappy preferences this talented director seems in danger of continuing to follow.

East of Eden is a film without a centre. One feels that Kazan has been impressed by the allegorical universals implied by the pretentious Biblical parallels of John Steinbeck's novel. . . . To the basic themes of the various natures of love (distorting, blinding, or satisfying, and the consuming loneliness of the boy who yearns for it), Kazan only ever offers a peripheral illustration. The most consistent quality of this is a virile assertiveness. The action of the story seems to be presented, explosively, moment by moment, and these separate stresses never make up a believable rhythmic flow. Relationships are never closely investigated, tables may be thumped and voices raised, but one is never imaginatively drawn or held. In particular, the pivotal jealousy between the two brothers appears almost naïvely unplotted, while in backgrounds busy with cleverness, small parts limp and twitch with such intensity of "character" that the mere business of being people is quite overlooked.

It is, then, this lack of a genuine response, and the consequent inability to convey to his actors the core and essence of the situations, which seems to lead Kazan to favour an acting style that discourages any direct expression. (pp. 32-3)

The film's failure to convey any credible existence in space and time is in fact responsible for its oppressive tedium, and the absence of a feeling of progression in the narrative. The following scene is a case in point. A group of characters are debating the workings of a 1917 motor-car; the scene is cleverly written, the resulting note should be one of humour and charm. But the relentlessly emphatic acting never takes the central object (the car) into account, and the dialogue, though interestingly delivered, is never allowed really to connect with the situation and soon becomes a meaningless onslaught of sound. (p. 33)

It is, of course, Kazan's undoubted talent that sets him so squarely in the line of critical fire. His own standards ask to be judged exactingly. That, in dramatic exposition, he has here bitten off more than he can chew, needs to be stated—as does the hope that he may return to the kind of material that evokes the best of his imagination. (p. 34)

Derek Prouse, "Film Reviews: 'East of Eden'," in Sight and Sound *(copyright © 1955 by The British Film Institute), Vol. 25, No. 1, Summer, 1955, pp. 32-4.*

PAULINE KAEL

The subject matter of *On the Waterfront* is alienation at the lowest social level. . . . Terry Malloy, the hero of *On the Waterfront,* is alienated at the instinctive level of the adolescent and the bum, and the drama, as those who made the film see it, is in his development of consciousness and responsibility, his taking his place as a man.

The attempt to create a hero for the mass audience is a challenge and a great big trap. *On the Waterfront* meets the challenge, falls into the trap. (p. 47)

On the Waterfront succeeds brilliantly in creating a figure out of the American lower depths, a figure simple in reasoning power but complicated in motivation and meaning; it fails to win complete assent when it attempts to make this figure into a social and symbolic hero—by fiat. (p. 48)

On the Waterfront is [an] ambitious film, though its moral scheme is that battle of good versus evil which is a film commonplace. No doubt those who made the film, and many of those who see it, view the conflict in the film not as a commonplace, but as a rendering of the "supreme" theme. But this "supreme" theme has never been the theme of great drama because it tends to diminish man's humanity, rather than to illuminate it. (p. 49)

The director, Elia Kazan, is undoubtedly a master of what is generally regarded as "good theater": all those movements, contrasts, and arrangements which have been developed to give inferior material the look of drama. (p. 50)

The advantages of Kazan's direction are in his fine eye for living detail (for example, in Terry's first interchange with the men from the crime commission); the disadvantages are that the best things are often overpowered by the emphasis given to the worst. . . . There are a few places where Kazan's dexterity fails completely: moving the union men around as a herd is too "staged" to be convincing. And even "good theater" doesn't allow for elements that are tossed in without being thought out (the ship owner, an oddly ambiguous abstraction, possibly cartooned in obeisance to the labor-union audience) or tossed in without being felt (the complacent, smiling faces of the priest and the girl at the end—converted, by a deficiency of artistic sensibility, into pure plaster). (p. 51)

The writer and director placed [the] imaginatively compelling figure [Terry] in a structure which, while theatrically fairly sound, is not the dramatic complement the figure deserves. Terry has his own kind of consciousness; he is *too* compelling to act out *their* consciousness and to fit the social role they assign him. Terry is credible until he becomes a social hero. Does moral awakening for a Terry mean that he acquires the ability to change the external situation, or does it mean simply an intensification and a broadening of his alienation? . . . Our social problems are much too complex to be dramatically rendered in a Christian parable. The artists who made the film have a remarkable negative similarity: they do not risk alienation from the mass audience. And they do not face up to the imaginative task—nor to the social risk—of creating fresh symbols. Have they earned the right to show their hero risking his life in order to save his soul?

The myth of the creation of a saint (or, indeed, a multiplicity of saints) which cripples the dramatic development of Terry's character, does an even more obvious disservice to the social questions the film raises. The myth structure forces a superficial answer to questions for which no one has a satisfactory answer. (pp. 52-3)

Would Terry seem so compelling if his behavior and attitudes did not express a profound mass cynicism and a social truth? More goes into his alienation than the activities of a John Friendly, and his character is powerful because it suggests much more—the desire of adolescents to find an acceptable ethic, quasi-homosexual elements in this ethic, adolescent hostility toward adult compromises, the identification with an antisocial code, the intensity of aspirations. Terry's scene with his brother in the cab is drama because these accumulated elements explode. These elements and many more derive, not merely from a corrupt union, but from the dislocation of youth in our society, and ultimately, if one takes a pessimistic view, they derive from the human condition. (pp. 53-4)

Despite its defects, and they are major, *On the Waterfront* provides an imaginative experience. If one regrets that the artists, having created an authentic image of alienation, failed to take that image seriously enough, one remembers also that most films provide no experience at all.

The alienated hero acquires a new dimension in *East of Eden*. . . . [Cal] is a romantic figure, decorated with all sorts of charming gaucheries, and set, anachronistically, in a violent reverie of pre-World War I youth. At one level he's the All-American boy (and the reverse of the usual image of the artist as a youth): he's not too good at school, he's sexually active, he's not interested in politics but has a childlike responsiveness to parades, he doesn't care about words or ideas. Yet this lack of intellectual tendencies is projected as evidence of sensitivity and purity of feeling; the strangled speech, the confused efforts at gesture, as poetry. (p. 55)

The film is overpowering: it's like seeing a series of teasers —violent moments and highly charged scenes without structural coherence (one begins to wonder if the teaser is Kazan's special genre?). (pp. 55-6)

If, after the film, the air outside the theater seems especially clean and fresh, it is not only from relief at escaping the cracker-barrel humanism, it's the restorative power of normal, uncoerced perspective: it's a little like coming out of a loony bin. A boy's agonies should not be dwelt on so lovingly: being misunderstood may easily become the new and glamorous lyricism. With *East of Eden*, Hollywood has caught up with the main line of American avant-garde cinema—those embarrassingly autoerotic twelve-minute masterpieces in which rejected, inexplicable, and ambiguous figures are photographed in tortured chiaroscuro, films which exude symbolism as if modern man were going to find himself by chasing the shadow of an alter ego in a dark alley. When alienation is exploited for erotic gratification, film catches up with the cult realities of city parks and Turkish baths; clear meanings or definite values would be too grossly explicit—a vulgar intrusion on the Technicolor night of the soul.

The romance of human desperation is ravishing for those who wish to identify with the hero's amoral victory: everything he does is forgivable, his crimes are not crimes at all, because he was so terribly *misunderstood*. (And who in the audience, what creature that ever lived, felt he was loved enough?). . . . Cal is the hero simply and completely because of his *need*, and his frenzied behavior, the "bad" things that he does, establish him as a hero by demonstrating his need. . . . This is a complete negation of previous conceptions of heroism: the hero is not responsible for his actions—the crazy, mixed-up kid becomes a romantic hero by being treated on an infantile level. (pp. 56-7)

The type of heroism entrenched in most older and routine films is based on the obscenity: "right makes might and might makes right." (The hero can back up his moral and ethical edge on the villain with stronger fists.) And an absurd corollary is attached: the girl loves the man who fights for the right. *East of Eden* introduces a rather dismaying new formula: need for love makes right, and the girl loves the boy who most needs to be loved. (p. 57)

Pauline Kael, "The Glamor of Delinquency: 'On the Waterfront,' 'East of Eden,' 'Blackboard Jungle' . . ." (1955), in her I Lost It at the Movies *(copyright © 1965 by Pauline Kael; reprinted by* *permission of Little, Brown and Company in association with the Atlantic Monthly Press), Atlantic-Little, Brown, 1965, pp. 44-61.**

ANDREW SARRIS

Baby Doll is a complex of mannerisms, some of which come perilously close to self-parody. Elia Kazan's uneasy blend of surface realism and theatrical exaggeration, Tennessee Williams' injection of the *commedia dell' arte* into the decaying corpus of the Deep South, and the unmotivated virtuosity of "method" acting give *Baby Doll* a dated, almost antique quality. This film is for Kazan what *The Sun Shines Bright* was for John Ford, *Meet John Doe* for Frank Capra . . . a stylistic throwback, too calculating in its effects, culturally anachronistic, and, as in all instances, a faithful reflection of the director's most popular weaknesses.

The violent climaxes that flawed Kazan's work in *On the Waterfront* and *East of Eden* are more pronounced, though less effective, in this curious chamber drama of avarice and cuckoldry, and the steady thematic drift from normality and logical characterization has culminated in the fantasy of aberration, a deplorable genre for an artist of Kazan's calibre. As a career setback, *Baby Doll* indicates not so much a technical regression as an unfortunate choice of subject matter. . . .

Kazan and Williams, who are famous in the theatre for revising plays from audience reactions, have obscured the fundamental drives of the original situation. It is now not clear whether Baby Doll is actually seduced, and this ambiguity is linked distastefully with the addition of the virgin wife who refuses to perform her conjugal duties until her husband refurnishes their empty home. With the introduction of a feeble-minded aunt, who is one arthritic step away from the poor farm, *Baby Doll* enters the grotesque world of Erskine Caldwell. . . .

The theatrical contrivances of *Baby Doll* are set against the authentic background of Benoit, Mississippi, a muddy backwater in the stream of American civilization. What little contact this society has with the modern world seems only to intensify the demoralization of its people. New cars emphasize the absence of unpaved roads; a picturesque river raft connotes a world devoid both literally and symbolically of bridges. (p. 19)

The background of *Baby Doll,* unlike that of *Giant,* cannot be isolated from the central plot. Kazan captures the *verismo* of Benoit's passive faces, but their range of observation is carefully limited to the unusually energetic conflict of passions in their midst. Archie Lee, Baby Doll, and Silva Vacarro do not emanate from their environment; they intrude upon it with their Gothic adventures. Even if they are considered as allegorical extensions of their time and place, they fail to be morally or psychologically consistent. Baby Doll is introduced as a simple-minded creature, who shrewdly withholds her voluptuous charms until she obtains the right price from her husband. . . . When she is deserted by the two men in her life, she assumes the wistful aura of a Southern belle waiting at Tara for someone to return. Archie Lee is an outrageous personification of ineffectual lechery and clutching avarice until he becomes inexplicably concerned with family honor. However, it is Vacarro, a unique literary creation, who poses the greatest mystery. A half-cousin of Williams' Serafina in *The Rose Tatoo,* Vacarro is by turns solicitous, sadistic, whimsical, relentless, considerate, callous, and generally much too literate for his milieu. He is overloaded with Williams' fanciful notions of a Sicilian vendetta in the alien soil of Mississippi, and his antecedents are invoked to justify his sudden, pseudo-dramatic shifts in feeling. The calculated alternations of wild farce and malignant intensity in the film are based to a great extent on the chromatic range of Vacarro's personality. (pp. 19-20)

It is misleading to condemn *Baby Doll* for its divergence from its original sources or for its failure to say more about race relations in the South. These are not the crucial issues. The absence of a consistent rationale for the characters is a more serious flaw, but it can be argued that unpredictability of human behavior is an adequate mystique for certain forms of storytelling. The fact that Williams and Kazan cheat on the sex and overdevelop the lecherous by-play is unfortunate, but, by now, thoroughly familiar. . . . The ultimate error of *Baby Doll* lies in its aesthetic assumptions which overrate the power of certain elliptical techniques in writing, acting, and direction to create valid emotional effects without the laborious processes of intellectual and thematic development. In this artistic context, the only area in which Kazan can be judged, the fact that *Baby Doll* succeeds as popular entertainment is almost irrelevant. (p. 20)

Andrew Sarris, "'Baby Doll'," in Film Culture *(copyright 1957 by* Film Culture*), Vol. 3, No. 1, 1957, pp. 19-20.*

FRANÇOIS TRUFFAUT

All great filmmakers aspire to be free from the constraints of drama; they dream of making a film without progression, without psychology, in which the spectators' interest would be aroused by means other than changes of place and time, the cleverness of the dialogue, or the characters' comings and goings. *Un Condamné à Mort s'est échappé (A Man Escaped), Lola Montès, Woman on the Beach,* and *Rear Window* all achieve a considerable amount in this tricky game, each one in its own way.

In *Baby Doll,* Kazan has succeeded almost completely, by means of a style of direction that is unique, in making this sort of film, while simultaneously mocking the emotions that are portrayed and analyzed in conventional films.

What bothers Kazan, what he cannot seem to manage, are the transition scenes involving several characters. In *Baby Doll* he succeeds in dodging them except at the beginning of the film, and from the moment the Sicilian starts to court the woman-child, we are watching a film in which each gesture and glance is made to count, so perfect is its precision. It is a film masterfully dominated by one man.

Kazan's talent, which is essentially of a decorative nature, is more effective with subjects of this type (those that come from Broadway, we could say quite simply) than those laborious social theses which are necessarily dishonest.

We know now that Elia Kazan has nothing more to say to us than what his screenplay writers have written for him, and at the same time that he is the man who knows best of all how to reveal actors to themselves.

The second time we see *Baby Doll,* we discover a second film which is still richer. Whether it is a work of genius or mere talent, whether decadent or generous, profound or brilliant, *Baby Doll* is fascinating. (pp. 112-13)

François Truffaut, "Elia Kazan: 'Baby Doll'" (1957), in his The Films in My Life, *translated by Leonard Mayhew (copyright © 1975 by, Flammarion; translation copyright © 1978 by Simon & Schuster; reprinted by permission of Simon & Schuster, a Division of Gulf & Western Corporation; originally published as* Les films de ma vie, *Flammarion, 1975), Simon & Schuster, 1978, pp. 110-13.*

HENRY GOODMAN

Considering the abundance of good story material for the screen contained in the social issues of the day, surprisingly few American films have tackled the public problems from which spring the personal dramas. Of the occasional ventures into this area Elia Kazan's have been among the best —for instance, *On the Waterfront, Panic in the Streets* and *A Face in the Crowd,* films which grew out of "documentary" materials and drew the private story from a wider social context. And now with *Wild River* Kazan explores a community issue and the private sorrows stemming from it. . . .

In Kazan's film the subject [the Tennessee Valley Authority] gives rise to a moral issue that is the surest stuff of tragedy: two rights clashing head on make a wrong. Here is the archetypal conflict of the state versus the individual that we find in *Antigone:* community need (the irresistible force) against personal conscience (the immovable object). . . .

The government's purpose is admittedly good—to control a destructive river and to provide cheap power for the inhabitants of the region. But Progress has a way of hurting while helping; with benevolence there is also tyranny. In the face of social necessity Ella Garth fights for those things which matter most to the individual: her identity, her roots, and her dignity. (p. 50)

[However, a] film excellent in many ways is wrenched out of shape by a love story that gets more space than it merits.

More pertinent to the main struggle and in keeping with the scope of social drama is the introduction of the racial issue. . . . The community, already disrupted and bewildered by depression, government relief projects, and the crush of history, becomes a confused mass of outraged bigotry. . . . The [racial] scene as a whole creates a nightmare experience mixing terror with absurdity.

Kazan has a talent for achieving poetic statement from even the most accidental naturalistic detail. The idle, uncomprehending stare of an old woman in a cheap hotel lobby becomes a powerful image. Again, as in *Panic in the Streets, Baby Doll,* or *A Face in the Crowd,* the camera explores scenes in a wonderful old-fashioned way to provide a rich environment for the immediate drama. Kazan recalls the depression years with poetic swiftness through a fleeting look at a WPA sign, a picture of Roosevelt, or a group of hotel residents gathered in the lobby at night to listen to the radio. Scraps of songs from the 'thirties or a giggling desk clerk quoting the comic tags of the day—"Wanna buy a duck?" and "Vas you dere, Sharlie?"—are at once documentary and intensely theatrical in impact.

Finally, Kazan's pictorial sense is magical: fishermen at the river, golden sunlight on dark branches or dried stalks in the field, and mist over the water are among the fine things in this good film marred only by a misshapen story. (pp. 50-1)

Henry Goodman, "Film Reviews: 'Wild River'," in Film Quarterly *(copyright 1960 by The Regents of the University of California; reprinted by permission of the University of California Press), Vol. XIII, No. 4, Summer, 1960, pp. 50-1.*

JOHN COLEMAN

Splendour in the Grass . . . comes from the canvas-backed chair of Kazan, the typewriter of William Inge and the camera of Boris Kaufman: it is accordingly a very glossy, punchy, expert piece of something or other. Unfortunately, it is also ludicrous. (p. 96)

The end of this packed film (there is an unjustified, recalcitrant air of jumbo novel about it, like *Giant*) brings together the two kids, now older and saner, in a wistful encounter. They lost that Wordsworthian 'splendour in the grass'—here interpreted as a roll in the hay—presumably for 'strength in what remains behind'. . . . In ways too devious to recount in full, this long film forfeits seriousness and sympathy by being either too sheerly arranged at crucial times—the girl's parents rocking on the porch in awful symmetry could be advertising anything from bungalows in Los Angeles to a capitalist vodka—or too thunderously repetitious, too Methodic, strenuous and symbolic. . . . There are large merits, too—a party that snares what one imagines to have been the spendthrift hysteria of the Twenties, superbly photographed in tastefully muted shades of violence. . . . [However,] the general prettifying and guile detract from belief. (p. 97)

John Coleman, "The Amis World," in New Statesman *(© 1962 The Statesman & Nation Publishing Co. Ltd.), Vol. LXIII, No. 1610, January 19, 1962, pp. 96-7.**

ERNEST CALLENBACH

Kazan is a director who gets powerful performances from his actors. . . . Where he has had strong scripts also, as in *Streetcar Named Desire,* the under-rated *East of Eden,* or *On the Waterfront,* his particular kind of talent has come through extraordinarily well; these are films which will last, though none of them is a really great work. Even Kazan's worst films are by no means the filmed plays turned out by lesser men coming from television or the stage; in fact, in avoiding that danger, Kazan tends to fall into a decoratively "cinematic" style in which strong effects are a little too obviously worked for, rather than allowed to rise out of the material, out of the structure of the work itself. In a nutshell, Kazan is a "pushy" director; his best films have been those in which he had a good story and good actors to push against.

In *America, America* he had total free rein; it is a personal film in every sense of the word. And hence I am forced to the unwilling conclusion that Kazan is not a director who gains by producing, writing, and directing, at least not on material so close to him. . . . Kazan here seems to have needed the harsh discipline of the check-and-balance system of filming. This method does not allow idiosyncratic masterpieces, and on this count the Hollywood producer certainly deserves the villainous character he has acquired; but at least it prevents excesses. And most of the troubles with *America, America* are excesses.

In a work which swings erratically from epic drama to psychological analysis, Kazan asks an excessive sympathy for his young hero with the "Anatolian smile"—Stavros is a stupid, gullible, vacantly ambitious, incompetently cynical youth, whose irrepressible smile turns out to be a mask rather than a redeeming naive virtue. (Good luck ultimately saves Stavros, but his own incorrigible schmuckery causes almost all his troubles.) (pp. 55-6)

We are asked to take an excessive interest in this hardly epic tale, and with progressively less reason. The grail Stavros seeks perhaps qualifies as epical, being suitably vague and ambiguous: America is at first a haven from oppression, but Stavros soon thinks of it chiefly as a place where he will be cleansed of all the sins he has committed in order to get there. His ill-starred jousts and reluctant wooing of maidens might have made a comic epic. But Kazan is being serious: he has drawn us Stavros the idiot hero, apt for all manner of lunacy, while thinking he was making a sentimental gesture toward his ancestors.

Indeed, one comes uncomfortably close to feeling that the film's real, latent subject is precisely the failures and humiliations which Stavros so largely brings upon himself. Kazan gives these episodes full dramatic play, with his accustomed energy. It is, of course, not unknown for minority group members to have a kind of fixation on traits that cause them grief; and one may grant Kazan many mixed feelings about his real-life uncle Stavros and his lost innocence. But why, then, the persistence in a heroic tone?

With such uncertainties of conception at its heart, it is no wonder that the film wanders unsurely and lacks balance. Individual episodes are impressive, but have a way of countering each other. (p. 56)

Ernest Callenbach, "Film Reviews: 'America, America'," in Film Quarterly *(copyright 1964 by The Regents of the University of California; reprinted by permission of the University of California Press), Vol. XVII, No. 4, Summer, 1964, pp. 55-6.*

ESTELLE CHANGAS

Kazan's career is marked by a striking progression from films expressing a detached, liberal social consciousness towards more personal and emotional films. His career reveals a basic tension: an intellectual desire to deal with social issues as viewed in his less satisfying *urban* films which utilize a broad and contemporary canvas, versus his instinctual response to the past and to the unworldly inhabitants of cohesive ethnic communities or simple agrarian environments. . . .

While his work would continue to be marked by a concern for social problems, Kazan's most interesting films—especially *East of Eden* (1955) and *Wild River* (1960), his richest works—combine a careful integration and balance between character development and social issues. These social concerns spring from the inner lives of the central figures themselves, rather than remaining the detached, objectified problems of crime and corruption that the heroes of Kazan's earlier films succeed in solving. (p. 9)

A child immigrant from Turkey, Kazan views America much as we would expect a foreigner to—with a sense of wonder and fascination at the eccentricities of this country. More and more Kazan was drawn to material involving characters from particularized areas of America, notably the South—Mississippi *(Baby Doll)*, Arkansas *(A Face in the Crowd)*, Tennessee *(Wild River)*—but also embracing the small towns of Kansas *(Splendor in the Grass)*, and the northern California communities of Salinas and Monterey *(East of Eden)*. These isolated worlds where change is slow in coming and values remain ultimately stable reveal Kazan's attraction to innocence and tradition.

The most stirring voice for his celebration of rural Americana and the primitive pioneer spirit is Ella Garth, the 80-year-old protagonist of *Wild River*. . . .

A moving chronicle of the Depression Thirties, *Wild River* reiterates Kazan's intellectual interest in American social phenomena which altered the face of the nation. By placing its basic conflict—technological progress versus a more traditional ethic—within the intimate, familial canvas of Ella Garth's dynamic history and personal struggle against the cold, passionless edicts of the New Deal, the film achieves a remarkable depth and power. . . .

Wild River caught a basic contradiction in American values which the Depression Thirties seemed to accentuate: an irreconcilability between the nation's belief in rugged individualism and the realities of social progress. . . .

East of Eden, his most beautiful and penetrating film, seemed to mark Kazan's first real attempt to examine his past; and as he has admitted, the film's painfully compelling father-son relationship was deeply personal to him. . . .

Most of Kazan's work up to this time had been firmly rooted in realistic detail and staging. He abandoned this in *East of Eden* for an audacious surrealism, a style whose own extremes appropriately met the demands of the idiosyncratic and reckless protagonist and the psychological depth of the writing. . . . The boy's changing moods are transmitted through sharply contrasting chiaroscuro images. We are immediately struck by the pale, dream-like quality of the film in its opening sequence, where Cal stalks his estranged mother through the town, determined to discover his origins. (p. 11)

Cal's agonized gestures are the visual symbols heightening the fury and anger of all Kazan's central figures—the alienated heroes who stand as the most distinguishing characteristic of his films. No director of recent times has given us such a gallery of magnetic, sexually dynamic men. They are usually characters without much education—outsiders, loners, but people of great energy and drive, great charisma. These heroes are deeply confused, uncertain how to express their longings and frustrations, often struggling to commit themselves, to channel their great passion for life into some socially constructive action. Kazan has captured the inarticulate, defiant protagonist in *A Streetcar Named Desire, Viva Zapata!, On the Waterfront, East of Eden, A Face in the Crowd,* and *America, America.* In their undirected anger, these characters reflect the deepest form of rebellion against society. These intense figures with their semi-articulated sounds and gestures, sometimes even paralyzed by the force of their anger and frustration and their inability to understand their own confusion, are the perfect metaphor for Kazan's concern with the individual's search for his identity. . . . The torment of characters like Terry Malloy *(On the Waterfront)* and Eddie Anderson *(The Arrangement)* results from their recognition that they have compromised and sold out to a corrupt system. On a more personal level, their inarticulateness springs from an inability to adjust the force of their personalities to the conventional strictures of society.

For Cal Trask and Terry Malloy, frustration and the struggle to express themselves in words spring from a bewilderment at the way life has dealt with them. Their sensitivity and vision of truth have immobilized them. By contrast, Stanley Kowalski in *A Streetcar Named Desire*—like Steve Railsback's Sergeant in *The Visitors*—represents the more destructive potentialities of the primitive, inarticulate hero. Stanley's brutal conquest of Blanche, triggered by his suspicion and hatred of her fragile, poetic vision of life, dramatizes a lust for power that will reaffirm his manhood. . . .

Kazan's heroes are not intellectuals. But their directness and immediacy do not make them simple figures by any means. They are complex in motivation, and surprisingly paradoxical—alienated on a personal level but often drawn towards conventional success out of their need to establish their identity. The two young men, Cal and Terry, hate themselves for what they think they are. Terry confesses that he is nothing but a bum; Cal, that he is quite simply "bad." Ironically, they are driven back into the society they have rejected because of their desperate desire to transcend this self-image. . . .

Like Kazan's male protagonists, the leading women characters in his films possess a striking individuality. These unusual and complex portraits are a startling departure from the majority of females depicted in American cinema. Women in American films are usually punished for exercising power, but Kazan applauds the women in his films because of their strength.

Unlike their groping, verbally paralyzed male counterparts, the women are amazingly adept at articulating their conflicts as well as those of the heroes. These women are not always worldly, but they are surprisingly insightful about defining their own desires and they serve a crucial dramatic function in clarifying for the troubled heroes *their* strengths and weaknesses. (p. 12)

Throughout much of his work Kazan has maintained an ultimate faith in the ability of the individual to overcome even the darkest obstacles of his life, and his earlier works were marked by a final patriotic affirmation of American institutions, with the hero triumphing over social evils. In this respect Kazan's work is representative of other major American directors who similarly affirmed their faith in America with their optimistic endings. But even Kazan's later films, which have a sense of bitterness and complexity lacking in his early work, often end with the implication that the most crucial conflicts can be resolved for the good of everyone.

East of Eden, which deals with one of the most disturbing images of adolescence we have seen and presents Cal not merely as a troubled teenager but as a tormented being, finally dispels its sense of doom in a sentimental, albeit moving, reconciliation between father and son. *Splendor in the Grass* presents an essentially tragic vision of youthful destruction only to resolve itself with a spiritually uplifting ending in which the heroine surmounts her tragedy and rises to dignity and maturity. In *On the Waterfront* one individual amazingly has the power to cleanse an entire system; and in *A Face in the Crowd,* Lonesome Rhodes, the symbol of the evil seductive powers of the mass media, is finally overwhelmed by the forces of goodness and reason. . . .

Kazan seems torn by tensions. Many appear to be rather classical Hollywood conflicts that spring from the pressure to survive as a film artist in this country. One is struck, for example, by Kazan's ambivalence towards America which emerges in much of his work. *On the Waterfront* and *A Face in the Crowd* contain an element of contempt for the ignorance and cultural vacuity of the masses of Americans. Yet much of Kazan's work is a celebration of American ideals. Kazan has been attacked by the right as well as the left and these assaults from both directions seem to illuminate the ways in which he is torn. He counters attacks from the right by defending films like *Viva Zapata!* and *Wild River* as pro-American and democratic:

> I've done more films about social issues in America than anybody. I don't see what films they've made that say anything. Look at the films they've done, and what have they done? I've made more films that deal with America by myself than all of them put together. They despise America, or seem to. I think America is in terrible trouble and difficulty now. But I think it's a wonderful country.

These ambivalences—the sentimentality about Americana, yet the strong strain of social criticism of American institutions and myths—really make Kazan's films remarkably revealing of changing social attitudes over the past 25 years, and at their best, give his work a dramatic intensity that has the power to move us. (p. 14)

Estelle Changas, "Elia Kazan's America," in Film Comment *(copyright © 1972 Film Comment Publishing Corporation; all rights reserved), Vol. 8, No. 2, Summer, 1972, pp. 8-14.*

JIM KITSES

Questions of personal conscience, individual freedom and social responsibility have often supplied Kazan with his material; in this sense Kazan can be said to have become the victim of his concerns when McCarthyism arose. Despite this ostensible continuity, however, fewer directors reveal sharper changes of emphasis in their careers than Kazan. . . .

In the films of the forties the treatment of moral and social issues is unexceptional. Kazan here is working within well-established genres and a general ethos of post-war optimism and conventional social awareness: *Boomerang* and *Panic in the Streets* are documentary thrillers after [Louis] de Rochement; *Pinky* and *Gentlemen's Agreement,* part of Hollywood's anti-prejudice cycle. In all of these, the personal sacrifices that idealism demands are only theoretically explored, the costs brought home to neither characters nor viewers. . . . Like many another liberal film of the era, Kazan's movies are morally complacent. Evil exists out there somewhere; principle and personal passion are reconciled easily; characters discover limitations and transcend them. The community, seen conventionally as small-minded or corrupt, is redeemed by the nobility and industry of the individual. In short, the American way wins out.

In the next decade the Cold War invades America and Kazan's very life. The result is that the attitudinizing gives way to propaganda, the didactic air of the earlier films growing into a desperate, often hysterical rhetoric that assaults the viewer. Often enough the meanings that are obscured add up to a denial of idealism. *Viva Zapata!* and *On the Waterfront,* two films that ostensibly reject the rule of force, both resort to the most violent tone and action. "Can a good thing come from a bad act?", asks a character in the earlier film. The credibility and internal logic of these films suffers in the strident way they make their simplistic points: power corrupts, people matter, principles are abstract and ideas of honor and loyalty must be weighed against human experience. What is remarkable is not the point of view but the extent to which the films seem forced into this stance. In general, the fifties films describe a world where older values are crumbling and the individual is forced to act wholly from within himself: passion, rather than morality, is prominent. . . .

Kazan's world is one of conflict and power relationships, a world of oppression, exploitation, manipulation. As with many American directors, Kazan's heroes are typically on the margins of society. However, the drama is not an existentialist one of the 'outsider'; nor is Kazan interested in moral or metaphysical conflicts arising from the traditions of American individualism. Intellectually a child of the thirties, Kazan everywhere reveals the impact of Marx and Freud, his films striving (often with only partial success) to strike a balance between social analysis and psychological exploration. . . .

Kazan is preoccupied with the individual as representative of a group: minority ethnic communities, the poor, the young, the middle class, the worker, the criminal. Kazan is not involved with what sociologists call contracultures: subversive groups whose goals and values are in conflict with the mainstream society, Kazan's characters live in communities whose values are mediated by the macro-culture; consequently, their struggle is for the legitimacy of social recognition, Kazan's movies typically describe a sub-culture in some detail, evoking the rituals, mores and allegiances that give the group, class or locale its distinctive identity. (p. 28)

Existence within the sub-culture is presented ambiguously. The economically depressed are seen to face daunting problems. Life at this level is repressive and violent, reductive of the human personality: the basic metaphor is that of the jungle. Kazan's films often employ animal references to characterize life at this extreme: peasants and workers are treated as sheep, characters function as beasts of burden. (pp. 28, 31)

In recent years Kazan has extended the metaphor to the bourgeoisie, suggesting that here the jungle mentality persists albeit masked by social role: a key sequence in *Splendor in the Grass* is built on this idea, Barbara Loden reduced to an animal to service a gang of tuxedoed rapists. . . .

[Such characters as Johnny Nolan, Dicey, Kowalski, and Lonesome Rhodes] carry a dignity earned in the struggle to retain a sense of roots and passion. They can be said to represent an experiential and psychological ideal for Kazan, that of the whole person living out an integrated emotional and physical existence, often in the face of the most punishing social and economic circumstances. It is towards this ideal that Kazan's characters, especially the young, reach out in their deep yearning for dignity. . . .

At their darkest, Kazan's films, especially in the fifties, seem to endorse the jungle code of survival of the fittest. However, this undercurrent is held in tension with Kazan's involvement with characters pursuing the ideal of full expression of a balanced personality. Kazan's films are strongest when characters affirm that ideal in the face of the complete knowledge that life, both inside the sub-culture and the larger community, is a dog-eat-dog affair.

For Kazan, American history is not so much class struggle as a war of cultures. . . . [The] tensions arising from Europe to America are more properly dialectical: close, often cramping village life as opposed to the privacy and loneliness of the modern city; fixed social roles, oppressive yet rooted in community and nature, versus mobility, change and possibilities of alienation; a moral and physical climate, austere and beautiful, that both breaks the back and inspires a spirit of joy and passion, versus the comforts and costs of technology, institutions and status.

If the turbulence of a conflict of allegiances is most explicit in Kazan's recent films (notably *America, America* and *The Arrangement*), elements of it are central to his whole career. For Kazan, the American dilemma of achieving a sense of individual identity is a well-defined one. Above all, it involves honoring one's roots, finding continuity with the values and feelings of the past, achieving an equilibrium that allows an expression of one's origins and nature. Within the sub-culture, the individual elaborates and lives out an idea of himself from his experience. . . . However, the main point is that the equilibrium a sub-culture can provide is temporary, the precarious balance between sustaining and diminishing, protecting and oppressing, the individual inevitably shifting as he or she grows and develops. At a certain point the individual must re-define himself, move on, change.

And it is the psychological pressures arising from the crossing of cultural boundaries that are often at the heart of Kazan's material. The movement may be away from, or back to, one's roots, an attempt to escape or live out original values. Either way, the adoption of values alien to the culture creates inner turmoil; it is also experienced by the family, the basic social unit, as invasion or betrayal. It is this trauma of cultural change that Kazan's films record—rebellion, rejection, exile—and the dramatic action is characteristically structured around family conflict. (p. 31)

Beyond the sub-culture, mediating and hence in constant tension with it, is the larger society, the institutionalized values and goals that make up a nation's idea of itself. The essence of the individual versus the essence of the civilization: more often than not, it is in this combat that Kazan's movies live and breathe. Increasingly, Kazan has been consistent in seeing ideology, tradition and culture as mechanistic forces that transmit enervating goals and principles; the individual, in short, is at war with the society. In contrast with the precarious experiential equilibrium possible within the sub-culture, the community at large ruthlessly forces the adoption of social roles that are cramping and reductive. Despite a few facile victories in the films of the forties, Kazan's career can be seen as a set of variations on the basic theme of the individual as victim of social pressures that demand a caricature of the self and betrayal of the past. . . .

A key opposition in Kazan is between being "human," usually associated with values arising from a character's roots, and being *processed.* Often, a role within the community is seen as psychic surrender to role playing in the literal sense. The dialectic between being and acting, inner reality and exterior pose, authenticity and role playing, is an old and persistent one in Kazan. Despite the neurotic violence that colors much of his earlier work, it is arguable that a dramatic irony arising from our awareness of a character's performing within the action, is the emotional tone most typical of Kazan. (p. 32)

A distillation of Kazan's extensive stage experience is increasingly the rule in his films, moments where facial expression, body movement, gesture, communicate the psychic interplay of inner reality and a whole culture. *America, America* is rich with this kind of detail: the finger held to the lips (carried over into *The Arrangement*), the Anatolian smile of servility, the wise-guy flip of the coin at the end. Given his temperament and background, such moments of nuance in Kazan are likely always to have a more calculated feel than with the more evocative style of a Ford or Renoir. As often as it discovers detail in the shot, Kazan's camera is likely to elide dramatic action and symbol, as in the cut from the lovers in *Splendor in the Grass* to the waterfall nearby. There is typically little natural depth in Kazan frame, few long takes, little freedom within the staging. Such control is at the heart of the emotional intensity that Kazan often achieves. However, so purposeful a style can mean that meetings become encounters, and characters needs or ideas (alongside of Freud, the influence of Ibsen and social theater traditions is often close to the surface in Kazan). Out to shock an audience he sees as insulated and dulled by the mass media, to plunge them into the midst of meaningful passions, Kazan is always in danger of being reductive, over-explicit, and insensitive to ambiguity. (p. 34)

As Kazan moves into the seventies (and his sixties), his cinema seems less one of effects and more one of personal style, a unified point of view rooted in psychological time. . . . Kazan's work is consequently more 'open' now, the characters more complex and ambiguous, the audience freer in its relationship with them. As Kazan's films have become more personal, they have also become increasingly subjective in style. . . .

Auteur theory, with its special emphasis on the 'small' director who tunnels his way through the industry, has created an unfortunate critical backlash against the filmmaker, like Kazan, who attacks "big themes." However, it is a fallacy to assume (as Claude Chabrol once argued) that a small subject and a large one are of equal importance, that realization is all. Although Kazan has uneven passages even in his most achieved works, the total weight of his achievement is impressive. (p. 36)

Jim Kitses, "Elia Kazan: A Structured Analysis" (©, 1972, by Spectator International, Inc.; copyright reassigned to the Author; ©, 1980, by the Kilimanjaro Corporation), in Cinema, *Vol. 7, No. 3, Winter, 1972-73, pp. 26-36.*

PETER BISKIND

On the Waterfront is one of the earliest and most effective attempts to suppress politics with morality and private values that the fifties produced. It takes an important first step in detaching the self from a larger social context so that the idea of self can be redefined in narrower, safer terms. *Splendor in the Grass, America, America,* and *The Arrangement* merely develop the notion of personality initially presented in *On the Waterfront*. . . .

Films like *Viva Zapata!* and *On the Waterfront* bear the marks, the *inscription,* as the French would say, of their historical context. They cannot be fully understood outside the passionate political controversies of which they were part. (p. 26)

[*On the Waterfront*] is political allegory cast in the form of a morality play. This requires a particularly skillful form of aesthetic footwork, since its success requires that the political allegory be simultaneously admitted and refused. To deny the allegorical level runs the risk that the message of the film will go unrecorded. To acknowledge the allegorical level runs the risk that the ideological project of the film will be unmasked. Films like *On the Waterfront* walk a tightrope between revelation and concealment, between clarity and mystification.

In *Viva Zapata!* (1952) . . . [Kazan] had shown that the exercise of individual power is either perverse or tragic. . . . Although the commonplace that power corrupts is a staple of Hollywood political wisdom, finding classic expression in the comedies of Frank Capra, in the fifties, and especially in the hands of Kazan, it became a weapon in the cold war struggle against the left in general, and Stalinism in particular. . . .

Where *Viva Zapata!* has aged quickly, *On the Waterfront* remains, after two decades, a tremendously powerful film, one of the best films of the fifties. In many ways, it was a child of the [House Un-American Activities Committee] investigations, a blow struck in the ideological and artistic battle between those who talked and those who didn't. . . .

It presents a situation in which informing on criminal associates is the only honorable course of action for a just man. The injunction against informing on friends and colleagues is axiomatic in most societies where the state does not exercise overwhelming moral authority, but the film's dialogue repeatedly defines squealing not as an absolute but a relative matter. It depends on where you stand. (p. 27)

[The opening title says, in part]: "The incidents portrayed in this picture were true of a particular area of the waterfront. They exemplify the way self-appointed tyrants can be fought and defeated by right-thinking men in a vital democracy."

This optimism regarding the democratic process is not so much a betrayal of the thirties, but a fulfillment of certain attitudes towards the state implicit in thirties radicalism. . . .

[The film's portrayal of union corruption is] very convincing. Although it is quite faithful to the texture of east-coast waterfront life, it falsifies the overall picture. Just as Kazan conveniently overlooks the larger social and political implications of the class structure of Mexico in *Viva Zapata!,* attributing the dependent position of the dispossessed peasants solely to the venal generals and politicians, so here he is careful to circumscribe the tumor of corruption so that it may be neatly excised without undue injury or embarrassment to the body politic. Despite one rhetorical gesture towards generality (a single shot shows "Mr. Upstairs" watching the Crime Commission hearings on television), Kazan emphasizes the limited and exceptional nature of his subject. He even goes so far as to have one of his dockers exclaim: "The waterfront . . . ain't part of America." (p. 28)

We can now turn to the critical question of the film's conception of power. What immediately becomes clear is that the film doesn't seem to deal with power at all. The arena of conflict in *On the Waterfront* which is, after all, a film about labor and unions, is not class but self. It is not without but within. It is Terry Malloy's interior struggle, his struggle to come to moral awareness and to act on his new perception of right and wrong.

The agent of Terry's awakening is the waterfront priest, Father Barry. . . .

Kazan apparently approves of this kind of moral agency, since all [the priest's] interventions turn out for the best, but they could have easily been catastrophic. What emerges is an alarming picture of a ruthless crusader who manipulates others like chess pieces in the name of a higher good for which no price is too high, no sacrifice too great.

That manipulation is not too strong a word for Father Barry's behavior is clear from the authority with which he employs his carrot-and-stick strategy to guide Terry through the intricate moral maze that Kazan has constructed for him. Although his interventions in the course of the action are frequently direct and forceful (at one point he knocks Terry down in order to prevent him from going gunning for Friendly), just as frequently this coercion is coyly denied or disguised. . . .

Father Barry is doing no more than applying manipulative methods of social control which have deep roots in the American past, in the Progressive movement in general and in the philosophy of John Dewey in particular. (p. 29)

In choosing to use persuasion rather than coercion, Barry is doing no more than acting in accord with the democratic ethos. . . .

What is the significance of a ruthless and powerful but apparently moral figure like Father Barry when Kazan had shown us in *Viva Zapata!* that power corrupts? Although the power-to-the-people moral of *Viva Zapata!* would lead us to expect that in a democracy, where power is shared among the demos (In America, "the people have a voice"), such a figure should be either evil or unnecessary. But in *On the Waterfront* the people are incapable of exercising power. They are a passive herd who invariably fail to act when put to the test. At best, they can follow the leader, or exercise their power in a negative refusal to act: "How 'bout Terry? He don't work, we don't work." The conclusion which inescapably emerges from the contradiction between the two films, is that when Kazan wishes to show the self-regenerative capacities of liberal capitalist society, through mass political action, effective yet circumscribed, leaders are *OK*. But when he is faced with a real social upheaval, as he is in *Viva Zapata!,* which threatens to exceed the bounds of decorous reform, he enforces a self-serving moral that leadership will always become corrupt.

Rather than the egalitarian society we might have expected after *Viva Zapata!, On the Waterfront,* like many other films of the fifties, offers an elitist model of society in which power is the prerogative of experts in the law and its enforcement. . . . Acting in concert, the official and unofficial agents of society curb the hero's cynical, self-interested asocial behavior by awakening in him, at the very most, a higher moral awareness (as in *On the Waterfront*) or, at the very least, a recognition that his own self-interest coincides with the larger purposes of the state. . . . The control exercised by these figures is indirect rather than direct, manipulative rather than coercive. . . . But Terry is in no sense free; he has merely exchanged one type of bondage for another. Authoritarian coercion exercised by the mob (he had to take a fall in a fixed fight) gives way to authoritarian manipulation exercised by the society.

Even though Terry rises bravely on his own two feet at the end, having successfully beaten Friendly in hand-to-hand combat, inspiring the men to defy the mob, his stance is an uncertain one; we have the feeling that Terry is still at the mercy of forces he cannot understand, forces much more subtle and dangerous than the ones he has overcome. . . . (p. 30)

Kazan's view of reform is as elitist as his conception of democracy. Both social reform and individual salvation are top-down affairs, conducted by experts, the Crime Commission in the one case, and the priest in the other. The initiative in both instances comes from the experts, from above. (p. 31)

Even though the main thrust of *On the Waterfront* is towards the socialization of Terry, it is necessary to pay close attention to the way this operation is carried out. It occurs through an apparently contradictory process of individuation. Terry is divested of old-world ethnic ties to immediate family ("they're asking me to put the finger on my own brother"), to the extended family of the union local ("Uncle" Johnny Friendly "used to take me to the ball games when I was a kid"), and to neighborhood. . . . He is systematically detached from the social tissue that forms his natural habitat, and gathered into a larger notion of community-as-nation. . . .

This transition is facilitated in several ways. First, it is rendered as a process of growth. Terry's testimony before the Crime Commission is an indication of self-knowledge ("I was ratting on myself all them years, and I didn't even know it") and the assumption of adulthood. The measure of his maturity is his decision to inform, to transcend local loyalties for larger and presumably higher ones. . . . Second, the mob, although in one sense Terry's family, is in another sense a false family. After all, it is an all-male group like the Golden Warriors, and it frequently acts to destroy family ties. . . . Third, Terry's private goals, like his boxing career that the mob had frustrated, are legitimized. And, finally, all these strands are gathered up in the nuclear family represented by Edie. It offers maturity and responsibility, adult sexuality, upward mobility (Edie has been educated in a suburb, Tarrytown, and her father has labored so that she will enjoy the advantages of which he was deprived), and satisfaction of "private" goals. . . .

Submerged in the valorization of romantic love, family, and "feminine" virtues is a new definition of what it meant to be a man in fifties America. The old-style immigrant morality of John Friendly, and the character structure that accompanied it, were obsolete. . . . Changed social circumstances required a new, softer, more pliable and trusting version of the male role. (p. 32)

Although, as we have seen, Kazan falsifies the larger picture in the interests of his own political position, it is important to come to terms with the reasons the film works as well as it does. Part of the answer to this question lies in the kind of world Kazan presents. . . . [In Kazan's world the] state of nature is not innocent, but a Hobbesian jungle. As Terry tells Edie: "You know this city's full of hawks . . . they hang around on top of the big hotels and they spot a pigeon in the park—right down on them." This predatory morality informs the ethics of the mob, and makes strong claims on Terry as well. . . . Opposed to this philosophy in which the strong (hawks) consume the weak (the pigeons) is Edie's morality ("Isn't everyone part of everybody else?") and Father Barry's Christianity which promises that the meek shall inherit the earth. The battleground on which these two conceptions of man's fate contend is American democracy, and when Terry decides to become a stool pigeon, he fuses the spiritual and secular realms. . . . In Christian terms, Terry voluntarily assumes the role of the meek (the dove); in secular terms, he assumes the role of the stool pigeon (the informer), and the one transfigures the other. . . .

If power in the hands of one man is always abused, as Kazan emphasized in *Viva Zapata!* and reminded us again in *On the Waterfront* (Friendly), it has to be disguised (Father Barry) or, as manifest in a character like Terry Malloy, a potentially more explosive figure than Barry, must be domesticated. . . . The significance of Terry's final walk down the pier to the shed is that his power has been chastened, transfigured and spiritualized into the endurance of the martyr. . . .

Like Leo McCarey and other anti-Communist directors of the period, Kazan not only made the implicit claim that those who named names before *HUAC* were Christian saints, but that fifties America was the secular City of God on earth. . . . *On the Waterfront* suggests that he shared with most Americans a belief in a providence that had saved America from the ravages of war, had given her the atomic bomb, and had delivered into her reluctant hands the responsibility for world leadership. (p. 33)

Kazan twists and turns to avoid confronting the implications of American power and power in America. He presents a picture of an ideal democratic society in which power, as such, does not exist. It is only the enemy which exercises (and abuses) power, the John Friendlies of the world. Nevertheless, since power is in fact exercised by agents with whom Kazan is sympathetic, it must be disguised in order to maintain the fiction of its absence. Power struggles in the public sphere are displaced into moral struggles in the private sphere. Manipulation replaces coercion, and power, to the extent that it cannot be denied, is transformed into the negative power of the martyr.

This is the portrait of America that the film intends to present. But the picture of America that actually emerges from the film is quite different. Power, rather than being dispersed throughout the whole society, is concentrated in the hands of an elite of experts, both official and unofficial, who wield it with a ruthless singleness of purpose for their own ends. These ends include the socialization, if possible, of dissident individuals and groups or, if necessary, their destruction. Socialization is achieved by redefining individual allegiances and goals so that they conform to those sanctioned by society.

The two antagonistic portraits of America (egalitarian and elitist) offered by *On the Waterfront* are not entirely contradictory. A view of society as run by technical elites is one way of achieving the masking of power required by the egalitarian fiction. The state is viewed as a politically neutral organization of administrators standing above the petty quarrels of competing interest groups, a servant of the people. (pp. 35-6)

Peter Biskind, "The Politics of Power in 'On the Waterfront'," in Film Quarterly *(copyright 1975 by The Regents of the University of California; reprinted by permission of the University of California Press), Vol. XXIX, No. 1, Fall, 1975, pp. 25-38.*

PAULINE KAEL

Monroe Stahr, the young hero of Scott Fitzgerald's *The Last Tycoon,* is meant to represent the last of a breed; he's an individualistic artist-businessman who runs his movie studio like a small grocery store. . . . [As] Fitzgerald sees him, Stahr has the heart and soul of an artist without the crazy weaknesses of artists. (p. 216)

Harold Pinter is said to have spent a year and a half working on the script [for "The Last Tycoon"]—presumably in reverent noodling, since he has rearranged the book's dialogue and hasn't added much. Kazan has been quoted as saying, "I didn't change any of Pinter's words." This is reverence piled upon reverence. If the movie is, as I think, a tragedy—a series of disastrous mistakes by intelligent, gifted, well-meaning people—probably the first mistake was to approach the book cap in hand, and the next was to hire Pinter. (pp. 217-18)

The film is bewilderingly mute and inexpressive. Kazan's work seems to be a reaction against the shrill energy he has sometimes used to keep a picture going. He's trying for something quiet and revelatory, but he seems to have disowned too much of his temperament. Though the picture certainly has promising characters, they remain potential, tentative. There's no impetus, so you question everything you see; you're aware of the lame discomfort of the performers. . . . (p. 218)

You can't really believe that Stahr is running a factory that's churning out pictures. The movie world that Kazan shows us has no hustle. The characters are so enervated that *The Last Tycoon* is a vampire movie after the vampires have left. . . . Kazan let Pinter get away with a Pinteresque dribbling-away finish: we don't learn what happens to Monroe Stahr—instead, we see him demonstrating once *again* how to tell a story in the movies. They must not have respected Stahr's crude, honest point: he was explaining how you hook an audience, not what you send it home with. The film's ending is the real confession of impotence. (pp. 218-19)

Pauline Kael, "Stallone and Stahr" (originally published in The New Yorker, *Vol. LII, No. 41, November 29, 1976), in her* When the Lights Go Down *(copyright © 1975, 1976, 1977, 1978, 1979, 1980 by Pauline Kael; reprinted by permission of Holt, Rinehart and Winston, Publishers), Holt, 1980, pp. 213-219.**

LOUIS MARCORELLES

As Elia Kazan acquires a measure of financial as well as artistic independence, the importance of the place he holds in the American cinema increases. Intentionally or not, he has become the spokesman of certain contemporary attitudes; and from *On the Waterfront* to *Baby Doll* we have the complete circle, the picture of *homo Americanus* as a victim of blindly destructive forces, painfully engaged in waging his battle of conscience.

Baby Doll is only indirectly and by implication a social drama: its real subject is the sexual awakening of a young girl married to a man twenty years older than herself. . . .

Like Blanche Dubois, like the paralysed heroine of *The Glass Menagerie,* Baby Doll lives on the edge of the real world, creating for herself an illusory world compounded of childhood memories, but also heavily charged with sensuality. She is not just a simple, romantic teenager: like any good Tennessee Williams heroine, she has already been marked by the stupidity and brutality of her surroundings. Sharing in the corruption of this world, she will finally succeed in adjusting herself to it—though without, in the process, questioning the social and moral assumptions which have almost brought her to disaster. Kazan consciously exploits the whole atmosphere of refined decadence characteristic of his writer. He uses all his technical skill to involve us in the film's dubious setting, to undermine the spectator's critical sense and to make him share, willingly or unwillingly, in its atmosphere of collective hysteria. It is not, I think, an exaggeration to say that the films and plays on which Kazan and Williams have collaborated depend to a great extent on this kind of sleight-of-hand, on trickery considered as a fine art.

The end determines the means, and Kazan ensures that the tone of his film stays wholly in line with its basic assumptions. . . . Baby Doll is tricked out with all the showy apparatus of sex: peroxided hair, sluttish clothes, a calculated laziness in gesture and attitude. . . . Baby Doll is really nothing more than another decorative element in the film, almost on a level with the crumbling old house where the action takes place, or the metal cot where she retreats into her erotic-infantile dreams. The player becomes in effect part of the symbolism of the film, and there is no better example of this than in the first shots of Baby Doll, lying back in her cot sucking her thumb, with one bare leg trailing, and with film magazines spread around her on the floor in an atmosphere of carefully calculated disorder. Even the actress's appearance helps to round off this characterisation heavy in Freudian over-tones: her rather square and childish face, her awkward movements, brilliantly convey the impression of a little girl who would steal her grandmother's sweets or pull her neighbour's hair in class. As created by Kazan, Baby Doll becomes the symbol of a sort of vicious innocence. (p. 150)

Kazan has endeavoured in his stage productions to break down the theatre's restrictions in space and time, to give the stage something of the cinema's greater freedom. His object has been the same as that of Bert Brecht—to attain a greater sense of reality—but his achievement has in fact been almost the reverse of Brecht's. Kazan's art is above all that of visual effect, style developed to the point of affectation. He heightens the spectator's sense of illusion, plunges him into a sort of no-man's land of art for art's sake where moral considerations no longer have any real meaning. It is worth making the comparison with Brecht, not for reasons of political opportunism, but to underline and clarify the present necessity for the Western artist to express himself in terms of conscience. The true artist cannot afford to add through his work to the general confusions and ambiguities of our time: rather, his job should be to question and consider the accepted standards. Brecht in the theatre, like Bresson in the cinema, affirms the pre-eminent importance of the artist's critical conscience, his questioning individualism.

Whatever revulsion one may feel from the decaying social climates of *On the Waterfront* and *Baby Doll,* one can deny neither Kazan's significance as an artist nor the extent to which his work expresses a characteristically American view of our time. One or two passages in *Baby Doll,* moreover, show a skill in the direction of actors that borders on genius. Kazan here relies less than previously on the kind of atmospheric tricks that jarred in *A Streetcar Named Desire*. In one astonishing scene (the explanation at the door of the house) he holds his two leading players for several minutes in a single close shot, achieving an intensity of dramatic expression that entirely justifies his own comment of a few years ago—"Acting in pictures is much more demanding than on the stage. The camera penetrates like a microscope". Finally, Kazan's work has the merit, even though it may seem a somewhat negative one, of holding up to us certain aspects of our civilisation, typifying its particular corruptions: of this gift, *Baby Doll* is a particularly striking example. (pp. 150-51)

Louis Marcorelles, "Film Reviews: 'Baby Doll'," in Sight and Sound *(copyright © 1976 by The British Film Institute), Vol. 26, No. 3, Winter, 1976-77, pp. 150-51.*

GORDON GOW

Gentle by comparison with the thrusting mainstream of current cinema, Elia Kazan's film of *The Last Tycoon* evokes a romanticism which persists and glows against the commercially orientated ethos of Hollywood in the 1930s. The spare and sensitive adaptation by Harold Pinter is respectful to the source material, the final and unfinished novel of Scott Fitzgerald—so respectful, indeed, as to eschew the profusion of indications left in the author's notes about the resolution of the story: the film is curtailed, only slightly rounded off, and therefore like what exists of the novel it places its main emphasis upon Monroe Stahr's vain efforts to recreate his former love life, while the fascinating social background and its relevance to Stahr can be savoured only as a kind of incidental factor instead of the more consequential element that Fitzgerald would presumably have developed had he lived to finish the work. . . .

[A] surprising amount of historical feeling seeps through, suggesting in the main the earlier half of the decade, and colouring the work very delicately and rather movingly.

If Fitzgerald had been able to do his customary polishing, the chances are that his emphasis in the structure would have been different, but I doubt whether the most fastidious of his admirers could wish for many amendments to the actual prose, nor to the talent for viable dialogue, so uncommonly speakable for a novel that Pinter understandably retains a deal of it exactly as Fitzgerald set it down. And just as the unfinished novel remains compelling to read, the film is constantly absorbing, although perhaps its intriguing apartness from today's norm strikes a bit oddly for a time until one adjusts to it. Kazan, of course, is a director incapable of doing much wrong, and here his control and balance are marvellously light, whether touching in details of the studio milieu—the back lot from waterfront to Western street, the passing trolley of bespangled chorus girls; the unpalatable executive lunch with shop talk, the elder at the feast being carried away from table like a babe in arms while still mouthing his sage opinion upon the latest project —or catching the ephemeral nature of the relationship between Stahr and Kathleen. (p. 41)

Gordon Gow, "Reviews: 'The Last Tycoon'" (© copyright Gordon Gow 1977; reprinted with permission), in Films and Filming, *Vol. 23, No. 6, March, 1977, pp. 41-2.*

Stanley Kubrick

1928-

American director and screenwriter.

Kubrick's are among the most ambitious and original films of the past three decades. A controversial director of outlandish subjects and eccentric cinematic styles, Kubrick derives an artistic identity from his natural bent for novelty and inventiveness. As a youth he took a keen interest in photography. While in high school he sold some of his photographs to *Look;* and after graduation became a staff photographer for that magazine. His first film short, *Day of the Fight,* was originally a picture story in *Look,* and his increasing preoccupation with cinema led to a second short documentary entitled *Flying Padre.* Kubrick sold these films to RKO at a slight profit and, after borrowing additional funds, made his first feature, *Fear and Desire.*

Stylishly imaginative camerawork and a somewhat erratic structure are the identifying traits of *Fear and Desire.* It received critical approval but not commercial success. *Killer's Kiss* is also characterized by an interesting visual style and structure supporting a conventional storyline. Less conventional is *The Killing,* a crime caper distinctive for relating its story with impersonal and efficient objectivity. Of the early films the most highly regarded is *Paths of Glory,* its favorable critical reception promoting Kubrick to the stature of an important American director. After directing *Spartacus,* a project on which he considered himself only hired talent, Kubrick chose to make a film from Vladimir Nabokov's controversial novel *Lolita.* Though criticized for its various divergences from the novel, Kubrick's film nonetheless proves artistically adventuresome in its own right, containing at times a surreal quality foretold by certain scenes in his early films and pursued further in his later ones.

The sometimes grotesque farce in *Lolita* is amplified in Kubrick's next film, *Dr. Strangelove; or, How I Learned to Stop Worrying and Love the Bomb.* This work, like all its successors in the Kubrick filmography, received dramatically varied critical estimates and interpretations. *2001: A Space Odyssey* is probably the most outstanding example of this mixed reception, being alternately viewed as a work of cosmic prophecy and an attempt at gratuitous mystification.

***A Clockwork Orange,* based on the novel by Anthony Burgess, is the third Kubrick film concerned with a hypothetical reality. Some critics see this story of ultra-violence in a decaying society as further evidence of the pessimistic undercurrents present in all of this director's films. After his three scenarios of the future, Kubrick recreated William Thackeray's novel of romance and adventure in the eighteenth century, *Barry Lyndon.* Despite the apparent departure from the previous themes and subjects of Kubrick's work, critics have observed in this film the same emphasis on stylization and strictly formal elements, along with a skeptical perspective on societal pretenses.**

Kubrick is an idiosyncratic artist whose work nevertheless has wide appeal. Perhaps his greatest strength as a filmmaker lies in his ability to make films that are readily accessible to the viewer while providing abundant matter for critical speculation. (See also *Contemporary Authors,* Vols. 81-84.)

GAVIN LAMBERT

The difference between [*Fear and Desire*] and [*Killer's Kiss*] is striking; although *Killer's Kiss* is a melodrama too full of familiar and not always skilful contrivances, it has a simplicity of outline, an atmospheric power, a directness in its characterisation, that suggests a maturing and distinctive personality. . . . [The] melodrama is the least successful, most derivative aspect of the film; its real originality lies in its approach to characterisation and atmosphere. . . .

By contrast the action sequences seem not only derivative but dramatically less strong. The attack on Davy's manager in the deserted yard at night reminds one too directly of *The Set-Up,* and the rooftop chase, apart from recalling *The Naked City,* fails to excite. One would be tempted to say that all this represents something more theoretical, obligatory, for the director, were there not some explosions of physical violence that seem personally characteristic, and also a restlessness, an occasional jaggedness, that contribute to the film's inner tension. At its most obvious and questionable this results in female models being weirdly truncated during the fight in the warehouse; the diversion with the two drunken conventioneers in the street, though, is a curious and effective touch. But when Gloria relates the story of her early life (which includes a starkly Freudian relationship with her father), and of her sister who became a dancer, Kubrick illustrates this simply by a series of shots of the dancer . . . performing on an empty stage, and the evocative lighting, the dancing and the choreography . . . are in themselves too interesting for one to be able to absorb what is being narrated on the soundtrack—apart from the irrelevance of the images for most of the time. All the same, this is the reverse side of the freedom, the experimentation, that runs through much of the film and affirms that its maker has a talent to watch.

Gavin Lambert, "In Brief: 'Killer's Kiss'," in Sight and Sound *(copyright © 1956 by The British Film Institute), Vol. 25, No. 4, Spring, 1956, p. 198.*

ARLENE CROCE

Stanley Kubrick's [*The Killing*] is an estimable entry into that small field of well-made crime films that expose the *modus operandi* of the colossal caper. Like *Rififi* and *The Asphalt Jungle* (after which it is principally patterned) its action is thickly and informatively plotted, possessed of that classic fatality that insures retribution, and dependent for its thrills upon a network of smooth calculation severed by fey circumstance and mislaid trusts. . . .

His film lacks the pervasive knowledge and control of John Huston's masterwork, and although his material has absorbed him utterly, he has been wise to remain detached from it. His camera is relentlessly objective, cool, economically observant, and capable of an unusual rhetoric, as when, at the film's end, the hero's captors advance upon him and are framed to remind us of the menacing gunman targets that had filled the screen a few reels before. . . . [The] visual authority of *The Killing* consistently dominates a flawed script. In a film that is largely a crescendo of detail and preparation, Kubrick has found it necessary at the peak of tension, to resort to cutbacks in order to fill in information and set his sprawling scene. Thus the action at its climax knots and unravels, knots and unravels. This is done in the name of clarity, but a certain cumulative suspense is thereby sacrificed. Kubrick has also used an off-screen narrator where one would have preferred an absolutely cinematic exposition. The documented effect that is obtained invades the unique privacy of events and becomes negligible when we are told what we do not really need to know. . . . (p. 30)

Professionally speaking, Stanley Kubrick has grown older. . . . [*The Killing*] bears evidence of a fresh and maturing talent and completely belies the impression given by his earlier efforts—that of a college boy who, in a semester's turning, had gone from comic books to *Oedipus Rex*. (p. 31)

Arlene Croce, "'The Killing'," in Film Culture *(copyright 1956 by* Film Culture*), Vol. 2, No. 3, 1956, pp. 30-1.*

GAVIN LAMBERT

There is much in [*Paths of Glory*] that powerfully illustrates the physical horrors of war, but even more impressive and frightening is the study of its social structure. The world seems cruelly divided into the leaders and the led. The officers conduct their foxy intrigues in the elegant rooms of a great chateau, and the setting somehow emphasizes their indifference to human life. The men go to the trenches and into battle as in peace-time they went to offices or factories. The sequence of the attack itself, done mainly in a series of vivid, inexorable, lateral tracking shots, is a fearful reminder that war, simply, kills a lot of people; and the film finds an eloquent visual contrast between the grim carnage of the battlefield and the spacious luxury of headquarters.

We are in fact a long way from the emotional pacificism of *All Quiet on the Western Front*, which was made twelve years after World War One. *Paths of Glory*, made twelve years after World War Two, never openly attacks war as an abstraction, neither does it examine causes. I suspect it will be the more lasting film, certainly it is difficult to imagine a film about war that could have a more stunning impact today. . . .

This is not only a film of unusual substance but a powerfully realised and gripping work of art. In *The Killing* Stanley Kubrick's talent was operating within the limits of familiar melodrama; *Paths of Glory* is meaningful as well as brilliant. (p. 144)

Gavin Lambert, "Film Reviews: 'Paths of Glory'," in Sight and Sound *(copyright © 1957 by The British Film Institute), Vol. 27, No. 3, Winter, 1957-58, pp. 144-45.*

JONATHAN BAUMBACH

In an age characterized on the one hand by a cult of happy mediocrity and on the other by the growing power, prestige, and necessity of the military, *Paths of Glory* is a specter from our unsophisticated past. . . .

Directed with obvious sincerity and restraint, *Paths of Glory* is an explosion upon our consciousness. The locale is France and the time is 1916 but the film has an insistent immediacy that is at once stunning and upsetting. Though unfashionable it is timely and also timeless, the especial qualities of art. The military, committed to the game of wholesale destruction for personal glory, is, by definition, petty and corrupt. But that is an irreverent thing to say about our fatted protector. *Paths of Glory* is only permissible, though deemed unfashionable, because it deals with the French army. . . . The American myth of military purity remains inviolate. . . .

Paths of Glory like no other film save *All Quiet on the Western Front* shows war in its naked ugliness, stripped of glory, heroics, and high-sounding causes. . . .

Stanley Kubrick seemed, on the basis of his three previous films, a young director of extraordinary facility and promise. But *Paths of Glory* is a notable advance, a fulfillment of earlier promise. The gratuitous virtuosity of his technique is less in evidence than before. He no longer demonstrates pyrotechnical brilliance for its own sake, and the emphasis is now on the whole rather than isolated parts. *Paths of Glory* is a dedicated, passionately honest, angry film told with great visual eloquence.

Jonathan Baumbach, "'Paths of Glory'," in Film Culture *(copyright 1958 by* Film Culture*), Vol. IV, No. 2, February, 1958, p. 15.*

NORMAN N. HOLLAND

It used to be idle—or scholarly—to compare films to the novels from which they were taken; now, one can scarcely avoid it. The index to the change is the difference between Stanley Kubrick's *The Killing* (1956) or *Paths of Glory* (1957) and his *Lolita* (1962). The earlier films were real films; *Lolita* is in the current style of the un-film.

The only truly cinematic effect I noticed was a cut from somebody's face to a face in a horror movie at a drive-in, a cut so drastic I cannot even remember what face Kubrick cut from. In the absence of cinema, such details as Charlie at the girls' camp or Dolly's husband's hearing-aid are dutifully lugged over from the novel; they make a *film à clef* for those who are "in" on the novel, but never become part of the film as such, and this, despite the fact that Nabokov himself did the script.

My respect for Nabokov makes me doubt my own judgement, but even so, it seems to me he tore down a richly redolent roadside diner to put up a Howard Johnson's. Lolita herself is putsched rather farther along the straits of puberty than her fictional counterpart. James Mason finely conveys the shyness and reticence of a cultured European (he reads "Ulalume") confronted with the barbaric yawp of American motel culture; but he projects no more passion for his erstwhile nymphet than a ping-pong paddle.

The novel seemed to me somewhat blurred in conception; the film has done nothing to clarify matters. As before, I got the feeling of some kind of dualism (Lo-Lo, Humbert Humbert, Humbert-Quilty, Europe-America) and there are double-entendres aplenty: Camp Climax for Girls, the lecherous town of Ramsdale, Charlotte's promise to Humbert (as he looks at Lolita) to make him "cherry pies"; her attempt to seduce him with "a magnificent spread." All that the film adds is the notion (new, I think) that Quilty has a sort of Oriental intelligence, so that maybe now it is not just Europe-confronts-America, but a Kiplingesque East-meets-West. Or is the film dealing with a sort of *Through the Looking-Glass* learning of the local folkways, the curious captivities in American freedom? I don't know, and probably I shouldn't ask.

The strength of the novel was its deft, swift satire of Americana, and this Nabokov and Kubrick do translate—no mean trick in film, where the slight exaggeration into satirical absurdity, when rendered forty feet across, can easily become too broad. . . . There are a few delightful bits, Lolita eating potato chips no-hands; a grandmotherly type in a plastic raincoat flitting over a fatal accident with a candid camera. But alas! in the nature of the case, most of what made the novel fun cannot be translated into film: Nabokov's sleight-of-pen and his lovingly physiological descriptions of Humbert's little ecstasies. Those made the novel a best-seller and therefore a movie—but, of course, they cannot be put in a movie. And this is the sorry and inevitable outcome in the game of the un-film. (pp. 411-12)

Norman N. Holland, "Film, Metafilm, and Un-Film" (copyright © 1962 by Norman N. Holland; reprinted by permission), in The Hudson Review, *Vol. XV, No. 3, Autumn, 1962, pp. 406-12.**

PAULINE KAEL

The surprise of *Lolita* is how enjoyable it is: it's the first *new* American comedy since those great days in the forties when Preston Sturges recreated comedy with verbal slapstick. *Lolita* is black slapstick and at times it's so far out that you gasp as you laugh. (p. 205)

Perhaps the reviewers have been finding so many faults with *Lolita* because this is such an easy way to show off some fake kind of erudition: even newspaper reviewers can demonstrate that they're read a book by complaining about how different the movie is from the novel. The movie *is* different but not *that* different, and if you can get over the reviewers' preoccupation with the sacredness of the novel . . . you'll probably find that even the characters that *are* different (Charlotte Haze, especially, who has become the culture-vulture rampant) are successful in terms of the film. (p. 208)

Lolita isn't a consistently good movie but that's almost beside the point: excitement is sustained by a brilliant idea, a new variant on the classic chase theme—Quilty as Humbert's walking paranoia, the madness that chases Humbert and is chased by him, over what should be the delusionary landscape of the actual United States. This panoramic confusion of normal and mad that can be experienced traveling around the country is, unfortunately, lost: the film badly needs the towns and motels and highways of the U.S. (pp. 208-09)

There *is* a paradox involved in the film *Lolita*. Stanley Kubrick shows talents in new areas (theme and dialogue and comedy), and is at his worst at what he's famous for. *The Killing* was a simple-minded suspense film about a race-track robbery, but he structured it brilliantly with each facet shining in place; *Paths of Glory* was a simple-minded pacifist film, but he gave it nervous rhythm and a sense of urgency. *Lolita* is so clumsily structured that you begin to wonder what was shot and then cut out, why other pieces were left in, and whether the beginning was intended to be the end; and it is edited in so dilatory a fashion that after the first hour, almost every scene seems to go on too long. It's as if Kubrick lost his nerve. If he did, it's no wonder; the wonder is, that with all the pressures on American moviemakers—the pressures to evade, to conceal, to compromise, and to explain everything for the literal-minded—he had the nerve to transform this satire on the myths of love into the medium that has become consecrated to the myths. *Lolita* is a wilder comedy for being, now, family entertainment. (p. 209)

Pauline Kael, "Broadcasts and Reviews, 1961-1963: 'Lolita'" (originally published in Partisan Review, *Vol. XXIX, No. 4, Fall, 1962), in her* I Lost It at the Movies *(copyright © 1955, 1962, 1963 by Pauline Kael; reprinted by permission of Little, Brown and Company in association with the Atlantic Monthly Press), Atlantic-Little, Brown, 1965, pp. 203-09.*

ROBERT BRUSTEIN

Dr. Strangelove possesses a great many distinctions as a work of the imagination, but I should like to cite it, first and foremost, for valor: I think it may well be the most courageous movie ever made. It is certainly one of the funniest. . . . [There] is something extraordinarily liberating in the nature of the movie itself. It is the kind of total theater that Antonin Artaud would have admired, with its dark humor, its physical and anarchic dissociation. Dr. Strangelove is a plague experienced in the nerves and the funny bone—a delirium, a conflagration, a social disaster.

What Stanley Kubrick has done is to break completely with all existing traditions of moviemaking, both foreign and domestic. While the European art film seems to be inexorably closing in on the spiritual lassitude of certain melancholy French or Italian aristocrats, *Dr. Strangelove* invests the film medium with a new exuberance, expansiveness, and broadness of vision; compared with the sweep of this masterpiece, the weary meanderings of Resnais, Fellini, and Antonioni seem solipsistic and self-indulgent. Moreover, Kubrick's film is fun—this is its one debt to Hollywood. It is enjoyable for the way it exploits the exciting narrative conventions of the Hollywood war movie—say, *Air Force* or *Thirty Seconds Over Tokyo*—and even more, for the way it turns these conventions upside down, and cruelly scourges them. This is what is arrestingly new about the film: its wry, mordant, destructive, and, at the same time, cheerful, unmoralistic tone. (pp. 3-4)

Dr. Strangelove is a work of comic anarchy, fashioned by a totally disaffected and disaffiliated imagination: it is thus the first American movie to speak truly for our generation. Kubrick has managed to explode the right-wing position without making a single left-wing affirmation: the odor of the Thirties, which clung even to the best work of Chaplin, Welles, and Huston, has finally been disinfected here. Disinfected, in fact, is the stink of all ideological thinking. For although *Dr. Strangelove* is about a political subject, its only politics is outrage against the malevolence of officialdom. . . . [It] releases, through comic poetry, those feelings of impotence and frustration that are consuming us all; and I can't think of anything more important for an imaginative work to do. (p. 4)

Robert Brustein, "Out of This World" (reprinted by permission of the author), in The New York Review of Books, *Vol. 1, No. 12, February 6, 1964, pp. 3-4.*

TOM MILNE

Some directors possess an instantly recognisable signature; others, merely a consistency of style and treatment; but the worrying thing about Stanley Kubrick was the way he once made excellent films which seemed to reveal so little of their director's personality that they might almost have come out of a vacuum. While admiring *The Killing* and, even more, *Paths of Glory,* one couldn't help wondering whether Kubrick might not turn out after all as simply a brilliant packager of artistically viable merchandise, giving the turn of the screw of his clever talent to the production of something several shades more incisive, but no more personal, than the gangster films or anti-war films which were in the commercial air. . . .

Looking back after *Lolita,* however (the film which, capped by *Dr. Strangelove,* finally removed any reservations about Kubrick as a director), the pattern of Kubrick's personality and its development emerged quite clearly. . . .

[Kubrick's] films tend, like Bergman's, to follow a characteristic pattern.

Most reviewers complained of *Lolita,* for instance, that it was too cold and calculating, that it completely missed the eroticism of Nabokov's novel. While true enough, this is irrelevant as criticism, because what Kubrick was after was not an evocation of Humbert's sensuous joy in his nymphet, but of his obsessive fear of what his tabooed love will bring. Nabokov's *Lolita* begins with Humbert's bitter-sweet recollection, his story already over, of his past joy and pain. . . . Kubrick's *Lolita* begins with the end itself, the brutal act of murder which is the inevitable outcome of Humbert's sense of guilt. And whereas the novel is in effect an epic poem on the love of Humbert and Lolita in which the ambiguous Quilty, who swells into an avenging Fury in Humbert's mind, appears only halfway through, in the film Quilty is an immediate, tangible presence throughout, teasing and terrifying Humbert into destroying him.

It is thus the nature of the obsession and its consequences which interest Kubrick; and each of his films charts an obsession—or, more precisely, charts an action in which a fatal flaw in human nature or in society brings disaster. In *Killer's Kiss* (1955), a young boxer falls in love, and because his girl is involved with a lecherous crook, becomes enmeshed in a round of violence and murder. In *The Killing* (1956), five men in desperate need of money plan a perfect robbery, and end in a maze of betrayals and killings. In *Paths of Glory* (1957), three soldiers involved in an impossible attack, initiated because a general's reputation is at stake, find themselves arbitrarily selected as scapegoats and shot for cowardice. In *Spartacus* (1959-60), the hero instigates a slave rebellion against Rome, the ranks close against him and he ends up crucified, his revolt a total failure. In *Lolita* (1961), Humbert Humbert indulges his forbidden love for his twelve-year-old stepdaughter, is caught up in a fantasy of retribution, and brings about his own doom by shooting his ambiguous pursuer. And in *Dr. Strangelove* (1963), of course, "a single slip-up" brings the end of the world.

If each of the films ends in defeat, it is not so much because Kubrick is cynical or pessimistic, as because the mechanism of human nature, operating within the structure of society, creates a vicious circle which can permit no other solution. If Spartacus, or Colonel Dax (in *Paths of Glory*), tries to right an injustice from the noblest of motives, then society in the shape of Roman senators and slave merchants, or the military hierarchy, will have to stifle the impulse in order to preserve its *status quo;* if Humbert Humbert loves a minor then, even though she technically seduced him, and even though he was not even her first lover, society must label him a criminal, a corrupter of youth; if a young boxer (*Killer's Kiss*) braves the underworld to rescue his girl, he will spark off a recoil of violence likely to strain her courage and make her betray him; if mutual trust and co-operation is required to carry out a plan, then conflicting interests and suspicion will wreck it (*The Killing*). (p. 69)

Life, in Kubrick's films, is a dilemma in which people are trapped by the mechanics of expediency—their own, other people's, or society's. The trap is set at the beginning of each film, and as we watch the mouse making his pitiful, obstinate attempts to steal the cheese before the steel closes in on him, we know that by the end the trap *will* be sprung. Although there is no point in pushing the comparison very far, it is perhaps worth noting the similarity of approach in Sophoclean tragedy, where malign Fate inexorably prevents the hero from escaping or attaining his goal; where a point of crisis is dramatised, and all action is pared down and deployed so as to illuminate the scope and significance of that crisis. . . .

Kubrick has often been called a cold director, but his purpose in *Paths of Glory* is not to make one weep for the three innocent puppets who are shot. In the condemned cell scenes, for instance, there is an almost Buñuelian avoidance of sentimental identification in the varying levels of hysteria in the three prisoners, in the pious platitudes of the priest, in the struggle which breaks out between the priest and one of the men; and above all in the preparation for execution of the prisoner with the fractured skull ("Pinch his cheeks a couple of times . . . it may make him open his eyes"), and the sudden squashing of the cockroach ("Now you got the edge on him") which Corporal Arnaud has just sadly remarked will be alive when they are dead tomorrow —the first mature examples of the *humour noir* which flowered in *Lolita* and *Strangelove*. Instead of tears, Kubrick wants his audience to break out in a cold sweat at the intricate, ruthless manipulations which make the three men's deaths inescapable. Throughout, therefore, he has adopted an almost mathematical style, fairly obviously though effectively in his use of contrasts (cutting from the elegance of the château to the mud and smoke of the trenches), and more subtly in his overall style. (p. 70)

Although *Killer's Kiss* is only partly successful, and meanders too much to achieve the taut, driving inevitability of the Kubrick "film as trap" which I have tried to define, it is a curiously attractive film, evidently made under the dual influence of neo-realism (the sequences in Davy's room, or when he wanders quietly in Gloria's room, looking and wondering at her things) and Wellesian baroque (the fight among the wax dummies hanging in a storeroom, the beating up in the alley, a good deal of chiaroscuro lighting in the dancehall scenes and elsewhere). The film, too, reveals Kubrick's brilliant talent for pictorial composition, here perhaps a little mannered, and later kept severely in check. . . .

[It] was with *Lolita* that Kubrick demonstrated that, despite the failure of *Spartacus,* it was possible to adapt his style to both complexity *and* blockbuster length. *Lolita,* in fact, is a perfect example of Kubrick's film as trap, with the added complexity that although society closes its ranks in disapproval of perverts like Humbert, in this case society is ignorant of his activities, and the trap which closes in on him is a product of his own mind. . . . [As] we see in the brilliant opening sequence following the credits, Humbert is already caught in his trap and is impelled to kill Quilty. These twin prologues—the airy toe-painting and the long, tortuous track through the baroque jumble of packing-cases, statues, bottles, glasses and paintings in Quilty's house—are the two halves of the film in microcosm as it drives through on its firmly single, though tortuous line of Humbert's fantasy/obsession. . . .

The film grows heavier, more abrupt in style, matching the increasing violence of Humbert's obsession, and culminating in the swift track along the loweringly dark facade of the hospital where he finally loses his Lolita for ever.

Here, and in *Dr. Strangelove,* with its brilliant balance between choppy newsreel urgency and the darkly brooding, flowing menace of its interiors, Kubrick has evolved a style which allows him to range with perfect freedom from utter seriousness to the wildest slapstick, without ever loosening the film's claw-like grip on the audience. (p. 72)

Tom Milne, "How I Learned to Stop Worrying and Love Stanley Kubrick," in Sight and Sound *(copyright © 1964 by The British Film Institute), Vol. 33, No. 2, Spring, 1964, pp. 68-72.*

JACKSON BURGESS

Kubrick films are very bloody and cruel. For savage assault upon the viewer's nerves and hopes, there is little in modern film to match the protracted death-march in *Paths of Glory,* and the Kubrick canon includes also *Lolita,* with its murder shown lovingly and lengthily not once but twice; the explosive massacre in *The Killing;* the *Spartacus* bloodbath; and the unforgettable "thump" of the dying general's nose hitting the floor in *Fear and Desire.* This virtually sadistic treatment of the audience must be accounted for, along with the numerous ambiguities of *Strangelove,* if Kubrick's particular brand of anti-militarism, and its effect on his work, is to be understood. One must account, above all, for the generally gloomy tone of his work. . . .

[Kubrick's first feature, *Fear and Desire,*] is a painfully amateurish picture. (p. 4)

Cinematically, *Fear and Desire* shows some of the rag-bag quality one expects from a novice director who has studied his art: a couple of *Rashomon* shots, a Renoir shot. But on the whole it is surprisingly personal and original. Despite its several particular badnesses and its general fuzziness, the film has a striking purity and honesty and is unmistakably the product of a single man's striving. Its processes are governed by decisions of thought and feeling rather than by formulae or the counsels of caution. (p. 5)

[In *Fear and Desire*] a powerful and complex emotion is conveyed, and a vision of the vexing conflicts of virtue and authority and the uncertainty which swathes every moral choice. It is a vision of clarity (despite the vapidity of the lines assigned the lieutenant) and depth and dignity, and it is conveyed by means of image. This vision, in fact, is more effectively and simply stated by one central shot from the film than by any possible paraphrase or declaration, and that is in the scene of the shooting of the general, who is the type of authority and age, by the lieutenant, the type of youth, rebellion and moral yearning. (pp. 5-6)

The figures of authority take it on the chin in *Dr. Strangelove.* . . . But at whose hands? . . .

The curious thing about *Dr. Strangelove* as a satire is that General Ripper, Col. Kong, "Bat" Guano—the ones who effectively blow up the world—are shown not as incompetents or villains but as lovable lunatics, and when the fireballs unfold in the final frames and the girl begins to sing "We'll Meet Again" the picture has allied itself with their lunacy, leaving the viewer all by himself with no place to stand. (p. 9)

Dr. Strangelove mocks not only militarism, Edward Teller, and the Pentagon, but all pretensions to moral judgment on the part of men (all of us) who have delivered their environment into the hands of totally amoral technological Science and their decisions (the very stuff of morality) to gamesmen aspiring through amorality to Science. (p. 10)

[If] *Dr. Strangelove* has a message I think it is that human fallibility is less likely to be fatal than pretensions to godlike infallibility, or abdication of moral responsibilities to "infallible," passionless, machines or machine-logic.

I think that what has drawn Kubrick to war as the subject-matter for three films is not anti-militarism, specifically, but a concern with public morality. . . .

[It] is not alone the size and seriousness and complexity of Kubrick's moral vision which makes him the finest of living American directors, but his ability to express his vision in a coherent structure of images: the "paths" of *Paths of Glory,* the maddening machines of *Strangelove,* belong to the poetry of the film. (p. 11)

Jackson Burgess, "The 'Anti-Militarism' of Stanley Kubrick," in Film Quarterly *(copyright 1964 by The Regents of the University of California; reprinted by permission of the University of California Press), Vol. XVIII, No. 1, Fall, 1964, pp. 4-11.*

ANDREW SARRIS

The great merit of *Dr. Strangelove* is its bad taste. It is silly to argue that we have the right to say anything we want but that to exercise this right is the height of irresponsibility. Responsible art is dead art, and a sane (no pun intended) film on the bomb would have been a deadly bore.

Given the basic premise of nuclear annihilation, the zany conception of Stanley Kubrick, Terry Southern, and Peter George has much to commend it. Where my critical fallout with most of my colleagues occurs is in the realm of execution. Aided by the tightest scenario since *Rashomon,* and the most deceptive as far as directorial exercises go, Kubrick has been hailed in many quarters as the greatest director since D. W. Griffith. (p. 181)

Since Kubrick's major shortcoming, like Kurosawa's, is in structuring (or rather in failing to structure) his films with a consistent camera viewpoint, a scenario like *Dr. Strangelove* comes as a godsend. All the action is divided neatly and plausibly into three main sections, separate in space and concurrent in time. With the fate of the world riding on every twist and turn of the plot, suspense is virtually built into the theme of the film. Kubrick could sit back and let the clock tick away without reducing the tension in the audience. In this context the feeblest jokes gain added vibrations from the nervous relief they provide. Still, Kubrick's direction is, on the whole, efficient without ever being inspired. . . .

Kubrick can be faulted occasionally for blatant overstatement. The sign reading PEACE IS OUR BUSINESS has an ironic kick, however obvious, the first time it is shown in a strife-torn Air Force base, but when repeated a half dozen times more, the effect crosses the thin line between satire and propaganda. (p. 182)

Some of Kubrick's most admired effects are not quite as original as they may seem to the unschooled eye. . . . The Hiroshima and Christmas Island explosions constitute the most dog-eared footage for "peace" movies on both sides of the Iron Curtain. Consequently it is never clear whether Kubrick's "doomsday" ending is actually representational or merely rhetorical in the time-honored symbolism of anti-bomb movies.

Dr. Strangelove is more effective, if less consistent, when it probes the irregular sexual motivations of its crazy generals. It is hilariously unfair to ridicule one officer for keeping a tootsy on the side and then ridicule the other for conserving his precious fluids from hordes of women seeking his depletion.

Ultimately, *Dr. Strangelove* is not a bad movie by any standards, and I would feel much more kindly toward it if it were not so grossly overrated. . . . As it is, *Dr. Strangelove* can serve as a comic testament to the death wish of many American intellectuals. The world may still come to an end, of course, but the current odds are not with a bang but a whimper. (pp. 182-83)

Andrew Sarris, "Dr. Strangelove," in The Village Voice *(reprinted by permission of* The Village Voice; *copyright © The Village Voice, Inc., 1964), February 13, 1964 (and reprinted in* The National Society of Film Critics on Movie Comedy, *edited by Stuart Byron and Elisabeth Weis, Grossman Publishers, 1977, pp. 181-83).*

F. ANTHONY MACKLIN

In all of the varied critical opinion, much has been said about the purposes of *Dr. Strangelove,* but a dominant theme that pervades the film from beginning to end has been ignored. . . . *Dr. Strangelove* is a sex allegory: from foreplay to explosion in the mechanized world. . . .

Like Jonathan Swift, who employed Master Bates in *Gulliver's Travels,* the creators of *Dr. Strangelove* . . . gave special significance to names that represent various aspects of sex. General Jack D. Ripper . . . , commander of Burpelson Air Force Base, initiates the attack on the Soviet Union. General Ripper, a sex fiend in his own way, is obsessed by the idea of "bodily fluids" and what is happening to them; he is certain that fluoridation is a Commie plot to destroy the strength of America by undermining her bodily fluids. Ripper's description of the act of love has been described by one woman I know as the sexiest moment in any movie she has seen.

Ripper possesses two objects that are obvious sex symbols. The first is his cigar, which is a dominant fixture. Secondly, there is his pistol. When the President discovers Ripper's attack plan, he orders Ripper's capture. Only Ripper's code can halt the planes heading toward the U.S.S.R. As the army tries to unseat him, Ripper barricades himself in with the unwilling Captain Mandrake, a British exchange officer. While the enemy fights toward him, Ripper enters the bathroom and commits suicide with his pistol. (See Seymour Glass's suicide in J. D. Salinger's *Perfect Day for Bananafish* for an interesting parallel). (p. 55)

Meanwhile, the womb-like War Room is the scene of other action. The President, Merkin Muffley, is trying to reach Premier Dmitri Kissoff in Moscow to tell him what is happening. Stanley Kauffmann, in his review in the *New Republic* has called attention to the President's name with the words "erotica students, observe." Merkin means female pudendum (Oxford English Dictionary), which shows the femininity of the President, illustrated by his lack of action. Premier Dmitri is off somewhere with female companionship. Eventually, Muffley gets through and gives Kissoff the news. Although Mandrake relays the code and Kissoff is warned, it is too late. (pp. 56-7)

Meanwhile, back at the War Room, Dr. Strangelove—and this name captures the essence of the film—has made his appearance. . . .

Strangelove is in a wheel chair, impotent. He is a product of German science, talking in a measured, clipped accent; he is mechanized, his arm snapping at his throat and his crotch in an uncontrollable attack. He is the end result of science. . . .

The film concludes with a panorama of beautiful mushroom clouds destroying the world, as Vera Lynn sweetly sings *We'll Meet Again.* Impotence is no more. Warped sex has been eased. Civilization can go back to its beginnings. *Dr. Strangelove: Or How I Learned to Stop Worrying and Love the Bomb* ends in an orgiastic purgation. . . . [The real Doomsday Machine is not men. The] real Doomsday Machine is sex. As King Kong, Buck Turgidson, and Dr. Strangelove himself would chorus, "What a Way to Go!" Love that bomb. (p. 57)

F. Anthony Macklin, "Sex and Dr. Strangelove," in Film Comment *(copyright © 1965 by Lorien Productions, Inc.; all rights reserved), Vol. III, No. 3, Summer, 1965, pp. 55-7.*

STANLEY KAUFFMANN

Stanley Kubrick's *2001: A Space Odyssey* took five years and $10 million to make, and it's easy to see where the time and the money have gone. It's less easy to understand how, for five years, Kubrick managed to concentrate on his ingenuity and ignore his talent. In the first 30 seconds, this film gets off on the wrong foot and, although there are plenty of clever effects and some amusing spots, it never recovers. Because this is a major effort by an important director, it is a major disappointment. . . .

2001 tells us, perhaps, what space travel will be like, but it does so with almost none of the wit of *Dr. Strangelove* or *Lolita* and with little of the visual acuity of *Paths of Glory* or *Spartacus*. What is most shocking is that Kubrick's sense of narrative is so feeble. Take the very opening (embarrassingly labelled *The Dawn of Man*). Great Cinerama landscapes of desert are plunked down in front of us, each shot held too long, with no sense of rhythm or relation. . . . [We] are painfully aware that this is not the Kubrick we knew. The sharp edge, the selective intelligence, the personal mark of his best work seem swamped in a Superproduction aimed at hard-ticket theatres. This prologue is just a tedious basketful of mixed materials dumped in our laps for future reference. What's worse, we don't need it. Nothing in the rest of the film depends on it. (p. 24)

[Kubrick] contrives some startling effects. . . . [And the] detail work throughout is painstaking. . . .

But all for what? To make a film that is so dull, it even dulls our interest in the technical ingenuity for the sake of which Kubrick has allowed it to become dull. He is so infatuated with technology—of film and of the future—that it has numbed his formerly keen feeling for attention-span. The first few moments that we watch an astronaut jogging around the capsule for exercise—really *around* the tubular interior, up one side, across the top, and down the other side to the floor—it's amusing. An earlier Kubrick would have stopped while it was still amusing. . . . High marks for Kubrick the special-effects man; but where was Kubrick the director? (p. 41)

Stanley Kauffmann, "Lost in the Stars" (reprinted by permission of Brandt & Brandt Literary Agents, Inc.; copyright © 1968 by Stanley Kauffmann), in The New Republic, *Vol. 158, No. 18, May 4, 1968, pp. 24, 41.*

TIM HUNTER, with STEPHEN KAPLAN and PETER JASZI

As a film about progress—physical, social, and technological—Stanley Kubrick's huge and provocative *2001: A Space Odyssey* remains essentially linear until its extraordinary ending. In the final transfiguration, director Kubrick and co-author Arthur Clarke . . . suggest that evolutionary progress may in fact be cyclical, perhaps in the shape of a helix formation. Man progresses to a certain point in evolution, then begins again from scratch on a higher level. Much of *2001*'s conceptual originality derives from its being both anti-Christian *and* anti-evolutionary in its theme of man's progress controlled by an ambiguous extra-terrestrial force, possibly both capricious and destructive. . . .

2001 is, among other things, a slow-paced intricate stab at creating an aesthetic from natural and material things we have never seen before. . . . (p. 12)

If Kubrick's superb film has a problem, it may simply be that great philosophical-metaphysical films about human progress and man's relationship to the cosmos have one strike against them when they attempt to be literally just that. Rossellini's radiant religious films or Bresson's meditative ascetiscism ultimately say far more, I think, than Kubrick's far-more-ambitious attempt at synthesizing genre and meaning.

Nevertheless, *2001: A Space Odyssey* cannot be easily judged if only because of its dazzling technical perfection. To be able to see beyond that may take a few years. When we have grown used to beautiful strange machines, and the wonder of Kubrick's special effects wears off by duplication in other Hollywood films, then we can probe confidently beyond *2001*'s initial fascination and decide what kind of a film it really is. (p. 20)

Tim Hunter, with Stephen Kaplan and Peter Jaszi, "'2001: A Space Odyssey'," in Film Heritage *(copyright 1968 by F. A. Macklin), Vol. 3, No. 4, Summer, 1968, pp. 12-20.*

ELIE FLATTO

Essentially, the space-odyssey described in *2001* represents, I believe, Man's eternal quest for spiritual meaning and self-renewal. Man, as such, seems to have come to the end of a long journey begun with his inception as a species on earth. Having maximized his control over nature, he has reached a deadend in the evolutionary process, and in a circuitous manner, he has returned to his primordial conditions. Man may continue to invent, create, discover—yet he is no longer capable of fulfilling and renewing himself. In short, Man is ready for a new step in the evolutionary process in order to re-experience the excitement and adventure of a meaningful life.

Going back in time, the film recreates the conditions from which Man originated, and it begins with the era when apes, the highest product of evolution, huddled about in collectivized security and were completely integrated in their surroundings. Despite their sporadic fights over territorial possession, their life had achieved a state of perfect stasis and boredom not unlike that to be experienced later by the overly sophisticated human community of the year 2001. . . . Suddenly, the stability of their drab environment is disturbed by the appearance of a strange, oblong and darkly luminous object, about which the apes crowd in fear and wonder—the first faint glimmering of an authentic emotion. This strange object, giving *2001* its structural unity and highly symbolic character, is one of the most controversial features of the film. . . . Although some may construe it as that eternal quotient of mystery before which Man and beast are alike helpless, I see it as a symbol (akin to the Jungian four-sided mandala, the most fundamental of all archetypes) of that inspirational force through which life eternally renews itself, for it is upon its appearance that the apes discover and perfect the use of the first tool—a skeletal relic shaped into a club. A perhaps crude beginning, yet in terms of what we know, one that ushers in a completely new evolutionary mode of existence characterized by intellectual development, political experimentation, spiritual growth, heroic action, and dominated by spiritual rather than instinctual impulses. (pp. 7-8)

The last part of the film, wherein the hero is catapulted from Jupiter into the infinite and undergoes a series of transformations—first into an old man, then into a new-born baby—defies precise analysis. . . . [However, we may surmise that the hero in the form of a new-born infant, catapulted back to earth, brings the message that] will usher in an age as different from ours as our own has been from that of the primates. Once again the eternal process of death and renewal, wherein evolution reaches out to new and higher forms, has been set in motion.

The intellectual content of the film, particularly its vision of evolution as a spiritual non-Darwinian process precipitated by mythical objects, visions and transformations, may strike some as quaintly poetic. Yet, in its sensitive probing of Man's desire for transcendence; in its artistic recreation of a future dominated by science and automation; in its view of evolutionary development and indeed of the cosmos itself as a single unit of which all processes are but parts—Kubrick's *2001* is one of the most entertaining as well as insightful films ever to have appeared on screen. (p. 8)

Elie Flatto, "'2001: A Space Odyssey': The Eternal Renewal," in Film Comment *(copyright © 1969 Film Comment Publishing Corporation; all rights reserved), Vol. 5, No. 4, Winter, 1969, pp. 7-8.*

STANLEY KAUFFMANN

In one way Stanley Kubrick's [*A Clockwork Orange*] is cheering. This time, as in all his work before *2001*, he sticks to a narrative, depicts character, opts for "literary humanism"—does all the things that some critics claimed he had deliberately abandoned, in the space picture, for a new esthetics. Perhaps the new esthetics *was* only a wobble? Revised editions of various pronunciamentos may now be in order.

But there isn't a great deal more to celebrate in *A Clockwork Orange*. Certainly there are some striking images; certainly there is some impudent wit, some adroitness. But the worst flaw in the film is its air of cool intelligence and ruthless moral inquiry, because those elements are least fulfilled. Very early there are hints of triteness and insecurity, and before the picture is a half-hour old, it begins to slip into tedium. Sharp and glittery though it continues to be, it never quite shakes that tedium.

The screenplay, by Kubrick, follows Anthony Burgess's novel fairly closely in story, but that's not much of an advantage. This novel of the near future hasn't got much of a story, as such; Burgess relies principally on an odd language he has devised. . . .

Kubrick's first mistake may have been to select a book whose very being is in its words. The film is inevitably much weaker. Kubrick uses the verbal texture as far as possible, which cannot be far. . . . The modest moral resonance of the book is reduced: partly because of certain small changes, like converting a murder victim from an old woman to a sexy broad and killing her with a giant ceramic phallus (thus changing sheer heartlessness into sex sensation); mostly because Kubrick has to replace Burgess's linguistic ingenuity with cinematic ingenuity, and he doesn't. The story as such is thin, so the picture thins. (p. 88)

Inexplicably the script leaves out Burgess's reference to the title: it's the title of a book being written by a character in the novel, with an excerpt provided to clarify. That author's book-inside-the-book is a protest against "the attempt to impose upon man, a creature of growth and capable of sweetness . . . laws and conditions appropriate to a mechanical creation," the attempt to make a growing thing into a mechanism, even—as Stanley Edgar Hyman said—to eliminate his freedom to sin.

Now this is hardly a staggeringly new concept or protest, but Burgess makes it mildly interesting because of the linguistic acrobatics he can perform while expounding it. Kubrick is stuck with the message and, for this work, the wrong medium. We simply see the working-out of the design, the spelling of the lesson, with very little esthetic increment along the 137-minute way. (pp. 89-90)

[The] one thing that, two films ago, I'd never have thought possible to say about a Kubrick film is true of *A Clockwork Orange:* it's boring. (p. 90)

Stanley Kauffmann, "'A Clockwork Orange'" (originally published in The New Republic, *Vol. 166, Nos. 1 & 2, January 1 & 8, 1972), in his* Living Images: Film Comment and Criticism *(copyright © 1971, 1972, 1973, 1974 by Stanley Kauffmann; reprinted by permission of Harper & Row, Publishers, Inc.), Harper, 1975, pp. 88-90.*

PAUL D. ZIMMERMAN

[At] its most profound level, "A Clockwork Orange" is an odyssey of the human personality, a statement on what it is to be fully human. Alex's adventures are, in one sense, the adventures of the id itself. Alex embodies all of man's anarchic impulses. Shorn of his individuality in the penitentiary and of his fantasy life in the conditioning program, he ceases to be a human being in any real sense. His resurrection at the end, as he regains his ability to act out his lusts and aggressions, represents an ironic triumph of the human psyche over the forces that seek to control or diminish it.

Control has been a continuing theme in Kubrick's movies: control of time and the environment by the gangsters who must rob a racetrack within the limits of a single race in "The Killing"; control of the men in the trenches by the officers in the chateau in "Paths of Glory"; Lolita's control of Humbert, Humbert's battle to control his passions and Quilty's playful manipulation of Humbert in "Lolita"; control of nuclear weaponry in "Dr. Strangelove"; the battle for control of the spaceship in "2001"; and, in "A Clockwork Orange," control of the human personality itself. (pp. 29-30)

Stanley Kubrick's unique contribution to contemporary film—what makes him loom larger than other directors who may make more "perfect" films—is [his] capacity to tackle essential and awesome questions that intimidate filmmakers of lesser nerve and intellect. From a young man fascinated by the power and technique of filmmaking, he has grown into an artist with a deep concern for the fate of a species increasingly caught between the sweet orange of humanity and the cold clockwork of technology. It is a tribute to his artistry that this concern produces, not an arid cinema of ideas, but an ironic, galvanizing vision of those aspects of modern life that frighten us all. (p. 33)

Paul D. Zimmerman, "Kubrick's Brilliant Vision," in Newsweek *(copyright 1972 by Newsweek, Inc.; all rights reserved; reprinted by permission), Vol. LXXIX, No. 1, January 3, 1972, pp. 28-33.*

CHARLES THOMAS SAMUELS

From the beginning, most American filmmakers have been *idiot-savants:* technically brilliant but unintelligent about life. (p. 439)

Although Stanley Kubrick began his career within [this] artistic tradition . . . , he soon displayed signs of rejection. After two obviously apprentice films . . . , Kubrick made a tightly plotted action movie that nevertheless subverts some of the genre's basic assumptions. So far from showing a meticulously planned heist as the expression of human adroitness, *The Killing* reveals how poignant an error it is to neglect needs and feelings in one's dependence on technique. Without departing from the crime-does-not-pay formula, *The Killing* humanizes its characters just enough to produce a modest critique of faceless organizational efficiency.

[In] *Paths of Glory,* Kubrick attacks one of American filmdom's most admired exponents of action. He depicts the army unheroically, as a vainglorious organism that thrives on the sacrifice of weaker members, adding vindictiveness to brutality when its methods fail. The particular army in question, however, is French rather than American; thus the native relevance of the criticism is somewhat qualified. . . .

Paths of Glory muffles its pacifism by locating evil in a single class. The result is a tendentiousness never quite overcome by the graphic portrayal of war's horrors. Timidity also mars Kubrick's . . . *Lolita.* Heeding some internalized form of conventional sanctions (with Nabokov's collusion), Kubrick prettifies Humbert's sordid obsession and captures the novel's grotesque comedy only in the secondary roles of Mrs. Haze and Quilty. The result is neither the pathetic May-December romance that major casting and composer Nelson Riddle's arpeggios seem designed to achieve nor Nabokovian satire, but an incompatible mixture of the two. . . .

Nevertheless, flawed as Kubrick's first films are, they clearly established him as more than an entertainer willing to adorn any project offered him with the standard quantity of kinetic thrills. His preeminence among American filmmakers was subsequently assured by a film consolidating all the best in its predecessors. *Dr. Strangelove* combines the critical plotting of *The Killing,* with the pacifist and anti-institutional themes expressed in *Paths of Glory,* by perfecting the comic style marginally evident in *Lolita.* As a result, *Dr. Strangelove* holds up to devastating ridicule values that a film like [Sam Peckinpah's] *Straw Dogs* deplorably celebrates.

Beginning with the shot of two bombers copulating in midair, *Dr. Strangelove* presents America's fascination with might as an absurd confusion of libido. (pp. 440-41)

Dr. Strangelove is exceptional not only for placing this self-criticism before us but for doing so with an hilarious relentlessness that takes us laughing right through Armageddon. Moreover, while exposing the ultimate destructiveness of a culture perversely in love with machines, the film itself avoids mechanical flourishes, making direction reticently serve the content. . . .

With some of the critical alertness displayed in *Dr. Strangelove,* Kubrick's . . . *2001* speculates about what life might become. Numerous details reveal the underside of futurist technology: the insipidity of cosmic cuisine, the colossally disproportionate effort and boring experience of space travel, the atavistically banal human behavior that makes the film's one colorful figure a computer programmed to feel. Yet, Kubrick's critical voice eventually seems to be crying in the wilderness, drowned out by the alluring special effects with which he fills up the vastness of space.

Thus, the last sequence suggests a faith that man will ultimately transcend whatever follies still cling to him as he enters the era of total mechanism. We are, however, never told why. Nor can we explain how an artist who distinguished himself by satirizing mindless, heartless mechanization can suddenly find it promising. . . .

Suggesting some fundamental ambivalence, *2001* is so obscure that it has become a cult object for those who argue that a film should not mean but be. It doesn't signal a shift in Kubrick's thinking so much as a new fascination with the sheer joy of making images.

This fascination renders Kubrick's [*A Clockwork Orange*] "sensational" in both senses of the term: "outstanding" and also a work dependent on "exaggerated or lurid details." . . .

But *A Clockwork Orange* is no *Straw Dogs;* love of violence is not its problem. Although detractors argue that Alex, the film's antihero, is too charming and clever, this charge is shortsighted. . . . Kubrick and Burgess want to make Alex sufficiently valuable, however, so that we can feel that the methods used to repress him may be as deplorable as Alex himself. (p. 441)

In *Straw Dogs* violence isn't charming; it is necessary. In *A Clockwork Orange* it lacks appeal because it is so manifestly unnecessary. . . . [Violence] is never presented as a response to any threat that might justify it. (pp. 441-42)

Kubrick's film . . . [is] artful for finding cinematic means to display Burgess' ironic equation between lawlessness and the presumed alternatives. Most strikingly, Kubrick signals a breakdown of value distinctions by accompanying the violence with musical and sometimes decorative elements that are ostentatiously benigh. A gang rape takes place to the strains of Rossini in a baroque theater. (pp. 442-43)

What Kubrick does not emphasize is the novel's theme; the unreality of goodness when not freely chosen. . . . But before he is charged, as he has been, with desecrating a superior work of fiction, we must remember how localized the theme is in Burgess' novel, where it exists alongside far more striking details that articulate a nearly contradictory point: good and evil have become equivalent. . . .

Kubrick finds brilliant cinematic equivalents for Burgess' gimmicks, but he is limited by the original's intellectual and emotional thinness. As a result, grand show that it is, *A Clockwork Orange* simply reminds us that Kubrick is a master visualizer. Visualization is, of course, the essence of cinema, but it is not the whole of the art. . . . Kubrick seems intent merely on showing us how to embody filmically a world first imagined in words. His expertise is undeniable, but it is also narrow and unedifying. If, as everyone claims, he is the best American filmmaker, this fact merely reminds us of the terribly limited achievement of his native context. Once in his career Kubrick transcended his tradition; now, entertainingly but to our ultimate disappointment, he seems to be going the way of his predecessors. (p. 443)

Charles Thomas Samuels, "The Context of 'A Clockwork Orange'" (copyright by the Estate of Charles Thomas Samuels; reprinted by permission), in The American Scholar, *Vol. 41, No. 3, Summer, 1972, pp. 439-43.*

NORMAN KAGAN

Fear and Desire is a fascinating effort containing a host of ideas, images, and themes which continue to appear in Kubrick's later films. (p. 18)

The first theme in *Fear and Desire,* stated in the poem at the opening, is that the story is made up of "imaginary worlds": each man's "war," "enemies," and "conflict" are his mind's way of dealing with the enigmatic events and inconsistent behavior that surround him. This is objectified throughout the film: in the powerful shocking images of animal-like passion, in the dreamlike retreats, chaotic killings, idle and absurd "philosophical" conversations. The images of the dead men are grotesque, eerily backlighted—they are no longer real men, but "pure enemies"—corpses stylized into ideas. In the end, Corby sums up life this way: "It's all a trick we perform, because we'd rather not die immediately." It recalls T. S. Eliot's "Human beings cannot stand very much reality."

Two other linked ideas are the futility of intelligence and the distrust of the emotions. The most intelligent man, Lieutenant Corby, is so detached he doesn't know why he is alive, but just collects reasons ("like butterflies"). He uses his brain mostly to make "intellectual jokes" nobody else gets. (pp. 18-19)

The emotions are equally useless to everyone in *Fear and Desire.* The boy, Sidney, is driven to assault and murder by his fear and lust. Kubrick's treatment of eroticism is embarrassingly grotesque and perverse, but not unrealistic—an attitude that persists through all his work, though the next few films are relatively sexless. Mac, obsessed by his desire to justify himself by killing a general, and the most effective soldier, is driven half-consciously to self-destruction. This pair of homicide-suicides—Sidney and Mac—is typical of nearly all of Kubrick's films: *Lolita* (Humbert Humbert, Quilty); *Dr. Strangelove* (General Ripper, Major Kong); and *2001: A Space Odyssey* (HAL-9000, Astronaut Bowman). But the portraits of such characters, driven by passions and compulsions they only half understand, are never so clear.

All these concepts—the world as a dream, intelligence as futile, emotion as suspect—are rather pessimistic. There are two more ideas in the film that are more encouraging.

One is the notion of a journey to freedom, an Odyssey. It is possible to move toward knowledge and safety, and though the men flounder and run in circles, their concern is always such an escape. Individually, each man travels along the road to self-knowledge. . . . In a way, the four soldiers are like the exploded fragments of a personality: intellectual thought and playfulness, emotional drives like lust and fear, emotional control and self-discipline, and the self-maintaining functions. At the end, they have triumphed, survived, and rejoined each other. (pp. 19-20)

Killer's Kiss is certainly the most untypical of Kubrick's films. It is a weak, naturalistic thriller, shot from Kubrick's own screenplay. The story line shows Kubrick's early errors as a dramatist: It wavers and lacks the obsessional drive and energy of the later films, as do the characters. *Killer's Kiss* is most successful at creating the ambiance of lower-class New York life, realistic touches and urban types. (p. 21)

An interesting aspect of *Killer's Kiss* is that, although straitjacketed by his genre, Kubrick still included [themes which would be found in his later films]:

The imaginary worlds. Though *Killer's Kiss* deals in the shabby details of lower-class life, the characters give little attention to their economic and social plights. They focus on dream worlds which provide specious relief. (p. 29)

Futility of intelligence, errors of emotions. Alice, the brilliant artist, kills herself. Vince's passion drives him to self-destruction. Davy almost dies for his love. His manager is destroyed by a coincidence. Gloria, who thought she could hurt her sister, degrades herself in remorse.

The journey to freedom. The train trip to Seattle is hopefully such a journey, but so is Davy's search for Gloria through shabby New York.

Triumph of obsessional dedicated hero. Davy's winning of Gloria.

The pair of suicide-homicides. Vince has the manager killed, then dies, and Davy (who kills Vince) is allowed to live on for a "happy ending." (pp. 30-1)

In the perspective of the seventies, both [Mike Nichols's] *Catch-22* and *Paths of Glory* can be seen as products of the stifling anti-intellectualism, smugness, and paranoia of the Eisenhower-McCarthy years. Both are full of pointless brutalization, absurd and arbitrary power, and smothering conformity. Criticism of *Catch-22* (both the book and the film) suggests the less obvious absurdity of Kubrick's hero: trying to stay always within the limits of the military system, Dax winds up arguing the defense of his men against the judge who arranged the trial so they would be put to death. You can't become more of an absurd hero than that! For better or worse, Dax can be seen as an absurd, impotent character who won't or can't rebel, even staring into the face of evil itself.

[A] heuristic critical approach is to see *Paths of Glory* as a dramatized model of society (clearly created by a brilliant nihilist). Gavin Lambert has pointed out the class structure of this society. Its cruel, dehumanizing, and pointless "work" is production in a consumer economy, allegorically intensified. The lives of its citizens are "mean, nasty, brutish and short"; they tend to advance in proportion to their wits, endurance, aggression, and tolerance for inflicting pain. The closer to the top, the worse they are. But the men on the bottom have no nobility—of the three chosen to die, the shrewd, vengeful hater endures the wait; the brave man chosen at random cracks up and becomes a babbling child; the criminal destroys himself in a clumsy escape attempt. There is no law or justice, of course, and the trappings of civilization—the exquisite chateau—are used for displays of vanity, ambition, treachery, and monstrous "public relations stunts" like the trial. (pp. 64-5)

Along with . . . this, Kubrick's [aforementioned] themes are present in full force. . . . (p. 66)

[In *Spartacus*] the character Spartacus is to me incompatible with Kubrick's films, for he is a man who undergoes a profound personal transformation, from good bright tough to heroic democrat-general. Such a character shift is unknown in all the director's films: The very most a person can change his point of view is to fall in love, and that is almost always fatal. (Sidney in *Fear and Desire,* Vince in *Killer's Kiss,* all the couples in *The Killing*). Kubrick's characters are driven or passive. They cannot change. It takes extraterrestrial intervention before a Kubrick person is significantly altered.

A second trouble with an all-Kubrick *Spartacus* is that the story violates his vision of human relations. Human relationships in Kubrick's films are rarely satisfactory, and never warmly democratic. Spartacus and his fleeing comrades, living in a sort of ideal socialism, are an optimistic comment on human community, a topic Kubrick always approaches with distrust, pessimism, and futility (the natural confluence of reason and emotion). (p. 80)

[*Dr. Strangelove* may] be considered as the logical extension of Kubrick's other two war films: *Fear and Desire* and *Paths of Glory*. The parallels between the Kirk Douglas film and *Dr. Strangelove* are striking: a catastrophic attack and the subsequent debacle; levels of command fighting and destroying each other; a comedy of irony and contradictory responses; the basic problem—the survival of anonymous individuals; a never-seen enemy.

In other ways, *Dr. Strangelove* resembles *Paths of Glory* driven to the ultimate limits, jet-propelled as it were: The emotional commander is now not just vain and spiteful but psychotic; the battlefield is again sundered—bomber, base, and War Room—without access or even communications among them until it's too late; the top command is divided into weak fragments—decent, powerless Mandrake, reasonable President Muffley, computerlike Dr. Strangelove; the prize in the balance is not three drab Everymen, but all humanity. (p. 138)

Kubrick's films are fascinating as consistent stories of one psycho-social model of the world. Each takes place in an ambiance of great tension and deviousness, typified by cover-ups, diversions, masquerades. Every film is a prolonged contest conducted under duress in which characters' beliefs are often mocked, exploded, or prove lethal.

Of all Kubrick's films, *Paths of Glory* and *A Clockwork Orange* are probably the most complete pictures of Kubrick's social vision; *Lolita* and the subsequent works dealing mostly with the elite, *The Killing* and those before mostly with the desperate and victimized dregs.

Life for the characters in thse films resembles an existence in a human version of an "environmental sink," in which animals are allowed to multiply and crowd together far beyond what is healthy. In such a situation, any social order disintegrates; instead of the life patterns involving courtship and pairing off, a few sleek, powerful animals collect harems in privileged territories, dominating and terrorizing the rest of the creatures, or crowd together in desperate uncertainty and fear, or wander about in a daze, refusing to accept the realities of their degenerate environment. A few, in their desperation, become predators on their own kind, clawing or sexually attacking at random.

Such is the society of *Paths of Glory, A Clockwork Orange,* and, to a large degree, all of Kubrick's films. The great masses of men live lives of quiet desperation and/or vulnerable twitchy unreality; Fletcher and Sidney in *Fear and Desire;* the hold-up gang in *The Killing;* the troops of *Paths of Glory;* the soldiers and the B-52 crew in *Dr. Strangelove;* Astronaut Poole and the killer man-apes of *2001: A Space Odyssey;* the droogs, bums, and civilians of *A Clockwork Orange*. Theirs is a hard lot; the worst or weakest become predators on their own: Sidney in *Fear and Desire,* Sherry Peatty in *Killer's Kiss;* Lieutenant Roget in *Paths of Glory;* Georgie, Dim, and the Leftist writer of *A Clockwork Orange*.

Dominating and controlling these submissive masses at the highest levels are the generals and politicians and communicators: Generals Broulard and Mireau in *Paths of Glory;* Quilty the television writer in *Lolita;* General Turgidson, President Muffley, and Dr. Strangelove in *Dr. Strangelove;* bureaucrat Heywood Floyd and HAL-9000 in *A Space Odyssey;* the chief psychologist and Minister of the Interior in *A Clockwork Orange*. These so-called leaders may be foolish, proud, sly, headstrong, brilliant, decisive, but they are all somehow tainted by their own knowledge and power—they are all either amoral or partly ineffectual, corrupt or corrupted.

Finally, between these two groups is a third, a sort of spirited middle class of characters—capable, intelligent, independent, from which most of Kubrick's heros are chosen: Johnny Clay in *The Killing;* Colonel Dax in *Paths of Glory;* Humbert Humbert in *Lolita;* Major Kong in *Dr. Strangelove;* Astronaut Bowman in *A Space Odyssey;* even Alex of *A Clockwork Orange*.

In terms of this psycho-social approach, all of Kubrick's films are really about just one subject—finding a third alternative to impotent weakness or the corruption of power. Johnny Clay doesn't want to be a working stiff or a cop; Colonel Dax won't resign his commission or try to be a general; Humbert Humbert isn't interested in an "ordinary marriage," but never uses Quilty-type tricks; Major Kong shows again and again the initiative that made him an officer, but wouldn't want a War Room post; astronaut Bowman carries out his mission, but wouldn't want Heywood Floyd's big job; Alex couldn't stand just staying home at night, but neither could he be a schemer in the Minister's government. In a world of very limited personal consciousness, where intelligence is often futile and emotion not to be trusted, Kubrick's obsessive hero searches for another way out.

In the end, nearly all are defeated: Johnny Clay loses both his new wealth and new freedom; Colonel Dax dooms his career in a vain search for nonexistent social justice; Humbert dedicates himself to true love and is left alone; Major Kong is vaporized because he blindly followed his social role. Mission Commander Bowman succeeds only in becoming a "star child," an eerie nonhuman being whose activities Kubrick does not reveal; Alex seems about to return to his life of perverse unmotivated violence, now with the unspoken toleration of society.

Kubrick's moral seems clear: *There is no "way out."* To find some pure purpose or meaning in life, one would seemingly have to become nonhuman, or, alternately, be so mentally disposed that, like Alex, the question never arises in the first place. While Alex may be seen as a living "psychological myth," he is surely at the same time the most rigid of Kubrick protagonists. Through betrayal, confinement, brainwashing, suicide, rebrainwashing, whitewashing, he never changes, never questions himself. . . . (pp. 189-91)

Kubrick has made his life into an artist's odyssey, a search for new freedoms and powers with which to illuminate the world. "The very meaninglessness of life," he has said, "forces man to create his own meanings. . . . However vast the darkness, we must supply our own light. . . ." (p. 192)

Norman Kagan, in his The Cinema of Stanley Kubrick *(copyright © 1972 by Norman Kagan; reprinted by permission of Holt, Rinehart and Winston, Publishers), Holt, 1972, 204 p.*

DANIEL De VRIES

One might often disagree with Kubrick's ideas, at times even find them a bit silly, but none of that detracts from the fact that Kubrick puts together picture shows which are entertaining, aesthetically pleasing, and provoking, all at the same time.

Kubrick is, among other things, a true screen poet. He knows how to use visual images to communicate. Movies should probably never communicate anything with words that could be communicated with a picture, and Kubrick's rarely do. Kubrick characterizes a gangster by the way he handles a gun in *The Killing,* a strange family triangle with a peck on the cheek in *Lolita,* a mad general by the way he chomps his cigar in *Dr. Strangelove.* What is wonderful about Kubrick's imagistic skill is that theme and image conjoin so naturally in his movies. In *Paths of Glory* soldiers attacking a hill called "The Anthill" really look like ants and Kubrick has the good sense not to have anyone verbalize the comparison. In *Dr. Strangelove* the top half of the screen above a group of government officials is completely black and one does not have to say or think "impending doom"—one feels it. The genius in all of this is that none of it is artificially imposed upon the movie. . . . This is one facet of Kubrick's genius—his ability to project theme without using symbols, by creating visual images which *are* the themes of his films. (pp. 5-6)

The Kubrick world is not exactly a pleasant place. It is marked by belief in the badness of human nature, and the suggestion that there is at work in the universe some malevolent force, whose chief aim is to destroy human beings and their expectations. Even in *2001: A Space Odyssey,* certainly his most optimistic film, salvation does not come to man as man, but through man's evolution into something else. In *Lolita* Quilty personifies that force, in *Dr. Strangelove* it is the film's namesake, but in other films it goes unspecified and unnamed. But one knows that it is there because things never work out. It is something like the Lord of the Flies. As the head asks Simon in Golding's novel, "I'm the reason why it's no go? Why things are what they are?" Maybe in Kubrick's work as in Golding's, the problem is that the beast is in all of us. Kubrick is a chess lover, and critics often point to chess motifs in his movies. In general the comparison holds up—Kubrick's movies are like chess games with an unseen opponent who always wins. (p. 6)

Because Kubrick's films are set in his own world, and because he sees man as a loser, one sometimes misses humanness in his characters. . . . Thus his movies are more stylized than realistic art. If one is partial (as I am) to humanist art, he tends to think of Kubrick's anti-humanism as a limitation, although, seen more objectively, it is probably merely a matter of taste. (p. 7)

Daniel De Vries, in his introduction to his The Films of Stanley Kubrick *(copyright © 1973 by William B. Eerdmans Publishing Company; used by permission), Eerdmans Publishing Co., 1973, pp. 5-7.*

HARRIET DEER and IRVING DEER

Stanley Kubrick's major films reveal his search for an unrestricted form through which he can communicate with his audience without coercing them into mistaking his particular structures for reality. Increasingly, he has come to use the popular arts as his central means for expressing that search. He does this by showing us the contradictory meanings and implications of the popular arts, their escapist as well as their life-asserting implications, the ways in which they reveal the contemporary tendencies to run away from the complex, concrete uniqueness of life, and the ways in which they reveal the desperation of our search for the complex, concrete, uniqueness of life, our search for being itself. Kubrick recognizes the primitive, vital roots of the life-asserting impulse itself, the roots that give rise to and are reflected in all the arts including the popular arts, as well as the contradictory tendencies so clearly expressed in the popular arts, the tendencies to conform, to give in to the accumulated baggage of public and traditional meanings and to lose the self in cliché and stereotyped responses to life. For Kubrick, the popular arts in fact become grand metaphors of contemporary experience, visions of contemporary man struggling desperately to reconcile his life-affirming and his life-denying drives. And in creating such metaphors, Kubrick miraculously creates art in a time most inimical to art out of the very material that would seem most hostile to it, the escapist fantasies of the popular arts. He achieves the paradoxical McLuhanesque mystery of transforming his medium, film, a popular art itself, into his message. (p. 234)

Kubrick takes sides in *Paths of Glory*. He sees things literally, to a significant extent, in terms of blacks and whites, good and evil. His uses of blacks and whites, light and darkness in the film illustrate this. Like Shakespeare in the destructive worlds of *Romeo and Juliet* and *Othello,* Kubrick reverses the conventional meanings of light and darkness. Light is associated with the generals, the men who destroy individuals, who send them to their deaths in battle or before firing squads. The chateau in which one almost always sees the generals is bathed in light in contrast to the darkness of the trenches and the prison in which the three men are waiting to die. (pp. 234-35)

What Kubrick is discovering in *Paths of Glory* is how to make his visual content express his theme. But the problem is that he does in fact see things in this film in terms of black and white, that is, in terms of having to choose between one side or the other. We are never allowed to see the complexities and contradictions of the French officers, never allowed to view the validity—at least from their perspective—of their struggle. The officers are evil, the men, even though imperfect, are good. In order to make his characters conform to his theme, he has had to rob them of complexity. He has had to show that creativity and complexity can reside only with the individual men, most specifically with Ralph Meeker as the Sisyphus-like individual who transcends his death at the hands of the firing squad by freely choosing death gracefully. The generals, on the other hand, are reduced to totally inhuman manipulators. (p. 237)

When Kubrick makes *Dr. Strangelove,* however, he substitutes archetypes from popular literature and film for institutions. In so doing, he frees himself to allow the complexities and contradictions implicit in his archetypes to be utilized to their fullest. *Dr. Strangelove* abounds with popular characters. Their very names imply their contradictory archetypal functions. General Jack D. Ripper suggests a guardian of order turned homicidal maniac; Bat Guano, a combination of Bat Masterson and manure; Mandrake, a sleight of hand artist. In fact, he is, because we see Peter Sellers, the actor who plays his part, playing two other parts, those of the president and of Dr. Strangelove. This shifting of roles by Sellers is a perfect expression of the way the use of archetypes from the popular arts frees Kubrick to indulge in invention and performance. He has shifted from visuals as expressions of thematic argument to visuals as expressions of sheer performance. (pp. 238-39)

[The character of Dr. Strangelove] allows for a synthesis of comic delights and horrible awareness. We recognize that any scientist who wears glasses and speaks in an ominous foreign accent must be a villain. We expect his villainy to emanate from his super-rationality. Instead, Dr. Strangelove's villainy derives from a series of Freudian slips and the movement of uncontrolled parts of his body. He speaks rationally, almost like a computer, but his arm and leg move irrationally, as if by their own will. And his speech adds up to a comic revelation of his own sexist consciousness. What we get is both a delight in the reversal of the stereotyped scientist-villain and a sudden horrible awareness of the subjectivity and arbitrariness that underlies supposedly objective and rational behavior.

In his treatment of Dr. Strangelove, Kubrick has stumbled on a technique that will become indispensable in his last two films. He has discovered a way to preserve and express the need embodied in the stereotype, the truth and vitality expressed in the popular arts, without succumbing to a stereotyped response. Paradoxically, he shows the validity of the stereotype of the scientist. According to the stereotype, we distrust the scientist because he dehumanizes through excessive objectivity. Kubrick shows that, paradoxically, what we take to be extreme objectivity and rationality is extreme subjectivity and irrationality. He has preserved the validity and vitality of our perception while expanding our consciousness of its underlying meaning and significance.

In *2001: A Space Odyssey,* he follows the same pattern, expanded to cover the whole story through its science-fiction metaphor. In following this pattern he is following the archetypal Odyssey plot from Homer through the frontiersman moving west, through the cowboy, through even the gangster. In essence, the hero moves out searching for knowledge of the external world, but ends by gaining awareness of the world inside himself. (pp. 239-41)

The archetype of the voyage tells us that discovery is never complete until it includes both external and internal revelation. It engages our vital, primitive responses, our sense of wonder, and if handled right as Kubrick handles it, it satisfies our longing for confrontation with the mysteries of existence. What is wrong with most science fiction stories is that they content themselves with external discovery or, at most, with a mere moral lesson. Kubrick, on the other hand, compels us in *2001* to desert the mechanistic, supposedly objective order of the world and to create our own subjective reality. (p. 241)

In *A Clockwork Orange,* Kubrick uses the con-man archetype from popular arts instead of the pure science fiction archetype, and superimposes it on a futurist base. (p. 242)

We like the hero, Alex, not for any sentimental reasons, but only because he embodies the primitive vitality captured in his stereotyped con-man role; he survives as sheer con-man, by his wits and vitality. Unlike the astronaut in *2001,* Alex may not discover himself, but we nevertheless discover ourselves in discovering the nature of the world in which he and we move. We are jarred into making this discovery for ourselves through the complex responses that Kubrick evokes in us. When we discover that a thief, rapist and murderer is more human than the supposedly sane and moral society in which he lives, we must become imaginatively engaged in making sense of the situation. . . .

Kubrick violates us, shocks us, into recognizing the violation of human vitality we practice, or at least condone, by sanctioning and creating a society in which the only way to survive, the only way to be vital, is to be a con man. (p. 243)

Kubrick is reducing life in this film literally to its primitive source, its very roots, survival and sexuality. In reducing Alex to the embodiment of this primitive source of human vitality, Kubrick shows us better than any other artist the essential vitality and limitation of the pornographic impulse. He shows us that sexuality is a vital impulse without which man cannot survive and yet one which, divorced from the total person, is merely destructive. As with all of his successful uses of the popular arts, Kubrick has now passed the supreme test. He has both affirmed the essential truth of the roots of man's vital impulses embodied in the popular arts, and he has shown us the perversions to which that truth can be twisted. He has achieved the miracle of using pornography, that most escapist and fantasy-inducing popular art, as a way of forcing us to confront the reality of our escapist behavior. In achieving this miracle, he has not only created a significant work of art, he has revealed to us the capacities and limitations of the popular tradition itself. (pp. 243-44)

Harriet Deer and Irving Deer, "Kubrick and the Structures of Popular Culture," in Journal of Popular Film *(copyright © 1974 by Sam L. Grogg, Jr., Michael T. Marsden, and John G. Nachbar), Vol. III, No. 3, 1974, pp. 232-44.*

JOHN RUSSELL TAYLOR

Kubrick's is a unified, coherent *oeuvre,* in the best *auteur* tradition. And yet, for myself I find there is always something in Kubrick's films, brilliant though most of them are, that seems to stop short of the total creative involvement of the true *auteur.* Is it perhaps that he is keeping back something vital of himself, that the films seem in a way like so many masks assumed by their maker rather than various aspects of his own face? . . .

Technically [*Fear and Desire*] leaves little to be desired: Kubrick's own camera work has considerable polish and a good professional finish spiced here and there with touches which suggest that his hours at the Museum of Modern Art were not ill spent—in particular the evocation of the dream-like forest landscape in a way which suggests some Japanese films, specifically Kurosawa's *Rashomon* for the sunlight flashing through the leaves; but also perhaps his *Tora-No-O* for the placing of the soldiery within this landscape.

Occasionally Kubrick goes a little overboard with flashy camera effects . . . , but, considering his youth and inexperience, the film has surprising coherence—even its lurches into melodrama are interesting and indicative, pointing the way (without the application of too much hindsight) to the mature Kubrick who has shown in *Dr. Strangelove* and *A Clockwork Orange* a unique gift for playing drama on and over the edge of melodrama into the sort of black farce which sometimes seems implicit in *Fear and Desire* if only he would or could let himself go. (p. 104)

The Killing (1956) is a disappointment. Not absolutely, for it is at the very least a superlatively well-crafted thriller, tight, sharp, and almost painfully vivid. But for all its virtues it comes across, particularly if seen again today, as the least personal of all Kubrick's films (except perhaps *Spartacus*). . . . (p. 107)

The Killing is a superior example [of the crime film] in its slickness, tautness, and ruthless machine-like precision. But it is not greatly superior to others in its genre, and it lacks (deliberately, no doubt) the ambiguity, the expansiveness, the unexpected touches of poetry which distinguished its nearest competitor, [John Huston's] *The Asphalt Jungle*. Nevertheless, there are moments vividly exemplifying Kubrick's taste for or interest in the bizarre and peculiar, the unreality or surreality lurking at the heart of the seemingly normal and everyday. . . . In general, though, *The Killing*, while perfectly acceptable and even distinguished within its own rather closely circumscribed genre, seems, because of its very perfection in its chosen form, curiously impersonal, an exercise and a demonstration rather than a personal statement.

[*Paths of Glory*, 1957] is a very different matter. It is as though Kubrick, having made two films with the accent on feeling, self-expression rather than precision, and then one film in which tightness, precision, and a rather cold, impersonal finish were of paramount importance, was able triumphantly to combine the two sides of his cinematic nature. *Paths of Glory* creates its extraordinary effect not only by the intensity of its feeling but, even more, by the way the intensity is kept under scrupulous control. The emotional Kubrick, the man who has an attitude toward life and its issues that he wishes to convey to his audience, is perfectly matched here by the technological Kubrick, the man who is fascinated by the sheer logistics of filmmaking, the way the pieces fit together, the adaptation of means to ends. (pp. 109-10)

[*Lolita*, 1962] stands up as the first full, mature expression of Kubrick's personality and point of view—more decisively, certainly, than *Paths of Glory*, fine though that is, because it enables us to appreciate fully for the first time the comic aspects of Kubrick's vision. Like Nabokov's, it is an anguished, violent, sometimes ugly comedy—the comedy of a man who has to laugh in order not to cry, who has to use a distancing frame of reference in order to make sense of an experience that could otherwise lead to black despair. (pp. 115-16)

Dr. Strangelove, or How I Learned to Stop Worrying and Love the Bomb (1964) is obviously in many ways . . . a logical sequel to *Lolita*. . . . (p. 119)

Kubrick's intention in *Dr. Strangelove* is clear enough—to express the absurdity of the arms race in a form equally absurd, taking up the theme of *Paths of Glory* in a fantastic register, or for that matter accepting the moments of *Fear and Desire* where the action declines from being existentially Absurd to being merely absurd in a more basic sense as a viable means of expression. . . . If the tone can be seen as deriving from *Lolita*, where Kubrick seems to have learned the secret of playing comedy in deadly earnest and not being afraid to plunge right into outrageous farce when it suited his purpose, the character outlines can be traced back to *Paths of Glory* and even more unmistakably to *Fear and Desire* (no doubt because the four characters there are intended as permanent stereotypes anyway). The intricate dovetailing of parallel actions into a clear piece of exposition refers back to the construction of *The Killing*, and indeed in all sorts of ways *Dr. Strangelove* has the air of being consciously a kind of summary of Kubrick's work to date, a rehearsal of the lessons he had learned from film to film throughout his career. (p. 122)

[But] *Dr. Strangelove* is frequently not funny enough to be accepted as really funny, and because of that, because it seems not to take its own comedy seriously enough, does not come across either as serious enough to be serious. (p. 124)

Up to [*2001: A Space Odyssey* Kubrick] had always been particularly remarkable for his skill in telling complicated stories on screen, juggling the elements of several intrigues at the same time, as in *The Killing* and *Dr. Strangelove*, or showing the pieces of a plot fall into place like a steel trap, as in *Paths of Glory* and *Lolita*. Certainly, either way his films had been very story-oriented. Now he was to go to the other extreme, to build a major film not on a complex intrigue, but on simple gestures with a minimum of words, and leave the psychological, emotional, and philosophical ramifications up to his audiences to provide. The master of the cut-and-dried, the precise, the forcefully explicit, had chosen to seek the vague, the general, the ambiguous; the filmmaker who had always approached his audiences very importantly through their minds was now looking to approach them "at an inner level of consciousness just as music does." (pp. 124-25)

[This] is a roundabout way of describing the self-transformation of a prose artist into a poet, a psychologist into a myth maker. I think that any lingering doubts I may have about the effect of the finished film come from one basic doubt—that of whether one can become a poet simply by taking an infinitude of pains. It seems to me that the one big distraction the film presents, as far as the operation of its intended mode of communication is concerned, is the underlying awareness one has that it is a construct, intellectually arrived at, with a certain design on us which the creator perfectly understands but we are supposed not to. (p. 125)

[In his best film, *A Clockwork Orange*,] Kubrick, back refreshed after his experiments with minimal plotting in *2001* to apply the skills of nonverbal filmic expression to a perfectly explicit story line, uses a technique which it is tempting to call comic-strip. Episode follows episode brusquely, with no lingering over transitions: the stages of our hero's accumulating misfortune following his indulgence with his three mates, or droogs, to use Burgess's argot, in a bout of ultra-violence—a therapeutic beating up of a shambling drunk, an all-out tangle with a rival group, a rape-cum-beating-up of a couple of country-dwelling intellectuals—are economically sketched in, with overwhelming logic. Each episode in the first half, when he is up, finds its mirror image in the second half, when he is down, drained of his violent and sexual impulses by a new conditioning course of cinematic forced feeding. (p. 133)

In *A Clockwork Orange* Kubrick seems to have found his ideal subject and his ideal form of expression. In all the lofty discussion occasioned by *2001* we have tended to forget . . . that Kubrick is essentially a *popular* artist, one skilled in adapting the latest techniques to the task of communicating complicated ideas to the largest possible audience. The look of *A Clockwork Orange,* contrasting the Pop/Op/Kinetic art trappings of the brave new world with the grubby makeshift of everyday life in a world run to seed, is smart and modern, but also perfectly functional, all there to convey something rather than indulged in for its own sake. Kubrick the master of dramatic-cinematic narrative is again functioning at full power, and it is arguable that *2001,* whatever one's reservations about its total success, was a step necessary for Kubrick to take in order to get to this point. Whether or not he has in the process proved himself an *auteur,* an inspired filmmaker, or merely, as I tend to believe, the brilliantly gifted cinematic intelligence who can occasionally turn out an inspired film, does not seem to matter too much at this point. (pp. 134-35)

John Russell Taylor, "Stanley Kubrick," in his Directors and Directions: Cinema for the Seventies *(reprinted by permission of Hill & Wang, a division of Farrar, Straus & Giroux, Inc.; in Canada, by A D Peters & Co Ltd; copyright © 1975 by John Russell Taylor), Hill and Wang, 1975, pp. 100-35.*

JOHN SIMON

Barry Lyndon is a curious choice for Kubrick, who has become more and more estranged from the taste and smell of human experience. . . .

[Watching] the movie is like looking at illustrations for a work that—partly through Thackeray's, but more through Kubrick's, negligence—has not been supplied. Striking as some of these illustrations, often in long or extreme long shot, are, they do not encourage our getting involved with the characters in the story. This has something to do with the episodic nature of the film, but mostly with the fact that the director seems more concerned with landscapes, architecture, period interiors, costumes, etc., than with what happens to the people in them. (p. 84)

[The] film is almost entirely cool to the point of near-tonelessness, exuding, along with visual splendor, an aura of detachment if not indifference out of which the death of Bryan resonates with a doubly plangent, and so particularly inappropriate, note. (p. 85)

John Simon, "Million-Dollar Blimps," in New York *Magazine (copyright © 1975 by News Group Publications, Inc.; reprinted with the permission of* New York *Magazine), Vol. 9, No. 1, December 29-January 5, 1975-76, pp. 84-7.**

STANLEY KAUFFMANN

Barry Lyndon very nearly accommodates Zeno's paradox of motion: it seems to remain—at least for long periods—in one place while actually it is moving ahead. Kubrick has produced three hours and four minutes of pictures. . . .

Why was Kubrick interested in [Thackeray's] book? I infer, not by remote psychoanalysis but from what we are shown on screen, that the warping of innocence by experience was not the concern of his screenplay. We are *told* by the narrator . . . , whose voice is important in the proceedings, that Barry became skillful in chicanery and guile. We see nothing of this process, any more than we see him become skillful in the swordsmanship he later displays. All through the film we are *told* a great deal about the changes in Barry's character; we see only his actions before and after. . . .

A certain lame rationale is soon apparent in Kubrick's method. Many sequences begin with a close shot of an object or person, then the camera pulls back slowly to set the initial subject in a vast environment. Over and over again this strophe is repeated. When it's not used, often a sequence *begins* with the subject in the middle distance of a broad vista. Kubrick has opted strongly for context as subject, possibly to create a tension between the heavenly serenity of the places and the intrigue-cum-butchery they contain, or possibly in the dubious belief that this perspective works against Romantic subjectivity and toward classical perspective. (But then why does he use so much Schubert on his sound-track?)

Even this method might have had some limited result if Kubrick showed any sense of rhythmic force—in effect, some awareness of the viewer's presence. Mile after mile of countryside rolls before us, scene after scene is played with a lengthy pause after almost every line. (I can hardly remember a cue that was promptly "picked up.") Scene after scene is written as extendedly as possible. (p. 22)

Sometimes we are told, and sometimes by Kubrick himself, that to dissent from the mode of his recent work is to show a "literary" bias, to lack response to cinema as such. My view is precisely the opposite. All this museum-imitation of 18th-century painters, all this adoration of the sheerly photographic seems to me destructive of the vitality and uniqueness of the *whole* film art, a kind of esthetic echolalia in the middle of a vast new linguistic possibility. It is all facile, glib, reductive, hobbling film's addition to our artistic means of dealing with experience. Beautiful pictures are not film style. . . . Kubrick's latter-day work is solipsist and smug, isolated and sterile. For me *Barry Lyndon* is an anti-film, a gorgeous, stultified bore. (p. 23)

Stanley Kauffmann, "Films: 'Barry Lyndon'" (reprinted by permission of Brandt & Brandt Literary Agents, Inc.; copyright © 1976 by Stanley Kauffmann), in The New Republic, *Vol. 174, Nos. 1 & 2, January 3 & 10, 1976, pp. 22-3.*

HAROLD ROSENBERG

The movies could make their maximum contribution to culture by following the lead of Stanley Kubrick's unread literature. (p. 1)

But Kubrick's "Barry" is a lot more than a substitute for an all-but-forgotten tale. The movie also translates the printed page into art for the eye and the ear by coordinatings, music and landscaping of the period. The adventures of Barry, by this time commonplace and threadbare, are delivered in a faultless esthetic package. . . . The laggard unfolding of the plot permits one to lose oneself in countrysides that imitate paintings, in classically composed and toned interiors, in the placement and lighting of the figures. Kubrick's salvage job turns out to be a vessel filled with brand new 18th-century treasures. I could have watched

"Barry Lyndon" for another two hours without the slightest interest in what was happening to its hero.... (p. 15)

Harold Rosenberg, "Notes on Seeing 'Barry Lyndon'," in The New York Times, *Section 2 (© 1976 by The New York Times Company; reprinted by permission), February 29, 1976, pp. 1, 15.*

HANS FELDMANN

In *Barry Lyndon,* Kubrick is making a significant statement about *his* age. In fact, along with *2001* and *A Clockwork Orange, Barry Lyndon* completes a trilogy on the moral and psychological nature of Western man and on the destiny of his civilization. *2001* itself is perhaps an emotionally and psychologically necessary response on Kubrick's part to the nihilism of *Dr. Strangelove.* The basic argument of the "Space Odyssey" is that mankind will survive the impending collapse of Western civilization. The film ends with an affirmation of life, an affirmation of the adventurous human spirit. Kubrick's affirmation, it is true, takes place outside of his cultural tradition, and the basic philosophical assumptions of the movie reject the Hebraic-Christian ideology that has functioned as the cohesive center of Western civilization for the past 2000 years. But if Kubrick rejects the Christian idea of God, he nevertheless believes a civilization can develop only if it is rooted in *an* idea of God.... The "Space Odyssey" predicts man's imminent effort to re-establish contact with that divine intelligence....

His view of man is clearly Freudian: the primal facet of the human personality is the id, the completely self-oriented structure that demands immediate gratification of its instinctual urges for food, shelter, and the propagation of itself. It is not moral or intellectual or sensitive to the needs or feelings of others. It simply is. Kubrick's fascination with this aspect of human personality can be traced from the prehuman creatures that achieve the miracle of conceptual thought at the beginning of *2001,* through the character of Alex in *A Clockwork Orange,* to the sublimated savages who inhabit the fashionable courts of Europe in *Barry Lyndon.*

Kubrick's trilogy is a disturbing study of a decadent civilization, decadent because the life-forms it has established for man to achieve the expression of his essential self are founded upon a false conception of the nature of man. Yet for all the bleakness that the critics have argued informs Kubrick's view of man, for all his negativism and pessimism, Kubrick is nevertheless struggling to strike an affirming note. Rebirth, renewal, the regeneration of the adventurous human spirit is the major dramatic point of *2001.* The civilization that begins when the prehuman creature, sitting before the skeleton of an animal, conceptualizes the thought that he can use an element in his environment as an extension of his will to gain dominion over his environment inevitably culminates with the astronauts voyaging through space on a mission to contact the suprahuman intelligence responsible for the monolith that has been uncovered on the moon. (pp. 12-13)

Conceptual thought, first used for the immediate gratification of the instinctual need for food, has ultimately delivered mankind to the threshold of some cataclysmic discovery about itself and about the universe which is its home. (p. 14)

The assumption upon which the argument of *2001* is based is that Western civilization is moribund, that its cultural forms and social institutions no longer provide man with the significant order that makes life meaningful experience. In his next two movies, Kubrick's principal interest is to study the relationship between the individual man and the cultural forms through which that individual must achieve the expression of himself. At the heart of *A Clockwork Orange* and *Barry Lyndon* is the great philosophical question that is at the heart of all great art: What is man, and what must he *do* with his life? ... Kubrick continues to sound the life-affirming note with which he concluded *2001* in both *A Clockwork Orange* and *Barry Lyndon.* (p. 15)

[Anthony Burgess] has lamented that Kubrick failed to understand the point of his novel. The fact is that Burgess, as well as the many movie critics who have appreciated the novel, has failed to understand the point of Kubrick's movie, which is grounded in a Freudian view of the dynamics of civilization.... Kubrick's discontents with civilization's forms are not only because they frustrate the instinctual man, but also because they deny that the instinctual self is intrinsic to man's nature. Kubrick insists upon this point throughout *A Clockwork Orange* by juxtaposing the brutal enactment of instinctual urges with sublimated expressions of those urges. The popular song "Singin' in the Rain," for example, is a sentimental, sublimated expression of the same urge that is compelling Alex to the act he commits while singing it. (pp. 15-16)

That the forms and institutions of Western civilization deny the Alex in every man, and therefore can only deform the social man as he seeks to express his essential self through them, is the central theme of *Barry Lyndon.* Redmond Barry's failure to achieve selfhood in the terms prescribed by his society is his tragedy, and by extension the tragedy of Western man. Eighteenth-century Europe, the world in which Barry must achieve self-hood, represents for Kubrick, as it had at the end of *2001,* Western civilization at its most formal stage of development. Conformity to the innumerable codes of ritualized social conduct was essential for any man wishing to establish his value as a man. Barry, in his effort to become a "gentleman," accepts the validity of all the institutions of his day. Only once does he fail to act according to form, and that once destroys all his efforts to achieve his peerage, the highest life-form then available to man. (p. 17)

The charge that Kubrick's later movies are devoid of meaning is ... nonsensical. The charge that he is ponderous and dull is comprehensible only if his ideas are ponderous and dull. The evidence of his trilogy on Western civilization supports the claim that he is one of America's top film directors. He is more than that. Stanley Kubrick is a critic of his age, one of its interpreters and one of its artists. (p. 19)

Hans Feldmann, "Kubrick and His Discontents," in Film Quarterly *(copyright 1976 by The Regents of the University of California; reprinted by permission of the University of California Press), Vol. XXX, No. 1, Fall, 1976, pp. 12-19.*

GENE YOUNGBLOOD

I think *Barry Lyndon* is the most intelligent, most amazing, most radical movie Stanley Kubrick has made—which is to say it's among the great achievements of contemporary cinema. I think the "failure" of this film is a failure of the collective imagination and I'm ashamed at the incomprehension and hostility with which our illustrious critics and noble citizens have dismissed it. Ashamed but not surprised. For at the heart of *Barry Lyndon* there's a silence that challenges the strength of the imagination, and imaginative courage is these days in exile. . . .

I can think of few films of such intrinsic existential power, sans ideology and melodrama. This is pure cinema at full force, miraculous to behold. It may be the most "beautiful" movie ever made, but the beauty is in its logic as much as its images—which are so colored and distinguished as to defy description. This is beauty carried to ecstatic extremes, and it makes the petty rituals of mere mortals seem as absurd as they are. The fops and fools in this movie play out their follies against an earth so resplendent, in rooms so overarching and vaulted, that anything they do becomes ludicrous, utterly insignificant. That, of course, is the "subject" of the film, if it has one at all. Kubrick doesn't think much of the human race but he does appreciate the quality of light; and it's the light dancing in the chambered air that this movie is really about. . . .

Never has color, light, and motion been employed more brilliantly in a narrative film to signify nothing, only to astonish, amaze, entrance. And that's what *Barry Lyndon* is for me: a trance film, a trip film, a luminous machine for meditation. It is irresistibly hypnotic and dreamy, transcendent in the classic sense of the word. This is a film that respects the sovereignty of the observer. Its vast silence is a gift, a place for the imagination to do its work.

Of course the independent experimental cinema has for decades been concerned with precisely these issues. In this sense *Barry Lyndon* is related more closely to Michael Snow's *Wavelength* or to Brakhage's *Text of Light* than it is to, say, *Tom Jones*. . . .

The similarities between *Karl May* and *Barry Lyndon* are uncanny. Both are three hours long, both examine in tedious detail the lives of characters who represent the descent of myth into popular form, both are transcendentally beautiful, both invite the observer to enter and make them complete.

Gene Youngblood, "Flamingo Hours: Luminous Machines," in Take One *(copyright © 1977 by Unicorn Publishing Corp.), Vol. 5, No. 6, January, 1977, p. 27.*

ALAN SPIEGEL

The events in *Barry Lyndon,* while dramatic in themselves, are not presented in the form of a drama, but rather in the form of a spectacle for the senses. A beguilement of eye and ear precedes the customary seizure of the emotions. As in so much of Kubrick's best work—indeed, it is perhaps his defining quality—the images that you see exist not simply as vehicles for a story, but as vibrant indicators of a film-maker's commitment to his medium. . . .

While all of this is true to some degree of each one of this director's films, it is true to the greatest degree of his present film: *Barry Lyndon* is Kubrick's most extravagantly beautiful creation. Opulent and solemn, jewel-like and lucid, profuse and lordly, the beauty of the film is not at all unlike the beauty of Handel's music (of which we hear the majestic and sweeping Sarabande in various guises and emotional contexts throughout the film). (p. 197)

[The] deliberation of the effort is matched and finally surpassed by the originality of the achievement. The source of this originality is the singularity of the film's beauty—to come back to this—the special way this beauty makes its meaning to eye and ear. By this I mean precisely the *strangeness* of the way things are seen and heard, and for this reason, the imperviousness of the film's beauty to a comfortable assimilation by the viewer. (p. 198)

Barry Lyndon isn't "a collection of paintings," but the invention of an autonomic culture. And what might otherwise have appeared as the woolgatherings of an archivist has been transmitted by a film-maker into a tribute to the farraginous nature of his medium.

Each image seals off direct access to its content by converting content into an object of formal admiration; the formalism, that is, insures the image as both visual enticement and proof against further intimacy. The beauty of the film is indeed strange as the formalism of the image sequestrates not only its dramatic, but also its historical utility. (p. 199)

What is true of history is equally true of the narrative that Kubrick has extracted from Thackeray's novel, *The Luck of Barry Lyndon:* neither history nor novel serves the film as its subject; rather, both provide materials out of which a subject is to be shaped. . . . Thackeray has made of these events a picaresque for cynics, a social satire which charts the rise and fall of a jackanapes. Kubrick, by contrast, has made not a satire, but a virtually abstract contemplation of human suffering and loss: the story of a man who cannot get what he wants or keep what he gets as the function of a formalist construction. The film's true subjects then become mortality and art, grief and cinematographics, human ruin "ingested" by the plenitude of an aural-visual ordering of film. Actually these motifs generalize upon a current of imagery that has flowed through all of Kubrick's work, and the dialectics of his present film recall sequences and icons from the past: for example, a great baroque chateau that harbors the death-dealing decisions of the French high command (in *Paths of Glory*), or a wizened and dying astronaut smashing a dish in a Louis XVI drawing room (in *2001*), or perhaps most memorably, a love-sick James Mason pumping bullet holes into a Gainsboroughlike portrait of a lady (in *Lolita*). But in *Barry Lyndon,* the fusion of art and human suffering is more than a matter of isolated images: it has become a structural concept that both determines and permeates the emotional ambience of an entire film. . . . (pp. 199-200)

The director has thoroughly neutralized his hero's identity to create neither a rogue nor an innocent, but a human shape that approaches the conditions of an artifact. Who Barry is, what he wants, and what we are to make of him, are issues of psychology and morality that resolve and finally conciliate themselves into how and where Barry stands in film time and film space; his career and character development translate into exteriorized patterns of posture, gesture, choreography within a frame, and position within a tableau. (p. 202)

Everywhere the methodology of the film attempts to transform a continuous action into a finished design, something happening into something remembered, a subject enacted into an object contemplated. To effect this transformation, the film makes special use of two devices—the camera and a narrator. Thackeray immerses the reader in the events of his novel by allowing Barry to tell his own story. Kubrick removes the viewer from the events of his film by rarely allowing the commentary of his anonymous narrator to synchronize precisely with any given action. The voice of the narrator, genial, ironic, and remote, is the voice of a collective memory, a public recollection of private passions. . . . The primary function of the commentary . . . qualifies, challenges, and "mutes" the present tense condition of the visualized action; finally determines the status of the action as the ineffable, transient, and sometimes irregular inflection of lives already packaged by memory. (pp. 202-03)

If the temporal provenance of the action is the present and that of the narrator is the past and the future (i.e., the historical overview), the stance of the camera itself—the third active presence in this multiplex work—seeks to elude the temporal continuum altogether, and reside in the condition of formal meditation, of timeless repose as a maker of self-reflexive images. The provenance of the camera is the provenance of art, and indeed at certain times, this provenance is threatened: during the boxing match, the fight with Bullingdon, and Lady Lyndon's attempted suicide, as if "overcome by grief" or "shattered by violence," the camera capitulates to the human turmoil, enacts its subject, shifts to hand-held position, and dramatizes a dizzy, rushing space. But once the moment is past, the camera quickly "composes" itself and proceeds, as before, to propitiate and formalize the action in a regular succession of elegant, even-keeled compositions. (p. 203)

Characters and situations are taken away from us even in the midst of their happening; the camera withdraws from that to which we would cleave close—and in this respect, our sorrow is collateral to Barry's: we too can never get what we want or keep what we get, and the motion of the camera is the measure of our bereavement. (p. 204)

Alan Spiegel, "Kubrick's 'Barry Lyndon'," in Salmagundi *(copyright © 1977 by Skidmore College), Nos. 38-39, Summer-Fall, 1977, pp. 194-208.*

PAULINE KAEL

[In Kubrick's "The Shining," though] we may admire the effects, we're never drawn in by them, mesmerized. When we see a flash of bloody cadavers or observe a torrent of blood pouring from an elevator, we're not frightened, because Kubrick's absorption in film technology distances us. Each shot seems rigorously calculated, meticulous, and he keeps the scenes going for so long that any suspense dissipates. Kubrick's involvement in film technology led to the awesomely impressive effects of "2001," and to the tableau style of "Barry Lyndon," which some people found hypnotic, but it works against him here. (p. 130)

It took nerve, or maybe something more like hubris, for Kubrick to go against all convention and shoot most of this gothic in broad daylight. . . . But the conventions of gothics are fun. Who wants to see evil in daylight, through a wide-angle lens? We go to "The Shining" hoping for nasty scare effects and for an appeal to our giddiest nighttime fears—vaporous figures, shadowy places. What we get doesn't tease the imagination. Visually, the movie often feels like a cheat, because most of the horror images are not integrated into the travelling shots; the horrors involved in the hotel's bloody past usually appear in inserts that flash on like the pictures in a slide show. . . . Clearly, Stanley Kubrick isn't primarily interested in the horror film as scary fun or for the mysterious beauty that directors such as Dreyer and Murnau have brought to it. Kubrick is a virtuoso technician, and that is part of the excitement that is generated by a new Kubrick film. But he isn't just a virtuoso technician; he's also, God help us, a deadly-serious metaphysician. (pp. 130, 132)

Kubrick seems to be saying that rage, uncontrollable violence, and ghosts spawn each other—that they are really the same thing. He's using Stephen King's hokum to make a metaphysical statement about immortality. The Torrances are his archetypes; they are the sources and victims of monsters that live on.

Kubrick mystifies us deliberately, much as Antonioni did in "The Passenger," though for different purposes. The conversations between Jack and his demons are paced like the exposition in drawing-room melodramas of fifty years ago; you could drop stones into a river and watch the ripples between words. . . . "The Shining" is also full of deliberate time dislocations. . . . The film is punctuated with titles: suddenly there will be a black frame with "Tuesday" on it, or "3 o'clock," or "Saturday;" after the first ones, the titles all refer to time, but in an almost arbitrary way. Jack says that he loves the hotel and wishes "we could stay here forever, ever, ever." And at the very end there's a heavy hint of reincarnation and the suggestion that Jack *has* been there forever, ever, ever. I hate to say it, but I think the central character of this movie is time itself, or, rather, timelessness. (pp. 139, 142)

But we don't know how to read Kubrick's signals; it may be that he simply doesn't know us well enough anymore to manipulate us successfully. Again and again, the movie leads us to expect something—almost promises it—and then disappoints us. Why give us a tour of the vast hotel kitchen, with an inventory of the contents of the meat locker, when nothing much takes place there? (p. 142)

"The Shining" seems to be about the quest for immortality—the immortality of evil. Men are psychic murderers: they want to be free and creative, and can only take out their frustrations on their terrified wives and children. . . . Apparently, [Jack] lives forever, only to attack his family endlessly. It's what Kubrick said in "2001": Mankind began with the weapon and just went on from there. . . . The bone that was high in the air has turned into Jack's axe, held aloft, and Jack, crouched over, making wild, inarticulate sounds as he staggers in the maze, has become the ape.

What's increasingly missing from Kubrick's work is the spontaneity, the instinct, the lightness that would make us respond intuitively. We're starved for pleasure at this movie; when we finally get a couple of exterior nighttime shots with theatrical lighting, we're pathetically grateful. (pp. 144, 147)

Pauline Kael, "The Current Cinema: Devolution," in The New Yorker *(© 1980 by The New Yorker Magazine, Inc.), Vol. LVI, No. 16, June 9, 1980, pp. 130-47.*

Akira Kurosawa

1910-

(Also Kurasawa) Japanese director and scriptwriter.

Until 1951 when Kurosawa's *Rashomon* won the Grand Prix at the Venice Film Festival, virtually no Japanese films were seen in the United States. The popularity of Kurosawa's film opened the way for Japanese masters like Yasujiro Ozu and Kenji Mizoguchi.

Kurosawa began as a painter, studying at the Tokyo Academy of Fine Arts. It was by chance that he became a director. Answering a newspaper advertisement, he was hired by Toho Studios. Kurosawa worked under Kajiro Yamamoto, who taught him not only directing but scriptwriting. Fully expecting to leave the industry and go back to painting, Kurosawa was surprised to find that he loved directing.

Kurosawa has professed a taste for Western art which is evident in his films. While this has made him readily popular in the West, he has been criticized in Japan for the occidental flavor of his films. Still, he has managed to bridge the gap between the oriental and occidental tastes and address himself to subjects that are universal: the futility of a selfish life (*Ikiru* and *Red Beard*), the subjective quality of truth (*Rashomon*), the power and beauty of love (*One Wonderful Sunday* and *No Regrets for Our Youth*). Yet each of his films is a multifaceted gem which defies classification by any one theme.

Kurosawa has directed many chambara (or sword-fight) films which are immensely popular. Often considered the best of these is *The Seven Samurai*. This film also boasts a fine performance by Tashiro Mifune. Mifune and Kurosawa have done some of their best work together and have become associated in the minds of many critics and film buffs.

Although some critics find Kurosawa's films overly emotional or stilted, it is to his credit that he has established a name for himself in countries whose philosophies and life-styles differ so much from his own. Audie Bock has written in her *Japanese Film Directors:* "If Kurosawa can begin making films in Japan that speak to the underlying spiritual needs of an overeducated, overfed nation—and he is one of the very few who have the potential for spiritual and intellectual leadership—not only will his own work be revitalized, but its international currency will be, if anything, reinforced."

JESSE ZUNSER

Rashomon is a symphony of sight, sound, light, and shadow, in celluloid. It is an extraordinary motion picture combination: a rarely beautiful film that forms a memorable visual setting for an absorbing drama—as brilliant in its multifaceted plot as a cut gem, as fascinating in the variety of its engrossing complexities as a chess problem, and as penetrating in its study of theoretical logic, human behavior, and playwright-plotting as any picture within recall. (p. 37)

Which story tells the truth—or even part of the truth—is left to the audience. The priest, who listens in silence to the astonishing tale on the steps of a towering, dilapidated gateway leading to the ancient capital of Kyoto, sits in a driving rain, seeking for the secret of what truly goes on in men's hearts. The priest believes that Truth—as the ultimate good that is in all men—will out. For, truly, men are, at heart, not evil; since evil is only a part—but not the whole part—of man's nature. The relating of this dramatic epic is exquisitely sensitive, cast in impressive cadences. Indeed the film itself is innately poetic, swinging in singing rhythms of mood, movement, music, and speech—merging time, space, and the eternal verities into graceful, measured, ineffably lovely photographic images. (p. 38)

Jesse Zunser, "Reviews: 'Rashomon'," in Cue *(copyright © Cue Publications, Inc., 1951; reprinted by permission of News Group Publications, Inc.), December 29, 1951 (and reprinted in* Focus on "Rashomon," *edited by Donald Richie, Prentice-Hall, Inc., 1972, pp. 37-8).*

MANNY FARBER

[*Rashomon* is a] torpid, stylish Japanese study in human frailty, like nothing so much as a tiny aquarium in which a few fish and a lot of plants have delicately been tinkered with by someone raised in Western art-cinema theaters and art galleries. Five characters, two unfrequented real-life sets—a ruined temple and a forest—and a script which is probably the first to describe a highly contrived sword-fight-and-seduction through the biased eyes of four different people. The villain is a conceited, slothful, bug-ridden bandit . . .—a type now familiar in Hollywood adventure-comedies about Mexico—who has a hard time pulling himself away from a good nap to ravish the wife of a traveling samurai. Makes its play for posterity with such carefully engineered actions as one in which the dozing barbarian scratches his crotch while the sword across his knees somehow rises (Maya Deren-fashion) as though it had just had a big meal of sex hormones. *Rashomon* is supposed to get down to the bedrock of such emotions as lust, fear, and selfishness, but actually it is a smooth and somewhat empty film whose most tiresome aspect is the slow, complacent, Louvre-conscious, waiting-for-prizes attitude of everyone who worked on it.

Manny Farber, "Reviews: 'Rashomon'," in The Nation *(copyright 1952 The Nation Associates, Inc.), Vol. 174, No. 3, January 19, 1952 (and reprinted in* Focus on "Rashomon," *edited by Donald Richie, Prentice-Hall, Inc., 1972, p. 47).*

TONY RICHARDSON

In *The Seven Samurai* . . . , and in the light it throws back on *Rashomon,* Kurosawa's method and personality emerge clearly. He is, above everything else, an exact psychological observer, a keen analyst of behaviour—in a fundamentally detached way. His handling of the young lovers is typical of this. He notes and traces with precision and truth their first, half-terrified awareness of each other sexually, the growth of mutual attraction, the boy's *gauche* admiration, the girl's aching and almost frantic abandonment; what he fails to do is to convey any feeling for, or identification with, the individuals themselves. He strives for this, he uses other images to heighten their scenes—the flower-covered hillside, the sun filtering through the tops of trees (an echo of its more successful use as an orgasm metaphor in *Rashomon*), the dappled light swarming like insects over them as they lie together in a bamboo hut—but somehow these remain perfunctory, a little cold, lacking in real poetry.

In this it is not unrewarding to compare Kurosawa with [John] Ford—by whom, report has it, he claims to have been influenced. There are many superficial resemblances —the reliance on traditional values, the use of folk ceremonies and rituals, the comic horseplay—to Ford in particular and to the Western in general. The fast, vivid handling of the action sequences, the staccato cutting, the variety of angles, the shooting up through horses rearing in the mud, are all reminiscent of recent films in this genre. But the difference is more revealing. The funeral of the first samurai, killed in a preliminary skirmish, is exactly the sort of scene to which Ford responds, with all his reverence and honour for times past and the community of beliefs and feelings which they embodied. Kurosawa uses the scene in two ways, first as a further observation of the character of the "crazy samurai"—who, in a defiant attempt to satisfy his own feelings of frustration and impotence, raises the flag the dead man had sewn—and secondly, as an effective incident for heightening the narrative tension: the bandits launch their first onslaught during the funeral. . . .

Of course, to say Kurosawa is not Ford is critically meaningless; the comparison has value only in so far as it is a way of gauging the film's intentions, and its realisation of them. What made *Rashomon* so unique and impressive was that everything, the subject, the formal structure, the playing, even perhaps the period, allowed for this exterior approach to behaviour. In *The Seven Samurai* Kurosawa is striving for something different, a re-creation, a bringing to life of the past and the people whose story he is telling. Here, for all the surface conviction of period, the perceptive observation, the raging vitality and the magnificent visual style, the film doesn't quite succeed. All the elements are there except the depth and the generosity of life. One feels that each incident is too carefully worked into the texture as a whole. (p. 195)

These ultimate reservations should not, however, prevent us from recognising the film's astonishing qualities. Incident after incident is created with biting precision. . . . Kurosawa is a virtuoso exponent of every technique of suspense, surprise, excitement, and in this he gives nothing to his Western masters. Only in his handling of the series of battles is there a hint of monotony. He knows exactly when to hold a silence; how to punch home an extraordinary fact with maximum effect; and his use of the camera is devastating. . . . Visually the film makes a tremendous impression. Kurosawa can combine formal grace with dramatic accuracy, and many scenes create a startling pictorial impact. (pp. 195-96)

Tony Richardson, "Film Reviews: 'The Seven Samurai'," in Sight and Sound *(copyright © 1955 by The British Film Institute), Vol. 24, No. 4, Spring, 1955, pp. 195-96.*

JAY LEYDA

The real threat [to the postwar Japanese film] was the suffocation of new or rebellious artistic tendencies . . . by the tight, successful patterns of the pre-war "sword films," a form precisely as unbending and as satisfying as our "western." This danger was heightened in recent years by an almost uncritical acceptance of any films made on this pattern exported to America and Europe. This is partly explained by the superficial resemblance of these sword films to the richness and movement of the great Japanese theatre forms; we were grateful for any tokens of that beauty. . . .

With such blocks it is clear that the greatest blessing to the postwar Japanese film is the imagination and courage of Akira Kurosawa. (p. 3)

[Kurosawa looks] at the raw material of the sword film with the same humanity and immediacy that he brought to his modern subjects. He says that he had dreamed of this since the beginning of his film career and now that he had his opportunity, he took a whole careful year of filming to realize his dream. The result, *The Magnificent Seven,* is as easily distinguished from the "normal" sword-swinging theatricalities as is *Stagecoach* from the usual run-of-the-ranch affairs. In the process of freshening and humanizing the sword film, Kurosawa performed another needed miracle: he has made this material more exciting, more dynamic, more dramatic than the patterns had ever permitted or hinted.

From the first seconds of *The Magnificent Seven*—the drums, the horses' hoofs, the threatening voices—the issues of the film are stated with more directness than we are accustomed to. (p. 4)

The film has a beauty all its own, quite dissimilar to Kurosawa's previous work as well as to other Japanese films; it is the beauty of actuality, of tangibility, of the thought behind the faces you see, and of the reasons behind the motions of the bodies. It takes more skill to produce such individual beauty than to astonish us with what we are usually shown as "photographic beauty". . . . The film reminds its audience, Japanese and American, that the term "samurai" originally meant "those who serve."

In breaking with the traditional Japanese film and its attitude to violence, Kurosawa strikes more deeply—at Shintoism, the hero-worship out of which the glorified sword film developed and froze. Kurosawa has saturated his film with a philosophy antagonistic to Shinto: Zen-Buddhism, a religious practice that abhors the hero-leader, and dedicates every act, even the edge of every sword, and the tip of every arrow, to the self-effacing mission of good. The distinction between the heroes of the film and its villains is shown in the mentality behind each lunge and stroke. . . . Even the style of the film reflects this peculiarly Japanese esthetic: its art conceals itself in a manner that increases its power. This may be the nearest cinema has come to "the artless art," the Zen ideal that has permeated the best Japanese arts of the past. (pp. 4-5)

This becomes a film of the behavior and heroism of men and women, any time, anywhere, in crises. . . . These people change and grow as you watch them; you even feel an eye-witness of social change. The samurai-stratum is no longer a static unit; individualities within it come to light, with varying motives and with varying means of attaining their aims. Though always stated with clarity and force (how clearly the strategy and fighting are shown!), there is nothing in the film that can be called simple. The conflicts among the allied peasants and samurai make a dramatic element as forceful as the conflict between allies and bandits, and has the effect of making the alliance firmer. In seeming contradiction of the film's universality, it offers more understanding of Japanese life and thought than has any other work to come to us from that extraordinary country. (p. 5)

Jay Leyda, "Modesty and Pretension in Two New Films," in Film Culture *(copyright 1956 by* Film Culture*), Vol. 2, No. 4, 1956, pp. 3-7.**

CHARLES FOX

It is hard for an Occidental to look at *Throne of Blood,* the Japanese version of *Macbeth,* with complete impartiality. . . .

Finding a familiar story within a new context often renders its motives curiously naked. Ambition, treachery, greed—in *Throne of Blood* these become freed of subtlety, unwrapped from the poetry that gave them orientation. And just as poetry, philosophy, even humour, are lost, so tragedy slides into melodrama. The tersest, the most pungent and violent of all Shakespeare's tragedies, *Macbeth* is made credible by its poetry; raw savagery rarely lifts *Throne of Blood* above hysteria. Yet if the film lacks the inevitability of tragedy, at least events follow their own grim logic. (p. 22)

In an article in *The Times* . . . , Kurosawa is quoted as saying that his aim is "to give people strength to live and to face life; to help them live more powerfully and happily." Only a fool would quarrel with such unexceptionable sentiments. Kurosawa has a moralist's approach, the only approach worthy of a serious artist. Yet in *Throne of Blood*—to a Western eye, at any rate—it is the absence of such a background that makes the drama meaningless. Shakespeare's play worked because its poetry evoked a world outside the wings of the theatre, a world whose values gave this pattern of events its significance. At this level *Throne of Blood* fails, a victim, oddly enough, of its own violence. (p. 23)

Charles Fox, "Reviews: 'Throne of Blood'," in Film *(reprinted by permission of British Federation of Film Societies), No. 15, January-February, 1958, pp. 22-3.*

JOSEPH L. ANDERSON and DONALD RICHIE

[In 1952 Kurosawa] made one of his finest films, *Living* (Ikiru)—known as *Doomed* in America—which the *Quarterly of Film, Radio, and Television* has called "one of the greatest films of our time." In it Kurosawa explored almost every potentiality of the film medium in illustrating his relatively simple story. . . . In this film Kurosawa's humanism was at its height. This discursive film is long and varied; it winds and unwinds; it shifts from mood to mood, from present to past, from silence to a deafening roar—and all in the most unabashed and absorbing fashion. Its greatest success may be in its revitalization of film technique. It, together with Kinoshita's *A Japanese Tragedy* (Nihon no Higeki) and *Carmen's Pure Love* (Karumen Junjosu), shows that when it wants to, Japanese film technique can be among the most dynamic in the world. The film's fault is perhaps that Kurosawa's genius flows unchecked and that sometimes he carries things too far. (pp. 187-88)

Kurosawa's 1950 film, the now world-famous *Rashomon,* which, though classified as a period-film since it is set in the early Heian period, is in actuality just about as far away from the standard Japanese period-film as one can get. It was a highly adventurous undertaking, extremely advanced for its audience, and quite experimental in its technique. Those in the West who instantly concluded that all Japanese films were "like *Rashomon*" were, as time richly proved, completely mistaken. (p. 223)

In [*Seven Samurai*], the director made many technical experiments, one of the most original being his use of super-powered telephoto lenses to get a feeling of intimacy. These lenses cause things on a line to and from the camera to "pile up," and this effect causes them to seem much closer than they really are. The intimacy was heightened by a frequent dependence on close-ups, often recalling their use in Carl Dreyer's *Jeanne d'Arc.* Kurosawa also used deep focus, low-key photography and slow motion to accent the death and killing scenes. Throughout, editing was used with a vigor that one thought had died out with the silent Soviet films. (p. 272)

In [*The Lower Depths*] Kurosawa tried a new production method. The cast and crew, with lights, full costume, make-up, and camera positions, rehearsed for forty days before starting the actual shooting. Another innovation was that there were no leading characters, the film being entirely a series of vignettes. One of the most important results was an ensemble effect rare on the screen, an acting unit, one part very carefully balanced against the other. Another result was that the film had a real style, a consistent set of rules governing characters, camera movement, formal composition, and editing. These rules all unified the film, making it a bit more consistent than life itself, and gave that higher realism which we usually call art. (p. 273)

In contrast to the artless simplicity of the average Japanese picture, Kurosawa's films are heavily calculated and enormously artful. His interest in technique may call occasional attention to itself, as in the huge close-ups of *Seven Samurai* or the perfectly balanced composition of set-ups in *The Lower Depths,* but more often than not the mechanics and techniques of cinema are used entirely for psychological effect. (p. 377)

While shooting, Kurosawa . . . thinks relatively little about continuity. He relies much more on editing to give continuity to his films. Also, rather like Kinoshita, he is sometimes apt to change his ideas on a film just before shooting it. (p. 378)

Ever since *Seven Samurai,* [Kurosawa] has favored the multi-camera technique, using it for even the most intimate scenes, which considerably decreases some editing problems, though creating others. The director believes that using several cameras is useful in creating atmosphere and tone, "the catching of the actors when they are at their peak [which] usually only occurs once. If you have to do the same scene for different set-ups you lose naturalness and the basic tone changes from shot to shot due to the difference of time and circumstance." (p. 379)

Yet, in the best of Kurosawa's films, [the] mastery of film style has but one purpose: it is meant to tell a story, and to tell it in the most striking manner possible. The director is frankly interested only in the psychological power carried by his images. . . .

He is concerned with the human lot above all else and he particularly insists upon the equality of all human emotion. All of his films share this basic assumption. . . .

This theme is essentially un-Japanese and it certainly runs completely contrary to the prevailing philosophy of the Japanese film. Perhaps it is for this reason that the films of Akira Kurosawa have taken so experimental and so original a form: the thought behind them, and the personality of the director, are so completely original that a new form had to be created to hold them. (p. 380)

Joseph L. Anderson and Donald Richie, in their The Japanese Film: Art and Industry *(copyright in Japan 1959 by Charles E. Tuttle Co.; reprinted by permission of Charles E. Tuttle Co., Inc., Tokyo, Japan), Tuttle, 1959, 456 p.*

VERNON YOUNG

[*The Hidden Fortress* has an] air of wild cogent invention, of visual shock and of abrupt outrage. Grandiose, raw, implausible (yet conventional in a sense), [the film] recapitulates and enlarges, in more than "aspect-ratio" terms, virtually every feature of the so-called entertainment film, as we know it, from the Fairbanks genre to *Treasure of the Sierra Madre,* while incorporating stylistic vestiges of the older Soviet masters and from a host of *samurai*-films. . . . Kurasawa re-affirms his already manifest command of the witness point and of its collaborative art, editing. . . . (p. 270)

Kurasawa's modes of action are seemingly inexhaustible, his bravura editing tireless. . . . Better than anyone now working in film, perhaps, he knows when to *hold* his camera position and exploit wide-screen, not simply as a theater tableau but as a magnitude wherein movement is never absent and space is viable. . . . Throughout the action, mainly unified by the trek of four characters bearing gold concealed in bundles of firewood, Kurasawa's sense of the exact faltering gasp and shift of weight, the side-steps of momentum and recovery, is infallible. Which makes more astonishing the information that he once envied [Shiro] Toyoda for that director's *physiological* emphasis. All the evidence we have defines Kurasawa as perhaps the *most physical* director in the history of the movies!

This, alone, may be thought of as a drawback if we're expecting another multi-level masterpiece of the *Rashomon* order. In *Seven Samurai (The Magnificent Seven),* which I don't see as the outstanding achievement critical opinion would make it, the exclusively kinetic emphasis vitiated, or just replaced, an implied interior drama (relating to the hero) never conveyed. However, I'm prepared to acknowledge that I've overstated the force of such an implication—in this case. But not in *Ikiru,* where Kurasawa's rage for excess was a seriously distracting indulgence. (pp. 271-72)

As a morality of the proto-human utilized by a disciplined elite, the story [of *The Hidden Fortress*] is no doubt open to complaint from those who consider themselves too sophisticated for delight in such fables. I wonder if dissenters on these grounds are willing to ask themselves honestly if the latest capers of Elia Kazan, John Ford or Stanley Kramer are any more worldly or if, to take hats-in-the-air examples, *A Place in the Sun* or *Look Back in Anger* say anything more pregnant about man's management of his destiny? . . . *The Hidden Fortress* is definitive of its kind and not to be identified with the latest western or ben-hurern: it honors the flow of events and quietly predicates an ethic. (p. 272)

Kurasawa, no matter what he claims about wanting to be honored for making films of *contemporary* Japan, is inevitably attracted by the feudal setting, wherein social man was more broadly, essentially, ethnically differentiated. And it is just this regressive, if you like, purity of vision which sustains the dramatic tensions of his comedy. When the imperious Princess cries or the stoical Rokurota smiles or the bondsmen cooperate reasonably, an inhibition of impulses has been temporarily released, and the surprise engendered is a basic element—dramatic relief. (p. 274)

The impassive samurai or loyal retainer unmoved by the sex appeal of the bare-legged (here) Princess he is defending, is a staple of the Japanese period-film. As such, Kurasawa makes no attempt to disguise it. He intensifies it. At one juncture all hope for the fugitive seems lost, in which eventuality death before dishonor, for the Princess above all, is an imperative. Before preparing a final desperate strategy, Rokurota offers her the weapon with which she may have to destroy herself—in a resolute straight-arm gesture. As he does so, their eyes meet and his expression, in a single closeup, is as nakedly complete as any half-dozen reaction shots could ever be: a wordless suffusion of his face with the emotions he has until then suppressed, in which the whole meaning and mettle of the man is made explicit. The human soul has entered the landscape where before there was a type, less human than zoological. . . . [By] such touches—in this instance a momentarily piercing recognition of the nobility which crouches in the cage of the heart—Kurasawa restores to man the quality that individualizes him, and reaffirms the actual as a vital ingredient of the unbelievable. (pp. 274-75)

Vernon Young, "'The Hidden Fortress': Kurasawa's Comic Mode," in The Hudson Review *(copyright © 1961 by The Hudson Review, Inc.; reprinted by permission), Vol. XIV, No. 2, Summer, 1961, pp. 270-83.*

AKIRA IWASAKI

The thing which distinguishes Akira Kurosawa from other Japanese directors—I would go so far as to call it his great achievement—is precisely that he is first and foremost a director of ideas. Kurosawa is fond of insisting that every artist has, ultimately, only one theme. In his own case, he says, it is the question of why men cannot live together more happily and with greater good will than they do. Of course, one should be wary of swallowing whole such self-revelations by artists, since the artist is prone to self-delusion and self-misinterpretation in peculiarly complex and involved forms. Nevertheless, Kurosawa's remark can be taken at its face value insofar as it suggests that all his works are born, originally, of an idea. Whereas Japanese film directors in the past have leaned heavily toward naturalism, basing their work on a narrow, personalized experience, Kurosawa's style is intellectual, and his emergence after the war marked the appearance of an utterly unfamiliar element in the Japanese film world.

The fact that his favorite author is Dostoevski is in itself enough to suggest his style. Most of his films have a theme expressible in one line, or even one word: good, evil, happiness, unhappiness, the beauty of love—problems that boil down in essence to the problems of the existence of man, its meaning and its forms. (p. 26)

Kurosawa is a research worker who places man in a test tube, provides certain conditions or applies certain stimuli, then waits to see his reaction. His films are the resulting case studies. For example, he unearths an honest workman who finds himself one Sunday morning with only 35 yen in his pocket, in a great city plagued with the inflation and black marketeering of the immediate postwar years. What joys and what sorrows will the day bring him and his sweetheart? This is the experiment that produced *Subarashiki Nichiyobi* (*One Wonderful Sunday,* 1947). (pp. 26-7)

Even the characters who appear in Kurosawa's films seem to be internalized, to have passed through the filter of his intellect, and in the actors Toshiro Mifune and Takashi Shimura he has found the ideal vehicles for his ideas. (p. 28)

Nor is it only Kurosawa's characters that are intellectually conceived. The settings in themselves seem somehow removed from the ordinary, everyday dimension. The very air is denser, the air pressure greater than in the atmosphere we normally breathe, sounds fall on the ear an octave higher than their usual pitch, and physical movements are speeded up or slowed down abnormally. Without such an atmosphere and such a setting, in fact, his characters would be incapable of acting freely or naturally. His films, simply described, are dramas of violent emotions, their traumatic effect heightened still further by exaggeration, emphasis, and extremes. Kurosawa himself admits to a preference for the harsher aspects of nature—for the glitter of high summer and the asperity of midwinter, for torrential rains and blizzards. They provide his films with their natural backdrop and, of course, with their psychological background as well. They are the reverse of the conventionally "Japanese"—of the equivocal, the understated and the unadorned. He rejects the traditional "boiled-rice-and-green-tea" austerity so beloved of Ozu and Naruse: "I want my films to be like a steak spread with butter and topped with good, rich, broiled eels."

I have described his style as intellectual, a label which he gives to his work himself. Yet, in another aspect, the excellence of his work derives from the acuteness with which he constantly observes, remembers, and records the external world. He keeps an avid eye on the society and men about him, ever ready to summon actuality to amend his ideas for him. (pp. 29-30)

When Kurosawa begins writing a scenario, he has no idea of what the final scene will be; intellectual though his first inspiration may be, he abhors intellectual conclusions. He creates the setting and gives his characters their personalities, but from then on it is the characters themselves who, with unpredictable results, take over the action. A single passing remark is enough to set his heroes and heroines on a completely different course, and he is obliged to follow them wherever they lead. It is this kind of realism in the course of creation that gives a sense of actuality to the non-realistic worlds he creates.

Unfortunately, a work produced in this fashion sometimes ends up at a point that conflicts with the film's original intellectual point of departure. At such times, the original idea is left stranded and without support. At the end of *Rashomon,* the itinerant priest who has listened to the whole story states that, thanks to the woodcutter [who has taken on the responsibility of adopting an abandoned baby], he has regained his temporarily shaken faith in humanity—a conclusion utterly out of keeping with the main theme the film has gone to such trouble to expound, the relativity of truth and the perfidy of man. At the end of *Seven Samurai* . . . , Kambei, the most clever strategist of the band, who has rid the farming village of the wandering samurai who have been preying on it, muses to himself as he rides away: The samurai have passed away like the wind, while the peasants, like the earth itself, go on forever—a patently forced moral that blends ill with what has gone so far. It is, as it were, a vestigial reminder of the original idea that moved Kurosawa to make the film. (pp. 30-1)

Akira Iwasaki, "Kurosawa and His Work," translated by John Bester, in Japan Quarterly *(© 1965, by the Asahi Shimbun), Vol. 12, No. 1, January-March, 1965 (and reprinted in* Focus on "Rashomon," *edited by Donald Richie, Prentice-Hall, Inc., 1972, pp. 21-31).*

DONALD RICHIE

[Kurosawa's] interest is in a certain kind of character. Since all men have much the same reasons for action, their only differentiation can be in how they act. The Kurosawa hero is a very special sort of person and since he (from film to film) shows the same characteristics, it is well to examine the first of the line.

Sugata [in Kurosawa's first film, *Sanshiro Sugata*] seems to be average in all ways. His only difference is that he wants to be different from what he is. It is he who searches for a teacher and, having found one, persists in learning. The path to inner wisdom, according to Kurosawa, is a very difficult one, so difficult indeed that very few are those who even manage its beginnings—and no one, of course, ever discovers its ending. Yet, difficult though it is, the Kurosawa hero is distinguished by his perseverance, by his refusal to be defeated. . . . [The] struggle is always an inner one. . . . This effort is spiritual—and all of Kurosawa's films have as their turning point a spiritual crisis. It is here —in the mind—that resolution takes place. The action which follows is usually the outcome of this resolution. It is, again, the practical aspect of the theoretical. (pp. 17-18)

[Kurosawa often prefers his villains.] His preference, however, should be understood in a particular way. The hero is man actively engaged in becoming himself—never a very reassuring sight. The villain, on the other hand, has already become something. . . .

Kurosawa's preference is the preference we all have for the formed man. In the ordinary film this man would be the hero. . . . [Kurosawa's] heroes, beginning with Sugata, . . . are all unformed. . . . For this reason, all of his pictures are about education—the education of the hero. (p. 19)

[The fight scene between Sugata and the villain] has become the most famous in all Japanese cinema and its influence continues until now. . . . It is silent but for the rushing wind and the sound of reeds trampled upon. It is motionless for almost a minute and then erupts into action so swift one can almost not follow it. As in the sword-fights in *Seven Samurai* and *Sanjuro,* we see two men, opposed, still as statues. Then the action is so sudden, so furious, that the two men become fused, welded into the very image of battle. . . .

After this superb battle—one which Sugata barely and only with the greatest difficulty wins—one might expect the picture to end with some kind of statement that he has at last grown-up, that he has arrived, that he has *become* something—the great judo champion. This would be the logical Western conclusion to a film about the education of a hero.

Kurosawa, however, has seen that this cannot be true. A hero who actually *becomes* is tantamount to a villain—for this was the only tangible aspect of the villain's villainy. To suggest that peace, contentment, happiness, follows a single battle, no matter how important, is literally untrue. . . . (p. 20)

[It is unusual that from his first film the elements of Kurosawa's style should be evident. Besides his] fondness for a certain kind of story, a certain kind of hero, for cyclic form, for theory and practice in parallel scenes, for the resultant implications of illusion and reality; and besides his liking for such punctuation marks as the wipe—there are many other elements of the Kurosawa style which are visible in *Sugata.*

Most important, since his craft is based directly upon it, are the various short-cuts, the many telescopings, the extraordinary economy of the way in which he shows his story. The Kurosawa film lacks any extraneous scenes, is without longeurs, and all unimportant transitions are missing. His craftsmanship and his economy are one. (p. 21)

One other element of the mature Kurosawa technique is also present in this film and this is his peculiar use of the flash-back—seen in its perfection in *Rashomon.* Unlike many directors, Kurosawa does not favor extended flashback, perhaps because it is too easy, and too expected. However, in many of his earlier films, there are looks backward which are really flashes and nothing more. They remind but, more than that, they are used either to establish plot points (as in *Stray Dog*) or—more important—to indicate emotional states, as in *No Regrets for Our Youth* and here. . . .

All of these innovations were, even in 1943, peculiar to Kurosawa and they make *Sugata* an extrordinary debut film—doubly extraordinary in that, a quarter of a century later, the picture is emotionally valid (which is more than one can say for some of the pictures in between) and still almost as surprising as the day it was released. In it, Kurosawa showed fully the profile which the entire world would come to know. (p. 23)

[*The Most Beautiful*] is extremely likeable and one of the reasons, certainly, is that Kurosawa's documentary is so enriched by the kind of beauty which only truth can give. The plot line is manipulated to a degree but, oddly, the characters are not. In this context of presumed actuality, of beautifully captured wartime stringency (the very conditions of which—not enough film, not enough lights, not enough sets—might account for the extreme economy and directness of the picture), the performances ring with a kind of truth that one finds usually only in real documentaries.

In this picture Kurosawa again sounded the major theme that had become his (as in *Sugata*: the problem of becoming oneself, the necessity of realizing this, the difficulty of persevering) but did so within the framework of the present (and, even now, he feels the present, the contemporary-life-film, to be the more important genre; feels, even now, that its actuality, its life-likeness makes it more important than the "period" genre) and, further, sounded it within the context of actuality itself—the documentary. Just as one may trace from *Sugata* many of the elements in the later films, in *The Most Beautiful,* can be found the beginnings of that intense concern for actuality which animates so many of his pictures. (p. 29)

Kurosawa thinks of himself as a socially-minded rather than as a politically-minded man. . . .

Scandal, Record of a Living Being, The Bad Sleep Well were all to have "some social significance" and yet this turns out to be the least important aspect of these pictures. Kurosawa's talent is stronger than his wish to be socially useful. This is one continuing aspect of all of his films and is seen at its strongest in *No Regrets for Our Youth.*

The picture is based upon the famous Takikawa Incident of 1933 which forced the resignation of Professor Yukitoki Takikawa from the faculty of Kyoto University for his supposed "Communistic thought," and caused a sensation among the nation's intellectuals. One of his pupils was Hidemi Ozaki, who became involved in the famous Sorge spy case, and was executed in Tokyo in 1944. What appealed to Kurosawa in the story was not the suppression of a certain kind of political thought, but the fact that thought of any kind was suppressed; not that a possible leftist was executed but that any man was executed.

His sense of injustice and outrage provided the initial decision to make the picture. . . . Yet, in the picture itself, there is very little direct emphasis upon either militaristic excess or lost freedom. This is because, as is usual with Kurosawa, he is so interested, is so engrossed in *how* something such as lack of freedom affects a person, how a living character reacts in all of its richness and humanity, that he forgets the social issue or, better, finds it irrelevant. (p. 36)

Kurosawa's political uninvolvement is nowhere better seen than in [the] farm sequences. The military, the heroes of the right, are monsters; the peasants, heroes of the left, are also monstrous. The world and both of its extremes are not good enough, and how can simple striving humanity exist in such a place? This question, which reverberates throughout all of Kurosawa's later films, never remains unanswered. In this picture, he gives an answer through simple example. (p. 39)

Kurosawa has said that the only way for Japan to make a new start was by respecting the "self," the individual, that "I wanted to show a woman who did just this." And so he has, but what he has shown is so much more serious, so much more truly responsible than anything we are used to seeing in life, let alone the movies, that the very hardness, the difficulty of what he is suggesting, almost repels. . . .

[*No Regrets for Our Youth* is a difficult film] because it is extremely personal and because it offers so little comfort. Belonging to the left or belonging to the right, these are comforting; *being* a peasant, *being* a well-off Kyoto girl, these too are comforting. They comfort because they suggest security, and Kurosawa in this film—as in *Ikiru,* as in *High and Low*—is insisting that there *is* no security, that all fancied security is only a form of blindness. Hence the picture moves, unnerves, and repels. . . .

What the critics and public alike resented most deeply [about *No Regrets for Our Youth*] was Kurosawa's daring to state that most fundamental and disturbing of all truths: the road to yourself is the hardest road of all and it is the only road which can justify life, since we humans believe justification necessary; the only road which can vindicate, since we insist upon vindication; the only road which—since we are living beings—allows us to live. (p. 40)

Just as the various sections of *Rashomon* are filmed and edited according to the content of the section . . . , so both filming and editing in this picture are devoted to the explication of the girl's character. Since this character is mercurial, given to violent and almost simultaneous extremes (in the first half of the film at any rate), Kurosawa has invented a kind of grammar to show this to us. . . .

[For example, the whole marriage of Setsuko and Fujita is seen in a series of fragments.] The sequence is built like a mosaic, little scenes sometimes no more than two seconds long placed among slightly longer ones. . . .

This has been their life together, this apparently disconnected series of tiny scenes leading from marriage to catastrophe, seen with none of the connecting links usually observed in classic screen grammar. One of the reasons for this extreme form of short-hand might be that Kurosawa, after all, had to show twelve years in two hours, but certainly the more important is that, by showing us in this way he not only telescopes the actions, moves the story, but, at the same time, and most important, shows how things appear *to* her. (p. 41)

This [subjective view] occurs very rarely in the work of Kurosawa. Usually an examination of character takes the form of repeated action (in *Rashomon* and *Ikiru*), or an investigation (the second half of *Ikiru*) or, as in the majority of his films, the orthodox method of a character's revealing himself through language and action. But then in no other film, not even *Ikiru,* was Kurosawa so concerned with a single character. . . .

One of Kurosawa's strongest attributes as a director is that he knows not only that the style is the man, he also knows that the man is continually changing, growing, and that therefore, style itself grows, changes, and it is this metamorphosis, this continual adaptation which is most necessary, most interesting, and most rewarding.

If he never returned to the style of *No Regrets for Our Youth* with its extraordinary freedom, its enormous power of evocation, it was because other stories demanded other styles. . . .

And it is for this reason that each of his films, though bound to the others by reason of certain stylistic affinities, by a continuing interest in a single and basic story, are at the same time completely different from each other. This gives his work a variety which is very rare in contemporary cinema. But equally rare is the perfection of those of his pictures which are perfect. *No Regrets for My Youth* is the first of these. (p. 42)

The beginnings of *Rashomon* lie in the stories of Ryunosuke Akutagawa. . . . He has always been extremely popular and also critically well-thought-of, almost despite his popularity. Yet he has never been considered in the "main stream" of Japanese literature. His defenders point out his inventive style; his detractors call him "Western" in his orientation. He *is* "Western" in the same way as Kurosawa: he is concerned with truths which are ordinarily outside pragmatic Japanese morality and, being concerned with them, he questions them. (p. 70)

[Akutagawa's] *In a Grove* opens abruptly with the testimony of a woodcutter before the police. This is followed by various testimonies: that of a priest, a police agent, an old woman who turns out to be the mother of the girl the bandit raped, the bandit himself, the girl herself, the murdered man through a medium, and there is no conclusion: the reader is presented with seven testimonies and given no indication of how he should think about them. Akutagawa's point was the simple one that all truth is relative, with the corollary that there is thus no truth at all.

Kurosawa's most significant addition (beside that of the abandoned baby in the last scenes) is the introduction of the character of the commoner, a cynical yet inquisitive man, whose questions and disbelief act as a comment upon all the various versions of the story. The commoner talks to both priest and woodcutter—since all three are found under the gate at the beginning of the film—and in a way acts as a moral (or amoral) chorus. (p. 71)

Having invented the character of the commoner, having chosen to frame all of his stories within the general story of the three conversing under the ruined gate, [Kurosawa] now invents a further incident. They hear a baby crying and the commoner finds it. He takes its clothes (a suggestion perhaps from the original *Rashomon* story), an act which horrifies the other two and which, in turn, makes him culpable. Throughout the picture he has not once acted, merely asked questions—now he acts and his act is immoral. The woodcutter picks up the naked child, saying he will take it home. The priest says that this single act has restored his faith in men and the picture concludes with the rain stopping, the sun breaking through, and the woodcutter going off with the baby.

Akutagawa is content to question all moral values, all truth. Kurosawa, obviously, is not. Neither anarchist nor misanthrope, he insists upon hope, upon the possibility of gratuitous action. Like the priest he cannot believe that men are evil—and, indeed, if Kurosawa has a spokesman in the film it is probably the priest: weak, confused, but ultimately trusting.

There is, however, much more to the film than this. There is an apparent mystery, an elliptical intent, which has fascinated audiences all over the world. . . . One of the most fascinating aspects of the film is just that it is extremely difficult to determine *what* it means. It shares with other modern art (abstract painting, free-form sculpture) an apparent lack of ostensible meaning. . . . (pp. 71-2)

One doubts very much that Kurosawa was deeply interested in objective truth in this or in any other film. This is because the *why* is always implied. And in none of his pictures is Kurosawa even slightly interested in the why of a matter. Instead, always, *how*. This offers a clue. The level of objective truth is not the truly interesting one. Much more interesting is the level of subjective truth. If the truth searched for becomes subjective, then no one lies, and the stories are wildly at variance. . . .

Five people interpret an action and each interpretation is different because, in the telling and in the retelling, the people reveal not the action but themselves. This is why Kurosawa could leave the plot, insofar as there is one, dangling and unresolved. The fact that it *is* unresolved is itself one of the meanings of the film.

In all of Kurosawa's pictures there is this preoccupation with the conflict between illusion (the reactions of the five and their stories) and reality (the fact of the rape and murder). . . .

One can now assign various reasons for the five having seen and heard the things that they thought they saw and heard. All the stories have in common one single element—pride. . . . They are proud of these actions and we know because they insist upon them. One confesses only what one is openly or secretly proud of, which is the reason that contrition is rarely sincere. (p. 75)

Rashomon is like a vast distorting mirror or, better, a collection of prisms that reflect and refract reality. By showing us its various interpretations . . . , he has shown first that human beings are incapable of judging reality, much less truth, and, second, that they must continually deceive themselves if they are to remain true to the ideas of themselves that they have.

Here then, more than in any other single film, is found Kurosawa's central theme: the world is illusion, you yourself make reality, but this reality undoes you if you submit to being limited by what you have made. The important corollary—you are not, however, truly subject to this reality, you can break free from it, can live even closer to the nature you are continually creating—this occurs only in the later films. (p. 76)

[In the adaptations done after *The Idiot, The Throne of Blood* and *The Lower Depths*], Kurosawa was much less personally involved with his material and did not feel it necessary to be literal. Macbeth could rise and fall in medieval Japan, Gorky's characters could be made to fit an Edo Period tenement. In *The Idiot* all the characters must inhabit a compromise country—Hokkaido; Mifune must talk anarchism, and Mori, Christianity—issues not burning to the Japanese; Kurosawa must take a nineteenth-century novel and lay it in contemporary Japan, hoping that this would preserve the immediacy of Dostoevsky, and—instead—obscures it. . . .

[His] desire to "preserve" Dostoevsky weakens the film at every turn because Kurosawa's faith in his author was so strong, and so blind, that he seemed to feel that the mere act of photographing scenes from the novel would give the same effect on the screen as they do on the page. What occurs, however, is merely a devastating simplification. (p. 82)

The interest in the film, then, is that despite its excesses (extreme even for a Japanese film: the first part of the picture, for example, has the grand title—*Love and Agony;* the second, the only slightly less grandiloquent *Love and Hatred*) or because of them, it shows the Kurosawa style evolving.

What we recognize in later pictures makes a first and often tentative appearance in this one. Kurosawa, who had long preferred action to talk, here forced himself to make room for talk in his cinematic vocabulary, and in this picture we see the extremely skillful movement of characters within the frame which became part of the visual style of *The Lower Depths* and *The Bad Sleep Well*. (p. 83)

The best scene in the film has no counterpart in Dostoevsky and indicates what the picture might have been had not respect paralyzed Kurosawa. Mifune [Rogozhin] and Mori [Myshkin] have been arguing. In the following scene Mifune will stalk Mori through the snow. In between, however, and for no logical reason, but apparently because it felt right, Kurosawa inserts an invented scene, a very lovely one where Mifune takes Mori to have tea with his mother. She is very deaf, very religious, realizes that she has no cakes and so, with the most gracious and charming of smiles, takes the offering from the family altar and they together eat it. Intellectually, this tender scene has no place in the film; emotionally, it is just right. It is so good and so strong that it even carries and for a time we "believe" the chase through the snow which follows.

Such interpolated scenes become more common in later Kurosawa . . . but this one remains one of the most beautiful. It is both ironic and telling that the best scene in *The Idiot* should be the single scene that is not in the novel. It is perfect for Dostoevsky and perfect for Kurosawa. (p. 84)

The transformation [of *The Lower Depths*] to film is literal. If one compares the play with the scenario, one is surprised how little is added, how little removed. . . . Kurosawa is in such basic agreement with Gorky that whole pages of dialogue and action remain the same. The difference is one of interpretation—action and dialogue may remain the same but Kurosawa's emphasis is different from Gorky's which is why the film may be seen as a comedy although the play is usually seen as something different from that. This is more clearly seen in Kurosawa's precise delineation of the major characters. . . .

His interest in the various problems of ensemble acting . . . —the meshing or clashing of various moods of intentions, the playing off of one character against another, usually within the same frame—began with *Record of a Living Being* and continued in this picture. It is perhaps for this reason that he saw in Gorky's play a collection of *individuals* and consequently failed to be saddened or disturbed by the sense of misery and waste which comes if you see the play as group-message or social comment or something of the sort. (p. 124)

The picture is, along with *Rashomon,* Kurosawa's major statement concerning his continual preoccupation with illusion versus reality. The other characters insist upon one illusion or another. Only the priest can endure naked reality. And this is why Kurosawa makes him comic—because the priest is very funny. . . . Comedy is certainly one of the results of believing in illusion to the point of incongruity; but another cause of high comedy, as Kurosawa will again indicate in *Yojimbo,* is being free of illusion. The glimpse of reality which all of us achieve from time to time can result either in suicide or in laughter. (pp. 129-30)

[In *Red Beard*] Kurosawa is, in effect, constructing a chain of good. The idea is a novel one. All of us believe in a chain of evil and are firmly convinced that bad begets bad. . . . In *Red Beard,* however, the director is offering the proposition (startling, even alarming) that good also begets good.

One can see what Kurosawa has had the bravery to do in this film. He is suggesting that, like the hospital, the world in which we live may indeed be a hell but that good, after all, is just as infectious as evil. We so firmly believe that "evil begets evil" that its contrary is quite dazzling. To consider such a proposition, in a cynical age (and modern Japan is as cynical as anywhere), seems almost shameful. But this is why Kurosawa has made the movie. . . .

Kurosawa's dilemma is rather similar to that of Dickens. Laconic realist though he is, he believes in the good; but the good is very difficult to dramatize. Difficult as it is, however, Dickens manages admirably in at least several novels. So does Griffith, a very Dickensian creator. In their best work, they affirm by refusing to sentimentalize—and that is what also Kurosawa does in this picture.

Dr. Red Beard, for example. He, like the doctor in *Drunken Angel,* is possessed by, consumed by, a rage for good. He will do anything to get at it, even—and again a parallel with *Drunken Angel*—things that he considers bad. When it appears that Akemi Negishi will be put into prison for trying to stab her husband, Mifune [as Red Beard] blackmails the magistrate by mentioning his knowledge of the magistrate's mistress. He is quite convinced of his badness in doing this. . . .

Mifune is a brother to the doctor in *Drunken Angel:* the one railing against ignorance and the hospital; the other, against poverty and the sump. They are men possessed. The difference from the suave, knowledgeable Dr. Kildare with his crotchety bedside-manner is apparent. The latter cannot afford to hate illness; he makes his living from it. Red Beard's hate of disease is one of the reasons that he is in a public clinic—the lowest of medical positions. And he doesn't care. He does more than merely devote himself to the good; he devotes himself to a fight against bad.

This is why the picture is not sentimental. To simply feel for, sympathize with, weep over—this is sentimental because it is so ridiculously disproportionate to what is needed. But to gird the loins and go out and do battle, to hate so entirely that good is the result: this is something else. (p. 175)

The film is both compassionate and hard-boiled—because Kurosawa's concern, like Red Beard's, is the opposite of indulgent. The film can carry its extraordinary weight of sentiment (including a happy ending) because it can carry us so far beyond the confines of our daily hells. The stake in Kurosawa's game is *us*—and he does everything he can to make us accept. One has a fleeting reminiscence of the girl in *One Wonderful Sunday* turning to the audience and pleading for, demanding acceptance. This 1965 picture is much more profound, personal, persuasive than the 1946 one, but the morality is the same. And so is the conclusion —if you accept yourself you are saved. Have courage enough to allow that you are moved, allow yourself respite from cynicism, from hate. Allow yourself to believe in yourself. (p. 177)

[All] Kurosawa films are about the same thing. In simplest terms, and shorn of all philosophy, his pictures are about character revelation. One of the reasons he has made so many suspense films either directly (*Stray Dog, The Bad Sleep Well, High and Low*) or indirectly (almost all the others, particularly *Rashomon* and *Ikiru*) is that the suspense-story, like the detective-story, is about revelation. Kurosawa takes the "crime" (the unrealized life or the problem of choosing among evils) and works out a "solution." The solution is usually the hero himself and his character and it is this which gives the film its final form.

Or forms, because Kurosawa has several favorites. One of them, for lack of any better name, I will call "sonata-form." The other (for the same reason) the "theme with variations." The latter is the simpler and *Rashomon* is an example. So, however, is *One Wonderful Sunday;* so is *Ikiru*. The "sonata-form" is more common in the later films and usually consists of (1) an introduction or prelude which usually sounds the major theme, (2) a bridge which is usually of major cinematic importance, (3) the main theme or *hauptsatz* (whether there is a *seitensatz* or not depends on the film) which is not a first "subject" so much as it is a complex of related ideas; it leads into (4) the development, of which it is also itself a part, and into (5) a recapitulation which may be separate from the (often ironic) (6) coda. (pp. 185-86)

This sonata-form need not be insisted upon but it is interesting that so many of the films exhibit the same pattern. Perhaps it is because these films are based upon conflict in a way that ordinary pictures are not. Since the conflict is usually one of character rather than of situation, it would naturally follow that a "recapitulation" (that is, a testing of the hero) would bring back to the film its own major idea in a new, different, or expanded form. The reason that one may refer to the form as similar to first-movement sonata-form is that both are about conflict. Music has never found a better way of presenting conflict than through the sonata-form, and Kurosawa's pictures falling into a somewhat similar pattern is another example of its validity.

Another aspect of form seen in many of Kurosawa's pictures is that of the full circle, or the spiral, the return to the beginning with a difference, the cyclic. (pp. 186-87)

Metamorphosis, the feeling for the circle, the sense of return, the recapitulation—all of these contribute to the form of the Kurosawa script and give the pattern of the picture. There are doubtlessly very personal reasons why this should be so, but another reason would be that Kurosawa is interested in the totality of a character, the totality of a situation. One of the few ways a narrative art may encompass a character is to circle him, to reveal one facet after another, to return continually to what is already known, to contrast what we saw then with what we know now. The most revealing of psychological fiction (Proust for example) continually circles and returns. Kurosawa's interest in character revelation insists upon a like movement—with the result of a like pattern. (p. 188)

"There are people," [Kurosawa] has said, "who criticize my work . . . and say it is not realistic. But I feel that merely copying the outward appearance of the world would not result in anything real—that is only copying. I think that to find what is real one must look very closely at one's world, to search for those things which contribute to this reality which one feels under the surface. These are few and one uses them to create. These are the core around which the world moves, the axis on which it turns. The novels of Dostoevsky, Tolstoy, and Turgenev show us what these things are. To be an artist means to search for, find, and look at these things; to be an artist means never to avert one's eyes."

In the films of Kurosawa one finds that these things include an awareness of oneself and an awareness of the world, and an awareness of the fact that the world and the self do not, cannot match. "I suppose all my films have a common theme. If I think about it though, the only theme I can think of is really a question: Why can't people be happier together?" To ask that question is to answer it—which is what Kurosawa has done in every one of his major films. They cannot be happy because they are people, *because* they are human.

Kurosawa is a philosopher who works with film, and who affirms that in this weakness lies the essentially human quality. But, though weak, man can hope and through this he can prevail. Samurai and robbers may be revealed as one and the same but there are always the villagers who, after the great deeds are done, will plant the new rice with hope and confidence. Man must fight to retain hope in the midst of this hopeless world and in this fight all men are brothers.

This is the central thesis of Kurosawa's films, most of which show the progress from despair to hope, and this is one of the reasons his films are so meaningful to the world. This thesis is also personal to the director, is an expression of himself as a man. (pp. 197-98)

Donald Richie, in his The Films of Akira Kurosawa *(reprinted by permission of the University of California Press), University of California Press, 1970, 223 p.*

JOAN MELLEN

Few [directors] have succeeded in reflecting a world-view which encompasses an entire society, an achievement that writers like Fielding and Tolstoy managed so well for the novel. The films of Akira Kurosawa have been seriously ignored by critics who favor more simplistically avant-garde directors like Fellini, Godard, Antonioni and Resnais. Even Luis Bunuel has called Kurosawa's work "superficial." Yet in the contemporary film only Kurosawa, in the tradition of Eisenstein and Pudovkin, has treated the epic as a dynamic, modern form. The epic appropriate to our time, as Brecht defines it, is a work centered around a human being who "is alterable and able to alter," whose thought has been determined by social being, and which appeals to the spectator only to "arouse his capacity for action" and "force him to take decisions" by "facing something." Kurosawa's conception of the epic comes close to Brecht's.

If Kurosawa's films seem more old-fashioned than Godard's, it is because he employs a more conventional narrative mode and because he is concerned with man's capacity to perform moral acts. Ironically more than any other major director, he resembles Bunuel. Bunuel tests the devotion of his people to moral principles by placing them in a world made grotesque by greed and rapacity. The paradigms of his hero are Nazarin and Viridiana, who are both finally defeated in their attempts to devote their lives to a suffering humanity. Their deepest sacrifices are only resented by their charges, and make no impact on the brutalizing conditions afflicting them. Neither can Kurosawa's hero, armed only with his own higher humanity, alter the direction of his society. This marks Kurosawa's adaptation of the epic genre to a world-view which finds individual acts in themselves of marginal consequence. . . .

Kurosawa portrays a social structure that is unfair and ruthless without making his films too narrowly topical. It is true that his Prince Myshkin in *The Idiot* (1951) and the young detective in *Stray Dog* (1949) have had to find new means of survival in their changed society after returning very specifically from the Second World War, but they could have found themselves jobless and alone during any period of historical upheaval. To treat a contemporary social conflict carries the danger of being either too polemical or didactic. Like Brecht, who frequently for this very reason set his works in the distant past or in far-away places, Kurosawa strives to use the historical to achieve a more universally compelling sociological approach. He also shares with Brecht the creation of characters who learn a strong class sense from the dilemma of their social alienation. However, he does not affect fashionable "Brechtian" detachment from his subject matter but, rather, he conveys an abiding sympathy with the less fortunate of his characters. . . .

In the cinema of Kurosawa there is always a struggle between a well-meaning individual and an evil collective which expresses its selfish nature in the crushing economic conditions inflicted upon his characters. . . .

Within the context of a society in which history seems frozen because changing events bring no relief to the oppressed, Kurosawa's heroes set out to live morally. (p.16)

The epic quality of Kurosawa's films comes in his representation of a hero larger than life, a moral individual recognizable as a social type. He may appear as a detective in modern society *(Stray Dog)*, a samurai declassé *(Seven Samurai, Yojimbo, Sanjuro)*, an industrialist *(I Live in Fear, High and Low)* or a dedicated doctor *(The Quiet Duel, Drunken Angel, Red Beard)*. These heroes confront circumstances which question the moral rectitude of the social role that they have taken for granted throughout their lives. The best of them attempt to rectify a life of tacit assent to injustice. They sacrifice their hard-earned respectability and economic security. But only in transcending norms they have accepted unquestioningly do they become, in Kant's sense, rational or moral agents. (pp. 16-17)

Another measure of the goodness of a man in Kurosawa's films is the degree to which he is able to form compassionate relationships with others and to make these a primary loyalty. He is never ironic in his admiration of the warmth with which some men can respond to each other. Three examples come to mind. Nishi, the hero of *The Bad Sleep Well* (1960), learns to love the lame girl whom he had married to avenge his father's murder by the girl's father. Sanjuro Kuwabatake *(Yojimbo,* 1961), seemingly a homeless *yojimbo* (bodyguard), is genuinely sorry for the young family he befriends, although his ethic demands that he show no emotion. The most winning of the seven samurai is easily Kikuchiyo, who becomes a peasant once more as he trains the farmers to defend themselves, and it is he who delightedly gives away the white rice reserved for the samurai to the hungry children.

The affection of the Kurosawa hero is always demonstrative and unabashed. Kurosawa never extols the good thought separated from the good action. He refuses to sanction the dilemma of the "noble" mind ambivalent about taking an action that would make him less than "pure." For this reason his films do not seem "intellectual" or "modern." Unlike Bergman, he never leaves an emotion in its abstract state, but quickly translates it into action. The plots of his films, dealing as they do, in the epic manner, with moments of crisis, make decisions imperative for his characters. (p.17)

High and Low might be considered the typical Kurosawa film. At its center is the good man, as heroic as an individual who must invariably act alone can be. In the background is a struggle between classes growing out of an unjust social structure. . . .

[In the satire *Yojimbo*], Kurosawa shows with much more bitterness the moral chaos attendant upon the fall of the old order and the rise of a ruthless and materialistic middle class surrounded by a lumpen proletariat which lives off its crimes. Two equally unscrupulous factions vie for economic control of a town, to be plagued by a down-and-out samurai who can return law and order only by slaying a majority of the citizenry. Kurosawa traces the rise of the middle class by moving his scenario from a rural to an urban setting. (p.18)

[In *Sanjuro* (1962), the sequel to *Yojimbo,*] Kurosawa allows his camera to impact his theme. He refuses didacticism or facile allegory. The unjust social structure is depicted. It breeds an Aeschylian revenge upon revenge: police upon criminal, ruling faction upon its opposition, outcast upon the "respectable."

Grafting one of the oldest genres, the epic, with its strong emphasis on the moral, onto the newest of the arts, Kurosawa uses a traditional narrative structure to pose essential moral questions. His films rarely experiment with time in a Proustian manner, nor do they, like the films of Antonioni (whom Kurosawa admires), withhold information necessary to the viewer's understanding. *Seven Samurai* is superficially an adventure melodrama of the destruction of bandits and the victory of the peasants. *High and Low* rises to two climaxes typical of the *roman policier* (George Simenon is one of Kurosawa's favorite novelists): the safe return of the kidnapped boy and the police dragnet closing in on the kidnapper.

Kurosawa's films, like nineteenth-century novels, are told in the third person, maintaining the objectivity which early novelists thought essential to verisimilitude. Like the old epic storytellers, he is confident of the truths his films impart. Primarily moral in their outlook, his films, as he says, "keep saying the same thing over and over again. Why, I ask, is it that human beings cannot get along with each other? Why can't they live with each other with more good will?" As Enoken, the poor carrier the nobles pick up along the way in *Men Who Tread On The Tiger's Tail,* asks, "Why can't two brothers not quarrel?" The nobility are embarrassed by his question.

Unlike the earlier creators of the epic, Kurosawa ends, not in praise of a permanence achieved through the efforts of the hero, but with the haunting suggestion that his heroes have been able to do little to redeem their social order, and that if profound structural changes are not forthcoming, chaos will result. Through the deeds of his heros, who appear as large as Ulysses or Aeneas, he points a way: concern for the less fortunate, kindness, tolerance, and repudiation of materialism, ambition and greed. Kurosawa does not anticipate the society capable of fulfilling these values. He rests with a moral vision which, he implies, is the perpetual concern of men—without which degeneration and suffering will never cease. (p.19)

Joan Mellen, "The Epic Cinema of Kurosawa," in Take One *(copyright © 1971 by Unicorn Publishing Corp.), Vol. 3, No. 4, March-April, 1971, pp. 16-19.*

ROGER GREENSPUN

"Dodes'ka-den" is Kurosawa's first color film, and he has adjusted his color to suit each vignette, from the childlike brightness of the streetcar motorman's fantasy, to the dull monochromes of the ragpicker's obsession, to the unreal abstract-expressionist behind the wrecked-car home of the beggar and his boy. In their dreams and their fate, this last pair defines the farthest imaginative reach of the movie, belonging more to the conventions of art than of life—and to an art that exhibits all the emotional and, indeed, the intellectual range of a wide-eyed child painted by Keane.

The beggar's is perhaps the saddest—and the most ludicrous—life in "Dodes'ka-den," but it is not much more gratuitous or suffocatingly sentimental than anything else in the film—which succeeds in little but the painful recall of better works in its type. I have in mind the lovely community-life films of Yasujiro Ozu or the great "Lower Depths" of Jean Renoir—but not the "Lower Depths" of Kurosawa.

For without a sustaining fiction or traditional fictional matter (as in "Rasho-Mon," 1951, or "Throne of Blood," 1961, or any of the samurai films), Kurosawa is thrown upon the resources of his own inventive vision, and those resources show themselves to be nothing much. The humor is strained, the ironies are easy and mostly unearned, and even the director's celebrated humanism seems artificially produced, to be hauled out as if for demonstration purposes at appropriate intervals. "Dodes'ka-den" is an immensely long, elaborately trivial movie in which the compassion does not compensate for the smallness of imaginative life.

Roger Greenspun, "Film Fete: Lives in a Junk Yard in Kurosawa's 'Dodes'ka-den'," in The New York Times *(© 1971 by The New York Times Company; reprinted by permission), October 6, 1971, p. 39.*

TOM MILNE

With his central metaphor of snow—the towering drifts that turn streets and houses into blind burrows where dark, scurrying figures, blanketed by the snow that never seems to stop falling, seek and momentarily find each other—Kurosawa instantly captures the essence of Dostoievsky's novel [*The Idiot*]: that sense of people as isolated units, reaching helplessly out with their sympathies but unable to tear down the barriers of understanding and intention which separate them from peace of the soul. . . . [Although Kurosawa simplifies the story, he] manages to convey the interlocking despair of human relationships, quite magnificently, through a simple stylistic device: the triangular grouping in which, usually in monologue, one person explains, one listens intently, and the third, marginally excluded, is baffled by the spellbinding emotional waves he cannot quite grasp. Used repeatedly, this geometrical composition leads almost mathematically to the extraordinary climax of the ice carnival—in itself an extraordinary visual conception with its swirling movement, torches flickering in the darkness and grotesque painted masks, all dominated by the huge ice sculpture of a brooding demon—where all the characters, as though summoned by demonic invocation, converge tangentially, at different moments, upon the fixed point of the Idiot. Yet for all its formality, *The Idiot* seems to lie outside the Japanese visual tradition; indeed, it has been criticised for being neither Russian nor Japanese. Movement and gesture are hieratic and abruptly stylised, certainly . . . , but there is a curious *décalage* between sound and image, almost a feeling that the actors are playing in pantomime accompanied by invisible doubles speaking their lines. The strange, almost oneiric effect is of watching a silent film and simultaneously listening to an operatic aria. . . . We are, literally, in a country of the soul, dark and inscrutable, watching these creatures suffering through their dark night in which we, suddenly and mysteriously, are somehow implicated at the end when Kameda returns and asks about Taeko: with Taeko lying dead in the next room, Akama does not reply, he simply turns to the camera and stares, accusing, uncomprehending. . . . Strange, poetic, clearly very personal to Kurosawa, it is certainly one of his best films.

Tom Milne, "Feature Films: 'Hakuchi' ('The Idiot')," in Monthly Film Bulletin *(copyright © The British Film Institute, 1974), Vol. 41, No. 482, March, 1974, p. 57.*

ALAN P. BARR

Kurosawa, as obsessively as any other artist, [explores] the nature and possibility of heroic action in a world that is basically corrupt, corrupt almost as a consequence of its human-ness. What likelihood for humanitarian commitment remains and what is its inexorable cost in such a society? Is man doomed to a kind of intellectualizing impotency, or can action be redemptive and rejuvenating? Is action necessarily violent? Film after film elaborates these conundra, using telephoto lenses to show us the minutia of faces and expressions far away, sharp (often perpendicular) angles and harshly contrasting lighting to accentuate the harshness of existence and the brittleness of human relations, and wide angle lenses to juxtapose opposing camps. Just as we see characters literally wiped out with a spectacular gesture of the sword, so does Kurosawa make the wipe one of his most characteristic camera transitions. (p. 158)

Despite its seeming simplicity, . . . Kurosawa's *Yojimbo* has remained an intractably large film. . . . The action and figures give the impression of being in the distance, and yet we get to know their looks intimately. Individual movements seem to be jerky and staccato-like, but the total impression of the movie is similar to that of a highly choreographed modern ballet. All of these perspectives or insights are correct enough, but none—nor all together—is adequate to account for the film's effect. In fact, the more carefully one probes, the larger the critical view necessary to encompass the numerous facets of *Yojimbo*. Kurosawa's extraordinary sense of action and plot only veils the detailed and cunning artistry ingredient in the film.

With impeccable judgment and artistry, Kurosawa weaves references to American Westerns, western art and its heroes, Christianity, the "generational conflict," the social turmoil in mid-nineteenth century Japanese life . . . into a thoroughly unified and forceful artistic statement. Life may not be worth a great deal, the film suggests, but still it is engaged at impressively high stakes. . . .

Perhaps the most frequent observation made about *Yojimbo* is that it is a parody of the American Western—of [Fred Zinnemann's] *High Noon* in particular. The comparison may be initially both facile and limited, but it can still be fruitful. (p. 159)

The divergences, though, are even more illuminating. I am very fond of both films and do not mean this evaluatively, but it is as if *Yojimbo* goes further than *High Noon* ("further" in the sense that the archetypal critics see comedy as going further than tragedy; it includes more, another dimension). It is almost as if for this "portion" of his film Kurosawa started with *High Noon* (I strongly suspect out of affection for it) and pondered where he could build to from there. . . . If much of the art of *Yojimbo* and its exquisitely chosen background music overlap the art of the ballet, then after it is all over we are capable of realizing how essential precise timing was—as essential to the picture as it was to the samurai's strategy and swordplay. The difference is that whereas in the Western the movements, dialog, and percussion sounds keep reminding us during the movie that the clock and therefore the train and the killers are closing in, in *Yojimbo* everything seems so absolutely jaunty and casual. (p. 160)

Kurosawa has managed to sustain a note of comedy throughout his film—largely through the way in which he uses the element of time. Compared with the very somber percussion sounds and the threatening clock in *High Noon*, is his bumbling, comic watchman, who timorously steals out to bang out the hour; rather than the clock being the agent that intimidates people, it is the watchman who panics when he sees Sanjuro, a figure from the past, return to the town. (p. 161)

The title *High Noon* refers back to the time when Christ was crucified and *Yojimbo* is set at the time 1860 when Japanese society was in the midst of a painful transition between the old world and its manners and values and the new world of technology and the gun. In both films the isolated hero is set against a town where evil threatens to consume all, and the result approaches genocide—especially in *Yojimbo*. Yet, unlike Zinnemann, Kurosawa can sustain a comic tone throughout his film and, better still, leave us on the note of a shrug. Both heroes may end up leaving their towns, but the way in which Sanjuro leaves puts the whole of the preceding action into perspective, all without in any way diminishing its magnitude or meaningfulness; there are other roads leading to other towns and other times. This is very different from the tone and emphasis of the traditional American Western, particularly of *High Noon*, and where Kurosawa seems to have exceeded it in his purview. (pp. 161-62)

Just as Kurosawa presents life as simultaneously serious and comic and even trivial, so too are the aspects of Sanjuro which parallel Christ simultaneously important and laughable. It would seem that for Kurosawa life is serious and meaningful enough without adding any supernatural fol-de-rol, and that it is rich enough and shoddy enough without imposing any unnatural somberness—or sobriety.

The broadest parallel or commonality between Christ and the samurai is that each of them, like so many other traditional heroes, finds himself in a world of corruption, where the gamblers and money-changers ride high and where life is devalued. Each then risks himself to restore the society and exorcise the pollution. So far Kurosawa is delivering his story without irony and the citing of a Christ parallel is unspecific and not very illuminating. When, however, he begins to invoke actual allusions to the Christian story, his tone changes to high comedy and the content of what Kurosawa is saying becomes richer for the fun he is now adding. As a Japanese, he can afford not to take religion too seriously—especially not ours and especially not its details, while still appreciating its mythic content and utility. (p. 162)

Denuded of its supernaturalism, the Christ story is humorous as well as fitting and useful for Kurosawa. The figure of the hero and the corrupt world he visits remain recognizably universal. But, like the American Western the director parodies, the god come to earth of Western religion provides Kurosawa with a means of commenting on our culture, the one which presumes benevolently to influence the rest of the world, as well as on his own. There is absolutely no notion of a world of eternity or immortality or of powers beyond the human in *Yojimbo*. It is entirely a world of the here and now. Morality, like retribution, remains a thoroughly human and practical affair. The damnation of *this* world and its realities seem abundantly sufficient for Kurosawa. (p. 163)

The carefully worked-in parallels to western films, culture heroes, and religion contribute undeniable intellectual and "literary" richness to *Yojimbo,* but it is with his images, as the camera and soundtrack convey them, that Kurosawa creates the real dramatic effectiveness of the film. An opening flip of a stick shows us that any road randomly chosen will reveal much the same story, as the accompanying soundtrack tells us "here's no great matter" and a good deal of well-executed fun.

Through depth of focus photography and wide-angle lenses, the film frequently manages, by high-lighting the foreground, middleground, and background almost equally vividly, to encompass the entire world of the film (the town) simultaneously. (pp. 164-65)

On every level Kurosawa portrays a world that is being fractured and dismembered. Set against the credits, the unemployed samurai thrusts himself into a society in transition, one that no longer needs and respects his class. In this transition the old order, which presumably prized the virtues his tradition embodies, has been replaced by a bestial, mercenary rapaciousness. (p. 167)

The trouble with a Christ is not only that his teachings depend so heavily on a redeeming next world, but that the whole notion of sacrificing oneself is absurd in a town where no one is worth it. . . . [From] the initial narration, which introduces the situation and the figure which Mifune is to portray, to his exiting gesture, Kurosawa has worked at defining or reworking the concept of the hero. We find neither the rigid code of honor of the old samurai, the sacrificing self-lessness and self-abnegation of the Christian, the emotional commitment of the humanist, or the generally lauded—at least in fiction—indifference to worldly gain adequate. The narration announces that Sanjuro lives by his wit and his sword, and the omission of any reference to a directing morality turns out not to be accidental. The hero is as adaptable in his ethics as he is in his movements. The only remnant of a morality is esthetic, his liability to be disgusted by certain people—particularly by their frailties. Far from seeing him as self-less, we never doubt the hero's very strong sense of self. Since trust, involvement, and caring are anathema to survival, Sanjuro becomes cynical and detached. He is casual about the predicaments the humans find themselves in, but fastidious about his own pecuniary rewards (though he is obviously capable of turning around and giving all away to the needy family). Most of all, he trusts himself and trusts to himself. (pp. 167-68)

Alan P. Barr, "Exquisite Comedy and the Dimensions of Heroism: Akira Kurosawa's 'Yojimbo'," in The Massachusetts Review *(reprinted from* The Massachusetts Review; *(© 1975 The Massachusetts Review, Inc.), Vol. XVI, No. 1, Winter, 1975, pp. 158-68.*

ANDREW SARRIS

[In *Kagemusha* the] screen is awash with one brilliant canvas after another, and all the Kurosawa obsessions are present, too: the stormy, psychological expressionism, the inner torment, the lordly absolution of mere mortals from their indecision. Drawn toward the tapestry of the Shakespearian chronicle plays and the Fordian cavalry westerns, Kurosawa dazzles the viewer's eye even when he is disorienting the viewer's sense of the plot. . . .

The central plot concerns a legendary leader who conceals his "double" until after his death so that the clan can survive without its enemies becoming aware of his passing. . . . I must confess that at one point in *Kagemusha* I thought that Kurosawa was priming himself to attain a Mizoguchian nobility. It is the scene in which the double unexpectedly provides an uncanny imitation of the leader. But I should have known better. Had I not written years ago that Mizoguchi was to Kurosawa as Sophocles was to Euripides? It would follow, therefore, that Kurosawa would not allow the double to become the leader in heroic fashion, but, rather, call into question the illusions of leadership itself. The film deals consequently with a comparatively incoherent spectacle of slaughter and madness, yet it never loses the gravity and sobriety associated with a major talent.

Andrew Sarris, "Cannes: A Last Hurrah," in The Village Voice *(reprinted by permission of* The Village Voice; *copyright © News Group Publications, Inc., 1980), Vol. XXV, No. 21, May 26, 1980, p. 49.**

George Lucas

1944-

American director and screenwriter.

Although critics have yet to evaluate Lucas's overall contribution to the cinema arts, box-office returns have unquestionably rendered a favorable judgment of his work. His *American Graffiti* and *Star Wars* have drawn more viewers than the life work of most filmmakers.

Lucas grew up in Modesto, California, which later served as the prototype for the teenage dreamworld portrayed in *American Graffiti.* His formal education in film began at the University of Southern California where he developed a bias for the visual rather than the narrative aspects of film.

As a graduate student at USC Lucas was granted a scholarship by Warner Brothers to observe films being made in the studio. It was under this auspice that he met Francis Coppola. Coppola served as artistic counselor to Lucas and supported the young director's future film projects.

Lucas's first commercial film, *THX 1138,* displays his early concern with technical proficiency, but its abstract handling of stock themes from science fiction evoked only a halfhearted response from critics and audiences. The script for his next film, *American Graffiti,* was rejected by several companies. Coppola's offer to produce the film lent the project economic credibility, and Universal Pictures consented to finance the new director. The success of *American Graffiti* surprised many, for the odds were against the acceptance of a film without a traditional narrative plot line. This story of coming of age in the early sixties flourished in an era of nostalgia, but the formal expertise of the film testifies to its value beyond the demands of popular culture.

Lucas's greatest financial success thus far has been *Star Wars,* a film for which he served as writer, director, producer, film editor, and cameraman. In contrast with the alien dystopia of *THX 1138, Star Wars* represents a technologically superior universe that is the battleground for a traditional and familiar conflict between good and evil. "I wanted to do a modern fairy tale, a myth," states Lucas. The elements of myth blended together in *Star Wars* have indeed led many critics to see Lucas as an adept handler of both mythical archetypes and modern cinematic technique. Lucas's most recent contribution to the cinematic field is *The Empire Strikes Back,* a sequel to *Star Wars,* for which he served as executive producer. *Star Wars* and *The Empire Strikes Back* are the central episodes of a projected nine-part space saga in which Lucas proposes to develop the epic potential of his fictional universe. Although he plans to remain solely in the capacity of producer for the series, it is expected that his artistic vision will inform the entire project. (See also *Contemporary Authors,* Vols. 77-80.)

STANLEY KAUFFMANN

[*THX 1138*] is a classic instance of what is right and wrong with many US film-school graduates. Lucas has good eyes, if no original vision, and he knows a lot about film technique; but what he does with it all is thin. He has acquired a lot of skills but not much self.

Would you believe one more story about the dehumanized future, where people have numbers instead of names, where Big Electronic Brother watches all, where everyone wears the same white uniform and all heads are shaved, where the unseen State disposes as it will, and where the great sin is—hold on, now—love? The script by Lucas and Walter Murch almost has an arrogance toward the *need* to have a fresh idea.

Lucas has clearly made his bet on his cinematic display, and to his credit, he sustains interest on that score for about fifteen minutes. Disregard the collegiate jape of beginning with a Buck Rogers clip and then having the credits roll downward—as if this departure from rolling them upward made a particle of difference—and then we get a pretty good initial display of splintery quick editing, with blue filters, white-on-white figures, computer printouts, wall-size TV, capsule meals, robot policemen, and so on. All this is somewhat entertaining for a while, despite the derivations from *2001,* despite the mimicking of *Alphaville* by using modern structures (garages, vehicular tunnels) as buildings of the future.

But Lucas would have to be one of the great geniuses of film history to hold us this way for 90 minutes, to keep us from discovering that he really doesn't have a clue as to why he made this picture, other than that he wanted to crack the whip at this cinema circus, and that he's patched together this old story as an arena. (pp. 24, 31-2)

"Shut your mind and open your eyes," films of this type suggest. "Nuts," is what I suggest in return. A great many good films ask us to keep our minds *and* eyes open; so why should we put up with this latter-day fiddle? (p. 32)

Stanley Kauffmann, "Films: 'THX 1138'" (reprinted by permission of Brandt & Brandt Literary Agents, Inc.; copyright © 1971 by Stanley Kauffmann), in The New Republic, *Vol. 164, No. 15, April 10, 1971, pp. 24, 31-2.*

STANLEY KAUFFMANN

[When artists use their young years as subject matter,] they have to prove that their young years can be fascinating to others. Broadly speaking, there are only two ways to do this: by showing that your young years were extraordinary or by finding depth and form that illuminate and *preserve* the commonplace. (p. 218)

George Lucas has tried for the latter. He has taken some familiar bull right by the horns and has wrestled it into a reasonably good film. A couple of years ago . . . Lucas made a "future" film called *THX 1138* in which he lavished impressive cinematic skills on material so trite that he made me feel he had "an arrogance toward the need to have a fresh idea" [see excerpt above]. This new script—by himself, Gloria Katz and Willard Huyck—still has no new ideas as such. But working close to what is apparently his own youthful experience, Lucas has so integrated methods and material that he finds some of the depth and form mentioned above; and, to some degree, he transforms the banalities of TV situation comedy into a small epiphany of a period. (pp. 218-19)

But the story is not the film—only its means of coming into being. (Which is what Lucas attempted, less successfully, in *THX 1138*.) The weakest parts are those that try to beef up the script, in plot and literary "theme" terms, like the mysterious blonde in a white T-bird who weaves symbolically through the film taunting one of the boys. . . . [The] pleasures of the picture are in the way it was made. There is no mere springboard of accurate decor, as in *Summer of '42*, which got all its details right, then wallowed ahead into syrup: the milieu, so to speak, *is* this film, or what is best about it.

Lucas has picked a moving medium for a moving picture. Most of it—seemingly—takes place in and around cruising automobiles in the town streets. (p. 219)

This mobility is of course fit for film, and it's an easy figure of sexual exploration and of social rite of passage—passage —to maturity. From dusk to dawn, yet. But Lucas sees the automobile as the focus of other cultural implications: the broadcast music of the time, the eating of the time (drive-ins, with waitresses on roller skates), even the hoodlumism of the time. When some not-so-juvenile delinquents want to scare one of the boys, what do they do? They take him for a ride!

So we see a group of late adolescents pinned to a target for cultural barrage. The drive-in food has funny names ("a double Chubby Chuck") that seem to feed them as much as the food itself. They are followed everywhere by the voice of a disc jockey whom they adore. (And he's a black man. When one boy goes to see him at his lonely early-morning studio, he denies his identity, saying that he's only the broadcaster of tapes. Lucas implies that it's not yet time for a black deity to reveal himself.) And of course there's the force of the movies themselves, who modeled the gang of hoods and the styles of kissing and romance.

As the picture floated and intertwined, it reminded me of Twyla Tharp's recent ballet *Deuce Coupe*—the phrase occurs in the dialogue—which used early '60s music from one of the same sources, the Beach Boys. The more it resembles ballet, the better *American Graffiti* is. The more it tries to delve into character and build climaxes (like an unbelievable prank on a police car), the thinner and more sitcom it gets.

Haskell Wexler, the accomplished cinematographer who was "visual consultant" on the film, saw the need for realistic abstraction. For instance an all-night stand called Mel's Drive-in is an oval neon temple with suggestions of the War Room in *Dr. Strangelove*. When *American Graffiti* concentrates like this, on *being* what it's about, it succeeds. (pp. 219-20)

Stanley Kauffmann, "'American Graffiti'" (originally published in The New Republic, *Vol. 169, No. 11, September 15, 1973), in his* Living Images: Film Comment and Criticism *(copyright © 1971, 1972, 1973, 1974 by Stanley Kauffmann; reprinted by permission of Harper & Row, Publishers, Inc.), Harper, 1975, pp. 218-20.*

MICHAEL DEMPSEY

[In *American Graffiti*] Lucas and his fellow writers, Gloria Katz and Willard Huyck, manage to be serious without portentous symbolism or heavy underlining. They slip on an end title which they should have let the audience write for itself but, otherwise, their poise is flawless; the car crash at the end, to take the most obvious example, has not been inflated into an apocalypse. Despite its crowded sound track and its mesmerizing flow of images, *American Graffiti* is a low-keyed, unpretentious movie. Yet it cuts to the heart of something serious and entangling in American life. . . .

Lucas has been amazingly thorough and technically dazzling in conjuring up this "last year of the fifties." Except for the final two sequences, the whole movie takes place after dark. Aided by his creative cast and camera crews supervised by Haskell Wexler, Lucas has spliced bits of San Francisco, San Rafael, and Petaluma into a ghost-dancing, iridescent nightgown, a galaxy of pranks, games, thrills, and lights through which the gaudy cars weave and cruise like phantoms. Maybe, after *THX 1138*, locking us into enclosed worlds is turning out to be a Lucas specialty, but *American Graffiti* has no trace of the earlier film's tired ideas and visual clichés out of tritely doom-laden student epics. It captures the humor and verve of youth that can, at least briefly, transform pop-schlock trash into an amusing, stylish constellation of codes and rituals. At the same time, it also finds some surprising emotions lurking behind them: each characterization catches us off guard with unexpected quirks and depths. . . . *American Graffiti* is not just a checklist of fifties memorabilia; it uses them to recapture the *attitudes* of the period, particularly the innocence that Vietnam, Oswald, hard drugs, birth-control pills, Nixon—the whole spectrum of sixties shake-ups—would alter, perhaps destroy, forever. (p. 58)

[The] surprising resonance of *American Graffiti* stems from its understated but trenchant criticism of nostalgia. . . . Lucas captures the sheer disposability of pop culture and its trappings. It's a jolt for anyone of his generation to see how quaint everything—clothes, cars, slang—now looks and sounds, nearly as archaic as the flivvers, phaetons, spats and idle rich of the twenties and thirties. Then you think, "But this was only eleven years ago." Those who thoughtlessly call this a "period picture," though it is one, unknowingly highlight its weird, unnerving distillation of future shock. Even those utterly inured to rapid change may feel a chill or two while they bellylaugh, when they experience firsthand how swiftly only yesterday has turned into long ago.

The movie is firmly plugged into the nostalgia boom that plays upon our desires for a sense of roots, for a more comprehensible world, for a half-fearful look back at our own innocence. The same media that bring disorienting change to our living rooms and thereby stimulate our urges to recapture the past usually reduce that past to safe, sentimental placebos: nostalgia peddlers chew up ever more recent chunks of yesterday and spit them out as flavorless, denatured pulp. But in *American Graffiti,* superman John—a wistful blend of machismo and charm, braggadocio and uneasiness—rebukes these merchandisers and those in thrall to them. He is living what they sell. . . .

John is part of an American syndrome whose victims litter our imaginative writing: the "big rods" in Dan Wakefield's novel of the fifties, *Going All The Way,* rudderless jocks fixated on the sham accomplishments of their youths; F. Scott Fitzgerald's Tom Buchanan, the aging polo player who will never outgrow his cheap emotions; the paunchy, tired American gargoyles of Jason Miller's play, *That Championship Season,* compulsively reenacting the Big Game because it has turned out to be the high point of their miserable lives. In some ways, John is a more complex character than any of these: he is younger, softer, more sympathetic. (p. 59)

In *American Graffiti,* none of the young people but Curt can abandon a hometown . . . that is incandescent by night but deadening in the glare of the following day. The movie is a poetic lament for the passing of their wondrous night and all that it seemed to promise. This and the sensitivity of Lucas, Katz, and Huyck to the blighting influence of social conditioning on life's most crucial steps lends to *American Graffiti,* for all its real exuberance, a strong undertone of heartbreaking pathos. (p. 60)

Michael Dempsey, "Reviews: 'American Graffiti'," in Film Quarterly *(copyright 1973 by The Regents of the University of California; reprinted by permission of the University of California Press), Vol. XXVII, No. 1, Fall, 1973, pp. 58-60.*

PAULINE KAEL

Using women (and not only women) as plot functions may be a clue to the shallowness of many movies, even of much better movies—*American Graffiti,* for example. The audience at *American Graffiti* appears to be ecstatically happy condescending toward its own past—how cute we were at seventeen, how funny, how lost—but for women the end of the picture is a cold slap. Set in 1962, *American Graffiti* compresses into one night the events from high school graduation to the opening of college in the fall. At the close, it jumps to the present and wraps up the fates of the four principal male characters—as if lives were set ten years after high school!—and it ignores the women characters. This is one of those bizarre omissions that tell you what really goes on in men filmmakers' heads and what women—who are now, for the first time in movie history, half the moviegoing audience—bitterly (or unconsciously) swallow. (p. 193)

Because of the energy of the performers, Laurie and Carol stay in the memory more vividly than the boys, but that chilling omission at the end is indicative of the limited male imagination of the picture. I don't think the director, George Lucas, who also worked on the script, ever wondered whether Laurie, who wants her boy-man Steve so fiercely and wants nothing else, could sustain the giving over of herself or whether her intensity would sour into neurosis. Was Steve really enough for her, and could he stand being her everything? These questions arise because of the shrill vibes in Cindy Williams' performance, not because of the context; the garish, overdrawn blond swinger Debbie (Candy Clark), who comes out of the comic strips, is probably meant to be as believable as Laurie. The facile wrap-up of the men's lives (so like the brisk, neat finishes of old movies—everything in place) is consistent with the naïve seriousness of the film which audiences find so appealing. I like the look of *American Graffiti,* and the feel of it. Lucas has a sensual understanding of film . . . , Lucas is a real filmmaker. But *American Graffiti* fails to be anything more than a warm, nice, draggy comedy, because there's nothing to back up the style. The images aren't as visually striking as they would be if only there were a mind at work behind them; the movie has no resonance except from the jukebox sound and the eerie, nocturnal jukebox look. And I don't like the pop narcissism of it—the way it invites the audience to share in a fond, jokey view of its own adolescence. (pp. 193-94)

The audiences allow the fifties jukebox tunes on the track to define their early lives for them. I think they can laugh so easily because the shared recognitions are all external; it's the giggle you get from looking at a false image of yourself. Though done with style, this is fake folk art, and the kids are stock characters. (p. 194)

[The protagonists of *American Graffiti*] don't know what they want; they're searching. The girls . . . want nothing but men. I raise this point not to make a feminist issue of it (though that's implicit) but to make an aesthetic one: mechanical people, including searching young men, are a blight on the movies—evidence that the filmmakers aren't thinking freshly, that they're resorting to the stockpile. (p. 195)

Pauline Kael, "Un-People" (originally published in The New Yorker, *Vol. XLIX, No. 36, October 29, 1973), in her* Reeling *(copyright © 1973 by Pauline Kael; reprinted by permission of Little, Brown and Company in association with the Atlantic Monthly Press), Atlantic-Little, Brown, 1976, pp. 263-70.**

ALICE SODOWSKY, ROLAND SODOWSKY, and STEPHEN WITTE

[*American Graffiti*] imports more than mere nostalgia for a past: it explores the consequences of technology upon an age that still has the need to understand experience through a mixture of epic, myth, and romance patterns. *American Graffiti*'s achievement—or near-achievement—is that it gives us a chance to satisfy this need, to find these patterns, in a mundane, all-too-familiar mechanized world.

The mythic land of *American Graffiti* is a country of city streets under the false day of relentless lights, of youths who live on wheels, where even the waitresses are on roller-skates and where all are electronically linked through the pulsating beat of their radios. The music (of the spheres?) is broadcast by Wolfman Jack, the mysterious surrogate god of this neon wasteland. Among its inhabitants are a few adults who are shadow figures, aliens briefly encountered with hostility or indifference by the true "citizens" of this country. . . . There is however an adult who remains ambiguous. She is the elusive blonde in the white Thunderbird, a woman who may be a prostitute or the wife of a jeweler, or both, or neither. Silently mouthing "I love you," she is a vision of beauty that Curt has seen through the double windows of the parallel cars. She is the dualistic symbol of romance and seduction, a figure of great appeal yet associated with societal decadence.

Defining the topography of this mythic country are the patterned streets of Modesto, California, which stretch into mazes of vibrating lines and harsh colors ending on one side at the wooded lake area where couples attempt to make love and where, as the story goes, the Goatman kills people. On the other side, however, a route extends beyond the boundaries of the country. It is Paradise Road, where two climactic actions occur: John Milner defeats the challenger from another town here, and Curt's last view of Modesto is of this road as his plane carries him away.

Within this closed "universe" moves John Milner, ducktailed driver of a chopped and channeled '32 Ford, the fastest car in town. John is the epic hero of *American Graffiti*'s society: he is the idealization of its code of conduct, the gloomy (because of his Beowulfian sense of his own impending doom) upholder of the "traditional" values of the high school set, the foremost of the Mel's Drive-In knights who, not unlike those of Arthur's Round Table, start out on their quests for adventure from the circular curbs of this Burger-and-Coke Camelot and return to recount their deeds, always accompanied and comforted by the omnipresent, seemingly omniscient voice of their local deity, Wolfman Jack. John's legs are too long for his torso, so that his walk is almost absurdly graceless; he cannot stand, but slouches against car fenders and walls, thumbs in pockets or belt loops. Only when he dons the "armor" of his squinting, visor-like hotrod coupe does he assume heroic proportions; like his literary antecedents, Milner is nothing unless encased in his battle dress. (pp. 47-8)

John cannot carry the entire burden of the hero in *American Graffiti,* however, because he is limited. He is capable of feats of derring-do only within the physical-social sphere of his "world." It remains for Curt, the anti-hero, whose consciousness increasingly includes more than John can comprehend, to reach beyond the apparent bounds toward a spiritual goal, symbolized by the woman in the Thunderbird. Curt is neither wholly within nor without the order: he drives a rickety Citroen, an obviously weak link to John's souped-up world. But despite the ambiguity of his relationship to the society, of which Curt alone seems aware, he is accepted and even esteemed by its members, as though they somehow sense his importance, as a kind of societal *Vates,* a poet-prophet, to them. John is his rough but sincere friend; a former girl friend still has affection for him; even the "Pharoah Gang" members eventually solicit his companionship after first threatening to kill him.

John and Curt's adventures during the night differ essentially in that John, having long since passed all initiatory tests and having no further ambitions, needs nothing and learns nothing. For Curt, everything is preparatory: the high school hop merely amuses him and he leaves, while another member of the peer group, Steve, remains—an action foreshadowing the fate of the two characters which is so mechanically proclaimed in the "epilogue" of the film. Curt engineers an abrupt leave-taking from a former girl friend while Laurie entices Steve to stay behind; in league with the Pharoah gang, Curt sabotages a police car then tactfully rejects them; he talks face-to-face with Wolfman Jack while the rest speak of the disc jockey as another-worldly figure. Unlike Curt's destiny, John's is heroic in the society's terms because it is identifiable; Curt's "destiny" has some parallels with John's but is unheroic because it is beyond the society's ken.

Curt and John, then, are hero and anti-hero around whom the episodes leading to the climactic drag race and Curt's departure revolve. John's rescue of Toad from . . . two thugs, his preliminary race with Bob Falfa, the issuing of challenges and counter-challenges, and the encounter with the cop are trivial activities from an adult's point of view or perhaps from Curt's, but, given the values of the world as John knows them, the episodes take on significance and thereby qualify as epic-heroic actions. In this sense John is not unlike the western gunfighter caught in a time and place by his role, sensing his own doom and unable to escape it. Curt's actions against adult or alien "enemies," such as the cops and the Moose Lodge members, are significant within the order; but he recognizes the meaninglessness of those actions. Reinforcing the idea of triviality within the system is Toad, who, like the original braggadocio, dons armor for which he is unfit and parodies—and thus cheapens—the actions of the real hero. Furthermore, Toad's too-eager acceptance of an armor for which he is unsuited prepares the audience for the stark announcement of his death in the Vietnam War. (pp. 49-50)

Curt and John make parallel visits into areas which have meanings beyond those which the hero and the anti-hero have previously explored. These areas take on significance because Curt and John are not accompanied by music and because they cannot come into these places by car. Milner takes Carol to a dark salvage lot, the equivalent of the epic romance underworld, where they walk in the quiet unlit shadows as Milner points out the dented and crushed armors of past heroes. The scene bodes not only Milner's eventual death but also the death of the world which sustains him.

Curt, on the other hand, makes his visit to the radio tower where, if he does not experience an ethereal vision, he at least begins to understand what is amiss in his blacktopped world. Curt "climbs the mountain" in search of Wolfman Jack, the elusive and mysterious disc jockey god to whom all the young knights and their ladies respond and whose music provides the background for all the film's errant adventures. Curt hopes that Wolfman Jack will send a radio message which will put him in touch with the nameless blonde in the Thunderbird. The tower, unlike the salvage lot, is brightly lighted, making it easy for Curt to find its only inhabitant, a corpulent man sucking popsicles. He tells Curt that he is not Wolfman Jack but that he will do what he can to get the message to him. Then, between slurps on his popsicle, he off-handedly advises Curt to leave town. He also offers Curt a popsicle (the wafer of the electronic temple) which Curt, significantly, refuses. As Curt leaves, he overhears the fellow taping a Wolfman Jack commercial and thus learns what no one else in his group knows, viz., that the sticky-fingered man is the pop god of the air. Curt returns from the tower; and although his quest cannot be granted by the turntable deity, Curt will act on his advice, thereby freeing himself from the world in which John Milner is both hero and victim.

Curt's increasingly frantic search for the woman in the white Thunderbird is like the other episodes of the film in that it has meaning only in context, and even there only for Curt's heightened awareness. Given these conditions, she—or the ideal she represents for Curt—gradually acquires a mythic significance; she is the Holy Grail of King Arthur's Knights, the romantic Daisy of *The Great Gatsby,* the powerful ring of *The Hobbit*—all of which are associated with the collapse of a society. Thus, Curt's quest is less spectacular but ultimately more profound in its impact than John's adventures; Curt cannot attain the White Vision in Modesto, but he can leave the "world"; and when he does so, he sees from the airplane window that if he has not yet achieved the goal of his quest he is at least headed in the right direction, away from the neon nights of Modesto and toward the sun of a larger world.

Thus these gasoline-powered experiences become, as they are translated into time-honored patterns, more than graffiti, more than isolated adventures in nostalgia. In looking at the two protagonists, John the inner hero, gloomy with a half awareness that he epitomizes the values of a world he no longer can belong to or escape from, and Curt, the anti-hero who is able to leave John's world, we are painfully aware of the kind of society being explored in this film. The land of techno-youth is as depressing a nether world as one could imagine. But the meshing, valid or not, of this four-wheeled world with the patterns in which our ancestors once found dignity and meaning offers us a bit of sanity, allows us to fulfill that singular human need to find form where there appears to be none. (pp. 53, 54-5)

Alice Sodowsky, Roland Sodowsky, and Stephen Witte, "The Epic World of 'American Graffiti'," in Journal of Popular Film *(copyright © 1975 by Sam L. Grogg, Jr., Michael T. Marsden, and John G. Nachbar), Vol. IV, No. 1, 1975, pp. 47-55.*

STANLEY KAUFFMANN

George Lucas has made three features: *THX 1138,* which was about the future; *American Graffiti,* which was about adolescents; and now *Star Wars,* which is a "future" film for adolescents. Neither of the earlier pictures was distinguished for novelty or depth, but *THX 1138* tried to compensate with visual and technical ingenuity, and *American Graffiti* found some good objective correlatives, in cinematic method, for its study of small-town teen-agers. *Star Wars* . . . doesn't have the technological cleverness of his first, and it's about nothing more than what it seems to be about.

This is Lucas' tribute to Flash Gordon, and is now enthralling all those who feel that Flash Gordon needs a two-hour, eight-million-dollar tribute. There's a glitzy attempt at profundity in the opening title which tells us that the story took place on a galaxy far away "a long time ago." It really takes place in the science-fiction future, a place which is as fixed and fictitious for bad sci-fi writers as the Old West is for bad Western writers. Lucas' script has Good Guys, Bad Guys, a princess, intergalactic imperialist war, staunch defenders of human and humanoid rights, secrets that will not be surrendered to the warlords—a whole spectrum of simplified earthly problems projected onto cardboard and illuminated with interminable ray-gun flashes and last-minute huge explosions.

About the dialogue there's nothing to be said. In fact the dialogue *itself* can hardly be said: it sticks in the actors' mouths like peanut butter. . . .

The only way that *Star Wars* could have been interesting was through its visual imagination and special effects. Both are unexceptional. I was not the world's biggest fan of Kubrick's *2001,* but surely after that picture and after the work of Jordan Belson that preceded it, space films have an ingenuity-mark to aim at before they can engage our wonder. In no way does Lucas come up to the Kubrick/Belson level, and, to rely on my memory, his work here seems less inventive than in *THX 1138.*

But I saw at last—after about, say, 20 minutes—that *Star Wars* wasn't meant to be ingenious in any way; it was meant to be exactly what it is. From Lucas' view it certainly has not failed. I kept looking for an "edge," to peer around the corny, solemn comic-book strophes; he was facing them frontally and full. This picture was made for those (particularly males) who carry a portable shrine within them of their adolescence, a chalice of a Self that was Better Then, before the world's affairs or—in any complex way—sex intruded. Flash Gordon, Buck Rogers and their peers guard the portals of American innocence, and *Star Wars* is an unabashed, jaw-clenched tribute to the chastity still sacred beneath the middle-aged spread. (p. 22)

Stanley Kauffmann, "Films: 'Star Wars'" (reprinted by permission of Brandt & Brandt Literary Agents, Inc.; copyright © 1977 by Stanley Kauffmann), in The New Republic, *Vol. 176, No. 5, June 18, 1977, pp. 22-3.*

RICHARD A. BLAKE

"Star Wars" is original and surprising. It is witty, not only in its comic dialogue, but in its ability to spoof itself and the science-fiction genre without going for the cheap laugh. . . .

Pointing out the "message" of such an avowedly entertaining film is to risk the humorless pomposity that plagues film journals. But even the most entertaining film can propose a message and, in fact, the message may even heighten the entertainment, as it does in "Star Wars."

Basically, the film is an expression of mid-20th-century romanticism, an act of faith and hope in the eventual triumph of old-fashioned humanity over the technology that surrounds it. The young actors are all rather dull characters, dehumanized by the society in which they live. They are extensions of their machines. As a parody of the humans, the robots are far more interesting people. . . . They argue, sulk, express affection, sacrifice themselves, have accidents and remain singlemindedly loyal to one another. C3PO, with his Jeeves English, and R2D2, with his buzzes and blips of computer talk, may be the best new comedy team since Rowan and Martin. In contrast to these sensitive marvels that man can create, man himself is pretty dull. (p. 568)

Richard A. Blake, "Two Histories of Film," in America *(© America Press, 1977; all rights reserved), Vol. 136, No. 25, June 25, 1977, pp. 568-69.**

ROBERT HATCH

Star Wars belongs to the sub-basement, or interstellar comic-strip, school of science fiction; *Terry and the Pirates* with astro-drive. The main participants are a princess in mortal peril, a splendid young Four-H type who is fated to rescue her, an irreverent free enterpriser with a space ship for hire, an aged mystic possessed of "the Force," and a gaggle of villains who, when they are not entirely encased in elegantly fitted plastic armor, look very much like extras borrowed from scenes of the Wehrmacht general staff plotting Hitlerian strategies. The princess . . . is spunky and in both manner and hair style somewhat resembles the Gish sisters; the young knight . . . is not quite bright but adroit with machinery; the freebooter . . . talks with shocking cynicism out of the side of his mouth, but has an honest heart; and the old mystic, survivor of a chivalric order that combined stunning swordsmanship with the ability to transmit psychic force by telepathy. . . .

These human actors are consistently upstaged by a pair of robots—one of them, an electronic improvement on the Tin Woodsman, seems to have derived his stilted vocabulary and obsequious manners from the servants' quarters of *Upstairs, Downstairs;* the other, shaped rather like a canister vacuum cleaner, but without the hose, is possessed (like the mind reader in *The Thirty-Nine Steps*) of the secret information that is causing all the fireworks, speaks in beeps, whistles and blinking lights and is as emotionally vulnerable as a motherless child.

This is the sort of thing that will leach one's brain, and I suspect that George Lukas . . . concocted the plot and personages deliberately to put us all in a slack-jawed state of mind suitable for maximum appreciation of his astonishing cinematic trickery. . . .

Years from now, long after the last bucket of popcorn has been eaten at the last neighborhood showing of *Star Wars,* film buffs will be regaling one another with recollections of their favorite scenes and persons. . . . All in all, it is an outrageously successful, what will be called a "classic," compilation of nonsense, largely derived but thoroughly reconditioned. I doubt that anyone will ever match it, though the imitations must already be on the drawing boards.

Robert Hatch, "Films: 'Star Wars'," in The Nation *(copyright 1977 The Nation Associates, Inc.), Vol. 224, No. 25, June 25, 1977, p. 794.*

ROBERT G. COLLINS

[A] film such as *Star Wars* proves anew that the descriptive capability of the camera can be effective, as words cannot, at a certain level of generalized and popular experience. (p. 1)

[Taken for what it is, *Star Wars*] functions as magic. With incredible audacity, it combines the stereotypes of modern pop literature and cinema with the Arthurian romance. Lucas deliberately and obviously steals from such movie antecedents as the original *Wizard Of Oz,* from the classic movie and pulp westerns based on the frontier tradition, from the old World War I and World War II flying battles. In fact, it is done so deliberately that a second considerations forces one to drop the word "steal" and substitute another verb; Lucas *weaves together* these elements of modern myth and ties them to earlier ones that have long since embedded themselves in our historical consciousness. The result is a new and effective narrative technique. Because he is creating visual literature, language becomes secondary, a simple supplement to the camera's flowing image out of which emerges the myth. The lines of dialogue, virtually all drawn from stock situations, are audible gestures, the phrasing so familiar that we need hear only half a sentence to know what the second half will be. And yet satire is clearly neither intended nor unwittingly achieved. Lines that, out of the context of their amalgamation in this work, would be absurdly hackneyed, here evoke only a smile of pleasure at their familiarity in an exotic world. Clichés, as often as not, are folk wisdom; they only become platitudes . . . when they occur in an irrelevant situation. Not infrequently humor depends on them. The difference between *Star Wars* and, say, Woody Allen's sci-fi film *Sleepers* is that *Star Wars* takes its frame of existence seriously at each step, although it includes at the same time a great amount of fun. It creates a world as separate as that of Spenser or the medieval romance. Through it we become voyeurs, visual eavesdroppers, on an alternate history from our own but one in which all of our emotional realities are recognizable. Undoubtedly there are less obvious others, but *Star Wars* confronts us as the first omnibus work of generalized myth in the film medium. (pp. 1-2)

[Much] has been made of the deliberate distancing of this work. It takes place, we are told, "long ago, in a galaxy far, far away." The classic fairy tale "once upon a time." Within the story are many sentient life forms, monsters to our view, who live in a communal pattern shared by human beings. Yet it is clearly a world in which surrogates for ourselves—recognizable human beings of the ordinary sort, going about mundane activities—live. As the story unfolds, we share their identity. On the other hand, the setting and technology are, from our point of view, clearly futuristic, involving space travel at speeds beyond that of light, interplanetary commerce and warfare, laser guns, and the like. In brief, their past is something that we view as our future.

The artistic advantages of such distancing are distinct. Whatever happens need not have been verified by our historical past, for instance. Moreover, the sense of it all having happened long ago, particularly when combined with the archtypal myth elements employed by George Lucas, suggest that as future it has a positive inevitability about it—fate, in an affirmative sense.

The controlling myth with which Lucas works, although it is nowhere referred to in the film, is the legend of Prince Arthur. Here, the cosmic avatar is the youth Luke Skywalker. . . . [*Star Wars*] is obviously a first chapter in a multiple-phase history—the initiation of the young hero. As with Uther Pendragon, the Red Cross Knight, and others, the surname is definitive: *Skywalker,* the champion who will traverse the aerial seas of the universe, fighting the remote and awesome forces of evil known as the Empire. The first name, *Luke,* as George Lucas himself must know, given his own surname, is one that means "Light," the visual life-nurturer of the cosmos. Another myth operates in complementary fashion at the outset: Luke is apparently a farm boy who yearns to get away from the monotony of daily life, doing domestic chores around the home place. A standard popular myth, that of the yokel who turns out to be a great natural fighter, it is also illusory and gives way before an older and more classical one: Luke is a prince in disguise. . . . As hero, Luke is thus certified by a dynastic heritage; and that, one which is related to the father, for the traditional saga hero is virtually motherless in contrast to the modern psychologically defined literary protagonist of involuted concerns. His release from his false identity (one of refuge while the child grows into the man) and the beginning of his initiation into the heroic mold comes about as a result of a desperate plea for help from a beautiful princess now imprisoned in a dungeon by the evil governor of an apparently impregnable space station (i.e. interstellar castle) which holds all planets in the galaxy in subjugation. The message, delivered by a loyal robot that has escaped capture and is now being pursued by the Imperial forces, is the occasion for bringing together Luke and the aged wise man who will be his mentor, the Merlin who will teach him the arcane secret of his warrior priesthood. . . . It is he who delivers to Luke the "magic sword," the ancient laser sword that was the traditional weapon of the Jedi Knights, passed on from the mythic father to the chosen son now grown to man's estate. It is, of course, Excalibur, the sword of Siegfried, the Armor of Achilles, the Singing Sword of Prince Valiant, to link modern pop literature with its forebears. As is true with all magic weapons, Luke must learn to master it and, as Ben Kenobi tells him, it is only by faith, a complete acceptance of "the Force" that this will eventually be possible. He must become pure, by freeing himself of doubt.

Ben Kenobi himself is very much of a Merlin parallel. First described as a "crazy old wizard" by the practical Owen, Ben Kenobi lives like all traditional saints and wise men as a hermit in the desert, held in awe by the rude and primitive Sand People from whom he rescues the youth, Luke. It is he who invests Luke with the Quest, the freeing of Princess Leia Organa, through which his destiny as a hero will be fulfilled. As guardian of the Secret, the old man is the means of the escape for the others from the Imperial Space Station known as the Death Star. In a battle with the Dark Lord of the Sith, Darth Vader, a Black Knight who was once his prize pupil but now, having chosen to use his magical power for evil, is chief warrior to the Imperial Governor, Ben Kenobi delivers his fateful prediction: though he must yield to the younger man's physical strength, in being struck down he takes on new spiritual strength and will rise in death more powerful than ever before. Though Time cannot be denied, neither can Truth. And when the Dark Lord strikes and Ben Kenobi falls, there is found on the floor only his sword and his empty clothes. Like Merlin, he has disappeared from this earth; but in time of greatest peril for the young prince of whom he has become the good spirit, he will return as a voice whispering the way to salvation. The aged Oedipus, Jesus, King Arthur in his turn, from Barbarossa to Quetzelcoatl the list could go on of those mythic heroes who, their immediate earthly task done, vanish without physical death and in so doing remain as active spirit whose return is promised in time of need. Darth Vader himself, a black-clad monstrous power, is a fallen archangel, a Miltonic Lucifer whose wings stretched out over chaos are those of a deadly space craft.

Luke, as we meet him, is an unshaped figure, virtually without a personal psychology, in place of which he displays a natural idealism and instinctive sense of responsibility. As the young untried knight in the tradition of Parsifal, Galahad, Spenser's Red Cross Knight (or the Once and Future King), he is predestined to become an embodiment of the community's best ideals emerging in heroic action. (pp. 2-4)

As Knight-initiate, Luke receives the magic laser sword, is instructed by his aged warrior-mentor, goes forth successfully on his first Quest of honor. Additionally, too, he has an entourage, beginning with Han Solo, the pragmatic, earthy, capable, amoral side-kick, whose ritual character has been defined in literature since Greek satyrdrama and Latin comedy. He is the noble youth's parasite who straightens out matters, Sancho Panza, the grumbling squire who, when all is said and done, will not abandon the foolhardy knight. Cowardice aside but humor included, he is Roderick Random's Strap, Tom Jones' Partridge, Pickwick's Sam Weller; he is Romeo's Mercutio, D'Artagnan's Three Musketeers, The Lone Ranger's Tonto, Tom Sawyer's Huck Finn, perhaps Huck Finn's Jim. The name of Han Solo (an echo of earlier television's Napoleon Solo?) with the unavoidable fusion of the two parts (Han/s/olo) suggests his freedom from the constrictive society under the Empire; he is, of course, lawless. . . . Solo himself has a side-kick, since even second knights must have their squires, his first mate, the giant monster Wookie, whose name, Chewbacca, is clearly one of authorial whimsy. Alternately brave and comically fearful, Chewbacca is one of the good monsters. Physically, he is a visual copy of Bert Lahr's Cowardly Lion in the early film version of *The Wizard of Oz*.

That film is further drawn upon for a more prominent character, the robot See-Threepio (C3 PO), who is a gilded version of Jack Haley's Tin Man, creaking along, worrying about rusting in the rain, in the original *Oz*. While no Judy Garland as Dorothy is around to sing about a rainbow, one of the early scenes in *Star Wars* shows See-Threepio and his little robot buddy Artoo-Detoo (R2 D2) on an equivalent of the yellow brick road, the sands of a golden desert, in search of the good wizard who will help them. This sequence, incidentally, is effectively structured to yield a warmth that will establish a peculiarly characteristic note of humor throughout the story; paradoxically, the two robots evoke a more affectionate response than do any of the human characters. (pp. 4-5)

In his mythic pastiche, Lucas draws heavily from modern popular adventure fiction, particularly that which was successfully adapted to early film interpretation. The most obvious one is that classic bit of romantic primitivism drawn earlier from the pulps, the frontier tradition of the western American hero. Luke's first name, conveniently, is not only latinate but evocative of a rural American identity that is more apt to remind the average modern reader/spectator of a cowboy than of the Biblical author. Through the ingenious use of stock dialogue in an exotic setting, the frontier planet Tatooine on which Luke is raised loses its strangeness for us and at moments might well be a Kansas homestead in the 1800s. . . . [Like] the standard frontier youth as potential hero, Luke is a boy who has through determined solitary practice become master of his mount, a rider (pilot) of surpassing skill as yet untested. Before we leave the frontier planet with him, we participate in "Indian" tracking among the desert canyons, surprise attack by the natives (Sand People) and rescue of the unconscious youth by the old white Shaman (Ben Kenobi) that the predatory natives regard with awe and fear. Then, too, the massacre of everyone at Luke's homestead in his absence, which frees him to go forth, and with the added motive of revenge, is a scene of fire and slaughter that resembles every Indian massacre of the past three hundred years in fact and fiction, a tradition of brutal murder come out of nowhere that has established itself as American myth from the actual smoking ruins at Deerfield to the cinematic ones in the latest Hollywood shoot-em-up. Typically, too, this one is fake in that it is staged by the brutal Imperial forces (for which, read: renegades, or bad soldiers), who massacre first the hooded Scavengers, then everyone at Luke's home farm, and try to make it look like an attack of the Sand People. But, says the shrewd old Ben Kenobi, "Sand People always travel single-file," not abreast. Shades of Zane Grey! Or, more appropriately, Fenimore Cooper.

Here, however, cliché situations and dialogue represent a double reverse. Rather than creating implausibility, their very familiarity leads us to an acceptance of the characters and of the setting that might otherwise be impossible. There are, one should note, strong echoes of the stock western in the previously mentioned Han Solo, who handles his laser gun with all the skill of Wyatt Earp in a number of shoot-outs. Appropriately, too, for this situation, the hackneyed nature of the incidents suggests at times the mock violence of a Tom-and-Jerry animated cartoon. . . . A further pop comic effect is achieved when the captive Princess Leia Organa, clad in classical white tunic though she is, turns out to be a tough-minded gal who, when they are trapped and her male would-be rescuers are milling around in confusion, snorts in exasperation, says "Let's blast our way out out of here," and grabbing a gun from one of them promptly fits her words to action by blowing a gaping hole in the nearest wall. A scrappy heroine, she plays the role of the suppliant maiden in the tradition of Una in Spenser's *Faerie Queen* with all the aplomb of Calamity Jane in Buffalo Bill's Original Wild West Show. (pp. 6-7)

[The] characters in *Star Wars,* with the slight exception of the robots, and that a comic one, have no psychology to cripple them. There is a clear-cut distinction between good and evil that makes *Star Wars* virtually a Manichean conflict. This clarity is reinforced by the full range of technical device, including some scenes that are aesthetically gorgeous and which serve as a contrast to the plastic, mechanical, and dehumanized character attributed to the Imperial forces. The result of such arbitrary distinctions might well have been the simpleminded, or even silly, actions that form the basis for much mass-consumer art, but we have been through a long period of spurious complexity of character, with sociologists and psychologists wending their way through soap operas the way that the good country doctor or the selfless minister plodded through nineteenth century fiction. In *Star Wars,* the moral distinction is so well handled that a freshness and innocence is achieved which virtually makes credible the call for a renewed faith in the underlying truth of things ("The Force") of which Ben Kenobi is the spokesman.

Moreover, the simplicity and beauty of the total experience yields a warm sense of delight. As told on film, the story is an example of that humor which underlies the best of all science fiction: the mind playing with possibilities, creating dangers to face, anticipating horrors that have not yet been born. Fear made incarnate and then controlled. (p. 8)

[What] has George Lucas achieved by bringing such older myths as the Arthurian hero together with the myths of twentieth century popular art forms? First of all, he rediscovers the old myths for us, of course. At the same time, he legitimizes the modern myths of popular art forms. By casting both into an exotic time and locale, he makes that setting plausible while fusing the earlier and later varieties of myth. A conservative impulse frequently has a revolutionary effect, and a resurgence of traditional myth at the popular level seems always to represent a yearning for a future in which former values will be reasserted, in which an idealized past (paradoxically seen as eternally youthful) returns to purge a decadent present. If the old myths had fallen into disuse, and new ones had not yet reached the dignity of legitimate art, in *Star Wars* we have a clear attempt to make them glitter with new life as they become one. (p. 9)

Robert G. Collins, "'Star Wars': The Pastiche of Myth and the Yearning for a Past Future," in Journal of Popular Culture *(copyright © 1977 by Ray B. Browne), Vol. XI, No. 1, Summer, 1977, pp. 1-10.*

ARTHUR LUBOW

If you want a loyal friend or a lethal weapon, try a machine. But when the revolution is sliding down the incinerator chute and there's only five seconds left to save it, you had better rely on the Life Force.

That's the unexpected message of *Star Wars,* a movie which manages to slap technology's face while celebrating the glories of gadgetry. This double-jointed maneuver gives the film its springy bounce. An anti-modern message in an ultra-modern wrapper: what could be more stylish? What could be more fun?

Much of *Star Wars'* success is simply the overflow from its excesses. Loaded with enough special features to equip a dozen lesser vehicles, hurtling along at a velocity close to light speed, George Lucas's movie breaks down all barriers of resistance. Like a radio serial, it begins at the middle, quickly summarizing previous events and starting right in with some sizzling action. The race is on, and there are no pit stops. No reflective pauses or digressing subplots are permitted to slow the progression of adventures. Any hints of romance are condensed into an offhand mumble of affection or a second's kiss before a daring leap. This is a boy's movie. (p. 20)

The technical achievements of *Star Wars* are so exciting that it's easy to overestimate their importance. The film's screenplay, for instance, can be dismissed as secondary. . . . Or so you think at first. But there's a sharp mind behind this mindlessness. Lucas knows exactly what he's doing.

Among the countless quotations from hack movies and comic books, one scene stands out as different. Several critics have remarked that the closing sequence of *Star Wars,* in which Luke, Han Solo, and the Wookie Chewbacca walk down a grand aisle to receive their medals, is a restaging of the march of Hitler, Himmler, and Lutze to the Nuremberg memorial monument in Leni Riefenstahl's *Triumph of the Will.* The quote is appreciated as a high-spirited joke by a former film student. If it means anything, it's merely a skeptical footnote to the heroism celebrated throughout the movie. . . . [The] reference to *Triumph of the Will* is a whispered self-criticism, a bite without teeth, a flaw smoothed away with a witticism.

Star Wars would seem to be light-years away from a celebration of Nazi power. Yet its subject is indeed the triumph of the will, and a reviewer from the *Volkische Beobachter* would find much to praise. "History is a sequence of many virile decisions," Josef Goebbels wrote in his novel, *Michael.* "Armies are not victorious, but men within armies." George Lucas has similar ideas about individual heroism. (pp. 20-1)

What we are watching is but another battle in the epic struggle between Mammon and idealism, matter and spirit. The one city depicted in *Star Wars* could be Hitler's vision of Weimar Berlin. Naturally, Luke is a farm boy of pure yeoman stock. He is justifiably sickened by the jabbering Jawas, bright-eyed itinerant merchants whom the Führer would have found familiar. No better are the Sand people, barbaric gypsies who lack culture and humanity. Against this sordid world of ugliness and corruption stand the power and the glory of the Force.

Obi-Wan defines the Force as the "energy field created by all living things . . . it binds the galaxy together." The Force is a version of Bergson's *élan vital* and Jung's collective unconscious. More to the point, it is an expression of a basic Nazi tenet: the fundamental unity of nature, the "ultimate interconnections" of all living things. To acquire enormous powers, you need only tap the Force. . . .

What are we to make of this mumbo-jumbo? Is it significant that beneath this film's futuristic skin there beats an unregenerate reactionary heart? The movie that duplicates the achievement of automation—replacing human protagonists with machines—is stridently anti-technological. *Star Wars* is a paean to mysticism and an attack on modern science. That message has a powerful appeal. It was the essence of the Nazi myth, and that's worth pointing out—not because the analogy makes *Star Wars* a "fascist movie" (its good humor and lack of rancor insure that it's not), but because it explains some of the buzz of excitement from the audiences leaving the movie theater. The Nazi mixture of heroism, self-sacrifice, and mysticism is heady stuff. When the old *Liebfraumilch* is poured into new bottles, it packs a powerful wallop. (p. 21)

Arthur Lubow, "A Space 'Iliad'—The 'Star Wars' War: I," in Film Comment *(copyright © 1977 by The Film Society of Lincoln Center; all rights reserved), Vol. 13, No. 4, July-August, 1977, pp. 20-1.*

TERRY CURTIS FOX

[The survival chances of *Star Wars*] are slim. The film defeats serious consideration. No matter how one looks at it, George Lucas has not only made a movie which is mindless where it would be mind-boggling, he has made a movie which is totally inept.

Never mind special effects. If you've seen one plastic starship you've seen them all. As for midgets in cute-suits, who remembers the amputees in *Soylent Green*? Consider instead the laser-sword which Lucas painfully spends forty-five minutes defining as an elegantly human weapon, emblematic of the life-sustaining Force. Not only is there nothing elegant, much less exciting, in the light-sword fight between Lord Darth Vader . . . and Ben/Obi-Wan Kenobi . . . , but Luke Skywalker . . . , the Force's young receiver, never gets to use the thing at all. Lucas has painfully constructed a payoff which never arrives. . . .

When it comes to extending the [science fiction] genre, Lucas hasn't done a thing. Consider Luke's return from the desert to find his surrogate parents blown away by an Imperial raiding party. The shot itself is a direct quote from *The Searchers* and, one expects, a particularly relevant quote at that. Martin Pauley's discovery of his massacred family not only occurs after a diversionary chase through a desert, but it forces Pauley to begin the redefinition of family which lies at the heart of that film. . . .

But unlike *The Searchers,* which Lucas quotes, the death of Luke's "family" causes neither pain nor a confrontation with difficult decisions. Rather than raising problems, it solves them. With his old surrogate parents conveniently killed off, Luke can follow his new surrogate father [Ben/Obi-Wan] to the ends of the universe. Between good and evil is an easy choice.

Even more revealing is the film's end quote—a hero's welcome for Luke, Han, and company which is a direct lift from Leni Reifenstahl's *Triumph of the Will.* Although there is talk about the death of a "republic" and the dismantling of a "senate," the alternative in *Star Wars* is at best a parliamentary monarchy. Not only does this world rely upon heroes, it is devoutly subservient to Princess Leia Organa. . . . The rebel forces seem to want restoration, not revolution.

This is not an idle ideological complaint. Unlike the detective novel, science fiction has yet to find its Hammett. . . . From H. P. Lovecraft's Cthulhu to Frank Herbert's Dune, SF is a genre whose strength comes from its imaginative powers, its ability to create societies in which alternative laws of action and behavior can be displayed.

Lucas, who was so successful at creating a social structure in both *THX 1138* and *American Graffiti,* seems here to have abandoned his most interesting talent. Subsumed by technology, he's lost control not only of his mechanics and metaphors but of his vision as well.

Examine, for a moment, the much praised robot comedy team of See Threepio . . . and Artoo-Detoo. . . . Like the spelling out of their names, See Threepio and Artoo-Detoo are in the throes of what Travis McGee calls "the terminal cutes." They've got everything but fur—everything, that is, except the ability to comment on human activity which makes real comedy teams (not to mention better anthropomorphizations) worthwhile.

Unlike HAL in *2001: A Space Odyssey* the robots of *Star Wars* are not the most human characters in the film. They are exactly what they pretend to be—mechanical figures endowed with a limited number of human characteristics. Like the dog with which W. C. Fields refused to appear, the robot-comics reveal nothing: they exist solely to steal scenes.

The fun-fun-fun brigade claims this is just the point. Looking at the movie closely is like throwing water on the Wicked Witch of the West—so why make it dissolve? Because Lucas has (or had) more potential and, box-office records notwithstanding, so did the film. I'd rather spend my time with a Barry Smith *Conan The Barbarian.* Smith is in control of both his material and medium; Lucas is not. (p. 23)

Terry Curtis Fox, "Star Drek—The 'Star Wars' War: II," in Film Comment *(copyright © 1977 by The Film Society of Lincoln Center; all rights re-*

served), Vol. 13, No. 4, July-August, 1977, pp. 22-3.

PAULINE KAEL

The loudness, the smash-and-grab editing, the relentless pacing drive every idea from your head; for young audiences "Star Wars" is like getting a box of Cracker Jack which is all prizes. This is the writer-director George Lucas's own film, subject to no business interference, yet it's a film that's totally uninterested in anything that doesn't connect with the mass audience. There's no breather in the picture, no lyricism; the only attempt at beauty is in the double sunset. It's enjoyable on its own terms, but it's exhausting, too: like taking a pack of kids to the circus. An hour into it, children say that they're ready to see it all over again; that's because it's an assemblage of spare parts—it has no emotional grip. "Star Wars" may be the only movie in which the first time around the surprises are reassuring. (Going a second time would be like trying to read "Catch-22" twice.) Even if you've been entertained, you may feel cheated of some dimension—a sense of wonder, perhaps. It's an epic without a dream. But it's probably the absence of wonder that accounts for the film's special, huge success. The excitement of those who call it the film of the year goes way past nostalgia to the feeling that now is the time to return to childhood.

Maybe the only real inspiration involved in "Star Wars" was to set its sci-fi galaxy in the pop-culture past, and to turn old-movie ineptness into conscious Pop Art. And maybe there's a touch of genius in keeping it so consistently what it is, even if this is the genius of the plodding. Lucas has got the tone of bad movies down pat: you never catch the actors deliberately acting badly, they just seem to be bad actors, on contract to Monogram or Republic, their klunky enthusiasm polished at the Ricky Nelson school of acting. In a gesture toward equality of the sexes, the high-school-cheerleader princess-in-distress talks tomboy-tough —Terry Moore with spunk. Is it because the picture is synthesized from the mythology of serials and old comic books that it didn't occur to anybody that *she* could get The Force? (p. 123)

Pauline Kael, "Contrasts," in The New Yorker *(© 1977 by The New Yorker Magazine, Inc.), Vol. LIII, No. 32, September 26, 1977, pp. 123-28, 131-33.**

MICHAEL PYE and LYNDA MYLES

[*THX-1138*] works at a near-abstract level. Its premise is classic in science fiction: an individual asserting himself against the social machine. Its first sequence is a quote from a Buck Rogers serial, with Our Hero "exploring the wonderful world of the twenty-fifth century." Its theme encompasses the same crushing of identity that is central to William Cameron Menzies's *Things to Come*. But Lucas works by different methods. The camera is often literally distanced from the action, to establish the weirdness and aridity of the underground world. Only for lovemaking does the camera close in on individuals; and then, it is in soft focus. The paraphernalia of the future world is voyeuristic, full of cameras that pry, screens that show, observers heard casually asking for tighter close-ups on THX as he is stunned into passivity. Its technology is as closely observed as the machines in *Star Wars*. Brisk, brash jet cars escape down endless tunnels, just as in the later film Luke Skywalker takes his jet car across the deserts of Tatooine. Electronic gauges show the robot police closing in on THX-1138 as he speeds for freedom; they resemble electronic games boards or the computer displays used in the attack on the Death Star. The delicate, spun probes that examine the body of THX are like the robot probe that threatens the Princess Leia in her cell. Parts of *THX-1138* have the same guts, panache, and vigor as the later film; they resemble a dress rehearsal. . . . One central trouble common to both films is the lack of character development; but at least in *THX-1138* the premise of the plot is that individuality has been suppressed, that the workers conform in shuffling herds like the geometric processions in Lang's *Metropolis*. Only two individuals are presented, because anonymity is the essence of the underground world.

THX-1138 plays off language in a way that is highly curious. [Co-scriptwriter Walter] Murch and Lucas evidently wanted to warn their audience of every possible route to nightmare, since the bland voices which control this bleak society are given a set of apparently conflicting clichés to recite. The constant, unfinished question of the authorities is: "Are you now, or have you ever been . . ." It echoes, obviously, the House Un-American Activities Committee at work. Yet an omnipresent voice also offers "the blessing of the State, the blessing of the Masses"; and the eye of God follows monklike figures who have power through faint suggestions of Catholic orthodoxy; there are confessionals where stand pictures of a face like Christ's, and there is a system of repentance and absolution. There is even a constant reminder—"Buy, Be Happy!"—that an affluent, consumer society has dangers too.

[*THX-1138* fails because it] is not enough of an idea, a theme, to carry a full-length film. (p. 119)

The tension between our dreams and Lucas's life is what makes [*American Graffiti*] work for so large an audience. The low light filming, with its curious, golden radiance, becomes a dream. Time is collapsed. All the central characters are confronted with a turning point in the course of a single night. Yet that night could be placed anywhere within a decade. Cars and music span ten years, an era rather than a date. The slogan for the film—"Where were you in '62?" —makes the setting seem fixed in time, but it is not. The reality, the underpinning, is the music; and that goes from the start of Eisenhower's second term to the end of Kennedy's more golden years. . . . [The film opens] on a giant amber light; as the camera pulls back we realize it is the marking on a radio dial. The structure of the film comes from the radio program, the songs that disc jockey Wolfman Jack plays. Characters take cues from the music. And Wolfman Jack is the unseen center of it all, father figure as much as circus master. (p. 121)

Like a father, he resolves problems, calms fears, and arranges for meetings that would otherwise be only longings. The one character who ever comes close to him is Curt; after confronting him, it is Curt who can escape the town, while the others stay fixed in their past. . . . On the surface we are watching a meticulous reproduction of the real teenage culture of California in the early 1960s. Beneath the surface is, in terms of Freudian psychology as developed by Jacques Lacan, something as strong and basic as the resolution of an Oedipal complex—that is, Curt learns to repair his sense of loss at separation from mother's earliest warmth. The force of *American Graffiti* comes from the fact that its dreamlike quality also contains reference to the real force of dreams.

American Graffiti is also funny; and it backtracks to the situations and shots of movies in the late 1950s. There are echoes of *High School Confidential,* of *Rock Around the Clock,* of Nicholas Ray's template for the high school film, *Rebel Without a Cause.* The film's climax, a drag race in which the sympathetic John Milner is forced to realize that he has been beaten by yet another generation that overtakes him, is visually close to the chicken run in *Rebel.* The difference is the quality of nostalgia, the knowledge of time passing. (p. 122)

The values of the film come from its social background. The group of teenage characters all have cars; and those who do not are outsiders like Terry the Toad who must be loved despite their obvious material failings. That is the message of dim, blonde Debbie's final commitment to the Toad. Ranking is by possessions; college education is a chance for everybody; there is a sense of democracy among the kids. The love of neighborhood and the profound sexism—the only characters whose fates are described at the film's end are men—suggest the link with suburban values that the film's context would lead us to expect. This is Middletown, in its sunny, golden California version. Women are invisible because they have given up their hard-won independence in wartime for the more stolid values of homemaking. Material goods eliminate the problems of class and aspirations; John Milner, car mechanic, has a machine of his own like Curt Henderson, the would-be writer. The nostalgia in *American Graffiti* is as much for social values that had lost their power by 1973 as it is for the externals of the rock 'n' roll generation. (p. 123)

Compared with *2001* . . . the special effects in *Star Wars* were cheap. Where Kubrick could allow his space stations to circle elegantly for a minute, Lucas always has to cut swiftly between individual effects. (p. 134)

[He] does not tell a story. It is the basic failing of the film. It lacks true narrative drive and force. It is a void, into which any mystic idea can be projected; an entertainment, brilliantly confected, which is quite hollow. Its only idea is individualism: that a man must take responsibility for others, even at great personal cost and peril. Its idea is, in classic form: "A man's gotta do what a man's gotta do."

The iconography is bizarre. Darth Vader, the dastardly villain, is black. That is common in science fiction. . . . But Darth Vader's forces are storm troopers, armored in white. The wicked Grand Moff Tarkin lives in a gray green world, with gray green uniforms; he is clearly a wicked Nazi. Yet when our heroes take their just reward at the very end, there are images that parallel the finest documentary of Nazism, Leni Riefenstahl's *Triumph of the Will.* . . . Critical confusion is not surprising when there are allusions to Nazism as both good and bad. French leftist critics thought the film was Fascist-oriented; Italian rightists thought it was clearly Communist-oriented.

Nor is the vague pantheism of the film coherent. *Star Wars* talks much of the Force, a field of energy that permeates the universe and can be used for both good and evil. It is passed on, with a sword, just as the sword Excalibur is passed on in Arthurian romance; the influence of chivalric stories is strong. But when the Force is used by Luke Skywalker to help him destroy the monstrous Death Star, he is urged only to relax, to obey instincts, to close his eyes and fight by feeling. The Force amounts to building a theology out of staying cool.

Star Wars has been taken with ominous seriousness. It should not be. The single strongest impression it leaves is of another great American tradition that involves lights, bells, obstacles, menace, action, technology, and thrills. It is pinball, on a cosmic scale. (pp. 135-37)

Michael Pye and Lynda Myles, "George Lucas," in their The Movie Brats: How the Film Generation Took Over Hollywood *(copyright © 1979 by Michael Pye and Lynda Myles; reprinted by permission of Holt, Rinehart and Winston, Publishers), Holt, 1979, pp. 113-39.*

Rouben Mamoulian

1898-

Armenian-born American filmmaker and theatrical director.

Mamoulian's films are successful and artistic; he is a master at employing innovative techniques. His first experience in the theater involved directing plays in London. Drawn to the United States by an offer from George Eastman to join his American opera company in Rochester, Mamoulian accepted but only stayed for two years. The Theatre Guild in New York hired him as a teacher and director and in 1927 he directed *Porgy*. The play was immediately successful. His style of direction was expressionistic, exemplified by the "Symphony of Noises" which provided the background for one of his scenes. One by one, the sounds of Catfish Row are introduced and eventually joined in perfect rhythm.

This style has not been abandoned in his films. Mamoulian has no taste for naturalism: "My aim was always rhythm and poetic stylization." It was this credo which prompted him to surpass the techniques of his time and become a remarkably innovative filmmaker. His first film, *Applause,* which he directed at the Astoria Studios in New York, exemplifies his daring. As an early sound film it was expected to follow its predecessors using a stationary camera, one sound track, and straight narrative. Mamoulian envisioned a scene with Helen Morgan singing a lullaby to her daughter while the girl recited a rosary. It was a significant scene, one which would show the disparity between the burlesque queen whose lullaby was one of her show tunes and the daughter whose upbringing had been in a convent. But it necessitated using two sound tracks, which was unheard of. Mamoulian insisted on it despite opposition from his crew and his own inexperience. From that point on, his techniques became more and more novel. He used mobile cameras, images with incongruous sounds to create emotional impact, superimposed images, and silent images with voice-over tracks. Although common practice now, these techniques originated with Mamoulian.

Not surprisingly, Mamoulian also led the way in color production. His *Becky Sharp* was the first feature film in Technicolor. Throughout, he uses color for artistic ends, especially in the Waterloo sequence. Despite the fact that one would expect soldiers to leave a ball before all the others, in the case of military emergency, Mamoulian directed them to leave last. Though this device defied logic, it left the screen flooded with the red of their uniforms. Later Mamoulian said: "Colour is such a strong emotional medium of such subconscious potency, that if the gradation were wrong here it could destroy the fundamental reality of the scene. . . . [No one] has ever remarked on [the soldiers leaving last], because it makes such sense dramatically."

Mamoulian's success has been attributed to his innate sense of staging musicals, his direction of actresses, his technical expertise. But he has been able to combine his artistic standards with universal appeal and his films were, and still are, remarkably entertaining. (See also *Contemporary Authors,* Vols. 25-28, rev. ed.)

ALEXANDER BAKSHY

There are two reasons why Rouben Mamoulian's "Applause" . . . is one of the most significant talking pictures that has yet been produced in this country. Its first claim to distinction is that rare thing the artist's touch, a quality which proclaims a cultured and sensitive mind attuned to the medium of its expression. Its second claim rests on its convincing demonstration of the ability of the talking picture to create drama which is not modeled after the stage. . . .

Perhaps the most striking achievement of Mr. Mamoulian is the sustained sense of unity, of an atmosphere, with which he infuses his play as a whole. The sordidness of its realistic detail is not to be gainsaid; yet how mordant and spicy it is, how different in its imaginative treatment from the countless scenes of chorus girls on the stage as found in even the best of Hollywood's films! Particularly striking, also, is the opening sequence showing a desolate street with bits of paper blown by the wind, then a solitary dog running this way and that, then groups of excited children and, finally, as a climax, the street parade of the burlesque troupe, with the volume of sound rising from scene to scene until it swells to a cacophonous blare of the actors' trumpets. Since Mr. Dudley Murphy's "St. Louis Blues," a very remarkable little picture in its own way, this is unquestionably the most satisfying instance of cinematic treatment of sound. Another instance, even more important in its implications because of the far-reaching developments it foreshadows, is to be found in Mr. Mamoulian's use of the "split screen"—that is, two independent scenes shown side by side. Taken as a whole, however, "Applause" is not free from some important defects. The dramatic values of its dialogue are not so well brought out as are those of the visual images, and there is a consequent loss of emotional effect. Nor is Mr. Mamoulian's almost continuous use of the moving camera wholly convincing. It slows up action where an imaginative "cutting," like that in Eisenstein's "Potemkin," would have given speed and concentration of interest. Besides, with its bouncing horizon and its emphasis upon the outline of the picture, the moving camera gives a view of the world as it might be seen by an elephant out of a closed car, rather than by a human being walking in the open.

Alexander Bakshy, "The Talkies Advancing," in The Nation *(copyright 1929 The Nation Associates, Inc.), Vol. 129, No. 3356, October 30, 1929, p. 503.*

[*Applause*] shows much that is distinctive by way of retaining the cinematic method of the silent screen and applying it to the screen of the sound film. In this one perceives a further step in blending the technique of both in that composite method which apparently is to furnish the picture art of the future. Finished composition in the photography has been striven for and camera invention to a very large degree retained for the narrative manner. Quite apart from sound and dialogue effects, this film "says it with pictures." Here a great superiority has been achieved over most of the current talkies. Were sound omitted from *Applause,* it would still have coherence and a story-telling power of its own through its pictorial interest. . . .

[The plot] is time worn, turned into a little different shape here and there. . . . The strings are pulled in the same old way and the mechanism of jazz and show girls, which proved so appealing to the populace in *Broadway Melody,* is not overlooked in the theatre sequences. But there is a difference, because these things are done with cinematic meaning as well as with sound enhancement. And the sound finds elaboration, and gains in naturalness, through subordinating to or mingling of dialogue with the pervading noises of the places where the action takes place.

Technically *Applause* is often surprising; the sound track has been carried through dissolves and fades and camera shifts with telling effect and gives almost the same flexibility aurally that the film possesses visually. The camera speech itself gets close to the virtuosity of a *Variety* or *The Last Moment,* and the speed, ease and fluidity of the film are among the marks of its cinematic virtue. . . .

[The] direction, given a story which is somewhat squalid and brutal, shows reluctance to over-state, dramatic judgment and tenderness. One of the loveliest sequences yet to find its way into the talkies is that composed of the shots of the boy and girl finding the shy utterance of their awakening love under the towering arches of Brooklyn Bridge, with the night sounds of the river coming up to them, becoming a part of their feelings, their reticent speech, so in keeping with their isolation, their shadowy selves, the dim city they have for this haunting and magic hour escaped.

"'Applause'," in National Board of Review Magazine *(copyright, 1929), Vol. IV, No. 9, November, 1929, p. 11.*

THORNTON DELAHANTY

[The] spoken word has placed a hardship on the cause of motion pictures simply because dialogue tends to slow up the action and to atrophy that panoramic fluidity of the camera which was a chief and startling virtue in the silent film days.

In view of which it is interesting to note how one director has succeeded, to an unusual degree, in freeing himself from the fetters of sound recording. The picture is "Applause" . . . and the director is Rouben Mamoulian. (p. 240)

[There is] constant evidence that a creative intelligence was responsible for the making of "Applause." Having been given a free rein, Mr. Mamoulian went about his business with nothing to rely on other than his own skill in showmanship and, I suspect, fairly good acquaintance with the best of the latter day silent pictures.

The fact that he had dialogue to deal with didn't disturb him at all. Instead of allowing the dialogue to intrude itself in the story or even to take a respectable place alongside of it, Mamoulian used his camera for all it was worth and made *it* tell the story.

The result is that "Applause" exists—to me, at any rate—as a cohesive, well integrated series of pictures. Its intensity, its sharp projections of tragedy, emerge from the eye of the camera; an omniscient, omnipresent eye that slides easily over the links of the story and emphasizes only the true and the relevant. (pp. 240-41)

Always there are artful touches, designed to illuminate the characters or to indicate the humors of the story. The opening sequence is deadly eloquent in its simplicity. There is the deserted street of a small town. Scattered bits of newspapers and bill posters are blown about by the wind. That is all. But you can feel the bleakness of the day, the chill November winds that sweep through the vacant street. And then one of the bill posters is flattened momentarily against the side of a building. It is the advertisement of Kitty Darling and the burlesque troupe coming to town. . . .

Certainly the mood of the picture is imparted without any waste of time and, I might add, without any waste of words. Taking a leaf from Mr. Mamoulian's book a rule for directors might be adduced to the effect that when you want to get a point over quickly to the audience, don't say it with words. As a matter of fact, the most telling sequences in "Applause" are done in pantomime. The dialogue is held to the subservient function of framing the story and heightening the characterizations.

In spite of the sordidness of its theme there is much pictorial beauty in "Applause." As far as I know, Mr. Mamoulian is the first director to utilize the photographic possibilities of the Brooklyn Bridge, with its delicate filigree of interlacing cables and the New York skyline in the distance. He has made his camera predominantly avid, which might be set down as rule Two for directors who would inject a future into the talkies. (p. 241)

Thornton Delahanty, "'Applause'," in The Arts *(copyright, 1929, by The Arts Publishing Corporation), Vol. XVI, No. 4, December, 1929, pp. 240-41.*

ALEXANDER BAKSHY

[Dulness] and flatness, I regret to say, are to be found in particularly irritating doses in "Love Me Tonight." Maurice Chevalier, who used to charm us with the roguishness of a young boy and the knowledgeable understanding of a man of the world that made him such a delightful screen lover, is revealed in this latest picture of his as a tired man who is trying his hardest to appear sprightly and irresistible. . . .

Even more disappointing to me, because of the expectations aroused by his earlier work, is Rouben Mamoulian's performance as the director of the picture. In his first picture, "Applause," made when the talkies were still in their infancy, Mr. Mamoulian was daring and original. Above all, he showed a quality of imagination that knew how to bring the unfamiliar and the significant out of the welter of photographic impressions. In "Love Me Tonight," a musical comedy romance with a touch of wilful extravaganza, he either failed to find a subject after his own heart, or failed to discover in himself the power of imagination that would have made its hackneyed story pointed and interesting. Only once, and then merely by repeating himself, does he succeed in striking a note of convincing inventiveness. This is in the opening scene, showing the sleepy Paris awakening to its daily labors in a swelling symphony of miscellaneous noises. In the rest of the picture he either attempts comedy in the style of Lubitsch, without the latter's flair for the bizarre, or follows the treatment of music in "Sous les Toits de Paris" by laborious repetition of the same song by various characters quite regardless of its dramatic relevance to the story. After hearing about a dozen versions of The Son of a Gun Is Nothing But a Tailor, at least one of the spectators was on the point of using a less printable language.

Alexander Bakshy, "Three Premature Births," in The Nation *(copyright 1932 The Nation Associates, Inc.), Vol. 135, No. 3506, September 14, 1932, p. 240.*

FRANCIS BIRRELL

The film industry has produced many men of talent, but few artists. Mamoulian has always seemed to me one of those rare men. The picture of first love in *Applause,* of crime in *City Streets,* of the macabre in *Dr. Jekyll and Mr. Hyde,* all had about them a distinction that transcended their Hollywood setting. His latest film *Love Me To-night* . . . shows what he can make of an old story in new dress, and more sensationally, perhaps, what he can make of Chevalier. *Love Me To-night* is a latter-day version of *The Sleeping Beauty,* with Chevalier as a tailor's apprentice, who bursts into a ducal château to get a bill paid, and carries off a princess dying of ennui and inbreeding.

Such a treatment of an old tale lends itself to facetiousness, the facetiousness of Mark Twain or of Will Rogers. But Mamoulian can keep this side of farce. He has the smile of comedy—a tender comedy—for the old fairy tale he is dressing up. Provided with the slop of the Hollywood studios, he has turned it into something almost sad. For Mamoulian is genuinely romantic without being sentimental. . . . A sequence in which the aristocratic guests play bridge so slowly that the cards can hardly fall on to the table recaptures the idiom of Grimm. The hunting scenes are as pretty as possible. The three duennas, bent over their tapestry, and sighing over the lover who never came to them, have a mediaeval charm. Though *Love Me To-night* is a hymn to democracy, Mamoulian does not too much "guy" the life of the château. So much for the distinction of Mamoulian's mind. As a technician he seems to me equally admirable. Chaplin has an unequalled eye for comic likenesses in physical objects, such as an ice-pudding and a bald head in *City Lights,* as the bear and the man in the bearskin in *The Gold Rush.* Mamoulian has a similar skill for the unsuspected resemblance of objects in motion, above all for the noise they make. Sound is the *terminus a quo* of his art. He can really construct a "noisy." Notice the resemblance between the yapping of dogs and the yapping of old women, and the ocular correlation, based on sound, between the legs of horses and the wheels of trains. The opening of this film, which shows Paris waking up in the morning, is a pure study in noises. This film is the opposite of a talkie. For the noise dictates the speech, not the speech the noise. The noise also dictates the movement, of which the speed is never for long the same. He uses the sound as the basis of everything. . . . The characters on occasion address each other in verse, as if to emphasise the liberty that is allowed the camera-man. Even in the hunting scenes the stag cannot run with a natural motion. Its stylised jumps remind us that we are after all listening to a fairy tale, which might have been woven on the tapestries of the "Gothick North." For Mamoulian is a civilised man, who can smile, inhabiting a world, of which most of the denizens can only laugh.

If would be pleasant to see Mamoulian less tied to Hollywood, not always making bricks out of other people's bad straw. . . . With complete freedom he might do anything; for he is a man of genuine invention. . . . Take, for instance, that one moment in *Dr. Jekyll,* when Mr. Hyde after his first translation sniffs the storm as he comes out of his house. I do not believe that there is another man in the film industry who would have thought of this or of the too-languid bridge in *Love Me To-night.* (pp. 657-58)

Francis Birrell, "The Art of Mamoulian," in The New Statesman & Nation *(© 1932 The Statesman & Nation Publishing Co. Ltd.), Vol. IV, No. 92, November 26, 1932, pp. 657-58.*

OTIS C. FERGUSON

Taking the subject of Christina, enlightened despot, Lesbian, free-lance adventuress, ["Queen Christina"] substitutes for all the strange facts bearing upon her reign and exile the considerably mildewed fictions of the Graustark cycle. To be sure, it borrows enough facts to make a setting; it indicates the Swedish court, and makes itself pleasant with glamor while it may. But then come the big scenes, the Od's-wounds-milady-'tis-but-a-scratch. In the end, it reduces the complex circumstances surrounding the abdication of a homosexual queen to a quick and wholesome elopement with the Gentleman from Spain. . . . So the whole play falls down, echoing falsely. Its essential crumbling, of course, has come about not because it is poor history but because it has nothing satisfactory to give in history's place.

Otis C. Ferguson, "Histories and a Travelogue," in The New Republic *(reprinted by permission of* The New Republic; *© 1934 The New Republic, Inc.), Vol. 77, No. 100, January 31, 1934, p. 336.*

JAMES SHELLEY HAMILTON

Queen Christina follows quite closely the career of Sweden's notorious seventeenth century queen as it was known to most of her contemporaries, without benefit of modern pathological psychology. The one serious concession it makes to presumed movie demands is in giving Christina an abiding passionate love for the Spanish ambassador, whereas the rumors of the time credited her with no more than a passing affair of scandal. . . . Where the film falls down as an historical picture is chiefly in its failure to suggest the cold and rugged Sweden of those rough days when the warrior sons of the Vikings took up the Protestant banner and made such a stir in Europe. Mamoulian's silken direction has a strangely softening effect on the scenes he is depicting, which distorts history far more than mere departures from recorded fact. (pp. 11-12)

James Shelley Hamilton, "Two Queens," in National Board of Review Magazine *(copyright 1934), Vol. 9 No. 2, February, 1934, pp. 10-12.**

ALBERTO CONSIGLIO

Mamoulian's latest film [*Queen Cristina*] is the result of a defect both of sentimental intuition and of culture. We should not need to speak of culture if sentimental intuition and the breath of art had inspired the producer or the actress [Greta Garbo] on behalf of the producer. Who cares whether Shaw's *Joan of Arc* is really the Joan burnt at the stake by the English or if Shakespeare's *Coriolanus* is really the tragic Roman patrician? Their strong artistic vitality excludes all possibility of criticism. The humanity of the characters gives them a superior reality of their own.

When, however, the producer is not inspired with a creative capacity, culture may save his work in another direction, another zone of ideal interests. Has not Mamoulian himself shown this to be the case both in the *Song of Songs* and *Dr. Jekyll?* He certainly did not rise to any special heights in revivifying and remoulding the material of this ancient German romance [*Song of Songs*]; but in his reconstruction of the atmosphere and conditions of Imperial Germany he observed a quantity of minute details and showed a precise knowledge of the bombastic baroque style of the "fin di siècle". (p. 329)

In *Dr. Jekyll* . . . , Mamoulian's illustrative and suggestive talent is well revealed in seeking to overcome the repugnance evoked by the grossness of the central idea of the plot as shown by means of an art which is capable of the subtlest tricks and devices. If we recall the atmosphere of Hyde Park, the hall of the University, the prostitute's house and, in general, the early Victorian air of Stevenson's time, one recognizes all the signs of the decorative and documentary temperament in which the Armenian's originality shows itself. Even in *Queen Cristina,* within these narrow limits, a certain scrupulousness of construction is shown. In this film, Mamoulian is . . . bound to an actress with a certain "type". . . . In addition, he chose or was given in default of a creative inspiration, an historical argument which called for a sense of responsibility, of which there is no trace in any aspect of *Queen Cristina*.

In *Queen Cristina,* one is struck by the poverty of the historical reconstruction, the utter lack of concern for truth or the significance of atmosphere. The intelligent wealth of detail manifest in the *Song* is forgotten if not banished. Did Mamoulian wish to return to the simple lines of the *Streets of the City?* If so, the comparison between the two pictures is appalling. Whilst the magnificent realism of the latter film results in a complete picture of modern life, the simplicity of *Queen Cristina* becomes the artificial lifelessness of the cardboard and plaster scenario of the old time historical drama.

This neglect of the structural elements of the film is certainly intentional. The scenario has been adapted and elaborated to throw into high relief the actress's personality and her interpretation of this historical personage. . . . Thus rather than criticizing a work by Mamoulian we have to analyse the complicity of the producer in a cinematographic hot-potch which is an offence to culture and art. Those who have the necessary experience should notice the first rapidly moving scenes which depict the death on the battlefield of Gustavus Adolphus. The lights, the atmosphere, the contrasting shadows, the gestures are happily reminiscent of the great Flemish painters of the 17th century. In this brief fragment the Mamoulian of the *Song of Songs* is easily recognised, and it is legitimate to imagine what he might and could have created in a reconstructive and documentary way, if he had been given full liberty. . . . (pp. 330-32)

It would thus be useless to dwell long over a description of a Sweden conceived in a commonplace manner, illustrated by ordinary snow scenes, and with pictures of seventeenth century Swedes whom we recognise as such owing to their enormous jugs of beer, Spaniards who are Spaniards because they have olive complexions and throw about "a few carambas".

Yet even these clumsy effects to which must be added the dull neutral tone of the scenery cannot be dismissed in one word. If we study them from another point of view than that of cinematography, they assume a certain logic. In fact, the importance of the actress and her interpretation of the part, was of such moment that an unhesitating and unregretful return was made to a typical theatrical mentality. (p. 332)

Queen Cristina as an historical drama, has a worth not much different from an improvised *commedia dell'arte*. It is not enough to say that the daughter of Gustavus Adolphus, as a physical being, has been obliged to help the Garbo. The unreasonable and unjustified falsification is carried to incredible extremes. The Garbo did not even give herself the trouble of altering her mannerisms or of showing any more intimate revelation of her art than that to which we have been accustomed for ten years. The life, passion, drama, the opposing forces in the Queen of Sweden are reduced to a miserable and feeble little play about a discontented, misunderstood lunatic of a woman, full of rhetoric and melancholy and the desperation usually attributed to the women of the North who are supposed to seduce the men of the South by their strangeness. (pp. 332, 334)

Leaving out of the case *Queen Christina,* what remains of Mamoulian's personality? His first famous picture was *City Streets*. This film belongs to that short list of works so full of clear modern poetry that they can be handled with the strictest technique.

But soon afterwards, in *Doctor Jekyll, Love me Tonight* and *The Song of Songs,* Mamoulian's personality is revealed in an ability to translate into cinematographic visions documents relative to a certain epoch. His principal source of inspiration lies in photographs, dagguereotypes, lithographs and the files of old illustrated papers. (p. 336)

Alberto Consiglio, "Rouben Mamoulian," in Intercine, *Vol. 7, No. 6, June, 1935, pp. 328-36.*

ANDRE SENNWALD

Science and art, the handmaidens of the cinema, have joined hands to endow the screen with a miraculous new element in "Becky Sharp," the first full-length photoplay produced in the three-component color process of Technicolor. . . .

Rouben Mamoulian and [color designer] Robert Edmond Jones have employed the new process in a deliberately stylized form, so that "Becky Sharp" becomes an animate procession of cunningly designed canvases. Some of the color combinations make excessive demands upon the eye. Many of them are as soothing as black and white. The most glaring technical fault, and it is a comparatively minor one, is the poor definition in the long shots, which convert faces into blurred masses. . . .

The major problem, from the spectator's point of view, is the necessity for accustoming the eye to this new screen element in much the same way that we were obliged to accustom the ear to the first talkies. The psychological problem is to reduce this new and spectacular element to a position, in relation to the film as a whole, where color will impinge no more violently upon the basic photographic image than sound does today. This is chiefly a question of time and usage. At the moment it is impossible to view "Becky Sharp" without crowding the imagination so completely with color that the photoplay as a whole is almost meaningless. That is partly the fault of the production and partly the inevitable consequence of a phenomenon. . . .

The real secret of the film resides not in the general feeling of dissatisfaction which the spectator suffers when he leaves the [theater], but in the active excitement which he experiences during its scenes. It is important and even necessary to judge the work in terms of its best—not its worst or even its average. "Becky Sharp" becomes prophetically significant, for example, in the magnificent color-dramatization of the British ball in Brussels on the eve of Waterloo.

Here the Messrs. Mamoulian and Jones have accomplished the miracle of using color as a constructive dramatic device, of using it for such peculiarly original emotional effects that it would be almost impossible to visualize the same scene in conventional black and white. From the pastel serenity of the opening scenes at the ball, the color deepens into somber hues as the rumble of Napoleon's cannon is heard in the ballroom. Thenceforward it mounts in excitement as pandemonium seizes the dancers, until at last the blues, greens and scarlets of the running officers have become an active contributing factor in the overwhelming climax of sound and photography.

If this review seems completely out of focus, it is because the film is so much more significant as an experiment in the advanced use of color than as a straightforward dramatic entertainment. Based upon Langdon Mitchell's old dramatization of "Vanity Fair," it is gravely defective. Ordinarily Mr. Mamoulian is a master of filmic mobility, but here his experimental preoccupation with color becomes an obstacle to his usual fluid style of screen narration. Thus a great deal of "Becky Sharp" seems static and land-locked, an unvarying procession of long shots, medium shots and close-ups. It is endlessly talkative, as well, which is equally a departure from Mr. Mamoulian's ordinary style.

Perhaps it was inevitable that Thackeray's classic tale of the ambitious Becky and her spangled career in English society would be reduced on the screen to a halting and episodic narrative. But the film is unconscionably jerky in its development and achieves only a minor success in capturing the spirit of the original. In many of the screened episodes, Thackeray's satirical portraits come perilously close to burlesque, and they barge over the line in several places. . . .

But one thing is certain about "Becky Sharp." Its best is so good that it becomes a prophecy of the future of color on the screen. It forced this column to the conclusion that color will become an integral motion picture element in the next few years.

Andre Sennwald, "The Radio City Music Hall Presents 'Becky Sharp,' the First Full-Length Three-Color Photoplay," in The New York Times *(© 1935 by The New York Times Company; reprinted by permission), June 14, 1935, p. 27.*

CHARLES DAVY

Nobody knows yet whether *Becky Sharp* will inaugurate a decisive new vogue for colour films. Nor does anybody know whether a general use of colour would enrich or impoverish the artistic resources of the cinema. I think it might do both.

Becky Sharp, loosely adapted from Thackeray's *Vanity Fair,* is the first full-length picture to use the new Technicolor process, and it establishes certain facts. . . .

One thing that colours can do on the screen is to intensify emotional moods. A powerful red can send an immediate emotional stimulus surging out over an audience, and all the audience need do is to submit to its intoxicating influence. Rouben Mamoulian, in directing *Becky Sharp,* has tried to make use of this possibility by building up to an ominous red climax—red uniforms, red lamps and a red glow in the distant sky—at a moment when the sound of guns breaks into the Duchess of Richmond's ball on the eve of Waterloo. Many of his colour effects here are vivid and expressive, but there is something false, I feel, in the application of this rather arbitrary device to real people and real events.

Charles Davy, "Films: 'Becky Sharp'," in The London Mercury, *Vol. XXXII, No. 190, August, 1935, p. 376.*

LEWIS JACOBS

Intelligence, an experimental willingness and aptitude, and an understanding of pictorial and sound effects (which springs both from his operatic experience and from his studies of other craftsmen) have raised Mamoulian into the first rank of directors. His awareness of pace, rhythm, movement, and music has made his musical films his best; in these more than in his dramatic pictures he has blended the cinematic elements into an excellent whole.

Mamoulian's first movie, *Applause* (1930), revealed a director who recognized the difference between stage and screen. In a day of readjustments, when the proper relation between the film and the microphone was being groped for consciously or, in many cases, unconsciously, *Applause* spoke in favor of camera mobility first, talk second. Audiences sat up and took notice; critics could not ignore the film's cinematic implications. Mamoulian's use of mobile sound was then novel: for instance, a chorus starting a song is left by the camera for a second scene, and the music continues through this second scene, being modulated so that a conversation can be heard above it. The camera moved freely, daringly, and even enthusiastically—sometimes, in fact, too much for the spectator's comfort.

One of the most effective moments in *Applause* comes when the lover of the fading burlesque queen tells her she is old, ugly, finished. The camera hovers for an instant over Miss Morgan's face, moves slowly to the framed picture of her in her lovely youth, and then comes back to her. The movement of the camera and the continuing bitter voice over it combine to intensify the effect enormously. (pp. 469-70)

In *Applause* Mamoulian endeavored to blend light, shadow, and sound imaginatively and dramatically, and whenever possible he introduced nature to heighten the mood. His love scenes were exquisitely lyrical, presaging those in all his later works. His young lovers on top of a skyscraper were played against the sky and the wind; later, in *City Streets,* his lovers were placed in a setting against the sea; many of his later films show them in the rain. Such scenes, stemming from his thorough knowledge of the stage, are indicative of Mamoulian's forethought and awareness of the dramatic elements at the disposal of a director.

Mamoulian's daring and perspicacity in moving the camera, while other directors' cameras were literally hand-tied, contributed much at the psychological moment to the mutual adaptation of sound and camera. Although *Applause* was a sensitive venture in the right direction, however, the lack of restraint in Mamoulian's use of the camera suggested immaturity, defective discrimination, a lack of understanding of filmic continuity. (p. 470)

Mamoulian's second undertaking, a melodramatic gangster film, *City Streets* . . . , displayed a firmer control of the medium. The film demonstrated Mamoulian's awareness of sound's possibilities and his intelligent application of the contributions of other directors (traits he has manifested ever since). In the episode where Sylvia Sidney is in jail, the audience hears in a sound flash-back a garbled repetition of her earlier conversation with her lover. The influence of Russian and German films is strongly evidenced in the symbolic use of inanimate objects to suggest or accent a character. Birds flying through the prison windows make the cell seem more confining than ever; the snuffing out of a match by a character just before he murders his rival portends the killing; the statues of cats in scenes of the jealous girl sharply point her characterization. Since *City Streets* such symbolism has become pronounced in Mamoulian's work. The cutting of this film on the whole showed a more balanced conception of the film medium.

Mamoulian's next assignment was a melodrama offering unusual opportunities: *Dr. Jekyll and Mr. Hyde*. In the silent films this story had already shown itself to be powerfully adaptable to the screen. Mamoulian brought to it his flair for the moving camera, eerie compositions, and unusual sound effects. His superior taste, feeling for mood, sense of the theatrical, and use of symbolism in this film were very pronounced, lifting the story well above the *Frankenstein* class if not into the class of the distinguished.

After these tries at melodramatic material, Mamoulian turned his hand to a musical film. He had directed opera and was well versed in sound accompaniments. Perhaps his outstanding merit as a film director, thus far, had been his intelligent and often original use of sound. . . . By [*Love Me Tonight*] a true appraisal of Mamoulian can be made, for it brings to light at its best his outstanding talent. In *Applause* that talent was suggested; in *City Streets* and *Dr. Jekyll and Mr. Hyde* it was approved; in *Love Me Tonight* it was acclaimed.

Love Me Tonight was in every way a delightful musical fantasy in real movie terms. So directly was it derived from René Clair and Lubitsch that had either of those names been affixed to the film no one would have been surprised: it was charming, fanciful, witty, sophisticated. The opening sequence, a symphonic montage of a city awakening; and the deer-hunt episode, a Disneyesque tour de force, were high-lights of a brilliant movie. Mamoulian has never equaled it; neither Lubitsch nor Clair ever surpassed it.

Having directed four pictures, of which at least three—*City Streets, Dr. Jekyll and Mr. Hyde,* and *Love Me Tonight*—were accomplished works, Mamoulian subsequently made a series of films which, if they were the only ones to his credit, would hardly earn him a reputation. *Song of Songs* (1933) glorified Marlene Dietrich; *Queen Christina,* made the same year, starred Greta Garbo; and *We Live Again* (1934) attempted to put Anna Sten in their class. None of these pictures compared with his previous efforts.

In 1935 Mamoulian made his first color film, *Becky Sharp,* the first full-length dramatic photoplay done by the Technicolor process. That Mamoulian was selected to direct this initial Technicolor feature was a signal recognition of his position. As a film it followed close upon the static style of his previous two pictures; as a color experiment, it had many exciting moments that presaged a brilliant future for color in films. The most outstanding instance was the device of using color dramatically for an emotional overtone. In the scenes of the ball, the color is at first somber; then, as the roar of the cannons is heard, the color intensifies with the excitement of the dancers, until at last, as the officers rush off to battle, it is vivid scarlet. Although it was considered by André Sennwald as, "coloristically speaking, the most successful [film] that ever has reached the screen," its endless talk and tableaux weakened it.

In 1936 Mamoulian once again showed himself to be a distinctive director with another musical film, *The Gay Desperado.* Under no obligation to be serious, he had gone seriously to work to produce a clever, satirical, flowing film that would be exceptional and more original than *Love Me Tonight.* A gay and colorful comedy about Mexican outlaws who ape the slang and tactics of American gangsters, it was exactly the type of satirical fantasy at which he excels. (pp. 470-72)

Mamoulian's most recent film, *High, Wide, and Handsome* (1937), was a spectacular and lavishly produced show which, while it had many qualities typical of his best work, was as a whole a second-rate concoction. . . . [It] had conflicting aims in trying to present, at the same time, a social and industrial development [of the oil industry] and a spectacular operetta of "atmosphere and songs." The best parts of the picture were those showing the early Titusville oil drillings; the worst were those of the ensuing battle between the railroad crowd and the circus, which arrives like the marines at the last minute and, with the aid of elephants, gets the pipe line through. The lively subject matter of the film was never co-ordinated: it was operatic one moment, serious the next, and confused the third.

Mamoulian has resolved his technique into musical rhythm, just as von Sternberg has resolved his into pictorialism. He believes that anything can be put to music, and apparently he is intent upon proving it in his movies. When his philosophy coincides with his material, as in *Love Me Tonight* and *The Gay Desperado,* we get a good musical film; when it is forced upon dramatic material with undue and unnatural emphasis, as in *High, Wide, and Handsome,* the result is not so successful. (pp. 472-73)

Lewis Jacobs, "Contemporary Directors," in his The Rise of the American Film: A Critical History *(copyright 1939 by Lewis Jacobs; reprinted by permission of the author), Harcourt Brace Jovanovich, Inc., 1939, pp. 453-95.**

THEODORE STRAUSS

"Blood and Sand" [is] opulently Technicolored, resplendently caparisoned in the gold and pink brocades of Spain, and languid as midafternoon. Such a succession of sumptuously colored stills has not dazzled Broadway in quite a while. With infinite care Rouben Mamoulian, the director, has arranged his cast in striking tableaux; lovingly the camera eye lingers on burnished candelabra, El Greco altarpieces and rococo interiors of Spanish haciendas. In themselves they are good calendar art; as film drama they are . . . hopelessly static. . . .

[There] is too little drama, too little blood and sand, in it. Instead the story constantly bogs down in the most atrocious romantic cliches, in an endless recital of proof that talented young bull-fighters are apt to become arrogant and successful; that Curro, the critic, will sing their praises, and that thereafter their love life becomes very complicated.

Now and again for brief moments the film takes on some of the harsh vitality it might have had. Sometimes the camera hovers far above the corrida to catch the pageantry of the entrance and later the precise dance of death between a flaring cape of scarlet and a charging bull. In the darkness of the entry to the ring itself a door opens and the afternoon light flashes like a sword upon taut faces of waiting matadors. Or again the camera catches the frenzy of the crowd at the "moment of truth" in a woman's hand smearing lipstick across her face. These are glimpses of a stunning romantic melodrama with somber overtones.

But most of the essential cruelty of the theme is lost in pretty colors and rhetorical speeches.

Theodore Strauss, "'Blood and Sand'," in The New York Times *(© 1941 by the New York Times Company; reprinted by permission), May 23, 1941, p. 3.*

DWIGHT MACDONALD

Mamoulian is a bright young Armenian. [His] productions are glib, imitative, chic, with a fake elegance, a pseudo-wit and a suggestion of Oriental greasiness. They are marked with that vulgarity which is continually straining for effect, which cannot express a simple thing simply. A Mamoulian production can be depended on to overstress the note, whether pitched to lyricism, melodrama, fantasy. Thus his *City Streets,* a gangster melodrama, is directed as heavily and pretentiously as if it were *Greed* or *Sunrise.* There are brooding shadows, shots of pigeons flying beyond prison bars (freedom—get it?), weird angle shots of sculpture. Thus, too, in *Applause,* a sentimental little backstage tragedy, he put Helen Morgan through her extremely limited paces with all the solemnity due a Sarah Bernhardt. The trashy emotionalism of the story, which a more honest director would have restrained, Mamoulian plays up for all it is worth. His *Dr. Jekyll and Mr. Hyde* is a cheaply sensational affair compared to the silent Barrymore version. The brutal exaggeration of Hyde's makeup, physically so much more revolting than Barrymore's, spiritually so much less so, is a typical Mamoulian touch.

To Mamoulian's other cinematic crimes must be added that of plagiarism. *City Streets* is almost pure Von Sternberg. And his latest film, *Love Me Tonight,* is a René Clair film plus some Lubitschisms and minus Clair's freshness, wit, and charm. To make up for Clair's wit, Mamoulian has gone in for bigness. His country house is an enormous castle in the most opulent Hollywood tradition, with swarms of aristocratic inmates, long lines of servants, acres of sparkling polished floors. There is not one comic old spinster—there are three, which of course makes it three times as amusing. (Mamoulian, by the way, has more of Cecil B. De Mille in him than his admirers suspect.) For Clair's freshness, Mamoulian substitutes a hectic experimentation with trick effects. Sometimes this is pleasing enough, as the use of slow motion in the hunting scene. But Mamoulian uses his tricks unintelligently, without taste. The shot of the horn-blowing huntsman, for example, taken from an Eisenstein angle, strikes a heroic note that is absurdly out of key in a musical comedy featuring Jeannette MacDonald and Maurice Chevalier. For Clair's casual charm Mamoulian can make no substitution. To be light and casual is simply not in him. (pp. 81-2)

Dwight Macdonald, "Notes on Hollywood Directors (as of 1933)," in his Dwight Macdonald on Movies *(copyright © 1969 by Dwight Macdonald; reprinted by permission of the author), Prentice-Hall, Inc., 1969, pp. 75-106.**

TOM MILNE

Open almost any history of the cinema or volume of criticism and the story is the same: high praise of [Mamoulian's] early films, total neglect of the later ones. Almost invariably, Mamoulian is valued chiefly as an innovator. . . . (p. 9)

Even Mamoulian himself seems to subscribe to the view that his films are important mainly because of their innovations and experiments. In interviews and in his comments made during personal appearances for a retrospective devoted to his work at the National Film Theatre in April 1968, he returns constantly to the same topics: the two separate sound channels mixed on a single track in *Applause,* the superimposition of Gary Cooper's voice over Sylvia Sidney's face in *City Streets,* the thunderous explosion accompanying the shattering of a vase in *Love Me Tonight,* the gradual suffusion of red over the screen during the Waterloo sequence in *Becky Sharp.* These technical advances, like the dramatic highlights which also recur in Mamoulian's reminiscences—the bedroom-stroking scene in *Queen Christina,* the transformations in *Dr Jekyll and Mr Hyde*—are undoubtedly important; but not to the exclusion of the films themselves, considered as a coherent, developing whole.

The purpose of this monograph is therefore dissent. And I take as my basic text a quotation from Mamoulian when he was describing the famous 'symphony of noises' which illustrated the awakening of Catfish Row in his 1927 production of *Porgy,* and which he later incorporated into *Love Me Tonight:* 'In direction and staging, I used my favourite principle of integrating all theatrical elements into one stylised rhythmic pattern.' (pp. 9, 12)

[Mamoulian took] to cinema like a duck to water . . . with *Applause,* bringing to it an impeccable control of that essential element of moving pictures: movement. No wonder the Mamoulian trade-mark, making its appearance somewhere or other in each of his films, is that most graceful of all creatures, the cat. Movement to Mamoulian is like a brush-stroke to a painter: the delicate, infinitely variable factor which can bring life to a still life, beauty to a human face, emotion to a landscape, transforming dross into gold. A rose is a rose until Renoir paints it. *The Mark of Zorro* is just another historical romance until Mamoulian films it. (p. 13)

[One] is almost tempted to say that every Mamoulian film is a musical. It isn't true, of course, but with every action and every line of dialogue conceived in terms of stylised rhythm —*choreographed* rather than directed—it feels as though it were. *The Mark of Zorro,* for instance, opens with an effortless sequence, no more than a dozen brief shots, in which two rows of cadets going through their paces on horseback at the military academy in Madrid suddenly become, just for a moment, dancers in an elegant quadrille. . . . Even in *Dr Jekyll and Mr Hyde,* as Jekyll sits absorbed in playing the organ at the beginning of the film and is interrupted by his butler entering to remind him of his lecture, the dreamy repetition of the butler's name ('What is it, Poole? . . . So it is, Poole, so it is. . . . You know, Poole, you're a nuisance. . . . All right, Poole, all right') makes a perfectly ordinary conversation echo like the introduction to a Rodgers and Hart song. (pp. 13-14)

Even as early as 1932, with *Love Me Tonight,* Mamoulian's camera was so adept at simulating dance and musical rhythms round the characters that when they do break into song and dance, there is virtually no perceptible transition. By 1957 and *Silk Stockings,* his inimitable method of conjuring action, dialogue, songs and dances out of one magical, all-purpose hat, and expressing plot, emotion and meaning as freely by one as by the other, was one of consummate mastery. (pp. 14-15)

[In *Dr Jekyll and Mr Hyde*], Mamoulian again tackled a popular genre, and his first and only venture into the world of horror remains by far the best of all the various adaptations of Stevenson's novella. One might perhaps argue that John Barrymore in 1920, or Jean-Louis Barrault in Renoir's *Testament du Docteur Cordelier,* had outdone Fredric March; but no one has come within miles of equalling the film's marvellous chiaroscuro vision of Stevenson's London as a fog-laden, gaslit warren of glistening streets, towering stairways and shabby dens, haunted by the shadow of Mr Hyde, alternately bestially small or towering like a giant, as he prowls with black cloak swirling like a matador's cape.

To anyone inured to Hollywood's long tradition of discreet evasion, the first thing that strikes one about Mamoulian's *Jekyll and Hyde* is its unequivocal sexual basis. Stevenson, of course, made no bones about the fact that Hyde indulged the unmentionable lusts that Jekyll only dreamed about, and the various adaptations have all seized on the point to explore Hyde's pleasures with varying degrees of gusto and frankness. But this version . . . is alone in openly tracing the cause of Jekyll's troubles to the frustration by society of his own perfectly natural, unorgiastic desires. (p. 39)

Jekyll reveals a curious moral confusion, illustrating Mamoulian's remark (interview with Jean Douchet and Bertrand Tavernier in *Positif*) that what interested him in Stevenson's story was not so much the conflict between Good and Evil, but between Nature and Civilisation. This subtle but important distinction is charted at the end of the conversation with Lanyon, when the latter, acknowledging the existence of man's baser instincts, urges the ostrich morality: 'We have to accept certain things.' Angrily, Jekyll retorts, 'I don't want to accept them. I want to be clean, not only in my conduct, but in my innermost thoughts and desires. And there's only one way to do it. . . . Separate the two natures in us.' (p. 41)

Mamoulian begins *Dr Jekyll and Mr Hyde* with the celebrated sequence seen from Jekyll's point of view, opening with a shot of organ pipes as a Bach fugue peals out, panning down to a close-up of hands on the keyboard, and remaining stubbornly subjective—sheet music on the organ, butler entering to remind him of his lecture, his reflection in the hall mirror as he puts on his hat and cloak, climbing into a carriage, arriving at the university—until he enters the lecture room, when the camera pans round in a 360° arc and, on the first word of his lecture, 'Gentlemen . . . ' cuts to the back of the auditorium for the first objective view of Jekyll himself. Many interpretations and justifications have been offered for this sequence, all valid. . . . Mamoulian himself has said that he wanted to draw the audience into Jekyll's brain, to create an experience in which—as with the transformations—'the audience does not see him—they *are* him'. But it is also, and perhaps most importantly, a subtle introduction to the Nature-Civilisation theme, with its unmistakable progression from moonstruck joyousness to straitlaced sobriety. At the outset, Jekyll's behaviour, the music, his inconsequential banter with Poole, are the paean of joy of a man in love; but from the moment he is glimpsed in the mirror, the celebrated Dr Jekyll arrayed for the public eye, the mood changes, constables and doormen bow obeisance, and the soundtrack rings with obsequious phrases. . . . (p. 45)

In any adaptation of Stevenson's story, the transformation scene is inescapable: the audience is sitting waiting for the moment when handsome Jekyll will be metamorphosed into the deformed and diabolical Hyde, and Mamoulian plays the game brilliantly. To this day he has refused to reveal the secret of how the transformations were achieved in front of the camera, but it is not difficult to guess that they were done with coloured filters, changed to reveal different layers of make-up, and given a hallucinatory sense of actually happening before our eyes by the extraordinary soundtrack. Our first glimpse of the completed transformation as Hyde stares at himself in the mirror, panting 'Free! Free at last!' or holds his face exultantly up to the rain on his first venture out, is of a devil incarnate. But the real chill of horror in the film comes at the end, after Jekyll's visit of farewell to Muriel. Unable to bear the thought of never seeing her again, he stands staring at her in the darkness outside the french windows, and a shot of his hands reveals that he is changing into the familiar, dwarfish figure of Hyde. Instead, the dark, cloaked figure at the window swells in stature, proud and erect, not Hyde but a Luciferian Jekyll.

Structurally, thematically and psychologically, *Dr Jekyll and Mr Hyde* is masterly, and superbly executed in Karl Struss's velvety, glowing camerawork. Here and there the tone falters—in the slightly overwrought transformation scenes (more Stevenson's fault than Mamoulian's) or in the scene where Jekyll reveals his secret to Lanyon, with the latter towering over him like a judge behind his desk in a sudden reversion to the heady expressionism of the earlier films. (p. 49)

For [*Love Me Tonight*], Rodgers and Hart wrote nine numbers, so brilliantly integrated into the witty script that they are all but inseparable from it; and Mamoulian at last had something which would permit him to 'combine all the elements of movement, dancing, acting, music, singing, décor, lighting' (though not yet colour). The result was one of the most enchanting musicals ever made, the Lubitsch film that Lubitsch was always trying to pull off but never quite did.

Mamoulian's critics have always tended to dismiss *Love Me Tonight* as a pallid imitation of Lubitsch and Clair. It is possible that there was an influence, though in the case of Clair it seems to be limited to a shot or two of Paris streets and rooftops, and of Lubitsch, to the general air of sophistication and the presence of Maurice Chevalier and Jeanette MacDonald, his ineffable stars from *The Love Parade*. If so, Mamoulian in any case left his masters far behind. Dialogue exchanges like Charlie Ruggles's 'Can you go for a doctor?' and Myrna Loy's lightning 'Certainly, bring him right in!'; stylistic tricks like the sudden cut into slow motion as the castle settles down for yet another exciting evening of bridge; sounds like the extraordinary whimper, neither human nor yet quite canine, made by the three old aunts at moments of stress; all are handled by Mamoulian with a deft, airy legerdemain which makes the famed Lubitsch touch fall like a dull thud. (pp. 51, 53)

[*High, Wide and Handsome*] is the most persistently underrated of all Mamoulian's films: a sort of musical Western which anticipates the serene and summery blend of fairy-tale, fact and fantasy of such post-war Renoir films as *French Cancan* and *Eléna et les hommes*.

The story, an original by Oscar Hammerstein II, concerns the true history of the discovery of the Pennsylvania oil-fields in 1859, and the epic struggle waged by the poor farmer-prospectors against the railroad freight tycoons who resorted to every means in their power, financial and physical, to prevent the completion of the pipelines which would bring oil to every home in America. Hammerstein, it seems, wrote a gay and fluffy musical comedy; Mamoulian rewrote it with him, putting its feet back on the ground with a good deal of accurate background detail. The result, as Richard Roud has said (National Film Theatre programme note), is 'an extraordinary fusion of Brecht and Broadway'.

Not that *High, Wide and Handsome* is particularly didactic in intent, but it does very effectively follow Brecht's principle outlined in the *Little Organum for the Theatre:* 'As we cannot invite the public to fling itself into the story as if it were a river, and let itself be swept vaguely to and fro, the individual events have to be knotted together in such a way that the knots are easily seen. The events must not succeed one another indistinguishably but must give us a chance to interpose our judgment.' On the one hand, there is the basically realistic treatment of the historical facts: the prospectors toiling to build the pipelines clear across the state through snow and forest and over mountains to the refineries; the chicanery of rising freight prices countered by farmers contributing their life savings; the gangs of mercenaries sent out to terrorise the builders and destroy their work. On the other, the rustic never-never village of Titusville, with its rose-covered cottages and dainty farmyards where hero and heroine conduct their idyllic romance. Knotting the two together, such splendid alienation effects as the pastoral wedding in which the guests parading in their gingham and frockcoat finery are showered by sprays of gushing oil, or the magnificent ride to the rescue of an entire circus troupe just as the heroes, within sight of success as they hoist the last pipes up a sheer mountain rock-face, are attacked by the villains brandishing whips and pickaxes. (pp. 106, 108)

To analyse the film in these terms, of course, is to be hopelessly ponderous about it—Mamoulian was not trying to make a Brechtian analysis of the human condition along the lines of *The Caucasian Chalk Circle* or *The Good Woman of Setzuan*—and I have done so simply because the attitude is so widespread that in *High, Wide and Handsome* he wrecked a good historical Western by getting frivolous about it, or alternatively, wrecked a good musical by getting too serious about it. The truth is that he has simply instilled a little reality and a little human feeling into the artificial world of the musical. (p. 110)

Mamoulian's second encounter with colour was almost as fruitful as his first. With its elegantly swirling capes and statuesque groupings, its rich romantic aura of love in the moonlight and death in the afternoon, and its superb colour effects setting the dusty ochres of the arena scenes against the glowing blues and crimsons of the costumes and interiors, *Blood and Sand* all but brings off the tricky task of dominating the melodrama inherent in Ibanez's story of a matador's progress from rags to riches and retribution. Only at the end does the plot begin to pile up and get out of hand. (p. 128)

Mamoulian has described how many sequences in the film were deliberately styled after certain painters. For instance, Murillo bronzes, browns and blacks for Juan's poverty-stricken childhood; Goya, of course, for the bullring; Velazquez for Doña Sol's mansion (in essential flavour rather than detail: Velazquez as the master of light and shadow, of the richness of court life); El Greco for the matador's chapel; fourteenth-century primitives for the death of Nacional (because he is a primitive); sixteenth-century Venetians for Juan's dressing-room, with the luxurious colour and bustling movement of Titian and Veronese in the ceremonial robing of Juan; Sorolla for the street and market scenes; and so on.

To anyone not particularly well versed in the history of art, most of these derivations will probably pass unnoticed; but not the reasons, emotional and visual, for their adoption. After the long childhood sequence, dominated by the drab browns and blacks of poverty, the first splash of colour comes with the shock of a window opening on a new world. Juan and his boyhood friends, having run away to Madrid to learn the art of the ring, are returning ten years later as fully fledged bullfighters. On the train taking them home they talk, and someone addresses a question to Juan, lying stretched out on the seat. He lowers his newspaper, and behind his head is a folded cape making a nimbus of brilliant, dazzling crimson. A symbol of his glory as a matador, the colour is soon to be appropriated by Doña Sol . . . , the free-loving society lady first seen striking a discordant note amid the soft blues and greens of the El Greco chapel as she sets her sights on Juan . . . while he prays before entering the ring. (pp. 128, 130)

Counterpointing these illusory splendours, a motif of soft, romantic purity centering on Carmen, the patient Grizelda who is lent a touch of Juliet by being the object of two balcony serenades: the first as a child, when young Juan arrives by moonlight to announce his departure to Madrid, and makes an undignified exit by falling off the creeper which has carried him to her window; and the second when he arrives with a full orchestra to announce his return. Heralded twice by the moonlight, generally dressed in downy white with gentle mantillas softening the contours of her face, Carmen is as much an illusion as the glittering Doña Sol. Briefly, in her shortlived happiness with Juan, in her visit (dressed in unrelenting black) to plead her cause with Doña Sol, she becomes a woman. For the rest she is a wraith, haunting Juan's imagination as a dream of love, and haunting the ethereally tormented El Greco chapel where he faces his fears and finally meets his death.

If these twin motifs had been allowed to have the field to themselves, *Blood and Sand* might have been a masterpiece to match *Becky Sharp*. Unfortunately they are backed—or, rather, undermined—by several others, some good, some bad. The worst is the note of heavy foreboding introduced by Juan's mother, . . . a *mater dolorosa,* usually seen on her knees gloomily scrubbing floors and for ever embarking on prophecies of doom as she recalls how she has seen it all before when Juan's father fell from fame to fear, and finally death. There is also the rather too pat circular construction, which has a matador named Garabato . . . riding the crest of the wave during Juan's boyhood; when Juan returns from Madrid, he is accosted by a beggar who turns out to be the same Garabato, and gives him a job as his dresser; and the circle is completed when Curro and Doña Sol, after Juan's fatal goring, grow ecstatic over the new and rising star of his rival, Manolo de Palma. . . . (p. 132)

With all of these dooms piling up—not to mention the sister and brother-in-law who batten on his earnings like vultures, and the numerous creditors who are more heard of than seen or felt—it is scarcely surprising that the film begins to founder. Nevertheless, for more than half its length, *Blood and Sand* is Mamoulian at his best, flowing easily along from the characteristic opening: a close-up of a poster, pan down, past a bull's head on the wall to a palliasse where young Juan lies sleepless, a sword on a cushion by his side. (pp. 132-33)

Despite the mounting melodrama of the second half, leading to the inevitable goring of Juan and his death, *Blood and Sand* remains so intelligently designed that the basic motifs still work to a climax. . . . Mamoulian holds back the full emblazonment of Doña Sol till the moment of her betrayal in the café where she abandons Juan for Manolo's rising star. While Juan glowers, Manolo asks her to dance: 'I'd love to,' she answers, and throws off her shawl to reveal for the first time the full glory of her crimson evening gown. Returning to the chapel before his last corrida, Juan is haunted once more by the vision incarnate of Carmen, who hovers faithfully in the shadows to pray for him. And the last shot, as Manolo stands in the ring to acknowledge the roar of the crowd, is a slow pan across the arena, past a bouquet of trampled roses, to rest on a dull stain spreading in the sand. (p. 134)

[Nineteen forty-seven] was the *annus mirabilis* which brought both *The Pirate* and *Summer Holiday,* each perfect in its own way, and sharing a common denominator in that neither used song and dance as decoration, but rather as part of the basic narrative structure.

Summer Holiday, indeed, uses both even more radically, with the irresistible gaiety of its songs, polkas and hayride dances forming a bedrock for the basic concept of *Ah, Wilderness!,* the Eugene O'Neill play on which it is based. *Ah, Wilderness!* is the exception to the rule of towering tragedy in O'Neill's work, a tender, nostalgic comedy in which he recalled (semi-autobiographically) and gently satirised the growing pains of adolescence. 'My purpose,' he wrote, 'was to write a play true to the spirit of the American large small-town at the turn of the century. Its quality depended upon atmosphere, sentiment, an exact evocation of the mood of a dead past.' He did so, of course, through dialogue and characterisation. Yet he was also strongly aware of the evocative power of popular music. . . . Nothing, in fact, could be more quintessentially O'Neill—who always had to labour so hard for his atmosphere amid a plethora of adjectives and exclamation-marks—than the 'Weary Blues' sung in the film by Marilyn Maxwell as the saloon girl who gives young Richard Miller his first taste of sin: with its age-old, yearning lament for hope and disillusionment, it almost sums up the whole of *Anna Christie.* (pp. 139-40)

The advantage Mamoulian has over O'Neill is that he can *show* the world of nostalgia instead of merely suggesting it: the radiantly green lawns which are inseparable from summer and young love not as they were but as they are remembered; the rows of ideally clean, bright and hopeful faces at the Graduation Day ceremony; the little street tidy and expectant with its rows of flags awaiting Independence Day. Oddly enough the film is least successful in one brief sequence where it attempts to re-create too faithfully in a series of tableaux vivants based on famous paintings by Grant Wood ('Daughters of the American Revolution'), Thomas Benton and John Curry; most successful when creating a pure Utopia of endless summer days, green grass, flowing meadows and simple pleasures in an untroubled land of peace and plenty. (pp. 142-43)

One of the complaints frequently laid against *Summer Holiday* is that it robs O'Neill's play of much of its warmth and genuine feeling by allowing Mickey Rooney to play the part of Richard Miller, the rebellious and impossibly arty adolescent, chiefly for farce. Actually, his cheerfully strident interpretation of the role as a minimal variant on Andy Hardy works remarkably well, despite the anachronism of his enthusiasms for Swinburne, Omar Khayyám and Carlyle's *French Revolution,* and despite the fact that he seems hardly likely to develop into the writer-poet envisaged by O'Neill. The yearning arrogance of adolescence, after all, doesn't change all that much from generation to generation; and with so much built-in sentiment present in the settings, songs and dances, his stridency is probably useful as a door-stop to prevent the film from succumbing to the ever-present danger attendant upon nostalgia: sentimentality.

The criticism, in any case, seems to miss the point of the film. Unlike *Meet Me in St Louis, Summer Holiday* is not simply a tender evocation of family life from a gentler, more leisurely age. It is an attempt to pin down that moment which comes in everyone's life when one sees things from a new perspective: you realise that your schooldays probably were the happiest days of your life even though you hated every moment of them; or that you loved your family even though you couldn't wait to leave home; or that the world is a marvellous place even if it seems to have no use for you. (pp. 143, 145)

Beautifully shot by Charles Schoenbaum in warm, soft colours, *Summer Holiday* equals *Love Me Tonight* in the mastery with which rhymed dialogue, songs and leisurely action are swept up by Mamoulian's cutting into one dynamic overall rhythm. It is with some surprise that one realises in examining the film in detail that, despite some admirable steps created by Charles Walters, there are really no formal dance numbers in the film at all. Mamoulian needs neither dances nor dancers to create choreography; but when he did finally use them, ten years later in *Silk Stockings,* the result was arguably his greatest film. (p. 146)

To draw comparisons between *Silk Stockings* and *Ninotchka* is as fruitless an occupation as complaining that *Kiss Me Kate* isn't *The Taming of the Shrew,* or, for that matter, that *Summer Holiday* isn't *Ah! Wilderness.* Much more to the point is the way in which Mamoulian has improved on the stage version by giving it an emotional depth in line with the original.

Broadly speaking, the stage musical follows the plot of the Lubitsch film fairly closely. Ninotchka still comes to Paris to discipline three defecting envoys, and she still falls in love with her decadent Western charmer. (pp. 147-48)

Mamoulian, while remaining very faithful to the stage version, made several important changes because, as he put it (interview with Douchet and Tavernier in *Positif*), 'I had two of the best dancers in the world, and what interested me was to give greater importance to the dancing than to the action proper, which was merely a repeat of *Ninotchka.* The psychological and dramatic development existed only in the dances. It was by dancing that the characters became aware of something or other. . . .' (p. 149)

In the stage version, when Ninotchka subsequently appears in her new, secretly acquired finery and Canfield sings his appreciation in 'Silk Stockings', it is little more than a neat capping of the earlier joke when Ninotchka, gazing at a window display of lingerie and adapting Garbo's line about the hat, exclaimed in prim disgust, 'How can such a civilisation survive which permits women to wear things like these?' In the film, it is much more. We watch Ninotchka dressing for her date with Canfield, and her slow, dreamy dance as she casts away her old clothes and lovingly draws out her silk stockings, ear-rings, filmy underwear and high heels one by one from their secret hiding-places all over the apartment, is as much an affirmation of love as the bedroom-stroking sequence in *Queen Christina* on which it is obviously patterned. And the finality of the gesture with which, once dressed and radiant in her silks and satins, she tosses her old black stockings away on to a chair, is curiously reminiscent in its self-abandonment of the moment when Christina slips off her doublet and waits for Antonio to acknowledge her femininity. (p. 151)

Quite apart from its use of dance to narrate the progress of the love story, *Silk Stockings* is so rich in invention that it gives the lie even more forcefully than *The Mark of Zorro, Blood and Sand* or *Summer Holiday* to the myth of Mamoulian's decline. Right from the opening his inimitable touch is evident in the series of foot-level shots which tracks Canfield from his room across a corridor, into a lift, pause to stare at a pair of pretty female feet, out of the hotel, into a taxi, and up the stage-door steps to the theatre where Boroff, just finishing a concert and having received a telegram summoning him back to Moscow, divides his time between threatening to commit suicide and dashing back on stage to keep the applause up to scratch. From there on, with some of Cole Porter's best numbers impeccably staged and looking as though they had been poured into the story, we are unquestionably watching a Mamoulian film. The ease with which he slips in and out of dialogue sequences and into musical numbers without any perceptible faltering in rhythm is incredible, as is the constant invention he brings to the action. (p. 158)

Above all, with its generous allowance of thirteen musical numbers, ranging from the enchanting 'Paris Loves Lovers' to the brassy 'Satin and Silk', *Silk Stockings* is enormously cheerful and cheering. And as Ninotchka gloomily puts it, 'Nobody can be so happy without being punished.' This, to date, is Mamoulian's last film. Perhaps, one day, critics, historians and those who write about the cinema will at last realise that it is one of the great musicals. (pp. 159-60)

Tom Milne, in his Rouben Mamoulian *(copyright © Tom Milne 1969; reprinted by permission of Martin Secker & Warburg Ltd), Thames and Hudson, 1969, 176 p.*

ROBIN WOOD

One of the most stimulating and valuable developments in recent film criticism has been the concern with ideology—particularly with the ideological content of Hollywood films, with the notion that the films are "determined" (or, at the very least, affected) at all levels by an ideology (definable roughly as "bourgeois Capitalist," but with specific inflections and emphases peculiar to America) so deeply entrenched as to be largely taken for granted, hence unnoticed and unchallenged, by filmmakers and audiences alike. . . .

Silk Stockings (Rouben Mamoulian's musical version of *Ninotchka*) offers itself as a convenient example precisely because its ideological project appears so clear, indeed blatant. (p. 28)

I discern in *Silk Stockings* four main ideological impulses, linked yet partly separable, listed in descending order of explicitness or obviousness:

1. The film's surface project, which could be summed up as "You're better off under Capitalism." The assumption is that all Communists would really rather live in Capitalist societies if they could, or if they knew about all the benefits from experience. The benefits are presented primarily in the form of material possessions, with a strong emphasis on luxury goods—perfume, champagne—the familiar Hollywood emblems of romance, success, and wealth. With this goes the upholding of beauty (Paris at night) against utility. Even on this simple, overt level, the film periodically produces elements or emblems that make the satire double-edged or ambiguous. An example is the absurdly dressed-up poodle in the restaurant which Charisse objects to as "useless" and Fred Astaire defends as "amusing." The connotations of poodles in American movies are, after all, primarily farcical-satirical; here the dog—de-animalized, prettified, constrained—inevitably stands for the sillier excesses of Capitalist society.

2. Less explicitly, but even more pervasively, the film is concerned with the ideological role of woman in Capitalist society—with woman-as-object, the mere embodiment of male wish-fulfillment. As a Communist, and with the sexually neutral title of Comrade, Charisse poses a threat to male supremacy; she must therefore learn in the course of the film to be a "real woman," and learn that that is what she *really* wants to be. (p. 29)

The richness of the film arises partly from the way in which the notion of woman-as-object is satirized in the overtly vulgar musical numbers involving Janis Paige, particularly "Satin and Silk," which at once enacts and parodies the idea that a woman's function is to be "a pleasure" for the male. The ideological project here, in fact, is somewhat called into question by the film's clear preference for Charisse as against Paige—the grounds for the preference being both the generic definition of the Paige role as comic support and its thematic definition as parody of the woman-object image.

One notes also the weight that is allowed Charisse's protest against the ludicrous musical film Astaire is producing, a moment which draws together a number of the ideological-thematic threads of the film. The musical itself parodies the mindless vulgarity and silliness of standard Capitalist popular entertainment. In it, Paige plays the Empress Josephine (with "titillating thighs"), her number reinforcing the woman-object parody. The score is a debased version of the music of the Soviet composer whose defection provided the starting-point for the action. Charisse's protest (which we are allowed to take unexpectedly seriously) is provoked partly by her recognition of the way Astaire has manipulated her and ignored her own feelings and commitments.

3. The validation of "entertainment" as against "art." "Entertainment"—as something to be passively absorbed rather than actively participated in, dedicated to the discouragement of awareness—is a central "bourgeois-Capitalist" concept and one inherent in the Hollywood musical as a genre, surfacing in the case of individual films as an explicit concern. (pp. 29-30)

A leading plot-thread [in *Silk Stockings*] is the conversion of the Russian composer's music (which is presented, rather awkwardly, as combining the highbrow with the Communist-utilitarian) into the score for an American musical; and one encounters the assumption that Borodin and Tchaikovsky were important composers because they supplied melodies for popular American songs. On the other hand, the tendency of Entertainment to trivialize and vulgarize is quite explicitly commented upon by the hilarious "Josephine" number; by the composer's outrage (which is treated as not at all unreasonable, and left unresolved and unmollified); and by the seriousness of Charisse's protest. One regrets that the ending of the film fails to find a satisfactory way of resolving these ideological tensions—it prefers to forget them.

4. The opposition between an inhibiting, depersonalizing system and freedom, self-expression, spontaneity. Dance is crucial here, and provides the vindication of transforming *Ninotchka* into a musical, dancing becoming not mere decoration but a leading thematic motif. Charisse's liberation comes when Astaire lures her into dancing. (Her learning to dance corresponds to the moment at the end of *Alphaville* when Anna Karina learns to say "I love you.") The implicit theme of dance-as-liberation, however, recurs throughout the film, starting from the splendid "We Can't Go Back to Moscow" number. Crucially, the emphasis in the *mise-en-scène* is on *individual* movement, in which even non-dancers like Peter Lorre find some physical means of expression.

A statement at this point from my own personal ideology: I find the first three of these projects (leaving aside for the moment the ways in which they are disturbed or undermined by certain elements) ideologically unacceptable, the fourth wholly admirable. Yet in the film, while the fourth is not simply or comprehensively identifiable with the other three (producing further tensions), it is also not cleanly separable from them.

The beautiful Charisse solo number, for example, gives unified expression to all four simultaneously. She surrenders to the various allures of Capitalistic luxury, dressing to transform herself into the object of male desire, and thereby incidentally providing an archetypal Entertainment number. At the same time, the grace and freedom of physical movement (both of dancer and camera) throughout the sequence movingly express the casting off of repressive constraints. (p. 30)

One might argue (keeping in view the opposed parodies of "Capitalism" and "Communism") that the film implicitly proposes a third ideology, necessarily rather vaguely defined, but based on values of freedom, spontaneity, movement, which is set against both the ideologies that are defined explicitly. Some attempt is made to balance the two discredited ideologies: the degenerate commercialism of the *Josephine* musical against the exploitation of Russian ballet and Russian films as cultural propaganda. But one must note that the two "false" ideologies are not—could not be—presented on equal terms. We are encouraged to laugh unambiguously *at* "Communism," while our attitude to "Capitalism" even at points of the most extreme satire (the Janis Paige numbers), is partly one of complicity. Similarly, the third ideology is decisively and explicitly opposed in the film to "Communism" but ambiguously related to "Capitalism."

Inevitably, the "Capitalist" ideology (and male supremacy) is firmly reimposed at the end of the film. Cyd Charisse is brought back to Paris by Astaire's machinations; the climax of which has her seated in a night club (La *Vieille* Russie) to watch admiringly Astaire's solo-with-chorus dance number ("The Ritz Roll 'n Rock") which is a blatant affirmation of the material rewards of Capitalism (though, again, not entirely free from elements of parody that call this into question). She then, after a brief misunderstanding has been cleared up, rather lamely submits to him. Her earlier stand (in reaction against the *Josephine* musical) is forgotten by the film, though not necessarily by the audience. We are left with, at the very least, a sense of dissatisfaction.

There seems to me an alternative way of dealing with the ideological issues posed by *Silk Stockings,* and countless other films. I would suggest—somewhat hesitantly, for it is the sort of suggestion that gets hooted down in contemporary film criticism—that, rather than talk in terms of a "third ideology," one might talk of certain aspects partially escaping ideological determination. I would suggest, in other words, that there are indeed certain fundamental drives and needs that are not ideological but universal—

drives which certain ideologies can suppress but which no ideology creates—and that such things as freedom of expression, delight in bodily movement, instinctual spontaneity, are among them.

Heretically, and despite Garbo, the Lubitsch touch, and the laughing scene, I enjoy *Silk Stockings* more than I enjoy *Ninotchka*—largely because of the extra dimension given by the musical numbers (or certain aspects of them), a dimension that affects the meaning and values of the film. (pp. 30-1)

The vitality of the musical numbers in *Silk Stockings* itself transcends their local ideological functions.

Consider the first number, "We Can't Go Back to Moscow." Its local function is to establish and celebrate the conversion of the three Soviet emissaries to the material delights of Capitalism, notably champagne and "available" women; every precise detail can be explained in relation to this function. What transcends the ideological purpose here is the energy of the realization, an energy expressed not merely in the physical movements of the actors but in the inventiveness of the *mise-en-scène*. . . .

The use of abstract words (energy, inventiveness) here is inevitable. I am arguing that Materialism is not enough; that, even when every concrete detail in a given work can be shown to be ideologically determined, the details may be the product of fundamental creative drives that transcend ideology. The prevailing ideology, in other words, may determine (to varying degrees according to the artist's level of awareness) the forms in which the drives find embodiment, but it can't account for the drives themselves. . . .

A part of the interest and richness of *Silk Stockings* lies . . . in its internal tensions and contradictions. If, for example, the element of parody of Capitalist ideology represented by the Janis Paige numbers, or the challenge to the image of woman-as-object represented by the Cyd Charisse dances, were absent—if there were no more to the film than the simple "Capitalism good—Communism bad" opposition on which it is nominally built—its interest would be severely diminished. Yet the film's creative vitality . . . cannot reasonably be reduced to its ideological contradictions. The inventions of the Cyd Charisse solo, for example the "silk stockings" dance—are almost entirely "within the ideology." . . .

The evaluation of works of art must always be a complex, delicate, and tentative business. Ideological issues cannot be irrelevant to it, yet no work can be justly evaluated on purely ideological grounds. Crucial, it seems to me, is the concept of creativity as at once transcending ideology, even when its concrete forms and details are ideologically determined. That is why it can transcend time and space, so that to listen to the music of Bach, or watch the films of Mizoguchi, can be an enriching experience however alien their cultural determinants; and why it is still permissible (and necessary)—the united efforts of Marxism and semiology to the contrary—to talk of "genius," of "personal expression," and of "individual creativity." (p. 31)

Robin Wood, "Art and Ideology: Notes on 'Silk Stockings'," in Film Comment *(copyright © 1975 by The Film Society of Lincoln Center; all rights reserved), Vol. 11, No. 3, May-June, 1975, pp. 28-31.*

Elaine May

1932-

American director, scriptwriter, and actress.

In her films, May's subtle humor, finely honed during her early days as a comedienne, is focused on human foibles. Throughout her work, she views her characters with a combination of sympathy and black humor.

While studying as an unenrolled student at the University of Chicago, May met Mike Nichols. They formed a comedy team generally conceded to combine unique acting abilities and wit. After a concert tour, several television appearances, and a Broadway run, they separated, and May began writing plays. Most critics were unenthusiastic about her efforts.

May next worked as an actress, appearing in two films. Her first attempt at directing, *A New Leaf,* was taken out of her hands after shooting ended. The studio's editing made it, in her eyes, "a cliché-ridden, banal failure." Though she sued to prevent its release, it opened to warmer reviews than she expected.

May received her first real recognition when she directed *The Heartbreak Kid,* which was scripted by Neil Simon. Beneath the light comedy of the film, May reveals the painful struggles of a young man in search of the perfect love. Most critics praise May's ability to temper Simon's usually blatant humor with compassion for her characters. But some critics conclude that her scorn of romantic illusions surfaces in the sharp-edged wit and the ambiguous ending of the film.

Although May has enjoyed moderate success, it is generally conceded that in her films she has not yet fully developed the talent that was evident in her days with Mike Nichols.

ELAINE ROTHSCHILD

A New Leaf is hackneyed comedy about an aging playboy who, having gone through his inheritance, decides to marry a rich innocent. Miss May, who wrote the script, directed, and played the role of the rich innocent, endeavors to enliven such plot clichés with the negative shibboleths currently considered "in", and loads her film down with other liabilities. (p. 232)

As for Miss May's noises, fully exploited by Paramount's flacks, about the final cut of this picture not conforming to her intention: Well, from the interior evidence, this picture couldn't have been cut any other way. Which means Miss May shot it this way. What way? To make as much money as possible. Why her alleged protest? To draw attention to her picture, and to delude the gullible that she is still anti-Establishment—all the way to the bank. (p. 233)

Elaine Rothschild, "Film Reviews: 'A New Leaf'," in Films in Review *(copyright © 1971 by the National Board of Review of Motion Pictures, Inc.), Vol. XXII, No. 4, April, 1971, pp. 232-33.*

RICHARD COMBS

[*A New Leaf*] has that rather plain and graceless look which combines the functional needs of stage and television comedy. Admittedly there is some dabbling with more respected models—the film opens with a visual gag of a type refined by Buster Keaton, and the storyline itself is vaguely reminiscent of Keaton's *Seven Chances.* But then the tragedy of Henry Graham, middle-aged bachelor and profligate of a now exhausted private income, and his efforts to find a marriageable heiress, to appropriate the fortune and then dispose of its owner, has its own classic status which Elaine May chooses not to update, or at least only for occasional and very specific comic effect. . . .

A New Leaf keeps the current phobias of American comedy firmly out of sight, with a rigour of approach that is more than just the artificially airtight conventions of its story. The society inhabited by Henry Graham, all hyper-refined and aristocratic tedium, has a perverse dislocation from any American reality. It is blandly characterised by Henry's vaguely English but perfectly generalised activities at his club, a languid canter along a bridle-path, or the exquisite boredom of hearing about the current blight in a friend's garden. . . .

[The cultural joke of Henry's drive through a New York ghetto, bemoaning his financial situation,] a wrenching and rearranging of social contexts—*The Great Gatsby* as written by P. G. Wodehouse—conditions its response to the characters. Peculiarly isolated and plainly ridiculous in their situation and their private obsessions, they are still permitted to be discreetly real in their absurdity. . . .

The wistful, fierce integrity of [the personalities of Henry and his wife], viewed with a detached amusement, allows the film to bypass the usual agenda of subjects (sex, the System, etc.) of current comedy concerned with vanishing human identity, and lends a particular vivacity to the comic set-pieces. . . .

[Henry] progresses from pillar of futility to bustling man of action. . . . While [his wife] Henrietta remains in a state of ignorance so blissful that it seems less than human, Henry returns to indolence with just a twinge of self-awareness.

The movement in fact is close to that of [Mike Nichols'] *The Graduate,* with the latter's furious acting out of roles, its bemused acceptance of the futility of both speech and action, and a final weary closing of the circle on a happy ending which is not quite that. Nichols' art suggests a ring-master's display of 'turns', a parading of masks, while Miss May organises her entertainment with very conscious touches of theatrical artifice (the romantic props of country lane, full moon, golden sunset are whisked on and off very quickly), and has her characters act out their obsessions with touching intensity and showmanship.

Richard Combs, "Film Reviews: 'A New Leaf'," in Sight and Sound *(copyright © 1971 by The British Film Institute), Vol. 41, No. 1, Winter, 1971-72, p. 52.*

PAULINE KAEL

Elaine May has the rarest kind of comic gift: the ability to create a world seen comically. Her satirist's malice isn't cutting; something in the befuddled atmosphere she creates keeps it mild—yet mild in a thoroughly demented way, mild as if impervious to sanity. It may be a trait of some witty women to be apologetic about the cruelty that is inherent in their wit; Miss May, all apologies, has a knack for defusing the pain without killing the joke. The dialogue sounds natural and unforced. The humor sneaks up on you, and it's surprisingly evenhanded and democratic; everybody in [*The Heartbreak Kid*] is a little cockeyed. . . .

Elaine May's tone often verges on the poignant (and is best when it does), but there are unkillable demons in her characters, and you never know what you'll discover next. Working almost entirely through the actors, she lets those demons come to the surface in a scene before she moves on. The characters don't seem to be middle-class survivors (though they are)—they seem to be crazy people in leaking boats, like other people. She supplies a precarious element of innocence that removes them from [the pandering, hard-core humor of the screenwriter, Neil Simon]. (p. 69)

Elaine May keeps the best of Neil Simon but takes the laugh-and-accept-your-coarseness out of it. She reveals without complacency, and so the congratulatory slickness of Neil Simon is gone. Lila and Lenny and Kelly have inadequate dreams; they're on their way to missing out because of these tinkly little dreams. In this sense, they're younger editions of the middle-aged failures Simon has been writing about in his latest plays. . . . *The Heartbreak Kid* is anarchically skeptical about the ways in which people bamboozle themselves; it gets at the unexpected perversity in that self-love. (p. 70)

However, the only actual flaw is that the picture just sort of expires, with an undersized "thought-provoking" ending when we're expecting something outrageous that would clarify the hero's new quandary. . . . [But] Elaine May's work has a note of uncertainty about people and their fates —things may change at any minute, you feel—and so an ambiguous ending isn't jarring, just a little disappointing. . . .

I guess what I like best about [*The Heartbreak Kid*] is that although Miss May's touch is very sure (and although the picture is, technically, in a different league from her wobbly first movie, *A New Leaf;* I mean it isn't shot in murkocolor, and the framing of the action—the whole look of it—is professional), sureness in her doesn't mean that mechanical, overemphatic style which is the bane of recent American comedy and is Broadway's worst legacy to the movies. That crackling, whacking style is always telling you that things are funnier than you see them to be. Elaine May underplays her hand. The element of uncertainty that results in a shambles when she isn't on top of the situation as a director can, as in this case, where she's functioning well, result in a special, distracted comic tone, which implies that you can't always tell what's funny. It is uncertainty as a comic attitude—a punchiness that comes from seeing life as a series of booby traps. (p. 71)

Pauline Kael, "New Thresholds, New Anatomies" (originally published in The New Yorker, *Vol. XLVIII, No. 43, December 16, 1972), in her* Reeling *(copyright © 1972 by Pauline Kael; reprinted by permission of Little, Brown and Company in association with the Atlantic Monthly Press), Atlantic-Little, Brown, 1976, pp. 68-74.**

WILLIAM S. PECHTER

For a considerable portion of its length, *The Heartbreak Kid* seems merely to be another mining of [the] lode of Jewish self-hatred. On brief acquaintance, Lenny Cantrow marries Lila Kolodny, and, almost as soon as she's been sexually demystified (she'd been making Lenny wait until the honeymoon), she is revealed to him as the proto-Jewish mother in all her gross vulgarity. Loud and inescapable, virtuoso of nonstop talking and eating undeterred even by sex . . . , her character, whatever one may think of the creation, *is* a creation. And anything the actress . . . fails to suggest of the character's insistently smothering presence, the film fills in by its sense of her encroachment on its space, from the narrow squeeze down the aisle at the opening wedding through her crowding in the car on the honeymoon trip to the hotel room where, laid up by a sunburn, she waits to pounce on Lenny each time he enters. Yet even as one admires the deftness with which all this is done, one is repelled by its cruelty; . . . [the] character seems drawn for no other purpose than to humiliate her, and, unappealing as the character may be, the film's treatment of her seems less appealing still. . . .

[For] a while, it looks like the film, after spending its first half humiliating Lila, will spend its second humiliating Lenny, a CCNY *shmuck* vainly aspiring to conquer [Kelly,] an all-American campus queen.

Up until the point in the film at which Lila is dumped, *The Heartbreak Kid* seemed . . . neither particularly distinguished nor particularly likable; what one sees in it soon after, however, is something I tend, given the formula-ridden character of most movies, to value highly: the capacity of a film to shift gears, and surprise us. For just as one fears that Lenny is going to have his head handed to him by one of the bull-necked jocks by whom Kelly is constantly surrounded, the worm turns with Bilko-like aplomb, and the film itself suddenly changes direction. And one sees that Lenny's talents as a manic liar, revealed earlier when he invents excuses to leave Lila alone in their hotel room, are born not merely of nervousness but of nerve, and bespeak real resources of daring and cunning.

From then on, the film becomes a much funnier one. . . . (p. 83)

The emptiness one feels at the end of *The Heartbreak Kid* seems to come not from the milieu, but rather from within Lenny himself, the gifted hustler suddenly revealed to be operating on nothing but hustle. At the end, Lenny, having gone through everyone else at the wedding reception, sits with a group of restless children, and incongruously hustles them with his standard line of patter; when Lenny asks their age, one of them says he is ten years old, and, a vacant look passing over his face. Lenny muses, "I was ten." . . . [One is left with] Lenny's incredulous contemplation of the distance he has traveled from being ten to being at that moment there, a journey on which he's shed all baggage. . . . This is a film in which, for all that one feels it couldn't be other than by and about Jews, the word "Jew" is not, to my recollection, spoken once; even Kelly's father's obdurate resistance to Lenny as a prospective son-in-law seems curiously without discernible anti-Semitic content. Yet though there is no sense that Kelly's Waspishness is in itself what Lenny desires in her, there is little doubt it is the condition which makes possible those qualities in her he finds desirable; she is, as even the best of all possible Lilas could never be, the all-American dream girl. It would be horrible to think of Lila as the sole content of Lenny's cultural heritage, the residue of his tradition; and yet the hollow sensation one is left with at the end feels like just that. It feels like deracination. (p. 84)

William S. Pechter, "A Mother's Vengeance," in Commentary *(reprinted by permission; all rights reserved), Vol. 55, No. 5, May, 1973, pp. 81-4.**

MITCHELL S. COHEN

That *The Heartbreak Kid* manages to synthesize May's improvisational satire, Simon's situation comedy, and [the bitterly black humor of Bruce Jay Friedman's "A Change of Plan," from which *The Heartbreak Kid* was adapted], and emerge as an occasionally brilliant, if indecisive, American comedy is an achievement very much out of the ordinary. Furthermore, Elaine May's second directorial effort is carried off with such a casual comfort and buoyant pace that the contrasting threads are only rarely visible. . . . [The] one consistent quality found in *The Heartbreak Kid* is the ability to take us by surprise—which is above all what makes this movie one of the few really enjoyable comedies by a young American director in recent years. (p. 60)

At the core of *The Heartbreak Kid* is a serious moral dilemma. This dilemma hinges on whether Lenny is correct in cruelly dumping Lila in order to pursue his dream girl. Neil Simon's traditional response to complex human relationships is to pass them off with a gag line, and it is to Elaine May's eternal credit that she did not allow *The Heartbreak Kid* to deteriorate into *Barefoot in the Park*. By lingering on the characters for a brief moment after the scene's punctuation with a joke, she enables us to see that the humor coincides with confusion and sadness. Framing the film with almost identical weddings, down to the music . . . , also reinforces the lack of resolution in the intervening comedy. The most disturbing aspect of Simon's comedic formula in the past has been his tendency to give his hand away, to anticipate his own punch line and rob us of the joy of discovery. May's gift has been quite the opposite; she lets us believe that she is guileless, totally distanced from the humor in the situation. In the role of innocent participant rather than sophisticated commentator, she allows humor to evolve where Simon's dissolves. *The Heartbreak Kid* permits Simon his pokes in the ribs, but May's emphasis falls on the side of the people involved. Like Lenny himself, *The Heartbreak Kid* manages to win one over by virtue of its surface charm. Unlike the film's rather dubious hero, however, the film has a lot going on beneath the exterior. (p. 61)

Mitchell S. Cohen, "Short Notices: 'The Heartbreak Kid'," in Film Quarterly *(copyright 1973 by The Regents of the University of California; reprinted by permission of the University of California Press), Vol. XXVI, No. 4, Summer, 1973, pp. 60-1.*

ERIC BRAUN

Elaine May has a considerable reputation for wit and perception and I viewed the beginning of *The Heartbreak Kid* —. . . with an expectant smile, which froze on my lips at the first wedding breakfast. I just cannot find anything inherently funny in Jewish weddings—still less in honeymoon nights in which the idiosyncrasies of either partner are held up to ridicule. By the time the stupid bride was writhing in the throes of sunstroke, which the groom was seizing as a Godsent opportunity to date another girl, my lips were tight indeed; not even Almira Sessions nor the late Edna May Oliver ever registered disapproval as wholeheartedly as I. The whole approach to the subject of the non-hero's emotional life—or lack of it, for there was never a more cold-blooded, self-indulgent creep than Lenny—seems to me too sadistic to be funny, and he himself too lacking in charm or any of the basic human qualities to be able to hold one's attention for longer than one unhappy honeymoon.

Neil Simon's comedy has always seemed to me in the past to mirror the American way of life with good humour and affection for his characters so that it was possible to laugh with their shortcomings rather than to be made uncomfortable by them, and Elaine May has made her witty shafts strike home without resorting to the pillory. Together, in this case, they have failed to create a single situation which does not smack of the cynical or a character with whom one can have sympathy. (p. 46)

Eric Braun, "Reviews: 'The Heartbreak Kid'" (© copyright Eric Braun 1973; reprinted with permission), in Films and Filming, *Vol. 19, No. 10, July, 1973, pp. 45-6.*

MARJORIE ROSEN

[Judging by *A New Leaf* and *The Heartbreak Kid,* Elaine May] is like an Uncle Tom whose feminine sensibilities are demonstrably nil. May enjoys broad caricatures, especially of her women characters, and there's something self-serving and snide about them. Their menacing "satire" recalls *The Women,* but Clare Boothe Luce's play, for better or worse, was written forty years ago; May works in the present. In *A New Leaf,* she directs herself as the classic drippy spinster, a weirdo rich botanist named Henrietta transformed into awkward loveliness by a money-hungry dilettante. *The Heartbreak Kid* is even more discomforting, exhuming fifties' stereotypes: the sloppy lower-class bride . . . , the shrewd loudmouthed groom . . . , who is marrying about half a notch down, and the Sunshine WASP. . . . Groom meets WASP on his honeymoon while he is being sufficiently soured by lower-class virgin's lovemaking (What did she *do* that was so bad?), by the sight of egg salad running out of her mouth, and finally by her blistering sun poisoning. After a piercing scene in which he tells her that not only the honeymoon but the marriage is over, he runs off to win the WASP. And we are supposed to feel, *How funny! How sad!* It's a tricky movie, because a lot of it *is* funny, the scenes are quick, and it's all treated casually. But May stands aside and chuckles at her misfit women. . . . The bride in *The Heartbreak Kid* gets special buffoon treatment, which reflects on the director's *idea* of characterization rather than the character herself. So what is essentially a grotesque story anyway becomes weighted, for the sake of comedy, against the girl. Everyone else is smooth America; she's a leftover from the Yiddish stage or Ellis Island.

There is, in all fairness, a possibility that May has simply not toned down her straight-faced self-parody. . . . In that case it is a stylistic rather than attitudinal handicap. On the other hand, when Nichols and May broke up [their comedy act], he emerged as Broadway's and then Hollywood's Golden Boy while she, a woman, found fewer opportunities as a director. How much of her toughness stems from bitterness, from denying her femaleness? But why not compassion instead? *She's been there,* as they say; she knows what's at stake. (pp. 363-64)

Marjorie Rosen, "Changing—Breakthrough or Backlash?" in her Popcorn Venus: Women, Movies & the American Dream *(adapted by permission of Coward, McCann & Geoghegan, Inc.; copyright © 1973 by Marjorie Rosen), Coward, McCann & Geoghegan, 1973, pp. 345-66.**

MOLLY HASKELL

Lenny, the hero of *The Heartbreak Kid,* . . . seems more the progeny of [Bruce Jay] Friedman, who wrote the story on which the film is based, than of Neil Simon, who wrote the screenplay, or Elaine May, who directed. But May has softened the edges, making Lenny more enchanting than he has any right to be, and brought into dramatic, if not completely resolved, focus, the surrounding characters. . . .

Elaine May's second feature is a funny and sometimes sidesplitting film whose whole never approaches the success of its best moments in which the two levels of romantic fantasy and satire are reconciled. It falls prey to the kind of tonal inconsistencies, or rather irresolutions, that one might expect from the collective effort of such similar, wittily urbane, but not identical sensibilities as May's, Simon's, and Friedman's.

The first half hour, and weakest section of the film, sets up in derisive, skit-like fashion, the marriage from which Lenny will be at least partially excused from wishing to escape. (p. 171)

The minute Kelly comes into view, or, more properly, eclipses the sun on a deserted Miami beach, the movie picks up—not just because of [her] Amazon beauty and slyly comical self-awareness, but because the WASPs are treated with hardly a trace of the caricature lavished on the Jews. They belong to a fantasy world and the question the film asks, without being able to answer, is, What happens when a fantasy comes true?

It plays on a reversal of the usual expectations: that fantasies don't come true, and that the Jewish hero will slink back, chastened to his ethnic bride. The problem—and this brings us back to the equivocal nature of the hero . . .—is that the film is predicated on the compelling nature of that fantasy, without any clear understanding of what is behind or ahead of it. He is not the usual intellectual hero or poor boy, driven by social or economic motives to reach beyond himself, and the whole notion of marriage loses its urgency. However else May, Simon, and Friedman may differ, they begin with the common assumption that marriage is ridiculous, an idea that not even society is at great pains to contradict these days. Hence, there is no real reason to make marriage crucial to the narrative except to make satirical points. But the fact is, there *is* a strong impulse to marry . . . , and if May and company had approached it with curiosity instead of derision, they might have come away with more satisfying (poetically and logically) reasons for its failure. She came closer to suggesting a feeling of complementary needs among the romantic oldsters of *A New Leaf* than she does here, where the egotistic male fantasies prevail.

The best scenes seem to bear her mark—scenes which combine satire, deadpan humor, and sheepish vulnerability, often with little or no dialogue, long takes, and three or four people in the frame. . . . For such touches and minor enchantments *The Heartbreak Kid* is well worth seeing. (pp. 171-72)

Molly Haskell, "'The Heartbreak Kid'," in her From Reverence to Rape: The Treatment of Women in the Movies *(copyright © 1973, 1974 by Molly Haskell; reprinted by permission of Holt, Rinehart and Winston, Publishers), Holt, 1974 (and reprinted in* The National Society of Film Critics on Movie Comedy, *edited by Stuart Byron and Elisabeth Weis, Grossman Publishers, 1977, pp. 171-72).*

JOAN MELLEN

[In *The Heartbreak Kid*] Elaine May presents us with two versions of "woman": the Jewish, gum-chewing Lila at home amidst the vulgarities of Miami Beach, and the Wasp Kelly, whose surface patina of blonde invulnerability and athletic grace bespeaks utter emotional emptiness. The hero, Lenny, is no better than either the woman he abandons nor the one he pursues to the wilds of the Mid-West. But his callow opportunism can in no way mitigate May's unfortunate offering of crudely stereotyped women, recognizable ethnic types presented at their worst for the sake of a few cheap laughs. . . . (p. 41)

[Lila is] an adolescent whose gratifications remain oral and a Jewish girl to whom a mouth stuffed with food is bliss. We know how soon she will triple her chins, already well on their way. Elaine May even has Lila a sloppy, disgusting eater who smears egg salad all over her face, spits, wipes with her hand and talks with her mouth full. Lacking all confidence or sense of herself, she must constantly be told that their lovemaking is wonderful. We are led by May to sympathize with the steady disillusionment of the young husband who moans, "it's difficult to give out bulletins in the heat of passion." Lila is so gross that her body and its carriage are used by May to revolt us all. It is a conception born of a considerable self-hatred—of women, Jews, and, at some level, her own daughter [, who plays Lila].

Thus we are meant to accept Lenny's flirtation with the blonde, gay and joyful Kelly. . . . If Lila can't swim, Kelly can. Lila turns beet red from the sun and must spend her days in the hotel room smeared with noxema, packing her jowls with chocolate. Kelly's skin has turned a golden brown. Lila is over-eager, anxious, self-deprecating, gushing and loud. Kelly, the American heroine, knows how to play it cool and how to make a man want her. She has style even if it is that of a cheer-leading Lolita.

Kelly is viciously, almost innocently amoral. When she learns that Lenny is married, this poses no obstacle: "What else is new?" She can manipulate both Lenny and her father with ease. Rich, spoiled and lacking nothing, she finds all men desirable as creatures to tease and bend to her bemused will. None can deny her. (pp. 42, 44)

[What] is striking about the film is the absence of any women capable of grace or substance. Lila's mother is an older version of herself grown heavy. Kelly's mother, more attractive as befitting her superior social station, and, May unconsciously suggests, her Anglo-Saxon appeal, is blonde, brittle, but stupid. She is forever in the shadow of her husband to whom she defers in all decisions. The younger women are simply their mothers twenty years earlier. Neither shows any sign of transcending the bleak vulgarity of her conditioning.

In fact, the two wives of Lenny are equally obnoxious. Lila's crudity is more obvious, but Kelly's is more sinister. It is the vulgarity of an utter incapacity to feel or make emotional commitments. The film leaves an emptiness that defies the rave reviews. All the human beings portrayed lack redeeming grace. . . . May, no less than Lila and Kelly, is a product of bourgeois society; she sees its excesses, but not its structure. She can register what it has done to women, but can neither desire nor imagine any means of change, nor the vision of an alternative. (p. 44)

Joan Mellen, "Bourgeois Woman: A Disturbance in Mirrors," in her Women and Their Sexuality in the New Film *(copyright 1973, reprinted by permission of the publisher, Horizon Press, New York), Horizon, 1973, pp. 15-54.**

STUART M. KAMINSKY

[May's] films—*A New Leaf* and *The Heartbreak Kid*—deal with dependent weak characters. . . . [Her] characters, male and female, are equal and both weak in some major, emotional way. They meet out of mutual need . . . , fall in love and support each other's weaknesses. . . . The films are less generic satires than rather traditional romances or man vs. women comedies of courtship.

The protagonists are both openly neurotic victims who, like the protagonists of Woody Allen's films, triumph, achieve what they want, a love relationship earned through pain. Secondary characters in May's films are generally pragmatists . . . , people who use other people. However, May sees this social pragmatism as a neurotic weakness behind which people hide. For May, like Allen, open vulnerability and weakness are virtues compared to a false pragmatic front of security.

Her plots deal with men who see women as objects to be used to fulfill a fantasy or from whom to gain something pragmatic. In both cases, [Henry Graham] in *A New Leaf* and [Lenny Cantrow] in *The Heartbreak Kid* . . . start out by being pragmatists seeking wealth, sex or security from the women and finding their pragmatic facade stripped away so they can have a mutually dependent agonized relationship with a woman. In both films, the woman starts out as the victim and, in both films, triumphs. (pp. 62-3)

Stuart M. Kaminsky, "Eight Comedy Directors of the Last Decade," in Film Reader *(copyright © 1975* The Silver Screen*), No. 1, 1975, pp. 59-65.**

STANLEY KAUFFMANN

[*Mikey and Nicky* is an] odd, biting, grinning, sideways-scuttling rodent of a picture. . . .

[The plot] sounds like the schema of a "character" crime picture, a so-called *film noir,* particularly since most of it is shadowy. (Virtually all of it takes place at night.) It is those things, but it is several things more. The first additional thing is, incredibly, that it's comic. Actual laughs are scattered, but the overall view of the two men is through a prism of comic detail. The script is by Elaine May, who also directed. Her previous scripts *A New Leaf* and *The Heartbreak Kid,* both adapted from other people's stories, were ungainly and ill-focused. *Mikey and Nicky* is her own work, and she sees its grimness through her well-known comic temperament. Nicky's neuroses, the squabbles, the horseplay that Mikey has to sustain in order to keep credible to Nicky, even the put-upon-drudge dialogue of the hit man, are seen by May as a kind of gallows-humor vaudeville. We get no sense that she thought up the plot and then decided to do it at a blackly comic angle: this is the way she saw the moral swamp from the start.

And the nature of the vaudeville, the fact that it's mostly a double act by two men, is also part of the film's difference. Among the most deeply ingrained American myths is the one of the two male friends. . . . May, possibly with bitter amusement at all those decades of male glorification of male bonding, may have wanted to treat this now-classic pair as latently homoerotic (one screws a woman while the other waits—just barely vicarious homosexuality); she may have wanted to show the hatred and envy she sees under this noble concept. (Envy and rejection are what motivate Mikey's betrayal.) . . .

Further to this theme, few will miss the point that the very title *Mikey and Nicky* echoes the name Mike Nichols, who was May's partner for years in a celebrated "mixed" double act. The play on Nichols' name may have no more significance than Orson Welles' private joke on the last name of that dear old Irish actor Whitford Kane. On the other hand May did choose this particular joke. Under this film's title the double act of male duplicities takes on some additional wicked gleam.

The overall shape of the story, a life in a night with the picture ending at dawn, is not new, which of course May knows. Surely she knows the peak antecedent *La Notte.* Whether or not she was consciously using Antonioni as a general model, she too has her "couple" recapitulate their lives together and, more important, delineate the society around them, to which they have succumbed. The two men move through as wide a range of memory and experience as could be credible in one night. . . . And underneath it all is the betrayal, mocking the bath in nostalgia, as we feel Mikey tacitly justifying it to himself out of Nicky's supposed rejection of his love.

The film moves from station to station like a medieval morality play except that there is absolutely no morality.

Every person in the picture, from the racket boss, who is apparently a lawyer, to the hit man, who complains about the money he's losing on this job, accepts the immoral landscape of his life as the norm. (p. 20)

But *Mikey and Nicky* is not a satire, nothing so fundamentally benevolent. . . . May has plunged her camera right into the sewer and closed the cover. The sewer creatures, harsh or less harsh, loyal by sewer standards or not, are seen as merely topographical gradations within the pit. The only hint of irony—there is no compassion—is between the author outside the work and the work itself.

May overstates the case, probably consciously, by telling us that these people "are" the world, but she must feel that, actually or symbolically, they represent a good deal of it; and this picture states her loathing. That loathing, somewhat sophomorically simple though it is, gives the picture its integrity. It is utter: nastiness fills the screen from edge to edge.

May has directed as intimately as possible. All through it I felt that she was trying to press me up against the two men in mimesis of the feeling between them (and thus with an implicit comment on what mere closeness is worth). Her editing, about the duration of which there has been much talk, is sometimes ragged. Whiskers disappear, reappear, and disappear again during the same sequence; likewise cigarettes. The picture could have been shorter: the second visit to the "easy" woman serves a merely formal purpose, it doesn't really hold us. (pp. 20-1)

[*Mikey and Nicky* is] a little furry film that first interests, then amuses, then bites you, then scurries away again, leaving you a bit sickened. But authentically sickened. (p. 21)

Stanley Kauffmann, "Films: 'Mikey and Nicky'" (reprinted by permission of Brandt & Brandt Literary Agents, Inc.; copyright © 1977 by Stanley Kauffmann), in The New Republic, *Vol. 176, Nos. 1 & 2, January 1 & 8, 1977, pp. 20-1.*

MOLLY HASKELL

Mikey and Nicky are so enclosed in their own mediocrity [in *Mikey and Nicky*] that their night-long binge of recrimination and reconciliation is . . . more obscuring than enlightening. And when the light does come, in a violent denouement—sunlight, the illumination of the sibling rivalry—it is too late and too bright and too neat.

Elaine May hasn't come any closer to mastering the basics of filmmaking or developing a feeling for the medium, and awkwardnesses that were incorporated into the daffiness of *A New Leaf* or partially covered by the professionalism of *Heartbreak Kid* here stand exposed, and there is no humor to redeem them. (pp. 36-7)

I think I wouldn't mind the film so much if it didn't seem constantly to be telling us (as [John] Cassavetes's films always do) how much more "real" and authentic it is than all those phony Hollywood films to which both directors feel so comfortably and erroneously superior. May reminds me of the feminist who refuses to so much as wash a dirty dish after herself because it stands for the traditions and the tyrannies she left suburbia to escape. There is something symbolically apt in the image of Elaine May stealing two reels of her film from Paramount at one point in their altercation. She makes films in the same way, as if each moment of an actor's jagged improvisation were truth seized from under the noses and against the wishes of evil Hollywood. The great fuss over the cutting seems ironic, since you could throw the pieces up in the air and they would settle down in some form that as much resembles a pattern or progression as this one does.

As for Mikey and Nicky, even though we don't like 'em, I think Elaine May does, or thinks she does, and the fact that she has not been able to transfigure them with her affection is significant. Perhaps, unwittingly, she has planted the kiss of death on the buddy myth, at least for a while. If so, I will forgive her anything, even the misogyny that binds her to her male characters and is so casually contemptuous of the females—the three women are all dim-witted doormats—as to make one *almost* appreciate the stylized grotesques of Lina Wertmuller. (p. 37)

Molly Haskell, "A Long Day's Journey into Buddy-Buddy Land," in The Village Voice *(reprinted by permission of* The Village Voice; *copyright © The Village Voice, Inc., 1977), Vol. XXI, No. 1, January 3, 1977, pp. 36-7.*

JOHN SIMON

[Elaine May, a gifted comic artist,] has chosen to make something impossible: a film about two horrid fellows alternately abusing and greasily cajoling each other (and equally repulsive either way) when not getting into fights with other men or, for a little variety, maltreating the hapless women in their lives. Awful as this premise is, there is worse to come. One of these two old buddies may have a contract out on his life; the other is trying either to save or to finger him. Our sympathies are manipulated in such a way that we must keep switching allegiances: Now we are dragged into feeling pity for an utter louse, now we are forced to recoil at the creepiness of a dedicated friend.

The idea seems to be to show us the relativity of emotional truths in a world where good and bad have become Gordianly entangled; where even the decent, long-suffering women are also frumps or doormats whom the swinish men exploit by means of that drop of charm or pathos mixed in with their meanness. It does not begin to work. Not just because you cannot be simultaneously Damon Runyon and Dostoevski, but also because you can't make us care about people whose sweetness is virtually indistinguishable from their beastliness, so that the range of feelings with which we view their interminable, degrading squabbles extends only from distaste to boredom. Can you imagine two hours' worth of film about love, hate, and death among the cockroaches? And even that might be more interesting than this endless dawdling among people whose very souls are sweaty under their collars.

What truly sets one's teeth on edge, though, is that Miss May cannot forgo that cuteness which, when used aptly in zany, satirical comedy, adds an extra flavor to the zestful brew. Superimposed on this morose and morbid mess, however, it is unendurable—rather like a cloying perfume fighting a losing battle with an acrid body odor. . . .

One becomes acutely aware of Miss May's endless, irresolute editing, of her unhealthy inability to be finished with something, to let go. On a more elementary level yet, the film never gives us the much needed exposition that would clue us in about who these characters really are, what their work is, and what Nicky has done or not done to incur his boss's lethal wrath. . . .

The only way to describe *Mikey and Nicky* is as a celluloid death wish, a desperate challenge to the audience to dare like anything about the film. . . . [Miss May's writing and direction are] not so much created as exuded or secreted, like some particularly nasty discharge. (p. 55)

John Simon, "May, Bogdanovich, and Streisand: Varieties of Death Wish," in New York *Magazine (copyright © 1977 by News Group Publications, Inc.; reprinted with the permission of* New York *Magazine), Vol. 10, No. 2, January 10, 1977, pp. 55-7.**

MICHAEL TARANTINO

Mikey and Nicky is a film about male camaraderie *in spite of itself*. . . . [It] is concerned with the fragile base upon which such relationships are built, rather than establishing the phenomenon itself. Thus, the emotional ties that have been formed through childhood and adolescence are taken for granted in order to concentrate on the differences which ultimately lead to betrayal: in this case, Mikey's sense of rational decorum as pitted against Nicky's predictable unpredictability.

May has managed the perfect blend, utilizing the improvisatory techniques of her actors in order to re-inforce the film's narrative thrust. As disjointed as it may seem, each stray piece of business belongs. Ultimately, the film's "look" reflects itself. . . .

Whereas *A New Leaf* and *The Heartbreak Kid suggested* malaise, *Mikey and Nicky* delivers. It opens with Nicky stretched out in a seedy hotel, his ulcers killing him from lack of food. The editing is extremely disjunctive, frustrating the viewer's attempt to define the space. When Mikey comes to help, he is locked out. This becomes the leitmotif which joins the disparate pieces as the night winds down. However, from this point on, it is Nicky who is refused entrance—to his lover's, to his wife's, and finally, to Mikey's front door. By reinforcing a particular theme, May invites us to rethink the ways in which it has been used. Thus, the scene in which Mikey is locked out of Nicky's hotel room may be viewed in reverse—it is Nicky who is locked *in*.

It is only because of the film's rambling sense of narrative that these types of strategies are allowed to work. It is that rare American film which defines the event in terms of its own essence. . . . This is a film with a question at its center, rather than a multitude of answers. Did Mikey waver in his assignment to set his friend up for the kill? Despite his actions at the end, there are no easy solutions. He tells his wife to go to bed, as if it were all a bad dream. The night has been reduced to a split second, and has started all over again. (p. 11)

Michael Tarantino, "Elaine May's 'Mikey and Nicky'," in Take One *(copyright © 1977 by Unicorn Publishing Corp.), Vol. 5, No. 8, March, 1977, pp. 10-11.*

Albert Maysles

1926-

David Maysles

1932-

American documentary filmmakers.

The films of the Maysles brothers mark the first clear attempt to use cinéma vérité (though they prefer the term "direct cinema") in a nondramatic fashion. Their work reflects the influence of the Drew Associates, where they learned the art of cinéma vérité before starting their own company. Typical of cinéma vérité, their films are characterized by a spontaneous and unstructured quality. This is facilitated by their use of hand-held cameras and their observation, rather than direction, of their subjects.

Albert Maysles was initiated into filmmaking in 1955 when he shot footage of mental hospitals in the Soviet Union. His film *Psychiatry in Russia* is a diary-like recording of his trip. While in Moscow in 1959, Albert met Richard Leacock and D. A. Pennebaker of Drew Associates and then worked for that company on several films. In 1962, Albert left Drew Associates and he and David formed their own company.

***Salesman* is considered their most important work to date for its attempt to capture an American experience without benefit of a famous personality or event of marked significance. David Maysles feels it is noteworthy because: "We proved you could take someone from everyday life and make a film about him." Many of their films developed from routine commercial assignments, and grew into their own projects. The most notable of these, *Gimme Shelter,* is the recording of the Rolling Stones's disastrous concert at Altamont. Because the film contains footage of an actual murder, critics generally feel that its fame is due to controversy and sensationalism rather than cinematic artistry.**

More than their other films, *Grey Gardens* raises the issue of the exploitative nature of cinéma vérité. While some critics find the Maysleses' examination of the Beales poignant and insightful, others feel *Grey Gardens* is a cruel invasion of privacy.

It is often felt that the Maysleses' quest for "truthfulness" is an act of indiscretion that dishonestly manipulates reality. Albert Maysles has said: "It's truth, the way we see it—in the shooting and the finishing. And in almost every case, that truth is shared by the people, by the subjects who see the film afterward." But, despite this avowal, the Maysles brothers are faced with opponents who feel their honesty often masks sensationalism. (For Albert Maysles, see also *Contemporary Authors,* Vols. 29-32, rev. ed.)

PATRICK MacFADDEN

[The salesmen of *Salesman*] are driven by an antic demonology: the ethic of individual entrepreneurialism rages like a hectic in the blood. The commanding heights of the economy already scaled by the faceless inter-locking directorates of the billion-dollar corps., only the marshlands are left to direct selling—encyclopedias, books of Knowledge, door-to-door Bibles—all the bric-a-brac of social improvement. But the salesmen have pride in their craft, their self-image that of cottage artisans deluged by an earlier shift in production relationships. (p. 12)

Selling is freedom; but it is also survival. One false cadence, an over-eager handshake, a too-familiar confidence and all is lost. Back out to the chilling street, briefcase obstinately full. . . .

The Maysles Brothers finally home in on Paul Brennan, the Thomas beginning to doubt. And doubters are not allowed. Kennie the sales supervisor knows that "one bad apple can destroy the whole barrel." (p. 13)

Paul is beginning to slip. The harvesting is thin, the glibness shows signs of wear-and-tear. He is losing "credibility," suffers from "negative thinking"—a thought process that Marcuse has fingered as the element most frightening to the social engineers of the manipulated society. . . .

Why is Paul coming to the end of the road? The Maysles record his spontaneous Joycean dialogue with himself, his uneasy humming, the silent half-hearted whistling—all the marks of the brooder, the loser, the professional victim. (p.14)

Is it that Brennan is disgusted with his own cheerful cynicism, with the reductiveness involved in the selling process? "All neighbourly content and easy talk are gone / He that's mounting up must on his neighbour mount . . ." Paul would understand the sexual ambience of Yeats' line; for his own situation is compounded by the erotic overtones of selling. Not of course the fantasies of the commercial traveller's tale, but the fear of being unmanned which is built into the very substance of the transaction itself. The approach, the stalking, the small insincerities, the faked interest, the final spasm as the contract is hammered home. Or, alternatively, the repulse that is more than a question of sales returns, the psychic buffeting of a slow castration. Hence Paul's growing self-hate as his crisis deepens, the defense-mechanism of the truly colonized.

This would suggest an awareness of his own condition. And perhaps only in fiction, or on the road to Damascus, do such flashes come. But there is no fictive arranging of experience in *Salesman;* if there are Gods from the machine, they've decided to stay there. (Indeed, the Maysles refer to *Salesman* as the cinematic equivalent of the nonfiction novel.) It is more probable then, that Paul is half in love with easeful rout, seeking out the stalemate, a conoisseur of what's sure to bomb. For Paul, as for so many brooders, nothing succeeds like failure.

By resolutely refusing to patronize their subjects, by insisting on the autonomy of the caught moment, the Maysles have elevated the tawdry activities of marginal commerce to the level of metaphor. It is a metaphor that calls all in doubt; for it raises a question and makes a statement about the ways in which our human dimension has been taken away from us. (p. 17)

Patrick MacFadden, "'Salesman'," in Film Society Review, *Vol. 4, No. 6, February, 1969, pp. 11-17.*

S. F.

Salesman, a film as exploitative as the practices it tries to expose, continues to sell audiences on that which looks like penetrating social commentary, but which is nothing more than anti-social non-commentary on a subject too far from our hearts to bring tears to our eyes. . . .

[The] only truly engrossing moment in *Salesman* is the one time that a conscious "dramatization" does take place, when the salesmen and their supervisor are "acting out" a hypothetical sales situation for self-instructive purposes. Here the supervisor plays the salesman, the salesmen play resistive clients, and men are engaged in the practices of their profession. Brennan and his associates are most interesting, most animated, when they are *not* themselves, and unintentionally this segment of the film makes as strong a case against Cinema Verité and its untarnished reality as I have seen. . . .

If the grainy images and noisy soundtrack of *Salesman* are too real to be true, it is perhaps a loophole in subject and attitude which clinches the film's objective emptiness. *Salesman* is a film about failure. . . . What are the insights in the point of view presented here? Obviously the revelations of the camera are applicable to any professional in any income bracket, and would be, in fact, more pointed and more poignant if seen in the framework of the really "big" businessmen in America, who revel in what looks like success. What value judgment is being made? Are we to believe that a salesman whose two necessities are 1) making a living and 2) justifying the means of that living is any "worse" than any other human being who is similarly compromising? Admittedly a film which instead dealt with the emptiness of success would be an encyclopedia of clichés, but a film about the failure of failure of failure is even less amusing and far less important. There is nothing funny, or sad, or even interesting in a chronicle of the lives of people in dull, competitive, empty professions who do indeed turn out to be dull, competitive and empty people. There *are* such, and they are, in *Salesman,* as particularly unexciting on film as they are in life.

S. F., "'Salesman'" (©, 1969, by Spectator International, Inc.; copyright reassigned to the Author; ©, 1980, by the Kilimanjaro Corporation), in Cinema, *Vol. 5, No. 2, 1969, p. 46.*

STANLEY KAUFFMANN

Much of [*Salesman*] is fascinating. How could it be otherwise? There isn't a person who passes in the street whose life we wouldn't spy on, at least for a time, if we had the chance. Intrusion into privacy is as human an urge as sex; and it's by no means prurience or itch for scandal that drives us. Somehow some Great Answer may be hidden behind those window shades. If we only *knew* more about others, we could at least be sure that our own insufficiencies aren't unique. A film that allows us to peek is bound to get our attention; and when, like *Salesman,* it also fixes irrefutably some facts about our whole society, it holds that attention longer than it might do otherwise. (pp. 151-52)

The picture continues interesting for a good deal of its hour and a half. When it begins to seem repetitious, we forgive it at first because these lives are more incessantly repetitious than most. But this is not life, this is a film; we are not coworkers, we are an audience. Kenneth Burke says: "There is in reality no such general thing as a crescendo." The Maysles brothers are aware of this; so, out of their material, they have quarried the particular story of one of the salesmen, Paul Brennan, and, using the models of fictional narrative, they have tried to give it dramatic structure. But life has not cooperated sufficiently. As drama, the figurative death of this salesman lacks the dimension that it needs to be completely engrossing. There is material missing—of character and conflict and variation—that a good scriptwriter could have supplied; and what we are left with is the consolation that there *was* no scriptwriter, that what we see is spontaneous and unacted.

Almost completely. In a few scenes it seems that voices from other shots—of these men—have been laid on the sound track. And there are indications of the camera's presence in other scenes. For instance, when Brennan comes back after his first bad day, he uses some profanity (the only time in the film). It has an air of bravado, unnatural for him, as if he knew he were being watched and would not be cowed. Some of the other men glance at the camera occasionally. In his car Brennan plays directly to it in the seat next to him. Heisenberg's law has to be trotted out yet again: the fact of observation in itself alters the phenomenon that is observed. The really surprising point is that there are moments—always solitary, always silent—when Brennan seems completely to have forgotten the camera and simply broods. For me, these were the best moments, not only most revealing of him but most supportive of this filming method.

Also—and perhaps this, too, is because the material is given, not made—the film's viewpoint is unclear. Does it mock the commercialization of religion? No. . . . Is the film an indictment of sales as the absolutely central American profession? No, the Maysles brothers have picked scenes that show selling at its grittiest (in poor homes), but the picture's tone is almost as compassionate as mocking. Do they attack selling as corrosive of individuality? No, the picture tries to show a lack of congruence between selling and one man's character. It's a chronicle of this man's failure, not his submersion in sales success. Brennan fails because, quite evidently, he has no histrionism, no con, which three of his fellows have; he has to pump away at it, lamely. Nor does he have the simpleton's sincerity that the fifth man has. *Salesman* is not a criticism of a vocation or the society that produced it. Insofar as it is focused, it's a portrait of a man in the wrong vocation. (pp. 152-53)

It is this fuzziness of viewpoint and the feeling of plateau that make us feel we are finished with the film before it is over. If "direct cinema" (the Maysles phrase) grabs us immediately with a reality that fiction takes time to manufacture, with the knowledge that we really are there, it has a harder time keeping us there. It lacks the resources that fiction can use to sustain *its* truth: emphasis, distortion, elision, variation, artifice. The most successful direct cinema is, usually, the film about an intrinsically dramatic subject: *Warrendale* (disturbed children), *The Queen* (a transvestite beauty contest), *A Face of War* (Vietnam combat). The daily grind is more difficult. (pp. 153-54)

Direct cinema is going to play an increasing part in film making because of its ease (not that it's easy to do well but it's easy to *do*) and because it seems like a blow at falseness. But there's one immediate paradox: direct cinema does not cut below facts to truth unless the techniques of fiction are applied. Another paradox: even though "eavesdropping" material is immediately gripping, very soon the content has to feed the basic phenomenon. The snooping into fact, in short, must reveal the content of art. In *Salesman* it does, and in considerable measure, but not enough. (p. 154)

Stanley Kauffmann, "'Salesman'" (originally published in The New Republic, *Vol. 160, No. 14, April 5, 1969), in his* Figures of Light: Film Criticism and Comment *(copyright © 1968, 1969, 1970 by Stanley Kauffmann; reprinted by permission of Harper & Row, Publishers, Inc.), Harper, 1971, pp. 150-54.*

PATRICK MacFADDEN

On a Saturday in early December of 1969 The Rolling Stones completed their American tour with an open-air concert at a speedway track in Altamont. . . .

[The] Hell's Angels were retained to preserve law and order at Altamont, amiably brutal *condottieri* from the badlands around San Jose, come to protect the princes of the new Renaissance. . . . The casualty list became a snake-dance. . . . Finally, one 18-year-old black, Meredith Hunter, bearing a gun and pursuing some lonely odyssey inside his own head, fell under the knives of the Angels and was hacked to death.

Of all this, Altamont and the preceding concert tour, Albert and David Maysles, co-directing with Charlotte Zwerin, have made *Gimme Shelter,* the title borrowed from a Stones song, a film which, in its own becoming, moves consistently towards that rare condition in which the subject-object hiatus merges and blurs and is gone. (p. 39)

Moods are caught and deftly played, one against another: the desperate gaiety of a vulnerable girl in the audience, who knows something's gone wrong, but continues to blow soap bubbles from an antic pipe. The bubble floats out over the hordes, the music investing it with all that might have been had the promises been kept. And then the bubble disappears. . . . And always, inevitably, [Mick] Jagger, by turns Byronic-demonic, *poete maudit* floating high in the red haze of a purgatorial filter, later petulant and slightly silly, ("C'mon now people, let's get it together,") strutting and grinding like a cockatoo that got into the Benzedrine, suddenly and terribly a working-class boy out of his depth, pathetically unaware that the fracas up-front is no longer a rumble between Mods and Rockers in South London on Saturday night, but a replay of How the West was Won. (pp. 40-1)

Between filming and final release, Altamont had become the first tombstone along the counter-culture route. Consequently, *Gimme Shelter* had been awaited with more than usual impatience. Apart entirely from its putative use in criminal proceedings—the actual murder is stop-framed through the movieola at Jagger's request, thus providing an instant replay as in the hockey games on tee-vee—it was felt that the film might provide a pinch of psychic absolution.

This the Maysles-Zwerin team has resolutely refused to provide. Not the least of their merits is to have understood the uneasy cohabitation at Altamont of both the significance and the total insignificance of the Hunter slaying, to have grasped the essential banality of this cut-rate *Walpurgisnacht,* to have pinned down the imbecility, not of the generation-culture gap, but of the star gap, to have shown a process, not an individual, characterized by what Auden once called "the concupiscence of the oppressor." . . .

Gimme Shelter is a technical knockout, a blindingly well-realized experience of the tensile furies that leap along the filament of human greed and aesthetic expression. And in so doing, serve to illumine a social process that courts disaster larger, potentially, than December at Altamont. (p. 42)

Patrick MacFadden, "'Gimme Shelter'," in Film Society Review, *Vol. 6, No. 3, November, 1970, pp. 39-42.*

PAUL SCHRADER

The disaster at Altamont threw the youth prophets and merchandisers into a painful dilemma; a new gruesome reality had suddenly emerged and had to be somehow confronted and, hopefully, packaged and sold. Caught in this crunch were several veteran *cinema-verite* documentarians, David and Albert Maysles and Charlotte Zwerin, whose cameras had captured all the action, including the murder. Like the dazed, bleeding hippies the Maysles were caught in the center of violent change. Altamont became for the Maysles, as it had for the hippies, a symbolic, watershed event. Altamont was the cauldron in which the Maysles' method of film-making, both vices and virtues, were tested and magnified and it is a test which they failed.

The Maysles brothers were probably not the best representatives of *cinema-verite* to take this test; even before Altamont, they had one of the shiftiest aesthetics going. When accused of altering reality, they would contend they were artists; when accused of being second-rate artists, they would contend they were simply documentarians. . . . Critics and viewers often found themselves caught in the classic double squeeze: did the Maysles' admitted intervention in and tampering with reality serve the Truth as they claimed, or did it serve their particular, and rather unrewarding, truth? . . .

[Now] the Maysles with *Gimme Shelter* have become the exclusive documentarians of a major event with serious ramifications, and [this] tired *cinema-verite* debate takes an urgent turn. (p. 52)

Even if the Maysles will not publicly admit it, they sensed the need for an artist overview in *Gimme Shelter.* At least they have applied more manipulations to the reality of

Gimme Shelter than they have to the reality of any of their previous films. The film shifts freely from three different times and places; Rolling Stones Jagger and Charlie Watts are allowed to comment on footage of both the Altamont and Madison Square Garden concerts; evaluative radio commentary about Altamont is introduced before the concert comes on screen. These are all obvious artistic organizing devices and because of them . . . the film can and should be judged artistically. . . .

In *Gimme Shelter* there are at least four definite artistic decisions which indicate the quality of the filmmakers. They are:

(1) *artificially created suspense. Gimme Shelter* is structured with both ends moving toward the middle. The Altamont concert occurred in the middle of the Stones' U.S. tour, and the film freely intercuts between the finish of the tour . . . and the beginning. . . . The chronology of the tour put the Maysles in an awkward position: if they had followed chronology everything after Altamont would have been a let down. Instead, the Maysles opted for another mistake, to hype the film toward the murder finale. In so doing they create phoney suspense (since everyone knows it's coming) and get neither distance nor involvement. After an hour and a half of artificial build-up, the murder itself is a let-down, just a scrap of film with one man stabbing another. The audience has great expectations for *Gimme Shelter,* and the Maysles in effect prey on those expectations rather than transcending them. . . .

(2) *montage cliches.* The Maysles shoot their montages as if they were laying out a special supplement for *Life*. . . . The montages fit into pre-existing categories and in no way enlarge upon the conventional myth of rock audiences. The concert audience is somehow expected to be the backboard for murder and tragedy, yet it is given little chance for resonance.

(3) *parallel cutting.* Perhaps the Maysles' most irresponsible artistic intervention occurs in their film juxtaposition. Many examples could be cited, but one stands out: the first section of *Gimme Shelter* contains footage of Tina Turner singing "I've Been Loving You Too Long" at Madison Square Garden. (p. 53)

Taken in its entirety, the scene is the most vicious, demeaning treatment of a person I have ever seen in a documentary. Seen apart from the film Tina Turner's act has a grinding, spine-chilling effect, but the act must be allowed to build in time with all attention riveted on the singer. By cutting Tina Turner off from both the attention and time span she requires, the Maysles have turned her into an obscene caricature. Such juxtaposition not only shows a bad sense of timing, but also a criminal disrespect for the raw material of the film itself—the power of music.

(4) *a bogus sense of perspective.* The editing table sequences in which David Maysles allows Jagger and Watts to comment on film footage does much more than permit a more dramatic chronology to the film. Maysles asks Jagger and Watts, not [anyone else] to comment on the Altamont footage; the film thereby implies that Jagger and Watts have a special perspective on the event. Yet any astute viewer of the film knows the opposite is true: the Stones had only a hint of what was actually happening. (pp. 53-4)

These failed artistic devices suggest that the Maysles sought to bring an organizing aesthetic to the film, yet were unable to successfully bring it under control. The result is a film which employs just enough artistic editorializing to accomplish its limited ends: to be "true" to the superficial reality of a time and place—the ultimate Altamount bummer. The events shown in the film certainly did happen, but the perspective given to them is misleading. *Gimme Shelter* makes dozens of inferences (about Tina Turner, Jagger, Hell's Angels, rock audiences) which simply cannot be taken at face value. In another time and place (and in another Maysles film) their face value might have had meaning, but in *Gimme Shelter* the viewer knows the face value all to well and seeks the lasting value. The shifting aesthetic shifts once too often: one cannot separate the event from the second-rate artistic vision.

The final image of *Gimme Shelter* is not, to my mind, the murder of Meredith Hunter, but the shot of David Maysles explaining to Jagger over the editing table, "This gives us complete freedom. We may only be on you for a minute, and then be somewhere else." *Gimme Shelter* shows the Maysles to be infatuated with what they *can* do, not concerned with what they *must* do.

Gimme Shelter remains a film of shallow intentions; its aesthetics seem those of possibility and opportunism rather than necessity and moral commitment. (p. 54)

Paul Schrader, "'Gimme Shelter'" (©, 1971, by Spectator International, Inc.; copyright reassigned to the Author; ©, 1980, by the Kilimanjaro Corporation), in Cinema, *Vol. 7, No. 1, Fall, 1971, pp. 52-4.*

STEPHEN MAMBER

It has been widely pointed out that *Gimme Shelter* is a highly structured film, intercutting events widely separated both spatially and temporally. This is a throwback to early Drew Associates techniques (especially in *Primary, Eddie, Football, The Chair,* and *Crisis*) of sending out as many camera teams as you can to get a larger view of an event than is possible for any single witness and then wait until editing to fit all the jigsaw pieces together. By adding the dimension of filmed participants viewing themselves some time later (a la Rouch-and-Morin's *Chronique d'un Été*), the Maysles further complicate the levels of action. At any rate, *Gimme Shelter*'s structure seems not so much complex as overly intricate. For some strange reason, however, no one has asked why *Gimme Shelter* is put together this way, especially in view of the structural simplicity of earlier Maysles work.

While it may seem to be begging the question of social responsibility, this structure seems to me to be an outgrowth of the Maysles's own confusion as to the significance of the event and partially as recognition of the difficulty in synthesizing such disjointed activities. . . . [If] Altamont were indeed the culmination of a logical progression of events, a simple chronological structure (like the one the Maysles have employed so often previously) would have been wholly appropriate and easily developed. Instead, I think the Maysles were torn between previous preoccupations in personality studies and an only partially felt need to deal with social issues. *Gimme Shelter* is a paradigm expression of the personality-issue tension in American *cinéma vérité* films.

Cinéma vérité tradition has a strong effect on *Gimme Shel-*

ter, well beyond the Drew-like method of heavy coverage. In fact, if the film is a synthesis of anything, it is as a compendium of ten years of c-v influences, styles, and subject interests. One cannot evaluate, for instance, the function of the Melvin Belli planning conferences by telephone (intercut throughout the movie) without considering the precedents for such scenes in earlier c-v work, primarily because it is earlier uses of similar material which probably motivated their inclusion here (rather than a concern for exploring another facet of the Altamont event). *Gimme Shelter* cannot be viewed as an accidental cultural artifact, simply an impersonal recording of an event. Instead, the film should be considered as a Maysles Brothers film, a personal response to people and events, one that draws heavily on their earlier work and the films of their past colleagues such as [Richard Leacock, Robert Drew, and D. A. Pennebaker]. (pp. 14-15)

Gimme Shelter also has more than accidental affinities to their *What's Happening! The Beatles in the U.S.A.*, a 1964 film about the group's first American concert tour. The prime similarity is not a happy one: both films are a by-product of the continuing exploitation (often with the film-maker's own impetus included) of *cinéma vérité* for the purpose of making publicity films about rock stars. This is not to deny such films the possibilities of genuine insight and merit, but it seems pretty clear that the Maysles are not wholly attuned to their subject, despite public statements about complete personal rapport with the Stones. . . .

A real strength of the film is that no conclusions are put forth; no excuses are offered. The film leaves itself open to the harsh criticisms of the Stones's at least partial responsibility for the violence that took place, offering its own version of the event (itself free of direct comment) through this added emphasis upon their deliberate selectivity. . . . The Maysles, drawing upon earlier lessons of their colleagues, seem to me to offer a great deal of latitude for interpretation of what took place. In the context of a film seriously compromised at the outset by its entertainment function, that's a reasonable accomplishment.

In terms of social concerns, then, *Gimme Shelter* leads to some limited conclusions. The Maysles were almost like spectators at native tribal rites, but without the knowledge of their subjects so basic to ethnographic work. Lacking this foundation, they fell back on interests and methods developed in ten years of American c-v work, their own and others. This reliance was a saving grace, for the film's feeling of tentativeness, its own admissions of selectivity, are a virtue not shared by the authoritative tone of many documentary films. . . . The Maysles, whatever their limitations in this film, were not lacking in self-awareness. (p. 15)

Stephen Mamber, "Cinéma Vérité and Social Concerns," in Film Comment *(copyright © 1973 Film Comment Publishing Corporation; all rights reserved), Vol. 9, No. 6, November-December, 1973, pp. 8-15.**

STEPHEN MAMBER

Showman is a landmark film, the first American cinema-verite work entirely free from the constraints of crisis situations and plot progression to a clear resolution. The Maysles' first film, it is literally a slice of life, a record of some time spent following Joe Levine, a film entrepreneur then rising to the top on the financial strength of his *Hercules*. While there are threads of narrative continuity, there is no real story or dramatic character change. Levine is no different at the end of the film than at the beginning, and he has not passed through a particularly climactic period. The film has the engaging quality of looking caught on the run, with events happening too quickly to be molded into a tightly ordered structure. *Showman* is an almost pure form of revelation through situation; each scene looks as though it was selected for nothing more than insight into the film's main character.

The film is not completely structureless, however. Its prime unifying force is the simple convention of chronological continuity, with arbitrary starting and ending points. . . . [*Showman* has a way of] making the possibly spectacular into the acceptably routine. (pp. 142-44)

Freed from plot advancement, the film is full of spontaneous moments unmatched in fiction films. The introduction given Levine at the Boston dinner, like the mayor's speech in Leacock's *Happy Mother's Day,* is the kind of florid banality that rings true in a way that a fictionalized incident could never get away with. ("The man with a golden touch has a heart of gold, too.") Cinema-verite can make cliché fresh: the ethic of noninterference means that everyday speech and typical relationships are again within the province of film. Levine's "yes men" are a fictional cliché, but their very presence in the film argues for a certain unmanipulated form of observation. . . .

Levine's complexity in *Showman* develops from the contradictions of his personality, which are expressed, not through a balance of scenes showing him in a "good" or a "bad" light (the typical "objectivity" of many television documentaries) but directly and discretely in each moment we observe him in action. If one were to take sides, one could conclude that Levine is either a monster destroying public taste or just a very ambitious guy who has won out over other ambitious guys, but whatever one's opinion of Levine, it could be supported by the entire film and not just by selected scenes. (p. 145)

The first full-length synch-sound cinema-verite film completely free of narration (no small accomplishment), [*What's Happening! The Beatles in the U.S.A.*] gives the impression of having been almost accidentally recorded, when in fact its structure and thematic concerns are surprisingly consistent.

The film seems so entirely objective, so free of external comment, that some accused it of being little more than a glorified newsreel. The view of Antony Jay, then Head of Features for BBC-TV, is typical of this attitude: ". . . as most documentary film-makers understand the term, it was hardly a film at all. . . . I think it will be hard for anyone who comes fresh to this film in ten years' time to believe that anything so unutterably tedious was ever transmitted: its viewability depended entirely on a nearly obsessive interest in everything to do with the Beatles. . . . Unless there is no difference at all between the documentary producer and the newsreel cameramen, it had almost no relevance to the development of documentaries. . . . It is not about art, it is about keyholes." (p. 146)

Maysles films do not attempt to "hide" a message in a surface of uninterpreted observation; they simply refuse to spoon-feed interpretation when the material itself is open to consideration from a number of points of view. This approach, rather than interfering with rationality, openly encourages it, since none of the thinking is done for you in the form of narration or an easily followed plot. . . .

The idea of The Beatles as a commodity, a marketable product, is certainly clear in the film, but even more apparent is the atmosphere of excessive commercialism that makes it impossible for them to function in any other way. Some critics have claimed that the film fails to differentiate among the four members of the group, but this is not so much a shortcoming of the film as an observation of how people in the film treat The Beatles. To say that the film could express distinct personal characteristics of each of the four would mean that the situations where they were observed would allow for such differentiation. (p. 147)

Theme is nonassertive in *What's Happening* for two reasons: the film lacks specific crisis situations to point up the tensions at work, and it refuses to press for a certain point of view through camera style (or narration). Al Maysles' camera simply follows action, rarely moving in on small details or gestures. (p. 148)

The Beatles, for the most part, refuse to pretend that the camera is invisible, accepting it as just another natural element of intrusion. They often perform directly to the camera, or at least mug occasionally in its direction. Sometimes, however, the probe goes on a little too long for their liking. . . . There are few such moments, but this element of open confrontation . . . is a far different approach from the concept of the camera as an invisible (or at least unobtrusive) recorder, as is the case in *Showman*.

Another departure from impersonal observation is the occasional tendency to select reactions rather than follow actions. (p. 149)

What's Happening is also the prototypical performer portrait, bearing close resemblances to Pennebaker's film on Bob Dylan, *Don't Look Back*. Both films deal with a performer's tour of a foreign country and are structured on that basis. The newness of the performer to the country he's visiting leads to many press interviews, a way of getting verbal response without the filmmakers' taking a direct hand. In both, the idea of performer as commodity is important, and consequently there are quite similar scenes of their managers negotiating deals (similar, too, to telephone deals in *Showman*). Both films invite interpretation of their subjects as social and cultural phenomena, exploring the milieu they travel through and the responses people make to them. Because these films take performers out of their usual environment, they can be viewed in several ways—as personality studies and as explorations of the stars as products of society. (p. 154)

The deliberately flat visual style, along with the minimal structure, makes *Meet Marlon Brando* one of the "purest" examples of American cinema-verite so far realized.

On first seeing the film, there's a certain astonishment, after one or two of the interviews, in realizing that the whole film is going to consist of nothing but these interviews. This structural audacity, though, appears less radical when defined and placed within the context of the Maysles' work to this point. The film can be viewed as a sort of controlled experiment where external variables are kept at a minimum. In each segment, Brando is put through the same process of having to "sell" a film he's not interested in to a person he doesn't like. Again, one could argue that we don't "know" any more about Brando at the end of the film than after the first interview, but in terms of the film's credibility (or, rather, Brando's), it is the very repetition, the lack of "new" information, that gives the film meaning. The absence of plot in the Maysles films discussed so far would be the first indication that the structure of the Brando film, while surprising at first, is only an extension of tendencies previously expressed.

The repetition of incidents in *Meet Marlon Brando* is a result of the tendency in Maysles films to separate personality from plot. (p. 156)

In the Maysles films, a tension usually exists between a person's "nature" and what he does to make money. (This is most true for Brando, Paul Brennan in *Salesman*, and The Beatles; least for Levine.) Because of this tension, we get a stronger sense than in the Drew films of people whose identities can be discussed apart from their professional activities. We do not necessarily think of Brando in the film as an actor but as a man who is also an actor. . . . This distinction is more important than it may seem, for it is the discrepancy between Brando's view of himself and the way others see him that most clearly defines the nature of his situation, and this discrepancy is developed and impressed on the observer by repetition. (p. 157)

In relation to structure, then, because Brando (as well as other Maysles subjects) is not defined by action, it is entirely illogical to say that "nothing" happens for thirty minutes except a repetition of identical situations. In fact, it is the structure itself that makes his predicament clear, in other words, that reveals his personality. One of the interviews alone, perhaps as a single episode in a *Showman*-type film of many different Brando activities, could only express these feelings in skeletal form. If we interpret "knowledge" in this film (using the word in answer to those who would say you don't "know" more about Brando by the end) as a better understanding of Brando's contradictory position, the depth of his compromise, then the form and length of the film are quite important.

The film can also be taken as an ironic comment on the interview process itself. American cinema-verite filmmakers have almost completely avoided the use of interviews, and this film is a useful index of the Maysles' probable feeling in this regard. By running so many short interviews in sequence, they demonstrate the equal inability of all to draw Brando out on matters he would like to discuss. (p. 160)

Meet Marlon Brando is further revealing in regard to the actual promotion routine—the curious form of torture that a movie star has to go through. Like *Showman* and *What's Happening* (and perhaps *Gimme Shelter*), the film is also about the merchandising of art or at least its business aspect. In all cases there is a feeling that the people in question have made compromises by giving in so readily to the lust for money. Brando's series of inane interviews, like The Beatles tour, is a crazy idea to begin with, endured only for personal commercial benefit.

Brando, like the others, is aware of his huckster role and of his function as a commodity. He tells one interviewer: "I'm like the hula hoop. It comes along and everybody buys it, and after awhile, nobody buys it any more." Like other Maysles personalities, it is Brando's degree of self-realization which makes him sympathetic. Maysles heroes, when we're not laughing at the absurdity of their situation (and *Meet Marlon Brando is* a hilarious film), achieve an almost tragic stature. (pp. 160-61)

Stephen Mamber, "The Maysles Brothers," in his Cinema Verite in America: Studies in Uncontrolled Documentary *(reprinted by permission of The MIT Press, Cambridge, Massachusetts; copyright © 1974 by The Massachusetts Institute of Technology), The MIT Press, 1974, pp. 141-72.*

CHARLES MICHENER

Grey Gardens [is] an extraordinarily crafty invasion into the lives of Edith Beale and her daughter Edie, better known as Jacqueline Onassis's impoverished aunt and first cousin, whose own fallen estate in East Hampton, Long Island, made gossipy headlines a few years ago. After a Wellesian nod to those headlines and the local scandal that generated them, and after a graceful, passing admission of their own presence as filmmakers, the Maysles brothers prowl the dilapidated Beale manse with an unblinking cool—underscored by an ironic, growing compassion—that achieves what *cinéma vérité* aims for but seldom conveys: a sense that the material is telling itself.

In the course of the film's feature-length running time, that material becomes hypnotic—as much so as the story of the stunted lives of Miss Havisham and her ward Estelle in *Great Expectations,* or of Faulkner's ghoulish spinster in "A Rose for Emily." . . .

Grey Gardens raises in high relief the usual, vexing questions of *cinéma vérité:* how much are the filmmakers manipulating, exploiting their subjects? and how much are the subjects manipulating, exploiting them? In the end, it resolves these Questions in one shattering moment. Suddenly, Edie advances toward the camera exclaiming with real passion to the filmmakers: "I love you." Scornful at first, then finally outraged as she sees her ward attempting to escape, Mrs. Beale rises from her bed and demands over and over again that Edie shut up. As the battle of nerves and wills rages, what has been implicit all along becomes clear: if the Maysles have been exploiting their subjects, the subjects have been exploiting them as well. And it's a tug-of-war of equals, for in Edith and Edie Beale, the Maysles are luckily contending with subjects that every *cinéma vérité* film must have to succeed—brilliant, genuine performers.

Charles Michener, "Film Festival Preview: 'Grey Gardens'," in Film Comment *(copyright © 1975 by The Film Society of Lincoln Center; all rights reserved), Vol. 11, No. 5, September-October, 1975, p. 38.*

MARJORIE ROSEN

["Grey Gardens"] is a film allowing us an extraordinary glimpse into [Edith and Edie Beale's] relationship, a glimpse which cuts as sharply as a machete to the core of a crippling human dependency.

Few films have spoken so poignantly about dependency, obligation, and guilt. About how a mother clips her daughter's wings in order to insure companionship and servitude in her own old age. About how a daughter masks fear of the adult world with familial duty. . . .

With relentless gusto the camera records lunatic attitudes and awesome psychological paralysis, and with equal gusto mother and daughter perform before the camera as though they've been waiting in the wings for 25 years. This is their moment before the klieg lights. They give it their all. (p. 28)

The filmmakers are unsparing in documenting the weakness, selfishness, and true madness that feed the Beale women's monstrous relationship. While their relationship is one of extremes, I found it to be rich in the kinds of psychological truths that the screen rarely probes. . . . The dynamics of nurturing and punishing that Big and Little Edie replay for themselves daily may be disconcerting, hostile, even horrifying; but "Grey Gardens" deserves serious attention for the directness of these revelations. (p. 29)

Marjorie Rosen, "'Grey Gardens': A Documentary about Dependency," in Ms. *(© 1976 Ms. Magazine Corp.), Vol. IV, No. 7, January, 1976, pp. 28-30.*

JOHN SIMON

[In *Grey Gardens* the Maysles concentrate their attention] on a mother who is, at the very least, eccentric, and a daughter who is, to put it mildly, spaced out, and who have made a modus vivendi out of confusing the past with the present, fantasy with reality, and communication with nonstop bickering. Direct cinema may always be an act of indiscretion; here, I think, it becomes also an act of indiscrimination and indecency. (p. 68)

[What] was the Maysleses' aim in recording the daily life of Edith and Edie, their interior and exterior messiness as it oozes out of and into them, even as day seeps into desolate day? Well, not entirely desolate, because old Edith, though mostly recumbent or semirecumbent, still has a good deal of fun; while middle-aged Edie skitters and fritters away an existence bitterly immured within a meaningless bustle. But, yes, totally disconsolate, when you consider that most of Edith's pleasure now stems from carping at, mocking, and lording it over Edie, to whose destruction she probably contributed very handsomely in concert with the departed and fondly remembered Mr. Beale.

How does scrutiny avoid becoming prying? Definitely not by getting its victims' wholehearted consent. For Edith is a born performer, always singing, reminiscing, philosophizing, bragging for an audience she needs more than anything else—the reason she retrieved Edie when she tried to make herself independent in New York City was, most likely, the need for a captive audience of at least 1 girl 1 over and above the hordes of cats and 'coons. And Edie also sings occasionally—not just tunelessly, but almost militantly antitunefully—and dances, horribly and ludicrously, sometimes trying to re-create her youthful drum-majorette routines. And when she does not dance, she wrangles with her mother, or flirts with the Maysleses, or yearns for the delivery boy whom she lures into tarrying in the house, or recites a litany of past and present grievances and absurd hopes for a better future. Now that the film is a mild *succès de scandale,* and Edie has been going around touting it, some of her dreams of glory may indeed seem to have been fulfilled, but at what price? (pp. 68, 71)

The only possible justifications for "direct cinema" are bringing us closer to people worth getting to know better, of the demonstration of a procedure, a *techne* (skill, craft, or art), or the clarification of a historical situation. But the hermits of *Grey Gardens* are not worth knowing—at least not in the very superficial way recorded in the film—nor do they shed light on artistic, political, or other important problems. Only the indirect cinema of a creative artist could have gotten at the inner truths of these women. The Maysles brothers, however, are merely pandering to morbid curiosity, sensationalism, and, worse yet, *schadenfreude:* look how these once fine-looking, wealthy, upper-class women have fallen, and rejoice, dear friends, in how much better off you are in your mediocrity. In one word: repugnant. (pp. 71-2)

John Simon, "Through a Lens Falsely," in New York *Magazine (copyright © 1976 by News Group Publications, Inc.; reprinted with the permission of* New York *Magazine), Vol. 9, No. 12, March 22, 1976, pp. 68, 71-3.**

JOEL E. SIEGEL

[*Grey Gardens,* the] portrait of a complex love-hate relationship, is compelling, but exposing these two peculiar, rather pathetic women to public scrutiny is somehow unseemly. The filmmakers invite us to look down on the Beales (who are, by birth and experience, superior to most of us) and encourage us to interpret our amusement at their eccentricities as sympathy. By any standards of charity and decency, *Grey Gardens* is opportunistic, voyeuristic, and exploitative of its vulnerable subjects. However absorbing the film may be, I suspect we are all a bit poorer in spirit for having seen it.

Joel E. Siegel, "'Grey Gardens'," in Film Heritage *(copyright 1976 by F. A. Macklin), Vol. 11, No. 3, Spring, 1976, p. 35.*

Yasujiro Ozu
1903-1963

Japanese director and scriptwriter.

Ozu, perhaps the foremost of traditional Japanese directors, was known for the spare cinematic style of his dramas of the Japanese middle class. His prolific career centered around films made in the *shomin geki* genre. These films study family relationships and reflect Ozu's pessimism about the endurance of the family as a cohesive unit. Typically devoid of plot, Ozu's films analyze characters rather than concentrating on action.

After studying at Waseda University, Ozu entered the film industry as an assistant to Tadamoto Okubo. Although Okubo was regarded as a director of little distinction, Ozu prospered from their association because of Okubo's willingness to let Ozu dominate production. At this time, Ozu met Kogo Noda, who became his screenwriter for most of Ozu's career. In 1927, Ozu directed *The Swords of Penitence,* his first feature. His prewar films were studies of external social conditions contributing to a family's disintegration. *I Graduated, But . . .* marks the emergence of Ozu's distinctive style, making the transition from light, simple comedy to more mature concerns. Ozu's first film to receive acclaim, *I Was Born, But . . . ,* is regarded as a definitive *shomin geki,* faithfully depicting the rigidity of Japanese society through its tale of two young boys who will not eat to protest their father's ingratiating attitude towards his employer. Like others of its genre, it celebrates innocence while combining elements of comedy and drama.

Ozu's interest in the family was a primary concern, and he preferred to present it in simple terms. Until the mid-1930's Ozu did not utilize sound. He also disregarded cinematic devices such as fades and dissolves, and kept his camera at a uniformly low level. Ozu's last film before the outbreak of war, *The Only Son,* served as an example of the *haha-mono* genre, the films about mothers. Ozu made such films because they were lucrative and also because his own life was reflected in them: he lived with his mother all his life and never married.

Because his staff diminished after the war, Ozu found it necessary to modify his style. He had previously utilized a company of actors and cameramen, all attuned to his disciplined, strict manner, and with many of them gone, Ozu branched out into a new realm of cinema. His first work of the new period, *Late Spring,* is regarded as "one of the most perfect studies of character ever achieved in Japanese cinema." It also marked his renewed collaboration with Kogo Noda, and signalled an even greater simplicity of style. After this Ozu showed an increased disinterest in plot and action.

In 1952, Ozu made *Tokyo Story,* his best known film. Perhaps more than any other film, it combines the pervasive theme of a family's disintegration with Ozu's perceptive, simple style, culminating in the essence of an Ozu film: an analysis of life's spiritual makeup.

Increasingly, Ozu's films became more introverted, dealing with the inner motivations of familial unrest rather than the social situations that caused them. The final films were starker, allowing nothing extraneous. *An Autumn Afternoon,* Ozu's final work, is a culmination of Japanese transcendental style, reflecting the Zen tenet that less is more. More than anything, Ozu's work represents traditional Japanese thought and art. His stark style reflected Ozu's opinion of life: it is a simple process that humans should not be allowed to complicate.

JOHN GILLETT

Ozu's understanding and compassion for [his characters] is evident in every scene of [*The Tokyo Story*]. The relationship between the old and the young is not only explored with considerable psychological insight, but cuts deeply into the heart of human experience. There are no strictly good or bad people here; much of the characterisation possesses an oblique ambiguous quality akin to certain 19th century novelists (the beautiful daughter-in-law, for example, has a kind of enigmatic personality rarely encountered in the Western cinema). Although the tone of the piece is undeniably sad, there are moments when a gentle, resigned humour makes itself felt. . . . Elsewhere, the intensity of its emotion echoes the famous concept of de Sica and Zavattini: "Our puspose is to make people see and feel." And for pure eloquence of feeling I think it would be hard to find a recent European parallel to the film's final passages depicting the funeral ceremony, the alternately helpful, tactless and bitter reactions of the relatives, and the inner grief of the old man, symbolised in one marvellous shot of his tottering figure returning to the house and the mourners. (pp. 20-1)

With the exception of three brief tracking shots, the film is made up of several scores of completely static set-ups. The lack of camera movement (there is, of course, action within the frame) has the effect of concentrating attention entirely upon the people and their backgrounds—the sets, incidentally, are always apt and meticulously designed. This self-imposed restriction on the cinema's freedom of movement occasionally appears forced and unnatural, but such is the strength of the total conception that one is soon absorbed into the texture of the story itself.

It is easy, however, to understand how the film's slowly paced cutting and unfamiliar idiom could quickly alienate an unresponsive audience. Not unnaturally, its approach is totally different from that of the West, although if one looks beneath the surface (where nothing apparently happens) there is plenty to see and learn. What Ozu is saying is important to all of us, and here he speaks in a voice free from vulgarity or compromise. (p. 21)

John Gillett, "Reviews: 'The Tokyo Story'," in Film *(reprinted by permission of British Federation of Film Societies), No. 13, September-October, 1957, pp. 20-1.*

LINDSAY ANDERSON

[*Tokyo Story*] is a film of relationships, a film about time, and how it affects human beings (particularly parents and children), and how we must reconcile ourselves to its working. Apart from the great fact of death, the incidents are all slight, and there is no chiaroscuro either in characterisation or mood. The tempo is all the way calm, leisurely, inevitable. There is only one element in the style which might seem at first to jar: the sequences do not fade into each other or dissolve. Every transition is effected by a cut, to some view of the new setting, a rooftop, a wall, a harbour vista, which then cuts again directly to the scene where the characters are going on with their living. But this is not jarring: on the contrary it is a way of conveying the essential unity of existence, of matter and spirit, which is intrinsic to the film's philosophy. (p. 132)

[What] we have here is a work that expresses in every image, and in the precise *growth* (as opposed to *force*) of its movement, a whole attitude to living, an attitude that comprehends, in the sense both of understanding and embracing, the painful necessities as well as the joys of existence. From our point of view this philosophy can be called, at least partly, humanistic; but this is by no means its essence. And it is here, I think, that even a reviewer as appreciative as John Gillett [see excerpt above] is in danger of missing the point. For with all its understanding and compassion, *Tokyo Story* is not a simple humanistic protest against the transience of life and the bitterness of experience. Specifically, in the "marvellous shot" (which it is) "of the tottering figure returning to the house and the mourners" it is *not* the "inner grief" of the old man that is being symbolised, but rather his wisdom and acceptance. (pp. 132, 160)

Even more than its humane virtues (I know one ought not to attempt the differentiation), it is the directness and clarity with which *Tokyo Story* reflects a whole philosophy of living that makes it so memorable an experience. (p. 160)

Lindsay Anderson, "Two Inches Off the Ground," in Sight and Sound *(copyright © 1957 by The British Film Institute), Vol. 27, No. 3, Winter, 1957-58, pp. 131-32, 160.**

TOM MILNE

It is difficult, without literally re-telling [*An Autumn Afternoon*], to convey the manner in which each scene is dependent on every other scene for its meaning. Perhaps the most illuminating comparison is with music: each sequence comes like the entry of a new subject in a sonata, which is then developed and counterpointed with the other themes already introduced. . . .

Each time the film moves from one locale to another, the new scene is introduced by its establishing shots, so that at any point in the film one knows not only where one is but where one is going to be. . . .

But these shots seem to have another function over and above "establishing". They are always of inanimate objects —a corridor, a block of flats, chimneys, a pile of petrol drums, a neon sign—and the first shot in an establishing sequence never contains human figures (though subsequent shots may—someone passing across the far end of the corridor, for example). The idea of the transience of human life is basic to Buddhist thought: human existence is a mere drop in the ocean of time. And herein lies, perhaps, one of the secrets of the tranquillity, the deep reconciliation, which pervades Ozu's work. Each of his scenes is introduced by an object, durable and immovable; against it, his characters live out their lives, and long after their suffering has ended, the object will endure. . . .

The application [of the principles of *haiku*] to Ozu's work is obvious, both in the relationship between establishing shot and subsequent scene, and in the relationship between the scenes themselves, which, like the images of the *haiku,* combine to create an interlinear meaning. At the same time, though, the *haiku* illustrates another facet of Japanese art which is particularly relevant to Ozu's method of *mise en scène* [tending toward the isolation of a single, significant, visual moment]. (p. 184)

In *An Autumn Afternoon,* for instance, there is a breathtakingly beautiful moment which, in the context of a European film, might well be a cliché of virtuosity. The daughter has just been told that she cannot marry the man she loves. . . . As the father leaves, a final shot observes the girl from behind, and after a moment she slowly raises a hand to tuck a stray lock of hair into place. The gesture, surely a "significant visual moment," vividly captures the girl's grief and helpless isolation. More particularly, however, it is worth noting that because there is no dissolve or fade, there is no tapering or artificial prolongation of the emotion: it is complete in itself. Moreover, because there is no pan from one character to the other, the shot of each of them retains its purity: energy (i.e. emotional content) is not drained from one to feed the other. And the cut comes at the very last moment, with Ozu holding the shot of the father until one feels that he *must* cut to the girl; a dynamic relationship is thus created between the shots which allows the emotional content of each to remain quite separate, held suspended as it were, shot against shot, scene against scene, awaiting their place in the pattern of the whole. (pp. 184-85)

Twenty-seven years later, Ozu remade, or rather reworked, the theme of *I Was Born, But . . .* in the 1959 *Good Morning (Ohayo).* Comparison between the two films is particularly interesting, as the later one reveals a distinct change of emphasis. *I Was Born, But . . .* concentrates almost entirely on the two boys, their pains and joys as they discover society and the difficulties it presents. . . . [We] feel by the end that we have shared a difficult experience with the children. . . .

In *Good Morning* the emphasis shifts from the boys to society in general. A whole host of characters is introduced—more parents, neighbours, a very ancient grandmother, a pedlar, a teacher—as well as certain episodes which have nothing to do with the boys at all. . . . The central situation still remains the same: in *I Was Born, But . . .* the boys rebel against their parents with a hunger strike because they cannot see why their father should kow-tow to anybody; in *Good Morning,* they rebel with a silence strike because they cannot see why they shouldn't have a television set like everybody else. But in *Good Morning* Ozu's concern is mainly satirical, and he uses the silence strike to spark off a series of malicious sketches about "keeping up with the Joneses" and the backbiting of neighbours who feel sure the parents have instructed the boys not to speak to them for snob reasons. Here Ozu is so little interested in his original and central theme that the boys' problems, as well as everybody else's, are solved all too simply and impermanently when their parents are finally driven to buy a television set. *Good Morning* is extremely funny (perhaps Ozu's funniest film), and often brilliantly sharp in its satire, but it has no real centre.

Failure of a more serious kind is illustrated by *Early Spring*. . . . Although *Early Spring* appears to be highly regarded in Japan, it seems to me to stray, heavily and uninspiringly.

The subject, slightly unusual for Oku, deals with a married man, bored with his wife, who embarks on an unsatisfactory affair with a free-and-easy girl; disillusioned with her, he accepts a transfer to a provincial branch of his firm; there, away from the bustle of Tokyo, he ponders his life, and is eventually reconciled to a forgiving wife. The first image of the film is one of emptiness and boredom, as the husband and wife get up in the morning to start their day; and Ozu—probably because the lasting communion of marriage is to him self-evident—never bothers to *demonstrate* the value of their marriage. Consequently the final reconciliation, shot in characteristically exquisite style, seems completely arbitrary. (p. 186)

Late Spring has a very similar theme to *An Autumn Afternoon*—a father's decision to marry off his only daughter—and is one of Ozu's most beautiful films. *Late Autumn* is a remake, considerably changed, in terms of a mother and daughter, and much less successful. As with *Good Morning,* many of the characters seem arbitrarily introduced merely to make a good scene: for example, the daughter's pert young office colleague who suddenly emerges to take a major role in the film, roundly telling off the matchmakers for their shady dealings, and rather unconvincingly becoming the mother's mainstay against loneliness by visiting her regularly after the daughter's marriage. In *Late Spring,* on the other hand, every character and every scene is perfectly integrated in the main theme (not a father's loneliness as in *Autumn Afternoon,* but rather a daughter's reconciliation to the idea of marriage), and the character of the daughter's friend is carefully established so that her final offer of friendship to the father is completely and convincingly in character.

The integration of character and incident is so exact throughout the film that is one of his great masterpieces, and the sequence in which father and daughter make a last trip together to Kyoto before her marriage is probably one of the most perfect in Ozu's work. . . . By comparison, the *Late Autumn* remake gives short change indeed, with a rather perfunctory conversation between mother and daughter on their last trip, and then, quite simply, a conventional studio photograph of bride and groom in their wedding clothes. It is as though Ozu, because it was a remake of a subject he had already explored, used bits and pieces without ever becoming involved.

Late Autumn, in fact, like *Good Morning* and like *Early Spring,* has no true centre, and therefore no dynamic growth: the sum of its scenes adds up to no more than the sum of its scenes. In the great films, on the other hand—*Late Spring, Tokyo Story, An Autumn Afternoon*—there is a subtle Ozu alchemy whereby the separate elements expand and coalesce to form a perfect whole. At the end of *Tokyo Story,* the old man mourning for his wife walks out on the terrace in the early morning. "It was a beautiful sunrise," he says quietly. "I think we're going to have another hot day." This is the point to which the entire film has been moving: it is a summation of experience. (pp. 186, 206)

Tom Milne, "Flavour of Green Tea over Rice," in Sight and Sound *(copyright © 1963 by The British Film Institute), Vol. 32, No. 4, Autumn, 1963, pp. 182-86, 206.*

STANLEY KAUFFMANN

It is possibly risky to say, but the chief reward in *Late Spring* is not in its materials, gratifying though they are. The highest benefit—as in *Tokyo Story,* though less strong—is appreciation of the artist himself. One is moved by a great deal in the film, but the ultimate and most moving of responses is one's regard for Ozu. This is in no way due to exhibitionism; most certainly it's not because of virtuosity à la Fellini. It's because everything in an Ozu film derives from his utter subscription to a view of life as infinitely sacred and of art as the most sacred exercise in life. He serves, rather than making anything serve him. (p. 127)

The motion of this quiet-motion picture is in the effort by which the widowed father, a professor, turns his daughter away from the security-and-resentment ambivalence of her life with him toward a life of her own, gently urging her toward a marriage which she both wants and dreads. Ozu's touch is so implicative that we never even see the fiancé; our last sight of the girl is in her traditional wedding dress. Our last sight of the father, which is the end of the film, is when he sits alone after the ceremony, peeling an apple, in one long peel; and by his daring in ending here, Ozu crystallizes retrospectively the design of his film. Another way to put it: we don't know how good the picture is until it finishes. When we see [the father] sitting there alone, we comprehend how much Ozu has staked on a simple design to contain a great deal, what courage he has, what indifference to conventional demands.

His method is one of non-drama, but not in any prosy, naturalistic, flattened sense. He believes, with many Japanese painters and draftsmen, that if you select the right details and present them realistically, you have created an abstraction that signifies a great deal more than detailed realism. The drama, for Ozu, is in life itself, and his task is not to contrive but to reveal. (p. 128)

Stanley Kauffmann, "'Late Spring'" (originally published in The New Republic, *Vol. 167, Nos. 6 & 7, August 19 & 26, 1972), in his* Living Images: Film Comment and Criticism *(copyright © 1971,*

1972, 1973, 1974 by Stanley Kauffmann; reprinted by permission of Harper & Row, Publishers, Inc.), Harper, 1975, pp. 127-29.

PAUL SCHRADER

The personal interpretation of Ozu's films has been encouraged by two misleading circumstances: one, that we simply happen to know much more about Ozu than we do about earlier traditional artists, and two, that Ozu, unlike a Zen poet or painter, must use living human beings as his raw material. The characters on screen are experiencing life. . . . But the characters who are emoting on screen may be no more or less representative of the film-maker than a nonhuman shot of a train or a building. The characters' individual feelings (sorrow, joy, introspection) are of passing importance: it is the surrounding form which gives them lasting value. (p. 26)

Much of Ozu's approach is derived from Japanese culture itself, and it is the traditional elements which make him the "most Japanese of all directors." The most appropriate analogy for the cultural elements in Ozu's films is Zen art. Zen is not an organized religion with physical and political concerns like Shintoism or Christianity, but a way of living which has permeated the fabric of Japanese culture. . . .

Perhaps the basic principle of Zen art is the first *koan* of Zen, *mu,* the concept of negation, emptiness, and void. Emptiness, silence, and stillness are positive elements in Zen art, and represent presence rather than the absence of something. . . . *Mu* is the character used to refer to the spaces between the branches of a flower arrangement; the emptiness is an integral part of the form. (p. 27)

Like the traditional Zen artist, Ozu directs silences and voids. Silence and emptiness are active ingredients in Ozu's films; characters respond to them as if they were audible sounds and tangible objects. Although such responses are usually quite subtle, a rather obvious use of active silence occurs in *Early Summer:* Setsuko Hara has just told her parents of her intention to marry, a decision which displeases them. After a polite argument the parents, despondent, go upstairs. In the next shot the father is staring into the camera while in the background the mother does some busywork and speaks to him. She makes a trivial remark, and he replies, "Ah." She makes another remark, he again replies, "Ah." The mother leaves the room and Hara walks noiselessly through the background. The father again says, "Ah." The silence has become electric, much more meaningful than anything the mother could have said. (p. 28)

But most of all, *mu* is expressed in Ozu's "codas." His films are structured between action and emptiness, between indoors and outdoors, between scene and coda. The conflicts are always explicated in indoors, usually in long dispassionate conversations. The settings may vary (home, office, bar, restaurant), but the story is rarely forwarded by anything but indoor conversations (and the one or two exceptions in each film are thematically crucial). These indoor discussions are set off by "codas": still-life scenes of outdoor Japanese life, empty streets and alleys, a passing train or boat, a distant mountain or lake. . . . Each of the codas sets off an Ozu "paragraph." . . . There are no chapters, only paragraphs and codas. . . . In Western art one would naturally assume that the codas are inserted to give weight to the paragraphs, but for Ozu, as for Zen, it is precisely the opposite: the dialogue gives meaning to the silence, the action to the still life. (p. 29)

"Nostalgia" in Ozu's films, such as the scene when the father in *An Autumn Afternoon* revisits the bar where the barmaid resembles his dead wife, is not so much a longing for the past in Western terms but is more likely an "expansion" of the present so familiar to Zen art. When Ozu focuses on a wall clock, watching the seconds tick futilely away, it is partially to contrast film time and psychological time, . . . but it is also to create the mood of total timelessness integral to Zen art. . . .

Ozu achieves the "eternal now" in the same manner as *cha-no-yu,* [the Zenta ritual] through ritual. Each possible event in an Ozu film can be reduced to a predetermined, limited and precise number of shots. If the tea bowl is of a certain color or texture, a certain type of conversation will ensue; if an Ozu character is in a certain location, a certain type of conversation will ensue. (p. 31)

In Zen painting the technique ritual evolved into an alphabet of brush strokes. There were a certain number of brush strokes used to represent natural objects; they were learned by rote, practiced piecemeal, and were meaningless until assembled. Similarly one may speak of Ozu's alphabet, a set of predetermined shots from which he would never depart. (p. 32)

Ritual in Oriental art is not structured around a single cathartic event (like the blinding of Oedipus, for instance), but is cyclic, with little rise and fall, revealing the timeless Oneness of man and nature. . . . The continuation is based on the infrastructure of ritual. A certain pattern of shots is repeatable within an Ozu paragraph, a certain pattern of Ozu paragraphs is repeatable with an Ozu film, and a certain number of Ozu films are repeatable within an Ozu career. The ritual is not separate from the form, which is not separate from the content. (p. 33)

The greatest conflict (and the greatest resulting disillusionment) in Ozu's films is not political, psychological, or domestic, but is, for want of a better term, "environmental." That the aged cannot communicate with the young, that the parents cannot communicate with their children, that the craftsmen cannot communicate with the office workers—these are all dimensions of the problem that the modern Japanese cannot communicate with his environment. During a disillusioning saké-drinking bout a character in *Late Autumn* says, "It is people who tend to complicate life. Life itself is very simple." . . . These statements reflect a breakdown in the traditional attitude toward nature in Zen art. How can man complicate life? How can the fish complicate the water? This for Ozu, is the great threat of modernization: it threatens the traditional Oneness, and when that unity wobbles the rest of the structures—home, office—come tumbling after. (p. 35)

Ozu responds to the disunity in Japanese life by evoking the traditional verities of Zen art in a contemporary, cinematic context. He is naturally more predisposed to the older generation because they are closer to traditional culture and because time itself evokes *aware,* the mood of autumn. . . . In the tradition of Zen art, Ozu does not forge an artificial synthesis between the old and the young, man and nature, but situates these elements within the larger context of the *furyu* [the four basic moods of Zen] which affects and encompasses everything. The runaway, *après-guerre* daughter of *Tokyo Twilight* (*Tokyo Boshoku,* 1957) manifests the same "sympathetic sadness" which permeates her respectable, misunderstanding father. *The Flavor of Green Tea Over Rice* is one of the least successful of Ozu's later films because he breaks his rule of situating seeming conflicts within the larger context of the *furyu*. (pp. 35-6)

The final shots of Ozu's films, like the codas, are reaffirmations of nature. These shots may depict something as traditional as a mountain, or it may incorporate such contemporary elements as a boat on a river, or a smokestack. These scenes are the final codas, the final silences and emptiness. (p. 37)

[Taken] as a whole Ozu's techniques are so similar to traditional Zen methods that the influence is unmistakable, and one must consequently assume that Ozu's personality, like that of the traditional artist, is only valuable to the extent that it expresses his thesis. His personality, like those of his characters, merges with an enveloping sense of *mono no aware,* and—the ultimate achievement of Zen art—finally becomes undistinguishable from it. (p. 38)

In Ozu, the stylization is near complete. Every shot is from the same height, every composition static, every conversation monotone, every expression bland, every cut forthright and predictable. (p. 41)

A potential disparity between man and nature underlies Ozu's films. He suggests that the flow of man and nature may be separate rather than unified, which, within the context of his traditional structure, certainly does create a schizoid reaction. This disparity becomes obvious when Ozu juxtaposes similar codas after contrasting family scenes. A shot of a snow-capped mountain inserted after a discussion by several parents plainly suggests the unity to which they aspire, but the same shot inserted after a parent-child quarrel suggests that the traditional unity may have little meaning within the postwar family structure. The codas cannot only be a positive statement on the unity of man and nature, but also a wry commentary on the lack of it.

For the most part, disparity in Ozu's films is conveyed by a strange human density which seems inappropriate to the clinically observed environment, and which, at the moment of decisive action, reveals itself to be a spiritual weight. Throughout his films there is an undercurrent of compassion which, although not overtly expressed, seems inherent in the treatment of the characters by each other and more importantly by their director. The viewer senses that there are deep, untapped feelings just below the surface. (pp. 43-4)

In a similarly ambivalent manner Ozu simultaneously evokes both laughter at and sympathy for his characters. Even when he makes fun of his characters, as in the drinking scene in *Tokyo Story* (*Tokyo Monogatori,* 1953), Ozu also evokes sympathy for them. His unblinking camera impresses the viewer with its fairness, its willingness to watch all of a man's conduct, both ludicrous and noble, without comment. . . . The nagging sense of disparity grows and grows.

In this mild form disparity is often reflected by a thoroughgoing sense of irony. In films of transcendental style, irony is the temporary solution to living in a schizoid world. The principal characters take an attitude of detached awareness, find humor in the bad as well as the good, passing judgment on nothing. (pp. 44-5)

Disparity, therefore, is a gradual process, each progressive step eating away at the solid veneer of everyday reality. At first, it is a "sense" of compassion which teases the viewer, making him believe that emotions are present but giving him no tangible proof. Finally, it is a *decisive action,* a totally bold call for emotion which dismisses any pretense of everyday reality. (p. 46)

Stasis is the end product of transcendental style, a quiescent view of life in which the mountain is again a mountain. (p. 49)

Complete stasis, or frozen motion, is the trademark of religious art in every culture. It establishes an image of a second reality which can stand beside the ordinary reality; it represents the Wholly Other. In Ozu, the image of stasis is represented by the final coda, a still-life view which connotes Oneness. It is the same restrictive view which began the film: the mountain has become a mountain again, but in an entirely different way. Perhaps the finest image of stasis in Ozu's films is the lengthy shot of the vase in a darkened room near the end of *Late Spring*. . . . The vase is stasis, a form which can accept deep, contradictory emotion and transform it into an expression of something unified, permanent, transcendent. (pp. 49, 51)

Paul Schrader, "Ozu," in his Transcendental Style in Film: Ozu, Bresson, Dreyer *(copyright © 1972 by The Regents of the University of California; reprinted by permission of the University of California Press), University of California Press, 1972, pp. 15-56.*

TOM ALLEN

Early Spring seems paced with the director's own life pulse. The cutting is totally unobtrusive: the gaze uncluttered by lens refractions, the camera shots delicately held until the naturalistic poet has made his impression. It is the deceptive simplicity of the artist, working within the most primitive articulation, to make his human drama that much more accessible to the widest possible audience, of which he is the primary spectator. In *Autumn Afternoon,* . . . the editing could be felt like precise, cutting whiplashes in a contracting expression. *Early Spring* is one of Ozu's longest, most expansive works, encompassing a larger milieu and interweaving many side characters into the fabric of the hero's life.

Early Spring has a tight thematic core in centering on the vague unrest of a salaried worker at a time of family crisis in a childless marriage and at a critical time of a job transfer; but it is also broad enough to enfold a time, a society, and a way of life. The hero's bleak expectations drag him down to his most bitter hour; but the optimistic credo of the film buoys him along until in a climactic moment with the graying Ozu figurehead, Chishu Ryu, the husband-worker acknowledges that a life can be regenerated and that any time is "the springtime of life." (p. 73)

Tom Allen, "Top Liner," in New York *Magazine (copyright © 1974 by News Group Publications, Inc.; reprinted with the permission of* New York *Magazine), Vol. 7, No. 39, September 30, 1974, pp. 72-3.**

DONALD RICHIE

[The tension in Ozu's films] derives from confrontations between men and women who are in different sections of the pattern, between, for example, parents who have returned to Japaneseness and children who are on their way out.

There is never any doubt where Ozu's essential sympathies lie in these confrontations, though as a moralist he is scrupulously fair, and for this reason some young Japanese have disliked his work, calling him old-fashioned, bourgeois, reactionary. And so he would appear, since he so continually celebrates those very qualities, the traditional virtues of their country, against which young Japanese must revolt. . . .

Ozu's films are among the most restrained, the most limited, controlled, and restricted. From early in his career, for example, Ozu used only one kind of shot: a shot taken from the level of a person seated in traditional fashion on the tatami. . . .

This traditional view is the view in repose, commanding a very limited field of vision. It is the attitude for listening, for watching. It is the same as the position from which one watches the Noh or the rising moon, from which one partakes of the tea ceremony or a cup of hot sake. It is the aesthetic attitude; it is the passive attitude. Less poetically, it also represents the viewpoint of a then-majority of Japanese. (p. xii)

Ozu's method, like all poetic methods, is oblique. He does not confront emotion, he surprises it. Precisely, he restricts his vision in order to see more; he limits his world in order to transcend these limitations. His cinema is formal and the formality is that of poetry, the creation of an ordered context that destroys habit and familiarity, returning to each word, to each image, its original freshness and urgency. . . .

The unique art of Ozu is very evident, but so is his common humanity. The Ozu character is among the most lifelike in cinema. Since character for its own sake is always a major subject in the Ozu film and since it is but rarely that a character must work to forward the ends of the story the director is determined to tell us, we are often given that rare spectacle of a character existing for himself alone. This we observe with the delight that precise verisimilitude always brings, and with a heightened awareness of the beauty and fragility of human beings. (p. xiii)

A similar duality occurs with respect to the sense of time in the Ozu film. His pictures are longer than most and at the same time have less "story" than most. What story there is, moreover, often seems more anecdote (which is why a précis of an Ozu film fails even more completely than usual to convey what the picture is like as an experience). Since the story is presented over a long period of time, and since there is little overt action to sustain the time values, unsympathetic critics complain about a pace that to them seems slow. They would have real grounds for complaint if this pace existed by and for itself. Yet Ozu's films are not slow. They create their own time and for the audience, drawn into Ozu's world, into a realm of purely psychological time, clock time ceases to exist. And what at first seems a world of stillness, of total inaction, is revealed as appearance. (p. xiv)

[Just] as technique restricted comes to make us see more, so tempo slowed comes to make us feel more. The effect of both is the same: characters come alive in a manner rare in film. And both means are the same: the spectator is led into the film, is invited to infer and to deduce. He gives of himself and of his time, and in so doing he learns to appreciate. What remains after an Ozu film is the feeling that, if only for an hour or two, you have seen the goodness and beauty of everyday things and everyday people; you have had experiences you cannot describe because only film, not words, can describe them; you have seen a few small, unforgettable actions, beautiful because real. You are left with a feeling of sadness, too, because you will see them no more. They are already gone. In the feeling of transience, of the mutability and beauty of all life, Ozu joins the greatest Japanese artists. It is here that we taste, undiluted and authentic, the Japanese flavor. (pp. xiv-xv)

Though the majority of all Ozu's films are about the dissolution of the family (as are a large number of Japanese novels and of Western novels too, for that matter) his emphasis changed during his nearly forty years of film-making. In his first important films the director emphasized the external social conditions impinging upon his characters: the strain in a family occasioned by the father's joblessness in difficult times, the children's inability to understand that their father must be subservient to his employer to keep his job, etc. It was only in later films that the director found more important the constraints on the human condition imposed from within. (p. 5)

Ozu's patterns are reflected in his stories. A character moves from security to insecurity; he moves from being with many to being alone; or, a group shifts, loses members, accommodates; or, conversely, a younger character moves into a new sphere with mixed emotions; or a person moves from his accustomed sphere and then returns with a new understanding. These patterns are stacked, as it were, one upon the other; it is the rare Ozu film that has only one pattern and one story. Through the similarities and differences of the patterns and stories with their parallels and perpendiculars, Ozu constructs his film, the sum of his thoughts on the world and the people living in it. (p. 9)

Not only did Ozu often use the same actor in the same kind of role, playing, generally, the same kind of character (Setsuko Hara and Chishu Ryu are notable examples), he also used the same story line in various films. *A Story of Floating Weeds* is the same as *Floating Weeds, Late Spring* is very similar to *Late Autumn,* which in turn resembles *An Autumn Afternoon.* (p. 10)

Character, too, is recurrent. The daughters in *Late Spring, Early Summer, Equinox Flower, Late Autumn,* and *An Autumn Afternoon* are, though played by different actresses, essentially the same character involved with the same problem—whether or not to get married and leave home. (p. 11)

Ozu's most potent device for nostalgia . . . is the photograph. Even though family pictures, class pictures, company pictures, remain in Japan something of the institution they once were in the West, there is a surprising amount of formal portrait-taking going on in Ozu's films. There is the group picture, of students and teacher, for example, in front of the Kamakura Buddha in *There Was a Father;* there is the wedding portrait, as in *Late Autumn;* there is the family portrait, as in *The Brothers and Sisters of the Toda Family, Early Summer, The Record of a Tenement Gentleman.* Except in the first example cited above, we do not see the finished picture. No one drags out the portrait of his dead mother and gazes fondly at it. Rather, we see the family gathered (invariably for the last time), smiling bravely into an uncertain future. Nostalgia lies not in later reflections, but in the very effort to preserve the image itself. (p. 15)

[Similarities] are many, and differences few in the extraordinarily limited world of the Ozu film. It is a small world, closed, governed by rules apparently inflexible, controlled by laws that are only to be deduced. Yet, unlike Naruse's narrow family-centered world, Ozu's does not provoke claustrophobia, nor do its apparently inflexible governing rules give rise to the romantic idea of destiny seen in the apparently wider world of Mizoguchi. What keeps Ozu's films from these extremes are Ozu's characters, the kind of people they are and the way they react to their life. (p. 16)

Human nature in all its diversity and variation—this is what the Ozu film is essentially about. It must be added, however, that as a traditional and conservative Asian, Ozu did not believe in any such essence as the term "human nature" may suggest to us. Each of his characters is unique and individual, based on known types though they all may be; one never finds "representative types" in his films. . . . By so restricting our view and confining our interest, Ozu allows us to comprehend the greatest single aesthetic paradox: less always means more. (p. 17)

As with most of his countrymen, Ozu's originality lay not in the material itself—it was always of the most mundane—but in the angle from which the material was viewed, the personal, even idiosyncratic way it was reassembled on film. Like most Japanese artists, Ozu was in this sense a formalist, and the pattern of events in a film was as important to him as the events themselves. (p. 18)

The conventionality of the events in the Ozu film is even by Japanese standards extreme. Marriage and death are the only conclusions permitted in many of the later pictures, and the appreciations or misunderstandings that mark the progress toward the conclusion are usually unexceptional. Truisms abound, as do both coincidence and the obvious, and Ozu's manner and method match his material. He never attempts to unsettle. (p. 19)

One of the key differences between Ozu and other film directors is the autonomy of the single scene in Ozu's films, and the enormous importance assigned to character-revealing dialogue. The conventional film-maker often decides first on location and plot, has a specific place for the scene within the film in mind, and only then tries to think of something for the characters to say that will forward the plot a bit. Ozu's method more closely resembled that of directors of animated films or musical comedies who construct their film around a finished sound track. One result of this method was the creation of characters that in no way depended upon the convolutions of plot or story. . . . These characters grew—or, rather, the dialogue through which they came to life grew—according to the personality that Ozu and his fellow writer discovered in them. The character became real with no reference to story or plot; he became real because all the words he spoke gave expression to those principles of his character which it was the writers' duty to discover.

The result was the invariable rightness of the Ozu character, a rightness based upon his being given an amount of freedom almost unknown to cinema characters. Since he had no work to do, no story to act out, no plot to advance, he could be contradictory, illogical—and always faithful to himself. (pp. 22-3)

Ozu's mode is one of heightened realism. The characters say just what they would say, yet the dialogue continually surprises because it is always unfolding facets of the character that we were hitherto unaware of. This is like life, but the tempo of the Ozu dialogue (as opposed to the tempo of the Ozu film) is so swift that we learn in seconds what in life takes months. Yet we are taught nothing, we merely observe, with a heightened awareness. As will later become evident, much is demanded of us when we watch an Ozu picture. We are presented with the evidence, as it were, but must put it together for ourselves. To be sure, the skill with which the film is made usually precludes our putting it together in any way but the one Ozu intended. (p. 24)

[Logical] incongruities form the basis of Ozu's humor. They are not only amusing in themselves, they contribute directly to the revelation of character. The people involved are rarely aware that what they have said or done is funny. They have simply been what seems to them logical and what seems to us funny. Their error was either in method or in the degree of application. From this rises irony, and also our own sudden interest in a character capable of such incongruities. Ozu uses such devices because in suggesting the complexity of the human character, he is unwilling to tell us anything. Rather, he would show us everything, and the success of this method depends upon our willingness to be shown. Ozu's invitation, when tendered through humor, is commonly amusing, logical, and questioning of our assumed values. (p. 30)

Good Morning, in some ways Ozu's most schematic film, certainly one of his least complicated formally, is an example of a film constructed around motifs. There are a number of motifs in the film, all easily recognized because they are underlined, as it were, in a manner one associates with the earlier rather than the later Ozu. We will examine two of them: the first is the breaking wind or farting motif, the second the one that gives the film its title.

It should surprise no one that farting has a place in Ozu's "world of stillness." Characters run off to the toilet on many occasions, children finger themselves, ladies pick their teeth and express themselves with occasional earthy vulgarity, sex is openly acknowledged. His reason for such earthy touches is always the same: it is at these moments that a person is often most human. A man who farts, a man having sex, is—among other things—acknowledging his similarity to all other men. Etiquette, a concept which suggests that we are more than merely human, obscures what is common to all human beings. (pp. 35-6)

[The] fart motif is experienced only in conjunction with the film's second principal motif.

The boys in this picture have decided to go on a hunger strike. The ostensible reason is that their father refuses to buy a television set. The real reason, however, is that they are at an age to be bored with themselves and those around them. Particularly they resent the sameness of their daily existence. As a focus for their discontent they pick on those meaningless phrases, such as "Good morning," that adults habitually use. One reason the boys are so taken with breaking wind, then, is that a fart is a spontaneous utterance pleasantly devoid of just that kind of predictable meaninglessness found in the everyday phrases they have decided to dislike. Specifically, they call such phrases unnecessary.

The adults understand their feeling. A teacher, talking to their aunt, says: "Well, what they say is true enough. But then everyone has to use words like that. And perhaps they aren't really so unnecessary after all. The world would be rather dreary otherwise." . . . The teacher's voice is Ozu's. He does not share youth's fierce criticism of the world; he accepts the world as it is, imperfections, unnecessary things, and all. (pp. 37-8)

Just as a character is never all bad or all good in an Ozu film, so never is an idea all right or all wrong. There are no absolutes in these films, only immutables. One is born, but . . . the rest of life is not certain in the slightest. Ozu's characters all have to make their own sense out of their lives. So, in *Good Morning* neither the boys nor the adults are wholly right. In the Ozu film we rarely if ever experience the fierce joy of certainty. The world of the Ozu film is a flowing world, in which little is ordained. The life we see in these films nonetheless makes more sense because one event visibly leads to another, parallels another, or presages another. (p. 38)

[A] minor motif of light romantic attachment parallels a major theme of [*Late Autumn*], one also concerning love and marriage: a girl's marrying and leaving her widowed mother, who allows her to think that she herself may remarry so the girl will feel free to go. Ozu, as always, resists all temptation to plot. . . . For his purposes it is quite enough to have two strains (and others) showing variations on a theme. The variations may be presented as contrasting with each other, e.g., romantic love versus conventional marriage. Or one variation may continue another, e.g., romantic love followed by conventional marriage. The canvas of the Ozu picture is filled with mutually supporting lines. (p. 39)

More often in an Ozu film, however, the parallels running side by side do not meet; they stretch into infinity, and if they do meet we are not shown the event. This is the position that best ensures their commenting upon each other without Ozu's having to overtly state that they do.

In *I Was Born, But* . . . , as well as many of the earlier films, there are direct visual parallels. A slow tracking shot along the desks of the sleepy pupils in the classroom is cut directly to a similar shot along the desks of the yawning businessmen, their fathers. Here the comment is only partly satiric: it is the parallel that is most important, a demonstration that the two scenes are identical. (pp. 40-1)

The most satisfying parallels in Ozu's films, and the few that are readily recognizable as parallels, are those which fit the film and amplify it but whose connection with the main theme remains elusive. They are mysterious; one recognizes a pattern but does not know what it means. Perhaps these are the most satisfying because they are the most life-like, the most recognizable from our own experience. Perhaps they are the most beautiful because they are the most apparently useless. (p. 43)

In Ozu's films as in life itself the seemingly antithetical live happily side by side. It is inconsistency which creates irony, and which also makes the father seem so human. Perhaps then, as Ozu so often indicates, it behooves us to regard humanity with irony; perhaps that is the only way to live in the world. (p. 49)

The irony with which we must observe the father in [*Equinox Flower*] is extreme; perhaps no other Ozu character demands so much. The film is, in part, the study of a man deep in self-deception. Yet Ozu's irony is always one of character. There is nowhere in his work a scene of which the real, intended meaning is contrary to the one seemingly expressed. Rather, a character reveals his beliefs to be the contrary of those he expresses, or maintains a belief different from the one reality quite apparently imposes. In Ozu's work, such self-deception is, as the father in *Equinox Flower* plainly states, proof of humanity.

Ozu's films are filled with such proof and this, in turn, is what makes his characters so human and consequently so real. He shows us the gulf between opinion or intent and reality, and then bridges it for us. (pp. 49-50)

One of the traditional functions, or perhaps results, of irony is that one keeps one's distance, that one finds a wholesale empathy impossible. Ozu's irony, however, like that of Chekhov or Jane Austen, is there for but one purpose: our detachment reveals a design of which the characters are unaware, and this makes us want to move closer to these warm and very human people. Perhaps it is for this reason that many of the ironies in Ozu's films are neither explained nor exploited. (pp. 50-1)

The philosophy of acceptance in the films of Ozu may be called this both because it is so deeply felt and because it has antecedents both in the Buddhist religion and in Japanese aesthetics. In basic Zen texts one accepts and transcends the world, and in traditional Japanese narrative art one celebrates and relinquishes it. The aesthetic term *mono no aware* is often used nowadays to describe this state of mind. The term has a long history . . . , and though its original meaning was more restricted, from the beginning it represented feeling of a special kind: "not a powerful surge of passion, but an emotion containing a balance; . . . on the whole, *aware* tended to be used of deep impressions produced by small things." Now it is used to describe the "sympathetic sadness" (Tamako Niwa's phrase) caused by the contemplation of this world, and is also used to describe a serene acceptance of a transient world. . . . (pp. 51-2)

Ozu did not, of course, set out self-consciously to capture this quality. To do so would have seemed to him artificial, just as the concept itself would have seemed to him old-fashioned and bookish. Nonetheless, his films are full of it, since he was. The many examples of *mono no aware* in his pictures, homely, mundane, often seemingly trivial, are none the less strong for all that. (p. 52)

The central figure in an Ozu film is often a character with the ability to contemplate, to remain for relatively long periods of time seemingly inactive, utterly given over to contemplation. Some scenes of Ozu characters in silent contemplation have become extremely well-known, most of them ones that occur at the film's end: the mother alone at the end of *The Only Son;* the son alone on the train carrying the ashes of his father in *There Was a Father;* mother alone in *Late Autumn,* fathers alone in *Late Spring, Tokyo Story, Tokyo Twilight, Equinox Flower,* etc. Other such moments occur at the end of scenes, and the long still shot of the character simply existing, no longer acting or reacting, is usually given some small reason; often it is the weather, or some other natural manifestation. (p. 56)

The message of an Ozu film—to the extent that one can be sorted out from the sum experience of the film itself—is, perhaps, that one is happiest living in accord with one's own imperfections and those of one's friends and loved ones; that these imperfections include aging, dying, and other calamities; that man's simple humanity must, in the end, be recognized and obeyed. (p. 65)

Life is a dream. This is a familiar Buddhist concept, radically updated. Originally the observation that the world is a mirage was meant to console the sufferer, but in Ozu's universe there is no afterlife. That life is a dream means one has had no life at all. We may feel that Ozu overstates the case, but he does so with compassion and even restraint. (p. 66).

The theme of the world in change is sounded again and again in the films of Ozu. In *Tokyo Story,* for example, the mother says when she sees her child: "I'm so glad I lived to see this day. The world has changed so." . . . To which the children reply: "But you haven't changed at all."

This is the way of the world, the old no longer change, the young continue to change, as the parents in this picture discover. Yet the parents never cease to hope that their lives will find some vindication in those of their children. The happiness they seek is a mirage. Most of Ozu's films are about parents and children, all of whom suffer a degree of disappointment. As Shuichi says in *Late Spring:* "Raise them and then off they go. If they don't get married you worry, and if they do you feel disappointed." . . . This disappointment is built into the human condition, as many an Ozu character learns during the course of the picture. They begin by hoping that all will be well, that things will turn out as they wish; they often end by consoling themselves that at least they have suffered less than others they know. (pp. 67-8)

Ozu shows in his films both the natural reluctance of the old to let go of the young and the natural impatience of the young to be rid of the old. He is not, however, interested in comparing the virtues of the one with the shortcomings of the other. What Ozu chronicles, rather, is the impossibility of accord. (p. 69)

[The] end is always there, staring us in the face. When asked why he seems so sad, Kawai in *An Autumn Afternoon* says, "Solitary, sad—after all, man is alone." . . . Man is alone, and as one of the characters toward the end of *The End of Summer* remarks, "Life *is* very short, isn't it?" . . . The conclusions of many Ozu films—*Late Spring, Tokyo Story, Late Autumn* among them—underline this common fate. It is so common, indeed, that its appearance in films as in literature always surprises. Loneliness and death are in a sense such banal facts of human experience that only a great artist, a Tolstoy, a Dickens, an Ozu, can restore to them something of the urgency and sadness that we all someday experience. Ozu does this through a deliberate description of the facts, a full display of them, and—surprisingly in one so often described as an apologist for the traditional—by confrontation. Ozu is one of the very few artists whose characters are aware of the great immutable laws that govern their lives. (pp. 69-70)

We watch the people in an Ozu film choosing and deliberating over and over again, usually in the knowledge that in choosing one forms one's character. (pp. 71-2)

Here, perhaps, is the reason why Ozu's characters have . . . no past. They may refer to times past, but we never see them. Ozu is one of the very few directors who never once in his entire career used a flashback. A person's past has done its work, but it is not interesting. Of his people you may truly say what is important is not what life has done to them, but what they do with what life has done to them.

One understands, then, Ozu's dislike and distrust of plot. Plot is possible only if it is agreed that a character is a certain kind of person with a certain kind of past who will therefore predictably do certain kinds of things and not others—that he is, in short, limited in a way people never are, before death. One understands also why inconsistency of character is so important to Ozu: it is a sign of life because it is a sign of choice. . . .

[This], finally, is what the Ozu film shows us—character being formed through choice. (p. 72)

Donald Richie, in his Ozu *(copyright © 1974 by The Regents of the University of California; reprinted by permission of the University of California Press), University of California Press, 1974, 275 p.*

JONATHAN ROSENBAUM

Devoted to both the profound necessity and the sublime silliness of gratuitous social interchange, *Ohayo* is a rather subtler and grander work than might appear at first. Commonly referred to as a remake of Ozu's silent masterpiece *I Was Born, But . . .* , it is as interesting for its differences as for its similarities. . . . [It] is the humiliations in the first film which provide much of the comedy, a subject assuming gravity only when it causes a rift between father and sons. But the more pervasive humour of *Ohayo* extends to the rebellion itself and all it engenders, as well as the various local intrigues surrounding it. Clearly one of Ozu's most commercially-minded movies—with its stately, innocuous muzak of xylophone and strings recalling Tati backgrounds, a similar tendency to keep repeating gags with only slight variations, and a performance of pure ham (quite rare in an Ozu film) by the delightful Masahiko Shimazu as the younger brother—its intricacy becomes apparent only when one realises that each detail intimately links up with every other. . . . In a context where banal greetings among neighbours, schoolboy farting contests and sweet nothings between a couple are treated as structural equivalents, and sliding doors and shot changes become integral facets of the same 'architecture'—an interrelating complex of adjacent, autonomous units—the fascination is how even throwaway details become part of the design. A poster for *The Defiant Ones,* for instance, alludes not only to the recalcitrant sons, but the sense of antagonistic parties chained together by circumstance which often seems to function just below the surface of the everyday pleasantries. . . . Mainly designed to look as casual and as inconsequential as its title, *Good Morning* gleefully embraces a world that *I was Born, But . . .* can acknowledge only painfully. With a father figure at the centre of its constellation . . . who is exempt from ridicule, it neither seeks nor finds any comparable reasons for serious doubts or despair. Yet thanks to the precision and consistency of the vision, Ozu can take up all the other grinning denizens of this discreetly closed world and pin their endearing absurdities neatly into place. (pp. 247-48)

Jonathan Rosenbaum, "'Ohayo' ('Good Morning')," in Monthly Film Bulletin *(copyright © The British Film Institute, 1975), Vol. 42, No. 502, November, 1975, pp. 247-48.*

DEREK ELLEY

In *Ohayo* the premise is [the same as in *I Was Born, But* . . .]: the young children are seen as free-thinking spirits, while the adults are portrayed as encumbered by gossip, status and meaningless small talk. The rebellion of Minoru and Isamu against their parents' apparent obsession with greetings like 'Good Morning', 'Good Evening', 'Hello', and the rest, takes the form of a refusal to talk to anyone; that this 'rebellion' is, in fact, motivated more by their desire to force their parents to buy a TV set so they can watch *sumo* wrestling than by any deep seated resentment or conviction provides the main comic base for the film—flimsy, insubstantial, but far from trivial in its own way. Ozu never makes his plot carry more weight than it is fit to bear, and one is consequently never aware of any dramatic strain. . . .

[One] is made very much more aware of the actors as people rather than directorial objects, and with either the *tatami* mat or ground level invariably in view, there is a powerful sense of being rooted to the action. . . . Ozu is concerned with the unspectacular and everyday—not necessarily in the sense of workaday, but rather in the sense of those areas often overlooked by film-makers for their supposed lack of dramatic malleability.

In *Ohayo* Ozu fixes on small-talk as a springboard for several matters: its temporary importance as a field for 'rebellion' by a maturing child, the devastating consequences when small-talk is placed under the microscope and taken seriously, and the equally serious consequences when it is overlooked as worthless (the parents' disregard of Minoru's stand). . . . The comedy of the boys' self-imposed silence has considerable charm: the young Isamu remaining mute to his schoolteacher's questions, or Minoru desperately trying to ask his parents for lunch-money but having his mimings totally misunderstood. (p. 29)

[The] abiding memory of *Ohayo* is as a portrait of a small community, one section of one street in a modern Tokyo housing estate: Ozu's opening gambit, which he uses to introduce his characters, is to blow up a small matter of missing dues paid to the local Women's Association into a major issue (parents not speaking to one another, etc); it is an accurate introduction to the children's later tantrum and shows that such matters are not merely the prerogative of the immature. With Ozu, however, there is no rancour and no bitterness. (pp. 29-30)

Derek Elley, "Reviews: 'Ohayo'" (© copyright Derek Elley 1975; reprinted with permission), in Films and Filming, *Vol. 22, No. 3, December, 1975, pp. 29-30.*

BEN BREWSTER

A great deal happens in [*Early Spring*], not much of it very remarkable. Of course, the cinema simply cannot avoid a level of detail unattainable in the most painstakingly naturalistic literature. However, the 'suspense' of the main plot of *Early Spring,* the marital and career problems of Sugiyama and his wife, is reduced not just by an accumulation of details but by the linking of these details across the text into a mass of minor chains of implication. . . . There is the same calculated casualness in the way important information about the characters, such as the death of the Sugiyamas' child, is introduced late and in fragments—even Masako's name is not mentioned until halfway through the film. . . . *Early Spring* is, perhaps surprisingly, considering Ozu's austere reputation, a very ideological film. The advantages and disadvantages of the statuses of 'salaryman', manual worker (tinker, electrician), and independent shop-owner are exhaustively discussed by the men, the position of the wife in the family by the women. The ostensible message is that despite a nostalgia for old, pre-war days, these are now gone forever, and despite the drawbacks of the wife's position, the family is not as cold as the office job. The reason for this is never explicitly discussed, but main plot and subplots, as well as Ozu's other films, suggest that it is children. The only children we see in the film are Onodera's, who call him away from his conversation with Sugiyama at Seta Bridge, the conversation which leads to the reconciliation of Sugiyama and Masako, driven apart by their dead child. And children do not represent a hope for the future; they are condemned in their turn, like Hattori's son, like Koichi, to office jobs or nothing better. Children are simply the compensation for accepting those jobs, all that life offers. The problem here is not that the film purveys a reactionary ideology. . . . But to provide a progressive reading of Ozu's films, one would have to be able to demonstrate the work involved in the imposition of this ideology. And the trouble is that *Early Spring,* at least, does not seem to offer very favourable material for this approach. (p. 178)

Ben Brewster, "Retrospective: 'Soshun' ('Early Spring')," in Monthly Film Bulletin *(copyright © The British Film Institute, 1976), Vol. 43, No. 511, August, 1976, pp. 177-78.*

DON WILLIS

Late Autumn is character as jigsaw puzzle, with tantalising missing pieces—the characters' silences, the film's empty spaces.

Ozu's film concerns the mystery of the human essence, and much of it is devoted to the surmises, opinions, machinations and viewpoints of those around the mother and daughter, including Aya's friend Yuriko and three friends of her late father. As in *Citizen Kane,* each observation or comment presents the two women in a new, slightly different light. The goal is not so much truth or completeness as an appreciation of the elusiveness of truth. The most 'dramatic' scene—Akiko 'rhapsodising' about her late husband when it is suggested she should remarry—is not even shown, only related in dialogue. We see the two main characters principally through the other people—further, the implication is that we see them through our eyes, or through Ozu and Noda's. Our conception or impression of a character in a film is ultimately just that—*our* conception —and not the character itself, who is necessarily filtered through our subjectivity and is thus distorted, however slightly. We can't quite know others (or ourselves): this is the sense of the character of the father in *Late Spring* . . . , and the sense of *Late Autumn* as a whole.

The four friends serve a dual purpose. They are half-callous, half-conscientious manipulators. Their scheming separates, unites, provokes Akiko and Aya. Fate-like, they determine the 'plot'. They are also extensions of the two women. Yuriko, for instance, shares their distaste for second marriages (her own father remarried), but is more 'realistic' on the subject. Her disloyalty to her mother, however, is balanced by loyalty to Aya and to *her* mother, whom she promises to visit often after Aya leaves. This sense of almost comically convoluted, conflicting loyalties to oneself, one's parents, one's offspring and one's friends is strangely crystallised in one simple action: angry at her for approving her mother's remarriage, Aya orders the concerned Yuriko out of the apartment. Reluctantly, Yuriko leaves, but as she walks away she whirls around, pausing momentarily, and only then departs for good.

That moment of hesitation is like a miniature of the conflicts of mother and daughter. It suggests, in its quirky conciseness, how it is possible for Aya, at two different times, to respond very differently to the idea of her mother remarrying; why Akiko wants does not want Aya to marry; why Ozu can't explain to us exactly why Aya cries. Taken separately, Aya, Akiko, Yuriko and the three older men reflect each other's inconsistencies and sense of divided loyalties, or split affinities. Together, they are like a fantastically detailed, permutated composite character—mutually enriching analogues of each other that form one master portrait. For all this detail, however, Ozu is finally forced to come back to Hara's suggestive smile at the end of the film, that ironic smile which intimates that there are still many details that he has left out of the portrait. . . .

[*An Autumn Afternoon*] is similar in story and structure to *Late Autumn*—too similar, perhaps. It is always a source of amazement how many formal and narrative elements Ozu repeats from film to film, and yet how distinctive each one is as a whole—no one, really, like another. Only *An Autumn Afternoon* of Ozu's later films seems to me to have no clear identity of its own; to be, in its almost rote reshuffling of the elements, simply reminiscent of earlier films in story, structure, scene and character. . . . Its closing note—Ryu sitting alone and drunk in the kitchen, in long shot, after his daughter's wedding—is a typically memorable Ozu ending. But even this coda has an air of forced variation, as though Ozu and Noda did not want to repeat themselves, or not *exactly*. What they do here they do well; it's just that they did it before and better, with more sense of form and purpose. . . .

In one unfortunate way, *An Autumn Afternoon* did represent a new departure for Ozu. Alone of his late films, it is almost exclusively peopled by the 'mean', 'mediocre' creatures that his detractors (and even some of his defenders) say always was Ozu's speciality. The ordinary, mean or simply less than extraordinary characters that appear in his earlier films—the children in *Tokyo Story,* say, or the mistress' daughter in *The End of Summer*—are merely part of the natural diversity of character in those films, a diversity that includes several Setsuko Hara characterisations which qualify as among the most extraordinary creations in film. But *An Autumn Afternoon* is filled with unthinking, peremptory fathers, brothers and husbands, whose 'selfishness' too schematically makes loving wives and daughters stern, snippy and pettily dictatorial, in turn driving the weak-willed men to drink. As with *There Was a Father* and its characters strait-jacketed by fate, this seems less a bleak or honest view of life than a narrow one. In the context of this circumscribed world, even Ozu's pay-off images—the daughter in her wedding gown, the father alone—lack their customary resonance. (p. 48)

A final point: all the people in the film talk about loneliness. One old man describes himself as 'all alone'. When he passes out drunk, a friend warns the father: 'Beware—that could be you.' His son tells him, 'You'll be lonesome when she goes.' Near the end a woman asks him, 'But won't you be lonely?' Finally, drunk, he admits to himself, 'Yes . . . all alone in the end.' These admonitions and admissions could be seen as the characters' collective, vain attempt to confront and dispel the fact of loneliness, but they seem closer to superfluous comments, a thematic tipping of the hand. In *Late Spring* the imminence of the father's solitude is submerged in the drama of cleaving father from daughter. His sudden solitariness is almost a shock, when of course it was the film's inevitable, *tacit* conclusion. The talk about loneliness in *An Autumn Afternoon* seems intended to fill a dramatic or aesthetic void—there is simply nothing else for the characters to talk about.

The End of Summer . . . is from one angle a justification of selfishness; from another, a statement about one's responsibility for one's own life; from yet another, a statement on the basic immutability of character. 'It's his character'; 'Character? You mean he can do as he pleases?'; 'It's your life': these are representative lines. Concepts of self, self-interest and responsibility intertwine. At the centre is the fact of death: because one has only one short life one cannot entrust it to another person.

The two key images isolate the two independent-minded sisters of the Kohayagawa family, Akiko . . . and Noriko. . . . The sisters refuse to marry simply for 'the good of the family', whose business is failing, and in relation to the family this refusal is seen as selfish and divisive. In relation to the fact of death, however, their refusal is seen as necessary, urgent. Their 'selfishness' is, on another level, an acceptance of responsibility for fashioning the shape of their lives. The periodic shots of the sisters side by side, kneeling or standing in unison, are exquisite yet ultimately ironic images of accord—ironic because their personal accord means discord for the family as a whole. Their smiles of mutual agreement are subtly inverted subversion: they agree to disagree.

The film is so light and charming on the surface—but the last three shots are of the crows [harbingers of death]. A peasant (Ryu) at one point comments, 'New lives replace old', but the film does not conclude with cyclical images of rebirth but, like *Citizen Kane,* with images of finality and death. New lives replace old, but they are *different* lives. In one scene the whole family rushes into the frame to see the old man, abruptly recovered from a severe heart attack, up and about and refreshed by his 'sleep'. Later, Ozu shows the family again crowding into the frame, this time to see the smoke from the crematorium. This 'double exposure' is like an image of the fact of death, and what it means in this one case. The idea of rebirth expressed by the peasant is an abstraction; death is a fact, and while the two sisters may recapitulate their father's life in spirit, Ozu implies that it is the fact of his death that is his chief legacy to them. (pp. 48-9)

Don Willis, "Yasujiro Ozu: Emotion and Contemplation," in Sight and Sound *(copyright © 1978 by The British Film Institute), Vol. 48, No. 1, Winter, 1978-79, pp. 44-9.*

Gordon Parks

1912-

American filmmaker, author, and photographer.

Parks overcame racial obstacles in Hollywood to become the first prominent black director. His work depicts his own struggle to conquer extreme poverty and prejudice rather than become embittered by them.

In 1937, in the midst of the Depression, Parks saw a portfolio of photographs taken for the Farm Security Administration, which inspired him to buy an inexpensive camera. He became a fashion photographer, but devoted his spare time to photographing the ghettos of Chicago. The resulting collection of photographs won him a Julius Rosenwald fellowship established for struggling artists. An apprenticeship with Roy Stryker in the Farm Security Administration led to a job as a photographer for *Life* magazine.

In 1963 Parks published his autobiographical novel, *The Learning Tree*. An extremely popular work, it was translated into nine languages and provided the vehicle for Parks's directing talents. Although critics find the story touching, they are most impressed by the visual beauty of the film version. Here Parks's talent as a photographer is in full flower.

This film was followed by *Shaft* and *Shaft's Big Score,* stories of a black private eye working in the ghetto. Despite the flash and slickness of these films, critics praised Parks for portraying blacks as unique individuals in contrast to common cinematic stereotypes.

***Leadbelly,* Parks's most recent film, has been criticized for depicting whites as unfavorably as blacks are usually depicted. It is charged that Parks's characterization of the protagonist is inaccurate. Parks, however, feels it is a director's prerogative to make judgments and character interpretations. In this case, Parks parallels his own life with Leadbelly's. The blues singer's battles with the law and his struggle to be accepted as an artist are similar to Parks's own difficulties. The lament Leadbelly sings is an apt description of Parks's attitude towards the hardships he has surmounted: "You ain't broke my mind. You ain't broke my body. And you ain't broke my spirit." (See also *CLC*, Vol. 1, *Contemporary Authors,* Vols. 41-44, rev. ed., and *Something About the Author,* Vol. 8.)**

SUSAN RICE

Gordon Parks is a still photographer. He directed *The Learning Tree,* his first motion picture. It is still born. Dare I say primitive? Gordon Parks is black. If he wasn't nobody would pay much attention to his picture. But he is, and everybody is giving the film much more attention and praise than it deserves. . . .

I am also sorry that the first massive, lavish, technicolor, mass distributed film by a black man should be so reassuring . . . like *Green Pastures*. Parks' remembrance of his boyhood is unaffected but middle-brow, like The Supremes doing Frank Sinatra tunes. The only charitable thing I can think of to say about it is that it is free of self-pity and bombast. . . . *The Learning Tree* has some of the stiltedness and some of the sensitivity of Truman Capote's childhood reminiscences. Does the idea of a black Truman Capote strike you as oddly as it does me? Does the world *need* another Capote of any color? Let's try another. I think Parks sees himself as a mini Orson Welles. In addition to directing, he wrote the screenplay, from his novel of the same name, and scored the film. I guess I am scoring it as well. Only God can make a tree.

Susan Rice, "Reviews: 'The Learning Tree'," in Take One *(copyright © 1969 by Unicorn Publishing Corp.), Vol. 2, No. 3, January-February 1969, p. 25.*

ARTHUR KNIGHT

[A] film that must be rated a failure despite its high aspirations is Gordon Parks's *The Learning Tree,* based upon his autobiographical novel. The fact that a Negro has been able to recall his own past with considerable affection and nostalgia is, I suppose, a good sign, and certainly the fact that a major studio . . . has encouraged him to do so is virtually a cause for celebration. But the celebration stops abruptly as cliché piles on cliché, as the past becomes bathed in the ineffable glow of homely virtues and self-sacrifices that transcend belief.

This is not to imply that Mr. Parks has saccharined his own life story to make it more palatable and acceptable to a general audience. . . . The hard core is there, but its edges are blurred, indistinct, often maudlin. It is odd, particularly at this time, to find a movie that surveys the life of the Negro in the Twenties with such deep underlying feelings of approbation. Even the film's solitary gesture of defiance—when at the end young Newt . . . refuses the white sheriff's proffered ride—seems to be accompanied by some rueful shaking of the head.

Arthur Knight, "Little Lulus," in Saturday Review *(copyright © 1969 by* Saturday Review; *all rights reserved; reprinted by permission), Vol. LII, No. 32, August 9, 1969, p. 22.**

JOSEPH MORGENSTERN

The pleasures of "The Learning Tree," an awkward but greatly affecting movie, are all bound up with nostalgia for a vanished land in which barefooted farm boys could do cartwheels through unbounded fields of yellow flowers, in which a preacher could implore the Lord to "deliver our young from cigarettes, from dancing, from drinking, from flapper skirts," in which an amorous young man could give his girl a bottle of violet water and a card, especially made up to go with it, that said: "Roses are red, violets are blue, sugar is sweet and so are you." . . .

Parks has made, among several other things, a predictably pictorial period piece in soft-spoken Technicolor. He has made a lovely small movie about boyhood; not black boyhood or white boyhood so much as human boyhood, the maybehood that follows babyhood. He has also made a movie about the perilous plight of a black boy, confronted constantly by the sudden, sometimes violent, death of friends and family, who's still naive enough or brave enough to believe in the future.

The outward trappings of his life are as reassuringly bourgeois as the outside of a Watts bungalow—a cohesive family dominated by a strong, warm mother, church picnics, white shirts to school, some white friends, even a white piano teacher for a privileged black few in his community. In reality, though, the whites have the upper hand —on occasion the upper fist—and blacks are firmly steered away from dangerously white aspirations. The gifted young high-school student learns from his white teacher, just as Malcolm Little did in "The Autobiography of Malcolm X," that Negro children are simply not college material.

With every reason in the world to lash out at the world, the younger Parks moves through it cleverly, carefully, while the older Parks recalls it as a world in which whites had no exclusive claim on vice and blacks had no exclusive claim on virtue. . . . "The Learning Tree" is an astoundingly even-tempered piece of autobiography, given the melodramatic violence of its author's youth. It is also an uneven piece of film craftsmanship. . . .

In a few minor roles and scenes . . . the performances are tentative and Parks's direction is sloppy or distracted. Surprisingly enough for a photographer of Parks's achievements, he relies heavily on dialogue where pictures alone would have turned the trick.

Apart from the sumptuous photography, "The Learning Tree" has little of the gloss and velocity we've come to expect from fashionably modern movies. At times it turns downright clumsy. I don't know what else to say about the clumsiness except that it's there and that it doesn't matter very much in the end. What matters most is the abiding presence of a good man telling a good story about a boy who was himself, a boy who remains alive, kicking and growing long after the movie ends.

Joseph Morgenstern, "Boy's Life," in Newsweek *(copyright 1969 by Newsweek, Inc.; all rights reserved; reprinted by permission), Vol. LXXIV, No. 6, August 11, 1969, p. 74.*

[There] are many images of startling beauty in Parks' film, like the dappled summer light shining through the trees on a country lane. *The Learning Tree*'s major problem is not with pictures but with people.

Adapting his own 1963 autobiographical novel about growing up as a black boy in the Kansas of the 1920s. Parks recollects the characters of his childhood as the sort of stereotypes that usually appear in elementary-school brotherhood pageants. . . .

The original novel was a reminiscence. Not a protest, a souvenir of a simpler time when a quiet bitterness was as good as a riot and the most drastic sort of racial demonstration was trying to buy a Coke at the drugstore soda fountain. Parks is not yet sufficiently sophisticated as a dramatist to make such an unquestioning life completely credible to a contemporary audience. . . .

Parks' meticulous photographic direction . . . only seems to underscore all [the] melodramatics, lending every character and scene an extra edge of unreality. His shimmering imagery creates a world of benign memory but imperfect drama, in which black is just too beautiful.

"Where Black Is Too Beautiful," in Time *(reprinted by permission from* Time, The Weekly Newsmagazine; *copyright Time Inc. 1969), Vol. 94, No. 9, August 29, 1969, p. 65.*

PHILIP T. HARTUNG

[Most] of our pictures with and about Negroes these days lack authentic black backgrounds and thinking—and are a disappointment. Instead of just making films with some Negro actors, the studios would be wise to begin their planning with Negro culture, realistic Negro themes, and then select their working staff who will make the picture and be in it.

To the credit of Warner Bros.-Seven Arts they did just that in signing the famous photographer Gordon Parks to film his autobiographical novel, *The Learning Tree*. . . . The film is incredibly beautiful as it captures this 1920 Kansas town and countryside; perhaps too beautiful. . . . Too often director Parks allows a scene to start with a stunning Technicolor picture, develop with movement, and then end as another stunning picture. This technique slows up the movie, which is crowded with incidents one after the other all illustrating injustice, intolerance, charity, kindness, the behavior of the good people and bad (too many of the episodes are smothered in clichés and sentimental corn). If "The Learning Tree" is somewhat disappointing it is so because it had so much going for it that we expected too much from Gordon Parks. He will do better in his next movie, especially if he learned from "The Learning Tree" that film-making is not a one-man job. (pp. 543-44)

Philip T. Hartung, "Black, White and Technicolor," in Commonweal *(copyright © 1969 Commonweal Publishing Co., Inc.; reprinted by permission of Commonweal Publishing Co., Inc.), Vol. XC, No. 20, September 5, 1969, pp. 543-45.**

MOIRA WALSH

Shaft (first name John) is a black private detective who is a cross between Sam Spade and James Bond. He is the hero of a modishly photographed, but rather old-fashioned, private-eye melodrama directed by black former photojournalist and still photographer Gordon Parks. Despite a difficult-to-follow plot—about the grudge kidnapping of the daughter of a black racketeer by the Mafia—and an unabashed racial militance in tone (tempered however by good humor), the film is a disarmingly entertaining piece of hokum, with just enough contemporary resonance and sting. (pp. 48-9)

Moira Walsh, "More Brief Takes," in America *(© America Press, 1971; all rights reserved), Vol. 125, No. 2, July 24, 1971, pp. 48-9.*

TOM MILNE

Humphrey Bogart is alive and well and living in Harlem. His skin is black, but he lives with it. His private eye affairs are still more quixotic than lucrative. His lip still curls when the police chief threatens to withdraw his licence unless he cooperates. Laconic, sardonic, and only just on the right side of the law, he is now called John Shaft. . . .

Dark alleys and red herrings, exotic sirens and prowling gunmen, sinister encounters and strange alliances, all the familiar icons come tumbling out as engagingly as they used to in the Forties thrillers, freshly minted by being seen through the eyes of a black director. Like *Cotton Comes to Harlem, Shaft* leaves the racial thing to take care of itself in some edgy observation, and lets in a welcome breath of fresh air by having its black characters behave like people rather than walking advertisements for Black Power or Liberal Conscience. The result is as wittily enjoyable as Ossie Davis's film and much more stylish.

It is perhaps a pity that Gordon Parks' first film, *The Learning Tree,* has yet to be released in Britain, since *Shaft* is so unpretentious that the excellence of his direction is likely to go unnoticed. Not that *The Learning Tree* is a masterpiece: its nostalgic recollection of a Southern childhood is a shade too bitter-sweet, too Carson McCullers-ish, for absolute comfort. But it reveals a sensitivity to actors and settings which is confirmed, less obviously, by *Shaft.*

Tom Milne, "'Shaft'," in Focus on Film *(© 1971 The Tantivy Press, London, Great Britain), October, 1971, p. 7.*

RICHARD COMBS

[*Shaft* is] quite a lively article—a straight forward, one-to-one transformation of the elements of 'forties' thrillers into contemporary terms. It is in between the action and the constant crackle of hip jargon that there is room for dissatisfaction. Although Parks has revitalised the clichés more thoroughly than many similar attempts—to the extent of a black private eye, Harlem locations, and so on—and has avoided nostalgia for a recreated style, retaining only a few small touches of parody, the new life is never altogether comfortable inside the old body.

Opening high-angle shots of Fun City establish the setting and society in a slickly stereotyped way. For the duration of the credits Shaft moves through these streets; his position as a self-elected rather than socially segregated outsider is noted before the sequence ends with a joke that anticipates all the subsequent ironies about the obvious, and not so obvious, conflicts of race and personality. . . . Shaft's encounters with the policeman, Androzzi, and with other negroes of different persuasions than his own, the hoodlum, Bumpy Jonas, the young militant, Ben Buford, support the view of Shaft as a solitary and aggressively non-aligned individual. They relate him, in one direction, to the tradition of private dicks with a chip on the shoulder, cynical about people and resentful of society, and in another, to a ghetto view of personal relationships as almost continual warfare, a tough, flip way with both friend and foe, that Shaft practises to perfection and which the film seems to use as an indication of his maturity, as opposed to the sullen, boyish resentment of the militant, Buford.

There is a less satisfactory meeting of past and present in the way the protagonist actually carries out his profession. . . . (pp. 52-3)

Away from the areas of battle, the sense of personal relations tends to be trite and awkward (the scene in which Shaft takes the runaway Buford to stay with a comfortable, middle-class acquaintance of his, and Shaft's relations with all his women), and in his generally well disciplined direction, Parks occasionally over-emphasises the mock-Chandler wisecracks and punch-lines. But despite the few elements that make for confusion, *Shaft* succeeds well enough within its own terms, given a ruthlessly dynamic hero and some splendidly engineered action. (p. 53)

Richard Combs, "'Shaft'" (© copyright Richard Combs 1972; reprinted with permission), in Films and Filming, *Vol. 18, No. 7, April, 1972, pp. 52-3.*

ARTHUR COOPER

John Shaft, private eye, aspires to be a steely black version of Sam Spade but more closely achieves an ironic, dimpled James Bond. *Shaft's Big Score* . . . clearly is no "Maltese Falcon" or even a "Goldfinger." . . . [However, the film is] a rousing and entertaining thriller, better than the original and far superior to all those imitations that Shaft's success has spawned. . . .

The film is directed with style and vigorous pace by Gordon Parks, who celebrates an apparent affection for Hitchcock by appearing in the film (as a croupier in a casino called Mother Clyde's) and by imitating the airplane chase sequence in "North by Northwest" (Parks uses a helicopter). An excellent still photographer, Parks sometimes indulges his fondness for the camera—one lyrically filmed seduction scene would seem more appropriate as a mouthwash ad.

Arthur Cooper, "Black Eye," in Newsweek *(copyright 1972 by Newsweek, Inc.; all rights reserved; reprinted by permission), Vol. LXXX, No. 3, July 17, 1972, p. 78.*

MARGARET TARRATT

[*Shaft's Big Score*] is a development rather than an imitation of the earlier film. . . .

To a greater extent than its predecessor, *Shaft's Big Score* is a film which stands or falls on its elaborate production sequences, notably the lengthy climactic chase at the end of the film. . . . (p. 55)

[It] is a film of the moment, something in the manner of Bond, lacking the fluctuating mood and style which mark the great gangster and private-eye classics. (p. 56)

Margaret Tarratt, "Reviews: 'Shaft's Big Score'" (© copyright Margaret Tarratt 1972; reprinted with permission), in Films and Filming, *Vol. 19, No. 1, October, 1972, pp. 55-6.*

HUBBELL ROBINSON

Shaft emerges in [*Shaft's Big Score*] as a highly lethal and effective weapon of destruction and not much else. . . .

Gordon Parks directed and keeps things moving at great speed to cover up the picture's emptiness. There is a chase sequence at the end which borrows from all the other successful chase sequences with which we've been peppered of late.

Shaft's Big Score's kinetic values are many. That's good because its creative assets are meager. (p. 505)

Hubbell Robinson, "Film Reviews: 'Shaft's Big Score'," in Films in Review *(copyright © 1972 by the National Board of Review of Motion Pictures, Inc.), Vol XXIII, No. 8, October, 1972, pp. 504-05.*

REX REED

In the hands of a less responsible filmmaker, Leadbelly's saga might have been just another tale of a poor, downtrodden Sambo butting his head against "The Man"; but it just didn't happen that way, and [in *Leadbelly*] Parks avoids Black clichés as if they were recruiting slogans for the Ku Klux Klan. (Too bad he didn't also avoid showing the whites in prison-guard assignments as stereotypical pot-bellied crackers.) . . .

Not a great movie, but there's more meaning and truth for Blacks here than *Mahogany* had in one of its lime-green sequined fake fingernails.

Rex Reed, "Movies: 'Leadbelly'," in Vogue *(courtesy* Vogue; *copyright © 1975 by The Condé Nast Publications Inc.), Vol. 166, No. 1, January, 1976, p. 33.*

KATRINE AMES

In spite of rich raw material, both factual and fanciful, ["Leadbelly"] falls a little flat. It moves, but never jumps. . . . Ernest Kinoy's screenplay is only adequate. Director Gordon Parks gets good but not memorable performances from his actors, and though he concentrates on what should be the film's greatest asset, the music, he fails to do it justice. . . . Visually, the movie is magnificent: Parks and cinematographer Bruce Surtees capture the look and feel of the old rural South. "Leadbelly" doesn't exploit its subject the way "Lady Sings the Blues" exploited Billie Holiday. This movie gets a hold on the legend of Ledbetter; it's too bad that no one involved ever really lets loose. (p. 96)

Katrine Ames, "Black Legend," in Newsweek *(copyright 1976 by Newsweek, Inc.; all rights reserved; reprinted by permission), Vol. LXXXVII, No. 16, April 19, 1976, pp. 95-6.*

JAY COCKS

It is good to remember the [rough and hard facts of Huddie Ledbetter's life] seeing *Leadbelly,* because in the movie Huddie has been considerably sanitized.

Thanks in large part to some good period detail by Director Gordon Parks . . . , *Leadbelly* at least maintains a degree of dignity and professionalism. . . . Parks shows a careful eye for small evocative details. . . . (p. 76)

Leadbelly [who was embarrassed by his rough past] might have found this movie . . . to his liking, which is part of the problem. The screenplay puts Huddie into situations where he seems to have no choice but to kill. He emerges as a man innocent, put-upon and perennially puzzled by the cruel vicissitudes of life, who would just like to get on with his singin' and his ramblin'. . . .

The violence, the bitterness and the reckless sensuality that make Leadbelly's music great can hardly be seen here for all the laundering. . . . The songs sound the way the whole movie feels: smooth, eager to please, defused. (p. 78)

Jay Cocks, "Cinema: 'Leadbelly'," in Time *(reprinted by permission from* Time, The Weekly Newsmagazine; *copyright Time Inc. 1976), Vol. 107, No. 22, May 24, 1976, pp. 76, 78.*

JOHN SIMON

In *Leadbelly,* Gordon Parks tries to tell the story of the black singer who spent years of his life on Southern chain gangs in a way that is one part moralizing primer for black children, and one part unpleasant facts transmuted into striking pictures for white coffee-table books. It is calculated . . . to disturb without upsetting, which means that the protagonist's seamy side must be prettified, and suffering must be represented in artfully staged images, as if it were *Washington Crossing the Delaware.* There must always be reaction shots of black faces in picturesque groupings, and, whenever possible, misty out-of-focus landscapes or sunsets turning the world into a place inhabited solely by blood oranges. I admire Parks's purpose and his fight to get the film made and exhibited, but I can react to the actual movie only with polite uninvolvement.

John Simon, "Head Ache," in New York *Magazine (copyright © 1976 by News Group Publications, Inc.; reprinted with the permission of* New York *Magazine), Vol. 9, No. 24, June 14, 1976, p. 66.**

JAMES MONACO

[Gordon Parks, Sr.] made a short, *Flavio,* about a boy in a Brazilian *favela,* in 1965. It was well received, but it took him more than three years to put together his first feature, *The Learning Tree*. . . . Finally Hollywood was ready for its first prominent Black director.

The Learning Tree (1968) based on Parks's own memoirs, is a visually stunning evocation of his childhood in Kansas in the twenties. Because the setting is Midwestern, the story is also rather novel, successfully avoiding the clichés and truisms of growing up Black in the South, or in a Northern ghetto. Yet, Parks's childhood wasn't particularly dramatic—no great traumas—and so *Learning Tree* is rather static, a fact which would have caused no problems if the film had been European, but which did not do much for his reputation as a bankable director in late-sixties Hollywood.

The emphasis in the moving-picture industry had always been on "moving" rather than "picture," and Parks's superb training as a still photographer wasn't of much use to him commercially in 1968, when Hollywood was just learning, through the use of new filmstock and techniques, that movies didn't have to be breathlessly paced to be attractive; that audiences would buy the "picture," too.

So Parks set out to show he could do "movies." The proof, *Shaft* (1971), was irrefutable. *Cotton Comes to Harlem* had introduced the form of Blaxploitation action films; *Shaft* added the all-important tone. The film was tough, lean, cool, hip, angry, and in the end even wise. Black audiences understood immediately that Richard Roundtree's heroic exploits as private eye John Shaft were a commentary on decades of white detective films as well as being entertaining in themselves. Most important: at last there was a real Black hero on the screen. Parks did one sequel, *Shaft's Big Score,* in 1972 . . . , and a more general urban cop film, *The Supercops* (1974), unusual in being one of extremely few non-Black films directed by a Black. Parks refused to be ghettoized as a filmmaker, just as he had refused to be ghettoized as a *Life* photographer.

Having paid his dues to the commercial film establishment, Parks was finally able to return to a more personal project. (pp. 196-97)

[*Leadbelly* is] a magnificent telling of an historical episode with strong mythic overtones. *Leadbelly* was just the sort of film Parks was meant to make. His experiences as photographer, musician, and novelist combine to create a film that works well on all three levels.

Like most mythic stories, this biography of Huddie Ledbetter—"Leadbelly"—the master of the twelve-string guitar, potentially verges on cliché. It takes someone of Parks's particular talents to avoid those pitfalls. He does so by confronting the mythic material head-on rather than apologizing for it. The film has a classic narrative structure: strong, simple, direct, and pointed. In short, it's very much like Leadbelly's own music.

It's grounded in humiliation. (Texas Governor Pat Neff comments after Leadbelly has performed for him: "Ain't nothin' can sing like a darkie when he puts his mind to it!") It opposes that oppression with the elemental politics of survival. (Dicklikker, Leadbelly's prison buddy, explains: "Ya suit yerself to the situation. When they wants to kill ya, just livin' is winning.") Ultimately, *Leadbelly* is a triumph of will. . . . *Leadbelly* provides a legitimate historical high of the sort we seldom get any longer from mainstream American movies, made by people who have lost (or never had) a sense of the vitality and meaning of the politics of existence.

Parks can bring it off because, first, he understands the strength of Leadbelly's music. He has also guided [the actors] . . . to an extraordinary level of performance. Along with his cinematographer, Bruce Surtees, he has in addition created a breathtakingly elemental imagery for the film—full of earth, air, sun, sweat, and color—that's almost insolent it is so powerful.

Most important, perhaps, is the groundbase of the film. What gave Leadbelly's songs their special power was the people whose stories they told. The same must be said for Parks's film. He made a movie about people, and the people give *Leadbelly* its mythic energy. (pp. 198-99)

James Monaco, "The Black Film (and the Black Image)," in his American Film Now: The People, the Power, the Money, the Movies *(copyright © 1979 by James Monaco; reprinted by arrangement with The New American Library, Inc., New York, New York), The New American Library, New York, 1979, pp. 185-214.**

Roman Polanski

1933-

Polish director, screenwriter, and actor.

Polanski's films are a compilation of assorted cinematic genres, encompassing surrealism, psychological thriller, the horror story and its parody, and the detective mystery.

He was born in Paris of Polish parents; the family moved to Kracow three years later. During World War II his parents were put in a concentration camp, where his mother died, and Polanski grew up in a series of Polish homes. He began acting professionally in theater when he was a teenager and later worked in films, including several with Polish director Andrzej Wajda. Polanski studied painting, sculpture, and graphics in Kracow and spent five years at the State Film College at Lódź, where he made *Two Men and a Wardrobe*. The film projects its maker's deep absorption with the tenets of surrealism and the Theater of the Absurd. About his early style, also informing *The Fat and the Lean*, Polanski has said: "I must confess that I was completely formed by surrealism."

Polanski's first full-length feature, *Knife in the Water*, initiated a career-long succession of films exploring the varieties of violence and estrangement. His second feature, *Repulsion*, has been likened to Alfred Hitchcock's definitive shocker *Psycho* for its study of inner torment that bursts into outward mayhem. *Cul-de-Sac* somewhat refines overt carnage into a surreal depiction of human chaos, drawing upon the absurdist tradition of Samuel Beckett and Harold Pinter. Some critics see a direct relationship between the turbulent background of this director's life and the array of unusual brutalities in his films, especially emphasizing this correlation after the bizarre murder of Sharon Tate, Polanski's second wife. Throughout his career Polanski has sought to articulate the extremes of human experience, leading necessarily to displays of violence in some form, though never limiting it to the single dimension of physical grue.

From the violence in the spiritual order of *Rosemary's Baby* to the violence of moral corruption in *Chinatown* and the psychological violence of *The Tenant*, Polanski investigates many levels of existential menace. More exactly, his concern is the atmospheric suggestion of potential havoc in the worlds in which his endangered protagonists exist. Polanski is adapting Thomas Hardy's novel *Tess of the D'Ubervilles* and Polanski feels his film *Tess* will be representative of a mature phase in his career. He has said of the film: "I have been influenced a great deal by surrealism and the theater of the absurd. . . . But now that the world itself has become absurd and almost surreal, I want to go back to the simplicity and essence of human relationships." (See also *Contemporary Authors*, Vols. 77-80.)

JONATHAN HARKER

[*Two Men and a Wardrobe*] juggles symbol and reality, lighthearted story and allegorical message in a casual manner we are hardly accustomed to. . . .

The film's success is largely in its expert manipulation of two levels of meaning and in the flexible, "open" quality of its symbolism. I interpret the wardrobe to represent all the ethical, moral, and religious values considered "outmoded" in pre-Gomulka Poland—and, for that matter, throughout the world. The [wardrobe closet's] mirror then represents man's conscience, reflecting his own self-criticism. (It is this mirror which gives away the adolescents as they are about to attack a girl, and provokes a fight in which the mirror is smashed.) One published interpretation of the film states that the two men get into trouble because they try to interest organized society in their wardrobe. This is simply inaccurate. Rather, the wardrobe is a heavy burden, which the two will not put down or abandon, but which in turn amuses, affronts, or enrages everybody else. I do not wish to insist on this single "translation." The story could, for example, be read as a variant on the legend of St. Christopher. Again, one scene opens with a fish apparently floating among clouds in the sky. One of the two men picks the fish up—it has been lying on the wardrobe mirror, which reflected the clouds overhead. The two proceed to eat the fish—or are they eating something else? It's not crucial; for one of the greatest virtues of the film lies in its literal, realistic level, admirably maintained throughout. There is no real need to translate the film at all to get something out of it. And of how many "symbolic," "Freudian," "experimental" films can this be said?

Indeed, *Two Men and a Wardrobe* can be taken as the perfect compendium of all that the ordinary experimental film is not—lengthy, confused, opaque, ill-proportioned, humorless, and technically inept. What it reveals about life in Poland is open to discussion, as is what it reveals of the Polish avant-garde school. But the superlative quality of Polanski's film is beyond question or qualification. I have no hesitation in stating that *Two Men and a Wardrobe* is the best film of its kind in thirty years. (p. 55)

Jonathan Harker, "Film Reviews: 'Two Men and a Wardrobe'," in Film Quarterly *(copyright 1959 by The Regents of the University of California; reprinted by permission of the University of California Press), Vol. XII, No. 3, Spring, 1959, pp. 53-5.*

RAYMOND DURGNAT

[In *Repulsion*] the murderer is dewily sensitive Catherine Deneuve. But, instead of discovering her through the eyes of others, as in the best of the preceding films, *Psycho,* we live life with her, look out on the world through her eyes—with the additional advantage that we can understand the ordinary human reactions to which she is blind. It's an admirable compromise between a conventional and a 'stream-of-consciousness' film.

I won't dwell . . . on the film's 'sensational' qualities which are considerable. More important is the film's whole atmosphere, exemplified by the shot of the angelic young murderess-to-be walking, unseeing, past a road accident. Her quiet deterioration is integrated with our everyday—London's familiar streets (in the exteriors), the routine of everyday living (steadily degenerating in the flat), the myopic goodwill of her friends (in the beauty parlour). Everybody must have wondered how it would *feel* to go, slowly, mad; how your friends would react to the warning symptoms; but above all how the world would seem, how you'd gradually withdraw into a kind of isolation and timelessness in which, steadily, hideous dreams acquired greater reality than reality and devoured your mind until time, place, life itself broke up into an incoherent succession of extreme states. Of all the films I've seen on the topic of madness this gives the most vivid picture of *being* mad. It is vivid because no verbal explanations, no pleas for understanding, get in the way; we simply watch her feelings, and identify, and share. (pp. 28-9)

Raymond Durgnat, "Film Guide: 'Repulsion'," (© copyright Raymond Durgnat 1965; reprinted with permission), in Films and Filming, *Vol. 11, No. 11, August, 1965, pp. 28-9.*

KENNETH TYNAN

Repulsion is *Psycho* turned inside out. In Hitchcock's film we see a double murder through the eyes of the victims—in Polanski's our viewpoint is the killer's. Polanski (coauthor, with Gerard Brach, of the original story) offers no psychiatric explanation for his heroine's behavior. He simply presents it, and if we choose to identify with her fears and her irrational ferocity that is our business, not his. . . .

Within its limits, *Repulsion* is a flawless exercise: it establishes Polanski as a master of the casual macabre. We know he can scare us to death—all that remains is for him to prove that he can also warm us to life.

Kenneth Tynan, "A Grisly Tour de Force of Sex and Suspense," in Life *(courtesy of* Life *Magazine; © 1965 Time Inc.; reprinted with permission of the author), Vol. 59, No. 15, October 8, 1965, p. 23.*

TOM MILNE

'Ah! Pinter' one cries, sniffing like a Bisto Kid at the heady aroma of *Cul-de-Sac*. . . . Then one remembers the odd, elliptical conversations of *Knife in the Water,* and wonders if Polanski was even then the Pinter of Poland. An unanswerable question, really, even if one knows Polish, as Pinter's English is so distinctive that it sounds like something else as soon as it is translated. Whatever the answer, the fact remains that Polanski's command of the English language has matured rapidly since the hesitancies of *Repulsion,* and the idiotic clichés of polite conversation, observed with hilarious exactness, form a permanent, twittering background to *Cul-de-Sac*.

For the rest, this is very much Polanski as we have come to know him: ghoulish black comedy; the pain of solitude; pride; a touch of masochism; and above all, people and objects at odds with a landscape (like the bandaged men against the snow in *Mammals,* the two men and a wardrobe in *Two Men and a Wardrobe,* the squabbling trio locked together by a boat in *Knife in the Water*). (p. 146)

Tom Milne, "Film Reviews: 'Cul-de-Sac'," in Sight and Sound *(copyright © 1966 by The British Film Institute), Vol. 35, No. 3, Summer, 1966, pp. 146-47.*

RAYMOND DURGNAT

The affinities of this 'black comedy' [*Cul-de-Sac*] with the Theatre of the Absurd hardly need underlining; and there's a spirit not unlike Ionesco's in his playing with the conventions of the genre, something of Beckett in his final image of sobbing nihilism.

To make these comparisons is far from suggesting that his work is derivative. On the contrary. . . . [Polanski's] films bring a new impetus to a now inbred, cult-ridden, mood. For he remains in contact with certain positive enthusiasms: a robust, amiable Surrealism; a sense of the weight and strain and pain of everyday, realistic experiences; and a huge, mischievous enjoyment of the melodramas which he parodies. . . . Polanski's humour, like the Polish cinema, is profoundly existentialist. His studies of minds cracking might carry as subtitle the title of one of Sartre's novels, *The Age of Reason;* and their common theme, of slowly decomposing rationality, is adumbrated in Sartre's short story *The Room*. (p. 18)

Cul-de-Sac is a case of style transcending subject: indeed, if the film is so difficult to write about . . . it's because so much of it is a meditation in the odd visual details through which Polanski keeps turning the everyday into a sort of fantasy-land—eg, the simple act of drinking is imbued with sinister overtones because the camera-angle stresses the muscles pulling away in the men's throats. The script concocts some brilliantly eccentric re-circuitings of the dramatic current—thus the suspense-making situation of friends and child calling for lunch with the gangster-dominated couple ends, not with a plea for rescue, but with hosts and friends venting all their long-pent-up hostility in one blazing row. In its construction the film has an inspired dottiness, as in the slow spiralling-down of the terror situation to a casual practical joke, which in its turn escalates through a sexually highly-charged situation to the final killings. (p. 51)

[It's] not just certain motifs (eggs, corpses, 'solidarity'), or the mad mood, that recalls Buñuel. What keeps his film lightweight, relatively, is the reliance on melodrama and parody; and Polanski may well match *The Exterminating Angel* (itself a title for *Repulsion!*) when he altogether dispenses with these ingredients and comes to trace the interweaving of madness and sanity, 'straight', in a world as unquivocally everyday as [Cesare] Zavattini's. (p. 52)

Raymond Durgnat, "New Films: 'Cul-de-Sak'" (© copyright Raymond Durgnat 1966; reprinted with permission), in Films and Filming, *Vol. 12, No. 10, July, 1966, pp. 18, 51-2.*

BRENDAN GILL

["Cul-de-Sac"] is the quintessence of fashionable, phony movie-making, and I am all the more impatient with it because of my admiration for Mr. Polanski's "Knife in the Water." . . . [In "Knife in the Water"] the test, conducted mainly in terms of a weekend sail on a remote Polish lake, gave the director an opportunity to deal with some of the oldest and most imperious emotions we know—fear, lust, rage, and jealousy—which he depicted with insouciant conviction, as if, despite their humble origins in prehistory, they were still worth paying strict attention to. The most notable thing about Polanski's ["Repulsion"] . . . was a lessening of this conviction. Like Hitchcock, and perhaps in homage to him, Polanski shifted his attention from the emotions of his characters to the emotions of his audience; he was plainly out to shock us at any cost, and the cost proved high. The heroine of "Repulsion" was a pretty girl who skittered hysterically away from any promise of a sexual relation, but we never learned why, the significant action of the movie having taken place before the movie began. Polanski cavalierly pretended to provide a clue to her madness by ending the movie with a stop-shot of a faded family photograph, in which the girl stares woebegonely out at us, already a victim. But a victim of what? Of whom? The family photograph is no "Rosebud"—indeed, it compounds the cheat of the movie by affecting to explain everything and explaining nothing. . . .

[In "Cul-de-Sac"] the lack of conviction is complete. A slick, gaudily Gothic movie, it seems bent on making our flesh creep, but not through the manipulation, however perverse, of any recognizable human emotion.

Brendan Gill, "Dead End," in The New Yorker *(© 1966 by The New Yorker Magazine, Inc.), Vol. XLII, No. 38, November 12, 1966, p. 115.*

STANLEY KAUFFMANN

[Polanski] is teaching us how to regard him. *Knife in the Water,* his fine first film, was a tight little Sartrean engine of internal forces. Since then, the horrors in his films have become much more external, at best merely entertaining. *Repulsion,* a chronicle of psychotic murders, was coolly frightening, if largely gratuitous. *Cul-de-Sac* was a far-out thriller-rag, less successful but sometimes ingenious. *The Fearless Vampire Killers,* which Polanski says was mutilated by the distributors, was an amusing idea for a *Dracula* spoof, but it completely misfired. *Rosemary's Baby* seems to settle in right where he wants to live: as a manufacturer of intelligent thrillers, clever and insubstantial. Only a director with wit could have made the witchcraft credible. Only a director with real cinematic gifts could have made a sequence like the one where Rosemary barricades herself in the apartment or the childbirth scene. Only a director satisfied with ephemera could have lavished his gifts on the whole project. (p. 85)

Stanley Kauffmann, "'Rosemary's Baby'" (originally published in The New Republic, *Vol. 158, No. 25, June 15, 1968), in his* Figures of Light: Film Criticism and Comment *(copyright © 1968, 1969, 1970 by Stanley Kauffmann; reprinted by permission of Harper & Row, Publishers, Inc.), Harper, 1971, pp. 83-5.*

HARLAN ELLISON

As a writer of fantasy, I cannot conceive of any way in which "Rosemary's Baby" could be improved. It is, for this reviewer, one of the very finest fantasy films ever made. The promise of Roman Polanski . . . remains undimmed. The talent he displayed with "Repulsion" is more controlled, more adroit, certainly more impressive here. . . .

It is the sort of film Hitchcock would be making today, had he not grown old along about "The Man Who Knew Too Much." Polanski has not taken on the Old Master's mantle, he has created his own, with the warp and woof of black magic, danger, the essence of fear and a sinister simplicity that is like all great Art—so deceptively simple looking, until one tries to take it apart and find out why it functions as well as it does, without any moving parts. (p. 41)

Polanski. Jesus, the man is good! Let me tell you a thing: in all the canon of fantasy writing, the very hardest job of all is the creation of a contemporary fantasy, using the elements of ancient myth or folklore—gnomes, witches, demonology, dragons, dryads, mermaids—in such a way that the old horrors have relevance for our times. . . . Polanski knows this. He has been constructing with his last three films a modern grimoire utilizing these ancient, dust-and-hoar-covered legends in their modern settings. And he has become a master at it. This is a task of great rigor, but Polanski has somewhichway tapped into the bubbling lava of fear down in the gut of us all. (pp. 41-2)

For those who need specific statements, who have not yet been able to grasp that this reviewer was knocked out by "Rosemary's Baby," let me conclude by saying quite boldly: this film will be looked back upon with growing recognition as the years pass. It is in every way and by every standard of critical judgment, a classic of that most intriguing of genres, the film of fear. (p. 42)

Harlan Ellison, "Film Reviews: 'Rosemary's Baby'" (©, 1968, by Spectator International, Inc.; copyright reassigned to the Author; ©, 1980, by the Kilimanjaro Corporation), in Cinema, *Vol. 4, No. 3, Fall, 1968, pp. 41-2.*

COLIN McARTHUR

[Roman Polanski's] surrealism is visceral rather than intellectual and he seems not to be aware of surrealist theory and revolutionary implications as set out in the writings of, for example, André Breton. It can be guessed from his work that the main filmic influence on him has been Buñuel. If *Two Men and a Wardrobe* is reminiscent in places of Dali's coastal deserts, it is also indebted . . . to *Los Olvidados. Repulsion,* in its presentation of a sexual obsessive and in its recurrent imagery, is the most Buñuelian of films. Indeed, it is explicitly a *hommage*.

The image behind the credits is a huge close-up of an eye with the credits moving at random across it. When the credit 'directed by Roman Polanski' comes up, it moves precisely from right to left across the centre of the eyeball, recalling the notorious opening sequence of *Un Chien Andalou* in which an eyeball is sliced by a razor. The first intimations of violence are conveyed by the juxtaposition within the frame of Carol . . . washing her legs, and her sister's lover's razor—two familiar Buñuelian images. Examples of surrealist imagery in Polanski's work could be multiplied almost indefinitely: the chicken feathers in *Mammals,* the raw meat in *Repulsion* and *Rosemary's Baby,* the white garden chair in the grave in *Cul de Sac,* plus very general surrealist traits such as his fascination with the sea with all its Freudian overtones.

A melange of influences does not of itself produce an artist, but Polanski has a good claim to be regarded as such primarily through the single-minded power of his vision. There is a strong thematic continuity in his feature films so far released in this country. All examine aspects of sexuality: *Knife in the Water* is a study of sexual rivalry, *Repulsion* of sexual disgust, and *Cul de Sac* of sexual humiliation. *Rosemary's Baby* tenses the audience with the possibility that it is a study in sexual hysteria.

Knife in the Water remains a striking first film, although in retrospect it seems Polanski's least personal work. . . . [It] shows a great deal of Polanski's strength and not a little of his weakness.

He has said that the quality which interests him most in cinema is 'atmosphere', the defining of a particular mood. This is practically a definition of what he has done so successfully in *Knife in the Water.* He sharpens the mood of potential violence with a striking array of visual and sound imagery: the initial calm of the Baltic haffs, the game the two men play with the younger man's knife, the sudden eruption of sound and movement as the boat is hauled through the reeds, the clatter of metal objects during the cooking scene, the burning of the young man's hands, the storm, the unseen fly which buzzes around the cabin—all leading up to the final violent confrontation. Polanski's sureness of touch in creating atmosphere, his ability to raise and release tension, contrasts with the playfulness, if not flippancy, of parts of the film. Critics have remarked on the Christ imagery surrounding the young man: he lies on the deck in the posture of the crucified Christ, a coil of rope making a halo behind his head, he walks on the water, he is resurrected, and so on. However, the recurrent Christ imagery in no way illuminates the central, sexual theme; and if, as has been suggested, it is part of a complex allegory on modern Poland, this must be accounted a weakness rather than a strength.

The weaknesses of *Repulsion* are few, and lack of relevance of the parts is not among them. Indeed, it is the most singleminded of Polanski's films, every element sucked into the sexual vortex at the centre. Moving outward from the central situation of the film, a young girl's disgust with sexuality and her descent into madness and violence, almost every character, relationship and situation is defined in sexual terms. . . .

Within this framework of thematic unity Polanski deploys a remarkable filmic technique, the closest analogy to which is Hitchcock's in *Psycho.* In addition to the obvious influences of that film (the recurrent eye imagery, the use of the tracking shot towards a potentially menacing area), Polanski unnerves and disorientates his audience principally in two ways. Apart from his more traditional surrealist imagery (razors, raw meat), the violent reference of which is absolutely precise, he presents other images which evoke a less precise, but none the less chilling, horror. The most striking is the image of the three buskers, one playing a banjo, the other two bent over hideously playing spoons, and all three advancing, crab-like, into the camera. More usually, Polanski offers an image which appears heavy with menace or horror and turns out to be innocent or banal, thus letting the audience, temporarily, off the hook. (p. 15)

Despite the single-mindedness of conception and Polanski's flawless technique, *Repulsion* exhibits weaknesses which are perhaps in the nature of the subject. In charting the path of a disintegrating mind, the most original sensibility would be taxed to find adequate images to convey the final stages. Inevitably, Polanski is at his most convincing depicting the early stages of Carol's collapse by subtle distortions in the visible world, the reflection of her face in a kettle, or the potatoes with ever more grotesque tentacles growing from them, the naturalism of which enhances their quality as images of a disordered mind. Where in these images the audience is aware of a whole world become sick, in the cracking walls and grasping, disembodied hands of the later stages of Carol's decline, we have no yardstick of normality and see only the ingenious products of the props department. Despite this reservation, however, *Repulsion* remains Polanski's most interesting achievement.

Compared with the tightly constructed *Repulsion, Cul de Sac* seems sprawling and formless. It would seem to have been conceived as a study of the sexual humiliation of George . . . by his young wife Teresa . . . and one of the interloping gangsters, Dickie. . . . Three key sequences underline this basic motif: the uproarious bedroom sequence in which Teresa forces George to act out her role in nightie, painted mouth and eyes, and turban; the beach sequence in which George, walking on his knees, confesses to Dickie his hopeless obsession with Teresa (this is restated in the numberless paintings he has done of her); and the sequence in which George discovers the sexual exhilaration of violence by killing Dickie. However, these sequences virtually become lost among the many unassimilated elements of the film. Of these the Pinteresque/Beckettian elements are the funniest. . . .

Despite its grave structural weaknesses, *Cul de Sac* is kept afloat by the power of its conception and, yet again, by Polanski's superb technique. What remains of *Cul de Sac* is the texture of sound and image: the phut of boat engines, the roar of a passing plane, seagulls' screams, the clucking of hens, the texture of [Teresa's] body, a decaying chair in an empty room, a blazing Jaguar.

It has been claimed that *Repulsion* holds up well as a documentary account of one kind of mental illness. *Rosemary's Baby* offers the audience the possibility that it is a study in pre-parturitional hysteria; but where in *Repulsion* the audience is certain that it is watching a mind falling apart and is disorientated by the horror of the imagery, in *Rosemary's Baby* it is disorientated by its inability to assess whether Rosemary . . . is mentally ill or whether her apparent imaginings are true. Our assessment veers from one side to another, sometimes approaching certainty that there is a witches' plot against Rosemary, at other times dismissing the apparent conjunction of events as a web spun by a hysterical girl anxious for the safety of her unborn child. This to and fro juggling of audience response is the main structural principle of the film. (p. 16)

Roman Polanski's vision is profoundly pessimistic. Exploring man's sexuality he finds humiliation, betrayal, violence and madness. It is fitting that the only birth in the Polanski canon should bring forth the child of Satan. (p. 17)

Colin McArthur, "Polanski," in Sight and Sound *(copyright © 1968 by The British Film Institute), Vol. 38, No. 1, Winter, 1968-69, pp. 14-17.*

BEVERLE HOUSTON and MARSHA KINDER

Rosemary's Baby is not merely a sophisticated horror film. The horror is only one aspect of a complex statement frightening in its relevance. Based on the novel by Ira Levin, the film remains extraordinarily faithful to its literary source. But Polanski deserves the credit for re-creating the meaning in visual terms. The film is about a girl who is trapped in a reality which she cannot believe. She must choose between not believing what appears to be real or believing what cannot be real. The irony is that in this film, Rosemary finally believes the fantastic because Polanski gives it the texture of an undeniable reality, however bizarre.

The story takes the traditional Christ myth and dresses it an its equally traditional Satanic disguise. The film's myth parallels the New Testament, with the divine figure as father of the child, Rosemary as the chosen vessel, the starting of the new era with the birth of the messiah, and the adoration of the child. It treats the myth in such a way that we are forced to accept its literal truth. Yet at the same time we the audience cannot accept what is being presented as real, because for centuries we have believed that the birth of the anti-christ is a detestable lie. Yet the film gives us evidence for its truth that is more convincing than any evidence on which Christian belief is based. The film is frightening because it forces us to examine the kinds and bases of belief. We confront the idea that the Christian myth is certainly no more believable than its mirror image, and possibly less so. And beyond this, we are also forced to realise that our mode of believing in Christianity is quite different from the one with which we perceive 'real' things. (p. 17)

[There is] a merging of competing mythologies in the film's imagery. In the extraordinarily powerful scene where Rosemary conceives the Son of Satan, there is a merging of images from at least three mythologies: Satan and the witches from the demonic, the Pope and Michelangelo's creation of Adam from traditional Christianity, and the Kennedyesque yachting captain from the modern myth of power. The images in Rosemary's dream are constantly transformed from one to the other. For example, Guy's face dissolves into the demon, and Hutch assumes the role of Pope. These mergings of the various myth figures are further complicated by three modes of reality in the scene itself. Are these images Rosemary's dream, a half-drugged waking vision, or the fantastic reality of the witches' coven? Ironically, the events which trigger the uncertain reality of Rosemary's response are just as fantastic as the images themselves. Rosemary's scream that this is real, and the marks on her body the next morning, attest to their undeniable reality. That Rosemary has responded to them with the mixing of the three myths shows their interchangeability. As modes and myths merge in these ways, the film insists that we believe or disbelieve them all. . . .

The film has forced us to face two things. First of all we claim to assign belief to our myths; yet if we do so, it is a different kind of belief than that which we assign to 'reality'. But our desire to hold belief is so powerful that under its pressure we can accept anything. (p. 19)

Beverle Houston and Marsha Kinder, "'Rosemary's Baby'," in Sight and Sound *(copyright © 1968 by The British Film Institute), Vol. 38, No. 1, Winter, 1968-69, pp. 17-19.*

ROBERT CHAPPETTA

Rosemary's Baby is a tolerably successful commercial movie, which is to say it isn't very good, and a clear disappointment to anyone who has admired—if only in part—Roman Polanski's earlier films. If it does fail as a horror film, however, it is, I think, because Polanski's main interest lies elsewhere: the humor of the film, especially the wit of the ending, makes the film worth considering. To begin with, any reasonably sophisticated person's response to the movie's ending is likely to be: but there are no witches. No effort is made to suspend your disbelief in witches; they are just a "given," a dramatic assumption never made compelling. This problem of belief is especially acute because the action of the film is here and now: the supernatural, the world of witches, is easier to believe in when it is made somehow remote, or removed from the present and the familiar, as in Henry James's *Turn of the Screw* or Murnau's *Nosferatu*. But to make the world of witches contemporary does give the tale a surface smartness, which whatever problems it raises, is a major asset of the film, an advance for Polanski over the banality of the world of *The Vampire Killers*. This very surface smartness indicates the level of the film: entertainment, not art. To use the new, the contemporary, even the avant-garde, to achieve an effect without working through the problems they raise, is the hallmark of the facile showman, the entertainer. What is wrong with *Rosemary's Baby*, however, is that these surface effects have not been used more richly and complexly to make a more successful entertainment.

Polanski's commitment to the pedestrian, pedestrianly executed, makes the film the least visually interesting of any Polanski has done. Polanski's talent, a not atypically Polish one, is for the baroque, for an oddness of the visual world, not only in decor, or angle of shot, or composition, but, as in the closing parts of *Cul-de-Sac*, in the very light itself, a crisply underlit, nondaylight world more awesome and madness-provoking than the weak, dull lighting of Bergman's *Hour of the Wolf*. . . . In *Rosemary's Baby*, the character of the material, largely the everyday-urban-real, would be negated if it were shaped in a sustained baroque style. Instead, Polanski falls back on blandness. . . . (p. 35)

In its modernization, *Rosemary's Baby* does not achieve anything comparable to the traditional gothic psychological tensions that reflect the resentments and pressures of the class system. . . . In *Rosemary's Baby*, the psychological tensions between people are a lot weaker, involving more a sense of annoyance than of menace. (p. 37)

Significantly, at the end Polanski . . . does not show us Rosemary's baby
extravagances in coincidence earlier in the film . . . established the reality of the supernatural power of the witches, here in the last scene, shorn of the final supernatural extravagance, the witches seem cut down to naturalistic size. It's as if at this point Polanski were twitting the audience for its readiness to believe in witches. . . . In the end, I seemed to be watching not so much a witch story, but a story which assumed the madness of the mass of humanity, who, with appropriate changes of names and descriptions, still believe in the prevalence of witches. (p. 38)

Robert Chappetta, "Film Reviews: 'Rosemary's Baby'," in Film Quarterly *(copyright 1969 by The Regents of the University of California; reprinted by permission of the University of California Press), Vol. XXII, No. 3, Spring, 1969, pp. 35-8.*

JOHN ALAN McCARTY

Although *Knife in the Water* actually emerges in retrospect as Polanski's least completely personal work . . . , it nevertheless does contain all that is thematically essential to him.

The expensive yacht, the beautiful young wife who shares it with him, and the private sea upon which it rides started out as status symbols which Andrzej felt compelled to attain. The film begins at that point where he has attained them and where their illusory protectiveness has created for him a private world, a world which is intruded upon by the student, and destroyed. This theme of isolation wherein the protagonist or antagonist's private world is intruded upon by strangers, a situation which always ends in some form of violence, self-destruction, or disaster is, in fact, the nucleus of all of Polanski's films. . . .

[In Polanski's films] couples are always significantly mismatched due to the neurotic obsession of one partner (or both) for his or her exact opposite, as witness the self-destructive attractions of: the intellectual George for the physical Teresa in *Cul-de-Sac,* the sexually insecure Andrzej for the self-assured Christine in *Knife in the Water,* the deeply religious and unselfish Rosemary for the agnostic and ambitious Guy in *Rosemary's Baby* all the way to the absurdly fatal pairing of the vampire killer Alfred with the Undead Anna in *The Fearless Vampire Killers.* (p. 19)

The subject of *Repulsion* is the deep and sometimes deadly relationship that exists between sex and fear.

An even more grotesque illustration of this relationship is to be found, oddly enough, in *The Fearless Vampire Killers,* a parody of the horror film genre which reveals more than a trace of Krafft-Ebing through its depiction of vampirism as a fundamentally sexual perversion. Indeed Alfred's seductive girlfriend and Count von Klocken's homosexual son . . . , each of whom use sex to ensnare blood victims, begin as parodies of a type, but wind up owing more to such real life "vampires" as Countess Elizabeth Bathory and Gilles de Rais than the fictional fiends of Bram Stoker and Sheridan LeFanu.

Although this implication does add greater thematic dimension, the strength of its bite proves ultimately lethal to the parody. Some of Polanski's gags are quite funny . . . , and yet the comedy overall suffers due to this internal conflict of approach. The finale in which the vampires rise from their tombs to come together in the castle's ballroom for a pre-conquest dance and celebration offers the best example of this conflict. As Alfred and the professor clumsily grope their way through the swirling crowd of waltzing Undead to find some route of escape, one is aware of the comic intent. But the figures of the vampires themselves dressed in moldy burial rags, their earth-gray flesh in various stages of decomposition, are nightmarish. Putting it simply, *The Fearless Vampire Killers* emerges more frightening than the kind of film it is trying to jest. . . .

[*Rosemary's Baby* is Polanski's] strongest surrealistic exercise since *Repulsion.* It also marks the first time he has based his work on already existing material. . . .

It is inevitable that an adaptation would emerge less personal than an original, but *less personal* does not mean *impersonal. Rosemary's Baby,* regardless of its origins, is a distinctly Polanskian film. While it retains all of [Ira] Levin's plot, most of his scenes, dialogue, and symbols, a close comparison of the two works reveals significant differences of intent between them. . . .

Like *Repulsion* [*Rosemary's Baby*] deals with a girl's subconscious mental conflict, in this case it is Rosemary's inner torment at being unable to reconcile her strict religious upbringing with her adult agnostic desires. Because we the audience, experience everything through Rosemary (as we did through Carol Ledoux), we also come to believe that what we are seeing is a terrifying fact ("This is no dream! This is really happening!"). But in the very last scene of the film, after Rosemary has accepted and begun to care for the demon child (the point at which the book ends), Polanski dissolves to a shot of the hotel's extreme where we see Rosemary and Guy walking hand in hand through the front entrance. It is, in fact, the same shot which began the film. What we have just been witness to was not reality, but the subconscious preliminaries to that reality—the destruction of Rosemary's soul.

This shot, however, would be no more than a meaningless trick ending were it not for the many visual correlatives that exist between Rosemary's behavior and Carol Ledoux's—a few of which are: (1) each girl's obliviousness to all but her own existence as she walks through the crowded city streets, (2) each girl's distorted view of others as she answers the door by first looking through the Juda hole, (3) and the disintegration of each girl's self-awareness when she comes across her unfamiliar reflection in a kitchen appliance.

Sex fear, too, plays an important role in Rosemary's psychological dilemma in that modern attitudes toward sex and Rosemary's desire to share them work in direct opposition to her inbred Catholicism.

The foremost criticism levelled at *Repulsion* was that it failed to deal satisfactorily with the hereditary and environmental origins of Carol's fear. In the film, Polanski places much visual emphasis on an old family portrait in the Ledoux living room which shows Carol's family gathered in the backyard of their Belgian home. Helene is kneeling at her father's side, her head resting on his knee; the mother is sitting in a chair close by; and Carol is standing behind them all alone, that same empty expression characterizing her face even as a child. Most reviewers felt, however, that while this photograph hinted at many things, it directly explained nothing, and therefore the film failed in completeness.

If this criticism were pertinent (and it is not), it could apply to the other Polanski films as well. *Cul-de-Sac* no more explains the genesis of the husband's maladjustment than does *The Fearless Vampire Killers* attempt to elucidate how its fanged predators first came to enjoy the taste of blood. And therein lie the short-comings not of Polanski, but of film critics who fail (or refuse) to study the characteristics of a filmmaker's overall work as a means toward understanding the basic intentions of each separate film.

The thematic province of Roman Polanski lies not in the causes of man's neuroses, but in the effects. (p. 20)

John Alan McCarty, "The Polanski Puzzle," in

Take One *(copyright © 1969 by Unicorn Publishing Corp.), Vol. 2, No. 5, May-June, 1969, pp. 18-21.*

LEN MASTERMAN

Though Polanski has often remarked upon the crucial importance of surrealism to his conception of the cinema, the extent of his commitment to surrealist philosophy in his feature films has never been satisfactorily examined. Indeed reviewers have tended to doubt Polanski's word and have regarded the observable surrealist elements in his major films as icing on the cake rather than as central to their conception (p. 44)

An examination of *Cul-de-Sac,* however, reveals a total commitment to the philosophy as well as the techniques of surrealism. The film's attacks on social conventions and institutions, and on logical thought processes; its veneration of the fool, the criminal, the primitive, and the insane as types who have escaped the deadening hand of social conformity; its anarchic humour and pervading ambiguity of tone; its devaluation of language as a means of communication; its stripping away of man's social persona to reveal the suffering being within; and finally its resolution of contradictions to attain what Breton called 'a kind of absolute reality'—all of these elements combine to make *Cul-de-Sac* a work whose whole *raison d'être* is inseparable from surrealist philosophy. The opening sequences of *Cul-de-Sac* serve as a brilliant exposition of the main elements of the plot, and are dominated by a landscape, which with its suggestion of freedom (open spaces) and sterility will be seen to have a thematic importance. (pp. 44-6)

The opening of *Cul-de-Sac* not only succeeds admirably in adumbrating the film's principal plot-elements, characters and images, but is stylistically characteristic of the remainder of the film. The sequences exemplify the familiar surrealist technique of divorcing characters and objects from their natural functions and normal connotations and placing them opposite one another so that new, more disturbing relationships are formed. The crashing of the car in such a deserted landscape; the very appearance of Albie, meek, soberly dressed and vulnerably peering through thick-lensed spectacles, making him resemble a bank-clerk rather than a criminal; the production of the huge unwieldy machine-gun from the small family car; the irony of Dickie —himself a professional menacer—feeling threatened as he wanders around the island; and the polite middle-class overtones of Dickie's words from the terrace, 'Anybody home? Hello! Anyone in?' coming as they do from his stock gangster-gravelled voice: all of these elements invest a familiar movie situation (wounded gangsters on the run) with a surrealist humour which constantly cheats our expectations and is from the outset part of the fabric of the film. Stylistically the opening sequences clearly establish *Cul-de-Sac* as part of the Line of Wit begun by *Un Chien Andalou.* (pp. 47-8)

The humour of *Cul-de-Sac* . . . is surreal in both method (illogical juxtapositionings) and intent (attacking social conventions, conformity, and logical thought). Here we may observe a third surrealist quality, closely connected with the other two, and one which will become increasingly evident during the remainder of the film: its ambiguous tone. There have already been hints of this in the film so far, though we may scarcely have been conscious of them. Our laughter has principally been derived from two sources. Firstly from our observance of George's failure to make the structures he has erected and upon which his life is built—his relationship with his wife, his fortress home, his money, his army reputation—work for him in any meaningful way. The comedy is transformed however, as we come to terms with its implications: for the structures represent George's unsuccessful attempts to conceal the meaninglessness of his existence. Secondly we are laughing at the expense of George's quite genuine terror. But it is not until we see George forced to drink alcohol . . . or Dickie shovel soil on George as he stands in Albie's grave, that we begin to recognize that we are witnessing one of the harshest of human realities, a situation in which the strong preys upon the weak and there is, in Hobbes' words, 'continual fear, and danger of violent death; and the life of man, solitary, poor, nasty, brutish, and short'. *Cul-de-Sac* constantly reminds us of Pinter's statement that 'tragedy is . . . *No longer funny.* It is funny, and then it becomes no longer funny'. (pp. 51-2)

Len Masterman, "'Cul-de-Sac': Through the Mirror of Surrealism," in Screen *(© The Society for Education in Film and Television 1970), Vol. 11, No. 6, November-December, 1970, pp. 44-60.*

RAYMOND DURGNAT

[*The Fat and the Lean* is a cynical slapstick tragedy that] evokes not only Samuel Beckett, but Hal Roach, and one thinks briefly of various American clowns: Laurel and Hardy, for the fat man bullying the thin one, Chaplin, for Polanski's fey, nimble pathos, Harold Lloyd, for the ingenuity of his eager-beaver attempts to please. If one hesitates to align the film alongside the great two-reel comedies (or early Tati), it's on account of spiritual and cinematic finesses, after which words can only clumsily grope. (p. 96)

It remains a deft, corrosive little parable on the theme of dominance absurdly accepted, of the volunteered slavery which is so paradoxical yet pervasive a feature of human society. In 1961 several critics wondered whether Katelbach represented a bourgeois capitalist or a communist bureaucrat, or both, or neither. In 1971 one thinks more easily of the Marcusian thesis, that in modern technological society, man is ostentatiously given freedom so that he will enthusiastically overfulfill the duties which make him a slave, and banish even dreams of escape (which, ironically, is from this rural Arcady to our office block world). To parody Rousseau: 'Man is born free; yet everywhere he chooses chains.' The co-ordinates of dominance and submission recur in Polanski's work, like the name Katelbach and the director's own role as an ingenuously trusting assistant. In one film after another Polanski plays with a virtuosity sometimes hilarious, sometimes sinister, on the pervasiveness of masochism, self-frustration and some equivalent of suicide, as much in complacency, murder and the master role as in hysterics and victims. . . .

[*The Fat and the Lean* is] certainly an early demonstration of Polanski's continuing gift for finding the common ground between apparently unlinkable genres (avantgarde tragedy and two-reel comedy) and parodying in a way which, far from being pastiche, is spiritually valid in its own right. There remains a subtle, perhaps finally unimportant, streak of the child prodigy, or eternal student, commenting on adult absurdities with devastating accuracy, yet lacking a certain depth of common experience. (p. 100)

Raymond Durgnat, "Reviews: 'The Fat and the Lean'" (© copyright Raymond Durgnat 1971; reprinted with permission), in Films and Filming, *Vol. 17, No. 8, May, 1971, pp. 96, 100.*

VERNON YOUNG

Roman Polanski's *Macbeth* [is] all but the worst Shakespeare ever filmed. If it wasn't as Now as Tony Richardson's *Hamlet* or as West-Side-Storyish as Zeffirelli's *Romeo and Juliet* . . . it was more blatant than either and distilled even less poetry, verbal or visual. (p. 170)

Polanski's setting is a panoramic slaughter-house in which the language is only impedimenta unreasonably holding up the "action." When, in a brief intercut moment, Banquo observes, "It will be rain tonight," and the murderer, felling him with a blow, remarks, "Let it come down," the director should cry, "Cut!—and print it!" To extend this encounter to a prolonged combat and knifings in the creekbed, like a Western sequence, is to dissipate hopelessly the terse irony of that inspired figure of speech. All the way, this film gets further and further out instead of driving steadily inward to the lining of the metaphor and the interior castle.

Why? Because Polanski and Kenneth Tynan, friends and partners in mischief and obscenity, were trading on the vogue for porno and spilled guts. . . . The few admirably directed minutes were those when Macduff, learning that his wife and children have been put to the sword, is unable to express instant wrath. Would that many others in the production had shared his restraint. (pp. 170-71)

Macbeth and *The Godfather* have much in common: in each the continuity is monomaniacal and accordion-pleated: murder, counter-murder, counter-counter-murder . . . ; in each a father-figure is to be avenged and the "hero" morally consents to be led by "witches" into an empire of the jackal and the werewolf. . . . If *The Godfather* has no verbal music to compensate for its unrelieved (but versatile) emphasis on assault and battery, decapitation and detonation, neither has *Macbeth* when, as I have pointed out, the words are mere obstructions to a wide-screen brawl. (p. 171)

Vernon Young, "Fat Shakespeare, Fat City, Lean Wilderness," in The Hudson Review *(copyright © 1973 by The Hudson Review, Inc.; reprinted by permission), Vol. XXVI, No. 1, Spring, 1973, pp. 170-76.**

NORMAND BERLIN

[With Roman Polanski's screen version of Shakespeare's *Macbeth,* we] may wish to regret that tragedy has become melodrama, that the camera has replaced the word, and that Shakespeare's play has been reduced both morally and metaphysically. But these regrets should not blind us to the virtues of the film, not only its energy and visual excitement, but its value as an interpretation of Shakespeare. How Polanski sees (or reads) *Macbeth* indicates the rich suggestiveness of Shakespeare's art; it also indicates Polanski's personal vision of the modern world. (p. 291)

[To illustrate] Polanski's use of Shakespeare, I would like to examine a specific poetic image in Shakespeare which becomes a visual sequence in Polanski. Hearing that Birnam Wood is coming to Dunsinane, ready to face his doom, Shakespeare's Macbeth utters these words: "They have tied me to a stake, I cannot fly / But bearlike I must fight the course." The reference here is to the sport of bearbaiting, much enjoyed by the Elizabethans, in which a bear, tied to a post by a long rope or chain, tries to retaliate against four or five large dogs who attack the bear. Shakespeare often uses the image in his plays, and here in *Macbeth* it perfectly suits a rugged bearlike Macbeth who realizes he is tied (the inevitability of tragedy) and soon to be attacked, but bravely faces his end. The poetic quality of Shakespeare's image is lost in Polanski's film, but its cinematic potentiality is fully exploited. In the banquet scene, when we see Macbeth as king and where we expect to find good cheer and merriment, as part of the entertainment a bear is brought in, chained to a stake (with Polanski giving us a single shot of the iron ring that holds the chain, forcing us to recall the ring that is a crown) and attacked by yelping mastiffs. We witness the bearbaiting for a few seconds before the camera moves to Macbeth talking to the murderers and then to the confrontation of Macbeth with the gory apparition of Banquo. After the banquet, which ends in disorder, the dead and bloodied bear and two of the dogs are seen dragged along the halls of the castle, a cinematic epiphany of violence in a Macbethian world. Shakespeare's poetic image at the end of his play becomes a visual image in the film's middle, allowing us to witness the condition of the world and foreshadowing the end of Macbeth, another bear tied to his own stake because of his murders, his ambition, his wife, and his mystical ties with those juggling fiends, the witches. Here is a perfect example, I think, of the rich suggestiveness of Shakespeare's art providing an intelligent director with a perfect cinematic image and idea.

Roman Polanski's *Macbeth,* although its form distorts Shakespeare and exploits Shakespeare's melodramatic side, is a valid modern interpretation of Shakespeare's play. Bloody, violent, unremitting in its horror, the film presents a vision of a world filled with confusions and madness, a world in which both brave Macbeth and limping Donalbain will always seek Satanic ties, a world containing only bears and dogs, a world where tomorrows are as brutal as todays. His filmic interpretation of Shakespeare's *Macbeth* allows Polanski to present a comment on our time. What seems to be his personal obsession with violence . . . has been objectified in an energetic piece of cinematic art. (pp. 297-98)

Normand Berlin, "'Macbeth': Polanski and Shakespeare," in Literature/Film Quarterly *(© copyright 1973 Salisbury State College), Vol. 1, No. 4, Fall, 1973, pp. 291-98.*

BEA ROTHENBUECHER

In *What?* Polanski again proves his sensitivity as an artist by giving us an ambiguous satire of life today, using sex as a metaphor for our lost sense of innocence. He makes full use of the new candor to push back the boundaries of cinema. . . . [But] his film is not about sex. It is about the abuse of sex. . . .

[Far] from being Hefnerian in its philosophy, *What?* is distinctly European in its origins. Its nakedness—the [American] girl's vulnerability—is completely appropriate to the absurd world of Franz Kafka, Samuel Beckett and others who have influenced Polanski. (p. 1179)

In the hands of Polanski, [Hugh] Griffith, who has made a career of playing the lecher, refines his role to a new pitch. And Polanski achieves an unusual juxtaposition of youth and age—life and death—and does it with great sensitivity.

Polanski manages to avoid ugly explicitness. When he has a couple making love on the floor, he places them under a large bedcover made of ostrich feathers. The effect is so bizarre that it distracts from the act itself, turning it into a satirical abstraction. Polanski as artist distances the viewer from the physical.

Although *What?* is concerned with the life style of a certain "chic" segment of society, Polanski makes clear that he is showing us a decadence symptomatic of our world. The lush Italian setting is perfect for the goings-on, but they could as well take place on the French Riviera or in any other "favored" locale. Polanski conveys his point of view with style and visual beauty. Unlike Bertolucci's *Last Tango in Paris,* Polanski's film presents its sexual material sensuously and with a certain good humor. The subject is serious but its treatment is not dead serious—an approach to sex that Americans find difficult to accept. . . .

What? is ironic, subtle, strangely surreal—ambiguous. The meaning of a contemporary Alice's adventures on the other side of the looking glass will depend pretty much on the viewer, and on whether he or she can believe in the survival of innocence in a depraved world. (p. 1180)

Bea Rothenbuecher, "'What?' Is Polanski Saying?" in The Christian Century *(copyright 1973 Christian Century Foundation; reprinted by permission from the November 28, 1973 issue of* The Christian Century*), Vol. XC, No. 43, November 28, 1973, pp. 1179-80.*

JAN DAWSON

The credit titles for Polanski's *What?* are in the form of signatures in a lined exercise book; and as the movie progresses and hindsight improves, they assume an increasing appropriateness. For despite its erratic moments of brilliance, the overall impression left by the film is of a rather puerile graffito scrawled in the margins of its literary antecedents. On the one hand, the pornographic tradition . . . of the violation of the perennially innocent; on the other, the more singular eccentricities of *Alice in Wonderland* whose best known incidents Polanski deliberately evokes. . . . In one sense, the two poles are not so very far apart: 'classical' pornography was the black-humoured expression of serious philosophical concerns, and one could argue that the prim product of the Victorian nursery provides the missing link between the elegant libertinism of the eighteenth century and the scatological permissiveness of the twentieth. They are none the less separated by the fact that the violated virgin has always been the vehicle for exploring the predominance of evil over good and for exposing various contemporary social hypocrisies, whereas the butts of Carroll's humour are more abstract and intellectual: the supposition of a relationship between cause and effect, and of a logically ordered universe; the concept of time itself. It takes a Colossus of Buñuel's stature to bestride the two, and this—on the present evidence—Polanski is not. His sexual notations and his surrealism remain (except for such occasional felicitious details as the heroine's blue leg) obdurately separate, and even detract from one another. The assorted huffings and puffings of the different species of the sexuawly obsessed are too literally rendered to sit easily with his featherweight reflections about the nature of time and the deceptiveness of the *déjà-vu:* his characters have too much density to convince us that they are mere figments of the troubled imagination, yet too little substance to impose themselves as individuals. (p. 95)

Jan Dawson, "'Che?' ('What?')," in Monthly Film Bulletin *(copyright © The British Film Institute, 1974), Vol. 41, No. 483, May, 1974, pp. 94-5.*

FRED KAPLAN

Chinatown has been praised to the heavens by almost all the critics and it's not difficult to see why. It is precisely the sort of film that apolitical (or pseudo-political) aesthetes would flip for. It presents politics as strictly an Evil Man's field of action. The Big Daddy in this thing has even committed incest, that's how Evil he is! Also laid out is that reassuring notion that politics is all too complicated, mysterious and even mystical for any of Us to understand. The political scandal and the incestuous scandal are, in fact, equated: the whole scene is beyond sense, completely irrational, utterly Evil. We are all controlled by a handful of Bad Guys and there's nothing We can do about it. . . . [It's] inspiring to literary-intellectuals who can cite Blake, Beckett and other trade-heroes in confirming that, (sigh) yes, there is nothing that one can do, the world is evil, so let us retreat into our blissful Art and Cinemah where only Beauty reigns.

There is no sense of political dynamics here, no sign of struggle or complexity (contrary to the event on which the film is loosely based, contrary, in fact, to any political phenomenon); there is virtually no historic, social, or any other sort of context. But this doesn't matter to grubby thieves like Polanski. He doesn't care. He's interested in titillating a crowd and making dough. (pp. 38-9)

He has made a technically impressive film but, ultimately, Polanski is on unfamiliar ground and, instead of attempting to explore the issues in any meaningful way, has simply decided to rub everyone's nose into as big a cosmic mess as he can drum up. As a result, he is doing nothing but exploiting a volatile public mood: a mood of anxiety, of paranoia, of dread and suspicion about politics, oil deals, and the like. These sentiments are, in good part, justified, as far as sentiments go. But what a film-maker (as opposed to a mere technician) would, or should, do, is to shape these sentiments, inform them, expand and direct them somewhere, illuminating roots of problems. (p. 39)

Fred Kaplan, "Film Reviews: 'Chinatown'," in Cinéaste *(copyright © 1974 by Gary Crowdus), Vol. VI, No. 3, Autumn, 1974, pp. 38-9.*

DAVID ELLIOTT

Chinatown is one of the most beautiful films ever made. It might not be art—that depends on your definition—but it is an object of beauty beyond all question. . . .

[Robert Altman's] *The Long Goodbye* may have defined the excitement [of the detective story], but *Chinatown* defines the values. (p. 44)

[Polanski] steers the story along so seductively, preparing us for every twist and shock so adroitly, that we are surprised and delighted to find that something this old-fashioned can still work so well. Remember the well-made story? Here it is again.

What's new is the atmosphere, which captures the '30s better than most '30s movies. This is the dark side of California we know from the books of [Ross] Macdonald and Raymond Chandler, but given a new burnish of style. . . .

For years Polanski has been prowling over the landscape of evil like a man who had discovered a new continent; he brings to the theme a fresh excitement no other director can match, at times jabbing deep (as in *Knife in the Water*), at times having fun (*Rosemary's Baby*), in his sinister way. Except for a few spry touches, *Chinatown* lacks the high-rolling humor of *The Maltese Falcon* and *The Long Goodbye,* but it has a feel for corruption and rot so convincing that it almost wraps up the subject.

Others have looked just as deep into the fens and bogs of American life—Orson Welles in his film *A Touch of Evil,* Mike Royko in his book *Boss*—but *Chinatown* makes the feeling of it crawl over your soul. . . .

The story finally turns on the oldest taboo in the world—incest—and Polanski asserts that the "real mystery" of the film is this private tragedy, this evil so offensive that people are wounded just thinking about it. It does give the film a terrific kicker, and maybe nothing less repellent would do the job. But Polanski still has a tendency to rely on shock, and—as in some of the Ross Macdonald stories—you feel that ancestral evil is being shot into the plot with a grease-gun, to lubricate melodrama.

And yet *Chinatown*—the title is a metaphor for corruption so deep that even a man like Gittes finds it hard to imagine—sums up the oppression that many people feel about modern life. . . . (p. 45)

David Elliott, "Film Reviews: 'Chinatown'," in Film Heritage *(copyright 1974 by F. A. Macklin), Vol. 10, No. 1, Fall, 1974, pp. 44-6.*

WAYNE D. McGINNIS

The moral climate of the U.S. has for some time been ripe for a work of art along the lines of the wasteland motif, the country plagued by its own ruler. . . . [With] Roman Polanski's outstanding film, *Chinatown,* an important segment of popular culture has fulfilled what might truly be called a need. . . .

The moral impact of *Chinatown* suggests another inspiration besides the modern detective story, a "detective story" of universal significance. Sophocles' *Oedipus Rex,* a work that itself uses a familiar story or cliché as framework. (p. 249)

The basic idea behind the comparison . . . lies in the atmosphere of decay that predominates in both works. There is an allusion in *Chinatown* with its 30's setting to . . . "the decadence of the 70's." . . . *Oedipus Rex,* too, alludes to a sterility of moral values in its own era, although the play symbolizes the drift in public life more subtly than the film. . . . *Oedipus Rex,* then, was staged in much the same sort of malaise it imitates in its action, and *Chinatown* is being shown in a decade which it alludes to as vastly corrupt. Polanski has simply emphasized the "badness" of the Oedipus figure, the corrupt ruler Noah Cross.

But Polanski has also split the Oedipus figure: the person in *Chinatown* who mirrors the "good" Oedipus, trying to figure out the source of the corruption, is the cool and suavely self-assured detective, Jake Gittes. Here again, the parallel with *Oedipus Rex* is striking. In confronting the web of evil perpetrated by [Noah] Cross, Gittes is reasonable and shrewd, the mock sophisticate detective. Yet the incest committed by Cross is essentially beyond his understanding, and the unfathomable aspect of human perversity is underscored thereby. Shortly before the climactic scene in Los Angeles' Chinatown in which Cross is reunited with his daughter/granddaughter, he tells Gittes concerning his incest, "Most people don't have to face the fact that at the right time and the right place, they're capable of anything." This is the climactic line and the core of the film. . . . Gittes is the Oedipus whose success, to use the words of Cleanth Brooks and Robert B. Heilman, "has tended to blind [him] to possibilities which pure reason fails to see." The incest touch is a masterful stroke in *Chinatown,* complicating as it does the political overtones and striking at the root of the human potential for evil and perversity. (p. 250)

The triumph of works like *Oedipus Rex*—or *Chinatown*—is that they, through displaying inevitable human weakness, whether in utter guilt or guiltlessness—or both at once—call on the deepest responses of the imagination. (p. 251)

Wayne D. McGinnis, "'Chinatown': Roman Polanski's Contemporary Oedipus Story," in Literature/Film Quarterly *(© copyright 1975 Salisbury State College), Vol. 3, No. 3, Summer, 1975, pp. 249-51.*

JOHN SIMON

There is scarcely a more depressing case in movies than that of Roman Polanski. A filmmaker of considerable talent and not just bad but downright repellent taste, he could well have become a major artist had he remained in his native Poland. Polanski, a naughty little fellow with bizarre preoccupations, desperately needs Big Brother to watch over him. Polish censorship provided him with just such a restraining superego, and never did curtailing of an artist's freedom yield more salutary results. His single Polish feature, *Knife in the Water* (1962), and the best of his Polish shorts, *Two Men and a Wardrobe* (1958), are original and pungent achievements, quite possibly major works. In these films, his taste for the perverse in life and (as he sees it) nature is confined within the boundaries of suggestion, saving him from his bent for grossness.

These early films contained also a certain amount of social criticism—Polanski's resentment of Communist restrictions on human and artistic self-expression—and this, too, happily deflected some of his attention from his favorite topic: sexual kinkiness, sometimes laced with supernatural overtones, though only as pretexts for greater sexual outrageousness. Yet even into these early Polish works Polanski could sneak references to his scabrous or obscene predilections; thus *When Angels Fall* (1959) takes place in a public latrine. His first Western work, a short called *The Fat and the Skinny* [or *The Fat and the Lean*], was already an outright piece of sadomasochism under its Beckettian veneer.

It is useful to recall how Polanski's faults were often transmuted by overindulgent fans and deluded reviewers into shining virtues. When his first Western feature, *Repulsion* (1965) came out, many serious critics were impressed by the fact that this study of a murderous female psychopath devoted little or no attention to why the girl got that way. . . . To me, the film was just one sensational effect after another, however occasionally brilliant; without psychoanalytical or some other form of humanistic insight, there was no human interest; without prime concern for human motivation, the violence of the film was as senseless as a mass murder, and just as inartistic. . . .

[*Cul-de-Sac* struck me as odious, as did *Rosemary's Baby*], despite scattered touches of dazzling dexterity. Quite aside from all other considerations, these films were so sensationalistic and exploitative that there was very little room for art in them. (p. 66)

[When Polanski made his quirky and overbrutal version of *Macbeth*], it was interesting to find Pauline Kael speculating on that excess of lovingly dwelt-on ferocity as an attempt to exorcise the memory of personal tragedy [the murder of Polanski's wife, Sharon Tate]. It seemed to me that Miss Kael was putting the cart before the horse; Polanski's by then legendary "unconventionality" seemed to be at the root of things, rather than some almost fortuitous consequence, a theory that appeared to gain confirmation by Polanski's electing to play the sadistic little punk in *Chinatown*. Yet with that film Polanski redeemed himself in part even for the deeply rotten *What?* that had preceded it, in which his appetite for kinky filmmaking, unmitigated by any artistry, reached its apogee.

Chinatown, however, was different: of all Polanski's later films it most closely resembled *Knife in the Water*. There was much criminal evil suffused through the movie, along with quite a lot of psychic cruelty; but it was all kept in check by wit and understatement, even by a certain kind of gutter romanticism, all of which may have been contributed by the screenplay of Robert Towne. . . . Though not quite a work of art, *Chinatown* comes close to being one in its best moments: it is, in any case, a well-made film, which is nothing to sneeze at, and shows no signs of sloppiness except for a few final improbabilities conveniently glossed over by good acting.

It is thus all the more surprising how thoroughly sloppy *The Tenant* . . . has turned out to be, even granted that he is reunited with his scenaristic nemesis, Gérard Brach. As always in Polanski's worst pictures, something that looks very much like stupidity takes over, though it may be nothing more than near-total lack of interest in whatever merely leads up to the kinky and maniacal sequences, the film's true *raison d'être*. We are given here the utterly improbable story of Trelkovsky, a little Parisian office worker of Polish origin who, for no convincing reason, rents expensively a small, dismal apartment without so much as a toilet to it on the top floor of a respectable-looking house, whose owner, concierge, and tenants, however, seem to be, at the very least, unappetizing, if not downright monstrous. (pp. 66-7)

[Even] technically the film is not well made. Thus Trelkovsky's fantasies are shot so explicitly and naïvely as to lose their chance at scariness. Some of them are holdovers from *Repulsion*, like that arm and hand coming out of nowhere; others are just too funny to be frightening. (p. 68)

John Simon, "Untenable Tenant," in New York *Magazine (copyright © 1976 by News Group Publications, Inc.; reprinted with the permission of* New York *Magazine), Vol. 9, No. 26, June 28, 1976, pp. 66-8.*

PENELOPE GILLIATT

"The Tenant" is no piece of whimsey about drag. It is a serious, exact film about the ache of exile. Exile from country. Exile from gender. Exile from the person whom others recognize as the self but whom the self, at times of extreme self-questioning or torment, can find quite foreign. It is a study of a man who, though small, feels he is a nuisance even to furniture. An occasional table, to his way of thinking, deserves courtesy and maneuver. He feels he is even more of an obstruction in the presence of people, and seems apologetic for his short unfurnished tenancy on his life. . . .

"The Tenant" has quite left behind the ethic of cool and the intent to shock which Polanski seemed to hanker after in his last few movies. It goes back to the days of "Knife in the Water" and "Cul-de-Sac." Trelkovsky is very Slav. There is a subtext of powerful humor and longing under every scene of the hero's, however much the film seems superficially to be a horror-thriller. It is a record of the sensibility of a man's tenancy of himself: a man about to be evicted, tinkling the bead curtains for a view of enemy officials, never sure that he is the certified leaseholder of the body he occupies. As in Dostoevski, and in Kafka, imaginary fears are matched uncannily by real forces. Bureaucracy enters with a warrant; the accused person admits to the required crime. "The Tenant" is a poetic nightmare about punishment imposed on an unguilty man who merely entertained great fear of guilt. (p. 62)

Penelope Gilliatt, "Only a Lodger," in The New Yorker *(© 1976 by The New Yorker Magazine, Inc.), Vol. 41, No. 20, July 5, 1976, pp. 62-3.**

MARTIN AMIS

The first hour of *The Tenant* could have gone on to become Polanski's most telling study to date of mental imbalance. Neurosis, anyway, *is* banal; and it is often wincingly funny: the nauseous cowering with which the neurotic reacts to the huff-and-puff of daily life can, as Polanski shows, make for a very intimate kind of dramatic irony. . . . Polanski's most sophisticated look at the horror genre was in the comedy *Dance of the Vampires*, where the conventions were reversed: frightful things are happening all about you, if only you'd turn the right way. In *The Tenant*, as to some extent in *Cul de Sac*, *Repulsion* and *Rosemary's Baby*, the baseless fears of distraught minds, once established, are abruptly given vulgar, tangible shape in the observed world. Psychosis is replaced by skull-football: this is the real banality behind a director who never quite dares to trust his wit. (p. 287)

Martin Amis, "Socket to Her," in New Statesman *(© 1976 The Statesman & Nation Publishing Co. Ltd.), Vol. 97, No. 2371, August 27, 1976, pp. 286-87.**

JONATHAN ROSENBAUM

Ever since *Knife in the Water*, [Roman Polanski's] career has largely gravitated round the problem of reconciling certain formal interests with the more 'saleable' sides of his artistic persona (principally black humour and a taste for Grand Guignol). It is significant that *What?*, the film where his formal concerns are probably most evident, might well be the least critically and commercially successful of his efforts to date; if satire, according to George S. Kaufman, is what closes in New Haven, formalism in 'mainstream' cinema can't even hope for an East Orange preview unless it sneaks in under another label, usually stylistic or thematic. In the case of Polanski, this taboo seems to have brought about a kind of schizophrenia no less troubling than some of his disordered characters—a sense of cross-purposes that finally splits *The Tenant* into virtually dissociated sections.

Film No. 1, roughly the first half, exhibits Polanski's formalist side, above all in its accumulation of *partis pris* and its ambiguous treatment of 'objective' facts and subjective states of mind. As in *What?*, many of these factors can be located in the soundtrack. The water dripping from Trelkovsky's kitchen tap, the rattle of pipes, the squeak of his cupboard door, the repetitive piano exercises heard from the stairway, the faint cooing of pigeons in the courtyard and the angry pounding of the neighbour upstairs all outline the space of a constricted consciousness; while the latter—always provoked by the sounds made in Trelkovsky's flat—draws particular attention to this register of awareness. And when Trelkovsky turns from cooking to answer an apparent knock at the door—only to find no one there—one may well wonder whether or not one *did* hear a knock. . . . Comparable uncertainties are created in visual terms: is the blonde girl Trelkovsky glimpses at the funeral the crippled daughter of his persecuted neighbour Mme. Gaderian . . . , whom we see later? Is her later appearance also an illusion —which is suggested when Mme. Dioz . . . , her mother's persecutor, flatly states that Mme. Gaderian has a son, not a daughter? At what stage do the strange appearances of figures standing in the toilet across from Trelkovsky's window stop being mysteries and start becoming hallucinations?

If Film No. 1 is largely devoted to posing such questions in the form of brilliant notations, Film No. 2—by establishing that the hero has gone mad—laboriously proceeds to answer others. A cut from Trelkovsky grasping his own throat to Mme. Dioz attempting to strangle him clearly labels the second shot as a hallucination; and countless other juxtapositions between real and imagined torments lead one straight into the clinical context of *Repulsion*. To put it as crudely as the film does, this is the kind of violence that audiences pay to see, with 'reality' and 'imagination' slotted into separate compartments so that one can watch the hero's agony from a safe voyeuristic distance. There is, to be sure, a moralistic point implied in much of this: the 'unexplained' ransacking of Trelkovsky's flat is later echoed by his own ransacking of Stella's flat in a paranoiac rage, suggesting that victims eventually take on the behaviour of their persecutors. And when, for instance, Trelkovsky flees to a hotel and gazes out of a window, where he and we see two workmen who *might* be looking up at him, the earlier terms of the film are briefly allowed to reverberate. But by this time it is too late: after Trelkovsky has gradually gone through the process of *becoming* Simone—even dressing up as a woman, and eventually jumping twice in succession from the same window—the see-sawing movement between 'truth' and 'illusion' has become too mechanical for either to carry much conviction. And when Polanski ends with a paraphrase of the previous hospital scene—Trelkovsky (apparently) encased like a mummy in bandages, looking up at Trelkovsky and Stella, then screaming while the camera zooms towards his mouth —formal interest has shrunk to the level of stylistic pirouette, and ambiguity becomes just the other side of apathy.

Jonathan Rosenbaum, "Film Reviews: 'The Tenant'," in Sight and Sound *(copyright © 1976 by The British Film Institute), Vol. 45, No. 4, Autumn, 1976, p. 253.*

ANDREW SARRIS

[*The Fearless Vampire Killers* (1967), an] absurdist spoof of *Dracula,* may still be as much ahead of its time as it was 13 years ago. . . . Whatever may be said about Polanski—and even his admirers have never mistaken him for Albert Schweitzer—he cannot be accused of hypocrisy. . . .

Polanski's films have always contained too much undigested clinical material for my taste, and he has never seemed capable of fashioning a coherently absurdist vision of the world. Consequently, he has been commercially successful on the megabucks level only when he has been working with, around, and under genre conventions in *Rosemary's Baby* and *Chinatown*. He has been modestly successful also with a pseudosociological exercise, *Knife in the Water,* and a pseudopsychoanalytical exercise, *Repulsion*. But when he has gone over the deep end with less conventionally structured efforts such as *Cul-de-Sac, What?* and *The Tenant,* critics and audiences, myself included, have forsaken him. In these comparatively uninhibited projects the sourness of his sensibility turns unendurably rancid as the pockmarks of nastiness begin to spread over the screen.

Yet who else but a first-hand acquaintance of the Holocaust in Poland during his childhood would dare present a Jewish vampire completely impervious to the barriers established since time immemorial by the brandishing of a cross? And who else but Polanski would have the comic insight to satirize the aristocratic posturings of vampires by packing them into a ballroom of dusty shabbiness? Still, if one is determined to detest Polanski at all costs, one can detect unmistakable tendencies toward sexism, misogyny, and homophobia in all his films. One can charge him even with exuding evil from every pore of his art. But no one has ever been able to accuse him of retreating into the kind of sanctimonious conformism that seems to be coming back into fashion out in Los Angeles. . . . [What] Hollywood can never forgive in Polanski are not his actions, but rather his dangerous habit as an artist of turning his camera on the dung heap itself without regard to the sensitivities of the Hollywood Babywonians attired in missionary costumes for their public.

I have not seen Polanski's treatment of *Tess of the D'-Urbervilles,* but I hope that it brings him back into the mainstream of filmmaking where his uncompromisingly cynical temperament is now sorely needed. In the meantime, *The Fearless Vampire Killers* provides a very lively reminder of his unique talents as a poetic gargoyle of the cinema.

Andrew Sarris, "Where Have All the Genres Gone?" in The Village Voice *(reprinted by permission of* The Village Voice; *copyright © News Group Publications, Inc., 1980), Vol. XXV, No. 14, April 7, 1980, p. 37.**

Satyajit Ray

1921-

Indian director, scriptwriter, critic, author, and composer.

Ray is the only Indian director to date to gain prominence in the Western world. His humanistic themes have earned him a small but enthusiastic following among intellectuals worldwide, while his films invariably retain Indian settings and situations. Ray's films explore the transitional state of Indian society and the resulting moral implications, and Ray's sympathy toward Old World values is rarely disguised.

When Ray studied fine arts at Tagore University, he wrote scenarios and saw as many films as possible. Working as an art director, he was sent to London in 1950, where he saw films almost daily and talked with many film critics. One film which particularly influenced Ray was Vittorio De Sica's *The Bicycle Thief,* in which human problems are graphically portrayed in natural settings. Back in Calcutta, Ray met Jean Renoir, who was then filming *The River,* and who encouraged Ray in his dream of filming *Pather Panchali,* a popular book in India. With virtually no financial backing, and using nonprofessional actors, Ray finished the film, but only after three years and several interruptions. Unlike most escapist Indian films, *Pather Panchali* employed the neorealist aspects Ray had found fascinating in De Sica and Renoir, and Ray achieved overnight success as a director as a result of its style and humanist themes. *Pather Panchali* won the grand prize at the Cannes Film Festival in 1956, and Ray gained a following among educated Indians and Western intellectuals.

Although Ray had not originally planned to film a trilogy, he saw the logical possibilities of following the development of his hero, Apu, and released *Aparajito* in 1957 and *Apur Sansar (The World of Apu)* in 1959. *Aparajito* was not as successful with the public as *Pather Panchali,* but *Apur Sansar* is generally regarded as a fine conclusion to the trilogy, showing clearly Ray's growing mastery of filmmaking.

Ray's later films are considered uneven, and critics are divided concerning the effectiveness of his portrayal of transition in Indian society. However, Ray branched out into other areas besides neorealism: *Devi (The Goddess)* has a particular focus on women's roles in society through a rather fantastical plot; *Kanchenjunga* is Ray's first color film, and also the first film for which he wrote the musical score (music is an aspect of major importance in all of Ray's films); *Gopi Gyne Bagha Byne (The Adventures of Goopy and Bagha)* is a musical fantasy, and Ray's most popular film in India; *Days and Nights in the Forest* is an expansion on the themes evident in the Apu trilogy; *Company Limited* is a detective thriller with political overtones; and *Distant Thunder* takes the political themes further, leading to much controversy as to its worth as a work of art.

Many critics find Ray's films boring or old-fashioned as a result of their lack of inventive plot. However, Ray considers plot less important than precise dramatization and characterization. He emphasizes in his actors the need for improvisation, naturalness, and spontaneity in order to portray effectively his themes and characters. He refuses to work outside of India, preferring the natural settings of his native land. Although his films are not popular successes in his own country and are not widely distributed in the United States, Ray's themes and methods of creating his films have established him as a major artist throughout the world.

GUIDO ARISTARCO

The influences of the Italian cinema on Satyajit Ray are quite clear. [*Aparajito* (*The Unconquered*)] . . . confirms the significance of the two influences we perceived two years ago at Cannes in *Pather panchali* (*The Song of the Road*), the first episode of the trilogy: first, the Zavattini and De Sica of *Bicycle Thief* and *The Children Are Watching Us* . . . , and, second, the lyric documentary quality of Flaherty and of the Renoir of *The River*. But Ray's "universities"—in the Gorkian sense—are wider and more extensive. . . .

Aparajito is not, in fact, the story of a maternal love, of a mother who sees the withdrawal of the object of her love, but a story, or, better, part of a story, of greater scope and views: it represents a portion of the "human comedy" of modern India. Ray's artistic method . . . is descriptive rather than narrative . . . and uncertainties of cinematic language are discernible here and there, though moments of great poetry are not lacking and there is an extremely apposite sound track in which music assumes a creative character in expressing situations and feelings. The final shot of Apu seated under the centuries-old tree, with its roots almost out of the ground, is unforgettable in its implied and expressed meanings: the mother is dead but there remains in the son the certainty of his having chosen the right road. (p. 9)

Guido Aristarco, "Three Tendencies: A Postscript to the Venice Film Festival," in Film Culture *(copyright 1957 by* Film Culture*), Vol. III, No. 5, December, 1957, pp. 7-9.**

DOUGLAS McVAY

Apart from suggesting an echo of the end of *Grapes of Wrath* in the closing compositions of *Pather Panchali,* I'd prefer to turn to one or two allegations of amateurism levelled against Ray—notably Paul Dehn's objection to the 'elementary' use in *Panchali* of long tracking shots. To me these shots are often among the most magical moments of the picture: the children pursuing the sweet-seller, the train sequence, or Apu running after Durga across the fields when they have quarrelled over the toy-box. And how many magical moments there are! . . .

[One can find nothing] amateurish in the visuals, the grey soft-dwelling close-ups and misty, luminous landscapes. Subrata Mitra may never have handled a camera before, but Ray has inspired him, just as he must have inspired Ravi Shankar, whose evocatively dissonant score was created in a night and is nowhere more perfectly employed than at the film's climax. The whole of the last two reels, indeed, are beyond praise. (p. 21)

In *Pather Panchali* desperate needs enforce desperate remedies. The family's existence, while it has its universal aspects and is frequently lightened by humour and small pleasures, seems a shade too impoverished to strike directly home to us: whereas the theme of *Aparajito* is psychological rather than documentary, applicable not merely to the poor but to every social plane.

I tend, in fact, to consider *Aparajito* the most profoundly sensitive panel of the triptych, for the central human bond of *World of Apu,* between husband and wife, springs from Apu's agreement to step into the shoes of a bridegroom who has become unhinged on his wedding day. Such an action—admittedly reluctant—may be excusable from an Indian outlook; to a Westerner, it appears a distasteful negation of sexual freedom. Because of it, the marital association isn't quite rooted in the normal, unlike the mother-son association of the preceding film. (p. 23)

Douglas McVay, "The Ray Trilogy," in Film *(reprinted by permission of British Federation of Film Societies), No. 24, March-April, 1960, pp. 20-4.*

JONATHAN HARKER

The World of Apu seems to me not only the most successful, the most brilliant, the most moving, and the most important of the three parts of Mr. Ray's trilogy, but also probably the most important single film made since the introduction of sound. (p. 53)

It's difficult to give the full flavor of this film; it's difficult to describe the extraordinary success with which Ray has succeeded in stripping away several more veils from reality than any film-maker has ever removed before. Moreover, here at last is a student of film history who is able to absorb the best of the heritage handed down to him by the great film-makers of the twenties' and thirties' and fifties', to re-digest and to improve on the originals. The dialogue is not only sophisticated but often genuinely surprising. The scenes at the end of the film involving Apu's five-year-old son and Apu's struggle to communicate with this boy whom he has never seen before represent perhaps the most moving portrayal of a father-son relationship in any motion picture ever made. Though they closely resemble some of the scenes in *The Bicycle Thief,* there is a surprising and even dazzling quality to them, which lifts them well above the DeSica-Zavattini work. (p. 54)

Jonathan Harker, "'The World of Apu'," in Film Quarterly *(copyright 1960 by The Regents of the University of California; reprinted by permission of the University of California Press), Vol. XIII, No. 3, Spring, 1960, pp. 53-5.*

ARLENE CROCE

[Roughly] two-thirds of *The World of Apu,* with which Ray closes his trilogy, are well worth the trouble, and some of this is as fine, in its own way, as the best of *Pather Panchali*. . . . Ray is so thoroughly in command of his material that for the first hour or so the reality of people, of their differentiated and changing worlds, leaps unquestioned from the screen.

Looking back over this film and back over the trilogy as a whole, you see that it was chiefly this reality of persons and backgrounds that spoke to Ray from the start. Where he deals most directly with its substance, he produces great cinema; where he deals with the pre-arranged reality of a conventional screenplay, he lapses into a rather unaccustomed second gear; and where he deals with outright artifice, his technique becomes faintly spurious or, at the very least, arguable. This isn't the mere truism of film making it sounds. Bergman, for example, works best with just the opposite strengths.

As in the two previous films, nothing much happens in *The World of Apu*—which is to say, the events of the scenario are extremely few and not especially extraordinary. (pp. 62-3)

The absence from the trilogy of any intricately developed dramatic interest is not a relevant point of criticism. Ray has obviously aimed for a poetic-realistic chronicle of the evolution of a boy into a man—or, to use Ray's own term—a "social being." As we know, he has adapted his films from an enormously popular serialized novel which had impressed him with its authenticity as a picture of Indian life. His avoidance of the factitious is to be commended as long as the chronicle sticks to those elements in his source which mirror the untamed individuality of an identifiable life and time. But the uncomfortable truth is that the final portion of *The World of Apu,* in spite of the great sincerity, trust and taste with which it is filmed, looks like a fairly accurate reflection of the unexamined stock attitudes of Western biographical fiction. . . . (pp. 63-4)

The beauty of *Panchali* was in the way every foot of it trembled with the wonder of its own distinctiveness. Sprung together in a rapture of poetic intuition, it had a blunt force and majesty which Ray has been unable completely to recapture since. The two subsequent scripts have lengthened and exercised his talent along more conventional lines of film making; he is still a poet, and an exceptionally sensitive one, but his best energies have gone into transcending the dramatic conceptions of his script rather than in embodying them. He is capable of a sensuousness and a symbolic imagery which often carry the drama well beyond its literal, "scripted" meaning. Take the scene where Apu, having fled his responsibilities as a father, is confronted by an erstwhile companion. The meeting takes place in desolate mining country at a crossroads. Both the overt symbolism and the pervasive dry ache of the landscape convey a meaning greater than the words the characters speak. And there are few directors who would have so dared to exalt the moment in which Apu destroys his book. Ray makes of this moment a deliberately stylized genre image, full of monumental echoes. I am not sure that the classical manner he has chosen for this, the crossroads scene, and many other shots in the film is the best under the circumstances, but I am sure that the resultant images are remarkable as the gentlest and most ingenuous attempts to transcend inflated literary generalities.

One instance where the classical manner fails is the scene in which Apu and the young woman he has just married are alone together for the first time. Ray shoots almost the whole of this scene in a stiff, reticent long shot, as though to convey (the way any film textbook will tell you you *must* convey) the painful distance between the two characters. By neither relaxing nor qualifying this initial tension the scene fails to satisfy our shifting curiosities, the screen goes dead. . . . Curiously enough, later in the film Ray loses another effect by making the opposite mistake—he comes in too soon. This is in the scene where Apu gets the news from a messenger of his wife's death. It occurs after an elaborate and tender build-up that prepares us for irony, but we are deprived of the full sense of ironic reversal because Ray yields it all up immediately in a series of close shots, in which, incidentally, the acting is not nearly good enough. Better to have let the action play itself out, wordless, in long shot.

It does no dishonor to Ray to pick holes in his technique or to question either his choice of material or the way he has chosen to film it. He is a practitioner of film art working hard and alone at what he knows and loves best. (pp. 64-5)

Arlene Croce, "'The World of Apu'," in Film Culture *(copyright 1960 by* Film Culture*), No. 21, Summer, 1960, pp. 62-5.*

CYNTHIA GRENIER

[Ray's first] films—*Pather Panchali, Aparajito,* and *The World of Apu,* form a kind of unified triptych of childhood, adolescence, and young manhood. *The Music Room* leisurely and patiently unfolds the story of the decline of the last member of a once mighty Indian noble family, revealing the man's character by quiet, ever-acute observation. The film has the quality and complexity usually reserved to an extremely good novel, without losing any of the visual beauty inherent to a first-rate motion picture. In its way, despite the foreign setting and details of Indian life which occasionally are quite alien to us, the film is, in its spirit, close to a number of Chekhov's later short stories or to Joyce's *Dubliners*: in it a man's life is epiphanized in an hour and a half of film. We are shown all the weaknesses of the man; his vanity, his self-deception, his total inability to adjust or adapt to any kind of life different from that to which he has always been accustomed. Yet we are also shown, with compassion and wisdom, a fellow human being whom we can understand, forgive, and with whom we can identify.

There is scarcely any plot at all in the conventional sense, yet at the end the viewer feels he has seen a man's entire life laid out before him and has come to understand not just the man's character, but something essential to life itself. Gently the film follows the shallow movements of this life; suddenly, from time to time, picking up a detail of almost frighteningly profound and true observation. Ray's view is serene, but never unmoved; deeply felt but never sentimental. (p. 42)

Ray has the unusual gift of creating, as perhaps no other film director does, a very real sense of the passing of time, of life, which is one of the most difficult problems for a filmmaker when faced with presenting a story which covers the span of many years. This, Ray achieves by an adroit selection of details and moments which serve, as it were, to sum up almost casually an attitude or phase of behavior which is indicative of an individual's entire character. (pp. 42-3)

The Music Room revealed for me, more than almost any other film I can think of, the wonderful, quite unexplored potential of its medium. Very few films have grasped and projected a man's character with such intelligence, simplicity, wit, and art. There's no sex, no sentimentality, really no action to speak of, certainly no chases, no shattering emotions, no big moments; none of the trappings with which even most of the best films today seem unfortunately to be hung in some form or other. Yet by the end of Ray's film, one knows and understands that man with an insight and comprehension that one rarely has for another human being. It makes something like Bergman's *Wild Strawberries* look like a terribly facile exercise—which it is, of course, compared to the rest of Bergman's work.

There probably won't be many films made in the near future which will resemble *The Music Room;* its serenity and sobriety pretty much rule it out as fare for contemporary audience tastes. But it's good to know such a film has been made, if only to prove that the motion picture is a much richer and subtler medium than we had thought. (p. 43)

Cynthia Grenier, "'The Music Room'," in Film Quarterly *(copyright 1960 by The Regents of the University of California; reprinted by permission of the University of California Press), Vol. XIII, No. 4, Summer, 1960, pp. 42-3.*

JOHN BURGESS

The World of Apu should not be qualified by the 'final part of a trilogy' tag. It stands surely on its own, prologue included, and this is not to overlook the fact that an extra dimension can be gained by seeing it after the earlier two films, *Pather Panchali* and *Aparajito*. This film is more than the sum of the successful contributions of a handful of technicians, and although its milieu is absolutely convincing and established without pretension it should not be patronised by being deemed significant for its peculiar relevance to the problems of contemporary India or Bengal. Its significance to India is that it confirms the emergence of a major creative talent who must be ceded a place beside the other contemporary greats Bergman and Fellini.

Stripped immodestly to essentials, *The World of Apu* explores the paradoxical business of death-in-life and the rebirth dependent upon it. (p. 83)

The film is constructed from dynamically linked movements, later ones containing reminders and overtones of the various states of innocence the former come to represent. . . .

Ray's personal vision fuses the unsophisticated narrative. A dynamic tightening is effected by various patterns of imagery, particularly a recurrence of child images and sounds. . . . [The] unobtrusive accumulation of sounds and images into suggestive patterns gives *The World of Apu* a most satisfying, yet in no way formal or artificial, structure.

Ray has rejected conventional time lapses, which he finds cheap and artificial, and *Apu* is an illustration of how brilliantly he has managed to convey a considerable stretch of time in which an important process is occurring. . . .

The restraint of Ray's camera is remarkable: closeups are handled religiously, their length governed by a sensitive discrimination. (p. 84)

John Burgess, "Films of the Quarter: 'The World of Apu'," in Film Journal *(copyright by Melbourne University Film Society), No. 16, August, 1960, pp. 83-5.*

JOHN GILLETT

The world-wide acclaim given to Satyajit Ray's Bengali trilogy has tended to overshadow his other films, none of which has received much of a showing in the West. In the case of *The Philosopher's Stone,* a mild comedy made as a commercial intermezzb, the loss is negligible; but *Jalsaghar* or *The Music Room* (made before *Apu*) was fobbed off with a minor prize at the 1959 Moscow Festival and then mysteriously disappeared. Fortunately, after two attempts, *Jalsaghar* was captured for last year's London Festival. Although it cannot be said to outclass the best parts of the trilogy, it proves to be an engrossing experiment in a deliberately minor key. (p. 35)

[This] is Ray's most romantic film, almost Gothic in its concentration on the crumbling spiritual and physical façade of its protagonist's existence. In it, Ray seems to be recording the loss of a certain kind of purity and idealism, but the comment is made without sentimentality. And there is no bitterness either—even the nobleman's *nouveau riche* rival is given a faintly ridiculous yet not unsympathetic pomposity. The gentle sadness and humour of the story sometimes bring it near to a Chekhovian tempo; certainly it is some distance from the eager striving forward of the *Apu* trilogy. But, despite the difference in subject matter, the style belongs unmistakably to Ray. Again, there is the atmospheric concentration on sounds and objects (a spider suddenly appearing on the nobleman's portrait, distant lightning flashing across a room), here used to re-create a crumbling world. In this respect, Ray has received excellent support from his usual collaborators. Banshi Chandra Gupta's décor (notably the music room itself, with its flaking columns and echoing musical ghosts) and Subatra Mitra's images of the bare landscape, with the sole remaining horse and elephant roaming idly in the midday dust, work towards an entirely unified mood.

Jalsaghar acts as a kind of bridge between the trilogy, with its universal appeal, and the more enclosed Indian cinema from which Ray revolted. In some ways it remains his most Indian film: the contemplative stillness of certain scenes is likely to prove too demanding for most Western audiences; several of the performances . . . are marred by the heavy make-up and over-emphasis of the commercial Indian film; and the final horse ride across the beach is most unconvincingly staged. Yet these are minor flaws in a work whose radiance places it firmly in the select list of the cinema's "chamber music."

In *The World of Apu* . . . we find the same intimacy, this time framed within a larger structure—Apu goes out into the world, marries, loses his wife and wanders aimlessly until he recovers both himself and his son. *Apu* is not only the logical last act of the trilogy but a unique work in its own right, in which Ray reveals his personal artistic gains and losses since *Pather Panchali*. The chief gain is an even richer feeling for relationships between people, expressed through a style again dependent on a careful accumulation of selected details. . . .

The losses are more difficult to categorise, since they largely depend on individual preferences and prejudices. For myself, they are to be found in the more consciously sophisticated editing style, in a few under-directed scenes near the beginning of the film and in the episode when Apu destroys his manuscript. Here Ray comes nearest to providing a stylistic set piece. Ravi Shankar's music and the glittering images of forest and mountain combine to underline the moment of defeat, yet the effect is a little worked out and academic. Ray's stature as an artist lies in the fact that he does not (or did not) need this kind of heightened statement to intensify his style. In striving for it, he has forsaken a little of the unforced expressiveness which still makes *Pather Panchali* his supreme achievement.

In other respects, however, *Apu* illustrates how backgrounds can be used to emphasise the central drama. Ray's groupings and Mitra's photography (which has improved steadily throughout the trilogy) bring a masterly density to a scene. . . . Echoes of the two preceding films can be found in an equally precise use of sound: the trains, once a symbol of release in *Pather Panchali,* become hissing monsters in *Apu* and the track constantly emphasises the rushing of water and the crying of babies. These sights and sounds are absorbed by Ray into his vision of an ever-recurring life force, in the same way that Apu is himself triumphant at the end. . . .

I have avoided using phrases like "poetic truth" in this review, because they have been over-indulged in some quarters until they have become devalued. But, on looking back on the work of Satyajit Ray, how else can one describe the forest scenes with the children in *Pather Panchali,* the mother's death in *Aparajito,* Aparna's farewell in *The World of Apu,* the final dance in *Jalsaghar*? These are the creations of a film-maker with an artistic sensibility rarely found in the cinemas of any country. He has emerged from an industry dedicated almost entirely to the perpetuation of fifth-rate ideas, but his influence has now spread and he is no longer an isolated pioneer. (p. 36)

John Gillett, "'Jalsaghar' and 'The World of Apu'," in Sight and Sound *(copyright © 1961 by The British Film Institute), Vol. 30, No. 1, Winter, 1960-61, pp. 35-6.*

ERIC RHODE

In general, Satyajit Ray's films embarrass the critics. Admirers go impressionistic, talk airily of Human Values, and look offended when asked to be more precise. Detractors are no less vague. Some of them call his work charming, in a tone which could hardly carry more weight of suspicion and distrust, or say they are not interested in the problems of the Indian peasantry. Only M. Truffaut, in describing *Pather Panchali* as Europeanised and insipid, has firmly placed himself in the opposition. This mustn't have taken him much trouble, since he apparently walked out of the film after the first two reels. Those who stayed on to the end, however, had every reason to be more hesitant; for the supposed simplicity of this work—and indeed of all Ray's films—disarms the critic. Only after close scrutiny do most of them turn out to be artefacts of the most subtle sort. It is a case of art concealing art, brought about by Ray's precise construction of plot—so that craftsmanship seldom shows—and by his ability while shooting to improvise against this structure in a way which gives his work a continual spontaneity. . . .

The myth of the Natural Genius, piping his native woodnotes wild, dies hard in certain quarters; and Ray it seems is to be the latest victim sacrificed upon its altars. He can only be made to play this part, however, if one ignores his robust plots and the density of his symbolism. Not that his best work is mannered, as this might suggest. His symbolism is not like that of [Ingmar] Bergman and [Georg] Pabst . . . , who are usually considered symbolist directors. All art in a sense is symbolic, and the success of symbolism lies in it being unobtrusive. This is not so with Bergman and Pabst, who, in trying to conceal the thinness of their material, let symbols sprout out of their feeble plots like straw out of a scarecrow. They fail because they are unable to construct suitable plots, which in turn is a failure properly to explore their material. In the best of Ray's films, on the other hand, the integration of symbol and action is so assured that we are hardly aware of the technical problems involved in such a feat. Yet Ray's continuing success has not been bought cheaply. After shooting *Pather Panchali* he went through a period—at about the time he was filming *Aparajito* and *Parash Pathar* (*The Philosopher's Stone*)—when he had great difficulty in making plots. It is part of his talent's strength that he managed to break through this sterile passage into the lucid and rich world of *Apur Sansar*.

What is so interesting about this talent is the limited means by which it has reached such richness. Ray's vision so far has been a narrow one. In his films there is no portrayal of evil (in the Christian sense), nor is there any sign of violence. The staple ingredients of the Occidental film—lust, murder and rape—play no part in his work. Most of his central characters are sensitive, often idealised people, usually scholars or rich men who have been dispossessed and therefore made vulnerable to poverty and suffering. (The trilogy could as well have been called *The Unprotected* as *The Unvanquished*.) Though this range is highly limited, I don't think it counts against him; for within it Ray has managed to deploy the old tragic conflicts with remarkable ease. What he has in fact done is to describe the relationship between art and life, duty and the emotions, free will and destiny, in very personal terms. And this he has brought off, I believe, by showing us how, in a most vivid way, these conflicts tie up to his major, almost obsessive, theme.

"In what way," asks Ray, "can man control the world, and what is the price he must pay for trying to do so . . . ?" This, as I would see it, is the Promethean theme behind all his films. (p. 133)

Aparajito is an uncertain film. There is no plot to it, only a series of episodes related to each other by the most tenuous of connections. Symptomatic of this is the restless shifting of location: Benares and the father's death, Dejaphur, a village, Calcutta, and another village—it is all very fragmentary, and Ray tries to obscure this by over-playing the train motif, by sensationalist cutting, and by a symbolism which is too often of the Bergman and Pabst sort. (p. 134)

The problem in making a sequel to a well-plotted film is that of finding another plot for the same characters in which they can, without strain, be put to a different use. In *Aparajito* Apu has become the protagonist, but has neither the personality of a child nor the character of an adult to sustain the role. The kind of adolescent problems which could interest us are beyond the range of Ray's fastidious talent, and the character is seen in middle distance. The mother, too, doesn't fulfil the new demands made on her as a central character. In *Pather Panchali* she was never more than a form of conscience, nagging away like an aching tooth. There was no need for her to be more than this. Naturally such a character can never develop into a major role. The consequence of this is that her part in *Aparajito* becomes an increasing embarrassment to Ray, until finally—she is so much at cross-purposes with the action—he forces disastrously the pathos of her death. To enact this scene expressionistic technique runs riot. The camera veers over the walls and lingers on ominous flames. It is all very embarrassing. (pp. 134-35)

These failures are a matter of more than one film. They relate to an overt self-consciousness in Ray himself, which manifests itself in the mannered facetiousness of his next film (*Parash Pathar*, 1958/59) and in the obtrusive symbolism of *Jalsaghar*. The latter is a curious piece . . . , but through being consistent it does work; and because of this such symbolism as the chandelier, representing the Tree of Life, is made plausible. But in *Aparajito* no such convention is sustained. The film is neither realistic nor symbolic: it is merely awkward. There is a sense of hiatus about it which only just manages not to be a sense of void. It is saved, in fact, by a number of typical Ray vignettes. . . . It would be wrong therefore to describe *Aparajito* as a failure. It manages (just) to hold our interest between the earlier masterpiece of *Pather Panchali* and the later, probably finer, masterpiece of *Apur Sansar*.

At this point, Ray conquered his self-consciousness by finding a way in which he could develop the themes of *Pather Panchali* into a new unity. By making Apu give up his study of science in order to become a writer, Ray puts him into a position which also tells us much about his own preoccupations with art at that time. Apu's failure as a novelist reflects on Ray's most serious problem: that of transforming the dialectic of his themes into a direct sensation of life. "He doesn't make it," says Apu to his friend Pulu, speaking of a character in his novel but referring unknowingly to himself. "He doesn't make it, but he doesn't turn away from life. He faces up to reality." Ray wants to do better than this. He wants both to face up to reality *and* to make a work of art that conveys such an apprehension. (p. 135)

It is not difficult to see behind [the] final scene [of *Apur Sansar*] the kind of criticism Ray must have been making of his own past work: how art without life leads to a kind of death, and how the artist should neither have a total control over his material nor be entirely controlled by it, but must in some way transcend this situation. One of the reasons why I think *Apur Sansar* is the best film of the trilogy is that in it Ray has managed to see how this can be done. He has brought it off, I believe, by raising his subject to a mythopoeic level without at any point destroying its realism. (pp. 135-36)

This account of Ray's films has so far neglected his originality as a director: his ability to apprehend experience in cinematic terms. There is his sense of cutting, for instance, which has developed from the clumsy opening sequences of *Pather Panchali,* where the figures often appear to be caught in the frame, into an unusual, implicatory style. This style falls somewhere between Eisenstein's anti-narrative montage and Hollywood's story-telling techniques. The success of Ray's symbolism, his ability to compress densely, is in part brought about by this style (see, for instance, Apu's attempted suicide, or his search for a job). Too often, though, Ray's diffidence in committing himself is helped by this implicatory—and therefore illogical—technique. We never learn, for example, if the nobleman in *Jalsaghar* has lost his fortune because of an obsessive interest in music, or because he has abandoned himself to mourning after the death of his family.

Ray's handling of actors is also exceptional. Like De Sica he knows how to winkle performances out of children, and how to create relationships in a quick though not a glib way through the use of the striking glance or the precisely right gesture. Unlike De Sica though, whose characters must always be up and doing something, he has (and I think this is an unique achievement) a sense of the inner poise of his characters, of a stillness which is never static. His frequently sustained shots of the *Jalsaghar* nobleman, as he sits meditating, do not bore us.

These accomplishments are technical, and as much the work of Ray's excellent and permanent team of collaborators (Mitra, the cameraman, Ravi Shankar, the composer) as of Ray himself. What first concerns us is the single-minded way in which he has grown as an artist. His achievement, for me anyway, has been that he has managed to find a rich connection between his own personal problems and the problems of a society. In coming to terms with his own creative powers, in other words, he has found it easier to understand the world about him. The duel between life and death, between manic control and hopeless abandonment, relates closely—if one can use Melanie Klein's psychological terms—to the artist's need to pass through the depressive (or mourning) phase in order to recreate his destroyed inner world. In discovering this in his own terms, Ray has temporarily managed to resolve the conflicts within himself and the conflicts between his various themes. (p. 136)

Eric Rhode, "Satyajit Ray: A Study," in Sight and Sound *(copyright © 1961 by The British Film Institute), Vol. 30, No. 3, Summer, 1961, pp. 132-36.*

GORDON GOW

[It] is right for a film to preserve the indigenous quality of its country of origin, but Ray is unique among Indian film-makers in that he has combined this with a cinematic idiom that is acceptable outside India. His films are very slow, but the influence of neo-realism and a flair for poetic imagery has brought them nearer to us than other Indian films have ever been. Even so, the slowness of Ray is less consistently cinematic than the slowness of, say, Antonioni. At times he is content to let the subject matter too much alone, and observe his characters, or in this case his almost solitary central character, in pictures that are often pretty dull. Yet, at other times, there are indications of his ability to present evocative images. . . . But [in *The Music Room*] there is never enough of this to outweigh the rest, the plodding part, the part that might mean much more to an Indian audience, perhaps, than it does to me.

Gordon Gow, "'The Music Room'" (© copyright Gordon Gow 1962; reprinted with permission), in Films and Filming, *Vol. 8, No. 10, July, 1962, p. 37.*

TONY MALLERMAN

Satyajit Ray can reveal reality as can no other director in the world. He can give us the squelch of mud so that our feet are sucked into it; and the sound of birds frantically chattering so that we might reach out and touch a wing in flight; and the nearness of a great sluggish river so that we, too, are governed by it. One feels it possible to touch a Ray film, to make real tactile contact with objects and people which, in other films, we might admire for the patterns they made or the attitudes they struck.

One might see a thousand well-intentioned documentaries about India, yet learn less from them than from either of the two stories in *Two Daughters.* And besides his benevolently accurate eye, Satyajit Ray has a heart he has not controlled in the interests of sophistication. Director, producer, writer, composer—Ray has credits for all these in *Two Daughters.* But at the risk of seeming arch I'd say it is for something uncredited that he earns our undying gratitude. Every frame in this film proclaims his love for his people and their environment. In neither of his treatments of the two Rabindranath Tagore stories on which he has based his film need we care about his direction, in the formal sense of the word. Or whether his lighting could be improved. Or whether his camera is at times too static. If he lingers on a close-up for what, in a western film might seem too long, it is because for every second that close-up is on screen, we learn a little more. It is as though his standards were arbitrary, having little to do with the *oeuvre* of the cinema, and almost everything to do with his marvellous intuition, and his love. (pp. 29-30)

Tony Mallerman, "'Two Daughters'" (© copyright Tony Mallerman 1963; reprinted with permission), in Films and Filming, *Vol. 9, No. 9, June, 1963, pp. 29-30.*

ERIC RHODE

On a first glance you might see *Devi* [*The Goddess*] . . . as no more than a film with a thesis, Ibsen in an Indian setting. . . .

The thesis, it seems, is clear; and in fact is nothing less than the latent theme of the Apu trilogy made articulate. . . .

On the level of a thesis . . . , the plot is both inexorable and tight. Ironies fall into place neatly—almost too neatly. A child is saved, so another child must die. Women are treated both as serfs *and* as idols; in any event, they are never allowed to be human beings. . . . In the Apu trilogy episodes were mainly related to each other by association; as the images of river and parched land recurred they took on the resonance, possibly the symbolism, of myth. In *Devi* episodes relate to each other with rationalist logic. So symbolism is played down; the river and landscape never become more than a beautiful backdrop to the action. Such a logic, moreover, requires motives to be highly plausible, a requirement which *Devi* doesn't entirely satisfy. . . .

But—fortunately—*Devi* is much more than a tract. As always, Ray shows sympathy for the old order as well as for the new. . . . On a closer look, indeed, *Devi* is anything but a tract. It has touches of a Greek tragedy in which Kali, the destroyer, enacts her necessary sacrifice; not without reason is Doyamoyee chased by furies across a sunlit field of flowers. Again, and most convincingly, you could see *Devi* as a study of the unconscious forces which hold a family together. (p. 195)

Devi is about a high-born family, and the atmosphere needs to be a little precious. Like Renoir, and unlike most other directors, Ray has a real understanding of every class. He describes his aristocrats generously and without bias; yet he misses none of their foibles. . . . As a structure *Devi* is deceptively lucid. (p. 196)

Eric Rhode, "'Devi'," in Sight and Sound *(copyright © 1964 by The British Film Institute), Vol. 33, No. 4, Autumn, 1964, pp. 195-96.*

PETER COWIE

The handful of Ray's films that one has been able to see reveal his major theme as being the conflict between the generations in India, between the older generation who lived under the British Raj, and the younger generation who have grown up in a modern, independent land. (pp. 28-9)

On paper [the plot of *The Goddess*] seems preposterous in this day and age. But Ray's handling of the characters is so discreet, and the acting of the father, son and his wife is so convincing that never once does the conception of Doya's being a goddess strike one as being altogether ridiculous. Instead it signifies the last stand of the older generations' beliefs in India, like the old man's house in *The Music Room*. The view of the new generation is expressed by Umaprasad's Professor in Calcutta. The question of belief, he says, is irrelevant; the tragedy is that a husband has been denied certain basic rights. When, in the final anguished scene, the feeble landowner collapses in the face of his son's accusations, his fall seems to symbolise the fall of an entire way of life.

Ray's style is impeccable. He weaves the timeless melancholy of the music, the serene life of the village on the river, and the elaborate ritual of the priests, into a study in depth of the essential India, the India that is absorbing up-to-date methods and dress without ever quite relinquishing the ceremonial *modus vivendi* of its forefathers. . . .

More successful dramatically than some of Ray's work, *The Goddess* is a minor masterpiece by virtue of the warmth of its director's vision, and the exquisite atmosphere evoked with apparent ease. A richly absorbing film. (p. 29)

Peter Cowie, "'The Goddess'" (© copyright Peter Cowie 1964; reprinted with permission), in Films and Filming, *Vol. 11, No. 1, October, 1964, pp. 28-9.*

PENELOPE HOUSTON

To attempt to annex Satyajit Ray as the last Victorian would be absurd. But it isn't merely because *Charulata* is set in 1880, and full of references to Gladstone and Macaulay, to English politics and the rotundities of nineteenth century leader writers, that one is made aware of the connections. The film brings together the two characters who seem most thoroughly to arouse Ray's sympathies, and who have appeared most persistently in his films. And neither of them is, in Western terms, quite of the present day.

Amal . . . , the literary-minded cousin who awakens Charu, the editor-publisher's wife, from the lethargy of the long Indian afternoons, is a variation on Ray's eternal student. (p. 31)

The second Ray character is the New Woman—and she deserves those Victorian capital letters. . . . [She] is very closely related to the heroine of *Mahanagar,* his preceding film. There the setting is modern, and the girl finds herself forced into unwilling competition with her husband: taking a job, and discovering that she actually enjoys it. . . .

Ray's women characters in themselves sum up a range of historical attitudes. The poor little wife in *Devi* is tradition personified: quietly submissive, classically patient, she is trapped into her appalling role of goddess. In *The World of Apu,* the wife is still submissive, though her docility is tempered by self-discovery; in *Two Daughters* the taming of the village tomboy is a contest between equals, largely because of the student's inadequacies as Petruchio; in *Kanchenjunga* the women are more modern, and have acquired the boredom of sophistication. And in *Mahanagar* the heroine is right out of the chrysalis. *Charulata* may look backwards in time, but the heroine herself is the most completely realised of all Ray's women. The wife in *Mahanagar* finds herself in a situation which her personality must expand to meet. Charu, however, is like an Ibsen heroine in that she knows too much about the sources of her own discontent. (p. 32)

The unresolved theme of old and new is of course an endlessly recurring one: from the first shots of the train in *Pather Panchali,* through *Jalsaghar,* with the old nobleman shoring up his palace against the inroads of the new men, and *Devi,* with its painful victory of superstition, to *Mahanagar* and *Charulata. Mahanagar* ultimately fails because it comes near to making a De Sica statement rather than allowing a situation to expand of itself. Towards the end of the film, the wife is busy selling her sewing-machines, and the husband is out of work. She defends an Anglo-Indian colleague against her employer (previously seen as rather an amiable man, he's now lit crudely from below in a manner too reminiscent of Soviet comments on capitalism), and loses her own job. Together, husband and wife walk off into the city crowd.

The ending of *Mahanagar* is generalised and sentimental: a flurry of plot to be got through, overtones of melodrama, and then a final shot which echoes too many scenes of little people lost in a big city. By contrast, the conclusion of *Charulata* is exact, particular, and beautiful: an ending which brings the film safely through a couple of melodramatic incidents and out on the other side. This time nothing is implied or imposed: the film stops where it must. In fact, there's a case for *Charulata* as the surest of all Ray's films in its emotional touch. Certainty about atmosphere he has always had, but in the past he has sometimes faltered over plot. His most successful films have been those like *Pather Panchali, Two Daughters* or *Jalsaghar,* in which what storyline there is can be carried atmospherically. *Mahanagar* fumbles its plot, and almost drops it. *Charulata* is only deceptive in that its story looks simple.

Critics of what are usually called the humanist directors

complain that they try to make us share a common experience ("universalise" it) by over-simplification. I don't think this has ever been true of Ray, and in *Charulata* the interplay of sophistication and simplicity is extraordinary. . . .

People have said, as they usually do of a Ray film, that *Charulata* is slow. "Full of unpregnant pauses," wrote Kenneth Tynan, in a review which damned with the remotest of praise. Certainly there are moments when nothing in particular happens, and the camera goes tracking down the corridors, or pauses in a kind of visual yawn at the cool, shaded emptiness. This isn't the impatient existentialist boredom of the West, but an expression of a world which has stopped waiting for something to happen: part of the large lethargy of India. (p. 33)

Penelope Houston, "'Charulata'," in Sight and Sound *(copyright © 1966 by The British Film Institute), Vol. 35, No. 1, Winter, 1965-66, pp. 31-3.*

RICHARD SCHICKEL

Satyajit Ray, the noted Indian director, is up to his usual lack of tricks in his latest film, *Kanchenjungha*. Once again he has dared to make a movie of such stately pace and conventionality of imagery that it—and the audience—always teeters on the brink of boredom. Once again his characters are fictional familiars—archetypes in danger of becoming stereotypes. Once again his story is little more than a cliché. And once again, by a magic that is peculiarly his own, he forces us to attend his deliberately difficult work closely and to care, perhaps more than common sense would dictate, about its outcome. (p. 77)

Some sketchy subplots underpin [the] central situation, but they are no more thrill-packed than the major premise. The Darjeeling setting is interesting, but Ray, who is no pictorialist, handles it routinely. The technical quality of the film is distractingly poor. What, then, is so fascinating about it?

I cannot fully answer that question, since I know the picture did its most forceful work on me below the conscious level, but I suspect it has to do with Ray's patient, insistent probing for the meanings of gestures and glances and silences, his search for the psychic realities that lie beneath conversational conventions and banalities. All these small matters carry a weight in this film that is far heavier than normal, and as we strain forward to catch their true meanings we are, almost against our wills, caught up in the mysteries, the psychopathology if you will, of everyday life. Almost imperceptibly the gentle flow of this film draws us beneath the surface of an ordinary situation, involving very ordinary people, and reveals unsuspected depths, material for speculation that lingers in the mind long after the film has ended.

In an era when most directors are exploiting the visual possibilities of their medium to the utmost, Ray, filming in a crude and even antique style, is perhaps the most daring of them all. He has deliberately cut himself off from all the gaudy gimmicks now available to help the director over the thin and through the rough spots of a script. By also avoiding the more traditional attention-grabbing devices—glamorized settings, décor, costumes, scenes highly charged with overt action and emotion—he has set himself extraordinarily narrow limits within which to work. His films are too "uncinematic" for the purists, too lacking in sensation to appeal much to the wide audience. Essentially, he is like a novelist of sensibility compelling us, through his sensitivity to nuance and the purity and economy of his art, to observe with him the small telling details that reveal the ways people relate—and fail to relate—to one another. Such artists are rarely popular, but they are valuable, reminding us that there are strengths in limitations, truths in subtleties. (pp. 78-9)

Richard Schickel, "'Kanchenjungha'" (originally published in Life, *August 12, 1966), in his* Second Sight: Notes on Some Movies, 1965-70 *(copyright © 1972 by, Richard Schickel; reprinted by permission of Simon and Schuster, a Division of Gulf & Western Corporation), Simon & Schuster, 1972, pp. 77-9.*

RICHARD SCHICKEL

It is always a trifle embarrassing to set down in unadorned outline the story of one of Satyajit Ray's films, for in that form they generally seem too small, too simple to support the critical enthusiasm they generate. (p. 126)

[In *The Big City*], it all seems rather banal. But it is perfectly wonderful when you see it unfold at Mr. Ray's customary unforced pace in his customary unfancy style. The real substance of his films lies between their plot lines, in the interaction of his almost Chekhovian characters. (p. 127)

I imagine that Mr. Ray sees the emergence of [the young wife] under trial as symbolic of India itself, emerging into the modern world after the long personality-crushing ordeal of colonialism, and I imagine, too, that he is urging upon his nation a course similar to that which his heroine pursues—neither clinging blindly to the past (like her unseeing father-in-law) nor clutching unthinkingly at the future as the other characters around her do. Rather, he seems to say, try to blend the forces of tradition with the forces of change thoughtfully, testingly, without panic or excessive passion. In such a way might a wholly new character—strong, supple, subtle—emerge in a wholly new world.

I have no wish, however, to imply that Mr. Ray is heavy or particularly dogged in pursuit of messages, symbolic or otherwise. He is, instead, a careful, ironic and always very specific observer of human character, patiently building his films out of the small gestures, inflections and silences of ordinary life, finding in its pains, problems and victories the stuff of an extraordinary art. (p. 128)

Richard Schickel, "'The Big City'" (originally published in Life, *August 18, 1967), in his* Second Sight: Notes on Some Movies, 1965-70 *(copyright © 1972 by, Richard Schickel; reprinted by permission of Simon and Schuster, a Division of Gulf & Western Corporation), Simon & Schuster, 1972, pp. 126-28.*

CHIDANANDA DAS GUPTA

It is in *Charulata* that both the statement and the art reach their height. For the first time since the trilogy, Ray has something different and important to say, and says it really well. It is, to me, his masterpiece since the trilogy. In a classically Indian fusion of decoration and expression, its miniature-painting-like images acquire an autonomy and poise. Its rhythm, gentle as in all Ray's films, never falters, and Ray's own musical score, competent and interesting in previous films, for the first time becomes a major instrument in making the statement of his film. (p. 44)

The exquisite period flavor is Ray's own, and distinguishes the film from the story, in which Tagore takes it for granted. The sunlit garden, the swing, the embroidery, the floral motifs on the doors and the walls, the horse-drawn carriage, the evocative settings . . . are, however, more than exquisite decorations; they frame the action and set it at a distance—the distance of contemplation. (p. 45)

Chidananda Das Gupta, "'Charulata'," in Film Quarterly *(copyright 1967 by The Regents of the University of California; reprinted by permission of the University of California Press), Vol. XXI, No. 1, Fall, 1967, pp. 42-5.*

ERNEST CALLENBACH

[*Mahanagar*] dramatizes a disconcerting shift in the roles of women, and hence in the patterns of family life and emotional life generally. (pp. 46-7)

American viewers, living in a culture which went through the emergence of women from the home a generation ago, will mostly find the film sentimental, and for them its appeal will be largely ethnographic: Ray is very good at catching the atmosphere of the Bengali household, the small glances and movements by which the inhabitants of the crowded apartment convey their love or disapproval or resentment. But this "humanist" appeal is not enough to preserve the film from charges of being an exotic soap-opera. (p. 47)

The comparison between Ray's *Charulata* and his preceding film *Mahanagar* shows how thin the dividing line [between soap-opera and art] may sometimes be. These films have the same actress at their center . . . ; they are both "women's pictures," focused on the domestic relations of husband and wife; they share Ray's gently humorous observation of manners. Such films stand or fall, then, on how delicately and intriguingly they are managed: how rich is the invention of character and incident, how skillful and nuanced the playing and dialogue, how interesting the *mise-en-scène*. *Mahanagar,* whether useful or regressive in its relation to the modernizing trend of present-day India, is simpler and more banal than the rather complexly ironic *Charulata* on the first two counts. It has, moreover, a fatal lapse in casting and playing, in the role of the Anglo-Indian girl who forms the chief pole of attraction drawing the wife from her old habits. But it is also dismaying to see that the director who once insisted on the minutest material reality of the village setting for *Pather Panchali* will now settle for shaky back-projection in office scenes shot in a studio. The camera positioning is lax and routine; the loving care which usually goes into Ray's lighting and framing is gone, and the handheld camera which follows the wife to her job interview is as shaky as anything out of New York. These weaknesses are unnerving in a director like Ray, whose *Music Room* is a quietly glorious masterpiece of the cameraman's art—the richness and fluidity of Subrata Mitra's lighting and camera work in that film being unsurpassed anywhere. And, unfortunately, such weaknesses produce a tedium which undermines the remarkable moments when, as often in Ray's films, small events take on large import: the wife sniffing the money in her first pay-envelope, her dispensing of presents to compensate her son for the loss of her presence, her husband's wry reaction to her success on the job. . . . These are in reality telling human events; what *Mahanagar* lacks is a fit telling of them. (pp. 47-8)

Ernest Callenbach, "'Mahanagar'," in Film Quarterly *(copyright 1968 by The Regents of the University of California; reprinted by permission of the University of California Press), Vol. XXI, No. 3, Spring, 1968, pp. 46-8.*

ELIZABETH SUSSEX

Satyajit Ray made *Mahanagar* . . . in Calcutta in 1963. It came to the London Film Festival in 1964, and we remembered it as lightweight Ray with an especially rich quota of humour. That is how it still seems, with the humour marvellously perceptive about the little things that are really the big things of life.

This conflict within the family between tradition and progress, between the old culture and the new enlightenment, that runs through all Ray's films, is after all a feature of the human condition not just in India but everywhere, and not just in our time but always. The need to overthrow things that conceivably still matter to us, and to taste the kind of knowledge that can sever us regretfully from our roots, recurs with each generation. What is so exciting about Ray's approach to this is that he actually shows us the ambivalence of people's attitudes. *Mahanagar* is about a young housewife . . . who goes out to work for the first time, and we can see on her face the mixture of nostalgia and anticipation, fear and courage, that this occasions. When a film can get as far inside people as this, there is no possibility of its losing anything with the passage of time.

This is not to deny the importance of the precise placing in space and time. For Ray, I think, the limitations imposed by his Bengali family settings provide the disciplined framework which, in one form or another, every artist needs. (p. 157)

The ending of the film is manipulated in a manner not characteristic of Ray, as if it had been clapped on in haste, but to complain of this is to judge him by the standards that he has set himself. On a less ideal plane, it is a flaw that we might almost overlook. (p. 158)

Elizabeth Sussex, "'Mahanagar'," in Sight and Sound *(copyright © 1968 by The British Film Institute), Vol. 37, No. 3, Summer, 1968, pp. 157-58.*

WILLIAM S. PECHTER

[Perhaps] the most remarkable aspect of Ray's body of work is its range and versatility. Even within the trilogy, each of the films is strikingly different from the others: *Pather Panchali,* a Dovzhenko-like poem of the earth and of human lives coming to definition against the anonymity of nature's cycles; *Aparajito,* owing less perhaps to De Sica than to Zavattini in the latter's call for an open form; and *The World of Apu,* in which a narrative of spiritual questing that reminds one of Hesse in its largeness of gesture is given an embodiment whose critical detachment and admittance of a natural world are as different from the emotional posturing of Hesse as they are again from any of the stereotypes of a film by Ray. Before completing the trilogy, Ray made two other works, *The Philosopher's Stone* (1957), a comic fantasy and the only one of Ray's films I would characterize as slight, and *The Music Room* (1958), a gothic study in obsession and decay that more nearly evokes the fateful cosmos of a Kleist (and of his "St. Cecilia, or The Power of Music," in particular) than it does any world of a perfectable human nature. Despite its backdrop of societal transformation, the essential force of *The Music Room* resides in the extent to which we are drawn into its protagonist's proud madness; the extent to which we are brought even to admire the declining aristocrat's compulsive sacrifice of all else to the thrall of a more perfect music. (p. 71)

[*Mahanagar* is] one of the least typical of Ray films in being one of the most visibly plotted. Like those farces it resembles, the action develops with a kind of independently propellent comic logic; when the wife is forced by family economics to go out into the world and get a job, we know her husband will eventually lose his; the logic of the situation demands it. But, even as this comedy of situation is allowed to run its traditional course, the characters in it are so fully fleshed out as to create of their relations a comedy of character that is both remarkably interactive with the farcical action and yet developmentally independent of its motoric drive. (pp. 71-2)

Whatever qualities talk of "humanism" may actually refer to in Ray, it seems to me that the salient quality of his work is its almost intoxicating sensuousness, its all but overwhelming apprehension of a physical world of flesh and fabrics, textures, tangible surfaces, material presences, odors, sexual vibrations, body heat; probably no other films convey to one as do Ray's the sense of an actual temperature emanated from the screen. What one can say critically of such an accomplishment, I do not know; perhaps one can only attempt to appreciate it. Ray's films defy analysis in the literal sense of being entities which it seems virtually impossible to separate into their component parts—that is to say, theme, style, etc.—even for purposes of discussion. They are narratives of such lucid simplicity that even art itself seems to disappear into their general transparency.

Ray's films are perhaps the supreme instance in film of a purely narrative art; one—like Chekhov's, in his stories—in which all abstract meaning is merged into a narrative whose reality seems to be confluent with our own; whose characters seem as fully alive, and whose events seem as wholly independent of artistic arrangement. Possibly one can say that much in Ray's films is touched by a sense of the primacy of life's natural rhythms over any plans which individuals may try to impose on them; but, if this sense does enter into the films, it is not as an abstract idea, or theme whose working out may be explicated by the action, but rather as something which the action is exactly equivalent to and which it celebrates. (p. 72)

William S. Pechter, "India's Chekhov," in Commonweal *(copyright © 1970 Commonweal Publishing Co., Inc.; reprinted by permission of Commonweal Publishing Co., Inc.), Vol. XCIII, No. 3, October 16, 1970, pp. 71-2.*

TOM MILNE

Days and Nights in the Forest . . . the very title rings with enchantment, and the old Ray magic is soon at work again. . . .

[Whereas] it would be impossible to detach Chekhov's characters, or indeed James's, from their very precise social contexts, Ray's characters seem to belong so essentially to no other time than their own that they could step quite easily out of *Charulata* into *Days and Nights in the Forest,* bridging three-quarters of a century in the process. Partly, of course, this is because aspects of Victoriana have survived quaintly in Indian life; partly because Ray has a respect for traditional (especially cultural) values which is hardly shared by modern society; but mostly because he withdraws so determinedly from the tempo of this technological age that time becomes almost as important a factor in his films as it is with Resnais. . . . (p. 48)

[It] is interesting that the most frequent criticism levelled against Ray by his detractors is that his films are too slow, and by his admirers, that he cannot handle melodrama (e.g. much of *Abhijan,* the end of *Mahanagar,* the assault on Hari in *Days and Nights in the Forest*). Opposite ends of the same candle, these criticisms arise because Ray's cinema is essentially one of contemplation in which both he and his characters like to ponder first, act afterwards. (p. 49)

Tom Milne, "'Days and Nights in the Forest'," in Sight and Sound *(copyright © 1972 by The British Film Institute), Vol. 41, No. 1, Winter, 1971-72, pp. 48-9.*

ROBIN WOOD

I should confront the problem . . . of the accessibility of Ray's films for western audiences: can we feel any confidence that we are adequately understanding, intellectually and emotionally, works which are the product of a culture very different from our own? The problem has two aspects. One is content, our intermittent sense that certain passages or details in the films may mean something more, or something different, to Indian audiences. The other is tempo: the chief explicit grumble in the West about Ray's films is that they move slowly.

The 'content' problem can easily be stood on its head: what is remarkable is how *seldom* in Ray's films the spectator is pulled up by any specific obstacle arising from cultural differences. Partly, this can be attributed to the fact that Ray appears to have learnt his art mainly from the western cinema. . . .

In terms of general subject-matter, Ray's films usually deal with human fundamentals that undercut all cultural distinctions. The subject-matter of the trilogy—family, the parent-child relationship, marriage, irreparable loss, reconciliation—is obviously universal in its accessibility. Even Ray's apparently more 'exotic' films like *Devi*—in which a young girl is mistaken by her father-in-law for a reincarnation of a goddess—can be reduced to conflicts (usually related to social change and the gulf between generations) that are certainly not restricted to one culture. When a specific cultural peculiarity *does* play a part in the narrative it often becomes evident that the attitude to it encouraged by the film as a whole is not all that far removed from our own. (pp. 6-7)

The 'tempo' problem presents more serious obstacles; it is also much more difficult to discuss or remove, depending as it does partly on subjective reaction, and on aspects of film it is impossible to cope with at all adequately in words. Even making allowances for possible national differences in expectation, there are passages in Ray which I feel to be 'stretched': within the trilogy, the later sequences of *Aparajito;* outside it, the later scenes of the second story of *Two Daughters*. In both these cases, we see where the film is moving long before it gets there, and feel we would accept a more elliptical treatment than Ray's painstaking analysis of each phase in the development of character and narrative.

Even here, however, we should be ready to allow for the fact that Ray is less interested in expressing ideas than in communicating emotional experience. In the West, we are conditioned primarily either by the classic American cinema with its taut narrative structures in which, when a scene has made its point, we are carried swiftly on to the next, or by the European 'art' cinema with its tendency to intellectual thematic structures. We may feel, with Ray, that we have already got the point when we are in fact continuing to miss it, for 'the point' may be not an extractable thematic or narrative issue but the total experience a character is undergoing.

More generally, the only answer to the complaint that Ray's films move 'slowly' is that this is surely their right. Rules cannot be applied externally to works of art, for each work defines its own rules. To ask Ray's films to move faster is like asking Brahms or Bruckner to be Stravinsky. This is not to say that either Brahms or Bruckner (or Ray) is necessarily beyond criticism, but the right to criticise is earned only by submitting to the work in question sufficiently to feel its movement, its rhythms, its breathing. Only then can we decide with any degree of authority whether or not a point is being laboured; the criterion is not the tempo adopted but our sense of the artist's success in realising his concepts, and, ultimately, the value of the concepts as realised. (pp. 7-8)

By aligning Ray, in my rough-and-ready analogy, with Brahms and Bruckner against Stravinsky, I may have seemed to concede the detractors' strongest point: Ray is, after all, a twentieth-century artist—isn't his cinema desperately old fashioned? To which one can imagine the hypothetical detractor adding, as an afterthought, the dread words 'literary' and 'academic'. . . . [To] call *Pather Panchali* old fashioned in relation to *L'Avventura* is as meaningless as to call *Broken Blossoms* old fashioned beside *Breathless*: of course it is, and the label does not reduce the film's value in the slightest. It is easy to guess that, in the context of the Bengali cinema, *Pather Panchali* was positively revolutionary. Ray's models were Renoir and the Italian neo-realists, but 'models' isn't really the right term because Ray's film does not in any real sense imitate them; rather, they gave Ray the kind of hints a great artist can take from others and use in his own way. It is true that Ray has not obviously extended the boundaries of cinematic expression, except perhaps in the context of Indian cinema; he is naturally conservative by temperament. . . . Ray hasn't been afraid to adopt the innovations of others when they suit his purposes (the use of the zoom lens and 'freeze' shots in *Charulata,* for example), but on the whole he has shown himself content with the film-maker's traditional means and methods, which he has turned to consistently personal use. The term 'academic' only has force if it implies a characterless following of rules, the safe reliance on repetition of what has been done before. Analysis will show, I think, that the decisions one can discern through Ray's *mise-en-scène* nearly always grow out of a personal response to the material. Nor is Ray in any real sense a 'primitive'. . . . The sensibility with which one makes contact through the films is notably refined and civilised, and the technique, within the limits of 'classical' *mise-en-scène* . . . , has a corresponding delicacy.

The charge of Ray's cinema being 'literary' might seem to carry rather more weight. Most of his films are adapted from novels and stories and most of the originals have the reputation of being respectable, distinguished works in their own right. His art clearly has affinities with that of the novelist, his most obvious concern being with the nuances of character-relationships and character development. Yet careful examination of almost any sequence in Ray's work will show that it has been conceived—or, when the literary original is closely followed, re-conceived—in terms that are essentially cinematic. This holds true even of simple dialogue-scenes taking place within a single set: camera-position, camera-movement and editing are not mere functional appendages but play a leading creative role, so that the overall effect is not only non-literary but non-theatrical. (pp. 9-10)

Ray's cinema is 'literary' only in the sense that it is firmly rooted in narrative. He thinks primarily in terms of plot and character, and the significance of the films grow naturally out of this, extractable ideas or themes being the product rather than the starting-point. . . . Ray's own statement (the specific reference is to *Mahanagar,* but the words can be taken to apply generally) is relevant here; indeed, several of the following remarks could be taken as texts for a dissertation on Ray's work.

> 'What I try to do in my films is to present certain situations. I try as far as possible not to comment—not to make didactic statements, not to be propagandist in any way. I merely show what it means for a family to have to change, what happens then; and certain problems are presented as clearly as possible showing all aspects, and then leave the public to draw their own conclusions. In a story like *Mahanagar,* I felt it was important to establish the fact that change was necessary, because in modern India certain ideas have to be put across. Important ideas, necessary ideas, you know. But nobody ever says in the film that you have to change or it's good to change. I merely present certain incidents, and through the incidents, and through the reaction of people to the incidents, certain facts emerge. Fairly complex facts, because there are always two sides to a thing. . . . And it makes for a kind of orderliness which helps an audience which is not used to intellectual subtleties. And yet it affords you to be subtle in other things.'

Such emphasis on plot and character, however, needs to be balanced and qualified by the 'pure cinema' aspects of Ray's art, those aspects that bring the cinema closer to music than to literature. From this point of view, *Two Daughters* marks an advance on the Apu trilogy, and Ray's subsequent films show further refinements. *Charulata* tells a story, certainly, but it can also be regarded as built on a complicated pattern of echoes and cross-references, both thematic and visual, with almost every incident finding an echo somewhere, down to details of camera-movement and set-up. Ray himself said of this:

> 'I'm very conscious at all times of the musical aspect of a film, of its rhythm, of its silences and of its general pattern. I'm a great lover of Mozart, and certainly I had Mozart in mind when I made *Charulata,* very much.

It's consciously planned, but not worked out like a mathematical problem. I find it's more and more what emerges naturally. It's conscious and subconscious at the same time I think.'

The reference to Mozart is an important clue to the nature of Ray's art. It points up his affinities with Renoir. It also helps us to connect the emphasis on the 'musical' aspects of his films with the awareness that 'there are always two sides to a thing'—*several* sides in a film like *Charulata* or *Days and Nights in the Forest*. The simultaneous awareness of different, even incompatible, viewpoints is a characteristic that finds supreme expression in Mozart's operas.

This emotional complexity, the delicate balancing of responses, what one might call the Mozartian aspect of Ray's art, which links him with Renoir, is already characteristic of *Pather Panchali*. It reaches fullest expression in *Days and Nights in the Forest,* the most recent of his films to reach the West at the time of writing, and perhaps his masterpiece to date—certainly the most 'musical' of his films. (pp. 12-13)

Except in the vague sense in which all major art is 'religious' (a reaching out towards a significance beyond the individual human life lived simply for itself), Ray is not a religious director. One guesses, however, that Hinduism has its importance in the background to his work, rather as Christianity is likely to have its importance for even a non-religious Western artist, as a generalised source and influence. (p. 14)

The central unifying thematic preoccupation of all Ray's work to date is change or 'progress': again and again he returns to an investigation of people's attitudes to change, how they cope with it (or fail to cope), the gaps it produces between generations or between people from cultural backgrounds at different stages of development. And the overall attitude to 'progress' is consistently ambivalent: what is created is always balanced (though not negated) by what is destroyed. . . .

Although a considerable time gap and two other films intervened between the shooting of *Aparajito* and the shooting of *The World of Apu;* although Apu himself is incarnated by three different actors in the course of the trilogy; and although each film makes sense if seen in isolation, it is nevertheless possible to trace a clear structure in the trilogy as a whole, and to view it as one long film in three parts.

Apu is the only character who appears in all three films, and (obviously enough) it is his development that provides the trilogy with its main unifying impulse. One striking overall structural feature is the way in which the focus is progressively narrowed, so that our attention is concentrated more and more exclusively on Apu himself. (p. 15)

This progressive concentration of focus on the trilogy's protagonist is accompanied by the removal through death of those nearest him. There are no less than five important deaths in the trilogy. . . . Each, at the time of her death, is the person emotionally closest to Apu. One special recurring circumstance in . . . three deaths heightens our sense of them as a leitmotiv running through the trilogy: each death takes place at a time of separation. It is true that we share intimately in the mother's experience of Durga's death, but the irrevocable fact of it is brought home most forcefully when Ray leads us sympathetically to share the father's shock when, returning home, he learns what has happened. Sarbojaya dies alone before Apu can get home to her. Aparna dies in childbirth several days' journey away from her husband. In each case the fact of absence greatly intensifies the sense of loss, of human helplessness in the face of death's abruptness and finality, and of life's terrible unpredictability.

But the deaths, felt as so terrible in themselves, are never merely negative in results. Throughout the trilogy loss is usually accompanied by gain, and each death leads, either immediately or indirectly, to progress. (p. 16)

The trilogy certainly encourages one to draw the inference that the progress from the primitive village of *Pather Panchali* to the city of *The World of Apu* constitutes an advance; but the point mustn't be allowed to stand unqualified. Ray is by no means a simple-minded believer in progress, and the sense of advance at the end of the trilogy will be modified for us, if we glance back over all that has led up to it, by, again, a sense of corresponding loss. If the life Apu has won through to is incomparably richer in potentialities than that into which he was born, it is also fraught with far greater problems and uncertainties. . . .

The ambivalence of the trilogy's attitude to 'progress' is epitomised rather beautifully in the development of its most obvious unifying motif: the train. There is nothing forced or arbitrary about Ray's use of train images as a unifying device. There is no simple symbolism involved. The meaning of the images shifts and changes and accumulates complex emotional overtones as the trilogy progresses. From the magical moment in *Pather Panchali* when the sound of a distant train first impinges on the child Apu's consciousness as the family sit in their home at night, to the adult Apu's attempted suicide on the railway tracks amid the squalor of a Calcutta slum in *The World of Apu,* is a movement that should remove any suspicion that the concept of 'progress' in the trilogy—and in Ray's work generally—is simple or naive. (p. 17)

Robin Wood, in his The Apu Trilogy *(© 1971 by Robin Wood; reprinted by permission of the author), Frederick A. Praeger, Publishers, 1971, 96 p.*

PAULINE KAEL

"It adds years to your life," the young men from Calcutta in Satyajit Ray's *Days and Nights in the Forest* say of the country quiet, and it's easy to believe. Ray's images are so emotionally saturated that they become suspended in time and, in some cases, fixed forever. Satyajit Ray's films can give rise to a more complex feeling of happiness in me than the work of any other director. I think it must be because our involvement with his characters is so direct that we are caught up in a blend of the fully accessible and the inexplicable, the redolent, the mysterious. We accept the resolutions he effects not merely as resolutions of the stories but as truths of human experience. Yet it isn't only a matter of thinking, Yes, this is the way it is. What we assent to is only a component of the pattern of associations in his films; to tell the stories does not begin to suggest what the films call to mind or why they're so moving. There is always a residue of feeling that isn't resolved. Two young men sprawled on a porch after a hot journey, a drunken group doing the Twist in the dark on a country road, Sharmila

Tagore's face lit by a cigarette lighter, her undulating walk in a sari—the images are suffused with feeling and become overwhelmingly, sometimes unbearably beautiful. The emotions that are imminent may never develop, but we're left with the sense of a limitless yet perhaps harmonious natural drama that the characters are part of. There are always larger, deeper associations impending; we recognize the presence of the mythic in the ordinary. And it's the mythic we're left with after the ordinary has been (temporarily) resolved. (p. 140)

On the surface, [*Days and Nights in the Forest*] is a lyrical romantic comedy about four educated young men from Calcutta driving together for a few days in the country, their interrelations, and what happens to them in the forest, which is both actual and metaphorical. As the men rag each other and bicker, we quickly sort them out. Ashim is a rising executive and the natural leader of the group. Lordly and disdainful to underlings, he is the worst-behaved; the most intelligent, he is also the most dissatisfied with his life and himself—he feels degraded. . . . Ashim is much like what Apu might have turned into if he had been corrupted, and he is played by Soumitra Chatterji, who was Apu in *The World of Apu*. On this holiday in the forest, Ashim meets Aparna, played by the incomparably graceful Sharmila Tagore. . . . In his fine book on the Apu Trilogy, Robin Wood wrote that the physical and spiritual beauty of Soumitra Chatterji and Sharmila Tagore seems "the ideal incarnation of Ray's belief in human potentialities." And I think they represent that to Ray, and inspire him to some of his finest work (he used them also in *Devi*) because they are modern figures with overtones of ancient deities. Unlike the other characters in *Days and Nights in the Forest*, they bridge the past and the future and—to some degree—India and the West. As Ray uses them, they embody more than we can consciously grasp. But we feel it: when Sharmila Tagore in her sunglasses and white slacks stands still for a second, she's a creature of fable—the image carries eternity. Even her melodious voice seems old and pure, as if it had come through fire. (p. 141)

Underneath their love story, and the stories of Ashim's companions, there's the melancholy and corruption of their class and country. In a quiet way, the subtext is perhaps the subtlest, most plangent study of the cultural tragedy of imperialism the screen has ever had. It is the tragedy of the bright young generation who have internalized the master race (like many of the refugees from Hitler who came to America); their status identity is so British that they treat all non-Anglicized Indians as non-persons. The caste system and the British attitudes seem to have conspired to turn them into self-parodies—clowns who ape the worst snobberies of the British. . . . We don't laugh at them, though, because they're achingly conscious of being anachronistic and slightly ridiculous. When we see them playing tennis in the forest, the image is so ambiguous that our responses come in waves. (pp. 141-42)

[Ray's] means as a director are among the most intuitively right in all moviemaking: he knows when to shift the camera from one face to another to reveal the utmost, and he knows how to group figures in a frame more expressively than anyone else. He doesn't butt into a scene; he seems to let it play itself out. His understatement makes most of what is thought of as film technique seem unnecessary, and even decadent, because he does more without it. (No Western director has been able to imitate him.) The story is told with great precision at the same time that the meanings and associations multiply. Ray seems to add something specifically Eastern to the "natural" style of Jean Renoir. Renoir, too, put us in unquestioning and total —yet discreet—contact with his people, and everything seemed fluid and easy, and open in form. But Renoir's time sense is different. What is distinctive in Ray's work (and it may be linked to Bengali traditions in the arts, and perhaps to Sanskrit) is that sense of imminence—the suspension of the images in a larger context. The rhythm of his films seems not slow but, rather, meditative, as if the viewer could see the present as part of the past and could already reflect on what is going on. There is a rapt, contemplative quality in the beautiful intelligence of his ideal lovers. (p. 142)

No artist has done more than Satyajit Ray to make us reëvaluate the commonplace. And only one or two other film artists of his generation—he's just past fifty—can make a masterpiece that is so lucid and so inexhaustibly rich. At one point, the four young blades and the two women sit in a circle on picnic blankets and play a memory game that might be called Let Us Now Praise Famous Men; it's a pity that James Agee didn't live to see the films of Satyajit Ray, which fulfill Agee's dreams. (p. 143)

Pauline Kael, "Lost and Found" (originally published in The New Yorker, *Vol. XLIX, No. 4, March 17, 1973), in her* Reeling *(copyright © 1973 by Pauline Kael; reprinted by permission of Little, Brown and Company in association with the Atlantic Monthly Press), Atlantic-Little, Brown, 1976, pp. 137-43.**

STANLEY KAUFFMANN

Neglect is benign for some artists. An American novelist named William March was thought by some to be a neglected fine writer until a large anthology of his work was published; that finished March. The Indian director, Satyajit Ray, is a first-class artist, until you see his films. As long as he isn't imported, one can talk about injustice and neglect. But then along comes a Ray film, and, allowing for such exceptions as *Aparajito* and *Charulata*, it is usually a mild and fairly dull item.

[*Days and Nights in the Forest*] is one of the milder and duller, wretchedly photographed, archaically edited, sentimental and superficial in style and theme. (p. 22)

Stanley Kauffmann, "Four for the Seesaw" (reprinted by permission of Brandt & Brandt Literary Agents, Inc.; copyright © 1973 by Stanley Kauffmann), in The New Republic, *Vol. 168, No. 16, April 21, 1973, pp. 22, 33.**

ALAN ROSS

Ray's films—arguably the most considerable achievement in the art of our time—have made only a modest impact in relation to their quality. What the curious but weary West has wanted from India has been its peripheral and largely discarded mysticism, not its human problems and statistics of defeat.

Where much of even the best cinema is a game, played in isolation and its interest dependent on awareness of cultural cross-references and its own improvizations, Ray's films have an organic growth, to which the actors in prescribed situations contribute, that makes discussions of technique and influence almost superfluous. (p. 150)

In *The Adversary* the visual and dialogue references to politics are more obvious than usual, but it is what Ray makes out of nothing, in purely cinematic terms, that is significant, not what his films can be reduced to in terms of theme and incident.

In fact, each of his films can be regarded as a series of beautifully conceived set-pieces, but so much are they part of a whole, so gently do they flow into each other, that anecdote or style are never obtrusive. Robin Wood and others have drawn attention to the Mozartian aspect of Ray's art [see excerpt above], to his debt to Renoir, to the stylish innovations he has borrowed from others, but ultimately the films quite simply *are*—aspects of growing, struggling, loving, dying, while the sun shines, the rains fall, the forms in offices are made out in triplicate, and the candidates wait. In the end the trains that are one of the most potent images of Indian life shunt their passengers separately away to new beginnings, new endings.

The Adversary is more or less this too; a few marvellously observed interviews in stifling heat, with hundreds of applicants overqualified for the most modest of jobs, some desultory walks about Calcutta, an unconsummated visit to a whore, the start of a love affair. It is a study, like nearly all Ray's films, in frustration and in hope, where only political references date it. (p. 151)

Alan Ross, "A Postscript in Bengal," in London Magazine *(© London Magazine 1973), Vol. 13, No. 1, April-May, 1973, pp. 149-51.*

TOM MILNE

Company Limited is an impeccable ideological tract detailing the exact price in human dignity and decency to be paid for a stake in the corridors of power. As always with Ray, the message is all the better and richer for being conveyed obliquely. . . . [The] secret motivation of *Company Limited* is the mournful yearning of Chekhov's characters, not this time for the seemingly unattainable city but for the 'provincial' life that has been lost. . . . *Company Limited* may not have the exquisite formal perfection of *Days and Nights in the Forest,* but it is considerably more successful than *The Adversary* in filtering the political demands of a situation which, as Ray says, "you feel every moment of the day in Calcutta", through the prism of his own vision. (p. 52)

Tom Milne, "Feature Films: 'Seemabaddha' ('Company Limited')," in Monthly Film Bulletin *(copyright © The British Film Institute, 1974), Vol. 41, No. 482, March, 1974, pp. 51-2.*

JOHN COLEMAN

Company Limited has a bleak, slightly off-key title to British ears and this quality of getting things just that shade wrong is an element in what it is all about. The film takes its place in a trio (the other two, *Days and Nights in the Forest* and *The Adversary*) concerned with the effects of what we did to India and Indians. We left them a language, English, and a way of life not unconnected with capitalism. These facts Mr Ray now occupies himself with stressing and, under their impact, he seems to be producing increasingly unnerved and unnerving movies. . . .

If one leans on the pictorial style, it is because it is nearly consistently ugly, harsh, almost as if Ray had decided (and, for heaven's sake, he worked under Renoir and himself made the visually ravishing *Charulata*) to send up a gamut of Hollywood postures. . . . Noises, the dialogue, the eerily clumsy or parody appearance of things begin to come together into a statement of sorts. This is Ray's bitterest work: that much is certain. He couldn't otherwise have permitted the visual going to get so rough.

And the script, which is credited to him, based on a novel by Shankar, is more replete with chucked-in English than any other of his I can remember. . . . Ray, who has no effective audience at home (where it is all song and dance), must make his films for himself or for an audience cautiously sensed as out there, which would be you and me. His predicament as an artist is unenviable and one sympathises with it.

John Coleman, "The Company He Keeps," in New Statesman *(© 1974 The Statesman & Nation Publishing Co. Ltd.), Vol. 87, No. 2241, March 1, 1974, p. 304.*

PENELOPE GILLIATT

"Charulata," Satyajit Ray's most nearly flawless film apart from his great Apu trilogy, is a flowing, opulent tale that seems to be lit from the inside like a velvet-lined carriage with a lantern in it rocked by a hot monsoon wind. The film carries an exquisite period flavor of the eighteen-seventies in Bengal. (p. 48)

The film leaves one with a sense of great things unfulfilled but never of mania. Like Ray's "The Music Room," which has tones of "The Cherry Orchard," it has a style that is songlike, beautiful, sometimes turning into an abrupt and comic rudeness that again seems very Russian. Grape-lipped men lapse into English as Chekhovians dreaming of revolution lapse into French.

"Charulata" is gentle to loneliness in the well-off, it is beautifully written, and sometimes it is very funny. The music was written by Ray himself. Along with everything else, the picture is a fascinating fable about the bequest of Empire in India. . . . Against the gaudy background of the Indian film industry, there may well appear to be something Europeanized about Ray's humor and his low tones. To Europeans or Americans, though, his Forsterish irony seems deeply embedded in his style, and he obviously works from within in his sight of the Indian character. The film is triumphant in its comprehension of a period. (pp. 49-50)

Penelope Gilliatt, "The Great Ray," in The New Yorker *(© 1974 by The New Yorker Magazine, Inc.), Vol. L, No. 20, July 8, 1974, pp. 48-51.*

PENELOPE GILLIATT

["Nayak the Hero"] is the achievement of a great film director working outside his usual style, fumbling sometimes with surrealism, using flashbacks that flaw the usual concord of his sense of storytelling, but sometimes illumining it by lines that suddenly show character in movement, like the glare of a torch catching a figure on a staircase. (p. 67)

Penelope Gilliatt, "The Fastest Anachronism in the West," in The New Yorker *(© 1974 by The New Yorker Magazine, Inc.), Vol. L, No. 23, July 29, 1974, pp. 66-7.*

JUDITH CRIST

[*The Hero* is] a witty and ironic film Ray made in 1966. It is quintessential Ray, a simple story moving at what has been so aptly described as "the pace of a majestic snail," its protagonist projected on a broad canvas so subtly crammed with insights, perceptions, and wry comment that its compassionate awareness of the human comedy sticks to the mind's ribs with surprising persistency. . . .

Ray provides a worldliness and sophistication to break the journey, with the tiniest of moments becoming significant drama, and gestures—like the quick, firm restoration of the hornrims—providing the breadth of character. We might, in fact, be riding the Twentieth Century again, a little less fliply and a lot more satisfyingly. It makes the erratic sound track and recurrence of white-on-white (but markedly literate) subtitles worth enduring.

Judith Crist, "Star's Trek," in New York *Magazine (copyright © 1974 by News Group Publications, Inc.; reprinted with the permission of* New York *Magazine), Vol. 7, No. 31, August 1, 1974, p. 53.*

TOM MILNE

Light shimmering on the water; what appears to be a dead hand floating just beneath the surface; then the hand idly begins to toy with the ripples, and the camera gently pans to reveal a girl dreamily bathing in the river and staring up at the sky as five fighter planes sweep by in formation: "How beautiful", she exclaims, "like a flight of cranes". This sequence of images immediately following the credits of *Distant Thunder* (themselves placed over images of tranquil nature and stormy winds starting to ruffle a field of waving corn) is Ray at his complex, evocative best. Long before we discover that this is some time after the fall of Singapore and that the distant thunder of World War Two will soon break over this remote Bengali village trailing a terrible man-made famine, that corpse-like hand already pollutes the placid river with its intimations of mortality. There is really no need for the complementary image later on in the film when order has begun to collapse in the village, two women save a third from attempted rape by beating her attacker to death, and a stream of blood flowing from a now unmistakably dead hand stains the same placid waters. The tautology here, or perhaps over-expressiveness in an attempt to encompass a vast theme would be a better term, is part of the problem with the film. "Five million starved in Bengal in what has come to be known as the man-made famine of 1943" reads the last, accusing title after an apocalyptic vision in which the hero and heroine are faced by a silhouetted horde of starving, skeletal people receding endlessly into the distance, converging on their front gate with arms stretched out in supplication. The effect here is a curious mixture of Russian agit-prop and expressionism, and moving as it is, it fits uncomfortably into the subtle intimacies where Ray is most at home. To prepare for it, he has to resort to the melodrama which (again in a rape scene) marred the perfection of *Days and Nights in the Forest,* this time not only with the rape sequence, but with the earlier, looming shot of a hideously scarred man who will eventually profit from social disaster by persuading a woman to sell her body for a measure of rice. The pity of it is that none of the melodrama is really necessary, since Ray tells the whole story, much more subtly, in the brilliant central section of the film where the Brahmin couple are pushed and pulled, with a delicate humour that is wholly persuasive, into an awareness of their true status as human beings. With the quiet, quizzical logic Ray deploys so effectively (*Distant Thunder* is particularly reminiscent of the "Postmaster" episode in *Three Daughters*), their horizons are widened and their privileged positions simultaneously whittled away from under them. The focal moment is perhaps the one in which the jaunty Brahmin, one of those Chekhovian figures Soumitra Chatterjee plays so well—an endearing mixture of dignity and absurdity as he plods through the mud with his rolled umbrella and his folded duster protecting his head from the sun, busily setting himself up as priest, physician and universal pundit all rolled into one—suddenly realises that for all his Sanskrit learning and the skimmed newspaper headlines with which he dazzles his illiterate flock, he really knows nothing. Hitherto he has explained the war, more or less, as "Our King is fighting the Germans and Japanese", but managed to locate Singapore somewhere in the remoter states of India. Then an old man, a beggar even though a Brahmin, casually tells him the true story, not only strategically (where the war is happening) but economically (why rice is scarce and soaring in price). Typically, Ray avoids any feeling of didacticism here by making the old man a whining misery, determined to cadge all he can from his hosts, and deserving of sympathy and respect only because he is starving; also typically, Ray makes the scene central not by stressing its ideological importance but by focusing on the secret, approving smile with which the wife (another of Ray's magical heroines) encourages her husband to listen and digest the lesson. The crux of the matter for these two good people, who are only just learning how to use their goodness, comes not with the open rhetoric of their vision of starving millions, but with their confrontation by a single victim immediately beforehand: the wife's friend, a low-caste peasant woman whom, as Brahmins, they cannot even touch as she lies dying outside their house. In Indian terms, the husband's decision to break the taboo by burying her to save her body from the jackals, and the wife's silent nod of approval, amounts to a revolution; and in his exploration of their evolving relationship to each other and to their community, Ray makes it more earth-shattering than all the global implications of his final image and title.

Tom Milne, "Feature Films: 'Ashani Sanket' ('Distant Thunder')," in Monthly Film Bulletin *(copyright © The British Film Institute, 1975), Vol. 42, No. 496, May, 1975, p. 99.*

PAULINE KAEL

The color imagery of Satyajit Ray's "Distant Thunder" is so expressive that I regretted the need to look down to the subtitles; it took precious time away from the faces and bodies, with their hint of something passive, self-absorbed —a narcissism of the flesh. . . .

The film is delicately, ambiguously beautiful; the shadowing comes from our knowledge . . . that the people we're looking at are endangered. It is a lyric chronicle of a way of life just before its extinction, and Ray gives the action the distilled, meditative expressiveness that he alone of all directors seems able to give. We're looking at something that we feel is already gone, and so the images throb. Or is it that *we* do? It comes to the same thing. (p. 169)

Ray is one of the most conscious artists who ever lived, and in this film he means to show us the subservient status of women. . . . Ray is not a vulgar chauvinist, exalting subservient women; quite the contrary. While the men in his films are weak and easily flattered—dupes, self-deceived by vanity and ambition—the women have conflicts that are larger, more dignified, involving a need for love, for independence, for self-expression. They are morally stronger than the men. This may, in part, reflect a belief that the women, having always been in a subservient position, were not corrupted by English rule in the way that the men were.

Still, in "Distant Thunder," in a village far removed from that emasculating Anglicization, Ray perceives the women with such love that they become figures in a vision, and since he sees the men without the etherealizing intensity, there's an imbalance—poetry and prose. In the Apu trilogy, the hero was the embodiment of poetry, but here it is only at the end, when Gangacharan accepts a group of famine victims as his family, that he becomes as compassionate (and as fully human) as the women were all along. For Ray, the source of their strength is humility. And although one wouldn't propose any other course of action for Gangacharan, the way Ray sees him—made whole by his passive, chivalrous acceptance of what's coming—suggests a rather attenuated attempt at universalizing his situation. Satyajit Ray has rarely before dabbled in having his characters do what he so obviously believes is symbolically right. . . . (p. 170)

The music, which Ray composed, is also used portentously, signalling "distant thunder." And Ray has developed an alarming affection for melodramatic angles and zoom-fast closeups; when there's a violent action—the scarred man's overtures to Chhutki, or a rapist's assault on Ananga—he wants us to feel the dislocation. But it's intrusive, pushy; his style can't accommodate this visual abrasion. When a movie director suddenly loses his tact, he can shock viewers right out of the movie: cameras are cruel to the disfigured, and when Ray forces us to look close at the enlarged burned face of the kiln worker, we don't understand why. . . . Ray's use of emphatic techniques to heighten the impact of his material actually lowers it. When Ananga first mistakes planes flying overhead for insects, that's naïve and halfway acceptable, but when, later, the noise of the planes drowns out her screams as she's being raped, that's ladling it on. The ironies are too charged, as in the situations that American television writers come up with; this cleverness is the dramatist's form of yellow journalism. In Ray's work, what remains inarticulate is what we remember; what is articulated seems reduced, ordinary.

"Distant Thunder" is not one of his greatest films, yet it's still a Satyajit Ray film, and in how many directors' films does one anticipate greatness? With Ray, you puzzle if a picture is a little less than a masterpiece. If this one lacks the undertones of a "Days and Nights in the Forest," it's probably because he's trying to do something that sounds straightforward but isn't quite clearly thought out. Ray wants to show us how war changes people (Bergman brought it off in "Shame"), but he also wants to make an indictment. And somehow he fails on both counts. Probably he fails on the first because he doesn't endow the villagers with enough complexity. And maybe he didn't think of them in complex enough terms because he had that second, social purpose in mind. . . . When we get the closing title, telling us that five million Bengalis died in the man-made famine of 1943, Ray uses the term "man-made" because it implies that the famine was a crime. But it looks more like a horrible pileup of accidents, plus some criminal greed, and thousands of years of no planning. His statement seems forced; his whole structure is forced, and yet the film is astonishingly beautiful. The character of Gangacharan—a mixture of slothful peacefulness and a sense of dissatisfaction which he takes out on the peasants and an inquisitive, modern mind—is a fine creation, except for terminal loftiness. . . . The film is more puzzling than it seems at first; Ray is such an imagist that even his poster art slips into ambiguities.

I don't know when I've been so moved by a picture that I knew was riddled with flaws. It must be that Ray's vision comes out of so much hurt and guilt and love that the feeling pours over all the cracks in "Distant Thunder" and seals them up. (pp. 171-72)

Pauline Kael, "A Dream of Women," in The New Yorker *(© 1975 by The New Yorker Magazine, Inc.), Vol. LI, No. 38, November 10, 1975, pp. 169-72.*

JOHN SIMON

[It] was indeed a miracle for even so modest a talent as Satyajit Ray's to emerge with *Pather Panchali* two decades ago. It is not so much that Ray's films are slow, or pallid, or derivative, or choppy, or technically rudimentary—though they are all of these things, too—as that they are, for the most part, dull. *Pather* and the other two films of the so-called Apu Trilogy seemed better than what followed, perhaps because of the novelty of seeing films from India. What impressed me in Ray's later films was the infallible gift for making things come out less varied, dimensional, moving (in both senses) than life.

Some of this is not the fault of Ray, but of the political mess and cultural wasteland, the underfinancing and over-censoring he must contend with. But all this oppressiveness works, in some ways, to his advantage: it precludes a lot of competition, excuses many crudities. And, true, there are cultural differences that may make it harder for us to apprehend Ray's meanings, yet given the bending over backward with which every supine bit of Indian mysticism is hailed by our budding Buddhists, yearning yogis, and transcendental meditators, Ray, for all his secularism and even socialism, cannot help benefiting indirectly from his Indianness. . . . [Such] recent films of his as *Days and Nights in the Forest* and *The Adversary* have demonstrated to me with how primitive, indeed nonexistent, a sense of humor he turns to comedy, with how insuperable an inability to get inside his characters he adverts to drama.

In *Distant Thunder,* Ray proposes to tell the story of some villagers during the 1943 famine, while World War II was rampaging across the border from India. The last image of the film is, in fact, a silhouette shot of dark figures advancing across a convex nocturnal horizon, while a title tells us that 5 million died during what some called "the man-made famine of 1943." That final image sums up Ray's inadequacies: it is, first, meretricious poster art, just as that title is sheer didacticism; secondly, it reminds us that the film did not show how this famine was any more man-made than any other in India's hunger-ridden history. (pp. 108, 113)

Ray's lack of acuity is everywhere apparent. The obvious thing to attack in India is inadequate birth control, but this

Ray flagrantly fails to do—indeed, he ends with a paean to philo-progenitiveness. . . . Nor does it seem to occur to Ray that India, even with a famine, might have been better off than those neighbors who were being bombed by the very planes his villagers gaze at with childish delight. In fact, it is not wars beyond or within the borders that cause famines; rather it is universal stupidity that causes war, famine, and films like *Distant Thunder*. (pp. 113-14)

John Simon, "Strictly from Hunger," in New York *Magazine (copyright © 1975 by News Group Publications, Inc.; reprinted with the permission of* New York *Magazine), Vol. 8, No. 46, November 17, 1975, pp. 106, 108, 113-14.*

JOHN RUSSELL TAYLOR

Ray is a great director, and *ipso facto* cannot be typical of anything, perhaps not even reliably himself (it is the prerogative of all great artists constantly to take us by surprise). But it seems reasonable to assume that he must have come from something and fit into some sort of context. And so of course he does. Not particularly a cinematic context: eighteen years after the appearance of *Pather Panchali*, the first of the Apu trilogy, he is still a solitary figure, a unique talent in Indian cinema, and the Indian cinema apart from him has hardly moved on from the kind of nonsense he gently satirizes in the filmgoing sequence of *Apur Sansar*, all trashy, theatrical, sentimental, and fantasticated. But a literary and artistic context is very much there. . . . (pp. 165-66)

Ray's first films, the Apu trilogy, at once place him in a certain tradition by being based on a modern classic of Bengali literature, the semi-autobiographical novels by Bibhuti Bhushan Bannerjee; a more personal kind of placing is implied by his much later filming of a famous children's book by his grandfather, *Goopy Gyne Bagha Byne*. The kind of cultural society from which the young Ray sprang can be observed more directly in his film *Charulata*, which shows something closely comparable to the cultural level and high-minded seriousness suggested in the works of Ibsen and Chekhov. If Ray seems in many ways the most Western of Oriental filmmakers, it is because the traditions in which he was brought up are most closely analogous to those of Western life.

Not only the literary side of Bengali culture has been influential in Ray's career, however. A trained musician, he has composed music for all his own films since *Teen Kanya*. . . . As a writer he has written not only all his own scripts but also a number of critical articles and has worked on and off as a journalist, as well as more recently blossoming into an author of children's stories. And during his filmmaking career he has acquired other skills—ever since *Charulata*, for instance, he has been his own camera operator. This is not to say that he was necessarily first-rate in any of these other, specialized fields of activity. . . . But an independent and proven ability in all these fields, as well as giving us some insight into the versatility of the man, has enabled him to exercise remarkably complete and detailed control over all aspects of his films—technicians such as the art director, cameraman, and editor come much closer in his films than in others', except perhaps in the films of Chaplin, to being pure executants of the director's ideas rather than contributors of their own creative personalities. (pp. 166-67)

The Apu trilogy is the work which first established Ray's fame, his style, and his approach to his subject matter. . . . It is difficult to believe that the three films were not conceived at the same time, as one unified work—even though Ray tells us the notion of the trilogy came to him gradually. They are based on two books, the materials of which are symmetrically divided among the three films. . . . In reshaping the material in cinematic terms Ray has imposed a different order, giving each section of his trilogy a dramatic center and point of its own—unobtrusively he has found or invented shape, or rather three shapes, out of the much more loosely organized material of a *roman-fleuve*.

It is useful to know this if we are to counter the supposition, current at the time the trilogy first came out, that Ray is a kind of primitive, instinctive creator who somehow manages to hit it right from time to time. Merely as adaptation of material from one medium to another, the Apu trilogy is an outstanding example of creative rethinking. And the result is three films each of which can perfectly well stand on its own and yet which gain immensely from being seen together, when the subtle lines of continuity, the recurrent yet constantly developing images and ideas, can be properly appreciated. (pp. 168-69)

The plot content of the films is, in fact, by Western standards very slight (and even more so in comparison with the average Indian film). The films are built up from a succession of little incidents, at first glance linked together by no more than the "and then . . . and then . . . and then . . ." of a children's story. But to counteract the danger of shapelessness Ray has devised a whole network of subtle pictorial and aural references to articulate his clear understanding of what, essentially, each film is about. However wayward the detail may seem to be, it is controlled by a strict criterion of relevance, which we can always feel to be guiding things even if we are not from moment to moment consciously aware of precisely what it is.

The first, and in many ways the subtlest, ensurer of consistency is the angle of regard Ray turns upon his characters and events. . . . One inference, which has been too readily drawn, is that Apu's is the eye we see through in the films, that we are seeing things from his point of view, as though this is a first-person narrative. But a moment's consideration shows that this is by no means true of the films as a whole. . . . (pp. 169-70)

Apu is always a character in the films, not an enveloping consciousness. And therefore there is no danger of the filmmaker becoming lost in his creation. This is as it should be, for Ray's theme is nearly always community, living together and finding ways of doing it without compromising the individual's individuality too much. We see Apu throughout as part of an evolving group, seeking solutions and finding answers. . . . For Ray, Apu truly exists only in relationships with others.

Given this unity of regard, each film is meticulously constructed to exemplify Ray's basic concept. . . . Everything in Ray is demonstrated, externalized in some way. This is not to say that his films lack richness or subtlety, but that their "poetry" is of a classical rather than a Romantic variety, depending on the exact management and constant redefinition of images, so that they take on a complex of associations without ever losing their immediacy and propriety as literal statements of fact. (pp. 170-71)

Aparajito, the second of the trilogy, seems to be generally considered the least satisfactory. Even many sympathetic critics feel that it is broken-backed and lacking in unity (especially since the period of time covered requires two different boy actors to play Apu), and that at best it makes formal sense only as a hinge between the two flanking films. I cannot agree with this—partly, I suppose, because by chance *Aparajito* was the first of the trilogy I saw, and I found then that it made perfect sense formally and intellectually taken by itself, without knowledge of *Pather Panchali* or of the yet unmade *Apur Sansar.* (pp. 175-76)

The form of the film is freer, more expansive than that of *Pather Panchali*. . . .

Everything is necessarily disconnected, impressionistic, though again it must be insisted that we are not seeing things through Apu's eyes: we are seeing him experience them. (p. 176)

The Apu trilogy is unmistakably Ray's longest and most ambitious work, and contains much that is unforgettable. But it is an early work by a beginner and for all its astonishing maturity and mastery it has weak points and fumblings, particularly in the third part—one has the feeling, very slightly, that Ray is more interested in Apu as a child and a youth than as a man. . . . Nor does the trilogy by any means exhaust the range of Ray's interests, sympathies, and abilities as a filmmaker. It is unfortunate, and quite unfair, that it has so often been used as a stick to beat Ray's later films.

Ray's next films after the first two parts were very different in subject matter and style, both from the trilogy and from each other. The trilogy so far might have helped to tag him as a rustic neo-realist concerned principally with the peasant classes, but *Paras Pathar* (1957) takes place entirely in the city, among the middle classes, and *Jalsaghar* (1958) is the first of a series of films dealing with the zamindar class, the rich landlords of British India. Moreover, *Paras Pathar (The Philosopher's Stone)* is of all things a satirical fantasy. . . . The first part of the film manages to tread its tightrope of whimsical fantasy with considerable grace and precision. . . . Later on, though, the comic tone is not kept up. . . . All the same, it is a pity *Paras Pathar* is not better known, for it shows a gift for fantasy in Ray which he was not to exploit again until *Goopy Gyne Bagha Byne* in 1969.

If *Paras Pathar* is unarguably minor, *Jalsaghar (The Music Room)* is a major work, and remains one of Ray's finest. It is curious that it should come immediately before the third part of the Apu trilogy, for while *Apur Sansar* is expansive, *Jalsaghar* is the most concentrated and restrained of his films, a long, lyrical meditation on a single theme, the decline of an aristocratic family. The film is deliberately underdramatized; the decline is a *fait accompli* from the first, and the whole story is told from the point of view of its principal victim . . . , an aged and solitary nobleman now near death. Above all, this is an atmospheric piece, set in the sad moldering remains of a once splendid country house on the edge of an empty, mournful estuary, almost the only sign of life apart from the few, slow remnants of the household being the one horse and the single elephant left to wander idly across the sandy flats. (pp. 181-83)

[The] entire film is a dying fall evoking a situation with the poet's sublime disregard for worldly whys and wherefores. Though there are one or two places, usually in action scenes . . . , where this leads to perfunctory handling (Ray has always been least sure in his direction of pure action, particularly violent action), in general *Jalsaghar* is one of Ray's most masterly films, exquisitely photographed and directed with a complete, unquestioning mastery of mood and tempo which matches the work of Jean Renoir at its best. Most wonderful of all, perhaps, are the two big sequences in the music room itself, that leading up to the storm in which the hero's son is lost and that in which with a grand gesture he spends the last of his money on just one more, crowning performance before he dies. In particular the first—with its long concentration on the mounting intensity of the Moslem singer's song, the physical signs of the rising storm in the shaking mirror and the swaying chandeliers, at first unnoticed by the rapt guests, the insect drowning in the zamindar's glass of wine, and then the full fury of the storm—is unforgettable as a piece of musical, dramatic, and visual construction. *Jalsaghar* is not the easiest of films, especially for a Western audience, since it lacks the more accessible appeals to sentiment of the Apu trilogy, but for those willing to place themselves under its hypnotic spell it offers pleasures of unique delicacy and refinement.

The same cannot be said of *Devi (The Goddess),* the film Ray made in 1960, immediately after *Apur Sansar.* Though some like it very much, it never seems to me to come through with the force and conviction that it should. Easy to feel, but hard to say exactly why. The plot is both interesting in itself and, for a Western audience, exotic enough to offer a bonus of Oriental glamour. . . . It is, in fact, an unusually coherent, tightly knit plot, one of the best-organized plots in Ray's *oeuvre,* and perhaps this is what is wrong with the film. Ray's is an expansive, rhapsodic talent, and it seems to blossom best when it has time to work by indirection, by the cumulative effect of recurrent images and delicate hints of character and motivation, and is least confined by a strict external form. *Devi* is more a matter of uncluttered storytelling than of atmosphere and the loving accumulation of detail. The story is, admittedly, quite well told, if a little slowly, but somehow in the process much of the life of the film, the life which we normally expect of Ray's films, seems to have drained away. Of course, there are remarkable things in *Devi* all the same, especially in the hypnotic scenes of the religious ceremonies in which the unfortunate heroine is involved, and these introduce another element into our knowledge of Ray's range of effects: his ability to handle successfully a florid style with flashy camera work and obtrusive editing effects. But by and large the film does not seem quite to live up to its ambitions, and it is interesting in Ray's progress mainly as marking a shift from a narrative to a more dramatic approach. (pp. 183-84)

Though a commissioned work, *Rabindranath Tagore* was obviously also in many ways a labor of love. As organized, it sets out to trace Tagore's life partly by the use of documents . . . and partly by reconstruction with live actors. On the whole, it reflects Ray's technical skill and superior tastes rather than his most personal gifts as a filmmaker, but even so it is often fascinating, with its glimpses of moldering architectural splendors and its revealing snapshots of both the great and the insignificant in the early years of this century. . . .

Teen Kanya is longer and more substantial, though its material is essentially slighter. In its original form the two primarily comic episodes known in the West as *Two Daughters* were separated by another new venture for Ray, a ghost story called "Monihara," which Ray felt would make the film, at nearly three hours, rather too much of a good thing for non-Indian audiences. *Two Daughters* is as it stands one of Ray's most wholly delightful films, showing his till then largely hidden gift for comedy to the full. (p. 185)

Ray's two ensuing films, *Kanchenjunga* (1962) his first color film, and *Abyijan* (162), *have had little showing in the West. This seems reasonable in the case of Abhijan,* a picaresque adventure story centering on a taxi driver and his romantic and dramatic entanglements, which apparently Ray undertook to direct at the last minute and has little to commend it apart from the interest of seeing Ray handle a subject much closer to the Indian commercial norm than any of his other films. But *Kanchenjunga* is one of Ray's subtlest and most personal films, and perhaps the most concentrated example of preoccupation with interrelations within the family and the difficulties as well as the joys of togetherness. It is, incidentally, the first film based on an original story by Ray himself. Essentially it is a conversation piece. Its action strictly observes the unities, the film taking exactly the one hundred minutes that the action it represefts takes. On one level the script is simple—merely eight members of one family drifting in and out of camera, talking often at random, with a couple of outsiders to influence the course of their meandering afternoon. But within this framework the drama is carefully and precisely patterned. (p. 188)

In a sense little happens; in a sense a great deal does. The drama here is much more interior than usual in Ray's films, and the surface is much more apparently literary, in that there is a lot of dialogue. But only apparently, for in this story the characters seldom say directly what they are thinking, or indeed anything particularly germane to the central issues of the drama, which are all thought and fought out beyond, between, and beneath the words they speak. The visuaw aspect of the film is cool and elegant, not overstuffed with effects or even images apart from the main one, which is an image of absence. . . . (p. 189)

Kanchenjunga is a high point in Ray's career; *Charulata,* which he made two years later, again basing his script on a story by Tagore, is another. In between comes *Mahanagar* (*The Big City*) (1963), which I do not find by any means so compelling, though it deals with a theme that obviously has some special importance for Ray, since he deals with it also in *Apur Sansar* and again in *Pratidwandi*: the search for work in a big city. (p. 190)

[The] second half of [*Mahanagar*] has too large an accumulation of bare happenings, some of them decidedly melodramatic and all of them losing conviction by their number and rapid succession. Ray still does not stage action well . . . and seems out of his element in a plot-bound situation which does not leave his characters enough room to grow and develop by interaction. He does not seem creatively involved with much of *Mahanagar,* however much importance he may as a man attribute to the ideas and attitudes expressed in it.

Charulata, on the other hand, is by any standard one of Ray's masterpieces. Dealing with a moneyed and highly literate section of the zamindar class in the 1870's, it is, to steal a phrase from the advertising campaign for a very different film, "almost a love story," concerning the elusive, implicitly emotional relationship between the young wife of a newspaper proprietor and her husband's artistic cousin. (p. 191)

The whole story is told in hints and sidewights; in fact, in a real sense nothing does happen: it is all atmosphere and suggestion and unstated, even unconscious, emotional responses. *Jalsaghar* had already demonstrated, if demon*stration were needed, how well capable of dealing with a* subject as sophisticated as this Ray was—the days, if they had ever existed, when he could reasonably be regardedsas a gifted but chancy primitive were long past—and in *Charulata* he brings the whole battery of his talents to bear, with sometimes breathtaking results. The sheer visual beauty of the film is extraordinary and the more showy technical devices—fast tracking shots, zoom lenses, etc.—are used with exemplary discipline and discretion. The acting of the principals too, on occasion the weak point in Ray's films, is here impeccable, catching exactly the Morrisian fervor relieved with heavy playfulness which makes this stratum of Indian life seem, oddly, more English than England itself. (pp. 191-92)

Charulata, it is tempting to say, is Ray's most Western film —in discussing it one thinks at once of Ibsen or Strindberg (more in this case than Chekhov, who so often seems to offer close parallels to Ray's dramatic practice). But that is begging the question whether most of Ray is not Western. Obviously there are qualities in his films, such as their frequently very measured tempo (slowness, unsympathetic critics would say), which are easiest to discuss as part of his Indianness. But apart from his subject matter it is hard to be sure that there is anything in his films that derives specifically from his Oriental background and heritage: he is very much a world filmmaker. . . . There is nothing in his films which has to be related to anything but his own artistic development and taste as an individual; like any artist, he is finally independent of his background, and whatever use he may choose to make of it is ultimately self-determined. (p. 193)

[*Goopy Gyne Bagha Byne*] is another attempt on Ray's part at something new—or at least something he had not ventured on since *Paras Pathar*—fantasy. . . . [As] well as being a fantasy, *Goopy Gyne* is a musical, with no fewer than eight full musical numbers in it, and the opportunity it offered Ray as a composer may well have tipped the balance unduly in its favor.

At least we can say that *Goopy Gyne* was a labor of love and no mere commercial chore. . . . One of the main pleasures to be derived from it is a sense of relief and relaxation —we feel that Ray is content to have fun with his subject, and though solemn analyses of the subject in relation to Ray's attitude toward war and violence have been produced, the feeling of the film is primarily that of a romp. . . . (pp. 194-95)

[It] is all very nice, if a bit long-drawn-out, with too many twists and turns of plot to try the audience's patience. It would be easy, reversing the judgment on *Charulata,* to say that *Goopy Gyne* is Ray's most Indian film, and in a sense this may be true—undoubtedly with its comedy and romance and fantasy, its songs and dances and spectacle, it is nearer than any of Ray's other films to the sort of Indian cinema best known n the West. . . . [But] a slight feeling remains that it is disappointing from Ray—less personal, less felt, less intensely realized than even the lightest of his other works, like *Teen Kanya* or *Kapurush-o-Mahapurush.* It is true, also, that purely technical limitation may have something to do with this: a fantasy of this kind has to be physically absolutely convincing, and suspension of disbelief is not aided here by shaky back projection and traveling matte or obvious economies in sets, costumes, and spectacular highlights. Nor indeed by the fact that the film, for financial reasons, had to be made in black-and-white (bursting into color only right at the end), when it obviously begs to be made in color throughout. (p. 196)

Aranyer Din Ratri (*Days and Nights in the Forest*) (1970) was a decided return to form, and enforced some clear rethinking of attitudes toward Ray which were beginning to become set in critics' minds. It has always been easy, too easy, to pull out the conventional epithets for Ray's films. "Measured," we say, to suggest that they are slow, but are obviously meant to be that way. "Poetic"—for Ray's approach to character and event is clearly far from documentary, and his films seem often to be built to music unheard as well as to his own heard, and highly expressive, scores. "Humane"—because his sympathy, and ours, goes out to even the most unlikely objects, realizing in practice that usually somewhat unrealistic maxim that to understand all is to forgive all. But these ready formulations leave the magic of his films unexpressed. (pp. 196-97)

[*Days and Nights in the Forest*] is not even, I would say, one of Ray's really top-notch films throughout: just a better-than-average middle-range work. There are sections, particularly in the first half, which are rather too measured for comfort, and the build-up to the appearance of the feminine interest is too long-drawn-out. But even this slight wearisomeness pays eventual dividends in that we really feel we have been living along with these people. There is, indeed, something Chekhovian about Ray's wayward, indirect means of character revelation. . . .

In the wake of *Days and Nights in the Forest,* Ray embarked on a film in which the political theme, implicit in *Days and Nights in the Forest,* came to the fore. And by the time he came to make his next film he became aware that what he had was a second trilogy, less closely-knit than the Apu trilogy, but united by recurrent themes indicative of social change in modern India. In *Pratidwandi* (*The Adversary*) (1970) we return to the theme and the world of the opening of *Apur Sansar* and *Mahanagar*. (p. 197)

In the following film, *Seemabadha* (*Company Limited*) (1971), we see as it were the reverse side of the medal. Back in Calcutta, Ray shows us the new bourgeoisie functioning in a Westernized setting of big business. (p. 198)

Company Limited is technically quite straightforward, particularly when compared to *The Adversary* and its elaborate structure, with its flashes forward and back, its adventures into negative in certain sequences, and its instantaneous glimpses of potential action going on in its characters' heads. It is also a lot funnier, with much mordant humor in its observation of business methods and the contrasts of social life in Calcutta. It is rather as though the satire present within the fantasy of *Paras Pathar* has been transmuted by contact with the realistic observation of, say, *Mahanagar* to produce a satisfying new tone in Ray's work. The sociopolitical observation of the new trilogy is consistent in its humor and its underlying sadness—sadness rather than bitterness, for Ray does not seem to be the stuff of which revolutionaries are made. He observes human follies and failings, but remains sympathetic and understanding toward his characters—his sympathies can embrace the young executive in *Company Limited* as well as the naïve, idealistic sister-in-law, and one feels that the revolutionary boy friend, if we ever saw him, would be no more likely to figure as an unequivocal all-round hero. Ray's is a world of complex human beings, in which most people mean more or less well, and nobody gets to carry the banner of Ray's sympathy or the stigma of his total disapproval; it is a fallible, human world we can all recognize.

If something of a new tone was perceptible in *Company Limited* . . . , *Ashani Sanket* (*Distant Thunder*) (1973), suggests a departure in quite a new direction for him, an extraordinary development in his talents. Though there are certain points of detail in common between it and some of his earlier works, these generally seem to be something in the nature of deliberate references. . . . What is different about *Distant Thunder* . . . is its whole tone, scope, and approach to character. It comes very near to being an epic drama in the Brechtian rather than the Hollywood sense of the term. (pp. 199-200)

There are details of great visual beauty in the film, particularly in its use of color, which Ray is here using in a feature for only the second time. But whereas Ray has often seemed in the past to be essentially a miniaturist, or at least an intimist, here it is the grand design of the whole which works on the spectator: the film is built on a monumental scale which belies its relatively modest length and overwhelms one as surely as the rising tide. (p. 201)

[Ray] has lived through, and lived down, a number of pigeonholing reputations. There was that of being an Indian filmmaker, *the* Indian filmmaker, as opposed to a filmmaker *tout court*: with its implication that he was a special case, requiring sympathy, tolerance, patronage, special standards of judgment. Then there was that of the neo-realist primitive, an instinctive artist whose first films just happened to come out right because of "sincerity" and humane values, rather than because of any conscious art. Then there was that of the poetic symbolist, dependent on the manipulation of obvious (and often too obvious) visual metaphors for his effects. Then there was that of the filmmaker of unfulfilled promise, who had shot his bolt with his earliest works and was now overproductive and disappointing—the Apu trilogy has often been used as a stick to beat his later films with, both because they are different and because they are not, even by critics who did not particularly like the trilogy when it first came out. And all this time Ray has continued to make films in his own time, according to the dictates of his own artistic development, and influenced as little as possible by critics or by commercial considerations.

Sometimes he may choose a deliberately simple, unadorned style, as in the "Postmaster" episode of *Teen Kanya,* when he feels that it matches the material, but in films like *Jalsaghar, Devi,* and the "Monihara" episode of *Teen Kanya,* his style can be as rich and highly wrought as any in the cinema today. Similarly, the pace of his films may often be slow (and not only to Western viewers), but the slowness nearly always justifies itself as the only way of adequately exploring the material, and when he wants to, Ray can pick up the pace with complete mastery and conviction, as in the swinging episode of *Charulata*. Admittedly, in his constant experimentation with new styles and materials, some weak points have emerged—he is not at home with the staging of violent physical action or of broad farce—but to balance this he has scored decisive successes in some unexpected genres, such as the horror film ("Monihara"), social comedy ("Samapti" and episodes of *Mahanagar* and *Days and Nights in the Forest*), and the highly sophisticated atmospheric conversation piece (*Kanchenjunga*)1 Understandably, the assumption which still crops up among Western critics, that he is a natural, untutored genius, unconscious of his art and unthinkingly warbling his wood-notes wild, rankles a little, but in spite of the critics, and in spite of commercial pressures at home, he goes on making films in his own fashion, with conscious and consciously developing art, on the principle that if they do not please him they are unlikely to please anyone else. (pp. 202-03)

John Russell Taylor, "Satyajit Ray," in his Directors and Directions: Cinema for the Seventies *(reprinted by permission of Hill and Wang, a division of Farrar, Straus & Giroux, Inc.; in Canada, by A D Peters & Co Ltd; copyright © 1975 by John Russell Taylor), Hill and Wang, 1975, pp. 165-203.*

CHRIS SCHEMERING

Distant Thunder, a rare color film by Satyajit Ray, is perhaps the master film-maker's loveliest, but it could take the cake as his most simple-minded and literal. . . .

Ray gets in a few social barbs at the huszling middle class. But while Ray plants the seed for satire, he doesn't go anywhere with it. It's a red herring—the calm before the storm.

After this point the narrative becomes an exposition of the theme: what war does to people, specifically what war does to Ray's innocents who will endure famine although the war never touches them directly. *Distant Thunder* has been compared with Bergman's *Shame* but the vivid images matched with heavy metaphors and tired plot bones brings it closer to *Cries and Whispers,* Bergman's awesome closet drama. . . . *Distant Thunder* begins as a fairy tale romance and ends on the same note; there's nowhere the film can go dramatically. . . . Nevertheless, the film moves forward so sensuously and lyrically and because all Satyajit Ray's films are invariably rubber-stamped with the critical catchword 'humanism', it's no wonder *Distant Thunder* could appeal to critics as varied as Vincent Canby, Molly Haskell and Pauline Kael. . . .

The ridiculously blunt symbolism comes down with the weight of a sledgehammer. Ray isn't giving an emotional nudge; it's a push. *Distant Thunder* contains some of Ray's worst ideas since *Nayak* where the hero, an insecure movie star, dreams of literally drowning in money.

I like Ray because his effects are usually so delicately and economically achieved. . . . The effects in *Distant Thunder* are all too obvious. . . .

Again Ray dramatically sets troubled, often confused and ineffective men against strong, instinctive women. Like Bergman he is mistakably in awe of women and shares with Bergman . . . the tendency for using the most obsessively lovely women set off against physically unattractive men. (p. 38)

Gangacharan's seemingly revealing comment when his wife tells him she has a job, "If we have to humble ourselves, it's best we do it together," is meaningless in the context of the ending. The change is fleeting, transitory. Perhaps it does not occur to them to question the system that sends the harvest the people reaped to far-off armies. In a fairy tale romance like this nothing much has really changed, not the couple's civic outlook and certainly not their plumply sensual appearance; neither is noticeably thinner by the end. They're still sacred cows. They have awakened only to social passivity. Their cock-eyed optimism—a mixture of empty bravery and political indifference—will see them through.

This is strange and disappointing coming from a director whose best films deal with the evolving social conscience, the psychology of change. Even stranger is the affectation of the art house equivalent of the Hollywood gloss. The horrible realism of hunger, emaciation, and death are eclipsed by the hypnotizing poetry of Ray's camera—the drifting lyricism, the white heat, the slowly changing rhythms, the softly colored images, and the floating, exotic sounds of the countryside. According to the reviewers it's the latest thing in ambiguity, as if ugliness is more threatening and hideous if it comes giftwrapped. It achieves the same end—they just starve beautifully, making it so much easier for critics in humanist cloak to be seduced by, rave about and forget. (p. 39)

Chris Schemering, "'Distant Thunder'," in Cinéaste *(copyright © 1976 by Gary Crowdus), Vol. VII, No. 2, 1976, pp. 38-9.*

WILLIAM S. PECHTER

That [*Distant Thunder*] falls short of Ray's best work is probably true enough, and worth saying. No less worth saying, however briefly and belatedly, is that I've seen no other film this year or last which seems to me to approach it.

[What] the film is about is less [the famine it depicts] than the transformations wrought by that famine on the lives of one couple. Characteristically, the principals aren't some neo-realist-style impoverished everyman-and-woman but a Brahmin teacher and his wife, accustomed by their caste to privilege, and taking deference as their due. It would have been easy to have made these characters, the man especially, more sympathetic. . . . And it would have been easy, also, to have set the film in some expressively ravaged and barren landscape rather than the film's verdantly beautiful one, and to have photographed it in stark black and white instead of sensuous color. But this is a film of *distant* thunder, in which the first words, said by the woman of some passing bombers, are, "How beautiful! Like a flight of cranes!"—a film about a world that's full of death, but a world in which death comes not with sudden violence so much as by stealth: stealing up on one in barely perceptible increments.

Distant Thunder has its faults. Though exquisitely delicate when it keeps to the intimate scale of the man and wife, it can be perfunctory and uninspired (montages of newspaper headlines) in sketching the larger social movements in the background. . . . (p. 78)

William S. Pechter, "Altman, Chabrol, and Ray" (copyright © 1976 by William S. Pechter; reprinted by permission of the author), in Commentary, *Vol. 62, No. 4, October, 1976, pp. 75-8 (and to be reprinted in his* Movies plus One, *Horizon Press, 1981).*

GEOFF BROWN

The Middleman is no exact sequel [to *Company Limited*], for Ray's portrait of the sad inter-relationship between amorality and success is painted in far greater detail and in darker colours. There is more explicit emphasis on the break-up of India's past traditions. . . . Religion is specifically degraded. . . . Unlike many other directors (Altman, for instance), Ray can depict sour and cynical characters or events without being sour himself: from the opening scenes the film bristles with the warm, involving comedy of everyday oddities and indignities, conveying Ray's moral and message with far more effectiveness than any strident tub-thumping. . . . Ray's camera observes the comic disasters and follies with his customary dry detachment: during a drive . . . , a dashboard compartment repeatedly flaps open every time the vehicle hits a pothole—an event deliciously signalled by shots of one of the car's wheels hurtling fatefully along the road. The film runs for a little over two hours, and the narrative drifts and drags its feet slightly; a couple of flashback scenes seem curious intrusions. But nothing can detract from the film's overall success and its penetrating charm.

Geoff Brown, "Feature Films: 'Jana-Aranya' ('The Middleman')," in Monthly Film Bulletin *(copyright © The British Film Institute, 1977), Vol. 44, No. 518, March, 1977, p. 43.*

TOM MILNE

Perhaps the most fascinating aspect of Satyajit Ray's *The Chess Players* . . . is the ambivalence with which Ray views the matter of politics and progress, recalling the fact that twenty years ago, in *Jalsaghar*, he demonstrated how an aristocratic landowner's irredeemable social negligence might yet aspire to a state of grace through his overruling delight in beauty. There, more overtly but no more inescapably than in the new film, Ray's direction recorded the death of a way of life, a suicide willingly undertaken because pure beauty cannot survive untarnished in a crassly material world. . . .

[Ray splits his viewpoint three ways.] Two of these, represented on the one hand by the montage sequence which sketches a concise but enormously expressive account of Britain's relationship with [the Nawabsof Oudh], and on the other by the tale of the two chess players, are governed by the historical determinants of British colonial arrogance and India's obliging submission to superior technology. . . . [Contrary] to his usual concern for the respect due to his characters' lives . . . , Ray treats both characters essentially as caricatures to match the cartoon basis of his historical montage.

In a sense, therefore, these two 'viewpoints' cancel each other out: if the march of progress is inevitable in the wake of the British Empire, equally inevitable is the fact—for all the chess players' stout insistence that they will play today but fight tomorrow—that India is not going to find the will to resist. And here Ray's third voice comes in, expressed by the arts whose fantastic flowering under the Nawab Wajid Ali Shah turned Lucknow into the treasure-house of Moslem culture. . . .

Ray, of course, is not naive enough to suggest that artistic talent compensates for misrule. . . .

Ray does not blame his two heroes for preferring the chess-board to the battlefield. Engagingly fantastical (much of the film is wonderfully funny, especially when, after losing their chess set to a disgruntled wife, the pair are frustrated in their attempts to borrow another by the untimely death of its owner and are reduced to improvising pieces out of fruit, nuts and spice bottles), their pursuit of pleasure and avoidance of strife is just as Wajid Ali Shah would have wished.

Tom Milne, "'The Chess Players'," in Sight and Sound *(copyright © 1979 by The British Film Institute), Vol. 48, No. 2, Spring, 1979, p. 125.*

J. HOBERMAN

American interest in Satyajit Ray appears to have peaked in the Peace Corps era of the early '60s. One wonders if he didn't forfeit his status as a Third World filmmaker once it became apparent that his theme was not the plight of India's landless masses but the social evolution of its Brahman bourgeoisie. That *The Middleman* (1975) . . . reiterates Ray's obsessive concern should be obvious from its title. What's uncharacteristic about the film—Ray's best since his chamber drama *Charluta* (1964)—is its bleak pessimism.

Shot during the early days of Indira Gandhi's "emergency rule" in the pressure cooker atmosphere of Ray's native Calcutta, *The Middleman* is played against a tatty backdrop of matter-of-fact chaos. The recurrent power failures and perpetually crossed phone wires are almost too routine to deserve comment. The lines of the unemployed snake through half the exterior scenes; the clamor of the street invades every interior. Nothing else can be taken for granted: Somnath . . . , the 24-year-old protagonist first seen in a hysterical crowd of students surging for their exam results, has his academic career wrecked because his test examiner is unable to borrow a pair of glasses from a neighbor. . . .

Ray is the most conservative of neo-realism's heirs and he spends the first hour of the film carefully establishing Somnath's relationships with his family, friends, and colleagues. At the same time he makes sure that we're one step ahead in contemplating the hero's fate from a distance. . . . Everything builds up to the bottom falling out. . . .

Somnath's father, a disciple of Gandhi, provides the film with a moral center—although it's clear that his values are hopelessly out of touch with the realities of modern India. Somnath, however, has broken through to that world of suffering and degradation which surrounds them, and, for this reason, *The Middleman* seems less a film of despair than disillusionment. But it is not depressing; Ray's characters are too rich, his criticism too sharp.

J. Hoberman, "Oy! Calcutta!" (reprinted by permission; copyright © J. Hoberman, 1980), in The Village Voice, *Vol. XXV, No. 8, February 25, 1980, p. 42.*

Alain Resnais

1922-

French director and actor.

A foremost filmmaker of the French New Wave, Resnais includes comic strips, Alfred Hitchcock, and Jerry Lewis among his influences. Fascinated with capturing the disjointed, yet fluid quality of time and memory, Resnais characteristically uses a non-narrative style and long tracking shots in his films.

Before directing, Resnais studied acting and editing at the Institut des Hautes Études Cinématographiques in Paris. His documentary experience commenced with several art films, *Van Gogh, Guernica,* and *Gauguin,* followed by a film on Nazi concentration camps, *Nuit et Brouillard.* Other short documentaries include studies of the plastics industry and the Bibliothèque Nationale. Resnais has often opted for collaboration with well-established writers. This, along with his taste for experimentation, formed the groundwork for his first feature, *Hiroshima Mon Amour* written by Marguerite Duras.

In *L'Année dernière à Marienbad* written with Alain Robbe-Grillet, Resnais shuns traditional plot in favor of focusing on psychological themes. This film is considered a milestone in the cinematic world. Jean de Baroncelli, called it the first cubist film, comparing it to Picasso's *Les Demoiselles D'Avignon.* *Marienbad* received limited popular acclaim, however, until it won the Great Golden Lion of the Venice Film Festival.

In *La Guerre est Finie,* Resnais sought to depict political reality. In addition, it was his first film concerning itself with a primary male character and the fusion of political and romantic lifestyles. *Je t'aime je t'aime,* on the other hand, represents a step into the science fiction world, telling the story of a man who must live his life twice. While examining the concept of time here, Resnais also had the opportunity to work with double imagery as a new form of narrative. *Providence* is his only attempt at comedy. However, *Providence* displays a strong Brechtian influence as well, and is generally considered to be Resnais's attempt to rediscover himself artistically.

Resnais's influence in the cinematic world has been chiefly noted of late in the new German cinema, whose exponents emulate his innovative forms of narrative. Though he is widely admired, he is not directly imitated; John Francis Kreidl said of Resnais, "There is no Resnaismania; he has no students because he is too difficult to copy; but he has become a sourcebook for the future."

NOEL BURCH

Though less ambitious, on the face of it, than *Toute la Mémoire du Monde,* Resnais's most recent short, *Le Chant du Styrène* . . . is perhaps even more brilliantly perfect. I say less ambitious because, in a sense, "it has all been done before": *le styrène* is a type of plastic—polystyrene. But rather than an industrial documentary, the film is a synthesis of visual abstraction and verbal lyricism, and as such it has probably never been equalled since the heyday of British documentary. (p. 59)

Alain Resnais and his cameraman, Sacha Vierny . . . , have performed a veritable *tour de force* in "industrial" camerawork. The acid contrast between candy-colored ribbons, pellets, and sheets of plastic as they pass through the gamut of presses and conveyor belts and the steely greys and browns of the machinery itself, is more than simply striking: it serves to create a perfectly coherent *abstract* universe, in which the sudden appearance of a line of workers shuffling oddly into the factory toward the end of the film—practically the only shot in which the "natural" spectrum is given full play—produces the shock of a rude awakening, as it recalls the irksome presence of mere humanity on the edge of this mechanical fairy-land. . . .

The most important element of synthesis in the film is the relationship between the metric structure of [the verse of the author, Raymond Queneau] and the relaxed rhythm with which Vierny's startling images are made to succeed one another. (p. 60)

Finally, as Queneau leads us farther and farther back towards the sources of polystyrene—coal, petroleum, etc.—he seems suddenly aware that there is no reason why this account should ever stop, and with a few speculative verses on the prehistoric origins of coal and petroleum he decides, still without breaking the meter, that further investigation is better left "à d'autres documentaires," and this provocative little masterpiece just seems to stop . . . on a close-up of the seething jade-green sea. (p. 61)

Noel Burch, "Four Recent French Documentaries," in Film Quarterly *(copyright 1959 by The Regents of the University of California; reprinted by permission of the University of California Press), Vol. XIII, No. 1, Fall, 1959, pp. 56-61.**

A. H. WEILER

If Alain Resnais, producer-director of "Hiroshima, Mon

Amour," may be classified a member of the French "new wave," then he also must be listed as riding its crest. For his delicately wrought drama . . . is a complex yet compelling tour de force—as a patent plea for peace and the abolition of atomic warfare; as a poetic evocation of love lost and momentarily found, and as a curiously intricate but intriguing montage of thinking on several planes in Proustian style.

Although it presents, on occasion, a baffling repetition of words and ideas, much like vaguely recurring dreams, it, nevertheless, leaves the impression of a careful coalescence of art and craftsmanship.

With the assistance of Marguerite Duras, one of France's leading symbolic novelists . . . , M. Resnais is not merely concerned with the physical aspects of a short (two-day) affair between a Gallic actress, in Hiroshima to make a film, and a Japanese architect. He also explores the meanings of war, the woman's first love and the interchange of thoughts as they emerge during the brief but supercharged romantic interlude.

A viewer, it must be stated at the outset, needs patience in order to appreciate the slow but calculated evolvement of the various levels of the film's drama. . . . Neither M. Resnais nor Mlle. Duras are direct in their approach. . . .

There is no doubt now that M. Resnais has chosen his proper metier. As a director who set himself an extremely difficult task, he expertly sustains the fragile moods of his theme most of the way. He also illustrates a rare expertise in his ability to show flashbacks. . . .

If "Hiroshima, Mon Amour" is any yardstick, M. Resnais seems to have assured himself a niche in the feature-film field, too.

A. H. Weiler, "'Hiroshima, Mon Amour'," in The New York Times *(© 1960 by The New York Times Company; reprinted by permission), May 17, 1960, p. 43.*

NORMAN N. HOLLAND

A brilliant, trying picture, at once sensitive and blunt, tender and savage, fleshy and spiritual, pacifist and politically realistic, [*Hiroshima, Mon Amour*] has something for everybody. For the film historian, not only does it provide another item to flesh out that increasingly meaningless label, *nouvelle vague;* it also uses some important new techniques of flashback. For the film critic, it is just a fine and meaningful film, to borrow a Bergman title, a lesson in love.

Hiroshima shows us a Frenchwoman and a Japanese having an impromptu affair in that city, which she tells us "was made for love." As they embrace, she drily and monotonously reconstructs from her tours of the city the world-wide horror of Hiroshima on August 6, 1945 and thereafter; later, she recalls as though on an analytic couch her personal horror—the French killing her German lover in the brisk process of liberation and her subsequent shames and sufferings. . . .

[The] complexity of Resnais' technique rules out the possibility he is dealing with anything so banal as a study in nationalities. (p. 593)

In joining the old love affair, the new one, and the bombing, Resnais insists on the essential sameness of human experience, specifically the bombing and the "liberation," love and war. Shots of her shorn head match shots of Japanese women pulling out their radiated hair after the bomb. They crawl out of ruins and cellars as she had done with her German lover. The lighting of her basement prison is the soot of Hiroshima. "Deform me, deform me," she cries to her new lover, "You destroy me—you are good for me." This sameness is implicit in the very technique of telling about the bombing and the German lover in the setting of the later love affair which fuses both episodes, Resnais' technique of unexplained flashbacks. (p. 594)

There is even a mythic quality to this oneness. Her Japanese lover tells her she is like a thousand women—the "She" herself identifies her German lover with her Japanese, speaking of his "German name" as though he were two incarnations of one man, crying out, "I shall triumph over you all." She is like a Venus (or Juliet or Perdita), to whom, after the canonical Frazerian round of fourteen years, her adversary Adonis returns. (pp. 594-95)

Yet, mythic or not, personal sorrows obviously cannot be the same order of thing as the world-tragedy of Hiroshima, and Resnais would be guilty of a grotesque sentimentality were not his images of the sameness of human experience completely overborne by images of its essential separateness (*"Tu n'as rien vu à Hiroshima"*) [You saw nothing at Hiroshima]. . . .

Hiroshima, Mon Amour, as the actress herself points out, defines an eternal *principe d'inégalité,* a world doomed to foin and fight because it is compounded of identities and contrasts, a world in which a Frenchwoman loves first a German, then a Japanese, in which love is like war, newsreel fact becomes cinematic memory, and madness, as she says, is the same as intelligence.

Resnais himself—this is his first feature-length film; till *Hiroshima* he had made only art shorts—says the picture is musically composed, an andante or theme and variations. In the last third of the film, this music, this uneasy and dialectic interplay of sameness and separateness, draws to a close and, in doing so, the theme of the opening comes clear again. (p. 595)

This section of the film, twenty almost wordless minutes, has been criticized as dull, and alas, it is. Yet, after the hectic of the bombing and the two love affairs, the emotional letdown is both unavoidable and supremely appropriate. It is precisely the feeling demanded by the paradoxical theme—that human union is neither permanent nor even, really, possible; we are separate even as we are inextricably entwined; one flesh is two. Thus, we the audience must pass through the same act of oblivion as "She" to learn what the film tells us. It is the very fact that she could forget the pain of her first love that makes her refuse to love again. . . .

The *"Ton nom est Hiroshima." "Ton nom est Nevers–en France,"* ["Your name is Hiroshima." "Your name is Nevers—in France"] speaks not *of* nationalities but *in* nationalities of all the irreducible separatenesses and samenesses, that drowsy melody of attractions and repulsions which binds into one world all the circling human monads—quite like the particles in an atom which, if they love, explode. (p. 596)

Norman N. Holland, "Two Films on Flesh," in The Hudson Review *(copyright © 1961 by The*

*Hudson Review, Inc.; reprinted by permission), Vol. XIII, No. 4, Winter, 1960-61, pp. 592-97.**

PENELOPE HOUSTON

[*L'Année Dernière à Marienbad*] is a study in persuasion, and one which involves the audience as much as the people on the screen; and it is a work in which the technique and the action are quite literally fused. If it were not told in this particular way, the film would not exist. . . .

[All] it can declare *is* itself—or, rather, the invitation to experience it contains.

L'Année Dernière opens, like *Hiroshima mon Amour,* with a sustained and elaborate introductory passage; in *Hiroshima* Resnais called it the 'opera'—here it is certainly not less than the overture. The music behind the credits fades, and before the last names come up on the screen a voice is heard, impersonal, grave, and at first very quiet. The voice becomes clearer as the first images appear: the long corridors of a big hotel, empty of people but suggesting a weight of habitation in their rich, arrogant decoration. Incantatory, the voice continues: "Once again I walk, once again, along these corridors, across these *salons,* these galleries, in this edifice from another century, this huge, luxurious, baroque hotel . . ." Organ music drowns the voice, then it returns, then the music rises over it again. The camera tracks slowly, inevitably, hovers over a theatre poster, a print of a formal garden, a row of numbered doors, moves down corridors, across baroque ceilings, gives such crystalline clarity to a section of moulding that it looks like a glistening bunch of fruit waiting to be picked. Then people: an audience for a play, gathered in a great *salon,* motionless and abstracted as they sit on their little gilt chairs and watch the stage. The voice of the actor on the stage takes over, as it were, from the narrator, "Voilà maintenant," says the actress, "Je suis à vous." Curtain.

The opening is entirely hypnotic. Like the beginning of a fairy tale, it draws us into an alien world, gives us no chance to get our bearings, hints at clues which may or may not turn out to have meaning. (p. 26)

The stranger's strength is in the sheer pressure of will: he wants it to be so; it will be so; it is so. Did they know each other, were they in love, if so, why does she resist the memory, if not, what is his motive? Are they patient and analyst, or does each achieve existence only in the imagination of the other? These are enticing though perhaps irrelevant questions. . . .

In their context, [the fantasy moments] are eerie, ominous, charged with tension. They are part of the whole elaborate process of involvement in the man's belief, catching us unaware, forcing us into a world in which the real is not quite real, the imagined not quite unreal; in which there are only a series of possibilities, which become actual once they are admitted and accepted. (p. 27)

L'Année Dernière, if written as a novel, would certainly seem nothing like as audacious or challenging as it does on the screen. Subjective time, recurring time, the gradations of reality and experience, are nothing strange to the modern novel. But the film can accommodate them more easily—or more suggestively; and since its essential ingredients are space and time it can manoeuvre in both at once, make both relative to its own purposes. In *Hiroshima mon Amour* Resnais explored time and memory from a fixed point of reference. Here there is no fixed point, and consequently the film imposes its own time. When it ends, it is over, apart from the echoes it sets reverberating in our minds. It has come full circle, from the scene on the stage at the beginning ("Je suis à vous") to the setting out into the dark garden; but how long has it taken to do so? An evening in the heroine's mind; a week of persuasive effort by the man? It has taken, one can only say, the time it needed on the screen. . . .

L'Année Dernière à Marienbad is a piece of persuasion; and the materials out of which it builds are those suggested by the setting itself: the quality of a dream hangs heavy over it. . . .

No picture could be more fully realised, less of a do-it-yourself kit for filmgoers, than *L'Année Dernière;* but it is a film which opens up perspectives, alternatives, and at the same time that it spreads them out before the filmgoer it also contains them. Think of a solution, and the film will probably have forestalled you; the meanings will be there, the clues offered, yet when you get to what seems to be the centre of the maze, there's still another path, and another . . . The meaning of the film is not, I would suggest, in some aphorism—the second half of the proverb—which you can bring out of the maze with you, but in this process of exploration, this containing of possibilities. Objective explanations can be sought but not imposed. We are being given not a comment on 'reality' but a series of mirror images, with the idea that this is how we apprehend—not reality, for that goes beyond the film's definition, but whatever it is we apprehend. And the involvement, finally, is in a shared dream: "Once again I walk, once again, along those corridors, across those *salons* . . .". (p. 28)

Penelope Houston, "Resnais: 'L'Année Dernière à Marienbad'," in Sight and Sound *(copyright © 1961 by The British Film Institute), Vol. 31, No. 1, Winter, 1961-62, pp. 26-8.*

BOSLEY CROWTHER

Be prepared for an experience such as you've never had from watching a film when you sit down to look at Alain Resnais' "Last Year at Marienbad." . . .

It may grip you with a strange enchantment, it may twist your wits into a snarl, it may leave your mind and senses toddling vaguely in the regions in between. But this we can reasonably promise: when you stagger away from it, you will feel you have delighted in (or suffered) a unique and intense experience.

And that, it appears, is precisely what M. Resnais means you to feel—the extreme and abnormal stimulation of a complete cinematic experience. . . . This is no lucid exposition of human behavior in terms of conventional dramatic situation, motivation and plot.

This is an eye-opening example of the use of the cinema device. . . .

To this observer's way of thinking (which we might as well recognize right now is going to be countered or challenged by others that may be just as good), it is not to be taken even as what it may seem to be. . . .

To our way of thinking and responding to the flow of sensuous stimuli, it is a web of complete imagination, a visualization of the thoughts, the mental associations, the wishes and fantasies that swirl through the mind of this fellow—the fellow conveying his dream to us—beneath the spell of an elegant palace that suggests all sorts of romantic things.

It suggests, as he walks us through it, looking at the decorated walls, the ballroom full of formal people, a stiff performance of Ibsen's "Rosmersholm," something of the cold, embalmed emotions that lived and died here in long-gone years. And as he picks up his married woman, his dream of love, and begins his pursuit, it suggests that time and emotions have no terminal points, that they whirl in fields of gravity surrounding material things and magnetize the sensitive people that come within these fields. . . .

[This] is not a picture in which a vital "message" is conveyed. It is a romantic excursion—or perhaps a serious sort of travesty on same. It is, in short, an experience, full of beauty and mood.

Take it thus and you should find it fascinating; try to make some sense of it—to discover some thread of proof or logic—and it is likely to drive you mad, like that clearly illogical match game that is played like a running gag through it.

Bosley Crowther, "'Last Year at Marienbad'," in The New York Times *(© 1962 by The New York Times Company; reprinted by permission), March 8, 1962, p. 26.*

WOLFGANG A. LUCHTING

[The structure of *Hiroshima Mon Amour* (*HMA*) is based on Resnais' concepts of time. The film not only deals with *exterior time* (the actual length of the film) but *interior time* (the time of the central action we see). Within Resnais' use of interior time, the series of dramatic entities have meaning contingent on the sequence in which they are presented. Each sequence of happenings might be called a *specific* time, a fraction of the interior one. They compose the *continuum* of action, the story of the film.]

These specific times, the circumstantial components of the interior *continuum,* are in *HMA* subdivided into two categories:

(a) One is *le temps réel,* the time in which the action in the city of Hiroshima takes place. *Le temps réel* is, then, the time in which the love story between the Japanese architect and the French actress develops.

(b) The other category is *le temps psychologique*—or even *le temps proustien,* for obvious reasons. This *temps psychologique* comprises the memories of and their effect within the *temps réel* on both hero and heroine. For him the memories are, primarily, *concentric,* that is to say: revolve around the complex of what Hiroshima as a historical fact means today, what the city's moment of destruction was like. Secondarily, his memories are *excentric,* in so far as they participate in her memories. For her, the memories of *le temps psychologique* are, primarily, *concentric* around her experience in Nevers. Secondarily, they are *excentric* in so far as they participate in his memories of Hiroshima.

Two things have to be mentioned here. First, that *le temps réel* and *le temps psychologique* interact. . . . [The] matter Alain Resnais set out to mold into a work of art, is the interaction between past and present. The spiritual effect of his work is to make us aware of the importance this interaction has on human behavior. This might be called the cathartic effect of the film, which does not, however, arise out of any climax, but out of the total, the accumulative impression the film makes: it is an epic film.

Here is one example of how complicated this interaction can become: Part of the story is the fact that the heroine, a French actress, has come to Hiroshima in order to do a picture about Hiroshima. Resnais' film also is about Hiroshima. We see, at the beginning, how a film-company shoots a picture about Hiroshima (the historical fact) in which the heroine acts. The people caught in the act of filming are Resnais' own people: Resnais thus films himself filming a film about Hiroshima. This is not so gratuitous as it may seem, for this procedure reminds one of Proust who also wrote seven volumes [*À la Recherche du temps perdu*] about how Marcel came to write seven volumes about how he came to write seven volumes. In both cases, with Resnais and with Proust, we find the creator describing how he created or came to create (often a topic of modern art). With Resnais the cause of the creation and the creation itself are the psychological complex of Hiroshima and what it represents in the history of mankind. (p. 301)

[Resnais and Duras] use what I should like to label time perspectives. . . . These time-perspectives are like aids for placing the story in, as it were, sudden temporal dimensions, for heightening some element of the story, making us fathom the invisible depths of the images visible on the screen. . . .

What then are some of these perspectives of time? According to their emphasis, the following are worth mentioning:

The film opens with images that immediately call to mind some sort of *Urschöpfung,* some cosmic creative process: the heaving of crude, raw, unformed masses, convulsions, it seems, of matter in the process of evolution. As the images become clearer and refine themselves, as words spoken by human beings become audible, we realize that those *Urmassen* in movement are nothing but the bodies of a man and a woman engaged in the sexual act. . . . What he evidently wishes to express by the gradual transformation of convulsing masses into recognizable human forms is that the sexual act, the physical symbol of human love, is something "eternal" and perhaps redemptive. . . . The perspective we are meant to glimpse is that of man and woman in love across mankind's, possibly life's, existence—in spite and because of Hiroshima. (p. 303)

[Directing] the audience's associations through the memories of Hiroshima and Nagasaki towards their immediate consequences in human destruction, visible here and now, before us, Resnais states another of the *Leitmotive* of his film: namely, that hearing of H-bombs and A-bombs and similar products of human genius, of their destructive power, and of all the horror that legend has accumulated since 1945 around the mere mention of them, is and has become so much of an everyday experience for us that we no longer associate it with its real consequences, of which burnt, shrinking, and stinking human flesh is one infinitesimally small part.

That the initial sequence, which reveals the present in its aspect of eternity by associating *Urmassen* in movement with the sexual act, is not an accidental time-perspective, can now clearly be seen. For, placing present events (love-making) in the perspective of the past (Urmassen) is as much a *Leitmotiv* in this film as bringing the viewer face to face with the atomic age in terms that he can understand and shudder at—in terms of what it can do to *him*. (pp. 303-04)

Knowing that life is not a handful of clearly and cleverly separate, separable, definable, or defined strands of *Leitmotive,* it can be assumed that those mentioned up till now will sooner or later be fused or recur in other constellations, constantly forming new patterns. Indeed, they do, revealing always other facets of Resnais' and Duras' "messages." One of the facets—and it is interesting to note its proximity to Proust's preocupations in *À la Recherche du temps perdu* . . .—is: No matter how intense a human experience is, it is always situated in time and therefore subject to oblivion, both by man as a historical *continuum* and by the individual as its manifestation in the present. In fact, this is one of Resnais' *universalia*. It teaches that forgetting is as necessary as living—which, among other things, consists precisely of experiences that seem unforgettable—is inevitable for man. (p. 304)

[A] rather interesting aspect of the film [is] the strangely neglected ethical problem that one would expect to arise immediately out of its love-story, namely that both protagonists are married. Their married life belongs to *le temps psychologique,* to the plane of memories. Its implications hardly ever manifest themselves in *le temps réel*. . . . This harsh suppression of an ethically highly explosive fact and its strange absence in the rest of the film are, of course, not due to any absented-mindedness of Mlle. Duras or M. Alain Resnais. They are intended. They are meant to reveal another *Leitmotiv* of the film:

I have said that both protagonists' *état civil* belongs to their memories. But so does the heroine's love affair with the German. Why then should the German lover be so intensely present in the *temps-réel* action, and the French husband, who waits for the heroine in Paris, so very little? I believe the answer is the following: their *état civil* is an integral part of their ordinary life. Not so their present love affair which is part of an extra-ordinary life. They are both different people. (pp. 304-05)

Resnais is less concerned with particular manifestations of routine—as would be the *état civil* of both protagonists—than with the general expression of routine, such as forgetting. . . . [In the *Leitmotives* of "love" and "oblivion"], Resnais brings together what ultimately are the basic factors of history: progressivism and conservatism. Resnais has made the bodies and the spirits of his protagonists the receptacles of time; the bodies, because through them love is experienced; the spirit, because through it the implications of this love are revealed and created: the memories. Love is history, memory also. Love, because it must needs be progressive; memory, because it must needs be resistant to love. From the struggle of the two results the development of the love-story on the plane of the *temps réel*. Leaving out the fact that both hero and heroine are married causes us to become aware of the ramifications that are contained in the juxtaposition between ordinary and extra-ordinary situations.

[Resnais] must make his protagonists' love "timeless," untroubled by the mediocrity of their married life, because he wants to achieve an effect that permits him to progress on to another of his *Leitmotive:*

Time asserting its rights: If we observe closely the "timelessness" of his protagonists, we notice that there is one way in which their past and their future (i.e., routine) may be permitted to intrude on it: paradoxically enough, through intensity, i.e., where earlier intense experiences equal or surpass their present intensity in *le temps réel:* her first love affair; his experience of the atomic explosion. This intrusion of intensities from the realm of *le temps psychologique* into that of *le temps réel* serves a very definite purpose. Resnais wishes to demonstrate that there exists a sort of cohesion of *situations extrèmes* across ordinary time. Again we enter the terrain of Proust, who also, in his novel, meant to save certain intensely experienced moments from the corrosion caused by the flux of time. (p. 306)

In HMA, action (on the *temps-réel* level) and flashbacks (onto the *temps-psychologique* plane) *are not essentially independent of each other*. There could be no action if there were no flashbacks, because the latter cause the former *and* the former cause the latter. Past and present are a sort of emulsion, little drops of past time being suspended in the present, and vice versa. . . . The method by which this effect of a perceptual present is achieved may best be circumscribed as a "flattening" of past and future into an even present. Undoubtedly, this denotes mankind's—or its antennae, the artists'—constant endeavor to fight against its becoming past and, by implication, to hold at a distance the approaching future, including, for them, that of Hiroshima's past. (p. 308)

Resnais' flashbacks are so organized and interwoven with the narration in the *temps réel* as to annul the normal time perspective and to create an effect of simultaneity. We are immediately reminded of Cubism which also dismantles the object, even destroys it, in order to permit us to see it in a new perspective, from different points of view at the same time, by recomposing it according to a new law. Resnais dismantles and mounts anew the traditional reality in order to create a new concept of time which is to traditional reality what the new love, in its intense moments (Nevers and Hiroshima), is to the traditional love in the protagonists' *état civil*. (pp. 309-10)

But could all this preoccupation with time not simply be overlooked? No. For, if we do, we do not understand the film: Time and its manifestations in man, forgetting, are the very theme of the film, as they were to be again in *L'année*. . . . In HMA, Resnais investigates above all the phenomenon of oblivion. In scene after scene he circles around this so essentially "timely" element of human life: forgetfulness—and its ethical implications. The film, it is true, does not have as its message "Thou shalt not forget!" Nor does it dictate "Thou shalt forget!" It simply does research on the subject of time as it becomes petrified in oblivion. The film, just as Proust, is *à la recherche du temps qu'on a perdu* . . . , and shows how with this loss also the lessons are lost that human experience has drawn and draws each day, incessantly, only to forget them. Resnais' film, in this light, represents a statement about man's attitude towards his history: history is the concrete record of all the lessons drawn from the experience of mankind, lessons whose usefulness for the present has been forgotten. In short, Resnais implies that it is wrong to say that history *teaches* anything. It never does, it never has. History only *explains*. The only "lesson" we can draw from this insight is that we never heed the lessons we have "learned."

To exemplify this, HMA has to interweave past and present, must show how the past affects the present and how the present even affects the past. Nowhere can this better be seen than in the famous restaurant scene. The heroine threatens to become mad again the very moment when past and present touch each other, when her memories become so strong that she confounds past and present. The Japanese architect slaps her! This is, theoretically, the most important movement of the film, for here Resnais leaves Proust behind, or at least goes farther than he. . . . [The] evocation of an impression of the past by events in the present, is, so to say, brusquely short-circuited: by slapping the heroine, the Japanese lover becomes the executor of Resnais' ultimate statement about time and man. The empirical order of things—i.e., past belongs to the past and present to the present—is reestablished, must be reestablished, else we become unfit for life—mad.

The order of things as we understand them asserts itself and its rights by all means: either we accept it and thus become capable of meeting life on our terms, or we refuse it and become insane, as the heroine did after the death of her first lover. (p. 310)

Forgetfulness, then, its necessity and its tragedy, are what the story of the film is about. In it Resnais and Mlle. Duras see an aspect of *la condition humaine*. In HMA, they decline the word "forgetfulness" in the forms of human grammar, exemplifying a universal quality in particular lives. That is why their film is a great work of art. . . .

If the heroine loves the Japanese and resigns herself to relegating her first lover to the gallery of inoperant memories, does she not also, implicitly and in the future, depreciate her present love? For, if in face of her present love she comes to renounce or to neutralize her earlier love, does this not imply the ephemeralness of love in general, no matter how strongly it may be felt? Again we are reminded of Proust: his hero's hopeless love for Gilberte.

But Resnais does not come to a halt there. He draws the conclusion on a universal level: if the heroine of the film can forget her first lover and, by implication, one day will surely forget her second, is this not proof that one day mankind, the Japanese nation, the people of the city of Hiroshima itself, will forget the disaster that befell them?

Applying this conclusion to the question of time, we come to the insight that, in accepting the power of the present we admit also the right of the future to *become* present. One might say: a sorrow (the heroine's forgetting of her first lover) and a joy (her acceptance of the present one) make for the reestablishment of the universal order of time and thus of history. This may be considered as Resnais' most memorable comment on modern time-consciousness. (p. 311)

[Everything] in this film, in one way or another, complements everything else and . . . from these complementary elements arise two important formal principles of HMA.

First, on the active side, the atomic explosion is symbolically equalled with the heroine's love for the German and the consequences of this love: insanity.

Second, on the passive side, her first love was a forbidden love, forbidden by the society she lived in. As in Greek tragedy the gods, so here, in Nevers, society reestablished its rights and its order by killing the German and thus driving the young girl to insanity. Only *time* heals her, i.e. forgetting. Hiroshima, i.e. Japan also did something the society of countries she lives in considered forbidden: it waged a war. Therefore, Japan, too, is punished by the society of other nations. And Japan, too, recuperates through time, as the last sequences of the film clearly indicate.

In conclusion, it seems advisable to point out the difference between Proust and Resnais in relation to their common subject, time.

Proust puts the emphasis on the change in people wrought by time. This change he records and saves from oblivion by remembering. *Resnais* cannot put the accent on the same elements—although he certainly shows his awareness of them—because he portrays a love-story. Lovers cannot live or love in the consciousness of forgetting. From this arises the film's problem. *Proust's* two main themes are, first, the time that destroys; second, the memory that conserves. *Resnais* treats these themes, too, but the other way round: first, for his protagonists, memory destroys; second, time restores. *Proust* is interested in memory. *Resnais* studies forgetting. In *Proust,* memories cause joy—the madeleine. In *Resnais'* film, memories cause sorrow and even terror. . . . In *both* artists the raw material of their works is the same: the tensions between past and present. But *Resnais* investigates two things: that which is being forgotten and why it is forgotten. *Proust* mainly studies that which has been forgotten. Besides, *Resnais* has a socio-political dimension in his film. *Proust* concentrates on the sociological dimension. (pp. 311-12)

Resnais does not wish the past to reside in the present, he pushes it back into its own realm. Proust celebrates the past, searches it, makes it into the present, and lives in it: *Le temps retrouvé* is the title of his last book. . . .

Proust, although he knew of course as well as Resnais that the past cannot be revived except in memories, prefers the memories and finds his redemption in them. Resnais believes one can keep on living only by forgetting, no matter how important is that which we have experienced and are going to forget—sooner or later. (p. 312)

Wolfgang A. Luchting, "'Hiroshima, Mon Amour', Time, and Proust," in The Journal of Aesthetics and Art Criticism *(copyright 1963 by The American Society for Aesthetics), Vol. XXI, No. 3, Spring, 1963, pp. 299-313.*

SUSAN SONTAG

Muriel is the most difficult, by far, of Resnais' three feature films, but it is clearly drawn from the same repertoire of themes as the first two. (p. 23)

The reason *Muriel* is difficult is because it attempts to do both what *Hiroshima* and what *Marienbad* did. It attempts to deal with substantive issues—war guilt over Algeria, the OAS, the racism of the colons—even as *Hiroshima* dealt with the bomb, pacifism, and collaboration. But it also, like burden of this double intention—to be both concrete and abstract—doubles the technical virtuosity and complexity of the film. . . .

Unlike *Hiroshima Mon Amour* and *L'Année Dernière à Marienbad, Muriel* directly suggests an elaborate plot and complex interrelationships. [Resnais] gives us a chain of short scenes, horizontal in emotional tone, which focus on selected undramatic moments in the four main characters. . . . *Muriel,* like *L'Année Dernière à Marienbad,* should not puzzle, because there is nothing "behind" the lean, staccato statements that one sees. They can't be deciphered, because they don't say more than they say. (p. 24)

[Although] the story is not difficult to follow, Resnais' techniques for telling it deliberately estrange the viewer from the story. Most conspicuous of these techniques is his elliptical, off-center conception of a scene. . . . In Resnais' films, all speech, including dialogue, tends to become narration—to hover over the visible action, rather than to issue directly from it. (pp. 24-5)

When Resnais cuts abruptly, he pulls the viewer away from the story. His cutting acts as a brake on the narrative, a form of aesthetic undertow, a sort of filmic alienation effect.

Resnais' use of speech has a similar "alienating" effect on the viewer's feelings. Because his main characters have something not only benumbed but positively hopeless about them, their words are never emotionally moving. . . . [The] firm prosiness of the dialogue in *Muriel* is not intended to *mean* anything different from the awful poetizing of the earlier two long films. Resnais proposes the same subject in all his films. All his films are about the *inexpressible.* (The main topics which are inexpressible are two: guilt and erotic longing). And the twin notion to inexpressibility is banality. In high art, banality is the modesty of the inexpressible (p. 25)

Resnais' techniques, despite the visual brilliance of his films, seem to me more literary than cinematic. . . .

Most literary of all is Resnais' love of formalism. Formalism itself is not literary. But to appropriate a complex and specific narrative in order deliberately to obscure it—to write an abstract text on top of it, as it were—is a very literary procedure. . . . *Muriel* is designed so that, *at any given moment of it,* it's not about anything at all. At any given moment it is a formal composition; and it is to this end that individual scenes are shaped so obliquely, the time sequence scrambled, and dialogue kept to a minimum of informativeness. (pp. 25-6)

The typical formula of the new formalists of the novel and film is a mixture of coldness and pathos: coldness enclosing and subduing an immense pathos. Resnais' great discovery is the application of this formula to "documentary" material, to true events locked in the historical past. Here—in Resnais' short films, particularly *Guernica, Van Gogh,* and, above all, *Nuit et Brouillard* (*Night and Fog*)—the formula works brilliantly, educating and liberating the viewer's feelings. . . . The triumph of *Nuit et Brouillard* is its absolute control, its supreme refinement in dealing with a subject that incarnates the purest, most agonizing pathos. For the danger of such a subject is that it can numb, instead of stir, our feelings. Resnais has overcome this danger by adopting a distance from his subject which is not sentimental, and which yet does not cheat the horror of its horrifyingness. *Nuit et Brouillard* is overwhelming in its directness, yet full of tact about the unimaginable.

But in Resnais' three feature films, the same strategy is not nearly so apt or satisfying. In *Hiroshima Mon Amour, L'-Année Dernière à Marienbad,* and *Muriel* the lucid and brilliantly compassionate documentarist has been superseded by the aesthete, the formalist. Noble sentiments—like guilt for the bomb (in *Hiroshima Mon Amour*) and for the French atrocities in Algeria (*Muriel*)—become the subject for aesthetic demonstration. Nostalgia itself becomes an object for nostalgia, the memory of an unrecapturable feeling becomes the subject of feeling. The method is to enclose a strong emotion—say, as in *L'Année Dernière à Marienbad,* the pathos of erotic frustration and longing—in a visual setting which has the character of an abstraction—say, that of a huge chateau peopled with *haute couture* mannequins. The aim of this formalism is to break up content, to *question* content. The questionable reality of the past is the subject of all Resnais' films. More exactly, for Resnais, the past is that reality which is both unassimilable and dubious. The new formalism of the French novels and films is thus a dedicated agnosticism about reality itself.

In the pursuit of these themes, *Muriel* is the most intelligent, the most original, and the most beautiful of Resnais' three feature films. But—fundamentally out of sympathy as I am with the formalist aesthetic that informs so many French novels and films today—I must admit to not really caring for *Muriel.* I admire the film, but I don't love it. . . . *Muriel* is somehow depressing, weighty. It's an extremely intelligent film, and an exciting one visually; but these virtues do not work together. There is much less in *Muriel* of that preciousness, that studied air, that damned artiness that nearly ruins what's good in *Hiroshima Mon Amour* and *L'Année Dernière à Marienbad.* But the film still lacks an essential ingredient of greatness in the cinema. (pp. 26-7)

A beautiful film, though, *Muriel* certainly is. First, in its visual composition. This is a strong point in all Resnais' films, but here he surpasses himself. (p. 27)

Susan Sontag, "Film Reviews: 'Muriel ou le temps d'un retour'," in Film Quarterly *(copyright 1963 by The Regents of the University of California; reprinted by permission of the University of California Press), Vol. XVII, No. 2, Winter, 1963-64, pp. 23-7.*

JOHN RUSSELL TAYLOR

[It was] in the field of short films that Resnais embarked on the experiment which has continued throughout his subsequent career and which makes him of particular interest to us now: the collaboration on equal terms with distinguished figures from the literary world. First, in *Nuit et Brouillard,* his documentary about concentration camps, it was Jean Cayrol. Then for *Le Chant du Styrène,* a commissioned piece about the manufacture of the plastic polystyrene, Raymond Queneau was called on for a characteristic punning verse commentary. In Resnais's first feature, *Hiroshima Mon Amour,* the original screenplay was by the novelist Marguerite Duras; in his second, *L'Année Dernière à Marienbad,* it was the turn of Alain Robbe-Grillet; and for the third, *Muriel, ou le Temps d'un Retour,* he returned to Jean Cayrol. It is an impressive enough list, and its consistency suggests that the succession is more than just chance. When questioned on the point Resnais is evasive, but talks of his interest in 'experiments' in the cinema, in trying out ideas which come to him, and expresses a conviction that the word is undervalued in the cinema today, hence his determined attempts to restore it to its proper place. As for the exact role of the script in the total ensemble, Resnais's remark about *Hiroshima Mon Amour* might stand for all the films: 'I encouraged Marguerite Duras to "faire littéraire" and not worry about it. I wanted to compose a sort of poem in which the images would work only as a counterpoint to the text.'

Which is all very well in theory—there is no reason in theory why anything should be ruled out before it has been tried. The only question is, how does it turn out in practice? My own feeling is that the system works well enough in documentary, if only because with documentary one tends to expect something rather more academic and unexciting than in the feature film; at any rate, one is more willing to accept it. The material of *Nuit et Brouillard* is in any case so highly charged emotionally that the cooling, endistancing effect of a very precise, formal, controlled montage establishing a clear, unequivocal relation between newsreel material of Auschwitz then and coloured film of the site now, between document and evocation, is a positive advantage, and the discreetly literary terms of Jean Cayrol's commentary have something of the same effect. As for *Le Chant du Styrène,* the effect here is largely humorous; against the highly coloured abstract patterns of the plastic as it is pushed backwards and forwards, stamped in presses, trimmed and shunted up and down the conveyor belt, the equally highly coloured patterns of Queneau's verbal fantasy (adequately indicated by the title itself) form an amusing counterpoint and help to dress up divertingly what is, at bottom, simply a very expert example of a rather dreary type of sponsored film.

It is with the features that we really come up against the problems that this sort of writer-director collaboration poses. Resnais's principal weakness as a director, even in his simplest documentaries, has always been an excessively chilling and intellectual approach. In the analytical art films this was quite in keeping, but elsewhere it sometimes showed through rather disturbingly, turning the films into private intellectual games. There is an excellent instance of this in *Toute la Mémoire du Monde,* a short about the Bibliothèque Nationale which Resnais made between *Nuit et Brouillard* and *Le Chant du Styrène*. (pp. 221-22)

The taint of academicism is just as strongly present in Resnais's feature films, and one cannot help thinking (perhaps unfairly; it would be difficult to make out a reasonable case for the thought) that the very idea of the sort of equal collaboration Resnais envisages would not occur to anyone but a born academic; it implies a deliberate withdrawal of self, a deliberate reduction of the film-director's role to that of faithful interpreter and repository of technical expertise which looks like the very opposite of the real creative temperament. And this is just what I at least find most difficult to take in Resnais's feature films. In *Hiroshima Mon Amour* . . . the trouble is particularly evident because, to state it in the simplest possible terms, the film is a love story, a story of sudden physical passion, and the treatment, formidably intelligent though it is, has not the slightest trace of sensuousness, let alone sensuality. Now though this is a film which has ambitions far beyond the love story at its centre ('I asked Marguerite Duras', Resnais tells us, 'for a love story set in Hiroshima which would not look too absurdly trivial in the context of the atomic bomb'), it does matter, because there is really something between the French film-star heroine and her Japanese lover, and we must believe that there is, or the progress of their affair against the great, past horror of Hiroshima and the less great but in some ways more immediate horror of her wartime experiences at Nevers will not make sense. Without this vital dimension of real feeling on some level, even if merely the physical, the film loses urgency and finally appears more than a little pretentious. Though meant, apparently, to be a film about both characters almost equally, it very rapidly becomes a film about the Frenchwoman only; on her life vaguely impinges a shadowy Japanese whom she little by little conflates in her mind with her wartime, German, lover and then, after the famous 'gifle' he delivers in the restaurant, rapidly disentangles again, but essentially this is her story. The attitudes and situation of the Japanese remain mysterious, even if we accept that the long 'documentary' introduction about Hiroshima does in some measure provide 'background' for him, even if only intellectual background, since the script makes it clear that he has not personally suffered Hiroshima as she has suffered Nevers. (pp. 223-24)

In fact, I feel that on the whole the illustration of the words in pictures—for too often it is illustration instead of the promised counterpoint—generally weakens what is already fully expressed in the text, and that only the flashbacks to wartime Nevers and the heroine's disastrous affair with a German soldier really serve the intended purpose of the film; they at least are powerfully evocative of romantic desolation and stay in one's mind when otherwise all one can remember is the words.

With Resnais's next film, *L'Année Dernière à Marienbad* . . . , at least there is no doubt about the efficacy of the pictures. Resnais and his cameraman, Sacha Vierny, seem to have set out deliberately to make the film as beautiful as possible to look at, judged simply as a series of elaborate art photographs, and in this at least they have succeeded: the look of the film is unforgettable. The main question the film has raised in critics' minds, though, is the value of visual beauty just by itself, without any apparent meaning or significance outside itself. For *L'Année Dernière à Marienbad* is in some ways less of a film than an intellectual trap. Certainly it is a trap if the spectator goes at it with the intellect, wanting to know what it means and determined to work out one explanation which will fit all the facts (if they are facts) the film offers, or at least enable him to distinguish the fact from the fiction. Some critics have plunged in straight away with intricate explanations; others have been provoked only to outbursts of outraged puritanism, announcing brusquely that of course the film is only a confidence trick and they, for their part, are not going to be taken in by it. But if a confidence trick is involved at all, it is a trick which the spectator persists, in spite of all warnings to the contrary, in playing on himself: neither the author, Alain Robbe-Grillet, nor the director gives him any reason, either explicitly, in their statements on the film, or implicitly, in the film itself, to suppose that it does all 'mean' anything, and if nevertheless he goes on rationalizing and worrying when he fails to rationalize, he has no one to blame but himself. (pp. 224-25)

[It] means many things partly, but means nothing when it is all put together? Yes and no. It all depends—to hedge tiresomely—on what you mean by 'mean'. Noticeably, nearly all the parallels one picks up are from romantic poetry—*The City of Dreadful Night, The Hound of Heaven* and the rest—and clearly the Symbolists could yield many more. And as in Romantic or Symbolist poetry, we are dealing with symbols, properly speaking, not allegories. There is no simple, complete equivalence for anything, and yet meanings hover in a cloud and each object presented to our attention—the hotel, the garden, even the curiously depersonalized characters—gradually accumulates significances which our minds hold simultaneously in suspension. And right down the middle of the film is a conflict which assumes various guises—present against past (real or imagined), freedom against convention, life against death—but remains appreciably the Romantic Agony at its last gasp. And this, finally, is what the film is 'about' (whatever that means): it is a series of variations on a romantic theme disguised as a film for film's sake, depending in the end on its power to enrapture us into suspending intellectual judgement.

Whether we are willing to do so, to capitulate at once to the beauty of the images and ask for nothing more than faint and perhaps rather pretentious hints of meaning, depends obviously very much on the temperament and mood of the individual spectator. There is no doubt that what is being done is being supremely well done, but one comes back always to the square but inescapable question, was it worth doing at all in the first place? In any case the whole thing turns finally on the writer and the script: *L'Année Dernière* is really a Robbe-Grillet film with sumptuous illustrations by Resnais rather than a Resnais film scripted by Robbe-Grillet. As such it is going firmly against the tide of the modern cinema to reach a sort of *ne plus ultra* of 'pure' *mise en scène* instead of fully integrated one-man film-creation.

Whether Resnais comes nearer to achieving this with his third feature film, *Muriel, ou le temps d'un retour,* is a question much debated, with no very decisive result. It is certainly a film which permits no critical half-measures: either you think it is a masterpiece or you cannot stomach it at all. My own feeling, I must confess, is closest to the latter position: the film seems to me essentially false, an elaborate piece of mystification built on, this time, a fairly straightforward story (by Jean Cayrol) which does not demand such oblique treatment and does not gain anything from it. (pp. 226-27)

[The story] is told in a remote and highly precious manner, with tricksy cutting, intricately oblique dialogue, some (apparently deliberately) dowdy and inexpressive colour photography, and a faintly grotesque score by Hans-Werner Henze featuring vocal interludes at climactic moments. Indeed, to me the whole thing approaches far too close to self-parody; it certainly resembles with uncanny accuracy the image of the highbrow cinema most lowbrow cinemagoers love to hate. There are, admittedly, striking moments in it, usually the most simple and direct: the exteriors of the town, the strange little scene in which Bernard goes riding along the clifftops, some of the unexplained glimpses of people on the fringes of the story—the waitress in the café, the girl Hélène meets on a park bench—going about their own separate lives. But I find this very little to compensate for the heaviness and pretention of the ensemble, its chilly, rigidly intellectual application of directorial ideas from here, there and everywhere to a basically quite interesting and original story-idea in such a way as to complicate it without making it more complex. But the film is, perhaps even more decisively than *L'Année Dernière à Marienbad,* one which you have to give in to totally or not at all; and about such films there is really very little point in arguing.

And yet, when all this is said, when all allowance has been made for Resnais's cool, academic side as a film-maker (he seems, unmistakably, more interested in solving intellectual and aesthetic problems than in film-making *per se*) there is still a strange consistency in his films: they are nearly all, even his art films, concerned with memory and the transmuting power of the imagination. Does this consistency of theme make him properly speaking an *auteur?* I doubt it, but perhaps it is still too early to pontificate. Up to now his film-making career has been almost entirely occupied with the conscientious attempt to produce film art with a capital 'A', an aim more often inhibiting than encouraging its actual appearance. (pp. 228-29)

John Russell Taylor, "The New Wave: Alain Resnais," in his Cinema Eye, Cinema Ear: Some Key Film-Makers of the Sixties *(reprinted by permission of Hill & Wang, a division of Farrar, Straus & Giroux, Inc.; in Canada, by AD Peters & Co Ltd; copyright © 1964 by John Russell Taylor), Hill & Wang, 1964, pp. 220-29.*

ANDREW SARRIS

[In *La Guerre est finie,* we] are no longer concerned with the pretentious counterpoint of Love and the Bomb, Past and Present, Illusion and Reality, Society and the Individual, etc. We are obsessed instead with the doubts of Diego, the fears of Diego, the hopes of Diego, the instincts of Diego, even the fantasies of Diego. . . .

For Resnais, it is enough to celebrate remembrance and mourn forgetfulness as fragments of personality and politics disintegrate in the void of time. . . . Cinema, like life, is a process of creating memories for the future. Resnais has always drawn on the past without paying for the future. His cinema has been hauntingly beautiful if dramatically improvident in its ghostliness. His characters have been paralyzed by the sheer pastness of their sensibilities. . . . Diego has become a hero of prudence and inaction. He has shown what it is to be a man without the obvious flourishes of virility so fashionable today. (Even the stately explicitness of the love-making is a measure of the hero's stature). To be a man, it is above all necessary to be patient as one's life dribbles away on the back streets, blind alleys and dead ends of political impotence. The at times agonizing slowness of *La Guerre est finie* achieves the pathos of patience by expressing a devotion to detail common to both Diego and Resnais. . . .

As for what the film actually "says," Jorge Semprun's script is explicit enough for the least sophisticated audiences. The meaning is in the title. The War Is Over, and Resnais, unlike Zinnemann in the grotesquely unfeeling *Behold a Pale Horse,* makes no attempt to reconstruct the agonies of antiquity with old newsreels. The ultimate tragedy of The Spanish Civil War is that all its participants are either dead or 30 years older. Spain still exists as a geographical entity, but it has been repopulated with an indifferent generation.

Andrew Sarris, "Ode to the Old Left," in Cahiers du Cinema in English *(copyright 1967 by Cahiers Publishing Company), No. 8, February, 1967, p. 67.*

RICHARD SCHICKEL

La Guerre Est Finie is an exciting movie on two counts. It is, I think, the most successful representation on film we have had so far of the archetypal political drama of our time, in which a man's psychological need to make ideological commitments wars with the disillusionment such commitments must inevitably bring. It is also the first truly well proportioned—and therefore the first truly satisfying—feature we have had from director Alain Resnais. . . .

[In] *La Guerre Est Finie,* story, style and symbols are much more carefully balanced [than in *Hiroshima Mon Amour* and *Last Year at Marienbad*]. Jorge Semprun's script is a model of intelligent character and thematic development, and Resnais, faced with the challenge of exploring a plot that is densely packed instead of wide-ranging, responds by digging deeply and carefully into his material. The result is an energetic, ironic and mature exploration of the sensibility of an aging revolutionary in an aging century. (p. 95)

La Guerre Est Finie is, in effect, a *Man's Fate* for the 1960s —a muted, thoughtful, truthful film about the way time betrays all revolutions and about the absurd, desperate, ennobling expedients men must take in order to escape the destruction of the self that is so often the by-product of the betrayal. The Franco government has objected to the film for obvious reasons, but in fact it quite transcends specific political realities and is a judiciously composed metaphor that says something essential about the human condition—not merely the Spanish one. This is a very important film, yet also a graceful and stylish one. (p. 97)

Richard Schickel, "La Guerre est finie" (originally published in Life, *Vol. 62, No. 10, March 10, 1967), in his* Second Sight: Notes on Some Movies, 1965-70 *(copyright © 1972 by, Richard Schickel; reprinted by permission of Simon and Schuster, a Division of Gulf & Western Corporation), Simon and Schuster, 1972, pp. 95-7.*

ROY ARMES

In all his film work Resnais constantly searches for new forms: "I want to make films that are experiments. All experiments are interesting." This implies a refusal of anything that seems like a mere repetition, yet despite this Resnais's work does have a unity. On the surface his short films form a heterogeneous agglomeration: films on art and the Spanish Civil War, negro culture, the concentration camps and the French national library, the prevention of accidents and the manufacture of polystyrene. . . . Resnais evolves his method of collaboration, lays down the basis of his style and clarifies his personal attitude to the issues raised. Above all the films are linked by the seriousness of mind with which each commission is approached. . . . (p. 37)

The content of Van Gogh's paintings [in his first short, *Van Gogh*] is selected and fused in the same way that a director might deal with real settings. . . . The story to be told in the film is dramatic enough and Van Gogh's paintings are sufficiently powerful to survive the kind of distortion inevitable with this approach. (p. 39)

The choice of subject-matter is also significant. As Resnais says, the film is not art criticism or scientific biography but 'an attempt to tell the imaginary life of a painter through his painting.' It tries to put us in Van Gogh's head and let us see the world not as it literally appeared to him (the photographic reality) but as it is transmuted by his vision (what is captured on his canvases). . . . Some of the parallels between *Van Gogh* and *Marienbad* are quite striking: in neither film do we get outside the images of mental life and into the fresh air of a real landscape. . . . (pp. 39-40)

To unify his material Resnais used two principal means. Firstly, he chose to make the film in black and white which allowed him to "create links between extremely disparate canvases" and . . . to treat the whole of the painter's output as a single immense picture. . . . A second and more positive means of linking the canvases was by the use of the musical score written by Jacques Besse. "The multiplicity of the shots (almost as many as in a feature film) forced us," Resnais wrote, "to give the music a predominant importance. It is no longer there to 'accompany the images' but to create the very backbone of the film". Where *Van Gogh* differs from most of Resnais's shorts is in the lack of interest of its commentary which in his later work came to be a further linking element. (pp. 40-1)

Resnais's second and much shorter documentary is almost universally regarded as his least interesting work and is the only one he himself has ever virtually rejected. . . . *Gauguin* was only a repetition of what Resnais had done before: "For a film to interest me, it must have an experimental side; that is what was lacking in *Gauguin* and that is why it is a bad film." (pp. 41-2)

'Guernica' has distinct advantages over Paul Gauguin's paintings as the subject for a black-and-white documentary, since it uses only black, white and gradations of grey. But the problems it posed were nonetheless real, for the subject-matter is vast and difficult to encompass in a short film of just over three hundred metres. *Guernica,* despite its considerable achievement, showed Resnais striving to get beyond the confines of the art film, for it is the destruction and suffering caused by war that forms the real subject of the film *Guernica,* not Pablo Picasso's technique or style. . . . In all his films Resnais approaches his documents with a desire for complete honesty and seeks an authentic voice to accompany them. . . . (p. 43)

There is no clear image of hope in Picasso's painting, the emphasis there, as in most of his paintings around that time, was on suffering and anguish, but the film does not accept this as a final comment. (p. 45)

Whereas the works of Van Gogh and Gauguin were fused to make a single whole, in the film *Guernica* one painting is broken down into jagged, isolated fragments, each representing an image of suffering. The film can disregard the spatial organisation of the painting (which is never shown in its entirety) because it recreates the elements in a temporal sequence which, thanks to the editing, acquires its own rhythm. . . . [Guernica is seen] not simply as a place of terrible suffering but as one of the 'capitals of living peace.' In some ways this message anticipates Resnais's later work where love is opposed to suffering and the city of Hiroshima becomes a place where love is found and experienced. Stylistically too *Guernica* represents for the director the first totally successful fusion of all the elements on which his mature style is based. Fragments of photographs, painting and sculpture are welded into a visual rhythm and set against an aural rhythm of music and verbal poetry bound together in a tone that combines documentary realism with pure lyricism. (pp. 45-6)

The pattern of [*Les Statues meurent aussi*] reflects this growing awareness of where the blame for the decline of negro culture lies. The significance of the film's title is revealed in the opening words: "When men are dead they enter history. When statues are dead they enter art. This botany of death is what we call culture." The negro art of the museums is dead because it no longer receives a living, understanding glance, because it has been killed by the impact of Western civilisation. Yet the two cultures, black and white, have basically the same aims. (p. 47)

[In *Nuit et Brouillard*] Resnais has his camera track through the derelict remains of Auschwitz as it is today, recording in realistic colour what is left of these places of horror. . . . The power and calm thoughtful rhythm of *Nuit et Brouillard* derive from the alternation of these two sets of images: the faded grey of the archive material contrasts with the colour of the present day shots, its immobility is set against the tracking movement of Resnais's camera, the rigidity of death opposed to the measured step of the contemporary investigator. As in his first feature, where Resnais dares to set his love story against the horrors of the atomic bomb, so here he has the audacity to make his film beautiful as well as terrible, in the belief that "if it is beautiful it can be more effective.' (pp. 49-50)

As in most of Resnais's shorts the music has an important part to play. . . . Resnais himself has explained that "the more violent the images are the gentler is the music. [The composer, Hanns Eisler,] wanted to show that the optimism and hope of man always existed in the background." (p. 52)

In *Nuit et Brouillard* Resnais fuses perfectly the talents of his photographers Cloquet and Vierny, his scriptwriter Cayrol and his composer Eisler and performs the almost impossible task of encompassing the worst horrors of the Nazi régime within a work of art. . . .

At first sight the subject of Resnais's next film, [*Toute la memoire du monde*], the Bibliothèque Nationale, might seem a surprising departure for the director. . . . But in fact this 'sentimental walk behind the scenes' was no more than a framework for Resnais's real interests. (p. 53)

Toute la mémoire du monde is a film that exists on several levels. Technically this is one of Resnais's most striking films with the camera continually tracking to and fro in the maze of passages and corridors. . . . On quite another level there are links with the concentration camp world of *Nuit et Brouillard*. Remo Forlani's script emphasises the prison aspect of the library: "In Paris it is in the Bibliothèque Nationale that words are imprisoned," and books are stamped "to indicate that a volume has entered the Bibliothèque Nationale, that never again will it be able to leave." (pp. 54-5)

Within the film too there are allusions to the world of comics and science fiction, beginning with the opening shots of a mysterious looking film camera and microphone. Like the factory of *Le Chant du Styrène* the library is a dehumanised world, with people appearing as no more than shadowy silhouettes. (p. 55)

In a sense the film uses the workings of the library as a symbol for the functioning of the mind: "Forlani and I wanted to insist on this very important notion of the usefulness of books and show the infinite, vertiginous aspect of memory." The very title of the film, chosen by Forlani, stresses this aspect and the work is a key one for those who wish to interpret Resnais as the 'cinéaste of memory'. . . . The books sought by readers are "fragments of a universal memory" which pieced together are a key to happiness. (pp. 56-7)

Alain Resnais's last documentary [*Le Chant du Styréne*] was made for the Péchiney organisation, which asked him "not to explain the manufacture of polystyrene but simply to show that it was a noble material since its manufacture was very complex, demanding a great deal of knowledge, because it was entirely created by man." Resnais's handling of this commission was startlingly unorthodox, frightening his sponsors at first. . . . Despite the terms of the commission, human beings play little part in this film, being no more than shadowy figures in a dehumanised world of pipes and machines, and the whole emphasis of the visuals is on colour, shape and pattern, making this perhaps the freest of Resnais's shorts. . . . Initially Resnais wanted the text to be sung and in this respect *Le Chant du Styréne* represents the fullest expression of his lyrical tendency, as *Nuit et Brouillard* most perfectly mirrors his commitment to a humanistic philosophy. (p. 60)

All the features have a precursor among the shorts: *Hiroshima mon Amour* is an expansion of the 'operatic' aspect of *Le Chant du Styréne; L'Année Dernière à Marienbad* a further exploration of the mental labyrinth of *Toute la mémoire du monde; Muriel* follows *Nuit et Brouillard* in recording a 'Lazarian' world. . . . and *La Guerre est finie* spells out in contemporary terms the lesson of *Guernica*. But the real importance lies even deeper than this, for through these documentaries one can trace the shaping of Resnais's mind and the formation of his style. The words of Emmanuelle Riva in *Hiroshima:* "Looking properly is something that can, I think, be learned" are borne out by these years. Resnais's interest in ideas follows a double flow. Firstly, turning away from photographic reality to find a substitute for it in painting, he initiates a move inwards: into the enclosed world of Van Gogh's madness or the labyrinth of the Bibliothèque Nationale. But to balance this there is an outward flow, for this same concern with documents leads him back into the world by confronting him with some of the central issues of twentieth century politics: total war, colonialism, racialism. On all these issues he maintains an independence of mind which is carried over into the feature films when he comes up against the equally intractable problems of the atomic bomb, Algeria and Fascism. If *Marienbad* is the supreme example of the inward 'evasion' into the mind, it is answered by the commitment of *La Guerre est finie*.

The documentary years are equally decisive in the establishment of Resnais's visual style. It is on the editing of images that his attention is concentrated from the very start. . . . (pp. 62-3)

It is noteworthy that Resnais takes his camera into his subject: into Picasso's painting, into Auschwitz to find traces of the past, into the library to get lost in the maze of its passages. . . . For Resnais, . . . reality is solid and tangible enough, if sometimes horrific, and his camera movement is his means of confrontation.

But for Resnais images alone do not make up a film. . . . So, to the visual rhythm of the images are added two further rhythms: a musical and a verbal one. The resulting synthesis of image, text and music is applied equally successfully to a prose subject like *Nuit et Brouillard* . . . and a poetic one like *Le Chant du Styrène*. . . . It is essentially a filmic conception of the cinema . . . but in the manner conceived by Sergei Eisenstein when he wrote in 'Film Form': "The cinema would seem to be the highest stage of embodiment for the potentialities and aspirations of each of the arts."

If Resnais's reputation rested solely upon his documentary films, he would still have a high place in the history of the French cinema, but what is particularly exciting about his work is that he used his short film achievements simply as a testing ground for methods later applied to feature length subjects. (pp. 64-5)

Hiroshima mon Amour has a marked dramatic structure, with the action falling into five distinct acts. The first, the prologue, comprises two parts. Firstly there are the opening shots of two embracing bodies "as if drenched with ashes, rain, dew or sweat" which form a poetic image, linking the ideas of love and death, pleasure and pain. . . . From these formless, anonymous shapes, the bodies of the lovers emerge, but initially the tone remains unreal, since the ensuing dialogue is incantatory. . . . To visit museums, to understand intellectually is not to grasp the essence of the catastrophe that Hiroshima represents. Together these two hypnotic sequences capture the mood of the whole film: the setting is revealed to us in what is, in effect, a documentary on the impossibility of comprehending, the central themes of memory and forgetfulness, love and death, mutilation by the bomb and deformation by love and stated, and the structural pattern of the film is made apparent. (pp. 70-1)

[The documentary aspects] are clearly used to counterpoint the personal story, heralding a fresh stage of recollection and becoming less pronounced as the memory grows stronger. Each time a distancing effect is brought to bear and the film contains no direct propaganda though it takes political issues seriously. Nevers is evoked not as an indictment of occupation and liberation, but as it might appear, fourteen years later, from the other side of the world. The case against the bomb is put in the form of a film within a film and since we are shown the organisation and contrivance of the peace rally scenes, Resnais avoids all trace of emotive pleading. . . . The characters in *Hiroshima* do not participate directly in the great events evoked but the documentary material does add weight to the two *leitmotifs* of the film, the names Hiroshima and Nevers. The love story gains by being set against a backcloth of death but as Duras's script tells us: "This personal story always dominates the necessarily demonstrative Hiroshima story." The characters of the film were conceived as people with political beliefs but these are left implicit. . . . (pp. 74-5)

Hiroshima mon Amour also follows naturally on the documentaries in the structural patterns it adopts. . . . [Resnais's] conception of the cinema as a combination of visual and aural rhythms in which the editor's role in juxtaposing the elements is a prime creative function is fully sustained in *Hiroshima* which is built around a series of contrasts and incongruities. . . . [The] Nevers episodes, which were shot last, are fitted into the Hiroshima framework in three successive phases: the initial flash shot, the balance of two moments of intense joy and finally the anguish of death out-weighing the sorrow of parting. (p. 76)

[Resnais] often derives impact from dual associations within a single image—as in the opening shot with its ideas of skin as the source both of pleasure and of pain or, more frequently still, within a single speech: "You destroy me. You're so good for me" or "I lie. And I tell the truth."

Basing his film on this kind of recurrent dichotomy rather than on traditional narrative preconceptions Resnais gives it a structural pattern that follows an essentially musical form. (p. 77)

Like a piece of music *Hiroshima mon Amour* depends entirely on its rhythmical structure. . . . (p. 78)

Set against music and images is Marguerite Duras's text, the tone of which is perhaps best defined as one of lyrical detachment: there is a surrender to feeling and emotion which permeates all the film and is allowed to dictate its shape and yet at the same time a lucid awareness of the corrosive effect of time and of the fourteen years that separate Nevers and Hiroshima. (p. 81)

In giving more weight to this lyrical tone than to plot development Resnais also makes largely irrelevant the conventional concept of character, for such a use of language has the effect of diverting the spectator's attention from individual idiosyncrasies to the flow of emotion, thereby preventing the normal identification with the protagonists to which we are accustomed in the cinema. (p. 82)

The key concept here, that of freedom, obviously has similarities with Brecht's preoccupations in the theatre but it also ties up with Resnais's literary tastes and perhaps helps to explain why he has always turned to novelists for his scripts. The modern novelist, as Resnais sees him, approaches his characters in such a way as to "show their acts in a raw state, such as they appear to him spontaneously as he writes. It is a way of provoking the reader by inviting him to justify these acts for himself." (pp. 82-3)

We have already seen how free from bias and propaganda the documentary sections of *Hiroshima* are, and it is clear Resnais does not say 'This is what the woman is like', he merely shows her to us and allows us to draw our own conclusions. Wide and important as the issues tackled in the short films had been, human beings are more complex still and give *Hiroshima* a richness that the rather abstract documentaries lacked. Resnais is deeply concerned with matters of form and style but only in so far as these allow him to present characters in their full complexity. (p. 83)

The characters are not naturalistically observed human beings—there are moments, especially at the beginning and end, when they cease to be 'real' people at all—but they come alive because they provoke the same mixture of sympathy and antagonism as the people we meet day by day. They are not in any way heroic, and if great events form a background to the story, the characters nonetheless remain apart from them: the actress experienced love, not the occupation, at Nevers and neither is directly connected with the disaster of Hiroshima. They hardly remember or recollect it in any meaningful way and in so far as the city is important it is as a further element of counterpoint: a background of death for a story of love. . . . (pp. 84-5)

It is in its handling of time that *Hiroshima mon Amour* proves its total originality, being a film that owes nothing to the conventions of narrative of other art forms but uses simply the cinema's ability to fuse past and present into a continuous flow. The stories of Nevers and Hiroshima develop simultaneously and with the heroine we move constantly from one to the other as they illuminate each other across the gulf of fourteen years. (p. 86)

L'Année Dernière à Marienbad is a realistic film, as Resnais has said, but it attempts an interior realism of mental processes, not the conventional realism of external events. If we submit to the emotional flow of the film, accepting it as occurring in the present without worrying about understanding it intellectually, then it emerges as a very simple and direct film containing nothing gratuitous and with a clear structural pattern. *Marienbad* is a love story but one that is not concerned with the external behaviour of the lovers. Its subject is the ebb and flow of their emotions, the turmoil into which love throws them and the event which the narrator describes as being in the past (Last Year) and in another place (at Marienbad) is in fact taking place here and now.

L'Année Dernière à Marienbad is in essence a continuous flow of images, words and music, but like a piece of musical composition it has a distinct shape, which gives it its emotional impact, and can be readily broken down into five movements or stages. Firstly, there is the long and hypnotic opening tracking shot which seems to take us away from the real world into an enclosed universe, with its isolation emphasised by the baroque setting. . . . (p. 95)

In the second section [the voice of the unseen narrator] mingles with the replies given in a play presented before the hotel guests and with the latter's conversation afterwards. It leads eventually to the words which may be said to conclude this part of the film: "You're still as beautiful . . . But you hardly seem to remember." All the elements of the story to follow are contained in this opening. (p. 96)

The film's third stage, that of the persuasion, begins with this, which comes with the first real conversation of the narrator, X, and the beautiful if statuesque woman A. . . . X explains, in a tone reminiscent of an art film commentary (shades of *Van Gogh*!), the detail of a moulding and then refers explicitly to the theme of memory: "You hardly seem to remember me." The first 'memory' is then evoked: in the gardens of Frederiksbad (or perhaps Karlstadt, Marienbad or Baden-Salsa) there was a discussion on a balcony about a statue to be found there of "a man and a woman in classical dress whose frozen gestures seemed to represent some specific scene." This statue, coming after the play and the story of Frank, represents the film's third main focal point. First the details of the statue are evoked verbally by X, then in a subsequent meeting with A (who is discovered reading a book in a little salon) it is successfully 'visualised' and the gestures of A in relation to it 'directed' by X, as if A were an actress rehearsing a role. A later discussion of the statue centred on an engraving of the subject hanging on the hotel wall is dominated by M . . . who authoritatively asserts that the statue is far from being mythological, allegorical or representing, as X has suggested, his relationship to A. This intervention of M's is typical of his somewhat mysterious role in the film. His precise relationship with A is left in doubt and yet he seems to be always somewhere in the background. His repeated contact with X in the film takes the form of a succession of games in which he invariably wins. Nevertheless he finally emerges as loser in the struggle for A's mind. The exact significance of the game is difficult to assess if one follows the authors' injunction to avoid hunting for symbols, yet it clearly serves several purposes: its constant return is a further rhythmical element and it demonstrates the basic inadequacy of a logical approach (it is a game of skill not chance) in this dream-world of *Marienbad.*

The visualisation and acceptance of the statue represent X's first victory, the base on which he builds his persuasion, and it is significant that it is A who now prompts further revelations, saying, albeit in an ironic tone: "Tell me the rest of our story." The next two 'memories' evoked seem insignificant ones—a trivial conversation with friends somewhere and an incident of walking in the gardens with a broken heel—and A apparently accepts them in the course of the evening's dancing. (pp. 97-8)

[When A accepts the garden,] the fourth stage, that of terror, begins. X's statement: "I've come now to take you away" still meets with a refusal but as if to prove his words we see the bedroom fully created, real, authentic, indubitably there. (p. 99)

Robbe-Grillet has conceived his film in terms of a verbal persuading, that the narrator's words are half the film, its backbone as it were. Absorbing them we imagine the film from his point of view, while the images, being described but not actually seen, are much less forceful. (p. 102)

The director, on the other hand, being primarily concerned with the images, was largely dealing with the woman's side of the affair, for the images belong to her principally, representing her thoughts and her relation to the man. From her point of view, and hence from the director's, there is no single certainty, rather the essence of the film lies in its ambiguity. (p. 103)

In so far as the film's images are a representation of the woman's stream of consciousness they contain varying shades of truth and *Marienbad* is indeed a "film about greater or lesser degrees of reality." Since the woman finally comes to accept the man's account of the past as real, the *mise en scène* must be conceived in terms of a real past, for the images represent what is subjectively true, not what is objectively real. . . .

In this way the approaches of Resnais and Robbe-Grillet diverged, indeed were bound to do so on account of their differing functions, but this divergence can only give the film an added power and impact, since its essence is the balance and opposition of image and text. (p. 104)

[We] witness the emergence of A and X out of the initial confusion and . . . by the end of the film they have disappeared again, for there is no sign of them in the final shot of the hotel exterior. Perhaps it is simplest to think of them not as people but as the complementary halves of a relationship, coming into existence when the relationship is born, being fused when it is resolved. Their total anonymity —they have no names, addresses, social ties etc. and the designations A, X and M are only adopted here, as in Robbe-Grillet's script, for convenience—is therefore their essence. (pp. 106-07)

The destruction of everyday logic and the creation of a new para-logic is achieved by the systematic and consistent reversal or extension of normal film techniques. To take a simple example, a flashback is conventionally used to take us into the past and then bring us back to our point of departure. In *Marienbad,* however, this clear cut division of past and present is blurred. For instance, there is a scene where X meets A reading in one of the salons. He talks about a meeting in the garden and we see A in a garden, wearing a different dress, but when we return to the salon we see A with her book again but retaining her outdoor clothes. A simple device like this makes the reconstruction of a 'real' chronology virtually impossible for the spectator but it does obey a logic of its own. (p. 108)

Marienbad represents the successful resolution of many of Resnais's stylistic preoccupations. . . . Its total removal from everyday existence frees the acting from the needs of mere reproduction of gesture and allows, even demands, a complete stylisation: it is the acted film *par excellence.* Finally, its total disregard of "anecdote, witty dialogue, explanation or chronology" throws into relief the rhythms of its images and soundtrack. In short *L'Année Dernière à Marienbad* is a film addressed simultaneously to eye and ear, satisfying to the emotions and stimulating to the intellect, a film in fact that "looks like a statue and sounds like an opera". (pp. 113-14)

The basic theme of *Muriel* is the interaction of past and present—Hélène experiencing first love and Hélène at forty, Bernard as a soldier in Algeria and Bernard back home. . . . The full title of the film, *Muriel ou le temps d'un retour,* shows the importance given to [the] aspect of attempted reintegration into life on the part of characters who have survived a shattering experience. (pp. 124-25)

The structure of *Muriel* was determined by the need to give adequate expression to these shattered and fragmentary existences. Despite the script's division into five distinct acts this is above all a jagged, abruptly edited film, full of jump cuts and startling transpositions. . . . (p. 125)

A further element of complexity and counterpoint in the film is that [the] half poetic, half banal dialogue is presented in a manner that is deliberately made to clash with the content. . . . [The film] follows *Hiroshima mon Amour* in preventing any sort of conventional identification with the characters: the lucidity of *Muriel* is in striking contrast to the hypnotic effect of *Marienbad* and in this respect anticipates the clear political commitment of *La Guerre est finie.* (pp. 131-32)

La Guerre est finie is the first of Resnais's films to be primarily about a man, and this change of focus brings with it a wider scope. Instead of being solely concerned with the emotional life of his characters, Resnais is here concerned with the relationship between love and masculine (and, more specifically, political) activity. There is a noticeable change of tone also: his earlier heroines had been played by Emmanuelle Riva and Delphine Seyrig, actresses trained in the theatre to compose a role, but here Diego Mora is portrayed by Yves Montand, to whom the customary filmic understatement and 'realistic' performance are second nature. The portrait that forms the central part of *La Guerre est finie* is complex, but only because of the large number of facets, the full range of attitudes and contradictions included, not because of any tension between dream and reality (as in *Marienbad* or *Hiroshima*) or between the character and the mode of portrayal (as in *Muriel*).

First of all, Diego is a Spaniard. . . . It is to Spain that he dreams of returning when it seems for a while that his political activity has come to a halt, yet his relationship with his native land is at best ambivalent. Long years of exile have cut him off from his roots and to the driver who comments on his perfect French, he admits that sometimes he forgets that he is Spanish.

The rootlessness of Diego is emphasised by the fact that Spain itself is never shown in the film. . . . Nevertheless a thesis about the future of Spain is propounded in *La Guerre est finie,* the thesis of Diego the revolutionary who has spent twenty years of his life working for the overthrow of Franco. The significance of the film's title is that while one form of fighting is finished, the struggle must continue, and the film is specifically concerned with how exactly this may best be done. (pp. 138-39)

La Guerre est finie aims to provoke the spectator, make him question his comfortable assumptions about Spain and the left, and in this it shares the same tone as Resnais's other films. But it also puts forward an assertion—that it is in Spain that things will happen—and this is unusual, for Resnais had previously been content to state the question and had not tried to offer solutions. (p. 140)

A further contributory factor to the somewhat negative effect of the film is that Diego, as well as being a Spanish exile and a revolutionary, has also reached the age of forty, a time of personal crisis when action for its own sake no longer proves automatically satisfying and certain questions seem unanswerable. He finds himself doubting the methods of his organisation, being tempted by the idea of opting out of the struggle, and lured into adventures that threaten his position. (p. 141)

One thing which [Diego's] political activity cannot give him . . . is a real identity. Before he reaches Marianne's apartment we have already seen him in several guises: as an anonymous passenger to Jude, as René Sallanches to the police, as Carlos to his comrade Antoine and as Domingo to Nadine. To the latter he admits: "Sometimes I jump when someone calls me by my real name", and then proceeds, almost automatically, to give a false name—the day of the week in Spanish—as they talk after making love. It is not until the scene of his meeting with Marianne, when she repeats his name, that he is seen in his true identity, with someone who knows who he really is. (p. 143)

Diego Mora, then, dominates the film with his thoughts, actions, memories and anticipations. Only once in *La Guerre est finie,* the single tracking shot following Marianne into the kitchen while he sleeps on, do we get a scene from which he is absent, elsewhere it is his "eyes, gestures and acts which give the world a structure, a psychological reality." Faced simultaneously with the problems of love and politics, Diego emerges as a complex character, ambiguous in the way that Resnais likes his heroes and heroines to be. . . . The use of anticipatory flashes, totally realistic because that is the way Diego sees life, is original and succeeds in giving the opening of the film a disorientating, thought-provoking atmosphere reminiscent of *Muriel.* (pp. 145-46)

What *La Guerre est finie* lacks is a certainty of tone. It is not by chance that this is Resnais's only feature film where filmic references are obvious, even obtrusive, or that the script needed to be entirely rewritten twice and was still changed quite extensively during shooting. . . . The subject and script with which he furnished Resnais demanded a purely realistic treatment: all scenes are timed, located and dated exactly. . . . [The] camera style with its seven hundred and fifty different set-ups, is bare and functional; even the imagined scenes are quite realistically presented. Yet this kind of approach is not Resnais's forte, and the film does not develop in any new way the stylistic concern with an interplay of text, image and music which has been the director's greatest contribution to contemporary cinema. . . . *La Guerre est finie*, a prosaic film *par excellence*, furnishes the counterbalance to the pure cinematic poetry of *L'Année Dernière à Marienbad* and though it undoubtedly reflects one side of its author's complex personality it is not altogether surprising that it left him dreaming of "a film where a language like that of Shakespeare of Giraudoux will be heard." (pp. 146-47)

Roy Armes, in his The Cinema of Alain Resnais *(copyright © 1968 by Roy Armes), A. S. Barnes & Co., Inc., 1968, 175 p.*

RICHARD M. BLUMENBERG

Last Year at Marienbad is a useful example of a film which attempts to show that cinema is able to describe psychological drama. The more detailed the description, the more "scientific" the forms; the more "scientific" the forms, the more abstracted from their environment the objects become. Resnais' documentary style (for example, long traveling shots) appears to work in this film visually to synthesize the "felt" with the "seen" object or objects. (p. 40)

Last Year at Marienbad occupies an important place in the history of narrative film, that it was a film that had to be made, and that—once done—new ideas about the possibilities of cinema can arise from a critical viewing of the film and its premises.

I think that *Marienbad* experimentally moves in a direction which is valid for showing off cinema's technology rather than for displaying its ability to "put life into action." The film's formal values inhibit direct expression of the human condition which arises from "empathy," from "accident," or from physical "response" to chance. Relying as much as it does on geometrical structures (the triangle, particularly as evidenced by the game, Nim; rectangles dimensionalizing into *trompe-l'oeil* frames) and using these structures almost scientifically to describe the behavior of the people who become subsumed under them, the film may in part support the theme Henry James and others used: "Lives lived too formally at the expense of feeling become hollow and meaningless; they are a type of death."

Marienbad's formalism perhaps destroys any significant qualitative response on the part of the viewer. Unable effectively to operate within the constraint of subjecting structure, the movie suggests that we need to escape from such forms to the more universal structures one can again attempt to build "essence" from. . . .

In a formal sense, however, *Marienbad* is about "death." Each shot in the film simply perishes. This does not mean that these shots have no experimental referents; nor does it mean that there is no governing form. The form is *imposed* on the actions, which are themselves objects, in motion or still, scientifically viewed (and hence "described" by the camera) rather than narrated. The many traveling shots attempt to dimensionalize the environment in order to make the rendition as objective as possible. The narrator's voice helps to substantiate this by continually describing emotions or events in time. The film's shots, then, are not causally connected to one another; rather, they are relative to one another in much the same way as objects in motion (*à la* Einstein) are relative to one another. (p. 41)

What the above seems to lead to in the case of *Marienbad* is a film which to an inordinate degree uses (or attempts to use) the objective structures of technological existence as structures for art. (p. 42)

In *Marienbad*, focusing upon one's interaction with others, the "love triangle" imposes itself as the geometrical design (the triangle) to symbolize constraint. In this sense, the structure (of which the triangle is only one possibility) becomes a labyrinth within which man peregrinates, lost to himself, his actions insignificant activities able to be described as objects in a laboratory are able to be described. These actions perish within the moments of their brief life. As with the editing in *Marienbad*, such shots do not inhibit further quantitative activity; they only effuse the despair of man, and his anguish. (pp. 42-3)

If man is to "act significantly," if he is going to be able to form "essence" from his existence rather than permit his "essence" to be determined for him, then he must, as A did in *Marienbad*, emotionally accept the form for, in Camus' language, his own absurdity), then break the balustrade and "escape." The escape from death which *Marienbad* presents is that not to the possibility of "freedom," but, rather, to that awareness of existence which is "life." As such, perhaps *Marienbad* becomes an allegory for man's contemporary "predicament," on an individual as well as on a universal basis. (p. 43)

Richard M. Blumenberg, "Ten Years after Marienbad," in Cinema Journal *(© 1971, Society for Cinema Studies), Vol. X, No. 2, Spring, 1971, pp. 40-3.*

GORDON GOW

With Resnais and his varied followers, the need for rationalised explanation has been modified, and audiences have come to accept the loose ends which are found in modern films as frequently (or almost) as they exist in real life.

This is very much the case in *Je t'aime, je t'aime*. One can see, from the lucid opening phases, that the 'story' is about a man named Claude who has attempted suicide and is discharged from hospital in very poor shape emotionally. . . .

Far from the stylised coolness of *Marienbad*, yet nowhere near the human warmth of *Hiroshima* and *Muriel*, this 1968 collaboration between Resnais and the writer Jacques Sternberg hardly succeeds at all with its characterisations. Claude is dull. . . . Catrine is hardly more than a cipher. And the other personages are *all* ciphers. . . . (p. 53)

Perhaps *Je t'aime, je t'aime* (a strange title in the circumstances) might be regarded as a mild swipe at scientists: the bunch set before us seem inept, and their environment less hygienic than Dr. Frankenstein's. . . . Frequent shots of the scientists themselves, fretting away and checking on their human guinea pig's mind, convey the same sense of man reaching dangerously beyond his own measure of knowledge that Kubrick imparted (far more strongly, of course) in the ambiguous closing sequences of *2001: A Space Odyssey*.

To this extent, but infrequently, our emotions are involved; and to a similar degree, we can enjoy the savour of make-believe, the 'comic-book' element to which Resnais disclosed his predilection as long ago as 1956 in the documentary *Toute la mémoire du monde*. Even then one could recognise the alignment of intellect and a kind of sensual joy in the medium of film: quite astonishing, really, that so much visual grace and mobility could be attained in a library.

In *Je t'aime, je t'aime,* however, it is the visual element that takes precedence, running away with the thematic ideas. The mysterious ride to the scientific research centre is technically a simple thing. . . . Yet, in conjunction with our knowledge of Claude's emotional condition and with some weirdly dreamy choral music, the passage becomes a fusion of realism and fantasy. . . . Recollected-events and imagined-events pass before us in apparently haphazard sequence. They never disguise the central flaw, the frugality of characterisation, especially in Catrine's case. What they do superbly well is to demonstrate the Resnais mastery of time-manipulation. Yet he gives me the feeling that he is trying a bit too hard to surpass his previous work in this line.

The human elements of uncertainty and persuasion, of the inconclusive choice between security and freedom, were abstracted magnificently in *Marienbad.* And humanity was decidedly more manifest in *Hiroshima, Muriel* and *La guerre est finie.* But, if there is a deficiency here in *Je t'aime, je t'aime,* there is also a perpetually enthralling journey of the mind; it is a film that keeps one alert every second, admiring its accomplished technique (which in its own right commands the respect of any thoroughgoing *cinéphile*). (pp. 53-4)

Gordon Gow, "'Je t'aime, je t'aime'" (© copyright Gordon Gow 1971; reprinted with permission), in Films and Filming, *Vol. 17, No. 12, September, 1971, pp. 52-4.*

JAMES MONACO

[The] romantic commerciality of *Stavisky* . . . is only emulsion deep. Like most of Resnais' previous films, this one is subtly deceptive. . . .

Stavisky . . . succeeds magnificently (as I've already suggested) as commodity: as a romantic evocation of the lost worlds of the twenties and thirties, entre deux guerres, it clearly out-Gatsbies [Jack Clayton's film version of *The Great Gatsby*]. . . .

[The] parallel with *Gatsby* extends deeper than their evident values as commodities in the film marketplace, for [Jorge] Semprun's script manages to catch some of the same mythic power which has made the novel a masterpiece (and which entirely eluded Jack Clayton's film). Stavisky, like his American cousin, is one of the last tycoons, the last of the grand self-made capitalist princes, building quite liveable castles in the air. But whereas Gatsby is only a vague homage to the old dream, *Stavisky* . . . gives us quite a precise analysis of its structure. (p. 24)

Like Fitzgerald's novel, Semprun and Resnais' film also gives a central position to its hero's *amour fou*. . . . [What] makes Resnais' film and Fitzgerald's novels classics is this simple structural trick they have of paralleling their heroes' sexual ardor with their equally obsessive adoration of cold hard cash. The process is reversed as we watch or read: our subconscious libidinous longing for money and the power and style which represent it is translated into more acceptable sexual and romantic feelings for the people of the story.

If *Stavisky* . . . stopped here it would still be a fairly intriguing film. . . . Resnais has complicated matters somewhat by showing us Alexandre Stavisky from a much more intricate point of view. This is a film about the legend, not the man, he explains, so he wanted a pulp fiction view of it because that is the way he had seen it as a kid. For the first time his *own* memories become part of the structure of a Resnais film; it is a logical advance for him. (pp. 24-5)

[This] is a very rich film, full of effective detail, but also strangely enough a film that is at first somewhat inaccessible. In one way or another this has been true of all of Resnais' films: they require repeated viewings before they yield up the intricate secrets of their structure. *Stavisky* . . . , at least, will have some immediate popular success simply on the basis of its gorgeous surface. But a real understanding of Resnais' accomplishment will depend on the precarious balance that eventually should emerge between the various dimensions of the film: the lush nostalgia commodity value, the importance of the myth of Stavisky, and —probably most important—Resnais' implicit and not quickly assimilated essay on cinematic and musical styles of the period and their urgent but only vaguely understood connection with that myth and that commodity. (p. 25)

James Monaco, "Reviews: Resnais' 'Stavisky . . .'," in Take One *(copyright © 1973 by Unicorn Publishing Corp.), Vol. 4, No. 6, July–August, 1973, pp. 24-5.*

PETER HARCOURT

Although the translucency of form in *La Guerre est finie* appeared to mark a new departure, the film still had much in common with Resnais's previous features. Central to the film is still the struggle on the part of Diego to come to grips with his own past. Related to this, in a way much like *Last Year At Marienbad,* Diego seems caught in a pattern of repetition. . . .

Diego's past, however, and this sense of repetition, are not simply matters of personal conjecture about the validity of some lost and private experience. They involve a public dimension as well. . . .

In *La Guerre est finie,* however, for the first time in his career, Resnais's two main characters *share* a common past; and they are both engaged, in varying degrees, in an actual political activity. They can reminisce romantically about their first encounter in Italy and make tentative plans for a future life in Spain. In fact, if Diego seems caught by the repetitions of his political activities, by the end of the film (though it is teasingly inconclusive about this matter), that final slow dissolve might imply that the hitherto *désengagée* Marianne might be caught in them as well, perhaps left to carry on. . . .

The split, then, which seeks to be resolved in *La Guerre est finie* is a split between the characters' private and their public lives. In this way, such distresses as the characters endure can in no way be described as neurotic. Their tensions are firmly placed in an actual place and time, and their attempts to deal with them are hopeful and, in terms of the film, realistic.

What seemed so fresh about *La Guerre est finie* when it first appeared was the bouyant beauty of the personal relationships and the way in which the greater simplicity of style allowed them to speak to us. . . . Certainly, it is a less complex film than *Muriel,* but beautifully handled. (p. 23)

Like *La Guerre est finie,* [*Je t'aime, je t'aime*] also has a compellingly charming character at its center plus the intermittent sense of many warm relationships. But the similarities end there. For one thing, unlike Diego, Claude Ridder is a man without a purpose, a man who lives (as Resnais himself has said) very much in the margins of life. This is one of the problems with the film, especially for a film supposedly concerned with time: Ridder is a man for whom time would be meaningless. . . . It is only the *form* of the film that thus lends an urgency to some of the moments of Ridder's life as we experience them for a second before they are flashed away again. . . .

We might *want* to be concerned, as Ridder himself is, with whether he actually killed his friend Catrine when they were away in Scotland together; but basically, I feel, the film holds us back from this. The film works more like a conventional thriller. . . . The sci-fi format seems chiefly an excuse for the chronologically jumbled exposition of a simple little story which in itself is rather thin. . . .

Like other Resnais characters, Ridder is caught up in a pattern of repetition. But with a difference. For Diego, as we have seen, the pattern was imposed from outside, the result of his public life. With previous Resnais characters, the pattern was almost totally internal, involving an obsession with some key moment of their past, generally a moment of idealized love, which they were attempting to reappropriate in the effort to understand. While this is *partly* true of Ridder, his will is not involved in the same way. Basically, Ridder seems caught up in the technological imperfections of his time-machine. He doesn't *choose* to go back into the past. He is sent back to live an arbitrarily chosen moment, chosen not by him but by the scientists in charge of him, and he gets stuck there. . . . Ridder cannot get free once he is thrown back into his own past experience. Nor can he make much sense of it. Nor can we.

If Ridder returns again and again to his concern with Catrine's death, he also returns to apparently trivial moments. . . . We also see him, sometimes very briefly, in marvellously warm and tender moments. . . . These moments provide the human center of *Je t'aime* and go a long way towards explaining my own patience with the film. At the same time, they do not provide the final justification for the form, a form that seems to present them in a willfully random way. . . .

There appears to be a conceptual weakness in the construction of *Je t'aime, je t'aime*. Here we find a harsh collision between the desire to create characters that might engage us and the desire to create a structure which, as in *L'année Dernière à Marienbad,* would make a predominently musical appeal. In direct contrast to *La Guerre est finie, Je t'aime* springs more from an idea than from a character, and the two don't really jell. (p. 25)

Hiroshima mon amour works best as a kind of liturgy, as a refined assault upon our sensibilities that tends to numb the precision of our minds. Repeatedly, the film startles and surprises, offering local delights which the mind cannot immediately grasp. And throughout it all, there is such an atmosphere of charged significance—Hiroshima, the bomb, the war, lost love, middle age, desperation, anxiety. Yet these elements remain separate. Indeed, they are not intended to jell. . . .

Somewhat similar to *Night and Fog,* Resnais' documentary meditation on the Nazi camps, the upshot of [his] rhetorical approach to the problem of characterization is that we get the sense on the human level that the characters are not in control of their own lives. The things they say do not necessarily relate to the things they do. Nowhere in the film do we get the sense of decisions being made. Things just happen. Like Nevers' first love: "At first we met in barns. Then among the ruins. And then in rooms. Like anywhere else."

At the same time, if these comments imply a generalized emotion as well as a personal lassitude, a fatalistic acceptance of things as they occur, the images accompanying them convey a much more particular emotion and create a more robust effect. In fact, the entire flashback sequence is full of truly magical effects, stunning artistic surprises. As we hear Nevers mention the ruins, we see her with her German lover posed against the gray sky with the wall of a ruin around them. It is held for the longest moment before slowly dissolving away. . . .

These local moments are very much of the essence of Resnais's basically interpretative, directorial art. They seem much more at the center of the film's achievement than the much discussed notions of memory and forgetfulness, responsibility and desire. They provide the music to the script's libretto. In their delicacy and originality, they reveal where Resnais's creative interest lies. In comparison with the specificity of these aesthetic effects; the concern with time in the film seems theoretical and conventional—one might even say perfunctory. (p. 26)

For Resnais, there is no continuity within the joy of life. There are moments of happiness, of intensely heightened awareness, but these are doomed to vanish away. Worse that that, they live on in one's memory, making one miserable, haunting one with the sense of something lost. . . .

In moral terms, in terms of what a work of art through its style affirms in life, the ending of *Hiroshima mon amour* is deeply pessimistic—hard set against life. The energy drains out of it as Nevers capitulates to a feeling of complete indecision, leading to an inability to act. The film ends on a scene not of rich ambiguity (as some people have claimed), but of moral and physical paralysis (against which may be contrasted the uncertain yet active ambiguity of *La Guerre est finie*). . . .

Like *Toute la mémoire du monde, Marienbad* sees our past life as a kind of confinement. Like *Hiroshima mon amour,* the characters in the film are uncertain about what really happened. . . . Throughout the film, the commentary often anticipates the appropriate images, which might seem once again like a kind of aesthetic teasing; but it also turns the whole film into a kind of dream.

However we might want to respond to them, the film hinges round three controlling images. First of all there is the hotel itself with its surrounding, shadowless gardens, where nothing ever changes, "without trees, without flowers, without growth of any kind." It is obviously a kind of geometric tomb into which the man keeps trying to lure the woman, to wander about forever, alone with him. . . .

The film builds for us an experience where there are no actual characters and no natural life. . . .

After the cold perfection of *Last Year at Marienbad, Muriel* seemed an exciting renewal of artistic energies. While it bears a strong stylistic and philosophical relationship to the films that preceded it, it offers us I think a far more satisfactory experience. It is demonstrably the most complex film that Resnais has yet made, even as *La Guerre est finie* remains the most accessible. (p. 27)

One of the real limitations of *Marienbad* is that its intentions seem to me to represent an invalid cimematic method. Films cannot *analyze* behavior; they can only *show* its outward manifestations. . . . To a large extent, *Muriel* invites us to respond in that way.

The film is dense in extraneous human details, details which are marginal to the main concern of the film but which nevertheless become part of its atmosphere. In a way that reminds me of Truffaut, these moments become part of the film's humanity. (p. 28)

More successfully than *Hiroshima mon amour,* more meaningfully than *Last Year at Marienbad,* the unity of *Muriel* is almost totally musical, quite literally so in the way that Hans Werner Henze's music serves to bind together the scattered fragments of Resnais's cinematic art. . . . *Muriel* seexs quite marvellously simultaneously centripetal and centrifugal, sending us outwards from the characters to create a sense of their actual environment, yet through the manner of this creation, giving us a sense of how the characters live their own lives.

Where, indeed, is the center of the town? What constitutes the center of any human character? This is it, the film seems to imply, this jumbled oscillation of expectation and memory, of the vain flight from the sense of past failure into the equally vain effort to recreate a more comforting reconstruction of the past. But without success. The characters in *Muriel* are as confined in their labyrinth of obsession and false memory as are the characters in *Marienbad* and the books in *Toute la mémoire du monde*. (pp. 28-9)

The film presents each of its characters as obsessed with a particular quest, whether it be a mate for a goat, the alleviation of guilt from an experience in Algeria, or simply the compulsion to prove that the past itself has been real. . . .

If we consider Resnais's films as a whole, what are the qualities that most stay with us? For me personally, there is the feeling of uncertainty—not only the uncertainty of the world that his characters inhabit (as in Godard), but also the uncertainty of himself as an artist, a gnawing sense of inadequacy before the problems which he chooses to deal with in his films. . . .

Cumulatively, the neurotic dread experienced by so many of Resnais's characters has to be related to Resnais himself —not necessarily Resnais the man, but Resnais the artist. There seems throughout his films a fascination with death and with various forms of self-destruction, plus a recurring passivity in the face of moral problems. . . .

I suggested earlier that Resnais's inventiveness was very different from Godard's. Godard's seems thrust upon him by the many new things he wants to say. Resnais's, on the other hand, seems related more to the ghostly gardens of *Marienbad*. It seems more the desire to create forms of such beauty and authority that they will be eternal, like the statue in *Marienbad*. . . . For Resnais, filmmaking is editing. . . . He certainly is an editor of genius, and he has made films which are among the most challenging of our time. Yet there is something missing from his work. There is a sense of coldness, something non-committal—perhaps a sense of fear. (p. 29)

Peter Harcourt, "Alain Resnais: Toward the Certainty of Doubt, Part II," in Film Comment *(copyright © 1974 Film Comment Publishing Corporation; all rights reserved), Vol. 10, No. 1, January-February, 1974, pp. 23-9.*

FREDERICK BUSI

In his latest film *Stavisky* Alain Resnais attempts to handle the peculiar climate of France during the 1930s, the years that paved the way for Laval and Pétain to come to power. For the Frenchman with a memory mention of the name Stavisky conjures up images of the worst civil disorders his country experienced since the Paris Commune of 1871. He would recall a government discredited by corruption and coverups, a country set adrift, demoralized by the great depression, domestic hopelessness and also mesmerized by the rise of Hitler.

Little of . . . political history is depicted in Resnais' "Stavisky." It could have been the ideal topic for a historical treatment but Resnais, despite the political tone of his early documentaries, has not been much given to Brechtian exposition. When considering how the subjects of *Hiroshima Mon Amour* and *La Guerre est Finie* could easily have lent themselves to cinemagraphic pamphleteering, it is not surprising that Resnais again prefers the esthetic approach to deal with history through the fantasy world of his main characters. In order to give free rein to his audience's imagination, Resnais offers a minimal dose of realism and maximal opportunity for reflection. This is the dominant tone of *Stavisky*.

Jorge Semprun, the author of this film's screen play, reveals just how far Resnais seemed to be removed from historical reality by identifying H. P. Lovecraft, of all writers, as one of the sources of inspiration for this work. (pp. 799-800)

Why not the gothic horror tale to serve as the setting for political scandals? Semprun argues that it is no less credible than the tale of Stavisky, a second confidence man whose schemes brought down the government of Europe's then most powerful state. Who would have believed that a high-class pimp and check forger would become the central figure in a scandal that ultimately led to the fall of the Third Republic?

What Resnais has retained from his excursion into Lovecraft country is the aura of mystery that also permeated public opinion during the Stavisky affair in 1934. In his film he is trying to suggest the sense of hysteria injected into the national consciousness by the yellow press. Lovecraft's talent consisted in beginning his tales in a naturalistic frame that runs parallel to the hidden world and then lapses into the underlying demonic current that propels his characters along. In fact Resnais seems to be using Lovencraftian techniques in reverse. Lovecraft tried to evoke the iridescent, silent, fantastic universe beneath the surface of the everyday world. Resnais, however, attempts to show the almost banal character, despite his posing, of the figure who was the focus of mass hysteria and horror in the outside world. (pp. 800-01)

Despite the dominant esthetic tone of this film, Resnais does not really forsake the political side of the affair, which is the feature remaining in the public mind down through the years. This aspect is evoked toward the end of his narrative in the scene depicting the government inquest on political and financial crimes. And all the way through this work Resnais interjects a subplot that reflects the activities of Trotsky who was in France at the same time when the scandal broke. One critic found this an awkward intrusion on the main plot. Like puppets, the "old man," his secretary and speechless minions keep popping up as if Resnais had spliced in snippets of Peter Weiss's *Trotsky in Exile*.

There are other reasons to justify this Trotskyite intrusion in the narrative. In his film credits Resnais has acknowledged his technical debts to Chester Gould and "Fearless Fosdick." . . . His use of the comic strip technique heightens the effects of the non-realistic method of narration by distorting and isolating a character from his surroundings and by creating the illusions of motion and action.

The distorting contrast of the comic strip perspective serves another purpose. More ambiguously, these references to Trotsky suggest a sequence of events running parallel to the Stavisky scandal itself. They also imply the revolutionary options available to a France suffering from the corrupt politics of bourgeois democracy. At the same time they suggest the theme of the "Jewish menace" that was associated with the scandal. (pp. 801-02)

At times Resnais' film appears designed to show off the cars and clothes of the period. For this reason it seems to some critics to be just another slick gangster movie. But this ostentation highlights the director's central concern: Stavisky's obsession with social standing and his fear of imminent death. (p. 802)

Though there are passing references to the political turmoil, Resnais is clearly committed to exploring Stavisky the man and not Stavisky the figure of public notoriety. As a director he deliberately turns away from merely reproducing reality. The focus is definitely inward to the closed world of Stavisky, away from the streets, the theater life and parties where he wielded so much influence. Resnais is mainly concerned with the private Stavisky, the Cagliostro of the financial world, when he is confined to back rooms and boudoirs with his cronies and lovers. But even here Resnais is not so much intent on developing the concept of character; he prefers to establish a lyrical atmosphere which is diffused throughout the narrative like a warm bath wherein Stavisky immerses his delicate, pampered body. (p. 803)

Most of the action of Resnais' film depicts the unravelling of Stavisky's last great operation which by the end of 1933 was well under way. His master plan was to defraud a chain of *crédits municipaux* or municipal pawn shops. (p. 804)

Stavisky was dead but the scandal that bears his name was just beginning. At this point in his film, toward the end of the narrative, Resnais moves back and forth chronologically to impart the feeling of malaise that had gripped public opinion. (p. 805)

This is precisely the image that Resnais wants to leave in the public's mind. His film is not just about one sensational scandal as Baron Raoul . . . makes clear in the film's last words: "I understood too late, but Stavisky was announcing his death to us . . . Not only his own, not only those of the February days: the death of an era . . ." The Stavisky affair was the agent of that deterioration and Resnais' latest film brings us face to face with the beginnings of the crisis and its repercussions. (p. 806)

Frederick Busi, "Alain Resnais' 'Stavisky': The Beginning of the End," in The Massachusetts Review *(reprinted from* The Massachusetts Review; *© 1975 The Massachusetts Review, Inc.), Vol. XVI, No. 4, Autumn, 1975, pp. 799-806.*

JUDITH CRIST

With varying success, Resnais has proved himself among the most adventurous of film artists, and certainly his present concept confirms it. Unfortunately, he has chosen as his collaborator for [*Providence*, an] exploration of what might best be termed a creative nightmare, David Mercer, the British playwright who last gave the screen *Morgan!*, based on his own play. In his first "original" screenplay, Mercer proves himself suffering major indigestion with the dialogue styles of Wilde, Coward, and Pinter; and it is indeed the English language itself . . . that is the stumbling block. . . .

It is Resnais's vision that holds the attention: the suggestion and shadow of environment, the lurking terrors of the night, the quick silver changes of character from flesh and blood to puppetry, the foisting of the narrator's suspicions and self-hatreds upon others. . . .

The dialogue becomes obvious, tedious, and intolerable in its stilted wordplay: "You have inner peace," "You have inner stagnation"; "Some people might say you're your own worst enemy, but I think you're your only best friend," on and on. And ultimately, with forays into the scatology of the novelist's ailments, the repetition and thereby the portentousness of the extermination-camp scenes and the recurrent land- and skyscapes combine to put a heavy-handed contrivance on what, in less self-conscious writing, would have been a tantalizing vision. In the last quarter there is a straightforwardness that is a blessed relief and refreshment. But as [a character] says early on: "If one has led a fatuous life one must have fatuous nightmares." As for Resnais—even a fatuous screenplay can become intermittently interesting in his hands. (p. 42)

Judith Crist, "'They Say In Harlan County, There Are No Neutrals There . . .'," in Saturday Review *(copyright © 1977 by Saturday Review; all rights reserved; reprinted with permission), Vol. IV, No. 11, March 5, 1977, pp. 39-42.**

JOHN FRANCIS KREIDL

Stavisky is the beginning film of Resnais' second period—a period forced into being by financial problems rather than artistic intent. It is his *Touch of Evil*, not in the sense of the closed structure of Orson Welles' film, but in the nature of its handling: like Welles', it suggests a "comeback," a nervous desire to make good and regain public attention. (pp. 172-73)

Stavisky makes perfectly clear that Resnais' love of comics is not "slumming" but one facet of his purism in style, a purism that can only allow itself to take ideas and building blocks from high art and from simplicity, and not from middlebrow culture or masscult love of one-dimensionality. . . .

Comics, well beyond the function of creative play, showed Resnais how to solve the problems of camera setup and cutting; for the comics were developed in parallel with the Hollywood school of continuity cutting and non-montage editing of the 1930s. In Resnais' own words: "The rules of shooting-script and editing are the same in the comics as in the cinema. What I know about the cinema, I have learned as much through comics as through the cinema." (p. 173)

[The techniques of comics] apply to a Resnais film because they frequently have commentary quite separate from the visual flow of the panels, narrating a different pace, in a line or two of print underneath the panel. . . . (p. 174)

Stavisky is a return to the uncluttered minimalism of his early documentaries; and while it does not have an overall comic book panel style, parts of it are totally set up as panels. The flashforwards of Arlette and the police inspector testifying at Stavisky's post-mortem parliamentary inquest are straight out of *Rex Morgan, M.D.* or *Mary Worth* in their coloration and flat focus, and *Dick Tracy* in their way of having their characters facing forward to address the spectator.

This stylistic use of the panel in *Stavisky* is formally justified. Serge Alexandre Stavisky is designed as an off-screen character—he is, for a character at the center of the film, rarely seen—a certain indication that the film is not about Stavisky but about something else: France in the 1930s? Time? Death? The character, Stavisky, is often just talked about, is dealt with by ellipsis. The characters who speak about him, are then brought forward—as in the device of the inquest—to narrate his story in comic strip frontal fashion. (pp. 180-81)

In *Stavisky,* Resnais . . . intends his strip-like characters to provoke our eavesdropping. In medium close-up admittedly these characters look a bit stiff on the screen. They never move anything but their lips (Resnais' admixture of comic panel and Bressonian style). . . .

If we see that the testifiers, the witnesses to the life of Stavisky, are all in panel form, we can see Resnais' use of the comic strip's method of handling time; often fast ellipsis takes the place of dissolves. . . .

The second element of narrative interest in *Stavisky* is Resnais' comics-like use of Belmondo, the actor who plays Stavisky. Belmondo comes out of elevators, runs out of doors. Belmondo bursts into a group, as if a cartoonist threw him there, and he runs off like a Captain America. (p. 181)

The third narrative element in *Stavisky* worth considering is how Resnais connects Stavisky and his friends with the parallel story of Trotsky, the fellow exile. No comic panalling is related to the story of Trotsky, a serious subject. The one time these two stories intersect, they are connected by a pan from one grouping to the other grouping, and where these two space-time located point spaces meet is shown with pictorial reality and classically fluid camera movement, not in comic strip fashion at all.

It seems Resnais intentionally structurally differentiated the three interrelated themes of *Stavisky:* Stavisky live, Stavisky legend, and Stavisky's parallel, Trotsky. Stavisky live is cut quickly, as is comic strip action. Stavisky legend is shown in isolated comic panels speaking back to us down the corridors of time. . . .

All of his use of the panel format in *Stavisky* is economical, displaying a minimalism that makes sense and redeems a film with what would otherwise be too slow a pace, a film that often threatens to use pictorialism for imagery's sake. By using the highly abbreviated panel style, Resnais changes the punctuation of the film. He also heightens the tragedy of the short, abbreviated life of Stavisky, the formal elements of the composition and the narrative intent of the film here becoming delightfully fused into one statement. (p. 182)

Stavisky is the first of Resnais' films to show his advancing age. It is peopled with a coterie of human and accessible characters, it abounds in chance conversations, with eavesdropping, and the characters' essences of the moment. *Stavisky* seems not to have been made from an existential or Marxist urge, but simply to show life out there. Stavisky's quest was his continual seeking of the answer to a question Resnais never lets him ask out loud, but which he transfers on to us. This question is: "to be or not to be?" That Stavisky's suicide ends the film shows that Resnais felt Stavisky's life was made tragic, that he died because there was never a chance for him to achieve an identity. The refugee's tragedy is that he often is denied the nobility of even posing Hamlet's question. (pp. 182-83)

Resnais, I should like to suggest, made *Providence* as a kind of homage to a uniquely American type of film comedy. Originating in the 1930s, the screwball comedy—its characters in tuxedos in drawing rooms—is Hawksian comedy, best illustrated by *20th Century* with Barrymore, for example. It is not the comedy of Chaplin or Harold Lloyd.

For a French director to translate this American subgenre, showing the world through comedy (the screwball comedy actually expressed an ontology: a laughing, self-confident response to the Great Depression) involves problems; for the type must be true to its American form, or it becomes a parody of a parody. It must be shorn of any quasi-sociological pretensions. It must simply be very witty and very funny to a mass audience. (p. 197)

One way to look at *Providence* is to take Resnais' "documentary" ending as a disjuntion, as just another of *Providence*'s many disjunctions, and assume, with it, that Resnais is again showing us "the impossibility of documenting." And, as *Providence* plays upon its own Proustian theme, Resnais makes his own film ironically comment upon itself. (p. 199)

[*Providence* ends], like *Marienbad,* by throwing a curtain upon itself. What we are left with is the urge to contemplate all the subsets of articulation of the valiant, struggling author, Langham. What we make of these subsets of Langham's articulation is in part influenced by the way Resnais has filmed them. Here, Resnais' influence on *Providence* becomes marked, if not paramount. (p. 200)

The basic structure of *Providence* is not so unlike that of *Muriel,* if we examine it carefully. There is a "suspension-of-disbelief" set of information, designed to make us believe there is a Clive Langham. This is accomplished by Resnais' showing us how much Langham loves to mix up fact and fiction. In the concentration camp sequences, for example, Resnais' visuals make Langham's thoughts seem vivid, as if Langham were really believing these fictions of his. (p. 201)

If we, however, appreciate *Providence*'s structure as Resnais intended it, we find that he and Mercer have taught us what fiction is. (Possibly Mercer has taught us what absurdity is as well.) Mercer and Resnais have taught us the linguistics of comedy. We can place *Providence* in the Jerry Lewis tradition of Jekyl-Hyde comedy. We can find some Gallic parallels to the bartender sequence in *The Nutty Professor* in Claud's confrontations with his wife in the kitchen of Providence Manor. We know Lewis was having fun; we should see that in *Providence,* Resnais was having fun. Mercer's peculiar Anglo-Saxon boffo humor filtered through Resnais' camera lens is especially amusing and transcends the Franco-English linguistic gap, plummetting *Providence* more genuinely into company with the Jerry Lewis films that Resnais so ardently admired. (p. 202)

The interplay of narrative in *Providence* is surreptitious, clandestine because Mercer thinks that is how life is if it is shown naked. It is an absurdist's garden, a personal bourgeois view, and as much of a personal *Welt* as Fritz Lang's Berlin, Bertolucci's Parma in *Before the Revolution,* or Antonioni's Ferrara in *The Red Desert.* Resnais then reinforces this notion that we are in a mind garden (but we are awake there and never dreaming) full of filmic points of view. (p. 204)

On the level of the image, disjunction reigns supreme. The integration between disjuncting images and comic punch lines is superb and combines the best of the continental and Hollywood styles. *Providence* is a masterpiece of comic timing. Resnais learned his Jerry Lewis well. (p. 205)

Are Mercer and Resnais soliloquizing on an author's death or on the death sensation an author feels after he is delivered of a novel? Are artists lonely by definition? Resnais' camera shows Langham mostly alone. At the end of the film, he is shown alone. Is *Providence* to the writer what *Blow-Up* was to the photographer: a study of limits?

Given the above, Resnais' self-appointed task in *Providence* was to get us to care about this world with loaded dice, this noncausal world. *Providence* in this sense approximated the pseudoclosed world of *Citizen Kane,* a favorite Resnais film, a film where just as one door seems to close on the findings about Kane, another door opens. Resnais' device in *Providence* seems to get us to care about its plot, not through Wellesian pathos but through Brechtian comic devices, giving us bursts of laughter. (p. 206)

[The] Brechtian devices in *Providence* which invite us to make a search for an answer to life do not lead us to any definite conclusions. *Providence,* from its Hitchcockian, *Rebecca*-like opening shot on, which shows the camera travelling in to investigate, informs us that we the spectators are going to have to participate. *Providence* tries in its final soliloquy to make this quest a bit easier for us, summing it up, and giving us some additional information almost as a sort of consolation prize for the film's not leading us to a firm answer. (p. 207)

The ending to *Providence* is not comic. The comedy is over. The comic first four-fifths of the film is life; the last fifth or less, only a quiet moment amidst life. Resnais at fifty-five has realized life is a lot of fun at the nodes amongst the chaos. Also, like Thomas Mann, who tried to be very liberal in his youth and ended as a bourgeois individualist, Resnais, too admits to and celebrates his middle class origins. (p. 208)

John Francis Kreidl, in his Alain Resnais *(copyright © 1978 by Twayne Publishers, Inc.; reprinted with the permission of Twayne Publishers, A Division of G. K. Hall & Co., Boston), Twayne, 1978, 250 p.*

WILLIAM F. VAN WERT

[*Providence*] is a meta-film, a film about the making of films, a work of art about the fabricating of art works. . . . It is a film dependent more upon the mechanics of the medium than upon any simple mimesis. . . .

Because a meta-film implies a simultaneous observation of the world and a meditation on itself, there is an unspoken tension, never resolved, within the work. Or, if resolved, it is only because the two functions have converged. The final scene of *Providence* is the only 'pure' scene in the film. We meet the real offspring of Clive Langham . . . , famous writer, liberated for the first time from his creative imagination. That liberation also implies the old man's death. The release of tension, on a structural level, comes from the fact that the spectator finally observes the author whose meditation is ended. If we use the mathematical construct of a topology, we have moved from the *inside* to the *outside* without, however, any change in the overall structure itself: Clive Langham has not changed personalities; his children are no better off in the 'real' world than they are in his mind; and his death is still inevitable. (p. 179)

Clive Langham is an old man dying and a creative writer creating. His vision contaminates everything else in *Providence.* His mind moves the other characters: they say the lines he gives them, they do what they are told. And the double role that Langham plays extends to all the other characters as well, so that they re-enact both his fantasies and his past experiences, even his nightmares, but never their own fantasies, experiences or nightmares. The result is that the spectator must constantly re-identify the characters in a symbolic way. . . . (pp. 179-80)

Resnais' *Providence* is an interesting meta-film, because it provides a kind of end-game to the form. . . . [It] is an example of montage as total *découpage,* the meta-film gobbling up the film itself, contaminating and finally eradicating the surface narrative, until the only thing left at the end of the film is the end of the film. . . .

There are two ways in which Resnais interrupts the text and imposes his own point of view, both involving the other characters. One is essentially cinematic, the other is literary. There are brief shots, violent in their content, unnarrated . . . and unassimilated by the rest of the text, which punctuate the soap-opera scenes involving characters speaking to each other. The first such shot is of an apparent madman pursued by soldiers with machine guns. . . . The shot is totally visual, cinematic, undiluted by any act of interpretation within the film. This and other shots involving the herding together and shooting of old people on a football field 'belong', of course, to Clive Langham. They are images of old age and death: hurried and violent, because Langham cannot comprehend his own death; unnarrated, because they are creations of the imaginary, creations which pop up in Langham's mind, but over which his mind has no control. Expressed in their brute state, with no voice-over commentary, they represent Langham's point of view as the creator manipulated and totally alone with his fears.

Impending death as repose, both peaceful and desirable, is also expressed uniquely in terms of images. I refer here to the two times in the film when Resnais' familiar forward-travelling camera moves into and over the tops of green trees. These images also stem from Langham's point of view, but again his conscious creating mind has no control over them. They are startling, both for their colour and for their silence.

All other images in which Langham is not visually present, representing the various combinations of Claude Langham [and Sonia, Woodford, and Helen] . . . and comprising most of the film's screen time, are contaminated in terms of literature more than film. . . . Clive Langham, the writer, imposes his point of view on that of his children, in written form: he steals their dialogue. He feeds them their lines. In the beginning, this symbolic superimposition in the dialogue seems to function on a double level: the spoken lines have meaning both in terms of the other characters and in terms of the father meddling in their lives or composing lines for a novel. But, as the scenes repeat themselves and the spatial integrity of the film is lost, we realise that all scenes, except the final scene, are re-enactments of Clive Langham's past, with Claude and Woodford serving as stand-ins for Clive and Sonia and Helen substituting for the absent Molly, who committed suicide. . . .

[The] face of . . . Langham is withheld for the first twenty minutes of the film, reminiscent of the withheld faces of the lovers in *Hiroshima mon Amour* (1959). The point here is that we associate point of view in film with a fixing of attention on characters' faces. We identify present tense, in a way, with the visual fixation on a face representing the whole body, the whole person. . . . [The] absence of that face (and the corresponding absence of a present tense) are crucial to the successful point of view superimposition, just as the lovers' faces being withheld in the long opening sequences of *Hiroshima mon Amour* established our identification, not with them but with their memories and reconstructions of Hiroshima and Nevers. (p. 180)

As Clive Langham comes full circle upon his failed past and as he approaches the inevitable death of the final scene, the doubling process breaks down. Characters begin to speak out of character, reversing each other's lines and, in some cases, speaking directly to the creator. . . .

The breakdown in role-playing after that would be completely confusing if Resnais' visuals did not hold the scenes together by their repetition. Helen, supposedly Claude's lover, repeats Molly's words to Woodford. And Woodford play-acts Claude cursing his father, now played (ironically) by Claude. . . .

Ingeniously, Resnais' repeated scenes function as a kind of revision process, a starting over for Clive Langham. The club scene, in which Sonia introduces Woodford to Claude, who has just tried in court to convict Woodford of murder, is Clive Langham's attempt as a writer/father to find a centre, to go back and begin again. Unfortunately, the decontamination process has already gone too far. Woodford says to Claude: 'What I'm searching for, Mr. Langham, is a moral language.' These were, in fact, Claude's words to his father, who now turns them back on his son in the composition process.

And suddenly the visuals break down as well. Claude and Sonia find themselves on the same patio as Helen and Claude, Helen and Woodford before them. In the background, the waves of the ocean are 'frozen', painted-on, a cardboard replication. As long as Clive Langham has control over the dialogue, the visuals in the scenes of conversation 'conform' to the composition. But his impending death, always expressed visually, destroys first the backdrop, then the foreground, from the frozen waves to the pursuit of Woodford. . . .

The transition from this scene to the final scene is an intertextual allusion. Woodford's body is dumped into a bin. The camera moves in for a close-up on his hand. Cut to a close-up of Clive Langham's hand in the final scene, with the sound of cicadas on the soundtrack for the first time and the sun shining for the first time in the entire film. The allusion is, of course, to the cutting by psychic association in *Hiroshima mon Amour,* from the Japanese lover's sleeping hand twitching on the bed in Hiroshima to the dying German lover's hand, twitching on the ground at Nevers. The sound of cicadas is also a reference to *Hiroshima mon Amour,* in which the same sound, the first 'natural' sound in the film, punctuates the first time that we see the lovers' faces, all sound accompanying their memories and reconstructions up to that point having been stylised sound: voice-over commentary of a recitative nature or discordant modern music. . . .

The resolution to this meta-film goes something like this: we finally see Clive Langham out in the open, objectified on his birthday and death-day. And, curiously, we as spectators assume the role of final creator. We now know the truth about the children that Clive Langham never knows: that he is loved, has been loved all along, and the only limits to that love are the terms that he himself has dictated. All the 'torture' of the rest of the film is exiled to the level of pure fiction, the creator duped by his own creation.

What prevents the film from being a simple 'it-was-all-a-dream' resolution, too facile a conclusion for Resnais' tastes, is that there are real victims in this story. The missing Molly remains missing, whether by actual suicide or accidental death. And Claude remains the estranged son of a prodigal father, no matter whose fault it is. Indeed, in retrospect (meaning that one has to see the film at least a second time, and maybe more, to piece it all together) Claude's is the most crucial role in the film, since his behaviour is the constant reminder of Molly, the mother. We are only given one glimpse of Molly in the film: a photograph. The photograph is of a woman we know in the film as Helen. Clive Langham's failure on both fronts (he was a womaniser in the marriage and he neglected Molly when he wasn't chasing women because he was writing) is photo-clear at the end. The sexual entanglement he has tried to create between Sonia and Woodford or between Claude and Helen never succeeds, precisely because incest prevents it from succeeding. Clive Langham's ultimate failure is that he never resolved his wife's death before his own. And he never re-created Molly in the fiction of his composition.

As film, *Providence* ends with the creator within the film becoming a character, a dying character at that. His point of view accedes to our own, and we have information/knowledge about him and the other characters that he will never have. As such, there is a kind of deflation or release of tension in this last scene. We are like the critics who only find out about a writer's life (and his intentional fallacy) after his death. But as meta-film, *Providence* has a very different ending. The intertextual allusions to *Hiroshima mon Amour* do cinematically what Clive Langham's comments about style in the dialogue have done throughout the film: they send us to Resnais, not Clive Langham. Product of a double-bind, the meta-film is a way for the director to go on creating, even while the failed artist dies within the film. Stated that way, *Providence* tells us a great deal about the enigmatic and usually silent Alain Resnais. (p. 181)

William F. Van Wert, "Meta-Film and Point of View: Alain Resnais's 'Providence'," in Sight and Sound *(copyright © 1979 by The British Film Institute), Vol. 48, No. 3, Summer, 1979, pp. 179-81.*

ANDREW SARRIS

Alain Resnais's *Mon Oncle d'Amerique* may be the funniest movie about the horrors of working since Charles Chaplin's *Modern Times*. I know this sounds strange, because Resnais's work never struck anyone as intentionally funny; his films have evoked, instead, a few giggles over the years for what has been alleged to be his failed seriousness or lame whimsy. . . .

The invidious critical catchword "didactic" will probably haunt the film for a long time, particularly in the unusually risky passages in which the characters reenact some of their scenes with the heads of white rats superimposed on their bourgeois-clad bodies. A more felicitous supplementary strategy is to identify each of the characters with a role model from the galaxy of French movie stars. . . .

[Failure] and disenchantment are very much the order of the day and night in [the film's] three interlocking stories. . . . Indeed, there are so many layers to the film that one almost feels the ground shifting under one's feet. . . .

The last shot of the picture consists of footage reportedly taken in the burned-down South Bronx. Whether or not this constitutes *L'Amerique* for Resnais is not clear. Nor is it clear where exactly Resnais is situated in the elaborate structure of the film. But time and again, I was reminded of every other film Resnais had ever made.

Andrew Sarris, "Waiting for Godard, Resnais, and Fuller," in The Village Voice *(reprinted by permission of* The Village Voice; *copyright © News Group Publications, Inc., 1980), Vol. XXV, No. 22, June 2, 1980, p. 41.**

Leni Riefenstahl

1902-

(Born Helene Riefenstahl) German director, scriptwriter, actress, author, and photographer.

Riefenstahl is best known for *Triumpf des Willens* (*Triumph of the Will*), a documentary of the 1934 Nazi Party rally in Nuremberg, Germany. More than a record of an event, *Triumph of the Will* is believed to be a masterpiece of propaganda that effectively persuaded many Germans to follow Hitler. Though her artistry is undeniable, Riefenstahl's alleged political affiliations handicapped her later career.

Riefenstahl was a student of director Arnold Fanck, the father of the German mountain cinema, and starred in several of his films. Her interest developed into a desire to make her own films, and Riefenstahl formed her own production company. She directed and starred in her first film, *Das Blaue Licht* (*The Blue Light*), the story of an ideal community versus a corrupted one—a theme that reemerged in her later works.

Hitler admired her work, and in 1934 approached her to make a film. The result, *Triumph of the Will*, is, according to Riefenstahl, "purely a historical film . . . a documentary." It is generally believed that Riefenstahl was more involved with the Nazi party and Hitler than she admits. Her next film, *Olympiad*, is considered by many to be an exceptional rendering of the 1936 Olympics, though some find it only a glorification of the Aryan ideal of physical perfection.

The end of World War II signalled the beginning of a long series of hardships for Riefenstahl, resulting from her affiliation with the Nazis. Only *Tiefland* (*Lowlands*), which Riefenstahl made before the war, was released after she became a figure of controversy. Various projects were started, then had to be abandoned. Undaunted, Riefenstahl traveled to Africa where, equipped with a small camera, she produced two books of photography. These books concerned critics because they view African tribesmen as idealized objects, an attitude reminiscent of Nazi ideology.

Riefenstahl presents an enigmatic figure in the history of the cinema. Although it is important to divorce the propagandist purposes to which her art was applied from the artistic quality of her work, it cannot be denied that Riefenstahl created works of sometimes frightening vision: frightening because the genius of her work lies in its emotive power, rather than its appeal to intellectual or humanistic ideals.

SIEGFRIED KRACAUER

[*Triumph of the Will*] represents the complete transformation of reality, its complete absorption into the artificial structure of the [Nuremberg] Party Convention. . . . [The] Convention could evolve literally in a space and a time of its own; thanks to perfect manipulation [on the part of the Nazis], it became not so much a spontaneous demonstration as a gigantic extravaganza with nothing left to improvisation. This staged show, which channeled the psychic energies of hundreds of thousands of people, differed from the average monster spectacle only in that it pretended to be an expression of the people's real existence. (p. 300)

It was Hitler himself who commissioned Leni Riefenstahl to produce an artistically shaped film of the Party Convention. In her book on this film, she incidentally remarks: "The preparations for the Party Convention were made in concert with the preparations for the camera work." This illuminating statement reveals that the Convention was planned not only as a spectacular mass meeting, but also as spectacular film propaganda. Leni Riefenstahl praises the readiness with which the Nazi leaders facilitated her task. Aspects open here as confusing as the series of reflected images in a mirror maze: from the real life of the people was built up a faked reality that was passed off as the genuine one; but this bastard reality, instead of being an end in itself, merely served as the set dressing for a film that was then to assume the character of an authentic documentary. *Triumph of the Will* is undoubtedly the film of the Reich's Party Convention; however, the Convention itself had also been staged to produce *Triumph of the Will*, for the purpose of resurrecting the ecstasy of the people through it. (p. 301)

Leni Riefenstahl made a film that not only illustrates the Convention to the full, but succeeds in disclosing its whole significance. The cameras incessantly scan faces, uniforms, arms and again faces, and each of these close-ups offers evidence of the thoroughness with which the metamorphosis of reality was achieved. . . . These particular close shots . . . seem to assume the function of removing things and events from their own environment into strange and unknown space. The dimensions of that space, however, remain entirely undefined. It is not without symbolic meaning that the features of Hitler often appear before clouds.

To substantiate this transfiguration of reality, *Triumph of the Will* indulges in emphasizing endless movement. The nervous life of the flames is played upon; the overwhelming effects of a multitude of advancing banners or standards are systematically explored. Movement produced by cinematic techniques sustains that of the objects. There is a constant panning, traveling, tilting up and down—so that spectators not only see passing a feverish world, but feel themselves uprooted in it. The ubiquitous camera forces them to go by way of the most fantastic routes, and editing helps drive them on. . . . [Here] total movement seems to have devoured the substance, and life exists only in a state of transition.

The film also includes pictures of the mass ornaments into which this transported life was pressed at the Convention. Mass ornaments they appeared to Hitler and his staff, who must have appreciated them as configurations symbolizing the readiness of the masses to be shaped and used at will by their leaders. The emphasis on these living ornaments can be traced to the intention of captivating the spectator with their aesthetic qualities and leading him to believe in the solidity of the swastika world. . . . *Triumph of the Will* not only explores the officially fabricated mass-ornaments, but draws on all those discovered by the wandering cameras: among them such impressive *tableaux vivants* as the two rows of raised arms that converge upon Hitler's car while it slowly passes between them; the bird's-eye view of the innumerable tents of the Hitler Youth; the ornamental pattern composed by torchlights sparkling through a huge cloth banner in the foreground. Vaguely reminiscent of abstract paintings, these shots reveal the propagandistic functions pure forms may assume.

The deep feeling of uneasiness *Triumph of the Will* arouses in unbiased minds originates in the fact that before our eyes palpable life becomes an apparition—a fact the more disquieting as this transformation affected the vital existence of a people. . . . This film represents an inextricable mixture of a show simulating German reality and of German reality maneuvered into a show. Only a nihilistic-minded power that disregarded all traditional human values could so unhesitatingly manipulate the bodies and the souls of a whole people to conceal its own nihilism. . . . [The] Reich's eagle, frequently detailed in the film, always appears against the sky like Hitler himself—a symbol of a superior power used as a means of manipulation. *Triumph of the Will* is the triumph of a nihilistic will. And it is a frightening spectacle to see many an honest, unsuspecting youngster enthusiastically submit to his corruption, and long columns of exalted men march towards the barren realm of this will as though they themselves wanted to pass away. (pp. 301-03)

Siegfried Kracauer, "Conflict with Reality," in his From Caligari to Hitler: A Psychological History of the German Film *(copyright 1947, © 1975 by Princeton University Press; reprinted by permission of Princeton University Press), Princeton University Press, 1947, pp. 297-307.**

DAVID GUNSTON

[A] slight story, diffuse script, and [Riefenstahl's] sheer inexperience, could hardly have failed to make the final result anything but weak and insipid. Yet *The Blue Light* retains a powerfully atmospheric impact, and remains an intense, dedicated, unique screen poem, "a film of extraordinary beauty." An anonymous contemporary critic pinpointed its great fault when he wrote "It is the cameraman's film, and therefore not a film at all." [Hans] Schneeberger met the natural beauties of the landscape with every artifice of careful composition, soft focus, time-lapse work (for the rising and setting of sun or moon) and coruscating filter-handling that gave rocks, trees, water, mist, sunshine, and peasant faces in close-up a magical effect. . . . All these intoxicating influences, whilst causing the tyro director to attempt the almost impossible task of making the film and taking the leading role, confirmed in her a tremendous ambition to be a film-maker of originality and power. (p. 12)

Leni Riefenstahl's first film for the Nazis was *Sieg des Glaubens* (*Victory of Faith*—1933), celebrating the first Nazi Party Congress after Hitler came to power. A short, powerful, yet compared with later productions a modest piece of screen propaganda, it revealed in its maker great gifts in the realm of editing for maximum mass effect. (p. 14)

Rarely has any film commission been so faithfully executed [as *Triumph of the Will*]. At this date, it is unnecessary to try to find anything fresh to say about this film which remains today both an historical document of the utmost importance, and an example of what screen propaganda can do, though it never did so before and probably will never do so again. Its tremendous impact can still arouse almost any audience: even those who profess to be profoundly bored with the whole thing are seldom reacting completely objectively, and must also admit to vague feelings of disquiet when the screening is over, the rantings and cheerings silenced, the banners and torches stilled. What can be stressed is the way it evolved naturally out of the mountain films, also how much the great [Nazi] Party Congress held at Nuremberg from September 4-10, 1934 was in fact a gigantic show staged for the making of this film. The use of cloud effects has already been mentioned; similarly the old houses and architectural details of the city of Nuremberg itself were used effectively in a way that had already been explored in *The Blue Light*. . . . We tend to forget, . . . that this Congress was "actually staged for the camera like some colossal Hollywood production," only more so. Kracauer's description of it as "an inextricable mixture of a show simulating German reality and of German reality manoeuvred into a show" is an apt one [see excerpt above]. . . . (pp. 14-15)

Two conclusions cannot escape anyone seeing *Triumph of the Will*: it could never have been made by anyone not fanatically at one with the events depicted, nor equally could it have been made by anyone not profoundly encompassed by the medium. (p. 15)

David Gunston, "Leni Riefenstahl," in Film Quarterly *(copyright 1960 by The Regents of the University of California; reprinted by permission of the University of California Press), Vol. XIV, No. 1, Fall, 1960, pp. 4-19.*

MARSHALL LEWIS

From the opening [of *Triumph of the Will*], a heavily mystical sequence of a lone airplane flying above a cloud bank and then dropping down to reveal the ancient spires of Nuremberg, to the final imposing shot of the massive swastika-clutching eagle, Miss Riefenstahl never allows a static moment. *Triumph*'s greatness as a film, then, is because of this woman who, before our eyes, constructs a world out of nothing and imbues it with an essence of reality so authentic that many times we are forced to shake ourselves out of the visual trance her superb virtuoso editing style places us in, and staggeringly accept the truth that the world we see was built out of segments of film and a powerhouse of cinematic talent. (p. 23)

Marshall Lewis, "'Triumph of the Will'," in Film Comment *(copyright © 1965 by Lorien Productions, Inc.; all rights reserved), Vol. III, No. 1, Winter, 1965, pp. 22-3.*

ULRICH GREGOR

[Junta was, so *The Blue Light*] would like to tell us, a child of the secretive world of nature, a person who stands apart and beyond the world of reason and civilization that could corrupt the better world of nature. Riefenstahl sharply separates a romantic, intuitive, nature-bound existence (glorified with all possible camera lyricism) from a more urban, civilized way of life that, of itself, smacks of decadence. And the mystical cult of a nature-mountain world is contrasted with profane, "plain" reason, the former being rather more holy, prior and predestined. . . .

[In *Triumph of the Will*] she succeeded in bringing to the screen the pomp of Naziism as a splendiferous and sacred spectacle. Above all, the film bestowed an aura of holy consecration on the personage of *Der Führer*. As the film opens, Hitler is likened to an Olympian god in a plane settling to earth through the clouds. The film suggests that the earth is awaiting its redemption, embodied in Hitler. The cameras . . . revel in ever-new, grandiose settings and in masses of people manipulated by dictatorial power. The dehumanizing that typified Nazi theatrics was stylized with great camera technique and formal pomp into a mendacious aesthetically embellished mystique. . . .

Leni Riefenstahl's films about the *Olympia Games, Fest Der Volker (Festival of the People)* and *Fest Der Schonheit (Festival of Beauty)* are, even in their purified versions that evade mention of Hitler and other Nazi leaders, still outspokenly fascistic in spirit. The films celebrate sport as an heroic, superhuman feat, a kind of ritual. This is especially apparent in the narration, which constantly resounds with words like "fight" and "conquest," and also in shots, for example, of marathon races through the forest that are stylized in Nordic mystery. Even *Tiefland* contains that demagogic contrast between the noble mountain people and the enchained, civilization-sick people of the city or lowlands. . . . These few illustrations should suffice to demonstrate the difficulty of separating Leni Riefenstahl's seemingly "unpolitical" films from her blatant propaganda works. Both emanate from a unified mind. . . .

[Riefenstahl's films are] typical products of a fascist (or pre-fascist) mentality. (p. 25)

Ulrich Gregor, "A Comeback for Leni Riefenstahl?" in Film Comment *(copyright © 1965 by Lorien Productions, Inc.; all rights reserved), Vol. III, No. 1, Winter, 1965, pp. 24-5.*

LENI RIEFENSTAHL

I knew that in all of my films, whatever they were, whether it concerned *Triumph of the Will, Olympia* or *Tiefland*, there was . . . yes: let us say purity. Yunta [in *The Blue Light*] was a young girl, intact and innocent, whom fear made retract at any contact with reality, with matter, with sex; and, later, in *Tiefland*, the character of Martha was nearly the same. But I didn't know this. I was searching. When I got somewhere, it was unconsciously.

I only know that I have a great love for beauty. The form taken by beauty, and not only its exterior form but its interior form. I only know how happy it makes me when I meet good men, simple men. But it repulses me so much to find myself faced with false men that it is a thing to which I have never been able to give artistic form. (p. 389)

[*Triumph of the Will*] is purely historical. I state precisely: it is *film-verite*. It reflects the truth that was then, in 1934, history. It is therefore a documentary. Not a propaganda film. Oh! I know very well what propaganda is. That consists of recreating certain events in order to illustrate a thesis or, in the face of certain events, to let one thing go in order to accentuate another. I found myself, me, at the heart of an event which was the reality of a certain time and a certain place. My film is composed of what stemmed from that. (pp. 392-93)

[We are now] able to consider the film with a purer eye and see it, as I said to you, as *film-verite*. From this point of view, the film had . . . such importance that it introduced a certain revolution in the style of newsreels, which were then filmed in a purely static fashion. I had sought to make a striking and moving film. A poetic and dynamic film. But it was while working on the film that I began to feel that I could do that. Previous to that I knew nothing at all about it. Everything came from the rhythm.

If you ask me today what is most important in a documentary film, what makes one see and feel, I believe I can say that there are two things. The first is the skeleton, the construction, briefly; the architecture. The architecture should have a very exact form, for the montage will only make sense and produce its effect when it is wedded, in some fashion, to the principle of this architecture. But that has no value as a general example, for one may also arrive at showing certain things in the opposite way, by making the montage and the architecture discordant. Can one explain everything? Perhaps these things basically come from a gift that one has or does not have. . . .

The second is the sense of rhythm. . . .

[The nature of the connection between the rhythm and the architecture is exemplified in *Triumph of the Will*.] I wanted to bring certain elements into the foreground and put certain others in the background. If things are all at the same level (because one has not known how to establish a hierarchy or chronology of forms) the film is doomed to failure from the start ("Kaput"). There must be movement. Controlled movement of successive highlight and retreat, in both the architecture of the things filmed and in that of the film. (p. 393)

Leni Riefenstahl, "Leni Riefenstahl" (1965), in an interview with Michel Delahaye, translated by Rose Kaplin, in Cahiers du Cinema in English *(translation copyright © 1966), No. 5, 1966 (and reprinted in* Interviews with Film Directors, *edited by Andrew Sarris, The Bobbs-Merrill Company, Inc., 1967, pp. 387-402).*

ROGER MANVELL and HEINRICH FRAENKEL

[Riefenstahl] lifts what would have been a dreary parade of rhetoric, marches, and mass spectacle into an evocation of what Hitler meant to her personally and to the German people, and it is this emotionalism which is conveyed through the whole tempo of [*Triumph of the Will*], with its rhythmic cutting, its carefully contrived sequences binding the ancient traditions of Germany (seen in the architecture of Nuremberg, for example) with the near-deification of Hitler as he is received by the assembled masses of his supporters. (p. 78)

Triumph of the Will remains a kind of spectacular curiosity, a mine of source material for the study of Hitler and the organization of the Nazi rallies, a social and psychological phenomenon reflecting all the emotional naiveté with which the German people responded to Hitler's nationalistic dictatorship during its initial stages. But *Olympiad* remains a monumental study in athletics, an unequalled record in its own right well over thirty years since its first release. The opening twenty minutes are brilliant as propaganda, either conscious or unconscious; the international tradition of the Olympic Games is exploited to create a grand climax with the arrival of the flame in Hitler's Germany. . . . (pp. 96-7)

Roger Manvell and Heinrich Fraenkel, "The Film in Nazi Germany–ii," in their The German Cinema *(© 1971 by Roger Manvell and Heinrich Fraenkel; reprinted by permission of Holt, Rinehart and Winston and Roger Manvell), Frederick A. Praeger Publishers, 1971, pp. 75-98.*

KEN KELMAN

Triumph of the Will did come to surpass *Potemkin* as the ultimate in cinema propaganda. This is for one essential reason: *Triumph* is a true documentary, completely made up of "actual" footage—the ultimate in incontrovertible credibility. The wonderful paradox here is that under any conditions but this absolute reportorial truth, the propaganda itself would be quite incredible. . . .

Riefenstahl creates a unique cinema: a cinema which transfigures "real life" while apparently recording it; which is essentially avantgarde while ostensibly conventional; which, in short, is dedicated to the creation of grand and ultimate illusion. (p. 162)

Triumph of the Will is structured straightforwardly enough, in the most literal documentary narrative tradition, events proceeding according to strict chronological order. . . . To the events themselves nothing is added (except some music), and apparently nothing left out save for purposes of economy. Yet Riefenstahl transfigures all, and this by the unobtrusive manipulation of standard cinema devices: camera set-ups and movement, editing, dissolves.

With these devices the basic images or motifs are varied, orchestrated. These motifs are: ancient things (buildings, statues, icons); the sky; clouds (or smoke); fire; the swastika; marching, the masses; Hitler. The central theme which they develop is that Hitler has come from the sky to kindle ancient Nuremberg with primal Teutonic fire, to liberate the energy and spirit of the German people through a dynamic new movement with roots deep in their racial consciousness.

Riefenstahl's choice of motifs to repeat and emphasize is greatly facilitated by the staged nature of the events, in which most of these images were deliberately conceived to function "live". (p. 163)

Animation, that is the imparting of spirit or life to matter, is achieved by close-up and angle of vision. Most remarkable here is the episode of flags parading, in which there are the merest glimpses of those bearing them. Close-up plunges the viewer into the midst of flags that seem to move of themselves, and in longer shots the camera angle obscures any human presence. Again, "reality" becomes figurative, things move as if charged with supernatural power, with a will of their own, or more precisely, the will of Hitler. . . .

[Hitler's] arrival on earth, the start of the film, is worthy of particular examination, being a statement of the key themes of *Triumph,* and an unusually inspired (even for Riefenstahl) development of them.

In the beginning all is without form and void. The documentary genre is maintained by making it clear we are in an airplane which is flying the Führer to Nuremberg. But the essential impact of the sequence is far, infinitely removed, from the merely reportorial. . . . The endless processions of clouds suggest both an eternal realm of the spirit and the primeval chaos out of which worlds are created. Soon the earth does emerge, born from the clouds. The ancient spires of Nuremberg are wrapped in mist like the afterbirth of the heavens. Hitler, the genius of the German renaissance, now nears the earth. The shadow or spirit of his airplane travels over the streets, touching the city, possessing it. The plane makes contact with the earth. The German people await their leader. The airplane door opens, there is mysterious, suspenseful emptiness. Crowds gape with expectation. Borne out of the heavens, Hitler now emerges, through the dark opening of his vessel, in the flesh.

Even in this most extravagant and romantic passage the technical bounds of "documentary" are never strained beyond the breaking point. The Führer's ministry on earth which follows—complete with speeches or sermons or prophecies, and vast throngs, titanic structures or miracles—never exceeds "correct" reportage. Thus Riefenstahl ultimately succeeds by virtue of her objective genre and material, combined with her intensely but subtly subjective vision, in creating perhaps the definitive cinematic obliteration of the division between fantasy and "reality". (p. 166)

Ken Kelman, "Propaganda as Vision–'Triumph of the Will'," in Film Culture *(copyright 1973 by* Film Culture*), Nos. 56 & 57, Spring, 1973, pp. 162-66.*

RICHARD MERAN BARSAM

Riefenstahl was critically praised for writing, producing, and directing [*The Blue Light*], but her real fulfillment came from playing the role of the young woman who has no contact with the real world and who is, therefore, destroyed by it. This unhappy story expresses Rienfenstahl's belief that the artist must, at all costs, remain independent of the material world. In her own life, she has achieved artistic freedom, but at a great cost. Like Junta, she had her own intuitive feelings about nature and was destroyed by her naive disregard of the real world around her, the world she set out to avoid. (p. 9)

[*Day of Freedom-Our Armed Forces (Tagder Freiheit-Unsere Wehrmacht)*, a beautifully photographed and edited film,] vaguely resembles *Triumph of the Will,* but it is little more than a skillful assemblage of factual footage and lacks any of the thematic or psychological interest of its famous predecessor. (p. 15)

Triumph of the Will is surprisingly free of reference to the specific evils which we associate with the Nazi doctrine. . . . Nonetheless, the film is a visual, sensual, kinetic, and cinematic marvel. In short, *Triumph of the Will,* like *Birth of a Nation,* embodies an overwhelming contradiction: it is cinematically dazzling and ideologically vicious. (pp. 17-18)

Tiefland [is] a romantic tale of poor peasants who rebel their oppresive landlords. Their struggle, with its Marxist implications, is symbolized on one side by a two-legged werewolf (the landlord) and on the other by four-legged predators (the wolves who attack the peasants' sheep). Set in eighteenth century Spain, it is a rich costume drama, notable for the strength of its story and for Riefenstahl's direction. . . . (p. 18)

In *Triumph of the Will,* Leni Riefenstahl imposes her vision upon realistic footage to achieve a wholly unique form of nonfiction film: the propaganda documentary. (p. 27)

As Wagner, Bruckner, and Mahler before her, Leni Riefenstahl gives artistic expression to an heroic conception of life. . . . The world of the Nazi leaders seems like Valhalla, a place apart, surrounded by clouds and mist, peopled by heroes, and ruled from above by gods. Much of the effectiveness of Riefenstahl's reinterpretation of German myth relies on the interplay of the heroic visual image and the heroic musical score. (pp. 27-8)

The slow, stately rhythm of the film is that of the imperial or religious procession. From beginning to end, we are aware of movement, a metaphor for progress. (p. 28)

[The] overall film is a triumph of organic unity. Themes are stated and restated, motifs are introduced and repeated, but all the individual elements of the film are subordinate to an overall structure which expresses and embodies the director's particular vision. All of the parts come together to create a whole, a crescendo of themes at the end, as the film moves from dawn to dawn, from air to earth, and back to air at the end. (p. 30)

In *Triumph of the Will,* the repeated use of the eagle, the swastika, and the "Horst Wessel" song both induces and helps to explain the emotional involvment of the leaders and their followers. (p. 32)

[There] is a discernible gap between the reality Riefenstahl records and the illusion she hopes to project. The myth. . . suggests that the *Führer* descends from the clouds, a region of light, and brings light with him; in turn, this light becomes energy in the food that he provides to fuel the activity of his men. . . .

After the meal, the focus shifts from the men to boys in a rapid montage of youthful fun and games. . . . [It] effectively suggests that there is joy, fun, and friendship to be found in all aspects of communal activity, and in the life of the people under Hitler's rule. The sequence ends with a wipe-down, again a thematic and visual transition. In this instance, the visual transition also links groups of people—soldiers and peasants. Riefenstahl's intention, . . . is to demonstrate solidarity behind Hitler and the party. (p. 36)

The shift . . . from the specific entity of the troops to the larger symbolic whole of the party leadership is significant because it serves to reinforce the strong connection between abstract symbol of the party itself and the specific men who form its ranks and lead its movement. . . . It is at this point that Riefenstahl begins to flex the political muscle of the film, to show the official magnitude of Hitler's power, to transform personal magnetism into political leadership. . . . (p. 38)

Here Riefenstahl's dynamic montage gives way to static propaganda necessities as the mythic world of her film yields to the prosaic meeting in the vast congress hall. The speeches are vague, overblown, obligatory; like many political speeches, they reassure, confirm, and satisfy the listener rather than provoke him. (pp. 38-9)

[The] dark, smoky mystique of the SA rally reinforces the men's blood brotherhood and suggests their mythic origins in fire; in the next scene, a sunlit youth rally, the emphasis is on the same political idea—massed troops in support of the *Führer*—but the atmosphere is different. The boys are fresh and uninitiated; they know nothing of smoke, fire, or purges of disloyal members from their ranks. Here, as in many places in the film, Riefenstahl juxtaposes light with dark, leaders with troops, boys with men, peace with war, and the kinetic with the static. (pp. 46-7)

[At an outdoor rally,] Leni Riefenstahl returns to the main theme of her film: the deification of Adolf Hitler. . . . Here the people are reduced to architectural patterns, deprived of their individuality in favor of some larger communal ideal. This is accomplished through the use of flags, as if they were costumes, to cover the participants. . . . From this point on, Riefenstahl continues to develop the godlike presence that began with motif and music in the early moments of the film. Now the controlling images are the recurrent shots of the huge architectural eagle and swastika and, of course, the forest of flags. Now while the canvas is crowded to the borders with men, we are given a clear picture of only one of them; the rest are supporting characters, faceless and unidentified. . . . (pp. 49-50)

Maintaining the consistent growth of her principal theme, Riefenstahl has now advanced Hitler to yet a higher level. In his speech, he makes reference to the "lord who has created our nation"; through the theater and film of this spectacle, he has become that lord of creation. Now the early sequences of the film assume an added significance; here, Riefenstahl suggests that the *Führer* is the lord, that he has descended to walk among his people, to bring them food, and to receive their vows. He gives life to the individual German and to the whole state in an ever-expanding sense of wholeness. (pp. 51-2)

Riefenstahl controls [a sequence portraying a memorial service] with consummate artistry, juxtaposing the dead with the living, the past with the present, the men with their leader, and finally, the spiritual with the material. The flags are consecrated with the leader's personal touch, while the booming cannons remind us both of the dead and of the military strength of the living Nazi power. In the beginning, Hitler emerged as if from the clouds, so now he moves among his men as if he were a god. Riefenstahl has created as apotheosis—and the reverse of it, too—for Hitler has come down to his people as the living embodiment of their beliefs.

In Riefenstahl's mythic conception, Hitler resembles a Christ figure, and in this second visit to Nuremberg since assuming power, a "second coming," he brings food (an action parallel to Christ's turning water into wine), he raises the dead (Christ and Lazarus), he drives the moneychangers from the temple (the purge of the dissident SA men), and he delivers a sermon from the mount (the last major speech in which the "dark shadow" is contrasted to the remaining faithful forces, the metaphorical "light" of his world). In her adaptation of German myth, Riefenstahl shows that Hitler is a political hero to his people, and by appealing to the viewer's familiarity with German myth and music, she further suggests that he is a culture hero. (p. 57)

The film does not end on this mythic note, as artistic structure and symbolism might suggest. The source of the party strength is embodied in Hitler's will and gestures and symbols are effective in conveying that strength, but the true source of Nazi power lies in the artillery and the troops. For propaganda purposes, it is that strength which must be paraded before the public and the film audience. The film has characterized Hitler as the Nazi spiritual leader; all that remains is to chronicle the physical measure of that strength. (p. 58)

Triumph of the Will demonstrates the power of the rhythmic montage to provide multi-leveled impressions of each scene, no matter how minor. This retains the viewer's attention; moreover, it creates the excitement and anticipation which give the film its essence. Furthermore, this montage is appropriate editing for propaganda films because it forces the viewer to see and to feel exactly what the director wishes. No single scene in the film exemplifies this better than this lengthy parade of German military forces. (p. 59)

Thematically, the parade sequence confirms the idea that Germany is a massed, marching column of men. Cinematically, the montage cuts the uninterrupted wholeness of the parade into pieces and then reassembles them to produce an even larger concept of wholeness. The space and the subject are fixed—a single roadway and a parade of men; Riefenstahl manipulates and redeems that prosaic space and subject with the omniscience of multiple camera positions and the dynamics of her editing. In sequence after sequence, the troops march past the *Führer;* anticipation builds, not to relief, but only to more anticipation. (pp. 59-60)

Between the end of the previous scene and the end of this one, the focus of the film has shifted from Hitler, as spiritual leader, to Hitler as head of the military forces. . . . In the final scene, Riefenstahl returns to focus on Hitler as party leader; but the last scene is really the penultimate—or next to last—element in the structure of the film, for it leads us not to the conclusion but back to the beginning. Moreover, it provides a vital insight into the dynamic theory of personality on which the film is based. (p. 61)

The text and delivery of [his closing speech] give Hitler the opportunity to proclaim his own deity, and he exploits the opportunity with histrionic techniques ranging from waving arms, to pounding fists, to visionary stares and enraptured ranting. But Riefenstahl's close-up view is extraordinary, too, for it appears to contradict the carefully made portrait that she has been creating until now. Obviously such a contradiction does not derive from any conscious attempt on the filmmaker's part, but rather emerges from the reality of the moment itself. . . . In order to emphasize the text of the speech, Riefenstahl focuses directly on the speaker and does not build any montage to give the moment extra significance. As a result, Hitler does not appear as an aloof, detached figure, or a spiritual power, or a fearful military leader; instead, he appears as an excited politician carried away with himself. (pp. 63-4)

[This speech] seems notable not for its length or content, but for its hollow phrases and empty vision. . . .

Riefenstahl does not dwell on this irony, but brings the film to its climax. (p. 64)

The final sequence is a return to a strong statement of unity and solidarity. . . . Here Riefenstahl returns to complete the theme of a German renaissance by suggesting a kind of spiritual resurrection through the *Führer's* leadership. The quest appears to be a slow, tedious one, requiring discipline, hard work, and a massed effort. Led by the spirit of their *Führer,* the men begin their quest; their goal—and the propaganda message of this film—is a triumph of the will. The cumulative effect of the film suggests that they will triumph over individuality, adversity, and disunity with the strength and determination of their will. Thus, the mass is related to the leader [and the quest to the goal] . . . and, with the titles, the film is completed. (p. 65)

Riefenstahl's art is to perceive the essence of a real situation and to transfer the form, content, and meaning of that essential moment to the screen. In short, she is a poet. Through her handling of myth, she extends the meaning of the immediate moment by enriching its cultural significance. In the history of world cinema, *Triumph of the Will* stands as Riefenstahl's brilliant fusion of prosaic film footage with her mythic vision of reality. (pp. 70-1)

Leni Riefenstahl's *Triumph of the Will* reminds us of Hitler's plans for creating a German renaissance through Nazi party unity and military strength. Unintentionally, it recalls our memories of a madman whose ideas of rebirth led to genocide. It reminds us of unspeakable evil, of the ghastly stillness that moves one now in the ruins of Dachau, Buchenwald, Mauthausen, Auschwitz, Sachsenhausen, Treblinka, and Belsen. It reminds us that man can be irrational, that people can follow false gods, and that it is all too humanly possible to make Hell seem like Heaven. The film does all of this and more, and yet it has another great power —cinematic power. The power and the paradox of *Triumph of the Will* is that it can repel us and attract us at the same time. (p. 72)

Richard Meran Barsam, in his Filmguide to "Triumph of the Will" *(copyright © 1975 by Richard Meran Barsam), Indiana University Press, 1975, 82 p.*

PAUL D. ZIMMERMAN

"The People of Kau" reflects a perfect marriage of artist and subject. The villagers seem to have built their village to suit Riefenstahl's specifications for scope and primitive mystery, their jumble of thatched towers rising from the rocks like magical mushrooms. The glistening, perfectly sculpted bodies satisfy her appetite for the sensual and the ideal. Perhaps not even a dreamer like Riefenstahl could have imagined the astonishing masking rituals that the warriors perform. Once, sometimes twice a day, out of a basically esthetic impulse, they paint their faces, transforming them into stunning abstract canvases. . . . Riefenstahl captures them like so many primitive Picassos, luminous against beautifully controlled backgrounds of remarkable depth.

Riefenstahl has also used her Leicas to document the stoicism of the Kau tattooing rituals, the bloody ballets of the gladiators and the sexual frenzy of the mating dances. But her interest is not really anthropological. There is no "family of man" here, no records of domestic intimacy, education or daily work. She is striving, instead, for heroic images—Africans transformed into idealized forms, heraldic figures, emblems of triumph and sacrifice. As a result, many critics have seen her African books as analogous to her Nazi propaganda films. . . .

[Riefenstahl's first film] "The Blue Light," dramatizes beautiful protagonists engaged in a heroic struggle against a mountain that is mystically Wagnerian. The film posits the vision of an ideal community and of a corrupted one. This same worship of beauty, strength, struggle and communal purity surely informs "Triumph of the Will" and the African books. This is not to say that "The People of Kau" is Fascist art per se. It does, however, signal the danger of an esthetic that ignores human complexities for a more primitive ethic—one that is fascinated by power rather than humanism, and therefore all the more ready to serve power.

Paul D. Zimmerman, "Leni's 'Triumph of the Will'," in Newsweek *(copyright 1976 by Newsweek, Inc.; all rights reserved; reprinted by permission), Vol. LXXXVIII, No. 22, November 29, 1976, p. 72.*

DAVID B. HINTON

[In] *The Blue Light,* Riefenstahl not only shifted from Fanck's realistic treatment of nature to a fantasized version; she also introduced the evil nature of man as a counter-force to the purity of nature. The mysterious blue light that appears on the mountain top is an idealized beauty; it becomes deadly only because of man's curiosity and greed. The mountain girl Junta, as an outcast from the village, represents the pure, trusting nature of man. The villagers are distrustful and hateful and persecute Junta because they do not understand her. Since the Nazis revered the villages as the cornerstone of their concept of the *Volksgemeinschaft*, Junta emerges as a rejection of that concept. Her purity is obtained not through living in society (or the *Volksgemeinschaft*), but through living outside it and away from its corruptions. Consequently, Junta is not the Savior or Messiah figure that Siegfried Kracauer always associates with Hitler in German films, but a martyr who suffers Christ-like persecution (rather than Hitlerian worship) by being stoned by a mob of the villagers. If there is a Hitler figure in the film, it is the Viennese painter (an interesting coincidence) who mistakenly believes that he is saving the village by removing the crystals, when the real result is to destroy one of nature's beauties and cause the death of Junta. In this sense, *The Blue Light* is a warning against Hitler, not a preparation for him. (p. 23)

Critics have often observed that the use of close-ups in the film is an insidious propaganda device. It has also been implied that these close-ups were staged to achieve the greatest effect. In reality, Riefenstahl [in *Triumph of the Will*] used telephoto lenses that were capable of putting in close-up one face out of a crowd at a distance of thirty to forty meters, which allowed her to record unnoticed the emotional reactions of members of the crowd. The fanaticism evident on the faces was already there, it was not created for the film. The medium should not be judged guilty merely because of what it records. Riefenstahl does use close-ups for more than cinéma vérité. At the end of the sequence, close-ups are used in a consciously artistic rather than documentary style. Here, they are of the S.S. bodyguard, lined up outside of Hitler's hotel. In close-up, their faces appear to be those of statues rather than living beings; they are reminiscent of the heroic faces found on the statues of the favorite Nazi sculptor, Arno Breker. Like a sculptor using clay, Riefenstahl molds reality on film until it becomes more than reality, a technique that can best be described as "statues on film," and which recurs not only throughout *Triumph of the Will,* but will also become the major motif for the prologue of *Olympia.* (p. 42)

[*Day of Freedom*] is an unexciting film, and the viewer can see immediately that Riefenstahl was only fulfilling a commitment and not trying to make a cinema classic. Only the very beginning of the film is worthy of note. It opens with a shot of marching soldiers, obviously filmed in a set, marching through foggy darkness. Then a distorted wall, done in true expressionistic style . . . is shown, with a soldier standing in front of two windows in the wall. The dark silhouette of the soldier is shown looming against the sky. This staging is a significant departure from Riefenstahl's documentary style in *Triumph of the Will,* but is an indication of what was to come in the prologue of *Olympia.*

The rest of the film could have been taken directly from *Triumph of the Will.* As Riefenstahl herself admits, the style is identical. (p. 59)

The rest of the film is devoted to scenes of war maneuvers involving light artillery, machine guns, tanks, and smoke bombs, all performed under the watchful eyes of Hitler. The final shot of the film shows planes flying overhead in a swastika formation, which is then superimposed on a swastika flag.

What survives of the film is of little interest after the accomplishments of *Triumph of the Will.* The central part of the film, which Riefenstahl claims is the only interesting part, is a speech by Hitler, and it is missing from the surviving print. *Day of Freedom* is precisely what Riefenstahl admits it to be: a minor film made to satisfy the petty jealousies of German generals. (p. 60)

[*Tiefland*] is a beautiful and captivating film that expands on the work [Riefenstahl] started in *The Blue Light.* It also contains explicitly stated social comment, perhaps Riefenstahl's personal reaction to her earlier political naiveté. (p. 83)

The opening shot of *Tiefland* establishes its debt to the mountain film genre: sharp, craggy mountain peaks are shot against a cloud backdrop, with day-for-night photography setting the scene in the night time. (p. 86)

In filming *Tiefland,* Riefenstahl had several ideas in mind. One was to contrast the Hochland (highlands) and the Tiefland (lowlands), both as to their place in nature, and their effect on humans. The Tiefland cannot exist on its own; it is a dry and barren land without the water from the Hochland. The Hochland, unlike the Tiefland, has everything it needs, and for man is a paradise on earth because he can escape from his fellow man into the solitude of the mountains. The missing footage not only obscures these concepts but changes the ending of the film. When Sebastian dies and the camera goes into a close-up of his body, the missing footage showed raindrops slowly starting to fall into the palm of his hand. With the death of Sebastian, life returns to the lowlands. The few raindrops become a pouring rainfall, and succeeding shots depicted nature springing back to life, with water filling the irrigation ditches and life returning to the fields. (pp. 102-03)

Critically, *Tiefland* can best be examined by comparing it with her first film, *The Blue Light*. Both films concern themselves with the same problems, and *Tiefland* can be regarded as a more mature, more fully developed continuation of the ideas initiated in the first film.

In *Tiefland*, Riefenstahl continues to contrast, this time with more emphasis than in *The Blue Light*, the purity of life in the mountains with living in society in the lowlands. This contrast is a standard trait of the mountain film genre.

The Blue Light, however, was content to deal merely with human failings: the intolerance of the villagers toward Junta and their persecution of her. But in *Tiefland*, Riefenstahl goes further than human failings and examines the failings of society: a leader who ignores the pleas of his people, who forces them into suffering for his own benefit; the injustice of a feudal system that allows one man to divert communal water for his own needs; and the peasants' inability to redress their grievances within the established system. (p. 104)

Marta is more integrated into society than was Junta, who was a complete outsider. Instead of being Junta's symbol of purity and innocence, however, Marta is morally ambiguous. Although she lives a life of good intentions, her exposure to the evils of the world has affected her reactions to life. Thus she can never accept Sebastian even though he loves her and can promise her a comfortable life. Nor can she bring herself to trust the innocent and well-intentioned Pedro. The true Junta role in *Tiefland* is not Marta, but Pedro. In adding more psychological motivations to her characters than was evident in *The Blue Light*, Riefenstahl reverses the sexual roles. Rather than being like Junta, Marta is reminiscent of Matias, the Viennese painter. Both have good intentions, but both are nevertheless a part of society and possess its imperfections. And though Pedro lives in the mountains, apart from society like Junta, their reception by the people in the lowlands is different. Junta is feared and scorned by the villagers, but Pedro is only mocked and laughed at.

The conflicts in both films not only revolve around the imperfections of man and society, but around threats posed by nature. In *The Blue Light*, the threat is the mysterious blue light emanating from Mount Cristallo. It is a benevolent threat; it is only dangerous because man's curiosity has made it so. Its origins, however, are still in nature. The threat from nature in *Tiefland* is more plain: it is the lack of water in the lowlands, further complicated by Sebastian's refusal to share it. The threat in each film lies in nature, and a human being holds the key to the threat. And in each film, the human being who holds the key perishes through the actions of his fellow man: Junta in *The Blue Light*, and Sebastian in *Tiefland*.The major difference between the two films is in their endings. *Tiefland* ends happily with the uniting of Marta and Pedro, and their ascent into the mountains away from the lowlands. *The Blue Light* ends in tragedy, with the separation of the two lovers through the death of Junta. *The Blue Light* was a romanticized legend, and a tragic ending is in keeping with the atmosphere of the legend. But *Tiefland*, intended as social comment with no legendary basis, requires an ending that is proper to the theme of the film: the triumph of purity. (pp. 105-06)

[Riefenstahl hoped *Penthesilea*] would not be dependent merely on dialogue for its stylization and departure from reality. The movements and gestures of the actors were to be stylized as well, setting off their differences from modern man. Their clothing would be as simple and basic as possible, imitating the manner of Greek statues where the clothing merely drapes the body, serving to accentuate rather than to hide the contours of the human form.

Although Riefenstahl attempted to make a stand for the artistic use of monochromy in *Tiefland*, she was not theoretically opposed to the use of color and planned to film *Penthesilea* in color. But where most early color films used color as an attempt to heighten realism, Riefenstahl's intention was to use it as yet another device to set the film apart from reality. Color was to be sparsely rather than elaborately used, and she hoped to use subtle shades of color to create a hued, stone-like effect. She would apply the same experimentations in filters and emulsions to color that she had done in black and white.

Not a single scene was to be realistically photographed. Even the battle scenes were to be filmed in such a way that they appeared much like the ancient Greek bas-reliefs. They were to be filmed against a cloudless blue sky with a filter causing a greyish tone on the battlefield. It would be the reverse of the *Olympia* Prologue; instead of bringing statues to life, she would convert life into statues.

The most significant change in Riefenstahl's approach was her decision to stylize nature as well. She would not only use nature, as she had done in *The Blue Light* and *Tiefland*, but would add to it. (pp. 115-16)

Had *Penthesilea* been filmed, it would have been the first time that Riefenstahl tampered with nature before the filming; for her other films, the stylization was not through the sets, but through the photography and the editing. (p. 116)

[The] word "stylized," or, more precisely, "stylized reality," becomes the key to understanding Riefenstahl's approach to the cinema. Riefenstahl takes the material of reality: rocks, mountains, trees, people, and using this material shapes reality until it transcends itself. Camera placements, selection of settings, the use of varying emulsions, lights, and filters are her instruments of stylization. . . .

Penthesilea also presents another important artistic concern found throughout Riefenstahl's films: the beauty of the human body, and the body's beauty enhanced through movement. . . .

Indeed, all of Riefenstahl's films are dominated by two concerns: either the beauty of nature and physical surroundings, or the beauty of the human body, and, as a corollary, the beauty of the body in movement, either single (as in *Olympia*) or in mass (as in *Triumph of the Will*). (p. 117)

[In *Penthesilea*] The beauty of the bodies would again be emphasized through movement as well as appearance. Particularly in the battle scenes, which Riefenstahl envisioned as strange atmospheric events transpiring in whirling clouds of fog and dust, the bodies of the actors and actresses would assume their most heroic roles. (p. 118)

David B. Hinton, in his The Films of Leni Riefenstahl *(copyright © 1978 by David B. Hinton), The Scarecrow Press, Inc., 1978, 162 p.*

Eric Rohmer

1920-

(Pseudonym of Jean Marie Maurice Scherer) French director, screenwriter, television producer, and film critic.

Rohmer, a nouvelle vague (new wave) director, is best known for his *contes moraux (Six Moral Tales),* each of which develop the same situation: a man is tempted by an alluring female after deciding on moral grounds to avoid a sexual relationship. Rohmer says of these films: "What I call a *conte moral* is not a tale with a moral, but a story which deals less with what people do than with what is going on in their minds while they are doing it. . . ."

In 1951, Rohmer became a critic for *Les Cahiers du Cinéma,* where he associated with the group of critics who became New Wave filmmakers, including Alain Resnais, Jean-Luc Godard, François Truffaut, and Claude Chabrol. He also coauthored a book with Chabrol on Alfred Hitchcock. Before his venture into fictional cinema, Rohmer made a series of educational biographical films.

Rohmer's first full-length feature, *Le Signe du lion,* was a commercial failure. The first two *contes, La Boulangere de Monceau* and *La Carrière de Suzanne* were short subjects, followed by *La Collectionneuse.* While agreeing that Rohmer's filmmaking talent is evident, most critics found the characters too corrupt to elicit their sympathies.

***Ma Nuit chez Maud* met with instant international acclaim, however, and Rohmer emerged as a major figure in French film. *Le Genou de Claire* and *L'Amour, L'Après-Midi* also received critical acclaim for Rohmer's understated way of dealing with his familiar moral dilemmas. His protagonists, who fend off their seductresses with protestations of moral seriousness are, in Rohmer's eyes, merely complacent rather than moral. They engage in endless philosophical discussions that resolve little. The series served as well to demonstrate Rohmer's belief that the director is an author, making his films a form of visual fiction. Narration is used frequently, and literary images, such as the novels in *Claire,* abound, reinforcing Rohmer's concept.**

His two recent films, *Die Marquise von O . . .* and *Perceval,* are period pieces, attempting to recreate a mood rather than make a statement. Though well received for the most part, they have not made the same impact as the *contes moraux.*

LOUIS MARCORELLES

[The framework of *Le Signe du Lion*] is fragile, and it should not be judged only on its probability. . . . [The] film shows its originality in its ultra-realistic technique, its extreme objectivity in portraying the friction set up between a human being and society, his wearing down, his slow degradation. This is not a descriptive but a rigorously visual art. It calls for the complete participation of the viewer and his submission to what he sees. One is reminded of Albert Camus's novel *L'Etranger,* because the situation of the main character is equally extreme: he is outside society. In this case he is up against not words but stone, water, the sky; and with him we make an infinite number of discoveries: the walls of Paris, its monuments, the Seine. At certain moments the hidden camera has caught ordinary people passing by, living in their own worlds, knowing nothing of the misery of the man they pass in the street. Jess Hahn rummages in a litter bin; the sole of his shoe flaps; no one takes any notice . . . A cruel study, but never a sentimental one. Rohmer makes his points objectively: "*ne prétendant que montrer, il nous dispense de la fraude de dire,*" as he once wrote himself about Buster Keaton. The dialogue is almost negligible; the interest is concentrated on human attitudes. It is a disquieting film. . . . (p. 85)

Louis Marcorelles, "Views of the New Wave," in Sight and Sound *(copyright © 1960 by The British Film Institute), Vol. 29, No. 2, Spring, 1960, pp. 84-5.**

PENELOPE HOUSTON

Rohmer's reluctance to dramatise gives *Le Signe du Lion* a sticky opening and a slightly muffed conclusion. But in the long central section the method not only justifies itself but creates the film. The maddening snatches of overheard conversations; the half-hearted attempts at stealing a bun or a packet of biscuits; the long passages in which the American simply sits, walks, fiddles with bits of string tying up a broken shoe, are not weighted or fictionalised. . . . They give the feeling of being filmed as they happen; and they happen to a man whose own reaction time is being slowed down by aimlessness as much as by starvation. The twist at the end . . . seems too tidy an ironic device for a film otherwise so resolutely (and sometimes amusingly) unstressed.

Penelope Houston, "'Le Signe du lion' and 'The Season for Love'," in Sight and Sound *(copyright © 1966 by The British Film Institute), Vol. 35, No. 4, Autumn, 1966, p. 199.**

BRIAN MURPHY

La Collectionneuse is a very private kind of film—not only in that it is clearly the work of an individual artist (any Bergman or Fellini film is that) but also in that it is about very special, very private problems. The first-person narrator, Adrien, . . . is a latter-day dandy, a kind of existentialist Oscar Wilde, who wants to achieve an elegant nullity and to talk about it in charming paradoxes reminiscent of Wilde or even the earlier Disraeli. His friend Daniel . . . is an artist who believes that the most difficult and important thing to achieve is an (existential) void. They are both intellectuals tired of thought, tired of effort, weary of the luxury of work, and impatient for the demanding rigors of idleness. . . .

In an odd way, the girl, Haydée, is already precisely what they want to be: she *is* 'natural', apparently uncomplicated and without thought. . . .

The relative peculiarity and privacy of the subject and treatment are matched by the film's structure. Although the film has some superb acting of an off-beat sort, imaginative, delicate direction, and beautiful photography, one hardly notices its obvious cinematic qualities. It is more like an intimate novel than (the more public, more theatrical) film. The extensive use of the first-person narrator, for example, is obviously more fictive than cinematic. . . . Much of what Adrien says is irritatingly sophomoric, and occasionally his problems are merely absurd, not Absurd. But, on the whole, Adrien and the film are engaging—even absorbing. The characters may be bizarre, but they are effectively realised personalities; their problems may be, to say the least, uncommon, but they are argued with wit and rendered with vigour. The conflicts among the three principal characters are, perhaps, tantalizingly obscure and understated, but the girl Haydée is so carefully, if subtly, drawn that one can well sympathise with Adrien's ambivalent feelings about her enigmatic attractiveness. And, moreover, it isn't every day that one can see a film in which a character remarks that work is just an easy way of buying a clear conscience.

Brian Murphy, "'La Collectionneuse'" (© copyright Brian Murphy 1969; reprinted with permission), in Films and Filming, *Vol. 15, No. 10, July, 1969, p. 42.*

CALVIN GREEN

Eric Rohmer's *Ma Nuit chez Maud* deals . . . explicitly with Jansenism; the characters discuss and analyze it in relation to modern Christianity, general moral attitudes, and the conduct of their own lives. Yet the film is by no means a turgid exegesis on the subject; the work is most interesting because of the way it reveals character and establishes relationships rather than for what is intellectualized. (p. 7)

Eric Rohmer's skill lies in his ability to lend aesthetic weight to visual understatement. He is sparse but not puritanical, since his use of black and white can be stunning in its unsensational candor. . . . (p. 9)

Rohmer is able to capture the sincerity and frankness of each gesture during conversations without arduous close-ups that call more attention to themselves than their subjects. His dialogue is neither cliched nor does it allude to pretensions beyond the limits of the film itself; his characters are not intellectuals and Rohmer is not trying to impress us with mannered profundities. Rohmer respects people and his story tells us this: he features them rather than Art. . . .

[In] a low-keyed fashion, Rohmer's engineer has a simplistic grace all his own. His earnest conviction that God has made a "good" world, that chance . . . can and *should* have a virtuous resolution gives his life a religious design which raises him above the pain of loss and frustration. His faith is indestructible without being arrogant.

It is irrelevant that Rohmer's hero is theologically more aware of what he believes or can rationalize his feelings, the obvious factor is that he did not gain his grace from lighting votive candles or by going through the charade of traditional ceremonies.

Rohmer's hero will never divorce himself from the world or make a fatalistic gesture. . . . (p. 10)

It is neither pompous nor self-consciously primed; he loves, remains loyal, and forgives because no other way is conceivable to him. His modesty even dictates that he pretend to have had an affair with Maud because he could not lord his moral affinities over his wife or anyone else. They would no longer be moral.

[Rohmer's vision] of the religious function is most concisely stated in one brief scene in *Ma Nuit chez Maud*. At a mass the engineer attends, the priest notes that although saints led exemplary lives in their renunciation, they were crazy. One should not be so quick to emulate them. So, paradoxically grace needn't be a thing of a mediocre man—one could say, Un Homme Doux—who lives a life which asks fulfillment of the mundane and receives it because he believes in its intrinsic goodness. (pp. 10, 36)

Calvin Green, "Ars Theologica: Man and God at the N.Y. Film Festival," in Cinéaste *(copyright © 1969 by Gary Crowdus), Vol. III, No. 2, Fall, 1969, pp. 7-10, 36.*

GRAHAM PETRIE

[In *Ma Nuit chez Maud*] Rohmer presents Jean-Louis and Françoise quite straight forwardly as people for whom principles are genuinely important and adultery and infidelity really matter. The film is all of a piece: characters, setting, and camera style constantly reinforce and interact with each other, yet within this apparent uniformity Rohmer creates effects of great subtlety and depth. Despite the fact that the film centers round the long conversation in Maud's apartment, filmed largely in long-held, almost static shots, and that this scene is paralleled, though more briefly, by the later dialogue in Françoise's room, it never loses visual interest. Rohmer controls the rhythm of the film perfectly, making the editing reflect all the facets of the debate—the flashes of intensity, the struggle for self-expression, the lapses into misunderstanding or confusion, the moments of slackness and tiredness. As the conversation develops we begin to see the characters from a variety of perspectives. . . . Rohmer shows great sensitivity to the ways in which behavior and even personality can shift according to situation or circumstance. . . . [Each] situation allows or forces a different facet to reveal itself. And behind each individual episode is the mingled austerity and joyfulness of the season, handled in such a way that the bleakness of the winter appears as a conditioning factor in the relationships. (pp. 57-8)

The structure of the film appears clear-cut, the images distinguish sharply between black and white, the rhythm is assured and self-confident, the settings are pared down so that they reinforce the argument rather than suggesting alternatives or variations of it. Yet within this framework people reveal themselves to be confused and hesitant, projects never work out in quite the way they were intended to, motives are mixed and muddled, and every act, however decisive and apparently self-sufficient, has its shadow. And over and above this is a final layer, in which the enclosures and limitations have their truth after all. The film moves through a series of clearly defined spaces—rooms, cars, streets, a church—within which each person has carved out his own personal space and within which the camera generally isolates him. In church the priest is rarely seen in relationship to his listeners: he is caught mainly in close-up, speaking into a void, while Jean-Louis and Françoise listen, each alone on the screen or focused sharply against a blurred group of fellow-worshippers. The same procedure holds true for the other scenes: Rohmer cuts between characters but seldom joins them. Jean-Louis's world is like that formed by the narrow streets of Clermont-Ferrand: ostensibly two-way, they allow effectively for movement in only one direction; to permit movement the other way, you have to abandon your own claims and pull aside. Two-way traffic is impossible, and this perhaps helps to account for the fact that one of the strongest impressions left by the ending of the film is a sense of lost opportunities. (p. 59)

Graham Petrie, "'Ma Nuit chez Maud'," in Film Quarterly *(copyright 1969 by The Regents of the University of California; reprinted by permission of the University of California Press), Vol. XXIII, No. 2, Winter, 1969-70, pp. 57-9.*

CARLOS CLARENS

Just as the narrator is in pursuit of a woman who, momentarily, seems to elude him, events bring him in contact with another. And, regardless of the charm and persuasion of the second, he will reject her in favour of the first, even when he is not yet assured of her possession. Thus, Eric Rohmer defines the recurred theme of his filmed *contes moraux*. . . .

Rohmer's aim is less to creiterary cinema than to enrich cinema with the techniques of literature, which accounts for the imprecise literary aura of his films. (p. 6)

[*Le Signe du Lion*] captures the intense physicality of a time and a place: Paris in the month of August, deserted by the natives and overrun by the tourists; the cosmopolitan *anomie* of the Left Bank, the sudden gust of desolation as night falls; but also, a feeling for bonds made and broken over a bottle of cheap red wine on a sunny *quai*.

There is hardly any feeling of regression in the hero's shifting fortune. Instead, the film suggests that the man succumbs less to the force of circumstance than to the ever-present lure of Bohemianism that Paris traditionally represents to the outsider, so that Wesselrin's six weeks in hell become as well the last summer in every man's youth. In documenting the passage from artist to mountebank, Rohmer builds a limpidly linear film, the ends of the story-line stretching outside the running time of the picture, almost beyond the director's control. Again . . . we have simply wandered into the characters' world, walked a short way together and taken our leave as they go on to live another moment of their lives. . . .

[Rohmer stated why he filmed his *contes moraux*:] 'I wanted to portray in film what seemed most alien to the medium, to express feelings buried deep in our consciousness. That's why they have to be told in the first person singular and why there has to be a commentary. The protagonist discusses himself and judges his actions. I film the process.' (p. 7)

[Of *La Collectionneuse*, he said:] 'The most fascinating aspect of the three characters is their *argot de caste* [individual way of speaking]. There were some allusions in Daniel's dialogue, for instance, that are still incomprehensible to me. It was indispensable for the picture that the actors collaborate in the *mise en scène:* I wanted very complex characters, not too black, not too white, impossible to define in a few words. Although they all belong more or less to the same generation, there are gaps of milieux, of sensibility. Each one had to have its own *vérité*.' . . .

La Collectionneuse becomes the intimate journal of a modern dandy with the soul of a Jansenist, the dilemma of a man wary of instinctual commitment and action (even in love), the portrayal of an artificial sensibility caught between emotion felt and emotion *literalised*. . . .

Adrien's flight from Haydée . . . is not to be interpreted, as Rohmer's more virulent detractors have done, as a refusal of passion or an apology for impotence and non-action. In reality, it is the refusal of love as imposed by a time and place: summer and the isolation of the villa in *La Collectionneuse*. . . . Other than sacrificing passion to principle, Adrien is also renouncing 'love from idleness' . . . for 'love from conviction', which brings Rohmer to the core of his theme, the problem of choice. (p. 8)

[All] four characters in [*Ma Nuit Chez Maud*] come fully equipped with religious/ideological principles. (Even Maud, a freethinker in a family of masonic aristocracy, wears her irreligiosity like a veil.) That's why the previous film lacks the gravity of the latter; why *Maud* had to be in black and white; why the characters, and not only the hero/narrator, have to bare their feelings one to another.

As usual in a Rohmer film, the opinions expressed by the characters engage the characters and them alone. . . . Their articulateness reduces narration to a minimum. . . . As every choice carries an implicit loss, Maud is made to appear the superior woman: she's generous, witty, passionate and . . . her erotic glow seems to light up Clermont-Ferrand in the dark of winter. She is not, however, a woman to be confined by the hero's moral limits. She loves well but not too wisely, and the epilogue finds her at sentimental loose ends once again. (pp. 8-9)

[Rohmer reaches back to the very source of moral conviction;] in his own measured, convincing manner, he talks to us about the joy and sorrow, the heartbreak and the triumph of *l'amour sage*. (p. 9)

Carlos Clarens, "Eric Rohmer: L'Amour Sage," in Sight and Sound *(copyright © 1969 by The British Film Institute), Vol. 39, No. 1, Winter, 1969-70, pp. 6-9.*

RICHARD SCHICKEL

[The] details of the story, if one can so dignify the skeleton over which Rohmer has stretched his movie [*My Night at Maud's*], are of less consequence than the remarkable manner in which these ordinarily pretentious, faintly foolish, incredibly *verbal* people compel our attention—the shifting of a glance or of a position in a chair becomes an event as important as, say, a murder or a cavalry charge in an ordinary movie.

How soberly involved everyone is! How comic is the care with which they examine themselves and each other about their motives and the effect their small statements and actions are having! (p. 307)

Is there, in fact, an American producer who [like Rohmer] understands that eroticism can be intellectual, may involve neither coupling nor stripping? Is there one who would risk a satire on the modern demi-intellectual's insistence on analyzing everything to death that you do not begin to laugh at until after you have left the theater and the lovely absurdity of the whole enterprise begins ticking like a time bomb in your brain? Is there one who would risk a dollar on a man whose style can only be described as classic formalism? (pp. 307-08)

[*My Night at Maud's* is a] dry, delicate, elegant novella of a film. . . . (p. 308)

Richard Schickel, "'My Night at Maud's'" (originally published in Life, *June 19, 1970), in his* Second Sight: Notes on Some Movies, 1965-70 *(copyright © 1972 by, Richard Schickel; reprinted by permission of Simon and Schuster, a Division of Gulf & Western Corporation), Simon & Schuster, 1972, pp. 307-08.*

PETER COWIE

At first glance, *Ma Nuit chez Maud* may appear intolerably stuffy, and removed from the realities of life in a French provincial town. *La Collectionneuse,* Eric Rohmer's other "conte morale" seen in this country, was altogether too much the work of an aesthete who rigorously eschewed any kind of emotional sympathy with his characters. But in *Ma Nuit chez Maud* we are scarcely aware of this intellectual standpoint. The film works simply because it lives up to its pretensions. It "cites" Pascal much as Bergman "cites" Mozart in *Hour of the Wolf,* but it is perfectly comprehensible to the viewer who is unfamiliar with the "Lettres Provinciales" or the "Pensées". . . .

Rohmer allows us to identify with Jean-Louis from the start. . . . His manner betrays dissatisfaction with his loneliness, and it is this vein of frustration that makes him vulnerable to all the events of the film. Yet secretly we relish identification with a man whose eyes glance eagerly at an attractive blonde during Mass. . . .

So to a certain extent we comply with Jean-Louis's decisions from now on. . . .

It is a measure of Rohmer's achievement that we still side with Jean-Louis against the somewhat mocking sophistication of Vidal and his attractive divorcee friend, Maud. (p. 11)

Conversation is vital in *Ma Nuit chez Maud.* It lays bare the four characters more cleanly and with less affectation than any violent action could. The long discussions on science, morals, and Pascal are not so rarefied as they might seem. Every argument raised has its counterpart—or its *demonstration*—in the film's proceedings. In Pascal, says Vidal, mathematician and metaphysician are one, and it is not long before we perceive why Jean-Louis shrinks from the Jansenist camp. For Pascal despised the relaxed morality of the Jesuits. In the "Pensées" he sided boldly with faith against reason, urging his readers to discipline the body to the outward observance of Christianity. But Jean-Louis is a Jesuit to his fingertips (this accounts for his appeal to our susceptibilities early in the picture). He is self-satisfied. . . . Thus religion for Jean-Louis is a convenient cloak of propriety beneath which he may shelter his desires. (p. 12)

[The] uncanny grasp of a character's response to a situation is Rohmer's principal forte here. He has built his film on a *contradiction:* the clash between rationalism and sensitivity-cum-intuition in Pascal. . . .

In the final analysis, Rohmer challenges our own ambivalent reaction to his film. We respond to Jean-Louis because he is not afraid to abandon his principles for something joyful and worthwhile; we reject him when he continues to assert those principles at the expense of other people's emotions. (p. 13)

Peter Cowie, "'Ma Nuit chez Maud'," in Focus on Film *(© 1971 The Tantivy Press, London, Great Britain), No. 1, January-February, 1971, pp. 11-13.*

STANLEY KAUFFMANN

Again [in *La Collectionneuse*] Rohmer gives us a protagonist who becomes interested in a younger woman and ends up with an older woman to whom he was linked originally. Again passion is more examined and discussed than created. Rohmer is more interested in the effect of desire on thought and action than in the creation of heat. . . .

He provides the extra dividend of all extraordinary film makers: the sense that an artist has made the medium his own, shaped it to his psyche and inquiries. In this case the tone is reflective and quiet—but only superficially quiet. (p. 55)

In *Claire's Knee,* a mature man's fancies about a nearly juvenile girl were distilled almost to disembodiment by his fantasy about her knee. Here the prologue tells us that Haydée's body is the figurative theater of this story and that intercourse, not fantasy, is the dynamics. I don't understand those who think that this difference between the two films is one of grossness. (p. 56)

Most of the film's tension comes from the contrast between the calm camaraderie of the trio in the villa, who are merely amiable much of the time, and the rationalized desires that are boiling in Adrien, particularly after the girl takes Daniel as a lover. (pp. 56-7)

All the elements are distilled by Rohmer into what must again be called a classic style: a view of art in which form is not only the preserver of experience but the ultimate insight into it. (p. 57)

Stanley Kauffmann, "'La Collectionneuse'" (originally published in The New Republic, *Vol. 164, No. 22, May 29, 1971), in his* Living Images: Film Comment and Criticism *(copyright © 1971, 1972, 1973, 1974 by Stanley Kauffmann; reprinted by permission of Harper & Row, Publishers, Inc.), Harper, 1975, pp. 55-7.*

CARLOS CLARENS

Le Genou de Claire is a summer film . . . whose only overt timeliness . . . is the lack on heavy religious, or metaphysical, preoccupations. . . . (p. 122)

Under cover of banality, Rohmer deepens his subtleties, splits his archetypes or keeps them off-stage, allows secondary readings to come to the surface. . . .

Except for Claire and her beau—from whom nothing is to be gleaned: what they say or think or feel exists merely to excite, provoke or seduce each other—Rohmer makes his people compulsive talkers; but this time the dialogue, witty and free of epigram as ever, takes on the dual function of alternately revealing and concealing the characters. . . . [The] more they explain themselves to us, the more one feels they're offering a counterfeit of motives and self-deception. . . .

There are other valid but less sunny readings to *Claire*. It's revealing that for the first time in a *conte moral,* Rohmer introduces a rapport of cruelty by bringing together in the same story characters from two different generations. . . . *Le Genou de Claire* throws in young and adults together, setting up a *vertical* relationship between the mature (Jerome, Aurora, perhaps Madame Wagner) and the juvenile (Claire, Laura, Gilles), and the subject of the film becomes then the progressive building, and inevitable resolution, of an erotic relationship between one and the other. Or, how the conflict between maturity (reflection, experience, self-control) and immaturity (impulse, desire) is resolved through an act of base childish spite: snitching. This abridging of the gap, this redressing of an imbalance, couldn't we read it as a metaphor for mutual, inevitable corruption? (p. 123)

Carlos Clarens, "'Le Genou de Claire'," in Sight and Sound *(copyright © 1971 by The British Film Institute), Vol. 40, No. 3, Summer, 1971, pp. 122-23.*

DAVID BROMWICH

[Rohmer's] subject has made him the master of what might be called the soft irony.

Unfortunately, his repertoire so far is narrowly circumscribed. His diapason is made of chords neither higher nor deeper than the soft ironic. . . . [In *Chloe* the ironies] turn to fluff, about to blow away. . . . [There is] the problem of style in Rohmer's films. . . . His movies . . . bear the same relation to the possibilities of cinema that closet drama bears to the possibilities of theater. . . . Still, the truth is that Rohmer's stories have not demanded anything beyond the means he uses, since every turn of a plot revolves around those small motions of grace in the eyes, the mouth, the voice of a character which might as well be seen occurring indoors. (pp. 222-23)

[Something] has gone awry, for Chloe is more fascinating than, according to Rohmer's moral, she has any right to be. Chloe is trying to charm the hero into infidelity; toward which end she must charm us as well, if the story is to be effective; but in fact she intrigues us far more than does the hero. . . .

[With] the gradual caving in of any substance in his tempted hero, Rohmer has made [this] boring soul the subject of *Chloe*. Films about this character, however much they try for the subtle or jostling ambiguity, are at last failures in persuasion. . . . Actually, we get not so much ambivalence as hesitation—the chronic and unnerving hesitation of a coward. . . .

The gap has widened between *Maud* and *Chloe:* no longer does the hero resist seduction for reasons of the heart which the mind will never understand. Rather, it is an affair of will, the merest velleity. This movie is good fun all the same, the way Rohmer always is. . . . (p. 223)

David Bromwich, "Angst-pushers & Austenites," in Dissent *(© 1973, by Dissent Publishing Corporation), Vol. XX, No. 2, Spring, 1973, pp. 222-23.*

WILLIAM JOHNSON

In trying to build the struggle [between Chloe and Frédéric in *Chloe in the Afternoon*] to a crisis, Rohmer slips into the one big pitfall of Cartesianism—instead of mapping reality onto a set of mental constructs, he imposes constructs arbitrarily on reality. When Chloe tells Frédéric outright that she loves him and intends to have a baby by him, he surely has to react *some* way: break with her, make it with her and to hell with fantasy, or at least get worried; but Rohmer, preoccupied with the pattern of his approach to the crisis, lets Frédéric go smiling along the same as ever.

At this point, too, the contrivance in Chloe's character begins to show. Earlier, when Frédéric says lightly that in another, imagined world he'd marry her, Chloe declares that she never has such daydreams. The contrast emerges briefly and believably. But in the last third of the film Chloe's character—disillusioned, blunt, depressive—seems too deliberately conceived as a challenge to Frédéric's. It's not clear why she persists with him—whether she really loves him or is simply playing a game. There are no independent clues to her deeper character, and in the end she is reduced from an intriguing mystery to a function of the plot.

Yet these signs of abstract contrivance are far outweighed by Rohmer's sensitivity to the richness of reality. . . . And the whole film develops into a rebuttal of Frédéric's assumption that his ordered view of life and of his relations with other people has any existence outside his mind.

Rohmer begins the rebuttal gently, almost imperceptibly. (p. 58)

[Although the scene when Frédéric decides to leave Chloe] misfires, it is certainly neither sentimental nor conventional. The sweater itself has no symbolic meaning: its removal is a nexus of tactile and kinesthetic sensations which suddenly connect Frédéric with reality. It is brought home to him physically that he can no longer rationalize his attraction to Chloe as an extension of his love for Hélène. At long last (if only temporarily) Frédéric breaks out of the imaginary world in his mind.

This is not an easy ending to accept, since it involves a denial of adventure and an apparent retreat into the security of the familiar. It's tempting to complain that Frédéric is merely playing it safe—and to extend this charge to Rohmer himself. . . . Yet Rohmer quietly works and reworks an extremely narrow territory of human behavior. (p. 59)

[With *Chloe* Rohmer takes a big] risk. In each of his previous Moral Tales, the woman who disturbs the protagonist's equanimity appears obviously attractive from the start. But the irruption of Chloe is so unexpected that it threatens the whole fabric of the film. If this had been Rohmer's first Moral Tale, I might assume he simply miscalculated. Since it is his last, I think he aimed at a bigger and more active clash between idea and reality than ever before—but within a concentrated framework that would still draw the viewer into his protagonist's experience. . . .

[Rohmer] occupies a small territory, but he fills it with the antinomies of coolness and intensity, calculation and surprise. (p. 60)

William Johnson, "'Chloe in the Afternoon'," in Film Quarterly *(copyright 1973 by The Regents of the University of California; reprinted by permission of the University of California Press), Vol. XXVI, No. 4, Summer, 1973, pp. 57-60.*

JOAN MELLEN

Eric Rohmer's *Contes Moraux* examine the withering away of feeling and genuine sentiment in the life of contemporary man. People for Rohmer subvert their intellects, using ideas as substitutes for feelings, and often to deny them. Thus the intellect works against man's deepest interests and desires, hiding from him his true self as well as the means by which he could satisfy the needs of that self. (p. 147)

Rohmer's heroes are all of a distinct moral type. Although Jean-Louis of *My Night At Maud's,* an ascetic Catholic, seems very different from the ebullient Jerome of *Claire's Knee* and the self-centered pleasure-loving Adrien of *Collectionneuse,* the three are very similar. Each represses spontaneous emotion preferring to live by calculation. Each is incapable of a relationship with a woman who is his equal because he is too self-centered to respond freely to the differentness of another. Moreover, the three have in common the fear of emotional risk and of having their true feelings "found out," as much by themselves as by others. In each film the hero feels a great need for a permanent love relationship. . . .

Jean-Louis of *My Night at Maud's* . . . sets out to find a woman who will complement his Catholic beliefs as well as his mundane, socially approved aesthetic standards. . . . His character emerges only in the course of the debate he has with his old Marxist friend, Vidal, over the meaning of Pascal. Having always subordinated body to mind, Jean-Louis expresses himself best in the world of abstractions. These conversations are the perfect objective correlative for a character whose life is so little oriented toward the satisfaction of primary, physical needs.

The cold Jean-Louis and the warm Vidal each find their own Pascal. (p. 148)

Rohmer is much more sympathetic to Vidal, although he is destined to be the loser, because Vidal sees in Pascal the notion that man is not man unless he is willing to take risks, for example, to commit himself to an uncertain if great end (Marxism or the love of Maud), even if he has only small chance of success. (p. 149)

Pascal's sense that "we do not possess true goodness" caused him to argue for ambiguity in the meaning man gives to his acts in the world. But Jean-Louis is too insensitive to recognize the essential ambivalence of human experience. Instead, fearing it, he imposes a rigid code upon himself by which he will live at all costs: that "love is eternal," that "self-respect" would make him love his wife forever, and that divorce for him would be impossible. He justifies his fear of risks with abstract principles which have nothing to do with his true desires. Hiding behind these ideas, he loses contact with what he feels. (pp. 149-50)

[Jerome of *Claire's Knee*] is, like Jean-Louis, totally self-absorbed, imperceptive of the feelings of others. Revealingly, at the end of the film he cannot remember the man whom his friend Aurora brought to visit him and whom she is now marrying. Jerome sees life only in terms of his image of himself. The frescoes of Don Quixote seated blindfolded on a wooden horse, believing he is flying, adorn Jerome's house and are his visual equivalent. Like Don Quixote and like Jean-Louis, Jerome believes he is actively choosing his destiny. In reality, these are timid men who become infatuated with the least intellectually threatening women—those incapable of offering them challenge. (pp. 150-51)

Rohmer's settings are visual manifestations of his heroes' personalities: the carefree life at St. Tropez defines the emptiness of Adrien whose sole object in life as we see him is "to do nothing well." (p. 151)

In *Claire's Knee* the setting too provides a judgment on the empty, idle existence of the haute-bourgeoisie personified by Jerome. . . . They reflect Jerome's boredom, and as in the case of Adrien, the superficiality of his emotions. (pp. 151-52)

The icy winter in the dreary French province of Clermont is a perfect analogue to the strained, closemouthed Jean-Louis [of *My Night at Maud's*]. The omnipresent snow and ice reflect his absence of feeling, his tendency toward jesuitical abstraction and the narrowness of his Catholicism. (p. 152)

In *My Night at Maud's* and *Claire's Knee* the cultural ideal, the blonde, coy, mindless coquette is placed beside an intellectual, witty woman, capable of humor and irony, but unappealing to the hero for her very independence and unique sense of self.

In *My Night at Maud's* Rohmer places before us two opposites: Maud and Françoise, the dark and the light. Maud is a woman of ideas. Knowing the ambiguities of life, she agrees with Pascal on the questionable value of marriage. . . . Like life, Maud is imperfect. . . . The images associated with Maud are meant to express the liberation of emotion whereas those with Françoise bespeak frigidity, duplicity, and the view that life is a game to be played with lies and cunning. (pp. 152-53)

Where Maud's every gesture expressed openness, Françoise's stifling of feeling creates barriers. . . .

[It] is inconceivable that with her stinginess of emotion [Françoise] should be capable of caring for others. (p. 153)

[However,] Maud, a loser at the end in a new marriage which "is not going well" is perhaps far from a moral paragon. . . . [She] loses both [Jean-Louis and Vidal] because her wager fails and because she chooses, unwisely, the men least likely to satisfy her needs. But Rohmer leaves little doubt that the Mauds of the world possessing imagination, spontaneity, a zest of life, are infinitely more desirable than the passive, dull Françoises, who lack culture, wit, and all charm.

Rohmer creates a similar opposition of types in the less intellectually realized *Claire's Knee* and *La Collectionneuse.* (p. 154)

Haydée is made the figure both desirable in a traditional way and the one representing risk and the wager. Sensing that Adrien will pervert his interest in her to deny all feeling, she wisely shows no awareness of him. . . . She despises his self-righteous and unfounded belief that in some mysterious way he is "better" than she.

More interesting are the trio of women of *Claire's Knee,* in which Rohmer breaks down the figure of Haydée into three distinct women. . . .

Claire is callow and narcissistic. A far more subtle woman is her sixteen-year-old half-sister, Laura, who unlike the sensuous Claire, has already felt the pangs of real love and who alone senses that Jerome's feeling for Lucinde is friendship, not love. Jerome argues that friendship and love are the same, thus justifying a discomforting recognition that he lacks all passion for his future bride. It is Laura who is right about him because, capable of spontaneous feeling, unlike Jerome, she knows that the experience of love affects one "totally," that one cannot be "happy" when in love.

Completing the trio is the older woman, Aurora, who looks on Jerome with irony. . . . Aurora presents, like Maud, a self-sufficient exterior, claiming that "solitude satisfies me. I enjoy it;" by the end of the film she belies her contention by marrying. As Aurora herself admitted earlier, speaking of Jerome, but also inadvertently about herself, "everyone has a blindfold." . . . Aurora needs the security of a man's presence, like Maud, who felt compelled to marry a second time, although intellectually she questioned the value of marriage as an institution.

Jean-Louis chooses Françoise, unconsciously obsessed with finding in woman an image of himself. (pp. 154-55)

Probability makes it equally possible for Jean-Louis to have chosen either Maud or Françoise. In Jean-Louis's case "chance" merely provides the opportunity for him to express his preconceived choice. (p. 158)

If Jean-Louis fights off Maud, Adrien of *Collectionneuse* cannot allow himself to yield to his desire for Haydée, as if pursuit of this careless female would undermine the idea he has of himself as a serious person whose life is carefully ordered and under his control. The "order" he seeks is antithetical to the spontaneous life. He fittingly sets for his vacation the goal of doing nothing well because what creates "meaning" for Adrien is the exercise of will alone where instinct can be subsumed by a preconceived notion. . . .

Like Jean-Louis of *Maud,* Adrien does not know what he wants. He has become too alienated from his feelings (which conflict with his self-image) even to recognize them. He returns to his mistress in London not out of choice, but to fill the void left by the gratifying self-deception that the sensuous Haydée really longed only for him. But he has felt nothing for either of the women in his life. . . .

The "ideas" of Adrien, his feeling that his life is his profession, are unrooted in purpose; they are empty of utility or commitment which would entail the risk of failure. (p. 160)

Seeing through Daniel and Adrien as poseurs, Haydée enjoys making them act contrary to their pretensions, exposing them as hypocrites. Fearing their essential "ugliness," the theme introduced in the prologue to the film, Adrien and Daniel assert that they are exceptional. Haydée reverses the roles, claiming that it is they who are easy and not she. . . . In reality, it is [Adrien] who is the predator, risking nothing in his relationships because his feelings are never involved.

Jerome in *Claire's Knee* risks nothing because he chooses as the object of his infatuation Claire herself, and neither Laura nor Aurora. In this film even more clearly than the others the ideas by which a man lives and defines himself are shown to be a mere facade, substituting for rather than expressing his innermost feelings.

Even when he acknowledges his desire for Claire, Jerome believes that he can retain command over his emotions with his intellect. (p. 161)

Jerome thus becomes a manipulator of feelings. . . .

Jerome transforms the reality of the little interlude with Claire into an intellectual construct, a fantasy. . . . Where emotions are inadequate, words can be marshalled to add the intrinsic importance the emotions lack. Jerome has learned nothing about himself from the revelation that he is indeed susceptible to "little girls," and the measure of his delusion is his continuing belief that he has done Claire "some good," having freed her from Gilles. . . . The verbal ruse Jerome has employed to avoid facing the meaning of his acts and choices is rendered ludicrous. Nothing changes except the weather: the men flee from women who are their intellectual equals, and the women, Maud in particular, from men who could accept the richness of response they have to offer.

Why men have become this way, burying their feelings, deceiving themselves with chimerical ideas, is the implied question buried in Rohmer's films. He leaves it unanswered. Despite the emphasis of his films on the process of conceptualization, how man hides behind intellectual constructs, his films are empty of prescription. They depend upon the visual—how man acts in the context of his world, and upon the verbal—how men reveal themselves in their relationships. There is no hint in Rohmer's moral tales of a world where men are fulfilled, where sexual relations are placed in the context of a useful, satisfying life. Jean-Louis, Jerome and Adrien have nothing to live for, neither values nor goals behind the narrow pursuit of self-interest.

The films judge and expose these men, but point to no path by which they might transcend their malaise. This weakens *Claire's Knee* and *La Collectionneuse* considerably. It makes of them art works in miniature, small statements. *My Night At Maud's* overcomes this weakness with its perspective of the wager as an alternative to the fear of "chance" and its sanctioning beyond the limited point of view of its hero Jean-Louis, the risking despite all odds of what is decidedly uncharacteristic of one's conscious self and motives. None of Rohmer's characters, men or women, find what they are looking for from life. Those who live most wisely are those willing to renounce absolutes and to pursue the image of their desire. If the wager fails, the life may yet have been meaningfully lived. (pp. 162-64)

In *Chloe In The Afternoon* Rohmer displays fatigue with the theme of a man in love with one woman but nearly successful in seducing (or being seduced by) another, an exhaustion under the weight of this mode of moral satire. Rohmer's own boredom reveals itself in his choice for the first time of a Parisian setting redolent of the ennui of afternoons spent at cafes and department stores. (pp. 164-65)

[Despite] considerable satire of the values and behavior of

the bourgeoisie, the bourgeois mode is affirmed [in *Chloe*]. Beside the disordered life of Chloe herself, moving in chaos and dirt from one dingy flat to another, Frédéric's sweet, sanitary existence with his wife Hélène signifies relief and a more viable way of living. (p. 165)

That the hero fails to be seduced for the first time in the *Contes Moraux* is a victory rather than a failure. For Frédéric the aborted affair with Chloe is not seen as a test exposing his poverty of imagination. . . . Rather, it is depicted as a narrow escape from intemperate yielding to an altogether undesirable temptation. . . . [It is] a love of safety in which the duality between bourgeois desire for certainties and the impulse to sensuality and adventure sinks beneath the burden of the habitual.

The difficulty with *Chloe In The Afternoon* is that Rohmer overly approves Frédéric's collapse into routine and a life without surprise. . . . Rohmer renders [Chloe] so spiritually unattractive precisely to elevate Frédéric's diminished life with Hélène and their two babies. (pp. 165-66)

Yet Rohmer relentlessly satirizes the bourgeois self-deceptions and hypocrisies of Frédéric. Like Rohmer's other male characters, he is a man who lives in his head. . . . In describing Frédéric's way of life, Rohmer's satire is sharp and to the point. He reveals that these twists to Frédéric's character serve only to enclose him more completely within his identity as a bourgeois, a man incapable of living by his impulses and deeper potential. In the end, despite afternoon fantasies of the Parisian girls he ogled on the streets, Frédéric cannot unite dream with reality. (p. 166)

Rohmer's wavering weakens the film because the conception, like the emotion, is trite. He wishes to ridicule the boyish, self-satisfied Frédéric, while at the same time the film moves toward a sense that an affair with Chloe . . . will yield pointless trouble rather than pleasure or discovery. Rohmer comes to the affirmation of a paltry marriage and reduces all the satire preceding it to a decorative embellishment not unlike Frédéric himself. (p. 167)

By confounding the superficiality of the bourgeois with the poignancy of passing youth, Rohmer softens and sentimentalizes both his larger theme and its moral resonance.

Because he presents it as undesirable that Frédéric *do* anything about his fantasies, the film is more static and slow-moving than the earlier *Contes Moraux*. Like the others, its interest lies in Rohmer's repeated exposure of the hero's lack of self-knowledge. . . .

No more than Frédéric is [Chloe] capable of spontaneous feeling. She says that it is important to her to be "free," but her freedom amounts to Don Juanism, vulgar, obvious and unenjoyed. Her distaste for the men she pursues to reject bespeaks an essential dislike of the heterosexual experience. Although she accuses Frédéric of being "bourgeois," she is as bourgeois as he. (p. 168)

The pessimism of this finale to the *Contes Moraux* flows from Rohmer's implied conclusion that none of us are capable of transcending ourselves. We have all lost the freedom to respond to the potential of the moment without dragging along the weight of the past. In the end, lapsing from the demands of his own theme, Rohmer decides that to be so vulnerable and committed to the sensual offerings of life is less desirable after all. Even a marriage diminished by our incapacity to be satisfied is better than the limbo of the transitory.

Rohmer's film is also weakened because no one depicted is capable of authenticity or an alternative vision. In the earlier films it was the free woman, but in Chloe freedom is reduced to license. (p. 171)

Chloe's role in the film is as some external, malevolent, Iago-like spirit, destined to play on Frédéric's susceptibilities, if only perversely to show she can ruin his life. She functions as well as Frédéric's unconscious impulse surfacing and destroying his pretension of being debonair and in control. . . .

Women too long at loose ends finally become demonic in Rohmer, their impulses perverse, their desires greedy, possessive and sadistic. (p. 174)

Toward the end of the film, primarily through the editing, Rohmer shows that while Frédéric seeks her as an answer, in reality Chloe has little to offer. At this point in the film the distance is most pronounced between Rohmer and his character. . . .

It is a loyalty that Rohmer has implicitly, if belatedly, affirmed in this film, suggesting that Pascal aside, life offers us little better. It is a despairing resolution and an intellectual defeat, reflected in the aesthetic failure of *Chloe In The Afternoon.* Rohmer satirizes Frédéric as he weakly leaves the water running in Chloe's bathroom and rushes down the stairs, an image of his sexual infantilism and lack of emotional command. Frédéric is finally sensible in fleeing home to Hélène, but for the wrong reasons. (p. 176)

To the end, Frédéric remains unaware of his own transparency; his "clever" lies have been frequently and easily exposed. . . . Thus even [the reunion of Frédéric and Hélène] seems as hollow as their marriage has been throughout the film.

In the last shot of the film Rohmer focusses on the accoutrements of bourgeois existence rather than on his characters: a table, a lamp and the suburban landscape stretching forth from their open window. These, Rohmer suggests, offer the only redeeming refuge we know from the temptations of the dirty Paris streets. The lack of excitement is made up for by order and tranquillity. (p. 177)

The game (it seems it was only a game after all) must ultimately tire us. It is even as if in the earlier [*contes moraux*] we were seduced by Rohmer into aspiring to and expecting more. What counts, Rohmer concludes, is what we have come to need, since we are members of the bourgeoisie all —stability, permanence and resignation to what we have been rather than commitment to what we might be. (p. 178)

Joan Mellen, "The Moral Psychology of Rohmer's Tales," in her Women and Their Sexuality in the New Film *(copyright 1973, reprinted by permission of the publisher, Horizon Press, New York), Horizon, 1973, pp. 147-78.*

PETER SOURIAN

Rohmer takes Pascal's *Pensées* for his text. According to Pascal we meet our sense of the void with nausea, ennui, anxiety: "All our unhappiness stems from the fact that we are incapable of sitting quietly by ourselves in a room." (pp. 132-33)

[In *Chloe in the Afternoon,* Chloe is, for Frédéric] the inauthentic diversion from mortality and from eternity, as represented by his marriage and embodied by his children.

For Frédéric, like many, fears the happiness of fulfillment; he tells us that he dreams madly of a life made of "first loves", that is to say—though he doesn't realize this—a life without death. In a stunning parade of impersonations, which Rohmer makes the most of visually, Chloe sees him in the afternoons, subtly giving him his wish, this safe feeling of constant newness, while his wife works on her graduate thesis. Like a knight in a mediaeval temptation he resists Chloe, yet is in thrall [until he realizes his mistake and returns to his wife.] (p. 133)

It is through the power of the human mind (operative even here, in such a trivial association) that Frédéric has finally managed to dare to replace an "inauthentic diversion" with a "true object of belief and love".

In *Claire's Knee* the inauthentic diversion would appear to be Claire's knee, an object of belief and love which Pascal would surely term a false one. Jerome, . . . engaged to be married, becomes obsessed by the knee of a young girl. But the film actually is concerned with the brilliant secret efforts of an entirely different person to cure herself of her fascination with the silly and cruel Jerome, who is *her* Claire's knee, *her* false object. Aurora is a gifted Romanian novelist who, cleverly encouraging Jerome to tell her step-by-step of how he cured himself of his obsession by literally touching Claire's knee, figuratively touches Jerome, proves to herself just how silly and cruel he is. This complex intellectual work which Rohmer forces us to follow with our own intellects thus releases her for marriage to a man whom she'd objectively respected deeply but from whom she'd been running.

Strong as these films are, they are not as strong as *My Night At Maude's*. . . . [In this film the] time is the present and the visible protagonists are flesh-and-blood, but no less alive for Rohmer is the mind of the great scientist and philosopher [Pascal], whose religious ideology systematically ordains the progress of this remarkably intellectual film. (pp. 133-34)

[Upon analyzing Jean-Louis's and Vidal's philosophical discussion, we] can understand why Jean-Louis would not find Jansenism attractive, and why Vidal might imagine himself a bit of a Jansenist. But if we observe carefully, Vidal's intense talk, brilliant and passionate, may be desperate bombast. And if we look carefully at the face of Jean-Louis, seeing a man who rather likes to indulge himself, we may also simultaneously see a man undergoing some deep process of difficult change, about to emerge in the breadth and light, or at least terrifiedly on the brink of it. (p. 136)

If Jean-Louis is "furious at Pascal's rigidity," it's because he may be about to find himself living it for the rest of his life. If Vidal is fascinated by it, it may be because it's academic for him, only a diversion from his real anguish. (p. 137)

Maude and Jean-Louis are not really in agreement at all [in their attitudes towards people]. Maude's become tired of seeing the same faces so she's looking for new ones. Jean-Louis draws a different conclusion from the same experience. He's learned that there are no "new" people. So, having experienced Pascal's stage of *the flesh* for what it's worth, he is now embarking perilously, purposefully, on a different endeavor.

Vidal, who is of the order of *mind,* is playing intellectual games with himself. He fancies he is suffering terribly over Maude's relative indifference. In fact, one of the three Misleading Powers as distinguished by Pascal, that of the Imagination, is hard at work in him (the other two being custom and self-love). As Pascal says, "Men often mistake their imaginations for their hearts." Vidal, after all, is not truly in bondage to Maude. (pp. 137-38)

Once it is established that Jean-Louis is a serious Catholic, yet seems neither stupid nor ugly, the game begins. That of setting out to prove he is not a serious man. Pascal is very clear on this psychological point—that as much as we fear the void, we tend to fear truth. Not only do we fear it, we meet it with underlying hatred. Jean-Louis has in effect said he believes there is meaning to life. The context of this meaning is, for him, the silly Catholic Church, but if he himself seemed really silly to them, they would dismiss him, whereupon their own emptiness would not seem so empty. After all, they would then tell themselves, what *is* there but emptiness? (p. 138)

[To test Jean-Louis, Vidal leaves him alone with Maude.] Now, like an archetypal hero, Jean-Louis will be put to the test. According to Jansen, after the Fall, man was thrown into a conflict between two "delectations"—one of worldly desires, and one of celestial enjoyment. Unless released by liberating Grace, man is in bondage to the more powerful appeal of worldly desire. (p. 139)

[One feels it was Jean-Louis's] night at damned Maude's which made it possible for him to pick up the lost trail to Françoise and his eternity. It was from Maude that he learned to recognize the claims of the finite, to accept human limitation along with perfect abstraction, and to pull these together. One feels that he has more or less come to grips with the demon of spiritual pride. Yet who is damned, and who is saved? According to Pascal, God does not tell. (p. 141)

Whom has Jean-Louis married? We do not know for certain after all. Jean-Louis has made his wager. Rohmer has left everything to the hidden God.

Rohmer is in rebellion against what is typified by Robbe-Grillet's statement that we live in a world of non-signification. In making a film that comes down on the side of a belief, he goes against a tiresomely persistent fashion, one which harks back to the one-dimensional polemics of Voltaire. Rohmer went back further, back past the eighteenth century, to find a believing type with whom a man of his ability and especially of his temperament might imaginatively identify. (pp. 141-42)

Though he is of course psychologically sophisticated in the modern sense, [Rohmer] has no respect for the passive sophistication common in our art, wherein much is sourly understood and little really happens. He is as purposeful as Jean-Louis; his tough-minded elegant films distinguish serious spiritual life from the multifarious mutations of superstition and sentimentality, inverted and otherwise, which substitute for it in filling the void.

If Rohmer's art does not wither in all this welter of ideas and ideology, it is because his feeling for the texture, the actual stuff of people is very strong. His highly organized fictions have real people in them. Of his characters he says, "I consider them to be free." (p. 142)

*Peter Sourian, "Starring ****** Blaise Pascal," in* The Transatlantic Review *(© copyright Transatlantic Review Inc. 1974), No. 48, January, 1974, pp. 132-42.*

PAULINE KAEL

In an explanatory title, Rohmer informs viewers that he has taken only a single liberty with the story [Heinrich von Kleist's "The Marquise of O . . .": in the film, instead of raping the Marquise during the fighting at the citadel, the Russian Count rapes her afterward, when she has been given a sleeping potion. Rohmer has written that this alteration makes the story more believable for moviegoers. But it can't be an accident that he's taken out the central mad, impulsive action. . . . What's lost is not only the sense of the narrow experience of the virgin-hearted Marquise but Kleist's spirit, what made him an avant-gardist and a modern—his acceptance of the id released by the chaos of war. In the movie, since the rape takes place through furtive calculation, the Count isn't Kleist's wild, natural man —he's a Rohmer character, slyly slipping his hand over Claire's knee. . . .

Attempting to achieve an objective version of Kleist's style, Rohmer gives us the surface—a quaintly amusing account of a woman whose idealism is betrayed. . . . The director missed the larger story, which was in the undercurrents (and, maddeningly, those who read the novella after seeing the movie are likely to get from it only what's in the movie). . . . In the movie, we fail to recognize that the Count, the foreigner, carrying the threat of what isn't understood, is a whole man; impetuousness hasn't been bred out of him, and if the widowed Marquise would just wake from her civilized trance she could begin to live. He's Prince Charming with a rape for a kiss, and she's too repressed to know it.

Rohmer isn't the director to bring us Kleist's hero—a precursor of Dostoevski's and Lawrence's. Rohmer's eventoned method precludes animal passion. The movies that Rohmer has written himself are generally compared to novels, but his "The Marquise of O . . . " is like a documentary film of a play. . . . The film is so formal it's like a historical work re-created for educational television; the costumes wear the actors. (p. 67)

Rohmer, with the help of his cinematographer, Nestor Almendros, keeps everything serenely pictorial. But without Kleist's demon sitting inside all that calm and mocking it, asking when the sleeping beauty is going to come to life, there's no urgency to this film. It's tame and archaic. (p. 68)

Pauline Kael, "No Id," in The New Yorker *(© 1976 by The New Yorker Magazine, Inc.), Vol. LII, No. 36, October 25, 1976, p. 67.*

J. P. STERN

Although much of the dialogue [in "Die Marquise von O . . ."] is taken word for word from Kleist's story, sometimes transferred from reported to direct speech, the director has also made use of the rare device of projecting whole sentences from the original on the screen, in print, to emphasize turning points in the story, and above all to convey those thoughts and guesses at motivation—those contents of *mind*—which action alone cannot intimate. Although the director follows the text closely in the film's mood and images, it is as if his veneration for Kleist's idiosyncratic style would not be satisfied with interpretation by actors and cameraman—the printed word must still be the vehicle of the creator's essential comments. . . .

The film brilliantly translates into visual experience the opening scene in which the nocturnal Russian attack on a North Italian citadel is endured by the occupants. Kleist's sense of domestic detail and of the helplessness of children, and the nightmare realism of scurrying, aimless flight inside a burning trap are brought to life in a few seconds of film which recall, and surpass, the effect of reading his few corresponding sentences of reportage. The subsequent slowing down of the film into an almost stately deliberation never becomes a beautiful bore, because a kind of stored energy has been generated in that first scene of eros and violence. Surprise is promised, and the promise is kept by the behaviour of the characters if not entirely by the plot (the Marquise von O . . . may be at a loss to understand how she became pregnant, but we are not). Eric Rohmer, like Kleist himself, makes full use of the genre-painting possibilities of the theme while keeping to a stage-sized perspective. . . .

With its tension between the incongruity, indeed the absurdity, of the story's central event, and its circumstantial, syntactically complex narrative—much of it is cast in the elaborate grammar of reported speech—"Die Marquise von O . . . " is an immensely German work; not only that: both its prose and its morality belong to the last years of the pre-Romantic age. M Rohmer is an eminently faithful interpreter: he takes us into the very heart of Kleist's story, yet he never allows this strangeness of time and place to lapse.

J. P. Stern, "Wanted: One Father," in The Times Literary Supplement *(© Times Newspapers Ltd. (London) 1976; reproduced from* The Times Literary Supplement *by permission), No. 3984, October 29, 1976, p. 1360.*

HAROLD CLURMAN

[*The Marquise of O . . .*] is a work of art so limpid and serene that one can hardly tell what it is about! Though there is no obscurity at all about the plot, the final impression created is not of a tale but of a mood or "music." The classic in this sense hides itself, it does not declare its point. It simply is. . . .

Kleist both accepts and teases the moral standards of the time. Ever so gently set forth is the incalculability of human destiny and the childishness of our behavior in regard to it. What gives the picture its special quality is the sober beauty of every shot, movement, setting, costume, performance. There is hardly any emphasis of detail: every moment is complete in itself. If the narration were to be suddenly arrested we would still feel that we had become part of a living experience, equivocal and fascinating like so much which goes unnoticed in our day-to-day traffic.

A German critic has found something of Kafka in Kleist. For my part, I find the film's "surface," pictorially and dramatically, so direct, burnished and *light*, that it eludes explanation while it says all.

Harold Clurman, "Films & Plays: 'The Marquise of O. . .'," in The Nation *(copyright 1976 The Nation Associates, Inc.), Vol. 223, No. 15, November 6, 1976, p. 475.*

STANLEY KAUFFMANN

The story [of *The Marquise of O. . .*] operates through the enclosure and reconciliation of contradictions: the Marquise's innocence, yet her pregnancy; her parents' belief in her, yet their doubt because of her condition; the Count's act of rescue, yet his act of ravishment. . . .

These contradictions create irony as well as complexity; and if you then add the straightforwardness of style and the sense that both the style and the irony are pushing the whole toward the sources of moral perception, you have a forerunner of Kafka. . . .

So there is an overarching contradiction in Kleist's novella: the paradox that through neoclassic means the beginnings of the modern age are becoming manifest. And thus the comparison of Kleist and Kafka is relevant to the continuing importance of Kleist. Rohmer's central achievement is that he has comprehended all these matters and has fixed them, beautifully, on the screen. (p. 20)

Rohmer has, necessarily, condensed Kleist, but he has served and honored him. He has once again dared to make a chaste film in an age of dazzle, an age in which frankness is dumped on us as an automatic equivalent of truth. Here Rohmer moves even further toward the perfection of his own cinema: of intelligent elegance and elegant intelligence, of pleasurable explicit patterns and implicit tensions, of faith in the value of every carefully selected atom that he shows us. Like all fine artists, he is forging a particular language out of a general lexicon. Like many fine artists, he has the courage not to be accessible to all as long as he is true to an inner music. (p. 21)

Stanley Kauffmann, "Films: 'The Marquise of O . . .'" (reprinted by permission of Brandt & Brandt Literary Agents, Inc.; copyright © 1976 by Stanley Kauffmann), in The New Republic, *Vol. 175, No. 19, November 6, 1979, pp. 20-1.*

JOHN SIMON

Eric Rohmer's film version of Heinrich von Kleist's 1808 novella, *The Marquise of O . . .*, is as intelligent and successful as such an undertaking can get. . . .

There is no way for a filmmaker to convey the Pyrrhic victory over chaos of Kleist's utterance on screen, even if, like Rohmer, he wisely makes the film in German and follows the text with almost fanatical fidelity. The very fact of Kleist's obsessively indirect discourse, with the wonderfully alienating device of those conditionals and subjunctives its use in German requires, cannot be rendered on film; it has to be put into direct discourse and into the characters' mouths, thus conventionalizing, de-electrifying, and slowing down the speed of thought to that of action. Rohmer's insistence on dissolves—which may be necessary to convey the passage of time—further delays what in the text hurtles ahead. . . .

Rohmer's . . . liberties taken with the text are minimal, and generally inventive as well as dramatically justifiable. (p. 76)

What does distract and detract is the comic tone Rohmer gives to a good many scenes that are absolutely earnest in the text. This may have been all but unavoidable: A mass audience cannot help being amused by the moral scruples, the fineness of compunction, the exaltation of etiquette evinced by a bygone age. Too bad, then, for the mass audience—if not, indeed, for our overpermissive society—but in turning, however unpreventably, *The Marquise of O* . . . into a proto-comedy from a rigorous study of individual moral growth to heroic dimensions, Kleist's work has been, charmingly and cogently, cheapened. . . .

Rohmer's direction is, as always, theatrical, but that fits in with the major part of this material. . . .

Rohmer's transposition of Kleist, then, is not without fault but generally impressive; it would have been even better, however, to have desisted. (p. 79)

John Simon, "Coming Close to Kleist," in New York *Magazine (copyright © 1976 by News Group Publications, Inc.; reprinted with the permission of* New York *Magazine), Vol. 9, No. 45, November 8, 1976, pp. 76, 79.*

ROBERT ASAHINA

Based on *Conte du Graal,* Chrétien de Troyes' 12th-century Arthurian romance about Perceval's quest for the Holy Grail, [*Perceval*] exhibits the meticulous antihistoricism evident in Rohmer's *The Marquise of O. . . .* Once again, the director's intent is to strip away our preconceptions and present the work as it appeared to its original audience.

The problem with such an endeavor, of course, is that cinema is a 20th-century medium. . . .

To counteract the modern inclination toward realism, he has set the movie on a sound stage with painted backdrops and artificial scenery; the highly stylized golden castles and silver trees give *Perceval* the look of an illuminated manuscript. (p. 19)

[This] does remove *Perceval* from our modern categories of drama and place it squarely in the middle of the medieval cosmos, at least as Rohmer perceives it. Yet in one respect the director has been too faithful to his material: The film, like the poem, contains as a subplot a lengthy tale about Gawain that has nothing to do with Perceval's adventures. But many scholars now believe that *Conte du Graal,* left unfinished after more than 9,000 lines, was actually two poems, combined only after Chrétien's death. In another respect Rohmer has not been faithful enough: Although Chrétien drew upon the tradition of the troubadours and *trouvères,* his tales were composed as literature to be read, not to be performed in dramatic recitations.

Even if we grant that this is correct 20th-century form for an Arthurian romance, the esthetic question would remain: Does *Perceval* succeed as *art,* not sorely as a solution to the intellectual problem of historicism? *The Marquise of O. . . .* certainly did; it was possibly the finest film adaptation of a literary work I have ever seen. *Perceval,* by contrast, requires so much literary knowledge and willful suspension of our modern conceptual framework that it left me wondering why in the world Rohmer chose to undertake such a curious project. (p. 20)

Robert Asahina, "On Screen: Filmed Fictions," in The New Leader *(© 1978 by the American Labor Conference on International Affairs, Inc.), Vol. LXI, No. 22, November 6, 1978, pp. 18-20.*

JAMES McCOURT

[*Perceval* is] a visually delirious, aurally seductive, tutorally exposed, exactly performed film version of Chretien de Troyes' romance. . . .

Perceval certainly is not a movie like *Ivanhoe,* or *The Sev-*

enth Seal, or *Lancelot du Lac.* It's a shut-up-tight-indoors experience, so contoured and so dazzling it amounts to a venereal assault. It's exigent ecstatic fabulism. Unhappily, it is a masterpiece to which subtitling is almost ruinous. (p. 57)

If "perfect of its kind" needs explanation, or if the question that can never be unanswered nevertheless still pleases as much as ever it may torment, *Perceval* will illustrate and will seduce. (p. 58)

James McCourt, "Percival and Other Knights" (copyright © 1978 by James McCourt; reprinted by permission of the author), in Film Comment, *Vol. 14, No. 6, November-December, 1978, pp. 57-65.*

DAVID SHAPIRO

Eric Rohmer has created a problematic *Perceval,* a rather intransigently autonomous work with many of the advantages of autonomy, and nonetheless a certain static delight in the Christology which is his topic. Rohmer has adapted the Chrétien de Troyes and maintained an almost didactically insistent rhyme-scheme throughout as part of the narration and dialogue. The sets are beautifully reduced, almost Kabuki versions of the real, as Rohmer insists on distancing us from any pathetic sense of mimesis. He is faithful to his form, committed, as Adorno has it, to the materiality of his art, and that paradoxically, is the political in Rohmer.

Perceval is "played" by a Buster Keatonish Fabrice Luchini. As a matter of fact, Rohmer has always displayed a particular affection for the master-comedian Keaton, and a certain expansive melancholy reigns over the work and sometimes mars its tone and at most moments induces both an elegiac and an anticipatory strain. . . . I perceived a montage of events with very little evolutionary zeal. This, for one viewer, was a wonderful anti-Aristotelian bonus. We have had enough student *Waste Land*'s and Wagnerian climaxes. . . .

One of the glories of the film is its use of music. There is a parody of 12th and 13th century themes by Guy Roberts and a Brechtian acceptance of music on stage. Rohmer's choruses produce lyrical interpolations, reminiscent sometimes of the canzones of Dante in his troubadour mode "interrupting" the prose in *Vita Nuova*. The music is a sudden swerve away from any attempt at mimesis again; it is part of the accepted artifice, even the *paradis artificiel* of this kingdom. But it is not mere; it is a major music that creates the norm of non-discursive, allegorical Existenz which is the film's poetry. . . .

The movie is a masterpiece of ironic deviations from direct address. The characters will often suddenly announce themselves in the third person, with the most excruciatingly conscious results. The whole business is as self-reflexive as consciousness permits. The discipline of this self-conscious narration becomes a kind of allegory for the very fidelities of Perceval. The movie concerns Concern, or *Sorge,* or Care; it is a *bildungsroman* of Perceval; but within the closed system of Christ's courteous passiveness. The film's obliqueness is a way of not permitting ourselves to be lulled by "content matter," in Meyer Schapiro's phrase, away from real "subject matter," form itself. As Webern said, "To live life is to defend a form." . . .

Rohmer made a very astute choice in constructing all sets deliberately and eschewing natural occasions. . . . To watch the lean horses drift past his little iron trees, no higher than a human, or enter obviously cardboard architecture, is to watch film aware of itself as film, metaphor announce itself as metaphor. Everything here is *en détail,* nothing is sacrificed to generality. Little speedy reductions in one-stroke battle scenes show his extraordinary willingness to learn from the medieval tropes themselves. And in place of verbal formulae, he reiterates his scenes with decorous and decorative talent. (p. 18)

Rohmer has achieved what he feels resides in the Chrétien text: "a subtle type of comedy." Maybe the central comedy is resolutely against the artist if he feels it serves final pietistic norms. The movie as a whole seems also Buñuel-like in its transgressions. While the *Marquise of O,* the director's last successful adaptation with theatrical style, suffered from an almost-too-resolute handling of Kleist's sublimely sublimated expressionism, called sick by Goethe, *Perceval* has been permitted to come forward with a little de-sublimation of the original. The devices of indirect discourse, that constant profiling of the dialogue, as it were, . . . here produces a de-familiarization, a difficulty, a slowing down.

We hear bird-song, we are about to respond to it with all the pathos of the familiar, but we immediately watch the musicians produce the sounds. There are no birds. We hear a sublime description of battle, but we immediately watch the musicians produce the sounds on little instruments, cymbals, and woodblocks. Art is produced in front of us as a process congruent with the virtuous life. . . . In an age of degraded public naturalisms, in an age that Adorno characterised as regressive in listening and fastened to fetishes, in an age that seeks to escape metaphor, Rohmer is relentlessly metaphorical and in his self-consciousness we find our truest relations. The cardboard forests Perceval rides through are more real than Riverside. . . .

It is part of Rohmer's effort and success, I think, to take the "commercial" film one step further towards being an adequately formal vehicle. He learned this at the knees of Chaplin, Murnau (on whom he did his doctoral thesis), and in collaboration with the more *gauchiste* Godard. His Perceval has camera shots of great length and concentration as inspired, as Rohmer admits, as much by television form as by Dreyer. The music is never background sentimentality, but represents a true juxtaposition and dialectic. Rohmer is attempting a certain rigor in what used to be thought of as "film form," now dissolved into a dessicated improvisatory representational zeal, in most American TV and movies. Rather than being a sociological symptom, his autonomous art regulates by extreme absence his critique. One applauds not simply the decorative charm of this movie, but its many negations of cheap whimsy and false irony. (p. 19)

David Shapiro, "Rohmer's 'Perceval': Film Form as Grail," in New York Arts Journal *(copyright © 1978 by Richard W. Burgin), No. 12, November-December, 1978, pp. 18-19.*

GEORGE MORRIS

[Eric Rohmer's *Perceval* is] unique in its virtual elimination of an intermediary, modern sensibility between the artist and the myth. Rohmer is so attuned to the virtues this story celebrates and the spirit it embodies that he transforms a potential curiosity into a movie at once immediate and vital. His oneness with this material erases a distance of eight centuries. . . .

The result of Rohmer's labor of love is a film that evokes the spirit of the Middle Ages in every frame. *Perceval* unfolds like a Book of Hours miraculously sprung to life. The physical movements and positioning of the actors even resemble those still life figures from engravings of the period, with their tilting bodies, inclined heads, and arms and hands extended in gestures of supplication. . . .

Rohmer has created a glorious paradox—a highly stylized theater piece which is conceived totally in cinematic terms. The self-imposed restrictions have actually liberated his imagination in a way that expands the potential of the medium. Like such great Renoir "theater" films as *The Golden Coach,* and *French Cancan, Perceval* plays with the contradictory impulses of theater and cinema. Its gleeful juggling of their similarities and differences modifies any preconceived definitions of either.

This movie revels in its theatricality. Nearly half the verse is sung to music that Guy Robert has culled from themes of the twelfth and thirteenth centuries. . . . Since the clarity of the text takes precedence over any inflection or vocal variation, the actors do not even attempt representational characterizations. The speaking of the rhymes is closer to an interpretative reading than a theatrical performance. (p. 9)

Rohmer's fidelity to the text has not smothered his own personal voice as a filmmaker. Like most of his films, *Perceval* is a contemplation of such outmoded concepts as faith, honour, love and moral rectitude. And like [the protagonists of *My Night at Maud's, Claire's Knee,* and *Chloë in the Afternoon,* the central character in] *Perceval* moves gradually from an initially narrow, selfish view of himself in relation to the world, toward a point approaching a measure of enlightenment. In the earlier Moral Tales, this interior journey is developed through those Platonic dialogues unique to Rohmer. In this film, however, Perceval's moral and spiritual progression is charted through his picaresque encounters. . . .

Perceval is shot through with the passion and moral commitment Rohmer brought to *My Night at Maud's* and *Claire's Knee.* This film trembles with a religious faith so awesome, so absolute, that even the staunchest atheist might pause. Rohmer also believes deeply in the code of chivalry which informed the Middle Ages. . . .

When Perceval's lack of perspicacity lets the mystery of the Holy Grail slip through his fingers, Rohmer abruptly deserts his hero at his lowest ebb and digresses to the tale of Sir Gawain, whose efforts to clear his good name return nobility to Arthurian folklore. Performing his deeds of chivalry with the purest of hearts, Gawain personifies the balance of humility, pride, and inner serenity that defines knighthood. . . .

Despite the seriousness of its concern, *Perceval* is consistently witty and invigorating. Rohmer infuses Perceval's naïveté and misdirected fervor with many humorous touches. . . .

Rohmer has generously shared his delight in this romance by turning it into a movie that recaptures the awe and magic a child discovers between the pages of his first storybook.

Eric Rohmer's *Perceval* is an astounding achievement. This seminal film literally extends the boundaries of the cinema. It simultaneously tests the limits of prevailing aesthetic criteria, and pushes most assumption of what constitutes a work of film art into unexplored areas. *Perceval* is more than an illustration of a medieval text; it is a joyful illumination of Eric Rohmer's very special universe. (p. 10)

George Morris, "'Perceval'," in Take One *(copyright © 1979 by Unicorn Publishing Corp.), Vol. 7, No. 2, January, 1979, pp. 9-10.*

Ken Russell

1921-

British director, scriptwriter, and photographer.

Russell is known for his idiosyncratic biographies of artists in which he both sensationalizes and psychoanalyzes his subject. He is a controversial filmmaker, for some critics find his vivid, often grotesque, depictions of humanity drastically overdone. In Russell's best work, such as *Song of Summer,* he is innovative, depicting the creative struggles of an artist combined with a perceptive understanding of the artist's personal life. Less successful attempts, like *Lisztomania,* are daring technically but as character studies superficial, relying on graphic details and shock appeal to win an audience.

One of Russell's first attempts at filmmaking was the creation of a television series on composers for BBC. Many of his stories such as those of Isadora Duncan and Richard Strauss, both awed and appalled audiences. As Russell continued making the films in the BBC series, each one became increasingly involved in the subject's psychological development.

His first full-length films were unsuccessful, until his adaptation of D. H. Lawrence's *Women in Love* established him as a film director. Later films, including the controversial *The Devils,* developed his increasing interest in decadence, perversion, cruelty, sexual repression, and sexual inadequacy. Russell's exaggerated, voyeuristic style is unique, owing creative inspiration to no previous directorial influence. Though a few of his films have received critical acclaim, Russell's talent is generally considered obscured by his taste for the outrageous. When Russell was asked why he wanted to shock people, he replied, "I want to make people extraordinary. Because the more people realize they're extraordinary, the better they are. Really, I want everyone to *freak out.*"

ALLEN EYLES

[*French Dressing* has a] flimsy story—and indeed a tired old script—but it has been made with spirit and gusto into an enjoyable spree that's running, jumping and hardly ever standing still.

Ken Russell has struck out boldly to create a broad, nutty world of his own that is given depth by the natural settings (mostly Herne Bay) but never compromised by awkward glimpses of real and unexaggerated behaviour. It's a world of 'What the Butler Saw' machines, paper Union Jacks, municipal bands and formal dress, sly sniggers and petty ideas, watched bemusedly from the Outside. . . . (p. 24)

But, as a whole, *French Dressing* lacks bite: its vision is blinkered and superficial, bashing at the same old inoffensive targets. Aren't the real Gormleighs ridiculous enough, or would some pressure group not like it? (p. 25)

Allen Eyles, "'French Dressing'" (© copyright Allen Eyles 1964; reprinted with permission), in Films and Filming, *Vol. 10, No. 10, July, 1964, pp. 24-5.*

RICHARD DAVIS

[The story of *Billion Dollar Brain* is apparently as confusing to the central character, Harry Palmer,] as it is to us. He drifts through the whole thing looking at times bewildered, at times merely bored, and quite honestly I wasn't surprised. . . .

Particularly sad is that this hotch-potch is directed by Ken Russell. . . . He has always embraced the complex structure in his work, and he is one of the few genuine stylists working in the British cinema. Nevertheless, I would rather have seen him tackling a more compatible subject. . . . [Harry Palmer] is the nearest thing to a Le Carre hero the comic-strip has yet thrown up. Now he is required to enter Bondland and he just can't cope. Perhaps the whole thing is just another symptom of the imminent demise of the cycle.

Richard Davis, "'The Billion Dollar Brain'" (© copyright Richard Davis 1968; reprinted with permission), in Films and Filming, *Vol. 14, No. 4, January, 1968, p. 24.*

IAN LESLIE CHRISTIE

[*Women in Love* emerges] not so much as an 'adaptation' of Lawrence's monumental novel, but as a kind of critical recreation. From the opening sequence, in which Gudrun and Ursula's half-sophisticated, half-innocent discussion of marriage is deftly punctuated by a passing couple with pram, the film develops as a dialogue between Lawrence's exploration of the freedom and submission of love and Russell's own distinctive vision. . . .

[Birkin has] been 'transposed' . . . but, more important, [he] has been re-created in terms of the film's own complex visual 'significance'. . . . *Of course* the novel has its unique significance and means of signification; it also exists as a cultural *fact* for both the film's makers and audiences. Merely to simplify and transpose it would be an impertinence. But what Russell and his scriptwriter producer Larry Kramer have made is a film *about* the novel, rather than *of* it.

Doubtless it will still offend many Lawrentians; for one strand of the film's response to the novel is to find a number of occasions for broad humour—as in a bemused miner's sudden collision with a hanging carcass in the market while Gudrun taunts him provocatively; or when Loerke, the materialistic sculptor, casually flicks ash on to Ursula's plate. But, more generally, it stands or falls as a structure of sharply individualised sequences exploiting the range of Russell's ability to convey his meaning in purely cinematic terms. (p. 50)

Ian Leslie Christie, "'Women in Love'," in Sight and Sound *(copyright © 1970 by The British Film Institute), Vol. 39, No. 1, Winter, 1969-70, pp. 49-50.*

GORDON GOW

A gift for hyperbole has been noted in Ken Russell's work before now, and it is argued both fulsomely and aptly to his remarkable film about Tchaikovsky [*The Music Lovers*]. Since much of this composer's work has been construed as a romantic compensation for the personal torments of his life, Russell's method is justified. Passages of great beauty are contrasted with a pronounced ugliness, as for example in Tchaikovsky's memory of the hot bath given his mother in a futile attempt to save her from death by cholera. This has its dramatically valid purpose, of course, because the same treatment was used without success when the son died of the same disease: therefore we get a double dose of grotesquerie. . . . Such incidents, to which Russell's film is rather prone, are not only pertinent to the hypersensitive state of mind he is depicting—they are also brilliantly cinematic. Yet, for my own taste, I find them in the long run too much. It would be unfair not to acknowledge their viability in a work that affords us an impression of the artist's psyche, as distinct from a mere documentation of the known facts about his life and work; nevertheless they have a tendency to outweigh the heady splendours of the passages which are superbly aligned with the music itself, the calculated flights of romanticism that echo visually the melodic graces and raptures of the composer's wishful imagination. (p. 47)

Rather an excess of footage . . . has been granted to [Nina,] the woman he married, and lived with for a short time. . . . Tchaikovsky's inability to copulate with her is demonstrated three times, and I should have thought once was enough. . . . Meantime, Nicholas Rubenstein . . . is reduced to a wisp of waspishness with barely any acknowledgment of his more benevolent moments in Tchaikovsky's career, and brother Modeste only once abandons spite for a hint of the affection and understanding that have been attributed to him in certain reference works. A number of things might aggravate sticklers for known fact, and fervently scholarly musicians: not least the derision with which Modeste supplies the name 'Pathetic' for the Sixth Symphony (the nuance of the word might well have been tender), and the indication in the same sequence that Tchaikovsky drank contaminated water intentionally, virtually committing suicide; possibly of lesser consequence is the implication that Mme von Meck withdrew her favours when she learned of Tchaikovsky's homosexuality, whereas some of her actual letters to him seem to suggest that she knew about it all along. (pp. 47-8)

Very frequently, though, music and visuals are truly exciting. . . . The *Nutcracker* explosion of revelry at a Moscow fair in 1875 is a wonderful prelude. And at the end of it all one comes away with images of torchlight in the snow and fireworks in the night, as well as the more gruelling visions. (p. 48)

Gordon Gow, "Reviews: 'The Music Lovers'" (© copyright Gordon Gow 1971; reprinted with permission), in Films and Filming, *Vol. 17, No. 6, March, 1971, pp. 47-8.*

ROBERT F. KNOLL

Ken Russell's film version of D. H. Lawrence's *Women in Love* is a love's labor's lost: much attention is paid to the letter and spirit of the original, yet the film accentuates the novel's weaknesses and doesn't suggest many of its (admittedly linear) riches and strengths. This film is a serious attempt at "art," for no exchange of dialogue is free from the burden of love, death, sex, or interpersonal relationships. . . .

Women in Love, as a film, achieves a gritty documentary-like authenticity when it explores the social milieu of the lower classes. The envious glances of bedraggled coal-gathers at the clothing of the Brangwen sisters; the grimy-faced occupants of the street car, who form a silent defeated backdrop to the dialogue capture in sheerly plastic terms Lawrence's quality of felt life. (p. 1)

The wealth of Lawrencian natural symbols, which serves more than anything else to vivify theme in the novel, is treated ambiguously by Russell and Larry Kramer, his producer and scenarist. The sexual content of the conversations about figs and catkins are blatantly illustrated in biology textbook fashion, while the use of chalice-like cups to stress the sacramental quality of nature in Birkin's concepts is handled almost unobtrusively.

The animal imagery employed indicates better the seemingly random selection of symbols from the novel. Gerald comes thundering up to a railroad crossing on horseback and lashes his beast repeatedly as it rears up against a bypassing train. The Brangwen sisters are witnesses to Gerald's brutality, yet, while Ursula cringes in revulsion, Gudrun's appetite for Gerald is literally whet. The sequence works well on the purely naturalistic and pictorial levels; furthermore, it is a forceful visualization of Gerald's attempting to subjugate nature, both in himself and in the horse, to the machine. In Lawrencian sexual terms, Gerald is both flaunting his phallus before Gudrun and also revealing his emasculation. (pp. 3-4)

Every symbol obviously cannot be translated in a cinematic treatment of a novel, but Russell and Kramer's choice of visual illustration makes obvious the more ludicrous purple passages of Lawrence's novel. The lush, even overripe, pastel tones used for Gudrun's encounter with the primeval cattle the Rite of Spring echoes in Georges Delerue's score, serve only to emphasize the absurdity of the scene. (p. 4)

Crosscutting from Rupert and Ursula in post-coital exhaustion to Gerald's drowned sister and her husband in a twisted death embrace, Russell reinforces a life/death struggle motif which he had utilized earlier in the film in a love soliloquy of Gudrun's while she is lying on a tombstone. While such is the antithetical tension of the novel, the filmic visualizations are rather flat and unimaginative. (p. 5)

The climactic episodes of the film and novel occur in the Alps, and once again the sheer technical accomplishment of the cinematography becomes a visual cliché. England, metaphor for fecundity and life, the natural environment of the lovers Rupert and Ursula, is facilely opposed to the Alps, a landscape of white death. It is in this environment that Gudrun fittingly destroys Gerald and accentuates the sexually ambivalent aspects of her personality by her involvement with the homosexual artist. (pp. 5-6)

The Lawrencian novel of psychic development is perhaps best understood in mystical terms: neither words nor images can do more than suggest the nature of the tangled relationships, particularly between Gerald and Rupert. As a desire for wholeness and completeness beyond, or in addition to, heterosexual love, the theory of Lawrence/Rupert can be seen by Ursula as a perversity, something unattainable. Open ended film and open ended novel leave the quest unfulfilled.

Russell's film must, however, be reckoned only a partial and sporadic success at best; his attempt is uneven in conception, casting, and recognition of the uniquely linear qualities of Lawrence's work. (p. 6)

Robert F. Knoll, "'Women in Love'," in Film Heritage *(copyright 1971 by F. A. Macklin), Vol. 6, No. 4, Summer, 1971, pp. 1-6.*

STANLEY KAUFFMANN

Seeing [*The Devils*] made me glad, for the first time, that both Huxley and Whiting are dead, so that they are spared this farrago of witless exhibitionism.

Russell has insured that, through every moment of the picture, we are paying attention not to the great themes of spirit and truth, morality and immorality, but to him. The camera whirls, the smoke wafts in and out, the lights flicker, the music whoops up the frequent climaxes, the editing palpitates, the angles of vision are mostly eccentric. . . .

And what is the self that Russell is so proud of? Part misunderstood German expressionism, part diluted Bergman (out of *The Seventh Seal*), part diluted Eisenstein (out of *Alexander Nevsky* and *Ivan the Terrible*), among other derivations. The only elements that seem *echt* Russell are the sadism posing as ruthless candor and the anxiety to be taken seriously. (p. 72)

Stanley Kauffmann, "'The Devils'" (originally published in The New Republic, *Vol. 165, No. 11, September 11, 1971), in his* Living Images: Film Comment and Criticism *(copyright © 1971, 1972, 1973, 1974 by Stanley Kauffmann; reprinted by permission of Harper & Row, Publishers, Inc.), Harper, 1975, pp. 72-3.*

GORDON GOW

Those who do not feel that they have supped quite full enough of sensationalism might find themselves more replete after savouring Ken Russell's latest dish. The policy of shocking people into awareness is applied very strongly in *The Devils;* a demonstration of the horrors that can be caused by excessive denial of the flesh. . . .

Russell could no doubt have gone to even more startling extremes, which would have been viable dramatically. As things stand, the visuals are pretty hair-raising. At the beginning, we have a balletic prelude given by Louis XIII for the delectation of Richelieu, who looks understandably impatient at the quality of the dance, and then we plunge into the potent stuff: on the outskirts of Loudon, skeletal shapes are rotting upon great wheels; inside the Convent, the nuns have clambered to windows to ogle Grandier as he passes by. The climate of frenzy is established fast. . . .

Relatively commonplace is the orgiastic sequence where nuns cast off their garments and disport themselves amid a rowdy throng: except for their nudity, which is alarmingly extended to their shaven heads, this is redolent of trad-epic cinema. The more fulsome devices of exorcism make a savage impact, however, and the final agonies of Grandier are potent.

Presumably to discourage us from dismissing it all as just a spot of ugly spice from the distant past, Russell throws in an occasional deliberate anachronism. . . . As an aid to continued relevance through the decades, this idea has worked quite well in other historical pieces. . . . But here the benefits are fitful: when occasion is found for Louis XIII to say 'Bye bye, blackbird' the mind begins to boggle a bit.

Gordon Gow, "'The Devils'" (© copyright Gordon Gow 1971; reprinted with permission), in Films and Filming, *Vol. 17, No. 12, September, 1971, p. 55.*

ALAN WARNER

Certainly one school of thought will disagree with the method by which the Sandy Wilson musical [*The Boy Friend*] has been transferred to the screen yet one must always remember to credit Ken Russell with an understanding of and a yearning for the cinema in its most flamboyant and visual form. The original setting of the 'twenties musical is used as the basis upon which the screenplay has been built. . . .

[The] much-publicised sequences are [those] in which Russell works [the 1930's film director and choreographer] Busby Berkeley kaleidoscopic formulas to an intense degree. . . . (p. 49)

Overall one feels that whilst Berkeley's routines were bordering on the self-indulgent, Ken Russell has endangered his tribute in that it tends to underline that they were much better suited to their original contexts and that to overload an idea can unintentionally step over the mark of appreciation. . . .

The picture will undoubtedly be viewed by many who will not appreciate the adulatery send-up which Ken Russell has unashamedly devoted his efforts to, but even these audiences cannot fail to be entertained by the assembled company and to this end, the film is a successful venture. (p. 50)

Alan Warner, "Reviews: 'The Boy Friend'" (© copyright Alan Warner, 1972; reprinted with permission), in Films and Filming, *Vol. 18, No. 7, April, 1972, pp. 49-50.*

PAULINE KAEL

It would be convenient to be able to say that Ken Russell's "Savage Messiah" is bad strictly on formal and technical grounds, but that would, I think, be fundamentally a lie. It is very poor technically; but that's not all that makes it bad. . . .

Is there any other movie director with the flair and imagination and, yes, the force of Ken Russell who has so little actual command of what is generally considered "film technique"? "Savage Messiah" starts by lunging into the middle of a situation and then just keeps throwing things at you. It's more hurried than his other films, and not so visually lush. You feel as if it were rushing through the projector at the wrong speed and with the sound turned up to panic level. Russell edits with a cleaver, and the frenetic intercutting is choppy and rhythmless. Nothing is prepared for, and the disjointed scenes are played as if they all had the same value; he charges from one to the next, and his inventiveness gets buried under the avalanche. (p. 225)

As a picture of bohemian life in Paris and London, "Savage Messiah" is about as convincing as "The Subterraneans" was about the Beats in San Francisco; but you understood the commercial pressures that shaped that, while with "Savage Messiah" the pressures are from Russell's insides. He's a one man marketplace, a compulsive Hollywoodizer, and his images of the artist's suffering are frantic versions of Hollywood's. This movie is like a continuation of "The Music Lovers," but now it's all random buffoonery. Russell seems to want something from them, but each time he gets close to them he dances away. His movies are charged with sex, but it's androgynous sex, and sterile. There's a giddy violence to the sensations of dislocation that this new film produces. The abrupt contrasts score points against the characters. Russell celebrates the pandemonium and senselessness of art and life. Yet in the middle of this lurid debauchery the virginal hero seems to be saving himself for something. . . . (pp. 225-26)

The title seems so appropriate to Ken Russell . . . that some people have thought the film . . . to be autobiographical. And in a sense it is, because Russell has wrested Gaudier-Brzeska's story from its place in art history and made it one move of his unstable satires on romanticism. Gentle, delicate-looking Gaudier. . . . becomes Russell's strutting, phallic artist assaulting society. His whole life builds up to the final Hollywood-style irony: he is taken up after death by the fashionable world, for its amusement. In a musical-comedy finale, Russell concocts a parade of rich and vapid young people with pink parasols who attend a posthumous exhibition of Gaudier-Brzeska's work and flirt and politely smile their approval. . . . [But] to suggest that his art was immediately taken up by smart young society people is to miss out on the meaning of his dedication to the avant-garde movement of his time, which was what kept him poor.

In Hollywood bios, the consummation of the artist's life was, of course, the romanticizing movie itself; Russell seems to be tormented by this convention—he keeps jabbing at it, angrily demonstrating that artists are not the ethereal dreamers those silly movies said they were, yet accepting the Hollywood myths of genius and "inspiration." This movie doesn't have the deliberate shocks and horrors of "The Music Lovers" or "The Devils"—the sores and the burning, bubbling flesh, and Rube Goldberg machines inserted into women. This time, Russell's full energy—a kind of mad zip—goes into parodics that burst out where they don't belong. The most inventive sequence is a freakily decadent erotic entertainment in a Vorticist night club in London. . . . Russell's jokes don't work, because they're so maniacally off target. The points aren't satirically valid; they're simply for kicks (though I imagine that Russell himself would defend them as valid, and would *also* say it's all meant to be a joke on us). . . . His hyperbolic method—going from climax to climax—is itself a form of ridicule, and it's orgiastic. And I think this is a large part of his fascination: some people can't resist his movies, because they can hardly wait to see what mad thing he'll do next. His films are preceded by puffery about the biographical research and the authentic incidents. But he removes those incidents from their human context; the attraction for him and for the audience is the porn of fame. . . . He's not trying to deal with the age any of his artist subjects lived in, or the appetites and satisfactions of that age, or the vision of a particular artist, but is always turning something from the artists' lives into something else—a whopping irony, a phallic joke, a plushy big scene. (pp. 226-28)

Russell is as crazed in his hatred of art lovers as some reactionary fantasists are about liberals. The world of the movie is made up of repulsive desiccated poseurs, who are mocked for the sensuality in their love of art. To Russell, love of art is an affection: these ghoulish art lovers really want the artist's flesh. . . . Russell seems to share with Hollywood the view that a supercilious manner and an aristocratic style and homosexuality equal decadence. For him, decadence is glitzy camp—which at one level he must love, because he compulsively turns everything into it. . . . [Those] who adore his movies say, "He's a genius." Genius is, of course, his subject—genius and possession. His possessed artists burn with an intensity that is so exhausting they seek death. But he can't help making them fools, too. He turns pop into highbrow pop. This is "art" for people who don't want to get close to human relationships, for those who feel safer with bravura splashiness. (pp. 228-31)

You never get to see what brought Henri Gaudier and Sophie Brzeska together, and you never get to understand why he needed the woman who called him her little son. There's one quiet moment in a shelter on the beach when Henri and Sophie talk together and you actually begin to feel something; but Russell doesn't trust it, and he throws it away. . . .

What is the sum total of his vision but a sham superiority to simple human needs a camp put-down of everything? Like *Yellow Book* diabolist of the eighteen-nineties, Russell lusts for a purity he doesn't believe in. He turns Gaudier-Brzeska into the virgin-artist raped in life by his dilettante admirers and raped in death by the fashionable world. One can't just dismiss Russell's movies, because they have an influence. They cheapen everything they touch—not consciously, I think, but instinctively. (p. 232)

Pauline Kael, "Hyperbole and Narcissus," in The New Yorker *(© 1972 by The New Yorker Magazine, Inc.), Vol. XLVIII, No. 39, November 18, 1972, pp. 225-32.*

PETER MEZAN

Russell's movies present something of an enigma, since nobody is too sure who likes them. While art-theatre habitués say that Russell is commercial, the studios seem to feel he is too stylized for the masses and must therefore, by elimination, be art theatre. Where the confusion arises is that Russell's stylizations, while undoubtedly very arty, aspire to the peculiarly unserious condition of a kind of scurrilous cartoon realism in which queening, transmogrified *Classics Illustrated* characters enacting fancy-dress charades speak lines so banal that nothing anybody says can make the slightest difference to anybody else; in which whole lifetimes are reduced to a handful of hyper-romanticized traumas, climaxes of the wonderful or the awful, whose psychology is abandoned to a few dopey formulae that it would be profane to call Freudian; in which fantasy is mistaken for imagination, and horror, masquerading as evil, is exalted by how seductively it is choreographed and photographed; in which all the subtle means by which humans hurt or please each other are reduced to the grossly physical; in which sexuality of any variety is everywhere and every time mortifying; in which nobody relates to anything outside his fantasies, inside which he is stuck like a fly in jam, and which, anyway, are like no fantasies anybody ever had, except maybe Bob Hope dreaming he was a sheik making Dorothy Lamour. (p. 167)

[For] the horror-show consciousness of the Sixties and Seventies to which bourgeois domestic realism meant obsession and degradation and doom, Russell . . . tailored a new naive romance, fixated on the pathetic, mortifying conclusion, on creativity not as renewal but as the climactic last kicks of the strangulating body: the Romance of the Bad Trip. So, instead of Genius being the ordinary, persevering Joe with a flare for divinity, he'd be the extraordinary obsessive with a flare for the diabolical—sick, drying up, terrified of boredom. . . .

[There] was a positive compulsion to Russell's films, a curious savior in being had by inverted, low-Hollywood, cliché junk consciously wielded into some kind of ersatz art form, always just outflanking the criteria by which film as "serious art" was usually judged. . . .

[Somehow], out of his passion to "make it all fantasy," Russell had cooked up a formidable marriage of medium and message, embracing exactly that sort of bijou dross to which the movie medium would most readily lend its powers—the mechanical titillations of isolating, self-enhancing daydreams and omnipotent fantasies, going nowhere in the guise of going everywhere. It was the fantasist's domain of comic-strip reality—passive, exclusive, and impervious to the imagination, for it had little to do with living, either in dream or in waking reality, and was of no symbolic value. And to it the movies lent their enormous power to command credence, to amplify the impact of even the most perfunctory effects into a passive, exclusive experience of abandon, exempt from the consequentiality of real events. Consequently, one didn't *have* a movie experience so much as *be* had by one. (p. 170)

Peter Mezan, "Relax, It's Only a Ken Russell Movie" (copyright © 1973, by Peter Mezan), in Esquire, *Vol. LXXIX, No. 5, May, 1973, pp. 167-204.*

ROBERT PHILLIP KOLKER

["Excess"] and an unrelentingly ironic point of view have probably been the qualities most responsible for the critical hatred of Russell's past work. His almost obsessive desire to destroy pretense and smash romantic icons seems to guarantee an adverse reaction. And an adverse reaction is bound to come each time he realizes this desire with vitality and an approach to cinema that does not admit of subtlety or moderation. But the reaction is quite unfounded. To be offended by a style without analyzing the reason for the style suggests critical self-satisfaction and cowardice, two qualities Russell is always attacking in his films.

Russell sees the artist as a man or woman of heightened sensibilities who is beleaguered both by his own neuroses or sense of mission and by an environment that is strained into madness as the artist tries to live out his life in it. Russell's inquiry (he says he approaches biography as a detective story) is into the ways his character might have dealt with his life, basing the material on existing facts, as Russell interprets them, but playing the "facts" against the romanticized myth that has grown up around the artist. Thus, the typical Russell subject is composed of three personae: the historical figure, the myth the figure has created, and Russell's own vision of the subject, which exaggerates the historical figure in order to pay it off against the myth. The result is, obviously, conflict. And it is a conflict in which no one wins: not the subject, not his contemporary world, not the popular myth, and certainly not the audience who come to a biographical film with certain expectations. Ultimately the biographical figure is turned into an actor in history and is destroyed by his act and the historical moment that cannot contain him. After his death he is further destroyed by his mythic persona, that *version* of himself created by the admirers of his art. (p. 42)

Somewhere along the line, he insists his subject must become comic . . . , the milieu foolish, and the whole film something other than high serious. With this in mind, the notion of hero as actor becomes even more complex; it becomes a matter of manipulation. The hero manipulates his life in an attempt to perform in the world and, as mentioned before, Russell manipulates the performer and his world together. In every sense of the word, Russell is the "director," and in the end the hero, be he poet, musician, dancer or priest is acting out the role Russell sets for him.

Consider *The Music Lovers,* basically a film about a bunch of neurotics imposing their fantasies on one another. On their mockery of a honeymoon, Tchaikovsky and Nina visit a camera obscura show. The camera picks up a pair of lovers in the grass outside the pavillion and reflects them to the voyeurs inside. Everyone is delighted, except Tchaikovsky, and the performance of the unexpecting lovers is roundly applauded. A parody of this scene will occur in the horrendous railroad car episode when Nina and Tchaikovsky return from their holiday. In this case we are the sole onlookers to this grotesque attempt by a homosexual and a nymphomaniac to consummate their marriage. We are no longer watching the voyeurs watching a candid camera. We *are* the voyeurs to a scene in which Tchaikovsky is forced into one of his many degrading performances. (pp. 43-4)

With the final overpowering images of Nina in the madhouse, and Tchaikovsky boiled like a lobster to cure his cholera, we are left with something other than a benign idea of the composer of beautiful melodies. The melodies remain; Russell has no intentions of debasing the art. He merely wants to dramatically de-romanticize the artist.

He wants to destroy simple emotions and wrong conclusions. He wants to undercut posturing and cure excessive sentiment. . . .

The Devils may be Russell's finest example of history as stage and hero as actor. . . . The interplay of modern sets and period "realism" sets up a counterpoint of medieval and modern prejudice, greed, and self-serving essential to the film's theme. Grandier moves about with an almost pompous self assurance, playing out the role of liberal Catholic and protector of his domain against political pressure. . . .

Games create stress. Acting roles to suit one's self-conceptions or to counter the games and tricks others are playing does violence to the self. Russell extrapolates stress and violence from the given situation; they saturate his *mise-en-scène*. Russell is nothing if not a showman. He loves his medium and is aware of its potential for violent action. But the violent action he loves to show is not laid over his subject. He is not "self-indulgent"; he only indulges the cinematic potentials of his subject for all they are worth. . . .

Savage Messiah [is] a tragicomedy whose characters Russell takes more seriously than any before. . . .

Russell exaggerates Gaudier's frenetic character in a way that makes it charming and attractive. He plays down Sophie's madness. (p. 44)

[The close of *Savage Messiah*] is the most understated, unmelodramatic close that Russell ever filmed, and it is in tone with the work as a whole. There is no violent action. . . . The comedy throughout is direct and genuine, not grotesque as in the Strauss film, or cute and campy as in *The Boy Friend*. Henri Gaudier-Brzeska postures and pontificates—in fact acts out a persona as do all Russell's subjects . . . , but there is a feeling he is aware of his posturing, and we can share in his vitality directly, without the discomfiting feeling that the joke is on him and on us. . . .

In *Savage Messiah* one doesn't find the shock cuts that seem to be one of Russell's trademarks. . . . Russell juxtaposes madness and sanity, violence and calm, attitudes and events cross cut, but eventually dove-tailing in a way that will undo the subject of the film. *Savage Messiah* moves in an orderly progression from sequence to sequence, and the few ironic juxtapositions it does contain occur within the sequence. . . . Gaudier succumbs to the world's demands, as do all of Russell's artists. But he does it with a grace and vitality and sanity that Russell heretofore has never permitted his subjects.

Are we to conclude from *Savage Messiah* that Russell has succumbed to restraint? Will the legion of critics, especially in England, who have chosen to hate him now say he has come to his senses? Probably not. Doubtless they will criticize him because he invents episodes in Gaudier's life that Ede never mentions, as if Russell's imagination had to be tied to an essentially dull book. And his ebullience and anger and sense of fun are not to be restrained. (p. 45)

Robert Phillip Kolker, "Ken Russell's Biopics: Grander and Gaudier," in Film Comment *(copyright © 1973 Film Comment Publishing Corporation; all rights reserved), Vol. 9, No. 3, May-June, 1973, pp. 42-5.*

MICHAEL DEMPSEY

Compared to other Russell movies, *Savage Messiah* is actually rather restrained, although like them it gets involved in role playing, theatrical behavior, comedy, madness, and the transcending of everyday life. As Tchaikovsky does in *The Music Lovers,* Gaudier equates life and art. Like Tchaikovsky's women or Sister Jeanne in *The Devils,* Sophie lives in an ethereal realm of fantasy harshly at odds with the surrounding material world—in this case, a world of starving artist's poverty that requires her to grub for half-rotten vegetables or menial jobs and to hole up in a hovel that roars with the din of trains and traffic overhead. But here things change. Insanity, self-destruction, death menace or annihilate people in the other films; even the ragged troupers of *The Boy Friend* . . . are almost macabre in their blindness to their own incompetence. None of these threats disappears from *Savage Messiah,* but the pattern established in the other films—the willful immersion in destructive, alluring illusion that is both exalted and condemned—has been altered.

For one thing, *Savage Messiah* contains *no* antiromantic satire. (pp. 10-11)

Nor is transcendence any longer a major issue, for when the film opens Gaudier and Sophie have already achieved it. Russell's previous heroes and heroines try to escape everyday banality by immersing themselves in love, art, religion, fantasy. The results in each case are ambiguous; in *Savage Messiah* they are not. The devotion of Gaudier and Sophie to their ideals gives them the courage to face their difficulties with grace, wit, and passion: the film emphasizes not their suffering but their *responses* to it. Nobody rapes either of them at any time. Who could?

Even the stress on death, likewise an important concern of the earlier films, undergoes a change in emphasis here. In the movies preceding *The Boy Friend* (in which death was metaphorical), Russell dwells on death and more or less religious concepts of immortality befitting a person with a Catholic background. In *Savage Messiah* he focuses on death and earthly life. The powerful drives of Gaudier and Sophie are certainly death defying; but neither, unlike Russell's version of Tchaikovsky, shows much interest in being remembered; neither turns art into a religion the way he and his fellow music lovers do. In this film, "death" indicates not just physical passing but killing approaches to art as well.

One of them is the sanctification of the creative act, the ascribing of it to some ineffable mechanism which only the lucky few can understand. With *Savage Messiah,* Russell explicitly (in his own way) joins Rossellini, the post-1968 Godard, and other filmmakers who have striven to demystify art and the making of art. (pp. 11-12)

To demystify is one thing; to deromanticize is another. Unlike those who demand the second along with the first, Russell remains a consummate romantic even when he scalds romanticism. (p. 12)

At other times, the film's demystification becomes more political. . . . (p. 13)

[The first draft of the] script fails to tell us why Sophie suddenly gets so political when she has not previously shown any interest in the subject. When in the film Gosh asks, "How many of the enemy will that kill?" she is clearly being presented as a jingoist loudmouth. But what are we to think when in the script Sophie asks this question? Are Sophie's political statements intended to rid herself of Gaudier by persuading him to go away to war? The script offers nothing but inconclusive hints: the way she muses about "thick, oily" sleep during a distracted monologue. In an effort to clarify things, the film adds the other influences on Gaudier's decision, plus scenes like Sophie writing to him, promising marriage and saying that she mistook his enlistment for another of his extravagant jokes. Her political remarks, now that the nastiest one has been put in Gosh's mouth instead, seem more consistent with her contempt for Shaw and her spiritualized opinions on the nature of art. These changes tend to suggest that she does not consciously desire Gaudier's death. Yet the contradictory hints from the first draft still remain; and the film fails to reconcile them with the newer material, undercutting as a result its treatment of how political and personal motives can merge.

Even so, the concluding sequence intercutting Gaudier's exhibition, Sophie's grief, photos from the trenches, and a wartime parade—brings the film's consideration of art and politics to a moving climax. . . . The images are poignant not only because they reveal the full range of Gaudier's art but also because they show the art still existing after he has died. Again, the first draft is crucially different, presenting this exhibition *before* Gaudier's death, having him be on hand for it, and supplying suggestions for the spectators' empty-headed chitchat, which Russell has entirely discarded. The chic cannibals appear in only a few shots, and even then our attention is directed to one woman, honestly affected by the work, who looks at it attentively.

The contradiction between the beauty of the sculpture and the social realities that make it what movie moguls call "product" remains unresolved, held in suspension. . . . Over the end titles, Russell adds a spirited march, and this final contrast between image and sound epitomizes the film's moral position. Undeceived by reactionary social structures, Russell acknowledges fully how transitory is the artist's victory over death in all its guises. Yet he rejoices in this victory nonetheless. (pp. 15-16)

Michael Dempsey, "'Savage Messiah'," in Film Heritage *(copyright 1973 by F. A. Macklin), Vol. 9, No. 2, Winter, 1973-74, pp. 9-16.*

JUDITH CRIST

The cinematic synthesis of Ken Russell and the Who's *Tommy* is a meeting of the mush-minds, a resplendent union of the rococo and the rock of which each is master. . . . If *Tommy,* still so completely satisfying an aural experience, must be turned into a visual one as well, it now seems that the opera and Russell were meant for each other, or at very least serve each other well.

"Experience" is the word for this two-hour film, a medley of literal bits and surreal pieces, of psychedelic effects and romantic realism, of crude comedy and sophisticated suggestions, all eye-catching, most mind-engaging, some simply stunning, and a few merely bemusing. . . .

The "mush-mindedness" of *Tommy* lies basically in its heavy-handed symbolism. . . .

In wading into this irresistibly lavish spread, Russell begins with an update of the story, from World War I to II, with 1951, rather than 1921, the "good year.". . . In detailing the cures sought for Tommy in his adolescence, Russell launches into orgies of imagination. . . . (p. 64)

Some of it is banal, some of it is mind-boggling, and all of it is pounded at the eyes as the music assaults the ears at an unvarying volume level. If you survive the first hour, you will relish the second. You will sit in awed (or battered) silence, absolutely dead-pan. . . . or you will . . . be simply boggled by the absolute ball Russell is so obviously having with every twist of the camera, trick of the lens, snip of the editing scissors. . . . It is, as noted, an "experience"—an interesting one to have had when you return, as indeed you should, for the purity of the pleasures, which are, first and last, musical. (pp. 64-5)

Judith Crist, "Opera on the Rocks, with a Twist," in New York *Magazine (copyright © 1975 by News Group Publications, Inc.; reprinted with permission of* New York *Magazine), Vol. 8, No. 14, April 7, 1975, pp. 64-5.**

STANLEY KAUFFMANN

Ken Russell seems to be the man for high school students of the '70s. His style is ultra-cinematic in the least demanding way—it can be called the TV commercial in excelsis, all split screens and star bursts and swiftly changing colors and anything else that's handy, all the time. For the adolescent, both young and old, who thinks that filmmaking virtuosity is all of filmmaking, he is ideal. His grotesqueries with the life of Tschaikowsky and with John Whiting's play *The Devils* were reticence itself compared with *Tommy*. . . . [For Russell's high school judgment of *Tommy* as "the greatest art work of the twentieth century,"] his film is the perfect cinematic equivalent. (p. 33)

Stanley Kauffmann, "Films: 'Tommy'" (reprinted by permission of Brandt & Brandt Literary Agents, Inc.; copyright © 1975 by Stanley Kauffmann), in The New Republic, *Vol. 172, No. 14, April 26, 1975, pp. 18, 33.*

DAVID WILSON

Intermittently inventive, always lively, [*Tommy*] remains a series of separate units linked only by a disparate if vigorous style. Which is a fair capsule description of Russell's film-making style.

Not surprising, then, that *Tommy* represents both the best and the worst of Ken Russell, often within the same sequence. . . . Russell's visual representations of the score (already, in 'Quintaphonic' sound, well into aural extravagance) are here merely aggravating annotations—in, out and zoom it all about like some nightmare conjunction of TV soap operatics and TV commericals. The rest, as nearly always in Russell's cinema, is bits and showpieces. And it would scarcely be worth noting did it not exemplify the familiar problem in responding to a Russell film: for all the tuppence-coloured banality (perhaps because of it), there is no denying the vitality of expression (it is hardly a style) which punctuates his films like an excess of exclamation marks.

And why should one deny it? Russell is rightly contemptuous of critics who have labelled (bludgeoned) him as 'tasteless', whatever that means, And if one index of a visual style is that it is irreducible to, or at best impoverished by, verbal exposition, it is not the only one. Russell's visual method is 'obvious' and 'banal' only in the sense that pop art is obvious and banal. Like pop art it can be both narcissistic and self-defeating; whether it is or not depends on whether the method, and its paraphernalia, is merely self-justifying or makes some discernible connection with the material. The analogy is not gratuitous. That frequently visited shrine of pop art, Marilyn Monroe, makes an appearance in *Tommy* in the shape of a grotesque plaster model, the centrepiece of the faith-healing carnival—a familiar Russell amalgam of religious hysteria and tame blasphemy—to which Tommy . . . is taken in the hope of finding a cure for his catatonic trance. Here, as with the cannon-ball sequence in *Music Lovers* or the Nazi emblems in the television 'biography' of Richard Strauss, the iconography seems both inapposite and superfluous, the more so for Russell's insistent illustration of it. The brash banality of this sequence contrasts tellingly with set pieces in which shrill decor and frenzied camera are more than simply eye-jarring adjuncts. (pp. 192-93)

In other words, this is the Russell mixture as before. In *Tommy,* though, there is a difference. Where previously the garish, only superficially outrageous display has obstinately remained just that, there is evidence enough here of subject and author making a genuine, if often troubled, marriage of like minds. Perhaps, after all, that is the key to Russell's film-making. Like any pop artist, he needs a special relationship with his material. When he finds it, as he does in several of the units of *Tommy,* the effect can be dazzling. When he doesn't, as he doesn't at intervals in *Tommy,* the result is mere discord. (p. 193)

David Wilson, "'Tommy'," in Sight and Sound *(copyright © 1975 by The British Film Institute), Vol. 44, No. 3, Summer, 1975, pp. 192-93.*

STEPHEN FARBER

[Even] Russell's bitterest enemies would not deny that he has his own distinctive vision. His baroque visual effects are easily identifiable. . . . Characters and episodes from one film are re-interpreted later. . . .

These relatively simple connecting links point to a more comprehensive thematic unity. Many of Russell's obsessions can be traced to his television films. One of the quintessential Russell images appears in *Dante's Inferno,* his film on Dante Gabriel Rossetti, when the poet, who has buried a volume of poetry with his first wife, goes to dig up the coffin and retrieve the poems—art snatched (quite literally) from the jaws of death. Russell is haunted by images of physical and mental disintegration; the tension between art and death accounts for much of the dramatic power of his films. . . .

Although Russell sympathizes with the struggle to transcend death, he wants to expose the artist's ruthlessness in pursuing his vision. In his eloquent television film *Song of Summer,* focusing on the relationship of Frederick Delius and Eric Fenby, a young music student who comes to transcribe his last works, Russell introduces another of his major themes: the sacrifice of a weaker individual to the over-weening ego of the artist. . . .

Russell's investigation of the moral failure of the artist is a major theme of his work, a theme explored most caustically in *Lisztomania.* The films of Russell that do not deal primarily with artists—*Billion Dollar Brain, The Boy Friend, Tommy,* even *Women in Love*—seem less characteristic, less urgent. *The Devils* occupies a more important position, partly because of its Catholic theme (Russell is a convert to Catholicism), but also because the radical priest, Grandier, is a heroic, tormented figure involved in the same kind of agonized struggle against death as the artist. Although *The Devils* has a stronger political subtext than most of Russell's films, he has very little interest in social and political issues, and that helps to explain what is missing from his striking but unsatisfying *Women in Love.* Russell does not begin to understand Lawrence's profoundly comprehensive vision of the Industrial Revolution and the class struggle; the images of poverty (like Gerald's white limousine moving through a line of blackened miners) are beautiful composed, but without the undercurrent of compassion and rage that animated the novel. (p. 41)

[*The Music Lovers*] is a pointed study of the decay of the nineteenth-century romanticism. At times the sensuous images and the soaring music reflect the breathtaking boldness and confidence of Tchaikovsky's aspirations, but there is usually a tinge of irony qualifying the composer's rapture. The images of idyllic family life that accompany the First Piano Concerto are luxurious, yet deliberately overripe. . . . Although precariously balanced between beauty and decay, romance and sexual nightmare, *The Music Lovers* ends with a harsh nihilistic vision of the triumph of chaos.

The Music Lovers feels like an exorcism of Russell's own fears. *Savage Messiah* is a sunnier companion piece, a more wholehearted tribute to the adventurousness of the romantic artist. It contains many of the same tensions as *The Music Lovers,* but it is a more jubilant work, with only a few muted reminders of the artist's delusions. (pp. 41-2)

Yet there are a few darker intimations even in this film. Russell cannot help observing that the same recklessness that fires Gaudier's art drives him to his death on the battlefield; his passion has its self-destructive side. The ending of the film is disturbingly ambivalent. At a posthumous exhibition of Gaudier's work, the smooth, gliding camera movements capture the beauty of the sculptures. In an earlier scene Gaudier said that art could not exist without an audience; yet the audience at his exhibition consists mainly of dilettantes who are titillated by his daring. The ending is a rousing tribute to Gaudier's art, shadowed by a nagging, barely perceptible sense of futility.

This ambiguous conclusion does not dispel the exuberant mood of *Savage Messiah,* but it suggests that Russell's vision of artistic fulfillment is always double-edged; he has a romantic spirit clouded by a sneaking sense of irony. Nevertheless, *Savage Messiah* is Russell's most relaxed and affectionate film, and possibly his best—less sensational, more evenhanded, mellow, and mature than anything else he has done in features. . . .

Mahler . . . is conceived almost like a burlesque tour of some high points of the composer's life. . . .

In *Mahler* Russell reduces plot to a minimum and develops an unorthodox surrealist style. . . . (p. 42)

Mahler does not have the dramatic or thematic unity of *The Music Lovers;* in this film Russell flings out ideas indiscriminately. . . . Obviously the film is a grab-bag; it doesn't all hang together, and one responds simply to the individual sequences, which are almost like the production numbers in a musical. . . . The depiction of Mahler's relationship with Alma is the major strength of the movie, and some of their scenes together have dramatic tension as well as emotional depth. . . .

Unfortunately, the relationship of Mahler and Alma, which could have made a film in itself, is only one element in this elaborate potpourri, and Russell gets distracted by other subjects just when we are most intrigued. (p. 43)

Tommy is inventive, but it is also exhausting, because it is so totally limited to scenes of horror and vulgarity. The feeling that comes through most strongly is one that was probably not intended—Ken Russell's feeling of revulsion from the modern world. *Tommy* at least helps to explain why Russell is ordinarily drawn to period films. He obviously cannot abide the contemporary world; he is a nineteenth-century romantic living out of his time. . . .

Most of the weaknesses of *Tommy* stem from the rock opera itself, a blend of sophomoric ideas, adolescent masochism, and bad music. It seems to me there is a basic conceptual problem with a rock opera in which the protagonist is deaf, dumb, and blind; Tommy must be the most passive, anemic hero ever created. . . .

Russell's impulses may be fundamentally at war with the Who's beatific conceptions, and that helps to explain why the film is such a mess. The mindless glorification of youth that is part of the original opera doesn't mesh with Russell's butting mockery of youthful delirium. His own confusions magnify the problem. Given the film's emphasis on torment, exploitation, and commercialization, the feeble affirmative ending rings especially false. . . . The film is cyclical in structure, beginning in innocence and ending in innocence reclaimed. There is obviously a Christian parable peeking out from beneath the glitter, and the ending is meant to echo the crucifixion and the resurrection.

It is hard to tell how seriously Russell takes this Christ symbolism. All of his work reveals an ambivalence on the subject of religion. He wants to condemn the commercialism of the church, the atrocities committed in the name of faith; but he also means to endorse spiritual values. In both *The Devils* and *Tommy,* however, the spiritual affirmation is less convincing than the attack on the abuses of religion. At least *The Devils* succeeds in creating an imposing spiritual leader. . . .

Lisztomania continues in the flamboyant circus style of *Tommy*. But this nineteenth-century comic opera . . . is not so relentlessly ugly, and Russell's satire has a lighter, more insolent tone. . . .

In this case Russell has an underlying conception and a unifying style—a pop-art comic-strip style, built on parodies of old movie genres. (p. 44)

Despite all these stylistic flourishes, *Listzomania* has something on its mind; the collage of wild comic images builds to a climax of unexpected intensity. This is a much more adventurous, imaginative film than *Tommy*. . . . (p. 45)

What [Russell] is really saying in *Lisztomania* is that once the artist surrenders to the rule of marketplace, he has violated the natural order of the universe and released demons that cannot be controlled. . . .

The paranoia in this view of the artist's responsibility is bizarre, but there is something irresistibly romantic in Russell's concern for the artist's integrity. In a world where everything has been debased and devalued, Russell still envisions art as the central creative act that brings order to a chaotic universe. The fact that most of his films examine the artist's betrayal of his vocation cannot obscure Russell's belief in the moral importance of art. His exalted view of art seems slightly insane and rather breathtaking.

The major problem with *Lisztomania* is formal. The pop art style is effective for dealing with Liszt's vulgar showmanship, but it limits the scope of the film. . . . Toward the end of the film, Russell seems to want to portray Liszt more sympathetically, but his style is not flexible enough to reflect this shift in attitude. . . .

As in *Tommy,* Russell tries to end on a note of Christian redemption. . . .

Perhaps this ending would have been more effective if the rest of the film had more mysterious romantic images to reflect Liszt's idealism. Russell's earlier films have a broader range of moods and emotions. . . . The loud, garish style of *Tommy* and *Lisztomania* is unrelieved by quieter moments. At its best *Lisztomania* is exceptionally powerful, but there are no shadings in the film, and that's why some of the spectacular set-pieces grow tiresome.

Both *Tommy* and *Lisztomania* are inventive but singularly unmoving; almost the only emotion they inspire is horror. In *Savage Messiah* Russell's affection for the characters is more important than any of his bravura effects. Even *Mahler,* which is closer to the style of a cartoon, has passionate feeling in some of the scenes between Mahler and Alma. The circus format of *Tommy* and *Lisztomania* is partly a function of the subject matter of these two films, but one cannot help feeling a measure of concern about Russell's increasing indifference to recognizable human emotions. (p. 46)

Russell's work is blemished by arrogance, self-indulgence, pomposity, and sensationalism. . . . Russell's work can be characterized as a series of vulgar, self-indulgent set-pieces without an organizing principle. . . .

[However,] Russell's daring but still imperfect experiments with kaleidoscopic, non-linear, operatic style are symptomatic of a formal quandary that affects all filmmakers. Russell is one of the few artists who is pushing forward, working to forge a purely visual vocabulary. His most compelling images and characters already have a place in film history. (p. 47)

Stephen Farber, "Russellmania," in Film Comment *(copyright © 1975 by The Film Society of Lincoln Center; all rights reserved), Vol. 11, No. 6, November-December, 1975, pp. 40-7.*

DEREK ELLEY

[*Lisztomania*] carries the photographic splendours of *The Devils* and *Tommy* to their absurdist limits. Russell's professed intention to deflate the pomposity of his musical subjects has taken many forms over the years. . . . *Lisztomania* again breaks new ground: this time there is no underlying affection for the artist in question, merely a desire to use his name, a few of his compositions, and some of the personalia of the period, to forge a celebration of the rock scene in nineteenth-century dress. Russell is still working in a post-*Tommy* haze, and it is almost coincidence that his subject is from the field of classical music. . . .

To parallel Liszt with the modern pop performer is not an idea original to Russell, but the glove fits well. Where Russell scores above others, however, is in taking the idea to its most outrageous limit—and beyond. . . .

Lisztomania is for much of the time a delight to watch, and even when the mind is left uncatered for, the eyeball is always amused. . . . The majority of the *clichés* are familiar from Russell's other films, and tell us more about him than his various subjects, but, as always, there is always a grain of truth (and little more than that) to support his fantasies. But while trading freely on popular myth, Russell also mixes in a strong amount of more factual material, seeking contemporary parallels to make the esoteric accessible to the general viewer. . . . For the rest, however, fantasy takes over, and much of this is superb. (p. 32)

Derek Elley, "'Lisztomania' and 'The Loves of Liszt'" (© copyright Derek Elley 1976; reprinted with permission), in Films and Filming, *Vol. 22, No. 4, January, 1976, pp. 31-3.**

JOSEPH A. GOMEZ

Ken Russell's methods of adaptation and his extravagant style of filmmaking have been grossly misunderstood, but the usual naive pronouncements of film critics can no longer be considered justified. Ken Russell is not a "compulsive Hollywoodizer" who distorts facts in order to outrage audiences for the sake of pure sensationalism. He does not "murder" his subjects, and his films are not examples of "bad art". He is not motivated by sadism or "egoistic frenzy". He is not driven by cruelty or insanity to embrace excessiveness, and his films are neither "degenerate" nor "despicable". True, they do cultivate a baroque vulgarity, and they are frequently punctuated with bizarre humor which manifests itself in "camp" images, but even to describe his films as notable illustrations of "kitsch" is to do them a serious injustice. (p. 204)

More often than not, the excessiveness and frenzy of Russell's films are derived from his original sources, and he often wisely selects material especially appropriate to his unique style of filmmaking. Subtlety does exist in his films—in the complexity of his allusions, the effectiveness of his *mise-en-scène,* the richness of his visual patterning, and the mastery of his matching images to music—but it is his shock editing, his obsessive camera movements, his penchant for theatricality and overblown performances, and his extraordinary, phantasmagoric images which overwhelm his audiences. For Russell, the art of gentle persuasion is lost in this present age; audiences have become complacent and therefore must be assaulted and jolted into awareness, or into sharing emotions of ecstasy or outrage about a particular subject.

To some extent, Russell's methods can be compared to those of D. H. Lawrence, another experimental artist too often dismissed as excessive and extravagant. Lawrence uncompromisingly, intemperately, and compulsively assaulted his readers in an attempt to alter their responses. He over-emphasized the power of the body and the "blood" because he claimed that this aspect had been denied by twentieth century man's over-dependence on abstract reasoning. His purpose, however, was not to tip the scale in favor of the flesh at the expense of the spirit. Instead, he used extremes to compensate for man's dominant preoccupations and to aid in the development of the total self. Russell's methods of assaulting his audience are not really dissimilar. He, too, goes to extremes to bring his audience to his position, which frequently rests somewhere between their conventional pieties or indifference and the presentation on the screen. (p. 206)

[Perhaps] the death scene of Grandier in *The Devils* becomes the quintessential Russell sequence. The skin on Grandier's face blisters and pops before the viewer's eyes as the flames consume him, but in his last moments, he looks out at the inhabitants of Loudun and at the audience of the film and cries out, "Don't look at me. Look at your city." It is a deep, strong, over-powering voice, but one which, like Russell's, cannot be denied or ignored.

Ken Russell possesses a remarkable visual flair, a trait uncommon among British filmmakers; as in the past, he continues to experiment with film as a fusion of various art forms at a time when most film critics are praising what could be called "pure film"; and finally he has changed and continues to change the ways of making and of viewing biographical films. When seen from this perspective, Ken Russell emerges as the most significant filmmaker presently working in Great Britain. (pp. 206-07)

Joseph A. Gomez, in his Ken Russell: The Adaptor as Creator *(copyright © Joseph A. Gomez 1976), Frederick Muller Limited, 1976, 223 p.*

PENELOPE GILLIATT

In these days, Russell bangs our noses against the conventional cinematic notion of genius as if it were a manic affliction that landed on someone because his wife was being ill-tempered and his mistress humbly believed in him. Russell has given us big-scale biographies of Tchaikovsky and Liszt, and now he fells us with his "Mahler." (p. 119)

Mahler's character doesn't seem to have been particularly melodramatic, but Russell's film asserts that it was. . . . The mind of the picture is dulled and Nietzschean. There is a long scene equating Wagner and Nazism through Cosima Wagner, and including a characteristically banal sequence in which Mahler abjures Judaism by eating pig's-head and drinking milk at the same time. He seems to regret his forsaken Judaism, but there is no historical documentation for this that I can find. . . . Some people may hold that Russell's devil-may-care technique has enough talent to override quibbles about the truth of historical facts. But there is no higher respect in biographical art . . . than respect for facts.

As Russell's film has it, Mahler's guilt about his cast-aside Judaism is extravagant. . . . Though there is much that is portentous in the film, there is absolutely nothing that is serious; and though there is much that is revved-up in the film, there is no insight into the tensity of Mahler's music, which perhaps owes less to Wagner than the sumptuousness of Russell's picture suggest.

So all we can know in our sane moments of which the lack in Ken Russell is enough to drive one up the wall—is what we knew before: that musical composition is entirely undramatic, not subject to glib psychoanalysis, both quite intolerable and uniquely rewarding, and, above all, extremely hard work, like a self-employed plumber's. Depictions of artists as dream-driven madmen do little service to the appreciation of Mahler's music. . . . All through this film, we have the feeling that we are not in Mahler's fantasies but in Russell's. (pp. 119-21)

Penelope Gilliatt, "Genius, Genia, Genium, Ho Hum," in The New Yorker *(© 1976 by The New Yorker Magazine, Inc.), Vol. LII, No. 10, April 26, 1976, pp. 119-21.*

ANWER BATI

Good news. *Valentino* . . . is Ken Russell's best film in years. . . .

I must say that I find it amazing that critics still treat Russell's "biographical" films as if they were *supposed* to be definitive, carefully researched screen representations of the lives of his subjects. Don't they realise that it is not simply beyond Russell to make films like that—it just isn't what he sets out to do. . . .

What Russell offers us in his films is a series of vivid cinematic dreams about his subjects. Known events are taken to bizarre conclusions and bizarre events are made even more nightmarish. In the case of *Valentino* the images are, on the whole, fairly restrained and Russell more or less confines his customary excessive and indulgent wallow in human degradation to the well-publicised [jail] scene. . . .

As with his other films, *Valentino* tells us more about Russell's own obsessions and insecurities than about his ostensible subject. . . .

Altogether *Valentino* is far more entertaining, moving and, yes, even illuminating (we do learn something of the problems of a male sex symbol who owes everything to women, is dominated by them and finally has his very virility challenged) than such recent yawnaramas as *Lizstomania* and *Tommy*.

Anwer Bati, "Rudi's Rudolf," in Punch *(© 1977 by Punch Publications Ltd.; all rights reserved; may not be reprinted without permission), Vol. CCLXIII, October 12, 1977, p. 670.*

GENE D. PHILLIPS

To say that Rudolph Valentino best embodies Russell's idea of a hero is not to imply that Valentino was genuinely heroic in every aspect of his life and character, but that the real-life Valentino provided Russell with the raw material out of which he could fashion a cinematic hero that approximated his concept of greatness without distorting the latter's life and character in the bargain. . . .

It may seem somewhat incongruous to compare a superstar of the primitive silent screen to composers and practitioners of other art forms which are all more exalted and sophisticated than silent movies ever were. But Russell's point seems to be that a man achieves greatness by living up to his personal code of behavior regardless of the circumstances in which he finds himself. (p. 131)

In his films Russell has often examined a problem that is endemic to all artists, regardless of their particular field of artistic endeavor: the conflict of illusion and reality in the artist's life. Because an artist devotes himself to manufacturing illusions for others, he runs the decided risk of confusing the world of illusion with which he is constantly involved with the real world in which he lives. This problem surfaces often in the present film, but is particularly evident in terms of Valentino's relationship with Natasha.

Although his screen image is that of an overwhelmingly strong-willed male, Valentino can be easily dominated by the women in his private life. Valentino seems unaware that Natasha has gradually managed to subjugate him not only in their personal relationship but by taking charge of his career as well. Perhaps because he has begun to believe in his own screen image, he refuses to believe that she has such a strong hold on him.

Russell illustrates the painful gap between reality and illusion in this instance by building a scene in which Natasha proves her power over Valentino. At the end of a day of shooting on *The Shiek,* Natasha entices Valentino into the shiek's tent on the set, where she coyly arouses his ardor and then coolly refuses his embraces. (pp. 138-39)

This portrayal of Natasha's conquest of Valentino the man is followed immediately by a scene from *The Shiek* in which Valentino the actor ravishes a helplessly passive female with all of the fiery passion and determination that was so conspicuously lacking in his foregoing real-life encounter with Natasha.

But Valentino is not alone in his inability to sort out fantasy and fact in his life. As June Mathis watches this seduction scene unreel on a movie screen, she tearfully fantasizes that it is she that is being crushed in the strong arms of the shiek. The implication is that no one in tinsel town, even the no-nonsense June Mathis, is completely free from this syndrome of mixing reality and illusion.

The Mathis sequence just described represents the only serious failure in narrative logic in the entire movie. The recollections in this part of the film are being narrated by Natasha Rambova; hence June Mathis's private fantasies about Valentino simply have no place in a flashback presented from Natasha's point of view. But this exception proves the rule that by and large Russell is careful to derive exposition in a given flashback only from the person whose memories are being depicted for the viewer at that point in the movie. (p. 139)

In discussing *Mahler* Russell made the point that, because screen time is so short, it is often necessary to say two things at once in a scene, "which is why I frequently introduce symbolism into scenes of reality." In the jail sequence Russell was indeed saying two things at once. First of all, he wished to comment on the callousness of a studio executive who would allow his biggest star to languish in a jail cell for the sake of free publicity. Secondly, the director wanted to use the scene to depict the enormous hostility which Valentino had unwittingly evoked in the American male population, which had become increasingly jealous of the sexual prowess which he exhibited on the screen. (p. 142)

As an object lesson in Russell's method of cutting across the biographical facts of a person's life to create a dramatic sequence in a biopic, it is well worth noting that he has dramatized the incidents surrounding this episode in Valentino's life into a spectacular manner which goes beyond the known facts in many details, but which nonetheless is faithful to the facts in essence. (p. 143)

Russell has mounted the prize fight so elaborately in the film in order to make it serve as an important metaphor for man's struggles in the contest of life. Valentino takes a lot of punishment in the battle of life, just as he does in the boxing ring; but he always goes down swinging and is the ultimate victor according to the standards of his venerable code of honor. Consequently, though the match which Valentino fought in real life was in private, the director had reason to orchestrate it in the grand manner which he employed in the motion picture to underline its importance to Valentino's personal honor and to his public image. (pp. 143-44)

In the film Valentino sees the boxing and drinking bouts as the twentieth-century equivalents of a traditional duel, whereby he can establish once and for all his masculinity and thus prove that he is no effeminate weakling offscreen who is unworthy to represent genuine masculinity on-screen. In making this point in the movie, however, Russell does not *ipso facto* resolve the questions surrounding Valentino's private life and personality. Russell implies but does not say for certain that Valentino was a latent homosexual whose sexual ambiguity caused the breakup of his unconsummated first marriage and left him prone to the domination of overbearing women like Natasha Rambova.

But what Russell does insist upon in his concept of Valentino is that this man was a professional artist devoted to his work, who transcended the personal problems of his private life to become one of the first legendary actors of the screen. In Russell's view, what makes a great artist is the ability to transcend one's personal inadequacies in practicing one's art; what makes a great man is the ability to transcend one's personal drawbacks in living one's life in harmony with one's principles. The Valentino who emerges from Russell's film gets high marks in both categories. (p. 144)

This, then, is the man and the artist who seems best to embody Russell's notion of a hero: someone who has more good qualities than bad and who uses the former to transcend the latter, not only to realize his artistic talent but also to mature as a human being. In creating a full-length portrait of a man and artist of this stature, Russell has in the bargain made a movie that will in time be recognized as one of his richest and warmest motion pictures. (p. 145)

Gene D. Phillips, in his Ken Russell *(copyright © 1979 by Twayne Publishers, Inc.; reprinted with the permission of Twayne Publishers, A Division of G. K. Hall & Co., Boston), Twayne, 1979, 200 p.*

Agnès Varda

1928-

French director and screenwriter.

Although her work is sometimes compared to that of her husband, filmmaker Jacques Demy, Varda is more often grouped with Alain Resnais and Chris Marker. These filmmakers are considered, along with others, the "Left Bank group," directors pursuing various experimental styles and emphasizing technique in film. Varda worked with Resnais in editing her first film, *La Pointe courte*. Resnais was hesitant to greatly alter the work Varda had done, for he saw in the film cinematic ideas which he himself intended to realize. Many critics have indeed called Varda a forerunner of the nouvelle vague (new wave) movement in film.

Varda worked on *La Pointe courte* with almost no prior experience and little formal knowledge of filmmaking. In some ways, however, she had already acquired an intuitive conception of contemporary film theory, and had definite ideas of what she wanted to accomplish with the medium. "I had the feeling . . . that the cinema was not free, above all in its form, and that annoyed me," Varda states.

She was a still photographer for the Theatre Nationale Populaire, and this experience is stylistically reflected in her films. She independently produced her first work, and was then commissioned to film three short travelogues for the French Tourist Office. The project had inherent limitations, but *O saisons, O châteaux* and *Du côté de la côte* nonetheless display the original artistic personality of their maker.

A distinguishing trait of Varda's cinematic method is her attempt to distance the viewer from characters in the film. Part of her objective with such films as *Cléo de 5 à 7* and *Le Bonheur* is to avoid establishing a relationship between the characters and the audience, so that the situation of the characters might be judged more than sympathized with. The focus on stylistic aspects in Varda's films, in addition, eclipses character and narrative content. Varda moves more toward narrative meaning and message in her recent work *Une chant et l'autre pas*. A study in feminism, the film has been termed simplistic but technically artful propaganda.

It is for her technical skill and innovation that Varda is most often praised by critics. The graceful artificiality of Varda's cinematic world adds a distinct style to contemporary film, as well as enlarging the possibilities of the art form.

FRANÇOIS TRUFFAUT

According to the advertisement—which, for once, is true to the work being promoted—[*La Pointe Courte*] is a "film essay to be read," made up of two accounts: one about a couple who have been married for four years, and another about a fishing village (La Pointe Courte, near Sète). The film doesn't try to reproduce an experience or to prove any point. It tells its stories slowly, in rhythm with the consuming, transforming passage of time, in rhythm with inexorable time, under the glow of time that is beautiful as well.

Behind the suspect simplicity of the project, a number of secret intentions are hidden, left unstated because they are almost impossible to articulate. Some might fear they bear only a distant relationship to the direction and the handling of the actors.

Since the heroine of the film is in touch only with iron, and her partner only with wood, there is an intense moment of crisis when, at a certain moment, the saw cuts into a plank of wood. That is the kind of idea—I would not have discovered this one unaided!—that recurs in *La Pointe Courte,* as images that have been a bit too carefully "framed" follow one another, accompanied by exchanges of dialogue that are straight out of the highly intellectual theater of Maurice Clavel.

It is difficult to form a judgment of a film in which the true and the false, the true-false and the false-true, are intermingled according to barely perceived rules. (pp. 308-09)

If, by the nature of its ambitions, *La Pointe Courte* joins the family of films that are *outside* cinema—*Minna de Venghel, Le Pain vivant, Huis Clos*—it is nonetheless superior to these because the result matches the director's intentions. Indeed, Agnès Varda may yet one day ask herself, and confront, the essential problems in filmmaking.

The main fault with this film, which in the end, I have not understood much better than my colleagues—those who praised it and those who did not—is that it is loosely directed. I am not speaking of the technique, which is surprisingly mature for a first film, but about the completely slack direction of the actors. The acting of Montfort and Noiret (whose resemblance to Varda is perhaps not accidental) remains uncertain. Their gestures, attitudes, looks, and tones of voice remain *deliberate and theoretical.*

At the end of this report on a film (which is itself a kind of report), I notice that I have dealt with the vehicle rather than the content. It was the best way of avoiding the ponderous remarks that this very cerebral director confidently expects. (p. 309)

François Truffaut, "Agnès Varda: 'La Pointe Courte'" (1956), in his The Films in My Life, *translated by Leonard Mayhew (copyright © 1975 by, Flammarion; translation copyright © 1978 by Simon & Schuster; reprinted by permission of Simon & Schuster, a Division of Gulf & Western Corporation; originally published as* Les films de ma vie, *Flammarion, 1975), Simon & Schuster, 1978, pp. 308-10.*

PARKER TYLER

[*L'Opéra Mouffe*] is a sensitive documentary, and, as such, "experimental" to the extent that it introduces imaginative moods into the documentary. We see lyrically, unaffectedly nude lovers; we see children playing monsters in masks; we see the pitifully old, the morally and physically misshapen. But is the method of showing these things imaginative *enough*? For one thing, it is uneven. At times, it is pretentious, arty, and banal (as in the young girl running slow-motion through a field and in the trapped dove) and at other times it simply "drifts" by adding one image statistically, rather than meaningfully, to another (as in the sequences of drunks and the people wiping their noses).... Image added to image without development or impetus is not true *montage* but picture-magazine journalism.... Technically, *L'Opéra Mouffe* is a "suite," a series of facets, but these facets possess no unifying principle either intellectual or sensuous. Supposedly, one thinks: "How human! how pitiful! how sweet! how strange! ... in brief: how lifelike!" Yet, however interesting and well-photographed in the conventional sense, the "anthology" attitude that life is an endless network of strange contradictions can never get, in terms of meaning, beyond the stage of clever reporting; it can never reach the stage of meaning that is art *as an efficient form;* it falls apart into the scattered materials of *potential* art.

Yet when, as presumably here, reporting *pretends* to be art, how undependable the reporting, as such, emerges! *L'Opéra Mouffe,* with its air of a jaunty café ballad, is deceptively "chic" and highly irresponsible in every way. The best reason for talking about it is that it represents a decided trend in way of contemporary thinking, insofar as these ways have a significant moral meaning.... The "trick" of placing lyric, exuberant, and happy images side by side with dreary, pathetic, and horrible ones is that we live in an age of special fear and tension, fed intimately by two world wars within half a century and the prospect of a third, ominously fatal, one. (p. 52)

L'Opéra Mouffe, substantially, is only a reporter's visual notebook about the backgrounds and conditions of significant human experience; it is inadequately processed studio material, playing a charade as an experimental film. (p. 53)

Parker Tyler, "New Images," in Film Quarterly *(copyright 1959 by The Regents of the University of California; reprinted by permission of the University of California Press), Vol. XII, No. 3, Spring, 1959, pp. 50-3.**

BOSLEY CROWTHER

[A] French film that fairly glitters with photographic and cinematic "style," yet fails to do more than skim the surface of a cryptic dramatic theme, is "Cleo From 5 to 7." ... Objectively, it might be favored as a fair example of the slick techniques of the French New Wave....

[The] film indicates at the outset that it is going to be a thing of fleeting moods, of casual illustration of the vagrant and fragile anxieties of a shallow girl....

Obviously, Mlle. Varda has wanted the changing scene to reflect the moods of her young woman, the encounters to counterpoint her thoughts. And, in some respects, she has succeeded, superficially but quite attractively. There are times when her girl is moving around Paris and picking up wisps of street music, or other times when she is listening to the chatter of her companions that flash little hints of haunting sorrow.

But, generally, Mlle. Varda is so absorbed with her camera stunts, as she is in that scene in the hat shop or when she is screening [a] comedy short, that the essential concentration on the heroine is neglected and the interest lost. The character becomes incidental to the techniques by which it is being explained.

Bosley Crowther, "'Cleo from 5 to 7'," in The New York Times *(© 1962 by The New York Times Company; reprinted by permission), September 5, 1962, p. 43.*

ROGER MANVELL

[*Cléo de 5 à 7*] is a film that very much depends on the extent and nature of the sympathy you can find for the particular girl with whom you are invited to spend a hundred minutes during a crucial period in her life. She has two hours to wait for the results of a medical examination which will confirm whether or not she has cancer and, if she has it, whether or not she can be saved from death.

Cléo is a vain, spoiled, revue artist at the beginning of a successful career as a popular singer.... Yet she is not altogether worthless; she is in fact still quite human, though the vanity of her life has given her neither the emotional nor the spiritual resources with which to face a period of endurance such as this. So at the point when we discover her she is pathetic and vulnerable, facing a particular test of character which any one of us might have to face at any time....

Cléo is discovering that everything that happens to her now is a heightened, almost symbolic experience. The streets that seem real and ordinary to us ... become alien and unreal to her; her lover comes and goes, but there is no human or physical contact; one of the new songs composed for her, *'Sans Toi'*, has a bitter and melancholy significance. Everything is *memento mori*....

[*Cléo de 5 à 7*] is a film of personal vision, and its strength lies in this. The structure to which Agnès Varda commits herself requires a minute by minute observation of events, and one's interest is sometimes threatened by the repetition involved in Cléo walking short distances in the streets and taking taxi and bus rides which tend to seem interminable because they literally mark time in the story and reveal nothing new. But these are small, incidental weaknesses set against the inner truth of the film as a whole. The passing characterisations are all good.... The lively Paris locations, which give constant meaning to the film, are admirably photographed. Cléo is, as it were, tethered to these streets like some sacrificial victim waiting the knife; her release from the torture of her familiar environment only comes when she goes away to the quiet park where she finds [a young soldier who is a cheerful and ironic observer of life].

But this is also a Latin film, and there are moments of cruelty and macabre shock, particularly the insistent, recurrent images of the street entertainer swallowing live frogs. But against this is the quite unsentimental humanity of Cléo's relationship with the soldier and the ambiguity of the end, when the doctor gives his enigmatic, dead-pan verdict on her future. . . .

[The film] gathers humanity as the minutes pass, and represents a considerable achievement for Agnès Varda.

Roger Manvell, "'Cleo, de 5 à 7'" (© copyright Roger Manvell 1962; reprinted with permission), in Films and Filming, *Vol. 9, No. 3, December, 1962, p. 38.*

GORDON GOW

[Agnès Varda's method in *Le Bonheur*] is the antithesis of the conventional scripted film: she has hoped that it will draw from its audience the kind of reactions she experiences herself when she looks at snapshots or at impressionist paintings: the ideas reside in the images, in the light and warmth and delicate shadows of summer, and later on in the maturity of autumn when sweaters worn by humans match the golden leaves but the idyll is modified by a chill fogging of the breath.

Happiness exists *en famille* at a picnic in the woods to celebrate Father's Day. The pictures have a gentle glow, and the careful planning of colour serves to remove us sufficiently from reality, into the small and personal world of a carpenter untouched by the social and political distractions of life around him. Placid at work amid his wood-shavings, weaving contentedly around trees in the square as he rides home on his bike, physically and emotionally fulfilled with his wife, he is not a man who must go searching for happiness. (pp. 30-1)

A minor tone-poem, [*Le Bonheur* is] about human nature and the seasons, at times almost somnolently quiet in its representation of happiness, isolated from the wider world: and in the long run about sadness as well. A brave try at making something fruitful of a wholly cinematic language; if it doesn't really work, that might be more a fault in our conditioning than in Agnès Varda's concept. It is the kind of thing that would be accepted, doubtless with cheers, as a ballet, but it intrudes a bit uncomfortably upon the hard-dying precepts of cinema as we know it.

It may be unfair to equate simplicity with carpenters, as well. One glances about for signs of deeper significance. When a television set functions unheeded in a room what are we to make of the fragment it is showing of Jean Renoir's *Le Déjeuner sur l' Herbe*? . . . [Should] we recall that the film of Renoir *fils* was a joke about the inadequacy of artificial insemination in the face of sexual humanity, and then see *Le Bonheur* as a lament for the natural urges which are inevitably undermined? Not a psychological study, Agnès Varda insists, striking again at the conditioned responses to anything resembling a triangle plot. Of course, it isn't a triangle: rather a *prolongement* of one man's happiness, which could have been resolved in several other ways, perhaps as a sophisticated jag in which the wife took a lover, or as a tear-jerker in which the children refused to accept the other woman. Agnès Varda plays it the hard way, allowing happiness to linger but in an altered form.

Her technique is intermittently provoking, but not displeasing, as she manipulates her colours with delicacy, influenced perhaps by her husband's [*Les Parapluies de Cherbourg*], matching clothes to settings and even, presumably, painting house fronts to fill the eye for a moment with one dominant hue. She fades her scenes not to black but to white or blue or red; yet nobody sings, although there is a deal of Mozart being played and somehow there is a hint of strain in this effort to show us that the story is not real but a heightened, and at the same time quietened, portrayal of nature and human nature. . . .

Despite shortcomings, *Le Bonheur* is an essential film for anyone who believes that the cinema can speak a language of its own. (p. 31)

Gordon Gow, "The New Films: 'Le Bonheur'" (© copyright Gordon Gow 1965; reprinted with permission), in Films and Filming, *Vol. 11, No. 12, September, 1965, pp. 30-1.*

ELIZABETH SUSSEX

When Resnais or Godard use a series of fragmented shots, they do it with a purpose that is visually cumulative; the whole sequence will stand for more than any one or two of its parts; style and content are inextricably linked. . . . [In *Le Bonheur*] fragmentation is simply a method of varying the presentation of a series of pretty pictures. It is style for style's sake: a symptom of all that is wrong with Varda's picture. (p. 200)

[With] every shot, reality recedes a little further from Varda's grasp. The film begins and ends with a picnic (picnics or making love or both are François's characteristic ways of being happy), and the very first scene is shot to extract, at least to some extent, a drooling response. . . . [Behind] it all there is the music of Mozart, an embarrassment of riches that, despite effective moments, rather suggests that for this purpose Michel Legrand might have been much better. The kind of happiness that one associates with a composer like Mozart has something just a little cerebral about it, which brings us to the worst aspect of Agnès Varda's film: the feeling that it is a kind of intellectual slumming.

Just as a picturesque shot of a shower of wood shavings precedes the first glimpse of the carpenter at work and sums up his happiness there, so everything in the film is exactly what it seems at first glance. These are simple people, Varda seems to be saying, who experience only simple pleasures. But the only reality that any artist can present convincingly is the reality within himself. Varda, who has somehow suppressed her sense of humour sufficiently to take a fool like François seriously, is so intent on reconstructing the appearance of happiness that the spirit of it has eluded her completely. . . . If one admired *Cléo de 5 à 7* less, one might have been prepared to like *Le Bonheur* more. (pp. 200-01)

Elizabeth Sussex, "Film Reviews: 'Le Bonheur'," in Sight and Sound *(copyright © 1965 by The British Film Institute), Vol. 34, No. 4, Autumn, 1965, pp. 200-01.*

Agnes Varda's study of marital and extramarital bliss, *Le Bonheur*, deserves a fighting chance for which it steadfastly refuses to fight. Instead of parading its virtues, which are many and varied, the film flaunts its defects, which are few but ostentatious. It is extremely easy pickings for people who delight in the destruction of fragile originality.

At first, Miss Varda seems to be trading in nothing but treacle. Her hero, a gentle young carpenter, spends a perfect Father's Day with his radiant wife and adorable children in the sunflowered sunshine of the French countryside. The scene, which might have been lifted bodily from "Picnic on the Grass," is a candid tribute to Renoir—both painter *père* and moviemaker *fils*. The family's happiness is transparently perfect, which makes it something of a bore for the onlookers, anxious to find a serpent or at least a dirty-minded cockroach in this dappled demi-Eden. . . .

But Miss Varda has tricks up her unruffled sleeves. Her studied simplicity and cool detachment are only a stylized way of showing that a man's happiness is not necessarily the same as a woman's. When the carpenter extends his candor campaign [about an extramarital affair] to his wife, she takes the news with something short of equanimity by drowning her sorrows in a stream along with herself. At this point, the husband . . . casts off his own sorrow and sets up a new ménage with his children and his uncaged-animal mistress.

The directress may be saying that life goes on, even though one-third of the triangle is unequal to the challenge of perfectly free love. She may also be saying, with irony pitched high as a dog whistle, that the damage such a man does to those who love him is incalculable, even though life may seem to go on despite it.

That she refuses to give pat answers to complex questions is all to the good. She takes a deceptively simple-seeming situation, peoples it with potentially fascinating characters and hires good actors to play the parts. . . . Then she pulls back, declining to give the audience any useful idea of what the hero is all about. The result is not the portrait of a pure spirit, or an impure spirit with pretensions to purity. It is the case history—curious, comely, refreshingly original but never really compelling—of a seeming psychopath who claims, eloquently but ambiguously, to be in love with two women, when his emotional responses are so shallow that he cannot love even one.

"Plants and Animals," in Newsweek *(copyright 1966 by Newsweek, Inc.; all rights reserved; reprinted by permission), Vol. LXVII, No. 24, June 13, 1966, p. 114.*

ROY ARMES

Drawing inspiration from William Faulkner's novel *The Wild Palms,* [Varda built *La Pointe Courte*] around the juxtaposition of two disparate themes. The first of these concerns the efforts of two young people . . . to revive their four-year-old marriage which is on the point of breaking up. . . . [In *La Pointe Courte* the] characters remain deliberately abstract, nameless and unpersonalised, and their conversation has a distinctly literary ring. One of the few weaknesses of *La Pointe Courte* is that the excessive theatricality of these two leading performances causes an unnecessary clash with the soberly handled background theme, which is concerned with the lives of the fishermen of La Pointe Courte, the village to which the couple has come. Varda shows a warm sympathy for the struggle which these people wage against poverty and the officialdom that keeps them from their traditional, but now polluted, fishing grounds; yet social problems have only a marginal interest here, as a comparison with Visconti's masterly *La Terra Trema* shows. As might be expected there is, in *La Pointe Courte,* a certain tendency to dwell on picturesque detail, and Varda's experience as a stills photographer is apparent in the way that the impact comes from the composition within a single frame rather than from a sequence of shots, but in its maintenance of a balance between the personal and the political, the theatrical and the documentary, the film fulfils to a remarkable extent the intentions and ambitions of its author. (pp. 80-1)

[*O Saisons, O Châteaux*] contains the obligatory architectural shots and historical references [of a publicity film], but Varda has sought to enliven this hackneyed material by including a number of original and satiric touches, among them a ballet by the castle gardeners, and fashion models in Jacques Heim dresses parading and posing like exotic birds in the castle courtyards. The director shows an ability to fuse contrasting material, lightly switch moods and compose beautiful shots, but there is no trace here of any depth or seriousness. (p. 81)

[*Opéra Mouffe*] is the freest of all Varda's films. . . . [It] gives a picture of the Mouffetard district of Paris, as seen through the eyes of a pregnant woman. Its range of material is wide: documentary shots, taken with a concealed camera, of the old people of this slum district shopping, gossiping, drinking; children playing in masks; images expressing symbolically the hopes, fears and preoccupations of pregnancy (gourds and doves, for instance); and some balletlike nude love scenes. There is no attempt to give a narrative link and related shots are simply grouped together under a suitable heading: "Lovers", "Pregnancy", "Drunkenness" etc. The true unity of *Opéra Mouffe* is provided by its subjective approach, the way in which the images and rhythms reflect the contradictory thoughts and feelings which dominate a woman at such a time. (p. 82)

[*Le Bonheur*] is a strange and in many ways disturbing work. For this investigation into the nature of happiness, the director has left aside as irrelevant all considerations of psychology and morality and chosen to make her hero an artisan simply to avoid social issues. We are left with something that is more of a symmetrical pattern than a plot in the conventional sense: François loves his wife and children dearly and enjoys a serenely contented home life, but this does not prevent him from falling in love with a pretty post-office clerk. When he tells his wife about this state of affairs, she commits suicide, but his happiness is preserved: after a decent interval his mistress moves in to look after him and his children and life goes on as before. The tone of *Le Bonheur* is uniformly idyllic, reinforced by the accompanying music of Mozart, and nothing could be further from realism than this make-believe world where children never cry and nobody utters an angry word. Though the characters are viewed with detachment and the whole film examines a lhilosophic notion, *Le Bonheur* is Varda's most decoratively resplendent work, showing perhaps the influence of her husband, Jacques Demy. There is an echo too of Renoir's use of landscape in *Le Déjeuner sur l'Herbe* . . . in the importance accorded to Nature: the film begins with a summer picnic which is the perfect picture of happiness and ends with an autumnal one in which the replacement of wife by mistress is the only alteration. Throughout colours are used symbolically and *Le Bonheur* remains in the memory as a film full of flowers and sunlight.

Agnes Varda, one of the few woman directors at work in the cinema today, has revealed a complex personality in the short and feature films she has made to date. She is in many ways typical of the new cinema and the exact antithesis of the "professional" director of the previous generation. Both independent and original, she is quite uncompromising in her approach and uninterested in expressing any views and insights but her own. (pp. 83-4)

Perhaps the most striking of the formal devices in Varda's films is the exploration of the possibilities of non-identification. None of her characters are fully rounded and often they are pruned of all individuality. . . . [In] *Le Bonheur* there is a total lack of psychology . . . and of concern with morality. It is this latter—the complete absence of any Christian awareness of sin—that gives the film its air of belonging to an alien age or culture. The particular relationship of audience and characters which Varda achieves in films like these is closely akin to that pursued by Resnais in all his features and by Marker in *La Jetée*. She shares too with Resnais a total detachment from her own characters, claiming, for instance, not to know whether the wife in *Le Bonheur* commits suicide or not, just as Resnais is doubtful about the outcome of *Hiroshima mon Amour*. As early as her first feature film, non-identification had been the theoretical basis of Varda's work: "I had the feeling that the spectator should remain outside, a feeling of alienation . . . I wanted to make a film where the spectator does not identify himself but, instead, judges—a cold film." It is this same desire to maintain distance that lies at the root of the formal patterns already noticed in *Cléo* and *Le Bonheur*.

The source of Agnès Varda's individuality and the sense of life and vitality one finds in her films is her training as a photographer. . . . All her films are impeccably shot, with a sharp grasp of detail and a keen interest in a documentary approach, most clearly apparent in the backgrounds of her films: the fishing village in *La Pointe Courte* and the Parisian settings of *Opéra Mouffe* and *Cléo*. She shows a great sensitivity to tiny variations of light and the atmosphere they produce (in *Cléo* for instance) and has made a bold and imaginative use of colour (in *Le Bonheur*). Despite her literary interest and tendency to abstraction Varda remains a true filmmaker whose central preoccupation is with seeing. . . . (pp. 84-5)

Roy Armes, "Agnès Varda," in his French Cinema since 1946: The Personal Style, Vol. II *(copyright © 1966 by Roy Armes), A. S. Barnes & Co., 1966, pp. 80-5.*

MAX KOZLOFF

After perhaps some initial confusion, a viewer might most profitably view Agnes Varda's *Le Bonheur* as a pastoral, in the old, even Renaissance sense of the word. Imbued with a simple gravity, nymph and shepherd enact a gracious courtship (here a self-refreshing marriage), which is yet miraculously attuned with nature. It is a genre convention as little current today as the implied vanity and death theme in Varda's earlier *Cléo de 5 à 7*. But it has the advantage of suspending the apparent implausibility of the wife's suicide in a mythic mold that would be totally unexplained in the usual narrative, or psychological context. Set in a modern Paris suburb, replete with high-rise housing projects, the picture quite magically evokes an ancient pantheism, a vegetable efflorescence, alien to tragedy. More than that, it is a celebration of all sensory pleasure, unaffected in what it depicts, yet subtle and willful in how it depicts it.

Part of the fascination here emerges in an improvised artifice that takes a bit of catching on for its comprehension. Unlike *The Umbrellas of Cherbourg* by her husband Jacques Demy, Varda's *Le Bonheur* does not announce itself as anything so hyper-stylized as operetta. The tale of a young carpenter, his wife, and the post-office girl he meets and loves—without surcease of desire or affection for the one, or guilt with the other—spins out in homely fragments. But their naturalism dissipates in the unfailing sweetness of the people involved. And though the animal bliss which is the picture's theme is leavened by domestic chores and workshop labors, none of them are connectable with care. More equivocally, while the characters often behave in accord with their ordinary stations in life—by most standards they're a rather dull lot—they sometimes unwittingly slip into a richer and more humane consciousness, as in the tersely poetic style of the husband. But this is not an oversight or pretension of the director. In her view, naiveté of utterance does not conflict with fineness of perception or capacity of response: a fact which complicates the film rather than its characters. The consistency which she imposes upon them is that of a fictional grace, running intermittently parallel rather than coincident with social morality.

That is why, when the husband misguidedly informs his wife of his affair (he can't stand lying), it is through a transcendant uxoriousness that he does so. Not being quite up to this, the wife drowns herself. That he is tremendously saddened, but neither crushed, nor prevented by his responsibility for her death from carrying on life with his mistress shortly thereafter, has raised many eyebrows. The torment he may have experienced between these two changes in his life is largely effaced. But this is surely to underline an earthly cycle of which one catches scattered glimpses; the beginning and ending of the film, the picnic in summer and autumn, delicately reiterate it. To obey that cycle which appears here almost in sonata form, is to exist considerably above, and yet below what are considered the normal claims of togetherness.

Far more insistently than the "plot," does the form of the film embody this issue. There is a Saturday night dance scene, for instance, which, in its movements, easily and inevitably enacts the psychological ritual of the pastoral. The camera oscillates from left to right of a dividing tree, and back again, complicating its lateral view of couples constantly changing partners (especially the husband, with wife and mistress) by regular shifts from near to far focus. Such a pan shot acts, not so much to convey the rhythms and gestures of bodies, as it does a larger dance of life. With a remarkable liquidity and impartiality, the lens switches depth of field and less noticeably, light and dark. Though obviously drawing attention to itself, it is an effect far more musical than gratuitous. One sees a charming spatial pingpong, punctuated by the bouncing motions of dancers, and the in-and-out of optical definition: all very gay, and impersonal. (pp. 35-6)

Between certain shots . . . Varda will flood the screen with a quick, unitary color chord that fades a trifle slowly at the dissolve. Such is the scarlet introduction to a group of shots, spotted with russets, and ending with a ruddy sunset. Immediately afterwards, a May green rinses out the red, and acts as a prelude for a new sequence. It is an explosion, then gradual fading or decaying of color, reminiscent of Bonnard. . . . Then too, there are various color accents made by passing trucks, or someone's sweater, that hover, or so it seems, between the composed and accidental. Never do they blanch a scene with obvious symbolism, as in Antonioni's *Red Desert,* or shamelessly decorate it, as in *The Umbrellas of Cherbourg.* With Varda, color can be used expressively, as in the contrast between the comfortable warm tones in the love scenes of husband and wife, and the cool, whiter ones of those of the husband and his mistress. And the many floral bouquets that flounce through countless shots are a kind of leitmotiv of the whole picture. But as a rule, color is a more or less tangible rhythmic element that inflects people's lives, sometimes by nothing more than variously delightful flesh-tinting patterns. (p. 36)

[In *Le Bonheur* there] are unexpected, almost subliminal jumps in continuity that convey snippets of a character's state of mind. A flirtatious young woman suddenly images herself playfully entwined with the man whose invitation for a stroll she has just accepted. Crouched over the drowned body of his wife, the husband pathetically "sees" her white arm going underwater. These touches are all the more poignant because seemingly involuntary. There has occurred a switch from external recording to a picturing of feeling—without characterization, or even severe dislocation. And this device is not a flashback so much as it is a fantasy inset, related to the differentiated consciousness pioneered more radically by Resnais in *Marienbad* and *Muriel.* Varda gives us little footnotes, or rather hypotheses about future and past—all the more radiant because frustratingly brief.

Yet here she will not go so far as her confrères in providing whole alternate constructions to an increasingly fragmented line. With Godard or Resnais, both quite influential on Varda in the recent past, inversion and false parallelism of incidents are not merely tokens of conceptual stress, but confessions of ambivalence that have found their way towards a quite widespread recreation of film form. Character and memory, as a result, precipitate into an opaque, troubling new compound. In the mixing of tenses, from which their characters suffer, history becomes an organism so confused as to weigh down emotion and stifle communication. By contrast, the people in *Le Bonheur* experience no crisis of identification whatsoever, but exist just as characteristically *outside* history. It is an eirenic vision Varda purveys, in which forgetfulness merges with regeneration. By siphoning off conflict into her lyric envelope, she is not so much interested in eliciting one's sympathy, as she is in offering a provisional resolution to the psychological questions raised earlier in the cinema around her. For if these characters feel gratification, and find happiness, it is largely in the context of a fairy tale. It is significant that she owes a debt to Truffaut here, especially the Truffaut who, in the warmth of his sensuous responses, was carrying on a tradition initiated by Jean Renoir. . . . Less earthy than Renoir, Varda with her rococo symmetries is also more disconcerting. In place of an older humanism, she gives a mechanistic view, undecoded, yet lovely. (pp. 36-7)

Max Kozloff, "Film Reviews: 'Le Bonheur'," in Film Quarterly *(copyright 1966 by The Regents of the University of California; reprinted by permission of the University of California Press), Vol. XX, No. 2, Winter, 1966-67, pp. 35-7.*

[At first glance Agnès Varda's work and her husband's, Jacques Demy,] seem totally different. While he conjures up pastel never-never lands, she broods over such weighty matters as morality, predestination and the nature of reality. But husband and wife do have in common two uncommon traits: the ability to reduce everything to playground platitudes and a stylistic pomposity that serves only to accent the vacuity of their scripts. In *Les Créatures* . . . [Varda] has fashioned a kind of portrait of the artist in finger paints, a childish and often embarrassing attempt to render life as the ultimate fiction.

The plot is the sort of thing that gives science fiction a bad name. A writer . . . and his mute wife . . . live in an abandoned fort on the coast of Brittany. She is pregnant; he is trying to write. . . . The writer's story becomes the film's own plot; illusion and reality are inextricably and ever so modishly mixed. With the bad guy getting killed, the baby getting born, and the wife regaining her voice, there is even a happy ending. . . .

Madame Demy has an unerring instinct for the stylishly avant-garde. She photographed *Les Créatures* as if it were a *Vogue* layout, and edited it elliptically. She even tinted the fantasy scenes to avoid confusion: red for those influenced by the mad engineer at his game board, a benign pink for the writer-hero. The trouble is that she seems to take the hero's fantasy as seriously as he does. As in her other films (*Cleo from 5 to 7, Le Bonheur*), she mistakes pulp for pith and winds up only with pretension.

". . . And Hers," in Time *(reprinted by permission from* Time, The Weekly Newsmagazine; *copyright Time Inc. 1969), Vol. 93, No. 11, March 14, 1969, p. 99.*

JONATHAN HOOPS

[*Lions Love* must be counted among] film weirdities. Agnes Varda abandons the sureties of the conventional film (like *Le Bonheur*) for what tries to be new, liberated, and honest and nearly succeeds. Story-telling is out: each scene connects to what has gone before as its significance unfolds in the viewer's mind—no plot guides us. The point is to enjoy what is at hand, as in *Cleo from 5 to 7.* No other choice except nonenjoyment or suicide exists for the three main characters, Viva, Jerome Ragni, and James Rado, who live in a rented house (metaphysical note: as the soul is said to do in the body) in Hollywood and wait for stardom (read "immortality," i.e., death). It should be clear that Varda intends something serious, a philosophy underlying all her films. Unfortunately, she flops. The film mixes contrivance (heavy directional hand) and spontaneity (underground "instant movies") with a result sometimes charming, but more often phony or confusing. For example, a terrible falseness pervades the argument with a Hollywood mogul over rights to the final cut of a film in the making by Shirley Clarke [who plays the lead character] who has happened into the life of our three lions. . . . *Lions Love* has a strong inclination toward the New York underground film, and the viewer's reaction will be determined largely by either an assumption that the underground deviates from or that it advances toward some desirable cinematic goal. Let's take choice two and give Varda credit despite *faux pas.* An Establishment film maker who recognizes the underground makes history, if not art. This aesthetic failure is a product of the director's confused intentions. The tension between spontaneity (never in full bloom until the last shot) and contrivance never satisfactorily resolves. With great courage and insufficient forethought Agnes Varda throws herself into strange waters where she struggles to appear composed while grasping desperately at the flotsam and jetsam of the wreck of the traditional film she has abandoned. (pp. 60-1)

Jonathan Hoops, "Short Notices: 'Lions Love'," in Film Quarterly *(copyright 1970 by The Regents of the University of California; reprinted by permission of the University of California Press), Vol. XXIII, No. 4, Summer, 1970, pp. 60-1.*

SUE LERMON

Some may feel that [*Daguerreotypes*] is too claustrophobic in its form, in its photography, and in its approach to the content, that more controversial issues should have been raised for discussion, that this section of the so-called silent majority might have been given a greater opportunity to condemn itself in the eyes of a sophisticated and radical audience, and that more of modern Paris might have been provided as a context. It would have been interesting, particularly for an English viewer, for whom much that was shown is already virtually of a bygone era, to have known how much such ways of life are in jeopardy and what kinds of danger are foreseen by the Daguerreotypes themselves. After all, the development around the tour Montparnasse is creeping none too slowly up the Avenue de Maine in their direction. But it is possibly because the film guarded its intimacy and because it did not inquire into sensitive matters that it held the confidence of its subjects, so that they relaxed and, paradoxically, gave more of themselves. . . .

If *Daguerreotypes* owes some of its attraction to its location with its unexpectednesses and eccentricities, it owes much more to perceptive direction and an eye for the details that make up people's minute to minute lives—things that can be found wherever people are living and working—and to a hesitancy to draw conclusions, to underline points uncovered, with its consequent avoidance of condescension and snap judgments. Interpretation is up to the spectator.

Sue Lermon, "How Do They Live?," in The Times Educational Supplement *(© Times Newspapers Ltd. (London) 1976; reproduced from* The Times Educational Supplement *by permission), No. 3162, January 9, 1976, p. 20.*

PAULINE KAEL

["Une chant et l'autre pas" or "One Sings, the Other Doesn't"] is all up front. It's a cheery, educational feminism-can-be-fun movie. Pomme and her combo tour provincial towns, performing songs with lyrics . . . such as "I'm neither a tough cookie nor a busy beaver nor a utopian dreamer—I'm a woman, I am me." Decked out in harlequin colors that suggest a French child's dream of what Haight-Ashbury was like, they chant "My Body Is Mine." Singing about the joys of pregnancy when it's "your choice and your pleasure," they wear pillows stuffed inside their long dresses—"It's beautiful to be a balloon." When these bubble dollies send actual balloons into the sky or sing about the "ovules," Varda brings a Disney touch to women's liberation. The sunshiny, masscult-hip simplicity of the feminist movement celebrated here is so laughable you can't hate the picture. You just feel that some of your brain cells have been knocked out.

Visually, the film has the glamorous real-unreal quality of the new feminine-hygiene ads—muted realism. Happiness here is a flower-print dress on a summer day in the country. The appeal of the film is of life seen as sensuous banality, in a pretty pastoral flow. Pomme has the look of an Auguste Renoir model with a bad dye job: a cherub with the frizzies. There's unforced charm in her complacent impudence. But she belts out her songs in a brass-lunged style, and she has a brute quality: her mind, like her lyrics, is a grab bag of feminist slogans. She swings ideas around like a baton twirler, and it's difficult to appreciate a struggle for self-expression which results in songs of the quality of hers. Pomme's middle-class hippie rebelliousness is contrasted with Suzanne's slow, hard-won self-education. Suzanne—reserved to the point of inexpressiveness—is a dimly performed, wan, Madonna-like character whose life seems to fit a traditional pattern. Circumstances force her to push beyond her youthful, Little Match Girl submissiveness, and she rises into the middle class, brings up her children with scrupulous devotion, and achieves the Sheila Levine goal: a doctor husband who loves her; i.e., what used to be called happiness and is now fulfillment.

The only real difference between Suzanne's life and the lives of countless poor, put-upon heroines of fiction who rose by their bootstraps is how colorless and humorless her fine doctor is. That's true of Pomme's Iranian, too; when you hear that he's an economist, you think there's been a mistake—he seems too vague to have acquired any skills. The men in the movie are shaded out. Varda doesn't appear to be antagonistic toward men; she just has no particular interest in them. The purpose of sex in this movie seems to be to have an abortion. That's the real high. Abortion is the new rite of passage, to be reported to one's friends with sad pride. Men are welcome in this balloons-and-sunshine land of the future. They're still needed to provide the plump, gurgling, freely chosen babies. Choice is what's important; the same women who choose abortion then choose pregnancy. There's no psychology in this movie—only sociology. The feminism here is a new form of asexual lyricism.

"One Sings" isn't sentimental in the manipulative manner of commercial movies. On the contrary, there's a whimsical randomness in Varda's approach. At times, as in the early sequence of Pomme's posing for Suzanne's photographer lover, the effect is so fresh it almost seems like luck. . . . [In "One Sings"] the skin-deep characters don't involve us in their predicaments. They don't seem to have any consciousness—they're just part of the traffic [Varda's] directing. Though we're told that this movie is about how these two women grow, that's exactly what we don't see. There are no perceptible connections between the two heroines, or between them and their parents or their lovers or their children. The way Varda skims over their lives, they could be butterflies or duckies. In Varda's earlier films ("Le Bonheur" especially), the shallowness was sometimes redeemed by physicality; she gave a special tactile feeling to bodies, fabrics, landscapes. It was possible to believe that the characters in "Le Bonheur," as in her "Cleo from 5 to 7," were made deliberately vapid, and so a viewer could get the impression that something complex and elusive was being suggested, even if one couldn't locate it. This time, there's nothing enigmatic about Varda's tone. When Pomme, who treats children as toys for adults, comes up with her solution—to trade off one baby and keep the next—we're meant to think she's sensible. In the terms of this movie, she *is:* her idyll works. . . . Agnès Varda is perfectly candid; everything is as practical and simple as Pomme's approach to maternity. Varda is proud of Pomme's and Suzanne's accomplishments in becoming women. (In this film, being a woman isn't a fact, it's a profession.) Yet experience has no weight in "One Sings"; there are no women in it—only girls. Its vision of the future is of a frolicsome adolescent matriarchy. One cannot accuse Varda of jumping on a bandwagon: her films have always had a sympathetic responsiveness to the women characters, and a polymorphous affection for them. This seems to have become drippier, though, now that she's officially expressing the new awareness, and commenting on the heroines with "Then she had time to cry" or "She went on singing, changing."

Varda's lyricism is trivializing. If there were twenty seconds of footage of an actual abortion in the movie, Pomme's chirrupy songs would be chilling. It seems never to have occurred to Varda that her characters have no depth—that they're amoebic in the way they react to stimuli. She's a lively, sophisticated film technician who thinks that this ode to superficiality is poetic truth. If a big American advertising agency had been given the job of devising a feminist film to offend the smallest number of people, this mindless, cosmetic movie is exactly what it would have come up with. Charming young girls setting their belligerent jaws and singing about their ovules. (pp. 75-8)

Pauline Kael, "Scrambled Eggs," in The New Yorker *(© 1977 by The New Yorker Magazine, Inc.), Vol. LIII, No. 39, November 14, 1977, pp. 75-8.*

JUDITH THURMAN

So much life is looked at in ["One Sings, the Other Doesn't"] that it has a certain old-fashioned and well-furnished vastness, like that of a family saga. It is, however, an extended family of women friends and children. Men are not excluded and they are not unimportant, but they are peripheral to the action. And this is neither inaccurate nor unfair. How many of our fathers have actively been there? (p. 26)

There is a spareness and lightness to Varda's decisions about her images which keep the melodrama contained to particular moments, balanced by dailiness and irony. She narrates the story herself in a quiet, editorial voice, and this makes it possible to read the film with a certain distance, to perceive Varda's captions, to see it as a work of imaginative criticism rather than pure fiction.

"One Sings, the Other Doesn't" is also a very clear and valuable account of a certain period. The two personal stories are in turn braided around a third strand—women's history between 1962 and 1977. Both women demonstrate for abortion at Bobigny. Apple [or Pomme] brings her feminist café-theater to the squares of provincial villages. Suzanne and the women factory and farm workers at her clinic have a political and sexual consciousness-raising group, and Varda, who shot the scenes in a real clinic, with "real" women, uses them to pose questions critical to her own narrative.

I felt at times that certain problems and impasses, personal and historical, had been simplified in the film and others passed over. But the strength and passion of the work lie in its refusal to wrap up these lives, to make a conclusive, celluloid package of their contradictions. Varda has had the confidence as an artist and the honesty as a woman to leave them unresolved. (pp. 26, 28)

Judith Thurman, "'One Sings, the Other Doesn't': Leaving the Loose Ends Intact," in Ms. *(© 1978 Ms. Magazine Corp.), Vol. VI, No. 7, January, 1978, pp. 26, 28.*

MARK ABLEY

[*One Sings, the Other Doesn't* is] full of virtues and empty of life. With a plot thicker than *The Edge of Night,* with stylish acting and memorable images, *One Sings, the Other Doesn't* sinks under the weight of its worthiness. (pp. 69-70)

There are some things Varda cares passionately about, notably a woman's right to abortion: When Pomme and Susanne meet after a long separation, it's at a pro-abortion rally where Pomme sings *Mon corps, c'est à moi*. But the movie is so cool and passive that you long for any sort of passion. If it lacks the stridency of a Lina Wertmüller movie, it also lacks the risk and flamboyance that made *Swept Away* or *Seven Beauties* compulsively watchable.

One Sings is unusually perceptive about children and friendship. And it's laden with telling moments such as Suzanne, forbidden from typing in her father's house, blowing on her freezing fingers as she learns to type in a shed, surrounded by cows. But the moments don't connect; there's no drive or fire. The music should have helped, only Mairesse is a woeful singer and Varda a dire lyricist. The real failure of this movie is that it doesn't make us care. It ends in a flush of sweetness and light; the New Wave is pumping old water onto familiar shores. (p. 70)

Mark Abley, "Fear of Flying beyond Feminism," in Maclean's Magazine *(© 1978 by* Maclean's Magazine; *reprinted by permission), Vol. 91, No. 28, November 20, 1978, pp. 69-70.*

Luchino Visconti

1906-1976

Italian film and stage director.

Visconti's international reputation was established with his first film, *Ossesione,* and despite a relatively small oeuvre, he has remained a major figure in Italian cinema. Of central importance to Visconti's early development as a filmmaker was his association with Jean Renoir, under whose tutelage he became involved with French film production and at whose suggestion he directed *Ossessione*. It is considered a masterpiece of Italian neorealistic cinema, characterized by a naturalistic, documentary approach. Visconti was born of an aristocratic Italian family, yet he early became a communist, and his concern with social and political values is manifested in his neorealist approach. In their desire to achieve *verisimo,* or verisimilitude in their films, the Italian neorealists sought to portray characters exploited by an unremitting social system.

It was in his next film, *La Terra Trema,* that Visconti most fully realized the neorealistic potential of his subject. Based on a novel by the nineteenth-century Sicilian novelist, Giovanni Verga, the film portrays the life of an Italian fisherman, a victim of the static social and economic system that perpetuates his poverty and hopeless existence. His next film, *Bellisima,* bears the influence of the neorealist school as well, but in its depiction of a young woman torn by the economic demands of a working class existence and her eventual capitulation to a life devoid of moral values, Visconti discovered what were to become major themes in his work: the disintegration of moral values and the struggle between one's sensual, passionate nature and one's spiritual character. Increasingly in the films that follow *Bellisima,* Visconti portrays a society in a state of decadence: the baroque splendors of his settings often betray the emptiness and hopelessness of human relationships, as well as the disintegration of European social structure.

Visconti's acknowledged indebtedness to the German romantic tradition is also mirrored in his themes of corruption and decadence. This influence was first evidenced in *Le Notti Bianche,* adapted from the novel *White Nights* by Dostoevsky. Many critics reacted with scorn to Visconti's romantic handling of his subject, and the film indeed signalled a further departure from his neorealist origins. This tendency was also demonstrated by Visconti's continued work in the theater, particularly in opera. His films took on an increasing visual lushness and opulence. It is apparent in *Il Gattopardo, Vaghe Stelle d'Orso,* and *La Caduti degli Dei,* and reaches its apex in his film version of Thomas Mann's *Death in Venice, Morte a Venezia*. This film brought together all of Visconti's essential themes: the destructive nature of passion, the fin-de-siècle malaise of Europe on the verge of a cataclysmic war, and the concerns of an artist mired in the decadence of his age. *Morte a Venezia* marks the evolution of Visconti's cinematic technique as well. The early films with their documentary style strove for a veristic portrayal of human beings whose fate was determined by their social and economic milieu. *Morte a Venzia,* with its elaborate, exaggerated cinematic sense, confirmed Visconti's turn from social to personal, and from simple to ornate cinematic structure. (See also *Contemporary Authors,* Vols. 81-84; obituary, Vols. 65-68.)

ALAIN TANNER

With *La Terra Trema,* Visconti developed the neo-realist approach to a dramatic subject in its most extreme form: the players, the lines they speak, the places they live in, the whole social background and motivation, depart hardly at all from reality. . . .

The basis of the story is Giovanni Verga's novel *I Malavoglia*—and Visconti's film remains surprisingly true to the letter of this original, however far it departs from it in spirit. *I Malavoglia* is a detailed and sombre study of the ruin of a family of fishermen, the disasters brought about by their own maladroit attempts to better their condition. "This sincere and dispassionate study", as Verga described it in his preface, seems to have been an end in itself for the novelist. He gives the reader a picture of a certain kind of life, but he is not concerned with suggesting solutions to the problems he raises. Many of the characters and situations of the film, as well as some of the dialogue and some passages in the Italian commentary, come directly from the novel, whose action is also set in the village of Trezza. But in Visconti's film all these elements serve another purpose. The artist is no longer content with the role of the objective, dispassionate observer: rather, he organises the facts of the situation for his own purpose, giving them their central place in his thesis.

Three quarters of a century separate the characters of *I Malavoglia* from the Valastro family of Visconti's film, and the two works in themselves sum up a period of historical change. Fatalism has given way to a struggle whose ends and means can now be clearly defined. The clearest example of this passage of time, from naturalism to neo-realism, can be found in the shift in the central character (in the novel it is the father, in the film the young nephew) and in the very different attitude he takes. The grandfather, who in the film symbolises the past, is an authentic Verga character. He is all for accepting things as they are; he represents a kind of antiquated "wisdom"; he talks only in proverbs which sound false and meaningless to his young relations. . . .

'Ntoni, the film's hero, is essentially a character developed by Visconti. He is the first to understand the methods of the dealers in the fish market, to realise just how the fishermen are being exploited by these middlemen. Though he makes only clumsy efforts to break the economic stranglehold, though his revolt ends in failure, it would be wrong to regard the film's conclusion as a wholly pessimistic one. *La Terra Trema* is not just the story of a defeat, but of the lessons learnt from defeat; and if 'Ntoni's ultimate victory has no place within the framework of the film, it is because Visconti has been careful not to anticipate events. 'Ntoni knows why he has failed, as his final dialogue with the little girls makes apparent: he sees clearly what is at stake. . . . (p. 214)

[The script] defines a pattern of interlocking social and economic forces which set a series of events in motion: once this process is started, the wheels turn automatically, the dramatic devices merely accelerating the working of the machinery. Once the characters and initial situation are established—'Ntoni's revolt, the setting up of the family business, its failure after the storm—the other disasters that strike the Valastros all follow logically and inevitably. The family's slow disintegration is not something imaginatively plotted by the screen-writer; instead, it results from a close analysis of the way in which a society, in a given set of circumstances, will reject those who try to resist its laws. (p. 215)

[The] script owes more to dialectic—to, it could be said, dialectical materialism—than to the working of imagination. It is an object lesson, even if superficially it seems an object lesson in failure. It is not surprising to learn that such a script was composed on the spot, day by day. As Visconti has himself said, it would have been preposterous to write these dialogues in a Roman drawing-room; and, at the same time, only deep and direct knowledge of the subject could make such a narrative feasible.

The film's characters, as a result, have nothing extraordinary about them. That they are put to the service of a particular thesis does not detract from their truth, nor the verisimilitude of what happens to them. They are, essentially, types representative of the society that has created them. (pp. 215-16)

[Visconti] developed neo-realist methods to their extreme limits. The same characteristic appears in the actual technique of the film, at least in the particular rhythm he has given it. This extreme slowness is not simply something designed to give the picture its special grandeur, its almost majestic pace. It may in the end achieve this effect, but its primary purpose is uncompromisingly to re-create the movement of life itself, to give to even the slightest gesture its proper duration and so its due significance and meaning. It should not be deduced from this, however, that the style of the film is a documentary one. *La Terra Trema* is not simply a fictionalised documentary on the lives of Sicilian fishermen. Its slow pacing, which permits it to explore situations so thoroughly, also serves a dramatic demand. . . .

Visconti, obviously enough, is not concerned only with the daily life of the village but with the moral and social situation of the people of Trezza. The actual work of fishing, for instance, is only suggested; the return of the men, coming back exhausted to their homes or going to the fish market to see what becomes of the fruits of their labour, is described at length. Similarly, when the Valastros and their friends salt their own fish for the first time, the emphasis is on their delight and triumph rather than the work itself.

This method of allowing actions to develop at their natural pace, rather than breaking them up for reconstruction in the cutting room, also indicates the director's steady control over the feelings he wants to express. He never allows emotion to take a free hand; he rejects the tactics by which the cinema habitually magnifies emotion, the underlining through a sharp editing technique. Sentimentality is rigorously excluded, and the film consistently addresses itself to the mind rather than the heart. (This, incidentally, is particularly noticeable in the treatment of the dealers, the exploiters, where the characterisation is wholly free from hatred.) Visconti is not here presenting an impassioned anecdote: he is painting a social fresco on a grand scale. The passion is there, certainly, but it is in the idea rather than its expression, and if the film seems detached it is simply because Visconti has taken that step backwards which enables the artist to see his subject in a true perspective. . . .

Without insisting on the technical skill needed to achieve such depth of focus within the confining walls of the little houses, or the takes lasting several minutes with complex camera movements in three directions, it is important to note that every shot is so designed as to extract the maximum value from its subject. Through this precise, direct composition, the whole setting comes to life for us. . . . The whole film vibrates with life, and in this sense Visconti makes positive his own statement: "The cinema that interests me is the anthropomorphic cinema". . . .

Visconti did not want merely to use nonprofessional players: he wanted his film to be acted by the fishermen of Trezza themselves. The distinction is between the usual method of using amateurs, mainly with the object of "deglamorising" the actor, and a method closer to that of documentary. Here again, though, the handling of the actors falls into line with the whole approach of the film: the transition is from pure realism to the most conscious stylistic refinement. (p. 216)

La Terra Trema's claim to greatness finally lies in its wonderful integration of form and content. Its theme, the lesson that experience teaches 'Ntoni, is grafted on to reality, and finds in reality its actual and historical justification. The form of the film is wholly directed towards the exaltation of man, of his pride and courage. The faces and everyday objects, for which Visconti finds so exact a place in the structure of his scenes, are there because of the value he attaches to them. The emotion that he so carefully restrains runs strongly beneath the surface of the action: it is only on leaving the cinema that we realise how deeply we have been moved. And the marvellous face of 'Ntoni reflects the desire to live, and to live justly, that is the essential spirit of the film. He is one of those characters who illuminate the history of the cinema. (p. 223)

Alain Tanner, "Rediscovery (2): 'La terra trema'," in Sight and Sound *(copyright © 1957 by The British Film Institute), Vol. 26, No. 4, Spring, 1957, pp. 213-16, 223.*

PETER JOHN DYER

When great directors consciously set out to create masterpieces, it always seems to end badly. The result is lifeless and remote, and often a throw-back to some old abandoned manner. . . . It has now happened to Luchino Visconti in *Notti Bianche*. . . . (p. 249)

This *conte,* for it is little more, survives only as a basis for an uneasy attempt—in aesthetic rather than human terms—to fuse a new, enclosed, and formal *mise en scène* with an old, irrevocably lost nostalgia. Exquisite in gesture, marooned in time, *Notti Bianche* has had a great number of the most studied simplicities and elaborate fabrications of the pre-1925 *avant-garde* lavished upon it. . . . In its stylised, artificial settings, its consistently beautiful camerawork and effects of chiaroscuro; its arabesques of movement; its emotional bric-a-brac and abstract, idealised passions; above all in its disenchanted expression of the illusory nature of love—*Notti Bianche* is a ghost from the past. . . .

After the themes of sexual fever, corruption, and fatality in *Ossessione* and *Senso,* this present exercise in "neo-romanticism" seems a natural enough development, if one bears in mind the hints of formalism and abstraction in Visconti's "neo-realism", as well as the pretty safe generalisation that the cinema's preoccupation with *le destin* and decay has never been more than one flight up from decadent cinema. *Notti Bianche* is decadent, and yet it could only have been made by a master. It moves slowly, but with complete exterior conviction. Visually it is an astonishing essay in black-and-white composition and architectural unity. . . . But within this assured, meticulous framework, the characters remain elusive symbols, part-real, part-dream, some eccentric, some capricious, their feelings intellectualised and their actions predestined. (p. 250)

Peter John Dyer, "Film Reviews: 'Notti bianche'," in Sight and Sound *(copyright © 1958 by The British Film Institute), Vol. 27, No. 5, Summer, 1958, pp. 249-50.*

GIANFRANCO POGGI

Visconti's search is not for novelties or "effects," and it does not occasion improvisations. Visconti's real concern is with the theme and style of his pictures, rather than with a display of cinematic prowess. "Neorealism," he once remarked, "is first and foremost a question of content, and that's what matters." His camerawork is generally sober, his cutting measured and harmonious. The tensions of his films are usually "inside the shot." In the rock 'n' roll sequence in *Le Notti Bianche,* for instance, the emotional and rhythmic impact of a very fast montage sequence is created by a perfectly static and very long take—in which the feeling of frenetic cutting is given by the whirling heads of the dancing couple which appear and reappear in big close-up. The quality of the photography in all of Visconti's films has been superb but unobtrusive, and cost him endless hours of meditation.

Visconti's concern with the narrative aspects of his films is a somewhat unusual trait in the context of the postwar Italian film. The tenor of neorealism has been to reject a primary concern with the story, at least with the contriving of a self-contained "plot." According to Cesare Zavattini, the ideal neorealist movie would be shot by an unseen camera on a street corner like any other, on a day like any other; it would not be a structure which builds up and then resolves itself, but a series of logically and chronologically connected episodes. (pp. 12-13)

By contrast, Visconti's films have been conceived as "historical" constructs: a line of events develops with a coherent logic toward a destiny, a dénouement. (p. 13)

In *Ossessione,* made in 1942-43, Visconti undertook to tell a story of sensual love and crime derived from James Cain's novel [*The Postman Always Rings Twice*] but set in the flatlands around the Po River in contemporary Italy. . . . In Visconti's treatment Cain's cynicism and violence were toned down; sensual passion, greed, human alienation, isolation, and guilt were brought to the foreground.

Three features stand out in *Ossessione.* One was the unusually frank treatment of sex in the relationship between the two protagonists. This was one of the reasons, together with the general turmoil that was sweeping the country, and objections of the censors to the movie's pessimistic, defeatist mood and political undertones, why *Ossessione* never made the normal distribution circuits in Italy. A second feature is the unprecedented formal care the director had given to all aspects of his job: photography, acting, settings, camerawork. . . . The final and critical feature of *Ossessione* was its new, vital, uncontrived and anti-rhetorical approach, which has made critics consider it a precursor of neorealism.

The break of *Ossessione* with the white-telephone manner which then dominated the "contact" of the film with the reality of contemporary Italian society could not be more complete. In an almost violent way, *Ossessione* really reestablished such contact—with bitter contempt for the fictional, utterly false way in which that reality had been so far avoided rather than sought. The heat and the sounds and the dust of the Po flatland; the drabness, the disorder of the house interiors, of the rooms for rent; the unkemptness in the train's third-class cars; the vulgar loudness of the local festivals and singing contests; the tired pace of life in this setting, the greed and the possessiveness of the people's life in it: all these traits of the bare everyday reality of a fairly typical corner of his country Visconti perceived with pitiless sharpness. (p. 14)

On the basis of Visconti's unmistakable success in making the film medium "meet the reality of the country" arose the misconception of *Ossessione* as a neorealist movie. The break with the pre-neorealist Italian film is indeed neat and full. . . . Perhaps the conditions for Visconti's taking that direction simply were not there; the rejuvenating experience of the Resistance, for instance, which Visconti was to live through later, was not yet a source of inspiration and of hope in the years when he made *Ossessione.* Whatever this or other factors—such as the oppressive political climate of dying Fascism—the basic approach of *Ossessione* was reminiscent of prewar French director Carné: not in dialogue, certainly, but in a certain calculation and formality. . . .

For one thing, there is none of the keen awareness of the historical, time-bound dimensions of the "human situations" found in the great neorealist films. For all the naturalism of its "geographic," "spatial" details, *Ossessione* could as well have been situated in another historical epoch.

Again, in the neorealist masterworks the characters derive their motivations, the logic and direction of their action from being construed as socially motivated, as members of historically conditioned and differentiated social groups. . . . But the protagonist of *Ossessione* is a marginal man, uprooted from his social *couche,* evolving his action only from a keenly idiosyncratic kernel of motivations and meanings. Also marginal is the only other character for whom Visconti feels any sympathy (he has hardly any for the woman, as is mostly the case in his pictures): a wandering actor called "lo Spagnolo," who bears some resemblance to Fellini's "Fool" in *La Strada.* But where as Fellini quite explicitly uses the Fool as a mythical semi-angelic figure, Visconti claimed for "lo Spagnolo" a full reality, but in utter contempt for what was going to be the central canon of the neorealistic conception of the character: its construction and development in terms of an identification with a wider, collective consciousness. (p. 15)

With *La Terra Trema* [1948] Visconti vigorously and unmistakably joined forces with [the neorealist movement] and posed his candidature to creative leadership in it.

Indeed *La Terra Trema,* a picture about a fishermen's village in Sicily, was designed from the beginning with an almost paradigmatic faithfulness to some of the expressed or unexpressed "canons" of neorealism. Apparently Visconti thought of it initially as a documentary—and this early inspiration has left unmistakable marks on the style of the film. . . . Even when that initial design changed into that of a "social epic," . . . Visconti stuck to methods which neorealism had in turn taken from the documentarist tradition. . . . Since "in Sicily Italian is not the language of the poor" his neorealist orthodoxy led him to put the dialogues exclusively in the local dialect. . . . The dialogues themselves were the actors' own phrasing, after Visconti had told them what the broad meaning of the line would have to be. The nature and content of the *story,* then, were meant to build into the picture that historical and collective awareness which had largely been missing in *Ossessione.* The social relationships of the fishermen to the fishmerchants were made the substance of the story, and each of the characters lived it as rooted in his socially determined condition. (pp. 15-16)

La Terra Trema is an almost completely successful work. It is a monumental picture, which inspires a feeling of awe. It brings to the screen, in images of splendid plastic beauty, the fullness of life of the village, the bitterness and the elation of its ever-repeated struggle with the sea. [Robert] Flaherty himself, in *Man of Aran,* hardly surpassed the mute sense of tragedy which Visconti gives to the waiting of the women after a storm. The social relationships whose pressure upon the fishermen Visconti wanted to reveal are made vivid in the scene of the market, where the camera finds its way on a track amid the voices and sounds of the crowd, to watch the transactions between the fishermen and the merchants. The fullness of these contacts with reality is possibly unparalled in Italian neorealism, with the exception perhaps of the last episode of *Paisà.* What is lacking is rather a feeling of *participation:* that alive, felt participation which makes DeSica virbrate along with the action in *Bicycle Thief,* and takes the spectator as he watches the scene of the maid in the kitchen in *Umberto D.* This is not to be found in *La Terra Trema.* It is not that Visconti only *watches* the action develop: on the contrary, he always construes it, step by step, and guides it unerringly toward its consummation. But his presence is always *mediate,* never *immediate.* Either a substantial "extraneity" to the drama itself, which Visconti may have felt in spite of himself, or an overwhelming preoccupation with the formal-stylistical job of making the movie (a preoccupation which was largely successful, of which Visconti was quite aware, and which he did not mind), or perhaps both these factors, make *La Terra Trema* a monumental picture which somehow does not get its message across. . . .

The story, the cast, the stylistic key of [*Bellisima* (1951)] (one without the arduous expressive flights of some parts of *La Terra Trema*) appeared to express a desire to play it safe, to make [the film] into a popular picture in rather a different sense from that of *La Terra Trema.* But it would be a mistake to infer that Visconti had simply thrown in the sponge, as so many actual or would-be movie creators have had to do at some time in their career. . . . Actually Visconti's ambitions had simply become more covert and more subtle. (p. 17)

[He] produced a splendid portrait of the protagonist, Maddalena, but he did not overcharge the figure with sympathy and stood somewhat aloof from her. . . . Visconti looked at Maddalena's own world, her Roman working-class milieu, with a sharp and perceiving eye: he dissected pitilessly its daily miseries and its occasional attempts at evasion: the big meals *all'aperto,* the soccer game, the unrealizable dream of owning one's house. In *Bellissima* Visconti also displayed his animosity toward women; with the exception of Maddalena, he showed them as greedy, twisted, arid figures. . . . Visconti looked with a shudder even at the sensuous surrender to her husband with which Maddalena at the end signified her frustrated withdrawal into her own world: she had learned her lesson, but Visconti gave her little sympathy for it. Such motifs, systematically evading the expectations one might have in such situations, are played quite subtly in *Bellissima.* It remains a rather puzzling picture, unamiable and unappealing, although its stylistic tone is quite high, and the portrait of Maddalena is clearly an achievement.

With *Senso,* which he made in 1951, Visconti took up a more overt, more complex challenge. . . . As the plot shows, Visconti was to deal with a historical theme. . . .

In Visconti's intentions, *Senso* was to prove that the reality which could be dealt with "realistically" in a film need not be limited, along one dimension, to strictly contemporary events, or along another, to lower- or middle-class milieux. . . .

It was an important challenge that lay in Visconti's intention to deal with a historical situation in the spirit of neorealism. The cinema has always felt the attraction of the "historical" film, and many times raised the claim that it had succeeded in bringing forth History as Reality. . . .

This is the challenge which *Senso* takes up. It does it through a complex strategy, not all the lines of which are successful. (p. 18)

Visconti seems to have judged that the first and major element of a realist film approach to history is a strenuous effort to recapture *from inside* the reality of the historical background. His was not simply a concern with exact reconstruction of settings; it was a serious philological effort to evoke the color, the feel, the proportion of the smallest detail. In his search for how the reality around them appeared to the characters of his story, he drew upon the painters, musicians, and writers of that age, as well as its historians. . . .

Senso is by far the best color movie ever made, as far as color goes: not only because it exploited more fully than ever before the technical potentialities of Technicolor; but mainly because it inexorably bent those potentialities to expressive goals: it used the color to bring forth meanings, references, undercurrents of feeling. (p. 19)

Another line of attack taken by Visconti to the task of a realistic historical film, was his attempt to maintain a complex and delicate balance between the "private" and the "public" side of the story: the affair between Countess Serpieri and Lieutenant Mahler on one side, the development of the Venetian independence movement and the war on the other. Such a balance, if successfully struck, would have helped avoid that flattening out of history into sheer oleography or breathless anecdote to which most historical movies have fallen victim. But the attempt was not successful: Visconti's attention is mainly on that knot of shame, of reckless egoism, of reciprocal betrayal, which is Livia's affair with Franz; the "public" line of events appears and disappears in the background, but is not integrated with the "private" line. (p. 20)

Finally, to avoid another common pitfall of "historical" films, the failure to *interpret* their characters, rather than just idolizing them or condemning them, Visconti projected a Marxian interpretation of his figures—interpreted them in class terms. . . . Not even this line of Visconti's effort is completely successful: the ruinous moral features of [Livia and Franz] so clearly verge on the monstrous, on the pathological, that we refuse to accept them as symbols of a class destiny.

Behind this weakness of *Senso* lies perhaps a fundamental ambiguity in Visconti's own attitude toward the world of Livia and Franz Mahler. As a Marxian intellectual Visconti condemns and rejects that world, and preaches the inevitability, the historical necessity, of its ruin. Yet, because of his links of blood and culture to that aristocracy, Visconti seems to feel a morbid fascination with its refined wealth, its manners, its destiny of decadence. (pp. 20-1)

A proud, incisive statement, [*Le Notti Bianche* (1957)] reveals rather clearly certain traits of the "uomo Visconti". . . . (p. 21)

The film derived a definite feel of irreality (in spite of Visconti's own contention to the opposite) from developing wholly at night, in a badly lit quarter of narrow lanes and steep bridges, which vaguely suggested an area in Leghorn. The set design, the lighting, and the photography were all aimed at creating a haunting atmosphere, while the drama, in a sense, went on inside the characters. There is a double remove from reality; one from the daytime reality of things and into the nocturnal reality of the selves; the other in dissolving even *that* reality either into a receding perspective which mixes memories and hopes (in Natalia's case) or into a frantic, self-defeating search for a response on the part of the Other (in Mario's case). The spectator—like Mario himself, in a way—is left to wonder whether the action he has seen develop was meant to have ever happened, or whether it was a nightmare to start with.

Thus, the negative side of Visconti's intention, the neat break with the neorealist formula, is fully embodied in *Le Notti Bianche*. But the nature of the "gate" Visconti is opening is much less clear. . . .

Visconti has, like Fellini, never been a "typical" neorealist; though he has led, he has at the same time always stood slightly aside. And while *Le Notti Bianche* is no doubt a slighter film than Visconti's previous works, he remains an innovating force in the cinema, ever able to go beyond himself. (p. 22)

Gianfranco Poggi, "Luchino Visconti and the Italian Cinema," in Film Quarterly *(copyright 1960 by The Regents of the University of California; reprinted by permission of the University of California Press), Vol. XIII, No. 3, Spring, 1960, pp. 11-12.*

ROBERT CONNELLY

Visconti has tried to encompass the whole of Lampedusa's novel in [*The Leopard*] and to include all its incidents and all its characters. He has succeeded in doing so. However, even three and a half hours aren't sufficient for such a task, and the result is that events and characters are sketchy. The American spectator unfamiliar with the details of the Italian Risorgimento [the movement for the liberation and unification of Italy between 1750 and 1870] is going to be a bit lost. This will not trouble the Italian spectator, who is fully acquainted with these characters, but for the rest of us they remain only puppet figures. . . .

Many of what seem at first to be faults in the film can be justified, or at least explained, by the novel itself. As the camera travels interminably up the walls of Palermo palazzi, lovingly scrutinizing gilded cherubs, frescoes, and damask draperies, one thinks—this is typical Visconti, with his usual lack of restraint, indulging his love for the beautiful, the baroque and the decadent. Turning to the book, however, we find that the author devotes page after page to describing the opulence surrounding a class for whom refinement and elegance were the only values that made life worth living. (p. 35)

The film's chief fault is its slowness and paucity of action, in keeping with the novel, which consists primarily of the inner thoughts of a perceptive man, the Prince. The sombre mood of the book was relieved by frequent flashes of wit. Lampedusa's prince had a subtle sense of humor apparently polished during frequent sojourns in London, and he was thus able to look with amused detachment on some aspects of his role of a Sicilian aristocrat. There is no hint of this in the film, humor being difficult for Visconti. Visconti has chosen not to go into the details of Sicily's role in the Risorgimento. Had he done so, the film doubtlessly would have had greater significance. Visconti, as a count and advocate of the Italian Communist Party, could easily have used this film as an attack on the aristocracy, its ideological deficiencies and its reactionary philosophy of history; instead, like the Prince of Salina, the aristocrat has won, and instead of an attack Visconti has given us an elegy on the passing of a way of life he loves. (pp. 35-6)

Robert Connelly, "3 Italian Films," in Film Comment *(copyright © 1963 by Lorien Produc-*

*tions, Inc.; all rights reserved), Vol. I, No. 6, Fall, 1963, pp. 34-8.**

TINO MENDES SARGO

The disappointment of seeing *The Leopard* is in direct proportion to the promises of the project. . . . [The] film had everything to make it a smashing success, even the excellent photography of [Giuseppe] Rotunno. . . .

[Unlike] most films made in this part of the world, [*The Leopard*] is not a producer's film. It is a director's film. . . . And, what's more, it is the film of a man with great experience in working from literary sources; also, this man is an aristocrat himself, coming from a most distinguished Italian family. (p. 35)

Visconti is a director whose films have largely derived from literary works; but he approached these works as a pretext, as it were, to make films that stand on their own feet and not to make films as mere illustrations or adaptations of the books. In viewing *The Leopard* one is astonished by the faithfulness with which the director follows Lampedusa's novel. . . . And yet, I submit, the success of the book is the film's failure. (p. 36)

The Prince has the centrality of a character whom everything is reflected upon, in the book and in the film. However, in the book there is a character, or rather, a supporting cast, as it were, that does not "appear" in the film: The historical background. . . . [The sequences in Palermo] are of an appalling mediocrity in their conception and directorial handling. (pp. 36-7)

The other important character is Don Calogero Sedara, the bourgeois on his way up the social ladder, upon whom Visconti, quite inexplicably, bestows farcical traits in a most arbitrary fashion. Maybe being an aristocrat and a Communist, the director does not see what is in the middle even if Don Calogero *is* a revolutionary force. . . .

Lampedusa gives us an historicist interpretation of history. Visconti, faithful to the book as he is, does not. The theme of the book somehow escapes the film: the flux of history, the fall of aristocracy, the rise of a new and vital class and the betrayal of a revolution. Visconti tries, but never quite succeeds. . . . Thus, on the one hand we have literal faithfulness which does not mean thematic faithfulness; on the other we have added scenes, subtle enough and timid enough not to give us the rendering of these themes.

Visconti oscillates between an historicist interpretation of history and a romantic view of the characters that make and are made by the same history. The theme of the flux of history is washed out by the theme of an aging man's foreknowledge of death. I have nothing against the intersection of biography and history. In fact, I am all for it, provided that biography and history do not annihilate each other, as is the case in *The Leopard*. Visconti's timidity is shown in the conventionality with which he approaches these themes. He is not bold enough to "recreate" the book in such a way that the film could be a great and autonomous work of art. . . .

The conventionality of this film lies precisely in the reduction of everything to a character. This is not only a question of structure, but also a question of scale, dictated by the supposed need of motion pictures to create characters with whom we can identify. We had the boy-next-door, now we shall have the Prince-next door! (p. 37)

This film, in all its merits (because it *has* merits: the ball at Ponteleone, the Plebiscite, the hunting scenes, etc.), was an effort and a great one that did not pay off, commercially or artistically. . . .

Thus, Luchino Visconti's talent for recreating works of literature on the screen, his immensely refined taste and his lucidity seem, in *The Leopard*, neutralized by romantic nostalgia and subserviency to motion picture myths. I said earlier that this was a director's film. But maybe inside every director there is a producer lurking. Given the fact that this was Visconti's most expensive film, I dread to think that the producer inside Visconti has taken over. The birth of a producer is usually the death of a director. (p. 38)

Tino Mendes Sargo, "Film Reviews: 'The Leopard'," in Film Quarterly *(copyright 1963 by The Regents of the University of California; reprinted by permission of the University of California Press), Vol. XVII, No. 2, Winter, 1963-64, pp. 35-8.*

RICHARD ROUD

[*Vaghe Stelle dell'Ora*] is a tragedy. Like Thebes, Volterra is a city dying, like human beings, of a mortal sickness; it is gradually crumbling away. Like Mycenae, it is perched high on a hill, surrounded by a cyclopean wall of stones, shaken by the winds of tragedy. Mycenae is very much to the point here, for it is not long after the return that the inevitable recognition scene takes place: Sandra . . . meets her brother Gianni . . . by the tomb of her father, and we realise suddenly that this is to be the story of Electra and Orestes, the House of Atreus. . . .

[No] real catharsis is possible, and the drama is never truly resolved. Does the film then suffer from the lack of any decisive satisfying action? Has Visconti failed, as so many others have failed before him, in the attempt to create a modern tragedy? I think not. For . . . he has succeeded in creating the climate of tragedy, which is perhaps as far as any modern artist can go. . . . Visconti has turned—as before—to opera. . . .

Senso, of course, was operatic, but that was an easier problem to solve—19th century Venice, colour, and the backdrop of the Risorgimento. *Rocco,* too, was in the same genre, but there I feel Visconti came to grief by trying to ally the operatic with social realism. This time, leaving realism behind, he seems to me to have succeeded. How? The tremendous contrast between the prologue and the drama proper points the way. From the open-plan room, from the broad highways, we suddenly are confronted with a dark palace. Never have so many doors been opened and shut in a film before: opened, shut, locked, forced, half-opened. But the darkness of the house is contrasted with the light outside: this is a summer tragedy. This light is bright, blinding, even. The contrast is accentuated by the way in which Visconti has lit and shot the film. . . .

In any case, Visconti has always gone against the prevailing fashions. (p. 40)

But sheer determination not to go along the well-travelled road has never been a guarantee of a successful work of art. What counts here is the tremendous conviction one feels behind the film, a conviction one did not always recognise in *Rocco.* There is also a dramatic intensity which was absent from *The Leopard,* a feeling that the film is all one massive whole, like the cyclopean blocks that make up the walls of Volterra. This solidity is of course contrasted with the nearly deliquescent nature of the drama; just as, in spite of the walls, Volterra is the centre of a slide area. We see the church with a gaping cleft in the façade, and Orestes tells us that slowly the whole town is crumbling away. This might be interpreted as a mild attempt by Visconti to inject an element of social comment—death of the aristocracy—but I do not think so. . . . (p. 41)

Richard Roud, "Film Reviews: 'Of a Thousand Delights'," in Sight and Sound *(copyright © 1965 by The British Film Institute), Vol. 35, No. 1, Winter, 1965-66, pp. 40-1.*

STANLEY KAUFFMANN

The sun—the Algerian sun—was an important part of Albert Camus's early being. . . . And it is integral to his first novel, *The Stranger:* the crucial moment of murder occurs when Meursault is in the grip of that same Algerian sun. Luchino Visconti has understood this essential thematic element perfectly. In his color film of *The Stranger*, apparently shot on location, Visconti has aimed to make the sun a benefaction, an oppression, an ambience. (p. 46)

This visual realization of the atmosphere is only the beginning of the film's achievements. Visconti has got a faithful screenplay. . . . However, to say that the script is faithful to Camus is both to praise it and to delimit it. It does the most, dramatically and cinematically, that is possible with the book, without any substantive alteration (which would have been intolerable), yet its fidelity gives it the same level dramatic plane as that of films about Jesus. Such films . . . always rise to a plateau and stay on it because there is no hero. A hero must have some illusions and must struggle as a result of them. Jesus is not deceived and will not struggle. So with Meursault.

This gives Visconti's film, like Camus's novel, a quality of observation and patience. The drama is not overt; it is internal, the inevitable abrasion between the protagonist's inner state and the world's protocol. But the film is at a disadvantage in comparison with the novel because of one central matter of technique: Camus evokes a pervasive somnambulistic quality by putting a good deal of Meursault's dialogue into indirect discourse. One example among dozens:

> "Why," [the chaplain] asked, "don't you let me come to see you?"
> I explained that I didn't believe in God.
> "Are you really so sure of that?"
> I said I saw no point in troubling my head about the matter; whether I believed or didn't was, to my mind, a question of little importance.

This technique is impossible in film. If Meursault's indirect answers were put on the soundtrack as narration, we would see his lips move as he replied. Or even if his face were not shown, the flip-flop from the chaplain's direct speech to Meursault's narrated replies would have the opposite of the intended effect. It would destroy the texture of the scene, whereas, in the novel, the device creates texture—suspended, dreamlike, *life*like.

But facing the book's difficulties and intent on rendering it authentically, Visconti has made a beautiful, discreet, perceptive film of this epochal work of the twentieth-century Western world. Pictures, in the specific sense, have never been difficult for him; on the contrary, he has tended to indulge himself by slapping pictures all over our eyeballs in films like *The Leopard* and *Sandra*. Here he has *used* his pictorial sense, rather than spewed it. There are plenty of extraordinary things to look at: the skylighted air of the mortuary in an old folks' home, the Algerian streets and rooms (with the smell almost visible), the sensual blending of sea and sun. And when Meursault is in his cell, Visconti (with [cinematographer] Rotunno) increases the isolation by increasingly isolating the prisoner's countenance until only his face is embodied out of the dark. But never is the picture merely pretty. Visconti was obviously deeply committed to Camus, and all his previously obtrusive virtuosity is here totally at Camus's service. (pp. 46-8)

Stanley Kauffmann, "'The Stranger'" (originally published in The New Republic, *January 13, 1968, Vol. 158, No. 2), in his* Figures of Light: Film Criticism and Comment *(copyright © 1968, 1969, 1970 by Stanley Kauffmann; reprinted by permission of Harper & Row, Publishers, Inc.), Harper, 1971, pp. 46-8.*

RICHARD SCHICKEL

Iconfess that I approached *The Stranger* with considerable trepidation. Albert Camus's novel, despite the vigor of its deceptively simple style, despite the marvelous clarity of its philosophy and psychology, seemed impossibly difficult to translate to the screen. (p. 163)

How wrong I was. Director Luchino Visconti, a team of screenwriters and, most especially, Marcello Mastroianni as Meursault have made from *The Stranger* a film that can only be described as excellent—thoughtful, moving and faithful. Above all, faithful, for theirs is the kind of modest, self-effacing craftsmanship that serves rather than exploits its basic material. Eschewing the temptation to overcinematize the story, they have concentrated with commendable discipline on allowing the grave voice of Albert Camus to speak to us in a medium that was not his own. It comes through firm and clear, and true. Since this was a voice that both summed up and shaped the sensibility of at least two postwar generations, it is well worth the close attention this film forces us to pay. (pp. 163-64)

Meursault is doomed by his lack of repentance and by a string of witnesses who testify that his indifference to death is only an extension of his indifference to the customary standards by which we judge a man's fitness to live in civilization. To decent right-thinking people he is a moral monster who must be condemned—if not for his crime, then for his thoughts.

But of course he is not a monster. He is merely a man in rebellion against the illusions which help the rest of us sustain our sanity, a man who has pressed rationalism to its outermost limits and is content to live on the brink of the darkest abyss, the place where even saints must fear to tread and which is, indeed, the take-off point for their sundry leaps of faith. Which makes him, perversely, ironically, a kind of tragic hero.

The artistic challenge such a figure presents is formidable. He is the embodiment not of observed human characteristics, as most fictional constructs are, but of a pure idea, the nature of which is such that our every instinct begs us to reject it. The problem is to humanize him so that we can open ourselves emotionally—not just intellectually—to his mind and his tragedy. I have never been certain that Camus himself solved this problem completely, especially for those who were not generally predisposed to his view of existence. The idea he represented clung unshakably to the mind, but Meursault the man had a way of slipping out of the reader's grasp.

The movie rectifies this defect. Meursault and his world are made palpable on film in a way they never were—for me, at least—on the page. This is not a matter of director or star adding a lot of helpful hints designed to cue our responses and make sure we get the point. It is, rather, an almost subliminal thing—the flicker of an expression in Mastroianni's face, the camera's eye falling briefly on a detail which helps concretize a story that is by its nature always in danger of becoming mythically abstract.

When, at the end, priest and Stranger meet in the condemned cell to discuss ultimate meanings, this attention to detail pays off. What seemed mainly an ideological duel in the novel here becomes a passionate struggle for the soul of an unpleasantly honest and courageous man we have come to care deeply about—not because we agree with him (we may or may not) but because we love him. He has already chosen death in preference to the conventional wisdom. Now he chooses damnation—if, indeed, there is a heaven. And this is a victory we can savor even if we believe he is wrong.

The Stranger is a muted, careful, even slow film that achieves *its* victory through an austere honesty that matches that of its hero. It is not a movie to engage casually and it may not please those for whom movies are primarily exercises in style or fashionable form. It does, however, place before us one of the key philosophical and artistic expressions of our time, and in illuminating it anew it inevitably illuminates the basic issues with which all of us must sooner or later grapple. It is, therefore, a film that any serious person must regard as inescapable. (pp. 164-66)

Richard Schickel, "'The Stranger'" (originally published in Life, *February 2, 1968), in his* Second Sight: Notes on Some Movies 1965-1970 *(copyright © 1972 by, Richard Schickel; reprinted by permission of Simon and Schuster, a Division of Gulf & Western Corporation), Simon & Schuster, 1972, pp. 163-67.*

MARGARET TARRATT

The kind of analogy which Visconti draws in [*The Damned*] between the history of the von Essenbecks and the rise of Nazism is by no means without precedent in literature. As artists, Visconti and Mann [particularly in his novel *Buddenbrooks*] have more than a little in common. The symbolic structure of Mann's novels in which 'characters and situations take on a representative symbolic character' incorporating a 'general human predicament' goes hand in hand with a minute attention to naturalistic detail. Both Mann and Visconti are stylists without being mere aesthetes. Mann's 'static and reflective' language and the distancing he achieves through his intrusion as a narrator might be said to be paralleled by Visconti's slow-moving camera which dwells on the remarkable textures and grouping he achieves in his work and which sometimes takes on an independent life of its own. In *The Damned,* for instance, during the scene of the birthday concert, the camera wanders amongst the spectators like an unseen guest lingering on individual faces in unhurried scrutiny. (pp. 47-8)

More specific parallels between *Buddenbrooks* and *The Damned* are to be found between Mann's conscious use of the Wagnerian leitmotif which becomes part of the symbolic structure of his work and Visconti's use of the same technique in this film. The strongest recurrent image in *The Damned* is that of fire. The opening and closing shots on an ominous fiery furnace is an image to which we often return, either directly or through analogy, as in the book-burning scene. Faces are frequently shown lit in a red glow, as if reflecting flames. (p. 48)

The suggestion of impending doom in the ominous smoke and flames of the opening shot, and the ill-fated marriage which leads to death, are straight out of Wagner's *Götterdämmerung* itself. We are reminded of the way Visconti uses Verdi in his earlier operatic film *Senso.* This begins with a performance of *Il Trovatore* in Venice—we are told it is Spring 1866 and that the Austrian occupation of Italy is coming to an end. The camera moves between stage and audience until the chorus begins a call to arms. The audience is roused to demonstrate in favour of the national cause and there is considerable confusion out of which an Italian patriot challenges an Austrian officer to a duel. The camera movement between stage and audience and the effect of the opera in inciting action amongst the audience sets the tone of the whole film. Visconti has said that he wished to show the way in which the melodrama of the stage carried over into the action of the audience and principal characters of the film.

In *The Damned,* Visconti once again makes use of this kind of interplay between the associations of Wagnerian romantic epic and the behaviour of those it inspires. Significantly, there is no musical reference to Wagner. The performance on stage which leads into a wider performance, again including the spectators, is an amateur concert. In place of the heroic Brunnhilde we are shown not merely a contemporary sex symbol, Dietrich, but a debased pastiche of her appearance and performance. The song Martin sings as Dietrich comes from *The Blue Angel,* a film which deliberately presents its characters as actors and is concerned with the sado-masochistic humiliation of a man by a woman. . . . [The] humiliation of Martin by his Mother, analogous to that of Herr Unrath by Lola-Lola, is a symptom of a state of mind peculiarly receptive to Nazism. Thus through its cinematic and literary associations, Martin's act symbolizes something of the state of German bourgeois society. (pp. 52-3)

Most of the music we hear in the film is popular and trivial. Visconti shows us something of a culture which has absorbed certain of the characteristics of Wagner's heroes—ambition, treachery, lust and ruthlessness without the vital redeeming element of the music itself. Similarly, Friederich, Visconti's Macbeth figure, inherits the ambition, guilt and weakness of his prototype without the intensity of imagination and power of verbal expression which lifts Shakespeare's character to the ranks of the tragic heroes.

The structure of *The Damned* is much closer to the theatrical *Macbeth* pattern than to the novelistic one of *Buddenbrooks,* since Friederich provides the central driving force against which the others react, and the phases of his rise and fall reflect those of Macbeth. Friederich loses control just as he seems most secure, at the family dinner to which Herbert Thallman's 'ghost' returns, when Bruckmann attempts to assert his headship of the family. But the signs of moral regeneration embodied in the figure of Malcolm at the end of *Macbeth* are ignored by Visconti in favour of an ironic Wagnerian ending in which the lovers are united in death, not with the exaltation of a Siegfried and Brunnhilde but with a hopeless resignation. (p. 53)

In *Vaghe Stelle dell'Orsa,* which was also an attempt to uncover the facts and resolve the guilt of the past era of fascism, Visconti made an analogy with the buried hatred, incestuous desires, madness and death-wishes of a family group. Such imagery is not arbitrarily chosen. In popular mythology, sexual decadence causes the decay of a culture, as with the destruction of Sodom and Gomorrah or the Fall of the Roman Empire. *The Damned* is structurally more complex than *Vaghe Stelle.* As opera, it highlights certain strongly drawn dramatic themes and ostensibly ignores 'irrelevant' incident and details. In *Senso,* Visconti made an implicit comparison between the simplified outlines of *Il Trovatore* and the history of Franz and Livia which is simultaneously grand and petty. In *The Damned* what is virtually ignored is shown to be of equal importance with what is emphasized. The grand passion and Wagnerian heroics of the Nazi order survive only through a studied blindness to what is going on beneath the surface. The Essenbeck house in which most of the action takes place is an enclosed world, protected on the whole by wealth and privilege. Visconti's use of colour throughout the film reflects this idea. . . . [The] avoidance of unsavoury detail forms another of the films leitmotifs. . . . The crime of ignoring what it is more comfortable not to see, reflects the familiar post-war German chorus that under the Nazis no one knew what was really going on.

The Damned is almost certainly not one of Visconti's major films. . . . Generally speaking, the script lacks the substance and complexity to match Visconti's dazzling style. . . . Nevertheless, *The Damned* does not deserve to be hawked around as a peg on which to hang the latest fashion any more than to be reviled as an irresponsible chronicle of sexual perversion and brutality. Visconti's characteristic strength in handling groups, creative use of colour and camera movement together with the absorbing use of visual and thematic leitmotif will undoubtedly lead to a reappraisal of his achievement in this film. (pp. 54-6)

Margaret Tarratt, "'The Damned': Visconti, Wagner and the 'Reinvention of Reality'," in Screen, *Vol. 11, No. 3, Summer, 1970, pp. 44-56.*

STEPHEN FARBER

Death in Venice is "visual" in the very worst sense—stuffed with extravagantly pretty pictures that only obscure the themes of Thomas Mann's novella. This film does a disservice to cinema as well as to literature. . . . (p. 643)

Mann's novella, published in 1911, is probably one of the central works of twentieth-century literature, dealing, as it does, with sexual ambiguities, the moral failures of art, and some of the disturbing tensions in the German temperament —extreme rigor and discipline contending with a strong, suppressed desire for sensual abandon. Very little of this is suggested in the film, which has become a monotonous, protracted study of a homosexual infatuation. . . . The film even loses the important reasons that Mann did have for giving the story a homosexual cast—that homosexuality has, associated with it, something of the thrill of breaking a tribal taboo, and that to a classical artist like Aschenbach an obsession with spiritual beauty is inevitably linked to the homoerotic ideals of Greek culture.

It is true that the film makes a feeble effort to raise some abstract questions about the artist's ambivalent relationship to physical beauty in a couple of flashback sequences in which Aschenbach conducts strenuous debates with an intellectual friend. These scenes are incredibly clumsy in themselves, with impossibly stilted dialogue . . . , and they are doubly embarrassing because they seem so arbitrarily imposed on the film. (pp. 643-44)

Visconti has heard the rumors that Mann based the character of Aschenbach on Mahler, and it is Mahler's music that floods the film's soundtrack. Aschenbach is supposed to be a classical artist, whose style is distinguished by "lofty purity, symmetry and simplicity"; over the years, we are told, it has grown increasingly rigid and formalized —it has become official state art. Even in the film, his friend attacks him as conservative, and accuses his music of being "stillborn." But the accusations cannot possibly apply to Mahler's music, which is unmistakably warm, passionate, imaginative. In one scene of the film Aschenbach is inspired by a vision of Tadzio to begin composing at a feverish pitch, but is that meant to suggest that he is creatively liberated by this confrontation with physical beauty? The music hardly sounds constipated. With this confusion the story loses its focus, for it is impossible to understand the impact of this sensual temptation on Aschenbach's art without having a much more precise idea of what his art was like before he came to Venice. Also, if we are meant to feel that for the first time in his life, freed of conventional morality, Aschenbach yields to his senses and experiments with what is socially forbidden, then what is the purpose of the flashback in which he visits a brothel—a scene suggesting that decadence and degradation are not in any way new to his experience? (pp. 644-45)

Perhaps if some of the undercurrents were captured, we wouldn't be so troubled by literal questions. Of course *Death in Venice* is a difficult work to adapt, and I am not sure that any film-maker could have found a fully satisfactory equivalent for the novella's intellectual complexity and psychological subtlety. But this is one literary classic with unusual cinematic potential. (p. 645)

On [the visual] level too, the film is a failure. Visconti has lavished a great deal of care on the hats and the table lamps, but in a larger sense, he has not found a meaningful visual style for the story. . . . If [Venice] had come alive visually, that might have helped to focus Mann's theme of the ambivalence of physical beauty and to dramatize Aschenbach's descent into Dionysian sensuality. In the novella there is a powerful dream sequence near the end in which Aschenbach sees himself participating in a bacchanal of lust and bestiality. The filmic equivalent is a brief sequence of Aschenbach in his hotel room, talking to himself about his degradation: "Wisdom, truth, human dignity . . . all finished." It seems a final irony that this "visual" film (probably no more than 30 of its 130 minutes have dialogue) has to express the climax of its story—an inherently cinematic climax—with a few feeble, inadequate *words.*

Many of the images in the film are admittedly quite lovely in themselves—but as still shots, not moving pictures. Even the loveliest are essentially hollow—high-class postcard art, images that serve as mere decoration. (pp. 645-46)

Death in Venice represents artistic bankruptcy, "visual cinema" without intelligence or imagination—movies as an animated form of interior decoration. (p. 646)

Stephen Farber, "Non-Talking Pictures," in The Hudson Review *(copyright © 1972 by The Hudson Review, Inc.; reprinted by permission), Vol. XXIV, No. 4, Winter, 1971-72, pp. 638-46.**

PAULINE KAEL

Ludwig II of Bavaria, the supreme childish fantasist among kings—and one of the most harmless of all kings—is such an obviously magical, gaudy subject for the movies that many people may look forward with glee to Visconti's *Ludwig*. But it's well to bear in mind that though Ludwig is remembered because of the pleasures his candied-rococo follies give us, Visconti's follies are grimly humorless. Of the major filmmakers, Luchino Visconti is certainly the most estranged from the audience. Sometimes, in his films, the vital connection between the material on the screen and us disappears, and Visconti doesn't seem to notice or to care—he just goes on without us, heavily treading water. This happens for almost the entire duration of *Ludwig,* which is two hours and fifty-three minutes long. The subject is so juicy and frivolous that bravura pageantry on its own, without much drama, might be enough, but, incredibly, this movie about the king's obsession with a mock-heroic fairy-tale mode of life has no *style*.

The translated, partly dubbed dialogue is neither formal and elegant nor colloquial; it's like an earnest translation of a dowdy libretto, and it makes the actors sound like the talking dead. The early portions of the film are shot in badly lighted compositions resembling those wide-canvas nineteenth-century academic Russian paintings of a convocation of stiff, important people. The continuity is a splatter of choppy, confused scenes; there are constant amputations, so we don't find out why we have been watching a sequence but simply move on to something else, and the arbitrary compositions and abrupt closeups destroy the sense of what's going on. Visconti has been able to photograph Ludwig's actual castles and to reproduce interiors he couldn't shoot in, and yet we don't have a chance just to rove around and luxuriate in them. We always seem to be driving up to the carriage entrance; then we're stuck in a room without finding out how we got there. The film gets better-looking, and every now and then there's a great shot, which goes by infuriatingly fast. The rhythmless, disruptive cutting does the movie in, even more than Visconti's usual failing—his lack of dramatic drive.

Typically, his allegorical melodramas, such as *Rocco and His Brothers* and *The Damned,* are pushed to such heights that they turn into epics—witless but passionate and strangely self-absorbed. There can be a grandeur in their hollow heaviness and languid monotony; they have generally had style, even when we couldn't be sure of anything else about them. Visconti's first epic, the lyrical yet austere and socially conscious *La Terra Trema,* is beautifully proportioned; I think it's one of the best boring movies ever made. . . . *Rocco* suggested an operatic spectacle with a libretto by Dostoevski based on the Warner Brothers social-protest films of the thirties; Visconti gave us not characters but highly theatrical, reminiscent images—Annie Girardot's scrawny, glamorous prostitute was like a young Bankhead, her murder out of *Wozzeck*. *The Damned* was a mixture of Wagner and Thomas Mann and the classical Greek crazies. Elements got slammed together that didn't quite make sense together, but they made thunder, and a flowing style can connect a lot. When the Visconti style collapses, you look for the links; they're still buried in the director's mind—in his Jacobean nostalgia. (pp. 144-45)

It seems characteristic of the private nature of Visconti's fantasies that the only sequence in [*Ludwig*] that has any kind of visual integrity is, at the end, the torchlight search for Ludwig's body, when a lake is dragged at night. Visconti is more carried away by the possibilities of operatic splendor in Ludwig's death than by the *opéra bouffe* of his life. (p. 146)

A disaster on the scale of *Ludwig* is a prodigy. I long to see the outtakes; and I'd love to know if there was any greater visual or dramatic logic in what Visconti shot than in what he wound up with. By ordinary dramatic standards, Visconti isn't a writer; his scripts (written in collaboration) seem to be blueprints for the big scenes he visualizes—obsessive scenes with overtones of other theatrical works—which are just loosely strung together. . . . Visconti's sense of length—that is, of the running time of his movies—may relate to opera; like the popular arias in dull operas, his overwrought, garish scenes (and a few funny scenes here) rouse us from apathy. My guess about why the continuity is so jumpy is that he rather magisterially goes on shooting scenes that fascinate him, and later finds he has no place for them. (pp. 146-47)

[If] *Ludwig* proves to be Visconti's last film—his swan song—this visual gibberish will appear to be the chaos he was always heading toward. Maybe the subject of Ludwig the dream king is just too close for a big moviemaker-dreamer to handle. . . . Could Griffith have tackled Ludwig, or could von Sternberg or von Stroheim or Gance or Welles or Fellini, without wallowing, and sinking in the wallow? An enigma like Ludwig, a king who disappears inside his fantasies of greater kings, might be a safe subject for a director of modest gifts, but it could be the ultimate dangerous subject for a movie king. (pp. 148-49)

Pauline Kael, "Kings" (originally published in The New Yorker, *Vol. XLIX, No. 5, March 24, 1973), in her* Reeling *(copyright © 1973 by Pauline Kael; reprinted by permission of Little, Brown and Company in association with Atlantic Monthly Press), Atlantic-Little, Brown, 1976, pp. 144-50.**

STANLEY KAUFFMANN

Ludwig is about two mad kings, Ludwig II of Bavaria and Luchino Visconti, who made the picture. The latter is only figuratively true, of course, but along with Ludwig's disintegration, we can see Luchino's.

The first mad symptom is the choice of this mad subject. This is a historical epic without a hero (like *Nicholas and Alexandra*), a central figure but no protagonist. Two hours and 53 minutes, acres of scenery, brigades of actors, all to detail what is only a case history, not a drama, let alone a tragedy. . . .

Is Visconti wreaking one-man revenge for the Axis? Or is

he, as an Italian friend of mine maintains, simply jealous of German grandeur?

The way of transgressors is hard, says the Old Testament, and Visconti doesn't make it any easier. We plunk plunk plunk along in a story without character or theme or narrative structure. Very obviously there has been a lot of chopping and patching of the film, which contributes to a general sense of lunacy. (p. 183)

[The] whole film seems as mad as its subject—in every way but one. It is gorgeous. (p. 184)

[Visconti,] former artist and latter-day mad charlatan, understands the theater in an old-fashioned sweeping-entrance and delayed-exit way. (See how Ludwig leaves the all-night drinking party with the young men—pausing in the open door and looking back.) Visconti miscalculated badly in his choice of subject but he understands that he's dishing up what used to be called "servant-girl theater": thrills of luxury for the lowly. He lays it on with a mink-covered trowel. (pp. 184-85)

Expect no sense. Shut your ears. (Besides the English, some Wagner gets murdered on the soundtrack.) Go to see a series of magnificent film-clips, and you can have a good time. It doesn't matter in the least when you come or go or how long you stay. (p. 185)

Stanley Kauffmann, "'Ludwig'" (originally published in The New Republic, *Vol. 168, No. 13, March 31, 1973), in his* Living Images: Film Comment and Criticism *(copyright © 1971, 1972, 1973, 1974 by Stanley Kauffmann; reprinted by permission of Harper & Row, Publishers, Inc.), Harper, 1975, pp. 183-85.*

ALEXANDER HUTCHISON

Form as a dimension of meaning has little to do with morality, and yet as the prize of discipline it is invested with ethical character. This is the central paradox of Visconti's *Death in Venice* just as it is of Mann's novella. I will discuss elements of form and dissolution in the film, the discrepancies between meaning and manner, between profits of the plague and the price of perfection. I assume a knowledge of both novel and film. The novel remains the best guide to the film's structure. . . .

In *Il Gattopardo* and *L'Étranger* Visconti worked close to respected literary texts. In *Death in Venice* he follows Mann's schema so faithfully at times that one inevitably attends to what he has chosen to omit or add or transform. The film takes up the action of the novel only as Aschenbach is approaching Venice; after that the significant omissions are few, but like the initial cut they provide insight into Visconti's choice of structure and the mood which is sustained throughout the film. Metaphoric structure takes precedence over action. Visconti has tightened that structure by selecting encounters which reproduce the *leitmotifs* Mann provides, but he de-emphasizes other elements which would disrupt the mood. Mann's original setting in Munich has been left out, including Aschenbach's encounter with the pug-nosed, red-haired foreigner on the steps of the Funeral Hall, his sudden desire to travel, the vision of the crouching tiger in the jungle, all mention of his "coldly passionate service" to his art, and any details of biography. The effect of this is to contain the landscape and the mythical dimension of the action: flashbacks relate to other times and places, but they all refer directly to Aschenbach's preoccupation during his term in Venice and introduce biographical information only within the chronology of his death in this city that echoes the name of the goddess of desire. (p. 31)

It is within [a] classical form of sea, city, music, and the masks of death, that the action of the film is contained.

Within that form are the elements of dissolution. Mann's exposure of the plague and its corruptions is more radical than Visconti's, and in his description of the *bacchantes* with their "blinding, deafening lewdness" he unleashes forces which would shatter the mood of the film as surely as they "crush and annihilate the substance of the man who dreams them." Mann restates with emphasis; Visconti reinforces with restraint. . . .

With regard to other signs of disorder, Mann lets us sense the plague with our noses in odors from the lagoon, the disinfected streets, the carbolic stink of the singer at the hotel; Visconti, predictably, emphasizes the visual aspects—showing the ubiquitous cautionary notices published by the unseen "authorities," and it is not the smell of the disinfectant that affects us (although it does Aschenbach) so much as the splashing of it in milky spurts on walls and sidewalks and by the fountains. (p. 32)

The film does not provide with regard to aesthetics, the subtlety, the depth of analysis that the novella *Death in Venice* can accommodate. Nor could we expect it. The film has nothing in terms of complexity to match the dialogues between Socrates and Phaedrus on the nature of desire and virtue, but we are given main points in the dispute. Aschenbach, in conversation with Alfred, has declared his belief in beauty as the product of labour. As he sits at dinner on the first evening at the hotel he recalls their discussion, and as he recollects his expression of this belief he nods his head in reinforcement. He still believes it. For Alfred beauty is spontaneous creation—it belongs to the senses. And the artist must find his inspiration in the ambiguous, even the degenerate: he must find joy in the affliction of genius. (p. 36)

The aesthetic question—the nature of beauty—is entangled with the moral vision. Alfred speaks for the gods of a drunken spirit, offering a "reflected" splendor which seduces the artist: it makes him "flare up in pain and hope" and sexual ecstasy then deserts him when lust has turned, inevitably, to ashes.

> Statute and mirror! . . . the beautiful itself, form as the thought of God, the one pure perfection which lives in the mind, and which in this symbol and likeness had been placed here quietly and simply as an object of devotion. . . .

This is the shape and likeness of the boy Tadzio, a Narcissus, a mirror and object of fate, a vessel, charming, enigmatic, spontaneous. "l'amour et la mort": the flute of Eros, the guide of the dead. . . .

It is in the matter of betrayal that Visconti makes his most important revisions on the text of *Death in Venice.* Mann's ironic pessimism centres on the consequences of Aschenbach's own falsehood to his art and ideals. Visconti dramatizes not only the composer's conspiracy against himself, but clearly makes others agents in that conspiracy. The main theme of *Ossessione* and *Senso*—a theme that touches all of Visconti's films—is the destructive power of sexual passion in relation to betrayal. It is a "permanent item." . . . To reinforce that theme, in addition to creating the character of Alfred, who begins by demonstrating his devotion to Aschenbach and ends by cruelly abusing him, Visconti very quickly makes Tadzio a "traitor," too. (p. 38)

Describing the incident in the novel, Mann is chiefly concerned to show Tadzio at close quarters for the first time and mentions that the boy looks anaemic, rather sickly—a thought that gratifies and reassures Aschenbach although he refuses to reckon with it. Mann even talks of Tadzio's modesty. There is almost no suggestion of a deliberate seduction. In the film, Aschenbach returns to his room in considerable distress: all his actions show his temper and humiliation. . . . Visconti makes it plain that Gustave's main reason for leaving Venice is his reaction to Tadzio. Mann does not give him that awareness until later, and initially lets him blame the "offensive sultriness" of the weather: he juxtaposes Tadzio's signs of frailty with the repulsive conditions in the city—"both stimulating and enervating." Visconti leaves Tadzio physically unflawed, but creates a conspirator. (pp. 38-9)

Again, Visconti has based the incident [of Tadzio's second betrayal] on circumstances described in the novella, but his presentation gives a very different picture of the relationship. In the novella Aschenbach is on the verge of speaking to Tadzio on the boardwalk, but Mann makes the writer "fail" in his effort to put the relationship on a "sound, free and easy" basis, and he "surrenders" to the impulse of license by passing the boy with bowed head. . . . A comparison of these parallel but dissimilar sequences reinforces the impression that, in the film, Tadzio rather than Aschenbach is at this point the agent of license—certainly he is not the "frail, unthinking object" described in the novella. His invitation is blatant. Aschenbach, confronted with it, is incapacitated. This makes his later declaration of love more poignant and desperate.

The embrace of Dionysus has another aspect, however, as both Mann and Visconti emphasize. Dionysian intoxication can also be creative: the affliction may become a stimulus toward productivity. Mann's Aschenbach produces a tract on a "certain large burning issue of culture and taste" which he models on the form of Tadzio's beauty. In the film, Aschenbach, inspired by the same model, turns to his score and works on a piece which I assume is the equivalent of the *Mittersnachtlied*. (pp. 39-40)

Coming when Aschenbach's spirits are highest during his stay in Venice, the *Mittersnachtlied* marks the aesthetic and moral centre, and in a film where the architecture of mood complements the architecture of form it is the highpoint of formal and emotive organization. What follows is dissolution—the slow descent to death. (p. 40)

Linking incidents, images, and details of characterization, Visconti borrows Mann's *leitmotifs* and develops them. Consider the "messengers of death." . . . Visconti eliminates the figure of wandering Death who appeared at the opening of the novella; he also transforms "the goatee from the inside cabin" into the old fop. But the other agents of malice and sickness he stations throughout the city as Mann did before him. He accentuates the sexual scuttle and cackling of the singer to add to his derision. He enlarges the role of the manager so that he presides over a more sinister field of operations. And from the ferryman who lost his fee, through the rigid hierarchy of the servants at the hotel, to the beggars who approach Aschenbach while he blindly follows Tadzio, he shows how all of these agents share in the plague and the profits of the plague.

When characters perform a literal and symbolic "office" in this way, one becomes aware of the creation of other formal patterns—for example, by attending to the pattern of sound and silence in relation to character as well as by noting speech content. The demonic abuse of language is traditional in scripture, myth and allegory, and it is pertinent to consider it here. Many of those who speak to Aschenbach confuse or attempt to deceive him. There are few who do not speak out of self-interest or malice. It is not that it is all gibberish—it is more sinister the more plausible it appears—but Aschenbach, harassed, often fails to make sense of it, and, when he believes it, he is betrayed. (pp. 41-2)

So temporal and psychological actuality are subordinated to moral sequence and duration. Visconti condenses time sequences, providing a reality which does not necessarily reflect verisimilitude. He consistently cuts directly from scene to scene without providing any sure indication of elapsed time. . . .

The film's flashbacks present important moral and aesthetic polarities: Alfred's devotion and betrayal; the love shown by Aschenbach's wife compared to the "grip" of Esmeralda; Aschenbach's assertions of will and balance, and his mocking defeat at the hands of the bourgeoisie; his own capacity for joy and love, and the presence of seductive evil. These sequences are condensed, self-contained, yet they provide an "imagined" or "retrospective" chronology which covers a much larger period of time than Aschenbach's stay in Venice but is contained within this lesser chronology. (p. 42)

At the close of Visconti's *Death in Venice* the presence of the camera on the beach appears to point to its own capacity for illusion. But the paradox goes beyond questions about artistic deception. . . . Form that is constantly threatened with formlessness: this is the irony that confronts Kierkegaard's "moralist incognito." And in every detail of this film—which records the dissolution not only of the central character, but of a city, of art, in fact, of civilized existence—there is evidence of the artist's determination to form. All artists attempt it; a few, like Mann and Visconti and those they emulate, convince us that they can shape it in their work. They show the last change of mind: how to win from the irremediable a measure of hope and time. (p. 43)

Alexander Hutchison, "Luchino Visconti's 'Death in Venice'," in Literature/Film Quarterly *(© copyright 1974 Salisbury State College), Vol. 2, No. 1, Winter, 1974, pp. 31-43.*

GIDEON BACHMANN

All of Visconti's films, even those dealing with history more or less remote, chronicle realistically the fate of individuals thrown into conflict with societies with which Visconti himself in some manner, either directly or through class ties, identifies.

Identification, on the other hand, has always been a

problem for Visconti; he has never carried it as far as recognition, inasmuch as there has really never been a character in his films that resembled its inventor. With *Death In Venice* the theme of loneliness begins to dominate, but one feels that his own experiences form the emotional base, not the source material. But now he quotes Flaubert's "*Madame Bovary c'est moi*" when asked about his latest film, adding "He who tries to share an idea, cannot but do it through himself." A Gestalt approach to film-making is evident in [*Conversation Piece*]. . . . It is tempting to compare his own life to that of its protagonist in the pattern of retreat from social contact that characterizes both. . . .

As a former communist and current sympathizer, positions are expected of him which he refuses to assume. *Conversation Piece* depicts Italian society in its decadence, but takes no sides, except on a purely human level. Practically every character in the film is both scum and victim; the shells peel off as we descend to the hell in those souls in our function as voyeurs. (p. 55)

As a concentrated introduction to the problems of today's Italy *Conversation Piece* is especially useful. Social, political, psychological, industrial, interpersonal, and economic aspects of the current crisis are reflected in the central situation of the film, which is the conflict of the generations. But it would be wrong to consider it important as a symptom of Italian society alone; in fact Visconti's fatalistic prognosis concerns us all. . . .

And yet one does not walk away from this work with a feeling of defeat. It is clear that, like his protagonist, Visconti is both repulsed and attracted by the ascending generation, and like him he attempts to come to terms with the sadness they inspire. He does not juxtapose, nor try condescendingly to understand. Here is a man at the end of his life who finds that everything he has believed in means nothing to those who follow. Just as his films have been criticized for a lack of concern for the answers society is seeking, so his professor finds no answers for his own ailing. One feels that a film about loneliness has hardly ever been made by a similarly lonely man. . . .

For a film which is basically a play inasmuch as it takes place in a single location and depends largely on dialogue, Visconti has succeeded in creating a style admirably suited to his concern. In dark browns and ochres and elaborate turn-of-the-century decor, paying minute attention to detail, both decorative and aural, and by delicately restraining the acting of the principals, he has underlined the claustrophobia and loneliness, and the hesitant steps, alas disastrous, to escape both. (p. 56)

"The old," Visconti says, "may well try to understand the young and to love them, but the gap between the generations cannot really be bridged. All I want to do with this film is show their relationship in all its sadness. I try to show the world the way it is. The old are either removed from it or have gone back to fascism. The young are corrupt or are exposed to corruption at every step. At the same time they are beautiful and attractive, and their corruption is not a conscious one. Life is short; one must live it without shame. It may end in a few minutes." He quotes Auden, as he does in the film. Because this is a film about impotence. Not an impotent film. (pp. 56-7)

Gideon Bachmann, "Film Reviews: 'Conversation Piece'," in Film Quarterly *(copyright 1975 by The Regents of the University of California; reprinted by permission of the University of California Press), Vol. XXIX, No. 2, Winter, 1975-76, pp. 55-7.*

GEOFFREY NOWELL-SMITH

Luchino Visconti's *L'Innocente* . . . opens with a shot of a book—Gabriele D'Annunzio's novel of that title—lying on a table. There is a zoom-in to get a closer look at the cover, a zoom-out, and then a gnarled and yet frail hand enters the frame and starts turning the pages. The hand is reputed to be in fact that of Visconti, but even if it were not its place in the fiction would be the same. It is the hand of the film author, an old yellowing hand on an old yellowing book, the two perhaps contemporary. What we are about to see, therefore, is not just a film of the book, but implicitly a restoration of a common past.

Nothing in the film quite fulfils the promise of the opening moment. . . . But *L'Innocente* is nevertheless a remarkable film, both in itself and in relation to Visconti's other work. It is first of all, it should be said, a triumph of décor—a décor beyond the dreams (or imagination) of MGM in its heyday, since so much of it is created in real locations. The concept of the décor is nevertheless theatrical, so that places become sets rather than sets being used to recreate places. . . . There is however no sense of enclosure, or a submergence of human figures in their setting, such as one finds in *Conversation Piece,* where the focus line tends to pass through the background figures and the soft—or unsharp—focus makes shadowy boundaries between person and place. Rather the settings form a concordant part of the rules of the game—a game which Tullio plays to the utmost, until destroyed by the incursion of an alien element into it.

Tullio, the central but not necessarily the most interesting character, is the empty D'Annunzian superman, a salon Nietzschean whose superiority and indifference take the form of a stylishness which masks an inability to decide his life. (pp. 123-24)

The absence of a sufficient psychology for the character is perhaps what has caused *L'Innocente* to be compared to Dreyer's *Gertrud.* But whereas in *Gertrud* the insufficiency is such as to undermine any sense of the film as a realistic fiction, here realism is maintained. If what Tullio does and what happens to him remain enigmatic, it is not because the film's construction refuses to the spectator evidence of the status of the events shown, but because Tullio is, simply, an enigmatic character. The character has motivations, but they are unclear to him, and unclear to us. A far more relevant comparison would be with *Lo Straniero,* Visconti's own 1967 adaptation of Camus' *L'Etranger.* Tullio is in many ways the character that Mastroianni's Meursault should have been in the earlier film, but was not. What Visconti did in *Lo Straniero* was to endow Meursault with a psychology—a 'character'—which Camus' text refuses to him. Meursault becomes a man who is inexplicable, whereas in the novel he is simply unexplained. In *L'-Innocente* the form of character creation is similar, but more successful. . . .

The construction of *L'Innocente* seems to me to run along dual lines. On the one hand there is the creation of an as it were autonomous fiction, with characters possessed of a certain degree of freedom and mobility and a certain degree of knowledge: characters, in other words, to be looked on as characters. And on the other hand there is an investigation of a world in which such characters are thought to exist. It is all too easy when trying to make sense of the film to elide those two lines into each other, and to see the world of the film as that of a decadent society, thereby missing the point, for what is in fact at stake is not a decadent society but a decadentist literature which provides the rules of the game which Visconti then scrutinises. The film is always striving towards the real-isation of something artificial, a fiction materialised with real actors in real places, which nevertheless constantly declares itself as a fiction. . . .

The film never really resolves itself in one way or the other —which has always been the weakness of Visconti's films but also their strength. (p. 124)

Geoffrey Nowell-Smith, "Film Reviews: 'L'Innocente'," in Sight and Sound *(copyright © 1978 by The British Film Institute), Vol. 47, No. 2, Spring, 1978, pp. 123-24.*

MICHAEL SEITZ

"The Innocent," despite a dated story, is a serious and masterfully made film, especially notable for its elegant *mise en scène* and visual sumptuousness. . . .

Although it cannot be said to represent Visconti's final testament, the film does reflect a mastery of the medium acquired over the course of a long and distinguished career. (p. R18)

The film's initial sequence of credits reveals an old but sensitive hand (Visconti's own) carefully turning the pages of a first edition of Gabriele D'Annunzio's *L'Innocente,* the 1892 novel from which the movie was adapted. This apparent reverence for the text would seem to suggest a faithful rendering of the novel, but this is not the case. All that has been rendered are the bare bones.

D'Annunzio's work is a rather tedious and highly introspective first-person narrative that, in its verbal indulgences and intellectual snobbishness, represents the Italian author at his worst. Visconti's film is more dramatic, more richly textured, and it places its action within a social setting that the novel largely ignores. Almost all of the film's most striking scenes and one of the major characters (the mistress is barely mentioned in the novel) are the creations of Visconti and his collaborators. . . . (pp. R19-R20)

Visconti, who has always had a special genius for staging, has endowed "The Innocent" with some of the most sumptuous scenes to be found in the cinema. Through the most careful attention to detail and period authenticity, and by means of an exquisite balancing and juxtapositioning of rich colors and textures, the film manages to make the material world of the *fin de siècle* European aristocracy startlingly palpable. . . .

The luxurious beauty of the settings is not, however, an end in itself, but a necessary context for the film's dramatic action. The estates and salons, with their silent, attentive servants, represent a world of apparent order and stability. Wealth and privilege insulate its members from the disruptive changes forming the modern world, and elaborate rules of decorum protect their society from internal disruption. . . .

The elegance and decorum we witness in "The Innocent" are only a veneer, barely concealing the disastrous lack of moral principle that underlies them. The substance of such traditional aristocratic values as faith, honor, and duty had been eroded by the Enlightenment and by the rise of capitalism, and there was nothing to replace them but a naïve belief in personal freedom—a belief that, in practical terms, translated into personal indulgence. It is this moral failure, embodied in Tullio Hermil, that Visconti has given cinematic dramatization. . . .

One of the most revealing sequences in "The Innocent" (it is repeated with some variations later in the film) takes place at a formal social gathering for a musical soirée. . . . It is an image of harmony—a privileged vision of privileged people in a moment of both physical and spiritual repose. In the midst of the performance, however, there are repeated exits and entrances, whispered conversations—movements and sounds that draw our attention away from the recital. It soon becomes clear that these interruptions are indicative of the inner agitations and personal worries that preoccupy the beautiful people who have gathered here.

The musical is little more than a pretext for assignations, for the formal display of marriageable young daughters, and for the verification of social status. It is a scene right out of Proust. . . .

I wish that Visconti had in fact been adapting Proust, and not a minor work of D'Annunzio. . . . He has, nonetheless, made a film of greater richness and strength than the literary work on which it is based. This is vintage Visconti, and that alone is sufficient cause for rejoicing. (p. R20)

Michael Seitz, "Two New Films from Italy Share the Same Star and Attitude, but the Similarities Are Only Skin Deep," in The Chronicle Review *(copyright © 1979 by The Chronicle of Higher Education, Inc.), March 5, 1979, pp. R18-R20.**

DONALD LYONS

The occasion of *The Leopard* is the bourgeois revolution of 1860, Garibaldi invading Sicily, and the tone of the film is one of detached pity for the follies of the liberators. . . .

The Prince's fastidious pride and melancholy valuing of past glory are Visconti's; there is no distancing. . . . The Prince's pride is earned in the film by sense, humor, kindness, rational authority, exemption from hysteria. . . . He is, the Prince, a man of the Enlightenment, a mathematician and astronomer, with a controlled intelligence akin to an artist's. But this pride must still be purged, and here is the function of the stupendous Ball that ends the film. It is a cosmic panorama of the old world and the new, as Sicily gathers to dance, the linear rhythms of the movie (driveway, battle, church, telescope) yielding to the circles of the dance. . . .

The function of the infinitely detailed background is to silhouette the lonely, aware protagonist; the crowd of people and things exists as foil to the solitary individual. (p. 11)

The Leopard is family history as tragedy; *The Damned* is family history as guignol. This preposterous phantasmagoria, pretentiously subtitled *Götterdammerung,* is uncontaminated by any character of sensitivity or sense, except for a few vague, vestigial liberals who are effortlessly eliminated or quickly converted to wickedness. I was surprised . . . how emptily rhetorical it is—a work of the will, from the outside, with no heart or point. It should have been played as comedy. (pp. 11-12)

[*Death in Venice*] has a stately, meditative gravity—smooth, unhurried tableaux of sea, boat, gondola, hotel, beach, sun. Ripeness is a key feeling. . . . Like the Prince at the end of *The Leopard* or Meursault in prison at the close of *The Stranger* . . . , [Aschenbach] gazes up and comprehends his own death as fulfillment and transcendence.

And what had brought Aschenbach to this comprehension is, above all, Tadzio, Polish *enfant de bonne famille*, object of the musician's loving obsession, and fatal magnet keeping him in the diseased city. And Visconti gives Tadzio an alert, amused, inviting complicity in the obsession. . . . Visconti has found space in Mann's tale to show the spirit of Romantic tragedy as the begetter of music. Art, inspired by passion, has triumphed over history.

German history was to Visconti what Italian was to Shakespeare: food for melodrama. If *The Damned* was a kind of bad dream of *The Leopard, Ludwig* is the German romanticism of *Death in Venice* as farce, though here brilliantly successful. *Ludwig* is an album of the South German royal families of Wittelsbach and Habsburg in their guttering twilight. With familiar dialectical deftness, Visconti gives us at once an irresistibly seductive dying elite and a devastating diagnosis of its fatal malady. History has stranded these pretties, these enchanted children, in their playpens; Ludwig's revenge is to build larger playpens. (p. 12)

To stand outside society and its chaining relationships is the impulse of the typical Visconti hero, from his first masterpiece, *Ossessione*, to his last, *Conversation Piece*. In *Ossessione*, the wanderer Gino . . . is tempted to the road by the figure of the Spaniard . . . , who proffers a Whitmanesque fantasy of male vagabondage. . . .

[Gino and Giovanna's journey] is an Orphic journey; they have passed through death into another, free dimension. The final car trip and accident are a kind of charade, a wrenching of the lovers back into an element they had left for good. Their liberation has already occurred. And so clearly, far from heralding a neo-realist apotheosis of environment, Visconti has already in *Ossessione* (though he encompasses it with a truly Renoiresque grace) structured the environment as stimulus and springboard to transcendence.

Conversation Piece—really called *Family Group in an Interior*, as many Visconti movies might have been—is permeated by an autumn melancholy, but laced as well with something akin to slapstick. . . . The result is, on one level, a very Italian comedy of mayhem in an apartment house; on another, a rich and unmistakably personal treatment of an old theme, the invasion of a refined and sensitive intelligence by the anarchic-erotic forces of the Id. It is *Bringing Up Baby*, as told from the side of Cary Grant and civilization.

The title, evoking genre painting of the eighteenth century, is given ironic point by the black-and-white-with-chrome décor that eventually emerges from the destructiveness upstairs, a graphic visualizing of the nervy chaos of modernity. The Professor's apartment below . . . perfectly evokes the culture—cluttered but human, impotent but irreplaceable—which is threatened by the attractive barbarians above. The Professor's paternal love for the gigolo, exasperated tolerance becoming anxious concern, is one of the most delicate successes of the movie; and it casts a retrospective light on the protectiveness with which Visconti has treated quasi-paternal relationships, from the Prince and Tancredi to Aschenbach and Tadzio. . . .

Conversation Piece is the quietest, the wisest, the most intimate of all the Visconti studies of the anguished solitary—the ironic visionary striving to awake from the nightmare of history. (p. 13)

Donald Lyons, "Visconti's Magnificent Obsessions" (copyright © 1979 by Donald Lyons; reprinted by permission of the author), in Film Comment, *Vol. 15, No. 2, March-April, 1979, pp. 9-13.*

PAULINE KAEL

Although [*Conversation Piece*] takes place entirely in the interior of a Roman house, one doesn't feel confined: Konrad and the Countess are such depraved beasties that when they start screaming insults at each other, who care about whether there's a sun outdoors? (p. 35)

The story mechanism is much like that of those old *Kind Lady* plays in which a gang of schemers moves in on a helpless person, but this troupe has no ulterior motive. These intruders simply use the Professor the way they use everybody, and he's more than willing to be used. It is the theme of Visconti's *Death in Venice* all over again. . . . It's a winning movie—Visconti has come back changed. When you laugh, you can't always be sure that you're meant to be laughing, but you feel certain that he wouldn't mind. He seems to have got past the point at which one minds being laughed at.

Visconti's pictures have often had an undercurrent of silliness (though the solemn pacing kept audiences respectful); this time, the silliness is so close to the surface that the Professor can ask Lietta, the Countess's daughter, if she sees him as a character in a comic opera. *We* do, because his situation is a joke. (pp. 35-6)

Yet Visconti (and his co-scenarists, Suso Cecchi D'Amico and Enrico Medioli) seem to see this drone as a noble and sympathetic figure. Opening with electrocardiagram tape spilling out under the titles, *Conversation Piece* has a special quality, rather like an *apologia pro vita sua*, and at times, particularly toward the end, the Professor stands in for the director. The Professor is like a somnambulist, powerless to alter anything; the interlopers—the family—go on doing whatever they feel like. Yet he presides over the movie, and Visconti places the camera so that the Professor is always looming up—not part of the action but above it all. It's almost as if his scenes were shot at a different time—as if he were in a movie house, standing near the screen observing the show. (pp. 37-8)

Visconti has often used "detached" figures (as far back as the movie director in *Bellissima*), and it may have been the theme of Meursault's detachment from his own life that attracted Visconti to *The Stranger*. But what an erratic development it is that he should combine a spinoff of Aschenbach with the idea of the detached observer. What it comes to is that the Professor doesn't need the sexual awakening we anticipate in the early part of the film—that he understands and accepts physical passion, even though he himself is a recluse. . . .

However, the inadvertent comedy of *Conversation Piece* comes from Visconti's *lack* of detachment. Audiences don't generally ask of artists that they resolve their conflicts, but political ideologues demand it of them, and Visconti seems to feel the pressure acutely. He can't seem to accept the contradictions that have always plagued him; he's still trying to find a way to prove that his "decadent" tastes and his Marxist politics are not really contradictory, and *Conversation Piece* turns into a carnival of special pleading. When Visconti has ideas he wants to get across, he simply gives the explanation to anyone at hand. (p. 38)

There's grandeur in the silliness: one comes away with visions of Marxist dukes cruising the boys on the barricades. Fortunately, Visconti's control is so serenely relaxed that the picture seems part charade anyway—a seriously intended *opera buffa,* like Sartre on Genet (and much more fun). Somehow, the sloppiness—even the ungainly shift to a closeup almost every time an actor speaks—doesn't bother one. . . . The hollow ring of the dialogue contributes to the thinness of the film's sensibility; no one in it has any depth, and even the memory scenes, when the Professor recalls his mother and his long-ago bride, lack resonance. . . .

It's idiosyncratic filmmaking, all right. The film's Audenesque argument is generous, but what's it doing here? Visconti sets up one of his howlingly decadent families and then claims sweet naturalness for the daughter and fiancé who are cavorting with the mother's lover. Maybe the film's flower-child rhetoric is meant to be double-edged, but more likely Visconti is so romantic that he wants to remove the stigma from whores like Konrad and to show that the men who fall in love with them aren't the ludicrous, deceived sugar daddies they're generally taken to be. . . . As for the victimization, Visconti seems a Marxist old dear to think that Konrad is a sensitive boy sacrificed to the lust of the industrialist class and that "society" is responsible. Konrad is too convincing a tart.

Visconti is an eccentric master who has earned the right to his follies, when he can make them as pleasurable as *Conversation Piece*. . . . (p. 39)

Pauline Kael, "Lazarus Laughs" (originally published in a different version in The New Yorker, *Vol. LI, No. 32, September 29, 1975), in her* When the Lights Go Down *(copyright © 1975, 1976, 1977, 1978, 1979, 1980 by Pauline Kael; reprinted by permission of Holt, Rinehart and Winston, Publishers), Holt, 1980, pp. 35-40.*

Andrzej Wajda

1926-

Polish director and scriptwriter.

Wajda is generally acknowledged to be one of Poland's greatest directors. He is not a popular figure with the public in Poland, however, due to his unsettling views of traditional values. His trilogy, as well as establishing Wajda as a major European director, proved to be a milestone in Polish cinema for its moving depiction of war and those it affects.

Wajda fought with the Polish resistance during World War II, then attended the Kraców Academy of Fine Arts before going on to the film school at Lódź. He assisted Aleksander Ford on *Five Boys from Barska Street,* an experience that prepared him for his first feature film, *Pokolenie (A Generation).*

This film, along with *Kanal* and *Popiol i Diament (Ashes and Diamonds),* formed Wajda's war trilogy, exposing the myths of national heroism and the conflicts Poland's young generation underwent as they watched their elders suffer. Caught up in a war they wanted no part of, these youths were confused and frustrated, and Wajda's films depicted this effectively. These films were stark and simple. In contrast, his films of the sixties were stylized period pieces that relied on elaborate imagery and symbolism and were, for the most part, unsuccessful artistically.

***Wszystko na Sprzedaz (Everything for Sale)* changed Wajda's style and, more significantly, altered his philosophy of filmmaking. Aside from being his most personal work, inspired by the death of a close friend and star of many of his films, it is also Wajda's acceptance of the "new cinema," the exchange of his stylized drama for a more personal realistic view of life.**

Wajda's earlier films were most successful when they did not stray from the Polish theme he knew best: the analysis of Poland's youth and their attitudes towards their situation. Later films embraced subjects not exclusively Polish, though Polish cinema asks to be judged in terms of its issues as much as its artistic merit. Though Wajda's work is occasionally flawed by a style some find ambiguous and baroque, his intensely personal vision makes him, according to Charles Higham, "the voice of Poland crying in its agony."

BOSLEY CROWTHER

[In his "Ashes and Diamonds," Andrzej Wajda] is doing a melancholy recapitulation on the political and social chaos at the end of the war.

As in his previous pictures, M. Wajda is putting forth here something more than a trenchant observation of a highly dramatic episode. . . .

Wajda has shaped the story in strong and striking visual images. His sharply etched black-and-white action has the pictorial snap and quality of some of the old Soviet pictures of Pudovkin and Eisenstein. Facial expressions are highlighted, bodily movements are swift and intense and the light that comes in from the outside in the shaky morning is as dense as luminous smoke.

Likewise, Wajda has created some vivid ideas through imagery—ideas that carry cynicism, melancholia, wistfulness and shock. There is a beautiful scene of the killers remembering dead comrades at a bar, marking each recollection with a glass of brandy set aflame. . . .

The mood of despair in this picture is as heavy as that in [his earlier work,] "Kanal," but the film itself is much more searching. . . .

Bosley Crowther, "'Ashes and Diamonds'," in The New York Times *(© 1961 by The New York Times Company; reprinted by permission), May 30, 1961, p. 8.*

ROGER MANVELL

Innocent Sorcerers is a charming, absorbing essay in the newer Polish sophistication. Sophistication has in any case its gradations of refinement in self-consciousness, and in Andrzej Wajda's film it is a little heavily played. . . .

Innocent Sorcerers has a conventionally happy ending that could have been far better left ambiguous. The sophistication of this night of verbal seduction is nicely, if, as I have said, a little obviously played; but in a way it becomes all the more poignant because of the essential amateurishness of these bourgeois pretensions in the rough surroundings of the war-scarred buildings. Our bourgeois eyes, sated by years of the Italian, French, German, Austrian and American variants of the old sentimental story of how what starts out as seduction can turn into the charms of true love, will find, I think, a certain pathos in this assertion by Polish youth that they, too, have the right to play at love once again now that the big freeze is more or less over and a new generation is claiming the right to create its own values.

Roger Manvell, "'Innocent Sorcerers'" (© copy-

right Roger Manvell 1962; reprinted with permission), in Films and Filming, *Vol. 8, No. 7, April, 1962, p. 31.*

CHARLES HIGHAM

Andrzej Wajda has only made a handful of films, not all of them good; yet already he is safely among the modern masters. The one director in the Polish cinema whose work one can study as a whole, he is, so far as one can see, its only romantic poet; his style—sombre, stark, elaborately symbolic, often laden with baroque decoration—exists to expose the dark passions of his heroes and their hopeless courage. (pp. 408-09)

The emphasis on courage, youth, physical strength and aspiration blazing like solitary beacons in the night of the world—this is at the centre of the lyrical-romantic Polish literary tradition. Mickiewicz, Stowacki—these poets with their powerfully evocative imagery, their hymns or elegies to the proud youth of Poland dead in war or revolution, are the spiritual godfathers of Wajda and of the late Andrzej Munk. And it is not too much to say that, like Mickiewicz, Wajda has been the voice of Poland crying in its agony, as well as a worthy singer of its eternal songs of freedom. (p. 409)

Disciplined and stark, *A Generation* has the fierce lyrical intensity of a Mickiewicz poem. . . . [It] stands in the mainstream of the Polish artistic tradition: it celebrates youth and beauty and courage, the struggle of the emergent warrior to conquer his fears, the final bursting into flower of manhood and strength. And in a sense, Wajda's personality is undergoing a similar purifying process in the development of the film; one can sense a determined attempt to spare himself nothing of his memories of 1942, of his thoughts of people and things seen, loved and lost. The austerity of the images [never falters]. . . .

A Generation remains Wajda's purest, most stripped and disciplined film. And its few moments of emotion—notably when Dorota is arrested, and Stach breaks into a sudden agony of grief—are all the more disturbing because of the tight-lipped sternness of the rest. In *Kanal* (1957), Wajda's style is already becoming more rhetorical, more baroque; nevertheless this, too, remains a powerfully haunting and beautiful film, and its technical skill shows a rapidly maturing grasp of the medium. (p. 410)

With *Ashes and Diamonds,* the third part of the trilogy (1958), Wajda emerged in the full romantic colors. The austere style of *A Generation* gives way completely to a dynamic virtuoso flair seldom found outside the American cinema. The film is—simply on the technical level—Wajda's most breathtaking achievement, its visuals and soundtrack orchestrated with triumphant skill. . . . (p. 411)

Occasionally the film tilts over into self parody—notably in the sequence when an inverted crucifix shifts and groans above the two lovers in a church (and much of the film suggests a talent strained beyond its resources) but *Ashes and Diamonds* still retains a seductive brilliance and power.

[In *Innocent Sorcerers* (1960)] the young Poles of the earlier films are discovered in a wholly contemporary world of motor-scooters, fast parties and willing girls, and the ravaged faces and bodies of the war years have filled out into the strength and beauty of a well-fed post-war generation. (p. 412)

At the end of the film, in the original version . . . planned by Wajda, comedy turns to tragedy: sophistication destroys love, and Magda walks away [from the doctor], their relationship unconsummated. But the producers, the Kadr Film Unit, forced a happy ending on them; after the doctor's desperate search for Magda through the streets, he finds her waiting for him in his room.

The last minute sell-out by no means destroys the impact of this fresh, graceful and quietly erotic film. It is full of wit and an edged, urbane charm, but the underlying dark poetry of Wajda is unmistakable. In the central characters, the whole nature of post-war youth is exposed: its sardonic common-sense, its self-destructive smartness and amorality, its permissive sensuality and moments of fierce disillusion. (pp. 412-13)

The character of Jakub Gold [in *Samson*]—fatalistically returning to certain death in the ghetto, only finding his Samson's powers by self-immolation for an heroic cause—is in direct line with Stach's in *A Generation,* and one sees Wajda's nostalgic need to return to a period when hopes and ideals were high. . . . But the film is severely flawed by the symbolism which is Wajda's curse; the Biblical parallels lie heavily on scene after scene, and too often the beautiful, bleak images—figures strikingly disposed in the Cinemascope frame—simply become melodramatic friezes, theatrical backdrops to a heavily overworked allegory. (p. 413)

[Contemporary] Poland remains a rather shadowy presence on the cultural map of the West and Wajda, poised between two worlds, dealing in the most powerful of international mediums, seems uniquely equipped to cast light on that darkness in the years to come. (p. 414)

Charles Higham, "Grasping the Nettle: The Films of Andrzej Wajda," in The Hudson Review *(copyright © 1965 by The Hudson Review, Inc.; reprinted by permission), Vol. XVIII, No. 3, Autumn, 1965, pp. 408-14.*

TOM MILNE

Bearing witness to the destruction of an ideal, *Lotna* is a deeply pessimistic film, built on an image of decay and obsessed by death. . . .

Almost all of Wajda's imagery here is bizarre—too bizarre, perhaps, for some tastes. . . . But *Lotna,* after all, is in itself something of a romantic gesture; its baroque excesses are also its strength, and one either likes them or one doesn't. . . .

With vivid strangeness, underlined by Wajda's extraordinary use of colour, *Lotna* records the passing of a civilisation. The night sequences are shot in sepia, with most of the day scenes dominated by the pale browns and greens of autumn exteriors (echoed in the cavalry uniforms), so that the more delicate tints—the blue of a Wedgwood vase, the red of an apple—seem to be gradually enveloped in a wash of drabness. (p. 42)

Tom Milne, "'Lotna'," in Sight and Sound *(copyright © 1965 by The British Film Institute), Vol. 35, No. 1, Winter, 1965-66, pp. 41-2.*

JOHN SIMON

Kanal seems to me, except for one minor flaw, as perfect an antiwar film as was ever made. (p. 21)

The wretched troop [of the Warsaw Uprising] sloshes about [in the sewers] waist-deep in muck, in abysmal darkness, and totally unsure of their way and of what will await them above, if they ever make it. Their sufferings, loyalties, weaknesses, quarrels, heroism, and hopes begotten on despair would suggest little fluctuation from the prevailing note of catastrophe. Yet Wajda is able to evoke such a range of human reactions to this overarching doom, he can show such various shadings of courage, such nuances of discouragement and grief, that we can all locate ourselves on this scale of human responses to disaster; and we are given both a foretaste of our individual dying and an overwhelming taste of our common mortality.

The one false note is struck by an artist and intellectual in the band who goes mad and blindly wanders about reciting passages from Dante's *Inferno*. This is redundant—carrying symbolism to the second power; within a concrete image of hell, we do not need an abstraction of it. But otherwise the film is utterly spare and chaste, and the inevitable tragedies, all different, all manage to surprise, shock, and, without any diminishing returns, shatter us. Contrary to the layman's belief, there are several shades of black, and *Kanal* explores and exemplifies them all. . . . *Kanal* comes as close as any work of art can to breaking the heart; if any films can prevent us, even temporarily, from shirking our humanity, this, surely, is one of them. (pp. 21-2)

John Simon, "Favorites," in his Private Screenings *(reprinted by permission of Wallace & Sheil Agency, Inc.; © 1967 by John Simon), Macmillan, 1967, pp. 17-37.**

COLIN McARTHUR

[*Everything for Sale*] is both public and private, a memorial to the dead actor [Zbigniew Cybulski], a personal testament of the director and, crucially, a work which shatters the artistic fetters which have bound Wajda throughout his career. Feeding both on reality and on film, *Everything for Sale* is Wajda's meditation on a theme, illusion and reality. . . . At one blow he has matured from an extremely interesting, visually exciting artist whose work was fully comprehensible only in the Polish context to an international artist who happens to be Polish. (p. 139)

[The very general question of illusion and reality appears in different terms throughout the film.] However, the most central expression of the appearance/reality theme is in terms of the truth or falsity of emotion, or, put in abstract, antinomic terms, whether life or art is the more important. (p. 140)

The abstract implication of the theme, the polarity of art and life, is realised in the complex scene in which the car driven by Andrzej brakes very suddenly, causing him to cut his head on the driving mirror. While Ela goes to moisten a handkerchief to wipe away the blood, Andrzej gets out a camera and photographs the wound. Like many of the crucial images in the film, this scene telescopes several themes. As well as stating the life versus art dichotomy, it reminds us that *Everything for Sale* is a film about Andrzej Wajda, and extremely frank confession of the stresses within his artistic sensibility and even within his psyche. Andrzej's photographing of his own wound carries sado-masochistic overtones, a charge often made, sometimes in crassly simplistic terms, against Wajda's work as a whole. Even allowing for the degree to which his preoccupation with heroism, defeat and death has pulled him towards images of violence. Wajda as artist seems to be fascinated to a remarkable extent with images of mutilation (the one-legged men in *A Generation, Siberian Lady Macbeth* and *Ashes* and the one-legged girl in *Kanal*) and with spectacular images of painful death (the killing of the cement workers and of Maciek in *Ashes and Diamonds*). At their most baroque, these images often incorporate their own obverse of life and beauty, like the corpse festooned with bandages in the bridal bed in *Lotna*. It is possible to read the scene in which Andrzej photographs his wound as Wajda's confession of this impulse in himself. . . .

Cybulski completely dominates the lives of the characters in *Everything for Sale* although he does not appear. Again, such is the integrity of the film that the portrait is presented warts and all. . . .

The legend, the relics, the devotion, all have mythic overtones, and the Cybulski myth is seen to be growing as Daniel, Beata and Ela seek out a resistance comrade of the dead actor to verify the story of his involvement with the Resistance. However, Wajda does not allow us to view the myth uncritically, as can be gauged from possibly the most striking scene in the film. After Cybulski's death has become known, the leading figures are seen in black, walking with downcast eyes. We assume that they are walking in his cortège until we see that they are in a film studio, and following a trolley bearing cans of film, as it turns out the film of Cybulski's funeral. Like so many of the images of *Everything for Sale,* this one is complex and resonant. It encapsulates the several expressions of the appearance/reality theme: in terms of the film's relationship with the audience, in terms of Wajda's preoccupation with the dichotomy between art and life, and in terms of the source of Cybulski's charisma; whether the myth is growing round the man or his celluloid image.

Everything for Sale exemplifies the eternal mystery of artistic creation. Out of a devastating personal tragedy Wajda has wrought a masterpiece. (p. 141)

Colin McArthur, "'Everything for Sale'," in Sight and Sound *(copyright © 1969 by The British Film Institute), Vol. 38, No. 3, Summer, 1969, pp. 139-41.*

KRZYSZTOF-TEODOR TOEPLITZ

Cybulski's sudden accidental death was the starting point for *Everything for Sale,* whose story concerns the disappearance of a famous actor during the shooting of a film. . . . The situation gives Wajda the occasion for confronting legend with reality, but he is aware of the danger of facile, shallow "debunking"; the film is far more complex than that. Instead, Wajda is interested in collecting the gestures, impressions, and various incidental fragments of personality or image which the dead actor scattered among the living, and showing how these "crumbs" constitute an awkward gift, like some heirloom one is dearly attached to and yet can do nothing with. The dead actor's legend persists among the living characters as a challenge; attempts to meet it result only in buffoonish or ludicrous gestures. A young actor, dreaming of taking the place of the deceased, hunts through the scraps of his life for materials with which to recreate and then usurp a legend which has already fatally dissolved. The actor's wife pitifully tries to promote a legend of their ideal marriage, which all know to be false. . . .

In *Everything for Sale* the focus shifts to the deceased actor's milieu—upon which his disappearance seems to throw a dazzling light. Among his colleagues, former girl-friends, and acquaintances the old heroic impulses have given way to personal, family, or erotic dramas. Nor does Wajda imply in the slightest degree that these are demeaning; on the contrary, it is the exaltation connected with the dead actor that seems anachronistic, and although the director figure goes through a crisis of conscience in deciding to finish his film, he is not portrayed unsympathetically. It turns out, in fact, that the actor-symbol had been dead long before his actual death. And thus in a literal as well as semimagical way Wajda manages to shift his point of view from identification with the actor to identification with his milieu. (p. 39)

The guiding formal idea of *Everything for Sale* is Wajda's own malicious destruction of his former stylization. The film consists of a series of pietistically constructed, pictorially beautiful images which again and again reveal their artificiality through ever so slight a shift in the point of view. . . . There is a magnificent cavalry charge, as in the best of historical reconstructions, yet at the same time we see the camera shooting the scene and we perceive all the fake details, as if in contrast to these beautiful artifacts. The film abounds in such images, always followed by an "exposure," as if the director wanted to demonstrate the ease of prearranging such scenes, and simultaneously to express his disapproval of their conventional vacuousness. In this way *Everything for Sale* becomes in a sense not only a film about film-making but it also expresses doubts whether film is at all possible.

In short, Wajda, like many other contemporary artists in cinematography as well as literature, faced the problem of self-conscious themes. These themes are both a seemingly indispensable stage of waking up to the peculiarity of one's own creation, and also a dangerous trap. (p. 40)

[*A Fly Hunt* or *Hunting Flies*] is a comedy situation, but Wajda uses it not so much as a traditional story but as a philosophical tale of a world in which women play an increasingly bigger role, subordinating men to their goals and ambitions. . . . In *A Fly Hunt* Wajda is interested in the paradoxical, often psychologically novel situations which result from the headlong emancipation of women, accompanied as it is by widespread emasculation and weakening of man's position. But perceptions of this complex worldwide social and historical process could be realized through diverse cases. *A Fly Hunt* is organized like a traditional story, but with a fabular tone, as of episodes illustrating a presupposed principle. (pp. 40-1)

What matters is the essential problem around which the film is woven, and if this proves credible even when we make the characters act in purposely exaggerated or fixed circumstances (maintaining of course some degree of believability) so much the better for the problem itself. Needless to add, such an assumption opens for Wajda, for the first time, possibilities of comedy. *A Fly Hunt* becomes a satirical comedy not only through the poignancy of its misogynism but also because of the director's facility in manipulating his protagonist's adventures. . . .

From this angle, too, the film attacks Wajda's problem of acceptable film form. He no longer attempts beautiful images, intended to suggest through their intensity some profound meaning. Film language now serves modestly to create a reality which is conventionalized enough to escape the demands of mimetic verisimilitude, while remaining sufficiently realistic and convincing to prevent an immersion in illusion. Wajda has noticed that the techniques introduced by the film avant-garde in the past decade—the new montage, techniques of manipulating the camera and focus, the ease of arranging scenes having the abstractness of modern painting, camera mobility combined with a penchant for the close-up—in short the entire language of the new cinema calls not for a challenge of the film as a fictional story but for subordinating the narration to an intellectual discipline which no longer needs to rely on plots that unfold step by step. If the traditional director assumed that only a few scenes truly mattered for him, whereas the rest of the film consisted of necessary explications and connections, the modern director can deal only with that which actually interests him—leaving out all the rest.

From this point of view the problem of "beautiful spectacle," always somewhat bothersome in Wajda's films, disappears or at least loses much of its significance. For here the picturesqueness or harsh brutality of imagery no longer relates in such a direct and univocal way to the subject matter; it is subsumed instead as part of the "handwriting" employed by the director—who may combine different elements of film reality according to his purposes.

Thus, in Wajda's new films, we witness the rare development of a director who attempts to escape—with great success—the magic circle of his own artistic achievements and the problems they inevitably raise. (p. 41)

Krzysztof-Teodor Toeplitz, "Wajda Redivivus," in Film Quarterly *(copyright 1969 by The Regents of the University of California; reprinted by permission of the University of California Press), Vol. XXIII, No. 2, Winter, 1969-70, pp. 37-41.*

PHILIP STRICK

While audiences outside Poland are unlikely to be aware of the historical echoes that resound through Andrzej Wajda's film of *The Wedding* . . . , and will certainly miss a fair number of its jokes and references, Wajda's achievement is to make the original event, extraordinary and uneasy as it must have seemed at the time, not only accessible but also hauntingly significant to the present. His film shudders with menace and regret, a lament for the Polish predicament both as it was in 1900 after yet another century of being used as Europe's doormat, and as it is now, its independence as elusive as ever. And setting aside nationalism entirely, *The Wedding* turns out to have its global metaphors as well, defined by the contrasts between the obsessive, raucous celebrations and the forces slowly gathering in the surrounding gloom.

The film begins with a torrent of jubilation and tumbling images before which the spirits shrink; the undisciplined racket and ill-aimed camera seem ugly and inept, an implausible attempt to simulate enthusiasm. But this proves to be exactly Wajda's intention. . . . [The] bedlam is overwhelming in a manner that feels characteristic of East European cinema, typified perhaps by the shots in which bride and groom spin round with the camera in the centre of the floor. . . .

The Wedding is a fascinating array of sudden nightmares. . . . Wajda's most disturbing image . . . is that of the house itself, a tiny outpost of warmth in a landscape of freezing terror. It is much the same contrast as between rubbish-dump and ballroom in *Ashes and Diamonds,* and one could argue that Wajda hasn't added to it appreciably. . . . But then the situation doesn't seem to have changed much either, since 1900.

Philip Strick, "Film Reviews: 'The Wedding'," in Sight and Sound *(copyright © 1973 by The British Film Institute), Vol. 42, No. 3, 1973, p. 174.*

BOLESŁAW MICHAŁEK

On the face of it, the story [of *A Generation*] appears to be fairly stereotyped. At the centre there is a character with the required hallmarks of the "positive hero": high-minded, uncompromising, dogged, with all the mandatory virtues and not a trace of doubts, complications or crises. (p. 19)

It is not enough to say that *A Generation* was made with such skill, feeling and power that it took these pitfalls in its stride. It deserves closer scrutiny to show where and how the shifting of its emphasis was brought about. Let me touch only on the most salient point: the characterisation of the two protagonists. It is a fair guess that the inner world to which Wajda personally felt most attuned was that of Jasio Krone—edgy, troubled, bewildered, switching from one extreme to another, and ultimately tragic—and not with Stach, the dour proletarian not to be deflected from his chosen course. So, against all the logic of the screenplay, it is Jasio who dominates the film—and with him the themes which have wound their way through all of Wajda's work: the sense of bitter defeat ("the heroes of this film are the people who lose, not the ones who win"); the tragic nature of human destiny (the man who dies is the one who most wanted to live); and beleaguerment (Jasio's line of escape is cut off by a barrier which leaves suicide as the only alternative, a *motif* which recurs in *Kanal*). (pp. 19-20)

Wajda's distinctive language was already minted: the characteristics unveiled in *A Generation* are recognisable from his other films—the love of shock contrasts, the vehemence bordering on brutality. . . . Equally evident in *A Generation* is a certain expressionist imagery. This is not so much a matter of an artist *manqué* straining after composition, elaborate harmony of shapes, outlines and light, as of a constant visual intensity, of images with dramatic bite: as the white trench-coat of the fleeing Jasio isolates him from the grey surroundings, the frame itself seems to be marking him down as doomed. This over-emphatic, highly-charged, often symbolic style of expression had critics already reaching for the adjective "baroque" with Wajda's very first film.

And yet . . . there is in *A Generation* a certain lightness of touch, a degree of ease in the *mise-en-scène,* a measure of relaxation in the acting. The film came over more like a captured fragment of reality than painfully re-created scenes from history. . . . (pp. 21-2)

In style [*Kanal*] is constructed as a steadily mounting crescendo. (p. 28)

Made with overpowering visual force, *Kanal* straddles a gulf between the realism of actual events with characters who are reasonably faithful portraits of the mentality and attitudes of the time, and an almost abstract vision of a sealed world whose inhabitants are doomed to extinction. Inevitably a parallel was drawn with Dante's "Inferno"—by Wajda himself as well as reviewers—and it is true that the film is permeated by a virtually unrelieved mood of despair, bitterness and resignation. The whole structure is pivoted on the idea that there is no way out, no hope, no chance of deliverance. As in Dante there is only a succession of narrowing circles of torment. What a contrast with *A Generation* with its variations of tone, its rays of hope, its surges of *joie de vivre* intermingling with the intimations of death! (pp. 29-30)

At first glance we have [in *Ashes and Diamonds*] a story of violence and love, deftly plotted and compulsively told: the assassin balks at his assignment, falters, thinks of backing out, but in the end goes through with it and is struck down shortly afterwards. At one level, *Ashes and Diamonds* is indeed a straightforward, suspenseful thriller; but there is more to its interest than that. (pp. 38-9)

[Deep down] *Ashes and Diamonds* has a broader meaning, sometimes missed by non-Polish audiences. The date of these fateful hours between the afternoon of one day and the morning of the next must be held in mind: it is the first day after the war, the first day of a new age. In this space of time it is more than the course of a single romance and single killing that reaches its breaking-point. The lives of these people and their nation stand at a crossroads between two eras. The occupation is over, but through those harrowing years of bloodshed, hardship and struggle, men's minds had been too pre-occupied with the necessities of battle and survival to give much thought to the exact shape of post-war realities. . . . A challenge was also being made to the nation's traditional moral and social hierarchies, beliefs and myths, and a different mentality, way of life and ideals propagated in their place. Long-suppressed aspirations broke through to the surface; so did apprehensions. This first day marked the onset, therefore, of a dramatic process which was to continue for many years. . . .

[The film] has, therefore, all the ingredients of a national epic, showing individual destinies being re-shaped in the turmoil of a great *débâcle*. (p. 39)

The heart of the matter lay in the social and political implications of *Ashes and Diamonds,* and these were traced to the presentation and confrontation of its two key figures: Maciek the assassin and Szczuka the representative of the new government. . . . [The] "representative" of the authorities is an old man, tired, soured, a little lackadaisical, while the "representative" of the anti-communist Underground is young, dynamic, captivating and unforgettable in every gesture and glance from behind his dark glasses. (p. 40)

Let us, however, take a closer look at these two figures. . . . [Szczuka] is an ageing, somewhat stolid man, possibly exhausted by the long years of political struggle (there is a suggestion that he also fought in the Spanish Civil War); in him lies a certain tolerant view of the surrounding events. . . . [He] views the turbulent new world not with the eyes of an energetic, robust and uncomplex-ridden Party organiser and outsider, but of a man who knows that, no matter what, everything must once again be started anew—but with whom and against whom? (pp. 41-2)

Despite the trappings of the late Fifties in [Maciek's] appearance—the dark glasses which serve as a kind of mask—he belongs to the generation which grew up under the Occupation, and is one of those people whom the writer Tadeusz Borowski called "contaminated by death" because they had seen and experienced too much. The love he finds in these brief hours regenerates him, crystallises all his honourable qualities and restores an attachment to life which had been drained out of him. (p. 42)

Can it be that these two men, who fell into each other's arms in a paradoxical embrace at the moment of assassination, are in fact brothers, regardless of all adversaries, careerists and dogmatists? Such an appeal for solidarity was implicit in [Jerzy] Andrzejewski's novel, and it is echoed in the film. (p. 45)

Lotna remains pure Wajda: if an anthology of Wajda's style were ever to be compiled, here would be the *locus classicus*. It may have been the thinness of the script and the absence of a firm narrative structure which led Wajda to give vent to a highly personal idiom far removed from any literary model. It is a language of great visual intensity which owes much to a certain type of painting he came to admire while still at art school, one which combines minute attention to reality with the shock effect of gruesome or absurd detail. This style . . . has affinities both with Nineteenth-century naturalism where it borders on *kitsch* and with the surrealism of the Twenties and Thirties. . . . The strange creatures glimpsed in *Lotna*— the expiring fish in the foreground of the love scene, the slit bodies of animals and people—are part of the same currency. (p. 50)

[It] was only in *Lotna* that the surrealist elements dotted around [Wajda's] films had at last been made to cohere [Zygmunt Kałużyński, in the weekly "Polityka", said that:] "This paradox can be explained by the moral of *Lotna:* it is in its way a cinematic epitaph to a dying world, and accordingly everything in it that is monstrous becomes a kind of symbolic elegy to the historical anachronism that now arouses our astonishment. Surrealism is the style of a civilisation in defeat, and so, strangely enough, it seems here to accord with the theme." (p. 53)

The most important thing omitted from [Kazimierz Brandys's novel *Samson*] was a view of history new to Wajda and one which coloured the whole treatment of human destiny. In his classic films—*Kanal* and *Ashes and Diamonds* —history was . . . seen as a blind, anonymous force smashing its way through life and leaving behind a trail of misery, pain and death. Wajda observed and registered the havoc but could not, or would not, look deeper into the machinery which caused it. It was only in *Samson* that, taking his cue from Brandys, he imposed some kind of logic and pattern on history and indicated its social, political and ideological mainsprings. Gold's fate is as tragic and inevitable as that of any of Wajda's other heroes; what is different is that the workings behind it are revealed, for the first time there is an intimation of the political, moral and class agencies responsible for his misfortunes. The sole opposition, not just to fascism, but to the terror and apathy of its victims, comes chiefly from the communists whom Gold first meets in prison and who later come to his rescue, rekindling his will to live and resist. It is worth noting, therefore, that we have not only a flat description of people who suffer and people who fight, but also an analysis of the forces which inflict these sufferings, of the people who bear guilt and responsibility. (p. 64)

[As Barthélemy Amengual noted in his study of Wajda in *Etudes Cinématographiques:*] "In *Ashes and Diamonds* and *Lotna* the acquittal is total: it is History which is guilty. But beginning with *Samson* Wajda embarks on a re-appraisal of the very idea of responsibility . . . He then stumbles upon the Sartrian proposition of 'on ne fait pas ce qu'on veut et cependant on est responsable de ce qu'on est.' ['one cannot do what one wishes and therefore one is responsible for what one is']." True enough: this new approach to the conformation of human destiny implies a new concept of responsibility—for oneself and for the world. In *Kanal* and *Ashes and Diamonds,* man pulverised by the juggernaut of history was seen only as an object, not as a subject; hence his passivity, his fatalistic acceptance of what is in any case inevitable. But once the mechanism of history has been laid bare and its undercurrents brought to light, man assumes a responsibility for himself, for his fellows and for his fate. The appearance of such a point of view in *Samson* should be regarded, therefore, as a new departure in the moral and philosophical content of Wajda's cinema, the elimination of a certain weakness or (as some critics had it) helplessness in its underpinning. (p. 65)

[*The Birch-Wood*'s] account of two brothers buried in the solitude of a remote forest brought into focus one of [Jarosław] Iwaszkiewicz's recurrent preoccupations: the theme of death, of life overshadowed by intimations of death, or—to put it in existentialist terms—the ubiquity of death in the structures of life. The only way, and at the same time the most natural one, of standing up to death, he seems to say, lies in romantic and physical love. Though love had appeared in *Siberian Lady Macbeth,* in *Ashes and Diamonds,* and in *Landscape after the Battle* as a force which could redeem from death, which regenerated human nature, these films never took on the makings of total existentialist dramas. In this respect *The Birch-Wood* is unique. (p. 135)

Iwaszkiewicz penetrates, in the psychological clashes, to the deeper layer of an existentialist drama. Wajda has followed this lead, developed the theme and pushed it further. There is no escape from death except in the consummation of the *libido*—love becomes a source of life, the one great force which can counteract the death instinct. Here, to use Freudian terminology, is an opposition between the life urge and the death urge, between Eros and Thanatos. The duel fought out in the birch-wood is between these two drives.

Eros and Thanatos: seeking the right visual key for this conflict, Wajda once again turned to painting, this time to the work of an artist similarly fascinated by this subject, Jacek Malczewski, an *art nouveau* painter recently rescued from oblivion. . . . His painting, "Thanatos," was loaned by the National Museum in Warsaw and hung in the forester's lodge, where it seems to preside over the drama and, like a tuning fork, establish the film's tone, shading and temperature.

The colour is certainly eerie, ugly in its way, "cadaverous" as it was called—a *mélange* of putrid yellows, greens and violets. These tones dominate the photography of human bodies with their faces splodged by sickly, sinister stains. The use of the same spectrum as Malczewski lent the film's images a disquieting, misty, but ever-present air of disease, decomposition and death. On the other hand, in the human shapes, in the naturalistic play of muscles, in the poses of figures towering over their surroundings and nature—and this was a recurrent feature in the composition of Malczewski's paintings—there is a clear sense of that vigour and vitality which opposes the deathly pallor of life. Again as with Malczewski, landscape also performs a distinctive function in the film: it is not simply a backdrop—its beauty, harmony and tranquillity act as a balm to the over-wrought characters torn between Eros and Thanatos.

The Birch-Wood was, therefore, carefully tuned to a specific visual style. The photography, art direction, *mise-en-scène,* even the performances, are all made to match. Only Bolesław, who begins with the smell of death and only later manages to shake it off, escapes these baleful hues. His face has the normal tan of a healthy, outdoor man.

Although this film appears at first glance a fleeting, marginal episode in Wajda's *oeuvre,* it marks a milestone in his career. From the outset he had picked subjects which were prickly, which sharply confronted national and social myths, and which argued with history. Here, for the first time, he made a success of a theme both universal and timeless, succeeding where previously defeated (working with a different story and a different kind of writing) in *Gates to Paradise*. To the eternal questions of love and death he brought a new dimension, a new emotional climate, and a fresh dramatic shape. It was for him a very enriching experience. (pp. 136-38, 140-41)

The film's touch of greatness comes not only from its aesthetic sophistication, its self-imposed restrictions, and concentration on three characters and their shared disquiets—all qualities completely new to Wajda—but above all from his first attempt to wrestle in earnest with the most deep-seated anxieties of human existence which for centuries have been art's most difficult material. (p. 141)

[Wajda suggested to his actors] a style of performance that departs quite markedly from the standard approach to [Stanislaw Wyspiański's play] "The Wedding," making them accentuate the commonplace aspect rather than the bewitchment of the occasion, and speak the verse as if it came naturally. Visually he gave the production distinct affinities with the art of the turn of the century, and particularly with the intriguing painting of Wyspiański himself: some of the frames with their soft lighting possess the same disturbing sweetness combined with piercing melancholy. The atmosphere of the party has been thickened and intensified: there is more movement, agitation, confusion, and alcoholic mist; although the stage has been opened out, it is more crowded. The confessions, conversations and apparitions which one after the other make up the meaning of the drama have been merged into the whole whirligig of the wedding revels. As the hours go by, moods change, and the atmosphere becomes steadily more charged until there is a feverish expectation of something about to happen, but which fades away in the hypnotic dance at dawn. Some of the conflicts latent in the play have been pointed up: when the peasants collect in response to their mysterious summons and find the Host asleep and dead to the world, they place their scythes to his neck. These scythes are not, therefore, just a part of folk-lore, a nostalgic reminiscence of the gallant scythe-bearers of the Kosciuszko Insurrection a hundred years earlier, but the threat hanging over the Kraków intelligentsia gathered at the wedding in Bronowice.

This is significant. Wajda seems to have mined from Wyspiański's play something that was certainly there but not always visible: the drama of the intelligentsia or, more broadly, of the *élite,* which for all its lumbering efforts to integrate with society, remains out of touch, locked up in myths, dreams and arguments which have no counterpart in real life. What comes to the surface in *The Wedding* is not only the drama of this *élite,* but also the drama of the culture of which it was the architect and prime beneficiary. For historical and other reasons culture in Poland has been a more fundamental factor of its existence and identity than in other societies. Yet the paradox is that it is deeply rooted in Nineteenth century themes and controversies, which, although often possessing an amazing relevance to contemporary conflicts and dilemmas, belong nevertheless to their own age. Andrzej Wajda's cinema is a good example of this paradox. One can therefore detect in *The Wedding* something of the drama of his art. (pp. 154-57)

Bolesław Michałek, in his The Cinema of Andrzej Wajda, *translated by Edward Rothert (© 1973 by The Tantivy Press, London, Great Britain and Bolesław Michałek), Tantivy, 1973, 175 p.*

JAN DAWSON

The most succinct way to describe *Man of Marble* . . . is as an East European *Citizen Kane*. Thematically, Andrzej Wajda's film is concerned with the mechanics of mythology: it explores the apparatus whereby a public image is created, modified and demolished, while simultaneously pursuing its own investigation into the reality behind the official myths. Like *Kane,* it is concerned with the power of the media to manipulate and even to manufacture truth; but where Welles was conducting a many-levelled enquiry into the power of the press, the medium with which Wajda is centrally concerned is that of the motion picture. His film, even more than *Kane,* becomes a technical demonstration of his subject matter: its virtuoso style has a total thematic relevance. And, as with Welles, the political sensitivity of Wajda's theme has scarcely helped ingratiate him with those who control domestic film production.

Where Kane himself was an American archetype, essentially a self-made man and myth, Wajda's hero is, as befits a socialist society, a pure product of the state. . . .

[His heroine] Agnieszka is a determinedly contemporary figure, striding at a more than manly pace in her blue denim suit, gracelessly abusing the male crew assigned to her, touting her worldly possessions around in a giant kit-bag. Her knowledge of the past appears as perfunctory as her knowledge of careerist politics (the TV producer's) or *realpolitik;* yet it is precisely this incautious ignorance (a survival of the spirit of '68?) which enables her to bludgeon her way through to the other truth she is seeking. Initially camouflaged by her surface of Westernised sophistication, her basic ingenuousness will prove to be a quality which she and her elusive subject have in common. . . .

Any implication that Wajda, by endorsing the stylistic preferences of his aggressive heroine ('Hand-held shots. Wide-angle lens. You've seen the latest American films, haven't you?'), is also suggesting that there's more truth and less manipulation with a mobile camera is neatly scotched within the film itself. The wide-angle shots of Burski's jet taxi-ing in to land are, as well as a political comment on the Americanisation of one of the film's more flagrant opportunists, also a timely demonstration of the ease with which the camera can inflate the significance of neutral events. There is an echo here of an early scene in which Agnieszka snatches the camera herself and, filming illegally in the museum vault for banished monuments, sits astride the fallen colossus of her missing hero. While Wajda's camera is ironically pointing out the sculptor's power to distort through magnification, Agnieszka's is busy reproducing these distortions through the latest fashionable means.

In emphasising that the *ars longa* maxim is particularly inapplicable to 'official' art, Wajda is, of course, also commenting on the ephemeral nature of political truths. His film explores the inextricable relationship between styles and politics, not merely through its own aesthetic but also through its treatment of time in relation to individuals. (p. 260)

Jan Dawson, "Film Reviews: 'Man of Marble'," in Sight and Sound *(copyright © 1979 by The British Film Institute), Vol. 48, No. 4, Autumn, 1979, pp. 260-61.*

STANLEY KAUFFMANN

[My] present opinion of Wajda grows, but does not differ, from what I thought 18 years ago. Wajda has now, quite evidently, the confidence that comes from extensive experience (he also directs in the theater) and from praise. To me, he is still honorably ambitious, still concerned with art that flourishes out of social tensions; also, he is still maladroit in method and selection, imitative, "unrecognizable" except in his excesses and faults. . . .

Without Anesthesia (1978) is a metaphoric, perhaps binary, film. . . . Politically *Without Anesthesia* doesn't say much more than that one can be in favor or disfavor, arbitrarily: the politics of the protagonist, a journalist-teacher, is not clear. But then neither is the marital split. The wife suddenly departs for a younger man without even leaving her address, and she takes their child with her. Why does she behave in this abrupt and cruel way, to a husband who clearly loves her? We never find out. His death at the end, through the explosion of a faulty stove, has nothing to do with his character, their situation, his politics. It's just a glibly ironic snapper.

But this is the best-directed film of Wajda's that I know. Fairly subtly, many of the scenes of mere dailyness are composed to suggest closure, confinement. . . .

[*The Girls of Wilko*] is Wajda's "Chekhov" picture, only he gives us five sisters instead of three. . . . In *The Girls of Wilko*, nothing goes deeper than mannerism: it's like a platitudinous director's idea of a Chekhov production applied to an inferior script—sighings and sentimental music. (p. 22)

The atmosphere [of *Land of Promise*] is well-enough evoked, and, so far as one can tell, the generally despicable characters are realistically written. . . . [However, Wajda's direction] seems frantic to impress. Whenever he wants to show a time lapse, he shoves in the belching smokestacks of Lodz. Whenever he goes to a country estate, he gives us shimmering leaves and sentimental music. When a sensual woman dines grandly, he almost shoves us down her gullet to prove her gluttony. When there's trouble in the streets, the camera gets erratically hand-held. When a stone is thrown by workers through a rich man's window, the camera plunks to floor level for a distorted close-up of the stone spinning on the floor—to make sure we know what happened. (Camera distortions are a feature of the film.) It's all the camera equivalent of ham acting.

The only tolerable character is the doting girl whom the adventurer declines to marry. Wadja plunges us into this almost unrelieved swamp of cynicism and greed to show us capitalism naked, I guess; but the result is *un*-naked, swaddled by his mannerisms.

He is often called the preeminent Polish director. Having no extraordinary knowledge of Polish films and admittedly having seen only 11 of Wajda's 23 to date, I nonetheless can think of three Polish films that I prefer to any of those 11: Polanski's *Knife in the Water*, Kawalerowicz's *Mother Joan of the Angels*, and (never released here) Konwicki's *Last Day of Summer*. Compared with them, and certainly compared with the best in the rest of the world, Wajda is far from the first rank, still a well-intentioned, energetically eclectic, somewhat loutish provincial. (p. 23)

Stanley Kauffmann, "Exploration of a Pole" (reprinted by permission of Brandt & Brandt Literary Agents, Inc.; copyright © 1979 Stanley Kauffmann), in The New Republic, *Vol. 181, No. 18, November 3, 1979, pp. 22-3.**

ELLIOTT STEIN

[*The Young Girls of Wilko*] is ironically elegiac, one of Andrzej Wajda's least vehement and most beautiful films. . . .

It is a film about lost opportunities and missed chances, of delicate undercurrents of the sort generally best left to literature. The shadowy, distant, and possibly affectless Wiktor never completely reveals himself to anyone; it is likely that his attraction is his emptiness—it can contain whatever those who love him wish to project.

Elliott Stein, "Reports from the New York Film Festival: 'The Young Girls of Wilko'" (copyright © 1979 by Elliott Stein; reprinted by permission of the author), in Film Comment, *Vol. 15, No. 6, November-December, 1979, p. 67.*

RYSZARD KONICZEK

[*Rough Treatment*] is the continuation of the line Wajda had adopted in the *Man of Marble*. A directly contemporary subject and a reporting style, quick, banal with no sophisticated symbols and in-frame compositions emphasise the shift in approach of the "romantic-baroque" plastic artist of the screen. . . . But in principle, Wajda is still deeply himself, a dramatic artist, violent, imposing his own philosophical point of view. The usual, the everyday, the trite—which are the essence of life—head toward tragedy in *Rough Treatment*. Wajda has never fitted into standard categories, Aristotle's logic, Cartesian motivation. His most epic subjects, such as *Ashes* or *Land of Promise*, as processed by him were seething internally. Those defiant, jarring, un-natural arrangements, are revealed again in *Rough Treatment*. The tempest of history—being the destructive moment, negation and calamity—are—as aesthetic and emotional principle—the inherent characteristic of Wajda's dramaturgy. In his new picture, Wajda is not modelling his hero slowly, nor is he developing his features from within. The character acquires features, colour and value only when he collides with life. . . . [It] is difficult to prove that the individual plans of action which add up to the drama are "improbable". The riddle of the wife's leaving for a weak *arrivist* is explained by her willingness to free herself of his domination; some personnel shifts, local manipulations in press circles, destroy the man's professional position; the mechanism of divorce is pushed forward by the technical "efficiency" of the lawyer and sealed by the soullessness of court procedures; and the explosion of the gas stove in the bathroom also results from the "necessity of coincidence." The basic question the film puts is not what *happened* but what is the protagonist's attitude toward the situation, how is he coping with it? Does he prove to be a hero, a conformist, or a coward? Through one catastrophic mechanism of his film Wajda has unveiled elementary, simple, basic questions. What would they mean without the magnifying glass of defeat and death? The outlines of the everyday would be blurred, meanings would become shallow, the power of telling things disappear. *Rough Treatment* is a drama of values expressed by a drama of existence; the eternal subjects in art, the ever-recurring subject of Wajda's works. (pp. 259-60)

Ryszard Koniczek, "Poland: 'Bez Znieczulenia' ('Rough Treatment')," in International Film Guide 1980, *edited by Peter Cowie (© 1979 by Thomas Yoseloff Ltd., London, Great Britain), The Tantivy Press, 1979, pp. 259-60.*

Lina Wertmüller

1928-

Italian director, and writer.

Wertmüller's tales of Italians victimized by their political system are variously termed feminist, antifeminist, capitalist, and communist. A controversial filmmaker who creates social satire in the tradition of Chaplin, it is evident that she encompasses many aspects of Italian life in her work. Her fellow countrymen are portrayed as torn between dignity and survival, often making choices that serve only to insure their preservation. While popularly received in the United States, Wertmüller's films have failed to gain critical acclaim in Italy, most likely due to a fluctuating political position that has little bearing on American thought. Her stance has been termed socialist-anarchist, though some find her a sociologist rather than a socialist. Alternately, she revels in and mocks the idiosyncrasies of the Italians, showing them as puppets of their country's faltering political system.

Wertmüller disdained her family's advice to pursue a career in law, choosing instead to study at the Academy of Theatre in Rome. Upon graduation, she traveled with an Italian puppet theater. Later positions resulted in a meeting with Federico Fellini, who asked her to assist him with his motion picture *8½*. Fellini's influence is strongly evident in her films, particularly in the way she utilizes ribald, vulgar humor. She also shares his interest in grotesque characters and his need to juxtapose reality and fantasy, creating an elaborate form of social disorder.

Her first independent film, *The Lizards*, was influenced by the neorealistic interest in social commitment to the lower classes, as well as being heavily indebted to Fellini's *I Vitelloni*. *Let's Talk About Men*, her next film, is considered a feminist film, though Wertmüller feels it is more general in tone, sexual roles serving rather as an analogy for the interaction of individuals in society. *Let's Talk About Men* reveals her droll humor, presenting her characters as both ridiculous and noble. *The Seduction of Mimi* proved to be Wertmüller's first major success. In this social parody of the disintegration of both society and industry, Wertmüller's comic treatment of a metal worker's struggles sharply delineates the way many Italians must prostitute themselves in order to survive. Mimi is the first of Wertmüller's anti heroes; by trying to avoid the system, he finally plays right into it. Her next film, *Love and Anarchy*, is considered by some a political doctrine of anarchism; others find it a study of political roots that uses a brothel as an analogy for fascism.

Later films became more controversial, such as *Swept Away by an Unusual Destiny in the Blue Sea of August*. It is the story of two people stranded on a desert island while locked into their servant-master roles. Ultimately, the roles are reversed, but only temporarily. Many found its portrayal of women degrading, though Wertmüller insists that the petty, vindictive, and demanding female, Rafaella, is intended to symbolize society in general rather than women in particular. Other critics, however, feel Wertmüller adopted this stance after the completion of the film, and claim she embraces whatever political school of thought seems convenient. However, *Swept Away* did not provoke the critical uproar of *Seven Beauties*. While popularly received, this story of a would-be ladies' man in a German prison camp has been accused of turning Nazi atrocities into cartoon fare. Many find it an insightful though horrible farce, but Wertmüller's technique of presenting situations that alternately amuse and shock the viewer disturbed several critics, who felt the film's popular reception was indicative of America's general insensitivity.

Though Wertmüller's political affiliations are ambiguous and seem to vary frequently, it appears that her essential political stance is humanistic, embracing no particular doctrine. She devotes her films to the masses, in her own words, and regards cinema, primarily, as 'tricks and fantasy."

ELIZABETH SUSSEX

[Like] so many of the current generation of Italian directors . . . , Lina Wertmüller is building on Italy's neorealist history [in *The Lizards*] and using as raw material the ambivalent face of a country that, in its infinitely varied sociology, is like a microcosm of the world. In the Italian cinema neorealism is no longer an idea but an instinct, an inherited gift that, coupled with a good script, can scarcely produce a bad film. It is not therefore as surprising as it would be anywhere else to find, in Italy, a new director who can perfectly evoke a way of life—especially when, like Lina Wertmüller, she can write her own quietly effective script. *The Lizards* . . . seems, in fact, so basically unassuming that it is very easy to fall into the error of regarding it as documentary instead of the very visual kind of drama that it is. . . . But Lina Wertmüller's personal contribution to a theme which at first glance seems very like that of *I Vitelloni* . . . is less marked in that to some extent she is still feeling her way. It is, however, enough to point to the sequence which begins with an elderly woman committing suicide because her daughter-in-law has ousted her authority in the home. . . . Nothing could be further from documentary than [the] succession of images [in this sequence]; nor is it symbolic except for those who like to think in symbols. To see it is, quite simply, to feel what the director wants to convey. The method might be described as impressionistic, and it is one which demands a cameraman as sensitive to visual nuances as the director herself. . . .

[The] camerawork always fits the mood. For the opening scenes at lunch and during siesta hour, the camera moves either in slow pans or not at all. When Francesco is making furtive advances to a peasant girl (it is the men and not the girls who fear being compromised), the camera enters joyfully into the spirit of intricate pursuit, swooping all over the place and catching the couple from every conceivable angle, including a fascinating vertical one; yet, in the manner of the south, its attention is easily distracted, so that even at the height of the chase it can turn away temporarily to tag on to a passer-by. All this exactly expresses the ephemeral enthusiasms of the south, for which Lina Wertmüller obviously has a kind of love-hate relationship. She shows, for instance, the bourgeois contempt for the peasantry and the claustrophobic class system as products not so much of viciousness as of the peasants' own rather disarming pride in being resigned to their inferior lot. Here nothing changes because no one has the energy to pursue anything wholeheartedly enough: flirtations with peasant girls always end in arranged marriages to someone like the chemist's fat and ugly daughter, and early ambitions are gently lulled to sleep. This is the mood for which Lina Wertmüller has tried to find visual expression, and there can be no doubt that she has succeeded. *The Lizards* may be a slight film, but it is a remarkably evocative one.

Elizabeth Sussex, "Film Reviews: 'The Lizards'," in Sight and Sound *(copyright © 1964 by The British Film Institute), Vol. 33, No. 2, Spring, 1964, p. 94.*

RAYMOND DURGNAT

Lina Wertmuller's *The Lizards* explores the urgent, if familiar, problem of the sloth and paralysis of the Italian South, the encrusted feudalism and snide Fascism. . . .

Because it's a good film let's tot up the debit side first, to get it over with. First of all the film hasn't enough to say that's new if one's seen *I Vitelloni* or *I Nuovi Angeli;* it's a more sensitive, more prolonged evocation, with a tinge of pessimistic irony. Second, Lina Wertmuller, like others in Italy's new wave of neo-neo-realism . . . , sometimes indulges a slowpaced aestheticism that saps the vitality of the story. . . .

Having said which, let's add that *The Lizards* has the virtues of its faults, and in abundance, developed to the nth degree of refinement. There are images so beautiful and so simple that one literally catches one's breath. The director has the quite uncanny precision, the magical control over location, of Agnes Varda. . . .

In its more intimate vignettes, the film easily has the edge on Visconti—the huddle of snoring bodies in a crowded room, a snoozing youth with legs jack-knifed up on a doorstep, a fat Momma cutting her husband's toenails while he monologues about the idleness of the rising generation. . . . (p. 30)

Something of an *onlooker's* film, it's a real delight for the connoisseur. (p. 31)

Raymond Durgnat, "'The Lizards'" (© copyright Raymond Durgnat 1964; reprinted with permission), in Films and Filming, *Vol. 11, No. 1, October, 1964, pp. 30-1.*

STANLEY KAUFFMANN

I thought [*Love and Anarchy*] crude in every way, particularly in its heavy use of reverse symbols: the brothel as a refuge of purity, the innocence of the would-be murderer and the whore and their sudden love, the whole clumsy good-for-bad pageant. There was, yet once more, much exploitation of '30s decor, and Wertmuller's camera movement was hyperthyroid.

The Seduction of Mimi . . . is a much better picture; so it's a bit depressing, because it was made before *Love and Anarchy.* Still, it lets us see the latter film as a slip, instead of a norm.

It's a much better script than *Love and Anarchy,* but it suffers somewhat from the same disease: the author's belief that mere choice of subject brings you halfway home. Over and over we watch scenes that are supposed to break us up, waiting for the moment that will take us over the line from intent to vitality. Wertmuller's camerawork is once again frenzied, muscular, near-hysterical—overhead shots for no reason, lots of zoom (*lots* of zooms), and the use of distorting lenses. . . .

Wertmuller's future seems now to rest on her ability to close, in her scripts, the gap between plan and realization; and her ability to make her steamy camera style serve her, instead of sweeping her along.

Stanley Kauffmann, "Films: 'The Seduction of Mimi'" (reprinted by permission of Brandt & Brandt Literary Agents, Inc.; copyright © 1974 by Stanley Kauffmann), in The New Republic, *Vol. 171, Nos. 4 & 5, July 27 & August 3, 1974, p. 20.*

COLIN L. WESTERBECK, JR.

Despite the abundant political activity in her films, Lina Wertmuller seems to have little regard for politics. In fact, she seems to dislike it altogether. In *Love and Anarchy,* for instance, neither of the two main characters has any political consciousness even though both are zealous Anarchists. . . .

[Whether] you see any political import in Wertmuller's films all depends on how the term "politics" is defined. You can't help wondering whether she isn't, like so many imaginative, self-assertive women these days, in the process of redefining it. When Mimi attacks Fiore sexually [in *The Seduction of Mimi*], his actions seem to parallel those of the rightwingers who attacked her a few scenes earlier on ideological grounds. We feel at least implicitly that she is involved in a more political struggle than she realizes—the old battle of the sexes transformed into a war of liberation. If the love life of these characters is being politicized, however, it's not something that Wertmuller approves, nor is it a result of the way the women in the film perceive life, Wertmuller herself included. (p. 430)

Women have always been thought to have some inherent incapacity for the purely abstract kinds of love and hate that politics requires. Women used to be rather proud of this, in fact. But they have become self-conscious about it lately because womanhood itself has been politicized. Among radical lesbians an ability to form only personal attachments is now held in such contempt that *even* personal attachments are supposed to be formed out of strictly ideological and impersonal motives. That is a form of emotional suicide, and if it is what's necessary to be a real feminist, then clearly Lina Wertmuller isn't one. Political lesbianism is behavior in a class with the revenge Mimi exacts for the betrayal of his honor. What distinguishes the heroines in Wertmuller's films is that they retain a womanish incapacity for abstract love or hate. That is what makes them so superior to the foolish men whom they have the misfortune to love. (pp. 430-31)

Colin L. Westerbeck, Jr., "The Screen: 'Love and Anarchy'," in Commonweal *(copyright © 1974 Commonweal Publishing Co., Inc.; reprinted by permission of Commonweal Publishing Co., Inc.), Vol. C, No. 18, August 9, 1974, pp. 430-31.*

PETER BISKIND

[*The Seduction of Mimi* and *Love and Anarchy*] reveal a mature and major talent, one which shows that Fellini's influence on the films of his own country has not been wholly malign but, in the hands of a disciplined disciple . . . , can be made to serve large and significant purposes. . . .

Wertmüller moves beyond bourgeois Italian modernism to demystify the experience of alienation by rendering transparent the clouded consciousness of private life. She picks up the pieces of Fellini's world, draws together the fragments of dream and memory on the one hand, and inert spectacle on the other, and shows that they are part of a whole. She reveals the peculiar historical circumstances which gave rise to the cleavage between private life and production, and thereby lays the bias for overcoming it. Unhappily, this vision of wholeness is unavailable to her characters, who perceive it, if at all, by its absence. They are destroyed, for the most part, by their own blindness or the incomprehension of others. (p. 10)

The Seduction of Mimi is a comic examination of the disintegration of a traditional society under the impact of industrial development and, at the same time, a demonstration of the superficiality of ideological change in the face of deeply ingrained culture patterns of behavior. (p. 11)

It is tempting to regard [the sequence depicting Mimi's seduction of the obese Amalia] as an explicit commentary on Fellini. It is introduced by a Saraghina-like figure (*8½*) who welcomes Mimi and lends her services to his designs; she functions, in short, as a kind of resident deity in the same way that Marx and Lenin preside over Fiore's home. More central, however, is the transformation of Amalia from person (albeit slightly ridiculous) to spectacle, that is, to an object with which we, as irresponsible spectators, are morally uninvolved. She has stepped out of *Satyricon* or *Roma*, a bloated and deformed freak. For Fellini, reality as spectacle is never classically proportioned, but is chaotic and incoherent, peopled with monstrosities, deprived of symmetry by the absence of consciousness or a principle of meaning. Unlike Fellini, however, and it is a crucial difference, Wertmüller shows us how Amalia came to be seen this way. Her transformation from subject to object is the end product of a voluntary act situated in a moral universe. (pp. 12-13)

Wertmüller's interrogation of Fellini is extended in her treatment of the relationship between subjective fantasy and reality. As Mimi's blindness to the political implications of his personal choices betrays him into the hands of the Mafia who manipulate private values like family honor for their own ends, in his imagination he attributes his misfortunes to the persecution of a ubiquitous and omnipotent Mafia chieftain whom he sees lurking behind every tree. (p. 13)

Like *The Conformist* and *The Investigation of a Citizen Beyond Suspicion, Love and Anarchy* deals with the fascist period, but Wertmüller avoids exotic studies of the psychosexual roots of the authoritarian personality which themselves perpetuate the alienation of personality from production, in favor of an examination of the motives of a common man, a "nobody". . . . *Love and Anarchy* is not so much an analysis of anarchism as a political doctrine, moral or immoral, practical or utopian, as a meditation on the sources of political action. It portrays the anarchist as saint, as the Dostoevskian Holy Fool, Prince Kropotkin as Prince Myshkin. (pp. 13-14)

In accord with its dualistic title, *Love and Anarchy* divides its world neatly in two. Public is set against private, politics against love, fascism against anarchism, men against women. (p. 14)

The interior of the brothel, dark and soft, is the compliment to the fascist world without. Here, the larger contradiction between politics and love is reproduced in the contrast between Salome and Tripolina. Salome is blonde, bawdy, and loud, a perfect match for Spatoletti whom she manipulates for her own political purposes as he uses her for his sexual ones. The antithesis of Salome is Tripolina, who gives voice to the demands of private life. She is, like her surroundings, soft, dark, and sensual. (pp. 14-15)

The brothel mirrors the regimentation of the fascist state. Female sexuality has been assimilated to the system of capitalist commodity exchange. For these women, family and private life have almost ceased to exist, thereby rendering their longing for love and personal satisfaction more pathetic and desperate. Under these circumstances, this aspiration becomes utopian and destructive, an end in itself and therefore an impossible illusion. As the film shows, there can be no love under Fascism. (p. 15)

Both Tripolina and Salome reflect, in opposite ways, the alienation of privacy from production. Both Tripolina and Salome divorce love from anarchy, life from politics, and consequently entertain a partial view of Tunin who becomes a sentimentalized reflection of their own needs. To Salome, Tunin is heroic political man: "I thought you were a saint, because you were ready to die for an ideal." To Tripolina, he is exclusively a lover, and a reminder of her own lost innocence. . . . The casual manner which has characterized the film's treatment of its themes is suddenly shattered by an entirely unexpected outburst of emotion [when Tripolina and Salome wrestle on the bathroom floor]. Tunin is revealed in all his contradictory fullness—humiliated and terrified to the point of imbecility, and at the same time exhibiting the capacity for a surprising and alarming amount of violence. (pp. 15-16)

What can we make of all this? On the level of the alienated culture of capitalism, which dictates the roles and perceptions of the principals, it seems indeed that love and anarchy don't mix. Like the mothers who hover at the fringes of the drama—Tunin's mother (at the beginning, baby Tunin's question: "What's an anarchist?" is answered by his mother with wry irony: "Someone who kills a prince or a king and is hanged for it") or the maternal figure nursing a baby outside the room (like his mother's room, Tunin remarks) where Tunin and Tripolina first make love—Tripolina plays a traditional conservative role. But she finds that to protect the males of the oppressed class from the oppressor, from prison or certain death, the mother must not only come between him and the oppressor, but between him and his own aspirations for self-respect, between him and history and life itself. For in reality, love and anarchy are not antagonistic, but indissolubly bound together. . . .

And what of Tunin? In a sense, the film offers an alternative to the flippant answer provided by his mother to the question which begins the film. Tunin, naked with fear, stripped of dignity, nauseated at the sight of the death inflicted with his own hand, humiliated by the failure even of his attempt to commit suicide, yet attains the unheroic but not immodest dignity of resistance—the refusal to talk under torture, the refusal to capitulate to overwhelming power. It is the heroism, in short, of the forgotten ones. (p. 16)

Peter Biskind, "Lina Wertmüller: The Politics of Private Life," in Film Quarterly *(copyright 1974 by The Regents of the University of California; reprinted by permission of the University of California Press), Vol. XXVIII, No. 2, Winter, 1974-75, pp. 10-16.*

PENELOPE GILLIATT

["Swept Away by an Unusual Destiny in the Blue Sea of August"] is a very Marxist film, beneath its complexion of comedy. Who belongs to whom? Is it the now unpaid wage earner to the rich employer separated from any bank? Or is it the burdensome complainer to the amused survivalist? The tenaciously habitual in arrogance to the newborn in command? The one who feels the greater need to the one who feels the freer?

Neither belongs to the other, says Lina Wertmüller, with characteristic political skepticism about emotional combat. (p. 94)

Lina Wertmüller's fine film is apparently a simple parable about a social irony, like J. M. Barrie's "The Admirable Crichton," in which the butler in a shipwrecked party of aristocrats is eventually called Gov because he is the most capable person. But "Swept Away by an Unusual Destiny in the Blue Sea of August" is about more than token amusements of paradox. It is about certain things' being swept away. The man, cast socially as a servant, regains in his native state his born worth, but he loses his heart; the woman, cast socially as the boss, is forced to admit her subservience, but as soon as she rejoins her husband and friends she loses her acquired pliancy. In other words, the hero is swept away by her. (pp. 94-5)

Penelope Gilliatt, "Vivid Doldrums," in The New Yorker *(© 1975 by The New Yorker Magazine, Inc.), Vol. LI, No. 31, September 22, 1975, pp. 94-5.*

JANET MASLIN

You really have to watch out, when it comes to women directors, for the extent to which they tend to be overrated and for the venomous quirk that prompts some to treat their heroines more nastily than any male director might. Though Lina Wertmüller has made a couple of interesting pictures (notably *The Seduction of Mimi,* a good sex comedy that managed to triumph over its political pretensions), her negligible *Swept Away* . . . has been . . . irrationally overpraised lately. . . .

[The opening sequence] means to show the Italian elite splashing around in the Mediterranean but is shot so unimaginatively (and scored with such irritating Muzak) that it looks like a travelogue about Hawaii. . . . After fifteen frenzied and excruciating minutes, [Raffaella and Gennarino] manage to get marooned on a lovely desert island and begin to indulge in some wonderfully broad comedy, when the script does them in. Gennarino, realizing he is suddenly in control of the situation, is called upon to starve, berate, beat, kick, rape (although he doesn't complete the act, for fear of her enjoying it), and generally abuse [Raffaella]. Even worse, *she* is called upon to like it. (p. 268)

Does it really matter that in the interim, as he slaps his prey, [Gennarino] is shouting things like "*This* is for causing inflation, and for not paying taxes . . . *this* is for high bus and train fares, and the high price of gas"? The bearing of this whole little fable on the political issues it name-drops is dubious at best.

You can search until you're blue, but you sure won't find any evidence to support claims that this is meant to be funny, either. True, the whole situation is clichéd enough to suggest deliberate parody, what with its role-reversal and desert-island motifs, not to mention its startling naïveté in relation to Wertmüller's other films. But the would-be tragic ending is too dragged-out and maudlin to be the result of even a light touch, let alone a clever or ironic one. And despite the numerous and unpleasant ways in which she makes [Gennarino] look foolish, Wertmüller is just sympathetic enough with her hero to throw off whatever balance her initial conception may have had. Hovering as it does between two genres as irreconcilable as overblown comedy and politically based cynicism, *Swept Away* . . . winds up being deeply annoying and not much else. Despite its wonderfully eye-catching poster shot of two bodies embracing in the surf, and despite a plethora of postcard sunsets and romantic-looking dunes, the picture is far too shrill to elicit any physical response except maybe a headache. (pp. 268-69)

Wertmüller's direction is no better than ordinary, with her few attempted bravura shots lavished on subjects that don't deserve them. (The fanciest one here swiftly circles a yacht, perhaps to show that it's surrounded by water.) And Wertmüller's abrupt cuts have an uncanny way of suggesting that the projectionist has slipped in the wrong reel. (p. 269)

Janet Maslin, "Lina Wertmüller: 'Swept Away . . .'," in Boston Phoenix, *1975 (and reprinted in* The National Society of Film Critics on Movie Comedy, *edited by Stuart Byron and Elisabeth Weis, Grossman Publishers, 1977, pp. 268-69).*

WILLIAM S. PECHTER

[Most] of *Love and Anarchy* is played as farce, and quite successfully. Apart from the ending, the film's two most effective sequences are both quite straightforwardly comic ones: a long Sunday outing in the country with Tunin, the two whores, and the security chief (hilariously caricatured by Eros Pagni, something of a Mussolini look-alike); and a boisterous scene of Tunin having his first meal in the brothel. . . . And though one's final impression of *Love and Anarchy* is of a work in a tragicomic mode, the film achieves this effect not so much by a true mixture of moods, but by their drastic alternation. Things in it aren't (as they are in, say, a *Seduced and Abandoned,* or the films of Buñuel) an inseparable fusion of the funny and the horrible; they are funny, and then they turn horrible. The ending of the film, in particular, is almost unbearably powerful; a sudden, swift, unrelenting outburst of sickening violence, the impact of which is such as to call into question the rampant use of prolonged slow motion as a means of intensifying the depiction of violence in films. And this stunning conclusion tends to leave one feeling that the film was all along more serious than it often seemed, a feeling reinforced by the work's being bracketed by, at one end, a photomontage of Mussolini and historical note on his rise to power and, at the other, a sober quotation from Enrico Malatesta to the effect that, though the use of murder as an instrument of political action is to be deplored, what will be remembered of the acts of assassins is not the acts themselves but rather the ideals that inspired them.

Yet the more one reflects on the film, the less satisfactory its swervings of moods and meanings seem to be. For one thing, Tunin really is portrayed throughout as too much of a comic figure to be dealt so savage a fate; it's rather as if *To Be or Not to Be* were to end with Jack Benny being dragged off, kicking and screaming, to face a firing squad. Moreover, though the closing quotation tends to impart a retrospective dignity and high-mindedness to all that's gone before, it seems singularly inappropriate to the case of Tunin, whose botched effort is made in the name of only the most generalized political sentiment ("Tyrants disgust me," he explains), and earns him only a newspaper obituary as an "unidentified" suicide. . . . [Throughout] most of the film, the joke seems to be Tunin's absolute unfitness for the task he's set himself, and the film's point that politics in general and tyrannicide in particular had best not be left to amateur bunglers. . . . Then, suddenly, we seem to be meant to see Tunin as a noble martyr to some ideological cause that will survive him. Nor is it really a case of these apparent contradictions in meaning tending to combine with and enrich each other, any more than the tragic and comic elements in the film finally jell into true tragicomedy. Rather—and it's this which I found most disturbing about the film—such things seem ultimately to have the effect of canceling each other out. (pp. 266-67)

William S. Pechter, "Lina Wertmüller: 'Love and Anarchy'" (copyright © 1976 by William S. Pechter; reprinted by permission of the author), in The National Society of Film Critics on Movie Comedy, *edited by Stuart Byron and Elisabeth Weis, Grossman Publishers, 1977, pp. 265-67 (and to be reprinted in his* Movies plus One, *Horizon Press, 1981).*

JOHN SIMON

There are, broadly speaking, two kinds of greatness in art: that of transcending previously known boundaries, of defying all norms; and that of perfect taste, of working with exquisite tact within one's limitations. In music, for example, this would be the difference between a Wagner or Mahler on the one hand, and a Fauré or Ravel on the other; in painting, between a Michelangelo or Picasso and a Botticelli or Degas. The artists of pure taste seem, rightly or wrongly, to possess a smaller greatness, though I often prefer them to the other sort. But there exists, fascinatingly, even a rare third kind that combines aspects of the two divergent greatnesses—artists who are, somehow, both big and small, fierce and civilized, beyond taste and yet also, miraculously, tasteful. . . .

Seven Beauties (Pasqualino Settebellezze), the new film by Lina Wertmüller, strikes me as the work of this third kind of artist: one who amazingly blends great force with something that, even if it is not exactly delicacy and finesse, is still a mischievous piquancy, a penetrating slyness that borders on a kind of refinement. If *Swept Away* marks a considerable step beyond Wertmüller's earlier, very fine films, *Seven Beauties* is an upward leap in seven-league boots that propels her into the highest regions of cinematic art, into the company of the major directors. (p. 25)

Wertmüller is a master both of camera placement and movement, and of editing, or montage. She would have delighted Bazin as much as Eisenstein. . . .

Faultless, too, is the rhythm with which the film shuttles between Germany and Italy. This always occurs when one story has become unendurable or stalemated, and any change is welcome. Even within individual episodes, though, the sense of contrast is marvelous. . . . And what of the glory of having the entire trial scene done in pantomime? In a baroque palace of justice, covered with grandiose frescoes, a puny mockery of justice takes place—and trust Wertmüller's camera to discover among the painted figures a bemused ostrich, the symbol of evasion of reality and truth. And what comic puppet's gestures everyone is making (Wertmüller started as a puppeteer), and how they're all gotten up! The ugly sisters have all dyed their hair blond, to convey the golden radiance of angelic purity; only it makes them look even more sluttish. And since people, separated by space, cannot talk to one another, what a veritable ballet of eyes! (p. 26)

Even the music backs up these points. *Träume* (Dreams), which the half-naked woman at the hunting lodge played in isolated yearning, is taken up again by the commander as she is serviced by Pasqualino. In between, however, when the prisoners are being brutalized in the death camp, we get "The Ride of the Valkyries." Well, those are the two extremes of Wagner's music, or of the Germanic soul: its most voluptuous sentimentality, and its most shrilling violence. . . .

There is more going on in a minute of this film than in an hour of *Hustle* or *Hester Street* or *Barry Lyndon.* By "more" I do not mean plot, of course. I mean things like symbolic geometry, the way the movements of the escaping Italians are opposed in direction and speed across the film frame to those of the Jews being herded to slaughter. . . .

Throughout the film, Miss Wertmüller's view moves in and out of her characters, creating a magnificent contrast between one shot in which things are seen subjectively, grandiosely, by a character, and the next, where they are perceived punily, objectively, by the eye of history. Thus in the brothel confrontation scene between Pasqualino and Totonno, which at one point is like the shootout in some John Ford Western, and at the next like some pratfall in a Germi comedy. . . .

The final sequences are the most moving. The Yankee liberators have made whores of everyone, from Pasqualino's mother down to the pure young girl; the prevailing jollity is as disturbing as it is gaudy. And when the Girl appears in the doorway—bedizened, soiled, ashamed—and still stares with unblemishable love at Pasqualino; and he, remembering uncomprehendingly Pedro's lesson, declares they must get married at once and have 30 children, so that when overpopulation and hunger set in, their family will be able to hang on to those apples, you are left in tears at what, after all, is a kind of happy ending. But oh the sadness of it. . . . (p. 27)

Just as at the start of the film historic stock footage imperceptibly changed into a personal story to the accompaniment of a satirical Wertmüller lyric worthy of Jacques Prévert, so the freeze frame at the end, showing Pasqualino's face as a compound of anguish and incomprehension, returns us to history, to mankind's danger of being frozen into misconceptions and headed for extinction, for all the shrewdness of dumb survival artists. How many comedies have ever made you cry?

That is the ultimate greatness of Wertmüller and her film—that it transcends all conventional categories. It is neither comedy nor tragedy (its saddest parts are funny; its funniest, heartbreaking), and it makes nonsense of the very need for classification. Above all, perhaps, it is grotesque—like a gargoyle that is ugly, beautiful, frightening, and ludicrous. It is even two entirely different kinds of filmmaking: the Italian scenes are early, prime Fellini; the German sequences are out of those somberly, tearingly sardonic Polish masters, Wajda and Munk. Yet the astonishing thing is that such divergent modes could be made to complement and nourish each other, bodying forth a most ancient wisdom about the ambiguity and self-contractoriness of things. For in this film there is no absolute right, except for the need for creative disorder and the New Man. . . .

Seven Beauties is also a film about the power and duality of love—love of sex, of passion, of survival—that is both bestial and angelic, both giving and selfish, gentle and terrible. (p. 28)

John Simon, "Wertmüller's 'Seven Beauties'-Call It a Masterpiece," in New York *Magazine (copyright © 1976 by News Group Publications, Inc.; reprinted with the permission of* New York *Magazine), Vol. 9, No. 5, February 2, 1976, pp. 25-31.*

STANLEY KAUFFMANN

[Lina Wertmüller has written and directed a tragic farce] in which the horrors are hung on a ludicrous plot. An Italian deserter, in a German prison that reeks with murder, uses his Neapolitan amatory wiles on the prison commandant—a woman built like a brewery horse—in order to save his life.

Can that be funny? Can it make us laugh when the Italian leers lecherously at the commandant as she stands in front of a hanging corpse, when he pulls that infamous prison cap down over one eye to make himself look dashing? The terrible answer is yes: because by this point in the picture farce has been interwoven with tragedy—we know we are in the hands of someone who uses farce to underscore the tragic, to complete a broad spectrum of connections. . . .

[In] spite of some flaws . . . *Seven Beauties* is an absolutely stunning piece of work. Wertmüller proves here more brilliantly than before that she is a somewhat erratic but individual, strong, fierce talent. . . .

Wertmüller has loaded her film on the back of a despicable, cowardly buffoon. She is far from saying that this is all of men or of humanity. . . . Pasqualino is the kind of man who, in a mental hospital, rapes a woman patient who is bound spreadeagled on a bed; and he doesn't change. Even such a man, Wertmüller implies, is grist for the power merchants; even in such a man the instinct for survival matters and takes what form it can within his character.

It matters because Wertmüller neither revels in his baseness nor shuns it. . . .

Wertmüller's eye is fantastic in both the loose and strict senses; she sees the world as a series of bizarre settings. Sometimes she takes this into what I would call the Bertolucci error, where *everything* is estheticized, nothing at all is seen simply. Even the assembly hall of the prison . . . looks like a misty cathedral. . . .

Wertmüller, in a culture where maleness dominates, uses maleness as the locus of tragedy because it is brutal; as the locus of farce because it is sexual and farce is inseparable from sex; as the locus of power analogies because, traditionally, male sex means conquest. . . .

[*All Screwed Up* (or, *Everything's in Place, Nothing's in Order*) is] strident, ecstatic, restless, perceptive, humane, comic, despairing. It takes banal material and sizzles it electrically into new life. . . .

Wertmüller is so *impatiently* talented that she tears into everything whether it quite needs it or not. . . . [She] whirls so energetically into her subject that her film ends with the camera submitting literally to the whirl of the city. She gets drunk on the rhythms of a slaughterhouse, of a huge restaurant kitchen. Yet in between, with tenderness and shame, she sees quietly the changes in people that are unperceived by themselves.

Wertmüller overdoes, empathically. . . . But you have to be able to do in order to overdo. (p. 23)

Stanley Kauffmann, "Film: 'Seven Beauties' and 'All Screwed Up'" (reprinted by permission of Brandt & Brandt Literary Agents, Inc.; copyright © 1976 by Stanley Kauffmann), in The New Republic, *Vol. 174, No. 7, February 14, 1976, pp. 22-3.*

PAULINE KAEL

["Seven Beauties"] is a grotesque vaudeville show. It's one act after another, with political labels stuck on the participants so you'll know what you're watching. The players come on at a sprint; they're overly spirited—the juice of life oozes out all over the place in a chorus of "*Mamma mia*"s. Wertmüller dances around with a hand-held camera and hauls the acts offstage fast, swinging from pathos to burlesque so that audiences won't become restless. . . .

"Seven Beauties" is a slapstick-tragedy investigation of an Italian common man's soul, set during the Second World War, with flashbacks to the thirties. (p. 104)

The satirical "Oh Yeah" song that opens the film has a good cabaret pungency (though the political montage that accompanies it is mediocre), and there is an imaginative moment of gallows-humor cheekiness when the emaciated

Pasqualino woos the commandant by humming a little love song. On the plus side, that's about it. . . .

In the tradition of broad popular theatre, "Seven Beauties" is all punctuation, and the Neapolitan scenes reinforce the clichés of Italian noisiness. In the German scenes, Wertmüller achieves the effect of liveliness through one whammy after another. . . . Past and present, Pasqualino's life is a comic strip of horrors. . . .

Pasqualino is everybody's dupe—a man who has swallowed all the lies that society hands out. He believes what the Mafia tells him, what Mussolini tells him, what anybody in authority tells him. . . .

He's the contemptible survivor. In "Swept Away," Wertmüller enthusiastically reactivated such audience-pleasers as the notion that a frigid rich woman gets her first sexual satisfaction when she has a working-class lover. In "Seven Beauties," she reactivates the entire comic-opera view of Italians as cowards who will grovel to survive. The commandant is an intelligent, dedicated idealist-sadist—a master-race superwoman. . . . Wertmüller's grotesqueries, such as the gross commandant, as bored as a sphinx, sitting, yawning, with her thighs spread while the scrawny, enfeebled Pasqualino tries to penetrate her, and the incessant, shrill obnoxiousness of the shrew on the yacht in "Swept Away," are appeals to the coarsest prejudices. . . . If it's easy to get laughs by sending the camera up fat women's thick legs and fleshy arms or by showing women as barnyard creatures—or as petit-bourgeois manipulators, like the women in the commune, or as rich teases, like Mariangela Melato's role in "Swept Away"—Wertmüller runs with the pack. (p. 107)

"Seven Beauties" might have had some comic shape if it had been structured so that Pasqualino's sugaring the commandant stirred a romantic response in her. But Wertmüller betrays her own comic premise, pushing for something big, and so we get prescient speeches by the commandant about how Nazism is doomed by its idealism and vision of order, and how worms like this little Italian will survive. . . .

The terrible thing about the movie is the absence of weight in these passages. The humiliations, the punishments, the horrors don't develop out of the characters or situations. They're just injected into the clowning-around atmosphere. They're hypes for us—kicky effects to give us a charge. But with that pious moralizing on top of them. So when the anarchist sinks in the muck, we're supposed to grin and shudder at the effect and, at the same time, think, Yes, he's doing that because life for him has become drowning in excrement. You don't feel a thing. . . . Wertmüller says she's a Socialist and/or an Anarchist, but the ugliness of the human material she shows us cannot all be blamed on economic oppression; the habitual closeups are merciless because the faces have no depth. (pp. 108-09)

For all the political babbling of her characters, the meaning of "Seven Beauties" is deeply reactionary and misogynous. It gets an audience response by confirming what people, in their most superstitious recesses, already believe: that "human nature" stinks and nothing can be done about it. The characters are squealing pigs and worms or else they're martyrs—a perfect dichotomy for the guilt-ridden in the audience who know damned well they don't want to be martyrs. Pasqualino the worm is also the most human of the characters. And, look, he isn't entirely soft and wormy: he can get an erection. All that's left at the end of the movie is his ability to procreate and bring more larvae into the world, which is a teeming bordello. Wertmüller presents all this in a goofy, ebullient mood. (p. 109)

Pauline Kael, "Seven Fatties," in The New Yorker *(© 1976 by The New Yorker Magazine, Inc.), Vol. LI, No. 52, February 16, 1976, pp. 104, 107-09.*

DIANE JACOBS

"Man in disorder—that's the only hope," announces a cherubic prisoner in *Seven Beauties;* and this about defines the breadth, if not the sophistication, of Lina Wertmuller's polemic thus far. . . . [She] deplores Hitler (and Mussolini) and is out of sorts with a System that traps her wide-eyed little man . . . somewhere between freely willed and predestined chagrin. Her throbbing camera is also not so secretly in love with this socio-political System, just as her neorealist predecessors were with the war-bruised and compromised city of Rome. For with what else would she justify her messy sexual romanticism or cloak and bawdy comedy and subliminal cruelty that are the backbones of an often redundant but increasingly provocative body of work? . . .

In Wertmuller vernacular, man usurps the classic female "receptacle" role in his relationship with the bullish lust of the political system. Women in turn are portrayed as either instruments or ornaments of that system. . . .

An exaggerated fondness for distortions is among the predilections Wertmuller has inherited from Fellini. . . . With Fellini, Wertmuller shares not only a flair for the ludicrous, but genuine empathy with the working-class Italian. . . .

But a cursory glance at *Cabiria vs. Swept Away* is sufficient to prove that there is very little sensibility overlap between Fellini's spiritual redemption through life and Wertmuller's survival through living. Up until *Seven Beauties* Wertmuller's strength was as comic director, the thrust of her humor pitting the hopelessness of the underdog . . . against the ferocity of his resilience. (p. 48)

While the counters vary in each successive film . . . , Wertmuller's preoccupations, like her cacophanous rhythm, have become richer, but no more ecclectic, with maturation. Even in the overtly political *Love and Anarchy* the importance of politics *per se* is conscientiously undermined. . . . Disorderly love wins out in the end, but, characteristically, sacrifice must be exacted, and the love object dies as grist for the System.

Capitulation is not seriously questioned until *Swept Away,* and it is more than coincidental that the pragmatist here is woman, not man. Molding oneself to society is the only pragmatic course, Wertmuller assures us, as Raffaella chooses the comforts of loveless marriage over the penury and squalor that would reward a life with island master Gennarino; but viscerally Wertmuller's sympathies are all with sexual romantic Gennarino, as they were with idealist Tunin. . . . Wertmuller's mind may be with the woman, but her heart is with the man. . . .

Seven Beauties is both the best and the most complex of Wertmuller's kinetic debates; but it too is little more than a denser variation on the more skeletal earlier works. . . . While the implications here are far more jarring than those of the earlier works, it is to Wertmuller's credit that she stoops neither to bathos nor to didacticism. *Seven Beauties* cleverly offsets Rossellini's *General Della Rovere:* whereas Rossellini portrays the hero as a function of the misfortune, Wertmuller suggests that the misfortune exists regardless of hero and coward alike. . . . That neither character is morally right or wrong is the most deftly portrayed of Wertmuller's non-conclusions thus far. . . .

Wertmuller's saving grace as a director is neither style nor dialectic, but a kinetic dexterity that allows her to carry on a subliminal dialogue between comedy and cruelty. . . .

In both *Swept Away* and *Seven Beauties,* Wertmuller maintains her options for comedy through cinematic conceit: the concentration camp is the yellowish gray of a Daumier cartoon, the island days are as sunny as Raffaella's well-lubricated skin is unbruisable. But there is a cruelty breeding in *Swept Away*'s pre-love island scenes that will assert itself again in the Teutonic prison of *Seven Beauties*. . . . Is Wertmuller insinuating that Gennario's male chauvinism is less fascistic than Raffaella's bourgois "ball-busting"? Superficially, the answer is no; but Wertmuller inserts details that suggest the contrary. For instance, Raffaella falls in love with Gennarino while watching him skin a rabbit, and their mating is forever predicated on his status as master. . . .

With *Seven Beauties* Wertmuller has found consummate expression for the themes of her earlier works. . . . It is now time for her to look past the rolling eyes of Giannini's failed humanity, either to find answers to her perennial question or to discover new questions to pose. (p. 50)

Diane Jacobs, "Lina Wertmüller: The Italian Aristophanes?" in Film Comment *(copyright © 1976 by The Film Society of Lincoln Center; all rights reserved), Vol. 12, No. 2, March-April, 1976, pp. 48, 50.*

BROOKS RILEY

At the heart of [Wertmuller's films] is formula—a very popular one, but a formula all the same. It may just be that when you've seen one Wertmuller, you've seen them all, or enough, or some permutation thereof. . . .

Wertmuller's formula may raise baby Wertmullers, but such a diet can be monotonous, something the director herself must realize as she strives to one-up herself from punchline to pratfall. The ingredients—politics, buffoonery, hubris, nemesis, pathos, bathos, comedy, tragedy, melodrama, psychodrama, Giancarlo Giannini, misplaced convictions, mismotivated sex, displaced honor, dialogue permeated with the comparisons of religion and politics to the remotest banalities—are all dumped in varying quantities into the vat and cooked just long enough to produce the sweet smell of excess. Wertmuller's timing isn't off; there's simply too much of everything. . . .

Wertmuller's formula requires the grand overview, a Message lurking obtrusively behind every turn of events, every churn of metaphor. This consciously-wielded Album of Great Ideas is what gives Wertmuller ballast with many critics who might otherwise be charmed but not awed. But what are these messages? and how much does she sacrifice of psychological continuity for comedy in order to get them across? In *Swept Away,* she chooses to ignore a profound psychological predicament between a man and a woman in favor of metaphor, by twisting and bending it to fit her political connotations, and thus co-opts a story rich with its own connotations and burning with possibilities far more devastating than Wertmuller is willing to follow through. (p. 49)

In *Seven Beauties,* it suits her purpose to have Pasqualino quiver before shooting his mortal enemy, while later, survival-obsessed, he shoots his best friend. The message of "survival first" is cynical enough, possibly true enough, but the character is a composite of conflicting reactions that doesn't quite add up to an interesting bundle of contradictions. Like nearly all of her messages, this one is pessimistic, indeed grim, delivered in rollicking nightmare scenes of concentration-camp compromises, with an irony born out of the scathing juxtapositions of bogus dignity and authentic betrayal. Only Wertmuller can force us to laugh at man's inhumanity to man—or to himself. . . . By making grotesquerie and overstatement her stock in trade, she bleeds the laughter from us at the cost of our sensibilities. Her considerable verbal wit and visual anomalies dare us to be outraged or outrageously amused. (pp. 49, 51)

Wertmuller may have put the situation back into comedy, but the effort of straining to extract significance from farce—and farce from significance—makes her films tiresome bundles of energy which could exhilarate only the most eager audience. Given a choice between the subtle and the profanely blatant, she always chooses the latter. . . .

Her vehicle is a comic bathosphere bulging with ideas, some good, some bad, some screaming to be edited out—An overeager synthesizer, she's gotten something from everyone: characters and comic grotesques from Fellini, theatrical lighting from Visconti, satire from de Filippo, that concentration-camp blue from Cavani. But the overriding influence is her own past. A former puppeteer, she's made living, breathing puppets, and tried to fit them into the naturalistic world of cinema. Her *commedia dell'arte* figures appear as incongruous in the settings they stalk as the first astronauts on the moon; and the result is imaginative artifice disguising itself as art. (p. 51)

Brooks Riley, "Lina Wertmüller: The Sophists' Norman Lear?" in Film Comment *(copyright © 1976 by The Film Society of Lincoln Center; all rights reserved), Vol. 12, No. 2, March-April, 1976, pp. 49, 51.*

CAROLYN PORTER and PAUL THOMAS

[*Swept Away by an Unusual Destiny in the Blue Sea of August*] is an original, a film unlike any other; the very length of its practically rococo title suggests that Lena Wertmüller wants us to be ready for anything. Yet it is not altogether without precedent; many of its ingredients are familiar enough. The recapture of some "state of nature" on a more or less conveniently placed desert island. . . .

Swept Away and Antonioni's *L'Avventura* start out, and in a very real sense conclude, in much the same way. Both films place their protagonists by means of an opening sequence depicting a luxury yacht full of rich, bitchy, bored Italian socialites, adrift sexually and socially in the Mediterranean. (p. 49)

Wertmüller is not content merely to make a point; she is concerned to engage, to disturb, to accuse, to involve, to implicate. We can all establish our distance from the world of *L'Avventura,* for Antonioni's own detachment shows us the way; but the extremity and shrill verbal violence of reactions to *Swept Away* . . . suggests something very different from forced detachment—that Wertmüller, by virtue of her own involvement in her film's themes, has succeeded not for the first time, in engaging almost viscerally the attention and emotions of her audience.

All these points—which, taken together, suggest that Wertmüller has succeeded in accomplishing what she set out to do—may be traced back to what is the most obvious difference between her film and Antonioni's: his is chill and humorless, hers not only funny but actually, even at its most uncomfortable moments on the verge of out-and-out hilarity. . . .

What saves *Swept Away* from its own comic brinkmanship is its constant, sustained proximity to *other* (emotional, social, sexual) brinks. Even before Rafaella and Gennarino reach the island, for example, her political prejudices (which have evident sexual overtones) have been matched by his less shrill and public, but no less obnoxious sexist prejudices (which have *political* overtones); the first revelation of sexism, in other words, is also and *by the same token* a version of class prejudice, a class prejudice that is also not uncoincidentally generously larded with sexual fantasy about the lives of the rich (orgies, drugs). This dialectic of sexism and class prejudice, and indeed of humor and insult, sets the tone of the film, which reverts to it again and again. Wertmüller is a cinematic diplomat, able to play them off against one another, though with an eye not to relieving but to heightening the tension involved in the exercise.

Swept Away is as emotionally charged as it is disturbingly funny because from its very beginning it is strung out on sexual tension and the impossibility of its final resolution. Every apparent relaxation of this tension raises it to a new level of intensity; and the tension in question is established, and sustained, both verbally and visually, which is why even the most elaborate linear plot summary cannot begin to do the film justice. Although *Swept Away* is shot in almost travelogue manner (with dreadful music to match—except for Gennarino's songs, perhaps), the orthodoxy of its visual style is used by Wertmüller to orchestrate her film according to the distance, within the frame or from sequence to sequence, between her protagonists. At the beginning of the film, Rafaella and Gennarino are at opposite ends of the boat (as though the social hierarchy separating them had been made horizontal); Wertmüller proceeds to draw together these seeming opposites by means of a verbal and visual counterpoint expressed in the signals each sends to the other. (p. 50)

Once Wertmüller has contracted the distance between her two central characters, by means of a pattern of attraction and repulsion, she throws them together into the close proximity of the dinghy, and then into the landscape of the island. Verbal gives way to physical brutality. Rafaella's beating is constructed around her own insults to Gennarino; he repays her, with interest, by throwing them back at her, literally and physically. . . .

Wertmüller is concerned that her audience cherish no illusions about how deeply rooted, sexually and psychically, these obstacles are. Most dramatically, Gennarino must enslave Rafaella; she is at her most cowed when, not without sadness in his eyes, he kills, skins, and runs a stick through a rabbit he has caught (what an image!) and she says she feels "just like that little rabbit." (p. 51)

The point about Gennarino and Rafaella's love is not that it is *ersatz* or superficial, let alone "natural" but that it is brief and precarious. When all the obstacles apparently have been transcended, Gennarino sights the ship that is to rescue them, which is all it takes to make him revert to form—that is, to socially conditioned *macho* form. (pp. 51-2)

This is a key moment in the film; despite the peace and freedom from rancor we have by now seen on his face, he *has to know,* he needs reaffirmation—not physical but social—of his male identity, just as the logic of Rafaella's identity compels her to try to dissuade him from taking this irrevocable step. Who is being "more realistic" is here beside the point; what they both perceive is that the sexual test now, by its very nature, has become a social test too. . . .

Wertmüller's film is about the interpenetration of sexual and class politics. Arguments about the "primacy" of one over the other are, whether we like it or not, on this view simply beside the point; the point is that she is not prepared to settle for the lame conclusion that the class struggle must take precedence over the struggle for women's liberation. The way in which Wertmüller broaches the relationship of sexual with class oppression makes it impossible to look at one without seeing the other. *Swept Away* is no simpleminded triumph of economics over love, because it is designed to prevent, and succeeds in preventing, our taking solace in the easy reduction of sex to politics or politics to sex; the film is about the impossibility of transcending *either* sexual or class roles, not because one predominates over the other, but because they work together, in tandem, to devastating effect. . . .

The very brutalization of Rafaella by Gennarino serves as a reminder that normally, in "civilization," she is protected against any such brutality or degradation by her class position. Significantly, upon her rescue, when she is reunited with her husband, Wertmüller portrays her as enshrined, serene, wearing a black scarf around her head like a nun. (p. 52)

The other pointed contrast—one which serves the same end—is that between Gennarino's wife and Rafaella's husband. . . . [At] one point, she sounds like a fascist—an unassuming enough observation, considering the diatribe she has just delivered; yet for all his lack of presence he has all the easy, abstract power at his command that his assured economic position can bring. It is this power that enables us to understand Wertmüller's statement that Rafaella "represents bourgeois society, therefore she represents the man." Bourgeois values themselves are defined by men, as Wertmüller is fully aware. . . .

[The] real measure of Rafaella's husband's power is that, thanks to it, the natural solution itself comes to seem artificial; Gennarino's almost laughable proposal—over the telephone from a gas station, a distance Wertmüller establishes with some poignancy—that Rafaella leave with him on a friend's boat and return to the island, is as impractical as it is inevitable.

Rafaella's response, by contrast, is *both* practical and inevitable. . . . We blame her for leaving, to be sure; but leave she must, by virtue of her economic status, by virtue of her easy dominance of the men who surround her—by virtue, in short, of the logic of her position and identity. . . .

Wertmüller is determined not even to give us the comfort of a cathartic ending. She refuses to end *Swept Away* with the helicopter shot of Gennarino on the pier, which is what a less unorthodox director with a message to push would have done. Instead, she traces Gennarino's steps back along the jetty to the quay—to the ugly urban civilization she has already depicted, to the side of his wife (whose bag he proceeds to carry!). The two worlds, of Gennarino and his wife and Rafaella and her husband, the two worlds Wertmüller's camera has separated before our very eyes, do not cease to exist; they remain in existence as arenas in which life must go on, despite, or *because of,* the anguish, both sexual and social, upon which they are built. (p. 53)

Carolyn Porter and Paul Thomas, "Reviews: 'Swept Away'," in Film Quarterly *(copyright 1976 by the Regents of the University of California; reprinted by permission of the University of California Press), Vol. XXIX, No. 3, Spring, 1976, pp. 49-53.*

AARON SULTANIK

In both [*The Seduction of Mimi* and *Love and Anarchy*] Wertmüller is concerned with the confrontation between social consciousness-mobility and personal desires, the battle between the mind and the heart, the linear, well-ordered road to success, and the volatile and inner emotional world. Throughout the two films Wertmüller's camera seems in perpetual motion, closing in on the characters' wild dramatic postures and affectations. . . . Wertmüller's exuberance and visceral lust for the physically overripe gesture interprets Giannini's intellectual romantic dilemma as a minor but comically effective derivative of Stendahl's numerous studies of politics and passion. (pp. 51-2)

[In *Love and Anarchy*] Wertmüller makes all her points through an elaborate, Rubens-like setting; her camera fluency rarely provides a static, visual metaphor.

But something happens in *All Screwed Up*. . . .

In *All Screwed Up,* the action is not so frantic or madcap. The comic nature of her work is toned down. . . .

Wertmüller's dramatic form is much more cryptic in *All Screwed Up*. . . . Wertmüller has stopped laughing at the world; she adopts a black humor perspective that no longer empathizes with her characters and the conflict between their emotional makeup and the grim, nonsensical rules and regulations they must abide by.

The battle of the sexes is seldom juxtaposed to the mores of family or church. Wertmüller, instead, ridicules the characters' grotesque attempts to secure happiness. . . .

But Wertmüller's descent into a modern hell is not radical enough in attacking the *mythos* of the "big city"; one does not sense the moral outrage so poignantly described in Celine's novels, or the cunning ploys of Brecht's work. Her emotional and stylistic commitment is no longer to the little guy, to the antihero whose zest for life will, if not neutralize the institution or environment he does battle with, put up one helluva of a performance before the curtain comes down. (p. 52)

Wertmüller has considerably sharpened her brush strokes, but instead of a more acute, piercing color and form, *All Screwed Up* seems to have been drawn with pincers. . . .

If *All Screwed Up* is a slight but morally critical jump in perspective and tone, *Swept Away* is a gargantuan leap from the world of Sennet's bathing beauties and mustachioed cops and robbers to Shaw's verbal demagogues, or those who render unto their native language what is naturally considered the province of God. . . .

Wertmüller has moved into the genre of social satire made famous from Sheridan to Shaw without providing the subtle cadences in speech and character development that is so abundant in English theater. Instead of the humorously contradictory meanings ascribed to the rakes and rich men, the idealists and the exploiters, the virtuous whores and the pretending virgins, the first part of *Swept Away* consists of Melato's petulantly dull harangues and Giannini's hound-dog mournfulness. . . .

Wertmüller treats the battle of the sexes with all the passion of a mortician looking at gonads in a bottle of ethyl alcohol. . . .

[*Seven Beauties*] is a much more ambitious film than *Swept Away*: it assimilates so many problems and personalities that nothing less than a Joycean (or Bachian) superstructure could contain its sundry motifs. . . .

In this film Wertmüller is attempting one of the grandest and most dangerous ironies ever committed in the name of film art: she is wagering everything on her antihero Pasqualino, who is not heroic, intelligent or tragic by nature. . . .

The irony is greatly compounded by the film's encyclopedic scope. Though it erroneously jumps back and forth in time and could have gained some clarity and force had the plot been developed in a straightforward manner, the awesomeness of the story is still readily apparent. From his initial decision to defend his sister's honor through his conquering of the commandant and her ensuing belittlement of Pasqualino, Wertmüller's story is that of the decline and fall of our civilization—not through the eyes of a Faustian figure or a Sancho Panza little guy, but the "face in the crowd." . . .

Whereas we laughed both with and at her protagonists in *The Seduction of Mimi* and *Love and Anarchy,* we are now dealing with a much more ponderous subject. And we must ultimately reject *Seven Beauties* as "the" socio-comic parody of our fall: neither the comedy nor the pain we experience is sufficiently nihilistic to make us cry out at this mirror image of our past. (p. 54)

Wertmüller has settled for a stultifying symbolic design that offers a veneer of reality but that, in essence, makes it easier for Pasqualino to be seen as a "survivor," or even worse, as Wilhelm Reich's "Little Man." The fact is, however, that Pasqualino is neither. (p. 56)

Aaron Sultanik, "How Lina Wertmüller Stopped Making Funny Films," in Midstream *(copyright © 1976 by The Theodor Herzl Foundation, Inc.), Vol. XXII, No. 6, June-July, 1976, pp. 51-6.*

PENELOPE GILLIATT

[The credits of "Let's Talk About Men"] take us back to an era that had a notably romantic view of differences between the sexes. But Wertmüller's gaudy, droll humor is not of a kind to indulge longing thoughts that the past was better. If her characters are sometimes showoffs, cowards, piratical buffoons, that is because they are of the multitude's making; they are the crowd's flunkies. Wertmüller sees her characters with a sense of context. They are struggling individuals held back by their origins: products poorly manufactured by society. (p. 82)

Sometimes the idea is cultivate now that Lina Wertmüller, simply because she is a woman, can be judged adequately only by women's-lib theorists, who tend to have literal minds about the activities of heroes and heroines in art. But she is not a didacticist; she is a filmmaker and a writer (she wrote this film, for instance), and she surely has the due to work above the yells of current sexual scraps. Her pictures make them seem philistine and parish-pump. She directs films as if she were any dramatist of old who put something of himself into every character: Lina Wertmüller puts an aspect of her energetically intelligent temperament into everyone in her films. The four women in this robust set of stories are the men's parallels; they are made different by circumstance, not by nature. . . . Lina Wertmüller understands the position in Italy of women in regard to men, of women in regard to women, of men in regard to men; more poetically, she understands and transmits the ache that can underlie their bombast, and the centuries of history that have created the social rules in Europe. She realizes that ancient regulations, apt for traditional puppet-show figures, can still govern modern characters, who often find the uniforms punishing to fit into. In the European countries that she understands very well, "politics" has no narrow meaning. It asks, "How are we to live together?" This is the question that has been running through her films ever since her first, "The Lizards." She is much moved by her characters' frequent indecision about apparently simple political issues; the people are prone to doubt because in fact the issues are not at all simple. (p. 85)

In the last episode of "Let's Talk About Men," Nino Manfredi discusses unemployment with friends. If we had men's work, we wouldn't be so dishonored. But there is no such work. How about a strike, though? There's an idea. If we struck, we'd be striking on principle. Wertmüller understands very well that there are many perplexities and fallacies in people's incessant hunt for principle.

She also knows that a good director, and a good writer, loves his characters equally, men and women. Wertmüller is not the balanced lover that Shakespeare was, but then who else ever has been? . . . Wertmüller has not yet done for her own sex what Shakespeare did with his opposite. Technically, "Let's Talk About Men" would probably have been a better film if it had been made up of fewer episodes, allowing more time for character and less for rough-and-tumble paradox. All the same, it is elating to see that such an early piece of work by this filmmaker is already capable of giving dignity to the ridiculous, and of creating heroes and heroines who, like Brecht's, are not heroic. (p. 86)

Penelope Gilliatt, "The Stronger Sex," in The New Yorker *(© 1976 by The New Yorker Magazine, Inc.), Vol. LII, No. 26, August 16, 1976, pp. 82, 85-7.**

KONRAD KELLEN

The stage direction is vast, the images are impressive, the spectacle is spectacular, the photography sensational. The content is filth, insanity, trash.

Lina [in *Seven Beauties*] generates her own world of insane, vicious, filthy *un*reality and palms off her own world to the moral and mental illiterates without number in the Western world as a hot piece of realism, a hot piece of art, a hot morality play.

Lina's *shtick* scores a number of firsts even in our era of bloody, sordid and raucous entertainment. What is outstanding is her using the victims of Nazism as mere props, background, scenery—extras. No matter how exploitative, and therefore counter-productive, past renditions of the victims of Nazi bestiality may have been, the victims were at least treated seriously, given center stage. . . . Not so in *Seven Beauties*. There, quaint corpses hang from meathooks, emaciated prisoners are whipped and brutalized, inmates are shot and driven to suicide, merely as decoration, as scenery designed to enhance the effect of what must be the most swinish and degrading sex scenes ever shown on screen, made all the more swinish and degrading *because* they are built upon that background. (p. 59)

Wertmuller uses the agony of Auschwitz not just as backdrop for some depraved and ridiculous sexual fantasy, but as a joke. This is something new, surpassing in intellectual and moral depravity all that "entertainers" have so far done. Even the Nazis did not treat the extermination camps as a joke. . . . Never before has anyone, no matter how foul his taste, how depraved his imagination, how unrestrained his lust for money and success, made audiences, while they put away their sodas and peanut brittle, laugh and giggle over a look into Hitler's chamber of horrors. (pp. 59-60)

Konrad Kellen, "'Seven Beauties': Auschwitz—The Ultimate Joke?" in Midstream *(copyright © 1976 by The Theodor Herzl Foundation, Inc.), Vol. XXII, No. 8, October, 1976, pp. 59-66.*

LUCY QUACINELLA

That Wertmuller is a thoroughly professional show-woman with an astonishing knack for the comic as well as the grotesque can hardly be denied. But is all the commotion about politically conscious cinema really justified?

Consider *Love and Anarchy*. Despite the quotation from Enrico Malatesta, a 19th Century anarchist, the film has no politically revolutionary moral. . . . The film may be sensitive to the interaction between the personal and the political, but the individualistic description it gives is thoroughly unrepresentative of the development of political consciousness among Italy's peasant and working classes, recognized as one of the most advanced in Western Europe. The film's focus on a politically naive individual carries the implication that the people are unaware and unprepared; it becomes a warning against the assumed irresponsibility of the masses, hardly a revolutionary attitude.

Swept Away takes the notion of irresponsibility a step further. From the opening moment when the Milanese industrialists are swimming and sunbathing, chattering about politics, taking jabs at the Right as well as the Left, the film works up to the idea that 'politics' boils down to talk, jibberish, confused babble. . . . Ostensibly, it's an allegory about the oppression of the masses by the ruling class; Gennarino is able to overwhelm Raffaela when he gets direct control of the means of production. But how is this newly-found power put to use? He rapes Raffaela and kicks her around the island. Raffaela, on her part, becomes a willing slave. Each reveals an inner personality completely in contradiction with the politics they outwardly profess. The implication is clear—politics is jive, deception, with each side trying to call the other's bluff. . . . *Swept Away's* treatment of the class contradictions in capitalist society is politically ambiguous, for although the fable runs along with the classic jargon about proletarians and bosses, oppressors and the oppressed, its twists and switches are such that one really isn't sure where the film-maker herself stands in the end.

The story of Mimi—a Southern worker who goes North, becomes radicalized in the factory but eventually gives up his Communist ideals under Mafia pressure—is far from the perceptive social commentary that most American critics have claimed it to be. Related only superficially to the tradition of Italian neo-realism—the post-war movement typified aesthetically and in terms of content by its social commitment and focus on the lower classes—*The Seduction of Mimi* is much closer to the series of long-titled *"commedie brillanti"* characterized by the familiar stereotyped image of the *"terrone"* (derogatory term for Southerner). All the basic ingredients are there—a ridiculously narrow-minded, hypocritical macho male is ultimately done in by his own shortcomings. (pp. 15-16)

In spite of its proletarian anti-hero, the film's political implications are clearly conservative. Mimi's path is a closed circle; it denies the possibility that the South can escape the oppressive, provincial mentality imposed by centuries of economic underdevelopment, the Church, the Mafia and Christian Democrats. Such pessimism is extremely anti-working class in view of the fact that it doesn't correspond to the actual political situation—Mimi in his ignorance is far from reflecting the Southern proletarians who have emigrated to the big industrial centers and have begun to collaborate with Northern workers. . . .

Much has been made of *Seven Beauties,* defined as a universal portrayal of the beast within us all, but again the stereotype of the ridiculous Southerner—a ruthless Neapolitan this time—imposes its limitations in terms of popular cinema "dedicated to the masses." The film tells us that you've got few choices if you're a small time gangster with a pack of ugly sisters to provide for, and that the insane asylum and concentration camp are horrific extensions of life on Naples' streets. The point is amply made, however, that Pasqualino ends up in one hell-hole after another essentially because of the personal choices he makes. At question is the issue of the individual's moral responsibility in the brutal face of history; but to play on the stereotype of the Neapolitan—a sly, crafty creature, dangerously antisocial, puffed up with self-importance and hung up on self-respect—in order to wring a symbol of the baseness of the human species out of him, seems at best to be in poor taste if you consider the fact that in Italy the problem of racial-like prejudice against the South is still far from resolved. . . .

Wertmuller's work may appear politically outrageous, ultra-committed or exceptionally sincere in America where political themes are rarely directly confronted on film; seen in her native context, she's just one among many talking, writing and filming about 'the exploited masses.' (p. 16)

Why have Americans been so swept away? The glitter of a well-wrapped package can draw attention from what's actually inside. American moviegoers are not accustomed to political situations—American, Italian or otherwise—being openly discussed on the screen. An interest in aesthetics fills in the void. Wertmuller's style is sophisticated and flashy, it dazzles; the color and composition of her images overwhelm, the pace leads you along at breakneck speed. Side-tracked by the force of such cinematic know-how, viewers might see Mimi's Sicilian machismo and cop-out on his co-workers, the class/sex war between Gennarino and Raffaela, and Pasqualino's apolitical lust for survival as bold and masterful synthesis of the political and the personal. A closer look, however, reveals the politics of these films to be shrewd manipulation of popular, 'in' notions about how cinema could or should be socially concerned, politically committed; Wertmuller makes an anti-hero out of a proletarian underdog and still manages to arrive at politically conservative conclusions. (p. 17)

Lucy Quacinella, "How Left Is Lina?" in Cinéaste *(copyright © 1976 by Gary Crowdus), Vol. VII, No. 3, 1976, pp. 15-17.*

DAVID BARTHOLOMEW

In *Let's Talk About Men,* a film made up of four short tales and a connective story, Lina Wertmuller talks about anarchy, love, seduction, beauty. And men, although the drive of this film—and of most of her films—is provided by its women. (p. 47)

Let's Talk About Men is a disappointment. Only the last story, with some notion of applying camera movement and *mise-en-scène* to theme, looks ahead to the sleek styling of later Wertmuller. The stories are all set-bound, talky and roughly edited. . . . The last story in the film is evidence that Wertmuller's talent needs only the shaping of experience.

Seen in retrospect, this early film remains one of Wertmuller's most pessimistic expressions of her consistently warring individuals, played out with little hope of appeasement or understanding on a grid of sex, politics, tradition, and economics. Unlike in the later films, the lines of good and evil are split along surprisingly morbid sexual boundaries alone. No other factors seem to matter. Her women here, excepting the peasant, have little to do but look pretty . . . and provide a toy-like sexual amusement for their men. All the men are unsuitable, unvarying from class to class, no matter their educational, societal, cultural, or economic strata. The film is a study of triumph-less women-forsaken, abused, suffering—their survival, even in a pietistic, 'Ma Joad' sense, can't be counted on. Even among the more traditionally down-trodden—the poor—there is no hope for revolt. The fourth tale does allow its women a community, although unlike the men's, based on leisure camraderie, it is formed of work and pain, enforcing its own powerlessness, and the two are totally separate, joined only during sex and then unwillingly.

This strident film's 'light' comedy—the touch-all-bases entertainment the producer may have hoped he was producing—is colored black. Over and beyond the end-title plays a furious Italian imitation of an American pop tune. Two of the lines read: "You're a cretin, baby . . . but that's how I like it." (p. 48)

David Bartholomew, "'Let's Talk About Men'," in Cinéaste *(copyright © 1977 by Gary Crowdus), Vol. VII, No. 4, 1977, pp. 47-8.*

ROBERT HATCH

The End of the World in Our Usual Bed in a Night Full of Rain—a title that cumbersome is as good a way as any to assure attention for a movie that otherwise might not attract much comment. In her latest work Lina Wertmuller refers to serious, not to say fashionable, topics of international concern: the women's drive for equality; the fact that, while a relatively few people are far too rich, the vast majority of people are far too poor; the savagery with which nations apply military sanctions at levels safely below the critical mass of nuclear warfare; the alleged imminent death by pollution of the only planet available to us. But the couple whose personal history evokes these considerations . . . are ill-suited for a rational exploration of large social issues. They are a pair of hysterics who communicate most readly by hitting, kicking, scratching, upending and generally bruising each other, to the accompaniment of uncontrolled weeping and breathless profanity, and by preference out of doors in a torrential downpour. . . . All of [their bouts] are terminated not by a reconciliation of views but by exhaustion. (p. 185)

Night Full of Rain is an energetic picture and I suspect cost a packet. . . . But it neglects to reveal anything worth knowing about its two characters (except that prudent acquaintances would avoid them), and it alludes to problems of genuine concern for no reason I could discover other than to appear topical. Wertmuller has described it as her most political film; in that case, if I now ask you to brood on the word "Trilateral," you may wish to judge this a highly political review. She is an accomplished, provocative, almost always interesting director. I have no clue to why, this time, she worked so hard but managed to be only provoking. (p. 186)

Robert Hatch, "Films: 'The End of the World in Our Usual Bed in a Night Full of Rain'," in The Nation *(copyright 1978 The Nation Associates, Inc.), Vol. 226, No. 6, February 18, 1978, pp. 185-86.*

STANLEY KAUFFMANN

Wertmuller's best work to date, such films as *Seven Beauties, All Screwed Up, The Seduction of Mimi* . . . had superb vigor, the zest of real assurance and real skill, and a rococo filigree that she had learned from Fellini. . . . Most of her film-making energies are in [*The End of the World in Our Usual Bed in a Night Full of Rain*], too, but unlike her past work, they are not applied to very much. Here we get little more than the energies. . . .

The picture begins and ends, as the title implies, in the marriage bed, with a number of flashbacks and excursions to explain what led up to it and what [the couple's] relations are. The story as such could hardly be more stale, but what keeps reminding us of its staleness is the lack of characterization. We get lots of (reminiscent) furiously romantic scenes. . . . and we got a lot of talk about [the wife's] troubles, but there is no dramatized realization of what these troubles are. They are simply stated, like items in a feminist pamphlet.

The odd fact is that, though Wertmuller is trying to say something about the perplexities of modern women, whatever characterization she achieves is with the husband. No, it's not so odd. Wertmuller knows him, knows that he's no less a male-chauvinist Italian husband for being a Communist. . . . But Wertmuller clearly does not know anything about the American woman: the character comes out conventional, undifferentiated, unexplored. We don't even know, really, what life the woman is being kept *from*. . . .

What makes the central weakness even more obvious is the feverish décor with which it's surrounded, as if something really momentous was being born. There's a recurrent chorus, a Fellinian gallery of overdressed women and a lesbian and eccentric men, all of whom hover symbolically in the bedroom and in other places, commenting in pseudo profundities about the main pseudo profundity. . . .

In her best previous pictures Wertmuller's very conscious style was a luscious way of providing a needed esthetic distance. Here there is little for which we need such distance. Her ostensible subject is a troubled marriage. Her real subject is a worse marriage—between her and her American producers. (p. 24)

Stanley Kauffmann, "High-class Hoopla" (reprinted by permission of Brandt & Brandt Literary Agents, Inc.; copyright © 1978 by Stanley Kauffmann), in The New Republic, *Vol. 178, No. 7, February 18, 1978, pp. 24-5.*

JOHN SIMON

That Wertmüller's new film, *The End of the World in Our Usual Bed in a Night Full of Rain,* is an almost total failure should, on reflection, not be surprising. This is the story of the courtship and marriage of a young American woman photographer and an Italian journalist . . . which has to carry several bone-crushing burdens. . . .

Though the film is adequately Englished, it has clearly been thought and felt in Italian, and thinking and feeling are much harder to translate than words. The result is a certain crude oversimplification of plot and character—to say nothing of dialogue—that is very different from Wertmüller's usual healthy vulgarity studded with flashes of poetry.

Secondly, for the first time in her film-making career, the director was creating something intended to be serious drama; yet her background in comedy obtruded comic timing, comic situations, vaguely comic turns of phrase on what was meant to express a sad reality: the realization that love grows tyrannical and onerous; that sex turns mechanical; that spouses become each other's jailers and victims, with the captive as much a tormentor as the turnkey. The Fellinian verbal and visual language proved simply inadequate to the Bergmanian theme. . . .

Furthermore, the project was too ambitious. The husband and wife are distinctly meant to assume symbolic dimensions. He is the Old World, she the New; their inability to thrive with each other brings about that preternatural rain that keeps raining throughout, until it becomes another Noah's Flood, from which no ark may sail forth. . . . [The effect of the chorus surrounding the couple] is particularly obtrusive, offensive, and essentially anti-cinematic. . . .

Another hurtful virtue here is that visual excellence Wertmüller's films consistently display. The splendid cinematography . . . merely [dwarfs] what goes on in front of [it], making it appear even more strident and trivial. Does this leave anything of value? Well, the first encounter of the future spouses at a religious procession in Padula has a few good moments; a scene in a San Francisco night spot in which Giannini jealously watches Bergen torment him as she clingingly dances with another man is effective. . . . Such rare good moments can, like the visual riches, contribute only sadness about what might have been—and what may again be in this gifted and undauntable woman's next picture. (p. 417)

John Simon, "Through Babel to the Flood," in National Review *(© National Review, Inc., 1978; 150 East 35th St., New York, NY 10016), Vol. XXX, No. 13, March 31, 1978, pp. 416-17.*

BRUNO BETTELHEIM

If ["Seven Beauties"] is to be taken for mere entertainment, I must state my disgust that the abomination of genocide and the tortures and degradations of the concentration camp are used as a special, uniquely macabre titillation to enhance its effectiveness. But I believe that Lina Wertmüller, the director, had more in mind, even though at certain moments the opportunities her story offered for sophisticated deathhouse comedy may have carried her away. . . .

I also believe that "Seven Beauties" is a somewhat uneasy, indirect, camouflaged—and therefore more dangerous, because more easily accepted and hence more effective—justification for accepting the world that produced concentration camps; it is a self-justification for those who readily accepted that world under these conditions and profited from it. (p. 31)

["Seven Beauties"], by truthfully suggesting that people remain more or less the same even under concentration-camp conditions, but also by showing the camp in all its gruesomeness, in all its brutality and horror, and then showing life outside the camp as being equally gruesome, brutal, and horrible, posits the argument that there is not much reason to get excited about the concentration-camp world or the Nazis and Fascists; after all, there is little difference between genocide and everyday life. (p. 47)

This disturbing debasement of life, inside and outside the concentration camp, is achieved in "Seven Beauties" through extremely clever and effective psychological play on our emotions. From the film's beginning, with the newsreels of Fascism and war, and the song accompanying them, scenes come in rapid succession, without any transition that would permit us to readjust emotionally. . . . We experience horror, then something grotesquely comic or funny, then scenes of brutality, then farcical humor again. With this technique, the horror becomes background for the comic scene, and the comic scene wipes out not the fact of the horror but its emotional impact, with the result that the horror adds, by contrast, to the effectiveness of the comic experience. Such quick manipulation of our emotions makes it impossible for us to go on taking seriously our emotional reaction to what we see on the screen, even though we do go on responding to it; it all changes too often, too radically, too rapidly. The film induces us to commit ourselves to not taking any event or situation seriously—not even one that would ordinarily upset us greatly or move us deeply. (pp. 47-8)

What is true for the most impressive events of the film also holds true for its most important figures. Although we know better, we cannot help having some liking for Pasqualino. . . . [This] portrait of the little man, which the film makes us believe in, is a lie. The world's little men do not rape or kill—not under Fascism or Communism or in a democracy. These little men do not think of or manage an erection and intercourse with an absolutely abhorrent woman, even if their lives are at stake. The little man is banal, but he is not evil. . . .

On first seeing Pasqualino on the screen, we rather like him, discovering only later what a mean scoundrel he is. We are immediately revolted by the commander, a ruthless and sadistic killer, apt boss of a pack of murderous guards and their man-eating dogs. The more we see of Pasqualino, the emptier he becomes as a person, while the opposite is true for the commander. The closer she gets to being a woman, the more grotesque this mass of flesh becomes, but also the more human, and the greater depth she reveals. . . . (p. 48)

But this portrayal of a concentration-camp commander is no less a lie than the portrayal of Pasqualino as a sometimes charming but always utterly unimportant little man. . . .

Even if we knew nothing about the concentration camps except what "Seven Beauties" shows us, we would be sure to sense that the portrayal of the commander, convincing though it might seem, could not be true. Somebody with so much insight into herself could not behave toward the prisoners as we see her do. So in regard to her, too, we become confused in our feelings by the film. Overall, unless one comes to distrust the film's story completely—and, if one can believe the reviewers, few do—then one distrusts one's feelings and is swept into the film's version of truth.

On thinking about this film after having seen it, we may well have strong reservations about how our emotions have been manipulated. But we cannot help admiring the consummate artistry with which we have been made to ride with furious speed the roller coaster of our ambivalent emotions as our feelings for the main characters change, and as comic humor is extracted out of abomination. (p. 49)

Bruno Bettelheim, "Surviving" (originally published in a different version in The New Yorker, *Vol. LII, No. 24, August 2, 1976) in his* Surviving and Other Essays *(copyright © 1979 by Bruno Bettelheim and Trude Bettelheim as Trustees; reprinted by permission of Alfred A. Knopf, Inc.), Knopf, 1979, pp. 274-314.*

ANDREW SARRIS

Lina Wertmuller has nowhere to go but up after her ill-fated English-language movie, *A Night Full of Rain* . . . , but I am not sure how far up *Blood Feud* . . . actually gets. The plot is a kind of Sicilian *Casablanca* in the style of *Seven Beauties* with accompanying lectures on feminism, fascism, radical chic, abortion, machismo, and the contradictions between personal and political morality. The style of presentation oscillates between grand opera and Punch and Judy. From the beginning of her career, Wertmuller's artistic strategies have exhausted me more than they have entertained me. . . .

By setting the film in the early period of Fascist rule in Italy, Wertmuller is able to transfigure characters who might otherwise be merely sordid and ridiculous in their flamboyantly carnal gropings, but I am a little suspicious of her facile equations of the Black Shirts and the Mafiosi. And by the time the gunplay reaches its ridiculous crescendo and the corpses are arranged in noble frescoes of big-star political allegory, I begin to get nostalgic for the good old days when Hollywood could dispense this kind of naive corn with much less self-consciousness. . . . [When the characters] begin to pontificate about life and politics and the paradoxes of the class struggle in Italy and America I do not feel that any of the half-baked rhetoric has been earned dramatically, cinematically, or psychologically. What I feel instead is that Lina Wertmuller seems to have been winging it as far back as I can remember.

Andrew Sarris, "Of Blood and Thunder and Despair," in The Village Voice *(reprinted by permission of* The Village Voice*; copyright © News Group Publications, Inc., 1980), Vol. XXV, No. 8, February 25, 1980, p. 39.**

ROGER ANGELL

Lina Wertmüller's concerns are large and unchanging—sex, honor, politics, survival—but her exploration of them is habitually so ironic, shifting, and ludicrous, and takes such unexpected turns, that people sometimes get her wrong. Her movies knock us off balance, because they can be appallingly funny or brutally satiric at one moment and wrenchingly sad at the next, or grotesque and exaggerated in their juxtapositions and suggestions but simple and reduced in their conclusions. . . . Miss Wertmüller's men and women—her men, particularly—are constantly being presented with farcically or gravely difficult questions, and I believe she presents a similarly hard choice to the moviegoer, which is whether to cling to the strong reactions one sometimes feels welling up in mid-movie and to stop and pull back at that point or to hear her out—to *live* her out—until the end and then begin to deal with the rich, conflicting blur of emotions she has imposed on us. When I do manage to stay with her, I find that she is not cheap or sexist or cynical but forgiving and generous. For me, she is a humanist (again and again, she is unexpectedly, wildly funny) who is amused and saddened by the ambiguities and distracting difficulties of life, including the unfair or unsatisfying nature of the questions we must answer. . . . Some of these difficult questions and issues reappear in Miss Wertmüller's new picture, "Blood Feud," which is in some ways the most striking movie she has made, but I don't mean it as a compliment when I venture the guess that it will outrage almost no one and that it will prove to be her most popular picture so far. It is an easy movie to enjoy, which is the whole trouble. (p. 112)

["Blood Feud"] never aggrieves us or takes us aback, never knocks us down with surprise and indignation. The picture, to be sure, is skilled and sometimes sharply interesting. . . . But the movie fails to drive us away—away from the screen and into our inner selves—with a switch or a shock, or even with sudden, startled laughter. (p. 115)

Which is not to say I did not almost love "Blood Feud." I had a wonderful time, most of the time, and my extreme disappointment over the absence of any real seriousness or surprise on the part of Lina Wertmüller did not do away with my continuing admiration for the splashiness and large dimensions of her cinema. She is never afraid to be excessive, and this time she has been excessively sensual and entertaining. (p. 116)

Roger Angell, "The Current Cinema: 'Three Beauties'," in The New Yorker *(© 1980 by The New Yorker Magazine, Inc.), Vol. LVI, No. 2, March 3, 1980, pp. 112-17.**

Appendix

THE EXCERPTS IN CLC, VOLUME 16, WERE REPRINTED FROM THE FOLLOWING PERIODICALS:

America
American Film
The American Scholar
Arts
The Arts
The Atlantic Monthly
Boston Phoenix
Cahiers du Cinema in English
The Canadian Forum
The Christian Century
The Chronicle Review
Cinéaste
Cinema
Cinema Journal
Collier's
Commentary
Commonweal
Cue
The Dial
Dissent
Encounter
Esquire
Film
Film Comment
Film Culture
Film Heritage
Film Journal
Film Library Quarterly
Film Literature Quarterly
Film News
Film Quarterly
Film Reader
Film Society Review
Films and Filming
Films in Review
Focus on Film
Harper's
Hollywood Quarterly
Horizon
The Hudson Review
The Humanist
Intercine
Japan Quarterly
The Journal of Aesthetic Education
The Journal of Aesthetics and Art Criticism
Journal of Modern Literature
Journal of Popular Culture
Journal of Popular Film
The Kenyon Review
Kulchur
Life
The Listener
Literature/Film Quarterly
London Magazine
The London Mercury
Maclean's Magazine
The Massachusetts Review
Midstream
Monthly Film Bulletin
Ms.
Musical America
The Nation
National Board of Review Magazine
National Review
New American Review
The New Leader
The New Republic
New Statesman
The New Statesman & Nation
New York Arts Journal
New York Magazine
The New York Review of Books
The New York Times
The New York Times Magazine
The New Yorker
Newsweek
The Observer
Partisan Review
Punch
The Quarterly of Film, Radio, and Television
Quarterly Review of Film Studies
Rolling Stone
Salmagundi
Saturday Night
Saturday Review
The Saturday Review of Literature
Scandinavian Studies
Screen
The Screen Writer
Sight and Sound
Southwest Review
The Spectator
Take One
Theatre Arts Monthly
Theatre Guild Magazine
Time
The Times Educational Supplement
The Transatlantic Review
The Tulane Drama Review
The Village Voice
Vogue
The Washington Post
Western Humanities Review
The Western Review
Yale French Studies

THE EXCERPTS IN CLC, VOLUME 16, WERE REPRINTED FROM THE FOLLOWING BOOKS:

Agee, James, Agee on Film, Vol. 1, *Grosset & Dunlap, 1969.*

Anderson, Joseph L., and Donald Richie, The Japanese Film: Art and Industry, *Charles E. Tuttle, 1959.*

Anstey, Edgar, ed., Shots in the Dark: A Collection of Reviewers' Opinions of Some of the Leading Films Released between January 1949 and February 1951, *Allan Wingate Ltd, 1951.*

Armes, Roy, The Cinema of Alain Resnais, *A. S. Barnes, 1968.*

Armes, Roy, French Cinema since 1946: The Great Tradition, Vol. I, *A. S. Barnes, 1970.*

Armes, Roy, French Cinema since 1946: The Personal Style, Vol. II, *A. S. Barnes, 1966.*

Barsam, Richard Meran, Filmguide to "Triumph of the Will," *Indiana University Press, 1975.*

Baxter, John, The Cinema of John Ford, *A. S. Barnes, 1971.*

Bazin, André, What Is Cinema?, *Hugh Gray, ed. and trans., University of California Press, 1967.*

Bazin, André, What Is Cinema?, Vol. II, *Hugh Gray, ed. and trans., University of California Press, 1971.*

Bergman, Andrew, We're in the Money: Depression America and Its Films, *New York University Press, 1971.*

Bettelheim, Bruno, Surviving and Other Essays, *Alfred A. Knopf, 1979.*

Breton, André, What Is Surrealism?: Selected Writings, *Franklin Rosemont, ed., Monad Press, 1978.*

Buache, Freddy, The Cinema of Luis Buñuel, *The Tantivy Press, 1973.*

Byron, Stuart, and Elisabeth Weis, eds., The National Society of Film Critics on Movie Comedy, *Grossman, 1977.*

Cowie, Peter, ed., International Film Guide 1980, *The Tantivy Press, 1979.*

Cowie, Peter, Sweden 2, *A. S. Barnes, 1970.*

De Vries, Daniel, The Films of Stanley Kubrick, *Eerdmans, 1973.*

Donner, Jörn, The Personal Vision of Ingmar Bergman, *Indiana University Press, 1964.*

Durgnat, Raymond, Luis Bunuel, *University of California Press, 1977.*

Fassbinder, Rainer Werner, Reihe Film 5: Claude Chabrol, *Peter W. Jansen and Wolfram Schütte, eds., Carl Hanser Verlag, 1975.*

Ferguson, Otis, The Film Criticism of Otis Ferguson, *Robert Wilson, ed., Temple University Press, 1971.*

Gibson, Arthur, The Silence of God: Creative Response to the Films of Ingmar Bergman, *Harper & Row, 1969.*

Glatzer, Richard, and John Raeburn, Frank Capra, *The University of Michigan Press, 1975.*

Gomez, Joseph A., Ken Russell: The Adaptor as Creator, *Frederick Muller, 1976.*

Greene, Graham, The Pleasure-Dome, *Secker & Warburg, 1972.*

Harcourt, Peter, Six European Directors: Essays on the Meaning of Film Style, *Penguin Books, 1974.*

Haskell, Molly, From Reverence to Rape: The Treatment of Women in the Movies, *Holt, Rinehart and Winston, 1974.*

Hinton, David B., The Films of Leni Riefenstahl, *Scarecrow Press, 1978.*

Hunter, William, Scrutiny of Cinema, *Wishart, 1932; Arno Press, 1972.*

Jacobs, Lewis, The Rise of the American Film: A Critical History, *Harcourt Brace Jovanovich, 1939.*

Johnson, Robert K., Francis Ford Coppola, *Twayne, 1977.*

Kael, Pauline, Deeper into Movies, *Atlantic-Little, Brown, 1973.*

Kael, Pauline, I Lost It at the Movies, *Atlantic-Little, Brown, 1965.*

Kael, Pauline, Reeling, *Atlantic-Little, Brown, 1976.*

Kael, Pauline, When the Lights Go Down, *Holt, Rinehart and Winston, 1980.*

Kagan, Norman, The Cinema of Stanley Kubrick, *Holt, Rinehart and Winston, 1972.*

Kass, Judith M., Robert Altman: American Innovator, *Popular Library, 1978.*

Kauffmann, Stanley, Figures of Light: Film Criticism and Comment, *Harper & Row, 1971.*

Kauffmann, Stanley, Living Images: Film Comment and Criticism , *Harper & Row, 1975.*

Kracauer, Siegfried, From Caligari to Hitler: A Psychological History of the German Film, *Princeton University Press, 1947.*

Kreidl, John Francis, Alain Resnais, *Twayne, 1978.*

LaValley, Albert J., ed., Focus on Hitchcock, *Prentice-Hall, 1972.*

Macdonald, Dwight, Dwight Macdonald on Movies, *Prentice-Hall, 1969.*

Mamber, Stephen, Cinema Verite in America: Studies in Uncontrolled Documentary, *The MIT Press, 1974.*

Manvell, Roger, and Heinrich Fraenkel, The German Cinema, *Frederick A. Praeger, 1971.*

McBride, Joseph, and Michael Wilmington, John Ford, *Secker & Warburg, 1974; Da Capo Press, 1975.*

Mellen, Joan, Women and Their Sexuality in the New Film, *Horizon Press, 1973.*

Mellen, Joan, ed., The World of Luis Buñuel: Essays in Criticism, *Oxford University Press, 1978.*

Michałek, Bolesław, The Cinema of Andrzej Wajda, *The Tantivy Press, 1973.*

Miller, Henry, The Cosmological Eye, *New Directions, 1939.*

Milne, Tom, Rouben Mamoulian, *Thames and Hudson, 1969.*

Monaco, James, American Film Now: The People, the Power, the Money, the Movies, *The New American Library, 1979.*

Monaco, James, The New Wave: Truffaut, Godard, Chabrol, Rohmer, Rivette, *Oxford University Press, 1976.*

Nash, Mark, Dreyer, *British Film Institute, 1977.*

The New York Times Biographical Edition, *The New York Times Company, 1973.*

Patterson, Lindsay, ed., Black Films and Film-Makers: A Comprehensive Anthology from Stereotype to Superhero, *Dodd, Mead, 1975.*

Pechter, William S., Twenty-Four Times a Second, *Harper & Row, 1971.*

Phillips, Gene D., Ken Russell, *Twayne, 1979.*

Poague, Leland A., The Cinema of Frank Capra: An Approach to Film Comedy, *A. S. Barnes, 1975.*

Pye, Michael, and Lynda Myles, The Movie Brats: How the Film Generation Took Over Hollywood, *Holt, Rinehart and Winston, 1979.*

Richie, Donald, The Films of Akira Kurosawa, *University of California Press, 1970.*

Richie, Donald, ed., Focus on "Rashomon," *Prentice-Hall, 1972.*

Richie, Donald, Ozu, *University of California Press, 1974.*

Rohmer, Eric, and Claude Chabrol, Hitchcock, the First Forty-four Films, *Frederick Ungar, 1979.*

Rosen, Marjorie, Popcorn Venus: Women, Movies & the American Dream, *Coward, McCann & Geoghegan, 1973.*

Rosenthal, Stuart, and Judith M. Kass, The Hollywood Professionals: Tod Browning & Don Siegel, *The Tantivy Press, 1975.*

Sarris, Andrew, ed., Interviews with Film Directors, *Bobbs-Merrill, 1967.*

Schickel, Richard, Second Sight: Notes on Some Movies, 1965-70, *Simon and Schuster, 1972.*

Schrader, Paul, Transcendental Style in Film: Ozu, Bresson, Dreyer, *University of California Press, 1972.*

Simon, John, Private Screenings, *Macmillan, 1967.*

Solomon, Stanley J., Beyond Formula: American Film Genres, *Harcourt Brace Jovanovich, 1976.*

Sontag, Susan, Against Interpretation and Other Essays, *Farrar, Straus & Giroux, 1967.*

Sontag, Susan, Styles of Radical Will, *Farrar, Straus & Giroux, 1969.*

Steene, Birgitta, ed., Focus on "The Seventh Seal," *Prentice-Hall, 1972.*

Steene, Birgitta, Ingmar Bergman, *Twayne, 1968.*

Taylor, John Russell, Cinema Eye, Cinema Ear: Some Key Film-Makers of the Sixties, *Hill & Wang, 1964*

Taylor, John Russell, Directors and Directions: Cinema for the Seventies, *Hill & Wang, 1975.*

Truffaut, François, The Films in My Life, *Simon and Schuster, 1978.*

Truffaut, François, with Helen G. Scott, Hitchcock, *Simon and Schuster, 1967.*

Wall, James M., ed., Three European Directors: François Truffaut by James M. Wall, Fellini's Film Journey by Roger Ortmayer, Luis Bunuel and the Death of God by Peter P. Schillaci, *Eerdmans, 1973.*

Willis, Donald C., The Films of Frank Capra, *Scarecrow Press, 1974.*

Wollen, Peter, Signs and Meaning in the Cinema, *Indiana University Press, 1969.*

Wood, Robin, The Apu Trilogy, *Frederick A. Praeger, 1971.*

Wood, Robin, and Michael Walker, Claude Chabrol, *Frederick A. Praeger, 1970.*

Wood, Robin, Hitchcock's Films, *A. S. Barnes, 1977.*

Wood, Robin, Ingmar Bergman, *Frederick A. Praeger, 1969.*

Yacowar, Maurice, Loser Take All: The Comic Art of Woody Allen, *Frederick Ungar, 1979.*

Young, Vernon, Cinema Borealis: Ingmar Bergman and the Swedish Ethos, *David Lewis, 1971.*

Young, Vernon, On Film: Unpopular Essays on a Popular Art, *Quadrangle Books, 1972.*

Zukofsky, Louis, Prepositions, *Rapp & Carroll, 1967.*

Cumulative Index to Authors

AUTHOR INDEX

AUTHOR INDEX

Cumulative Index to Critics

CRITIC INDEX

CRITIC INDEX

CRITIC INDEX

CRITIC INDEX

CRITIC INDEX

CRITIC INDEX

CRITIC INDEX

CRITIC INDEX

CRITIC INDEX

CRITIC INDEX

CRITIC INDEX

CRITIC INDEX

CRITIC INDEX

CRITIC INDEX

CRITIC INDEX

CRITIC INDEX

CRITIC INDEX

CRITIC INDEX

CRITIC INDEX

CRITIC INDEX

CRITIC INDEX

CRITIC INDEX

CRITIC INDEX

CRITIC INDEX

CRITIC INDEX

CRITIC INDEX

CRITIC INDEX

CRITIC INDEX

CRITIC INDEX

CRITIC INDEX

CRITIC INDEX

CRITIC INDEX

CRITIC INDEX

CRITIC INDEX

CRITIC INDEX

CRITIC INDEX

CRITIC INDEX

CRITIC INDEX

CRITIC INDEX

CRITIC INDEX

CRITIC INDEX

CRITIC INDEX